Criminal Procedure

Criminal Procedure

Constitutional Constraints Upon Investigation and Proof

EIGHTH EDITION

James J. Tomkovicz

Edward F. Howrey Professor of Law
University of Iowa College of Law

Welsh S. White

1940–2005

CAROLINA ACADEMIC PRESS

Durham, North Carolina

LCCN: 2016952077
ISBN: 978-1-5221-0544-2
eISBN: 978-1-52210-546-6

Carolina Academic Press, LLC
700 Kent Street
Durham, North Carolina 27701
Telephone (919) 489-7486
Fax (919) 493-5668
www.cap-press.com

Printed in the United States of America

Dedication

J.J.T.
To Nancy, Vivian, Michelle, Henry, and, of course, Welsh

W.S.W.
To Linda, Kathy, and Ryan

Contents

Preface

The eighth edition of CRIMINAL PROCEDURE: CONSTITUTIONAL CONSTRAINTS UPON INVESTIGATION AND PROOF marks the third time I have revised the casebook without the invaluable collaboration of my partner and friend, Welsh White. I hope I have been guided by his spirit and abiding wisdom. Ours was a remarkably respectful, conflict-free relationship. We rarely disagreed and, on the rare occasions when we did not see matters identically, we found constructive ways to resolve disagreements. As in the previous two editions, I have tried hard to be faithful to the vision and goals that first prompted the two of us to develop a new casebook three decades ago.

From the outset, this book has been intended for use in an introductory Criminal Procedure course that focuses entirely on issues raised by pretrial law enforcement investigatory practices. The principal topics covered are searches and seizures, entrapment, confessions, identification procedures, and the courtroom rules that command the suppression of evidence. The eighth edition adheres to the same overall structure and addresses the same subjects. Many of the changes made are predictable, due to new developments in the law of constitutional criminal procedure. Other modifications are the result of some new thoughts about how to present the essential subjects most economically and efficiently.

This revision incorporates only three new main cases. Two of them, *Riley v. California* (searches of cell phones incident to arrests) and *Maryland v. King* (taking and testing DNA samples from arrestees for purposes of "identification") were decided since the publication of the last edition. One new main opinion, *Kentucky v. King* (application of the "exigent circumstances" exception to police-created exigencies), was decided before the last edition. Reflection upon advice from a colleague who has adopted the casebook persuaded me that *King* is a better vehicle for teaching the "exigent circumstances" exception than *Vale v. Louisiana*, an opinion that has been in the text since the first edition. New decisions that are captured in notes include: *Florida v. Jardines; Grady v. North Carolina; Florida v. Harris; Missouri v. McNeely; Fernandez v. California; Navarette v. California; Heien v. North Carolina; Rodriguez v. United States;* and *Bailey v. United States.*

Because there are limits on how much the text can grow, I have had to make some difficult decisions about how to trim the material to make room for the additions described in the previous paragraph. *Vale v. Louisiana*, which has been supplanted as a main case by *Kentucky v. King*, is now a note. In addition, *New York v. Belton* and *Dunaway v. New York* have been reduced to note status. I have eliminated entirely former Chapter 9 — a brief treatment of the right to the assistance of counsel at trial that has always served as a predicate for the two ensuing chapters that discuss important pretrial extensions of the trial counsel guarantee. In lieu of that foundational chapter, I have written a substantial introductory note that appears at the beginning of Chapter 10. That note summarizes the most important lessons taught by the deleted chapter. I believe that the new note provides an ample, and much more economical, predicate for understanding the two pretrial right to counsel doctrines that are the subjects of Chapters 9 and 10 (formerly Chapters 10 and 11). I realize that some may disagree with my editorial decisions, particularly the omission of Chapter 9. Instructors who wish to assign and teach any of the material that no longer appears in the text are welcome to reproduce the versions that appear in the seventh edition.

Because many subjects addressed by this casebook have not been the focus of any (or any significant) decisions in the past four years, many chapters have changed little, if at all, in this edition. I do not believe in change for the sake of change. I have added a few supplemental notes and done some minor reorganization here and there in the hope of bringing additional clarity to certain issues and doctrines.

This casebook has always sought to strike an appropriate balance — to furnish enough material for students to gain a clear understanding of the basic topics, but not to overwhelm and confuse them with excessive, unnecessary, or distracting details. The cases presented are limited to those decided by the United States Supreme Court. The primary aim remains the same — to facilitate students' appreciation of the richness and complexity of the issues pertaining to each topic. Moreover, while it endeavors to be relatively comprehensive, the eighth edition makes no attempt to address every significant question or to present every Supreme Court decision relating to the topics that are covered.

From the start, the aim of this text has not been merely to explain the currently governing constitutional doctrine. Instructors will still find not only the most recent answers to the questions but also some of the prior approaches that have been supplanted or refined. Seminal decisions remain because students are enriched by insights into the historical roots and the evolution of the constitutional doctrines. Moreover, these decisions enable students to reach their own conclusions about the appropriate resolutions of important issues.

Welsh and I always preferred to allow the Supreme Court to speak for itself as much as possible. Although most of the opinions have been edited substantially,[1] core analytical elements of the majority opinions have been retained. Moreover, the

---

1. Substantive deletions have been indicated by ellipses. Although citations to cases and other sources have frequently been deleted, there are no indications of those deletions.

text presents the conclusions and the basic reasoning of significant concurrences and dissents.

There are two noteworthy features that have always distinguished this text from competing criminal procedure casebooks. First, the textual material at the beginnings of chapters and between main opinions has been, and still is, limited — although there has again been some growth of the introductory and interstitial text for purposes of economy and clarification. One belief that Welsh and I shared — a tenet that once again guided my choices — is that detailed scholarly or analytical discussions are better left to treatises, hornbooks, and law review articles. The preference has always been to include *focused* questions and *brief* comments that encourage students to do their own thinking. I once again made my best effort to restrict the Notes and Questions to the most germane issues related to the main opinions. Updated bibliographies of pertinent articles appear at the ends of chapters and/or subsections. Students interested in pursuing more extensive discussions of the subjects dealt with in this text might wish to consult the scholarly pieces listed in these bibliographies.

The second distinctive feature of the text is the inclusion of "problems" at the end of every lengthy section. The problems, all of which are based on actual federal and state cases, can serve several functions. By highlighting specific facets of the doctrine, some of the problems focus attention upon and reinforce important principles and limitations announced in the Court's decisions. Other problems highlight unresolved or debatable issues generated by those decisions — issues that are the focus of disputes in the lower courts. The problems furnish vehicles for testing and fleshing out students' awareness and understanding of doctrinal nuances. They afford opportunities to apply governing principles to different fact patterns, thereby refining and exercising exam-taking skills. While a large majority of the problems in the prior edition have been retained, I have made an effort to "refresh" most of the problem collections with new situations that raise interesting, challenging, sometimes novel or cutting-edge, issues.

From the start, the primary objective of this casebook has been to provide a pragmatic and flexible instructional tool that is adaptable for a variety of pedagogical approaches. Welsh and I believed that the inclusion of the most significant decisions, the preservation of the critical elements of the Justices' reasoning, and the incorporation of problem situations would prove useful to a wide range of criminal procedure professors. Instructors who prefer the more traditional, Socratic approach will have the necessary opinion material. Those who emphasize a problem-oriented methodology should find a sufficient number of problems to enable exploration and development of the students' understanding. Teachers who blend the case and problem approaches should also find the book suitable for their needs. Any of the classroom approaches facilitated by the text should enable professors and students to gain a comprehensive understanding of the relevant doctrine and to explore the vital policy considerations and value choices that underlie our Constitution and its interpretation.

I wish to express my sincere appreciation and gratitude to two conscientious and talented research assistants, Caleb Copley and Grant Taylor, who worked very hard on this revision, and to my longtime, dedicated administrative assistant, Jackie Hand. Indeed, I would be remiss not to express my gratitude to all research and administrative assistants who have contributed their labors to prior editions of the casebook. This eighth edition stands on the shoulders of its seven predecessors.

James J. Tomkovicz
October, 2016

JUSTICES OF THE UNITED STATES SUPREME COURT[1]

	(1)[2]	(2)	(3)	(4)	(5)	(6)	(7)	(8)	(9)
	Warren (1953)[3]	Black (1937)	Frankfurter (1939)	Douglas (1939)	Clark (1949)	Harlan (1955)	Brennan (1956)	Whittaker (1957)	Stewart (1958)
1960									
			Goldberg (1962–65)[4]					White (1962–93)	
			Fortas (1965–69)						
					Marshall (1967–91)				
1970	Burger (1969–86)		Blackmun (1970–94)						
		Powell (1972–87)				Rehnquist (1972–86)			
				Stevens (1975–2010)					
1980									O'Connor (1981–2006)
	Rehnquist (1986–2005)					Scalia (1986–2016)			
		Kennedy (1988–present)							
1990							Souter (1990–2009)		
					Thomas (1991–present)			Ginsburg (1993–present)	
			Breyer (1994–present)						
2000									
	Roberts (2005–present)								Alito (2006–present)
2010				Kagan (2010–present)			Sotomayor (2009–present)		

[1] Starting with membership as of 1958
[2] Chief Justice
[3] Year of Appointment
[4] Years on Court

xvii

Introduction

This brief Introduction is intended to familiarize students with two foundational subjects: the typical processes of and participants in the American criminal justice system and the constitutional source of restraints upon state law enforcement officers. The excerpt in Part A describes the operation of the criminal justice system. Part B contains a brief history and summary of the regulation of state conduct by Bill of Rights guarantees incorporated through the Due Process Clause.

[A] An Overview of the Criminal Justice System
National Advisory Commission on Criminal Justice Standards and Goals: Courts 11–15 (1973)*

Arrest

The first formal contact of an accused with the criminal justice system is likely to be an arrest by a police officer. In most cases, the arrest will be made upon the police officer's own evaluation that there is sufficient basis for believing that a crime had been committed by the accused. However, the arrest may be made pursuant to a warrant: in this case, the police officer or some other person will have submitted the evidence against the accused to a judicial officer, who determines whether the evidence is sufficient to justify an arrest. In some situations, the accused may have no formal contact with the law until he or she had been indicted by a grand jury. Following such an indictment, a court order may be issued authorizing police officers to take the accused into custody. But these are exceptional situations. Ordinarily, the arrest is made without any court order and the court's contact with the accused comes only after the arrest.

Even if there has been no court involvement in the initial decision to arrest the defendant, courts may have been involved in the case at an earlier stage. The requirement of the Fourth Amendment to the U.S. Constitution that all searches be reasonable has been interpreted to mean that a warrant be obtained from a judicial officer before all searches unless there are specific reasons for not obtaining a war-

---

* Reprinted with the permission of the United States Department of Justice Office of Justice Programs.

rant. Thus investigations that precede arrest sometimes involve searches made pursuant to a search warrant issued by a court. The court role in criminal investigation is broadening in other areas, and procedures are being developed whereby suspects may be compelled to submit to photographing, fingerprinting, and similar processes by court order. The potential for court involvement in the criminal justice system, then, extends to early parts of the police investigatory stage.

Initial Judicial Appearance

In all jurisdictions, a police officer or other person making an arrest must bring the arrested person before a judge within a short period of time. It is at this initial appearance that most accused have their first contact with the courts. This initial appearance is usually before a lower court — a justice of the peace or a magistrate. Thus in prosecutions for serious cases the initial appearance (and some further processes) occur in courts that do not have jurisdiction to determine the guilt or innocence of the accused. Often by the time of the initial appearance, the prosecution will have prepared a formal document called a complaint, which charges the defendant with a specific crime.

At the initial appearance, several things may occur. First, the defendant will be informed of the charges against him, usually by means of complaint. Second, the defendant will be informed of his or her rights, including the constitutional privilege against self-incrimination. Third, if the case is one in which the accused will be provided with an attorney at state expense, the mechanical process of assigning the attorney at least may begin at this stage. Fourth, unless the defendant is convicted of an offense at this point, arrangement may be made concerning the release of the defendant before further proceedings. This may take the traditional form of setting bail, that is, establishment of an amount of security the defendant himself or a professional bondsman whom the defendant may hire must deposit with the court (or assume the obligation to pay) to assure that the defendant does appear for later proceedings. Pretrial release, in some jurisdictions, also may take the form of being released on one's own recognizance, that is, released simply upon the defendant's promise to appear at a later time. Other forms of encouraging a released defendant's later appearance sometimes are used.

In addition to these matters collateral to the issue of guilt, it is at the initial appearance that judicial inquiry into the merits of the case begins. If the charge is one the lower court has authority to try, the defendant may be asked how he or she pleads. If the defendant pleads guilty, the defendant may be convicted at this point. If the defendant pleads not guilty, a trial date may be set and trial held later in this court.

However, if the charge is more serious, the court must give the defendant the opportunity for a judicial evaluation to determine whether there is enough evidence to justify putting the defendant on trial in the higher court. In this type of case, the judge at the initial appearance ordinarily will ask the defendant whether he or she wants a preliminary hearing. If the defendant does, the matter generally is continued, or postponed to give both the prosecution and the defense time to prepare their cases.

The matter will be taken up again later in the lower court at the preliminary hearing. At this proceeding, the prosecutor introduces evidence to try to prove the defendant's guilt. The prosecutor need not convince the court of the defendant's guilt beyond a reasonable doubt, but need only establish that there is enough evidence from which an average person (juror) could conclude that the defendant was guilty of the crime charged. If this evidence is produced, the court may find that the prosecution has established probable cause to believe the defendant guilty.

At this preliminary hearing the defendant may cross-examine witnesses produced by the prosecution and present evidence himself. If the court finds at the end of the preliminary hearing that probable cause does not exist, it dismisses the complaint. This does not ordinarily prevent the prosecution from bringing another charge, however. If the court finds that probable cause does exist, it orders that the defendant be bound over to the next step in the prosecution. As a practical matter, the preliminary hearing also serves the function of giving the defendant and his attorney a look at the case the prosecution will produce at trial. It gives a defense attorney the opportunity to cross-examine witnesses the attorney later will have to confront. This informal previewing function may be more valuable to defendants than the theoretical function of the preliminary hearing.

Filing of Formal Criminal Charge

Generally, it is following the decision of the lower court to bind over a defendant that the formal criminal charge is made in the court that would try the case if it goes to formal trial. If no grand jury action is to be taken, this is a simple step consisting of the prosecutor's filing a document called an information. However, in many jurisdictions the involvement of the grand jury makes the process more complex. There, the decision at the preliminary hearing simply is to bind the defendant over for consideration by the grand jury. In these areas, the prosecutor then must go before the grand jury and again present the evidence. Only if the grand jury determines that there is probable cause does it act. Its action — consisting of issuing a document called an indictment — constitutes the formal charging of the defendant. If it does not find probable cause, it takes no action and the prosecution is dismissed.

In some jurisdictions, it is not necessary to have both a grand jury inquiry and a preliminary hearing. In most federal jurisdictions, for example, if a defendant has been indicted by a grand jury the defendant no longer has a right to a preliminary hearing, on the theory that the defendant is entitled to only one determination as to whether probable cause exists.

Although the defendant is entitled to participate in the preliminary hearing, the defendant has no right to take part in a grand jury inquiry. Traditionally, he has not been able to ascertain what went on in front of the grand jury, although increasingly the law has given him the right, after the fact, to know.

Following the formal charge — whether it has been by indictment or information — any of a variety of matters that require resolution may arise. The defendant's competency to stand trial may be in issue. This requires the court to resolve the question of whether the defendant is too mentally ill or otherwise impaired to participate meaningfully in his trial. If he is sufficiently impaired, trial must be postponed until the defendant regains competency.

The defendant also may challenge the validity of the indictment or information or the means by which they were issued. For example, the defendant may assert that those acts with which he or she is charged do not constitute a crime under the laws of jurisdiction. Or, if the defendant was indicted by a grand jury, the defendant may assert that the grand jury was selected in a manner not consistent with state or federal law and, therefore, that the indictment is invalid.

A defendant also may—and in some jurisdictions must—raise, before trial, challenges to the admissibility of certain evidence, especially evidence seized by police officers in a search or statements obtained from the defendant by interrogation. In view of the rapid growth of legal doctrine governing the admissibility of statements of defendants and evidence obtained by police search and seizure, resolution of the issues raised by defendants' challenges to the admissibility of such evidence may be more complex and time-consuming than anything involved in determining guilt or innocence.

The criminal law also is increasingly abandoning the traditional approach that neither side is entitled to know what evidence the other side is going to produce until the other side actually presents it at trial. In the main, this has taken the form of granting defendants greater access to such things as physical evidence (e.g., fingerprints) that will be used against them. Access to witness[es'] statements sometimes is required, and some jurisdictions are compelling the defendant to grant limited disclosure to the prosecution.

Arraignment

In view of the potential complexity of pretrial matters, much of the significant activity in a criminal prosecution already may have occurred at the time the defendant makes his or her first formal appearance before the court that is to try him or her. This first appearance—the arraignment—is the point at which the defendant is asked to plead to the charge. The defendant need not plead, in which case a plea of not guilty automatically is entered for the defendant. If the defendant pleads guilty, the law requires that certain precautions be taken to assure that this plea is made validly. Generally, the trial judge accepting the plea first must inquire of the defendant whether the defendant understands the charge against him or her and the penalties that may be imposed. The judge also must be assured that there is some reasonable basis in the facts of the case for the plea. This may involve requiring the prosecution to present some of its evidence to assure the court that there is evidence tending to establish guilt.

Trial

Unless the defendant enters a guilty plea, the full adversary process is put into motion. The prosecution now must establish to a jury or a judge the guilt of the defendant beyond a reasonable doubt. If the defendant elects to have the case tried by a jury, much effort is expended on the selection of a jury. Prospective jurors are questioned to ascertain whether they might be biased and what their views on numerous matters might be. Both sides have the right to have a potential juror rejected on the ground that the juror may be biased. In addition, both have the right to reject a limited number of potential jurors without having to state any reason. When the jury has been selected and convened, both sides may make opening statements explaining what they intend to prove or disprove.

The prosecution presents its evidence first, and the defendant has the option of making no case and relying upon the prosecution's inability to establish guilt beyond a reasonable doubt. The defendant also has the option of presenting evidence tending to disprove the prosecution's case or tending to prove additional facts constituting a defense under applicable law. Throughout, however, the burden remains upon the prosecution. Procedurally, this is effectuated by defense motions to dismiss, which often are made after the prosecution's case has been presented and after all of the evidence is in. These motions in effect assert that the prosecution's case is so weak that no reasonable jury could conclude beyond a reasonable doubt that the defendant was guilty. If the judge grants the motion, the judge is, in effect, determining that no jury could reasonably return a verdict of guilty. This not only results in a dismissal of the prosecution but also prevents the prosecution from bringing another charge for the same crime.

After the evidence is in and defense motions are disposed of, the jury is instructed on the applicable law. Often both defense and prosecution lawyers submit instructions which they ask the court to read to the jury, and the court chooses from those and others it composes itself. It is in the formulation of these instructions that many issues regarding the definition of the applicable law arise and must be resolved. After — or sometimes before — the instructions are read, both sides present formal arguments to the jury. The jury then retires for its deliberations.

Generally, the jury may return only one of two verdicts: guilty or not guilty. A verdict of not guilty may be misleading; it may mean not that the jury believed that the defendant was not guilty but rather that the jury determined that the prosecution had not established guilt by the criterion — beyond a reasonable doubt — the law imposes. If the insanity defense has been raised, the jury may be told it should specify if insanity is the reason for acquittal; otherwise, there is no need for explanation. If a guilty verdict is returned, the court formally enters a judgment of conviction unless there is a legally sufficient reason for not doing so.

The defendant may attack the conviction, usually by making a motion to set aside the verdict and order a new trial. In the attack, the defendant may argue that evidence was improperly admitted during the trial, that the evidence was so weak that no reasonable jury could have found that it established guilt beyond a reasonable doubt, or that there is newly discovered evidence which, had it been available at the time of trial, would have changed the result. If the court grants a motion raising one of these arguments, the effect generally is not to acquit the defendant but merely to require the holding of a new trial.

Sentencing

Sentencing then follows. (If the court has accepted a plea of guilty, this step follows acceptance of the plea.) In an increasing number of jurisdictions, an investigation called the presentence report is conducted by professional probation officers. This involves investigation of the offense, the offender and the offender's background, and any other matters of potential value to the sentencing judge. Following submission of the report to the court, the defendant is given the opportunity to comment upon the appropriateness of sentencing. In some jurisdictions, this has developed into a more extensive court hearing on sentencing issues, with the defendant given the opportunity to present evidence as well as argument for leniency. Sentencing itself generally is the responsibility of the judge, although in some jurisdictions juries retain that authority.

Appeal

Following the conclusion of the proceeding in the trial court, the matter shifts to the appellate courts. In some jurisdictions, a defendant who is convicted of a minor offense in a lower court has the right to a new trial (trial de novo) in a higher court. However, in most situations — and in all cases involving serious offenses — the right to appeal is limited to the right to have an appellate court examine the record of the trial proceedings for error. If error is found, the appellate court either may take definitive action — such as ordering that the prosecution be dismissed — or it may set aside the conviction and remand the case for a new trial. The latter gives the prosecution the opportunity to obtain a valid conviction. Generally, a time limit is placed upon the period during which an appeal may be taken.

Collateral Attack

Even if no appeal is taken or the conviction is upheld, the court's participation in the criminal justice process is not necessarily ended. To some extent, a convicted defendant who has either exhausted all appeal rights or declined to exercise them within the appropriate time limits can seek further relief by means of collateral attack upon the conviction. This method involves a procedure collateral to the standard process of conviction and appeal.

Traditionally, this relief was sought by applying for a writ of habeas corpus on the ground that the conviction under which the applicant was held was invalid. Many jurisdictions have found this vehicle too cumbersome for modern problems and have developed special procedure for collateral attacks. Despite variations in terminology and procedural technicalities, however, opportunities remain for an accused convicted in federal court to seek such collateral relief from his conviction in federal courts and for those convicted in state courts to seek similar relief in state and, to a somewhat more limited extent, in federal courts.

The matter has become an increasingly significant point of the state-federal friction as issues of federal constitutional law have become more important parts of criminal litigation. Defendants convicted in state courts apparently have thought that federal courts offered a more sympathetic forum for assertions that federal constitutional rights were violated during a state criminal prosecution. State judges and prosecutors have indicated resentment of the actions of federal courts in reversing state convictions for reasons state courts either considered of no legal merit or refused to consider for what they felt were valid reasons.

In any case, because the collateral attack upon a conviction remains available until (and even after) the defendant has gone through the correctional process, the courts' role in the criminal justice process extends from the earliest points of criminal investigation to the final portions of the correctional process.

[B] Due Process and Incorporation of the Bill of Rights

There can be no question that the Fourth, Fifth, and Sixth Amendment guarantees treated in this casebook were intended to govern the actions of federal law enforcement officers. With respect to state law enforcement officers, an important preliminary question is whether the guarantees of the Bill of Rights regulate state action. Early on, in *Barron v. Baltimore*, 32 U.S. (7 Pet.) 243, 8 L. Ed. 672 (1833), the United States Supreme Court answered that question, holding that the Bill of Rights governs only the federal government and not the states. That holding endures today. Nevertheless, due to the Fourteenth Amendment Due Process Clause, a provision specifically designed to control state action, today the states are generally not free to do that which the Bill of Rights proscribes.

For many years, the members of the Supreme Court debated the extent to which the liberties reflected in various Bill of Rights provisions are a part of the "due process of law" that the Fourteenth Amendment prohibits states from denying. Initially, the prevailing view was that the Due Process Clause required only those rights and procedures that were "implicit in the concept of ordered liberty." *Palko v. Connecticut*, 302 U.S. 319, 58 S. Ct. 149, 82 L. Ed. 2d 288 (1937); *see also Adamson v. California*, 332 U.S. 46, 677 S. Ct. 1672, 91 L. Ed. 2d 1903 (1947). This "ordered liberty" approach to interpretation of the Fourteenth Amendment yielded a number of holdings that permitted states to afford fewer rights and liberties than provided for in the Bill of Rights.

Over the years, however, a different approach to the issue evolved. In *Duncan v. Louisiana*, 391 U.S 145, 88 S. Ct. 1444, 20 L. Ed. 2d 491 (1968), the Court, in an opinion by Justice White, endorsed and explained that approach. The Court explained that a provision of the Bill of Rights is applicable to the states as an integral part of due process if it is "essential to an Anglo-American regime of ordered liberty" or "fundamental to the American scheme of justice." Moreover, in determining whether a particular provision qualifies, the Court will not consider the provision in the abstract, but, rather, will evaluate it against the backdrop of the common-law system of criminal procedure that has developed "contemporaneously in England and in this country." Thus, in deciding that the right to jury trial is applicable to the states, the *Duncan* Court emphasized the historical role of the jury in England and in this country, noting that for centuries the jury had served as a buffer between the individual and the government.

That approach to deciding whether the substance of a particular Bill of Rights entitlement applies to the states has been called "selective incorporation."[1] While the approach has been "selective" in demanding individual evaluation of each provision, over time it has resulted in the effective "incorporation" of most of the Bill of Rights guarantees.[2] Moreover, the Court has generally refused to dilute those guarantees, but, instead, has found that the content of the Due Process Clause is identical to the content of specific Bill of Rights provisions.

For purposes of the subjects in this casebook, students need to appreciate two basic matters. First, the actual constitutional source of the controls on *state* law enforcement is the Fourteenth Amendment Due Process Clause. Second, the Fourth, Fifth, and Sixth Amendment regulations on law enforcement activity considered in this book have been fully and exactly "incorporated" and applied to the states through that Due Process Clause.

---

1. For a discussion of the approach, see Israel, *Selective Incorporation Revisited*, 71 Geo. L.J. 253 (1982).

2. For a summary of the historical development of the Supreme Court's different approaches to deciding whether a provision of the Bill of Rights is a part of the due process of law guaranteed against the states by the Fourteenth Amendment, *see McDonald v. City of Chicago, Illinois*, 561 U.S. 742, 759-765, 130 S. Ct. 3020, 177 L. Ed. 2d 894 (2010) (holding that the Second Amendment right to bear arms is applicable against the states because it is "among those fundamental rights necessary to our system of ordered liberty"). According to the Court, the only provisions of the Bill of Rights pertaining to the criminal process that have not been "fully incorporated" by the Due Process Clause are "the Sixth Amendment right to a unanimous jury verdict," "the Fifth Amendment[] grand jury indictment requirement," and "the Eighth Amendment[] prohibition on excessive fines." *See McDonald*, 561 U.S. at 765 n. 13. The Justices have never addressed whether the excessive fines ban governs states. *Id.* The holding in *Hurtado v. California*, 110 U.S. 516, 4 S. Ct. 111, 28 L. Ed. 232 (1884), that states need not adhere to the grand jury requirement long predates the era of selective incorporation. *Id.* The only modern ruling that due process of law does not require the states to provide a safeguard contained in the Bill of Rights is the decision that 12-person juries need not render unanimous verdicts in state courts. *See Apodaca v. Oregon*, 406 U.S. 404, 92 S. Ct. 1628, 32 L. Ed. 2d 184 (1972); *see also Johnson v. Louisiana*, 406 U.S. 356, 92 S. Ct. 1620, 32 L. Ed. 2d 152 (1972). With the exception of this single detail, the Sixth Amendment right to trial by jury in criminal prosecutions is binding on the states by virtue of the Fourteenth Amendment. *See Duncan v. Louisiana*, 391 U.S. 145, 88 S. Ct. 1444, 20 L. Ed. 2d 491 (1968).

What is the sequence of events in the criminal justice system?

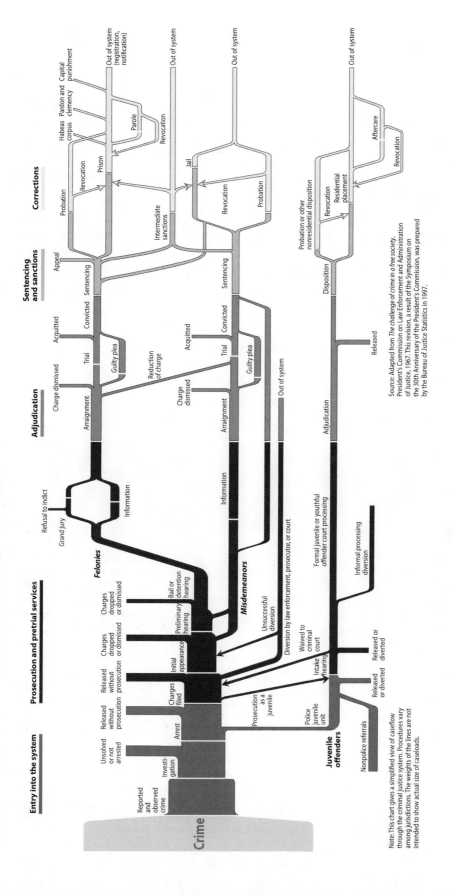

Note: This chart gives a simplified view of caseflow through the criminal justice system. Procedures vary among jurisdictions. The weights of the lines are not intended to show actual size of caseloads.

Source: Adapted from *The challenge of crime in a free society.* President's Commission on Law Enforcement and Administration of Justice, 1967. This revision, a result of the Symposium on the 30th Anniversary of the President's Commission, was prepared by the Bureau of Justice Statistics in 1997.

Entry into the system

Reported and observed crime

Crime

Investigation

Unsolved or not arrested

Released without prosecution

Arrest

Prosecution and pretrial services

Released without prosecution

Charges filed

Charges dropped or dismissed

Initial appearance

Charges dropped or dismissed

Preliminary hearing

Bail or detention hearing

Felonies

Refusal to indict

Grand jury

Information

Information

Misdemeanors

Unsuccessful diversion

Diversion by law enforcement, prosecutor, or court

Out of system

Prosecution as a juvenile

Waived to criminal court

Police juvenile unit

Intake hearing

Juvenile offenders

Nonpolice referrals

Released or diverted

Released or diverted

Formal juvenile or youthful offender court processing

Informal processing diversion

Adjudication

Charge dismissed

Arraignment

Trial

Guilty plea

Acquitted

Reduction of charge

Charge dismissed

Arraignment

Trial

Guilty plea

Acquitted

Adjudication

Released

Sentencing and sanctions

Convicted

Sentencing

Appeal

Convicted

Sentencing

Disposition

Corrections

Probation

Revocation

Prison

Habeas corpus

Pardon and clemency

Capital punishment

Parole

Revocation

Out of system (registration, notification)

Revocation

Out of system

Intermediate sanctions

Jail

Probation

Revocation

Out of system

Probation or other nonresidential disposition

Revocation

Residential placement

Aftercare

Revocation

Out of system

Part I

Searches and Seizures

Chapter 1

The "Threshold" of the Fourth Amendment Right to Be Secure against Searches

Introductory Note

By its terms, the Fourth Amendment applies only to official "searches and seizures." Accordingly, when an individual challenges government conduct on Fourth Amendment grounds, there may be a "threshold" question — whether that conduct constitutes a "search" or a "seizure." Although the Court has devoted some attention to the issues of when persons or property have been "seized," the body of doctrine spawned by the threshold "seizure" question is modest compared to that engendered by the issue of whether a "search" has occurred. The important question of when a person has been "seized" for Fourth Amendment purposes is treated in Chapter Five (see *infra* Chapter 5, subsection [A][1]). The more complex inquiry into whether a "search" has occurred is the central concern of all of the cases in this chapter.

Over the years, the Supreme Court has endorsed different criteria for resolving threshold "search" issues. It first addressed the question in the earliest Fourth Amendment landmark case, *Boyd v. United States*, 116 U.S. 616, 6 S. Ct. 524, 29 L. Ed. 746 (1886). At issue in *Boyd* was an order requiring an individual to produce business invoices. The Court concluded that the order to produce the documents qualified as a search because it was "a material ingredient and effect[ed] the sole object and purpose of" a search, which was "forcing from a party evidence against himself."

Forty-two years later, in *Olmstead v. United States*, 277 U.S. 438, 48 S. Ct. 564, 72 L. Ed. 944 (1928), the Court changed its approach. A majority concluded that wiretapping from outside a building did *not* constitute a search because, unlike the quintessential searches known to our Constitution's Framers, there was no "actual physical invasion" and no trespass upon a protected location. Without such an invasion, there could be no Fourth Amendment search.

In three cases between 1952 and 1966, the Court addressed situations involving the government's use of undercover agents (also known as "false friends") to obtain inculpatory statements from suspects. Each of the suspects claimed that the government had crossed the border of Fourth Amendment territory. In *On Lee v. United States*, 343 U.S. 747, 72 S. Ct. 967, 96 L. Ed. 1270 (1952), the Court rejected the claim that an informant's electronic transmission of statements to a nearby law enforcement officer amounted to a search. The Court reasoned that the Fourth Amendment did not govern the situation because the speaker's consent to the presence of the informant precluded a trespass, and, additionally, because the speaker was "talking confidentially and indiscreetly with one he trusted, and he was overheard." In *Lopez v. United States*, 373 U.S. 427, 83 S. Ct. 1381, 10 L. Ed. 2d 462 (1963), the Court declared that a known Internal Revenue Service agent's recording of a bribe offer was outside the borders of the Fourth Amendment because the suspect had consented to the agent's presence in his office, and had taken the risk of recording and reproduction in court by willingly speaking to the agent. Finally, in *Hoffa v. United States*, 385 U.S. 293, 87 S. Ct. 408, 17 L. Ed. 2d 374 (1966), the Court concluded that an informant who listened to, reported, and testified about Hoffa's inculpatory remarks did not "search" within the meaning of the Fourth Amendment because "no interest legitimately protected by the Fourth Amendment [was] involved." According to the Court, Hoffa had not relied "upon the security of his hotel room," for he had allowed the informant to enter and listen. Rather, he had relied "upon his misplaced confidence that [the informant] would not reveal his . . . voluntarily confide[d] wrongdoing."

Between 1942 and 1964, the Court decided three electronic eavesdropping cases that did not involve "undercover agents." In *Goldman v. United States*, 316 U.S. 129, 62 S. Ct. 993, 86 L. Ed. 1322 (1942), the Court held that the government did not trigger Fourth Amendment coverage by placing a "detectaphone" against an outer wall and listening to conversations inside a building. In *Silverman v. United States*, 365 U.S. 505, 81 S. Ct. 679, 5 L. Ed. 2d 734 (1961), however, law enforcement agents did tread upon Fourth Amendment territory by inserting a "spike mike" into a "party wall" and picking up conversations passing through heating ducts. The physical intrusion was deemed sufficient to cross the constitutional threshold, even though it did not effect a technical "trespass." Finally, in *Clinton v. Virginia*, 377 U.S. 158, 84 S. Ct. 1186, 12 L. Ed. 2d 213 (1964), the Court found that when the government attached a listening device to a wall by means that caused a "thumbtack-sized" penetration, it had "searched" within the meaning of the Fourth Amendment. Although *Olmstead*'s physical intrusion requirement still survived, the Court proved that it had been serious in *Silverman* when it had "decline[d] to go beyond [the physical intrusion boundary] by even a fraction of an inch." By 1964, the *Olmstead* criterion for resolving the threshold question had clearly become a fragile, tenuous barrier to Fourth Amendment regulation.

This historical sketch of cases and doctrine sets the stage for the revolutionary entrance of *Katz v. United States*, 389 U.S. 347, 88 S. Ct. 507, 19 L. Ed. 2d 576 (1967), the first case in this chapter. The majority and concurring opinions in *Katz* are the wellspring of most modern Fourth Amendment "search" doctrine. Most of the remainder of the opinions in this chapter are interpretations and applications of the

Katz decision. Their task has been to develop, refine, and delimit the boundaries of the rudimentary doctrine at the core of the landmark decision. Students should endeavor to identify the content of the contribution made by each of these cases. Moreover, they should consider whether that content is faithful to *Katz* and to the spirit of the Fourth Amendment.

Katz v. United States

United States Supreme Court

389 U.S. 347, 88 S. Ct. 507, 19 L. Ed. 2d 576 (1967)

MR. JUSTICE STEWART delivered the opinion of the Court.

The petitioner was convicted in the District Court for the Southern District of California under an eight-count indictment charging him with transmitting wagering information by telephone from Los Angeles to Miami and Boston in violation of a federal statute. At trial the Government was permitted, over the petitioner's objection, to introduce evidence of the petitioner's end of telephone conversations, overheard by FBI agents who had attached an electronic listening and recording device to the outside of the public telephone booth from which he had placed his calls. In affirming his conviction, the Court of Appeals rejected the contention that the recordings had been obtained in violation of the Fourth Amendment, because "[t]here was no physical entrance into the area occupied by [the petitioner]." We granted certiorari in order to consider the constitutional questions thus presented.

The petitioner has phrased those questions as follows:

A. Whether a public telephone booth is a constitutionally protected area so that evidence obtained by attaching an electronic listening recording device to the top of such a booth is obtained in violation of the right to privacy of the user of the booth.

B. Whether physical penetration of a constitutionally protected area is necessary before a search and seizure can be said to be violative of the Fourth Amendment to the United States Constitution.

We decline to adopt this formulation of the issues. In the first place, the correct solution of Fourth Amendment problems is not necessarily promoted by incantation of the phrase "constitutionally protected area." Secondly, the Fourth Amendment cannot be translated into a general constitutional "right to privacy." That Amendment protects individual privacy against certain kinds of governmental intrusion, but its protections go further, and often have nothing to do with privacy at all.[4] Other provisions of the Constitution protect personal privacy from other forms of

---

4. "The average man would very likely not have his feelings soothed any more by having his property seized openly than by having it seized privately and by stealth .... And a person can be just as much, if not more, irritated, annoyed and injured by an unceremonious public arrest by a policeman as he is by a seizure in the privacy of his office or home." *Griswold v. State of Connecticut*, 381 U.S. 479, 509, 85 S. Ct. 1678, 1695, 14 L. Ed. 2d 510 (dissenting opinion of MR. JUSTICE BLACK).

governmental invasion.[5] But the protection of a person's *general* right to privacy — his right to be let alone by other people — is, like the protection of his property and of his very life, left largely to the law of the individual States.

Because of the misleading way the issues have been formulated, the parties have attached great significance to the characterization of the telephone booth from which the petitioner placed his calls. The petitioner has strenuously argued that the booth was a "constitutionally protected area." The Government has maintained with equal vigor that it was not. But this effort to decide whether or not a given "area," viewed in the abstract, is "constitutionally protected" deflects attention from the problem presented by this case. For the Fourth Amendment protects people, not places. What a person knowingly exposes to the public, even in his own home or office, is not a subject of Fourth Amendment protection. But what he seeks to preserve as private, even in an area accessible to the public, may be constitutionally protected.

The Government stresses the fact that the telephone booth from which the petitioner made his calls was constructed partly of glass, so that he was as visible after he entered it as he would have been if he had remained outside. But what he sought to exclude when he entered the booth was not the intruding eye — it was the uninvited ear. He did not shed his right to do so simply because he made his calls from a place where he might be seen. No less than an individual in a business office, in a friend's apartment, or in a taxicab, a person in a telephone booth may rely upon the protection of the Fourth Amendment. One who occupies it, shuts the door behind him, and pays the toll that permits him to place a call is surely entitled to assume that the words he utters into the mouthpiece will not be broadcast to the world. To read the Constitution more narrowly is to ignore the vital role that the public telephone has come to play in private communication.

The Government contends, however, that the activities of its agents in this case should not be tested by Fourth Amendment requirements, for the surveillance technique they employed involved no physical penetration of the telephone booth from which the petitioner placed his calls. It is true that the absence of such penetration was at one time thought to foreclose further Fourth Amendment inquiry, [citing *Olmstead* and *Goldman*], for that Amendment was thought to limit only searches and seizures of tangible property. But "[t]he premise that property interests control the right of the Government to search and seize has been discredited." *Warden v. Hayden*, 387 U.S. 294, 304. Thus, although a closely divided Court supposed in

---

5. The First Amendment, for example, imposes limitations upon governmental abridgment of "freedom to associate and privacy in one's associations." *NAACP v. Alabama*, 357 U.S. 449, 462, 78 S. Ct. 1163, 1172, 2 L. Ed. 2d 1488. The Third Amendment's prohibition against the unconsented peacetime quartering of soldiers protects another aspect of privacy from governmental intrusion. To some extent, the Fifth Amendment too "reflects the Constitution's concern for" the right of each individual "to a private enclave where he may lead a private life." *Tehan v. Shott*, 382 U.S. 406, 416, 86 S. Ct. 459, 465, 15 L. Ed. 2d 453. Virtually every governmental action interferes with personal privacy to some degree. The question in each case is whether that interference violates a command of the United States Constitution.

Olmstead that surveillance without any trespass and without the seizure of any material object fell outside the ambit of the Constitution, we have since departed from the narrow view on which that decision rested. Indeed, we have expressly held that the Fourth Amendment governs not only the seizure of tangible items, but extends as well to the recording of oral statements, overheard without any "technical trespass under . . . local property law." *Silverman v. United States*, 365 U.S. 505, 511, 81 S. Ct. 679, 682, 5 L. Ed. 2d 734. Once this much is acknowledged, and once it is recognized that the Fourth Amendment protects people — and not simply "areas" — against unreasonable searches and seizures, it becomes clear that the reach of that Amendment cannot turn upon the presence or absence of a physical intrusion into any given enclosure.

We conclude that the underpinnings of *Olmstead* and *Goldman* have been so eroded by our subsequent decisions that the "trespass" doctrine there enunciated can no longer be regarded as controlling. The Government's activities in electronically listening to and recording the petitioner's words violated the privacy upon which he justifiably relied while using the telephone booth and thus constituted a "search and seizure" within the meaning of the Fourth Amendment. The fact that the electronic device employed to achieve that end did not happen to penetrate the wall of the booth can have no constitutional significance.

[The Court then proceeded to the next stage of Fourth Amendment analysis and concluded that Mr. Katz had been searched unreasonably.]

[The concurrence of Justice Douglas is omitted.]

Mr. Justice Harlan, concurring.

I join the opinion of the Court, which I read to hold only (a) that an enclosed telephone booth is an area where, like a home, and unlike a field, a person has a constitutionally protected reasonable expectation of privacy; (b) that electronic as well as physical intrusion into a place that is in this sense private may constitute a violation of the Fourth Amendment; and (c) that the invasion of a constitutionally protected area by federal authorities is, as the Court has long held, presumptively unreasonable in the absence of a search warrant.

As the Court's opinion states, "the Fourth Amendment protects people, not places." The question, however, is what protection it affords to those people. Generally, as here, the answer to that question requires reference to a "place." My understanding of the rule that has emerged from prior decisions is that there is a twofold requirement, first that a person have exhibited an actual (subjective) expectation of privacy and, second, that the expectation be one that society is prepared to recognize as "reasonable." Thus a man's home is, for most purposes, a place where he expects privacy, but objects, activities, or statements that he exposes to the "plain view" of outsiders are not "protected" because no intention to keep them to himself has been exhibited. On the other hand, conversations in the open would not be protected against being overheard, for the expectation of privacy under the circumstances would be unreasonable.

The critical fact in this case is that "[o]ne who occupies it [a telephone booth], shuts the door behind him, and pays the toll that permits him to place a call is surely entitled to assume" that his conversation is not being intercepted. The point is not that the booth is "accessible to the public" at other times, but that it is a temporarily private place whose momentary occupants' expectations of freedom from intrusion are recognized as reasonable.

In *Silverman v. United States*, 365 U.S. 505, we held that eavesdropping accomplished by means of an electronic device that penetrated the premises occupied by petitioner was a violation of the Fourth Amendment. That case established that interception of conversations reasonably intended to be private could constitute a "search and seizure," and that the examination or taking of physical property was not required. In *Silverman* we found it unnecessary to re-examine *Goldman v. United States*, 316 U.S. 129, which had held that electronic surveillance accomplished without the physical penetration of petitioner's premises by a tangible object did not violate the Fourth Amendment. This case requires us to reconsider *Goldman*, and I agree that it should now be overruled. Its limitation on Fourth Amendment protection is, in the present day, bad physics as well as bad law, for reasonable expectations of privacy may be defeated by electronic as well as physical invasion.

. . . .

[The concurrence of JUSTICE WHITE is omitted.]

MR. JUSTICE BLACK, dissenting.

. . . .

My basic objection is twofold: (1) I do not believe that the words of the [Fourth] Amendment will bear the meaning given them by today's decision, and (2) I do not believe that it is the proper role of this Court to rewrite the Amendment in order "to bring it into harmony with the times" and thus reach a result that many people believe to be desirable.

While I realize that an argument based on the meaning of words lacks the scope, and no doubt the appeal, of broad policy discussions and philosophical discourses on such nebulous subjects as privacy, for me the language of the Amendment is the crucial place to look in construing a written document such as our Constitution . . . . The first clause [of the Fourth Amendment] protects "persons, houses, papers, and effects, against unreasonable searches and seizures . . . ." These words connote the idea of tangible things with size, form, and weight, things capable of being searched, seized, or both. The second clause of the Amendment still further establishes its Framers' purpose to limit its protection to tangible things by providing that no warrants shall issue but those "particularly describing the place to be searched, and the persons or things to be seized." A conversation overheard by eavesdropping, whether by plain snooping or wiretapping, is not tangible and, under the normally accepted meanings of the words, can neither be searched nor seized. In addition the language of the second clause indicates that the Amendment refers not only to something tangible so it can be seized but to something already in existence so it can be described. Yet the Court's interpretation would have the Amendment apply to over-hearing future conversations which by their very nature are nonexistent until they take place . . . . Rather than using language in a completely artificial way, I must conclude that the Fourth Amendment simply does not apply to eavesdropping.

Tapping telephone wires, of course, was an unknown possibility at the time the Fourth Amendment was adopted. But eavesdropping (and wiretapping is nothing more than eavesdropping by telephone) was . . . "an ancient practice which at com-mon law was condemned as a nuisance. IV Blackstone, COMMENTARIES § 168. In those days, the eavesdropper listened by naked ear under the eaves of houses or their windows, or beyond their walls seeking out private discourse." [Berger,] 388 U.S., at 45. There can be no doubt that the Framers were aware of this practice, and if they had desired to outlaw or restrict the use of evidence obtained by eavesdropping, I believe that they would have used the appropriate language to do so in the Fourth Amendment . . . . Under these circumstances it strikes me as a charge against their scholarship, their common sense and their candor to give to the Fourth Amend-ment's language the eavesdropping meaning the Court imputes to it today.

. . . The Fourth Amendment was aimed directly at the abhorred practice of breaking in, ransacking and searching homes and other buildings and seizing people's personal belongings without warrants issued by magistrates. The Amend-ment deserves, and this Court has given it, a liberal construction in order to protect against warrantless searches of buildings and seizures of tangible personal effects. But until today this Court has refused to say that eavesdropping comes within the ambit of Fourth Amendment restrictions.

   . . . .

Since I see no way in which the words of the Fourth Amendment can be con-strued to apply to eavesdropping, that closes the matter for me. In interpreting the Bill of Rights, I willingly go as far as a liberal construction of the language takes me, but I simply cannot in good conscience give a meaning to words which they have never before been thought to have and which they certainly do not have in common ordinary usage. I will not distort the words of the Amendment in order to "keep the Constitution up to date" or "to bring it into harmony with the times." It was never meant that this Court have such power, which in effect would make us a continu-ously functioning constitutional convention.

With this decision the Court has completed, I hope, its rewriting of the Fourth Amendment, which started only recently when the Court began referring inces-santly to the Fourth Amendment not so much as a law against *unreasonable* searches and seizures as one to protect an individual's privacy. By clever word juggling the Court finds it plausible to argue that language aimed specifically at searches and seizures of things that can be searched and seized may, to protect privacy, be applied to eavesdropped evidence of conversations that can neither be searched nor seized. Few things happen to an individual that do not affect his privacy in one way or an-other. Thus, by arbitrarily substituting the Court's language, designed to protect privacy, for the Constitution's language, designed to protect against unreasonable searches and seizures, the Court has made the Fourth Amendment its vehicle for holding all laws violative of the Constitution which offend the Court's broadest concept of privacy. As I said in *Griswold v. Connecticut*, 381 U.S. 479, "The Court talks about a constitutional 'right of privacy' as though there is some constitutional provision or provisions forbidding any law ever to be passed which might abridge the 'privacy' of individuals. But there is not." (Dissenting opinion, at 508.) I made clear in that dissent my fear of the dangers involved when this Court uses the "broad, abstract and ambiguous concept" of "privacy" as a "comprehensive substitute for the Fourth Amendment's guarantee against 'unreasonable searches and seizures.'" (See generally dissenting opinion, at 507–527.)

The Fourth Amendment protects privacy only to the extent that it prohibits unreasonable searches and seizures of "persons, houses, papers, and effects." No general right is created by the Amendment so as to give this Court the unlimited power to hold unconstitutional everything which affects privacy . . . .

For these reasons I respectfully dissent.

Notes and Questions

(1) The Court acknowledged that its pre-*Katz* doctrine had required a physical intrusion or trespass into a "constitutionally protected area." Why might this factor have been deemed an appropriate determinant of Fourth Amendment coverage? Why did the *Katz* Court reject that criterion and hold that the protections of the Fourth Amendment could be triggered in the absence of physical intrusion? With what criterion did the Court replace the "intrusion" requirement?

(2) The dissent reflects a fundamentally different approach to the threshold issue. How does Justice Black's view of constitutional interpretation differ from the majority's?

(a) Justice Black complained that the majority's approach to electronic eavesdropping was wholly inconsistent with the words of the Fourth Amendment and ignored the historical impetus for its adoption. The majority did not answer those challenges directly. What plausible constitutional responses might have been made?

(b) Is it fair to accuse the *Katz* majority of rewriting the Constitution to suit changeable, modern notions of desirable individual rights and undesirable law enforcement practices?

(3) The *Katz* majority dealt a decisive blow to the *Olmstead* decision's threshold requirement of a physical intrusion into a constitutionally protected area. In its place, the Court proffered a relatively rudimentary and unquestionably vague standard for discerning searches. Most of the remaining cases in this chapter reflect the Supreme Court's attempts to flesh out and clarify that standard.

United States v. White

United States Supreme Court

401 U.S. 745, 91 S. Ct. 1122, 28 L. Ed. 2d 453 (1971)

Mr. Justice White announced the judgment of the Court and an opinion in which The Chief Justice, Mr. Justice Stewart, and Mr. Justice Blackmun join.

In 1966, respondent James A. White was tried and convicted under two consolidated indictments charging various illegal transactions in narcotics. He was fined and sentenced as a second offender to 25-year concurrent sentences. The issue before us is whether the Fourth Amendment bars from evidence the testimony of governmental agents who related certain conversations which had occurred between defendant White and a government informant, Harvey Jackson, and which the agents overheard by monitoring the frequency of a radio transmitter carried by Jackson and concealed on his person. On four occasions the conversations took place in Jackson's home; each of these conversations was overheard by an agent concealed in a kitchen closet with Jackson's consent and by a second agent outside the house using a radio receiver. Four other conversations — one in respondent's home, one in a restaurant, and two in Jackson's car — were overheard by the use of radio equipment. The prosecution was unable to locate and produce Jackson at the trial and the trial court overruled objections to the testimony of the agents who conducted the electronic surveillance. The jury returned a guilty verdict and defendant appealed . . . .

I

. . . .

Katz v. United States finally swept away doctrines that electronic eavesdropping is permissible under the Fourth Amendment unless physical invasion of a constitutionally protected area produced the challenged evidence . . . . [T]he Court overruled *Olmstead* and *Goldman* and held that the absence of physical intrusion into the telephone booth did not justify using electronic devices in listening to and recording Katz'[s] words, thereby violating the privacy on which he justifiably relied while using the telephone in those circumstances.

The Court of Appeals understood *Katz* to render inadmissible against White the agents' testimony concerning conversations that Jackson broadcast to them. We cannot agree. *Katz* involved no revelation to the Government by a party to conversations with the defendant nor did the Court indicate in any way that a defendant has a justifiable and constitutionally protected expectation that a person with whom he is conversing will not then or later reveal the conversation to the police.

Hoffa v. United States, 385 U.S. 293, 87 S. Ct. 408, 17 L. Ed. 2d 374 (1966), which was left undisturbed by *Katz*, held that however strongly a defendant may trust an apparent colleague, his expectations in this respect are not protected by the Fourth Amendment when it turns out that the colleague is a government agent regularly communicating with the authorities. In these circumstances, "no interest legitimately protected by the Fourth Amendment is involved," for that amendment affords no protection to "a wrongdoer's misplaced belief that a person to whom he voluntarily confides his wrongdoing will not reveal it." *Hoffa v. United States*, at 302. No warrant to "search and seize" is required in such circumstances, nor is it when the Government sends to defendant's home a secret agent who conceals his identity and makes a purchase of narcotics from the accused, *Lewis v. United States*, 385 U.S. 206, 87 S. Ct. 424, 17 L. Ed. 2d 312 (1966), or when the same agent, unbeknown to the defendant, carries electronic equipment to record the defendant's words and the evidence so gathered is later offered in evidence. *Lopez v. United States*, 373 U.S. 427, 83 S. Ct. 1381, 10 L. Ed. 2d 462 (1963).

Conceding that *Hoffa, Lewis*, and *Lopez* remained unaffected by *Katz*, the Court of Appeals nevertheless read both *Katz* and the Fourth Amendment to require a different result if the agent not only records his conversations with the defendant but instantaneously transmits them electronically to other agents equipped with radio receivers. Where this occurs, the Court of Appeals held, the Fourth Amendment is violated and the testimony of the listening agents must be excluded from evidence.

To reach this result it was necessary for the Court of Appeals to hold that *On Lee v. United States* was no longer good law. In that case, which involved facts very similar to the case before us, the Court first rejected claims of a Fourth Amendment violation because the informer had not trespassed when he entered the defendant's premises and conversed with him. To this extent the Court's rationale cannot survive *Katz. See* 389 U.S., at 352–353. But the Court announced a second and independent ground for its decision; for it went on to say that overruling *Olmstead* and *Goldman* would be of no aid to On Lee since he "was talking confidentially and indiscreetly with one he trusted, and he was overheard . . . . It would be a dubious service to the genuine liberties protected by the Fourth Amendment to make them bedfellows with spurious liberties improvised by farfetched analogies which would liken eavesdropping on a conversation, with the connivance of one of the parties, to an unreasonable search or seizure. We find no violation of the Fourth Amendment here." 343 U.S., at 753–754, 72 S. Ct., at 972. We see no indication in *Katz* that the Court meant to disturb that understanding of the Fourth Amendment or to disturb the result reached in the *On Lee* case, nor are we now inclined to overturn this view of the Fourth Amendment.

Concededly a police agent who conceals his police connections may write down for official use his conversations with a defendant and testify concerning them, without a warrant authorizing his encounters with the defendant and without otherwise violating the latter's Fourth Amendment rights. *Hoffa v. United States*, 385 U.S., at 300–303. For constitutional purposes, no different result is required if the agent, instead of immediately reporting and transcribing his conversations with defendant, either (1) simultaneously records them with electronic equipment which he is carrying on his person, *Lopez v. United States, supra*; (2) or carries radio equipment which simultaneously transmits the conversations either to recording equipment located elsewhere or to other agents monitoring the transmitting frequency. *On Lee v. United States, supra.* If the conduct and revelations of an agent operating without electronic equipment do not invade the defendant's constitutionally justifiable expectations of privacy, neither does a simultaneous recording of the same conversations made by the agent or by others from transmissions received from the agent to whom the defendant is talking and whose trustworthiness the defendant necessarily risks.

Our problem is not what the privacy expectations of particular defendants in particular situations may be or the extent to which they may in fact have relied on the discretion of their companions. Very probably, individual defendants neither know nor suspect that their colleagues have gone or will go to the police or are carrying recorders or transmitters. Otherwise, conversation would cease and our problem with these encounters would be nonexistent or far different from those now before us. Our problem, in terms of the principles announced in *Katz*, is what expectations of privacy are constitutionally "justifiable"—what expectations the Fourth Amendment will protect in the absence of a warrant. So far, the law permits the frustration of actual expectations of privacy by permitting authorities to use the testimony of those associates who for one reason or another have determined to turn to the police, as well as by authorizing the use of informants in the manner exemplified by *Hoffa* and *Lewis*. If the law gives no protection to the wrongdoer whose trusted accomplice is or becomes a police agent, neither should it protect him when that same agent has recorded or transmitted the conversations which are later offered in evidence to prove the State's case. *See Lopez v. United States*, 373 U.S. 427, 83 S. Ct. 1381, 10 L. Ed. 2d 462 (1963).

Inescapably, one contemplating illegal activities must realize and risk that his companions may be reporting to the police. If he sufficiently doubts their trustworthiness, the association will very probably end or never materialize. But if he has no doubts, or allays them, or risks what doubt he has, the risk is his. In terms of what his course will be, what he will or will not do or say, we are unpersuaded that he would distinguish between probable informers on the one hand and probable informers with transmitters on the other. Given the possibility or probability that one of his colleagues is cooperating with the police, it is only speculation to assert that the defendant's utterances would be substantially different or his sense of security any less if he also thought it possible that the suspected colleague is wired for sound. At least there is no persuasive evidence that the difference in this respect between the electronically equipped and the unequipped agent is substantial enough to require discrete constitutional recognition, particularly under the Fourth Amendment which is ruled by fluid concepts of "reasonableness."

Nor should we be too ready to erect constitutional barriers to relevant and probative evidence which is also accurate and reliable. An electronic recording will many times produce a more reliable rendition of what a defendant has said than will the unaided memory of a police agent. It may also be that with the recording in existence it is less likely that the informant will change his mind, less chance that threat or injury will suppress unfavorable evidence and less chance that cross-examination will confound the testimony. Considerations like these obviously do not favor the defendant, but we are not prepared to hold that a defendant who has no constitutional right to exclude the informer's unaided testimony nevertheless has a Fourth Amendment privilege against a more accurate version of the events in question.

It is thus untenable to consider the activities and reports of the police agent himself, though acting without a warrant, to be a "reasonable" investigative effort and lawful under the Fourth Amendment but to view the same agent with a recorder or transmitter as conducting an "unreasonable" and unconstitutional search and seizure.

. . . .

The judgment of the Court of Appeals is reversed.

It is so ordered.

[Justice Black concurred for the reasons set forth in his *Katz* dissent.]

[Justice Brennan concurred in the result. The dissent of Justice Douglas is omitted.]

Mr. Justice Harlan, dissenting.

. . . .

II

. . . .

A

On Lee involved circumstances virtually identical to those now before us. There, Government agents enlisted the services of Chin Poy, a former friend of Lee, who was suspected of engaging in illegal narcotics traffic. Poy was equipped with a "minifon" transmitting device which enabled outside Government agents to monitor Poy's conversations with Lee. In the privacy of his laundry, Lee made damaging admissions to Poy which were overheard by the agents and later related at trial. Poy did not testify . . . . [T]he Court concluded that in the absence of a trespass, no constitutional violation had occurred.

The validity of the trespass rationale was questionable even at the time the decision was rendered . . . .

It is, of course, true that the opinion in *On Lee* drew some support from a brief additional assertion that "eavesdropping on a conversation, with the connivance of one of the parties" raises no Fourth Amendment problem. 343 U.S., at 754. But surely it is a misreading of that opinion to view this unelaborated assertion as a wholly independent ground for decision. At the very least, this rationale needs substantial buttressing if it is to persist in our constitutional jurisprudence.

. . . .

III

A

That the foundations of *On Lee* have been destroyed does not, of course, mean that its result can no longer stand. Indeed, the plurality opinion today fastens upon our decisions in *Lopez, Lewis v. United States*, 385 U.S. 206, 87 S. Ct. 424, 17 L. Ed. 2d 312 (1966), and *Hoffa v. United States*, 385 U.S. 293, 87 S. Ct. 408, 17 L. Ed. 2d 374 (1966), to resist the undercurrents of more recent cases emphasizing the warrant procedure as a safeguard to privacy. But this category provides insufficient support. In each of these cases the risk the general populace faced was different from that surfaced by the instant case. No surreptitious third ear was present, and in each opinion that fact was carefully noted.

. . . .

The plurality opinion seeks to erase the crucial distinction between the facts before us and these holdings by the following reasoning: if A can relay verbally what is revealed to him by B (as in *Lewis* and *Hoffa*), or record and later divulge it (as in *Lopez*), what difference does it make if A conspires with another to betray B by contemporaneously transmitting to the other all that is said? The contention is, in essence, an argument that the distinction between third-party monitoring and *other* undercover techniques is one of form and not substance. The force of the contention depends on the evaluation of two separable but intertwined assumptions: first, that there is no greater invasion of privacy in the third-party situation, and, second, that uncontrolled consensual surveillance in an electronic age is a tolerable technique of law enforcement, given the values and goals of our political system.

The first of these assumptions takes as a point of departure the so-called "risk analysis" approach of *Lewis*, and *Lopez*, and to a lesser extent *On Lee*, or the expectations approach of *Katz*. While these formulations represent an advance over the unsophisticated trespass analysis of the common law, they too have their limitations and can, ultimately, lead to the substitution of words for analysis. The analysis must, in my view, transcend the search for subjective expectations or legal attribution of assumptions of risk. Our expectations, and the risks we assume, are in large part reflections of laws that translate into rules the customs and values of the past and present.

Since it is the task of the law to form and project, as well as mirror and reflect, we should not, as judges, merely recite the expectations and risks without examining the desirability of saddling them upon society. The critical question, therefore, is whether under our system of government, as reflected in the Constitution, we should impose on our citizens the risks of the electronic listener or observer without at least the protection of a warrant requirement.

This question must, in my view, be answered by assessing the nature of a particular practice and the likely extent of its impact on the individual's sense of security balanced against the utility of the conduct as a technique of law enforcement. For those more extensive intrusions that significantly jeopardize the sense of security which is the paramount concern of Fourth Amendment liberties, I am of the view that more than self-restraint by law enforcement officials is required and at the least warrants should be necessary.

B

The impact of the practice of third-party bugging, must, I think, be considered such as to undermine that confidence and sense of security in dealing with one another that is characteristic of individual relationships between citizens in a free society. It goes beyond the impact on privacy occasioned by the ordinary type of "informer" investigation upheld in *Lewis* and *Hoffa*. The argument of the plurality opinion, to the effect that it is irrelevant whether secrets are revealed by the mere tattletale or the transistor, ignores the differences occasioned by third-party monitoring and recording which insures full and accurate disclosure of all that is said, free of the possibility of error and oversight that inheres in human reporting.

Authority is hardly required to support the proposition that words would be measured a good deal more carefully and communication inhibited if one suspected his conversations were being transmitted and transcribed. Were third-party bugging a prevalent practice, it might well smother that spontaneity — reflected in frivolous, impetuous, sacrilegious, and defiant discourse — that liberates daily life. Much offhand exchange is easily forgotten and one may count on the obscurity of his remarks, protected by the very fact of a limited audience, and the likelihood that the listener will either overlook or forget what is said, as well as the listener's inability to reformulate a conversation without having to contend with a documented record. All these values are sacrificed by a rule of law that permits official monitoring of private discourse limited only by the need to locate a willing assistant.

. . . .

The interest *On Lee* fails to protect is the expectation of the ordinary citizen, who has never engaged in illegal conduct in his life, that he may carry on his private discourse freely, openly, and spontaneously without measuring his every word against the connotations it might carry when instantaneously heard by others unknown to him and unfamiliar with his situation or analyzed in a cold, formal record played days, months, or years after the conversation. Interposition of a warrant requirement is designed not to shield "wrongdoers," but to secure a measure of privacy and a sense of personal security throughout our society.

The Fourth Amendment does, of course, leave room for the employment of modern technology in criminal law enforcement, but in the stream of current developments in Fourth Amendment law I think it must be held that third-party electronic monitoring, subject only to the self-restraint of law enforcement officials, has no place in our society.

IV

. . . .

What this means is that the burden of guarding privacy in a free society should not be on its citizens; it is the Government that must justify its need to electronically eavesdrop.

. . . .

I would hold that *On Lee* is no longer good law and affirm the judgment below.

[The dissent of Justice Marshall is omitted.]

Notes and Questions

(1) In *Katz*, the government's electronic listening was deemed a "search." In *White*, similar electronic surveillance was not. What was the critical factual distinction between the electronic surveillance in *Katz* and that in *White*? Why should that distinction make a constitutional difference?

(2) Both Katz and White probably had the same basic expectations regarding the privacy of their conversations. Katz's expectations were constitutionally protected, while White's were not. In light of both *Katz* and *White*, what expectations concerning the privacy of our conversations with others are sheltered by the Fourth Amendment? What expectations are not protected? As a constitutional matter, what risks do we assume in conversing with others?

(3) In dissent, Justice Harlan was concerned that "communication" would be "inhibited," that "spontaneity" might be "smother[ed]," and that the "security" of "individual relationships between citizens" would be "undermine[d]." Should the Fourth Amendment be concerned with potential threats to free speech and association? Why?

Smith v. Maryland

United States Supreme Court

442 U.S. 735, 99 S. Ct. 2577, 61 L. Ed. 2d 220 (1979)

Mr. Justice Blackmun delivered the opinion of the Court.

This case presents the question whether the installation and use of a pen register[1] constitutes a "search" within the meaning of the Fourth Amendment, made applicable to the States through the Fourteenth Amendment. *Mapp v. Ohio*, 367 U.S. 643, 81 S. Ct. 1684, 6 L. Ed. 2d 1081 (1961).

I

On March 5, 1976, in Baltimore, Md., Patricia McDonough was robbed. She gave the police a description of the robber and of a 1975 Monte Carlo automobile she had observed near the scene of the crime. After the robbery, McDonough began receiving threatening and obscene phone calls from a man identifying himself as the robber.

---

1. A pen register is a mechanical device that records the numbers dialed on a telephone by monitoring the electrical impulses caused when the dial on the telephone is released. It does not overhear oral communications and does not indicate whether calls are actually completed. *United States v. New York Tel. Co.*, 434 U.S. 159, 161 n. 1, 98 S. Ct. 364, 366 n. 1, 54 L. Ed. 2d 376 (1977). A pen register is "usually installed at a central telephone facility [and] records on a paper tape all numbers dialed from [the] line" to which it is attached. *United States v. Giordano*, 416 U.S. 505, 549 n. 1, 94 S. Ct. 1820, 1842 n. 1, 40 L. Ed. 2d 341 (1974) (opinion concurring in part and dissenting in part).

On one occasion, the caller asked that she step out on her front porch; she did so, and saw the 1975 Monte Carlo she had earlier described to police moving slowly past her home. On March 16, police spotted a man who met McDonough's description driving a 1975 Monte Carlo in her neighborhood. By tracing the license plate number, police learned that the car was registered in the name of petitioner, Michael Lee Smith.

The next day, the telephone company, at police request, installed a pen register at its central offices to record the numbers dialed from the telephone at petitioner's home. The police did not get a warrant or court order before having the pen register installed. The register revealed that on March 17 a call was placed from petitioner's home to McDonough's phone. On the basis of this and other evidence, the police obtained a warrant to search petitioner's residence. The search revealed that a page in petitioner's phone book was turned down to the name and number of Patricia McDonough; the phone book was seized. Petitioner was arrested, and a six-man lineup was held on March 19. McDonough identified petitioner as the man who had robbed her.

Petitioner was indicted in the Criminal Court of Baltimore for robbery. By pre-trial motion, he sought to suppress "all fruits derived from the pen register" on the ground that the police had failed to secure a warrant prior to its installation. The trial court denied the suppression motion, holding that the warrantless installation of the pen register did not violate the Fourth Amendment. Petitioner then waived a jury, and the case was submitted to the court on an agreed statement of facts. The pen register tape (evidencing the fact that a phone call had been made from petitioner's phone to McDonough's phone) and the phone book seized in the search of petitioner's residence were admitted into evidence against him. Petitioner was convicted and was sentenced to six years.

. . . .

II
A

The Fourth Amendment guarantees "[t]he right of the people to be secure in their persons, houses, papers, and effects, against unreasonable searches and seizures." In determining whether a particular form of government-initiated electronic surveillance is a "search" within the meaning of the Fourth Amendment,[4] our lodestar is *Katz v. United States*, 389 U.S. 347 (1967).

. . . .

---

4. In this case, the pen register was installed, and the numbers dialed were recorded, by the telephone company. The telephone company, however, acted at police request. In view of this, respondent appears to concede that the company is to be deemed an "agent" of the police for purposes of this case, so as to render the installation and use of the pen register "state action" under the Fourth and Fourteenth Amendments. We may assume that "state action" was present here.

Consistently with *Katz*, this Court uniformly has held that the application of the Fourth Amendment depends on whether the person invoking its protection can claim a "justifiable," a "reasonable," or a "legitimate expectation of privacy" that has been invaded by government action. This inquiry, as Mr. Justice Harlan aptly noted in his *Katz* concurrence, normally embraces two discrete questions. The first is whether the individual, by his conduct, has "exhibited an actual [subjective] expectation of privacy," 389 U.S., at 361 — whether, in the words of the *Katz* majority, the individual has shown that "he seeks to preserve [something] as private." *Id.*, at 351. The second question is whether the individual's subjective expectation of privacy is "one that society is prepared to recognize as 'reasonable,'" *id.*, at 361 — whether, in the words of the *Katz* majority, the individual's expectation, viewed objectively, is "justifiable" under the circumstances. *Id.*, at 353.[5]

B

In applying the *Katz* analysis to this case, it is important to begin by specifying precisely the nature of the state activity that is challenged. The activity here took the form of installing and using a pen register. Since the pen register was installed on telephone company property at the telephone company's central offices, petitioner obviously cannot claim that his "property" was invaded or that police intruded into a "constitutionally protected area." Petitioner's claim, rather, is that, notwithstanding the absence of a trespass, the State, as did the Government in *Katz*, infringed a "legitimate expectation of privacy" that petitioner held. Yet a pen register differs significantly from the listening device employed in *Katz*, for pen registers do not acquire the *contents* of communications. This Court recently noted:

> Indeed, a law enforcement official could not even determine from the use of a pen register whether a communication existed. These devices do not hear sound. They disclose only the telephone numbers that have been dialed — a means of establishing communication. Neither the purport of any communication between the caller and the recipient of the call, their identities, nor whether the call was even completed is disclosed by pen registers.

United States v. New York Tel. Co., 434 U.S. 159, 167, 98 S. Ct. 364, 369, 54 L. Ed. 2d 376 (1977). Given a pen register's limited capabilities, therefore, petitioner's argument

---

5. Situations can be imagined, of course, in which *Katz's* two-pronged inquiry would provide an inadequate index of Fourth Amendment protection. For example, if the Government were suddenly to announce on nationwide television that all homes henceforth would be subject to warrantless entry, individuals thereafter might not in fact entertain any actual expectation of privacy regarding their homes, papers, and effects. Similarly, if a refugee from a totalitarian country, unaware of this Nation's traditions, erroneously assumed that police were continuously monitoring his telephone conversations, a subjective expectation of privacy regarding the contents of his calls might be lacking as well. In such circumstances, where an individual's subjective expectations had been "conditioned" by influences alien to well-recognized Fourth Amendment freedoms, those subjective expectations obviously could play no meaningful role in ascertaining what the scope of Fourth Amendment protection was. In determining whether a "legitimate expectation of privacy" existed in such cases, a normative inquiry would be proper.

that its installation and use constituted a "search" necessarily rests upon a claim that he had a "legitimate expectation of privacy" regarding the numbers he dialed on his phone.

This claim must be rejected. First, we doubt that people in general entertain any actual expectation of privacy in the numbers they dial. All telephone users realize that they must "convey" phone numbers to the telephone company, since it is through telephone company switching equipment that their calls are completed. All subscribers realize, moreover, that the phone company has facilities for making permanent records of the numbers they dial, for they see a list of their long-distance (toll) calls on their monthly bills. In fact, pen registers and similar devices are routinely used by telephone companies "for the purposes of checking billing operations, detecting fraud and preventing violations of law." *United States v. New York Tel. Co.*, 434 U.S., at 174–175. Electronic equipment is used not only to keep billing records of toll calls, but also "to keep a record of all calls dialed from a telephone which is subject to a special rate structure." *Hodge v. Mountain States Tel. & Tel. Co.*, 555 F.2d 254, 266 (9th Cir. 1977) (concurring opinion). Pen registers are regularly employed "to determine whether a home phone is being used to conduct a business, to check for a defective dial, or to check for overbilling." Note, *The Legal Constraints Upon the Use of the Pen Register as a Law Enforcement Tool*, 60 Cornell L. Rev. 1028, 1029 (1975) [footnotes omitted]. Although most people may be oblivious to a pen register's esoteric functions, they presumably have some awareness of one common use: to aid in the identification of persons making annoying or obscene calls. *See, e.g., Von Lusch v. C & P Telephone Co.*, 457 F. Supp. 814, 816 (Md. 1978); Note, 60 Cornell L. Rev., at 1029–1030, n. 11; Claerhout, *The Pen Register*, 20 Drake L. Rev. 108, 110–111 (1970). Most phone books tell subscribers, on a page entitled "Consumer Information," that the company "can frequently help in identifying to the authorities the origin of unwelcome and troublesome calls." *E.g.*, Baltimore Telephone Directory 21 (1978); District of Columbia Telephone Directory 13 (1978). Telephone users, in sum, typically know that they must convey numerical information to the phone company; that the phone company has facilities for recording this information; and that the phone company does in fact record this information for a variety of legitimate business purposes. Although subjective expectations cannot be scientifically gauged, it is too much to believe that telephone subscribers, under these circumstances, harbor any general expectation that the numbers they dial will remain secret.

Petitioner argues, however, that, whatever the expectations of telephone users in general, he demonstrated an expectation of privacy by his own conduct here, since he "us[ed] the telephone *in his house* to the exclusion of all others." Brief for Petitioner 6 (emphasis added). But the site of the call is immaterial for purposes of analysis in this case. Although petitioner's conduct may have been calculated to keep the contents of his conversation private, his conduct was not and could not have been calculated to preserve the privacy of the number he dialed. Regardless of his location, petitioner had to convey that number to the telephone company in precisely the same way if he wished to complete his call. The fact that he dialed the number on his home phone rather than on some other phone could make no conceivable difference, nor could any subscriber rationally think that it would.

Second, even if petitioner did harbor some subjective expectation that the phone numbers he dialed would remain private, this expectation is not "one that society is prepared to recognize as 'reasonable.'" *Katz v. United States*, 389 U.S., at 361. This Court consistently has held that a person has no legitimate expectation of privacy in information he voluntarily turns over to third parties. *E.g., United States v. Miller*, 425 U.S., at 442–444; *Couch v. United States*, 409 U.S., at 335–336; [*White, Hoffa,* and *Lopez*]. In *Miller,* for example, the Court held that a bank depositor has no "legitimate 'expectation of privacy'" in financial information "voluntarily conveyed to . . . banks and exposed to their employees in the ordinary course of business." 425 U.S., at 442. The Court explained:

> The depositor takes the risk, in revealing his affairs to another, that the information will be conveyed by that person to the Government . . . . This Court has held repeatedly that the Fourth Amendment does not prohibit the obtaining of information revealed to a third party and conveyed by him to Government authorities, even if the information is revealed on the assumption that it will be used only for a limited purpose and the confidence placed in the third party will not be betrayed.

Id., at 443.

Because the depositor "assumed the risk" of disclosure, the Court held that it would be unreasonable for him to expect his financial records to remain private.

This analysis dictates that petitioner can claim no legitimate expectation of privacy here. When he used his phone, petitioner voluntarily conveyed numerical information to the telephone company and "exposed" that information to its equipment in the ordinary course of business. In so doing, petitioner assumed the risk that the company would reveal to police the numbers he dialed. The switching equipment that processed those numbers is merely the modern counterpart of the operator who, in an earlier day, personally completed calls for the subscriber. Petitioner concedes that if he had placed his calls through an operator, he could claim no legitimate expectation of privacy. We are not inclined to hold that a different constitutional result is required because the telephone company has decided to automate.

 . . . .

We therefore conclude that petitioner in all probability entertained no actual expectation of privacy in the phone numbers he dialed, and that, even if he did, his expectation was not "legitimate." The installation and use of a pen register, consequently, was not a "search," and no warrant was required. The judgment of the Maryland Court of Appeals is affirmed.

It is so ordered.

MR. JUSTICE POWELL took no part in the consideration or decision of this case.

MR. JUSTICE STEWART, with whom MR. JUSTICE BRENNAN joins, dissenting.

I am not persuaded that the numbers dialed from a private telephone fall outside the constitutional protection of the Fourth and Fourteenth Amendments.

In *Katz v. United States*, 389 U.S. 347, 352, 88 S. Ct. 507, 512, 19 L. Ed. 2d 576, the Court acknowledged the "vital role that the public telephone has come to play in private communication[s]." The role played by a private telephone is even more vital, and since *Katz* it has been abundantly clear that telephone conversations carried on by people in their homes or offices are fully protected by the Fourth and Fourteenth Amendments.

. . . .

Nevertheless, the Court today says that those safeguards do not extend to the numbers dialed from a private telephone, apparently because when a caller dials a number the digits may be recorded by the telephone company for billing purposes. But that observation no more than describes the basic nature of telephone calls. A telephone call simply cannot be made without the use of telephone company property and without payment to the company for the service. The telephone conversation itself must be electronically transmitted by telephone company equipment, and may be recorded or overheard by the use of other company equipment. Yet we have squarely held that the user of even a public telephone is entitled "to assume that the words he utters into the mouthpiece will not be broadcast to the world." *Katz v. United States, supra*, 389 U.S., at 352.

The central question in this case is whether a person who makes telephone calls from his home is entitled to make a similar assumption about the numbers he dials. What the telephone company does or might do with those numbers is no more relevant to this inquiry than it would be in a case involving the conversation itself. It is simply not enough to say, after *Katz*, that there is no legitimate expectation of privacy in the numbers dialed because the caller assumes the risk that the telephone company will disclose them to the police.

I think that the numbers dialed from a private telephone — like the conversations that occur during a call — are within the constitutional protection recognized in *Katz*. It seems clear to me that information obtained by pen register surveillance of a private telephone is information in which the telephone subscriber has a legitimate expectation of privacy. The information captured by such surveillance emanates from private conduct within a person's home or office — locations that without question are entitled to Fourth and Fourteenth Amendment protection. Further, that information is an integral part of the telephonic communication that under *Katz* is entitled to constitutional protection, whether or not it is captured by a trespass into such an area.

The numbers dialed from a private telephone — although certainly more prosaic than the conversation itself — are not without "content." Most private telephone subscribers may have their own numbers listed in a publicly distributed directory, but I doubt there are any who would be happy to have broadcast to the world a list of the local or long distance numbers they have called. This is not because such a list might in some sense be incriminating, but because it easily could reveal the identities of the persons and the places called, and thus reveal the most intimate details of a person's life.

I respectfully dissent.

Mr. Justice Marshall, with whom Mr. Justice Brennan joins, dissenting.

. . . .

Applying the standards set forth in *Katz v. United States*, 389 U.S. 347, 361, 88 S. Ct. 507, 516, 19 L. Ed. 2d 576 (1967) (Harlan, J., concurring), the Court first determines that telephone subscribers have no subjective expectations of privacy concerning the numbers they dial. To reach this conclusion, the Court posits that individuals somehow infer from the long-distance listings on their phone bills, and from the cryptic assurances of "help" in tracing obscene calls included in "most" phone books, that pen registers are regularly used for recording local calls. But even assuming, as I do not, that individuals "typically know" that a phone company monitors calls for internal reasons,[1] it does not follow that they expect this information to be made available to the public in general or the government in particular. Privacy is not a discrete commodity, possessed absolutely or not at all. Those who disclose certain facts to a bank or phone company for a limited business purpose need not assume that this information will be released to other persons for other purposes. *See California Bankers Ass'n v. Shultz, supra*, 416 U.S., at 95–96 (Marshall, J., dissenting).

The crux of the Court's holding, however, is that whatever expectation of privacy petitioner may in fact have entertained regarding his calls, it is not one "society is prepared to recognize as 'reasonable.'" In so ruling, the Court determines that individuals who convey information to third parties have "assumed the risk" of disclosure to the government. This analysis is misconceived in two critical respects.

Implicit in the concept of assumption of risk is some notion of choice. At least in the third-party consensual surveillance cases, which first incorporated risk analysis into Fourth Amendment doctrine, the defendant presumably had exercised some discretion in deciding who should enjoy his confidential communications. By contrast here, unless a person is prepared to forgo use of what for many has become a personal or professional necessity, he cannot help but accept the risk of surveillance. *Cf. Lopez v. United States, supra*, 373 U.S., at 465–466 (Brennan, J., dissenting). It is idle to speak of "assuming" risks in contexts where, as a practical matter, individuals have no realistic alternative.

More fundamentally, to make risk analysis dispositive in assessing the reasonableness of privacy expectations would allow the government to define the scope of

---

1. Lacking the Court's apparently exhaustive knowledge of this Nation's telephone books and the reading habits of telephone subscribers, I decline to assume general public awareness of how obscene phone calls are traced. Nor am I persuaded that the scope of Fourth Amendment protection should turn on the concededly "esoteric functions" of pen registers in corporate billing, functions with which subscribers are unlikely to have intimate familiarity.

Fourth Amendment protections. For example, law enforcement officials, simply by announcing their intent to monitor the content of random samples of first-class mail or private phone conversations, could put the public on notice of the risks they would thereafter assume in such communications. *See* Amsterdam, *Perspectives on the Fourth Amendment,* 58 Minn. L. Rev. 349, 384, 407 (1974). Yet, although acknowledging this implication of its analysis, the Court is willing to concede only that, in some circumstances, a further "normative inquiry would be proper." No meaningful effort is made to explain what those circumstances might be, or why this case is not among them.

In my view, whether privacy expectations are legitimate within the meaning of *Katz* depends not on the risks an individual can be presumed to accept when imparting information to third parties, but on the risks he should be forced to assume in a free and open society. By its terms, the constitutional prohibition of unreasonable searches and seizures assigns to the judiciary some prescriptive responsibility. As Mr. Justice Harlan, who formulated the standard the Court applies today, himself recognized: "[s]ince it is the task of the law to form and project, as well as mirror and reflect, we should not . . . merely recite . . . risks without examining the desirability of saddling them upon society." *United States v. White, supra,* 401 U.S. at 786 (dissenting opinion) . . . .

The use of pen registers, I believe, constitutes . . . an extensive intrusion. To hold otherwise ignores the vital role telephonic communication plays in our personal and professional relationships, *see Katz v. United States,* 389 U.S., at 352, as well as the First and Fourth Amendment interests implicated by unfettered official surveillance. Privacy in placing calls is of value not only to those engaged in criminal activity. The prospect of unregulated governmental monitoring will undoubtedly prove disturbing even to those with nothing illicit to hide. Many individuals, including members of unpopular political organizations or journalists with confidential sources, may legitimately wish to avoid disclosure of their personal contacts. Permitting governmental access to telephone records on less than probable cause may thus impede certain forms of political affiliation and journalistic endeavor that are the hallmark of a truly free society. Particularly given the Government's previous reliance on warrantless telephonic surveillance to trace reporters' sources and monitor protected political activity, I am unwilling to insulate use of pen registers from independent judicial review.

Just as one who enters a public telephone booth is "entitled to assume that the words he utters into the mouthpiece will not be broadcast to the world," *Katz v. United States, supra,* 389 U.S., at 352, so too, he should be entitled to assume that the numbers he dials in the privacy of his home will be recorded, if at all, solely for the phone company's business purposes. Accordingly, I would require law enforcement officials to obtain a warrant before they enlist telephone companies to secure information otherwise beyond the government's reach.

Notes and Questions

The majority opinion in *Smith* reflects a significant development of the *Katz* threshold doctrine. Justice Blackmun clearly and unequivocally announced that the Court had adopted as its "lodestar" for Fourth Amendment threshold analysis the standards proposed in Justice Harlan's *Katz* concurrence. He took pains to demonstrate the roots of those standards in the *Katz* majority opinion. He then reasoned that Smith's claim that governmental use of a pen register ought to be regulated by the Fourth Amendment failed to satisfy the Harlan threshold test.

(1) Suppose that Smith had provided convincing evidence that he had always possessed a strong, personal expectation of complete privacy in the content of the numbers he dialed from his home phone. Would the Court's conclusion regarding the first prong of the Harlan test have changed?

(2) How did the Court know that "society" was not prepared to recognize the "reasonableness" of actual expectations regarding the privacy of numbers dialed? If a public opinion poll had revealed that a large majority of citizens would recognize the legitimacy of such an expectation, would the Court's analysis and conclusion have been different?

California v. Ciraolo

United States Supreme Court

476 U.S. 207, 106 S. Ct. 1809, 90 L. Ed. 2d 210 (1986)

CHIEF JUSTICE BURGER delivered the opinion of the Court.

. . . .

On September 2, 1982, Santa Clara Police received an anonymous telephone tip that marijuana was growing in respondent's backyard. Police were unable to observe the contents of respondent's yard from ground level because of a 6-foot outer fence and a 10-foot inner fence completely enclosing the yard. Later that day, Officer Shutz, who was assigned to investigate, secured a private plane and flew over respondent's house at an altitude of 1,000 feet, within navigable airspace; he was accompanied by Officer Rodriguez. Both officers were trained in marijuana identification. From the overflight, the officers readily identified marijuana plants 8 feet to 10 feet in height growing in a 15-by-25 foot plot in respondent's yard; they photographed the area with a standard 35mm camera.

On September 8, 1982, Officer Shutz obtained a search warrant on the basis of an affidavit describing the anonymous tip and their observations; a photograph depicting respondent's house, the backyard, and neighboring homes was attached to the affidavit as an exhibit. The warrant was executed the next day and 73 plants were seized; it is not disputed that these were marijuana.

. . . .

II

The touchstone of Fourth Amendment analysis is whether a person has a "constitutionally protected reasonable expectation of privacy . . . ."

Clearly — and understandably — respondent has met the test of manifesting his own subjective intent and desire to maintain privacy as to his unlawful agricultural pursuits . . . . It can reasonably be assumed that the 10-foot fence was placed to conceal the marijuana crop from at least street level views . . . . Yet a 10-foot fence might not shield these plants from the eyes of a citizen or a policeman perched on the top of a truck or a two-level bus. Whether respondent therefore manifested a subjective expectation of privacy from *all* observations of his backyard, or whether instead he manifested merely a hope that no one would observe his unlawful gardening pursuits, is not entirely clear in these circumstances . . . .

We turn, therefore, to the second inquiry under *Katz, i.e.,* whether that expectation is reasonable. In pursuing this inquiry, we must keep in mind that "[t]he test of legitimacy is not whether the individual chooses to conceal assertedly 'private' activity," but instead "whether the government's intrusion infringes upon the personal and societal values protected by the Fourth Amendment." *Oliver, supra*, 466 U.S., at 181–183.

Respondent argues that because his yard was in the curtilage of his home, no governmental aerial observation is permissible under the Fourth Amendment without a warrant.[11] The history and genesis of the curtilage doctrine is instructive. "At common law, the curtilage is the area to which extends the intimate activity associated with the 'sanctity of a man's home and the privacies of life.'" *Oliver, supra,* 466 U.S., at 180 (quoting *Boyd v. United States,* 116 U.S. 616, 630, 6 S. Ct. 524, 532, 29 L. Ed. 746 (1886)). *See* 4 Blackstone, COMMENTARIES *225. The protection afforded the curtilage is essentially a protection of families and personal privacy in an area intimately linked to the home, both physically and psychologically, where privacy expectations are most heightened. The claimed area here was immediately adjacent to a suburban home, surrounded by high double fences. This close nexus to the home would appear to encompass this small area within the curtilage . . . .

That the area is within the curtilage does not itself bar all police observation. The Fourth Amendment protection of the home has never been extended to require law enforcement officers to shield their eyes when passing by a home on public thoroughfares. Nor does the mere fact that an individual has taken measures to restrict some views of his activities preclude an officer's observations from a public vantage point where he has a right to be and which renders the activities clearly visible. *E.g.,*

---

11. Because the parties framed the issue in the California courts below and in this Court as concerning only the reasonableness of aerial observation generally without raising any distinct issue as to the photograph attached as an exhibit to the affidavit in support of the search warrant, our analysis is similarly circumscribed. It was the officer's observation, not the photograph, that supported the warrant. Officer Shutz testified that the photograph did not identify the marijuana as such because it failed to reveal a "true representation" of the color of the plants: "you have to see it with the naked eye."

United States v. Knotts, 460 U.S. 276, 282, 103 S. Ct. 1081, 1085–1086, 75 L. Ed. 2d 55 (1983). "What a person knowingly exposes to the public, even in his own home or office, is not a subject of Fourth Amendment protection." *Katz, supra*, 389 U.S., at 351.

The observations by Officers Shutz and Rodriguez in this case took place within public navigable airspace . . . in a physically nonintrusive manner; from this point they were able to observe plants readily discernable to the naked eye as marijuana. That the observation from aircraft was directed at identifying the plants and the officers were trained to recognize marijuana is irrelevant. Such observation is precisely what a judicial officer needs to provide a basis for a warrant. Any member of the public flying in this airspace who glanced down could have seen everything that these officers observed. On this record, we readily conclude that respondent's expectation that his garden was protected from such observation is unreasonable and is not an expectation that society is prepared to honor.

The dissent contends that the Court ignores Justice Harlan's warning in his concurrence in *Katz v. United States*, 389 U.S., at 361–362, that the Fourth Amendment should not be limited to proscribing only physical intrusions onto private property. But Justice Harlan's observations about future electronic developments and the potential for electronic interference with private communications, *see Katz, supra*, at 362, 88 S. Ct., at 517, were plainly not aimed at simple visual observations from a public place . . . .

As Justice Harlan emphasized,

> a man's home is, for most purposes, a place where he expects privacy, but objects, activities, or statements that he exposes to the "plain view" of outsiders are not "protected" because no intention to keep them to himself has been exhibited. On the other hand, conversations in the open would not be protected against being overheard, for the expectation of privacy under the circumstances would be unreasonable.

Katz, supra, 389 U.S., at 361.

. . . In an age where private and commercial flight in the public airways is routine, it is unreasonable for respondent to expect that his marijuana plants were constitutionally protected from being observed with the naked eye from an altitude of 1,000 feet. The Fourth Amendment simply does not require the police traveling in the public airways at this altitude to obtain a warrant in order to observe what is visible to the naked eye.

Reversed.

JUSTICE POWELL, with whom JUSTICE BRENNAN, JUSTICE MARSHALL, and JUSTICE BLACKMUN join, dissenting.

Concurring in *Katz v. United States*, 389 U.S. 347, 88 S. Ct. 507, 19 L. Ed. 2d 576 (1967), Justice Harlan warned that any decision to construe the Fourth Amendment as proscribing only physical intrusions by police onto private property "is, in the present day, bad physics as well as bad law, for reasonable expectations of privacy may be defeated by electronic as well as physical invasion." *Id.*, at 362. Because the Court today ignores that warning in an opinion that departs significantly from the standard developed in *Katz* for deciding when a Fourth Amendment violation has occurred, I dissent.

I

As the Court's opinion reflects, the facts of this case are not complicated . . . . In my view, the Court's holding rests on only one obvious fact, namely, that the airspace generally is open to all persons for travel in airplanes. The Court does not explain why this single fact deprives citizens of their privacy interest in outdoor activities in an enclosed curtilage.

II
A

The Fourth Amendment protects "[t]he right of the people to be secure in their persons, houses, papers, and effects, against unreasonable searches and seizures." While the familiar history of the Amendment need not be recounted here, we should remember that it reflects a choice that our society should be one in which citizens "dwell in reasonable security and freedom from surveillance." *Johnson v. United States*, 333 U.S. 10, 14, 68 S. Ct. 367, 369, 92 L. Ed. 436 (1948) . . . .

As the decision in *Katz* held, and dissenting opinions written by Justices of this Court prior to *Katz* recognized, a standard that defines a Fourth Amendment "search" by reference to whether police have physically invaded a "constitutionally protected area" provides no real protection against surveillance techniques made possible through technology. Technological advances have enabled police to see people's activities and associations, and to hear their conversations, without being in physical proximity. Moreover, the capability now exists for police to conduct intrusive surveillance without any physical penetration of the walls of homes or other structures that citizens may believe shelter their privacy. Looking to the Fourth Amendment for protection against such "broad and unsuspected governmental incursions" into the "cherished privacy of law-abiding citizens," *United States v. United States District Court*, 407 U.S., at 312–313 [footnote omitted], the Court in *Katz* abandoned its inquiry into whether police had committed a physical trespass.

. . . .

The second question under *Katz* has been described as asking whether an expectation of privacy is "legitimate in the sense required by the Fourth Amendment." *Oliver v. United States*, 466 U.S. 170, 182, 104 S. Ct. 1735, 1742, 80 L. Ed. 2d 214 (1984). The answer turns on "whether the government's intrusion infringes upon the personal and societal values protected by the Fourth Amendment." *Id.*, at 182–183. While no single consideration has been regarded as dispositive, "the Court has given weight to such factors as the intention of the Framers of the Fourth Amendment, . . . the uses to which the individual has put a location, . . . and our societal understanding that certain areas deserve the most scrupulous protection from government invasion." *Id.*, at 178 [citations omitted]. Our decisions have made clear that this inquiry often must be decided by "reference to a 'place,'" *Katz v. United States, supra*, 389 U.S., at 361 (Harlan, J., concurring); *see Payton v. New York*, 445 U.S., at 589, and that a home is a place in which a subjective expectation of privacy virtually always will be legitimate, *ibid.*; *see, e.g., United States v. Karo*, 468 U.S. 705, 713–715 (1984); *Steagald v. United States*, 451 U.S., at 211–212. "At the very core [of the Fourth Amendment] stands the right of a [person] to retreat into his own home and there be free from unreasonable governmental intrusion." *Silverman v. United States*, 365 U.S. 505, 511, 81 S. Ct. 679, 683, 5 L. Ed. 2d 734 (1961).

B

This case involves surveillance of a home, for as we stated in *Oliver v. United States*, the curtilage "has been considered part of the home itself for Fourth Amendment purposes." 466 U.S., at 180 . . . . [S]ociety accepts as reasonable citizens' expectations of privacy in the area immediately surrounding their homes.

. . . .

III
A

The Court begins its analysis of the Fourth Amendment issue posed here by deciding that respondent had an expectation of privacy in his backyard. I agree with that conclusion because of the close proximity of the yard to the house, the nature of some of the activities respondent conducted there, and because he had taken steps to shield those activities from the view of passersby. The Court then implicitly acknowledges that society is prepared to recognize his expectation as reasonable with respect to ground-level surveillance, holding that the yard was within the curtilage, an area in which privacy interests have been afforded the "most heightened" protection. As the foregoing discussion of the curtilage doctrine demonstrates, respondent's yard unquestionably was within the curtilage. Since Officer Shutz could not see into this private family area from the street, the Court certainly would agree that he would have conducted an unreasonable search had he climbed over the fence, or used a ladder to peer into the yard without first securing a warrant.

The Court concludes, nevertheless, that Shutz could use an airplane—a product of modern technology—to intrude visually into respondent's yard. The Court argues that respondent had no reasonable expectation of privacy from aerial observation. It notes that Shutz was "within public navigable airspace," when he looked into and photographed respondent's yard . . . .

The Court's holding . . . must rest solely on the fact that members of the public fly in planes and may look down at homes as they fly over them. The Court does not explain why it finds this fact to be significant. One may assume that the Court believes that citizens bear the risk that air travelers will observe activities occurring within backyards that are open to the sun and air. This risk, the Court appears to hold, nullifies expectations of privacy in those yards even as to purposeful police surveillance from the air. The Court finds support for this conclusion in *United States v. Knotts*, 460 U.S. 276, 103 S. Ct. 1081, 75 L. Ed. 2d 55 (1983).

This line of reasoning is flawed. First, the actual risk to privacy from commercial or pleasure aircraft is virtually nonexistent. Travelers on commercial flights, as well as private planes used for business or personal reasons, normally obtain at most a fleeting, anonymous, and nondiscriminating glimpse of the landscape and buildings over which they pass. The risk that a passenger on such a plane might observe private activities, and might connect those activities with particular people, is simply too trivial to protect against. It is no accident that, as a matter of common experience, many people build fences around their residential areas, but few build roofs over their backyards. Therefore, contrary to the Court's suggestion, people do not "knowingly expos[e]" their residential yards "to the public" merely by failing to build barriers that prevent aerial surveillance.

The Court's reliance on *Knotts* [which involved electronic monitoring of an individual's travels] reveals the second problem with its analysis. The activities under surveillance in *Knotts* took place on public streets, not in private homes. 460 U.S., at 281–282. Comings and goings on public streets are public matters, and the Constitution does not disable police from observing what every member of the public can see. The activity in this case, by contrast, took place within the private area immediately adjacent to a home. Yet the Court approves purposeful police surveillance of that activity and area similar to that approved in *Knotts* with respect to public activities and areas. The only possible basis for this holding is a judgment that the risk to privacy posed by the remote possibility that a private airplane passenger will notice outdoor activities is equivalent to the risk of official aerial surveillance. But the Court fails to acknowledge the qualitative difference between police surveillance and other uses made of the airspace. Members of the public use the airspace for travel, business, or pleasure, not for the purpose of observing activities taking place within residential yards. Here, police conducted an overflight at low altitude solely for the purpose of discovering evidence of crime within a private enclave into which they were constitutionally forbidden to intrude at ground level without a warrant. It is not easy to believe that our society is prepared to force individuals to bear the risk of this type of warrantless police intrusion into their residential areas.[10]

B

Since respondent had a reasonable expectation of privacy in his yard, aerial surveillance undertaken by the police for the purpose of discovering evidence of crime constituted a "search" within the meaning of the Fourth Amendment . . . .

---

10. The Court's decision has serious implications for outdoor family activities conducted in the curtilage of a home. The feature of such activities that makes them desirable to citizens living in a free society, namely, the fact that they occur in the open air and sunlight, is relied on by the Court as a justification for permitting police to conduct warrantless surveillance at will. Aerial surveillance is nearly as intrusive on family privacy as physical trespass into the curtilage. It would appear that, after today, families can expect to be free of official surveillance only when they retreat behind the walls of their homes.

IV

... Rapidly advancing technology now permits police to conduct surveillance in the home itself, an area where privacy interests are most cherished in our society, without any physical trespass. While the rule in *Katz* was designed to prevent silent and unseen invasions of Fourth Amendment privacy rights in a variety of settings, we have consistently afforded heightened protection to a person's right to be left alone in the privacy of his house. The Court fails to enforce that right or to give any weight to the longstanding presumption that warrantless intrusions into the home are unreasonable. I dissent.

Notes and Questions

(1) Just two years prior to *Ciraolo*, in *Oliver v. United States*, 466 U.S. 170, 104 S. Ct. 1735, 80 L. Ed. 2d 214 (1984), the Court addressed the "open fields doctrine" first announced in *Hester v. United States*, 265 U.S. 57, 44 S. Ct. 445, 68 L. Ed. 898 (1924). According to that doctrine, the "special protection accorded by the Fourth Amendment to the people in their 'persons, houses, papers, and effects,' is not extended to the open fields." *Hester*, 265 U.S. at 59. The *Oliver* majority reaffirmed *Hester*'s interpretation of the Fourth Amendment, "conclud[ing] that the open fields doctrine . . . is consistent with the plain language of the Fourth Amendment and its historical purposes" and that it also "accords with the 'reasonable expectation of privacy' analysis developed in subsequent decisions of the Court." According to the Court, one cannot possess a reasonable expectation of privacy in open fields because they

> do not provide the setting for those intimate activities that the Amendment is intended to shelter from government interference or surveillance. There is no societal interest in protecting the privacy of those activities, such as the cultivation of crops, that occur in open fields. Moreover, as a practical matter these lands usually are accessible to the public and the police in ways that a home, an office, or commercial structure would not be.

Consequently, no matter what precautions one might take to preserve privacy, there is no Fourth Amendment protection in "open fields" because "no expectation of privacy attaches to open fields."

(2) The *Oliver* Court did *not* hold that Fourth Amendment protection ceases once one passes beyond the walls of the home. The Court acknowledged that "the common law distinguished 'open fields' from the 'curtilage,' the land immediately surrounding and associated with the home" and observed that "the curtilage," unlike "the neighboring open fields, warrants the Fourth Amendment protections that attach to the home. At common law, the curtilage is the area to which extends the intimate activity associated with the 'sanctity of a man's home and the privacies of life,' *Boyd v. United States*, 116 U.S. 616, 630, 6 S. Ct. 524, 532, 29 L. Ed. 746 (1886), and therefore has been considered part of the home itself for Fourth Amendment

purposes." (In a footnote, the Court did note that it was not "necessary in this case to consider" whether curtilage is entitled to the same "degree of Fourth Amendment protection" accorded "the home itself." It remains uncertain whether both norms of reasonableness that govern searches of the home — probable cause and a search warrant — also govern searches of curtilage.)

The line between the "curtilage" and "open fields," therefore, is of considerable constitutional significance. The former enjoys Fourth Amendment shelter against unreasonable searches, while the latter can claim none. While the *Oliver* Court specifically declined to define the "scope" of the area that constitutes curtilage, just three years later, in *United States v. Dunn*, 480 U.S. 294, 107 S. Ct. 1134, 94 L. Ed. 2d 326 (1987), the Court announced that the four variables pertinent to determining whether an area is "curtilage" are: (1) the area's proximity to the home; (2) the existence of an enclosure around the area; (3) the nature of the use to which the area is put; and (4) the precautions taken to exclude others from the area. There is no "bright-line" standard for deciding whether a particular location is situated in the "curtilage" or in "open fields." Instead, all four variables must be considered to determine whether the location falls within "the area to which extends the intimate activity associated" with the home, and, therefore, is a place in which a person may have a "reasonable expectation of privacy."

(3) In *Ciraolo*, the police discovered marijuana within an area clearly deserving of constitutional protection — the curtilage of the defendant's home. Why, then, was the officer's warrantless aerial surveillance that led to the discovery constitutionally permissible?

(a) If Officer Shutz had climbed a ladder or nearby telephone pole and peered down into Ciraolo's backyard, would the result have been the same? Why? *Compare West v. State*, 588 So. 2d 248 (Fla. Dist. Ct. App. 1991), *with State v. Sarantopoulos*, 604 So. 2d 551 (Fla. Dist. Ct. App. 1992); *see also Sarantopoulus v. State*, 629 So. 2d 121 (Fla. 1993) (approving the decision in *State v. Sarantopoulus* and disapproving the decision in *West v. State*).

(b) If Officer Shutz had peered through a knothole in Ciraolo's fence and seen the marijuana growing in his backyard, would the Fourth Amendment have been implicated? If he had stuck his head through a larger hole in the fence? If he had unlatched an unlocked gate and stepped six inches inside the fence to get a clear look at the character of the plants growing there? Why?

(c) What if he had hovered over the yard in a helicopter or hot air balloon at an altitude of 400 feet? 100 feet? 50 feet? Why? For a later decision holding that aerial surveillance from a helicopter hovering at 400 feet did not constitute a "search," but indicating that 400 feet could well be the boundary of Fourth Amendment territory, see *Florida v. Riley*, 488 U.S. 445, 109 S. Ct. 693, 102 L. Ed. 2d 835 (1989).

(4) In footnote 11, the Court observed that the photographic surveillance by Officer Shutz was not challenged. Should photographic surveillance be analyzed and treated differently than the "naked eye" surveillance approved in *Ciraolo*? Why? *See*

Dow Chemical Co. v. United States, 476 U.S. 227, 106 S. Ct. 1819, 90 L. Ed. 2d 226 (1986), a companion case to *Ciraolo*, in which the Court addressed aerial photographic surveillance of the "commercial curtilage" of a large chemical manufacturing facility.

(5) In *United States v. Knotts*, 460 U.S. 276, 103 S. Ct. 1081, 75 L. Ed. 2d 55 (1983), government agents attached an electronic tracking device known as a "beeper" to a container of chemicals. The beeper enabled the agents to monitor the container's movements and location. Although the precise duration of the monitoring was not specified, it apparently lasted no longer than one or two hours. The reasoning supporting the Court's conclusion that the agents' surveillance of the public movements of the container was not a search was essentially the same as the reasoning in *Ciraolo*. In essence, the possessor of the container could not claim a reasonable expectation of privacy in those movements because he had exposed them "to anyone who wanted to look" from a lawful public vantage point. It did not matter that the agents had in fact used an electronic monitoring device because the information secured *could have* been obtained by "visual surveillance from public places." According to Justice Rehnquist, "Nothing in the Fourth Amendment prohibited the police from augmenting the sensory faculties bestowed upon them at birth with such enhancement as science and technology afforded them in this case."

(6) A SUPPLEMENTAL ALTERNATIVE THRESHOLD DOCTRINE

(a) In *United States v. Jones*, 565 U.S. ____, 132 S. Ct. 945, 181 L. Ed. 2d 911 (2012), officers installed a Global Positioning System (GPS) tracking device on a vehicle and monitored its movements on public roads for 28 days. The government contended that no warrant was necessary because the officers' conduct did not constitute a search or seizure. A unanimous Supreme Court concluded that the officers' actions qualified as a "search" under the Fourth Amendment. The Justices divided sharply, however, over the reasoning supporting that conclusion. A bare majority of five Justices agreed with the reasoning and the supplemental alternative to *Katz*'s threshold standards contained in Justice Scalia's majority opinion. The other four members of the Court agreed that a search had occurred, but reached that conclusion by relying on the *Katz* doctrine.

According to the majority, by installing the GPS device on the defendant's vehicle — "an 'effect'" within the meaning of the Fourth Amendment — officers had "physically occupied private property for the purpose of obtaining information." A "physical intrusion" of that sort "would have been considered a 'search'" at the time the Fourth Amendment was adopted. The "close connection" of the Fourth Amendment "to property" is reflected in its text and was evident in the Court's jurisprudence prior to "the latter half of the 20th century," which "was tied to common-law trespass."

Although later decisions, beginning with *Katz*, "deviated from th[e] exclusively property-based approach," focusing instead on reasonable expectations of privacy, they "did not repudiate" the historical understanding of the Fourth Amendment — that it "embod[ies] a particular concern for government trespass upon the areas ('persons, houses, papers, and effects') it enumerates." The Court has the obligation to preserve the "'degree of privacy . . . that existed'" at the adoption of the Fourth Amendment. The intent of *Katz* was not to "'withdraw'" any protection that was originally afforded; it "did not narrow the Fourth Amendment's scope." Rather, "the *Katz* reasonable-expectation-of-privacy test [was] *added to*, not *substituted for*, the common-law trespassory test" for whether conduct constitutes a Fourth Amendment search. According to the majority, the trespass standard must remain in effect in order to "provide *at a minimum* the degree of protection . . . afforded" at the adoption of the Fourth Amendment. If the *Katz* standard were the exclusive measure of that guarantee's reach, "rights that previously existed" might be eliminated.

Based on this understanding of the Fourth Amendment, the majority held "that the Government's installation of a GPS device on a target's vehicle, and its use of that device to monitor the vehicle's movements, constitutes a 'search.'" According to Justice Scalia, "[w]here . . . the Government obtains information by physically intruding on a constitutionally protected area, . . . a search has . . . occurred." A "[t]respass alone" is not sufficient to trigger Fourth Amendment application, but "must be conjoined with . . . an attempt to find something or to obtain information." In fact, neither a trespass upon a home or effect nor "a *Katz* invasion of privacy" constitutes "a search unless it is done to obtain information; and the obtaining of information is not alone a search unless it is achieved by such a trespass or invasion of privacy."

When the officers attached the GPS device to the defendant's vehicle, they "encroached on a protected area" in order to obtain information. When they used the device to monitor the vehicle's movements, they did obtain information. They conducted a search subject to the Fourth Amendment's reasonableness demand.

By relying on the trespassory installation of the device, the majority was able to avoid "'vexing'" problems raised by application of the reasonable expectation of privacy standard to determine whether monitoring the vehicle's movements alone constituted a search. Justice Scalia noted that "mere visual observation" is not a search. Thus, if the surveillance in *Jones* had been accomplished by "'a large team of agents'" without electronic assistance, the "cases suggest that [their] visual observation" would have been "constitutionally permissible." Although it is *possible* that "achieving the same result through electronic means, without . . . trespass" could be an "invasion of privacy" triggering Fourth Amendment scrutiny, because of the trespass in *Jones* the Court did not have to address that difficult issue. Nor was it necessary to confront the "thorny problems" involved in distinguishing between electronic monitoring of public movements that is constitutionally regulated and electronic monitoring that is not.

As noted above, the remaining four Justices agreed that a search had occurred but rejected the majority's analysis and reasoning. In a concurrence in the judgment authored by Justice Alito, they explained why the majority's holding, resting on the trespass involved in installing the GPS device, was "unwise," "strain[ed]" Fourth Amendment "language," had "little" precedential "support," and was "highly artificial." In their view, *Katz* "did away with the old approach," rendering trespassory intrusions neither necessary *nor sufficient*. According to the concurring Justices, the determination had to turn on "whether . . . reasonable expectations of privacy were violated by the long-term monitoring of the movements of the vehicle." They believed that the "expectation-of-privacy test avoid[ed] . . . problems and complications" generated by the majority's approach, but they acknowledged that the *Katz* standard has "its own difficulties." It is somewhat "circular[]," entails a risk that judges will simply rely upon "their own expectations of privacy," and assumes "stable . . . privacy expectations" in a world where emerging technologies "can change those expectations" — particularly an individual's "expectations about the privacy of his or her daily movements."

Despite all of these difficulties, the best option available was "to apply existing Fourth Amendment doctrine" to the monitoring that occurred in *Jones*. *Knotts* made it clear that "relatively short-term monitoring" of public movements does not violate reasonable expectations of privacy. On the other hand, "longer term GPS monitoring" of all of a person's public movements "in investigations of most offenses impinges on expectations of privacy." The four-week tracking of Jones's "every movement" while driving his vehicle clearly intruded on his reasonable expectations of privacy. Justice Alito deemed it unnecessary to pinpoint the point in time during the 28-day surveillance when the tracking "became a search" or to "consider whether prolonged GPS monitoring" of public movements to investigate "extraordinary offenses" would violate protected privacy interests.

Justice Sotomayor joined the majority opinion. In a separate opinion, however, she emphasized the need to apply the *Katz* reasonable expectation of privacy standard to GPS monitoring that does not involve a trespassory installation. Moreover, she expressly "agree[d] with" the concurring Justices "that, at the very least, 'longer term GPS monitoring in investigations of most offenses impinges on expectations of privacy.'" Consequently, five Justices endorsed the conclusion that longer term technological monitoring of public movements, with or without a physical intrusion by the government, can constitute a search. Justice Sotomayor went even further, observing that "even short-term monitoring" might be subject to constitutional scrutiny because of "some unique attributes of GPS surveillance."

(b) Just one year later, the Court relied upon the alternative to *Katz* promulgated in *Jones* to resolve another threshold "search" question. In *Florida v. Jardines*, 569 U.S. ____, 133 S. Ct. 1409, 185 L. Ed. 2d 495 (2013), the question was "whether using a drug-sniffing dog on a homeowner's porch to investigate the contents of a home is a 'search' within the meaning of the Fourth Amendment." Based on "an unverified tip" about in-home marijuana growing, detectives took a trained canine to Jardines' front porch. The dog alerted, indicating the presence of narcotics. Marijuana plants were found during a search of the home pursuant to a warrant issued on the basis of what had been learned from the dog sniff. A 5–4 majority of the

Court concluded that the initial investigation with the dog was a Fourth Amendment search.

Relying on the analysis in *Jones*, Justice Scalia observed that *Katz* had "add[ed] to the baseline" of the Fourth Amendment, which provides protection when "'the Government obtains information by physically intruding' on persons, houses, papers, or effects." Based on the baseline "principle," *Jardines* was "a straightforward" case. The officers "gathered ... information by physically entering and occupying" the curtilage of the home "to engage in conduct not explicitly or implicitly permitted by the homeowner." Their intrusion into that "constitutionally protected area" was "unlicensed," — that is, Jardines had not "given his leave (even implicitly) for them to do" what they did.

Ordinarily, an "implicit license" permits a visitor "to approach [a] home by the front path, knock promptly, wait briefly to be received, and then (absent invitation to linger longer) leave." On the other hand, "[t]here is no customary invitation" to bring "a trained police dog to explore the area around the home in hopes of discovering incriminating evidence" — that is, "to engage in canine forensic investigation." The "scope of a license — express or implied — is limited not only to a particular area but also to a specific purpose." The "behavior" in this case — the "use of the dog" to sniff for drugs, unlike a knock on the front door, was not "routine." Justice Scalia conceded that an officer does not conduct "a Fourth Amendment search" by "approach[ing a] home in order to speak with the occupant, *because all are invited to do that.*" The fact that the officer has the "'purpose of discovering information'" while engaged in such "permitted conduct" does not alter that conclusion. Bringing a drug-sniffing dog to the door, however, is different because the "background social norms that invite a visitor to the front door do not invite him there to conduct a search."

In sum, the resolution of the threshold issue in *Jardines* "depend[ed] upon whether the officers had an implied license to enter the porch, which in turn depend[ed] upon the purpose for which they entered." Because "their behavior objectively reveal[ed] a purpose to conduct a search, which is not what anyone would think he had a license to do[,]" it was subject to Fourth Amendment regulation.

Having concluded that the *Jones* standard for whether a search had occurred was satisfied, the Court did not "need [to] decide whether the ... investigation of [the] home violated [the homeowner's] expectation of privacy under *Katz.*" It was "enough" that "officers learned what they learned only by physically intruding on [the] property to gather evidence."

In a separate concurrence, three members of the majority, Justices Kagan, Ginsburg, and Sotomayor, agreed that the officers' "activity" was a search because it was "a trespass." In their view, however, even without the physical intrusion, the use of the dog to detect narcotics in the home would have constituted a search because it was "an invasion of privacy" that met the *Katz* standard.

Justice Alito authored a dissent joined by Chief Justice Roberts, Justice Kennedy, and Justice Breyer. According to the dissenters, neither "trespass law" nor "the reasonable-expectations-of-privacy test" of *Katz* supported the conclusion that the officers conducted a search. The majority's reasoning was flawed because its "interpretation of the scope of [the officers'] license" to approach the house was "unfounded." The dissenters conceded that a license to approach a home, "has certain spatial and temporal limits." In their view, the acknowledgment that officers may knock on a door "to obtain evidence" shows that "gathering evidence . . . is a lawful activity that falls within the scope" of that license. The Court had provided "no meaningful" distinction between "the 'objective purpose'" of a "'knock and talk'" by the officers and the "'objective purpose'" of officers who bring a drug-sniffing canine to a front door. Consequently, "the Court's 'objective purpose' argument [could not] stand." Because the officers in *Jardines* stayed on "the customary path" to the front door, "did not approach in the middle of the night," and "remained . . . for only a short period," they did not "exceed the scope of the license to approach [the] front door."

Justice Alito pointed out that the majority's holding did not govern situations where "a dog alerts while on a public sidewalk or street or in the corridor of a building to which the dog and handler have been lawfully admitted." The concurrers' privacy-based analysis, however, "would have a much wider reach" and would deem dog sniffs of homes to be searches in the absence of physical intrusions into protected spaces. In the dissent's view, this analysis was misguided because "occupants of a dwelling" do not have "a reasonable expectation of privacy in odors that emanate from the dwelling and reach spots where members of the public may lawfully stand." There was no reason to "draw a line between odors that can be smelled by humans and those that are detectible only by dogs."

(c) Two years later, a unanimous Court, in a per curiam opinion, relied solely upon the *Jones* physical intrusion doctrine to resolve another interesting threshold question. In *Grady v. North Carolina*, 575 U.S. ____, 135 S. Ct. 1368, 191 L. Ed. 2d 459 (2015), a man who had been convicted of sex offenses and had served his sentence was ordered to appear for a hearing to determine whether he should be subjected to satellite-based monitoring as a recidivist sex offender. He argued that the monitoring program — which would force him to wear tracking devices at all times — would violate his Fourth Amendment right to be free from unreasonable searches and seizures. The North Carolina courts rejected his claim, concluding essentially that there was no search involved. The Supreme Court reversed.

According to the Justices, *Jones* and *Jardines* held that where "'the Government obtains information by physically intruding on a constitutionally protected area, . . . a search'" occurs. Consequently, a state conducts a search when it "attaches a device to a person's body, without consent, for the purpose of tracking that individual's movements." It did not matter that the monitoring program was "civil in nature." Precedent made it clear that "the government's purpose in collecting information does not control whether the method . . . constitutes a search." Moreover, both the name of the monitoring program ("satellite-based monitoring") and the text of the statute authorizing the monitoring, (which specified that the "program shall use a system that provides . . . [t]ime-correlated and continuous tracking of the geographic location of the subject" and "reporting of [the] subject's violations of . . . schedule or location requirements") belied the state's contention that there was no evidence that it was "acting to obtain information." The program was "plainly designed to obtain information," and because "it [did] so by physically intruding on a subject's body, it effect[ed] a Fourth Amendment search."

Bond v. United States

United States Supreme Court

529 U.S. 334, 120 S. Ct. 1462, 146 L. Ed. 2d 365 (2000)

CHIEF JUSTICE REHNQUIST delivered the opinion of the Court.

Petitioner Steven Dewayne Bond was a passenger on a Greyhound bus that left California bound for Little Rock, Arkansas. The bus stopped, as it was required to do, at the permanent Border Patrol checkpoint in Sierra Blanca, Texas. Border Patrol Agent Cesar Cantu boarded the bus to check the immigration status of its passengers. After reaching the back of the bus, having satisfied himself that the passengers were lawfully in the United States, Agent Cantu began walking toward the front. Along the way, he squeezed the soft luggage which passengers had placed in the overhead storage space above the seats.

Petitioner was seated four or five rows from the back of the bus. As Agent Cantu inspected the luggage in the compartment above petitioner's seat, he squeezed a green canvas bag and noticed that it contained a "brick-like" object. Petitioner admitted that the bag was his and agreed to allow Agent Cantu to open it. Upon opening the bag, Agent Cantu discovered a "brick" of methamphetamine. The brick had been wrapped in duct tape until it was oval-shaped and then rolled in a pair of pants.

Petitioner was indicted for conspiracy to possess, and possession with intent to distribute, methamphetamine in violation of 84 Stat. 1260, 21 U.S.C. § 841(a)(1). He moved to suppress the drugs, arguing that Agent Cantu conducted an illegal search of his bag. Petitioner's motion was denied, and the District Court found him guilty on both counts and sentenced him to 57 months in prison. . . . [T]he Court of Appeals affirmed the denial of the motion to suppress, holding that Agent Cantu's manipulation of the bag was not a search within the meaning of the Fourth Amendment. We granted certiorari, and now reverse.

The Fourth Amendment provides that "[t]he right of the people to be secure in their persons, houses, papers, and effects, against unreasonable searches and seizures, shall not be violated. . . ." A traveler's personal luggage is clearly an "effect" protected by the Amendment. Indeed, it is undisputed here that petitioner possessed a privacy interest in his bag.

But the Government asserts that by exposing his bag to the public, petitioner lost a reasonable expectation that his bag would not be physically manipulated. The Government relies on our decisions in *California v. Ciraolo*, [476 U.S. 207 (1986)] and *Florida v. Riley*, 488 U.S. 445 (1989), for the proposition that matters open to public observation are not protected by the Fourth Amendment. In *Ciraolo*, we held that police observation of a backyard from a plane flying at an altitude of 1,000 feet did not violate a reasonable expectation of privacy. Similarly, in *Riley*, we relied on *Ciraolo* to hold that police observation of a greenhouse in a home's curtilage from a helicopter passing at an altitude of 400 feet did not violate the Fourth Amendment. We reasoned that the property was "not necessarily protected from inspection that involves no physical invasion," and determined that because any member of the public could have lawfully observed the defendants' property by flying overhead, the defendants' expectation of privacy was "not reasonable and not one 'that society is prepared to honor.'" *See Riley, supra*, at 449 (explaining and relying on *Ciraolo*'s reasoning).

But *Ciraolo* and *Riley* are different from this case because they involved only visual, as opposed to tactile, observation. Physically invasive inspection is simply more intrusive than purely visual inspection. For example, in *Terry v. Ohio*, 392 U.S. 1, 17–18 (1968), we stated that a "careful [tactile] exploration of the outer surfaces of a person's clothing all over his or her body" is a "serious intrusion upon the sanctity of the person, which may inflict great indignity and arouse strong resentment, and is not to be undertaken lightly." Although Agent Cantu did not "frisk" petitioner's person, he did conduct a probing tactile examination of petitioner's carry-on luggage. Obviously, petitioner's bag was not part of his person. But travelers are particularly concerned about their carry-on luggage; they generally use it to transport personal items that, for whatever reason, they prefer to keep close at hand.

Here, petitioner concedes that, by placing his bag in the overhead compartment, he could expect that it would be exposed to certain kinds of touching and handling. But petitioner argues that Agent Cantu's physical manipulation of his luggage "far exceeded the casual contact [petitioner] could have expected from other passengers." The Government counters that it did not.

Our Fourth Amendment analysis embraces two questions. First, we ask whether the individual, by his conduct, has exhibited an actual expectation of privacy; that is, whether he has shown that "he [sought] to preserve [something] as private." *Smith v. Maryland*, 442 U.S. 735, 740 (1979) (internal quotation marks omitted). Here, petitioner sought to preserve privacy by using an opaque bag and placing that bag directly above his seat. Second, we inquire whether the individual's expectation of privacy is "one that society is prepared to recognize as reasonable." *Ibid.* (internal quotation marks omitted). When a bus passenger places a bag in an overhead bin, he expects that other passengers or bus employees may move it for one reason or another. Thus, a bus passenger clearly expects that his bag may be handled. He does not expect that other passengers or bus employees will, as a matter of course, feel the bag in an exploratory manner. But this is exactly what the agent did here. We therefore hold that the agent's physical manipulation of petitioner's bag violated the Fourth Amendment.

The judgment of the Court of Appeals is

Reversed.

Justice Breyer, with whom Justice Scalia joins, dissenting.

Does a traveler who places a soft-sided bag in the shared overhead storage compartment of a bus have a "reasonable expectation" that strangers will not push, pull, prod, squeeze, or otherwise manipulate his luggage? Unlike the majority, I believe that he does not.

Petitioner argues — and the majority points out — that, even if bags in overhead bins are subject to general "touching" and "handling," this case is special because "Agent Cantu's physical manipulation of [petitioner's] luggage 'far exceeded the casual contact [he] could have expected from other passengers.'" But the record shows the contrary. Agent Cantu testified that border patrol officers (who routinely enter buses at designated checkpoints to run immigration checks) "conduct an inspection of the overhead luggage by squeezing the bags as we're going out." On the occasion at issue here, Agent Cantu "felt a green bag" which had "a brick-like object in it." He explained that he felt "the edges of the brick in the bag," and that it was a "[b]rick-like object . . . that, when squeezed, you could feel an outline of something of a different mass inside of it." Although the agent acknowledged that his practice was to "squeeze [bags] very hard," he testified that his touch ordinarily was not "[h]ard enough to break something inside that might be fragile." Petitioner also testified that Agent Cantu "reached for my bag, and he shook it a little, and squeezed it."

How does the "squeezing" just described differ from the treatment that overhead luggage is likely to receive from strangers in a world of travel that is somewhat less gentle than it used to be? I think not at all. The trial court, which heard the evidence, saw nothing unusual, unforeseeable, or special about this agent's squeeze. It found that Agent Cantu simply "felt the outside of Bond's softside green cloth bag," and it viewed the agent's activity as "minimally intrusive touching." The Court of Appeals also noted that, because "passengers often handle and manipulate other passengers' luggage," the substantially similar tactile inspection here was entirely "foreseeable."

The record and these factual findings are sufficient to resolve this case. The law is clear that the Fourth Amendment protects against government intrusion that upsets an "'actual (subjective) expectation of privacy'" that is objectively "'reasonable.'" *Smith v. Maryland*, 442 U.S. 735, 740 (1979) (quoting *Katz v. United States*, 389 U.S. 347, 361 (1967) (Harlan, J., concurring)). Privacy itself implies the exclusion of uninvited strangers, not just strangers who work for the Government. Hence, an individual cannot reasonably expect privacy in respect to objects or activities that he "knowingly exposes to the public."

Indeed, the Court has said that it is not objectively reasonable to expect privacy if "[a]ny member of the public . . . could have" used his senses to detect "everything that th[e] officers observed." *California v. Ciraolo*, 476 U.S. 207, 213–214 (1986). Thus, it has held that the fact that strangers may look down at fenced-in property from an aircraft or sift through garbage bags on a public street can justify a similar police intrusion. The comparative likelihood that strangers will give bags in an overhead compartment a hard squeeze would seem far greater. *See Riley, supra*, at 453 (O'Connor, J., concurring in judgment) (reasonableness of privacy expectation depends on whether intrusion is a "sufficiently routine part of modern life"). . . .

Of course, the agent's *purpose* here — searching for drugs — differs dramatically from the intention of a driver or fellow passenger who squeezes a bag in the process of making more room for another parcel. But in determining whether an expectation of privacy is reasonable, it is the *effect*, not the purpose, that matters. Few individuals with something to hide wish to expose that something to the police, however careless or indifferent they may be in respect to discovery by other members of the public. Hence, a Fourth Amendment rule that turns on purpose could prevent police alone from intruding where other strangers freely tread. And the added privacy protection achieved by such an approach would not justify the harm worked to law enforcement — at least that is what this Court's previous cases suggest.

Nor can I accept the majority's effort to distinguish "tactile" from "visual" interventions, even assuming that distinction matters here. Whether tactile manipulation (say, of the exterior of luggage) is more intrusive or less intrusive than visual observation (say, through a lighted window) necessarily depends on the particular circumstances.

If we are to depart from established legal principles, we should not begin here. At best, this decision will lead to a constitutional jurisprudence of "squeezes," thereby complicating further already complex Fourth Amendment law, increasing the difficulty of deciding ordinary criminal matters, and hindering the administrative guidance (with its potential for control of unreasonable police practices) that a less complicated jurisprudence might provide. At worst, this case will deter law enforcement officers searching for drugs near borders from using even the most non-intrusive touch to help investigate publicly exposed bags. At the same time, the ubiquity of *non*-governmental pushes, prods, and squeezes (delivered by driver, attendant, passenger, or some other stranger) means that this decision cannot do much to protect true privacy. Rather, the traveler who wants to place a bag in a shared overhead bin and yet safeguard its contents from public touch should plan to pack those contents in a suitcase with hard sides, irrespective of the Court's decision today.

For these reasons, I dissent.

Notes and Questions

(1) In *California v. Ciraolo*, the aerial surveillance of the defendant's backyard was not a "search" because "[a]ny member of the [flying] public *could have seen* everything that the[] officers observed." In *Bond*, why didn't the fact that any member of the traveling public *could have felt* everything that the officer felt lead to the conclusion that the physical manipulation of the defendant's bag was not a "search"? Isn't the dissent correct to suggest that it is more likely that a member of the traveling public will squeeze a soft-sided bag on a bus than observe the contents of a backyard

from navigable airspace? Are the majority's bases for distinguishing *Ciraolo* persuasive?

(2) Consider whether any or all of the following variations on the facts in *Bond* is governed by the Fourth Amendment:

(a) An officer squeezes a soft-sided bag that has been checked by a bus passenger and stored in the luggage compartment of a bus as firmly as Officer Cantu squeezed Bond's bag;

(b) An officer squeezes a soft-sided carry-on bag in the overhead bin of a bus more gently than Officer Cantu squeezed Bond's bag;

(c) An officer puts his face within an inch or two of a soft-sided carry-on bag and smells an aroma emanating from the contents;

(d) An officer puts his face within an inch or two of a soft-sided carry-on bag, squeezes the bag very gently, and smells the aroma of the air expelled by the squeeze.

(3) Consider also how the alternative "physical intrusion" threshold doctrine that dictated the holdings in *Jones*, *Jardines*, and *Grady* might affect the analysis of whether a search occurred in *Bond* or in any of the hypotheticals in note (2).

Kyllo v. United States

United States Supreme Court

533 U.S. 27, 121 S. Ct. 2038, 150 L. Ed. 2d 94 (2001)

JUSTICE SCALIA delivered the opinion of the Court.

. . . .

I

In 1991 Agent William Elliott of the United States Department of the Interior came to suspect that marijuana was being grown in the home belonging to petitioner Danny Kyllo, part of a triplex on Rhododendron Drive in Florence, Oregon. Indoor marijuana growth typically requires high-intensity lamps. In order to determine whether an amount of heat was emanating from petitioner's home consistent with the use of such lamps, at 3:20 a.m. on January 16, 1992, Agent Elliott and Dan Haas used an Agema Thermovision 210 thermal imager to scan the triplex. Thermal imagers detect infrared radiation, which virtually all objects emit but which is not visible to the naked eye. The imager converts radiation into images based on relative warmth — black is cool, white is hot, shades of gray connote relative differences; in that respect, it operates somewhat like a video camera showing heat images. The scan of Kyllo's home took only a few minutes and was performed from the passenger seat of Agent Elliott's vehicle across the street from the front of the house and also from the street in back of the house. The scan showed that the roof over the garage and a side wall of petitioner's home were relatively hot compared to the rest of the home and substantially warmer than neighboring homes in the triplex. Agent Elliott concluded that petitioner was using halide lights to grow marijuana in his house, which indeed he was. Based on tips from informants, utility bills, and the thermal imaging, a Federal Magistrate Judge issued a warrant authorizing a search of petitioner's home, and the agents found an indoor growing operation involving more than 100 plants. Petitioner was indicted on one count of manufacturing marijuana, in violation of 21 U.S.C. § 841(a)(1). He unsuccessfully moved to suppress the evidence seized from his home and then entered a conditional guilty plea.

The Court of Appeals for the Ninth Circuit remanded the case for an evidentiary hearing regarding the intrusiveness of thermal imaging. On remand the District Court found that the Agema 210 "is a non-intrusive device which emits no rays or beams and shows a crude visual image of the heat being radiated from the outside of the house"; it "did not show any people or activity within the walls of the structure"; "[t]he device used cannot penetrate walls or windows to reveal conversations or human activities"; and "[n]o intimate details of the home were observed." Based on these findings, the District Court upheld the validity of the warrant that relied in part upon the thermal imaging, and reaffirmed its denial of the motion to suppress. A divided Court of Appeals initially reversed, 140 F.3d 1249 (1998), but that opinion was withdrawn and the panel (after a change in composition) affirmed, 190 F.3d 1041 (1999), with Judge Noonan dissenting. The court held that petitioner had shown no subjective expectation of privacy because he had made no attempt to conceal the heat escaping from his home, *id.*, at 1046, and even if he had, there was no objectively reasonable expectation of privacy because the imager "did not expose any intimate details of Kyllo's life," only "amorphous 'hot spots' on the roof and exterior wall," *id.*, at 1047. We granted certiorari. 530 U.S. 1305, 121 S. Ct. 29, 147 L. Ed. 2d 1052 (2000).

II

The Fourth Amendment provides that "[t]he right of the people to be secure in their persons, houses, papers, and effects, against unreasonable searches and seizures, shall not be violated." "At the very core" of the Fourth Amendment "stands the right of a man to retreat into his own home and there be free from unreasonable governmental intrusion." *Silverman v. United States*, 365 U.S. 505, 511, 81 S. Ct. 679, 5 L. Ed. 2d 734 (1961). With few exceptions, the question whether a warrantless search of a home is reasonable and hence constitutional must be answered no.

On the other hand, the antecedent question of whether or not a Fourth Amendment "search" has occurred is not so simple under our precedent. The permissibility of ordinary visual surveillance of a home used to be clear because, well into the 20th century, our Fourth Amendment jurisprudence was tied to common-law trespass. Visual surveillance was unquestionably lawful because "'the eye cannot by the laws of England be guilty of a trespass.'" *Boyd v. United States*, 116 U.S. 616, 628, 6 S. Ct. 524, 29 L. Ed. 746 (1886) (quoting *Entick v. Carrington*, 19 How. St. Tr. 1029, 95 Eng. Rep. 807 (K.B. 1765)). We have since decoupled violation of a person's Fourth Amendment rights from trespassory violation of his property, but the lawfulness of warrantless visual surveillance of a home has still been preserved. As we observed in *California v. Ciraolo*, 476 U.S. 207, 213, 106 S. Ct. 1809, 90 L. Ed. 2d 210 (1986), "[t]he Fourth Amendment protection of the home has never been extended to require law enforcement officers to shield their eyes when passing by a home on public thoroughfares."

One might think that the new validating rationale would be that examining the portion of a house that is in plain public view, while it is a "search" despite the absence of trespass, is not an "unreasonable" one under the Fourth Amendment. But in fact we have held that visual observation is no "search" at all—perhaps in order to preserve somewhat more intact our doctrine that warrantless searches are presumptively unconstitutional. *See Dow Chemical Co. v. United States*, 476 U.S. 227, 234–235, 239, 106 S. Ct. 1819, 90 L. Ed. 2d 226 (1986). In assessing when a search is not a search, we have applied somewhat in reverse the principle first enunciated in *Katz v. United States*, 389 U.S. 347, 88 S. Ct. 507, 19 L. Ed. 2d 576 (1967). . . . As Justice Harlan's oft-quoted concurrence described it, a Fourth Amendment search occurs when the government violates a subjective expectation of privacy that society recognizes as reasonable. We have subsequently applied this principle to hold that a Fourth Amendment search does *not* occur—even when the explicitly protected location of a *house* is concerned—unless "the individual manifested a subjective expectation of privacy in the object of the challenged search," and "society [is] willing to recognize that expectation as reasonable." *Ciraolo, supra*, at 211, 106 S. Ct. 1809. We have applied this test in holding that it is not a search for the police to use a pen register at the phone company to determine what numbers were dialed in a private home, *Smith v. Maryland*, 442 U.S. 735, 743–744, 99 S. Ct. 2577, 61 L. Ed. 2d 220 (1979), and we have applied the test on two different occasions in holding that aerial surveillance of private homes and surrounding areas does not constitute a search, *Ciraolo, supra; Florida v. Riley*, 488 U.S. 445, 109 S. Ct. 693, 102 L. Ed. 2d 835 (1989).

The present case involves officers on a public street engaged in more than naked-eye surveillance of a home. We have previously reserved judgment as to how much technological enhancement of ordinary perception from such a vantage point, if any, is too much. . . . . .

III

It would be foolish to contend that the degree of privacy secured to citizens by the Fourth Amendment has been entirely unaffected by the advance of technology. For example, as the cases discussed above make clear, the technology enabling human flight has exposed to public view (and hence, we have said, to official observation) uncovered portions of the house and its curtilage that once were private. *See Ciraolo, supra*, at 215, 106 S. Ct. 1809. The question we confront today is what limits there are upon this power of technology to shrink the realm of guaranteed privacy.

The *Katz* test—whether the individual has an expectation of privacy that society is prepared to recognize as reasonable—has often been criticized as circular, and hence subjective and unpredictable. While it may be difficult to refine *Katz* when the search of areas such as telephone booths, automobiles, or even the curtilage and uncovered portions of residences is at issue, in the case of the search of the interior of homes — the prototypical and hence most commonly litigated area of protected privacy — there is a ready criterion, with roots deep in the common law, of the minimal expectation of privacy that *exists*, and that is acknowledged to be *reasonable*. To withdraw protection of this minimum expectation would be to permit police technology to erode the privacy guaranteed by the Fourth Amendment. We think that obtaining by sense-enhancing technology any information regarding the interior of the home that could not otherwise have been obtained without physical "intrusion into a constitutionally protected area," *Silverman*, 365 U.S., at 512, 81 S. Ct. 679, constitutes a search — at least where (as here) the technology in question is not in general public use. This assures preservation of that degree of privacy against government that existed when the Fourth Amendment was adopted. On the basis of this criterion, the information obtained by the thermal imager in this case was the product of a search.[2]

The Government maintains, however, that the thermal imaging must be upheld because it detected "only heat radiating from the external surface of the house," Brief for United States 26. The dissent makes this its leading point, contending that there is a fundamental difference between what it calls "off-the-wall" observations and "through-the-wall surveillance." But just as a thermal imager captures only heat emanating from a house, so also a powerful directional microphone picks up only sound emanating from a house — and a satellite capable of scanning from many miles away would pick up only visible light emanating from a house. We rejected such a mechanical interpretation of the Fourth Amendment in *Katz*, where the eavesdropping device picked up only sound waves that reached the exterior of the phone booth. Reversing that approach would leave the homeowner at the mercy of advancing technology — including imaging technology that could discern all human activity in the home. While the technology used in the present case was relatively crude, the rule we adopt must take account of more sophisticated systems that are already in use or in development. The dissent's reliance on the distinction between "off-the-wall" and "through-the-wall" observation is entirely incompatible with the dissent's belief, which we discuss below, that thermal-imaging observations of the intimate details of a home are impermissible. The most sophisticated thermal imaging devices continue to measure heat "off-the-wall" rather than "through-the-wall";

---

2. The dissent's repeated assertion that the thermal imaging did not obtain information regarding the interior of the home is simply inaccurate. A thermal imager reveals the relative heat of various rooms in the home. The dissent may not find that information particularly private or important, but there is no basis for saying it is not information regarding the interior of the home. The dissent's comparison of the thermal imaging to various circumstances in which outside observers might be able to perceive, without technology, the heat of the home — for example, by observing snowmelt on the roof, is quite irrelevant. The fact that equivalent information could sometimes be obtained by other means does not make lawful the use of means that violate the Fourth Amendment. The police might, for example, learn how many people are in a particular house by setting up year-round surveillance; but that does not make breaking and entering to find out the same information lawful. In any event, on the night of January 16, 1992, no outside observer could have discerned the relative heat of Kyllo's home without thermal imaging.

the dissent's disapproval of those more sophisticated thermal-imaging devices is an acknowledgment that there is no substance to this distinction. As for the dissent's extraordinary assertion that anything learned through "an inference" cannot be a search, that would validate even the "through-the-wall" technologies that the dissent purports to disapprove. Surely the dissent does not believe that the through-the-wall radar or ultrasound technology produces an 8-by-10 Kodak glossy that needs no analysis (*i.e.*, the making of inferences). And, of course, the novel proposition that inference insulates a search is blatantly contrary to *United States v. Karo*, 468 U.S. 705, 104 S. Ct. 3296, 82 L. Ed. 2d 530 (1984), where the police "inferred" from the activation of a beeper that a certain can of ether was in the home. The police activity was held to be a search, and the search was held unlawful.[4]

The Government also contends that the thermal imaging was constitutional because it did not "detect private activities occurring in private areas," Brief for United States 22. It points out that in *Dow Chemical* we observed that the enhanced aerial photography did not reveal any "intimate details." 476 U.S., at 238, 106 S. Ct. 1819. *Dow Chemical*, however, involved enhanced aerial photography of an industrial complex, which does not share the Fourth Amendment sanctity of the home. The Fourth Amendment's protection of the home has never been tied to measurement of the quality or quantity of information obtained. In *Silverman*, for example, we made clear that any physical invasion of the structure of the home, "by even a fraction of an inch," was too much, 365 U.S., at 512, 81 S. Ct. 679, and there is certainly no exception to the warrant requirement for the officer who barely cracks open the front door and sees nothing but the nonintimate rug on the vestibule floor. In the home, our cases show, *all* details are intimate details, because the entire area is held safe from prying government eyes. Thus, in *Karo, supra*, the only thing detected was a can of ether in the home; and in *Arizona v. Hicks*, 480 U.S. 321, 107 S. Ct. 1149, 94 L. Ed. 2d 347 (1987), the only thing detected by a physical search that went beyond what officers lawfully present could observe in "plain view" was the registration number of a phonograph turntable. These were intimate details because they were details of the home, just as was the detail of how warm — or even how relatively warm — Kyllo was heating his residence.

Limiting the prohibition of thermal imaging to "intimate details" would not only be wrong in principle; it would be impractical in application, failing to provide "a

---

4. The dissent asserts that we have misunderstood its point, which is not that inference *insulates* a search, but that inference alone is *not* a search. If we misunderstood the point, it was only in a good-faith effort to render the point germane to the case at hand. The issue in this case is not the police's allegedly unlawful inferencing, but their allegedly unlawful thermal-imaging measurement of the emanations from a house. We say such measurement is a search; the dissent says it is not, because an inference is not a search. We took that to mean that, since the technologically enhanced emanations had to be the basis of inferences before anything inside the house could be known, the use of the emanations could not be a search. But the dissent certainly knows better than we what it intends. And if it means only that an inference is not a search, we certainly agree. That has no bearing, however, upon whether hi-tech measurement of emanations from a house is a search.

workable accommodation between the needs of law enforcement and the interests protected by the Fourth Amendment," *Oliver v. United States*, 466 U.S. 170, 181, 104 S. Ct. 1735, 80 L. Ed. 2d 214 (1984). To begin with, there is no necessary connection between the sophistication of the surveillance equipment and the "intimacy" of the details that it observes — which means that one cannot say (and the police cannot be assured) that use of the relatively crude equipment at issue here will always be lawful. The Agema Thermovision 210 might disclose, for example, at what hour each night the lady of the house takes her daily sauna and bath — a detail that many would consider "intimate"; and a much more sophisticated system might detect nothing more intimate than the fact that someone left a closet light on. We could not, in other words, develop a rule approving only that through-the-wall surveillance which identifies objects no smaller than 36 by 36 inches, but would have to develop a jurisprudence specifying which home activities are "intimate" and which are not. And even when (if ever) that jurisprudence were fully developed, no police officer would be able to know *in advance* whether his through-the-wall surveillance picks up "intimate" details — and thus would be unable to know in advance whether it is constitutional.

The dissent's proposed standard — whether the technology offers the "functional equivalent of actual presence in the area being searched" — would seem quite similar to our own at first blush. The dissent concludes that *Katz* was such a case, but then inexplicably asserts that if the same listening device only revealed the volume of the conversation, the surveillance would be permissible. Yet if, without technology, the police could not discern volume without being actually present in the phone booth, JUSTICE STEVENS should conclude a search has occurred. The same should hold for the interior heat of the home if only a person present in the home could discern the heat. Thus the driving force of the dissent, despite its recitation of the above standard, appears to be a distinction among different types of information — whether the "homeowner would even care if anybody noticed." The dissent offers no practical guidance for the application of this standard, and for reasons already discussed, we believe there can be none. The people in their houses, as well as the police, deserve more precision.[6]

We have said that the Fourth Amendment draws "a firm line at the entrance to the house," *Payton*, 445 U.S., at 590, 100 S. Ct. 1371. That line, we think, must be not only firm but also bright — which requires clear specification of those methods of surveillance that require a warrant. While it is certainly possible to conclude from

---

6. The dissent argues that we have injected potential uncertainty into the constitutional analysis by noting that whether or not the technology is in general public use may be a factor. That quarrel, however, is not with us but with this Court's precedent. *See Ciraolo, supra*, at 215, 106 S. Ct. 1809 ("In an age where private and commercial flight in the public airways is routine, it is unreasonable for respondent to expect that his marijuana plants were constitutionally protected from being observed with the naked eye from an altitude of 1,000 feet"). Given that we can quite confidently say that thermal imaging is not "routine," we decline in this case to reexamine that factor.

the videotape of the thermal imaging that occurred in this case that no "significant" compromise of the homeowner's privacy has occurred, we must take the long view, from the original meaning of the Fourth Amendment forward.

> "The Fourth Amendment is to be construed in the light of what was deemed an unreasonable search and seizure when it was adopted, and in a manner which will conserve public interests as well as the interests and rights of individual citizens." *Carroll v. United States*, 267 U.S. 132, 149, 45 S. Ct. 280, 69 L. Ed. 543 (1925).

Where, as here, the Government uses a device that is not in general public use, to explore details of the home that would previously have been unknowable without physical intrusion, the surveillance is a "search" and is presumptively unreasonable without a warrant.

Since we hold the Thermovision imaging to have been an unlawful search, it will remain for the District Court to determine whether, without the evidence it provided, the search warrant issued in this case was supported by probable cause — and if not, whether there is any other basis for supporting admission of the evidence that the search pursuant to the warrant produced.

. . . .

The judgment of the Court of Appeals is reversed; the case is remanded for further proceedings consistent with this opinion.

It is so ordered.

JUSTICE STEVENS, with whom THE CHIEF JUSTICE, JUSTICE O'CONNOR, and JUSTICE KENNEDY join, dissenting.

There is, in my judgment, a distinction of constitutional magnitude between "through-the-wall surveillance" that gives the observer or listener direct access to information in a private area, on the one hand, and the thought processes used to draw inferences from information in the public domain, on the other hand. The Court has crafted a rule that purports to deal with direct observations of the inside of the home, but the case before us merely involves indirect deductions from "off-the-wall" surveillance, that is, observations of the exterior of the home. Those observations were made with a fairly primitive thermal imager that gathered data exposed on the outside of petitioner's home but did not invade any constitutionally protected interest in privacy. Moreover, I believe that the supposedly "bright-line" rule the Court has created in response to its concerns about future technological developments is unnecessary, unwise, and inconsistent with the Fourth Amendment.

I

. . . . "'What a person knowingly exposes to the public, even in his own home or office, is not a subject of Fourth Amendment protection.'" *California v. Ciraolo*, 476 U.S. 207, 213, 106 S. Ct. 1809, 90 L. Ed. 2d 210 (1986) (quoting *Katz v. United States*, 389 U.S. 347, 351, 88 S. Ct. 507, 19 L. Ed. 2d 576 (1967)). That is the principle implicated here.

. . . [T]his case involves nothing more than off-the-wall surveillance by law enforcement officers to gather information exposed to the general public from the outside of petitioner's home. All that the infrared camera did in this case was passively measure heat emitted from the exterior surfaces of petitioner's home; all that those measurements showed were relative differences in emission levels, vaguely indicating that some areas of the roof and outside walls were warmer than others. As still images from the infrared scans show, no details regarding the interior of petitioner's home were revealed. Unlike an x-ray scan, or other possible "through-the-wall" techniques, the detection of infrared radiation emanating from the home did not accomplish "an unauthorized physical penetration into the premises," *Silverman v. United States*, 365 U.S. 505, 509, 81 S. Ct. 679, 5 L. Ed. 2d 734 (1961), nor did it "obtain information that it could not have obtained by observation from outside the curtilage of the house," *United States v. Karo*, 468 U.S. 705, 715, 104 S. Ct. 3296, 82 L. Ed. 2d 530 (1984).

Indeed, the ordinary use of the senses might enable a neighbor or passerby to notice the heat emanating from a building, particularly if it is vented, as was the case here. Additionally, any member of the public might notice that one part of a house is warmer than another part or a nearby building if, for example, rainwater evaporates or snow melts at different rates across its surfaces. Such use of the senses would not convert into an unreasonable search if, instead, an adjoining neighbor allowed an officer onto her property to verify her perceptions with a sensitive thermometer. Nor, in my view, does such observation become an unreasonable search if made from a distance with the aid of a device that merely discloses that the exterior of one house, or one area of the house, is much warmer than another. Nothing more occurred in this case.

Thus, the notion that heat emissions from the outside of a dwelling is a private matter implicating the protections of the Fourth Amendment (the text of which guarantees the right of people "to be secure *in* their . . . houses" against unreasonable searches and seizures (emphasis added)) is not only unprecedented but also quite difficult to take seriously. Heat waves, like aromas that are generated in a kitchen, or in a laboratory or opium den, enter the public domain if and when they leave a building. A subjective expectation that they would remain private is not only implausible but also surely not "one that society is prepared to recognize as 'reasonable.'" *Katz*, 389 U.S., at 361, 88 S. Ct. 507 (Harlan, J., concurring).

To be sure, the homeowner has a reasonable expectation of privacy concerning what takes place within the home, and the Fourth Amendment's protection against physical invasions of the home should apply to their functional equivalent. But the equipment in this case did not penetrate the walls of petitioner's home, and while it did pick up "details of the home" that were exposed to the public, it did not obtain "any information regarding the *interior* of the home." In the Court's own words, based on what the thermal imager "showed" regarding the outside of petitioner's home, the officers "concluded" that petitioner was engaging in illegal activity inside the home. It would be quite absurd to characterize their thought processes as "searches," regardless of whether they inferred (rightly) that petitioner was growing marijuana in his house, or (wrongly) that "the lady of the house [was taking] her daily sauna and bath." . . . For the first time in its history, the Court assumes that an inference can amount to a Fourth Amendment violation.

. . . .

. . . [T]he . . . privacy interest [involved here] is at best trivial. After all, homes generally are insulated to keep heat in, rather than to prevent the detection of heat going out, and it does not seem to me that society will suffer from a rule requiring the rare homeowner who both intends to engage in uncommon activities that produce extraordinary amounts of heat, and wishes to conceal that production from outsiders, to make sure that the surrounding area is well insulated. The interest in concealing the heat escaping from one's house pales in significance to the "the chief evil against which the wording of the Fourth Amendment is directed," the "physical entry of the home," *United States v. United States Dist. Court for Eastern Dist. of Mich.*, 407 U.S. 297, 313, 92 S. Ct. 2125, 32 L. Ed. 2d 752 (1972), and it is hard to believe that it is an interest the Framers sought to protect in our Constitution.

Since what was involved in this case was nothing more than drawing inferences from off-the-wall surveillance, rather than any "through-the-wall" surveillance, the officers' conduct did not amount to a search and was perfectly reasonable.

II

. . . [T]he Court's new rule is at once too broad and too narrow, and is not justified by the Court's explanation for its adoption. As I have suggested, I would not erect a constitutional impediment to the use of sense-enhancing technology unless it provides its user with the functional equivalent of actual presence in the area being searched.

Despite the Court's attempt to draw a line that is "not only firm but also bright," the contours of its new rule are uncertain because its protection apparently dissipates as soon as the relevant technology is "in general public use." Yet how much use is general public use is not even hinted at by the Court's opinion, which makes the somewhat doubtful assumption that the thermal imager used in this case does not satisfy that criterion.[5] In any event, putting aside its lack of clarity, this criterion is somewhat perverse because it seems likely that the threat to privacy will grow, rather than recede, as the use of intrusive equipment becomes more readily available.

. . . .

The application of the Court's new rule to "any information regarding the interior of the home" is . . . unnecessarily broad. If it takes sensitive equipment to detect

---

5. The record describes a device that numbers close to a thousand manufactured units; that has a predecessor numbering in the neighborhood of 4,000 to 5,000 units; that competes with a similar product numbering from 5,000 to 6,000 units; and that is "readily available to the public" for commercial, personal, or law enforcement purposes, and is just an 800-number away from being rented from "half a dozen national companies" by anyone who wants one. App. 18. Since, by virtue of the Court's new rule, the issue is one of first impression, perhaps it should order an evidentiary hearing to determine whether these facts suffice to establish "general public use."

an odor that identifies criminal conduct and nothing else, the fact that the odor emanates from the interior of a home should not provide it with constitutional protection. The criterion, moreover, is too sweeping in that information "regarding" the interior of a home apparently is not just information obtained through its walls, but also information concerning the outside of the building that could lead to (however many) inferences "regarding" what might be inside. . . .

Because the new rule applies to information regarding the "interior" of the home, it is too narrow as well as too broad. Clearly, a rule that is designed to protect individuals from the overly intrusive use of sense-enhancing equipment should not be limited to a home. If such equipment did provide its user with the functional equivalent of access to a private place — such as, for example, the telephone booth involved in *Katz*, or an office building — then the rule should apply to such an area as well as to a home.

The final requirement of the Court's new rule, that the information "could not otherwise have been obtained without physical intrusion into a constitutionally protected area" (internal quotation marks omitted), also extends too far as the Court applies it. As noted, the Court effectively treats the mental process of analyzing data obtained from external sources as the equivalent of a physical intrusion into the home. As I have explained, however, the process of drawing inferences from data in the public domain should not be characterized as a search.

. . . [T]he Court suggests that its rule is compelled by our holding in *Katz*. . . . In *Katz*, the electronic listening device attached to the outside of the phone booth allowed the officers to pick up the content of the conversation inside the booth, making them the functional equivalent of intruders because they gathered information that was otherwise available only to someone inside the private area; it would be as if, in this case, the thermal imager presented a view of the heat-generating activity inside petitioner's home. By contrast, the thermal imager here disclosed only the relative amounts of heat radiating from the house; it would be as if, in *Katz*, the listening device disclosed only the relative volume of sound leaving the booth, which presumably was discernible in the public domain. Surely, there is a significant difference between the general and well-settled expectation that strangers will not have direct access to the contents of private communications, on the one hand, and the rather theoretical expectation that an occasional homeowner would even care if anybody noticed the relative amounts of heat emanating from the walls of his house, on the other. . . .

. . . .

III

Although the Court is properly and commendably concerned about the threats to privacy that may flow from advances in the technology available to the law enforcement profession, it has unfortunately failed to heed the tried and true counsel of judicial restraint. Instead of concentrating on the rather mundane issue that is actually presented by the case before it, the Court has endeavored to craft an all-encompassing rule for the future. It would be far wiser to give legislators an un-impeded opportunity to grapple with these emerging issues rather than to shackle them with prematurely devised constitutional constraints.

I respectfully dissent.

Notes and Questions

(1) Why did a majority of the Court conclude that the government's use of a thermal imager in *Kyllo* was a search subject to Fourth Amendment regulation? Four Justices were of the view that because "the case . . . merely involve[d] indirect deductions from 'off-the-wall' surveillance" and not the use of "through-the-wall" technology, the Fourth Amendment threshold had not been crossed. Why did the majority disagree? Whose logic reflects a more persuasive interpretation of the reach of the Fourth Amendment?

(2) The majority stressed the importance of drawing not only a "firm," but also a "bright" line that constitutes a "clear specification of the methods of surveillance that require a warrant." What line did the Court draw? Does it constitute a clear and constitutionally justifiable specification of the technological methods of surveil-lance governed by the Fourth Amendment?

(3) The Court stressed that the thermal imager in *Kyllo* was used to discern in-formation about a "home" and that the device employed was not "in general public use." Are either or both of these elements critical to the outcome? Should they be? For a discussion of these and other issues generated by *Kyllo*, see James J. Tomkov-icz, *Technology and the Threshold of the Fourth Amendment: A Tale of Two Futures*, 72 Miss. L.J. 317 (2002).

(4) The Court has identified several variables that are relevant to assessing the "reasonableness" of privacy expectations. The cases in this chapter illustrate the op-eration of some of the more influential variables. Factors in these cases that counted against reasonableness include the "voluntary disclosure" of information to a third party who conveys it to the government, the "failure to take precautions" to safe-guard one's privacy and/or the knowing "public exposure" of one's activities, and the fact that society has no "interest in protecting the privacy" of the activities jeop-ardized by the government conduct at issue.

In *United States v. Jacobsen*, 466 U.S. 109, 104 S. Ct. 1652, 80 L. Ed. 2d 85 (1984), yet another factor played a critical role. Therein, the defendants claimed that two different actions by the government had amounted to "searches." The first was a government agent's reopening of a package that had previously been opened by Fed-eral Express employees who qualified as "private parties." The second was a chemi-cal "field test" that identified a substance found inside the package as cocaine. The Court disagreed with both claims, concluding that neither action qualified for Fourth Amendment coverage.

First, the reopening did not violate a legitimate privacy expectation primarily because "there was a virtual certainty that nothing else of significance [other than what had already been described by the private parties] was in the package and that a manual inspection of the . . . contents would not tell [the agent] anything more than he already had been told." Put another way, the removal and visual inspection of the contents "enabled the agent to learn nothing that had not previously been learned during the private search."

Second, the "field test" was outside Fourth Amendment control because it "could disclose only one fact previously unknown to the agent — whether or not a suspicious white powder was cocaine." That disclosure could "not compromise any legitimate interest in privacy" because: (1) the fact that a "substance is something other than cocaine" is "nothing of special interest," and (2) the fact that "a substance is cocaine," possession of which is "illegitimate," is not something in which one can have a "legitimate privacy interest."

In essence, the *Jacobsen* Court reasoned that a governmental action does not threaten protected privacy interests if the government is almost certain to learn no information at all or if the information that it will learn is either insignificant ("nothing of special interest") or "illegitimate." For other decisions resting on similar logic to that underlying the holding that the "reopening" of the package was not a search, see *Illinois v. Andreas*, 463 U.S. 765, 103 S. Ct. 3319, 77 L. Ed. 2d 1003 (1983) (the reopening of a large container that government agents had previously searched and then delivered to the defendant was not a search because there was no "substantial likelihood . . . that the contents [of the container had] . . . changed") and *United States v. Karo*, 468 U.S. 705, 104 S. Ct. 3296, 82 L. Ed. 2d 530 (1984) (the mere transfer to an individual of a container to which a tracking beeper had been attached was not a search because such conduct "conveyed no information at all"). For another decision concluding that no search occurred based upon essentially the same reasoning as the *Jacobsen* Court's holding that the "field test" was not a "search," see *United States v. Place*, 462 U.S. 696, 103 S. Ct. 2367, 77 L. Ed. 2d 110 (1983), *infra* at Chapter 5[A][4].

(5) In *Katz v. United States*, the first case in this chapter and the source of reasonable expectation of privacy doctrine, the Court pointedly, but vaguely, observed that the Fourth Amendment only "protects individual privacy against certain kinds of governmental intrusion." Do the subsequent cases in Chapter One make it possible to identify with precision the *kinds* of intrusions that constitute "searches" within the meaning of the Fourth Amendment?

"Threshold" Problems

1–1: Between November and July, Ging robbed several banks at gunpoint, netting over $56,000. In August, his son, Jared, who works as a police officer in another town, read a newspaper article about a serial bank robber in the area. The article caught his attention because the description of the perpetrator — five foot eight, two hundred pounds, and a male in his late fifties — sounded a lot like his father, and a description of the get-away car matched one owned by his parents. When he viewed surveillance camera photographs of the perpetrator on the Internet, Jared recognized the person in the photographs as his father.

Jared called his older brother, Garrett, to tell him about the website. Garrett agreed that the person in the photographs was their father. When Garrett said that he was going to the town where their parents lived, Jared said that he wanted to go along. He arranged for Garrett to pick him up at his house so that he could change out of his uniform. After Garrett picked up Jared, he called their younger brother, Clay, who lived near their parents. Clay also agreed that the man in the surveillance photos was their father.

The three brothers met at the fire station in the town where their parents lived. They agreed that for their father's safety and the safety of the people in their community, the robberies had to be stopped. They decided to go to their parents' house, confront their father, and convince him to turn himself in. If he refused, they planned to take him in forcibly. The brothers proceeded with their plan. Jared wore a bulletproof vest and brought his gun and police badge. He wore the vest because he knew that his father was armed and did not know his father's state of mind. Clay first entered the unlocked house, followed by Garrett and Jared. Garrett looked for his father on the first floor, and Clay and Jared searched upstairs, but their father was not home. During the course of the search, Jared and Clay saw a pair of shoes, pants, and a shirt that matched those worn by the robber in the photographs. Based on the brothers' observations, the local police obtained a search warrant. When they executed it, they found the clothes matching those worn by the robber as well as cards and journals which revealed that Ging was cheating on his wife and spending the robbery proceeds on his mistress.

Did the entry of the home by the brothers infringe upon Ging's Fourth Amendment rights?

1–2: Carly Warn rented a ground floor unit in a large apartment building at 381 Edgewood Avenue. In the fall of 1994, James began paying Warn $125 per week in exchange for the privilege of using the bedroom of Warn's nine-year-old son to cook and cut crack cocaine. James had a key to the apartment and used the bedroom frequently.

At 7:00 p.m. on December 15, James and his friend, Christopher, arrived at the apartment and went to the bedroom. At 7:45, Police Lieutenant White, a narcotics investigator, received a telephone call from a "known and reliable" informant. The informant told White that James and Christopher were bagging crack at the rear apartment on the first floor of a woman's house located at 381 Edgewood, that their activities were visible through a window, and that they might be leaving soon.

Lieutenant White and a fellow officer arrived at the address at 8:25. Because they could not see into the windows of Warn's apartment from the public sidewalk or from the street, the officers entered the fenced-in rear yard of the building and proceeded to the fenced-in side yard — common areas accessible to all other tenants —

in order to see into the building. While in the side yard, the officers spotted a window whose venetian blinds were raised five or six inches. Without standing on tiptoes or leaning against the apartment, they were able to look through the window. They saw James and Chris in a well-lit bedroom bagging what appeared to be crack.

Did the officers engage in activity that is regulated by the Fourth Amendment?

1-3: Six armed robberies occurred at various business establishments. The first was at a Dollar Tree store; the second and third, on the same day, were at a jewelry store and a 7-Eleven store; the fourth was at a Shell gas station; the fifth and sixth robberies, committed on the same evening, were at a Burger King restaurant and a McDonald's restaurant. Several of the robberies involved the use of violence against victims. Witnesses at several of the scenes described a similar dark pickup truck used by the robbers. While investigating the Burger King robbery, Officer Cork received reports describing the robber, his clothing, and the pickup truck. Shortly thereafter, a radio call concerning the McDonald's robbery indicated that the pickup truck might be headed toward Cork's location. Upon leaving the Burger King, Cork spotted a pickup truck matching the descriptions he had received and observed that a passenger inside the vehicle wore a jacket matching the description of the one reportedly worn by the Burger King robber. Cork stopped the truck, securing and arresting Jordy, the driver, and Gram, the front seat passenger. Employees of Burger King and McDonald's identified Gram as the robber.

During a post-arrest investigation, Detective Werner applied for and obtained a search warrant for the pickup truck. During a search of the truck, Werner found two cell phones. The phone numbers associated with the two phones matched the numbers disclosed by Gram and Jordy after their arrests.

Pursuant to the "Stored Communications Act" ("SCA"), the government applied for and obtained two court orders requiring Sprint/Nextel to disclose "cell site location information" ("CSLI") for calls and text messages transmitted to and from both phones. The initial application sought CSLI for four periods: August 10–15, 2010; September 18–20, 2010; January 21–23, 2011; and February 4–5, 2011. A second application sought information for a much broader timeframe: July 1, 2010 through February 6, 2011. Sprint/Nextel provided records listing CSLI for this 221-day period for each cell phone,

Historical CSLI identifies cell sites, or "base stations," to and from which a cell phone has sent or received radio signals, and the particular points in time at which these transmissions occurred, over a given timeframe. Cell sites are placed at various locations throughout a service provider's coverage area and are often placed on towers with antennae arranged in sectors facing multiple directions to better facilitate radio transmissions. A cell phone connects to a service provider's cellular network through communications with cell sites, occurring whenever a call or text message is sent or received by the phone. The phone will connect to the cell site with which it shares the strongest signal, typically the nearest cell site. The connecting cell site can change over the course of a single call as the phone travels through the coverage area. When the phone connects to the network, the service provider auto-matically captures and retains certain information about the communication, includ-ing identification of the specific cell site and sector through which the connection is made. By identifying the nearest cell tower and sector, CSLI can be used to approxi-mate the whereabouts of the cell phone at the particular points in time in which transmissions are made. The cell sites listed can be used to interpolate the path the cell phone, and the person carrying the phone, traveled during a given period.

Prior to trial, Gram and Jordy filed motions to suppress the historical CSLI ob-tained from Sprint/Nextel, claiming that the government acquired it by means of an unreasonable search. The trial judge denied the motions. At trial, the prosecution used the CLSI to establish Gram's and Jordy's locations at various times before and after most of the robberies.

Did the required production of the cell phone company records constitute a search?

1–4: A cordless telephone consists of a base unit, attached to the land-based line, and a mobile unit which transmits and receives the radio signals that carry the actual conversation to and from the base unit. Early models broadcasted on fre-quencies that could be intercepted by conventional radios. Most modern cordless phone models, however, broadcast over radio frequencies that are not capable of in-terception by conventional radios. A "radio scanner" is a highly-specialized piece of electronic equipment that is capable of monitoring the frequencies used by most current cordless phone models. Only a small number of members of the public own and operate radio scanners.

David Smith conducted illicit narcotics dealings by means of his cordless tele-phone. His neighbor, using a "Bearcat" radio scanner, listened in on Smith's tele-phone conversations. After eavesdropping upon the conversations, the neighbor reported his findings to the local police. The police then provided him with blank tapes and asked that he record future conversations. Prosecutors used the evidence captured on these tapes to convict Smith of drug trafficking.

Did the neighbor conduct a "search" governed by the Fourth Amendment?

1–5: To further his investigation of crimes involving sexual exploitation of children, Detective Laughlin of the Keen Police Department placed a profile on an Internet social networking site. The profile, which indicated that he was a 14-year-old boy, included a photograph of a boy approximately that age. In October, Mellow added Laughlin's fictitious profile to his friend list on the social networking site. Mellow's profile on the site included several photographs of nude male children, some of which were pornographic. Laughlin and Mellow subsequently engaged in several e-mail and real-time chat exchanges in mid-October. Many of the exchanges were sexually explicit, and Mellow sent pornographic images of male children to Laugh-lin by e-mail and real-time chat.

Using Mellow's e-mail address, "wildbill911," Laughlin ascertained his corresponding Internet Protocol (IP) address. Laughlin's check of the IP address enabled him to identify the city where the subscriber lived and his Internet service provider, Comcast. On October 20, Laughlin obtained a search warrant authorizing a search for subscriber information associated with Mellow's IP address. The warrant stated that Comcast was in possession of that information. Laughlin faxed the warrant to Comcast, prompting Comcast to respond by faxed letter, providing the subscriber's name, address, telephone number, type of service, account number, account status, IP assignment, e-mail user IDs, and method of payment.

Based upon this information, Laughlin applied for and received an additional warrant to search Mellow's home for certain computer-related equipment. Laughlin and the Nashua Police Department executed the warrant and seized evidence that led to the indictment of Mellow on four counts of delivery of child pornography. Mellow filed a motion to suppress all evidence obtained as a result of the initial search warrant. The judge determined that this warrant was defective.

Does Mellow have a valid Fourth Amendment claim?

1–6: In November, Inspector Marcus, along with Agents Steven and Franks, arrested Lonnie near his home pursuant to an arrest warrant obtained in connection with an investigation into a scheme to fraudulently obtain unemployment benefits from a state agency. After Lonnie's arrest, federal agents learned from Lonnie's accomplice, Albert, that Lonnie stored a laptop computer and a cardboard box containing documents and debit/credit cards related to the suspected fraud at the apartment of his girlfriend, Erica.

Agent Heather visited Erica's apartment to inquire about Lonnie and the items he had left in her home. During the course of the visit, Erica "readily and willingly" handed over Lonnie's cardboard box and laptop. Some time thereafter, Heather examined the contents of the box, finding "a ziplock bag containing credit cards, a white envelope containing identification cards, a notebook with the words 'business information' on the front cover, and some loose paperwork." Much of the information inside the box pertained to identities used to file fraudulent unemployment benefit claims, and many debit cards found belonged to victims identified in the fraud investigation. Heather found some of the information after opening and reading the contents of the notebook, which had a loose piece of paper containing a victim's name and identifying information protruding from its side. Heather prepared an affidavit in support of a warrant to search the laptop. Along with other pertinent information, Heather included in the affidavit the facts she had learned from searching the cardboard box. After a warrant was issued, Heather searched Lonnie's laptop, finding additional incriminating data.

Prior to his trial for mail fraud and aggravated identity theft, Lonnie moved to suppress the evidence found in the cardboard box and laptop searches. Erica testified at the hearing on the motion to suppress. She reported that prior to the visit from Agent Heather she and Lonnie had been dating for several weeks. He had sometimes stayed as an overnight guest in her apartment and had left personal belongings—including the box and laptop—at the apartment. Erica stated that she first became aware of the cardboard box when, prior to an out-of-town trip, Lonnie had informed her that he had left it under her bed. Although the box was not taped, he had cautioned her not to "mess with" or "touch" it. Subsequently, Lonnie had moved the box from underneath the bed into her dining room. According to Erica, after Lonnie had not been in contact for several days, she decided to look through the box for information that would enable her to reach him. She had found a notebook but had not opened it. She had also found a ziplock bag containing credit cards, a white envelope containing identification cards, and other loose paperwork resembling tax documents. Later that same day, Agent Heather came to her apartment asking about Lonnie. Erica testified that when she gave the box to Heather she did not disclose that she had searched through its contents.

Does Lonnie have a Fourth Amendment claim regarding Heather's search of the box?

1–7: The Drug Enforcement Agency (DEA) was conducting an ongoing investigation of narcotics trafficking in Spring Valley. The DEA relied on the services of Lorenzo, a confidential informant who arranged narcotics purchases from suspected distributors in the area.

On December 26, the DEA directed Lorenzo to call an individual named Jerry. Lorenzo previously had obtained narcotics from Jerry. When Lorenzo called Jerry's home, Mary answered the phone. She told Lorenzo that Jerry was not home, but that she knew about Lorenzo from Jerry. Mary informed Lorenzo that she would be able to obtain whatever he needed and instructed Lorenzo to call her again later that day. Law enforcement agents then met with Lorenzo, providing him with money to purchase the drugs, a small audio transmitter which could be clipped to a belt or held in a pocket, and a portable video camera to be concealed in his jacket. The electronic devices were intended to transmit images and sounds to a nearby government vehicle during the drug transaction.

The narcotics purchase occurred later that day. Mary instructed Lorenzo to come to 350 Rose Avenue, an address where Lorenzo had met Jerry for past narcotics purchases. Upon arrival, Lorenzo informed Mary that he wanted to buy 10 grams of cocaine. After making a telephone call, Mary stated that her source was on his way. David arrived shortly thereafter. While inside the house, Lorenzo handed David $500, and David gave Lorenzo a tinfoil package containing a crystallized substance later determined by the DEA laboratory to contain approximately 9.5 grams of cocaine base. The transaction was captured by Lorenzo's hidden video camera and transmitted to a nearby vehicle where law enforcement agents watched.

Did Lorenzo's use of the video camera constitute a "search" within the meaning of the Fourth Amendment?

1-8: By means of aerial observation, officers saw a single marijuana plant growing in a brushy area behind Delbert's residence, just outside his back yard. This observation prompted State Trooper Strong and other members of the Governor's Marijuana Eradication Detail to conduct a "knock and talk" at Delbert's residence. Strong and another officer knocked at the front door of the home. When Delbert opened the door, Strong noted a scent of smoked marijuana coming from the residence. Trooper Strong then asked Delbert for consent to search his home, but Delbert refused. At the same time, another member of the Detail walked through Delbert's property to inspect the brushy area where the marijuana plant had been spotted from the air. No fencing, gates, or postings impeded his access to this area, which was visible from the road. Nine marijuana plants were discovered in this area.

After Delbert had denied permission to search his home, Trooper Strong walked around the house and across the back yard. He saw "10 small marijuana plants in a tray sitting at the end of the fence behind the residence, near two dog kennels and a clothesline containing freshly laundered clothes." The 10 plants were "in the open, approximately 35 yards from" Delbert's home. The lawn in the area was "well-kept and mowed. A low, two-plank fence separated the back of this yard from the adjoining brushy area" where the single marijuana plant was spotted. Trooper Strong did not have to move anything in order to see the 10 small plants. The area where those plants were situated was visible from the road if viewed from the right side of the house, but not from the left side of the house. The plants were not identifiable as marijuana from the road.

Which of the officers' actions, if any, were regulated by the Fourth Amendment?

1–9: Corporal Douglas, a State Trooper, spotted Pice speeding on I-95 and signaled for him to pull over. After Pice stopped his vehicle on the shoulder, Douglas radioed a request that Corporal Alison, a narcotics dog handler, come to the scene to perform "a K9 examination" of the vehicle. Douglas then parked his car behind Pice's, approached, and spoke to Pice through the open front passenger window. Douglas observed "stains, trash, papers, and discarded food wrappers in the passenger seat area," which "gave the car a lived-in look." A number of "cell phones and small electronic devices, mostly disassembled, and an open box of No-Doz were on the passenger seat. Bird seed and children's toys were scattered in the back seat."

When asked, Pice supplied a driver's license with the name "Rickard Tech III." When asked for the car's registration and insurance, Pice said that his girlfriend had rented the car and that he did not have the rental documents. After Douglas instructed Pice to step out and walk to the rear of the car, Pice complied, leaving the driver's door open. During an exchange that followed, Pice extracted a car rental agreement from his pocket that listed "Tamara Lundy" as the renter and described the rented car as a grey Intrepid — not the car Pice was driving. When Douglas asked him the name of his girlfriend, Pice could not give her last name. Douglas instructed Pice to sit by the guardrail behind the car while he ran a background check on the driver's license.

By this point, Corporal Alison had arrived at the scene with "K-9 Cole." Alison and Cole had been certified as a team for four years. Alison gave Cole the command to sniff the vehicle but did not direct his movements further, allowing the canine "to take the lead." Cole "responded to" the trunk area, then proceeded to the front passenger side door. He "jumped up onto his hind legs and reached his nose into the vehicle toward the dashboard through the open passenger side window," indicating that he "had an odor" and "was onto something." He then retreated toward the trunk and proceeded to the driver's side, jumping in through the open door. Cole sniffed at "the seams of the glove box and around the air vents," then leaped into the back seat and "continued to sniff the area." At that point, Alison concluded the K-9 examination, informing Douglas that Cole had "alerted" and that she "was certain that he had detected the odor of narcotics."

After the two officers discussed the information gained from Pice and Cole's examination, they decided to search the car. When they found one kilogram of cocaine and over $20,000 in cash in the glove box, Douglas arrested Pice.

Was the K-9 examination of the car governed by the Fourth Amendment's reasonableness requirement?

1–10: Detective J.A. Hack, a police officer assigned to the Metropolitan Drug Enforcement Network Team (MDENT), was performing a package interdiction — attempting to identify packages that could contain narcotics — at a U.S. Post Office. One parcel had several indicia of a typical narcotics package: it was an Express Mail envelope; it had a hand-written label; it was shipped overnight from a known drug source state; and no signature was required upon delivery. After picking up the soft-sided envelope, Hack felt a smaller box inside of the envelope. He squeezed or pressed on that box and felt a crunch or the moving of what he thought to be pills. The objects that he felt move were similar to pills he had felt before. Hack discovered that the sender's name and address did not coincide.

Hack arranged a controlled delivery of the envelope to the intended recipient. Postal Inspector Dome took it to the front door of the home to which it was addressed. After Dome knocked, Carl opened the door and accepted delivery of the envelope. Hack, who was watching from a nearby car, approached and identified himself. Carl invited Hack and Dome to come inside. Detective Hack informed Carl and his wife, Patty, that he was there because of the envelope and asked Carl if he had been expecting it. Carl replied that a friend had sent the envelope, which contained "medicine."

After Carl consented to Hack's request to search the envelope, Hack opened it and found a rectangular cardboard Priority Mail box approximately an inch and a quarter thick and several inches in length and width. Inside the box was a soft gift-wrapped envelope, within which was a Ziploc bag containing oxycodone pills. Hack asked Carl if they were the pills he was expecting, and he replied that they were.

Both Carl and Patty then consented to a search of their residence. Hack, Dome, and other officers thoroughly searched the home. During that search, which led to the discovery of additional contraband, both Carl and Patty made incriminating admissions about their involvement in oxycodone distribution. Carl and Patty were charged with conspiracy to distribute oxycodone. Prior to trial, they have moved to suppress the pills found in the envelope and all other evidence acquired as a result of the discovery of the pills. They contend that Detective Hack's initial inspection of the package at the post office was an unreasonable search.

Did Hack's inspection of the express mail package constitute a search?

1–11: Detective Schneider was assigned to investigate a report by Officer Larson that his flashlight had been stolen from the men's locker room of the police department building. Schneider had heard rumors that other items had also been stolen from the locker room. As part of his investigation, Schneider arranged to have a surveillance camera installed behind a ceiling tile near one of the locker room entrances. The camera, which was concealed from view and connected to a time-lapse video cassette recorder (VCR), recorded only the area around Larson's locker. However, Schneider was aware that it would capture images of male officers changing their clothes.

Every male officer had a locker in the men's locker room. Officers regularly changed, showered, and used the sinks, toilets, and urinals in the locker room. The general public used restroom facilities located in the lobby of the building and had very little access to most other areas of the building, especially the locker room. Suspects, arrestees, and persons being questioned had no access to the locker room or to the hallway outside the locker room. Persons in the hallway outside the locker room could not see into it, unless one of the doors was held open. Individuals who were not police department employees might enter the locker room to perform maintenance functions or to use the facilities when performing services in the communications room. At least one female officer was permitted to use the male locker room. However, she took precautions to make sure that no men were present in the locker room before she entered and that no one would enter the locker room while she was changing.

There were no signs in the locker room or anywhere else in the building announcing that the locker room was subject to video, audio, or photographic surveillance. Police department employees were never informed, either orally or in writing, that they might be subject to video, audio, or photographic surveillance while in the locker room.

Several years after the taping began, while moving police department equipment out of the building, Officer Harris found a tape in the VCR and brought it to the attention of other officers. The tape included images from multiple days and focused exclusively on the area around Officer Larson's locker. A number of police officers appeared on the tape in various states of undress. Based on these occurrences, police officers who used the locker room filed a civil suit against the city and Detective Schneider, alleging violation of their Fourth Amendment rights.

Did the videotaping in the locker room intrude upon rights protected by the Fourth Amendment?

Selected Bibliography

Susan Bandes, *Power, Privacy, and Thermal Imaging,* 86 Minn. L. Rev. 1379 (2002)

Patricia L. Bellia & Susan Freiwald, *Fourth Amendment Protection for Stored E-Mail,* 2008 U. Chi. Legal F. 121 (2008)

Marc Jonathan Blitz, *Video Surveillance and the Constitution of Public Space: Fitting the Fourth Amendment to a World that Tracks Image and Identity,* 82 Tex. L. Rev. 1349 (2004)

Susan W. Brenner, *The Fourth Amendment in an Era of Ubiquitous Technology,* 75 Miss. L.J. 1 (2005)

Thomas K. Clancy, *What is a "Search" Within the Meaning of the Fourth Amendment?,* 70 Alb. L. Rev. 1 (2006)

Sherry F. Colb, *What Is a Search? Two Conceptual Flaws in Fourth Amendment Doctrine and Some Hints of a Remedy,* 55 Stan. L. Rev. 119 (2002)

Donald L. Doernberg, *"Can You Hear Me Now?": Expectations of Privacy, False Friends, and the Perils of Speaking Under the Supreme Court's Fourth Amendment Jurisprudence,* 39 Ind. L. Rev. 253 (2006)

Martin R. Gardner, *Rediscovering Trespass: Towards a Regulatory Approach to Defining Fourth Amendment Scope in a World of Advancing Technology,* 62 Buffalo L. Rev. 1027 (2014)

David Gray & Danielle Citron, *The Right to Quantitative Privacy,* 98 Minn. L. Rev. 62 (2013)

Christian M. Halliburton, *How Privacy Killed* Katz: *A Tale of Cognitive Freedom and the Property of Personhood as Fourth Amendment Norm,* 42 Akron L. Rev. 803 (2009)

Catherine Hancock, *Warrants for Wearing a Wire: Fourth Amendment Privacy and Justice Harlan's Dissent in* United States v. White, 79 Miss. L.J. 35 (2009)

Stephen E. Henderson, *Beyond the (Current) Fourth Amendment: Protecting Third-Party Information, Third Parties, and the Rest of Us Too,* 34 Pepp. L. Rev. 975 (2007)

Stephen E. Henderson, *Nothing New Under the Sun? A Technologically Rational Doctrine of Fourth Amendment Search,* 56 Mercer L. Rev. 507 (2005)

Renee McDonald Hutchins, *The Anatomy of a Search: Intrusiveness and the Fourth Amendment,* 44 U. Rich. L. Rev. 1185 (2010)

Orin S. Kerr, *Searches and Seizures in a Digital World,* 119 Harv. L. Rev. 531 (2005)

Orin S. Kerr, *The Fourth Amendment and New Technologies: Constitutional Myths and the Case for Caution,* 102 Mich. L. Rev. 801 (2004)

Tracey Maclin, Katz, Kyllo, *and Technology: Virtual Fourth Amendment Protection in the Twenty-First Century,* 72 Miss. L.J. 51 (2002)

Richard H. Seamon, Kyllo v. United States *and the Partial Ascendance of Justice Scalia's Fourth Amendment,* 79 Wash. U. L.Q. 1013 (2001)

Brian J. Serr, *Great Expectations of Privacy: A New Model for Fourth Amendment Protection*, 73 Minn. L. Rev. 583 (1989)

Ric Simmons, *From Katz to Kyllo: A Blueprint for Adapting the Fourth Amendment to Twenty-First Century Technologies*, 53 Hastings L.J. 1303 (2002)

David A. Sklansky, *Back to the Future: Kyllo, Katz, and Common Law*, 72 Miss. L.J. 143 (2002)

Daniel J. Solove, *Digital Dossiers and the Dissipation of Fourth Amendment Privacy*, 75 S. Cal. L. Rev. 1083 (2002)

Katherine J. Strandburg, *Home, Home on the Web and Other Fourth Amendment Implications of Technosocial Change*, 70 Md. L. Rev. 614 (2011)

James J. Tomkovicz, *Beyond Secrecy for Secrecy's Sake: Toward an Expanded Vision of the Fourth Amendment Privacy Province*, 36 Hastings L.J. 645 (1985)

James J. Tomkovicz, *Technology and the Threshold of the Fourth Amendment: A Tale of Two Futures*, 72 Miss. L.J. 317 (2002)

Chapter 2

Unreasonableness and the Probable Cause Requirement

Introductory Note

Chapter One addressed the breadth of the Fourth Amendment's regulation of searches. The remaining chapters in PART I are primarily concerned with the substance of the protection provided by the Fourth Amendment. That protection is contained within two separate clauses, the first, known as the "unreasonableness" clause, and the second, known as the "warrant" clause.

In the first clause, the Framers enshrined a vague, deceptively simple prohibition upon "unreasonable" searches and seizures. As will be seen, the Supreme Court has discerned substantial content within that prohibition and has developed an extensive and complex doctrinal framework for expressing that content. The "warrant" clause is both more specific in content and narrower in scope. Nonetheless, the particular constraints it imposes upon the issuance and content of warrants have been the subject of debate, interpretation, and some doctrinal development. Chapters Two through Five each focus upon a distinct aspect of the Supreme Court's interpretation of these two Fourth Amendment clauses.

Chapter Two treats the concept of "probable cause." The Fourth Amendment states explicitly that "no warrant shall issue, but upon probable cause." The constitutional text, therefore, specifies that probable cause is an essential precondition for a valid warrant to search or to seize. Chapters Four and Five will explore in detail the circumstances in which warrants are not required. For present purposes, suffice it to say that a variety of types of warrantless searches and seizures are constitutionally acceptable. The Fourth Amendment's text does not explicitly mandate probable cause as a precondition for such warrantless searches and seizures. The Supreme Court, however, has concluded that probable cause is also a norm of reasonableness for searches and seizures without warrants. *See Wong Sun v. United States*, 371 U.S. 471, 479–80, 83 S. Ct. 407, 413, 9 L. Ed. 2d 441, 450 (1963).

Typically, questions of probable cause arise in connection with two basic, and distinguishable, law enforcement practices — arrests and searches. Because the natures and objects of arrests and searches are different, the definitions of probable cause to arrest and probable cause to search are different.

Probable cause to arrest "exists where 'the facts and circumstances within [the officers'] knowledge and of which they [have] reasonably trustworthy information [are] sufficient in themselves to warrant a man of reasonable caution in the belief that' *an offense has been or is being committed" by the person to be arrested. Brinegar v. United States*, 338 U.S. 160, 175–76, 69 S. Ct. 1302, 1311, 93 L. Ed. 1879, 1890 (1949) (quoting *Carroll v. United States*, 267 U.S. 132, 162, 45 S. Ct. 280, 288, 69 L. Ed. 543, 555 (1925)) (emphasis added). In essence, probable cause to arrest a person requires that there be a certain quantum of likelihood that: (1) that particular individual (2) has committed or is committing a particular offense.

Probable cause to search "exists if 'the facts and circumstances within [the officers'] knowledge and of which they [have] reasonably trustworthy information [are] sufficient in themselves to warrant a man of reasonable caution in the belief that' *an item subject to seizure will be found in the place to be searched." United States v. Garza-Hernandez*, 623 F.2d 496, 499 (7th Cir. 1980) (quoting *Brinegar v. United States*, 338 U.S. 160, 175–76, 69 S. Ct. 1302, 1311, 93 L. Ed. 1879, 1890 (1949)) (emphasis added). Probable cause to search an area demands that there be a certain quantum of likelihood that: (1) something that is properly subject to seizure by the government, i.e., contraband or fruits, instrumentalities, or evidence of a crime, (2) will be in the specific place to be searched when the search occurs. Ordinarily, this involves a showing that such an item is currently in that place, but probable cause can also be established by a showing of sufficient likelihood that the item not presently located in the place will be there in the future, at the time a search is carried out. See *United States v. Grubbs, infra*, Chapter 3[C].

Probable cause does not require certainty, but only a sufficient likelihood. Consequently, a showing of probable cause is not undermined if the conclusions drawn turn out, in fact, to have been mistaken. *See Hill v. California*, 401 U.S. 797, 804, 91 S. Ct. 1106, 1110–111, 28 L. Ed. 2d 484, 490 (1971); *see also Los Angeles County, California v. Rettele*, 550 U.S. 609, 127 S. Ct. 1989, 167 L. Ed. 2d 974 (2007). Because certainty is not demanded, both probable cause to search and probable cause to arrest raise the issue of the necessary quantum or level of probability required by the Fourth Amendment.[1]

One issue that can arise with regard to probable cause to *search* is "staleness." This refers to situations in which the facts at one time did establish sufficient likelihood that an object or person would be found in a particular place to satisfy the

---

1. The Court has repeatedly indicated that the standard of probable cause for warrant-authorized searches and seizures is slightly less demanding than the standard of probable cause for warrantless searches and seizures. *See United States v. Ventresca*, 380 U.S. 102, 106, 85 S. Ct. 741, 744, 13 L. Ed. 2d 684, 687 (1965). However, the Court has never specified the precise difference.

probable cause demand. The passage of time, however, has made the likelihood that the object is still in that place too low to satisfy the constitutional standard. Information that establishes probable cause to search can go stale and fail to clear the constitutional bar because objects and people by their nature do not remain permanently in one place. Rather, they move from one place to another. For example, if officers have probable cause that a package of contraband is in a home, but they delay applying for a search warrant while conducting a month-long investigation, it is entirely possible that their probable cause showing will have gone stale and will not support issuance of a valid warrant. Similarly, information in support of a warrantless search might go stale after sufficient time passes and no longer justify the warrantless search that would have been reasonable at an earlier time. If officers have adequate reasons to believe that the proceeds of a robbery are in the trunk of a vehicle, but do not search the vehicle for some reason until a week has elapsed, their search may well be unreasonable because the probable cause that existed earlier no longer does. Moreover, even if officers apply for and obtain a valid search warrant at a time when the facts are fresh and do establish a likelihood high enough to satisfy the Fourth Amendment probable cause norm, if they delay execution of the warrant for too long, time may cause the warrant to go stale. A warrant that once furnished valid authority for a search of a place no longer can because time has diminished the probability that the object or objects of the search are in the place specified in the warrant. Suppose, for example, that a judge issues a search warrant for an office based on an affidavit that recites facts making it very probable that a murder weapon is in that office. Officers postpone execution of the warrant while they investigate further and ultimately search the office six weeks after the warrant was issued. Even if they do find the weapon in the office, it is arguable that the search was unreasonable because the warrant went stale during the six-week delay.[2]

Two of the three main cases in this chapter are concerned with a particularly troublesome source of information for probable cause determinations — "hearsay from informants." In this context, "hearsay" means that the information was not acquired first-hand by the officer or other individual who related it to the magistrate or to the trial court — i.e., it was not within the personal knowledge of that officer or individual. "Informants" include known and anonymous suppliers of information. Concerns that are not present when officers or others provide first-hand information arise when the information said to support probable cause is personally known only to an absent, possibly anonymous, informant.

---

2. Despite suggestions to the contrary, *see United States v. Watson*, 423 U.S. 411, 432, 96 S. Ct. 820, 832, 46 L. Ed. 2d 598, 614 (1976) (Powell, J., concurring), probable cause to arrest does not go stale. In rare cases, the subsequent discovery of contradictory information regarding the likelihood that a person has committed an offense can nullify a previously established basis for an arrest. The passage of time alone, however, does not diminish that likelihood, and, therefore, does not undermine a showing of probable cause to arrest. *See Watson*, 423 U.S. at 449, 96 S. Ct. at 840, 46 L. Ed. 2d at 624 (Marshall, J., dissenting).

Draper v. United States, 358 U.S. 307, 79 S. Ct. 329, 3 L. Ed. 2d 327 (1959), is a pre-1960s case in which the Court dealt with the probable cause issues that arise when the basis for police action is an informer's tip. The *Draper* opinion is particularly significant because, as will be seen in the first two cases in this chapter, its holding has been used as a benchmark in later decisions.

In *Draper*, a known informant, one Hereford, told a federal narcotics agent that the defendant had gone to Chicago by train on September 6 and would be returning to Denver with three ounces of heroin on the morning of September 8 or 9 by train. Hereford provided a detailed description of Draper and his clothing, said that he would be carrying a tan bag, and reported that he "walked real fast." The agent and a police officer saw a man meeting the description in all respects arrive on the morning train from Chicago on September 9. They arrested and searched Draper, finding heroin and a syringe.

The Court quickly dismissed the defendant's claim that hearsay could not be the basis of a finding of probable cause, noting that precedent had already "settled the question the other way." The majority then concluded that there had, in fact, been probable cause to arrest Draper. First, the hearsay came "from one ... whose information had always been found accurate and reliable" in the past. Moreover, when the agent

> saw a man, having the exact physical attributes and wearing the precise clothing and carrying the tan zipper bag ... alight from one of the very trains from the very place stated by Hereford and start to walk at a "fast" pace toward the station exit, [he] had personally verified every facet of the information given him by Hereford except whether [Draper] had accomplished his mission and had three ounces of heroin on his person or in his bag. And surely, with every other bit of Hereford's information being thus personally verified, Marsh had "reasonable grounds" to believe that the remaining unverified bit of Hereford's information — that Draper would have the heroin with him — was likewise true.

In the 1960s, a majority of the Court concluded that hearsay-based findings of probable cause raised problems and issues meriting closer scrutiny, more detailed analysis, and more refined doctrine. Dissatisfaction with *Draper*'s approach gave rise to the analysis discussed and developed in *Spinelli*, the first case in this brief chapter. In time, however, dissatisfaction with perceived deficiencies in the *Spinelli* approach led the Court to chart a new course in *Illinois v. Gates*, the other main hearsay case in Chapter Two.

The opinions in *Spinelli* and *Gates* reflect dramatically different perspectives on the constitutional questions raised by reliance on hearsay from informants. Each makes important historical and theoretical contributions to the debate and resolution of significant probable cause issues. Each should inform analyses of the issues that remain unresolved today. Students should try to identify and describe the distinct phases of doctrinal development embodied in the two decisions and should reflect upon the nature and significance of the constitutional concerns that have made this area of probable cause law so unstable and problematic.

Spinelli v. United States

United States Supreme Court

393 U.S. 410, 89 S. Ct. 584, 21 L. Ed. 2d 637 (1969)

MR. JUSTICE HARLAN delivered the opinion of the Court.

William Spinelli was convicted under 18 U.S.C. § 1952 of traveling to St. Louis, Missouri, from a nearby Illinois suburb with the intention of conducting gambling activities proscribed by Missouri law. At every appropriate stage in the proceedings in the lower courts, the petitioner challenged the constitutionality of the warrant which authorized the FBI search that uncovered the evidence necessary for his conviction.... Believing it desirable that the principles of [*Aguilar v. Texas*, 378 U.S. 108, 84 S. Ct. 1509, 12 L. Ed. 2d 723 (1964)], should be further explicated, we granted certiorari....

In *Aguilar*, a search warrant had issued upon an affidavit of police officers who swore only that they had "received reliable information from a credible person and do believe" that narcotics were being illegally stored on the described premises. While recognizing that the constitutional requirement of probable cause can be satisfied by hearsay information, this Court held the affidavit inadequate for two reasons. First, the application failed to set forth any of the "underlying circumstances" necessary to enable the magistrate independently to judge of the validity of the informant's conclusion that the narcotics were where he said they were. Second, the affiant-officers did not attempt to support their claim that their informant was "credible" or his information "reliable." The Government is, however, quite right in saying that the FBI affidavit in the present case is more ample than that in *Aguilar*. Not only does it contain a report from an anonymous informant, but it also contains a report of an independent FBI investigation which is said to corroborate the informant's tip. We are, then, required to delineate the manner in which *Aguilar's* two-pronged test should be applied in these circumstances.

In essence, the affidavit, reproduced in full in the Appendix to this opinion, contained the following allegations:[3]

1. The FBI had kept track of Spinelli's movements on five days during the month of August 1965. On four of these occasions, Spinelli was seen crossing one of two bridges leading from Illinois into St. Louis, Missouri, between 11 a.m. and 12:15 p.m. On four of the five days, Spinelli was also seen parking his car in a lot used by residents of an apartment house at 1108 Indian Circle

---

3. It is, of course, of no consequence that the agents might have had additional information which could have been given to the Commissioner. "It is elementary that in passing on the validity of a warrant, the reviewing court may consider only information brought to the magistrate's attention." *Aguilar v. Texas*, 378 U.S. 108, 109, n. 1, 84 S. Ct. 1509, 1511....

Drive in St. Louis, between 3:30 p.m. and 4:45 p.m.[4] On one day, Spinelli was followed further and seen to enter a particular apartment in the building.

2. An FBI check with the telephone company revealed that this apartment contained two telephones listed under the name of Grace P. Hagen, and carrying the numbers WYdown 4–0029 and WYdown 4–0136.

3. The application stated that "William Spinelli is known to this affiant and to federal law enforcement agents and local law enforcement agents as a bookmaker, an associate of bookmakers, a gambler, and an associate of gamblers."

4. Finally it was stated that the FBI "has been informed by a confidential reliable informant that William Spinelli is operating a handbook and accepting wagers and disseminating wagering information by means of the telephones which have been assigned the numbers WYdown 4–0029 and WYdown 4–0136."

There can be no question that the last item mentioned, detailing the informant's tip, has a fundamental place in this warrant application. Without it, probable cause could not be established. The first two items reflect only innocent-seeming activity and data. Spinelli's travels to and from the apartment building and his entry into a particular apartment on one occasion could hardly be taken as bespeaking gambling activity; and there is surely nothing unusual about an apartment containing two separate telephones. Many a householder indulges himself in this petty luxury. Finally, the allegation that Spinelli was "known" to the affiant and to other federal and local law enforcement officers as a gambler and an associate of gamblers is but a bald and unilluminating assertion of suspicion that is entitled to no weight in appraising the magistrate's decision. *Nathanson v. United States*, 290 U.S. 41, 46, 54 S. Ct. 11, 12, 78 L. Ed. 159 (1933).

So much indeed the Government does not deny. Rather, following the reasoning of the Court of Appeals, the Government claims that the informant's tip gives a suspicious color to the FBI's reports detailing Spinelli's innocent-seeming conduct and that, conversely, the FBI's surveillance corroborates the informant's tip, thereby entitling it to more weight. It is true, of course, that the magistrate is obligated to render a judgment based upon a common-sense reading of the entire affidavit. *United States v. Ventresca*, 380 U.S. 102, 108, 85 S. Ct. 741, 745, 13 L. Ed. 2d 684 (1965). We believe, however, that the "totality of circumstances" approach taken by the Court of Appeals paints with too broad a brush. Where, as here, the informer's tip is a necessary element in a finding of probable cause, its proper weight must be determined by a more precise analysis.

The informer's report must first be measured against *Aguilar*'s standards so that its probative value can be assessed. If the tip is found inadequate under *Aguilar*, the

---

4. No report was made as to Spinelli's movements during the period between his arrival in St. Louis at noon and his arrival at the parking lot in the late afternoon. In fact, the evidence at trial indicated that Spinelli frequented the offices of his stockbroker during this period.

other allegations which corroborate the information contained in the hearsay report should then be considered. At this stage as well, however, the standards enunciated in *Aguilar* must inform the magistrate's decision. He must ask: Can it fairly be said that the tip, even when certain parts of it have been corroborated by independent sources, is as trustworthy as a tip which would pass *Aguilar*'s tests without independent corroboration? *Aguilar* is relevant at this stage of the inquiry as well because the tests it establishes were designed to implement the long-standing principle that probable cause must be determined by a "neutral and detached magistrate," and not by "the officer engaged in the often competitive enterprise of ferreting out crime." *Johnson v. United States*, 333 U.S. 10, 14, 68 S. Ct. 367, 369, 92 L. Ed. 436 (1948). A magistrate cannot be said to have properly discharged his constitutional duty if he relies on an informer's tip which — even when partially corroborated — is not as reliable as one which passes *Aguilar*'s requirements when standing alone.

Applying these principles to the present case, we first consider the weight to be given the informer's tip when it is considered apart from the rest of the affidavit. It is clear that a Commissioner could not credit it without abdicating his constitutional function. Though the affiant swore that his confidant was "reliable," he offered the magistrate no reason in support of this conclusion. Perhaps even more important is the fact that *Aguilar*'s other test has not been satisfied. The tip does not contain a sufficient statement of the underlying circumstances from which the informer concluded that Spinelli was running a bookmaking operation. We are not told how the FBI's source received his information — it is not alleged that the informant personally observed Spinelli at work or that he had ever placed a bet with him. Moreover, if the informant came by the information indirectly, he did not explain why his sources were reliable. In the absence of a statement detailing the manner in which the information was gathered, it is especially important that the tip describe the accused's criminal activity in sufficient detail that the magistrate may know that he is relying on something more substantial than a casual rumor circulating in the underworld or an accusation based merely on an individual's general reputation.

The detail provided by the informant in *Draper v. United States*, 358 U.S. 307, 79 S. Ct. 329, 3 L. Ed. 2d 327 (1959), provides a suitable benchmark. While Hereford, the Government's informer in that case, did not state the way in which he had obtained his information, he reported that Draper had gone to Chicago the day before by train and that he would return to Denver by train with three ounces of heroin on one of two specified mornings. Moreover, Hereford went on to describe, with minute particularity, the clothes that Draper would be wearing upon his arrival at the Denver station. A magistrate, when confronted with such detail, could reasonably infer that the informant had gained his information in a reliable way.[5] Such an inference cannot be made in the present case. Here, the only facts supplied were that

---

5. While *Draper* involved the question whether the police had probable cause for an arrest without a warrant, the analysis required for an answer to this question is basically similar to that demanded of a magistrate when he considers whether a search warrant should issue.

Spinelli was using two specified telephones and that these phones were being used in gambling operations. This meager report could easily have been obtained from an offhand remark heard at a neighborhood bar.

Nor do we believe that the patent doubts *Aguilar* raises as to the report's reliability are adequately resolved by a consideration of the allegations detailing the FBI's independent investigative efforts. At most, these allegations indicated that Spinelli could have used the telephones specified by the informant for some purpose. This cannot by itself be said to support both the inference that the informer was generally trustworthy and that he had made his charge against Spinelli on the basis of information obtained in a reliable way. Once again, *Draper* provides a relevant comparison. Independent police work in that case corroborated much more than one small detail that had been provided by the informant. There, the police, upon meeting the inbound Denver train on the second morning specified by informer Hereford, saw a man whose dress corresponded precisely to Hereford's detailed description. It was then apparent that the informant had not been fabricating his report out of whole cloth; since the report was of the sort which in common experience may be recognized as having been obtained in a reliable way, it was perfectly clear that probable cause had been established.

We conclude, then, that in the present case the informant's tip — even when corroborated to the extent indicated — was not sufficient to provide the basis for a finding of probable cause. This is not to say that the tip was so insubstantial that it could not properly have counted in the magistrate's determination. Rather, it needed some further support. When we look to the other parts of the application, however, we find nothing alleged which would permit the suspicions engendered by the informant's report to ripen into a judgment that a crime was probably being committed. As we have already seen, the allegations detailing the FBI's surveillance of Spinelli and its investigation of the telephone company records contain no suggestion of criminal conduct when taken by themselves — and they are not endowed with an aura of suspicion by virtue of the informer's tip. Nor do we find that the FBI's reports take on a sinister color when read in light of common knowledge that bookmaking is often carried on over the telephone and from premises ostensibly used by others for perfectly normal purposes. Such an argument would carry weight in a situation in which the premises contain an unusual number of telephones or abnormal activity is observed, but it does not fit this case where neither of these factors is present. All that remains to be considered is the flat statement that Spinelli was "known" to the FBI and others as a gambler. But just as a simple assertion of police suspicion is not itself a sufficient basis for a magistrate's finding of probable cause, we do not believe it may be used to give additional weight to allegations that would otherwise be insufficient.

The affidavit, then, falls short of the standards set forth in *Aguilar, Draper,* and our other decisions that give content to the notion of probable cause. In holding as we have done, we do not retreat from the established propositions that only the probability, and not a *prima facie* showing, of criminal activity is the standard of probable cause, *Beck v. Ohio*, 379 U.S. 89, 96, 85 S. Ct. 223, 228, 13 L. Ed. 2d 142 (1964); that affidavits of probable cause are tested by much less rigorous standards than those governing the admissibility of evidence at trial, *McCray v. Illinois*, 386 U.S. 300, 311, 87 S. Ct. 1056, 1062 (1967); that in judging probable cause issuing magistrates are not to be confined by niggardly limitations or by restrictions on the use of their common sense, *United States v. Ventresca*, 380 U.S. 102, 108, 85 S. Ct. 741, 745 (1965); and that their determination of probable cause should be paid great deference by reviewing courts, *Jones v. United States*, 362 U.S. 257, 270–271, 80 S. Ct. 725, 735–736 (1960). But we cannot sustain this warrant without diluting important safeguards that assure that the judgment of a disinterested judicial officer will interpose itself between the police and the citizenry.

Reversed and remanded.

Mr. Justice Marshall took no part in the consideration or decision of this case.

Mr. Justice White, concurring.

An investigator's affidavit that he has seen gambling equipment being moved into a house at a specified address will support the issuance of a search warrant. The oath affirms the honesty of the statement and negatives the lie or imagination. Personal observation attests to the facts asserted — that there is gambling equipment on the premises at the named address.

But if the officer simply avers, without more, that there is gambling paraphernalia on certain premises, the warrant should not issue, even though the belief of the officer is an honest one, as evidenced by his oath, and even though the magistrate knows him to be an experienced, intelligent officer who has been reliable in the past . . . .

What is missing . . . is a statement of the basis for the affiant's believing the facts contained in the affidavit . . . . If an officer swears that there is gambling equipment at a certain address, the possibilities are (1) that he has seen the equipment; (2) that he has observed or perceived facts from which the presence of the equipment may reasonably be inferred; and (3) that he has obtained the information from someone else. If (1) is true, the affidavit is good. But in (2), the affidavit is insufficient unless the perceived facts are given, for it is the magistrate, not the officer, who is to judge the existence of probable cause. With respect to (3), where the officer's information is hearsay, no warrant should issue absent good cause for crediting that hearsay. Because an affidavit asserting, without more, the location of gambling equipment at a particular address does not claim personal observation of any of the facts by the officer, and because of the likelihood that the information came from an unidentified third party, affidavits of this type are unacceptable.

Neither should the warrant issue if the officer states that there is gambling equipment in a particular apartment and that his information comes from an informant, named or unnamed, since the honesty of the informant and the basis for his report are unknown. Nor would the missing elements be completely supplied by the officer's oath that the informant has often furnished reliable information in the past. This attests to the honesty of the informant, but *Aguilar v. Texas, supra,* requires something more — did the information come from observation, or did the informant in turn receive it from another? Absent additional facts for believing the informant's report, his assertion stands no better than the oath of the officer to the same effect. Indeed, if the affidavit of an officer, known by the magistrate to be honest and experienced, stating that gambling equipment is located in a certain building is unacceptable, it would be quixotic if a similar statement from an honest informant were found to furnish probable cause. A strong argument can be made that both should be acceptable under the Fourth Amendment, but under our cases neither is. The past reliability of the informant can no more furnish probable cause for believing his current report than can previous experience with the officer himself.

If the affidavit rests on hearsay — an informant's report — what is necessary under *Aguilar* is one of two things: the informant must declare either (1) that he has himself seen or perceived the fact or facts asserted; or (2) that his information is hearsay, but there is good reason for believing it — perhaps one of the usual grounds for crediting hearsay information. The first presents few problems: since the report, although hearsay, purports to be first-hand observation, remaining doubt centers on the honesty of the informant, and that worry is dissipated by the officer's previous experience with the informant. The other basis for accepting the informant's report is more complicated. But if, for example, the informer's hearsay comes from one of the actors in the crime in the nature of admission against interest, the affidavit giving this information should be held sufficient.

I am inclined to agree with the majority that there are limited special circumstances in which an "honest" informant's report, if sufficiently detailed, will in effect verify itself — that is, the magistrate when confronted with such detail could reasonably infer that the informant had gained his information in a reliable way. Detailed information may sometimes imply that the informant himself has observed the facts. Suppose an informant with whom an officer has had satisfactory experience states that there is gambling equipment in the living room of a specified apartment and describes in detail not only the equipment itself but also the appointments and furnishments in the apartment. Detail like this, if true at all, must rest on personal observation either of the informant or of someone else. If the latter, we know nothing of the third person's honesty or sources; he may be making a wholly false report. But it is arguable that on these facts it was the informant himself who has perceived the facts, for the information reported is not usually the subject of casual day-to-day conversation. Because the informant is honest and it is probable that he has viewed the facts, there is probable cause for the issuance of a warrant.

So too in the special circumstances of *Draper v. United States*, 358 U.S. 307, 79 S. Ct. 329, 3 L. Ed. 2d 327 (1959), the kind of information related by the informant is not generally sent ahead of a person's arrival in a city except to those who are intimately connected with making careful arrangements for meeting him. The informant, posited as honest, somehow had the reported facts, very likely from one of the actors in the plan, or as one of them himself. The majority's suggestion is that a warrant could have been obtained based only on the informer's report. I am inclined to agree, although it seems quite plain that if it may be so easily inferred from the affidavit that the informant has himself observed the facts or has them from an actor in the event, no possible harm could come from requiring a statement to that effect, thereby removing the difficult and recurring questions which arise in such situations.

Of course, *Draper* itself did not proceed on this basis. Instead the Court pointed out that when the officer saw a person getting off the train at the specified time, dressed and conducting himself precisely as the informant had predicted, all but the critical fact with respect to possessing narcotics had then been verified and for that reason the officer had "reasonable grounds" to believe also that Draper was carrying narcotics. Unquestionably, verification of arrival time, dress, and gait reinforced the honesty of the informant — he had not reported a made-up story. But if what *Draper* stands for is that the existence of the tenth and critical fact is made sufficiently probable to justify the issuance of a warrant by verifying nine other facts coming from the same source, I have my doubts about that case.

In the first place, the proposition is not that the tenth fact may be logically inferred from the other nine or that the tenth fact is usually found in conjunction with the other nine. No one would suggest that just anyone getting off the 10:30 train dressed as Draper was, with a brisk walk and carrying a zipper bag, should be arrested for carrying narcotics. The thrust of *Draper* is not that the verified facts have independent significance with respect to proof of the tenth. The argument instead relates to the reliability of the source: because an informant is right about some things, he is more probably right about other facts, usually the critical, unverified facts.

But the Court's cases have already rejected for Fourth Amendment purposes the notion that the past reliability of an officer is sufficient reason for believing his current assertions. Nor would it suffice, I suppose, if a reliable informant states there is gambling equipment in Apartment 607 and then proceeds to describe in detail Apartment 201, a description which is verified before applying for the warrant. He was right about 201, but that hardly makes him more believable about the equipment in 607. But what if he states that there are narcotics locked in a safe in Apartment 300, which is described in detail, and the apartment manager verifies everything but the contents of the safe? I doubt that the report about the narcotics is made appreciably more believable by the verification. The informant could still have gotten his information concerning the safe from others about whom nothing is known or could have inferred the presence of narcotics from circumstances which a magistrate would find unacceptable.

The tension between *Draper* and the *Nathanson-Aguilar* line of cases is evident from the course followed by the majority opinion. First, it is held that the report from a reliable informant that Spinelli is using two telephones with specified numbers to conduct a gambling business plus Spinelli's reputation in police circles as a gambler does not add up to probable cause. This is wholly consistent with *Aguilar* and *Nathanson:* the informant did not reveal whether he had personally observed the facts or heard them from another and, if the latter, no basis for crediting the hearsay was presented. Nor were the facts, as Mr. Justice Harlan says, of such a nature that they normally would be obtainable only by the personal observation of the informant himself. The police, however, did not stop with the informant's report. Independently, they established the existence of two phones having the given numbers and located them in an apartment house which Spinelli was regularly frequenting away from his home. There remained little question but that Spinelli was using the phones, and it was a fair inference that the use was not for domestic but for business purposes. The informant had claimed the business involved gambling. Since his specific information about Spinelli using two phones with particular numbers had been verified, did not his allegation about gambling thereby become sufficiently more believable if the *Draper* principle is to be given any scope at all? I would think so, particularly since information from the informant which was verified was not neutral, irrelevant information but was material to proving the gambling allegation: two phones with different numbers in an apartment used away from home indicates a business use in an operation, like bookmaking, where multiple phones are needed. The *Draper* approach would reasonably justify the issuance of a warrant in this case, particularly since the police had some awareness of Spinelli's past activities. The majority, however, while seemingly embracing *Draper*, confines that case to its own facts. Pending full-scale reconsideration of that case, on the one hand, or of the *Nathanson-Aguilar* cases on the other, I join the opinion of the Court and the judgment of reversal, especially since a vote to affirm would produce an equally divided Court.

MR. JUSTICE BLACK, dissenting.

In my view, this Court's decision in *Aguilar v. Texas*, 378 U.S. 108, 84 S. Ct. 1509, 12 L. Ed. 2d 723 (1964), was bad enough. That decision went very far toward elevating the magistrate's hearing for issuance of a search warrant to a full-fledged trial, where witnesses must be brought forward to attest personally to all the facts alleged. But not content with this, the Court today expands *Aguilar* to almost unbelievable proportions. Of course, it would strengthen the probable-cause presentation if eyewitnesses could testify that they saw the defendant commit the crime. It would be stronger still if these witnesses could explain in detail the nature of the sensual perceptions on which they based their "conclusion" that the person they had seen was the defendant and that he was responsible for the events they observed. Nothing in our Constitution, however, requires that the facts be established with that degree of certainty and with such elaborate specificity before a policeman can be authorized by a disinterested magistrate to conduct a carefully limited search.

. . . In this case a search warrant was issued supported by an oath and particularly describing the place to be searched and the things to be seized. The supporting oath was three printed pages . . . .

... [T]he affidavit given the magistrate was more than ample to show probable cause of the petitioner's guilt.

. . . .

The existence of probable cause is a factual matter that calls for the determination of a factual question .... It cannot be said that the trial judge and six members of the Court of Appeals committed flagrant error in finding from evidence that the magistrate had probable cause to issue the search warrant here. It seems to me that this Court would best serve itself and the administration of justice by accepting the judgment of the two courts below. After all, they too are lawyers and judges, and much closer to the practical, everyday affairs of life than we are.

. . . .

I believe the Court is moving rapidly, through complex analyses and obfuscatory language, toward the holding that no magistrate can issue a warrant unless according to some unknown standard of proof he can be persuaded that the suspect defendant is actually guilty of a crime. I would affirm this conviction.

Mr. Justice Fortas, dissenting.

. . . .

We may well insist upon a sympathetic and even an indulgent view of the latitude which must be accorded to the police for performance of their vital task; but only a foolish or careless people will deduce from this that the public welfare requires or permits the police to disregard the restraints on their actions which historic struggles for freedom have developed for the protection of liberty and dignity of citizens against arbitrary state power.

. . . .

Aguilar v. Texas, 378 U.S. 108, 84 S. Ct. 1509, 12 L. Ed. 2d 723 (1964), holds that the reference in an affidavit to information described only as received from "a confidential reliable informant," standing alone, is not an adequate basis for issuance of a search warrant. The majority agrees that the "FBI affidavit in the present case is more ample than that in Aguilar," but concludes that it is nevertheless constitutionally inadequate. The majority states that the present affidavit fails to meet the "two-pronged test" of Aguilar because (a) it does not set forth the basis for the assertion that the informer is "reliable" and (b) it fails to state the "underlying circumstances" upon which the informant based his conclusion that Spinelli was engaged in bookmaking.

The majority acknowledges, however, that its reference to a "two-pronged test" should not be understood as meaning that an affidavit deficient in these respects is necessarily inadequate to support a search warrant. Other facts and circumstances may be attested which will supply the evidence of probable cause needed to support the search warrant. On this general statement we are agreed. Our difference is that I believe such facts and circumstances are present in this case, and the majority arrives at the opposite conclusion.

Aguilar expressly recognized that if, in that case, the affidavit's conclusory report of the informant's story had been supplemented by "the fact and results of . . . a surveillance . . . this would, of course, present an entirely different case." 378 U.S., at 109, n. 1, 84 S. Ct., at 1511. In the present case, as I view it, the affidavit showed not only relevant surveillance, entitled to some probative weight for purposes of the issuance of a search warrant, but also additional, specific facts of significance and adequate reliability: that Spinelli was using two telephone numbers, identified by an "informant" as being used for bookmaking, in his illegal operations; that these telephones were in an identified apartment; and that Spinelli, a known bookmaker,[5] frequented the apartment. Certainly, this is enough.

A policeman's affidavit should not be judged as an entry in an essay contest. It is not "abracadabra." As the majority recognizes, a policeman's affidavit is entitled to common-sense evaluation . . . .

MR. JUSTICE STEWART, dissenting.

For substantially the reasons stated by my Brothers BLACK and FORTAS, I believe the warrant in this case was supported by a sufficient showing of probable cause. I would therefore affirm the judgment.

Notes and Questions

(1) The *Spinelli* majority observed that its opinion constituted a significant development of the doctrine introduced by the Court's important earlier opinion in *Aguilar v. Texas*, 378 U.S. 108, 84 S. Ct. 1509, 12 L. Ed. 2d 723 (1964). *Aguilar* dealt with hearsay alone. *Spinelli* involved a considerably more complex factual mixture of hearsay and police investigation. Together, these two decisions gave rise to standards that came to be known as the "*Aguilar-Spinelli* two-pronged test."

(a) Justice White suggested that the *Aguilar-Spinelli* test is clearly different from the Court's prior approach to evaluating hearsay exemplified by the opinion in *Draper*. In what ways is the *Aguilar-Spinelli* approach distinguishable from its predecessor? Which approach to analyzing hearsay information is more faithful to the Fourth Amendment's probable cause demand?

(b) Why is each of the "two prongs" arguably essential to the proper analysis of hearsay information? What showing is necessary to satisfy each of the prongs?

(c) If an informant's tip that is an essential component of a probable cause showing fails to pass the "two-pronged test," can probable cause still be found? If so, of what significance is the test?

(2) For a post-*Spinelli* decision that discusses specific criteria relevant to the application of *Aguilar-Spinelli*, see *United States v. Harris*, 403 U.S. 573, 91 S. Ct.

---

5. Although Spinelli's reputation standing alone would not, of course, justify the search, this Court has held that such a reputation may make the informer's report "much less subject to scepticism [sic] than would be such a charge against one without such a history." *Jones v. United States*, 362 U.S. 257, 271, 80 S. Ct. 725, 736, 4 L. Ed. 2d 697 (1960).

2075, 29 L. Ed. 2d 723 (1971). For a thoughtful discussion and explanation of the two-pronged test, see Charles E. Moylan, *Hearsay and Probable Cause: An* Aguilar *and* Spinelli *Primer*, 25 Mercer L. Rev. 741 (1974).

Illinois v. Gates

United States Supreme Court

462 U.S. 213, 103 S. Ct. 2317, 76 L. Ed. 2d 527 (1983)

JUSTICE REHNQUIST delivered the opinion of the Court.

. . . .

II

. . . Bloomingdale, Ill., is a suburb of Chicago located in DuPage County. On May 3, 1978, the Bloomingdale Police Department received by mail an anonymous handwritten letter which read as follows:

> "This letter is to inform you that you have a couple in your town who strictly make their living on selling drugs. They are Sue and Lance Gates, they live on Greenway, off Bloomingdale Rd. in the condominiums. Most of their buys are done in Florida. Sue his wife drives their car to Florida, where she leaves it to be loaded up with drugs, then Lance flys down and drives it back. Sue flys back after she drops the car off in Florida. May 3 she is driving down there again and Lance will be flying down in a few days to drive it back. At the time Lance drives the car back he has the trunk loaded with over $100,000.00 in drugs. Presently they have over $100,000.00 worth of drugs in their basement.
>
> They brag about the fact they never have to work, and make their entire living on pushers.
>
> I guarantee if you watch them carefully you will make a big catch. They are friends with some big drugs dealers, who visit their house often.
>
> Lance & Susan Gates
>
> Greenway
>
> in Condominiums"

The letter was referred by the Chief of Police of the Bloomingdale Police Department to Detective Mader, who decided to pursue the tip. Mader learned, from the office of the Illinois Secretary of State, that an Illinois driver's license had been issued to one Lance Gates, residing at a stated address in Bloomingdale. He contacted a confidential informant, whose examination of certain financial records revealed a more recent address for the Gateses, and he also learned from a police officer assigned to O'Hare Airport that "L. Gates" had made a reservation on Eastern Airlines flight 245 to West Palm Beach, Fla., scheduled to depart from Chicago on May 5 at 4:15 p.m.

Mader then made arrangements with an agent of the Drug Enforcement Administration for surveillance of the May 5 Eastern Airlines flight. The agent later reported to Mader that Gates had boarded the flight, and that federal agents in Florida had observed him arrive in West Palm Beach and take a taxi to the nearby Holiday Inn. They also reported that Gates went to a room registered to one Susan Gates and that, at 7:00 a.m. the next morning, Gates and an unidentified woman left the motel in a Mercury bearing Illinois license plates and drove northbound on an interstate frequently used by travelers to the Chicago area. In addition, the DEA agent informed Mader that the license plate number on the Mercury registered to a Hornet station wagon owned by Gates. The agent also advised Mader that the driving time between West Palm Beach and Bloomingdale was approximately 22 to 24 hours.

Mader signed an affidavit setting forth the foregoing facts, and submitted it to a judge of the Circuit Court of DuPage County, together with a copy of the anonymous letter. The judge of that court thereupon issued a search warrant for the Gateses' residence and for their automobile . . . .

At 5:15 a.m. on March [sic] 7th, only 36 hours after he had flown out of Chicago, Lance Gates, and his wife, returned to their home in Bloomingdale, driving the car in which they had left West Palm Beach some 22 hours earlier. The Bloomingdale police were awaiting them, searched the trunk of the Mercury, and uncovered approximately 350 pounds of marijuana. A search of the Gateses' home revealed marijuana, weapons, and other contraband . . . .

The Illinois Supreme Court concluded — and we are inclined to agree — that, standing alone, the anonymous letter sent to the Bloomingdale Police Department would not provide the basis for a magistrate's determination that there was probable cause to believe contraband would be found in the Gateses' car and home. The letter provides virtually nothing from which one might conclude that its author is either honest or his information reliable; likewise, the letter gives absolutely no indication of the basis for the writer's predictions regarding the Gateses' criminal activities. Something more was required, then, before a magistrate could conclude that there was probable cause to believe that contraband would be found in the Gateses' home and car. See *Aguilar v. Texas*, 378 U.S. 108, 109, n. 1, 84 S. Ct. 1509, 1511, n. 1, 12 L. Ed. 2d 723 (1964); *Nathanson v. United States*, 290 U.S. 41, 54 S. Ct. 11, 78 L. Ed. 159 (1933).

The Illinois Supreme Court also properly recognized that Detective Mader's affidavit might be capable of supplementing the anonymous letter with information sufficient to permit a determination of probable cause. See *Whiteley v. Warden*, 401 U.S. 560, 567, 91 S. Ct. 1031, 1036, 28 L. Ed. 2d 306 (1971). In holding that the affidavit in fact did not contain sufficient additional information to sustain a determination of probable cause, the Illinois court applied a "two-pronged test," derived from our decision in *Spinelli v. United States*, 393 U.S. 410, 89 S. Ct. 584, 21 L. Ed. 2d 637 (1969). The Illinois Supreme Court, like some others, apparently understood *Spinelli* as requiring that the anonymous letter satisfy each of two independent requirements before it could be relied on. According to this view, the letter, as supplemented by Mader's affidavit, first had to adequately reveal the "basis of knowledge" of the letter writer — the particular means by which he came by the information given in his report. Second, it had to provide facts sufficiently establishing either the "veracity" of the affiant's informant, or, alternatively, the "reliability" of the informant's report in this particular case.

The Illinois court, alluding to an elaborate set of legal rules that have developed among various lower courts to enforce the "two-pronged test," found that the test had not been satisfied . . . .

We agree with the Illinois Supreme Court that an informant's "veracity," "reliability" and "basis of knowledge" are all highly relevant in determining the value of his report. We do not agree, however, that these elements should be understood as entirely separate and independent requirements to be rigidly exacted in every case, which the opinion of the Supreme Court of Illinois would imply. Rather, as detailed below, they should be understood simply as closely intertwined issues that may usefully illuminate the common-sense, practical question whether there is "probable cause" to believe that contraband or evidence is located in a particular place.

III

This totality of the circumstances approach is far more consistent with our prior treatment of probable cause than is any rigid demand that specific "tests" be satisfied by every informant's tip. Perhaps the central teaching of our decisions bearing on the probable cause standard is that it is a "practical, nontechnical conception." *Brinegar v. United States*, 338 U.S. 160, 176, 69 S. Ct. 1302, 1311, 93 L. Ed. 1879 (1949). "In dealing with probable cause, . . . as the very name implies, we deal with probabilities. These are not technical; they are the factual and practical considerations of everyday life on which reasonable and prudent men, not legal technicians, act." *Id.*, at 175, 69 S. Ct., at 1310.

  . . . .

As these comments illustrate, probable cause is a fluid concept — turning on the assessment of probabilities in particular factual contexts — not readily, or even usefully, reduced to a neat set of legal rules. Informants' tips doubtless come in many shapes and sizes from many different types of persons . . . . Rigid legal rules are ill-suited to an area of such diversity. "One simple rule will not cover every situation." [*Adams v. Williams*, 407 U.S. 143, 147, 92 S. Ct. 1921, 1924, 32 L. Ed. 2d 612, 617 (1972).]

Moreover, the "two-pronged test" directs analysis into two largely independent channels — the informant's "veracity" or "reliability" and his "basis of knowledge." There are persuasive arguments against according these two elements such independent status. Instead, they are better understood as relevant considerations in the totality-of-the-circumstances analysis that traditionally has guided probable cause determinations: a deficiency in one may be compensated for, in determining the overall reliability of a tip, by a strong showing as to the other, or by some other indicia of reliability.

If, for example, a particular informant is known for the unusual reliability of his predictions of certain types of criminal activities in a locality, his failure, in a particular case, to thoroughly set forth the basis of his knowledge surely should not serve as an absolute bar to a finding of probable cause based on his tip.[8] Likewise, if an unquestionably honest citizen comes forward with a report of criminal activity — which if fabricated would subject him to criminal liability — we have found rigorous scrutiny of the basis of his knowledge unnecessary. Conversely, even if we entertain some doubt as to an informant's motives, his explicit and detailed description of alleged wrongdoing, along with a statement that the event was observed first-hand, entitles his tip to greater weight than might otherwise be the case. Unlike a totality-of-the-circumstances analysis, which permits a balanced assessment of the relative weights of all the various indicia of reliability (and unreliability) attending an informant's tip, the "two-pronged test" has encouraged an excessively technical dissection of informants' tips, with undue attention being focused on isolated issues that cannot sensibly be divorced from the other facts presented to the magistrate.

As early as *Locke v. United States*, 3 L. Ed. 364, 7 Cranch. 339, 348 (1813), Chief Justice Marshall observed, in a closely related context, that "the term 'probable cause,' according to its usual acceptation, means less than evidence which would justify condemnation.... It imports a seizure made under circumstances which warrant suspicion." More recently, we said that "the quanta ... of proof" appropriate in ordinary judicial proceedings are inapplicable to the decision to issue a warrant. *Brinegar, supra*, 338 U.S., at 173. Finely-tuned standards such as proof beyond a reasonable doubt or by a preponderance of the evidence, useful in formal trials, have no place in the magistrate's decision. While an effort to fix some general, numerically precise degree of certainty corresponding to "probable cause" may not be helpful, it is clear that "only the probability, and not a *prima facie* showing, of criminal activity is the standard of probable cause." *Spinelli, supra*, 393 U.S., at 419.

We also have recognized that affidavits "are normally drafted by nonlawyers in the midst and haste of a criminal investigation. Technical requirements of elaborate specificity once exacted under common law pleadings have no proper place in this area." *Ventresca, supra*, 380 U.S., at 108. Likewise, search and arrest warrants long have been issued by persons who are neither lawyers nor judges, and who certainly do not remain abreast of each judicial refinement of the nature of "probable cause."

---

8. *Compare Stanley v. State*, 19 Md. App. 507, 313 A.2d 847, 861 (Md. Ct. Spec. App. 1974), reasoning that "even assuming 'credibility' amounting to sainthood, the judge still may not accept the bare conclusion of a sworn and known and trusted police-affiant."

The rigorous inquiry into the *Spinelli* prongs and the complex superstructure of evidentiary and analytical rules that some have seen implicit in our *Spinelli* decision, cannot be reconciled with the fact that many warrants are — quite properly — issued on the basis of nontechnical, common-sense judgments of laymen applying a standard less demanding than those used in more formal legal proceedings. Likewise, given the informal, often hurried context in which it must be applied, the "built-in subtleties," *Stanley v. State*, 19 Md. App. 507, 313 A. 2d 847, 860 (Md. Ct. Spec. App. 1974), of the "two-pronged test" are particularly unlikely to assist magistrates in determining probable cause.

Similarly, we have repeatedly said that after-the-fact scrutiny by courts of the sufficiency of an affidavit should not take the form of *de novo* review. A magistrate's "determination of probable cause should be paid great deference by reviewing courts." *Spinelli, supra*, 393 U.S., at 419. "A grudging or negative attitude by reviewing courts toward warrants," *Ventresca, supra*, 380 U.S., at 108, is inconsistent with the Fourth Amendment's strong preference for searches conducted pursuant to a warrant; "courts should not invalidate warrant[s] by interpreting affidavit[s] in a hypertechnical, rather than a commonsense, manner." *Id.*, at 109.

If the affidavits submitted by police officers are subjected to the type of scrutiny some courts have deemed appropriate, police might well resort to warrantless searches, with the hope of relying on consent or some other exception to the warrant clause that might develop at the time of the search. In addition, the possession of a warrant by officers conducting an arrest or search greatly reduces the perception of unlawful or intrusive police conduct, by assuring "the individual whose property is searched or seized of the lawful authority of the executing officer, his need to search, and the limits of his power to search." *United States v. Chadwick*, 433 U.S. 1, 9, 97 S. Ct. 2476, 2482, 53 L. Ed. 2d 538 (1977). Reflecting this preference for the warrant process, the traditional standard for review of an issuing magistrate's probable cause determination has been that so long as the magistrate had a "substantial basis for . . . conclud[ing]" that a search would uncover evidence of wrongdoing, the Fourth Amendment requires no more. *Jones v. United States*, 362 U.S. 257, 271, 80 S. Ct. 725, 736, 4 L. Ed. 2d 697 (1960). *See United States v. Harris*, 403 U.S. 573, 577–583, 91 S. Ct. 2075, 2079–2082, 29 L. Ed. 2d 723 (1971).[10] We think reaffirmation of this standard better serves the purpose of encourag-

---

10. We also have said that "Although in a particular case it may not be easy to determine when an affidavit demonstrates the existence of probable cause, the resolution of doubtful or marginal cases in this area should be largely determined by the preference to be accorded to warrants," *Ventresca, supra*, 380 U.S., at 109. This reflects both a desire to encourage use of the warrant process by police officers and a recognition that once a warrant has been obtained, intrusion upon interests protected by the Fourth Amendment is less severe than otherwise may be the case. Even if we were to accept the premise that the accurate assessment of probable cause would be furthered by the "two-pronged test," which we do not, these Fourth Amendment policies would require a less rigorous standard than that which appears to have been read into *Aguilar* and *Spinelli*.

ing recourse to the warrant procedure and is more consistent with our traditional deference to the probable cause determinations of magistrates than is the "two-pronged test."

Finally, the direction taken by decisions following *Spinelli* poorly serves "the most basic function of any government": "to provide for the security of the individual and of his property." *Miranda v. Arizona*, 384 U.S. 436, 539, 86 S. Ct. 1602, 1661, 16 L. Ed. 2d 694 (1966) (White, J., dissenting). The strictures that inevitably accompany the "two-pronged test" cannot avoid seriously impeding the task of law enforcement, *see, e.g.*, n. 9 *supra*. If, as the Illinois Supreme Court apparently thought, that test must be rigorously applied in every case, anonymous tips would be of greatly diminished value in police work. Ordinary citizens, like ordinary witnesses, *see* Federal Rules of Evidence 701, Advisory Committee Note (1976), generally do not provide extensive recitations of the basis of their everyday observations. Likewise, as the Illinois Supreme Court observed in this case, the veracity of persons supplying anonymous tips is by hypothesis largely unknown, and unknowable. As a result, anonymous tips seldom could survive a rigorous application of either of the *Spinelli* prongs. Yet, such tips, particularly when supplemented by independent police investigation, frequently contribute to the solution of otherwise "perfect crimes." While a conscientious assessment of the basis for crediting such tips is required by the Fourth Amendment, a standard that leaves virtually no place for anonymous citizen informants is not.

For all these reasons, we conclude that it is wiser to abandon the "two-pronged test" established by our decisions in *Aguilar* and *Spinelli*. In its place we reaffirm the totality-of-the-circumstances analysis that traditionally has informed probable cause determinations. The task of the issuing magistrate is simply to make a practical, common-sense decision whether, given all the circumstances set forth in the affidavit before him, including the "veracity" and "basis of knowledge" of persons supplying hearsay information, there is a fair probability that contraband or evidence of a crime will be found in a particular place. And the duty of a reviewing court is simply to ensure that the magistrate had a "substantial basis for . . . conclud[ing]" that probable cause existed. *Jones v. United States, supra*, 362 U.S., at 271. We are convinced that this flexible, easily applied standard will better achieve the accommodation of public and private interests that the Fourth Amendment requires than does the approach that has developed from *Aguilar* and *Spinelli*.

Our earlier cases illustrate the limits beyond which a magistrate may not venture in issuing a warrant. A sworn statement of an affiant that "he has cause to suspect and does believe that" liquor illegally brought into the United States is located on certain premises will not do. *Nathanson v. United States*, 290 U.S. 41, 54 S. Ct. 11, 78 L. Ed. 159 (1933). An affidavit must provide the magistrate with a substantial basis for determining the existence of probable cause . . . . Sufficient information must be presented to the magistrate to allow that official to determine probable cause; his action cannot be a mere ratification of the bare conclusions of others. In order to ensure that such an abdication of the magistrate's duty does not occur, courts must continue to conscientiously review the sufficiency of affidavits on which warrants are issued. But when we move beyond the "bare bones" affidavits present in cases such as *Nathanson* and *Aguilar*, this area simply does not lend itself to a prescribed set of rules, like that which had developed from *Spinelli*. Instead, the flexible, common-sense standard articulated in *Jones, Ventresca*, and *Brinegar* better serves the purposes of the Fourth Amendment's probable cause requirement.

. . . .

The real gist of Justice Brennan's [dissent is an argument] . . . that magistrates should be restricted in their authority to make probable cause determinations by the standards laid down in *Aguilar* and *Spinelli*, and that such findings "should not be authorized unless there is some assurance that the information on which they are based has been obtained in a reliable way by an honest or credible person." However, under our opinion magistrates remain perfectly free to exact such assurances as they deem necessary, as well as those required by this opinion, in making probable cause determinations. Justice Brennan would apparently prefer that magistrates be restricted in their findings of probable cause by the development of an elaborate body of case law dealing with the "veracity" prong of the *Spinelli* test, which in turn is broken down into two "spurs" — the informant's "credibility" and the "reliability" of his information, together with the "basis of knowledge" prong of the *Spinelli* test. That such a labyrinthine body of judicial refinement bears any relationship to familiar definitions of probable cause is hard to imagine . . . .

. . . "Fidelity" to the commands of the Constitution suggests balanced judgment rather than exhortation. The highest "fidelity" is achieved neither by the judge who instinctively goes furthest in upholding even the most bizarre claim of individual constitutional rights, any more than it is achieved by the judge who instinctively goes furthest in accepting the most restrictive claims of governmental authorities. The task of this Court, as of other courts, is to "hold the balance true," and we think we have done that in this case.

IV

Our decisions applying the totality-of-the-circumstances analysis outlined above have consistently recognized the value of corroboration of details of an informant's tip by independent police work . . . .

Our decision in *Draper v. United States*, 358 U.S. 307, 79 S. Ct. 329, 3 L. Ed. 2d 327 (1959) . . . is the classic case on the value of corroborative efforts of police officials.

. . . .

The showing of probable cause in the present case was fully as compelling as that in *Draper*. Even standing alone, the facts obtained through the independent investigation of Mader and the DEA at least suggested that the Gateses were involved in drug trafficking. In addition to being a popular vacation site, Florida is well-known as a source of narcotics and other illegal drugs. Lance Gates' flight to West Palm Beach, his brief, overnight stay in a motel, and apparent immediate return north to

Chicago in the family car, conveniently awaiting him in West Palm Beach, is as suggestive of a prearranged drug run, as it is of an ordinary vacation trip.

In addition, the magistrate could rely on the anonymous letter, which had been corroborated in major part by Mader's efforts—just as had occurred in *Draper*.[13] The Supreme Court of Illinois reasoned that *Draper* involved an informant who had given reliable information on previous occasions, while the honesty and reliability of the anonymous informant in this case were unknown to the Bloomingdale police. While this distinction might be an apt one at the time the police department received the anonymous letter, it became far less significant after Mader's independent investigative work occurred. The corroboration of the letter's predictions that the Gateses' car would be in Florida, that Lance Gates would fly to Florida in the next day or so, and that he would drive the car north toward Bloomingdale all indicated, albeit not with certainty, that the informant's other assertions also were true. "Because an informant is right about some things, he is more probably right about other facts," *Spinelli, supra*, 393 U.S., at 427, 89 S. Ct., at 594 (White, J., concurring)—including the claim regarding the Gateses' illegal activity. This may well not be the type of "reliability" or "veracity" necessary to satisfy some views of the "veracity prong" of *Spinelli*, but we think it suffices for the practical, common-sense judgment called for in making a probable cause determination. It is enough, for purposes of assessing probable cause, that "corroboration through other sources of information reduced the chances of a reckless or prevaricating tale," thus providing "a substantial basis for crediting the hearsay." *Jones v. United States, supra*, 362 U.S., at 269, 271.

Finally, the anonymous letter contained a range of details relating not just to easily obtained facts and conditions existing at the time of the tip, but to future actions

---

13. The Illinois Supreme Court thought that the verification of details contained in the anonymous letter in this case amounted only to "the corroboration of innocent activity," and that this was insufficient to support a finding of probable cause. We are inclined to agree, however, with the observation of Justice Moran in his dissenting opinion that "In this case, just as in *Draper*, seemingly innocent activity became suspicious in the light of the initial tip." And it bears noting that all of the corroborating detail established in *Draper, supra*, was of entirely innocent activity—a fact later pointed out by the Court in both *Jones v. United States*, 362 U.S. 257, 269–270, 80 S. Ct. 725, 735–736, 4 L. Ed. 2d 697 (1960), and *Ker v. California*, 374 U.S. 23, 36, 83 S. Ct. 1623, 1631, 10 L. Ed. 2d 726 (1963). This is perfectly reasonable. As discussed previously, probable cause requires only a probability or substantial chance of criminal activity, not an actual showing of such activity. By hypothesis, therefore, innocent behavior frequently will provide the basis for a showing of probable cause; to require otherwise would be to *sub silentio* impose a drastically more rigorous definition of probable cause than the security of our citizen's demands. We think the Illinois court attempted a too rigid classification of the types of conduct that may be relied upon in seeking to demonstrate probable cause. *See Brown v. Texas*, 443 U.S. 47, 52, n. 2, 99 S. Ct. 2637, 2641, n. 2, 61 L. Ed. 2d 357 (1979). In making a determination of probable cause the relevant inquiry is not whether particular conduct is "innocent" or "guilty," but the degree of suspicion that attaches to particular types of noncriminal acts.

of third parties ordinarily not easily predicted. The letter writer's accurate information as to the travel plans of each of the Gateses was of a character likely obtained
only from the Gateses themselves, or from someone familiar with their not entirely
ordinary travel plans. If the informant had access to accurate information of this
type a magistrate could properly conclude that it was not unlikely that he also had
access to reliable information of the Gateses' alleged illegal activities. Of course, the
Gateses' travel plans might have been learned from a talkative neighbor or travel
agent; under the "two-pronged test" developed from *Spinelli*, the character of the
details in the anonymous letter might well not permit a sufficiently clear inference
regarding the letter writer's "basis of knowledge." But, as discussed previously, probable cause does not demand the certainty we associate with formal trials. It is enough
that there was a fair probability that the writer of the anonymous letter had obtained his entire story either from the Gateses or someone they trusted. And corroboration of major portions of the letter's predictions provides just this probability.
It is apparent, therefore, that the judge issuing the warrant had a "substantial basis
for ... conclud[ing]" that probable cause to search the Gateses' home and car existed. The judgment of the Supreme Court of Illinois therefore must be

Reversed.

JUSTICE WHITE, concurring in the judgment.

. . . .

I continue to believe that the exclusionary rule is an inappropriate remedy where
law enforcement officials act in the reasonable belief that a search and seizure was
consistent with the Fourth Amendment . . . . In this case, it was fully reasonable for
the Bloomingdale, Illinois police to believe that their search of respondents' house
and automobile comported with the Fourth Amendment as the search was conducted pursuant to a judicially-issued warrant. The exclusion of probative evidence
where the constable has not blundered not only sets the criminal free but also fails
to serve any constitutional interest in securing compliance with the important requirements of the Fourth Amendment. On this basis, I concur in the Court's judgment that the decision of the Illinois Supreme Court must be reversed.

. . . .

III

Since a majority of the Court deems it inappropriate to address the good faith issue,
I briefly address the question that the Court does reach — whether the warrant authorizing the search and seizure of respondents' car and home was constitutionally
valid. Abandoning the "two-pronged test" of *Aguilar v. Texas*, 378 U.S. 108, 84 S. Ct.
1509, 12 L. Ed. 2d 723 (1964), and *Spinelli v. United States*, 393 U.S. 410, 89 S. Ct. 584,
21 L. Ed. 2d 637 (1969), the Court upholds the validity of the warrant under a new
"totality of the circumstances" approach. Although I agree that the warrant should
be upheld, I reach this conclusion in accordance with the *Aguilar-Spinelli* framework.

A

. . . .

In the present case, it is undisputed that the anonymous tip, by itself, did not furnish probable cause. The question is whether those portions of the affidavit describing the results of the police investigation of the respondents, when considered in light of the tip, "would permit the suspicions engendered by the informant's report to ripen into a judgment that a crime was probably being committed." *Spinelli, supra,* at 418. The Illinois Supreme Court concluded that the corroboration was insufficient to permit such a ripening.

. . . .

In my view, the lower court's characterization of the Gateses' activity here as totally "innocent" is dubious. In fact, the behavior was quite suspicious. I agree with the Court that Lance Gates' flight to West Palm Beach, an area known to be a source of narcotics, the brief overnight stay in a motel, and apparent immediate return north, suggest a pattern that trained law-enforcement officers have recognized as indicative of illicit drug-dealing activity.

Even, however, had the corroboration related only to completely innocuous activities, this fact alone would not preclude the issuance of a valid warrant. The critical issue is not whether the activities observed by the police are innocent or suspicious. Instead, the proper focus should be on whether the actions of the suspects, whatever their nature, give rise to an inference that the informant is credible and that he obtained his information in a reliable manner.

. . . .

As in *Draper*, the police investigation in the present case satisfactorily demonstrated that the informant's tip was as trustworthy as one that would alone satisfy the *Aguilar* tests. The tip predicted that Sue Gates would drive to Florida, that Lance Gates would fly there a few days after May 3, and that Lance would then drive the car back. After the police corroborated these facts, the magistrate could reasonably have inferred, as he apparently did, that the informant, who had specific knowledge of these unusual travel plans, did not make up his story and that he obtained his information in a reliable way. It is theoretically possible, as respondents insist, that the tip could have been supplied by a "vindictive travel agent" and that the Gateses' activities, although unusual, might not have been unlawful. But *Aguilar* and *Spinelli*, like our other cases, do not require that certain guilt be established before a warrant may properly be issued . . . . I therefore conclude that the judgment of the Illinois Supreme Court invalidating the warrant must be reversed.

B

The Court agrees that the warrant was valid, but, in the process of reaching this conclusion, it overrules the *Aguilar-Spinelli* tests and replaces them with a "totality of the circumstances" standard. As shown above, it is not at all necessary to overrule *Aguilar-Spinelli* in order to reverse the judgment below. Therefore, because I am inclined to believe that, when applied properly, the *Aguilar-Spinelli* rules play an appropriate role in probable cause determinations, and because the Court's holding may foretell an evisceration of the probable cause standard, I do not join the Court's holding.

The Court reasons that the "veracity" and "basis of knowledge" tests are not independent, and that a deficiency as to one can be compensated for by a strong showing as to the other. Thus, a finding of probable cause may be based on a tip from an informant "known for the unusual reliability of his predictions" or from "an unquestionably honest citizen," even if the report fails thoroughly to set forth the basis upon which the information was obtained. If this is so, then it must follow *a fortiori* that "the affidavit of an officer, known by the magistrate to be honest and experienced, stating that [contraband] is located in a certain building" must be acceptable. *Spinelli*, 393 U.S., at 424 (White, J., concurring). It would be "quixotic" if a similar statement from an honest informant, but not one from an honest officer, could furnish probable cause. *Id.* But we have repeatedly held that the unsupported assertion or belief of an officer does not satisfy the probable cause requirement. Thus, this portion of today's holding can be read as implicitly rejecting the teachings of these prior holdings.

The Court may not intend so drastic a result. Indeed, the Court expressly reaffirms the validity of cases such as *Nathanson* that have held that, no matter how reliable the affiant-officer may be, a warrant should not be issued unless the affidavit discloses supporting facts and circumstances. The Court limits these cases to situations involving affidavits containing only "bare conclusions" and holds that, if an affidavit contains anything more, it should be left to the issuing magistrate to decide, based solely on "practical[ity]" and "common-sense," whether there is a fair probability that contraband will be found in a particular place.

Thus, as I read the majority opinion, it appears that the question whether the probable cause standard is to be diluted is left to the common-sense judgments of issuing magistrates. I am reluctant to approve any standard that does not expressly require, as a prerequisite to issuance of a warrant, some showing of facts from which an inference may be drawn that the informant is credible and that his information was obtained in a reliable way. The Court is correctly concerned with the fact that some lower courts have been applying *Aguilar-Spinelli* in an unduly rigid manner. I believe, however, that with clarification of the rule of corroborating information, the lower courts are fully able to properly interpret *Aguilar-Spinelli* and avoid such unduly-rigid applications. I may be wrong; it ultimately may prove to be the case that the only profitable instruction we can provide to magistrates is to rely on common sense. But the question whether a particular anonymous tip provides the basis for issuance of a warrant will often be a difficult one, and I would at least attempt to provide more precise guidance by clarifying *Aguilar-Spinelli* and the relationship of those cases with *Draper* before totally abdicating our responsibility in this area. Hence, I do not join the Court's opinion rejecting the *Aguilar-Spinelli* rules.

Justice Brennan, with whom Justice Marshall joins, dissenting.

. . . .

I

. . . .

In recognition of the judiciary's role as the only effective guardian of Fourth Amendment rights, this Court has developed over the last half century a set of coherent rules governing a magistrate's consideration of a warrant application and the showings that are necessary to support a finding of probable cause. We start with the proposition that a neutral and detached magistrate, and not the police, should determine whether there is probable cause to support the issuance of a warrant.

. . . .

The use of hearsay to support the issuance of a warrant presents special problems because informants, unlike police officers, are not regarded as presumptively reliable or honest. Moreover, the basis for an informant's conclusions is not always clear from an affidavit that merely reports those conclusions.

. . . .

Although the rules drawn from [*Aguilar, Spinelli*, and other cases] are cast in procedural terms, they advance an important underlying substantive value: Findings of probable cause, and attendant intrusions, should not be authorized unless there is some assurance that the information on which they are based has been obtained in a reliable way by an honest or credible person. As applied to police officers, the rules focus on the way in which the information was acquired. As applied to informants, the rules focus both on the honesty or credibility of the informant and on the reliability of the way in which the information was acquired. Insofar as it is more complicated, an evaluation of affidavits based on hearsay involves a more difficult inquiry. This suggests a need to structure the inquiry in an effort to insure greater accuracy. The standards announced in *Aguilar*, as refined by *Spinelli*, fulfill that need. The standards inform the police of what information they have to provide and magistrates of what information they should demand. The standards also inform magistrates of the subsidiary findings they must make in order to arrive at an ultimate finding of probable cause. *Spinelli*, properly understood, directs the magistrate's attention to the possibility that the presence of self-verifying detail might satisfy *Aguilar*'s basis of knowledge prong and that corroboration of the details of a tip might satisfy *Aguilar*'s veracity prong. By requiring police to provide certain crucial information to magistrates and by structuring magistrates' probable cause inquiries, *Aguilar* and *Spinelli* assure the magistrate's role as an independent arbiter of probable cause, insure greater accuracy in probable cause determinations, and advance the substantive value identified above.

Until today the Court has never squarely addressed the application of the *Aguilar* and *Spinelli* standards to tips from anonymous informants. Both *Aguilar* and *Spinelli* dealt with tips from informants known at least to the police. And surely there is even more reason to subject anonymous informants' tips to the tests established by *Aguilar* and *Spinelli*. By definition nothing is known about an anonymous informant's identity, honesty, or reliability . . . . In any event, there certainly is no basis for treating anonymous informants as presumptively reliable. Nor is there any basis for assuming that the information provided by an anonymous informant has been obtained in a reliable way. If we are unwilling to accept conclusory allegations from the police, who are presumptively reliable, or from informants who are known, at least to the police, there cannot possibly be any rational basis for accepting conclusory allegations from anonymous informants.

To suggest that anonymous informants' tips are subject to the tests established by *Aguilar* and *Spinelli* is not to suggest that they can never provide a basis for a finding of probable cause. It is conceivable that police corroboration of the details of the tip might establish the reliability of the informant under *Aguilar*'s veracity prong, as refined in *Spinelli*, and that the details in the tip might be sufficient to qualify under the "self-verifying detail" test established by *Spinelli* as a means of satisfying *Aguilar*'s basis of knowledge prong. The *Aguilar* and *Spinelli* tests must be applied to anonymous informants' tips, however, if we are to continue to insure that findings of probable cause, and attendant intrusions, are based on information provided by an honest or credible person who has acquired the information in a reliable way.

In light of the important purposes served by *Aguilar* and *Spinelli*, I would not reject the standards they establish . . . .

II

. . . .

. . . [O]ne can concede that probable cause is a "practical, nontechnical" concept without betraying the values that *Aguilar* and *Spinelli* reflect. As noted, *Aguilar* and *Spinelli* require the police to provide magistrates with certain crucial information. They also provide structure for magistrates' probable cause inquiries . . . . Neither the standards nor their effects are inconsistent with a "practical, nontechnical" conception of probable cause. Once a magistrate has determined that he has information before him that he can reasonably say has been obtained in a reliable way by a credible person, he has ample room to use his common sense and to apply a practical, nontechnical conception of probable cause.

. . . *Aguilar* and *Spinelli* do not stand as an insuperable barrier to the use of even anonymous informants' tips to establish probable cause . . . .

The Court also insists that the *Aguilar-Spinelli* standards must be abandoned because they are inconsistent with the fact that non-lawyers frequently serve as magistrates. To the contrary, the standards help to structure probable cause inquiries and, properly interpreted, may actually help a non-lawyer magistrate in making a probable cause determination. Moreover, the *Aguilar* and *Spinelli* tests are not inconsistent with deference to magistrates' determinations of probable cause.

. . . .

At the heart of the Court's decision to abandon *Aguilar* and *Spinelli* appears to be its belief that "the direction taken by decisions following *Spinelli* poorly serves 'the most basic function of any government: to provide for the security of the individual and of his property.'" This conclusion rests on the judgment that *Aguilar* and *Spinelli* "seriously imped[e] the task of law enforcement," and render anonymous tips valueless in police work. Surely, the Court overstates its case. But of particular concern to all Americans must be that the Court gives virtually no consideration to the value of insuring that findings of probable cause are based on information that a magistrate can reasonably say has been obtained in a reliable way by an honest or credible person. I share Justice White's fear that the Court's rejection of *Aguilar* and *Spinelli* and its adoption of a new totality-of-the-circumstances test, "may foretell an evisceration of the probable cause standard . . . ."

III

The Court's complete failure to provide any persuasive reason for rejecting *Aguilar* and *Spinelli* doubtlessly reflects impatience with what it perceives to be "overly technical" rules governing searches and seizures under the Fourth Amendment. Words such as "practical," "nontechnical," and "commonsense," as used in the Court's opinion, are but code words for an overly permissive attitude towards police practices in derogation of the rights secured by the Fourth Amendment. Everyone shares the Court's concern over the horrors of drug trafficking, but under our Constitution only measures consistent with the Fourth Amendment may be employed by government to cure this evil . . . .

Rights secured by the Fourth Amendment are particularly difficult to protect because their "advocates are usually criminals." *Draper v. United States*, 358 U.S. 307, 314, 79 S. Ct. 329, 333, 3 L. Ed. 2d 327 (1959) (Douglas, J., dissenting). But the rules "we fashion [are] for the innocent and guilty alike." *Id.* By replacing *Aguilar* and *Spinelli* with a test that provides no assurance that magistrates, rather than the police, or informants, will make determinations of probable cause; imposes no structure on magistrates' probable cause inquiries; and invites the possibility that intrusions may be justified on less than reliable information from an honest or credible person, today's decision threatens to "obliterate one of the most fundamental distinctions between our form of government, where officers are under the law, and the police-state where they are the law." *Johnson v. United States*, 333 U.S. 10, 17, 68 S. Ct. 367, 370, 92 L. Ed. 436 (1948).

[The dissenting opinion of JUSTICE STEVENS has been omitted.]

. . . .

Notes and Questions

(1) In *Massachusetts v. Upton*, 466 U.S. 727, 732, 104 S. Ct. 2085, 2087–88, 80 L. Ed. 2d 721, 726–27 (1984), the Supreme Court corrected Massachusetts's "misunderstanding" of the import of *Gates*. The Court's remarks provide additional insight into the meaning and significance of the *Gates* opinion:

> . . . [T]he Supreme Judicial Court of Massachusetts misunderstood our decision in *Gates*. We did not merely refine or qualify the "two-pronged test."

We rejected it as hypertechnical and divorced from "the factual and practical considerations of everyday life on which reasonable and prudent men, not legal technicians, act." Our statement on that score was explicit. The [Massachusetts] court did not consider [the] affidavit in its entirety, giving significance to each relevant piece of information and balancing the relative weights of all the various indicia of reliability (and unreliability) attending the tip. Instead, the court insisted on judging bits and pieces of information in isolation against the artificial standards provided by the two-pronged test.

(2) For many years prior to 1983, lower courts debated and differed over the quantum of probability contemplated by the Fourth Amendment. Some adopted a "more probable than not" approach, while others concluded that the phrases "reasonable cause" and "more than a mere possibility" described the constitutional level of likelihood. In *Gates*, the Court offered insight into the constitutionally required quantum of probability. What level did the Court prescribe? Is its choice consistent with the reasons for a probable cause requirement?

(3) *Maryland v. Pringle*, 540 U.S. 366, 124 S. Ct. 795, 157 L. Ed. 2d 769 (2003), addressed whether there was *probable cause to arrest a passenger* in an automobile when there was probable cause to believe that felony narcotics possession had been committed by someone in the vehicle. During a lawful search of the vehicle, an officer found a substantial amount of cash in the glove compartment and several packages of cocaine between the back-seat armrest and the back seat. When none of the three men in the car admitted ownership of the items, the officer arrested all three. Pringle, the front-seat passenger, contended that there was an inadequate basis for believing that *he* possessed the drugs. The Court of Appeals of Maryland agreed. A unanimous Supreme Court first recounted the facts it deemed important: that Pringle was one of three men riding in a car at 3:16 a.m., that the glove compartment directly in front of him contained $763, that five baggies of cocaine "were behind the back-seat armrest and accessible to all three men," and that when questioned "the three men failed to offer any information" about ownership of the drugs or money. The Court then held that it was "an entirely reasonable inference from these facts that *any or all three of the occupants* had knowledge of, and exercised dominion and control over, the cocaine. Thus, a reasonable officer could conclude that there was probable cause to believe Pringle committed the crime of possession of cocaine, *either solely or jointly*." (Emphasis added.) In distinguishing the situation in which a number of individuals are present in a large, public location, the Court pointed out that the three men were present "in a relatively small automobile," that "'a car passenger ... will often be engaged in a common enterprise with the driver, and have the same interest in concealing the fruits or the evidence of their wrongdoing'" and that it was "reasonable ... to infer a common enterprise among the three men" here because the "quantity of drugs and cash ... indicated the likelihood of drug dealing, an enterprise to which a dealer would be unlikely to admit an innocent person with the potential to furnish evidence against him."

(4) "Hearsay" information can come from a variety of types of "informant." Upstanding citizens, paid, confidential informants with criminal histories, and anonymous individuals, for example, have all been known to furnish information to law enforcement officers. In making probable cause determinations, should there be any distinctions based on the type of informant involved? Why?

(5) Despite the *Gates* holding, a number of state courts continue to adhere to the *Aguilar-Spinelli* doctrine. In our federal system, federal and state courts are bound by the Supreme Court's interpretation of the United States Constitution. They can discern no more and no less privacy protection in interpreting the Fourth Amendment than the Supreme Court did in *Gates*. See *Arkansas v. Sullivan*, 532 U.S. 769, 121 S. Ct. 1876, 149 L. Ed. 2d 994 (2001) (Arkansas Supreme Court may not interpret the Fourth Amendment "to provide greater protection" than the Supreme Court's own precedents provide). However, state courts are free and entitled to interpret state constitutional guarantees that are identical, equivalent, or similar to the Fourth Amendment more or less expansively than *Gates* interprets the Fourth Amendment. *See Michigan v. Long*, 463 U.S. 1032, 103 S. Ct. 3469, 77 L. Ed. 2d 1201 (1983). Specifically, states are free to grant their citizens the greater privacy and liberty protection afforded by the *Aguilar-Spinelli* two-pronged test.

The state courts that have proclaimed the continuing vitality of the two-pronged test have found the *Gates* approach to the problems posed by reliance on informant hearsay to be unsatisfactory. The potential for independent, and more expansive, state constitutional interpretation reflected in those state decisions highlights the importance of studying and understanding overruled precedents and dissenting views. They provide ammunition for arguments to state courts and can furnish the foundations for state court opinions. Although divergent state court interpretation is certainly not the norm, it is a definite possibility. It has been rendered all the more significant by the conservative approach to federal constitutional rights that has characterized the Supreme Court's opinions since the end of the 1960s. *See* William J. Brennan, *State Constitutions and the Protection of Individual Rights*, 90 Harv. L. Rev. 489 (1977).

(6) The issue in *Florida v. Harris*, 568 U.S. ____, 133 S. Ct. 1050, 185 L. Ed. 2d 61 (2013), was "how a court should determine if the 'alert' of a drug-detection dog . . . provides probable cause to search." The Florida Supreme Court had concluded that "to demonstrate a dog's reliability" the "'State must present . . . the dog's training and certification records, an explanation of the meaning of the particular training and certification, field performance records (including any unverified alerts), and evidence concerning the experience and training of the officer handling the dog, as well as any other objective evidence known to the officer about the dog's reliability.'" Florida had "stressed the need for 'evidence of the dog's performance history,' including records" of alerts that did not result in the discovery of drugs. According to a unanimous Supreme Court, these demands were "inconsistent with the 'flexible, common-sense standard' of probable cause." Florida's approach was the "antithesis of [the] totality-of-the-circumstances analysis" prescribed in *Gates* and other opinions.

The Court reasoned that it had "consistently . . . rejected rigid rules, bright-line tests, and mechanistic inquiries in favor of a more flexible, all-things-considered approach." *Gates* had abandoned an "inflexible checklist" method for determining the "reliability" of "human informants." A checklist approach was equally inappropriate for assessments of a canine's "reliability." Although records of a dog's performance in the field "may sometimes be relevant," Florida's treatment of those records "as the gold standard in evidence" was misguided because "in most cases they have relatively limited import." A "better measure of a dog's reliability" is his performance "in controlled testing environments." In fact, a canine's "satisfactory performance in a certification or training program can itself provide sufficient reason to trust his alert." "If a bona fide organization has certified a dog after testing his reliability in a controlled setting," or, even without "formal certification, if the dog has recently and successfully completed a training program that evaluated his proficiency in locating drugs, a court can presume (subject to . . . conflicting evidence . . .) that the dog's alert provides probable cause to search." Of course, a defendant "must have an opportunity to challenge . . . evidence of a dog's reliability" in general or in his or her particular case.

In sum, when a probable cause determination depends on a dog's alert to the presence of contraband, a court should "evaluate . . . all the circumstances," avoiding "inflexible . . . evidentiary requirements." Ultimately, "[t]he question . . . is whether all the facts surrounding a dog's alert, viewed through the lens of common sense, would make a reasonably prudent person think that a search would reveal contraband or evidence of a crime. A sniff is up to snuff when it meets that test."

Whren v. United States

United States Supreme Court

517 U.S. 806, 116 S. Ct. 1769, 135 L. Ed. 2d 89 (1996)

JUSTICE SCALIA delivered the opinion of the Court.

In this case we decide whether the temporary detention of a motorist who the police have probable cause to believe has committed a civil traffic violation is inconsistent with the Fourth Amendment's prohibition against unreasonable seizures unless a reasonable officer would have been motivated to stop the car by a desire to enforce the traffic laws.

I

On the evening of June 10, 1993, plainclothes vice-squad officers of the District of Columbia Metropolitan Police Department were patrolling a "high drug area" of the city in an unmarked car. Their suspicions were aroused when they passed a dark Pathfinder truck with temporary license plates and youthful occupants waiting at a stop sign, the driver looking down into the lap of the passenger at his right. The truck remained stopped at the intersection for what seemed an unusually long time — more than 20 seconds. When the police car executed a U-turn in order to head back toward the truck, the Pathfinder turned suddenly to its right, without signaling, and sped off at an "unreasonable" speed. The policemen followed, and in a short while overtook the Pathfinder when it stopped behind other traffic at a red light. They pulled up alongside, and Officer Ephraim Soto stepped out and approached the driver's door, identifying himself as a police officer and directing the driver, petitioner Brown, to put the vehicle in park. When Soto drew up to the driver's window, he immediately observed two large plastic bags of what appeared to be crack cocaine in petitioner Whren's hands. Petitioners were arrested, and quantities of several types of illegal drugs were retrieved from the vehicle.

Petitioners were charged in a four-count indictment with violating various federal drug laws, including 21 U.S.C. §§ 844(a) and 860(a). At a pretrial suppression hearing, they challenged the legality of the stop and the resulting seizure of the drugs. They argued that the stop had not been justified by probable cause to believe, or even reasonable suspicion, that petitioners were engaged in illegal drug-dealing activity; and that Officer Soto's asserted ground for approaching the vehicle — to give the driver a warning concerning traffic violations — was pretextual. The District Court denied the suppression motion, concluding that "the facts of the stop were not controverted," and "[t]here was nothing to really demonstrate that the actions of the officers were contrary to a normal traffic stop." App. 5.

Petitioners were convicted of the counts at issue here. The Court of Appeals affirmed the convictions. . . .

II

The Fourth Amendment guarantees "[t]he right of the people to be secure in their persons, houses, papers, and effects, against unreasonable searches and seizures." Temporary detention of individuals during the stop of an automobile by the police, even if only for a brief period and for a limited purpose, constitutes a "seizure" of "persons" within the meaning of this provision. . . . As a general matter, the decision to stop an automobile is reasonable where the police have probable cause to believe that a traffic violation has occurred.

Petitioners accept that Officer Soto had probable cause to believe that various provisions of the District of Columbia traffic code had been violated. *See* 18 D.C. Mun. Regs. §§ 2213.4 (1995) ("An operator shall . . . give full time and attention to the operation of the vehicle"); 2204.3 ("No person shall turn any vehicle . . . without giving an appropriate signal"); 2200.3 ("No person shall drive a vehicle . . . at a speed greater than is reasonable and prudent under the conditions"). They argue, however, that "in the unique context of civil traffic regulations" probable cause is not enough. Since, they contend, the use of automobiles is so heavily and minutely regulated that total compliance with traffic and safety rules is nearly impossible, a police officer will almost invariably be able to catch any given motorist in a technical violation. This creates the temptation to use traffic stops as a means of investigating other law violations, as to which no probable cause or even articulable suspicion exists. Petitioners, who are both black, further contend that police officers might decide which motorists to stop based on decidedly impermissible factors, such as the race of the car's occupants. To avoid this danger, they say, the Fourth Amendment test for traffic stops should be, not the normal one (applied by the Court of Appeals) of whether probable cause existed to justify the stop; but rather, whether a police officer, acting reasonably, would have made the stop for the reason given.

A

Petitioners contend that the standard they propose is consistent with our past cases' disapproval of police attempts to use valid bases of action against citizens as pretexts for pursuing other investigatory agendas. We are reminded that in *Florida v. Wells*, 495 U.S. 1, 4, 110 S. Ct. 1632, 109 L. Ed. 2d 1 (1990), we stated that "an inventory search must not be used as a ruse for a general rummaging in order to discover incriminating evidence"; that in *Colorado v. Bertine*, 479 U.S. 367, 372, 107 S. Ct. 738, 93 L. Ed. 2d 739 (1987), in approving an inventory search, we apparently thought it significant that there had been "no showing that the police, who were following standard procedures, acted in bad faith or for the sole purpose of investigation"; and that in *New York v. Burger*, 482 U.S. 691, 716–717, n. 27, 107 S. Ct. 2636, 96 L. Ed. 2d 601 (1987), we observed, in upholding the constitutionality of a warrantless administrative inspection, that the search did not appear to be "a 'pretext' for obtaining evidence of . . . violation of . . . penal laws." But only an undiscerning reader would regard these cases as endorsing the principle that ulterior motives can invalidate police conduct that is justifiable on the basis of probable cause to believe that a violation of law has occurred. In each case we were addressing the validity of a search conducted in the *absence* of probable cause. Our quoted statements simply explain that the exemption from the need for probable cause (and warrant), which is accorded to searches made for the purpose of inventory or administrative regulation, is not accorded to searches that are *not* made for those purposes.

. . . .

. . . Petitioners' difficulty is not simply a lack of affirmative support for their position. Not only have we never held, outside the context of inventory search or administrative inspection (discussed above), that an officer's motive invalidates objectively justifiable behavior under the Fourth Amendment; but we have repeatedly held and asserted the contrary. . . . In *United States v. Robinson*, 414 U.S. 218, 94 S. Ct. 467, 38 L. Ed. 2d 427 (1973), we held that a traffic-violation arrest (of the sort here) would not be rendered invalid by the fact that it was "a mere pretext for a narcotics search," *id.*, at 221, n. 1, 94 S. Ct. at 470, n. 1; and that a lawful postarrest search of the person would not be rendered invalid by the fact that it was not motivated by the officer-safety concern that justifies such searches, *see id.*, at 236, 94 S. Ct., at 477. *See also Gustafson v. Florida*, 414 U.S. 260, 266, 94 S. Ct. 488, 38 L. Ed. 2d 456 (1973). And in *Scott v. United States*, 436 U.S. 128, 138, 98 S. Ct. 1717, 56 L. Ed. 2d 168 (1978), in rejecting the contention that wiretap evidence was subject to exclusion because the agents conducting the tap had failed to make any effort to comply with the statutory requirement that unauthorized acquisitions be minimized, we said that "[s]ubjective intent alone . . . does not make otherwise lawful conduct illegal or unconstitutional." We described *Robinson* as having established that "the fact that the officer does not have the state of mind which is hypothecated by the reasons which provide the legal justification for the officer's action does not invalidate the action taken as long as the circumstances, viewed objectively, justify that action." 436 U.S., at 138, 98 S. Ct. at 1723.

We think these cases foreclose any argument that the constitutional reasonableness of traffic stops depends on the actual motivations of the individual officers involved. We of course agree with petitioners that the Constitution prohibits selective enforcement of the law based on considerations such as race. But the constitutional basis for objecting to intentionally discriminatory application of laws is the Equal Protection Clause, not the Fourth Amendment. Subjective intentions play no role in ordinary, probable-cause Fourth Amendment analysis.

B

Recognizing that we have been unwilling to entertain Fourth Amendment challenges based on the actual motivations of individual officers, petitioners disavow any intention to make the individual officer's subjective good faith the touchstone of "reasonableness." They insist that the standard they have put forward — whether the officer's conduct deviated materially from usual police practices, so that a reasonable officer in the same circumstances would not have made the stop for the reasons given — is an "objective" one.

But although framed in empirical terms, this approach is plainly and indisputably driven by subjective considerations. Its whole purpose is to prevent the police from doing under the guise of enforcing the traffic code what they would like to do for different reasons. Petitioners' proposed standard may not use the word "pretext," but it is designed to combat nothing other than the perceived "danger" of the pretextual stop, albeit only indirectly and over the run of cases. Instead of asking whether the individual officer had the proper state of mind, the petitioners would have us ask, in effect, whether (based on general police practices) it is plausible to believe that the officer had the proper state of mind.

Why one would frame a test designed to combat pretext in such fashion that the court cannot take into account *actual and admitted pretext* is a curiosity that can only be explained by the fact that our cases have foreclosed the more sensible option. If those cases were based only upon the evidentiary difficulty of establishing subjective intent, petitioners' attempt to root out subjective vices through objective means might make sense. But they were not based only upon that, or indeed even principally upon that. Their principal basis — which applies equally to attempts to reach subjective intent through ostensibly objective means — is simply that the Fourth Amendment's concern with "reasonableness" allows certain actions to be taken in certain circumstances, *whatever* the subjective intent. But even if our concern had been only an evidentiary one, petitioners' proposal would by no means assuage it. Indeed, it seems to us somewhat easier to figure out the intent of an individual officer than to plumb the collective consciousness of law enforcement in order to determine whether a "reasonable officer" would have been moved to act upon the traffic violation. While police manuals and standard procedures may sometimes provide objective assistance, ordinarily one would be reduced to speculating about the hypothetical reaction of a hypothetical constable—an exercise that might be called virtual subjectivity.

Moreover, police enforcement practices, even if they could be practicably assessed by a judge, vary from place to place and from time to time. We cannot accept that the search and seizure protections of the Fourth Amendment are so variable and can be made to turn upon such trivialities. The difficulty is illustrated by petitioners' arguments in this case. Their claim that a reasonable officer would not have made this stop is based largely on District of Columbia police regulations which permit plainclothes officers in unmarked vehicles to enforce traffic laws "only in the case of a violation that is so grave as to pose an *immediate threat* to the safety of others." Metropolitan Police Department—Washington, D. C., General Order 303.1, pt. 1, Objectives and Policies (A)(2)(4) (Apr. 30, 1992), reprinted as Addendum to Brief for Petitioners. This basis of invalidation would not apply in jurisdictions that had a different practice. And it would not have applied even in the District of Columbia, if Officer Soto had been wearing a uniform or patrolling in a marked police cruiser.

. . . .

III

In what would appear to be an elaboration on the "reasonable officer" test, petitioners argue that the balancing inherent in any Fourth Amendment inquiry requires us to weigh the governmental and individual interests implicated in a traffic stop such as we have here. That balancing, petitioners claim, does not support investigation of minor traffic infractions by plainclothes police in unmarked vehicles; such investigation only minimally advances the government's interest in traffic safety, and may indeed retard it by producing motorist confusion and alarm—a view said to be supported by the Metropolitan Police Department's own regulations generally prohibiting this practice. And as for the Fourth Amendment interests of the individuals concerned, petitioners point out that our cases acknowledge that even ordinary traffic stops entail "a possibly unsettling show of authority"; that they at best "interfere with freedom of movement, are inconvenient, and consume time" and at worst "may create substantial anxiety," [*Delaware v.*] *Prouse*, 440 U.S., at 657, 99 S. Ct. at 1398. That anxiety is likely to be even more pronounced when the stop is conducted by plainclothes officers in unmarked cars.

It is of course true that in principle every Fourth Amendment case, since it turns upon a "reasonableness" determination, involves a balancing of all relevant factors. With rare exceptions not applicable here, however, the result of that balancing is not in doubt where the search or seizure is based upon probable cause. . . .

. . . .

Where probable cause has existed, the only cases in which we have found it necessary actually to perform the "balancing" analysis involved searches or seizures conducted in an extraordinary manner, unusually harmful to an individual's privacy or even physical interests—such as, for example, seizure by means of deadly force, *see Tennessee v. Garner*, 471 U.S. 1, 105 S. Ct. 1694, 85 L. Ed. 2d 1 (1985), unannounced entry into a home, *see Wilson v. Arkansas*, 514 U.S. 927, 115 S. Ct. 1914, 131 L. Ed. 2d 976 (1995), entry into a home without a warrant, *see Welsh v. Wisconsin*, 466 U.S. 740, 104 S. Ct. 2091, 80 L. Ed. 2d 732 (1984), or physical penetration of the body, *see Winston v. Lee*, 470 U.S. 753, 105 S. Ct. 1611, 84 L. Ed. 2d 662 (1985). The making of a traffic stop out-of-uniform does not remotely qualify as such an extreme practice, and so is governed by the usual rule that probable cause to believe the law has been broken "outbalances" private interest in avoiding police contact.

Petitioners urge as an extraordinary factor in this case that the "multitude of applicable traffic and equipment regulations" is so large and so difficult to obey perfectly that virtually everyone is guilty of violation, permitting the police to single out almost whomever they wish for a stop. But we are aware of no principle that would allow us to decide at what point a code of law becomes so expansive and so commonly violated that infraction itself can no longer be the ordinary measure of the lawfulness of enforcement. And even if we could identify such exorbitant codes, we do not know by what standard (or what right) we would decide, as petitioners would have us do, which particular provisions are sufficiently important to merit enforcement.

For the run-of-the-mine case, which this surely is, we think there is no realistic alternative to the traditional common-law rule that probable cause justifies a search and seizure.

. . . .

Here the District Court found that the officers had probable cause to believe that petitioners had violated the traffic code. That rendered the stop reasonable under the Fourth Amendment, the evidence thereby discovered admissible, and the upholding of the convictions by the Court of Appeals for the District of Columbia Circuit correct.

Judgment affirmed.

Notes and Questions

(1) If an officer admits that he arrested a driver for speeding because he had an unfounded hunch that the driver was in possession of narcotics, is the arrest invalid under the Fourth Amendment? Under any other constitutional provision? What if the officer admits that the real reason for the speeding arrest was that the driver was a member of a racial minority group? Should that arrest be held to violate either the Fourth Amendment or any other constitutional provision?

(2) If an officer *searches* a vehicle based on probable cause to believe that the owner is in possession of fireworks, a petty misdemeanor, can the owner succeed with a claim that the officer was not actually interested in finding the fireworks, but, rather, was hostile to the owner because of a brutality claim the owner had filed against him? Is the result different if the owner establishes that other officers would not have searched the vehicle for fireworks?

(3) After *Whren*, when will an officer's actual, subjective motivation for an arrest or search be relevant to the validity of her conduct under the Fourth Amendment?

(4) Suppose that an officer alleges that he arrested a woman based on probable cause to believe that she had stolen the vehicle she was driving. In fact, the objective facts known to the officer fell short of probable cause to arrest the woman for theft, but did support an arrest for reckless driving. Is the arrest valid under the reasoning and holding of *Whren?*

In *Devenpeck v. Alford*, 543 U.S. 146, 125 S. Ct. 588, 160 L. Ed. 2d 537 (2004), the Supreme Court addressed the question of whether an arrest is constitutional when an officer lacks probable cause to arrest a person for the offense he stated to be the basis for the arrest, but has probable cause to arrest the person for another offense that is *not* "'closely related'" to the stated offense. Relying heavily upon *Whren*, a unanimous Court held that such an arrest is consistent with the probable cause demand.

In *Devenpeck*, officers arrested Alford for violating the state's Privacy Act by tape recording his conversations with them. They apparently lacked probable cause to arrest for that offense, but might have had probable cause to arrest for either impersonating or obstructing a law enforcement officer. According to the Court "[w]hether probable cause exists depends upon the reasonable conclusion to be drawn from the facts known to the arresting officer at the time of the arrest." There was "no basis in precedent or reason" for further limiting "the probable-cause inquiry . . . to the known facts bearing upon the offense actually invoked at the time of arrest" and for demanding that "the offense supported by these known facts must be 'closely related' to the offense that the officer invoked." *Whren* had made it "clear that an arresting officer's state of mind (except for the facts that he knows) is irrelevant to the existence of probable cause" and that "his subjective reason for making the arrest need not be the criminal offense as to which the known facts provide probable cause."

A "rule" that the offense for which probable cause does exist "must be 'closely related' to, and based on the same conduct as, the offense identified by the arresting officer at the time of arrest" is irreconcilable with these established principles. Such a rule would "make[] the lawfulness of an arrest turn upon the motivation of the arresting officer," excluding both facts that did not play a "part in the officer's expressed subjective reason for making the arrest" and "offenses that are not 'closely related' to that subjective reason." *Whren*, however, concluded that "[s]ubjective intent of the arresting officer, *however* it is determined . . . is simply no basis for invalidating an arrest. Those are lawfully arrested whom the facts known to the arresting officers give probable cause to arrest."

Probable Cause Problems

2–1: On January 29, 1992, Mark Dove informed Officer Pace that his wife, Susan Dove, had gone shopping the previous evening and had not returned home and that he had just discovered her car, a Cavalier, across the street from the Stop and Shop Market. After completing a missing person report, Dove drove his wife's car home. Shortly thereafter, the police learned that a woman's body was in a soccer field near the Stop and Shop. Dove was summoned to the location. Without showing emotion, he identified his wife's body. On the back of Mrs. Dove's body police observed numerous wood fragments and some synthetic fibers.

Later that day, Dove consented to a search of his home and the Cavalier. Although officers found no evidence linking him to his wife's death, they noticed that Dove's entire home had recently been thoroughly cleaned and vacuumed. They also spotted sawdust on the garage floor, most of which had been swept up and deposited in a small metal container. On the passenger seat of the Cavalier, the officers observed several wood chips.

On May 8, 1992, Detectives Gifford and Raucci obtained a warrant to search Dove's home for "wood particles and synthetic fibers resembling carpet similar to those found on the victim's clothing." In addition to the preceding facts, the affidavit in support of the warrant included facts supporting the inference that the victim had been strangled in her home and dragged through the house and into the garage. The affidavit stated that numerous wood fragments had been found on the clothing covering the victim's back; that Dove had told the police that the sawdust on the garage floor was the result of the construction of a deck that was going to be installed on the rear of his home; and that the deck was seen to be leaning up against the rear of Dove's home on May 5.

Upon executing the warrant on May 11, the police seized wood fragments from the garage that matched those on the victim's clothing. Dove has challenged the search, claiming that the warrant was not supported by probable cause.

Should the court sustain Dove's claim? Why?

2–2: On June 7, Detectives Kelly and Martin drove to Veer Park to investigate a complaint of suspicious activity involving a young child. The child's uncle told the detectives that he had observed a man interacting with his five-year-old niece, pushing her on a swing and talking about movies and videos he had at his home. The child and two other witnesses described the man's vehicle — a blue sedan with rear antennas resembling those of a police cruiser. Upon receiving a radio report, two patrol officers identified and stopped the vehicle. When Kelly and Martin arrived at the scene, Bert, the driver, consented to a search of his sedan. Inside Bert's car, the detectives found a police scanner, handcuffs, and a hat bearing the phrase "N. Y. P. D." Bert reported that he had the handcuffs because he had been employed as a security guard four years earlier. He admitted speaking to the girl about movies he had at his apartment. The detectives took Bert to the police station for questioning.

Detective Kelly relayed the information they had learned to Detective Mark. Mark drafted a warrant application for a warrant to search Bert's residence for "child pornography, including books, photos, videos, and other electronic media depicting minors engaged in a prohibited sexual act or in the simulation of a prohibited sexual act." The affidavit in support of the warrant application set forth the following information:

- On June 7 officers responded to a Veer Park reference to a suspicious subject;
- During the investigation it was determined that Bert, who lived at 512 E Lucas St., Apt #3, attempted to lure a five-year-old female to his apartment;
- Bert had a 40-minute conversation with the girl in which he told her that he had movies and videos at his apartment that she would like to watch and other things for the girl to do;
- Bert's license plate 511NYG was provided by a witness and the vehicle was located by officers near Bert's apartment;
- Bert consented to a search of his vehicle where officers observed a police scanner, binoculars, a police-type hat, handcuffs; and the vehicle was equipped with CB antennas making it similar to a police vehicle.

A judge issued a search warrant for Bert's apartment for child pornography. During the search of the apartment, officers found children's movies, a computer, and numerous compact discs containing child pornography.

Was the search warrant supported by probable cause?

2–3: Fifty-three-year-old James Curdy hosted a graduation party for his nephew. When the party ended at midnight, Curdy and others, including Roger and Heath, continued a card game in Curdy's apartment. Curdy consumed alcohol during both the party and the card game. Around 5:00 a.m., Curdy walked Roger and Heath to their cars. As the three men, who were African-American, were talking, Officer Cole, who was on "routine patrol" in his cruiser, drove past very slowly, then circled around and drove past the group a second time. Cole stopped his car, and, to get the men's attention, asked, "What's up, gentlemen?" Curdy responded, "What the fuck do you want?"

Cole got out of his car and asked why Curdy had used profane language. When Curdy asked why the officer had approached them, Cole asserted, "It's my job to see what's going on if somebody's standing out here at five in the morning." Curdy asked, "What the fuck is your job?" Officer Cole then requested identification from the men. Curdy responded that he was in front of his own home, that he had no identification, and that neither he nor his friends needed to show any.

Officer Cole then asked Curdy if he had been drinking. When Curdy said that he had, Cole ordered him to go inside his home because he lacked identification and was obviously intoxicated. Curdy asserted that he did not have to go inside and did not have to do "shit" that Officer Cole ordered. The officer warned that if Curdy did not return to his home immediately, he would be arrested and taken to jail. Curdy asked about the grounds for arrest, but Cole simply repeated that if Curdy did not go inside, he would be arrested. Curdy again refused, whereupon Cole took him into custody for "disorderly conduct." The "disorderly conduct" statute provides that: "No person, while voluntarily intoxicated, shall engage in conduct or create a condition that presents a risk of physical harm to the offender or another or to the property of another."

Curdy subsequently sued Officer Cole and Montgomery County, asserting that he had been arrested in violation of the Fourth Amendment. At the trial, Officer Cole testified concerning his reasons for arresting Curdy. According to Cole: "When a person is intoxicated to that level, to my training and experience, under law, they essentially become my responsibility once I come in contact with them. If I let that person go, I cannot tell what's going to happen to him. I can only, unfortunately, speculate what could happen to him. It becomes my responsibility to make sure that one of a million things does not happen to him."

Is there merit in Curdy's Fourth Amendment claim?

2–4: On October 25, Agent Dennis applied for a warrant to search the premises at 397 Taz Road. In the supporting affidavit, Dennis recited the following information, which was provided to him by Drug Enforcement Administration (DEA) Special Agent Hard, a 20-year veteran of the DEA:

1. SA Hard with the Drug Enforcement Administration (DEA) recently met with a Confidential DEA Informant (CI). The CI provided information regarding an indoor marijuana grow operation at 397 Taz Road. According to SA Hard, the CI had also furnished reliable information within the past year leading to the successful arrests, prosecutions, and convictions of three subjects.

2. The CI informed SA Hard that J. Thomas had a reputation within the marijuana community for the past two to three years as being a successful producer of not only "leaf" marijuana, but the more sought after "bud" of the plant, which is more expensive and produces a greater high for the user. One ounce of the "hydroponically" produced bud can sell for as much as $250.00 per ounce.

3. The CI informed SA Hard that Thomas lived at 397 Taz Road. SA Hard confirmed that Thomas's driver's license indicated 397 Taz Road as his address, and discovered that Thomas had an active gun permit with that address. On October 18, at approximately 10:15 am, SA Hard drove by the residence at 397 Taz Road and observed Thomas standing in the driveway smoking a cigarette.

4. The CI reported that he/she has been to the residence on at least three occasions and observed Thomas conduct narcotic transactions and that he/she has observed Thomas take marijuana from the residence and sell it to customers on at least three occasions. All of the CI's information about Thomas and the grow operation was more than eight months old.

5. Electric company records list Sandra Brum, Thomas's girlfriend, as the subscriber for 397 Taz Road, and County Property Records list Brum as the owner. SA Hard obtained the electricity bills for the property from March through September of the current year. They ranged from $350 to $530 and increased over time. A neighboring residence, which is 50% larger than the residence on Brum's property, had bills ranging between $125 and $230 during the same period. SA Hard and I believe that the bills for 397 Taz Road are indicative of "high" electricity usage — which is typical for indoor marijuana cultivation because of the special light systems used.

6. Property records indicate at least two "out buildings" on the property which are not visible from the front. Those records do not indicate the presence of any other structures that would account for the high electricity usage — such as a heated pool or air conditioned buildings other than the residence.

The judge issued a search warrant. When the officers arrived at the property on October 26 to execute the warrant, they discovered that Thomas, his girlfriend, and their two children lived in a freestanding trailer home behind the main residence. In the trailer they found and seized 128 living marijuana plants growing in soil, five pounds of processed marijuana, and equipment for growing marijuana indoors.

Was the search warrant supported by probable cause?

2–5: Plaintiff Jerry Mack sold products referred to as "potpourri" from a roadside stand. The products had brand names such as "Funky Green Stuff," "Purple Haze," and "Cannabus." Packaging container labels stated that the potpourri was not to be used for human consumption and was not intended for use by minors. An ounce sold for $200 and up. Officers Jack, William, and Leo came to the stand and seized the product. Mack filed a civil suit, claiming violation of the Fourth Amendment because the officers lacked probable cause to confiscate his product.

The officers who seized the potpourri had received numerous citizen complaints about "sons and daughters" buying and smoking the potpourri. On the day of the seizure, Jack and William had stopped a vehicle in the vicinity of the stand. Believing the driver to be under the influence of "something," they arrested him. In the glove compartment they found a small package of potpourri purchased from Mack's stand. Potpourri is a form of "synthetic marijuana." After this incident, Officer Jack contacted County Prosecutor Colleen to discuss law enforcement authority concerning synthetic marijuana. Colleen informed Jack that the law criminalizing synthetic marijuana was not yet in effect. She instructed Jack, however, that he could seize the potpourri as a "hallucinogenic substance."

Officers Jack and William met Officer Leo at the roadside stand. They informed Jerry Mack that he would be cited for the sale of hallucinogenic substances and that his potpourri would be confiscated. Based on Officer Jack's conversation with Prosecutor Colleen and the belief that the potpourri constituted a hallucinogenic substance, the officers seized 355 bags and 55 bottles of Jerry Mack's product.

In fact, there was no statute that addressed the possession or sale of "hallucinogenic substances." Moreover, Colleen was correct that the recently adopted prohibition on "synthetic marijuana" had not yet taken effect. The official report filed after the seizure did include a statement that the potpourri had been seized as a "harmful intoxicant," but that was not the actual reason the officers confiscated the potpourri, and it is uncertain whether potpourri qualifies as a "harmful intoxicant" under the provision prohibiting dispensing or distributing "harmful intoxicants." According to the definition in that provision, a "harmful intoxicant" does not include beer or liquor, but means "any compound or substance the gas, fumes, or vapor of which when inhaled can induce intoxication, excitement, giddiness, irrational behavior, depression, stupefaction, paralysis, unconsciousness, asphyxiation, or other harmful physiological effects, and includes, but is not limited to, any of the following: organic solvents, plastic or model cement, fingernail polish, aerosol propellant, fluorocarbon refrigerant, and anesthetic gas." Jerry Mack was not charged with violation of this provision or with any other criminal offense.

Did the officers violate Jerry Mack's Fourth Amendment rights?

2–6: Kenneth and Brandon were driving through South Carolina on Interstate 77 in a rental vehicle. It was raining at the time. Officers Vines and Scott observed Kenneth following a truck too closely. The officers initiated a traffic stop as he pulled into a gas station. After obtaining his license and registration, Vines asked Kenneth to accompany him to the police cruiser. As Vines ran Kenneth's license, he asked several questions about where the two men were traveling from and what they did there. Kenneth replied that they went "to see some girls" in Atlanta and were on their way back to North Carolina. Brandon told Scott that they were returning from Atlanta after going to see a cousin play basketball.

Vines radioed for a K–9 unit. While waiting for the dog to arrive, Scott searched Kenneth pursuant to consent and found no contraband. After Kenneth stated repeatedly that he had to use the restroom, Scott escorted him to the restroom. Brandon also asked to use the restroom. He consented to a search of his person by Officer Vines. No contraband was found. Vines told him he would have to wait to use the restroom until Kenneth returned. Vines asked if Brandon had smoked marijuana earlier in the day, stating that he "smelled marijuana when Brandon got out of the car." Brandon replied that the smell was from a cigar and that he did not smoke marijuana.

When the canine unit arrived, minutes later, Officer Gibbs twice led "Justice," a drug-detecting dog, around the exterior of the vehicle. Justice did not alert. Although Kenneth and Brandon had refused to consent to a search, Vines decided to search the car, beginning with the interior and proceeding to the trunk. He discovered a plastic bag in the trunk containing 393 ecstasy pills concealed within a small gift bag. Kenneth and Brandon were placed under arrest. During a more thorough search after the arrests, officers discovered a plastic bag containing a half a pound of marijuana underneath the spare tire.

Kenneth and Brandon were indicted on charges of trafficking in ecstasy and possession of marijuana with intent to distribute. Prior to trial, Morris moved to suppress the drugs as the fruit of an illegal search and seizure. At the hearing, Officer Vines testified that he had "smelled an odor of marijuana when I first approached the vehicle" and that he had observed "several hollowed out Phillies Blunt cigars in the center console of the vehicle, and loose blunt tobacco scattered over the frontal interior of the vehicle." (Phillies Blunts are "an inexpensive brand of cigar." Marijuana smokers are known to hollow them out, replacing the tobacco with marijuana to conceal what they are smoking.) Vines also saw "several empty cans of Red Bull." Vines conceded that Justice had not alerted, but stated the canine had "failed to keep his nose on the vehicle as he usually did during a search and instead frequently stopped to shake the water off." Vines assumed "he did not like being out in the rain."

The trial court denied the motion to suppress. After they were convicted, Kenneth and Brandon appealed the judge's ruling.

How should the appellate court rule?

2–7: Sergeant Steven Gaudy, acting on a tip from a confidential informant that "James" was dealing cocaine in front of an abandoned house in the 2100 block of LaSalle, went to the location with Officers Lamp and Snap. The officers observed a hand-to-hand transaction between two men who were standing across the street from the abandoned home. The officers immediately placed the two men, Scott and Bryant, under arrest and searched them. Bryant had a single bag of cocaine; Scott had 19 bags of cocaine.

While Officer Lamp was handcuffing Scott and advising him of his rights, Scott informed Lamp that he did not want to go to jail. He reported that the cocaine had been given to him to sell by a man named Samhill, and described Samhill's clothing. He then motioned with his head to the apartment behind and above him, indicating that Samhill resided there. He informed the officers that Samhill had more cocaine stashed on the premises. While looking up at the apartment, Sergeant Gaudy observed a man who fit Scott's description of Samhill duck his head out of the doorway to the second story apartment at least three times. According to Gaudy, the man looked "as if he were monitoring our activities."

Shortly thereafter, the officers saw two young men exit from the apartment and enter a black Nissan parked on the street. An older woman also left the apartment, sat briefly in the Nissan, and then returned upstairs. Moments later, the officers observed Samhill, in the company of the woman, at the head of a winding iron staircase that connected the second-story apartment to the ground. They appeared to be leaving. Gaudy and Lamp stopped the pair on the stairs, advised Samhill that he was under investigation for a possible narcotics violation, and read him his rights. The officers then took Samhill and the woman back to the apartment. At the same time, Officer Snap retrieved the two young men from the Nissan and escorted them to the apartment. At this point, Samhill said that he did not want his family to go to jail.

He directed the officers to a plastic bag containing 25 smaller bags of cocaine hidden underneath the stairway outside the apartment.

Sergeant Gaudy subsequently prepared an application for a search warrant and returned with a drug-sniffing dog. He discovered two small bags of cocaine and a small bag of marijuana in an ice bucket on top of the refrigerator in the kitchen. Samhill was charged with narcotics offenses and moved to suppress the contraband, claiming that it was discovered as a result of his illegal arrest.

How should the trial court rule on Samhill's motion?

2–8: Brendan was two months shy of his nineteenth birthday and had an eleventh-grade education. He lived with his cousin and cousin's wife, Aaron and Angie Haw, and their three boys, ages one, three, and five, as a live-in babysitter. On the evening of June 21, Angie brought her three-year-old son to the Community Hospital ("Hospital") emergency room ("ER") to be examined. She told medical personnel that the three-year-old had claimed that Brendan had "touched his pee-pee" and that Brendan's "pee-pee had touched his butt." The doctor who examined the child found no physical evidence of trauma or sexual penetration.

Investigator Ford, who was on duty the evening of June 21, was notified of a possible sexual assault. He went to the Hospital to investigate, arriving at approximately 11:20 p.m. Ford met initially with Nurse Slaughter, who told him what Angie had said. He then spoke with Angie, who repeated the allegation, but did not interview or speak with the child. Ford then called Special Agent Rebecca Gan, told her he was investigating a sexual assault, and asked her to join him at the Hospital. After Gan arrived, she spoke with Angie, then asked her to come to the police station. Angie was concerned about needing to drop off her child at a neighbor's. She indicated that she did not want to have any kind of confrontation with Brendan and did not want her children to see him. Consequently, Gan directed Ford to "[go] over and get Brendan." Sometime after midnight, Ford, who was not in uniform but was armed, went to the Haw family's "quarters" in an unmarked police car. Sergeant Burn and his working dog arrived on the scene shortly after Ford.

At the Haw residence, Ford and Burn found Brendan standing in front of the house. Without telling him why, Ford informed Brendan that "they needed to talk to him down at the station." Ford did not place Brendan under formal arrest, but he also did not tell Brendan that he was not under arrest. Instead, he frisked and handcuffed Brendan before placing him in the backseat of his police car. Brendan was fully clothed, but was not wearing shoes or socks. Ford did not permit Brendan to go inside the Haw residence and put shoes on before placing him in the car and taking him to the police station.

Did Investigator Ford violate the Fourth Amendment by taking Brendan to the police station?

2–9: Trooper Wagner was an eight-year veteran of the State Police who had written hundreds of traffic citations and warnings. As part of his patrol duties, Wagner participated in a Department of Homeland Security overtime program named "STOP," which requires officers zealously to enforce traffic laws. On May 27, Wagner was working a "STOP" overtime shift. At 8:00 a.m., he was tasked to perform traffic control at a traffic incident that occurred on Interstate 80. While performing these duties, Wagner observed Delf driving a red pickup truck. As he approached the truck, Wagner "noticed what appeared to be a 'necklace' or 'pendant' hanging from the rear view mirror." He perceived this item to be low hanging, but "not quite touching the dashboard." Wagner believed that the item had the potential to "obscure the driver's vision" and to "be a distraction" because the item was not stationary. Wagner believed that the object hanging from the rearview mirror violated Section 4524(c) of the State Statutes which he understood to prohibit hanging "anything" from a rearview mirror. Wagner's understanding of Section 4524(c) was erroneous, however. In fact, an object hanging from the inside rearview mirror does not violate that provision unless it is positioned in such a way as to "materially obstruct, obscure or impair the driver's vision through the front windshield."

Based on his understanding of the law, Wagner stopped the pickup truck. He obtained Delf's identification document (a Mexican driver's license) as well as identification documents (Mexican election cards) from other occupants of the truck. Wagner then advised Delf that he had been stopped because of the object — which Wagner had discovered to be a crucifix — which was dangling from the rearview mirror. At this point, the front-seat passenger volunteered that he was a native of Puerto Rico, but that the rest of the truck's occupants were illegal aliens. Wagner then ordered Delf to follow him to the State Police barracks.

Delf was subsequently charged with knowingly transporting an illegal alien. Prior to trial, he filed a motion to suppress evidence, arguing that the traffic stop was pretextual and also that it was made without probable cause because "the religious pendant which hung from Delf's rearview mirror was, in fact, no obstruction to his visibility and safe driving."

Does Delf have a valid claim under the Fourth Amendment?

2–10: In August 2001, an FBI agent discovered a website called "Lolitas.com." The site contained images of nude and partially-dressed girls, some prepubescent, along with this text: "Lolitas.com offers hard to find pics! Weekly updates and high quality pix inside. You can't go wrong if you like young girls!" Some images displayed the genital areas of minors and included a caption that read: "Lolitas age 12–17. Over one thousand pictures of girls age 12–17! Naked Lolita girls with weekly updates!" For $19.95 per month, the FBI agent purchased and maintained a membership in the website from August to December 2001. Members received unlimited access and were allowed to download images directly from the website. By browsing the site, the agent captured "hundreds of images" that "included both legal adult pornography and illegal child pornography." Although possessing child pornography is a serious offense, merely viewing it online does not seem to be prohibited by the relevant statutes.

In January 2002, the FBI executed a search warrant at the premises of the owner and operator of Lolitas.com. They seized his computer, which contained illegal child pornography that had been posted to the website. The owner admitted to agents that Lolitas.com was a website that contained child pornography. In response to a subpoena, the company that handled credit card transactions for the website provided the FBI with records of Lolitas.com subscribers. The records listed Micah as a member and provided his home address, date of birth, email address, and the fact that he had subscribed from November 2001 until January 2002. The FBI shut down the site at the end of January, while Micah was still a member.

In May 2002, the FBI applied for a search warrant for Micah's home and computer. The supporting affidavit contained the preceding facts. Citing FBI computer experts, the affidavit also explained that if a computer had ever received or downloaded illegal images, they would remain on the computer for an extended period. If the user sent the images to "recycle" and then deleted the files in the recycling bin, the files were not actually erased but were kept in the computer's "slack space" until randomly overwritten. Even deleted files could be retrieved by computer forensic experts. The affidavit also stated that "[p]aid subscription websites are a forum through which persons with interests in child pornography can view and download images in relative privacy." It described how collectors and distributors of child pornography use the free email and online storage services of Internet portals to operate anonymously because these websites require little identifying information. The affidavit also asserted that most child pornography collectors "are sexually attracted to children," that they "collect sexually explicit materials" including digital images for their own sexual gratification, and that they, "rarely, if ever, dispose of their sexually explicit materials."

The affidavit concluded with the following observations: (1) Micah "took steps to affirmatively join Lolitas.com"; (2) that website "advertised pictures of young girls" and "offered images of young girls engaged in sexually explicit conduct"; (3) Micah remained a member for over two months, although he could have canceled at any time; (4) Micah had access to hundreds of images, including historical postings to the website; and (5) any time Micah visited the website, he had to have seen images of "naked prepubescent females with a caption that described them as twelve to seventeen-year-old girls." There is a strong likelihood that if they had examined the computer seized from the website owner the FBI could have ascertained whether or not Micah had, in fact, downloaded illegal images from the Lolitas.com website.

Based on the affidavit, the magistrate issued a warrant to search Micah's residence and computer. The FBI searched Micah's house and seized his computer, which contained over 100 images of child pornography.

Was there probable cause to conduct the searches authorized by the warrant?

2–11: At approximately 10:00 p.m., Officer Leonard Fog saw a Sport Utility Vehicle ("SUV") that was illegally parked. Observing that there was no one sitting in the driver's seat, he approached the vehicle. As he approached, he saw a front-seat pas-

2 · UNREASONABLENESS AND THE PROBABLE CAUSE REQUIREMENT   111

senger, a rear-seat passenger (H.T.), and multiple boxes of fireworks in the back compartment that was behind the rear passenger seat where H.T. was sitting. H.T. could have reached the compartment if he had pivoted in his seat and faced the rear of the SUV.

The officer asked H.T. and the front seat passenger who owned the fireworks. Both of them replied that the fireworks belonged to the absent driver. The officers then ordered H.T. and the passenger to get out of the vehicle, and they complied. At that point, the officers handcuffed both H.T. and the front seat passenger and arrested them for possession of the fireworks. H.T. did not make any furtive gestures at any point during the encounter. During a subsequent search, the officers found a handgun inside a small zipped bag that was in H.T.'s pocket. H.T. claims that the police did not have probable cause to arrest him.

Is H.T. correct regarding the lack of probable cause for the arrest?

Selected Bibliography

Bruce A. Antkowiak, *Saving Probable Cause*, 40 Suffolk U. L. Rev. 569 (2007)

Ronald J. Bacigal, *The Fourth Amendment in Flux: The Rise and Fall of Probable Cause,* 1979 U. Ill. L.F. 763 (1979)

Ronald J. Bacigal, *Making the Right Gamble: The Odds on Probable Cause*, 74 Miss. L.J. 279 (2004)

Eugene Cerruti, *The Demise of the* Aguilar-Spinelli *Rule: A Case of Faulty Reception*, 61 Denv. U. L. Rev. 431 (1984)

Gabriel J. Chin and Charles J. Vernon, *Reasonable but Unconstitutional: Racial Profiling and the Radical Objectivity of* Whren v. United States, 83 Geo. Wash. L. Rev. 882 (2015)

Erica Goldberg, *Getting Beyond Intuition in the Probable Cause Inquiry*, 17 Lewis & Clark L. Rev. 789 (2013)

Joseph D. Grano, *Probable Cause and Common Sense: A Reply to the Critics of* Illinois v. Gates, 17 U. Mich. J.L. Reform 465 (1984)

Yale Kamisar, Gates, *"Probable Cause," "Good Faith," and Beyond*, 69 Iowa L. Rev. 551 (1984)

Wayne R. LaFave, *Probable Cause From Informants: The Effects of Murphy's Law on Fourth Amendment Adjudication*, 77 U. Ill. L.F. 1 (1977)

Tracy Maclin, *Race and the Fourth Amendment*, 51 Vand. L. Rev. 333 (1998)

Edward G. Mascolo, *Probable Cause Revisited: Some Disturbing Implications Emanating from* Illinois v. Gates, 6 W. New Eng. L. Rev. 331 (1983)

Charles E. Moylan, Illinois v. Gates, *What It Did and What It Did Not Do*, 20 Crim. L. Bull. 93 (1984)

Timothy P. O'Neill, *Beyond Privacy, Beyond Probable Cause, Beyond the Fourth Amendment: New Strategies For Fighting Pretext Arrests,* 69 U. Colo. L. Rev. 693 (1998)

Anthony C. Thompson, *Stopping the Usual Suspects: Race and the Fourth Amendment*, 74 N.Y.U. L. Rev. 956 (1999)

Chapter 3

Unreasonableness and the Warrant Requirement

Introductory Note

This chapter is concerned with two topics: (1) the relationship between warrants and the Fourth Amendment reasonableness requirement and (2) the specific dictates of the Fourth Amendment's "warrant" clause. It is noteworthy that the Fourth Amendment text does not explicitly demand a warrant to search or to seize. Moreover, the historical origins of the Amendment do not reveal a concern with threats posed by *warrantless* searches or seizures. *See* Telford Taylor, TWO STUDIES IN CONSTITUTIONAL INTERPRETATION 41, 43 (1969). What history does demonstrate is that it was not the prospect of warrantless searches and seizures, but, rather, the *abusive use of warrants* to search and seize, that troubled and galvanized the Framers of our Constitution.

"[O]ur constitutional fathers were . . . concerned . . . about overreaching warrants . . . . Far from looking at the warrant as a protection . . . , they saw it as an authority for unreasonable and oppressive searches, and sought to confine its issuance and execution in line with the stringent requirements applicable to common-law warrants for stolen goods . . . ." The Framers' "prime purpose was to prohibit the oppressive use of warrants . . . ." *Id.;*[1] *see also* Akhil Reed Amar, THE CONSTITUTION AND CRIMINAL PROCEDURE 10–13 (1997).

The instruments of oppression that generated our colonial ancestors' desire to confine the issuance and regulate the content of warrants were known as "general warrants" and "writs of assistance." Those warrants and writs were issued without a

---

1. In fact, as proposed and agreed to by the House, the text of the Fourth Amendment was *solely* concerned with prohibiting abusive warrants. The modification of the text that resulted in an "unreasonableness clause" and, thus, in a Fourth Amendment that was not restricted to regulating warrants was apparently the work of the "Committee of Three" whose role was "to arrange the amendments," not to make substantive changes never agreed to by the House. *See* N. Lasson, THE HISTORY AND DEVELOPMENT OF THE FOURTH AMENDMENT TO THE UNITED STATES CONSTITUTION 101 (1937).

showing of probable cause. Moreover, they conferred upon their holders untempered discretion to select the places to be searched and the persons and things to be seized. To the colonists, the authority those devices bestowed upon law enforcers was objectionably broad and insufficiently constrained. Taylor, *supra*, at 53–54.

The second clause of the Fourth Amendment — the "warrant clause" — was designed to prevent the threats and eliminate the abuses generated by general warrants and writs of assistance. Toward those ends, it explicitly demands "probable cause, supported by Oath or affirmation" as a prerequisite for the issuance of a warrant. It also specifies that warrants must "particularly describe the place to be searched, and the persons or things to be seized." In construing the Fourth Amendment, the Supreme Court has also discerned certain implicit restrictions upon the issuance and execution of warrants.

The first opinion in this chapter discusses whether a warrant is a "procedural" precondition for a reasonable search — i.e., whether it is necessary to secure a warrant prior to searching a place. The second and third cases address two important issues that pertain to the constitutionality of arrests — whether officers ordinarily need warrants to take suspects into custody for offenses and whether it is reasonable to arrest individuals for minor offenses. The last three cases consider the content required for a valid warrant and explore some specific constraints upon the issuance and execution of facially valid warrants. Students should consider whether the current rules and restrictions regarding warrants are consistent with the Framers' original fears and objectives.

[A] The Warrant Requirement and Searches of Persons, Houses, Papers, and Effects

Johnson v. United States

United States Supreme Court

333 U.S. 10, 68 S. Ct. 367, 92 L. Ed. 436 (1948)

MR. JUSTICE JACKSON delivered the opinion of the Court.

. . . .

At about 7:30 p.m. Detective Lieutenant Belland, an officer of the Seattle police force narcotic detail, received information from a confidential informer, who was also a known narcotic user, that unknown persons were smoking opium in the Europe Hotel. The informer was taken back to the hotel to interview the manager, but he returned at once saying he could smell burning opium in the hallway. Belland communicated with federal narcotic agents and between 8:30 and 9 o'clock went back to the hotel with four such agents. All were experienced in narcotic work and recognized at once a strong odor of burning opium which to them was distinctive and unmistakable. The odor led to Room 1. The officers did not know who was occupying that room.

They knocked and a voice inside asked who was there. "Lieutenant Belland," was the reply. There was a slight delay, some "shuffling or noise" in the room and then the defendant opened the door. The officer said, "I want to talk to you a little bit." She then, as he describes it, "stepped back acquiescently and admitted us." He said, "I want to talk to you about the opium smell in the room here." She denied that there was such a smell. Then he said, "I want you to consider yourself under arrest because we are going to search the room." The search turned up incriminating opium and smoking apparatus, the latter being warm, apparently from recent use. This evidence the District Court refused to suppress before trial and admitted over defendant's objection at the trial. Conviction resulted and the Circuit Court of Appeals affirmed.

The defendant challenged the search of her home as a violation of the rights secured to her in common with others, by the Fourth Amendment to the Constitution. The Government defends the search as legally justifiable, more particularly as incident to what it urges was a lawful arrest of the person.

I

. . . .

Entry to defendant's living quarters, which was the beginning of the search, was demanded under color of office. It was granted in submission to authority rather than as an understanding and intentional waiver of a constitutional right.

At the time entry was demanded the officers were possessed of evidence which a magistrate might have found to be probable cause for issuing a search warrant. We cannot sustain defendant's contention, erroneously made, on the strength of *Taylor v. United States*, 286 U.S. 1, 52 S. Ct. 466, 76 L. Ed. 951, that odors cannot be evidence sufficient to constitute probable grounds for any search. That decision held only that odors alone do not authorize a search without warrant. If the presence of odors is testified to before a magistrate and he finds the affiant qualified to know the odor, and it is one sufficiently distinctive to identify a forbidden substance, this Court has never held such a basis insufficient to justify issuance of a search warrant. Indeed it might very well be found to be evidence of most persuasive character.

The point of the Fourth Amendment, which often is not grasped by zealous officers, is not that it denies law enforcement the support of the usual inferences which reasonable men draw from evidence. Its protection consists in requiring that those inferences be drawn by a neutral and detached magistrate instead of being judged by the officer engaged in the often competitive enterprise of ferreting out crime.[3] Any assumption that evidence sufficient to support a magistrate's disinterested de-

---

3. In *United States v. Lefkowitz*, 285 U.S. 452, 464, 52 S. Ct. 420, 423, 76 L. Ed. 877, 82 A.L.R. 775, this Court said: ". . . the informed and deliberate determinations of magistrates empowered to issue warrants as to what searches and seizures are permissible under the Constitution are to be preferred over the hurried action of officers and others who may happen to make arrests. Security against unlawful searches is more likely to be attained by resort to search warrants than by reliance upon the caution and sagacity of petty officers while acting under the excitement that attends the capture of persons accused of crime . . . ."

termination to issue a search warrant will justify the officers in making a search without a warrant would reduce the Amendment to a nullity and leave the people's homes secure only in the discretion of police officers.[4] Crime, even in the privacy of one's own quarters, is, of course, of grave concern to society, and the law allows such crime to be reached on proper showing. The right of officers to thrust themselves into a home is also a grave concern, not only to the individual but to a society which chooses to dwell in reasonable security and freedom from surveillance. When the right of privacy must reasonably yield to the right of search is, as a rule, to be decided by a judicial officer, not by a policeman or Government enforcement agent.

There are exceptional circumstances in which, on balancing the need for effective law enforcement against the right of privacy, it may be contended that a magistrate's warrant for search may be dispensed with. But this is not such a case. No reason is offered for not obtaining a search warrant except the inconvenience to the officers and some slight delay necessary to prepare papers and present the evidence to a magistrate. These are never very convincing reasons and, in these circumstances, certainly are not enough to bypass the constitutional requirement . . . .

If the officers in this case were excused from the constitutional duty of presenting their evidence to a magistrate, it is difficult to think of a case in which it should be required.

[In PART II of its opinion, the Court rejected the government's claim that the warrantless search could be justified as incident to Ms. Johnson's arrest. The search could not be so justified because there was no probable cause to arrest her "until [the officer] had entered her room and found her to be the sole occupant."]

Reversed.

THE CHIEF JUSTICE, MR. JUSTICE BLACK, MR. JUSTICE REED and MR. JUSTICE BURTON dissent.

Notes and Questions

(1) The Court has continued to adhere firmly to the basic principle that controlled its decision in *Johnson*. In *Katz v. United States*, 389 U.S. 347, 88 S. Ct. 507, 19 L. Ed. 2d 576 (1967), discussed *supra* in Chapter One, the government contended that even if its electronic eavesdropping was a search, it was a reasonable search. The Court agreed that if the surveillance was conducted as described by the government, it "was so narrowly circumscribed that a duly authorized magistrate, properly notified of the need for such investigation, specifically informed of the basis on which it was to proceed, and clearly apprised of the precise intrusion it would entail, could constitutionally have authorized . . . the very limited search and seizure that the Government

4. "Belief, however well founded, that an article sought is concealed in a dwelling house, furnishes no justification for a search of that place without a warrant. And such searches are held unlawful notwithstanding facts unquestionably showing probable cause." *Agnello v. United States*, 269 U.S. 20, 33, 46 S. Ct. 4, 6, 70 L. Ed. 145, 51 A.L.R. 409.

asserts . . . took place." However, to the government's argument that its conduct should be validated because "its agents did no more . . . than they might properly have done with prior judicial sanction," the Court responded,

> It is apparent that the agents in this case acted with restraint. Yet the inescapable fact is that this restraint was imposed by the agents themselves, not by a judicial officer. They were not required, before commencing the search, to present their estimate of probable cause for detached scrutiny by a neutral magistrate. They were not compelled, during the conduct of the search itself, to observe precise limits established in advance by a specific court order. Nor were they directed, after the search had been completed, to notify the authorizing magistrate in detail of all that had been seized. In the absence of such safeguards, this Court has never sustained a search upon the sole ground that officers reasonably expected to find evidence of a particular crime and voluntarily confined their activities to the least intrusive means consistent with that end. Searches conducted without warrants have been held unlawful "notwithstanding facts unquestionably showing probable cause," *Agnello v. United States*, 269 U.S. 20, 33, 46 S. Ct. 4, 6, 70 L. Ed. 145, for the Constitution requires "that the deliberate, impartial judgment of a judicial officer . . . be interposed between the citizen and the police . . . ." *Wong Sun v. United States*, 371 U.S. 471, 481–482, 83 S. Ct. 407, 414, 9 L. Ed. 2d 441. [S]earches conducted outside the judicial process, without prior approval by judge or magistrate, are *per se* unreasonable under the Fourth Amendment — subject only to a few specifically established and well-delineated exceptions.

> . . . Omission of [judicial] authorization

> "bypasses the safeguards provided by an objective predetermination of probable cause, and substitutes instead the far less reliable procedure of an after-the-event justification for the . . . search, too likely to be subtly influenced by the familiar shortcomings of hindsight judgment." *Beck v. Ohio*, 379 U.S. 89, 96, 85 S. Ct. 223, 228, 13 L. Ed. 2d 142.

> And bypassing a neutral predetermination of the *scope* of a search leaves individuals secure from Fourth Amendment violations "only in the discretion of the police." *Id.*, at 97, 85 S. Ct. at 229.

For want of a warrant, the Court held that the electronic surveillance constituted an unreasonable search and seizure and that Katz's conviction had to be reversed.

(2) The search warrant requirement (or "*per se* rule") that dictated the holdings in *Johnson* and *Katz* has long been the subject of heated debate. While some judges and scholars have strenuously argued that the requirement lacks textual and historical bases and is not logically defensible, others have contended that the Court's adherence to the requirement is a legitimate and sensible interpretation of the Fourth Amendment. For an exchange over the merits of the warrant rule, see Akhil

Reed Amar, *Fourth Amendment First Principles,* 107 Harv. L. Rev. 757 (1994) (criticizing the warrant requirement), and Carol S. Steiker, *Second Thoughts About First Principles,* 107 Harv. L. Rev. 820 (1994) (defending the warrant requirement).

[B] The Warrant Requirement and Seizures of Persons

United States v. Watson

United States Supreme Court

423 U.S. 411, 96 S. Ct. 820, 46 L. Ed. 2d 598 (1976)

MR. JUSTICE WHITE delivered the opinion of the Court.

. . . .

I

The relevant events began on August 17, 1972, when an informant, one Khoury, telephoned a postal inspector informing him that respondent Watson was in possession of a stolen credit card and had asked Khoury to cooperate in using the card to their mutual advantage. On five to 10 previous occasions Khoury had provided the inspector with reliable information on postal inspection matters, some involving Watson. Later that day Khoury delivered the card to the inspector. On learning that Watson had agreed to furnish additional cards, the inspector asked Khoury to arrange to meet with Watson. Khoury did so, a meeting being scheduled for August 22.[1] Watson canceled that engagement, but at noon on August 23, Khoury met with Watson at a restaurant designated by the latter. Khoury had been instructed that if Watson had additional stolen credit cards, Khoury was to give a designated signal. The signal was given, the officers closed in, and Watson was forthwith arrested. He was removed from the restaurant to the street where he was given the warnings required by *Miranda v. Arizona,* 384 U.S. 436, 86 S. Ct. 1602, 16 L. Ed. 2d 694 (1966). A search having revealed that Watson had no credit cards on his person, the inspector asked if he could look inside Watson's car, which was standing within view. Watson said, "Go ahead," and repeated these words when the inspector cautioned that "[i]f I find anything, it is going to go against you." Using keys furnished by Watson, the inspector entered the car and found under the floor mat an envelope containing two credit cards in the names of other persons. These cards were the basis for two counts of a four-count indictment charging Watson with possessing stolen mail in violation of 18 U.S.C. § 1708.

. . . Watson was convicted of illegally possessing the two cards seized from his car.

---

1. In the meantime the inspector had verified that the card was stolen.

A divided panel of the Court of Appeals for the Ninth Circuit reversed, 504 F.2d 849 (1974), ruling that the admission in evidence of the two credit cards found in the car was prohibited by the Fourth Amendment . . . .

II

. . . .

Contrary to the Court of Appeals' view, Watson's arrest was not invalid because executed without a warrant. Title 18 U.S.C. § 3061(a)(3) expressly empowers the Board of Governors of the Postal Service to authorize Postal Service officers and employees "performing duties related to the inspection of postal matters" to

> make arrests without warrant for felonies cognizable under the laws of the United States if they have reasonable grounds to believe that the person to be arrested has committed or is committing such a felony.

make warrantless arrests!

By regulation, 39 C.F.R. § 232.5(a)(3) (1975), and in identical language, the Board of Governors has exercised that power and authorized warrantless arrests. Because there was probable cause in this case to believe that Watson had violated § 1708, the inspector and his subordinates, in arresting Watson, were acting strictly in accordance with the governing statute and regulations. The effect of the judgment of the Court of Appeals was to invalidate the statute as applied in this case and as applied to all the situations where a court fails to find exigent circumstances justifying a warrantless arrest. We reverse that judgment. *THEY REVERSE THIS EFFECT*

Under the Fourth Amendment, the people are to be "secure in their persons, houses, papers, and effects, against unreasonable searches and seizures, . . . and no Warrants shall issue, but upon probable cause . . . ." Section 3061 represents a judgment by Congress that it is not unreasonable under the Fourth Amendment for postal inspectors to arrest without a warrant provided they have probable cause to do so. This was not an isolated or quixotic judgment of the legislative branch. Other federal law enforcement officers have been expressly authorized by statute for many years to make felony arrests on probable cause but without a warrant . . . .

Because there is a "strong presumption of constitutionality due to an Act of Congress, especially when it turns on what is 'reasonable,'" "[o]bviously the Court should be reluctant to decide that a search thus authorized by Congress was unreasonable and that the Act was therefore unconstitutional." *United States v. Di Re*, 332 U.S. 581, 585, 68 S. Ct. 222, 224, 92 L. Ed. 210 (1948). Moreover, there is nothing in the Court's prior cases indicating that under the Fourth Amendment a warrant is required to make a valid arrest for a felony. Indeed, the relevant prior decisions are uniformly to the contrary.

"The usual rule is that a police officer may arrest without warrant one believed by the officer upon reasonable cause to have been guilty of a felony . . . ." *Carroll v. United States*, 267 U.S. 132, 156, 45 S. Ct. 280, 286, 69 L. Ed. 543 (1925). In *Henry v. United States*, 361 U.S. 98, 80 S. Ct. 168, 4 L. Ed. 2d 134 (1959), the Court dealt with an FBI agent's warrantless arrest under 18 U.S.C. § 3052, which authorizes a warrantless arrest where there are reasonable grounds to believe that the person to be arrested has committed a felony. The Court declared that "[t]he statute states the constitutional standard . . . ." *Id.*, at 100, 80 S. Ct., at 170. The necessary inquiry, therefore, was not whether there was a warrant or whether there was time to get one, but whether there was probable cause for the arrest. In *Abel v. United States*, 362 U.S. 217, 232, 80 S. Ct. 683, 693, 4 L. Ed. 2d 668 (1960), the Court sustained an administrative arrest made without "a judicial warrant within the scope of the Fourth Amendment." The crucial question in *Draper v. United States*, 358 U.S. 307, 79 S. Ct. 329, 3 L. Ed. 2d 327 (1959), was whether there was probable cause for the warrantless arrest. If there was, the Court said, "the arrest, though without a warrant, was lawful . . . ." *Id.*, at 310, 79 S. Ct., at 331. *Ker v. California*, 374 U.S. 23, 34–35, 83 S. Ct. 1623, 1630, 10 L. Ed. 2d 726 (1963) (opinion of Clark, J.), reiterated the rule that "[t]he lawfulness of the arrest without warrant, in turn, must be based upon probable cause . . ." and went on to sustain the warrantless arrest over other claims going to the mode of entry. Just last Term, while recognizing that maximum protection of individual rights could be assured by requiring a magistrate's review of the factual justification prior to any arrest, we stated that "such a requirement would constitute an intolerable handicap for legitimate law enforcement" and noted that the Court "has never invalidated an arrest supported by probable cause solely because the officers failed to secure a warrant." *Gerstein v. Pugh*, 420 U.S. 103, 113, 95 S. Ct. 854, 862, 43 L. Ed. 2d 54 (1975).

The cases construing the Fourth Amendment thus reflect the ancient common-law rule that a peace officer was permitted to arrest without a warrant for a misdemeanor or felony committed in his presence as well as for a felony not committed in his presence if there was reasonable ground for making the arrest. 10 HALSBURY'S LAWS OF ENGLAND 344–345 (3d ed. 1955); 4 W. Blackstone, COMMENTARIES *292; 1 J. Stephen, A HISTORY OF THE CRIMINAL LAW OF ENGLAND 193 (1883); 2 M. Hale, PLEAS OF THE CROWN *72–74; Wilgus, *Arrest Without a Warrant*, 22 Mich. L. Rev. 541, 547–550, 686–688 (1924); *Samuel v. Payne*, 1 Doug. 359, 99 Eng. Rep. 230 (K.B. 1780); *Beckwith v. Philby*, 6 Barn. & Cress. 635, 108 Eng. Rep. 585 (K.B. 1827). This has also been the prevailing rule under state constitutions and statutes.

. . . .

Because the common-law rule authorizing arrests without a warrant generally prevailed in the States, it is important for present purposes to note that in 1792 Congress invested United States marshals and their deputies with "the same powers in executing the laws of the United States, as sheriffs and their deputies in the several states have by law, in executing the laws of their respective states." Act of May 2, 1792, c. 28, § 9, 1 Stat. 265. The Second Congress thus saw no inconsistency between the Fourth Amendment and legislation giving United States marshals the same power as local peace officers to arrest for a felony without a warrant . . . . That provision . . . was supplemented in 1935 . . . [to] empower[] marshals to make felony arrests without warrant and on probable cause . . . .

The balance struck by the common law in generally authorizing felony arrests on probable cause, but without a warrant, has survived substantially intact. It appears in almost all of the States in the form of express statutory authorization.

This is the rule Congress has long directed its principal law enforcement officers to follow. Congress has plainly decided against conditioning warrantless arrest power on proof of exigent circumstances. Law enforcement officers may find it wise to seek arrest warrants where practicable to do so, and their judgments about probable cause may be more readily accepted where backed by a warrant issued by a magistrate. *See United States v. Ventresca*, 380 U.S. 102, 106, 85 S. Ct. 741, 744–745, 13 L. Ed. 2d 684 (1965); *Aguilar v. Texas*, 378 U.S. 108, 111, 84 S. Ct. 1509, 1512, 12 L. Ed. 2d 723 (1964); *Wong Sun v. United States*, 371 U.S. 471, 479–480, 83 S. Ct. 407, 412–413, 9 L. Ed. 2d 441 (1963). But we decline to transform this judicial preference into a constitutional rule when the judgment of the Nation and Congress has for so long been to authorize warrantless public arrests on probable cause rather than to encumber criminal prosecutions with endless litigation with respect to the existence of exigent circumstances, whether it was practicable to get a warrant, whether the suspect was about to flee, and the like.

Watson's arrest did not violate the Fourth Amendment, and the Court of Appeals erred in holding to the contrary.

III

Because our judgment is that Watson's arrest comported with the Fourth Amendment, Watson's consent to the search of his car was not the product of an illegal arrest. To the extent that the issue of the voluntariness of Watson's consent was resolved on the premise that his arrest was illegal, the Court of Appeals was also in error.

. . . .

In consequence, we reverse the judgment of the Court of Appeals.

So ordered.

Reversed.

MR. JUSTICE STEVENS took no part in the consideration or decision of this case.

MR. JUSTICE POWELL, concurring.

. . . .

I

. . .

In reversing the Court of Appeals, the Court concludes that nothing in our previous cases involving warrantless arrests supports the position of respondent and the Court of Appeals. *See e.g., Gerstein v. Pugh*, 420 U.S. 103, 113, 95 S. Ct. 854, 862, 43 L. Ed. 2d 54 (1975). But it is fair to say, I think, that the prior decisions of the Court have assumed the validity of such arrests without addressing in a reasoned way the analysis advanced by respondent.[1] Today's decision is the first square holding that the Fourth Amendment permits a duly authorized law enforcement officer to make a warrantless arrest in a public place even though he had adequate opportunity to procure a warrant after developing probable cause for arrest.

On its face, our decision today creates a certain anomaly. There is no more basic constitutional rule in the Fourth Amendment area than that which makes a warrantless search unreasonable except in a few "jealously and carefully drawn" exceptional circumstances. *Jones v. United States*, 357 U.S. 493, 499, 78 S. Ct. 1253, 1257, 2 L. Ed. 2d 1514 (1958) . . . .

Since the Fourth Amendment speaks equally to both searches and seizures, and since an arrest, the taking hold of one's person, is quintessentially a seizure, it would seem that the constitutional provision should impose the same limitations upon arrests that it does upon searches. Indeed, as an abstract matter an argument can be made that the restrictions upon arrest perhaps should be greater. A search may cause only annoyance and temporary inconvenience to the law-abiding citizen, assuming more serious dimension only when it turns up evidence of criminality. An arrest, however, is a serious personal intrusion regardless of whether the person seized is guilty or innocent . . . . Logic therefore would seem to dictate that arrests be subject to the warrant requirement at least to the same extent as searches.

But logic sometimes must defer to history and experience. The Court's opinion emphasizes the historical sanction accorded warrantless felony arrests. In the early days of the common law most felony arrests were made upon personal knowledge and without warrants . . . . There is no historical evidence that the Framers or proponents of the Fourth Amendment, outspokenly opposed to the infamous general warrants and writs of assistance, were at all concerned about warrantless arrests by local constables and other peace officers . . . .

The historical momentum for acceptance of warrantless arrests, already strong at the adoption of the Fourth Amendment, has gained strength during the ensuing

---

1. None of the decisions cited by the Court today squarely faced the issue. In *Henry v. United States*, 361 U.S. 98, 80 S. Ct. 168, 4 L. Ed. 2d 134 (1959), for example, the Court declared that 18 U.S.C. § 3052, which authorizes an FBI agent to make a warrantless arrest when he has reasonable grounds to believe that a person has committed a felony, "states the constitutional standard." 361 U.S., at 100, 80 S. Ct., at 170. But that declaration was made without discussion, and the issue actually presented to and addressed by the Court was whether there was in fact probable cause for the arrest in that case. Similarly, *Draper v. United States*, 358 U.S. 307, 79 S. Ct. 329, 3 L. Ed. 2d 327 (1959), stands only for the validity of a warrantless arrest made with probable cause to believe that the arrestee had committed an offense in the arresting officer's presence. *See id.*, at 313, 79 S. Ct., at 333. As this Court had noted in an earlier case, such an arrest presents no danger that an innocent person might be ensnared, since the officer observes both the crime and the culprit with his own eyes; there thus would be no reason to require a warrant in that particular situation even if there might be in others. *Trupiano v. United States*, 334 U.S. 699, 705, 68 S. Ct. 1229, 1232, 92 L. Ed. 1663 (1948) . . . .

two centuries. Both the judiciary and the legislative bodies of this Nation repeatedly have placed their imprimaturs upon the practice and, as the Government emphasizes, law enforcement agencies have developed their investigative and arrest procedures upon an assumption that warrantless arrests were valid so long as based upon probable cause. The decision of the Court of Appeals in this case was virtually unprecedented. Of course, no practice that is inconsistent with constitutional protections can be saved merely by appeal to previous uncritical acceptance. But the warrantless felony arrest, long preferred at common law and unimpeached at the passage of the Fourth Amendment, is not such a practice . . . .

Moreover, a constitutional rule permitting felony arrests only with a warrant or in exigent circumstances could severely hamper effective law enforcement. Good police practice often requires postponing an arrest, even after probable cause has been established, in order to place the suspect under surveillance or otherwise develop further evidence necessary to prove guilt to a jury.[4] Under the holding of the Court of Appeals such additional investigative work could imperil the entire prosecution. Should the officers fail to obtain a warrant initially, and later be required by unforeseen circumstances to arrest immediately with no chance to procure a last-minute warrant, they would risk a court decision that the subsequent exigency did not excuse their failure to get a warrant in the interim since they first developed probable cause. If the officers attempted to meet such a contingency by procuring a warrant as soon as they had probable cause and then merely held it during their subsequent investigation, they would risk a court decision that the warrant had grown stale by the time it was used.[5] Law enforcement personnel caught in this squeeze could ensure validity of their arrests only by obtaining a warrant and arresting as soon as probable cause existed, thereby foreclosing the possibility of gathering vital additional evidence from the suspect's continued actions.

In sum, the historical and policy reasons sketched above fully justify the Court's sustaining of a warrantless arrest upon probable cause, despite the resulting

---

4. . . . Whatever evidence may be necessary to establish probable cause in a given case . . . it is clear that it never need rise to the level required to prove guilt beyond a reasonable doubt. The different standards for arrest and conviction reflect a recognition of society's valid interest in the earliest detention of suspected criminals that is consistent with the individual's interest in freedom from arbitrary interference with his liberty. But society's equally valid interest in ultimate conviction of the guilty requires the police sometimes to continue their investigation after establishing probable cause to arrest, even if doing so means they have to leave a suspect at large pending such investigation.

5. The probable cause to support issuance of an arrest warrant normally would not grow stale as easily as that which supports a warrant to search a particular place for particular objects. This is true because once there is probable cause to believe that someone is a felon the passage of time often will bring new supporting evidence. But in some cases the original grounds supporting the warrant could be disproved by subsequent investigation that at the same time turns up wholly new evidence supporting probable cause on a different theory. In those cases the warrant could be stale because based upon discredited information.

divergence between the constitutional rule governing searches and that now held applicable to seizures of the person.[6]

. . . .

[The concurrence in the result of Mr. Justice Stewart has been omitted.]

Mr. Justice Marshall, with whom Mr. Justice Brennan joins, dissenting.

. . . .

I

Before addressing what the Court does today, I note what it does not do. It does not decide this case on the narrow question that is presented. That is unfortunate for this is, fundamentally, a simple case.

. . . .

The signal of the reliable informant that Watson was in possession of stolen credit cards gave the postal inspectors probable cause to make the arrest. This probable cause was separate and distinct from the probable cause relating to the offense six days earlier, and provided an adequate independent basis for the arrest. Whether or not a warrant ordinarily is required prior to making an arrest, no warrant is required when exigent circumstances are present. When law enforcement officers have probable cause to believe that an offense is taking place in their presence and that the suspect is at that moment in possession of the evidence, exigent circumstances exist. Delay could cause the escape of the suspect or the destruction of the evidence. Accordingly, Watson's warrantless arrest was valid under the recognized exigent-circumstances exception to the warrant requirement, and the Court has no occasion to consider whether a warrant would otherwise be necessary.[1]

This conclusion should properly dispose of the case before us . . . . I would reverse the Court of Appeals on the legality of the arrest, vacate its judgment, and remand the case to that court for further proceedings.

---

6. I do not understand today's decision to suggest any retreat from our longstanding position that such an arrest should receive careful judicial scrutiny if challenged . . . .

1. The Court of Appeals did not recognize this independent probable cause to arrest petitioner, perhaps because one of the arresting officers testified that the arrest was made for the earlier, rather than the contemporaneous, offense. That testimony should not limit the inquiry into contemporaneous probable cause. Where the good faith of the arresting officers is not at issue, and where the crime for which a suspect is arrested and that for which the officers have probable cause are closely related, courts typically use an objective rather than subjective measure of probable cause. *Ramirez v. Rodriguez*, 467 F.2d 822 (10th Cir. 1972); *United States v. Martinez*, 465 F.2d 79 (2d Cir. 1972); *United States v. Atkinson*, 450 F.2d 835, 838 (5th Cir. 1971). Since the objective facts demonstrably show probable cause as to the contemporaneous offense as well as the earlier offense, Watson's arrest is properly justified by reference to those facts.

II

Since, for reasons it leaves unexpressed, the Court does not take this traditional course, I am constrained to express my views on the issues it unnecessarily decides.

. . . .

... There is no doubt that by the reference to the seizure of persons, the Fourth Amendment was intended to apply to arrests. *Ex parte Burford*, 2 L. Ed. 495, 3 Cranch 448 (1806). Indeed, we have often considered whether arrests were made in conformity with the Fourth Amendment. However, none of the cases cited by the Court, nor any other warrantless arrest case in this Court, mandates the decision announced today . . . . [T]he dicta relied upon by the Court in support of its decision today are just that — dicta. They are no substitute for reasoned analysis of the relationship between the warrant requirement and the law of arrest.

The Court next turns to history. It relies on the English common-law rule of arrest and the many state and federal statutes following it. There are two serious flaws in this approach. First, as a matter of factual analysis, the substance of the ancient common-law rule provides no support for the far-reaching modern rule that the Court fashions on its model. Second, as a matter of doctrine, the longstanding existence of a Government practice does not immunize the practice from scrutiny under the mandate of our Constitution.

... To apply the rule blindly today ... makes as much sense as attempting to interpret Hamlet's admonition to Ophelia, "Get thee to a nunnery, go,"[2] without understanding the meaning of Hamlet's words in the context of their age.[3] For the fact is that a felony at common law and a felony today bear only slight resemblance, with the result that the relevance of the common-law rule of arrest to the modern interpretation of our Constitution is minimal.

Both at common law and today, felonies find definition in the penal consequences of crime rather than the nature of the crime itself. At common law, as this Court has several times recognized, "No crime was considered a felony which did not occasion a total forfeiture of the offender's lands or goods or both." *Kurtz v. Moffitt*, 115 U.S., at 499, 6 S. Ct., at 152 . . . . At present, on the other hand, "Any offense punishable by death or imprisonment for a term exceeding one year is a felony." 18 U.S.C. § 1(1).[5] This difference reflects more than changing notions of penology. It reflects a

---

2. W. Shakespeare, HAMLET, act iii, sc. 1, line 142.

3. Nunnery was Elizabethan slang for house of prostitution. 7 OXFORD ENGLISH DICTIONARY 264 (1933).

5. In the States the most common rule is that any crime punishable by death or imprisonment in the state prison is a felony. *See Kurtz*, at 571. *See also e.g.*, Ark. Stat. Ann. § 41–103 (1964); 22 Fla. Stat. Ann. § 775.08 (Supp. 1975); Ill. Ann. Stat. § 2–7 (Supp. 1975); Ky. Rev. Stat. Ann. § 431.060 (1970); Mass. Gen. Laws Ann., c. 274, § 1 (1970); Okla. Stat. Ann., Tit. 21, § 5 (1958); Wash. Rev. Code § 9.01.020 (1974).

substantive change in the kinds of crimes called felonies. *Carroll v. United States, supra*, 267 U.S., at 158, 45 S. Ct., at 287. Only the most serious crimes were felonies at common law, and many crimes now classified as felonies under federal or state law were treated as misdemeanors.

. . . .

To make an arrest for any of these crimes at common law, the police officer was required to obtain a warrant, unless the crime was committed in his presence. Since many of these same crimes are commonly classified as felonies today, however, under the Court's holding a warrant is no longer needed to make such arrests, a result in contravention of the common law.

Thus the lesson of the common law, and those courts in this country that have accepted its rule, is an ambiguous one. Applied in its original context, the common-law rule would allow the warrantless arrest of some, but not all, of those we call felons today. Accordingly, the Court is simply historically wrong when it tells us that "[t]he balance struck by the common law in generally authorizing felony arrests on probable cause, but without warrant, has survived substantially intact." *Ante*, at 827. As a matter of substance, the balance struck by the common law in accommodating the public need for the most certain and immediate arrest of criminal suspects with the requirement of magisterial oversight to protect against mistaken insults to privacy decreed that only in the most serious of cases could the warrant be dispensed with. This balance is not recognized when the common-law rule is unthinkingly transposed to our present classifications of criminal offenses. Indeed, the only clear lesson of history is contrary to the one the Court draws: the common law considered the arrest warrant far more important than today's decision leaves it.

I do not mean by this that a modern warrant requirement should apply only to arrests precisely analogous to common-law misdemeanors, and be inapplicable to analogues of common-law felonies. Rather, the point is simply that the Court's unblinking literalism cannot replace analysis of the constitutional interests involved. While we can learn from the common law, the ancient rule does not provide a simple answer directly transferable to our system. Thus, in considering the applicability of the common-law rule to our present constitutional scheme, we must consider both of the rule's two opposing constructs: the presumption favoring warrants, as well as the exception allowing immediate arrests of the most dangerous criminals. The Court's failure to do so, indeed its failure to recognize any tension in the common-law rule at all, drains all validity from its historical analysis.

Lastly, the Court relies on the numerous state and federal statutes codifying the common-law rule. But this, too, is no substitute for reasoned analysis. True enough, the national and state legislatures have steadily ratified the drift of the balance struck by the common-law rule past the bounds of its original intent. And it is true as well, as the Court observes, that a presumption of constitutionality attaches to every Act of Congress. But neither observation is determinative of the constitutional issue, and the doctrine of deference that the Court invokes is contrary to the principles of constitutional analysis practiced since *Marbury v. Madison*, 2 L. Ed. 60, 1 Cranch 137 (1803).

. . . .

III

. . . .

One of the few absolutes of our law is the requirement that, absent the presence of one of a few "jealously and carefully drawn" exceptions, *Jones v. United States*, 357 U.S. 493, 499, 78 S. Ct. 1253, 1257, 2 L. Ed. 2d 1514 (1958), a warrant be obtained prior to any search . . . .

The rule the Court announces today for arrests is the reverse of this approach . . . .

The Court has typically engaged in a two-part analysis in deciding whether the presumption favoring a warrant should be given effect in situations where a warrant has not previously been clearly required. Utilizing that approach we must now consider (1) whether the privacy of our citizens will be better protected by ordinarily requiring a warrant to be issued before they may be arrested; and (2) whether a warrant requirement would unduly burden legitimate governmental interests.

The first question is easily answered. Of course, the privacy of our citizens will be better protected by a warrant requirement. We have recognized that "the Fourth Amendment protects people, not places." *Katz v. United States, supra*, 389 U.S., at 351 . . . . Thus a warrant is required in search situations not because of some high regard for property, but because of our regard for the individual, and *his* interest in his possessions and person.

. . . .

A warrant is required in the search situation to protect the privacy of the individual, but there can be no less invasion of privacy when the individual himself, rather than his property, is searched and seized. Indeed, an unjustified arrest that forces the individual temporarily to forfeit his right to control his person and movements and interrupts the course of his daily business may be more intrusive than an unjustified search.

. . . .

A warrant requirement for arrests would, of course, minimize the possibility that such an intrusion into the individual's sacred sphere of personal privacy would occur on less than probable cause. Primarily for this reason, a warrant is required for searches. Surely there is no reason to place greater trust in the partisan assessment of a police officer that there is probable cause for an arrest than in his determination that probable cause exists for a search . . . .

We come then to the second part of the warrant test: whether a warrant requirement would unduly burden legitimate law enforcement interests . . . . Indeed, the argument that a warrant requirement for arrests would be an onerous chore for the police seems somewhat anomalous in light of the Government's concession that "it is the standard practice of the Federal Bureau of Investigation (FBI) to present its evidence to the United States Attorney, and to obtain a warrant, before making an arrest." Brief for United States 26 n. 15. In the past, the practice and experience of the FBI have been taken as a substantial indication that no intolerable burden would be presented by a proposed rule of procedure.

The Government's assertion that a warrant requirement would impose an intolerable burden stems, in large part, from the specious supposition that procurement of an arrest warrant would be necessary as soon as probable cause ripens. There is no requirement that a search warrant be obtained the moment police have probable cause to search. The rule is only that present probable cause be shown and a warrant obtained before a search is undertaken.[14] The same rule should obtain for arrest warrants, where it may even make more sense. Certainly, there is less need for prompt procurement of a warrant in the arrest situation. Unlike probable cause to search, probable cause to arrest, once formed, will continue to exist for the indefinite future, at least if no intervening exculpatory facts come to light.

This sensible approach obviates most of the difficulties that have been suggested with an arrest warrant rule. Police would not have to cut their investigation short the moment they obtain probable cause to arrest, nor would undercover agents be forced suddenly to terminate their work and forfeit their covers. Moreover, if in the course of the continued police investigation exigent circumstances develop that demand an immediate arrest, the arrest may be made without fear of unconstitutionality, so long as the exigency was unanticipated and not used to avoid the arrest warrant requirement. Likewise, if in the course of the continued investigation police uncover evidence tying the suspect to another crime, they may immediately arrest him for that crime if exigency demands it, and still be in full conformity with the warrant rule. This is why the arrest in this case was not improper.[15] Other than where police attempt to evade the warrant requirement, the rule would invalidate an arrest only in the obvious situation: where police, with probable cause but without exigent circumstances, set out to arrest a suspect. Such an arrest must be void, even if exigency develops in the course of the arrest that would ordinarily validate it; otherwise the warrant requirement would be reduced to a toothless prescription.

---

14. The police will, however, encounter problems of "staleness" of their information if they delay too long in seeking a search warrant. *E.g., Sgro v. United States*, 287 U.S. 206, 53 S. Ct. 138, 77 L. Ed. 260 (1932); *United States v. Sawyer*, 213 F. Supp. 38, 40 (E.D. Pa. 1963). *See generally* Annot., 100 A.L.R.2d 525 (1965). *But see People v. Wright*, 367 Mich. 611, 116 N.W.2d 786 (1962). This problem relates, however, to the existence at the time the warrant is applied for of probable cause to believe the object to be seized remains where it was, not to whether the earlier probable cause mandated immediate application for a warrant. Mascolo, *The Staleness of Probable Cause in Affidavits for Search Warrants: Resolving the Issue of Timeliness*, 43 Conn. B.J. 189 (1969). This problem has no bearing, of course, in connection with a warrant to arrest.

15. Although the postal inspectors here anticipated the occurrence of the second crime, they could not have obtained a warrant for Watson's arrest for that crime until probable cause formed, just moments before the arrest. A warrant based on anticipated facts is premature and void. *United States v. Roberts*, 333 F. Supp. 786 (E.D. Tenn. 1971).

. . . .

It is suggested, however, that even if application of this rule does not require police to secure a warrant as soon as they obtain probable cause, the confused officer would nonetheless be prone to do so. If so, police "would risk a court decision that the warrant had grown stale by the time it was used." *Ante* (Powell, J., concurring) [footnote omitted]. This fear is groundless. First, as suggested above, the requirement that police procure a warrant before an arrest is made is rather simple of application. Thus, there is no need for the police to find themselves in this "squeeze." Second, the "squeeze" is nonexistent. Just as it is virtually impossible for probable cause for an arrest to grow stale between the time of formation and the time a warrant is procured, it is virtually impossible for probable cause to become stale between procurement and arrest . . . .

Thus, the practical reasons marshaled against an arrest warrant requirement are unimpressive. If anything, the virtual nonexistence of a staleness problem suggest[s] that such a requirement would be less burdensome for police than the search warrant rule. And given the significant protection our citizens will gain from a warrant requirement, accepted Fourth Amendment analysis dictates that a warrant rule be imposed . . . .

. . . .

I respectfully dissent.

Notes and Questions

(1) Under the *per se* rule of *Johnson* and *Katz*, if the postal inspector who arrested Watson had wanted to search his home instead he would have needed a warrant. The Court rejected Watson's claim that a parallel rule should apply to his arrest. What are the material differences between searches of homes and arrests of felons? Why don't the same reasons that underlie the search warrant requirement dictate an arrest warrant requirement?

(2) Would the postal inspector have needed a warrant to arrest Watson inside a restaurant or theater? In his fenced backyard? In "open fields" he owned? Would he have needed a warrant to arrest Watson in public for a misdemeanor postal theft? Why?

(3) If the logic of the warrant requirement is to be believed, the *Watson* Court's refusal to require officers "engaged in the competitive enterprise of ferreting out crime" to secure judicial authorization prior to an arrest means that a greater number of mistaken deprivations of liberty will occur. In evaluating the magnitude of those potential deprivations, the Court's holdings in *Gerstein v. Pugh*, 420 U.S. 103, 95 S. Ct. 854, 43 L. Ed. 2d 54 (1975), cited in *Watson,* and in the subsequently decided case of *County of Riverside v. McLaughlin,* 500 U.S. 44, 111 S. Ct. 1661, 114 L. Ed. 2d 49 (1991), are pertinent.

In *Gerstein,* the Court held "that the Fourth Amendment requires a judicial determination of probable cause as a prerequisite to extended restraint on liberty following arrest." While rejecting the claim that an adversary hearing is required, the Court observed that states "must provide a fair and reliable determination of probable cause as a condition for any significant pretrial restraint of liberty, and [that] this determination must be made by a judicial officer either before or promptly after arrest."

The *McLaughlin* "case require[d the Court] to define what is 'prompt' under *Gerstein*." The case involved a systemic challenge to the County of Riverside's policy regarding probable cause determinations. The County's policy provided for probable cause determinations to be made at the time of arraignment and specified that arraignments had to "be conducted without unnecessary delay and, in any event, within two days of arrest," excluding weekends and holidays.

Justice O'Connor, writing for a five-Justice majority, observed that "the Fourth Amendment does not compel an immediate determination of probable cause upon completing the administrative steps incident to arrest." Instead, jurisdictions are permitted to delay probable cause determinations in order to "incorporate" them "into other pretrial procedures." The majority concluded "that a jurisdiction that provides judicial determinations of probable cause within 48 hours of arrest will, as a general matter, comply with the promptness requirement [announced in *Gerstein*] . . . [and that] such jurisdictions will be immune from systemic challenges." If an arrested individual is detained for a period shorter than 48 hours prior to a probable cause determination, he or she can still establish a Fourth Amendment violation by proving "that his or her probable cause determination was delayed unreasonably." Delay to gather "additional evidence to justify the arrest," or "motivated by ill will against the" arrestee, or simply "for delay's sake" would be unreasonable. On the other hand, if "an arrested individual does not receive a probable cause determination within 48 hours" of his or her arrest, the delay is unreasonable unless the government carries the burden of "demonstrat[ing] the existence of a *bona fide* emergency or other extraordinary circumstance."

The majority decided that Riverside's policy of combining probable cause determinations with arraignments was permissible under *Gerstein*, but nonetheless found "that the County's . . . policy and practice [did] not comport fully with" Fourth Amendment "principles." Because the policy excluded weekends and holidays, "the County's regular practice exceed[ed] the 48-hour period [that the majority had] deem[ed] constitutionally permissible." Consequently, it was "not immune from systemic challenge[]."

Four Justices concluded that delay for purposes of combining probable cause determinations with other pretrial proceedings was constitutionally impermissible. Justice Marshall, joined by two other Justices, asserted that "a probable cause hearing is sufficiently 'prompt' . . . only when provided immediately upon completion of the 'administrative steps incident to arrest.'" In a separate dissent, Justice Scalia opined that "the period of warrantless detention must be limited to the time necessary to complete the arrest and obtain [a] magistrate's review." The only delays allowed are those needed to complete "the administrative steps incident to arrest" and to arrange "for a magistrate's probable-cause determination." In his view, "absent extraordinary circumstances," it is unreasonable "to delay a determination of probable cause for [an] arrest either (1) for reasons unrelated to arrangement of the probable-cause determination or completion of the steps incident to arrest, or (2) beyond 24 hours after the arrest."

Atwater v. City of Lago Vista

United States Supreme Court
532 U.S. 318, 121 S. Ct. 1536, 149 L. Ed. 2d 549 (2001)

JUSTICE SOUTER delivered the opinion of the Court.

The question is whether the Fourth Amendment forbids a warrantless arrest for a minor criminal offense, such as a misdemeanor seatbelt violation punishable only by a fine. We hold that it does not.

[margin note: 4th Amend dN FoRBid it = It is allowed w/o a warrant!]

[margin note: ✓ NOPE ✓]

I

A

In Texas, if a car is equipped with safety belts, a front-seat passenger must wear one, Tex. Transp. Code Ann. § 545.413(a) (1999), and the driver must secure any small child riding in front, § 545.413(b). Violation of either provision is "a misdemeanor punishable by a fine not less than $25 or more than $50." § 545.413(d). Texas law expressly authorizes "[a]ny peace officer [to] arrest without warrant a person found committing a violation" of these seatbelt laws, § 543.001, although it permits police to issue citations in lieu of arrest, §§ 543.003–543.005.

In March 1997, Petitioner Gail Atwater was driving her pickup truck in Lago Vista, Texas, with her 3-year-old son and 5-year-old daughter in the front seat. None of them was wearing a seatbelt. Respondent Bart Turek, a Lago Vista police officer at the time, observed the seatbelt violations and pulled Atwater over. According to Atwater's complaint (the allegations of which we assume to be true for present purposes), Turek approached the truck and "yell[ed]" something to the effect of "[w]e've met before" and "[y]ou're going to jail." He then called for backup and asked to see Atwater's driver's license and insurance documentation, which state law required her to carry. Tex. Transp. Code Ann. §§ 521.025, 601.053 (1999). When Atwater told Turek that she did not have the papers because her purse had been stolen the day before, Turek said that he had "heard that story two-hundred times."

Atwater asked to take her "frightened, upset, and crying" children to a friend's house nearby, but Turek told her, "[y]ou're not going anywhere." As it turned out, Atwater's friend learned what was going on and soon arrived to take charge of the children. Turek then handcuffed Atwater, placed her in his squad car, and drove her to the local police station, where booking officers had her remove her shoes, jewelry, and eyeglasses, and empty her pockets. Officers took Atwater's "mug shot" and placed her, alone, in a jail cell for about one hour, after which she was taken before a magistrate and released on $310 bond.

Atwater was charged with driving without her seatbelt fastened, failing to secure her children in seatbelts, driving without a license, and failing to provide proof of insurance. She ultimately pleaded no contest to the misdemeanor seatbelt offenses and paid a $50 fine; the other charges were dismissed.

B

Atwater and her husband, petitioner Michael Haas, filed suit in a Texas state court under 42 U.S.C. § 1983 against Turek and respondents City of Lago Vista and Chief of Police Frank Miller. So far as concerns us, petitioners (whom we will simply call Atwater) alleged that respondents (for simplicity, the City) had violated Atwater's Fourth Amendment "right to be free from unreasonable seizure," and sought compensatory and punitive damages.

The City removed the suit to the United States District Court for the Western District of Texas. Given Atwater's admission that she had "violated the law" and the absence of any allegation "that she was harmed or detained in any way inconsistent with the law," the District Court ruled the Fourth Amendment claim "meritless" and granted the City's summary judgment motion. A panel of the United States Court of Appeals for the Fifth Circuit reversed. 165 F.3d 380 (1999). It concluded that "an arrest for a first-time seat belt offense" was an unreasonable seizure within the meaning of the Fourth Amendment, *id.*, at 387, and held that Turek was not entitled to qualified immunity, *id.*, at 389.

Sitting en banc, the Court of Appeals vacated the panel's decision and affirmed the District Court's summary judgment for the City. 195 F.3d 242 (5th Cir. 1999). . . .

 . . . .

II

The Fourth Amendment safeguards "[t]he right of the people to be secure in their persons, houses, papers, and effects, against unreasonable searches and seizures." In reading the Amendment, we are guided by "the traditional protections against unreasonable searches and seizures afforded by the common law at the time of the framing," *Wilson v. Arkansas*, 514 U.S. 927, 931, 115 S. Ct. 1914, 131 L. Ed. 2d 976 (1995), since "[a]n examination of the common-law understanding of an officer's authority to arrest sheds light on the obviously relevant, if not entirely dispositive, consideration of what the Framers of the Amendment might have thought to be reasonable," *Payton v. New York*, 445 U.S. 573, 591, 100 S. Ct. 1371, 63 L. Ed. 2d 639 (1980) (footnote omitted). Thus, the first step here is to assess Atwater's claim that peace officers' authority to make warrantless arrests for misdemeanors was restricted at common law (whether "common law" is understood strictly as law judicially derived or, instead, as the whole body of law extant at the time of the framing). Atwater's specific contention is that "founding-era common-law rules" forbade peace officers to make warrantless misdemeanor arrests except in cases of "breach of the peace," a category she claims was then understood narrowly as covering only those nonfelony offenses "involving or tending toward violence." Although her historical argument is by no means insubstantial, it ultimately fails.

A

We begin with the state of pre-founding English common law and find that, even after making some allowance for variations in the common-law usage of the term "breach of the peace," the "founding-era common-law rules" were not nearly as clear as Atwater claims; on the contrary, the common-law commentators (as well as the sparsely reported cases) reached divergent conclusions with respect to officers' warrantless misdemeanor arrest power. Moreover, in the years leading up to American independence, Parliament repeatedly extended express warrantless arrest authority to cover misdemeanor-level offenses not amounting to or involving any violent breach of the peace.

1

. . . [S]tatements about the common law of warrantless misdemeanor arrest simply are not uniform. Rather, "[a]t common law there is a difference of opinion among the authorities as to whether this right to arrest [without a warrant] extends to all misdemeanors." American Law Institute, Code of Criminal Procedure, Commentary to § 21, p. 231 (1930).

[The Court then discussed the conflicting British authorities, some of which supported a "breach of the peace" condition and others of which supported the view that a "breach of the peace" was not required for a warrantless misdemeanor arrest.]

. . . .

We thus find disagreement, not unanimity, among both the common-law jurists and the text writers who sought to pull the cases together and summarize accepted practice. Having reviewed the relevant English decisions, as well as English and colonial American legal treatises, legal dictionaries, and procedure manuals, we simply are not convinced that Atwater's is the correct, or even necessarily the better, reading of the common-law history.

2

A second, and equally serious, problem for Atwater's historical argument is posed by the "divers Statutes," M. Dalton, COUNTRY JUSTICE ch. 170, § 4, p. 582 (1727), enacted by Parliament well before this Republic's founding that authorized warrantless misdemeanor arrests without reference to violence or turmoil. Quite apart from Hale and Blackstone, the legal background of any conception of reasonableness the Fourth Amendment's Framers might have entertained would have included English statutes, some centuries old, authorizing peace officers (and even private persons) to make warrantless arrests for all sorts of relatively minor offenses unaccompanied by violence. . . . .

[The Court then described the relevant statutes.]

. . . .

. . . The point is that the statutes riddle Atwater's supposed common-law rule with enough exceptions to unsettle any contention that the law of the mother country would have left the Fourth Amendment's Framers of a view that it would necessarily have been unreasonable to arrest without warrant for a misdemeanor unaccompanied by real or threatened violence.

B

An examination of specifically American evidence is to the same effect. Neither the history of the framing era nor subsequent legal development indicates that the Fourth Amendment was originally understood, or has traditionally been read, to embrace Atwater's position.

1

To begin with, Atwater has cited no particular evidence that those who framed and ratified the Fourth Amendment sought to limit peace officers' warrantless misdemeanor arrest authority to instances of actual breach of the peace, and our own review of the recent and respected compilations of framing-era documentary history has likewise failed to reveal any such design. Nor have we found in any of the modern historical accounts of the Fourth Amendment's adoption any substantial indication that the Framers intended such a restriction. Indeed, to the extent these modern histories address the issue, their conclusions are to the contrary.

The evidence of actual practice also counsels against Atwater's position. During the period leading up to and surrounding the framing of the Bill of Rights, colonial and state legislatures, like Parliament before them, regularly authorized local peace officers to make warrantless misdemeanor arrests without conditioning statutory authority on breach of the peace.

. . . . A number of state constitutional search-and-seizure provisions served as models for the Fourth Amendment, and the fact that many of the original States with such constitutional limitations continued to grant their own peace officers broad warrantless misdemeanor arrest authority undermines Atwater's contention that the founding generation meant to bar federal law enforcement officers from exercising the same authority. Given the early state practice, it is likewise troublesome for Atwater's view that just one year after the ratification of the Fourth Amendment, Congress vested federal marshals with "the same powers in executing the laws of the United States, as sheriffs and their deputies in the several states have by law, in executing the laws of their respective states." Act of May 2, 1792, ch. 28, § 9, 1 Stat. 265. Thus, as we have said before in only slightly different circumstances, the Second Congress apparently "saw no inconsistency between the Fourth Amendment and legislation giving United States marshals the same power as local peace officers" to make warrantless arrests. *United States v. Watson*, 423 U.S. 411, 420, 96 S. Ct. 820, 46 L. Ed. 2d 598 (1976).

The record thus supports Justice Powell's observation that "[t]here is no historical evidence that the Framers or proponents of the Fourth Amendment, outspokenly opposed to the infamous general warrants and writs of assistance, were at all concerned about warrantless arrests by local constables and other peace officers." *Id.*, at 429, 96 S. Ct. 820 (concurring opinion). We simply cannot conclude that the Fourth

Amendment, as originally understood, forbade peace officers to arrest without a warrant for misdemeanors not amounting to or involving breach of the peace.

2

Nor does Atwater's argument from tradition pick up any steam from the historical record as it has unfolded since the framing, there being no indication that her claimed rule has ever become "woven . . . into the fabric" of American law. *Wilson, supra,* at 933, 115 S. Ct. 1914. The story, on the contrary, is of two centuries of uninterrupted (and largely unchallenged) state and federal practice permitting warrantless arrests for misdemeanors not amounting to or involving breach of the peace.

First, there is no support for Atwater's position in this Court's cases. . . . Although the Court has not had much to say about warrantless misdemeanor arrest authority, what little we have said tends to cut against Atwater's argument. In discussing this authority, we have focused on the circumstance that an offense was committed in an officer's presence, to the omission of any reference to a breach-of-the-peace limitation.[11]

Second, . . . it is not the case here that "[e]arly American courts . . . embraced" an accepted common-law rule with anything approaching unanimity. *Wilson v. Arkansas,* 514 U.S., at 933, 115 S. Ct. 1914. . . .

. . . [N]umerous early- and mid-19th-century decisions expressly sustain[ed] (often against constitutional challenge) state and local laws authorizing peace officers to make warrantless arrests for misdemeanors not involving any breach of the peace.

Finally, both the legislative tradition of granting warrantless misdemeanor arrest authority and the judicial tradition of sustaining such statutes against constitutional attack are buttressed by legal commentary that, for more than a century now, has almost uniformly recognized the constitutionality of extending warrantless arrest power to misdemeanors without limitation to breaches of the peace.

Small wonder, then, that today statutes in all 50 States and the District of Columbia permit warrantless misdemeanor arrests by at least some (if not all) peace officers without requiring any breach of the peace, as do a host of congressional enactments. . . . This, therefore, simply is not a case in which the claimant can point to "a clear answer [that] existed in 1791 and has been generally adhered to by the traditions of our society ever since." *County of Riverside v. McLaughlin,* 500 U.S. 44, 60, 111 S. Ct. 1661, 114 L. Ed. 2d 49 (1991) (Scalia, J., dissenting).

---

11. We need not, and thus do not, speculate whether the Fourth Amendment entails an "in the presence" requirement for purposes of misdemeanor arrests. Cf. *Welsh v. Wisconsin,* 466 U.S. 740, 756, 104 S. Ct. 2091, 80 L. Ed. 2d 732 (1984) (White, J., dissenting) ("[T]he requirement that a misdemeanor must have occurred in the officer's presence to justify a warrantless arrest is not grounded in the Fourth Amendment").

III

While it is true here that history, if not unequivocal, has expressed a decided, majority view that the police need not obtain an arrest warrant merely because a misdemeanor stopped short of violence or a threat of it, Atwater does not wager all on history.[14] Instead, she asks us to mint a new rule of constitutional law on the understanding that when historical practice fails to speak conclusively to a claim grounded on the Fourth Amendment, courts are left to strike a current balance between individual and societal interests by subjecting particular contemporary circumstances to traditional standards of reasonableness. Atwater accordingly argues for a modern arrest rule, one not necessarily requiring violent breach of the peace, but nonetheless forbidding custodial arrest, even upon probable cause, when conviction could not ultimately carry any jail time and when the government shows no compelling need for immediate detention.

If we were to derive a rule exclusively to address the uncontested facts of this case, Atwater might well prevail. She was a known and established resident of Lago Vista with no place to hide and no incentive to flee, and common sense says she would almost certainly have buckled up as a condition of driving off with a citation. In her case, the physical incidents of arrest were merely gratuitous humiliations imposed by a police officer who was (at best) exercising extremely poor judgment. Atwater's claim to live free of pointless indignity and confinement clearly outweighs anything the City can raise against it specific to her case.

But we have traditionally recognized that a responsible Fourth Amendment balance is not well served by standards requiring sensitive, case-by-case determinations of government need, lest every discretionary judgment in the field be converted into an occasion for constitutional review. *See, e.g., United States v. Robinson*, 414 U.S. 218, 234–235, 94 S. Ct. 467, 38 L. Ed. 2d 427 (1973). Often enough, the Fourth Amendment has to be applied on the spur (and in the heat) of the moment, and the object in implementing its command of reasonableness is to draw standards sufficiently clear and simple to be applied with a fair prospect of surviving judicial second-guessing months and years after an arrest or search is made. Courts attempting to strike a reasonable Fourth Amendment balance thus credit the government's side with an essential interest in readily administrable rules.

At first glance, Atwater's argument may seem to respect the values of clarity and simplicity, so far as she claims that the Fourth Amendment generally forbids warrantless arrests for minor crimes not accompanied by violence or some demonstrable threat of it (whether "minor crime" be defined as a fine-only traffic offense, a

---

14. And, indeed, the dissent chooses not to deal with history at all. As is no doubt clear from the text, the historical record is not nearly as murky as the dissent suggests. History, moreover, is not just "one of the tools" relevant to a Fourth Amendment inquiry. . . . Because here the dissent "claim[s] that [a] practic[e] accepted when the Fourth Amendment was adopted [is] now constitutionally impermissible," the dissent bears the "heavy burden" of justifying a departure from the historical understanding.

fine-only offense more generally, or a misdemeanor). But the claim is not ultimately so simple, nor could it be, for complications arise the moment we begin to think about the possible applications of the several criteria Atwater proposes for drawing a line between minor crimes with limited arrest authority and others not so restricted.

One line, she suggests, might be between "jailable" and "fine-only" offenses, between those for which conviction could result in commitment and those for which it could not. The trouble with this distinction, of course, is that an officer on the street might not be able to tell. It is not merely that we cannot expect every police officer to know the details of frequently complex penalty schemes, but that penalties for ostensibly identical conduct can vary on account of facts difficult (if not impossible) to know at the scene of an arrest. Is this the first offense or is the suspect a repeat offender? Is the weight of the marijuana a gram above or a gram below the fine-only line? Where conduct could implicate more than one criminal prohibition, which one will the district attorney ultimately decide to charge? And so on.

But Atwater's refinements would not end there. She represents that if the line were drawn at nonjailable traffic offenses, her proposed limitation should be qualified by a proviso authorizing warrantless arrests where "necessary for enforcement of the traffic laws or when [an] offense would otherwise continue and pose a danger to others on the road." (Were the line drawn at misdemeanors generally, a comparable qualification would presumably apply.) The proviso only compounds the difficulties. Would, for instance, either exception apply to speeding? At oral argument, Atwater's counsel said that "it would not be reasonable to arrest a driver for speeding unless the speeding rose to the level of reckless driving." But is it not fair to expect that the chronic speeder will speed again despite a citation in his pocket, and should that not qualify as showing that the "offense would . . . continue" under Atwater's rule? And why, as a constitutional matter, should we assume that only reckless driving will "pose a danger to others on the road" while speeding will not?

There is no need for more examples to show that Atwater's general rule and limiting proviso promise very little in the way of administrability. It is no answer that the police routinely make judgments on grounds like risk of immediate repetition; they surely do and should. But there is a world of difference between making that judgment in choosing between the discretionary leniency of a summons in place of a clearly lawful arrest, and making the same judgment when the question is the lawfulness of the warrantless arrest itself. It is the difference between no basis for legal action challenging the discretionary judgment, on the one hand, and the prospect of evidentiary exclusion or (as here) personal § 1983 liability for the misapplication of a constitutional standard, on the other. Atwater's rule therefore would not only place police in an almost impossible spot but would guarantee increased litigation over many of the arrests that would occur. For all these reasons, Atwater's various distinctions between permissible and impermissible arrests for minor crimes strike us as "very unsatisfactory line[s]" to require police officers to draw on a moment's notice. *Carroll v. United States*, 267 U.S., at 157, 45 S. Ct. 280.

One may ask, of course, why these difficulties may not be answered by a simple tie breaker for the police to follow in the field: if in doubt, do not arrest. The first answer is that in practice the tie breaker would boil down to something akin to a least-restrictive-alternative limitation, which is itself one of those "ifs, ands, and buts" rules, *New York v. Belton*, 453 U.S., at 458, 101 S. Ct. 2860, generally thought inappropriate in working out Fourth Amendment protection. Beyond that, whatever help the tie breaker might give would come at the price of a systematic disincentive to arrest in situations where even Atwater concedes that arresting would serve an important societal interest. An officer not quite sure that the drugs weighed enough to warrant jail time or not quite certain about a suspect's risk of flight would not arrest, even though it could perfectly well turn out that, in fact, the offense called for incarceration and the defendant was long gone on the day of trial. Multiplied many times over, the costs to society of such underenforcement could easily outweigh the costs to defendants of being needlessly arrested and booked, as Atwater herself acknowledges.

Just how easily the costs could outweigh the benefits may be shown by asking, as one Member of this Court did at oral argument, "how bad the problem is out there." The very fact that the law has never jelled the way Atwater would have it leads one to wonder whether warrantless misdemeanor arrests need constitutional attention, and there is cause to think the answer is no. So far as such arrests might be thought to pose a threat to the probable-cause requirement, anyone arrested for a crime without formal process, whether for felony or misdemeanor, is entitled to a magistrate's review of probable cause within 48 hours, *County of Riverside v. McLaughlin*, 500 U.S., at 55–58, 111 S. Ct. 1661, and there is no reason to think the procedure in this case atypical in giving the suspect a prompt opportunity to request release, *see* Tex. Transp. Code Ann. § 543.002 (1999) (persons arrested for traffic offenses to be taken "immediately" before a magistrate). Many jurisdictions, moreover, have chosen to impose more restrictive safeguards through statutes limiting warrantless arrests for minor offenses. It is of course easier to devise a minor-offense limitation by statute than to derive one through the Constitution, simply because the statute can let the arrest power turn on any sort of practical consideration without having to subsume it under a broader principle. It is, in fact, only natural that States should resort to this sort of legislative regulation, for, as Atwater's own *amici* emphasize, it is in the interest of the police to limit petty-offense arrests, which carry costs that are simply too great to incur without good reason. Finally, and significantly, under current doctrine the preference for categorical treatment of Fourth Amendment claims gives way to individualized review when a defendant makes a colorable argument that an arrest, with or without a warrant, was "conducted in an extraordinary manner, unusually harmful to [his] privacy or even physical interests." *Whren v. United States*, 517 U.S., at 818, 116 S. Ct. 1769.

The upshot of all these influences, combined with the good sense (and, failing that, the political accountability) of most local lawmakers and law-enforcement officials, is a dearth of horribles demanding redress. Indeed, when Atwater's counsel was asked at oral argument for any indications of comparably foolish, warrantless misdemeanor arrests, he could offer only one. We are sure that there are others, but just as surely the country is not confronting anything like an epidemic of unnecessary minor-offense arrests.[25] That fact caps the reasons for rejecting Atwater's request for the development of a new and distinct body of constitutional law.

Accordingly, we confirm today what our prior cases have intimated: the standard of probable cause "applie[s] to all arrests, without the need to 'balance' the interests and circumstances involved in particular situations." *Dunaway v. New York*, 442 U.S. 200, 208, 99 S. Ct. 2248, 60 L. Ed. 2d 824 (1979). If an officer has probable cause to believe that an individual has committed even a very minor criminal offense in his presence, he may, without violating the Fourth Amendment, arrest the offender.

IV

Atwater's arrest satisfied constitutional requirements. There is no dispute that Officer Turek had probable cause to believe that Atwater had committed a crime in his presence. She admits that neither she nor her children were wearing seat belts, as required by Tex. Transp. Code Ann. § 545.413 (1999). Turek was accordingly authorized (not required, but authorized) to make a custodial arrest without balancing costs and benefits or determining whether or not Atwater's arrest was in some sense necessary.

Nor was the arrest made in an "extraordinary manner, unusually harmful to [her] privacy or . . . physical interests." *Whren v. United States*, 517 U.S., at 818, 116 S. Ct. 1769. As our citations in *Whren* make clear, the question whether a search or seizure is "extraordinary" turns, above all else, on the manner in which the search or seizure is executed. Atwater's arrest was surely "humiliating," as she says in her brief, but it was no more "harmful to . . . privacy or . . . physical interests" than the normal custodial arrest. . . . The arrest and booking were inconvenient and embarrassing to Atwater, but not so extraordinary as to violate the Fourth Amendment.

The Court of Appeals's en banc judgment is affirmed.

It is so ordered.

JUSTICE O'CONNOR, with whom JUSTICE STEVENS, JUSTICE GINSBURG, and JUSTICE BREYER join, dissenting.

---

25. The dissent insists that a minor traffic infraction "may serve as an excuse" for harassment, and that fine-only misdemeanor prohibitions "may be enforced" in an arbitrary manner. Thus, the dissent warns, the rule that we recognize today "has potentially serious consequences for the everyday lives of Americans" and "carries with it grave potential for abuse." But the dissent's own language (*e.g.*, "may," "potentially") betrays the speculative nature of its claims. Noticeably absent from the parade of horribles is any indication that the "potential for abuse" has ever ripened into a reality. In fact, as we have pointed out in the text, there simply is no evidence of widespread abuse of minor-offense arrest authority.

The Fourth Amendment guarantees the right to be free from "unreasonable searches and seizures." The Court recognizes that the arrest of Gail Atwater was a "pointless indignity" that served no discernible state interest and yet holds that her arrest was constitutionally permissible. Because the Court's position is inconsistent with the explicit guarantee of the Fourth Amendment, I dissent.

I

. . . .

We have "often looked to the common law in evaluating the reasonableness, for Fourth Amendment purposes, of police activity." *Tennessee v. Garner*, 471 U.S. 1, 13, 105 S. Ct. 1694, 85 L. Ed. 2d 1 (1985). But history is just one of the tools we use in conducting the reasonableness inquiry. *See id.*, at 13–19, 105 S. Ct. 1694; *see also Wilson v. Arkansas*, 514 U.S. 927, 929, 115 S. Ct. 1914, 131 L. Ed. 2d 976 (1995); *Wyoming v. Houghton*, 526 U.S. 295, 307, 119 S. Ct. 1297, 143 L. Ed. 2d 408 (1999) (Breyer, J., concurring). And when history is inconclusive, as the majority amply demonstrates it is in this case, we will "evaluate the search or seizure under traditional standards of reasonableness by assessing, on the one hand, the degree to which it intrudes upon an individual's privacy and, on the other, the degree to which it is needed for the promotion of legitimate governmental interests." *Wyoming v. Houghton, supra*, at 300, 119 S. Ct. 1297. In other words, in determining reasonableness, "[e]ach case is to be decided on its own facts and circumstances." *Go-Bart Importing Co. v. United States*, 282 U.S. 344, 357, 51 S. Ct. 153, 75 L. Ed. 374 (1931).

. . . [T]he majority allows itself to be swayed by the worry that "every discretionary judgment in the field [will] be converted into an occasion for constitutional review." It therefore mints a new rule that "[i]f an officer has probable cause to believe that an individual has committed even a very minor criminal offense in his presence, he may, without violating the Fourth Amendment, arrest the offender." This rule is not only unsupported by our precedent, but runs contrary to the principles that lie at the core of the Fourth Amendment.

. . . .

. . . The Court's thorough exegesis makes it abundantly clear that warrantless misdemeanor arrests were not the subject of a clear and consistently applied rule at common law. . . . We therefore must engage in the balancing test required by the Fourth Amendment. While probable cause is surely a necessary condition for warrantless arrests for fine-only offenses, any realistic assessment of the interests implicated by such arrests demonstrates that probable cause alone is not a sufficient condition.

. . . .

. . . . [W]hen there is probable cause to believe that a person has violated a minor traffic law, there can be little question that the state interest in law enforcement will justify the relatively limited intrusion of a traffic stop. It is by no means certain, however, that where the offense is punishable only by fine, "probable cause to believe the law has been broken [will] 'outbalanc[e]' private interest in avoiding" a full custodial arrest. *Whren v. United States, supra*, at 818, 116 S. Ct. 1769. Justifying a full arrest by the same quantum of evidence that justifies a traffic stop — even though the offender cannot ultimately be imprisoned for her conduct — defies any sense of proportionality and is in serious tension with the Fourth Amendment's proscription of unreasonable seizures.

A custodial arrest exacts an obvious toll on an individual's liberty and privacy, even when the period of custody is relatively brief. The arrestee is subject to a full search of her person and confiscation of her possessions. If the arrestee is the occupant of a car, the entire passenger compartment of the car, including packages therein, is subject to search as well. The arrestee may be detained for up to 48 hours without having a magistrate determine whether there in fact was probable cause for the arrest. Because people arrested for all types of violent and nonviolent offenses may be housed together awaiting such review, this detention period is potentially dangerous. And once the period of custody is over, the fact of the arrest is a permanent part of the public record.

We have said that "the penalty that may attach to any particular offense seems to provide the clearest and most consistent indication of the State's interest in arresting individuals suspected of committing that offense." *Welsh v. Wisconsin*, 466 U.S. 740, 754, n. 14, 104 S. Ct. 2091, 80 L. Ed. 2d 732 (1984). If the State has decided that a fine, and not imprisonment, is the appropriate punishment for an offense, the State's interest in taking a person suspected of committing that offense into custody is surely limited, at best. This is not to say that the State will never have such an interest. A full custodial arrest may on occasion vindicate legitimate state interests, even if the crime is punishable only by fine. Arrest is the surest way to abate criminal conduct. It may also allow the police to verify the offender's identity and, if the offender poses a flight risk, to ensure her appearance at trial. But when such considerations are not present, a citation or summons may serve the State's remaining law enforcement interests every bit as effectively as an arrest.

Because a full custodial arrest is such a severe intrusion on an individual's liberty, its reasonableness hinges on "the degree to which it is needed for the promotion of legitimate governmental interests." *Wyoming v. Houghton*, 526 U.S., at 300, 119 S. Ct. 1297. In light of the availability of citations to promote a State's interests when a fine-only offense has been committed, I cannot concur in a rule which deems a full custodial arrest to be reasonable in every circumstance. Giving police officers constitutional carte blanche to effect an arrest whenever there is probable cause to believe a fine-only misdemeanor has been committed is irreconcilable with the Fourth Amendment's command that seizures be reasonable. Instead, I would require that when there is probable cause to believe that a fine-only offense has been committed, the police officer should issue a citation unless the officer is "able to point to specific and articulable facts which, taken together with rational inferences from those facts, reasonably warrant [the additional] intrusion" of a full custodial arrest. *Terry v. Ohio*, 392 U.S., at 21, 88 S. Ct. 1868.

The majority insists that a bright-line rule focused on probable cause is necessary to vindicate the State's interest in easily administrable law enforcement rules. Probable cause itself, however, is not a model of precision. "The quantum of information which constitutes probable cause — evidence which would 'warrant a man of reasonable caution in the belief' that a [crime] has been committed — must be measured by the facts of the particular case." *Wong Sun v. United States*, 371 U.S. 471, 479, 83 S. Ct. 407, 9 L. Ed. 2d 441 (1963) (citation omitted). The rule I propose — which merely requires a legitimate reason for the decision to escalate the seizure into a full custodial arrest — thus does not undermine an otherwise "clear and simple" rule.

While clarity is certainly a value worthy of consideration in our Fourth Amendment jurisprudence, it by no means trumps the values of liberty and privacy at the heart of the Amendment's protections. . . .

At bottom, the majority offers two related reasons why a bright-line rule is necessary: the fear that officers who arrest for fine-only offenses will be subject to "personal [42 U.S.C.] § 1983 liability for the misapplication of a constitutional standard" and the resulting "systematic disincentive to arrest . . . where . . . arresting would serve an important societal interest." These concerns are certainly valid, but they are more than adequately resolved by the doctrine of qualified immunity.

[The dissent explained that "qualified immunity" shields officials from civil liability for Fourth Amendment violations as long as they do "not violate clearly established statutory or constitutional rights of which a reasonable person would have known" and "thus allays any concerns about liability or disincentives to arrest."]

. . . .

. . . . As we have said, "officials will not be liable for mere mistakes in judgment." *Butz v. Economou*, 438 U.S. 478, 507, 98 S. Ct. 2894, 57 L. Ed. 2d 895 (1978). Of course, even the specter of liability can entail substantial social costs, such as inhibiting public officials in the discharge of their duties. *See, e.g., Harlow v. Fitzgerald, supra*, at 814, 102 S. Ct. 2727. We may not ignore the central command of the Fourth Amendment, however, to avoid these costs.

II

The record in this case makes it abundantly clear that Ms. Atwater's arrest was constitutionally unreasonable. Atwater readily admits — as she did when Officer Turek pulled her over — that she violated Texas'[s] seatbelt law. While Turek was justified in stopping Atwater, neither law nor reason supports his decision to arrest her instead of simply giving her a citation. The officer's actions cannot sensibly be viewed as a permissible means of balancing Atwater's Fourth Amendment interests with the State's own legitimate interests.

There is no question that Officer Turek's actions severely infringed Atwater's liberty and privacy. Turek was loud and accusatory from the moment he approached Atwater's car. Atwater's young children were terrified and hysterical. Yet when Atwater asked Turek to lower his voice because he was scaring the children, he responded by jabbing his finger in Atwater's face and saying, "You're going to jail." Having made the decision to arrest, Turek did not inform Atwater of her right to remain silent. He instead asked for her license and insurance information.

Atwater asked if she could at least take her children to a friend's house down the street before going to the police station. But Turek — who had just castigated Atwater for not caring for her children — refused and said he would take the children into custody as well. Only the intervention of neighborhood children who had witnessed the scene and summoned one of Atwater's friends saved the children from being hauled to jail with their mother.

With the children gone, Officer Turek handcuffed Ms. Atwater with her hands behind her back, placed her in the police car, and drove her to the police station. Ironically, Turek did not secure Atwater in a seatbelt for the drive. At the station, Atwater was forced to remove her shoes, relinquish her possessions, and wait in a holding cell for about an hour. A judge finally informed Atwater of her rights and the charges against her, and released her when she posted bond. Atwater returned to the scene of the arrest, only to find that her car had been towed.

Ms. Atwater ultimately pleaded no contest to violating the seatbelt law and was fined $50. Even though that fine was the maximum penalty for her crime, and even though Officer Turek has never articulated any justification for his actions, the city contends that arresting Atwater was constitutionally reasonable because it advanced two legitimate interests: "the enforcement of child safety laws and encouraging [Atwater] to appear for trial."

It is difficult to see how arresting Atwater served either of these goals any more effectively than the issuance of a citation. . . .

    . . . .

The city's justifications fall far short of rationalizing the extraordinary intrusion on Gail Atwater and her children. . . . The majority's assessment that "Atwater's claim to live free of pointless indignity and confinement clearly outweighs anything the City can raise against it specific to her case" is quite correct. In my view, the Fourth Amendment inquiry ends there.

III

. . . The *per se* rule that the Court creates has potentially serious consequences for the everyday lives of Americans. A broad range of conduct falls into the category of fine-only misdemeanors. . . .

. . . Under today's holding, when a police officer has probable cause to believe that a fine-only misdemeanor offense has occurred, that officer may stop the suspect, issue a citation, and let the person continue on her way. Cf. *Whren v. United States*, 517 U.S., at 806, 116 S. Ct. 1769. Or, if a traffic violation, the officer may stop the car, arrest the driver, search the driver, *see United States v. Robinson*, 414 U.S., at 235, 94 S. Ct. 467, search the entire passenger compartment of the car including any purse or package inside, *see New York v. Belton*, 453 U.S., at 460, 101 S. Ct. 2860, and impound the car and inventory all of its contents, *see Colorado v. Bertine*, 479 U.S. 367, 374, 107 S. Ct. 738, 93 L. Ed. 2d 739 (1987); *Florida v. Wells*, 495 U.S. 1, 4–5, 110 S. Ct. 1632, 109 L. Ed. 2d 1 (1990). . . . [T]he majority gives officers unfettered discretion to choose that course without articulating a single reason why such action is appropriate.

Such unbounded discretion carries with it grave potential for abuse. The majority takes comfort in the lack of evidence of "an epidemic of unnecessary minor-offense arrests." But the relatively small number of published cases dealing with such arrests proves little and should provide little solace. Indeed, as the recent debate over racial profiling demonstrates all too clearly, a relatively minor traffic infraction may often serve as an excuse for stopping and harassing an individual. After today, the arsenal available to any officer extends to a full arrest and the searches permissible concomitant to that arrest. An officer's subjective motivations for making a traffic stop are not relevant considerations in determining the reasonableness of the stop. *See Whren v. United States, supra*, at 813, 116 S. Ct. 1769. But it is precisely because these motivations are beyond our purview that we must vigilantly ensure that officers' poststop actions — which are properly within our reach — comport with the Fourth Amendment's guarantee of reasonableness.

. . . .

The Court neglects the Fourth Amendment's express command in the name of administrative ease. In so doing, it cloaks the pointless indignity that Gail Atwater suffered with the mantle of reasonableness. I respectfully dissent.

Notes and Questions

(1) The majority concedes that Ms. "Atwater's claim to live free of pointless indignity and confinement clearly outweighs anything the City can raise against it specific to her case." In that case, how can her warrantless arrest for violating Texas's seatbelt law not be "unreasonable" within the meaning of the Fourth Amendment?

(2) The *Atwater* majority accords history a prominent role in its analysis of the Fourth Amendment issue at the core of the case. The dissenters suggest that history should be somewhat less influential, opining that it is merely "one of the tools" used to assess reasonableness. Which attitude toward the lessons of history seems preferable? Why?

(3) The majority also expresses genuine concern that any alternative rule would undermine "the values of clarity and simplicity." Why is it important that Fourth Amendment rules be clear and simple? Is the majority's rule decidedly clearer and simpler than any plausible alternative?

(4) The *Atwater* dissent expresses concern with the expansive arrest power authorized in the majority opinion in part because of the searches that are constitutionally reasonable as a routine matter after a lawful arrest. The merits of this concern

should be evaluated after studying the opinions that explain and explore the scope of the privacy invasions that may legitimately follow upon an arrest. Those opinions appear in Chapter 4, subsections [A] and [D].

[C] The Issuance, Content, and Execution of Warrants

United States v. Grubbs

United States Supreme Court

547 U.S. 90, 126 S. Ct. 1494, 164 L. Ed. 2d 195 (2006)

JUSTICE SCALIA delivered the opinion of the Court.

. . . .

I

Respondent Jeffrey Grubbs purchased a videotape containing child pornography from a Web site operated by an undercover postal inspector. Officers from the Postal Inspection Service arranged a controlled delivery of a package containing the videotape to Grubbs'[s] residence. A postal inspector submitted a search warrant application to a Magistrate Judge for the Eastern District of California, accompanied by an affidavit describing the proposed operation in detail. The affidavit stated:

> "Execution of this search warrant will not occur unless and until the parcel has been received by a person(s) and has been physically taken into the residence . . . . At that time, and not before, this search warrant will be executed by me and other United States Postal inspectors, with appropriate assistance from other law enforcement officers in accordance with this warrant's command."

In addition to describing this triggering condition, the affidavit referred to two attachments, which described Grubbs'[s] residence and the items officers would seize. These attachments, but not the body of the affidavit, were incorporated into the requested warrant. The affidavit concluded:

> "Based upon the foregoing facts, I respectfully submit there exists probable cause to believe that the items set forth in Attachment B to this affidavit and the search warrant, will be found [at Grubbs'[s] residence], which residence is further described at Attachment A."

The Magistrate Judge issued the warrant as requested. Two days later, an undercover postal inspector delivered the package. Grubbs'[s] wife signed for it and took the unopened package inside. The inspectors detained Grubbs as he left his home a few minutes later, then entered the house and commenced the search. Roughly 30 minutes into the search, Grubbs was provided with a copy of the warrant, which included both attachments but not the supporting affidavit that explained when the warrant would be executed. Grubbs consented to interrogation by the postal inspectors and admitted ordering the videotape. He was placed under arrest, and various items were seized, including the videotape.

A grand jury for the Eastern District of California indicted Grubbs on one count of receiving a visual depiction of a minor engaged in sexually explicit conduct. *See* 18 U.S.C. § 2252(a)(2). He moved to suppress the evidence seized during the search of his residence, arguing as relevant here that the warrant was invalid because it failed to list the triggering condition. After an evidentiary hearing, the District Court denied the motion. Grubbs pleaded guilty, but reserved his right to appeal the denial of his motion to suppress.

The Court of Appeals for the Ninth Circuit reversed. Relying on Circuit precedent, it held that "the particularity requirement of the Fourth Amendment applies with full force to the conditions precedent to an anticipatory search warrant." 377 F.3d, at 1077–1078 (citing *United States v. Hotal*, 143 F.3d 1223, 1226 (9th Cir. 1998)). An anticipatory warrant defective for that reason may be "cur[ed]" if the conditions precedent are set forth in an affidavit that is incorporated in the warrant and "presented to the person whose property is being searched." 377 F.3d, at 1079. Because the postal inspectors "failed to present the affidavit — the only document in which the triggering conditions were listed" — to Grubbs or his wife, the "warrant was . . . inoperative, and the search was illegal." *Ibid.* We granted certiorari.

II

Before turning to the Ninth Circuit's conclusion that the warrant at issue here ran afoul of the Fourth Amendment's particularity requirement, we address the antecedent question whether anticipatory search warrants are categorically unconstitutional. An anticipatory warrant is "a warrant based upon an affidavit showing probable cause that at some future time (but not presently) certain evidence of crime will be located at a specified place." 2 W. LaFave, SEARCH AND SEIZURE § 3.7(c), p. 398 (4th ed. 2004). Most anticipatory warrants subject their execution to some condition precedent other than the mere passage of time — a so-called "triggering condition." The affidavit at issue here, for instance, explained that "[e]xecution of th[e] search warrant will not occur unless and until the parcel [containing child pornography] has been received by a person(s) and has been physically taken into the residence." App. to Pet. for Cert. 72a. If the government were to execute an anticipatory warrant before the triggering condition occurred, there would be no reason to believe the item described in the warrant could be found at the searched location; by definition, the triggering condition which establishes probable cause has not yet been satisfied when the warrant is issued. Grubbs argues that for this reason anticipatory warrants contravene the Fourth Amendment's provision that "no Warrants shall issue, but upon probable cause."

We reject this view, as has every Court of Appeals to confront the issue, *see, e.g., United States v. Loy*, 191 F.3d 360, 364 (3d Cir. 1999) (collecting cases). Probable cause exists when "there is a fair probability that contraband or evidence of a crime will be found in a particular place." *Illinois v. Gates*, 462 U.S. 213, 238, 103 S. Ct. 2317, 76 L.

Ed. 2d 527 (1983). Because the probable-cause requirement looks to whether evidence will be found *when the search is conducted,* all warrants are, in a sense, "anticipatory." In the typical case where the police seek permission to search a house for an item they believe is already located there, the magistrate's determination that there is probable cause for the search amounts to a prediction that the item will still be there when the warrant is executed. *See People v. Glen,* 30 N.Y.2d 252, 258, 331 N.Y.S.2d 656, 282 N.E.2d 614, 617 (1972) ("[P]resent possession is only probative of the likelihood of future possession.").[2] The anticipatory nature of warrants is even clearer in the context of electronic surveillance. *See, e.g., Katz v. United States,* 389 U.S. 347, 88 S. Ct. 507, 19 L. Ed. 2d 576 (1967). When police request approval to tap a telephone line, they do so based on the probability that, during the course of the surveillance, the subject *will* use the phone to engage in crime-related conversations .... Thus, when an anticipatory warrant is issued, "the fact that the contraband is not presently located at the place described in the warrant is immaterial, so long as there is probable cause to believe that it will be there when the search warrant is executed." *United States v. Garcia,* 882 F.2d 699, 702 (2d Cir. 1989) (quoting *United States v. Lowe,* 575 F.2d 1193, 1194 (6th Cir. 1978); internal quotation marks omitted).

Anticipatory warrants are, therefore, no different in principle from ordinary warrants. They require the magistrate to determine (1) that it is *now probable* that (2) contraband, evidence of a crime, or a fugitive *will be* on the described premises (3) when the warrant is executed. It should be noted, however, that where the anticipatory warrant places a condition (other than the mere passage of time) upon its execution, the first of these determinations goes not merely to what will probably be found *if* the condition is met. (If that were the extent of the probability determination, an anticipatory warrant could be issued for every house in the country, authorizing search and seizure *if* contraband should be delivered — though for any single location there is no likelihood that contraband will be delivered.) Rather, the probability determination for a conditioned anticipatory warrant looks also to the likelihood that the condition will occur, and thus that a proper object of seizure will be on the described premises. In other words, for a conditioned anticipatory warrant to comply with the Fourth Amendment's requirement of probable cause, two prerequisites of probability must be satisfied. It must be true not only that *if* the triggering condition occurs "there is a fair probability that contraband or evidence of a crime will be found in a particular place," *Gates, supra,* at 238, 103 S. Ct. 2317, but

---

2. For this reason, probable cause may cease to exist after a warrant is issued. The police may learn, for instance, that contraband is no longer located at the place to be searched. *See, e.g., United States v. Bowling,* 900 F.2d 926, 932 (6th Cir. 1990) (recognizing that a fruitless consent search could "dissipat[e] the probable cause that justified a warrant"). Or the probable-cause showing may have grown "stale" in view of the time that has passed since the warrant was issued. *See United States v. Wagner,* 989 F.2d 69, 75 (2d Cir. 1993) ("[T]he facts in an affidavit supporting a search warrant must be sufficiently close in time to the issuance of the warrant and the subsequent search conducted so that probable cause can be said to exist as of the time of the search and not simply as of some time in the past."); *see also Sgro v. United States,* 287 U.S. 206, 210–211, 53 S. Ct. 138, 77 L. Ed. 260 (1932).

also that there is probable cause to believe the triggering condition *will occur*. The supporting affidavit must provide the magistrate with sufficient information to evaluate both aspects of the probable-cause determination.

In this case, the occurrence of the triggering condition — successful delivery of the videotape to Grubbs'[s] residence — would plainly establish probable cause for the search. In addition, the affidavit established probable cause to believe the triggering condition would be satisfied. Although it is possible that Grubbs could have refused delivery of the videotape he had ordered, that was unlikely. The Magistrate therefore "had a 'substantial basis for . . . conclud[ing]' that probable cause existed." *Gates*, 462 U.S., at 238–239, 103 S. Ct. 2317 (quoting *Jones v. United States*, 362 U.S. 257, 271, 80 S. Ct. 725, 4 L. Ed. 2d 697 (1960)).

III

The Ninth Circuit invalidated the anticipatory search warrant at issue here because the warrant failed to specify the triggering condition. The Fourth Amendment's particularity requirement, it held, "applies with full force to the conditions precedent to an anticipatory search warrant." 377 F.3d, at 1077–1078.

The Fourth Amendment, however, does not set forth some general "particularity requirement." It specifies only two matters that must be "particularly describ[ed]" in the warrant: "the place to be searched" and "the persons or things to be seized." We have previously rejected efforts to expand the scope of this provision to embrace unenumerated matters . . . . The language of the Fourth Amendment is . . . decisive here; its particularity requirement does not include the conditions precedent to execution of the warrant.

Respondent, drawing upon the Ninth Circuit's analysis below, relies primarily on two related policy rationales. First, he argues, setting forth the triggering condition in the warrant itself is necessary "to delineate the limits of the executing officer's power." Brief for Respondent 20. This is an application, respondent asserts, of the following principle: "[I]f there is a precondition to the valid exercise of executive power, that precondition must be particularly identified on the face of the warrant." *Id.*, at 23. That principle is not to be found in the Constitution. The Fourth Amendment does not require that the warrant set forth the magistrate's basis for finding probable cause, even though probable cause is the quintessential "precondition to the valid exercise of executive power." Much less does it require description of a triggering condition.

Second, respondent argues that listing the triggering condition in the warrant is necessary to "'assur[e] the individual whose property is searched or seized of the lawful authority of the executing officer, his need to search, and the limits of his power to search.'" *Id.*, at 19 (quoting *United States v. Chadwick*, 433 U.S. 1, 9, 97 S. Ct. 2476, 53 L. Ed. 2d 538 (1977)) . . . . This argument assumes that the executing officer must present the property owner with a copy of the warrant before conducting his search. *See* 377 F.3d, at 1079, n. 9. In fact, however, neither the Fourth Amendment nor Rule 41 of the Federal Rules of Criminal Procedure imposes such a requirement. *See Groh v. Ramirez*, 540 U.S. 551, 562, n. 5, 124 S. Ct. 1284, 157 L. Ed. 2d 1068 (2004) .... The Constitution protects property owners not by giving them license to engage the police in a debate over the basis for the warrant, but by interposing, *ex ante*, the "deliberate, impartial judgment of a judicial officer ... between the citizen and the police," *Wong Sun v. United States*, 371 U.S. 471, 481–482, 83 S. Ct. 407, 9 L. Ed. 2d 441 (1963), and by providing, *ex post*, a right to suppress evidence improperly obtained and a cause of action for damages.

. . . .

Because the Fourth Amendment does not require that the triggering condition for an anticipatory search warrant be set forth in the warrant itself, the Court of Appeals erred in invalidating the warrant at issue here. The judgment of the Court of Appeals is reversed, and the case is remanded for further proceedings consistent with this opinion.

It is so ordered.

Justice Alito took no part in the consideration or decision of this case.

[The opinion of Justice Souter, concurring in part and concurring in the judgment, has been omitted.]

Notes and Questions

(1) How are anticipatory search warrants different from other search warrants?

(a) Are anticipatory warrants consistent with the Fourth Amendment's explicit requirement that "no Warrants shall issue, but upon probable cause," as the Court concludes? Why?

(b) Are anticipatory warrants consistent with both the letter and the spirit of the Fourth Amendment's "particularity" requirement? What logic supports the contention that an anticipatory warrant is invalid unless it specifies the "triggering condition" for the search authorized by the warrant?

(2) The text of the "warrant clause" clearly and specifically provides that warrants are not valid unless they are supported by a showing of "probable cause."

(a) As noted in Chapter Two, probable cause does not require certainty; a "fair probability" will suffice. Consequently, a probable cause showing is not invalidated by the fact that the conclusions it supports turn out to have been "mistaken." If an individual is arrested pursuant to an arrest warrant supported by facts giving rise to a fair probability that she committed an offense, the fact that she did not commit the offense will not undermine the warrant or the arrest. If officers enter a home pursuant to a search warrant supported by probable cause to believe that contraband is present, but no contraband is found, neither the warrant nor the search is unconstitutional. In sum, a warrant is not subject to attack as improperly issued either because the conclusion on which it is based or the information supporting that conclusion ultimately proves to be erroneous. *See Los*

Angeles County v. Rettele, 550 U.S. 609, 127 S. Ct. 1989, 167 L. Ed. 2d 974 (2007) ("The Fourth Amendment allows warrants to issue on probable cause, a standard well short of absolute certainty. Valid warrants will issue to search the innocent, and people [who are not in fact involved in criminal activity] unfortunately bear the cost . . . . When officers execute a valid warrant and act in a reasonable manner . . . , however, the Fourth Amendment is not violated.").

(b) On the other hand, a warrant is subject to a Fourth Amendment challenge if the officer supplying the basis for the warrant *intentionally or recklessly* furnishes false information to the issuing magistrate. In *Franks v. Delaware*, 438 U.S. 154, 98 S. Ct. 2674, 57 L. Ed. 2d 667 (1978), the Court held that it is permissible to challenge the truthfulness of statements made in an affidavit supporting application for a warrant. According to the majority, "where the defendant makes a *substantial preliminary showing that a false statement knowingly and intentionally, or with reckless disregard for the truth*, was included by the affiant in the warrant affidavit, *and if the allegedly false statement is necessary to the finding of probable cause*, the Fourth Amendment requires that a *hearing* be held at the defendant's request. In the event that at that hearing the allegation of perjury is established . . . *by a preponderance of the evidence, and*, with the affidavit's false material set to one side, the affidavit's *remaining content is insufficient to establish probable cause, the search warrant must be voided* and the fruits of the search excluded to the same extent as if probable cause was lacking on the face of the affidavit." (Emphasis added.)

Dissenting Justice Rehnquist did not think that affidavits of probable cause should be subject to attack on the basis of the falsity of the information provided. According to his reasoning, "[i]f the function of the warrant requirement is to obtain the determination of a neutral magistrate as to whether sufficient grounds have been urged to support the issuance of a warrant, that function is fulfilled at the time the magistrate concludes that the requirement has been met."

Andresen v. Maryland

United States Supreme Court
427 U.S. 463, 96 S. Ct. 2737, 49 L. Ed. 2d 627 (1976)

Mr. Justice Blackmun delivered the opinion of the Court.

. . . .

I

In early 1972, a Bi-County Fraud Unit, acting under the joint auspices of the State's Attorneys' Offices of Montgomery and Prince George's Counties, Md., began an investigation of real estate settlement activities in the Washington, D.C., area. At the time, petitioner Andresen was an attorney who, as a sole practitioner, specialized in real estate settlements in Montgomery County. During the Fraud Unit's investigation, his activities came under scrutiny, particularly in connection with a transaction involving Lot 13T in the Potomac Woods subdivision of Montgomery

County. The investigation, which included interviews with the purchaser, the mortgage holder, and other lienholders of Lot 13T, as well as an examination of county land records, disclosed that petitioner, acting as settlement attorney, had defrauded Standard-Young Associates, the purchaser of Lot 13T. Petitioner had represented that the property was free of liens and that, accordingly, no title insurance was necessary, when in fact, he knew that there were two outstanding liens on the property. In addition, investigators learned that the lienholders, by threatening to foreclose their liens, had forced a halt to the purchaser's construction on the property. When Standard-Young had confronted petitioner with this information, he responded by issuing, as an agent of a title insurance company, a title policy guaranteeing clear title to the property. By this action, petitioner also defrauded that insurance company by requiring it to pay the outstanding liens.

The investigators, concluding that there was probable cause to believe that petitioner had committed the state crime of false pretenses, *see* Md. Ann. Code, Art. 27, § 140 (1976), against Standard-Young, applied for warrants to search petitioner's law office and the separate office of Mount Vernon Development Corporation, of which petitioner was incorporator, sole shareholder, resident agent, and director. The application sought permission to search for specified documents pertaining to the sale and conveyance of Lot 13T. A judge of the Sixth Judicial Circuit of Montgomery County concluded that there was probable cause and issued the warrants.

The searches of the two offices were conducted simultaneously during daylight hours on October 31, 1972. Petitioner was present during the search of his law office and was free to move about. Counsel for him was present during the latter half of the search. Between 2% and 3% of the files in the office were seized. A single investigator, in the presence of a police officer, conducted the search of Mount Vernon Development Corporation. This search, taking about four hours, resulted in the seizure of less than 5% of the corporation's files.

. . . .

At trial, the State proved its case primarily by public land records and by records provided by the complaining purchasers, lienholders, and the title insurance company. It did introduce into evidence, however, a number of the seized items. Three documents from the "Potomac Woods General" file, seized during the search of petitioner's corporation, were admitted. These were notes in the handwriting of an employee who used them to prepare abstracts in the course of his duties as a title searcher and law clerk. The notes concerned deeds of trust affecting the Potomac Woods subdivision and related to the transaction involving Lot 13T. Five items seized from petitioner's law office were also admitted. One contained information relating to the transactions with one of the defrauded home buyers. The second was a file partially devoted to the Lot 13T transaction; among the documents were settlement statements, the deed conveying the property to Standard-Young Associates, and the original and a copy of a notice to the buyer about releases of liens. The third item was a file devoted exclusively to Lot 13T. The fourth item consisted of a copy of a deed of trust, dated March 27, 1972, from the seller of certain lots in the Potomac Woods subdivision to a lienholder. The fifth item contained drafts of documents and memoranda written in petitioner's handwriting.

. . . .

[In PART II the Court discussed petitioner's Fifth Amendment claim.]

III

We turn . . . to petitioner's contention that rights guaranteed him by the Fourth Amendment were violated because the descriptive terms of the search warrants were so broad as to make them impermissible "general" warrants, and because certain items were seized in violation of the principles of *Warden v. Hayden*, 387 U.S. 294, 87 S. Ct. 1642, 18 L. Ed. 2d 782 (1967).[9]

The specificity of the search warrants. Although petitioner concedes that the warrants for the most part were models of particularity, he contends that they were rendered fatally "general" by the addition, in each warrant, to the exhaustive list of particularly described documents, of the phrase "together with other fruits, instrumentalities and evidence of crime at this [time] unknown." The quoted language, it is

---

9. Petitioner also contends that the affidavits do not establish probable cause . . . . The bases of petitioner's argument that the affidavits failed to establish probable cause are two: The affidavits, in violation of *Aguilar v. Texas*, 378 U.S. 108, 84 S. Ct. 1509, 12 L. Ed. 2d 723 (1964), did not establish the reliability of the information or the credibility of the informants; and the information on which they were based was so stale that there was no reason to believe that the documents sought were still in petitioner's possession. The affidavits clearly establish the reliability of the information related and the credibility of its sources. The complainants are named, their positions are described, and their transactions with petitioner are related in a comprehensive fashion. In addition, the special-agent affiants aver that they have verified, at least in part, the complainants' charges by examining their correspondence with petitioner, numerous documents reflecting the transactions, and public land records. Copies of many of these records and documents are attached to the affidavits; others are described in detail. Finally, the agents aver that they have interviewed, with positive results, other persons involved in the real estate transactions that were the object of the investigation. Rarely have we seen warrant-supporting affidavits so complete and so thorough. Petitioner's probable-cause argument is without merit. *See United States v. Ventresca*, 380 U.S. 102, 85 S. Ct. 741, 13 L. Ed. 2d 684 (1965). It is also argued that there was a three-month delay between the completion of the transactions on which the warrants were based, and the ensuing searches, and that this time lapse precluded a determination that there was probable cause to believe that petitioner's offices contained evidence of the crime. This contention is belied by the particular facts of the case. The business records sought were prepared in the ordinary course of petitioner's business in his law office or that of his real estate corporation. It is eminently reasonable to expect that such records would be maintained in those offices for a period of time and surely as long as the three months required for the investigation of a complex real estate scheme. In addition, special investigators knew that petitioner had secured a release on Lot 13T with respect to one lienholder only three weeks before the searches and that another lien remained to be released. All this, when considered with other information demonstrating that Potomac Woods was still a current concern of petitioner, amply supports the belief that petitioner retained the sought-for records . . . .

argued, must be read in isolation and without reference to the rest of the long sentence at the end of which it appears. When read "properly," petitioner contends, it permits the search for and seizure of any evidence of any crime.

General warrants of course, are prohibited by the Fourth Amendment. "[T]he problem [posed by the general warrant] is not that of intrusion *per se*, but of a general, exploratory rummaging in a person's belongings . . . . [The Fourth Amendment addresses the problem] by requiring a 'particular description' of the things to be seized." *Coolidge v. New Hampshire*, 403 U.S. 443, 467, 91 S. Ct. 2022, 2038, 29 L. Ed. 2d 564 (1971). This requirement "makes general searches . . . impossible and prevents the seizure of one thing under a warrant describing another. As to what is to be taken, nothing is left to the discretion of the officer executing the warrant." *Stanford v. Texas*, 379 U.S. 476, 485, 85 S. Ct. 506, 512, 13 L. Ed. 2d 431 (1965), quoting *Marron v. United States*, 275 U.S., at 196, 48 S. Ct. at 76.

In this case we agree with the determination of the Court of Special Appeals of Maryland that the challenged phrase must be read as authorizing only the search for and seizure of evidence relating to "the crime of false pretenses with respect to Lot 13T." 24 Md. App., at 167, 331 A.2d, at 103. The challenged phrase is not a separate sentence. Instead, it appears in each warrant at the end of a sentence containing a lengthy list of specified and particular items to be seized, all pertaining to Lot 13T.[10] We think it clear from the context that the term "crime" in the warrants refers only to the crime of false pretenses with respect to the sale of Lot 13T. The "other fruits"

---

10. "[T]he following items pertaining to sale, purchase, settlement and conveyance of lot 13, block T, Potomac Woods subdivision, Montgomery County, Maryland: title notes, title abstracts, title rundowns; contracts of sale and/or assignments from Raffaele Antonelli and Rocco Caniglia to Mount Vernon Development Corporation and/or others; lien pay-off correspondence and lien pay-off memoranda to and from lienholders and noteholders; correspondence and memoranda to and from trustees of deeds of trust; lenders instructions for a construction loan or construction and permanent loan; disbursement sheets and disbursement memoranda; checks, check stubs and ledger sheets indicating disbursement upon settlement; correspondence and memoranda concerning disbursements upon settlement; settlement statements and settlement memoranda; fully or partially prepared deed of trust releases, whether or not executed and whether or not recorded; books, records, documents, papers, memoranda and correspondence, showing or tending to show a fraudulent intent, and/or knowledge as elements of the crime of false pretenses, in violation of Article 27, Section 140, of the Annotated Code of Maryland, 1957 Edition, as amended and revised, together with other fruits, instrumentalities and evidence of crime at this [time] unknown."

Petitioner also suggests that the specific list of the documents to be seized constitutes a "general" warrant. We disagree. Under investigation was a complex real estate scheme whose existence could be proved only by piecing together many bits of evidence. Like a jigsaw puzzle, the whole "picture" of petitioner's false-pretense scheme with respect to Lot 13T could be shown only by placing in the proper place the many pieces of evidence that, taken singly, would show comparatively little. The complexity of an illegal scheme may not be used as a shield to avoid detection when the State has demonstrated probable cause to believe that a crime has been committed and probable cause to believe that evidence of this crime is in the suspect's possession . . . .

clause is one of a series that follows the colon after the word "Maryland." All clauses in the series are limited by what precedes that colon, namely, "items pertaining to . . . lot 13, block T." The warrants, accordingly, did not authorize the executing officers to conduct a search for evidence of other crimes but only to search for and seize evidence relevant to the crime of false pretenses and Lot 13T.[11]

. . . .

The judgment of the Court of Special Appeals of Maryland is affirmed.

It is so ordered.

MR. JUSTICE BRENNAN, dissenting.

[In the first part of his opinion, JUSTICE BRENNAN discussed the Fifth Amendment issue.]

. . . .

II

Even if a Fifth Amendment violation is not to be recognized in the seizure of petitioner's papers, a violation of Fourth Amendment protections clearly should be, for the warrants under which those papers were seized were impermissibly general. General warrants are specially prohibited by the Fourth Amendment. The problem to be avoided is "not that of intrusion *per se*, but of a general, exploratory rummaging in a person's belongings." *Coolidge v. New Hampshire*, 403 U.S. 443, 467, 91 S. Ct. 2022, 2038, 29 L. Ed. 2d 564 (1971). Thus the requirement plainly appearing on the face of the Fourth Amendment that a warrant specify with particularity the place to be searched and the things to be seized is imposed to the end that "unauthorized invasions of 'the sanctity of a man's home and the privacies of life'" be prevented. *Berger v. New York*, 388 U.S. 41, 58, 87 S. Ct. 1873, 1883, 18 L. Ed. 2d 1040 (1967). "'As to what is to be taken, nothing is left to the discretion of the officer executing the warrant.'" *Stanford v. Texas*, 379 U.S. 476, 485, 85 S. Ct. 506, 512, 13 L. Ed. 2d 431 (1965) (quoting *Marron v. United States*, 275 U.S. 192, 196, 48 S. Ct. 74, 76, 72 L. Ed. 231, Treas. Dec. 42528 (1927)).

The Court recites these requirements, but their application in this case renders their limitation on unlawful governmental conduct an empty promise. After a lengthy

---

11. The record discloses that the officials executing the warrants seized numerous papers that were not introduced into evidence. Although we are not informed of their content, we observe that to the extent such papers were not within the scope of the warrants or were otherwise improperly seized, the State was correct in returning them voluntarily and the trial judge was correct in suppressing others. We recognize that there are grave dangers inherent in executing a warrant authorizing a search and seizure of a person's papers that are not necessarily present in executing a warrant to search for physical objects whose relevance is more easily ascertainable. In searches for papers, it is certain that some innocuous documents will be examined, at least cursorily, in order to determine whether they are, in fact, among those papers authorized to be seized. Similar dangers, of course, are present in executing a warrant for the "seizure" of telephone conversations. In both kinds of searches, responsible officials, including judicial officials, must take care to assure that they are conducted in a manner that minimizes unwarranted intrusions upon privacy.

and admittedly detailed listing of items to be seized, the warrants in this case further authorized the seizure of "other fruits, instrumentalities and evidence of crime at this [time] unknown." The Court construes this sweeping authorization to be limited to evidence pertaining to the crime of false pretenses with respect to the sale of Lot 13T. However, neither this Court's construction of the warrants nor the similar construction by the Court of Special Appeals of Maryland was available to the investigators at the time they executed the warrants. The question is not how those warrants are to be viewed in hindsight, but how they were in fact viewed by those executing them. The overwhelming quantity of seized material that was either suppressed or returned to petitioner is irrefutable testimony to the unlawful generality of the warrants. The Court's attempt to cure this defect by *post hoc* judicial construction evades principles settled in this Court's Fourth Amendment decisions. "The scheme of the Fourth Amendment becomes meaningful only when it is assured that at some point the conduct of those charged with enforcing the laws can be subjected to the more detached, neutral scrutiny of a judge . . . ." *Terry v. Ohio*, 392 U.S. 1, 21, 88 S. Ct. 1868, 1880, 20 L. Ed. 2d 889 (1968). *See Berger v. New York, supra*, at 54, 87 S. Ct. at 1881; *Johnson v. United States*, 333 U.S. 10, 13–14, 68 S. Ct. 367, 368–369, 92 L. Ed. 436 (1948). It is not the function of a detached and neutral review to give effect to warrants whose terms unassailably authorize the far-reaching search and seizure of a person's papers especially where that has in fact been the result of executing those warrants.

[The dissenting opinion of MR. JUSTICE MARSHALL has been omitted.]

Notes and Questions

(1) In *Groh v. Ramirez*, 540 U.S. 551, 124 S. Ct. 1284, 157 L. Ed. 2d 1068 (2004), Groh, an agent for the Bureau of Alcohol, Tobacco, and Firearms prepared an application for a warrant to search a ranch for automatic firearms, automatic weapons parts, destructive devices, and receipts pertaining to the purchase of these items. He submitted the application, a detailed affidavit, and a completed warrant form to a magistrate, who signed the warrant form. Although the application described the contraband that was sought, the warrant itself did not. In the section of the form calling for a description of the items to be seized, Groh had typed in a description of the house to be searched. The warrant did not incorporate by reference the items described in the application, but did "recite that the Magistrate was satisfied the affidavit established probable cause to believe that contraband was on the premises and that sufficient grounds existed for the warrant's issuance." Groh led a team of officers in a search of the premises which "uncovered no illegal weapons or explosives."

The owners of the ranch filed a civil action, claiming that the search had violated their Fourth Amendment rights. The district court granted summary judgment for Groh, but the Ninth Circuit reversed. The Supreme Court affirmed, holding that the warrant was invalid and that the search had been unreasonable. The majority opinion sheds additional light on the meaning, significance, and objectives of the Fourth Amendment's particularity requirement.

According to the Court,

> [t]he Fourth Amendment states unambiguously that "no Warrants shall issue, but upon probable cause, supported by Oath or affirmation, and *particularly describing* the place to be searched, and *the persons or things to be seized*." (Emphasis added.) The warrant in this case complied with the first three of these requirements: it was based on probable cause, supported by a sworn affidavit, and it described particularly the place of the search. On the fourth requirement, however, the warrant failed altogether. . . .

> The fact that the *application* adequately described the "things to be seized" does not save the *warrant* from its facial invalidity. The Fourth Amendment by its terms requires particularity in the warrant, not in the supporting documents. And for good reason: "The presence of a search warrant serves a high function," *McDonald v. United States*, 335 U.S. 451, 455 (1948), and that high function is not necessarily vindicated when some other document, somewhere, says something about the objects of the search, but the contents of that document are neither known to the person whose home is being searched nor available for her inspection. We do not say that the Fourth Amendment forbids a warrant from cross-referencing other documents. Indeed, most Courts of Appeals have held that a court may construe a warrant with reference to a supporting application or affidavit if the warrant uses appropriate words of incorporation, and if the supporting document accompanies the warrant. But in this case the warrant did not incorporate other documents by reference, nor did either the affidavit or the application . . . accompany the warrant.

Groh argued that even though the warrant was invalid, the search itself was still reasonable considering the particular circumstances of the case. The Court disagreed because

> [the] warrant did not simply omit a few items from a list of many to be seized, or misdescribe a few of several items. Nor did it make what fairly could be characterized as a mere technical mistake or typographical error. Rather, in the space set aside for a description of the items to be seized, the warrant stated that the items consisted of a "single dwelling residence . . . blue in color." In other words, the warrant did not describe the items to be seized *at all*. In this respect the warrant was so obviously deficient that we must regard the search as "warrantless" within the meaning of our case law.

After reciting the "firmly established" principle that warrantless searches of homes are presumptively unreasonable, the Court stated that it had "clearly stated that the presumptive rule against warrantless searches applies with equal force to searches whose only defect is a lack of particularity in the warrant." In response to Groh's contention that "a search conducted pursuant to a warrant lacking particularity should be exempt from the presumption of unreasonableness if the goals served by the particularity requirement are otherwise satisfied," the Court asserted that unless the particular items described in the affidavit are also set forth in the warrant itself (or at least incorporated by reference, and the affidavit present at the search), there can be no written assurance that the Magistrate actually found probable cause to search for, and to seize, every item mentioned in the affidavit. . . .

We have long held, moreover, that the purpose of the particularity requirement is not limited to the prevention of general searches. A particular warrant also "assures the individual whose property is searched or seized of the lawful authority of the executing officer, his need to search, and the limits of his power to search." *United States v. Chadwick*, 433 U.S. 1, 9 (1977).

The Court concluded that

[i]t is incumbent on the officer executing a search warrant to ensure the search is lawfully authorized and lawfully conducted. Because [Groh] did not have in his possession a warrant particularly describing the things he intended to seize, proceeding with the search was "unreasonable" under the Fourth Amendment.

(2) "Particularity" is a matter of degree. How particular must a warrant description be to satisfy the constitutional command? Suppose police officers sought and secured a warrant to search for "property stolen [on a specified date] during a burglary of the Ace Department Store on State Street." That description would appear to be as particular as "other fruits, instrumentalities and evidence of crime at this [time] unknown," the warrant description that the *Andresen* Court found constitutional. Is the hypothetical search warrant distinguishable? How?

(3) One issue that has troubled lower courts is whether a search warrant that contains both sufficiently particular and too general sections should be treated as "severable" and, therefore, partially valid, or should be considered wholly invalid due to the general portion. The Supreme Court has yet to confront the question. Which approach seems more consistent with the Warrant Clause? *See United States v. Kow*, 58 F.3d 423 (9th Cir. 1995); *United States v. Brown*, 984 F.2d 1074 (10th Cir. 1993); *United States v. George*, 975 F.2d 72 (2d Cir. 1992).

(4) In *Maryland v. Garrison*, 480 U.S. 79, 107 S. Ct. 1013, 94 L. Ed. 2d 72 (1987), the Court addressed issues raised by a search warrant that was mistaken or ambiguous in its description of the place to be searched. The warrant in the case, which *was* supported by probable cause, authorized the search of Mr. "McWebb and 'the premises known as 2036 Park Avenue, third floor apartment.'" Both at the time they obtained the warrant and at the time of its execution, the police mistakenly believed that the third floor of the building described contained only one apartment. Consequently, in executing the warrant, they searched throughout the third floor. In fact, there were two separate apartments on the third floor, McWebb's and Garrison's. By the time officers realized that was the case, however, they had already entered Garrison's apartment and discovered contraband.

Garrison challenged the search of his apartment pursuant to the warrant, contending that it violated the Fourth Amendment. The "two separate constitutional issues" were whether the warrant was *valid when issued* and whether it was *executed in a reasonable manner*. With regard to the validity of the warrant, the Court found no violation of the particularity or probable cause requirements. The Court acknowledged that the warrant's description of the place to be searched turned out to be "broader than appropriate because it was based on the mistaken belief that there was only one apartment on the third floor," but asserted that "the discovery of facts demonstrating that a valid warrant was unnecessarily broad does not retroactively invalidate [a] warrant." Instead, a warrant's validity "must be assessed on the basis of the information that ... officers disclosed, or had a duty to discover and to disclose, to the issuing Magistrate." If the officers in *Garrison* "had known, or even if they should have known, that there were two separate dwelling units on the third floor," the warrant they obtained would not have been valid. However, because their mistaken belief about the configuration of the third floor was reasonable, "the warrant, insofar as it authorized a search that turned out to be ambiguous in scope, was valid when it issued."

As for the execution of the warrant, if "the officers had known, or should have known, that the third floor contained two apartments before they entered [Garrison's apartment], and thus had been aware of the error in the warrant, they would have been obligated to limit their search to McWebb's apartment." In general, officers' conduct must be judged "based on the information available" to them at the time they act, and it is necessary "to allow some latitude for honest mistakes" in executing warrants. In this case, "the validity of the search of [Garrison's] apartment pursuant to a warrant authorizing the search of the entire third floor depend[ed] on whether the officers' failure to realize the overbreadth of the warrant was objectively understandable and reasonable. Here it unquestionably was" because the "objective facts available to the officers at the time suggested no distinction between McWebb's apartment and the third-floor premises." Moreover, "even if the warrant" were to be read "as authorizing a search limited to McWebb's apartment rather than the entire third floor," the entry of Garrison's apartment was reasonable because at the time of that entry, the officers "perceived McWebb's apartment and the third-floor premises as one and the same." In sum, "[u]nder either interpretation of the warrant, the officers' conduct was consistent with a reasonable effort to ascertain and identify the place intended to be searched within the meaning of the Fourth Amendment."

Justice Blackmun authored a dissent that was joined by Justices Brennan and Marshall. He suggested that because the search authorized by the warrant was limited to McWebb's apartment, the search of Garrison's apartment "was warrantless and ... presumed unreasonable." To Justice Blackmun, it did not make "sense to excuse a reasonable mistake" when the victim of an error is someone whom officers have no probable cause to arrest or search. Moreover, he found it "questionable whether" the officers' mistaken belief about the third floor in this case was "reasonable" either at the time the warrant was secured or at the time it was executed. Thus, "even if a reasonable error on the part of police officers prevents a Fourth Amendment violation, the mistakes here, both with respect to obtaining and executing the warrant, [were] not reasonable and could easily have been avoided."

(5) One requirement that is not specified in the text of the Fourth Amendment, but that is critical to the validity of warrants, according to the Court, is the "neutral and detached magistrate" demand. The individual who issues warrants must be "neutral" — that is, not biased or partial toward the approval of a warrant application. Consequently, in *Connally v. Georgia*, 429 U.S. 245, 97 S. Ct. 546, 50 L. Ed. 2d 444 (1977), the Court held that a magistrate who received five dollars for issuing a warrant, but no compensation for refusing to issue a warrant, was not constitutionally qualified. The individual must also be "detached," that is, not affiliated with law enforcement. Therefore, in *Coolidge v. New Hampshire*, 403 U.S. 443, 91 S. Ct. 2022, 29 L. Ed. 2d 564 (1971), the Court declared a warrant issued by a state Attorney General in his capacity as a "justice of the peace" to be unconstitutional.

Finally, while individuals charged with the issuance of warrants need not be trained lawyers, according to *Shadwick v. City of Tampa*, 407 U.S. 345, 92 S. Ct. 2119, 32 L. Ed. 2d 783 (1972), they "must be capable of determining whether probable cause exists for the arrest or search." In *Shadwick*, the Court sustained a scheme in which municipal court clerks were authorized to issue arrest warrants for violations of city ordinances. The Court observed that it had not been shown that the tasks entrusted to the clerks were "too difficult . . . for a clerk to accomplish. Our legal system has long entrusted nonlawyers to evaluate more complex and significant factual data . . . ." To what sorts of evaluations was the Court referring?

Wilson v. Arkansas

United States Supreme Court

514 U.S. 927, 115 S. Ct. 1914, 131 L. Ed. 2d 976 (1995)

Mr. Justice Thomas delivered the opinion of the Court.

At the time of the framing, the common law of search and seizure recognized a law enforcement officer's authority to break open the doors of a dwelling, but generally indicated that he first ought to announce his presence and authority. In this case, we hold that this common-law "knock and announce" principle forms a part of the reasonableness inquiry under the Fourth Amendment.

I

During November and December 1992, petitioner Sharlene Wilson made a series of narcotics sales to an informant acting at the direction of the Arkansas State Police. In late November, the informant purchased marijuana and methamphetamine at the home that petitioner shared with Bryson Jacobs. On December 30, the informant telephoned petitioner at her home and arranged to meet her at a local store to buy some marijuana. According to testimony presented below, petitioner produced a semiautomatic pistol at this meeting and waved it in the informant's face, threatening to kill her if she turned out to be working for the police. Petitioner then sold the informant a bag of marijuana.

The next day, police officers applied for and obtained warrants to search petitioner's home and to arrest both petitioner and Jacobs. Affidavits filed in support of the warrants set forth the details of the narcotics transactions and stated that Jacobs had previously been convicted of arson and firebombing. The search was conducted later that afternoon. Police officers found the main door to petitioner's home open. While opening an unlocked screen door and entering the residence, they identified themselves as police officers and stated that they had a warrant. Once inside the home, the officers seized marijuana, methamphetamine, valium, narcotics paraphernalia, a gun, and ammunition. They also found petitioner in the bathroom, flushing marijuana down the toilet. Petitioner and Jacobs were arrested and charged with delivery of marijuana, delivery of methamphetamine, possession of drug paraphernalia, and possession of marijuana.

Before trial, petitioner filed a motion to suppress the evidence seized during the search. Petitioner asserted that the search was invalid on various grounds, including that the officers had failed to "knock and announce" before entering her home. The trial court summarily denied the suppression motion. After a jury trial, petitioner was convicted of all charges and sentenced to 32 years in prison.

The Arkansas Supreme Court affirmed petitioner's conviction on appeal. 317 Ark. 548, 878 S.W.2d 755 (1994). The court noted that "the officers entered the home *while they were identifying themselves*," but it rejected petitioner's argument that "the Fourth Amendment requires officers to knock and announce prior to entering the residence." *Id.*, at 553, 878 S.W.2d, at 758 . . . .

II

The Fourth Amendment to the Constitution protects "[t]he right of the people to be secure in their persons, houses, papers, and effects, against unreasonable searches and seizures." In evaluating the scope of this right, we have looked to the traditional protections against unreasonable searches and seizures afforded by the common law at the time of the framing. "Although the underlying command of the Fourth Amendment is always that searches and seizures be reasonable," *New Jersey v. T.L.O.*, 469 U.S. 325, 337, 105 S. Ct. 733, 83 L. Ed. 2d 720 (1985), our effort to give content to this term may be guided by the meaning ascribed to it by the Framers of the Amendment. An examination of the common law of search and seizure leaves no doubt that the reasonableness of a search of a dwelling may depend in part on whether law enforcement officers announced their presence and authority prior to entering.

Although the common law generally protected a man's house as "his castle of defence and asylum," 3 W. Blackstone, COMMENTARIES *288 (hereinafter Blackstone), common-law courts long have held that "when the King is party, the sheriff (if the doors be not open) may break the party's house, either to arrest him, or to do other execution of the K[ing]'s process, if otherwise he cannot enter." *Semayne's*

Case, 5 Co. Rep. 91a, 91b, 77 Eng. Rep. 194, 195 (K.B. 1603). To this rule, however, common-law courts appended an important qualification:

> But before he breaks it, he ought to signify the cause of his coming, and to make request to open doors . . . , for the law without a default in the owner abhors the destruction or breaking of any house (which is for the habitation and safety of man) by which great damage and inconvenience might ensue to the party, when no default is in him; for perhaps he did not know of the process, of which, if he had notice, it is to be presumed that he would obey it. . . . *Ibid.*, 77 Eng. Rep., at 195–196.

Several prominent founding-era commentators agreed on this basic principle. . . .

The common-law knock-and-announce principle was woven quickly into the fabric of early American law. Most of the States that ratified the Fourth Amendment had enacted constitutional provisions or statutes generally incorporating English common law, and a few States had enacted statutes specifically embracing the common-law view that the breaking of the door of a dwelling was permitted once admittance was refused. Early American courts similarly embraced the common-law knock-and-announce principle.

Our own cases have acknowledged that the common-law principle of announcement is "embedded in Anglo-American law," *Miller v. United States*, 357 U.S. 301, 313, 78 S. Ct. 1190, 2 L. Ed. 2d 1332 (1958), but we have never squarely held that this principle is an element of the reasonableness inquiry under the Fourth Amendment. We now so hold. Given the longstanding common-law endorsement of the practice of announcement, we have little doubt that the Framers of the Fourth Amendment thought that the method of an officer's entry into a dwelling was among the factors to be considered in assessing the reasonableness of a search or seizure. Contrary to the decision below, we hold that in some circumstances an officer's unannounced entry into a home might be unreasonable under the Fourth Amendment.

This is not to say, of course, that every entry must be preceded by an announcement. The Fourth Amendment's flexible requirement of reasonableness should not be read to mandate a rigid rule of announcement that ignores countervailing law enforcement interests. As even petitioner concedes, the common-law principle of announcement was never stated as an inflexible rule requiring announcement under all circumstances.

Indeed, at the time of the framing, the common-law admonition that an officer "ought to signify the cause of his coming," *Semayne's Case*, 5 Co. Rep., at 91b, 77 Eng. Rep., at 195, had not been extended conclusively to the context of felony arrests. The common-law principle gradually was applied to cases involving felonies, but at the same time the courts continued to recognize that under certain circumstances the presumption in favor of announcement necessarily would give way to contrary considerations.

Thus, because the common-law rule was justified in part by the belief that announcement generally would avoid "the destruction or breaking of any house . . . by which great damage and inconvenience might ensue," *Semayne's Case, supra,* at 91b, 77 Eng. Rep., at 196, courts acknowledged that the presumption in favor of announcement would yield under circumstances presenting a threat of physical violence. Similarly, courts held that an officer may dispense with announcement in cases where a prisoner escapes from him and retreats to his dwelling. Proof of "demand and refusal" was deemed unnecessary in such cases because it would be a "senseless ceremony" to require an officer in pursuit of a recently escaped arrestee to make an announcement prior to breaking the door to retake him. Finally, courts have indicated that unannounced entry may be justified where police officers have reason to believe that evidence would likely be destroyed if advance notice were given.

We need not attempt a comprehensive catalog of the relevant countervailing factors here. For now, we leave to the lower courts the task of determining the circumstances under which an unannounced entry is reasonable under the Fourth Amendment. We simply hold that although a search or seizure of a dwelling might be constitutionally defective if police officers enter without prior announcement, law enforcement interests may also establish the reasonableness of an unannounced entry.

III

Respondent contends that the judgment below should be affirmed because the unannounced entry in this case was justified for two reasons. First, respondent argues that police officers reasonably believed that a prior announcement would have placed them in peril, given their knowledge that petitioner had threatened a government informant with a semiautomatic weapon and that Mr. Jacobs had previously been convicted of arson and firebombing. Second, respondent suggests that prior announcement would have produced an unreasonable risk that petitioner would destroy easily disposable narcotics evidence.

These considerations may well provide the necessary justification for the unannounced entry in this case. Because the Arkansas Supreme Court did not address their sufficiency, however, we remand to allow the state courts to make any necessary findings of fact and to make the determination of reasonableness in the first instance. The judgment of the Arkansas Supreme Court is reversed, and the case is remanded for further proceedings not inconsistent with this opinion.

It is so ordered.

Notes and Questions

(1) The *Wilson* Court concluded that the "common-law 'knock and announce' principle forms a part of the reasonableness inquiry under the Fourth Amendment." That conclusion led the Court to "hold that *in some circumstances* an officer's unannounced entry into a home *might be unreasonable* under the Fourth Amendment." (Emphasis added.)

(a) What are those circumstances? If an officer cannot furnish a reason for failing to knock and announce, will an unannounced entry ever be reasonable?

(b) What must an officer do to comply with the "knock and announce" principle? How long must he or she wait for a response before entering a home?

(2) If knocking and announcing can increase the dangers to police officers and can enhance the likelihood that occupants will take actions that frustrate the very purposes of the search anticipated by a warrant, why did the Court conclude that the knock and announce principle is implicit in the Fourth Amendment's text?

(3) Are there general categories of cases that justify exemption from the knock and announce requirement? For example, may officers always enter unannounced in cases that involve easily disposable or destructible contraband such as narcotics?

In *Richards v. Wisconsin*, 520 U.S. 385, 117 S. Ct. 1416, 137 L. Ed. 2d 615 (1997), the Court resolved that question.

In *Richards*, the Wisconsin Supreme Court upheld an unannounced entry based on its conclusion that police officers never need to knock and announce their presence when executing a search warrant in a felony drug investigation. The court reasoned that the danger to officers and threat of contraband destruction present in such cases justified a *per se*, categorical exception to the knock and announce rule.

The Supreme Court disagreed. According to the Court, "creating exceptions to the knock-and-announce rule based on the 'culture' surrounding a general category of criminal behavior presents at least two serious concerns. First, the exception contains considerable overgeneralization. . . . [Second,] the reasons for creating an exception in one category can, relatively easily, be applied to others. If a *per se* exception were allowed for each category of criminal investigation that included a considerable — albeit hypothetical — risk of danger to officers or destruction of evidence, the knock-and-announce element of the Fourth Amendment's reasonableness requirement would be meaningless."

"Thus, the fact that felony drug investigations may frequently present circumstances warranting a no-knock entry cannot remove from the neutral scrutiny of a reviewing court the reasonableness of the police decision not to knock and announce in a particular case. Instead, in each case, it is the duty of a court confronted with the question to determine whether the facts and circumstances of the particular entry justified dispensing with the knock-and-announce requirement."

(a) *What kinds* of dangers justify "dispensing with the knock-and-announce requirement"? *How likely* must it be that the danger will come to pass if announcement is given? According to the *Richards* Court, "[i]n order to justify a 'no-knock' entry, the police must have a *reasonable suspicion* that knocking and announcing their presence, under the particular circumstances, would be *dangerous or futile*, or that it would *inhibit the effective investigation of the crime* by, for example, allowing the destruction of evidence. This standard — as opposed to a probable cause requirement — strikes the appropriate balance between the legitimate law enforcement concerns at issue in the execution of search warrants and the individual privacy interests affected by no-knock entries. This showing is not high, but the police should be required to make it whenever the reasonableness of a no-knock entry is challenged." For further discussion of the nature and meaning of a "reasonable suspicion" and how it is different from probable cause, see, *infra*, Chapter 5, section [A][3].

(b) May a magistrate issue a search warrant that authorizes officers to enter a dwelling without knocking and announcing? On that question, the *Richards* Court observed that "[a] number of States give magistrate judges the authority to issue 'no-knock' warrants if the officers demonstrate ahead of time a reasonable suspicion that entry without prior announcement will be appropriate in a particular context. The practice of allowing magistrates to issue no-knock warrants seems entirely reasonable when sufficient cause to do so can be demonstrated ahead of time."

(4) In *United States v. Ramirez*, 523 U.S. 65, 118 S. Ct. 992, 140 L. Ed. 2d 191 (1998), the Court addressed the question of whether the "reasonable suspicion" standard that the *Richards* Court announced for "no-knock" entries applies when the entry results in the destruction of property. Without knocking and announcing, the officers in *Ramirez* broke a window in the defendant's garage. The Ninth Circuit held that a "heightened standard" governs unannounced entries "when property is destroyed" and that the heightened "standard had not been met on the facts of this case."

The Supreme Court rejected the Ninth Circuit's refinement of the knock and announce doctrine. According to the unanimous Court,

> Neither [*Wilson* nor *Richards*] explicitly addressed the question whether the lawfulness of a no-knock entry depends on whether property is damaged in the course of the entry. It is obvious from their holdings, however, that it does not. Under *Richards*, a no-knock entry is justified if police have a "reasonable suspicion" that knocking and announcing would be dangerous, futile, or destructive to the purposes of the investigation. Whether such a "reasonable suspicion" exists depends in no way on whether police must destroy property in order to enter. This is not to say that the Fourth Amendment speaks not at all to the manner of executing a search warrant. The general touchstone of reasonableness which governs Fourth Amendment analysis governs the method of execution of the warrant. *Excessive or unnecessary destruction of property* in the course of a search *may violate the Fourth Amendment, even though the entry itself is lawful and the fruits of the search are not subject to suppression.* (Emphasis added.)

In other words, an unannounced entry is permissible based on a "reasonable suspicion," and the constitutionality of the entry is not altered by the fact that property was damaged or destroyed during the entry. Consequently, anything found during a subsequent search is lawfully obtained. The "seizure" involved in damaging or destroying property during a "no-knock" entry could, however, be constitutionally unreasonable and could support a claim for damages.

(5) The Court discussed the knock and announce requirement once again in *United States v. Banks*, 540 U.S. 31, 124 S. Ct. 521, 157 L. Ed. 2d 343 (2003). Armed with a search warrant for cocaine, officers arrived at Banks's two-bedroom apartment at two o'clock on a weekday afternoon. They called out "police search warrant" and rapped hard on the front door. After waiting "15 to 20 seconds," and with "no indication whether anyone was home," the officers "broke open the front door with a battering ram." Banks, who was in the shower, heard "the crash of the door" and emerged "dripping to confront the police." A search of his apartment produced contraband. A trial judge denied Banks's motion to suppress, but the Court of Appeals reversed in an opinion specifying eight factors that officers should consider in deciding when to enter premises "after knocking and announcing." The appellate court also delineated "four categories of intrusion following knock and announcement," concluding that different standards of reasonableness applied to each category. Because the forced entry in *Banks* was not based on exigent circumstances, required the destruction of property, and did not follow an explicit refusal of admittance, the officers' 15 to 20 second delay was deemed constitutionally insufficient.

The Supreme Court unanimously reversed, pointedly rejecting the categorical scheme devised by the Court of Appeals and emphasizing that the reasonableness of warrant execution must be determined "case by case" based on "the totality of circumstances." The Court observed that it had previously decided that the obligation to knock and announce "gives way" when officers have a "reasonable suspicion of exigency or futility." It had also previously ruled that officers "may damage premises so far as necessary for a no-knock entrance without demonstrating the suspected risk in any more detail than the law demands" for an unannounced entry involving no property damage. The *Banks* Court made it clear that the identical "reasonable suspicion" standard dictates whether officers are exempt from the ordinary obligation to wait before entering premises *following* a knock and announcement.

Conceding that *Banks* was a "close" case, the Court agreed with the government's contention "that after 15 to 20 seconds without a response, police could fairly suspect" that the cocaine would be disposed of "if they were reticent any longer." This reasonable suspicion of exigency was supported by the assumption that "a prudent dealer will keep [contraband] near a commode or kitchen sink," the fact that police arrived "during the day when anyone inside would probably have been up and around," and "the sufficiency of 15 to 20 seconds for getting to the bathroom or the kitchen to start flushing cocaine down the drain." The fact that Banks was actually in the shower was irrelevant because "the facts known to the police are what count in judging reasonable waiting time," and there was "no indication that the police knew that Banks was in the shower." In sum, "15 to 20 seconds [did] not seem an unrealistic guess about the time someone would need to get in a position to rid his quarters of cocaine. Once the exigency matured, . . . the officers were not bound to learn anything more or wait any longer before going in."

Two general observations in *Banks* further illuminate the knock and announce rule. *First*, the Court indicated that when officers justify an entry after a knock and announcement on the ground that an occupant's "failure to admit them fairly suggested a refusal to let them in," the reasonableness of suspecting refusal turns on whether "an occupant has had time to get to the door." The Court noted that the time needed to respond "will vary with the size of the establishment, perhaps five seconds to open a motel room door, or several minutes to move through a townhouse," and added that 15 seconds probably is adequate time to "walk the length" of a "small apartment." *Second*, the Court asserted that the need to damage property in order to enter premises *does* play a role in assessing the reasonableness of entry in cases "with no reason to suspect an immediate risk of frustration or futility in waiting at all." In those cases, "the reasonable wait time may well be longer when the police make a forced entry, since they ought to be more certain the occupant has had time to answer the door. . . . Suffice it to say that the need to damage property in the course of getting in is a good reason to require more patience than it would be reasonable to expect if the door were open. Police seeking a stolen piano may be able to spend more time to make sure they really need the battering ram."

(6) For a recent, significant opinion discussing whether the exclusionary rule is applicable to evidence found in a home after officers enter in violation of the Fourth Amendment knock and announce, see *Hudson v. Michigan*, 547 U.S. 586, 126 S. Ct. 2159, 165 L. Ed. 2d 56 (2006), *infra* Chapter 13, subsection [C].

(7) Although a warrant is valid, the "execution" of the warrant might also be unreasonable because officers have exceeded the "scope" of their authority under the warrant. For example, a warrant to search a home for a stolen computer authorizes a search of places within the home where the computer could be found. Searches of places that are too small to contain the computer are unreasonable because the privacy invasions entailed in those searches are not justified under the terms of the warrant.

Officers can also exceed the scope of their authority under a properly issued warrant by permitting other individuals to accompany them during a search. In *Wilson v. Layne*, 526 U.S. 603, 119 S. Ct. 1692, 143 L. Ed. 2d 818 (1999), "police officers invited representatives of the media to accompany them" while they were "executing an arrest warrant in a private home." The Court unanimously held that "such a 'media ride-along' does violate the Fourth Amendment."

Wilson involved a federal operation known as "'Operation Gunsmoke,' a special national fugitive apprehension program." Acting pursuant to this program, officers identified Dominic Wilson as a potential target. Wilson, who had violated probation, was considered likely to be armed, to resist arrest, and to assault the police. The officers secured three arrest warrants for Wilson based on his probation violations. Although the officers did not know it, the address for Wilson specified in computer records was actually the home of his parents.

In the early morning hours, a team of federal and state officers, accompanied by a reporter and a photographer from the Washington Post, who had been invited to accompany the officers as part of a "ride-along policy," entered the home of Charles and Geraldine Wilson, Dominic Wilson's parents. Upon hearing the entry, Charles Wilson, who was dressed only in a pair of briefs, got out of bed and went into the living room to investigate. He angrily demanded that the officers state their business. Believing that he was Dominic, the officers subdued Charles. Geraldine, who was wearing only a nightgown, entered at that point and saw armed officers restraining her husband. Upon completing a protective sweep and learning that Dominic was not present, the officers left. During the search, the photographer took numerous pictures, but none were published by the Post. The print reporter observed the confrontation between Charles Wilson and the police, but neither of the media representatives took part in executing the arrest warrant. The Wilsons filed a civil suit seeking damages for violations of their Fourth Amendment rights.

The Court began by emphasizing the critical importance of home privacy. It then noted that the arrest warrant authorized the officers to enter Dominic's parents' home to search for him, but that "it does not necessarily follow that they were entitled to bring [media representatives] with them." A search that is otherwise reasonable can be rendered unconstitutional because "'the scope of the search exceeds that permitted by the terms of a validly issued warrant.'" Put simply, "the Fourth Amendment does require that police actions in execution of a warrant be related to the objectives of the authorized intrusion." It was conceded that the presence of the reporter and photographer in *Wilson* "was not related to the objectives of the authorized intrusion. . . . This [was] not a case in which the presence of the third parties directly aided in the execution of the warrant."

The defendants argued that the reporters "nonetheless served a number of legitimate law enforcement purposes." They suggested that "media ride-alongs [may] further the law enforcement objectives of the police in a general sense" and that officers should have "reasonable discretion" to decide when media presence would advance their missions. The Court concluded that if "such generalized 'law enforcement objectives' themselves [were] sufficient to trump" the important residential privacy interests at the core of the Fourth Amendment, then "that Amendment's text would be significantly watered down." Defendants also maintained that the presence of third parties could publicize government efforts to combat crime and facilitate accurate reporting on law enforcement activities. The Court replied that while First Amendment values are important, "the Fourth Amendment also protects a very important right," that "the possibility of good public relations for the police is simply not enough, standing alone, to justify the ride-along intrusion into a private home," and that "the need for accurate reporting on police issues in general bears no direct relation to the constitutional justification for the police intrusion into a home in order to execute a felony arrest warrant."

Finally, the defendants contended that media presence could serve "to minimize police abuses and protect suspects, and also to protect the safety of officers." The Court responded by noting that the media representatives were not present in this case to serve those interests, but, rather, were present for "private purposes." Thus, "although the presence of third parties during the execution of a warrant may in some circumstances be constitutionally permissible, the presence of *these* third parties was not."

In sum, the Court held "that it is a violation of the Fourth Amendment for police to bring members of the media or other third parties into a home during the execution of a warrant when the presence of the third parties in the home [is] not in aid of the execution of the warrant." In such cases, if the warrant is valid, the presence of the police is lawful, but the Fourth Amendment is violated by the presence of the media.

Warrant Problems

3–1: Arnold was under surveillance by the Drug Enforcement Administration (DEA) after making a controlled sale of cocaine to a police informant. The day of Arnold's arrest, the agents had reason to believe that he would participate in another drug deal that evening. When they saw him leave his mobile home at 6:30 p.m. in a tan Hummer, they alerted the local sheriff. A deputy stopped the Hummer for a traffic violation. Arnold unsuccessfully fled. Marijuana was in plain view and the ensuing search of the Hummer uncovered nine ounces of cocaine.

One hour later, several law enforcement officers returned to Arnold's residence for an investigative "knock and talk." They knocked on the front door of the mobile home and announced themselves. They received no verbal response. Instead, they saw an occupant look at them through the window, watched that person retreat, and heard several persons "scuffling" and moving hurriedly inside toward the back of the residence. The officers quickly concluded that the occupants were likely destroying drugs and other evidence of narcotics. The officers immediately entered the home. During their protective sweep of the residence they found marijuana and drug paraphernalia in plain sight, as well as several plastic baggies floating in the toilet in a bathroom towards the back of the residence. The toilet bowl's water was still rotating from a recent flush.

The officers detained Aggie, who was not a resident, but had been a guest in the mobile home for 10 days. DEA Special Agent David applied for a warrant to search the mobile home. All of the information in the affidavit filed in support of the warrant application was known before the officers entered the mobile home. Specifically, the affidavit recited that Arnold had been under surveillance by the DEA and had been arrested for carrying "substantial amounts of cocaine" and marijuana in his car immediately after leaving his residence. It stated that Agent David's experience as an investigator had confirmed that drug dealers are likely to keep records of their trafficking activities in their homes. The magistrate issued a warrant authorizing a search of the mobile home for illegal narcotics and paraphernalia and for various items "used to facilitate drug sales and trafficking, including records, sales and/or purchase invoices, and financial records including books, records, correspondence, and documentation evidencing the acquisition, concealment, transfer and expenditure of money or assets." The warrant authorized the search of "personal papers, including address books and telephone directories, and personal assets including computers, disks, printers and monitors utilized in the drug trafficking operation."

With this warrant in hand, officers searched the mobile home, finding cocaine, marijuana, six marijuana pipes, three grinders, three digital scales, 14 cell phones, one shotgun, and one revolver. Aggie's cell phone, which was lying on her bed, was among the phones seized. It was protected by a password. When asked for the password, Aggie provided it. A search of the text messages on the cell phone uncovered several communications discussing "white" and "green," terms believed to refer to cocaine and marijuana, respectively.

Aggie moved to suppress all evidence obtained in the search of the mobile home, including her cell phone and its incriminating text messages. The judge ruled that the search of the home and the phone were constitutional. Aggie has appealed.

Should the trial court's rulings regarding the search of the home and Aggie's cell phone be reversed?

3–2: On a Friday morning, Susan Hallstrom's vehicle was stopped by an officer of the Garden City Police Department for a broken taillight. When she refused to show her license or proof of liability insurance coverage, she was arrested and taken to jail.

While in custody, she was cited for motor vehicle violations. She repeatedly requested presentation to a magistrate and refused to answer routine booking questions or submit to routine booking procedures. She repeatedly and consistently refused to supply satisfactory evidence of her identity. She was taken before a judicial officer on Monday afternoon, at which time she was arraigned before a state court judge and released on bail.

Hallstrom sued the County, the Sheriff, and the Jail Commander, claiming that they had violated her constitutional rights.

Is there merit to Hallstrom's claim?

3–3: On October 29, Officer Brandon of the Hillville Police Department went to the home Logan shared with his mother to serve her with a notice against trespass and harassment. While lawfully inside the home, Officer Brandon saw "three long guns" near a staircase. He was aware that Logan's mother was a convicted felon and, thus, was prohibited by state law from possessing a variety of weapons, including any "firearm." Brandon proceeded to apply for a warrant to search the home. In his affidavit in support of the application, he described the guns he had seen as follows:

> One appeared to be a shotgun with a dark colored stock, possibly a single shot. I did not observe a packing rod under the barrel indicating it was a black powder rifle and it appeared to have a chamber. Another appeared to be a .22 caliber with a wooden stock. The barrel on the rifle appeared to be too large to be a pellet gun and was longer than any pellet guns I recall ever seeing.

The magistrate issued a warrant authorizing the police to search Logan's home for "firearms." On October 31, three officers, including Brandon, searched the home pursuant to the warrant. Not long after beginning their search, the officers learned that the three guns near the staircase were, in fact, "BB" guns. It was not unlawful for Logan's mother to possess BB guns because they do not qualify as "firearms" under the state law that prohibits convicted felons from possessing weapons. The officers continued to search, asking Logan whether there were "any additional guns in the house." Logan stated that he had a "muzzle loader rifle," then took the officer to his bedroom to show it to them. While in the room, Brandon observed a lock box large enough to contain a handgun, but too small to contain a long gun. He told Logan to unlock it, stating that the officers would open it by force if necessary. Logan protested, asserting that the police had no reason or authority to look in the box. When officers insisted, Logan unlocked the box. The officers opened it, finding cocaine inside.

The trial court denied Logan's motion to suppress the contraband, and, after a bench trial, convicted him of cocaine possession. Logan has appealed, claiming the search violated his Fourth Amendment rights.

Does Logan have a valid claim?

3–4: Police Officers in Davenport received a tip that Terry Rodriguez was trafficking in controlled substances. They placed Rodriguez's residence under surveillance. A couple of days later, a police informer purchased cocaine at the residence as part of a "controlled buy."

Within 48 hours of the buy, officers submitted a sworn warrant application reciting the facts surrounding the buy. They also asserted that, two years previously, Rodriguez had been charged with possession with intent to distribute cocaine and that he had associated with well-known drug dealers. The judge issued a warrant authorizing a search of the Rodriguez premises and of "the persons and vehicles of any other subjects at the residence after the signing of the search warrant."

Almost immediately after the warrant was signed, officers conducting surveillance at the residence were notified by phone and radio that it had been issued. They maintained a log of vehicles stopping by the house after the warrant was issued. The first car to do so eluded pursuing officers. One hour after issuance of the warrant, Jamie's car became the second to arrive. He entered the house and left seven minutes later. Officers stopped him a few blocks away and found cocaine in a specially folded wrapper cut from a travel magazine later found at the Rodriguez residence.

Jamie moved to suppress the narcotics from his trial.

What arguments should Jamie make in support of his motion? Should the trial court suppress the narcotics?

3–5: Undercover officers learned that Perr had substantial libraries of "kiddie porn" in California and Seattle. A Seattle vice detective applied for a search warrant for Perr's residence based on an affidavit in which he averred that California officers had viewed 17 of 82 films obtained from Perr. Nine of the films were described. Five showed children in sexually explicit activity, and four showed adult females involved in sexual bestiality. Although possession of materials depicting children under the age of 16 engaged in "sexually explicit conduct" is unlawful, possession of adult pornography, pornographic drawings of adults or of children, and sexual paraphernalia is not unlawful.

The warrant obtained authorized the search for and seizure of: "Child or adult pornography; photographs, movies, slides, videotapes, magazines or drawings of children or adults engaged in sexual activities or sexually suggestive poses; correspondence or papers with names, addresses, and phone numbers which tend to identify any juvenile; camera equipment, video equipment, and sexual paraphernalia; records of safe deposit boxes and storage facilities; computer hardware and software used to store mailing list information or other information on juveniles; papers of dominion and control establishing the identity of the person in control of the premises; and correspondence or papers which tend to identify other pedophiles."

Execution of the warrant resulted in the seizure of 197 films, numerous books and magazines, and projection equipment. Some of the films depicted children under the age of 16 engaged in sexual conduct. Twelve of the magazines seized depicted children under 16 years of age engaging in sexual acts.

Perr challenged the search of his home, claiming that the warrant was constitutionally infirm.

What bases are there for Perr's contention? How should the state respond? Was the search constitutional?

3–6: Based on Deputy Wolf's affidavit stating that marijuana stems, seeds, and particles had been retrieved from Terry's garbage, a magistrate issued a search warrant for Terry's apartment, unit #5 at 729 Timberline Trail. Deputy Wolf and Officer Boudry, accompanied by a drug-detecting dog, went to the apartment, knocked, and were admitted by Terry's son. In the hallway of the apartment, the officers encountered Andy, a friend of Terry who had been studying with her in the master bedroom. Andy informed the officers that he did not live at the apartment and that he owned a duffel bag which was in the master bedroom. The officers told him to wait at the dinette table while they searched the apartment.

Officer Boudry took the dog to the master bedroom. When the canine reacted positively to the duffel bag found in the room, Deputy Wolf opened and searched it. Underneath notebooks and papers, he found a large plastic bag with smaller baggies of marijuana inside. He also found a hand-held scale and other drug paraphernalia. When he opened the duffel bag, Deputy Wolf believed that it belonged to Terry. A few minutes later, however, other officers told Deputy Wolf that it belonged to Andy. At that point, Wolf arrested Andy for possession of a controlled substance.

Did the search of Andy's duffel bag violate the Fourth Amendment?

3–7: Detective Hart prepared a six-page, typewritten affidavit in support of an application for a warrant to search Michael Gal's residence. In the affidavit, Hart outlined his investigation into a conspiracy to murder Barl and Pay, two security supervisors at "Angel Incorporated." Hart asserted that specified individuals employed by Angel had informed him that Gal and Byron Doro, two security guards at Angel, planned to use explosives at the Angel facility and had specifically threatened to shoot Barl and Pay; that Gal had claimed to have used explosives in the past and claimed to have an AK-47 high-powered rifle, an AR-15 rifle, and a Beretta handgun; that Gal had explained to others how to make a bomb; that Angel supervisors had found a five-page computer printout in Doro's paperwork box that contained Barl's address, detailed directions to Barl's residence, multiple references to AR-15 and AK-47 rifles and other weapons, and laudatory comments about the mass shooting at Columbine High School; that the printout was addressed to "Mike"; that Gal was the only employee at Angel whose first name was "Mike"; and, finally, that Gal and Doro had expressed anger that Angel's security guards were soon to be replaced by another security service.

Based on Hart's affidavit, a magistrate issued a search warrant for Gal's residence. The warrant specifically authorized the search for and seizure of: "Any and all firearms and ammunition; any and all explosives or incendiary devices, or parts; any and all written or printed material which provides instructions or examples concerning the production or use of any firearms, ammunition, and explosive or incendiary devices or parts; any and all written or printed material which shows an intent to do physical harm or physical damage against any person or building; any documents or materials that show the occupier or possessor of the premises and vehicle."

Detective Hart executed the search warrant. He seized hundreds of written documents, two desktop model computers, and five laptop computers. When the laptop computers were determined to be stolen, Gal was charged with theft. He moved to suppress the laptops, claiming that they had been unconstitutionally seized.

Were the detective's seizures of the laptop computers constitutional?

3–8: On August 17, Kyle was walking on a sidewalk when a speeding car nearly hit him. As the car slowed at a stop sign, Kyle loudly admonished the driver. After briefly responding, the driver took off again. Kyle called the Police Department and reported that a white male with a dark complexion in a red shirt was driving a white 2008 Dodge Avenger, dealer license plate #866 M88, at 65 to 70 miles per hour in a 20 miles per hour zone. Kyle also reported that the driver appeared intoxicated because he was bobbing his head and briefly closed his eyes. Officer Bradley was dispatched and, within minutes, met Kyle near where Kyle first encountered the driver.

Kyle repeated his story, and Officers Bradley and Dollar began canvassing the neighborhood in search of the vehicle. Within five minutes, they located the vehicle in the backyard of a nearby home. When Michael answered Officer Bradley's knock on his door, Bradley explained Kyle's report regarding the vehicle in Michael's backyard. Michael accompanied Bradley to the backyard, where Bradley felt the car's hood with his hand. It was hot to the touch. Michael volunteered that the car belonged to his employer, a local car dealer, and pulled a key out of his pocket. Officer Bradley recognized it as a Dodge or Chrysler key. Officer Bradley observed that Michael had a strong odor of alcohol on his breath, his eyes were bloodshot and glassy, and his speech was "thick-tongued and slurred." Michael stated that he had been drinking earlier in the day and had just arrived home. Michael failed a "horizontal gaze field sobriety test," which the officer administered.

Officer Bradley then issued *Miranda* warnings and requested that Michael accompany him to the police station. Michael agreed but asked if he could call his wife. He explained that his teenage child, who was restricted to a wheelchair, would be left home alone if he went to the police station. Officer Bradley refused because "his wife had no bearing on the situation" and because the fact that the child was home alone while Michael was previously out of the house indicated that he was capable of staying by himself. During the ride to the police station, Michael was handcuffed. Upon arriving at the station and after another recitation of *Miranda* warnings, Officer Bradley interviewed Michael and requested that he take a breathalyzer test. The breathalyzer indicated an alcohol concentration of 0.20. Michael was subsequently charged with operating a vehicle while under the influence of alcohol, a misdemeanor.

What Fourth Amendment claims should Michael raise? How should the government respond?

3–9: On the evening of March 20, Mr. Radley was home, working on a car in his backyard with the help of an unidentified man. There were two other unidentified people in the fenced-in backyard. Mr. Radley's girlfriend was upstairs inside the house, putting their five-year-old daughter to bed.

Between eight and 16 police officers — a team trained to execute search warrants — arrived at Radley's home at 9:41 p.m. The officers wore dark paramilitary uniforms like a SWAT team and at least some of them had masks or covers over their faces. They had a warrant to search the home. Several officers were deployed to the rear of the house. They immediately confronted Mr. Radley and the unidentified man, ordering them to the ground. It is uncertain whether the officers knew at that time that one of the men was Mr. Radley or that he was a primary resident of the home.

There were two doors at the front entrance of the home. The first door was a standard wood or metal door to an enclosed porch. The second door was an iron-bar security door between the porch and living room. The officers organized an "entry team" in a line at the front of the house. The officer in charge of the team knocked and announced their presence when the officers reached the first door, yelling as loudly as he could and banging on that door. As soon as he finished this process, he instructed his fellow officers to "set off an explosive detonation device," which makes a very loud noise and produces a flash of light if set off during evening hours. He then waited about 10 seconds before ordering officers who carried a battering ram to break the door open. It took a few more seconds to break through the second door. Counting the time that the officers were actually using the battering ram to break down the two doors, the time between the initial knock and announcement and the entry through the second door was approximately 15 seconds.

When the officers entered the home, they found evidence of drugs. They also found Radley's girlfriend and daughter upstairs. There were no other occupants. Radley's girlfriend reported that she had heard the distraction device but had not heard the officer knock and announce.

Did the officers execute the search warrant in a reasonable manner?

3–10: United States Postal Inspector Carr learned that Land had filled out and mailed a questionnaire distributed by a sexually-oriented business. In the questionnaire, Land expressed an interest in child pornography — specifically mentioning incest, pedophilia, and transvestites. Land provided his name and the address of a private post office box. Three years later, Carr targeted Land in a child pornography sting operation. He mailed to Land's post office box a brochure with a picture of a young girl on a bicycle and the caption "New in Colorado!!! Not your typical Fantasy!!! Forbidden Lifestyles!!!" The brochure provided a telephone number and an email address. Within days, Land called the number and left a message indicating an interest in young girls, videotapes, magazines, and "possibly meetings." He provided the address of his post office box.

In response, Carr sent a letter to Land, thanking him for calling the "Family Affairs Hotline." The letter described sexually explicit videotapes and magazines and had an order form attached. Land filled out the order form and mailed it the next day. He requested two videotapes, enclosing a money order for $125 to pay for them. Government agents then set up surveillance of Land's post office box to determine where he went after he collected his mail. They also secured a description of Land, learned that he worked for the Colorado Department of Revenue, and ascertained his home address.

Soon thereafter, the agents applied for and secured a warrant to install a "beeper" (an electronic tracking device) in a package containing the two videotapes ordered by Land. The package was to be delivered to Land's post office box. The agents also obtained a warrant that authorized them to search Land's residence "once the package containing the videotapes is brought into the residence." The next day, the package with the videotapes and beeper was delivered to Land's post office box. At 10:30 a.m., agents saw Land pick it up and walk back to his office. As he walked, the beeper indicated the package had been opened. Land left work for lunch at one point, but the beeper indicated that the package remained inside the building.

Before Land left work, the beeper's batteries stopped functioning. Agents observed him leave his office around 4:30, carrying a backpack and plastic bag. They could not determine whether he was carrying the tapes. Land got in his car and drove off, followed by the agents. He went about six blocks, then turned around, went back to his office, parked his car, and reentered the building for a couple of minutes. He then reemerged, got into his car, and drove home. Shortly after Land entered his home, Inspector Carr and three or four police officers knocked on the front door. Land's wife came to the door, whereupon Carr identified himself and asked to speak to Land. When Land appeared, Carr asked him about the package he had received in the mail. Although Land was evasive at first, eventually he told Carr that the package was still at his office and that the videotapes were in the backpack he had brought home. The backpack was sitting four or five feet away in Land's living room. Carr displayed the warrant for the home and told Land that the officers were going to conduct a search. During the search, they found the videotapes in the backpack. They also found a number of other items in Land's home, including sexually-oriented magazines and books. Land was charged with knowingly receiving child pornography through the U.S. mail. He challenged the search of his home.

Did the search of Land's home violate the Fourth Amendment?

3–11: Larry Whitt and Rose Bourne had been romantically involved for some time, had lived together for nearly a year, and had a young child together. At the time, Bourne was married to Muhammed. Sometime after 9:15 p.m., on September 17, Bourne and Muhammed met at Riverfront Park. Bourne had driven to the park in a yellow Ford truck that was owned by her husband, and Muhammed had driven to the park in a vehicle Bourne owned. While they were at the park, Muhammed suffered three forceful blows to his head. Bourne called the County 911 Center and reported that her husband had been attacked by an unknown assailant. According to Bourne, the man had asked Muhammed for a cigarette and had then, for no apparent reason, struck him in the head with a hammer multiple times. Police officers and emergency personnel responded to the call. Muhammed was pronounced dead at the scene.

Officers transported the yellow Ford truck and Bourne's vehicle to the city maintenance garage. They then applied for and obtained a warrant to search the truck for "evidence of a crime." The warrant authorized the seizure of "any personal property . . . belonging to [Muhammed] or his wife Rose Bourne." During the search of the truck, officers found and seized a cellular telephone. They were unaware that the phone was owned by Whitt, but was being used by Bourne. Investigators searched through the contents of the telephone, finding information that led them to Whitt. They learned that he was currently in Indiana. In addition, by accessing Whitt's cellular telephone account information, they discovered that on the day of the murder there had been 59 calls between Whitt and Bourne, and that seven of those calls had occurred very close in time to the murder. Information from a cellular telephone tower indicated that at the time of Muhammed's murder Whitt was in the area of Riverfront Park.

Officers traveled to Indiana to take a statement from Whitt. During a six-hour interview, he eventually confessed to killing Muhammed by striking him in the head with a hammer enclosed in a plastic bag. A grand jury indicted Whitt and Bourne for murder in the first degree and conspiracy to commit murder in the first degree.

What Fourth Amendment claims should Whitt raise? Did officers comply with the Fourth Amendment?

3–12: Iowa City, Iowa, Police Officer Brotherton was told by Officer Billingsley in Phoenix, Arizona, that a package being shipped to Jacob via Federal Express was suspicious. Billingsley suspected the package contained drugs for the following reasons: it was well-wrapped and had been delivered to Federal Express just in time to make a shipment; the person who brought it in (not the sender) did not know the zip code for the return address; the fee was paid in cash; and Jacob allegedly was involved in drug distribution. Iowa City officers decided to inspect the package.

The next morning, a group of officers went to the Federal Express office in Iowa City to intercept the package while Brotherton went to a magistrate with a warrant application. At the Federal Express office, the package and five to seven others were isolated in a room. "Turbo," a drug detection dog, was brought in; he showed some interest in the defendant's package by pushing it around with his nose and scratching it. This behavior, however, did not amount to an alert, so the dog's handler was unsure whether the package contained drugs.

Officer Henderson called Brotherton and told him of the dog's "interest in, but failure to fully alert to," the package. Brotherton typed on the warrant application that the dog "was presented with eight different packages including the one being sent to Jacob. The canine expressed *interest* in only the package addressed to Jacob."

The police then arranged for a second dog to examine the package. That dog failed to alert or show an interest in the package. Henderson again called Brotherton in the magistrate's chambers. He learned that the warrant had already been issued. He did not tell Brotherton the results of the second sniff. Instead, he reported that a second dog had arrived and said that the team was going to wait for this dog to conduct a sniff before executing the warrant.

After they received the search warrant, the officers in possession of the package opened it. It contained cocaine. They rewrapped the package, made a "controlled delivery" to Jacob's residence, and then executed a second search warrant at the residence about 15 minutes after the delivery. The package and other evidence were recovered.

Should Jacob's challenge to the validity of the search warrant for the package be upheld? Why?

3–13: In September 1999, Keith Baran, a licensed firearms dealer, began importing machine guns from Eastern European countries. He imported the guns through a bonded customs warehouse owned by Harley Larson and located in Louisville, Kentucky. Federal law required Baran to keep the guns in the Louisville warehouse until he could sell them to eligible law enforcement departments. Instead of selling the guns to eligible buyers, however, Baran obtained forged letters of interest from a police chief located in Missouri, so that he could remove the weapons from the warehouse and could sell them illegally. Bureau of Alcohol, Tobacco and Firearms (BATF) Agent Michael Johns uncovered the scheme when he found documents in a Missouri gun dealer's shop that linked Baran to the dealer and when he learned that one of Baran's letters of interest was forged.

On April 10, 2001, Johns applied for a search warrant to allow him to search for and seize "about 425" weapons still being held by Baran at the Larson warehouse. As part of the warrant application, Johns prepared an affidavit explaining Baran's scheme, detailing the probable cause for the search, identifying the bonded section of the warehouse as the place to be searched and identifying the machine guns as the items to be seized. In the location on the search warrant provided for describing the things to be seized, the warrant did not separately list those items but said "See Attached Affidavit." The affidavit did describe the guns that were the object of the search. That same day, the magistrate approved the warrant, separately signing both the search warrant and the attached affidavit. He sealed the affidavit, however, in order to protect the confidential BATF sources.

On April 11, 2001, Johns led approximately 20 BATF agents to the Larson warehouse to execute the warrant. Upon reaching the warehouse, the agents were met by Sahid Zadeh, an attorney for Larson. Zadeh asked to see the warrant. After reading it, he asked to see the affidavit. The agents informed him that it was under seal. One agent then informed Zadeh that they were looking for firearms owned by Baran that were located in the bonded section of the warehouse. Zadeh complained that the search was illegal because the warrant was invalid. He nonetheless cooperated with the agents. Zadeh escorted the agents to the basement of the building where the bonded warehouse was located. The agents seized 372 machine guns and 12 crates of firearm accessories belonging to Baran. Upon leaving the warehouse, the agents handed Zadeh an inventory of the seized items and a copy of the search warrant.

On July 5, 2001, Baran and Larson filed a civil action for damages in federal court, claiming that the search violated their Fourth Amendment rights.

What arguments support the claim raised by Baran and Larson? Does their claim have merit?

3–14: Assad and RJ, his 17-year-old son, lived in the back portion of a building in which Assad also operated the Roadview Bar. One evening, Assad and RJ got into a heated argument that escalated into physical violence. RJ went to the house of his friend, Robert Cono (Cono), and reported that he had hit his father repeatedly over the head with a baseball bat. Cono, a first responder, drove to the Roadview Bar to check on Assad's welfare. He found Assad talking on the phone, and asked whether Assad was all right. Cono noticed a shotgun sitting nearby. Assad said he was all right and ordered Cono to leave.

Cono returned home, called 911, and told the police of the evening's events. Deputies Skill, Wagner, and Wall proceeded to Cono's home. From talking to Cono and RJ the deputies learned that Assad had sustained head injuries from a baseball bat, that he had been drinking alcohol, and that he had once "fired a shot at some teenagers who were peering in the windows of his bar." RJ provided a key to the Assad home for the deputies to use. He asked Cono to inform the deputies that they needed to declare who they were when they entered or else his father would think that they were burglars, but Cono neglected to do so. The deputies went to the Assad home both to check on Assad's condition and to investigate the altercation between Assad and RJ.

When the deputies arrived at Assad's building, they shined flashlights in the windows, announcing that they were law enforcement officers while they walked around the building's perimeter. Assad, who had retired to his residence by this time, did not see flashlights or hear any announcements. He did believe that he "heard intruders enter his bar." The deputies decided to enter the building through the front door with their weapons drawn, making a conscious effort to enter "very quietly." Deputy Wall inserted and turned the front door key provided by RJ, but discovered that the door was already unlocked. The room where the deputies entered was dark. Deputies Skill and Wagner immediately noticed a laser light targeted on Wall's face. Knowing that the laser was consistent with a gun sight device, they announced repeatedly and loudly that they were police officers, and continually ordered Assad to drop his weapon. When Assad maintained the laser sight on Wall, Wall fired a gun in Assad's direction.

The deputies then retreated from the building. When Assad did not emerge, they established a perimeter and medical staging area outside the building. Attempts to communicate with Assad and convince him to leave the building throughout the night were unsuccessful. A SWAT team shot tear gas into the residence around five o'clock the next morning. This prompted Assad to come out. Law enforcement agents transported him to a local hospital where he received treatment for a gunshot wound to his abdomen, a bullet fragment in his upper right chest, and multiple injuries from the encounter with his son. Assad sued the deputies, claiming they had violated his Fourth Amendment rights.

Did the deputies violate the Fourth Amendment?

3–15: In the early morning hours of February 18, a fight broke out downtown. Two men were seen firing guns. Vossey was killed and Washington was severely injured. Tillman, who was apprehended by Officer Sark while running from the scene, was identified by eyewitnesses as one of the shooters. The other shooting suspect was not apprehended. Forensic analyses showed that bullets and casings at the scene had been fired from a gun found on Tillman and a gun he had tossed away while fleeing and that blood on Tillman's clothes was Vossey's.

At the time of Tillman's arrest, Sark took a cell phone from his possession. Officer Davis, a homicide detective investigating the shootings, prepared an application for a warrant to search the contents of the cell phone. In the application, in order "to assist in a homicide investigation," Davis requested a warrant to search "[a]ny and all information" contained on the cell phone. He specifically listed contacts, cell phone call lists, text messages, and voicemails, and he also requested authority to search for "any other information that can be gained from the internal components and/or memory cards." In the affidavit filed in support of the warrant, Davis stated that police had been dispatched to the scene where two victims had suffered gunshot wounds, that witnesses had seen two men firing at a victim, that an officer saw two men running from the scene, that one of the two men was later identified as Tillman, that the officer chased him and saw him throw a handgun under a vehicle, and that officers searched Tillman and found a handgun in his pocket and a cell phone in his possession. He asserted that, from his experience as a detective, he knew that suspects used cell phones to communicate about shootings they have been involved in before, during, and after the shootings and that such communications could be by means of voice or text messages or social media.

The county court issued a search warrant. The warrant did not refer to the crime that was being investigated. The terms of the warrant did list some types of data for which a search was authorized, specifying "cell phone calls and text messages," then added that officers could search for "any other information that can be gained from the internal components and/or memory cards."

Detective Nicks conducted the search. He downloaded information from the phone, including the contact list, call history, and text messages. Included in the information downloaded was a series of text messages exchanged between the cell phone and another number between 2:34 a.m. and 3:11 a.m. on February 18. Messages coming from the other number included two that stated, "That N____ that stab JB up here" and "After hour on Harney downtown." Messages sent from the searched cell phone included two that stated, "On my way keep close eye" and "I'm outside what up?" Other messages appear to indicate that the two persons exchanging the messages were attempting to meet up with one another outside the location mentioned in earlier messages. Nicks also found a picture of a man that was used as "wallpaper," or the background on the cell phone's screen. Nicks recognized the man in the picture as Jimmy Lever and knew him as "an infamous gang member."

Was the warrant to search Tillman's phone constitutionally valid?

Selected Bibliography

James A. Adams, *Anticipatory Search Warrants: Constitutionality, Requirements, and Scope,* 79 Ky. L.J. 681 (1990–91)

Akhil Reed Amar, *Fourth Amendment First Principles,* 107 Harv. L. Rev. 757 (1994)

Oren Bar-Gill & Barry Friedman, *Taking Warrants Seriously,* 106 Nw. U. L. Rev. 1609 (2012)

Phyllis T. Bookspan, *Reworking the Warrant Requirement: Resuscitating the Fourth Amendment,* 44 Vand. L. Rev. 473 (1991)

Josh Bowers, *Probable Cause, Constitutional Reasonableness, and the Unrecognized Point of a "Pointless Indignity,"* 66 Stan. L. Rev. 987 (2014)

Richard S. Frase, *What Were They Thinking? Fourth Amendment Unreasonableness in* Atwater v. City of Lago Vista, 71 Fordham L. Rev. 329 (2002)

Joseph D. Grano, *Rethinking the Fourth Amendment Warrant Requirement,* 19 Am. Crim. L. Rev. 603 (1982)

Tonja Jacobi & Jonah Kind, *Criminal Innovation and the Warrant Requirement: Reconsidering the Rights-Police Efficiency Trade-Off,* 56 Wm. & Mary L. Rev. 759 (2015)

Orin S. Kerr, *Search Warrants in an Era of Digital Evidence,* 75 Miss. L.J. 85 (2005)

Nelson B. Lasson, THE HISTORY AND DEVELOPMENT OF THE FOURTH AMENDMENT TO THE UNITED STATES CONSTITUTION (1937)

Wayne A. Logan, *Reasonableness as a Rule: A Paean to Justice O'Connor's Dissent in* Atwater v. City of Lago Vista, 79 Miss. L.J. 115 (2009)

Tracey Maclin, *The Central Meaning of the Fourth Amendment,* 35 Wm. & Mary L. Rev. 197 (1993)

Tracey Maclin, *When the Cure is Worse Than the Disease,* 68 S. Cal. L. Rev. 1 (1994)

Tracey Maclin, *The Complexity of the Fourth Amendment: A Historical Review,* 77 B.U. L. Rev. 925 (1997)

George R. Nock, *The Point of the Fourth Amendment and the Myth of Magisterial Discretion,* 23 Conn. L. Rev. 1 (1990)

Carol S. Steiker, *Second Thoughts About First Principles,* 107 Harv. L. Rev. 820 (1994)

David E. Steinberg, *Zealous Officers and Neutral Magistrates: The Rhetoric of the Fourth Amendment,* 43 Creighton L. Rev. 1019 (2010)

William J. Stuntz, *Warrants and Fourth Amendment Remedies,* 77 Va. L. Rev. 881 (1991)

Paul Sutton, *The Fourth Amendment in Action: An Empirical View of the Search Warrant Process,* 22 Crim. L. Bull. 405 (1986)

Adina Swartz, *Homes As Folding Umbrellas: Two Recent Supreme Court Decisions on "Knock and Announce,"* 25 Am. J. Crim. L. 545 (1998)

Telford Taylor, TWO STUDIES IN CONSTITUTIONAL INTERPRETATION (1969)

Chapter 4

Reasonable Searches Without Warrants: The Nature and Scope of the Exceptions to the Warrant Requirement

Introductory Note

Supreme Court opinions assert that the search warrant requirement is one of the most fundamental principles in Fourth Amendment law. Indeed, Justice Marshall once referred to the warrant rule as "[o]ne of the few absolutes of our law." *United States v. Watson*, 423 U.S., 411, 444, 96 S. Ct. 820, 837, 46 L. Ed. 2d 598, 621 (1976) (Marshall, J., dissenting). A majority of the Court remains committed to the view that the search warrant requirement is a "'cardinal principle.'" *California v. Acevedo*, 500 U.S. 565, 580, 111 S. Ct. 1982, 1991, 114 L. Ed. 2d 619, 638 (1991) (quoting *Mincey v. Arizona*, 437 U.S. 385, 98 S. Ct. 2408, 57 L. Ed. 2d 290 (1978)).

The traditional statement of the warrant requirement acknowledges that it is subject to "a few, specifically established and well-delineated exceptions." *Katz v. United States*, 389 U.S. 347, 357, 88 S. Ct. 507, 514, 19 L. Ed. 2d 576, 585 (1967). Those exceptions are the topics of this Chapter. They include searches incident to arrest, exigent circumstances searches, automobile doctrine searches, inventory searches, consent searches, and plain view seizures.[1]

---

1. This list is not exhaustive. The *Terry* frisk doctrine, which is considered in depth in Chapter 5, is also recognized as an exception to the warrant requirement. In addition, the school search doctrine of *T.L.O. v. New Jersey*, 469 U.S. 325, 105 S. Ct. 733, 83 L. Ed. 2d 720 (1985), and the "drug testing" authorized by *Skinner v. Railway Labor Association*, 489 U.S. 602, 109 S. Ct. 1402, 103 L. Ed. 2d 639 (1989), also treated in Chapter 5, constitute exceptions to the *per se* rule. All of these doctrines, however, particularly the *Terry* doctrine, are much more than mere exceptions to the warrant requirement. For that reason, and because of the importance of their theoretical contributions to and practical impact upon Fourth Amendment jurisprudence, these topics are explored in a distinct chapter. The doctrines considered in the present chapter are primarily, if not exclusively, significant as exceptions to the search warrant requirement.

Students should endeavor to analyze each exception to the warrant requirement individually. The logical underpinnings of each exception and the resulting doctrine are distinct and should not be confused. Still, the exceptions are not mutually exclusive. In one situation, multiple doctrines might simultaneously justify exemption from the warrant demand. For each exception, at least three basic aspects should be identified and explored: (1) the underlying *rationale* of the exception; (2) the precise *showing* necessary to invoke the exception; and (3) the *scope* of the warrantless authority conferred by the exception.

As a consequence of the several, expansive exceptions to the warrant requirement, law enforcement agents are frequently able to justify warrantless searches. It is arguable that the "cardinal" *per se* rule is honored more often in the breach than in the observance. At the conclusion of this Chapter and again at the conclusion of Chapter 5, students should consider whether the Court's descriptions of the exceptions as "few" and "well-delineated" are accurate and fair, and whether it is appropriate to continue to proclaim the importance of a constitutional principle that is so riddled with qualifications.

[A] Searches Incident to Arrests and Searches for Arrestees

Chimel v. California

United States Supreme Court

395 U.S. 752, 89 S. Ct. 2034, 23 L. Ed. 2d 685 (1969)

Mr. Justice Stewart delivered the opinion of the Court.

. . . .

Late in the afternoon of September 13, 1965, three police officers arrived at the Santa Ana, California, home of the petitioner with a warrant authorizing his arrest for the burglary of a coin shop. The officers knocked on the door, identified themselves to the petitioner's wife, and asked if they might come inside. She ushered them into the house, where they waited 10 or 15 minutes until the petitioner returned home from work. When the petitioner entered the house, one of the officers handed him the arrest warrant and asked for permission to "look around." The petitioner objected, but was advised that "on the basis of the lawful arrest," the officers would nonetheless conduct a search. No search warrant had been issued.

Accompanied by the petitioner's wife, the officers then looked through the entire three-bedroom house, including the attic, the garage, and a small workshop. In some rooms the search was relatively cursory. In the master bedroom and sewing room, however, the officers directed the petitioner's wife to open drawers and "to physically move contents of the drawers from side to side so that [they] might view any items that would have come from [the] burglary." After completing the search, they seized numerous items — primarily coins, but also several medals, tokens, and a few other objects. The entire search took between 45 minutes and an hour.

. . . .

Without deciding the question, we proceed on the hypothesis that the California courts were correct in holding that the arrest of the petitioner was valid under the Constitution. This brings us directly to the question whether the warrantless search of the petitioner's entire house can be constitutionally justified as incident to that arrest. The decisions of this Court bearing upon that question have been far from consistent, as even the most cursory review makes evident.

Approval of a warrantless search incident to a lawful arrest seems first to have been articulated by the Court in 1914 as dictum in *Weeks v. United States*, 232 U.S. 383, 34 S. Ct. 341, 58 L. Ed. 652, in which the Court stated:

> What then is the present case? Before answering that inquiry specifically, it may be well by a process of exclusion to state what it is not. It is not an assertion of the right on the part of the Government, always recognized under English and American law, to search the person of the accused when legally arrested to discover and seize the fruits or evidences of crime.

Id., at 392, 34 S. Ct., at 344. That statement made no reference to any right to search the *place* where an arrest occurs, but was limited to a right to search the "person." Eleven years later the case of *Carroll v. United States*, 267 U.S. 132, 45 S. Ct. 280, 69 L. Ed. 543, brought the following embellishment of the *Weeks* statement:

> When a man is legally arrested for an offense, whatever is found upon his person *or in his control* which it is unlawful for him to have and which may be used to prove the offense may be seized and held as evidence in the prosecution.

Id., at 158, 45 S. Ct., at 287. (Emphasis added.) Still, that assertion too was far from a claim that the "place" where one is arrested may be searched so long as the arrest is valid. Without explanation, however, the principle emerged in expanded form a few months later in *Agnello v. United States*, 269 U.S. 20, 46 S. Ct. 4, 70 L. Ed. 145 — although still by way of dictum:

> The right without a search warrant contemporaneously to search persons lawfully arrested while committing crime and to search the place where the arrest is made in order to find and seize things connected with the crime as its fruits or as the means by which it was committed, as well as weapons and other things to effect an escape from custody, is not to be doubted. *See Carroll v. United States*, 267 U.S. 132, 158, 45 S. Ct. 280, 69 L. Ed. 543; *Weeks v. United States*, 232 U.S. 383, 392, 34 S. Ct. 341, 58 L. Ed. 652; *Agnello*, 269 U.S., at 30, 46 S. Ct., at 5.

And in *Marron v. United States*, 275 U.S. 192, 48 S. Ct. 74, 72 L. Ed. 231, Treas. Dec. 42528, two years later, the dictum of *Agnello* appeared to be the foundation of the Court's decision. In that case federal agents had secured a search warrant authorizing the seizure of liquor and certain articles used in its manufacture. When they arrived at the premises to be searched, they saw "that the place was used for retailing and drinking intoxicating liquors." *Id.*, at 194, 48 S. Ct., at 75. They proceeded to arrest the person in charge and to execute the warrant. In searching a closet for the items listed in the warrant they came across an incriminating ledger, concededly not covered by the warrant, which they also seized. The Court upheld the seizure of the ledger by holding that since the agents had made a lawful arrest, "[t]hey had a right without a warrant contemporaneously to search the place in order to find and seize the things used to carry on the criminal enterprise." *Id.*, at 199, 48 S. Ct., at 77.

That the *Marron* opinion did not mean all that it seemed to say became evident, however, a few years later in *Go-Bart Importing Co. v. United States*, 282 U.S. 344, 51 S. Ct. 153, 75 L. Ed. 374, and *United States v. Lefkowitz*, 285 U.S. 452, 52 S. Ct. 420, 76 L. Ed. 877. In each of those cases the opinion of the Court was written by Mr. Justice Butler, the author of the opinion in *Marron*. In *Go-Bart*, agents had searched the office of persons whom they had lawfully arrested, and had taken several papers from a desk, a safe, and other parts of the office. The Court noted that no crime had been committed in the agents' presence, and that although the agent in charge "had an abundance of information and time to swear out a valid [search] warrant, he failed to do so." 282 U.S., at 358, 51 S. Ct., at 158. In holding the search and seizure unlawful, the Court stated:

> Plainly the case before us is essentially different from *Marron v. United States*, 275 U.S. 192, 48 S. Ct. 74, 72 L. Ed. 231, Treas. Dec. 42528. There, officers executing a valid search warrant for intoxicating liquors found and arrested one Birdsall who in pursuance of a conspiracy was actually engaged in running a saloon. As an incident to the arrest they seized a ledger in a closet where the liquor or some of it was kept and some bills beside the cash register. These things were visible and accessible and in the offender's immediate custody. There was no threat of force or general search or rummaging of the place. 282 U.S., at 358, 51 S. Ct., at 158.

This limited characterization of *Marron* was reiterated in *Lefkowitz*, a case in which the Court held unlawful a search of desk drawers and a cabinet despite the fact that the search had accompanied a lawful arrest. 285 U.S., at 465, 52 S. Ct., at 423.

The limiting views expressed in *Go-Bart* and *Lefkowitz* were thrown to the winds, however, in *Harris v. United States*, 331 U.S. 145, 67 S. Ct. 1098, 91 L. Ed. 1399, decided in 1947. In that case, officers had obtained a warrant for Harris' arrest on the basis of his alleged involvement with the cashing and interstate transportation of a forged check. He was arrested in the living room of his four-room apartment, and in an attempt to recover two canceled checks thought to have been used in effecting the forgery, the officers undertook a thorough search of the entire apartment. Inside a desk drawer they found a sealed envelope marked "George Harris, personal papers." The envelope, which was then torn open, was found to contain altered Selective Service documents, and those documents were used to secure Harris' conviction for violating the Selective Training and Service Act of 1940. The Court rejected Harris'

Fourth Amendment claim, sustaining the search as "incident to arrest." *Id.*, at 151, 67 S. Ct., at 1101.

Only a year after *Harris*, however, the pendulum swung again. In *Trupiano v. United States*, 334 U.S. 699, 68 S. Ct. 1229, 92 L. Ed. 1663, agents raided the site of an illicit distillery, saw one of several conspirators operating the still, and arrested him, contemporaneously "seiz[ing] the illicit distillery." *Id.*, at 702, 68 S. Ct. at 1231. The Court held that the arrest and others made subsequently had been valid, but that the unexplained failure of the agents to procure a search warrant — in spite of the fact that they had had more than enough time before the raid to do so — rendered the search unlawful. The opinion stated:

> It is a cardinal rule that, in seizing goods and articles, law enforcement agents must secure and use search warrants wherever reasonably practicable .... This rule rests upon the desirability of having magistrates rather than police officers determine when searches and seizures are permissible and what limitations should be placed upon such activities .... To provide the necessary security against unreasonable intrusions upon the private lives of individuals, the framers of the Fourth Amendment required adherence to judicial processes wherever possible. And subsequent history has confirmed the wisdom of that requirement.

> A search or seizure without a warrant as an incident to a lawful arrest has always been considered to be a strictly limited right. It grows out of the inherent necessities of the situation at the time of the arrest. But there must be something more in the way of necessity than merely a lawful arrest.

Id., at 705, 708, 68 S. Ct., at 1232, 1234.

In 1950, two years after *Trupiano*, came *United States v. Rabinowitz*, 339 U.S. 56, 70 S. Ct. 430, 94 L. Ed. 653, the decision upon which California primarily relies in the case now before us. In *Rabinowitz*, federal authorities had been informed that the defendant was dealing in stamps bearing forged overprints. On the basis of that information they secured a warrant for his arrest, which they executed at his one-room business office. At the time of the arrest, the officers "searched the desk, safe, and file cabinets in the office for about an hour and a half," *id.*, at 59, 70 S. Ct., at 432, and seized 573 stamps with forged overprints. The stamps were admitted into evidence at the defendant's trial, and this Court affirmed his conviction, rejecting the contention that the warrantless search had been unlawful. The Court held that the search in its entirety fell within the principle giving law enforcement authorities "[t]he right 'to search the place where the arrest is made in order to find and seize things connected with the crime ....'" *Id.*, at 61, 70 S. Ct., at 433. *Harris* was regarded as "ample authority" for that conclusion. *Id.*, at 63, 70 S. Ct., at 434. The opinion rejected the rule of *Trupiano* that "in seizing goods and articles, law enforcement agents must secure and use search warrants wherever reasonably practicable." The test, said the Court, "is not whether it is reasonable to procure a search warrant, but whether the search was reasonable." *Id.*, at 66, 70 S. Ct., at 435.

Rabinowitz has come to stand for the proposition, *inter alia*, that a warrantless search "incident to a lawful arrest" may generally extend to the area that is considered to be in the "possession" or under the "control" of the person arrested. And it was on the basis of that proposition that the California courts upheld the search of the petitioner's entire house in this case. That doctrine, however, at least in the broad sense in which it was applied by the California courts in this case, can withstand neither historical nor rational analysis.

Even limited to its own facts, the *Rabinowitz* decision was, as we have seen, hardly founded on an unimpeachable line of authority. As Mr. Justice Frankfurter commented in dissent in that case, the "hint" contained in *Weeks* was, without persuasive justification, "loosely turned into dictum and finally elevated to a decision." 339 U.S., at 75, 70 S. Ct., at 439. And the approach taken in cases such as *Go-Bart, Lefkowitz,* and *Trupiano* was essentially disregarded by the *Rabinowitz* Court.

Nor is the rationale by which the State seeks here to sustain the search of the petitioner's house supported by a reasoned view of the background and purpose of the Fourth Amendment. Mr. Justice Frankfurter wisely pointed out in his *Rabinowitz* dissent that the Amendment's proscription of "unreasonable searches and seizures" must be read in light of "the history that gave rise to the words" — a history of "abuses so deeply felt by the Colonies as to be one of the potent causes of the Revolution . . . ." 339 U.S., at 69, 70 S. Ct., at 436. The Amendment was in large part a reaction to the general warrants and warrantless searches that had so alienated the colonists and had helped speed the movement for independence. In the scheme of the Amendment, therefore, the requirement that "no Warrants shall issue, but upon probable cause," plays a crucial part.

. . . .

Clearly, the general requirement that a search warrant be obtained is not lightly to be dispensed with, and "the burden is on those seeking [an] exemption [from the requirement] to show the need for it . . . ." *United States v. Jeffers*, 342 U.S. 48, 51, 72 S. Ct. 93, 95, 96 L. Ed. 59.

. . . .

When an arrest is made, it is reasonable for the arresting officer to search the person arrested in order to remove any weapons that the latter might seek to use in order to resist arrest or effect his escape. Otherwise, the officer's safety might well be endangered, and the arrest itself frustrated. In addition, it is entirely reasonable for the arresting officer to search for and seize any evidence on the arrestee's person in order to prevent its concealment or destruction. And the area into which an arrestee might reach in order to grab a weapon or evidentiary items must, of course, be governed by a like rule. A gun on a table or in a drawer in front of one who is arrested can be as dangerous to the arresting officer as one concealed in the clothing of the person arrested. There is ample justification, therefore, for a search of the arrestee's person and the area "within his immediate control" — construing that phrase to mean the area from within which he might gain possession of a weapon or destructible evidence.

There is no comparable justification, however, for routinely searching any room other than that in which an arrest occurs — or, for that matter, for searching through all the desk drawers or other closed or concealed areas in that room itself. Such searches, in the absence of well-recognized exceptions, may be made only under the authority of a search warrant. The "adherence to judicial processes" mandated by the Fourth Amendment requires no less.

. . . .

It is argued in the present case that it is "reasonable" to search a man's house when he is arrested in it. But that argument is founded on little more than a subjective view regarding the acceptability of certain sorts of police conduct, and not on considerations relevant to Fourth Amendment interests. Under such an unconfined analysis, Fourth Amendment protection in this area would approach the evaporation point. It is not easy to explain why, for instance, it is less subjectively "reasonable" to search a man's house when he is arrested on his front lawn — or just down the street — than it is when he happens to be in the house at the time of arrest. As Mr. Justice Frankfurter put it:

> To say that the search must be reasonable is to require some criterion of reason. It is no guide at all either for a jury or for district judges or the police to say that an "unreasonable search" is forbidden — that the search must be reasonable. What is the test of reason which makes a search reasonable? The test is the reason underlying and expressed by the Fourth Amendment: the history and experience which it embodies and the safeguards afforded by it against the evils to which it was a response.

United States v. Rabinowitz, 339 U.S., at 83, 73 S. Ct., at 443 (dissenting opinion) . . . .

It would be possible, of course, to draw a line between *Rabinowitz* and *Harris* on the one hand, and this case on the other. For *Rabinowitz* involved a single room, and *Harris* a four-room apartment, while in the case before us an entire house was searched. But such a distinction would be highly artificial. The rationale that allowed the searches and seizures in *Rabinowitz* and *Harris* would allow the searches and seizures in this case. No consideration relevant to the Fourth Amendment suggests any point of rational limitation, once the search is allowed to go beyond the area from which the person arrested might obtain weapons or evidentiary items. The only reasoned distinction is one between a search of the person arrested and the area within his reach on the one hand, and more extensive searches on the other.[12]

---

12. It is argued in dissent that so long as there is probable cause to search the place where an arrest occurs, a search of that place should be permitted even though no search warrant has been obtained. This position seems to be based principally on two premises: first, that once an arrest has been made, the additional invasion of privacy stemming from the accompanying search is "relatively minor"; and second, that the victim of the search may "shortly thereafter" obtain a judicial determination of whether the search was justified by probable cause. With respect to the second premise, one may initially question whether all of the States in fact provide the speedy suppression

The petitioner correctly points out that one result of decisions such as *Rabinowitz* and *Harris* is to give law enforcement officials the opportunity to engage in searches not justified by probable cause, by the simple expedient of arranging to arrest suspects at home rather than elsewhere. We do not suggest that the petitioner is necessarily correct in his assertion that such a strategy was utilized here, but the fact remains that had he been arrested earlier in the day, at his place of employment rather than at home, no search of his house could have been made without a search warrant. In any event, even apart from the possibility of such police tactics, the general point so forcefully made by Judge Learned Hand in *United States v. Kirschenblatt*, 16 F.2d 202 (2d Cir.), remains:

> After arresting a man in his house, to rummage at will among his papers in search of whatever will convict him, appears to us to be indistinguishable from what might be done under a general warrant; indeed, the warrant would give more protection, for presumably it must be issued by a magistrate. True, by hypothesis the power would not exist, if the supposed offender were not found on the premises; but it is small consolation to know that one's papers are safe only so long as one is not at home.

Id., at 203.

Rabinowitz and *Harris* . . . are no longer to be followed.

Application of sound Fourth Amendment principles to the facts of this case produces a clear result. The search here went far beyond the petitioner's person and the area from within which he might have obtained either a weapon or something that could have been used as evidence against him. There was no constitutional justification, in the absence of a search warrant, for extending the search beyond that area. The scope of the search was, therefore, "unreasonable" under the Fourth and Fourteenth Amendments and the petitioner's conviction cannot stand.

Reversed.

[The concurring opinion of Mr. Justice Harlan has been omitted.]

Mr. Justice White, with whom Mr. Justice Black joins, dissenting.

Few areas of the law have been as subject to shifting constitutional standards over the last 50 years as that of the search "incident to an arrest." There has been a re-

---

procedures the dissent assumes. More fundamentally, however, we cannot accept the view that Fourth Amendment interests are vindicated so long as "the rights of the criminal" are "protect[ed] . . . against introduction of evidence seized without probable cause." The Amendment is designed to prevent, not simply to redress, unlawful police action. In any event, we cannot join in characterizing the invasion of privacy that results from a top-to-bottom search of a man's house as "minor." And we can see no reason why, simply because some interference with an individual's privacy and freedom of movement has lawfully taken place, further intrusions should automatically be allowed despite the absence of a warrant that the Fourth Amendment would otherwise require.

markable instability in this whole area, which has seen at least four major shifts in emphasis. Today's opinion makes an untimely fifth. In my view, the Court should not now abandon the old rule.

. . . .

II

The rule which has prevailed, but for very brief or doubtful periods of aberration, is that a search incident to an arrest may extend to those areas under the control of the defendant and where items subject to constitutional seizure may be found. The justification for this rule must, under the language of the Fourth Amendment, lie in the reasonableness of the rule . . . . [T]he Court must decide whether a given search is reasonable. The Amendment does not proscribe "warrantless searches" but instead it proscribes "unreasonable searches" and this Court has never held nor does the majority today assert that warrantless searches are necessarily unreasonable.

Applying this reasonableness test to the area of searches incident to arrests, one thing is clear at the outset. Search of an arrested man and of the items within his immediate reach must in almost every case be reasonable. There is always a danger that the suspect will try to escape, seizing concealed weapons with which to overpower and injure the arresting officers, and there is a danger that he may destroy evidence vital to the prosecution. Circumstances in which these justifications would not apply are sufficiently rare that inquiry is not made into searches of this scope, which have been considered reasonable throughout.

The justifications which make such a search reasonable obviously do not apply to the search of areas to which the accused does not have ready physical access. This is not enough, however, to prove such searches unconstitutional. The Court has always held, and does not today deny, that when there is probable cause to search and it is "impracticable" for one reason or another to get a search warrant, then a warrantless search may be reasonable. This is the case whether an arrest was made at the time of the search or not.

This is not to say that a search can be reasonable without regard to the probable cause to believe that seizable items are on the premises. But when there are exigent circumstances, and probable cause, then the search may be made without a warrant, reasonably. An arrest itself may often create an emergency situation making it impracticable to obtain a warrant before embarking on a related search. Again assuming that there is probable cause to search premises at the spot where a suspect is arrested, it seems to me unreasonable to require the police to leave the scene in order to obtain a search warrant when they are already legally there to make a valid arrest, and when there must almost always be a strong possibility that confederates of the arrested man will in the meanwhile remove the items for which the police have probable cause to search. This must so often be the case that it seems to me as unreasonable to require a warrant for a search of the premises

as to require a warrant for search of the person and his very immediate surroundings.

This case provides a good illustration of my point . . . . There was doubtless probable
cause not only to arrest petitioner, but also to search his house. He had obliquely
admitted, both to a neighbor and to the owner of the burglarized store, that he had
committed the burglary. In light of this, and the fact that the neighbor had seen other
admittedly stolen property in petitioner's house, there was surely probable cause on
which a warrant could have issued to search the house for the stolen coins. Moreover,
had the police simply arrested petitioner, taken him off to the station house, and later
returned with a warrant,[5] it seems very likely that petitioner's wife, who in view of petitioner's generally garrulous nature must have known of the robbery, would have
removed the coins. For the police to search the house while the evidence they had
probable cause to search out and seize was still there cannot be considered unreasonable.

III

This line of analysis, supported by the precedents of this Court, hinges on two
assumptions. One is that the arrest of petitioner without a valid warrant was constitutional as the majority assumes; the other is that the police were not required to
obtain a search warrant in advance, even though they knew that the effect of the
arrest might well be to alert petitioner's wife that the coins had better be removed
soon. Thus it is necessary to examine the constitutionality of the arrest since if it
was illegal, the exigent circumstances which it created may not, as the consequences of a lawless act, be used to justify the contemporaneous warrantless search.
But for the arrest, the warrantless search may not be justified. And if circumstances
can justify the warrantless arrest, it would be strange to say that the Fourth Amendment bars the warrantless search, regardless of the circumstances, since the invasion and disruption of a man's life and privacy which stem from his arrest are
ordinarily far greater than the relatively minor intrusions attending a search of his
premises.

. . . .

In light of the uniformity of judgment of the Congress, past judicial decisions, and
common practice rejecting the proposition that arrest warrants are essential wherever it is practicable to get them, the conclusion is inevitable that such arrests and
accompanying searches are reasonable, at least until experience teaches the contrary.

---

5. There were three officers at the scene of the arrest, one from the city where the coin burglary
had occurred, and two from the city where the arrest was made. Assuming that one policeman from
each city would be needed to bring the petitioner in and obtain a search warrant, one policeman
could have been left to guard the house. However, if he not only could have remained in the house
against petitioner's wife's will, but followed her about to assure that no evidence was being tampered
with, the invasion of her privacy would be almost as great as that accompanying an actual search.
Moreover, had the wife summoned an accomplice, one officer could not have watched them both.

It must very often be the case that by the time probable cause to arrest a man is accumulated, the man is aware of police interest in him or for other good reasons is on the verge of flight. Moreover, it will likely be very difficult to determine the probability of his flight. Given this situation, it may be best in all cases simply to allow the arrest if there is probable cause, especially since that issue can be determined very shortly after the arrest.

. . . .

IV

If circumstances so often require the warrantless arrest that the law generally permits it, the typical situation will find the arresting officers lawfully on the premises without arrest or search warrant. Like the majority, I would permit the police to search the person of a suspect and the area under his immediate control either to assure the safety of the officers or to prevent the destruction of evidence. And like the majority, I see nothing in the arrest alone furnishing probable cause for a search of any broader scope. However, where as here the existence of probable cause is independently established and would justify a warrant for a broader search for evidence, I would follow past cases and permit such a search to be carried out without a warrant, since the fact of arrest supplies an exigent circumstance justifying police action before the evidence can be removed, and also alerts the suspect to the fact of the search so that he can immediately seek judicial determination of probable cause in an adversary proceeding, and appropriate redress.

. . . .

Notes and Questions

(1) The *Chimel* Court attempted to bring clarity, rationality, and a measure of finality to the "search incident to arrest" exception to the warrant requirement. What is the justification for recognizing that exception? What must officers establish to justify a search incident to an arrest? Why does that make the search "reasonable"? What areas may officers search incident to an arrest?

(2) Should the area subject to search under the *Chimel* exception be affected by the degree of restraint to which an arrestee is subjected? Suppose, for example, that an arrestee is surrounded by several officers with drawn firearms. Suppose instead that an arrestee is securely handcuffed immediately after arrest. In either case, should the authority to conduct a warrantless search diminish?

(3) More than 20 years after *Chimel* tightly restricted the scope of searches incident to arrest, a majority of the Court announced a small expansion of the search incident to arrest doctrine that applies to in-home arrests. According to *Maryland v. Buie*, 494 U.S. 325, 110 S. Ct. 1093, 108 L. Ed. 2d 276 (1990), when officers arrest a person within a dwelling they may, "as a precautionary matter and without probable cause or reasonable suspicion, look in closets and other spaces immediately adjoining the place of arrest from which an attack could be launched" by associates of the

arrestee. Because the sole object is to enable officers to protect themselves against attacks by dangerous persons, the search authorized by *Buie* involves a limited inspection to determine if there are persons in the specified spaces.

United States v. Robinson

United States Supreme Court

414 U.S. 218, 94 S. Ct. 467, 38 L. Ed. 2d 427 (1973)

Mr. Justice Rehnquist delivered the opinion of the Court.

. . . .

On April 23, 1968, at approximately 11 p.m., Officer Richard Jenks, a 15-year veteran of the District of Columbia Metropolitan Police Department, observed the respondent driving a 1965 Cadillac near the intersection of 8th and C Streets, N.E., in the District of Columbia. Jenks, as a result of previous investigation following a check of respondent's operator's permit four days earlier, determined there was reason to believe that respondent was operating a motor vehicle after the revocation of his operator's permit. This is an offense defined by statute in the District of Columbia which carries a mandatory minimum jail term, a mandatory minimum fine, or both. D.C. Code Ann. § 40–302(d) (1967).

Jenks signaled respondent to stop the automobile, which respondent did, and all three of the occupants emerged from the car. At that point Jenks informed respondent that he was under arrest for "operating after revocation and obtaining a permit by misrepresentation." It was assumed by the Court of Appeals, and is conceded by the respondent here, that Jenks had probable cause to arrest respondent, and that he effected a full custody arrest.

In accordance with procedures prescribed in police department instructions,[2] Jenks then began to search respondent. He explained at a subsequent hearing that

---

2. The Government introduced testimony at the evidentiary hearing upon the original remand by the Court of Appeals as to certain standard operating procedures of the Metropolitan Police Department. Sergeant Dennis C. Donaldson, a Metropolitan Police Department Training Division instructor, testified that when a police officer makes "a full custody arrest," which he defined as one where an officer "would arrest a subject and subsequently transport him to a police facility for booking," the officer is trained to make a full "field type search":

> Q. Would you describe the physical acts the officer is instructed to perform with respect to this field search in a full custody arrest situation?
> A. (Sgt. Donaldson). Basically, it is a thorough search of the individual. We would expect in a field search that the officer completely search the individual and inspect areas such as behind the collar, underneath the collar, the waistband of the trousers, the cuffs, the socks and shoes. Those are the areas we would ask a complete thorough search of.
> Q. What are the instructions in a field type search situation when an officer feels something on the outside of the garment?
> A. If it is a full custody arrest and he is conducting a field search, we expect him to remove anything and examine it to determine exactly what it is.

he was "face-to-face" with the respondent, and "placed [his] hands on [the respondent], my right-hand to his left breast like this (demonstrating) and proceeded to pat him down thus [with the right hand]." During this patdown, Jenks felt an object in the left breast pocket of the heavy coat respondent was wearing, but testified that he "couldn't tell what it was" and also that he "couldn't actually tell the size of it." Jenks then reached into the pocket and pulled out the object, which turned out to be a "crumpled up cigarette package." Jenks testified that at this point he still did not know what was in the package:

> As I felt the package I could feel objects in the package but I couldn't tell what they were . . . . I knew they weren't cigarettes.

The officer then opened the cigarette pack and found 14 gelatin capsules of white powder which he thought to be, and which later analysis proved to be, heroin. Jenks then continued his search of respondent to completion, feeling around his waist and trouser legs, and examining the remaining pockets. The heroin seized from the respondent was admitted into evidence at the trial which resulted in his conviction in the District Court.

. . . .

THE COURT: That is a full custody arrest. What is the last part of it?

THE WITNESS: In conducting a field search, which is done any time there is a full custody arrest, we expect the officer to examine anything he might find on the subject.

THE COURT: Would he do the same thing in a pat-down search?

WITNESS: If he could determine in his pat-down or frisk by squeezing that it was not, in fact, a weapon that could be used against him, then we don't instruct him to go further.

THE COURT: But in a field search, even though he may feel something that he believes is not a weapon, is he instructed to take it out?

THE WITNESS: Yes, sir.

Sergeant Donaldson testified that officers are instructed to examine the "contents of all of the pockets" of the arrestee in the course of the field search. It was stated that these standard operating procedures were initiated by the police department "[p]rimarily, for [the officer's] own safety and, secondly, for the safety of the individual he has placed under arrest and, thirdly, to search for evidence of the crime." While the officer is instructed to make a full field search of the person of the individual he arrests, he is instructed, and police department regulations provide, that in the case of a full-custody arrest for driving after revocation, "areas beyond [the arrestee's] immediate control should not be searched because there is no probable cause to believe that the vehicle contains fruits, instrumentalities, contraband or evidence of the offense of driving after revocation." Those regulations also provide that in the case of some traffic offenses, including the crime of operating a motor vehicle after revocation of an operator's permit, the officer shall make a summary arrest of the violator and take the violator, in custody, to the station house for booking. D.C. Metropolitan Police Department General Order No. 3, series 1959 (Apr. 24, 1959). Such operating procedures are not, of course, determinative of the constitutional issues presented by this case.

I

It is well settled that a search incident to a lawful arrest is a traditional exception to the warrant requirement of the Fourth Amendment. This general exception has historically been formulated into two distinct propositions. The first is that a search may be made of the person of the arrestee by virtue of the lawful arrest. The second is that a search may be made of the area within the control of the arrestee.

Examination of this Court's decisions shows that these two propositions have been treated quite differently. The validity of the search of a person incident to a lawful arrest has been regarded as settled from its first enunciation, and has remained virtually unchallenged until the present case. The validity of the second proposition, while likewise conceded in principle, has been subject to differing interpretations as to the extent of the area which may be searched.

. . . .

Throughout the series of cases in which the Court has addressed the second proposition relating to a search incident to a lawful arrest — the permissible area beyond the person of the arrestee which such a search may cover — no doubt has been expressed as to the unqualified authority of the arresting authority to search the person of the arrestee. In *Chimel*, . . . full recognition was again given to the authority to search the person of the arrestee:

> When an arrest is made, it is reasonable for the arresting officer to search the person arrested in order to remove any weapons that the latter might seek to use in order to resist arrest or effect his escape. Otherwise, the officer's safety might well be endangered, and the arrest itself frustrated. In addition, it is entirely reasonable for the arresting officer to search for and seize any evidence on the arrestee's person in order to prevent its concealment or destruction.

395 U.S., at 762–763, 89 S. Ct. at 2040.

. . . .

Thus the broadly stated rule, and the reasons for it, have been repeatedly affirmed in the decisions of this Court since *Weeks v. United States, supra,* nearly 60 years ago. Since the statements in the cases speak not simply in terms of an exception to the warrant requirement, but in terms of an affirmative authority to search, they clearly imply that such searches also meet the Fourth Amendment's requirement of reasonableness.

II

In its decision of this case, the Court of Appeals decided that even after a police officer lawfully places a suspect under arrest for the purpose of taking him into custody, he may not ordinarily proceed to fully search the prisoner. He must, instead, conduct a limited frisk of the outer clothing and remove such weapons that he may, as a result of that limited frisk, reasonably believe and ascertain that the suspect has in his possession. While recognizing that *Terry v. Ohio*, 392 U.S. 1, 88 S. Ct. 1868, 20 L. Ed. 2d 889 (1968), dealt with a permissible "frisk" incident to an investigative stop based on less than probable cause to arrest, the Court of Appeals felt that the principles of that case should be carried over to this probable-cause arrest for driving while one's license is revoked. Since there would be no further evidence of such a crime to be obtained in a search of the arrestee, the court held that only a search for weapons could be justified.

Terry v. Ohio did not involve an arrest for probable cause, and it made quite clear that the "protective frisk" for weapons which it approved might be conducted without probable cause. *Id.*, at 21–22, 24–25, 88 S. Ct. at 1879–1880, 1881–1882. This Court's opinion explicitly recognized that there is a "distinction in purpose, character, and extent between a search incident to an arrest and a limited search for weapons."

> The former, although justified in part by the acknowledged necessity to protect the arresting officer from assault with a concealed weapon, *Preston v. United States*, 376 U.S. 364, 367, 84 S. Ct. 881, 883, 11 L. Ed. 2d 777 (1964), is also justified on other grounds, *ibid.*, and can therefore involve a relatively extensive exploration of the person. A search for weapons in the absence of probable cause to arrest, however, must, like any other search, be strictly circumscribed by the exigencies which justify its initiation. *Warden v. Hayden*, 387 U.S. 294, 310, 87 S. Ct. 1642, 1652, 18 L. Ed. 2d 782 (1967) (Mr. Justice Fortas, concurring). Thus it must be limited to that which is necessary for the discovery of weapons which might be used to harm the officer or others nearby, and may realistically be characterized as something less than a "full" search, even though it remains a serious intrusion.
>
> . . . An arrest is a wholly different kind of intrusion upon individual freedom from a limited search for weapons, and the interests each is designed to serve are likewise quite different. An arrest is the initial stage of a criminal prosecution. It is intended to vindicate society's interest in having its laws obeyed, and it is inevitably accompanied by future interference with the individual's freedom of movement, whether or not trial or conviction ultimately follows. The protective search for weapons, on the other hand, constitutes a brief, though far from inconsiderable, intrusion upon the sanctity of the person.

Id., at 25–26, 88 S. Ct., at 1882 [footnote omitted]. *Terry*, therefore, affords no basis to carry over to a probable-cause arrest the limitations this Court placed on a stop-and-frisk search permissible without probable cause.

. . . .

III

Virtually all of the statements of this Court affirming the existence of an unqualified authority to search incident to a lawful arrest are dicta. We would not, therefore, be foreclosed by principles of *stare decisis* from further examination into history and practice in order to see whether the sort of qualifications imposed by the Court of Appeals in this case were in fact intended by the Framers of the Fourth Amendment . . . .

. . . .

The Court of Appeals in effect determined that the *only* reason supporting the authority for a *full* search incident to lawful arrest was the possibility of discovery of evidence or fruits. Concluding that there could be no evidence or fruits in the case of an offense such as that with which respondent was charged, it held that any protective search would have to be limited by the conditions laid down in *Terry* for a search upon less than probable cause to arrest. Quite apart from the fact that *Terry* clearly recognized the distinction between the two types of searches, and that a different rule governed one than governed the other, we find additional reason to disagree with the Court of Appeals.

The justification or reason for the authority to search incident to a lawful arrest rests quite as much on the need to disarm the suspect in order to take him into custody as it does on the need to preserve evidence on his person for later use at trial. The standards traditionally governing a search incident to lawful arrest are not, therefore, commuted to the stricter *Terry* standards by the absence of probable fruits or further evidence of the particular crime for which the arrest is made.

Nor are we inclined, on the basis of what seems to us to be a rather speculative judgment, to qualify the breadth of the general authority to search incident to a lawful custodial arrest on an assumption that persons arrested for the offense of driving while their licenses have been revoked are less likely to possess dangerous weapons than are those arrested for other crimes.[5] It is scarcely open to doubt that the danger to an officer is far greater in the case of the extended exposure which follows the taking of a suspect into custody and transporting him to the police station than in the case of the relatively fleeting contact resulting from the typical *Terry*-type stop. This is an adequate basis for treating all custodial arrests alike for purposes of search justification. But quite apart from these distinctions, our more fundamental disagreement with the Court of Appeals arises from its suggestion that there must be litigated in each case the issue of whether or not there was present one of the reasons sup-

---

5. Such an assumption appears at least questionable in light of the available statistical data concerning assaults on police officers who are in the course of making arrests. The danger to the police officer flows from the fact of the arrest, and its attendant proximity, stress, and uncertainty, and not from the grounds for arrest. One study concludes that approximately 30% of the shootings of police officers occur when an officer stops a person in an automobile. Bristow, *Police Officer Shootings — A Tactical Evaluation*, 54 J. Crim. L. C. & P. S. 93 (1963), cited in *Adams v. Williams*, 407 U.S. 143, 148, 92 S. Ct. 1921, 1924, 32 L. Ed. 2d 612 (1972). The Government in its brief notes that the Uniform Crime Reports, prepared by the Federal Bureau of Investigation, indicate that a significant percentage of murders of police officers occurs when the officers are making traffic stops. Brief for the United States 23. Those reports indicate that during January-March 1973, 35 police officers were murdered; 11 of those officers were killed while engaged in making traffic stops. *Id.*

porting the authority for a search of the person incident to a lawful arrest. We do not think the long line of authorities of this Court dating back to *Weeks*, or what we can glean from the history of practice in this country and in England, requires such a case-by-case adjudication. A police officer's determination as to how and where to search the person of a suspect whom he has arrested is necessarily a quick *ad hoc* judgment which the Fourth Amendment does not require to be broken down in each instance into an analysis of each step in the search. The authority to search the person incident to a lawful custodial arrest, while based upon the need to disarm and to discover evidence, does not depend on what a court may later decide was the probability in a particular arrest situation that weapons or evidence would in fact be found upon the person of the suspect. A custodial arrest of a suspect based on probable cause is a reasonable intrusion under the Fourth Amendment; that intrusion being lawful, a search incident to the arrest requires no additional justification. It is the fact of the lawful arrest which establishes the authority to search, and we hold that in the case of a lawful custodial arrest a full search of the person is not only an exception to the warrant requirement of the Fourth Amendment, but is also a "reasonable" search under that Amendment.

IV

The search of respondent's person conducted by Officer Jenks in this case and the seizure from him of the heroin, were permissible under established Fourth Amendment law. While thorough, the search partook of none of the extreme or patently abusive characteristics which were held to violate the Due Process Clause of the Fourteenth Amendment in *Rochin v. California*, 342 U.S. 165, 72 S. Ct. 205, 96 L. Ed. 183 (1952). Since it is the fact of custodial arrest which gives rise to the authority to search,[6] it is of no moment that Jenks did not indicate any subjective fear of the respondent or that he did not himself suspect that respondent was armed.[7] Having in the course of a lawful search come upon the crumpled package of cigarettes, he was entitled to inspect it; and when his inspection revealed the heroin capsules, he was entitled to seize them as "fruits, instrumentalities, or contraband" probative of criminal conduct. The judgment of the Court of Appeals holding otherwise is reversed.

---

6. The opinion of the Court of Appeals also discussed its understanding of the law where the police officer makes what the court characterized as "a routine traffic stop," i.e., where the officer would simply issue a notice of violation and allow the offender to proceed. Since in this case the officer did make a full-custody arrest of the violator, we do not reach the question discussed by the Court of Appeals.

7. The United States concedes that "in searching respondent, [Officer Jenks] was not motivated by a feeling of imminent danger and was not specifically looking for weapons." Brief for the United States 34. Officer Jenks testified, "I just searched him [Robinson]. I didn't think about what I was looking for. I just searched him." As previously noted, Officer Jenks also testified that upon removing the cigarette package from the respondent's custody, he was still unsure what was in the package, but that he knew it was not cigarettes.

Reversed.

MR. JUSTICE MARSHALL, with whom MR. JUSTICE DOUGLAS and MR. JUSTICE BRENNAN join, dissenting.

. . . .

II

. . . .

The majority . . . suggests that the Court of Appeals reached a novel and unprecedented result by imposing qualifications on the historically recognized authority to conduct a full search incident to a lawful arrest. Nothing could be further from the truth . . . .

. . . .

The majority's attempt to avoid case-by-case adjudication of Fourth Amendment issues is not only misguided as a matter of principle, but is also doomed to fail as a matter of practical application. As the majority itself is well aware, the powers granted the police in this case are strong ones, subject to potential abuse. Although, in this particular case, Officer Jenks was required by police department regulations to make an in-custody arrest rather than to issue a citation, in most jurisdictions and for most traffic offenses the determination of whether to issue a citation or effect a full arrest is discretionary with the officer. There is always the possibility that a police officer, lacking probable cause to obtain a search warrant, will use a traffic arrest as a pretext to conduct a search. I suggest this possibility not to impugn the integrity of our police, but merely to point out that case-by-case adjudication will always be necessary to determine whether a full arrest was effected for purely legitimate reasons or, rather, as a pretext for searching the arrestee.

. . . .

III

The majority states that "[a] police officer's determination as to how and where to search the person of a suspect whom he has arrested is necessarily a quick *ad hoc* judgment which the Fourth Amendment does not require to be broken down in each instance into an analysis of each step in the search." No precedent is cited for this broad assertion — not surprisingly, since there is none. Indeed, we only recently rejected such "a rigid all-or-nothing model of justification and regulation under the Amendment, [for] it obscures the utility of limitations upon the scope, as well as the initiation, of police action as a means of constitutional regulation. This Court has held in the past that a search which is reasonable at its inception may violate the Fourth Amendment by virtue of its intolerable intensity and scope." *Terry v. Ohio*, 392 U.S., at 17–18, 88 S. Ct., at 1878. As we there concluded, "in determining whether the seizure and search were 'unreasonable' our inquiry is a dual one — whether the officer's action was justified at its inception, and whether it was reasonably related in scope to the circumstances which justified the interference in the first place." *Id.*, at 19–20, 88 S. Ct., at 1879.

As I view the matter, the search in this case divides into three distinct phases: the patdown of respondent's coat pocket; the removal of the unknown object from the pocket; and the opening of the crumpled-up cigarette package.

A

No question is raised here concerning the lawfulness of the patdown of respondent's coat pocket. The Court of Appeals unanimously affirmed the right of a police officer to conduct a limited frisk for weapons when making an in-custody arrest, regardless of the nature of the crime for which the arrest was made . . . .

B

With respect to the removal of the unknown object from the coat pocket, the first issue presented is whether that aspect of the search can be sustained as part of the limited frisk for weapons. The weapons search approved by the Court of Appeals was modeled upon the narrowly drawn protective search for weapons authorized in *Terry*, which consists "of a limited patting of the outer clothing of the suspect for concealed objects which might be used as instruments of assault." *See Sibron v. New York*, 392 U.S., at 65.

It appears to have been conceded by the Government below that the removal of the object from respondent's coat pocket exceeded the scope of a *Terry* frisk for weapons, since, under *Terry*, an officer may not remove an object from the suspect's pockets unless he has reason to believe it to be a dangerous weapon.

In the present case, however, Officer Jenks had no reason to believe and did not in fact believe that the object in respondent's coat pocket was a weapon. He admitted later that the object did not feel like a gun. In fact, he did not really have any thoughts one way or another about what was in the pocket. As Jenks himself testified, "I just searched him. I didn't think about what I was looking for. I just searched him." Since the removal of the object from the pocket cannot be justified as part of a limited *Terry* weapons frisk, the question arises whether it is reasonable for a police officer, when effecting an in-custody arrest of a traffic offender, to make a fuller search of the person than is permitted pursuant to *Terry*.

The underlying rationale of a search incident to arrest of a traffic offender initially suggests as reasonable a search whose scope is similar to the protective weapons frisk permitted in *Terry*. A search incident to arrest, as the majority indicates, has two basic functions: the removal of weapons the arrestee might use to resist arrest or effect an escape, and the seizure of evidence or fruits of the crime for which the arrest is made, so as to prevent their concealment or destruction.

The Government does not now contend that the search of respondent's pocket can be justified by any need to find and seize evidence in order to prevent its concealment or destruction, for, as the Court of Appeals found, there is no evidence or fruits of the offense with which respondent was charged. The only rationale for a search in this case, then, is the removal of weapons which the arrestee might use to harm the officer and attempt an escape. This rationale, of course, is identical to the rationale of the search permitted in *Terry*. As we said there, "The sole justification of the search in the present situation is the protection of the police officer and others nearby, and it must therefore be confined in scope to an intrusion reasonably designed to discover guns, knives, clubs, or other hidden instruments for the assault of the police officer." *Terry v. Ohio*, 392 U.S., at 29, 88 S. Ct., at 1884. Since the underlying rationale of a *Terry* search and the search of a traffic violator are identical, the Court of Appeals held that the scope of the searches must be the same. And in view of its conclusion that the removal of the object from respondent's coat pocket exceeded the scope of a lawful *Terry* frisk, a conclusion not disputed by the Government or challenged by the majority here, the plurality of the Court of Appeals held that the removal of the package exceeded the scope of a lawful search incident to arrest of a traffic violator.

The problem with this approach, however, is that it ignores several significant differences between the context in which a search incident to arrest for a traffic violation is made, and the situation presented in *Terry*. Some of these differences would appear to suggest permitting a more thorough search in this case than was permitted in *Terry;* other differences suggest a narrower, more limited right to search than was there recognized.

The most obvious difference between the two contexts relates to whether the officer has cause to believe that the individual he is dealing with possesses weapons which might be used against him. *Terry* did not permit an officer to conduct a weapons frisk of anyone he lawfully stopped on the street, but rather, only where "he has reason to believe that he is dealing with an armed and dangerous individual . . . ." 392 U.S., at 27, 88 S. Ct. at 1883. While the policeman who arrests a suspected rapist or robber may well have reason to believe he is dealing with an armed and dangerous person, certainly this does not hold true with equal force with respect to a person arrested for a motor vehicle violation of the sort involved in this case.

Nor was there any particular reason in this case to believe that respondent was dangerous. He had not attempted to evade arrest, but had quickly complied with the police both in bringing his car to a stop after being signaled to do so and in producing the documents Officer Jenks requested. In fact, Jenks admitted that he searched respondent face to face rather than in spread-eagle fashion because he had no reason to believe respondent would be violent.

While this difference between the situation presented in *Terry* and the context presented in this case would tend to suggest a lesser authority to search here than was permitted in *Terry*, other distinctions between the two cases suggest just the opposite. As the Court of Appeals noted, a crucial feature distinguishing the in-custody arrest from the *Terry* context "is not the greater likelihood that a person taken into custody is armed, but rather the increased likelihood of danger to the officer *if* in fact the person is armed." 153 U.S. App. D.C., at 130, 471 F.2d, at 1098, quoting *People v. Superior Court of Los Angeles County*, 7 Cal. 3d, at 214, 101 Cal. Rptr., at 857, 496 P.2d, at 1225 (Wright, C.J., concurring) (emphasis in original). A *Terry* stop involves a momentary encounter between officer and suspect, while an in-custody arrest places the two in close proximity for a much longer period of time. If the individual happens to have a weapon on his person, he will certainly have much more opportunity to use it against the officer in the in-custody situation. The prolonged proximity also makes it more likely that the individual will be able to extricate any small hidden weapon which might go undetected in a weapons frisk, such as a safety pin or razor blade. In addition, a suspect taken into custody may feel more threatened by the serious restraint on his liberty than a person who is simply stopped by an officer for questioning, and may therefore be more likely to resort to force.

Thus, in some senses there is less need for a weapons search in the in-custody traffic arrest situation than in a *Terry* context; while in other ways, there is a greater need. Balancing these competing considerations in order to determine what is a reasonable warrantless search in the traffic arrest context is a difficult process, one for which there may be no easy analytical guideposts. We are dealing with factors not easily quantified and, therefore, not easily weighed one against the other. And the competing interests we are protecting — the individual's interest in remaining free from unnecessarily intrusive invasions of privacy and society's interest that police officers not take unnecessary risks in the performance of their duties — are each deserving of our most serious attention and do not themselves tip the balance in any particular direction.

As will be explained more fully below, I do not think it necessary to solve this balancing equation in this particular case. It is important to note, however, in view of the reasoning adopted by the majority, that available empirical evidence supports the result reached by the plurality of the Court of Appeals, rather than the result reached by the Court today.

The majority relies on statistics indicating that a significant percentage of murders of police officers occurs when the officers are making traffic stops. But these statistics only confirm what we recognized in *Terry* — that "American criminals have a long tradition of armed violence, and every year in this country many law enforcement officers are killed in the line of duty, and thousands more are wounded." *Terry v. Ohio*, 392 U.S., at 23, 88 S. Ct. at 1881. As the very next sentence in *Terry* recognized, however, "[v]irtually all of these deaths and a substantial portion of the injuries are inflicted with guns and knives." *Id.*, at 24, 88 S. Ct. at 1881. The statistics relied on by the Government in this case support this observation. Virtually all of the killings are caused by guns and knives, the very type of weapons which will not go undetected in a properly conducted weapons frisk. It requires more than citation to these statistics, then, to support the proposition that it is reasonable for police officers to conduct more than a *Terry*-type frisk for weapons when seeking to disarm a traffic offender who is taken into custody.

C

The majority opinion fails to recognize that the search conducted by Officer Jenks did not merely involve a search of respondent's person. It also included a separate search of effects found on his person. And even were we to assume, *arguendo*, that it was reasonable for Jenks to remove the object he felt in respondent's pocket, clearly there was no justification consistent with the Fourth Amendment which would authorize his opening the package and looking inside.

To begin with, after Jenks had the cigarette package in his hands, there is no indication that he had reason to believe or did in fact believe that the package contained a weapon. More importantly, even if the crumpled-up cigarette package had in fact contained some sort of small weapon, it would have been impossible for respondent to have used it once the package was in the officer's hands. Opening the package, therefore, did not further the protective purpose of the search . . . .

It is suggested, however, that since the custodial arrest itself represents a significant intrusion into the privacy of the person, any additional intrusion by way of opening or examining effects found on the person is not worthy of constitutional protection. But such an approach was expressly rejected by the Court in *Chimel.*

. . . .

The Government argues that it is difficult to see what constitutionally protected "expectation of privacy" a prisoner has in the interior of a cigarette pack. One wonders if the result in this case would have been the same were respondent a businessman who was lawfully taken into custody for driving without a license and whose wallet was taken from him by the police. Would it be reasonable for the police officer, because of the possibility that a razor blade was hidden somewhere in the wallet, to open it, remove all the contents, and examine each item carefully? Or suppose a lawyer lawfully arrested for a traffic offense is found to have a sealed envelope on his person. Would it be permissible for the arresting officer to tear open the envelope in order to make sure that it did not contain a clandestine weapon — perhaps a pin or a razor blade? Would it not be more consonant with the purpose of the Fourth Amendment and the legitimate needs of the police to require the officer, if he has any question whatsoever about what the wallet or letter contains, to hold on to it until the arrestee is brought to the precinct station?

I, for one, cannot characterize any of these intrusions into the privacy of an individual's papers and effects as being negligible incidents to the more serious intrusion into the individual's privacy stemming from the arrest itself. Nor can any principled distinction be drawn between the hypothetical searches I have posed and the search of the cigarette package in this case. The only reasoned distinction is between warrantless searches which serve legitimate protective and evidentiary functions and those that do not.

The search conducted by Officer Jenks in this case went far beyond what was reasonably necessary to protect him from harm or to ensure that respondent would not effect an escape from custody. In my view, it therefore fell outside the scope of a properly drawn "search incident to arrest" exception to the Fourth Amendment's warrant requirement. I would affirm the judgment of the Court of Appeals holding that the fruits of the search should have been suppressed at respondent's trial.

MR. JUSTICE POWELL, concurring [in both *Robinson* and the companion case of *Gustafson v. Florida*, 414 U.S. 260, 94 S. Ct. 488, 38 L. Ed. 2d 456 (1973)].

Although I join the opinions of the Court, I write briefly to emphasize what seems to me to be the essential premise of our decisions.

The Fourth Amendment safeguards the right of "the people to be secure in their persons, houses, papers, and effects, against unreasonable searches and seizures . . . ." These are areas of an individual's life about which he entertains legitimate expectations of privacy. I believe that an individual lawfully subjected to a custodial arrest retains no significant Fourth Amendment interest in the privacy of his person. Under this view the custodial arrest is the significant intrusion of state power into the privacy of one's person. If the arrest is lawful, the privacy interest guarded by the Fourth Amendment is subordinated to a legitimate and overriding governmental concern. No reason then exists to frustrate law enforcement by requiring some independent justification for a search incident to a lawful custodial arrest. This seems to me the reason that a valid arrest justifies a full search of the person, even if that search is not narrowly limited by the twin rationales of seizing evidence and disarming the arrestee. The search incident to arrest is reasonable under the Fourth Amendment because the privacy interest protected by that constitutional guarantee is legitimately abated by the fact of arrest.

Notes and Questions

(1) In *Chimel*, the dispute was over the scope of the area around an arrestee that could be searched incident to his arrest. In *Robinson*, the argument focused on the permissible scope of the search of the arrestee's person. After *Robinson*, what is the legitimate scope of the search of the person of an arrestee? What specific showing is necessary to justify such a search? Is there any arrestee who is *not* subject to such a search?

(2) In the companion case of *Gustafson v. Florida*, 414 U.S. 260, 94 S. Ct. 488, 38 L. Ed. 2d 456 (1973), a defendant contended that the search of a "cigarette box" found on his person was not reasonable. He attempted to distinguish *Robinson* on the ground that in his case there were no police regulations requiring the officer to take him into custody and no police department policies requiring a full-scale body search of an arrestee. The Court rejected his argument, finding *Robinson* indistinguishable. According to the majority, a warrantless search of the arrestee equivalent to that authorized by *Robinson* was reasonable because "the officer had probable cause to arrest . . . and . . . he lawfully effectuated the arrest and placed the [defendant] in custody."

(3) Suppose an officer who has discretion to take a person into custody for an offense chooses to issue the person a citation instead. Does the officer have the same authority to search that person that she would have had if she had effected a custodial arrest? In *Knowles v. Iowa*, 525 U.S. 113, 119 S. Ct. 484, 142 L. Ed. 2d 492 (1998), the Court addressed the constitutionality of searching an individual incident to the issuance of a citation for a traffic offense.

In *Knowles*, a police officer stopped the defendant for speeding. Although Iowa law authorized the officer to arrest the defendant for the offense, the officer decided to issue a citation in lieu of arrest. An Iowa statute provided that an officer who chose to cite a traffic offender could conduct a search of the same magnitude that he could conduct incident to the arrest of such an offender. Acting pursuant to that statute and without any articulable reason to believe that anything incriminating would be found, the officer searched both the driver and his vehicle. Under the passenger seat, the officer discovered marijuana and a "pot pipe." The defendant challenged the search, claiming that the "search incident to citation" authorized by Iowa law and conducted in his case violated the Fourth Amendment.

The Supreme Court unanimously agreed. The Court first "noted the two historical rationales for the 'search incident to arrest' exception: (1) the need to disarm the suspect in order to take him into custody, and (2) the need to preserve evidence for later use at trial." It then concluded that "neither of these underlying rationales for the search incident to arrest exception is sufficient to justify" a full search incident to a traffic citation. While "the concern for officer safety is [not] absent in the case of a routine traffic stop," that concern "does not by itself justify the . . . intrusion attending a full field-type search." Moreover, "the need to discover and preserve evidence" cannot justify a full search incident to a citation for speeding because once a driver is "stopped for speeding and issued a citation, all the evidence necessary to prosecute that offense ha[s] been obtained. No further evidence of excessive speed [is] going to be found" on his person or in the car. "As for destroying evidence of other crimes, the possibility that an officer would stumble onto evidence wholly unrelated to the speeding offense seems remote." In sum, the Court "decline[d]" to extend the "bright-line rule" of *Robinson* "to a situation where the concern for officer safety is not present to the same extent and the concern for destruction or loss of evidence is not present at all."

The *Knowles* Court did not discuss whether it is constitutional to subject an individual to a full custodial arrest based on probable cause to believe that he has committed a minor traffic offense. The Court resolved that question in *Atwater v. City of Lago Vista, see supra*, Chapter 3[B], holding that "[i]f an officer has probable cause to believe that an individual has committed *even a very minor criminal offense* in his presence, he may, without violating the Fourth Amendment, arrest the offender." In *Atwater*, a custodial arrest for violations of a seatbelt law was deemed reasonable.

The holding of the *Atwater* Court restricts the significance of the Court's holding in *Knowles*. If full arrests for certain minor offenses were unreasonable, officers would not be able to invoke the broad authority to conduct searches incident to arrest for those offenses. Because *Atwater* authorizes arrests for all minor *criminal* offenses, an officer can avoid the strictures of *Knowles* by arresting a minor offender. Moreover, *Whren v. United States, see supra* Chapter 2, seems to make it clear that a search incident to arrest is not unreasonable under the Fourth Amendment simply because an officer decided to arrest an individual in order to exercise the authority to search incident to that arrest.

(4) Suppose that state law authorizes the issuance of a citation for an offense but forbids the arrest of an offender. Are an arrest and a search incident to arrest for that offense unreasonable under the Fourth Amendment? In *Virginia v. Moore*, 553 U.S. 164, 128 S. Ct. 1598, 170 L. Ed. 2d 559 (2008), the issue was "whether a police officer violates the Fourth Amendment by making an arrest based on probable cause but prohibited by state law." The Supreme Court found no support for the contention that the constitutionality of an arrest depends on its validity under state law in either history or "traditional standards of reasonableness."

According to an eight-Justice majority, an arrest based on probable cause serves interests sufficient to justify a seizure whether or not the state has chosen to forego the option of arrest. In addition, the interest in readily administrable rules — i.e., "the need for a bright-line constitutional standard" — supports a refusal to tie the constitutionality of an arrest to the dictates of state law. Finally, linking reasonableness to state law would cause Fourth Amendment protections to vary based on the time and place of an arrest, an undesirable state of affairs. For all these reasons, "[w]hen officers have probable cause to believe that a person has committed a crime in their presence, the Fourth Amendment permits them to make an arrest." An arrest based on probable cause is a "lawful arrest," and a search of an arrestee incident to a lawful arrest is constitutionally reasonable.

(5) Under the search incident to arrest exception to the warrant rule, explained in *Chimel*, *Robinson*, and other opinions that follow, significant privacy intrusions are constitutionally permissible as a routine matter following lawful arrests. As will be seen in subsection [D] of this chapter, arrestees may also be subject to reasonable routine "inventory searches" at jails and, in some circumstances, to strip searches, visual body cavity searches, and to the taking of DNA samples for the purpose of "identifying" them as the perpetrators of other offenses.

Arizona v. Gant

United States Supreme Court

556 U.S. 332, 129 S. Ct. 1710, 173 L. Ed. 2d 485 (2009)

JUSTICE STEVENS delivered the opinion of the Court.

. . . .

I

On August 25, 1999, acting on an anonymous tip that the residence at 2524 North Walnut Avenue was being used to sell drugs, Tuscon police officers Griffith and Reed knocked on the front door and asked to speak to the owner. Gant answered the door and, after identifying himself, stated that he expected the owner to return later. The officers left the residence and conducted a records check, which revealed that Gant's driver's license had been suspended and there was an outstanding warrant for his arrest for driving with a suspended license.

When the officers returned to the house that evening, they found a man near the back of the house and a woman in a car parked in front of it. After a third officer arrived, they arrested the man for providing a false name and the woman for possessing drug paraphernalia. Both arrestees were handcuffed and secured in separate patrol cars when Gant arrived. The officers recognized his car as it entered the driveway, and Officer Griffith confirmed that Gant was the driver by shining a flashlight into the car as it drove by him. Gant parked at the end of the driveway, got out of his car, and shut the door. Griffith, who was about 30 feet away, called to Gant, and they approached each other, meeting 10-to-12 feet from Gant's car. Griffith immediately arrested Gant and handcuffed him.

Because the other arrestees were secured in the only patrol cars at the scene, Griffith called for backup. When two more officers arrived, they locked Gant in the backseat of their vehicle. After Gant had been handcuffed and placed in the back of a patrol car, two officers searched his car: One of them found a gun, and the other discovered a bag of cocaine in the pocket of a jacket on the backseat.

Gant was charged with two offenses — possession of a narcotic drug for sale and possession of drug paraphernalia (*i.e.*, the plastic bag in which the cocaine was found). He moved to suppress the evidence seized from his car on the ground that the warrantless search violated the Fourth Amendment . . . .

The trial court . . . denied the motion to suppress. Relying on the fact that the police saw Gant commit the crime of driving without a license and apprehended him only shortly after he exited his car, the court held that the search was permissible as a search incident to arrest. A jury found Gant guilty on both drug counts, and he was sentenced to a 3-year term of imprisonment.

After protracted state-court proceedings, the Arizona Supreme Court concluded that the search of Gant's car was unreasonable within the meaning of the Fourth Amendment . . . . Relying on . . . *Chimel* [*v. California*], the court observed that the search-incident-to-arrest exception to the warrant requirement is justified by interests in officer safety and evidence preservation. 216 Ariz., at 4, 162 P.3d, at 643. When "the justifications underlying *Chimel* no longer exist because the scene is secure and the arrestee is handcuffed, secured in the back of a patrol car, and under the supervision of an officer," the court concluded, a "warrantless search of the arrestee's car cannot be justified as necessary to protect the officers at the scene or prevent the destruction of evidence." *Id.*, at 5, 162 P.3d, at 644. . . .

The dissenting justices would have upheld the search of Gant's car based on their view that "the validity of a . . . search [under *New York v. Belton*] . . . clearly does not depend on the presence of the *Chimel* rationales in a particular case." *Id.*, at 8, 162 P.3d, at 647. . . .

The chorus that has called for us to revisit *Belton* includes courts, scholars, and Members of this Court who have questioned that decision's clarity and its fidelity to Fourth Amendment principles. We therefore granted the State's petition for certiorari.

II

Consistent with our precedent, our analysis begins, as it should in every case addressing the reasonableness of a warrantless search, with the basic rule that "searches conducted outside the judicial process, without prior approval by judge or magistrate, are *per se* unreasonable under the Fourth Amendment — subject only to a few specifically established and well-delineated exceptions." *Katz v. United States,* 389 U.S. 347, 357, 88 S. Ct. 507, 19 L. Ed. 2d 576 (1967) (footnote omitted). Among the exceptions to the warrant requirement is a search incident to a lawful arrest. The exception derives from interests in officer safety and evidence preservation that are typically implicated in arrest situations.

In *Chimel,* we held that a search incident to arrest may only include "the arrestee's person and the area 'within his immediate control' — construing that phrase to mean the area from within which he might gain possession of a weapon or destructible evidence." [395 U.S. 752, 763, 89 S. Ct. 2034 (1969)]. That limitation, which continues to define the boundaries of the exception, ensures that the scope of a search incident to arrest is commensurate with its purposes of protecting arresting officers and safeguarding any evidence of the offense of arrest that an arrestee might conceal or destroy. If there is no possibility that an arrestee could reach into the area that law enforcement officers seek to search, both justifications for the search-incident-to-arrest exception are absent and the rule does not apply.

In *Belton,* we considered *Chimel*'s application to the automobile context. A lone police officer in that case stopped a speeding car in which Belton was one of four occupants. While asking for the driver's license and registration, the officer smelled burnt marijuana and observed an envelope on the car floor marked "Supergold" — a name he associated with marijuana. Thus having probable cause to believe the occupants had committed a drug offense, the officer ordered them out of the vehicle, placed them under arrest, and patted them down. Without handcuffing the arrestees,[1] the officer "'split them up into four separate areas of the Thruway ... so they would not be in physical touching area of each other'" and searched the vehicle, including the pocket of a jacket on the backseat, in which he found cocaine. [453 U.S. 454, 456, 101 S. Ct. 2860, 69 L. Ed. 2d 768 (1981)].

. . . .

In its brief [in *Belton*], the State argued that the Court of Appeals erred in concluding that the jacket was under the officer's exclusive control. Focusing on the number of arrestees and their proximity to the vehicle, the State asserted that it was reasonable for the officer to believe the arrestees could have accessed the vehicle and

---

1. The officer was unable to handcuff the occupants because he had only one set of handcuffs. See Brief for Petitioner in *New York v. Belton,* O.T.1980, No. 80-328, p. 3 (hereinafter Brief in No. 80-328).

its contents, making the search permissible under *Chimel*. Brief in No. 80-328, at 7–8. The United States, as *amicus curiae* in support of the State, argued for a more permissive standard, but it maintained that any search incident to arrest must be "'substantially contemporaneous'" with the arrest—a requirement it deemed "satisfied if the search occurs during the period in which the arrest is being consummated and before the situation has so stabilized that it could be said that the arrest was completed." Brief for United States as *Amicus Curiae* in *New York v. Belton*, O.T.1980, No. 80-328, p. 14. There was no suggestion by the parties or *amici* that *Chimel* authorizes a vehicle search incident to arrest when there is no realistic possibility that an arrestee could access his vehicle.

After considering these arguments, we held that when an officer lawfully arrests "the occupant of an automobile, he may, as a contemporaneous incident of that arrest, search the passenger compartment of the automobile" and any containers therein. *Belton*, 453 U.S., at 460, 101 S. Ct. 2860 (footnote omitted). That holding was based in large part on our assumption "that articles inside the relatively narrow compass of the passenger compartment of an automobile are in fact generally, even if not inevitably, within 'the area into which an arrestee might reach.'" *Ibid.*

. . . .

III

. . . *Belton* . . . has been widely understood to allow a vehicle search incident to the arrest of a recent occupant even if there is no possibility the arrestee could gain access to the vehicle at the time of the search. This reading may be attributable to JUSTICE BRENNAN's dissent in *Belton*, in which he characterized the Court's holding as resting on the "fiction . . . that the interior of a car is *always* within the immediate control of an arrestee who has recently been in the car." 453 U.S., at 466, 101 S. Ct. 2860. Under the majority's approach, he argued, "the result would presumably be the same even if [the officer] had handcuffed Belton and his companions in the patrol car" before conducting the search. *Id.*, at 468, 101 S. Ct. 2860.

Since we decided *Belton*, Courts of Appeals have given different answers to the question whether a vehicle must be within an arrestee's reach to justify a vehicle search incident to arrest, but JUSTICE BRENNAN's reading of the Court's opinion has predominated . . . . JUSTICE SCALIA has . . . noted that, although it is improbable that an arrestee could gain access to weapons stored in his vehicle after he has been handcuffed and secured in the backseat of a patrol car, cases allowing a search in "this precise factual scenario . . . are legion." [*Thornton v. United States*, 541 U.S. 615, 628, 124 S. Ct. 2127 (2004)] (opinion concurring in judgment) (collecting cases). Indeed, some courts have upheld searches under *Belton* "even when . . . the handcuffed arrestee has already left the scene." 541 U.S., at 628, 124 S. Ct. 2127 (same).

Under this broad reading of *Belton*, a vehicle search would be authorized incident to every arrest of a recent occupant notwithstanding that in most cases the vehicle's passenger compartment will not be within the arrestee's reach at the time of the search. To read *Belton* as authorizing a vehicle search incident to every recent occupant's arrest would thus untether the rule from the justifications underlying the *Chimel* exception — a result clearly incompatible with our statement in *Belton* that it "in no way alters the fundamental principles established in the *Chimel* case regarding the basic scope of searches incident to lawful custodial arrests." 453 U.S., at 460, n. 3, 101 S. Ct. 2860. Accordingly, we reject this reading of *Belton* and hold that the *Chimel* rationale authorizes police to search a vehicle incident to a recent occupant's arrest only when the arrestee is unsecured and within reaching distance of the passenger compartment at the time of the search.[4]

Although it does not follow from *Chimel*, we also conclude that circumstances unique to the vehicle context justify a search incident to a lawful arrest when it is "reasonable to believe evidence relevant to the crime of arrest might be found in the vehicle." *Thornton*, 541 U.S., at 632, 124 S. Ct. 2127 (Scalia, J., concurring in judgment). In many cases, as when a recent occupant is arrested for a traffic violation, there will be no reasonable basis to believe the vehicle contains relevant evidence. See, *e.g., Atwater v. Lago Vista*, 532 U.S. 318, 324, 121 S. Ct. 1536, 149 L. Ed. 2d 549 (2001); *Knowles v. Iowa*, 525 U.S. 113, 118, 119 S. Ct. 484, 142 L. Ed. 2d 492 (1998). But in others, including *Belton* and *Thornton*, the offense of arrest will supply a basis for searching the passenger compartment of an arrestee's vehicle and any containers therein.

Neither the possibility of access nor the likelihood of discovering offense-related evidence authorized the search in this case. Unlike in *Belton*, which involved a single officer confronted with four unsecured arrestees, the five officers in this case outnumbered the three arrestees, all of whom had been handcuffed and secured in separate patrol cars before the officers searched Gant's car. Under those circumstances, Gant clearly was not within reaching distance of his car at the time of the search. An evidentiary basis for the search was also lacking in this case. Whereas Belton and Thornton were arrested for drug offenses, Gant was arrested for driving with a suspended license — an offense for which police could not expect to find evidence in the passenger compartment of Gant's car. Cf. *Knowles*, 525 U.S., at 118, 119 S. Ct. 484. Because police could not reasonably have believed either that Gant could have accessed his car at the time of the search or that evidence of the offense for which he was arrested might have been found therein, the search in this case was unreasonable.

IV

.... The State argues that *Belton* searches are reasonable regardless of the possibility of access in a given case because that expansive rule correctly balances law enforcement interests, including the interest in a bright-line rule, with an arrestee's limited privacy interest in his vehicle.

---

4. Because officers have many means of ensuring the safe arrest of vehicle occupants, it will be the rare case in which an officer is unable to fully effectuate an arrest so that a real possibility of access to the arrestee's vehicle remains. Cf. 3 W. LaFave, Search and Seizure § 7.1(c), p. 525 (4th ed. 2004) (hereinafter LaFave) (noting that the availability of protective measures "ensur[es] the non-existence of circumstances in which the arrestee's 'control' of the car is in doubt"). But in such a case a search incident to arrest is reasonable under the Fourth Amendment.

For several reasons, we reject the State's argument. First, the State seriously undervalues the privacy interests at stake. Although we have recognized that a motorist's privacy interest in his vehicle is less substantial than in his home, the former interest is nevertheless important and deserving of constitutional protection, see *Knowles*, 525 U.S., at 117, 119 S. Ct. 484. It is particularly significant that *Belton* searches authorize police officers to search not just the passenger compartment but every purse, briefcase, or other container within that space. A rule that gives police the power to conduct such a search whenever an individual is caught committing a traffic offense, when there is no basis for believing evidence of the offense might be found in the vehicle, creates a serious and recurring threat to the privacy of countless individuals. Indeed, the character of that threat implicates the central concern underlying the Fourth Amendment — the concern about giving police officers unbridled discretion to rummage at will among a person's private effects.

At the same time as it undervalues these privacy concerns, the State exaggerates the clarity that its reading of *Belton* provides. Courts that have read *Belton* expansively are at odds regarding how close in time to the arrest and how proximate to the arrestee's vehicle an officer's first contact with the arrestee must be to bring the encounter within *Belton*'s purview and whether a search is reasonable when it commences or continues after the arrestee has been removed from the scene. The rule has thus generated a great deal of uncertainty, particularly for a rule touted as providing a "bright line." See 3 LaFave, § 7.1(c), at 514–524.

Contrary to the State's suggestion, a broad reading of *Belton* is also unnecessary to protect law enforcement safety and evidentiary interests. Under our view, *Belton* and *Thornton* permit an officer to conduct a vehicle search when an arrestee is within reaching distance of the vehicle or it is reasonable to believe the vehicle contains evidence of the offense of arrest. Other established exceptions to the warrant requirement authorize a vehicle search under additional circumstances when safety or evidentiary concerns demand. For instance, *Michigan v. Long*, 463 U.S. 1032, 103 S. Ct. 3469, 77 L. Ed. 2d 1201 (1983), permits an officer to search a vehicle's passenger compartment when he has reasonable suspicion that an individual, whether or not the arrestee, is "dangerous" and might access the vehicle to "gain immediate control of weapons." *Id.*, at 1049, 103 S. Ct. 3469 (citing *Terry v. Ohio*, 392 U.S. 1, 21, 88 S. Ct. 1868, 20 L. Ed. 2d 889 (1968)). If there is probable cause to believe a vehicle contains evidence of criminal activity, *United States v. Ross*, 456 U.S. 798, 820–821, 102 S. Ct. 2157, 72 L. Ed. 2d 572 (1982), authorizes a search of any area of the vehicle in which the evidence might be found. Unlike the searches permitted by JUSTICE SCALIA's opinion concurring in the judgment in *Thornton*, which we conclude today are reasonable for purposes of the Fourth Amendment, *Ross* allows searches for evidence relevant to offenses other than the offense of arrest, and the scope of the search authorized is broader. Finally, there may be still other circumstances in which safety or evidentiary interests would justify a search. Cf. *Maryland v. Buie*, 494 U.S. 325, 334, 110 S. Ct. 1093, 108 L. Ed. 2d 276 (1990) (holding that, incident to arrest, an officer may conduct a limited protective sweep of those areas of a house in which he reasonably suspects a dangerous person may be hiding).

These exceptions together ensure that officers may search a vehicle when genuine safety or evidentiary concerns encountered during the arrest of a vehicle's recent occupant justify a search. Construing *Belton* broadly to allow vehicle searches incident to any arrest would serve no purpose except to provide a police entitlement, and it is anathema to the Fourth Amendment to permit a warrantless search on that basis. For these reasons, we are unpersuaded by the State's arguments that a broad reading of *Belton* would meaningfully further law enforcement interests and justify a substantial intrusion on individuals' privacy.

V

Our dissenting colleagues argue that the doctrine of *stare decisis* requires adherence to a broad reading of *Belton* even though the justifications for searching a vehicle incident to arrest are in most cases absent. The doctrine of *stare decisis* is of course "essential to the respect accorded to the judgments of the Court and to the stability of the law," but it does not compel us to follow a past decision when its rationale no longer withstands "careful analysis." *Lawrence v. Texas*, 539 U.S. 558, 577, 123 S. Ct. 2472, 156 L. Ed. 2d 508 (2003).

We have never relied on *stare decisis* to justify the continuance of an unconstitutional police practice. And we would be particularly loath to uphold an unconstitutional result in a case that is so easily distinguished from the decisions that arguably compel it. The safety and evidentiary interests that supported the search in *Belton* simply are not present in this case. Indeed, it is hard to imagine two cases that are factually more distinct, as *Belton* involved one officer confronted by four unsecured arrestees suspected of committing a drug offense and this case involves several officers confronted with a securely detained arrestee apprehended for driving with a suspended license. This case is also distinguishable from *Thornton*, in which the petitioner was arrested for a drug offense . . . .

We do not agree with the contention in JUSTICE ALITO's dissent (hereinafter dissent) that consideration of police reliance interests requires a different result. Although it appears that the State's reading of *Belton* has been widely taught in police academies and that law enforcement officers have relied on the rule in conducting vehicle searches during the past 28 years, many of these searches were not justified by the reasons underlying the *Chimel* exception. Countless individuals guilty of nothing more serious than a traffic violation have had their constitutional right to the security of their private effects violated as a result. The fact that the law enforcement community may view the State's version of the *Belton* rule as an entitlement does not establish the sort of reliance interest that could outweigh the countervailing interest that all individuals share in having their constitutional rights fully protected. If it is clear that a practice is unlawful, individuals' interest in its discontinuance clearly outweighs any law enforcement "entitlement" to its persistence . . . .

The dissent also ignores the checkered history of the search-incident-to-arrest exception. [The Court then recounted the vacillation in its own interpretation of the breadth of the exception.] . . . Notably, none of the dissenters in *Chimel* or the cases that preceded it argued that law enforcement reliance interests outweighed the interest in protecting individual constitutional rights so as to warrant fidelity to an unjustifiable rule.

The experience of the 28 years since we decided *Belton* has shown that the generalization underpinning the broad reading of that decision is unfounded. We now know that articles inside the passenger compartment are rarely "within 'the area into which an arrestee might reach,'" 453 U.S., at 460, 101 S. Ct. 2860, and blind adherence to *Belton*'s faulty assumption would authorize myriad unconstitutional searches. The doctrine of *stare decisis* does not require us to approve routine constitutional violations.

VI

Police may search a vehicle incident to a recent occupant's arrest only if the arrestee is within reaching distance of the passenger compartment at the time of the search or it is reasonable to believe the vehicle contains evidence of the offense of arrest. When these justifications are absent, a search of an arrestee's vehicle will be unreasonable unless police obtain a warrant or show that another exception to the warrant requirement applies. The Arizona Supreme Court correctly held that this case involved an unreasonable search. Accordingly, the judgment of the State Supreme Court is affirmed.

It is so ordered.

Justice Scalia, concurring.

. . . . When an arrest is made in connection with a roadside stop, police virtually always have a less intrusive and more effective means of ensuring their safety [than a search of the vehicle] — and a means that is virtually always employed: ordering the arrestee away from the vehicle, patting him down in the open, handcuffing him, and placing him in the squad car.

Law enforcement officers face a risk of being shot whenever they pull a car over. But that risk is at its height at the time of the initial confrontation; and it is *not at all* reduced by allowing a search of the stopped vehicle after the driver has been arrested and placed in the squad car. I observed in *Thornton* that the government had failed to provide a single instance in which a formerly restrained arrestee escaped to retrieve a weapon from his own vehicle, 541 U.S., at 626, 124 S. Ct. 2127; Arizona and its *amici* have not remedied that significant deficiency in the present case.

. . . .

Justice Stevens acknowledges that an officer-safety rationale cannot justify all vehicle searches incident to arrest, but asserts that that is not the rule *Belton* and *Thornton* adopted. (. . . I read those cases differently). Justice Stevens would therefore retain the application of *Chimel v. California*, 395 U.S. 752, 89 S. Ct. 2034, 23 L. Ed. 2d 685 (1969), in the car-search context but would apply in the future what he believes our cases held in the past: that officers making a roadside stop may search the vehicle so long as the "arrestee is within reaching distance of the passenger compartment at the time of the search." *Ante*, at 1723. I believe that this standard fails to provide the needed guidance to arresting officers and also leaves much room for manipulation, inviting officers to leave the scene unsecured (at least where dangerous suspects are not involved) in order to conduct a vehicle search. In my view we should simply abandon the *Belton-Thornton* charade of officer safety and overrule those cases. I would hold that a vehicle search incident to arrest is *ipso facto* "reasonable" only when the object of the search is evidence of the crime for which the arrest was made, or of another crime that the officer has probable cause to believe occurred. Because respondent was arrested for driving without a license (a crime for which no evidence could be expected to be found in the vehicle), I would hold in the present case that the search was unlawful.

Justice Alito insists that the Court must demand a good reason for abandoning prior precedent. That is true enough, but it seems to me ample reason that the precedent was badly reasoned and produces erroneous (in this case unconstitutional) results . . . .

Justice Alito argues that there is no reason to adopt a rule limiting automobile-arrest searches to those cases where the search's object is evidence of the crime of arrest. I disagree. This formulation of officers' authority both preserves the outcomes of our prior cases and tethers the scope and rationale of the doctrine to the triggering event. *Belton*, by contrast, allowed searches precisely when its exigency-based rationale was least applicable: The fact of the arrest in the automobile context makes searches on exigency grounds *less* reasonable, not more. . . . .

No other Justice, however, shares my view that application of *Chimel* in this context should be entirely abandoned. It seems to me unacceptable for the Court to come forth with a 4-to-1-to-4 opinion that leaves the governing rule uncertain. I am therefore confronted with the choice of either leaving the current understanding of *Belton* and *Thornton* in effect, or acceding to what seems to me the artificial narrowing of those cases adopted by Justice Stevens. The latter, as I have said, does not provide the degree of certainty I think desirable in this field; but the former opens the field to what I think are plainly unconstitutional searches — which is the greater evil. I therefore join the opinion of the Court.

Justice Breyer, dissenting.

I agree with Justice Alito that *New York v. Belton*, 453 U.S. 454, 101 S. Ct. 2860, 69 L. Ed. 2d 768 (1981), is best read as setting forth a bright-line rule that permits a warrantless search of the passenger compartment of an automobile incident to the lawful arrest of an occupant — regardless of the danger the arrested individual in fact poses. I also agree with Justice Stevens, however, that the rule can produce results divorced from its underlying Fourth Amendment rationale. . . . .

The matter, however, is not one of first impression, and that fact makes a substantial difference. . . . . Principles of *stare decisis* must apply, and those who wish this Court to change a well-established legal precedent — where, as here, there has been considerable reliance on the legal rule in question — bear a heavy burden. I have not found that burden met. . . . . I consequently join JUSTICE ALITO's dissenting opinion with the exception of Part II-E.

JUSTICE ALITO, with whom THE CHIEF JUSTICE and JUSTICE KENNEDY join, and with whom JUSTICE BREYER joins except as to Part II-E, dissenting.

Twenty-eight years ago, in *New York v. Belton*, 453 U.S. 454, 460, 101 S. Ct. 2860, 69 L. Ed. 2d 768 (1981), this Court held that "when a policeman has made a lawful custodial arrest of the occupant of an automobile, he may, as a contemporaneous incident of that arrest, search the passenger compartment of that automobile." (Footnote omitted.) Five years ago, in *Thornton v. United States*, 541 U.S. 615, 124 S. Ct. 2127, 158 L. Ed. 2d 905 (2004) — a case involving a situation not materially distinguishable from the situation here — the Court not only reaffirmed but extended the holding of *Belton*, making it applicable to recent occupants . . . .

To take the place of the overruled precedents, the Court adopts a new two-part rule under which a police officer who arrests a vehicle occupant or recent occupant may search the passenger compartment if (1) the arrestee is within reaching distance of the vehicle at the time of the search or (2) the officer has reason to believe that the vehicle contains evidence of the offense of arrest. *Ante*, at 1723–1724. The first part of this new rule may endanger arresting officers . . . . The second part of the new rule is taken from JUSTICE SCALIA's separate opinion in *Thornton* without any independent explanation of its origin or justification and is virtually certain to confuse law enforcement officers and judges for some time to come. The Court's . . . reasoning undermines *Chimel*. I would follow *Belton*, and I therefore respectfully dissent.

I

Although the Court refuses to acknowledge that it is overruling *Belton* and *Thornton*, there can be no doubt that it does so.

In *Belton*, ... [t]he Court acknowledged that articles in the passenger compartment of a car are not always within an arrestee's reach, but "[i]n order to establish the workable rule this category of cases requires," the Court adopted a rule that categorically permits the search of a car's passenger compartment incident to the lawful arrest of an occupant. 453 U.S., at 460, 101 S. Ct. 2860.

The precise holding in *Belton* could not be clearer. The Court stated unequivocally: "[W]e hold that when a policeman has made a lawful custodial arrest of the occupant of an automobile, he may, as a contemporaneous incident of that arrest, search the passenger compartment of that automobile." *Ibid.* (footnote omitted).

Despite this explicit statement, the opinion of the Court in the present case curiously suggests that *Belton* may reasonably be read as adopting a holding that is narrower than the one explicitly set out in the *Belton* opinion, namely, that an officer arresting a vehicle occupant may search the passenger compartment "*when* the passenger compartment is within an arrestee's reaching distance." *Ante*, at 1717–1718 (emphasis in original) . . . .

. . . In *Thornton*, the Court recognized the scope of *Belton*'s holding. See 541 U.S., at 620, 124 S. Ct. 2127 . . . . This "bright-line rule" has now been interred.

II

Because the Court has substantially overruled *Belton* and *Thornton*, the Court must explain why its departure from the usual rule of *stare decisis* is justified . . . . [T]he Court has said that a constitutional precedent should be followed unless there is a "'special justification'" for its abandonment. *Dickerson v. United States*, 530 U.S. 428, 443, 120 S. Ct. 2326, 147 L. Ed. 2d 405 (2000). Relevant factors identified in prior cases include whether the precedent has engendered reliance, whether there has been an important change in circumstances in the outside world, whether the precedent has proved to be unworkable, whether the precedent has been undermined by later decisions, and whether the decision was badly reasoned. These factors weigh in favor of retaining the rule established in *Belton*.

A

Reliance . . . . [T]he Court has recognized that reliance by law enforcement officers is . . . entitled to weight . . . .

. . . The *Belton* rule has been taught to police officers for more than a quarter century. Many searches — almost certainly including more than a few that figure in cases now on appeal — were conducted in scrupulous reliance on that precedent. It is likely that, on the very day when this opinion is announced, numerous vehicle searches will be conducted in good faith by police officers who were taught the *Belton* rule.

. . . The Court states that "[w]e have never relied on *stare decisis* to justify the continuance of an unconstitutional police practice," *ante*, at 1722, but . . . cites no authority for the proposition that *stare decisis* may be disregarded or provides only lesser protection when the precedent that is challenged is one that sustained the constitutionality of a law enforcement practice.

. . . .

B

Changed circumstances. Abandonment of the *Belton* rule cannot be justified on the ground that the dangers surrounding the arrest of a vehicle occupant are different today than they were 28 years ago. The Court claims that "[w]e now know that articles inside the passenger compartment are rarely 'within "the area into which an arrestee might reach,"'" *ante*, at 1723–24, but surely it was well known in 1981 that a person who is taken from a vehicle, handcuffed, and placed in the back of a patrol car is unlikely to make it back into his own car to retrieve a weapon or destroy evidence.

C

Workability. The *Belton* rule has not proved to be unworkable. On the contrary, the rule was adopted for the express purpose of providing a test that would be relatively easy for police officers and judges to apply. The Court correctly notes that even the *Belton* rule is not perfectly clear in all situations. Specifically, it is sometimes debatable whether a search is or is not contemporaneous with an arrest, but that problem is small in comparison with the problems that the Court's new two-part rule will produce.

The first part of the Court's new rule — which permits the search of a vehicle's passenger compartment if it is within an arrestee's reach at the time of the search — reintroduces the same sort of case-by-case, fact-specific decisionmaking that the *Belton* rule was adopted to avoid. As the situation in *Belton* illustrated, there are cases in which it is unclear whether an arrestee could retrieve a weapon or evidence in the passenger compartment of a car.

Even more serious problems will also result from the second part of the Court's new rule, which requires officers making roadside arrests to determine whether there is reason to believe that the vehicle contains evidence of the crime of arrest. What this rule permits in a variety of situations is entirely unclear.

D

Consistency with later cases. The *Belton* bright-line rule has not been undermined by subsequent cases. On the contrary, that rule was reaffirmed and extended just five years ago in *Thornton*.

E

Bad reasoning. The Court is harshly critical of *Belton*'s reasoning, but the problem that the Court perceives cannot be remedied simply by overruling *Belton*. *Belton* represented only a modest — and quite defensible — extension of *Chimel*, as I understand that decision.

. . . .

Unfortunately, *Chimel* did not say whether "the area from within which [an arrestee] might gain possession of a weapon or destructible evidence" is to be measured at the time of the arrest or at the time of the search, but unless the *Chimel* rule was meant to be a specialty rule, applicable to only a few unusual cases, the Court must have intended for this area to be measured at the time of arrest.

This is so because the Court can hardly have failed to appreciate the following two facts. First, in the great majority of cases, an officer making an arrest is able to handcuff the arrestee and remove him to a secure place before conducting a search incident to the arrest. Second, because it is safer for an arresting officer to secure an arrestee before searching, it is likely that this is what arresting officers do in the great majority of cases. (And it appears, not surprisingly, that this is in fact the prevailing practice.) Thus, if the area within an arrestee's reach were assessed, not at the time of arrest, but at the time of the search, the *Chimel* rule would rarely come into play.

Moreover, if the applicability of the *Chimel* rule turned on whether an arresting officer chooses to secure an arrestee prior to conducting a search, rather than searching first and securing the arrestee later, the rule would "create a perverse incentive for an arresting officer to prolong the period during which the arrestee is kept in an area where he could pose a danger to the officer." *United States v. Abdul-Saboor*, 85 F.3d 664, 669 (CADC 1996) . . . .

I do not think that this is what the *Chimel* Court intended. Handcuffs were in use in 1969. The ability of arresting officers to secure arrestees before conducting a search — and their incentive to do so — are facts that can hardly have escaped the Court's attention. I therefore believe that the *Chimel* Court intended that its new rule apply in cases in which the arrestee is handcuffed before the search is conducted.

The *Belton* Court, in my view, proceeded on the basis of this interpretation of *Chimel*. Again speaking through Justice Stewart, the *Belton* Court reasoned that articles in the passenger compartment of a car are "generally, even if not inevitably" within an arrestee's reach. 453 U.S., at 460, 101 S. Ct. 2860. This is undoubtedly true at the time of the arrest of a person who is seated in a car but plainly not true when the person has been removed from the car and placed in handcuffs. Accordingly, the *Belton* Court must have proceeded on the assumption that the *Chimel* rule was to be applied at the time of arrest. And that is why the *Belton* Court was able to say that its decision "in no way alter[ed] the fundamental principles established in the *Chimel* case regarding the basic scope of searches incident to lawful custodial arrests." 453 U.S., at 460, n. 3, 101 S. Ct. 2860. Viewing *Chimel* as having focused on the time of arrest, *Belton*'s only new step was to eliminate the need to decide on a case-by-case basis whether a particular person seated in a car actually could have reached the part of the passenger compartment where a weapon or evidence was hidden. For this reason, if we are going to reexamine *Belton*, we should also reexamine the reasoning in *Chimel* on which *Belton* rests.

F

The Court, however, does not reexamine *Chimel* and thus leaves the law relating to searches incident to arrest in a confused and unstable state. The first part of the Court's new two-part rule — which permits an arresting officer to search the area within an arrestee's reach at the time of the search — applies, at least for now, only to vehicle occupants and recent occupants, but there is no logical reason why the same rule should not apply to all arrestees.

The second part of the Court's new rule, which the Court takes uncritically from Justice Scalia's separate opinion in *Thornton*, raises doctrinal and practical problems that the Court makes no effort to address. Why, for example, is the standard for this type of evidence-gathering search "reason to believe" rather than probable cause? And why is this type of search restricted to evidence of the offense of arrest? It is true that an arrestee's vehicle is probably more likely to contain evidence of the crime of arrest than of some other crime, but if reason-to-believe is the governing standard for an evidence-gathering search incident to arrest, it is not easy to see why an officer should not be able to search when the officer has reason to believe that the vehicle in question possesses evidence of a crime other than the crime of arrest.

Nor is it easy to see why an evidence-gathering search incident to arrest should be restricted to the passenger compartment. The *Belton* rule was limited in this way because the passenger compartment was considered to be the area that vehicle occupants can generally reach, but since the second part of the new rule is not based on officer safety or the preservation of evidence, the ground for this limitation is obscure.[2]

III

. . . I would . . . leave any reexamination of our prior precedents for another day, if such a reexamination is to be undertaken at all. In this case, I would simply apply *Belton* and reverse the judgment below.

Notes and Questions

(1) A majority of Justices (Justice Scalia and the four dissenting Justices) believe that the predominant understanding of *New York v. Belton* that granted officers broad authority to search vehicles incident to the arrest of an occupant was an accurate reading of *Belton*'s holding. The majority opinion in *Gant* suggests that Justice Brennan's dissent in *Belton* may be the source of this expansive interpretation of *Belton*. In fact, the *Belton* majority opinion, while hardly the picture of clarity, contains ample support for that interpretation. According to the understanding of *Belton* that prevailed in the lower courts, when was it reasonable for officers to search vehicles incident to the arrest of an occupant?

The majority opinion in *Gant* (joined by Justice Scalia to avoid the uncertainty that could result from a 4-to-1-to-4 split), "reject[ed]" the prevailing "reading of *Belton*" as incorrect. It held that under a proper interpretation of that decision, the authority to search vehicles incident to the arrest of an occupant is somewhat narrower. Why did the majority conclude that the authority recognized by the prevailing reading of *Belton* was constitutionally unacceptable? After *Gant*, when may officers conduct warrantless searches of vehicles incident to arrests of occupants? How does the holding in *Gant* limit the authority officers had under the prevailing understanding? Why are the two, distinct varieties of warrantless vehicle searches authorized by *Gant* reasonable?

---

2. I do not understand the Court's decision to reach the following situations. First, it is not uncommon for an officer to arrest some but not all of the occupants of a vehicle. The Court's decision in this case does not address the question whether in such a situation a search of the passenger compartment may be justified on the ground that the occupants who are not arrested could gain access to the car and retrieve a weapon or destroy evidence. Second, there may be situations in which an arresting officer has cause to fear that persons who were not passengers in the car might attempt to retrieve a weapon or evidence from the car while the officer is still on the scene. The decision in this case, as I understand it, does not address that situation either.

(2) THE SIGNIFICANCE OF *BELTON* AFTER *GANT*: Although the *Gant* majority rejected the broad authority to search a vehicle incident to the arrest of an occupant recognized in the prevailing understanding of *Belton*, there are several aspects of the *Belton* doctrine that the Court did not modify.

(a) The majority clearly endorsed *Belton*'s holding that a search incident to arrest is permissible when the arrestee is either an occupant or a *recent* occupant of the vehicle. In other words, officers have authority to search a vehicle even if an arrestee is not still inside the vehicle at the time of the arrest as long as he or she was an occupant "recently" — i.e., was inside the vehicle not long before being arrested. If the arrestee has been outside the vehicle too long to be considered a "recent" occupant, a search is unreasonable. How long is too long is a matter of some uncertainty, but the *Belton* Court noted that Belton qualified because he was an occupant "just before he was arrested." Moreover, the Court's holding in *Thornton v. United States*, 541 U.S. 615, 124 S. Ct. 2127, 158 L. Ed. 2d 905 (2004), makes it clear that the authority to search a vehicle is not "limited to situations where the officer makes contact with the occupant while the occupant is inside the vehicle." As long as the arrestee was a recent occupant, a vehicle may be searched incident to an arrest "even when an officer does not make contact until the person arrested has left the vehicle."

If an arrestee is *not* a recent occupant, the *Belton-Gant* doctrine does not authorize a search of a vehicle incident to his or her arrest. Suppose a person gets out of a car in the parking lot at a stadium, sets up a folding chair right next to his open car door, and consumes a few beers. An hour or two later, an officer arrests him in that location. Would a search of the vehicle incident to the arrest be reasonable under *Chimel*? Does *Gant* provide any insights?

(b) *Belton* prescribed the *scope* of the vehicle searches that were permissible incident to the arrest of a recent occupant. The *Gant* majority did not address the breadth of the vehicle searches that may be conducted under either branch of the search incident to arrest authority recognized in its opinion. Until the Justices say otherwise, it seems fair to assume that *Belton*'s pronouncements concerning scope continue to govern all searches of vehicles incident to arrest.

(1) A Temporal Limit: The Court has long adhered to the view that a search incident to arrest cannot be "remote in time" from an arrest. *Belton* confirmed that limitation, observing that a search of a vehicle must be "a contemporaneous incident of th[e] arrest" and upholding the search in that case because it "followed immediately upon th[e] arrest." This means that search incident to arrest authority will end at some point in time following the arrest. The amount of time that makes a search insufficiently "contemporaneous" or too "remote" is uncertain.

(2) A Spatial Limit: In *Atwater v. City of Lago Vista, supra*, Chapter 3[B], the "essential interest in readily administrable rules" was the critical factor that tipped the balance in favor of allowing arrests for even minor criminal offenses in an officer's presence. *Belton* was among the first significant Fourth

Amendment decisions to rely, in large measure, on the need for law enforcement officers to have clear, comprehensible rules to guide their search and seizure decisions. In order to provide such bright-line guidance for officers and because all the articles "inside the relatively narrow compass of the passenger compartment of an automobile are in fact generally, even if not inevitably, within" reaching distance of an occupant of the vehicle, the *Belton* Court held that an officer may "search the [entire] passenger compartment." In addition, an officer may "examine the contents of any containers found within the passenger compartment" because all such containers will "also . . . be within [an occupant's] reach." *Belton* noted that a container may be searched whether it is "closed or open," but did not indicate whether locked spaces or containers are subject to search. The Court stated that *only* the "interior of the passenger compartment" falls within the scope of search incident to arrest authority, cautioning that its bright-line "holding" regarding scope did "not encompass the trunk" of a vehicle. The Court did not discuss whether the entire interiors of vehicles that do not have trunks — station wagons, hatchbacks, and vans, for example — are within the scope of the searches allowed.

(3) What ramifications might the reasoning and holding in *Gant* have for search incident to arrest authority in contexts not involving vehicles? If an officer arrests a suspect while he is seated at his desk in his office, handcuffs the suspect, takes him outside into the hallway, and leaves him in the custody of other officers, may she return to the desk and search a drawer that was in front of the suspect at the time of the arrest?

Riley v. California

United States Supreme Court

573 U.S. ____, 134 S. Ct. 2473, 189 L. Ed. 2d 430 (2014)

CHIEF JUSTICE ROBERTS delivered the opinion of the Court.

These two cases raise a common question: whether the police may, without a warrant, search digital information on a cell phone seized from an individual who has been arrested.

I

A

In the first case, petitioner David Riley was stopped by a police officer for driving with expired registration tags. In the course of the stop, the officer also learned that Riley's license had been suspended. The officer impounded Riley's car, pursuant to department policy, and another officer conducted an inventory search of the car. Riley was arrested for possession of concealed and loaded firearms when that search turned up two handguns under the car's hood.

An officer searched Riley incident to the arrest and found items associated with the "Bloods" street gang. He also seized a cell phone from Riley's pants pocket. According to Riley's uncontradicted assertion, the phone was a "smart phone," a cell phone with a broad range of other functions based on advanced computing capability, large storage capacity, and Internet connectivity. The officer accessed information on the phone and noticed that some words (presumably in text messages or a contacts list) were preceded by the letters "CK" — a label that, he believed, stood for "Crip Killers," a slang term for members of the Bloods gang.

At the police station about two hours after the arrest, a detective specializing in gangs further examined the contents of the phone. The detective . . . [discovered gang-related videos and some] photographs of Riley standing in front of a car [that officers] suspected had been involved in a shooting a few weeks earlier.

Riley was ultimately charged, in connection with that earlier shooting, with firing at an occupied vehicle, assault with a semiautomatic firearm, and attempted murder. The State alleged that Riley had committed those crimes for the benefit of a criminal street gang, an aggravating factor that carries an enhanced sentence. Prior to trial, Riley moved to suppress all evidence that the police had obtained from his cell phone. He contended that the searches of his phone violated the Fourth Amendment, because they had been performed without a warrant and were not otherwise justified by exigent circumstances. The trial court rejected that argument. At Riley's trial, police officers testified about the photographs and videos found on the phone, and some of the photographs were admitted into evidence. Riley was convicted on all three counts and received an enhanced sentence of 15 years to life in prison.

The California Court of Appeal affirmed. . . .

The California Supreme Court denied Riley's petition for review and we granted certiorari.

B

In the second case, a police officer performing routine surveillance observed respondent Brima Wurie make an apparent drug sale from a car. Officers subsequently arrested Wurie and took him to the police station. At the station, the officers seized two cell phones from Wurie's person. The one at issue here was a "flip phone," a kind of phone that is flipped open for use and that generally has a smaller range of features than a smart phone. Five to ten minutes after arriving at the station, the officers noticed that the phone was repeatedly receiving calls from a source identified as "my house" on the phone's external screen. A few minutes later, they opened the phone and saw a photograph of a woman and a baby set as the phone's wallpaper. They pressed one button on the phone to access its call log, then another button to determine the phone number associated with the "my house" label. They next used an online phone directory to trace that phone number to an apartment building.

When the officers went to the building, they saw Wurie's name on a mailbox and observed through a window a woman who resembled the woman in the photograph on Wurie's phone. They secured the apartment while obtaining a search warrant and, upon later executing the warrant, found and seized 215 grams of crack cocaine, marijuana, drug paraphernalia, a firearm and ammunition, and cash.

Wurie was charged with distributing crack cocaine, possessing crack cocaine with intent to distribute, and being a felon in possession of a firearm and ammunition. He moved to suppress the evidence obtained from the search of the apartment, arguing that it was the fruit of an unconstitutional search of his cell phone. The District Court denied the motion. Wurie was convicted on all three counts and sentenced to 262 months in prison.

A divided panel of the First Circuit reversed the denial of Wurie's motion to suppress and vacated Wurie's convictions for possession with intent to distribute and possession of a firearm as a felon. . . .

We granted certiorari.

II

. . . .

. . . "[T]he ultimate touchstone of the Fourth Amendment is 'reasonableness.'" *Brigham City* v. *Stuart*, 547 U. S. 398, 403 (2006). Our cases have determined that "[w]here a search is undertaken by law enforcement officials to discover evidence of criminal wrongdoing, . . . reasonableness generally requires the obtaining of a judicial warrant." *Vernonia School Dist. 47J* v. *Acton*, 515 U. S. 646, 653 (1995). . . . In the absence of a warrant, a search is reasonable only if it falls within a specific exception to the warrant requirement. See *Kentucky* v. *King*, 563 U. S. 452, 460 (2011).

The two cases before us concern the reasonableness of a warrantless search incident to a lawful arrest. In 1914, this Court first acknowledged in dictum "the right on the part of the Government, always recognized under English and American law, to search the person of the accused when legally arrested to discover and seize the fruits or evidences of crime." *Weeks* v. *United States*, 232 U. S. 383, 392. Since that time, it has been well accepted that such a search constitutes an exception to the warrant requirement. Indeed, the label "exception" is something of a misnomer in this context, as warrantless searches incident to arrest occur with far greater frequency than searches conducted pursuant to a warrant. See 3 W. LaFave, Search and Seizure §5.2(b), p. 132, and n. 15 (5th ed. 2012).

Although the existence of the exception for such searches has been recognized for a century, its scope has been debated for nearly as long. See *Arizona* v. *Gant*, 556 U. S. 332, 350 (2009) (noting the exception's "checkered history"). That debate has focused on the extent to which officers may search property found on or near the arrestee. Three related precedents set forth the rules governing such searches:

[The Court then reviewed and summarized *Chimel*, *Robinson*, and *Gant*.]

. . . .

III

These cases require us to decide how the search incident to arrest doctrine applies to modern cell phones, which are now such a pervasive and insistent part of daily life that the proverbial visitor from Mars might conclude they were an important feature of human anatomy. A smart phone of the sort taken from Riley was unheard of ten years ago; a significant majority of American adults now own such phones. Even less sophisticated phones like Wurie's, which have already faded in popularity since Wurie was arrested in 2007, have been around for less than 15 years. Both phones are based on technology nearly inconceivable just a few decades ago, when *Chimel* and *Robinson* were decided.

Absent more precise guidance from the founding era, we generally determine whether to exempt a given type of search from the warrant requirement "by assessing, on the one hand, the degree to which it intrudes upon an individual's privacy and, on the other, the degree to which it is needed for the promotion of legitimate governmental interests." *Wyoming* v. *Houghton*, 526 U. S. 295, 300 (1999). Such a balancing of interests supported the search incident to arrest exception in *Robinson*, and a mechanical application of *Robinson* might well support the warrantless searches at issue here.

But while *Robinson*'s categorical rule strikes the appropriate balance in the context of physical objects, neither of its rationales has much force with respect to digital content on cell phones. On the government interest side, *Robinson* concluded that the two risks identified in *Chimel*—harm to officers and destruction of evidence— are present in all custodial arrests. There are no comparable risks when the search is of digital data. In addition, *Robinson* regarded any privacy interests retained by an individual after arrest as significantly diminished by the fact of the arrest itself. Cell phones, however, place vast quantities of personal information literally in the hands of individuals. A search of the information on a cell phone bears little resemblance to the type of brief physical search considered in *Robinson*.

We therefore decline to extend *Robinson* to searches of data on cell phones, and hold instead that officers must generally secure a warrant before conducting such a search.

A

We first consider each *Chimel* concern in turn. In doing so, we do not overlook *Robinson*'s admonition that searches of a person incident to arrest, "while based upon the need to disarm and to discover evidence," are reasonable regardless of "the probability in a particular arrest situation that weapons or evidence would in fact be found." 414 U. S., at 235. Rather than requiring the "case-by-case adjudication" that *Robinson* rejected, *ibid.*, we ask instead whether application of the search incident to arrest doctrine to this particular category of effects would "untether the rule from the justifications underlying the *Chimel* exception," *Gant, supra*, at 343.

1

Digital data stored on a cell phone cannot itself be used as a weapon to harm an arresting officer or to effectuate the arrestee's escape. Law enforcement officers remain free to examine the physical aspects of a phone to ensure that it will not be used as a weapon—say, to determine whether there is a razor blade hidden between the phone and its case. Once an officer has secured a phone and eliminated any potential physical threats, however, data on the phone can endanger no one.

Perhaps the same might have been said of the cigarette pack seized from Robinson's pocket. Once an officer gained control of the pack, it was unlikely that Robinson could have accessed the pack's contents. But unknown physical objects may always pose risks, no matter how slight, during the tense atmosphere of a custodial arrest. The officer in *Robinson* testified that he could not identify the objects in the cigarette pack but knew they were not cigarettes. Given that, a further search was a reasonable protective measure. No such unknowns exist with respect to digital data. . . .

The United States and California both suggest that a search of cell phone data might help ensure officer safety in more indirect ways, for example by alerting officers that confederates of the arrestee are headed to the scene. There is undoubtedly a strong government interest in warning officers about such possibilities, but neither the United States nor California offers evidence to suggest that their concerns are based on actual experience. The proposed consideration would also represent a broadening of *Chimel*'s concern that an *arrestee himself* might grab a weapon and use it against an officer "to resist arrest or effect his escape." 395 U. S., at 763. And any such threats from outside the arrest scene do not "lurk[ ] in all custodial arrests." *Chadwick*, 433 U. S., at 14–15. Accordingly, the interest in protecting officer safety does not justify dispensing with the warrant requirement across the board. To the extent dangers to arresting officers may be implicated in a particular way in a particular case, they are better addressed through consideration of case-specific exceptions to the warrant requirement, such as the one for exigent circumstances.

2

The United States and California focus primarily on the second *Chimel* rationale: preventing the destruction of evidence.

Both Riley and Wurie concede that officers could have seized and secured their cell phones to prevent destruction of evidence while seeking a warrant. See Brief for Petitioner in No. 13–132, p. 20; Brief for Respondent in No. 13–212, p. 41. That is a sensible concession. See *Illinois* v. *McArthur*, 531 U. S. 326, 331–333 (2001); *Chadwick*, *supra*, at 13, and n. 8. And once law enforcement officers have secured a cell phone, there is no longer any risk that the arrestee himself will be able to delete incriminating data from the phone.

The United States and California argue that information on a cell phone may nevertheless be vulnerable to two types of evidence destruction unique to digital data — remote wiping and data encryption. Remote wiping occurs when a phone, connected to a wireless network, receives a signal that erases stored data. This can happen when a third party sends a remote signal or when a phone is preprogrammed to delete data upon entering or leaving certain geographic areas (so-called "geofencing"). Encryption is a security feature that some modern cell phones use in addition to password protection. When such phones lock, data becomes protected by sophisticated encryption that renders a phone all but "unbreakable" unless police know the password.

As an initial matter, these broader concerns about the loss of evidence are distinct from *Chimel*'s focus on a defendant who responds to arrest by trying to conceal or destroy evidence within his reach. With respect to remote wiping, the Government's primary concern turns on the actions of third parties who are not present at the scene of arrest. And data encryption is even further afield. There, the Government focuses on the ordinary operation of a phone's security features, apart from *any* active attempt by a defendant or his associates to conceal or destroy evidence upon arrest.

We have also been given little reason to believe that either problem is prevalent. The briefing reveals only a couple of anecdotal examples of remote wiping triggered by an arrest. Similarly, the opportunities for officers to search a password-protected phone before data becomes encrypted are quite limited. Law enforcement officers are very unlikely to come upon such a phone in an unlocked state because most phones lock at the touch of a button or, as a default, after some very short period of inactivity. This may explain why the encryption argument was not made until the merits stage in this Court, and has never been considered by the Courts of Appeals.

Moreover, in situations in which an arrest might trigger a remote-wipe attempt or an officer discovers an unlocked phone, it is not clear that the ability to conduct a warrantless search would make much of a difference. The need to effect the arrest, secure the scene, and tend to other pressing matters means that law enforcement officers may well not be able to turn their attention to a cell phone right away. Cell phone data would be vulnerable to remote wiping from the time an individual anticipates arrest to the time any eventual search of the phone is completed, which might be at the station house hours later. Likewise, an officer who seizes a phone in an unlocked state might not be able to begin his search in the short time remaining before the phone locks and data becomes encrypted.

In any event, as to remote wiping, law enforcement is not without specific means to address the threat. Remote wiping can be fully prevented by disconnecting a phone from the network. There are at least two simple ways to do this: First, law enforcement officers can turn the phone off or remove its battery. Second, if they are concerned about encryption or other potential problems, they can leave a phone powered on and place it in an enclosure that isolates the phone from radio waves. . . .

To the extent that law enforcement still has specific concerns about the potential loss of evidence in a particular case, there remain more targeted ways to address those concerns. If "the police are truly confronted with a 'now or never' situation," — for example, circumstances suggesting that a defendant's phone will be the target of an imminent remote-wipe attempt — they may be able to rely on exigent circumstances to search the phone immediately. *Missouri* v. *McNeely*, 569 U. S. ____, ____ (2013) (quoting *Roaden* v. *Kentucky*, 413 U. S. 496, 505 (1973); some internal quotation marks omitted). Or, if officers happen to seize a phone in an unlocked state, they may be able to disable a phone's automatic-lock feature in order to prevent the phone from locking and encrypting data. . . . . .

B

The search incident to arrest exception rests not only on the heightened government interests at stake in a volatile arrest situation, but also on an arrestee's reduced privacy interests upon being taken into police custody. . . .

The fact that an arrestee has diminished privacy interests does not mean that the Fourth Amendment falls out of the picture entirely. Not every search "is acceptable solely because a person is in custody." *Maryland* v. *King*, 569 U. S. ____, ____ (2013). To the contrary, when "privacy-related concerns are weighty enough" a "search may require a warrant, notwithstanding the diminished expectations of privacy of the arrestee." *Ibid.* . . .

Robinson is the only decision from this Court applying *Chimel* to a search of the contents of an item found on an arrestee's person. . . . Lower courts applying *Robinson* and *Chimel*, however, have approved searches of a variety of personal items carried by an arrestee. See, *e.g., United States* v. *Carrion*, 809 F. 2d 1120, 1123, 1128 (CA5 1987) (billfold and address book); *United States* v. *Watson*, 669 F. 2d 1374, 1383–1384 (CA11 1982) (wallet); *United States* v. *Lee*, 501 F. 2d 890, 892 (CADC 1974) (purse).

The United States asserts that a search of all data stored on a cell phone is "materially indistinguishable" from searches of these sorts of physical items. That is like saying a ride on horseback is materially indistinguishable from a flight to the moon. Both are ways of getting from point A to point B, but little else justifies lumping them together. Modern cell phones, as a category, implicate privacy concerns far beyond those implicated by the search of a cigarette pack, a wallet, or a purse. A conclusion that inspecting the contents of an arrestee's pockets works no substantial additional intrusion on privacy beyond the arrest itself may make sense as applied to physical items, but any extension of that reasoning to digital data has to rest on its own bottom.

1

Cell phones differ in both a quantitative and a qualitative sense from other objects that might be kept on an arrestee's person. The term "cell phone" is itself misleading shorthand; many of these devices are in fact minicomputers that also happen to have the capacity to be used as a telephone. They could just as easily be called cameras, video players, rolodexes, calendars, tape recorders, libraries, diaries, albums, televisions, maps, or newspapers.

One of the most notable distinguishing features of modern cell phones is their immense storage capacity. Before cell phones, a search of a person was limited by physical realities and tended as a general matter to constitute only a narrow intrusion on privacy. Most people cannot lug around every piece of mail they have received for the past several months, every picture they have taken, or every book or article they have read—nor would they have any reason to attempt to do so. And if they did, they would have to drag behind them a trunk of the sort held to require a search warrant in *Chadwick, supra*, rather than a container the size of the cigarette package in *Robinson*.

But the possible intrusion on privacy is not physically limited in the same way when it comes to cell phones. The current top-selling smart phone has a standard capacity of 16 gigabytes (and is available with up to 64 gigabytes). Sixteen giga-bytes translates to millions of pages of text, thousands of pictures, or hundreds of videos. Cell phones couple that capacity with the ability to store many different types of information: Even the most basic phones that sell for less than $20 might hold photographs, picture messages, text messages, Internet browsing history, a calendar, a thousand-entry phone book, and so on. We expect that the gulf be-tween physical practicability and digital capacity will only continue to widen in the future.

The storage capacity of cell phones has several interrelated consequences for pri-vacy. First, a cell phone collects in one place many distinct types of information — an address, a note, a prescription, a bank statement, a video — that reveal much more in combination than any isolated record. Second, a cell phone's capacity allows even just one type of information to convey far more than previously possible. The sum of an individual's private life can be reconstructed through a thousand photographs labeled with dates, locations, and descriptions; the same cannot be said of a photo-graph or two of loved ones tucked into a wallet. Third, the data on a phone can date back to the purchase of the phone, or even earlier. A person might carry in his pocket a slip of paper reminding him to call Mr. Jones; he would not carry a record of all his communications with Mr. Jones for the past several months, as would routinely be kept on a phone.

Finally, there is an element of pervasiveness that characterizes cell phones but not physical records. Prior to the digital age, people did not typically carry a cache of sensitive personal information with them as they went about their day. Now it is the person who is not carrying a cell phone, with all that it contains, who is the excep-tion. According to one poll, nearly three-quarters of smart phone users report being within five feet of their phones most of the time, with 12% admitting that they even use their phones in the shower. A decade ago police officers searching an arrestee might have occasionally stumbled across a highly personal item such as a diary. But those discoveries were likely to be few and far between. Today, by contrast, it is no exaggeration to say that many of the more than 90% of American adults who own a cell phone keep on their person a digital record of nearly every aspect of their lives — from the mundane to the intimate. Allowing the police to scrutinize such records on a routine basis is quite different from allowing them to search a personal item or two in the occasional case.

Although the data stored on a cell phone is distinguished from physical records by quantity alone, certain types of data are also qualitatively different. An Internet search and browsing history, for example, can be found on an Internet-enabled phone and could reveal an individual's private interests or concerns — perhaps a search for certain symptoms of disease, coupled with frequent visits to WebMD. Data on a cell phone can also reveal where a person has been. Historic location information is a standard feature on many smart phones and can reconstruct someone's specific movements down to the minute, not only around town but also within a particular building.

Mobile application software on a cell phone, or "apps," offer a range of tools for managing detailed information about all aspects of a person's life. There are apps for Democratic Party news and Republican Party news; apps for alcohol, drug, and gambling addictions; apps for sharing prayer requests; apps for tracking pregnancy symptoms; apps for planning your budget; apps for every conceivable hobby or pastime; apps for improving your romantic life. There are popular apps for buying or selling just about anything, and the records of such transactions may be accessible on the phone indefinitely. There are over a million apps available in each of the two major app stores; the phrase "there's an app for that" is now part of the popular lexicon. The average smart phone user has installed 33 apps, which together can form a revealing montage of the user's life.

. . . [A] cell phone search would typically expose to the government far *more* than the most exhaustive search of a house: A phone not only contains in digital form many sensitive records previously found in the home; it also contains a broad array of private information never found in a home in any form — unless the phone is.

2

To further complicate the scope of the privacy interests at stake, the data a user views on many modern cell phones may not in fact be stored on the device itself. Treating a cell phone as a container whose contents may be searched incident to an arrest is a bit strained as an initial matter. But the analogy crumbles entirely when a cell phone is used to access data located elsewhere, at the tap of a screen. That is what cell phones, with increasing frequency, are designed to do by taking advantage of "cloud computing." Cloud computing is the capacity of Internet-connected devices to display data stored on remote servers rather than on the device itself. . . .

The United States concedes that the search incident to arrest exception may not be stretched to cover a search of files accessed remotely — that is, a search of files stored in the cloud. Such a search would be like finding a key in a suspect's pocket and arguing that it allowed law enforcement to unlock and search a house. But officers searching a phone's data would not typically know whether the information they are viewing was stored locally at the time of the arrest or has been pulled from the cloud.

. . . The possibility that a search might extend well beyond papers and effects in the physical proximity of an arrestee is yet another reason that the privacy interests here dwarf those in *Robinson*.

C

Apart from their arguments for a direct extension of *Robinson*, the United States and California offer various fallback options for permitting warrantless cell phone searches under certain circumstances. Each of the proposals is flawed and contravenes our general preference to provide clear guidance to law enforcement through categorical rules. . . .

The United States first proposes that the *Gant* standard be imported from the vehicle context, allowing a warrantless search of an arrestee's cell phone whenever it is reasonable to believe that the phone contains evidence of the crime of arrest. But *Gant* relied on "circumstances unique to the vehicle context" to endorse a search solely for the purpose of gathering evidence. 556 U. S., at 343. JUSTICE SCALIA's *Thornton* opinion, on which *Gant* was based, explained that those unique circumstances are "a reduced expectation of privacy" and "heightened law enforcement needs" when it comes to motor vehicles. 541 U. S., at 631; see also *Wyoming* v. *Houghton*, 526 U. S., at 303–304. For reasons that we have explained, cell phone searches bear neither of those characteristics.

At any rate, a *Gant* standard would prove no practical limit at all when it comes to cell phone searches. In the vehicle context, *Gant* generally protects against searches for evidence of past crimes. See 3 W. LaFave, Search and Seizure §7.1(d), at 709, and n. 191. In the cell phone context, however, it is reasonable to expect that incriminating information will be found on a phone regardless of when the crime occurred. Similarly, in the vehicle context *Gant* restricts broad searches resulting from minor crimes such as traffic violations. See *id.,* §7.1(d), at 713, and n. 204. That would not necessarily be true for cell phones. It would be a particularly inexperienced or unimaginative law enforcement officer who could not come up with several reasons to suppose evidence of just about any crime could be found on a cell phone. Even an individual pulled over for something as basic as speeding might well have locational data dispositive of guilt on his phone. An individual pulled over for reckless driving might have evidence on the phone that shows whether he was texting while driving. The sources of potential pertinent information are virtually unlimited, so applying the *Gant* standard to cell phones would in effect give "police officers unbridled discretion to rummage at will among a person's private effects." 556 U. S., at 345.

The United States also proposes a rule that would restrict the scope of a cell phone search to those areas of the phone where an officer reasonably believes that information relevant to the crime, the arrestee's identity, or officer safety will be discovered.

This approach would again impose few meaningful constraints on officers. The proposed categories would sweep in a great deal of information, and officers would not always be able to discern in advance what information would be found where.

We also reject the United States' final suggestion that officers should always be able to search a phone's call log, as they did in Wurie's case. . . . There is no dispute here that the officers engaged in a search of Wurie's cell phone. Moreover, call logs typically contain more than just phone numbers; they include any identifying information that an individual might add, such as the label "my house" in Wurie's case.

. . . .

IV

We cannot deny that our decision today will have an impact on the ability of law enforcement to combat crime. Cell phones have become important tools in facilitating coordination and communication among members of criminal enterprises, and can provide valuable incriminating information about dangerous criminals. Privacy comes at a cost. Our holding, of course, is not that the information on a cell phone is immune from search; it is instead that a warrant is generally required before such a search, even when a cell phone is seized incident to arrest. Our cases have historically recognized that the warrant requirement is "an important working part of our machinery of government," not merely "an inconvenience to be somehow 'weighed' against the claims of police efficiency." *Coolidge* v. *New Hampshire*, 403 U. S. 443, 481 (1971). Recent technological advances similar to those discussed here have, in addition, made the process of obtaining a warrant itself more efficient.

Moreover, even though the search incident to arrest exception does not apply to cell phones, other case-specific exceptions may still justify a warrantless search of a particular phone. "One well-recognized exception applies when ' "the exigencies of the situation" make the needs of law enforcement so compelling that [a] warrantless search is objectively reasonable under the Fourth Amendment.' " *Kentucky* v. *King*, 563 U. S., at 460 (quoting *Mincey* v. *Arizona,* 437 U. S. 385, 394 (1978)). . . .

. . . The critical point is that, unlike the search incident to arrest exception, the exigent circumstances exception requires a court to examine whether an emergency justified a warrantless search in each particular case.

. . . .

Our cases have recognized that the Fourth Amendment was the founding generation's response to the reviled "general warrants" and "writs of assistance" of the colonial era, which allowed British officers to rummage through homes in an unrestrained search for evidence of criminal activity. Opposition to such searches was in fact one of the driving forces behind the Revolution itself. . . .

Modern cell phones are not just another technological convenience. With all they contain and all they may reveal, they hold for many Americans "the privacies of life," *Boyd,* [*v. United States,* 116 U. S. 616, 630 (1886)]. The fact that technology now allows an individual to carry such information in his hand does not make the information any less worthy of the protection for which the Founders fought. Our answer to the question of what police must do before searching a cell phone seized incident to an arrest is accordingly simple — get a warrant.

We reverse the judgment of the California Court of Appeal in No. 13–132 and remand the case for further proceedings not inconsistent with this opinion. We affirm the judgment of the First Circuit in No. 13–212.

It is so ordered.

[JUSTICE ALITO's opinion, concurring in part and concurring in the judgment, has been omitted.]

Notes and Questions

(1) How does the holding in *Riley* restrict the scope of the searches authorized by the search incident to arrest exception to the warrant rule? Why does the Court reject the government's claim that the searches at issue in *Riley* should be considered valid under the search incident to arrest exception? Does the *Riley* restriction apply

to searches of anything other than cell phones? In other words, what is the dividing line between the searches permitted by the Court's holding in *Robinson* and the searches forbidden by the Court's holding in *Riley*? May officers examine the detailed contents of a written journal carried by an arrestee?

(2) When an officer finds a cell phone on a person lawfully arrested for any offense, what search is constitutionally reasonable? Under what circumstances, if any, may the officer conduct the more extensive type of search at issue in *Riley*?

(3) If an officer discovers a cell phone in a vehicle during a lawful search incident to arrest under *either* of the two distinct branches of search incident to arrest authority recognized in *Gant*, is a search of the data contained in the phone constitutionally valid?

(4) In *Birchfield v. North Dakota*, 579 U.S. ____, ____ S. Ct. ____, ____ L. Ed. 2d ____ (2016), the Justices again addressed the scope of the authority to search a person incident to a lawful arrest. A majority concluded that "incident to a lawful arrest for drunk driving" it is reasonable to administer "a breath test, but not a blood test" for evidence of intoxication. The Court reached this conclusion based on the balancing approach employed in *Riley*. According to the *Birchfield* majority, both breath and blood tests constitute searches. Breath tests are reasonable incident to arrests because the state interest in preventing drunk driving outweighs the intrusion on the individual. "The impact of breath tests on privacy is slight, and the need for [blood alcohol concentration] testing is great." Blood tests, however, are unreasonable incident to arrests because they are "significantly more intrusive," and, "in light of the availability of the less invasive alternative of a breath test," the state's interest in and need for a blood test do not outweigh that intrusion. Blood tests are permissible only if officers secure a search warrant or another exception to the warrant rule — the exigent circumstances exception, for example — applies. The Justices also concluded that a warrantless blood draw could not be justified on the basis of a motorist's "implied consent." In their view, "motorists may [not] be deemed to have consented" to "an intrusive blood test" on the basis of "a decision to drive on public roads."

Because breath tests are constitutional incident to lawful drunk driving arrests, it is permissible to impose criminal penalties for refusing to submit to such tests. On the other hand, the unconstitutionality of blood tests incident to arrest means that jurisdictions may not impose criminal penalties for refusing those tests.

Justices Sotomayor and Ginsburg expressed the view that neither blood nor breath tests were reasonable incident to lawful arrests. Justice Thomas asserted that the majority's search incident to arrest analysis was misguided, and that, as a *"per se* rule," both breath and blood tests of "driver[s] suspected of drunk driving are constitutional under the exigent-circumstances exception to the warrant requirement."

(5) The Court's opinion in *Washington v. Chrisman*, 455 U.S. 1, 102 S. Ct. 812, 70 L. Ed. 2d 778 (1982), introduced an additional, distinct exception to the warrant requirement that arises in the context of arrests. *Chrisman* held that an officer could enter the dormitory room of an arrested student without a warrant because "it is not 'unreasonable' under the Fourth Amendment for a police officer, as a matter of rou-

tine, to monitor the movements of an arrested person, as his judgment dictates, following the arrest." Insofar as the monitoring requires a warrantless entry into a private place, the Court concluded that an "exception" is justified by the officer's compelling needs "to ensure his own safety" and "the integrity of his arrest."

Chrisman involved an arrestee who desired to enter his dormitory room and acquiesced when the officer stated that he would have to accompany him. The Court has not decided whether *Chrisman* would apply if an officer *requested* or *commanded* an arrestee to enter a private area. In addition, the Court has not discussed whether an officer has any authority to search areas nearby while exercising the authority to monitor an arrestee's movements — that is, whether there is any authority to search all of the areas that come within the "immediate control" of an arrestee who has entered a private place.

Dissenters in *Chrisman* argued that there is "no justification for . . . a *per se* rule that an officer . . . [can] always enter [a private place] and stay at [an] arrestee's elbow." They contended that such entries should be based on case-by-case showings of the necessity for officers to enter in order to maintain control and protect themselves.

Payton v. New York
United States Supreme Court
445 U.S. 573, 100 S. Ct. 1371, 63 L. Ed. 2d 639 (1980)

Mr. Justice Stevens delivered the opinion of the Court.

These appeals challenge the constitutionality of New York statutes that authorize police officers to enter a private residence without a warrant and with force, if necessary, to make a routine felony arrest.

. . . .

I

On January 14, 1970, after two days of intensive investigation, New York detectives had assembled evidence sufficient to establish probable cause to believe that Theodore Payton had murdered the manager of a gas station two days earlier. At about 7:30 a.m. on January 15, six officers went to Payton's apartment in the Bronx, intending to arrest him. They had not obtained a warrant. Although light and music emanated from the apartment, there was no response to their knock on the metal door. They summoned emergency assistance and, about 30 minutes later, used crowbars to break open the door and enter the apartment. No one was there. In plain view, however, was a .30-caliber shell casing that was seized and later admitted into evidence at Payton's murder trial.

In due course Payton surrendered to the police, was indicted for murder, and moved to suppress the evidence taken from his apartment. The trial judge held that the warrantless and forcible entry was authorized by the New York Code of Criminal Procedure,[6] and that the evidence in plain view was properly seized. He found that exigent circumstances justified the officers' failure to announce their purpose before entering the apartment as required by the statute. He had no occasion, however, to decide whether those circumstances also would have justified the failure to obtain a warrant, because he concluded that the warrantless entry was adequately supported by the statute without regard to the circumstances . . . .

On March 14, 1974, Obie Riddick was arrested for the commission of two armed robberies that had occurred in 1971. He had been identified by the victims in June 1973, and in January 1974 the police had learned his address. They did not obtain a warrant for his arrest. At about noon on March 14, a detective, accompanied by three other officers, knocked on the door of the Queens house where Riddick was living. When his young son opened the door, they could see Riddick sitting in bed covered by a sheet. They entered the house and placed him under arrest. Before permitting him to dress, they opened a chest of drawers two feet from the bed in search of weapons and found narcotics and related paraphernalia. Riddick was subsequently indicted on narcotics charges. At a suppression hearing, the trial judge held that the warrantless entry into his home was authorized by the revised New York statute,[9] and that the search of the immediate area was reasonable under *Chimel v. California*, 395 U.S. 752, 89 S. Ct. 2034, 23 L. Ed. 2d 685.

---

6. "At the time in question, January 15, 1970, the law applicable to the police conduct related above was governed by the Code of Criminal Procedure. Section 177 of the Code of Criminal Procedure as applicable to this case recited: 'A peace officer may, without a warrant, arrest a person . . . 3. When a felony has in fact been committed, and he has reasonable cause for believing the person to be arrested to have committed it.' Section 178 of the Code of Criminal Procedure provided: 'To make an arrest, as provided in the last section [177], the officer may break open an outer or inner door or window of a building, if, after notice of his office and purpose, he be refused admittance.'" 84 Misc. 2d 973, 974–975, 376 N.Y.S.2d 779, 780 (Sup. Ct., Trial Term, N.Y. County, 1974).

9. New York Crim. Proc. Law § 140.15(4) (McKinney 1971) provides, with respect to arrest without a warrant: "In order to effect such an arrest, a police officer may enter premises in which he reasonably believes such person to be present, under the same circumstances and in the same manner as would be authorized, by the provisions of subdivisions four and five of section 120.80, if he were attempting to make such arrest pursuant to a warrant of arrest." Section 120.80, governing execution of arrest warrants, provides in relevant part:

4. In order to effect the arrest, the police officer may, under circumstances and in a manner prescribed in this subdivision, enter any premises in which he reasonably believes the defendant to be present. Before such entry, he must give, or make reasonable effort to give, notice of his authority and purpose to an occupant thereof, unless there is reasonable cause to believe that the giving of such notice will:

   (a) Result in the defendant escaping or attempting to escape; or
   (b) Endanger the life or safety of the officer or another person; or
   (c) Result in the destruction, damaging or secretion of material evidence.

5. If the officer is authorized to enter premises without giving notice of his authority and purpose, or if after giving such notice he is not admitted, he may enter such premises, and by a breaking if necessary.

. . . .

Before addressing the narrow question presented by these appeals, we put to one side other related problems that are not presented today . . . .

[T]hese cases [do not] raise any question concerning the authority of the police, without either a search or arrest warrant, to enter a third party's home to arrest a suspect. The police broke into Payton's apartment intending to arrest Payton, and they arrested Riddick in his own dwelling. We also note that in neither case is it argued that the police lacked probable cause to believe that the suspect was at home when they entered. Finally, in both cases we are dealing with entries into homes made without the consent of any occupant. In *Payton*, the police used crowbars to break down the door and in *Riddick*, although his 3-year-old son answered the door, the police entered before Riddick had an opportunity either to object or to consent.

II

It is familiar history that indiscriminate searches and seizures conducted under the authority of "general warrants" were the immediate evils that motivated the framing and adoption of the Fourth Amendment. Indeed, as originally proposed in the House of Representatives, the draft contained only one clause, which directly imposed limitations on the issuance of warrants, but imposed no express restrictions on warrantless searches or seizures.[22] As it was ultimately adopted, however, the Amendment contained two separate clauses, the first protecting the basic right to be free from unreasonable searches and seizures and the second requiring that warrants be particular and supported by probable cause.[23] . . .

It is thus perfectly clear that the evil the Amendment was designed to prevent was broader than the abuse of a general warrant. Unreasonable searches or seizures conducted without any warrant at all are condemned by the plain language of the first clause of the Amendment . . . .

The simple language of the Amendment applies equally to seizures of persons and to seizures of property. Our analysis in this case may therefore properly commence with rules that have been well established in Fourth Amendment litigation involving tangible items. As the Court reiterated just a few years ago, the "physical entry of

---

22. "'The rights of the people to be secure in their persons, their houses, their papers, and their other property, from all unreasonable searches and seizures, shall not be violated by warrants issued without probable cause, supported by oath or affirmation, or not particularly describing the places to be searched, or the persons or things to be seized.' Annals of Cong., 1st Cong., 1st sess., p. 452." [N. Lasson, The History and Development of the Fourth Amendment to the United States Constitution 100 (1937)] (Footnote omitted.)

23. "The general right of security from unreasonable search and seizure was given a sanction of its own and the amendment thus intentionally given a broader scope. That the prohibition against 'unreasonable searches' was intended, accordingly, to cover something other than the form of the warrant is a question no longer left to implication to be derived from the phraseology of the Amendment." [N. Lasson, *supra* at 103.]

the home is the chief evil against which the wording of the Fourth Amendment is directed." *United States v. United States District Court*, 407 U.S. 297, 313, 92 S. Ct. 2125, 2134, 32 L. Ed. 2d 752. And we have long adhered to the view that the warrant procedure minimizes the danger of needless intrusions of that sort.

It is a "basic principle of Fourth Amendment law" that searches and seizures inside a home without a warrant are presumptively unreasonable. Yet it is also well settled that objects such as weapons or contraband found in a public place may be seized by the police without a warrant. The seizure of property in plain view involves no invasion of privacy and is presumptively reasonable, assuming that there is probable cause to associate the property with criminal activity. The distinction between a warrantless seizure in an open area and such a seizure on private premises was plainly stated in *G.M. Leasing Corp. v. United States*, 429 U.S. 338, 354, 97 S. Ct. 619, 629, 50 L. Ed. 2d 530:

> It is one thing to seize without a warrant property resting in an open area or seizable by levy without an intrusion into privacy, and it is quite another thing to effect a warrantless seizure of property, even that owned by a corporation, situated on private premises to which access is not otherwise available for the seizing officer.

As the late Judge Leventhal recognized, this distinction has equal force when the seizure of a person is involved. Writing on the constitutional issue now before us for the United States Court of Appeals for the District of Columbia Circuit sitting *en banc, Dorman v. United States*, 435 F.2d 385, 140 U.S. App. D.C. 313 (1970), Judge Leventhal first noted the settled rule that warrantless arrests in public places are valid . . . .

His analysis of this question then focused on the long-settled premise that, absent exigent circumstances, a warrantless entry to search for weapons or contraband is unconstitutional even when a felony has been committed and there is probable cause to believe that incriminating evidence will be found within. He reasoned that the constitutional protection afforded to the individual's interest in the privacy of his own home is equally applicable to a warrantless entry for the purpose of arresting a resident of the house; for it is inherent in such an entry that a search for the suspect may be required before he can be apprehended. Judge Leventhal concluded that an entry to arrest and an entry to search for and to seize property implicate the same interest in preserving the privacy and the sanctity of the home, and justify the same level of constitutional protection.

We find this reasoning to be persuasive and in accord with this Court's Fourth Amendment decisions.

The majority of the New York Court of Appeals, however, suggested that there is a substantial difference in the relative intrusiveness of an entry to search for property and an entry to search for a person. It is true that the area that may legally be searched is broader when executing a search warrant than when executing an arrest warrant in the home. *See Chimel v. California*, 395 U.S. 752, 89 S. Ct. 2034, 23 L. Ed.

2d 685. This difference may be more theoretical than real, however, because the police may need to check the entire premises for safety reasons, and sometimes they ignore the restrictions on searches incident to arrest.

But the critical point is that any differences in the intrusiveness of entries to search and entries to arrest are merely ones of degree rather than kind. The two intrusions share this fundamental characteristic: the breach of the entrance to an individual's home. The Fourth Amendment protects the individual's privacy in a variety of settings. In none is the zone of privacy more clearly defined than when bounded by the unambiguous physical dimensions of an individual's home — a zone that finds its roots in clear and specific constitutional terms: "The right of the people to be secure in their . . . houses . . . shall not be violated." That language unequivocally establishes the proposition that "[a]t the very core [of the Fourth Amendment] stands the right of a man to retreat into his own home and there be free from unreasonable governmental intrusion." *Silverman v. United States*, 365 U.S. 505, 511, 81 S. Ct. 679, 683, 5 L. Ed. 2d 734. In terms that apply equally to seizures of property and to seizures of persons, the Fourth Amendment has drawn a firm line at the entrance to the house. Absent exigent circumstances, that threshold may not reasonably be crossed without a warrant.

III

. . . New York argues that the reasons that support the *Watson* holding require a similar result here. In *Watson* the Court relied on (a) the well-settled common-law rule that a warrantless arrest in a public place is valid if the arresting officer had probable cause to believe the suspect is a felon; (b) the clear consensus among the States adhering to that well-settled common-law rule; and (c) the expression of the judgment of Congress that such an arrest is "reasonable." We consider each of these reasons as it applies to a warrantless entry into a home for the purpose of making a routine felony arrest.

A

. . . .

. . . [O]ur study of the relevant common law does not provide the same guidance that was present in *Watson*. Whereas the rule concerning the validity of an arrest in a public place was supported by cases directly in point and by the unanimous views of the commentators, we have found no direct authority supporting forcible entries into a home to make a routine arrest and the weight of the scholarly opinion is somewhat to the contrary. Indeed, the absence of any 17th- or 18th-century English cases directly in point, together with the unequivocal endorsement of the tenet that "a man's house is his castle," strongly suggests that the prevailing practice was not to make such arrests except in hot pursuit or when authorized by a warrant . . . .

B

. . . .

In this case, although the weight of state-law authority is clear, there is by no means the kind of virtual unanimity on this question that was present in *United*

States v. Watson, with regard to warrantless arrests in public places. *See* 423 U.S., at 422–423, 96 S. Ct., at 827–828. Only 24 of the 50 States currently sanction warrantless entries into the home to arrest, and there is an obvious declining trend. Further, the strength of the trend is greater than the numbers alone indicate. Seven state courts have recently held that warrantless home arrests violate their respective *State* Constitutions. That is significant because by invoking a state constitutional provision, a state court immunizes its decision from review by this Court. This heightened degree of immutability underscores the depth of the principle underlying the result.

C

No congressional determination that warrantless entries into the home are "reasonable" has been called to our attention. None of the federal statutes cited in the *Watson* opinion reflects any such legislative judgment. Thus, that support for the *Watson* holding finds no counterpart in this case.

. . . In this case, . . . neither history nor this Nation's experience requires us to disregard the overriding respect for the sanctity of the home that has been embedded in our traditions since the origins of the Republic.

IV

The parties have argued at some length about the practical consequences of a warrant requirement as a precondition to a felony arrest in the home. In the absence of any evidence that effective law enforcement has suffered in those States that already have such a requirement, we are inclined to view such arguments with skepticism. More fundamentally, however, such arguments of policy must give way to a constitutional command that we consider to be unequivocal.

Finally, we note the State's suggestion that only a search warrant based on probable cause to believe the suspect is at home at a given time can adequately protect the privacy interests at stake, and since such a warrant requirement is manifestly impractical, there need be no warrant of any kind. We find this ingenious argument unpersuasive. It is true that an arrest warrant requirement may afford less protection than a search warrant requirement, but it will suffice to interpose the magistrate's determination of probable cause between the zealous officer and the citizen. If there is sufficient evidence of a citizen's participation in a felony to persuade a judicial officer that his arrest is justified, it is constitutionally reasonable to require him to open his doors to the officers of the law. Thus, for Fourth Amendment purposes, an arrest warrant founded on probable cause implicitly carries with it the limited authority to enter a dwelling in which the suspect lives when there is reason to believe the suspect is within.

Because no arrest warrant was obtained in either of these cases, the judgments must be reversed and the cases remanded to the New York Court of Appeals for further proceedings not inconsistent with this opinion.

It is so ordered.

[The concurring opinion of Mr. Justice Blackmun has been omitted.]

Mr. Justice White, with whom The Chief Justice and Mr. Justice Rehnquist join, dissenting.

The Court today holds that absent exigent circumstances officers may never enter a home during the daytime to arrest for a dangerous felony unless they have first obtained a warrant. This hard-and-fast rule, founded on erroneous assumptions concerning the intrusiveness of home arrest entries, finds little or no support in the common law or in the text and history of the Fourth Amendment. I respectfully dissent.

I

As the Court notes, the common law of searches and seizures, as evolved in England, as transported to the Colonies, and as developed among the States, is highly relevant to the present scope of the Fourth Amendment.

A

. . . .

[According to Justice White, one common law school of thought allowed warrantless home entries to arrest "on probable suspicion" while another simply imposed "a somewhat more stringent requirement of probable cause for arrests in the home." Neither, however, barred "nonexigent, warrantless home arrests in all circumstances, as the Court does today."]

. . . .

B

The history of the Fourth Amendment does not support the rule announced today. At the time that Amendment was adopted the constable possessed broad inherent powers to arrest. . . . . [T]he institution of the warrant was used to expand that authority by giving the constable delegated powers of a superior officer such as a justice of the peace. Hence at the time of the Bill of Rights, the warrant functioned as a powerful tool of law enforcement rather than as a protection for the rights of criminal suspects.

. . . .

. . . [T]he background, text, and legislative history of the Fourth Amendment demonstrate that the purpose was to restrict the abuses that had developed with respect to warrants; the Amendment preserved common-law rules of arrest. Because it was not considered generally unreasonable at common law for officers to break doors to effect a warrantless felony arrest, I do not believe that the Fourth Amendment was intended to outlaw the types of police conduct at issue in the present cases.

. . . .

D

. . . .

. . . . [A]lthough the Court purports to find no guidance in the relevant federal statutes, I believe that fairly read they authorize the type of police conduct at issue in these cases.

II
A

Today's decision rests, in large measure, on the premise that warrantless arrest entries constitute a particularly severe invasion of personal privacy. I do not dispute that the home is generally a very private area or that the common law displayed a special "reverence . . . for the individual's right of privacy in his house." *Miller v. United States, supra*, at 313, 78 S. Ct., at 1198. . . . .

Today's decision ignores the carefully crafted restrictions on the common-law power of arrest entry and thereby overestimates the dangers inherent in that practice. At common law, absent exigent circumstances, entries to arrest could be made only for felony. Even in cases of felony, the officers were required to announce their presence, demand admission, and be refused entry before they were entitled to break doors. Further, it seems generally accepted that entries could be made only during daylight hours. And, in my view, the officer entering to arrest must have reasonable grounds to believe, not only that the arrestee has committed a crime, but also that the person suspected is present in the house at the time of the entry.[13]

These four restrictions on home arrests — felony, knock and announce, daytime, and stringent probable cause — constitute powerful and complementary protections for the privacy interests associated with the home. The felony requirement guards against abusive or arbitrary enforcement and ensures that invasions of the home occur only in case of the most serious crimes. The knock-and-announce and daytime requirements protect individuals against the fear, humiliation, and embarrassment of being aroused from their beds in states of partial or complete undress. And these requirements allow the arrestee to surrender at his front door, thereby maintaining his dignity and preventing the officers from entering other rooms of the dwelling. The stringent probable-cause requirement would help ensure against the possibility that the police would enter when the suspect was not home, and, in searching for him, frighten members of the family or ransack parts of the house, seizing items in plain view. In short, these requirements, taken together, permit an individual suspected of a serious crime to surrender at the front door of his dwelling and thereby avoid most of the humiliation and indignity that the Court seems to believe necessarily accompany a house arrest entry. Such a front-door arrest, in my view, is no more intrusive on personal privacy than the public warrantless arrests which we found to pass constitutional muster in *Watson*.

. . . . The Court substitutes, in one sweeping decision, a rigid constitutional rule in place of the common-law approach, evolved over hundreds of years, which achieved a

---

13. I do not necessarily disagree with the Court's discussion of the quantum of probable cause necessary to make a valid home arrest. The Court indicates that only an arrest warrant, and not a search warrant, is required. To obtain the warrant, therefore, the officers need only show probable cause that a crime has been committed and that the suspect committed it. However, under today's decision, the officers apparently need an extra increment of probable cause when executing the arrest warrant, namely, grounds to believe that the suspect is within the dwelling.

flexible accommodation between the demands of personal privacy and the legitimate needs of law enforcement.

. . . .

B

While exaggerating the invasion of personal privacy involved in home arrests, the Court fails to account for the danger that its rule will "severely hamper effective law enforcement." *United States v. Watson,* 423 U.S., at 431, 96 S. Ct., at 831 (Powell, J., concurring); *Gerstein v. Pugh,* 420 U.S., at 113, 95 S. Ct., at 862. . . . .

[P]olice officers will often face the difficult task of deciding whether the circumstances are sufficiently exigent to justify their entry to arrest without a warrant. This is a decision that must be made quickly in the most trying of circumstances. If the officers mistakenly decide that the circumstances are exigent, the arrest will be invalid and any evidence seized incident to the arrest or in plain view will be excluded at trial. On the other hand, if the officers mistakenly determine that exigent circumstances are lacking, they may refrain from making the arrest, thus creating the possibility that a dangerous criminal will escape into the community. The police could reduce the likelihood of escape by staking out all possible exits until the circumstances become clearly exigent or a warrant is obtained. But the costs of such a stakeout seem excessive in an era of rising crime and scarce police resources.

The uncertainty inherent in the exigent-circumstances determination burdens the judicial system as well. In the case of searches, exigent circumstances are sufficiently unusual that this Court has determined that the benefits of a warrant outweigh the burdens imposed, including the burdens on the judicial system. In contrast, arrests recurringly involve exigent circumstances, and this Court has heretofore held that a warrant can be dispensed with without undue sacrifice in Fourth Amendment values. The situation should be no different with respect to arrests in the home . . . .

. . . I cannot join the Court in declaring unreasonable a practice which has been thought entirely reasonable by so many for so long. It would be far preferable to adopt a clear and simple rule: after knocking and announcing their presence, police may enter the home to make a daytime arrest without a warrant when there is probable cause to believe that the person to be arrested committed a felony and is present in the house. . . . .

MR. JUSTICE REHNQUIST, dissenting.

. . . .

. . . . There is significant historical evidence that we have over the years misread the history of the Fourth Amendment in connection with searches, elevating the warrant requirement over the necessity for probable cause in a way which the Framers of that Amendment did not intend. *See* T. Taylor, TWO STUDIES IN CONSTITUTIONAL INTERPRETATION 38–50 (1969). But one may accept all of that as *stare decisis,* and still feel deeply troubled by the transposition of these same errors into the area of actual arrests of felons within their houses with respect to whom there is probable cause to suspect guilt of the offense in question.

Steagald v. United States

United States Supreme Court

451 U.S. 204, 101 S. Ct. 1642, 68 L. Ed. 2d 38 (1981)

JUSTICE MARSHALL delivered the opinion of the Court.

. . . .

I

In early January 1978, an agent of the Drug Enforcement Administration (DEA) was contacted in Detroit, Mich. by a confidential informant who suggested that he might be able to locate Ricky Lyons, a federal fugitive wanted on drug charges. On January 14, 1978, the informant called the agent again, and gave him a telephone number in the Atlanta, Ga. area where, according to the informant, Ricky Lyons could be reached during the next 24 hours. On January 16, 1978, the agent called fellow DEA Agent Kelly Goodowens in Atlanta and relayed the information he had obtained from the informant. Goodowens contacted Southern Bell Telephone Co., and secured the address corresponding to the telephone number obtained by the informant. Goodowens also discovered that Lyons was the subject of a 6-month-old arrest warrant.

Two days later, Goodowens and 11 other officers drove to the address supplied by the telephone company to search for Lyons. The officers observed two men standing outside the house to be searched. These men were Hoyt Gaultney and petitioner Gary Steagald. The officers approached with guns drawn, frisked both men, and, after demanding identification, determined that neither man was Lyons. Several agents proceeded to the house. Gaultney's wife answered the door, and informed the agents that she was alone in the house. She was told to place her hands against the wall and was guarded in that position while one agent searched the house. Ricky Lyons was not found, but during the search of the house the agent observed what he believed to be cocaine. Upon being informed of this discovery, Agent Goodowens sent an officer to obtain a search warrant and in the meantime conducted a second search of the house, which uncovered additional incriminating evidence. During a third search conducted pursuant to a search warrant, the agents uncovered 43 pounds of cocaine. Petitioner was arrested and indicted on federal drug charges.

. . . .

II

[In Part II, the Court dealt with the government's contention that Steagald lacked "standing."]

III

The question before us is a narrow one.[6] The search at issue here took place in the absence of consent or exigent circumstances. Except in such special situations, we have consistently held that the entry into a home to conduct a search or make an arrest is unreasonable under the Fourth Amendment unless done pursuant to a warrant. *See Payton v. New York*, 445 U.S. 573, 100 S. Ct. 1371, 63 L. Ed. 2d 639 (1980); *Johnson v. United States*, 333 U.S. 10, 13–15, 68 S. Ct. 367, 368–369, 92 L. Ed. 436 (1948). Thus, as we recently observed: "In terms that apply equally to seizures of property and to seizures of persons, the Fourth Amendment has drawn a firm line at the entrance to the house. Absent exigent circumstances, that threshold may not reasonably be crossed without a warrant." *Payton v. New York, supra*, 445 U.S., at 590, 100 S. Ct., at 1382. Here, of course, the agents had a warrant — one authorizing the arrest of Ricky Lyons. However, the Fourth Amendment claim here is not being raised by Ricky Lyons. Instead, the challenge to the search is asserted by a person not named in the warrant who was convicted on the basis of evidence uncovered during a search of his residence for Ricky Lyons. Thus, the narrow issue before us is whether an arrest warrant — as opposed to a search warrant — is adequate to protect the Fourth Amendment interests of persons not named in the warrant, when their homes are searched without their consent and in the absence of exigent circumstances.

The purpose of a warrant is to allow a neutral judicial officer to assess whether the police have probable cause to make an arrest or conduct a search . . . . However, while an arrest warrant and a search warrant both serve to subject the probable-cause determination of the police to judicial review, the interests protected by the two warrants differ. An arrest warrant is issued by a magistrate upon a showing that probable cause exists to believe that the subject of the warrant has committed an offense and thus the warrant primarily serves to protect an individual from an unreasonable seizure. A search warrant, in contrast, is issued upon a showing of probable cause to believe that the legitimate object of a search is located in a particular place, and therefore safeguards an individual's interest in the privacy of his home and possessions against the unjustified intrusion of the police.

Thus, whether the arrest warrant issued in this case adequately safeguarded the interests protected by the Fourth Amendment depends upon what the warrant authorized the agents to do. To be sure, the warrant embodied a judicial finding that there was probable cause to believe that Ricky Lyons had committed a felony, and the warrant therefore authorized the officers to seize Lyons. However, the agents sought to do more than use the warrant to arrest Lyons in a public place or in his home; instead, they relied on the warrant as legal authority to enter the home of a third person based on their belief that Ricky Lyons might be a guest there. Regardless of how reasonable this belief might have been, it was never subjected to the detached scrutiny of

---

6. Initially, we assume without deciding that the information relayed to Agent Goodowens concerning the whereabouts of Ricky Lyons would have been sufficient to establish probable cause to believe that Lyons was at the house searched by the agents.

a judicial officer. Thus, while the warrant in this case may have protected Lyons from an unreasonable seizure, it did absolutely nothing to protect petitioner's privacy interest in being free from an unreasonable invasion and search of his home. Instead, petitioner's only protection from an illegal entry and search was the agent's personal determination of probable cause. In the absence of exigent circumstances, we have consistently held that such judicially untested determinations are not reliable enough to justify an entry into a person's home to arrest him without a warrant, or a search of a home for objects in the absence of a search warrant. *Payton v. New York, supra*; *Johnson v. United States, supra*. We see no reason to depart from this settled course when the search of a home is for a person rather than an object.[7]

A contrary conclusion — that the police, acting alone and in the absence of exigent circumstances, may decide when there is sufficient justification for searching the home of a third party for the subject of an arrest warrant — would create a significant potential for abuse. Armed solely with an arrest warrant for a single person, the police could search all the homes of that individual's friends and acquaintances. Moreover, an arrest warrant may serve as the pretext for entering a home in which the police have a suspicion, but not probable cause to believe, that illegal activity is taking place. *Cf. Chimel v. California*, 395 U.S. 752, 767, 89 S. Ct. 2034, 2042, 23 L. Ed. 2d 685 (1969). The Government recognizes the potential for such abuses, but contends that existing remedies — such as motions to suppress illegally procured evidence and damages actions for Fourth Amendment violations — provide adequate means of redress. We do not agree. As we observed on a previous occasion, "[t]he [Fourth] Amendment is designed to prevent, not simply to redress, unlawful police action." *Chimel v. California, supra*, at 766, n. 12, 89 S. Ct., at 2042, n. 12. Indeed, if suppression motions and damages actions were sufficient to implement the Fourth Amendment's prohibition against unreasonable searches and seizures, there would be no need for the constitutional requirement that in the absence of exigent circumstances a warrant must be obtained for a home arrest or a search of a home for objects. We have instead concluded that in such cases the participation of a detached magistrate in the probable-cause determination is an essential element of a reasonable search or seizure, and we believe that the same conclusion should apply here. In

---

7. Indeed, the plain wording of the Fourth Amendment admits of no exemption from the warrant requirement when the search of a home is for a person rather than for a thing . . . . In *Payton*, of course, we recognized that an arrest warrant alone was sufficient to authorize the entry into a person's home to effect his arrest . . . . Because an arrest warrant authorizes the police to deprive a person of his liberty, it necessarily also authorizes a limited invasion of that person's privacy interest when it is necessary to arrest him in his home. This analysis, however, is plainly inapplicable when the police seek to use an arrest warrant as legal authority to enter the home of a third party to conduct a search. Such a warrant embodies no judicial determination whatsoever regarding the person whose home is to be searched. Because it does not authorize the police to deprive the third person of his liberty, it cannot embody any derivative authority to deprive this person of his interest in the privacy of his home. Such a deprivation must instead be based on an independent showing that a legitimate object of a search is located in the third party's home. We have consistently held, however, that such a determination is the province of the magistrate, and not that of the police officer.

sum, two distinct interests were implicated by the search at issue here — Ricky Lyons' interest in being free from an unreasonable seizure and petitioner's interest in being free from an unreasonable search of his home. Because the arrest warrant for Lyons addressed only the former interest, the search of petitioner's home was no more reasonable from petitioner's perspective than it would have been if conducted in the absence of any warrant. Since warrantless searches of a home are impermissible absent consent or exigent circumstances, we conclude that the instant search violated the Fourth Amendment.

IV

The Government concedes that this view is "apparently logical," that it furthers the general policies underlying the Fourth Amendment, and that it "has the virtue of producing symmetry between the law of entry to conduct a search for things to be seized and the law of entry to conduct a search for persons to be seized." Yet we are informed that this conclusion is "not without its flaws" in that it is contrary to common-law precedent and creates some practical problems of law enforcement. We treat these contentions in turn.

A

. . . .

While the common law . . . sheds relatively little light on the narrow question before us, the history of the Fourth Amendment strongly suggests that its Framers would not have sanctioned the instant search. The Fourth Amendment was intended partly to protect against the abuses of the general warrants that had occurred in England and of the writs of assistance used in the Colonies. The general warrant specified only an offense — typically seditious libel — and left to the discretion of the executing officials the decision as to which persons should be arrested and which places should be searched. Similarly, the writs of assistance used in the Colonies noted only the object of the search — any uncustomed goods — and thus left customs officials completely free to search any place where they believed such goods might be. The central objectionable feature of both warrants was that they provided no judicial check on the determination of the executing officials that the evidence available justified an intrusion into any particular home. *Stanford v. Texas*, 379 U.S. 476, 481–485, 85 S. Ct. 506, 509–512, 13 L. Ed. 2d 431 (1965). An arrest warrant, to the extent that it is invoked as authority to enter the homes of third parties, suffers from the same infirmity . . . .

B

The Government also suggests that practical problems might arise if law enforcement officers are required to obtain a search warrant before entering the home of a third party to make an arrest. The basis of this concern is that persons, as opposed to objects, are inherently mobile, and thus officers seeking to effect an arrest may be forced to return to the magistrate several times as the subject of the arrest warrant moves from place to place. We are convinced, however, that a search warrant requirement will not significantly impede effective law enforcement efforts.

First, the situations in which a search warrant will be necessary are few. [A]n arrest warrant alone will suffice to enter a suspect's own residence to effect his arrest. Furthermore, if probable cause exists, no warrant is required to apprehend a suspected felon in a public place. *United States v. Watson*, 423 U.S. 411, 96 S. Ct. 820, 46 L. Ed. 2d 598 (1976). Thus, the subject of an arrest warrant can be readily seized before entering or after leaving the home of a third party. Finally, the exigent-circumstances doctrine significantly limits the situations in which a search warrant would be needed. For example, a warrantless entry of a home would be justified if the police were in "hot pursuit" of a fugitive . . . .

Moreover, in those situations in which a search warrant is necessary, the inconvenience incurred by the police is simply not that significant. First, if the police know of the location of the felon when they obtain an arrest warrant, the additional burden of obtaining a search warrant at the same time is minuscule. The inconvenience of obtaining such a warrant does not increase significantly when an outstanding arrest warrant already exists . . . .

Whatever practical problems remain, however, cannot outweigh the constitutional interests at stake. Any warrant requirement impedes to some extent the vigor with which the Government can seek to enforce its laws, yet the Fourth Amendment recognizes that this restraint is necessary in some cases to protect against unreasonable searches and seizures. We conclude that this is such a case. The additional burden imposed on the police by a warrant requirement is minimal. In contrast, the right protected — that of presumptively innocent people to be secure in their homes from unjustified, forcible intrusions by the Government — is weighty. Thus, in order to render the instant search reasonable under the Fourth Amendment, a search warrant was required.

Accordingly, the judgment of the Court of Appeals is reversed, and the case is remanded to that court for further proceedings consistent with this opinion.

So ordered.

THE CHIEF JUSTICE concurs in the judgment.

JUSTICE REHNQUIST, with whom JUSTICE WHITE joins, dissenting.

. . . .

. . . [The Court's] "reasoning" not only assumes the answer to the question presented — whether the search of petitioner's dwelling could be undertaken without a search warrant — but also conveniently ignores the critical fact in this case, the existence of an arrest warrant for a fugitive believed on the basis of probable cause to be in the dwelling. The Court assumes that because the arrest warrant did not specifically address petitioner's privacy interest it is of no further relevance to the case. Incidental infringements of distinct Fourth Amendment interests may, however, be reasonable when they occur in the course of executing a valid warrant addressed to other interests . . . .

. . . .

The government's interests in the warrantless entry of a third-party dwelling to execute an arrest warrant are compelling. The basic problem confronting police in such situations is the inherent mobility of the fugitive. By definition, the police have probable cause to believe that the fugitive is in a dwelling which is not his home. He may stay there for a week, a day, or 10 minutes. Fugitives from justice tend to be mobile, and police officers will generally have no way of knowing whether the subject of an arrest warrant will be at the dwelling when they return from seeking a search warrant. Imposition of a search warrant requirement in such circumstances will frustrate the compelling interests of the government and indeed the public in the apprehension of those subject to outstanding arrest warrants.

The Court's responses to these very real concerns are singularly unpersuasive . . . .

At the same time, the interference with the Fourth Amendment privacy interests of those whose homes are entered to apprehend the felon is not nearly as significant as suggested by the Court. The arrest warrant serves some of the functions a separate search warrant would. It assures the occupants that the police officer is present on official business. The arrest warrant also limits the scope of the search, specifying what the police may search for — i.e., the subject of the arrest warrant. No general search is permitted, but only a search of those areas in which the object of the search might hide. Indeed there may be no intrusion on the occupant's privacy at all, since if present the suspect will have the opportunity to voluntarily surrender at the door. Even if the suspect does not surrender but secretes himself within the house, the occupant can limit the search by pointing him out to the police.

. . . .

While I cannot subscribe to the Court's decision today, I will not falsely cry "wolf" in this dissent. The decision rests on a very special set of facts, and with a change in one or more of them it is clear that no separate search warrant would be required even under the reasoning of the Court.

On the one side *Payton* makes clear that an arrest warrant is all that is needed to enter the suspect's "home" to effect the arrest. 445 U.S., at 602–603. If a suspect has been living in a particular dwelling for any significant period, say a few days, it can certainly be considered his "home" for Fourth Amendment purposes, even if the premises are owned by a third party and others are living there, and even if the suspect concurrently maintains a residence elsewhere as well. In such a case the police could enter the premises with only an arrest warrant. On the other side, the more fleeting a suspect's connection with the premises, such as when he is a mere visitor, the more likely that exigent circumstances will exist justifying immediate police action without departing to obtain a search warrant. The practical damage done to effective law enforcement by today's decision, without any basis in the Constitution, may well be minimal if courts carefully consider the various congeries of facts in the actual case before them.

The genuinely unfortunate aspect of today's ruling is not that fewer fugitives will be brought to book, or fewer criminals apprehended, though both of these consequences will undoubtedly occur; the greater misfortune is the increased uncertainty imposed on police officers in the field, committing magistrates, and trial judges, who must confront variations and permutations of this factual situation on a day-to-day basis . . . .

Notes and Questions

Insofar as they involve felony arrests, *Payton* and *Steagald* are related to *United States v. Watson*, 423 U.S. 411, 96 S. Ct. 820, 46 L. Ed. 2d 598 (1976), encountered in Chapter 3. Unlike *Watson*, however, *Payton* and *Steagald* involved the validity of warrantless *entries* of dwellings to effect such arrests. The *Steagald* majority found the *search* warrant requirement applicable to the entry challenged in that case, while the *Payton* majority concluded that an *arrest* warrant would have satisfied the Fourth Amendment.

(1) What is the factual distinction that led the Court to impose different constitutional demands in *Payton* and *Steagald*? What is the practical difference between the warrant requirements imposed by the two decisions? Which is potentially more protective of the homeowner's privacy? What is the justification for the difference in constitutional privacy protection?

(2) Suppose that one individual objects to the entry of her dwelling to effect the arrest of another individual who shares the same dwelling. What showing must the government make to sustain such an entry?

(3) What is required for an officer to arrest a suspected felon in a hotel room? In the suspected felon's office? In the threshold of the doorway to his or her home? In connection with the latter question, see *United States v. Santana*, 427 U.S. 38, 96 S. Ct. 2406, 49 L. Ed. 2d 300 (1975), in which the Court held that a suspected felon who stood precisely in the threshold of the front door of her home was subject to warrantless arrest under the *Watson* holding. According to the Court, Ms. Santana "was in a 'public' place" for purposes of the Fourth Amendment, "not in an area where she had any expectation of privacy. . . . She was not merely visible to the public but was as exposed to public view, speech, hearing, and touch as if she had been standing completely outside her house." For those reasons, a warrantless arrest was valid under *Watson*.

The Court's holding about the propriety of a warrantless arrest in *Santana* is arguably a narrow one, limited by the specific facts of the case. From the Court's opinion, it appears that there was no barrier or obstruction that impeded the public from seeing, speaking to, hearing, or even touching Ms. Santana as she stood in her front doorway. Moreover, when the officers stopped their vehicle in front of the Santana home, they were a mere 15 feet from that doorway. Would a warrantless arrest have been permissible if the front yard of the Santana home had a fence that prevented public access? What if the yard had been fenced, but a private sidewalk that was accessible to the public led from the public sidewalk up to the front door of the home? Would the result change if Ms. Santana had been standing within her fenced front yard, in a place that could only be accessed by trespassing on her property. If she had been standing in the fenced or unfenced rear yard of her home? In which of these circumstances does it make sense to consider a person to be "in a public place" for Fourth Amendment purposes? In connection with these questions, reconsider the Court's discussions of the Fourth Amendment protection afforded privacy interests within the "curtilage" of private homes. *See Oliver v. United States*, 466 U.S. 170, 104 S. Ct. 1735, 80 L. Ed. 2d 214 (1984); *California v. Ciraolo, supra*, Chapter One.

Arrestee Search Problems

4A-1: On the evening of April 29, 2010, Thomas stopped at a gas station to refuel his Charger — a car for which he had paid $36,000. He had also purchased a special set of custom wheel rims for the vehicle. When he pulled into the station, Thomas noticed two men. As he filled his gas tank, one of the men approached and asked if he wanted to buy "some weed." He declined, but when he turned to get in his car, the other man was standing in his way. The first man put a gun to his side while the second took his wallet, cash, and phone. The men then drove away in his Charger.

The next day, Thomas and his girlfriend spotted his Charger in a parking space at a strip mall. Thomas asked his girlfriend to summon the police while he blocked the Charger with the vehicle he was driving. Through the window of a barbershop in the strip mall, Thomas spotted Ronald, the man who had offered to sell him marijuana and put a gun to his side. Ronald repeatedly looked at Thomas.

Shortly thereafter, Officer Kevin, who had responded to the gas station the previous night, was dispatched to the shopping center. He verified that the Charger was Thomas's car, and waited with Thomas for Ronald to leave the barber shop. Forty-five minutes later, Ronald came out of the barber shop and got into a car that pulled up to the curb. Kevin stopped the car and ordered the occupants to get out. He saw bags of marijuana on the floor boards where Ronald had been sitting. Although Kevin had instructed Thomas to keep his distance, Thomas walked up to Ronald and announced that Ronald was the man who had stolen his car. Officer Kevin arrested Ronald and recovered cash, cocaine, and a cell phone from his pockets.

The cell phone was a Samsung "flip" phone. Shortly after taking it from Ronald, the officer opened the phone and saw a screen saver image (sometimes also referred to as "wallpaper") of a wheel rim and fender that matched the wheel rims and color of the stolen car. The officer scrolled through the photos inside the phone. In the photo library, he discovered a photo of wheel rims matching Thomas's custom wheel rims. In scrolling through the phone, he also discovered a "properties screen" that contained "metadata" concerning the second photo. Included in the metadata was the date "4/30/10" and the time "7:00." Officer Kevin took photographs of the screen saver photo, the photo he found in the library, and the properties screen. The government intended to introduce these three photographs into evidence at Ronald's carjacking trial. Ronald moved to suppress the photographs.

Did the officer obtain the photographs by violating Ronald's Fourth Amendment rights?

4A–2: At approximately 3:45 p.m., State Trooper Jeff Wall stopped a truck driven by Rasky in Scott County. Wall had reason to believe that Rasky was driving without a proper license, so he brought Rasky to his patrol car and inquired. After Trooper Wall determined that Rasky's license had been suspended and that Rasky had twice before been convicted of driving with a suspended license, he handcuffed Rasky and placed him in the back of his patrol car. When Wall informed Rasky that he would not be released with a citation, Rasky said he did not want to go to jail and asked whether he could instead speak with a narcotics investigator to tell what he knew about drug crimes in the area. Trooper Wall summoned Investigator Low, a member of the Narcotics Group Task Force. Low arrived shortly after 4:00 p.m. He entered Wall's patrol car to speak with Rasky.

Low spoke with Rasky for approximately 45 minutes about becoming a confidential informant. During that time, Wall was undecided about whether he would take Rasky into custody. If Low reached an agreement with Rasky to serve as an informant, Wall was prepared to consider giving Rasky a ticket and releasing him. Ultimately, it became apparent to Low that Rasky was "not in a position or not ready to make" a commitment to help law enforcement. Low informed Wall that there would be no agreement, and that Wall should proceed as he would have done before Rasky offered to cooperate.

At approximately 5:05 p.m., Wall and Low began to search Rasky's truck. While searching the passenger area of the truck's extended cab, Low encountered a loose plastic insert covering a small cubby hole. Low pulled up the insert, discovering two handguns beneath the plastic. After the search was completed, Trooper Wall called a tow truck. The tow truck arrived at 5:50 p.m., and Rasky was then taken to jail.

Was the search of the truck reasonable under the Fourth Amendment?

4A–3: On November 19, Deputy Kevin proceeded to Heather's home, intending to arrest her pursuant to two arrest warrants and to question her regarding certain stolen checks. One of the warrants was for unpaid traffic fines. While he was en route, Kevin noticed a vehicle driven by Danny, Heather's spouse, and recognized the passenger in the vehicle as Heather. As he was observing the vehicle, he saw Heather's "head go down into the seat."

After Kevin stopped the vehicle, he discovered that Heather was no longer in the passenger compartment. Upon noticing that there was a small gap between the rear seats of the vehicle and the trunk, Kevin's suspected that Heather had lowered the rear seats and climbed into the trunk. This suspicion was confirmed when Danny admitted that his wife was in the trunk. Kevin then proceeded to lower the rear seats, remove Heather from the trunk, and execute the two outstanding warrants for her arrest.

Upon securing Heather in the back of his cruiser, Kevin searched the vehicle, finding a purse, a small leather bag, and a change purse. A search of those items yielded checks, which Heather admitted were stolen from the mail.

Subsequently, the state charged Heather with possession of stolen mail. She pleaded not guilty and moved to suppress the contents of the purse, bag, and change purse, arguing that they were the products of an unconstitutional search.

How should the trial judge rule on the motion to suppress?

4A–4: The police department received a tip that Carlos would arrive by train on November 3. The tipster mentioned that there was an active warrant for his arrest. Officers Kreger and Nyman, who were assigned to a multijurisdictional unit focused on gangs and drug activity, investigated the tip. They learned that Carlos was a member of the "Satan Disciples" gang. They also confirmed that he was the subject of an outstanding arrest warrant for failure to pay child support. Kreger, Nyman, and a third officer went to the train station at the time Carlos was scheduled to arrive. They saw him disembark and enter the train station. He was carrying a "laundry bag" over his shoulder and pulling a "wheeled luggage bag" behind him. The officers approached and placed Carlos under arrest, handcuffing him immediately. According to Officer Kreger, Carlos's friend, Lindsey, arrived at the scene after the arrest had been effected. According to Officer Nyman, however, Lindsey had walked up to Carlos before the officers approached and arrested him.

Carlos asked the officers if Lindsey could take his bags. The officers informed him that they "had to check the bags out first." Because gang members are known to carry weapons, the officers were concerned for their safety. Without removing the handcuffs, Kreger escorted Carlos an unspecified distance over to the side of the train station. Nyman carried and wheeled Carlos's bags to the same area. The officers then began to search the two bags. In one bag, Kreger found a jar of hair gel. He opened the jar and found inside a bag containing powder cocaine. Carlos was charged with possession of cocaine.

Was the search a valid search incident to Carlos's arrest?

4A–5: At approximately 2:22 a.m., two police officers were dispatched to 18th Avenue on a report of a crying, unclothed female. They found D.L., who was naked, wrapped in a blanket, shaking, crying uncontrollably, and "obviously terrified." Her face was bruised and bloody. She had bruises to her stomach and back and scrape marks on her arms and legs. She stated that she had been forced to have oral sex in the garage across the street and pointed toward 2801 18th Avenue. She told the officers that the suspect was in the basement of the residence, describing him as a "fat white guy" in his twenties, with "short, dark hair wearing no shirt, black pants and smelling of alcohol." Neighbors told the officers that Josh, a 23- to 24-year-old male, had been at 2801 18th Avenue earlier in the evening and had been very intoxicated. He commonly stayed at the residence. The neighbors believed that he "would either be inside the garage or inside the residence . . . because he was too intoxicated to leave."

The officers approached the garage at 2801 18th Avenue and noticed that an access door was wide open. They saw two chairs knocked over outside the access door and female clothing including a bra, a shirt, and a woman's shoe as well as condom wrappers strewn about on the ground. They also saw a pair of jeans hanging off the garage roof, a "make-shift bed on the floor of the garage," and "what appeared to be blood on the floor adjacent to the bed." One officer entered the garage to determine if the suspect was inside.

After they had been at the scene for approximately an hour, the officers knocked on two doors to the residence for approximately three to five minutes, but received no response. After they forced entry into the residence, they located Luss, who matched the description that D.L. had provided, sleeping on a couch on the main floor. They arrested him and placed him in the back of a squad car. They noted that he had numerous scratches on his chest, stomach, back, arms, and hands, that he had blood on his hands, that his shirt was on inside-out, and that his pants and belt were undone. The officers swabbed respondent's hands to take a sample of the blood.

Officers drove Luss to the hospital for a sexual assault examination. At the hospital, his clothing and undergarments were collected for evidence, his pubic hair was combed, pubic-hair samples were taken, and his cheek, hands, and penis were swabbed. Luss contends that the entry of the residence and the examination at the hospital violated his Fourth Amendment rights.

How should the government respond to Luss's contentions? Are his contentions valid?

4A–6: On October 23, Fish bought two 12-packs of beer and settled in for an evening of watching the World Series and cleaning his WWII gun collection. Around midnight, Leo, a security guard at Fish's apartment complex, was investigating a noise complaint. By looking through his sliding glass door, Leo saw that Fish was in his apartment. Leo summoned him outside. Fish walked out, carrying a rifle he had been cleaning. When Leo asked Fish whether he had heard noise coming from upstairs, Fish was unresponsive. Eventually, he changed the subject to the Second Amendment. Leo suspected that Fish was intoxicated. Because of the liquor, the gun, and the reaction to his questions, Leo called the police.

Sergeant Ryan arrived around 2:00 a.m. After speaking with Leo, Ryan went to Fish's apartment. Fish came to the door, but did not answer Ryan's questions. Instead, he rambled on about his Second Amendment rights. Ryan believed that Fish was intoxicated. Many more officers soon arrived at the scene. Some telephoned Fish's apartment. When Fish's wife, Sandra, answered the phone, the officers instructed her to leave the apartment. She did so. It is not clear whether she put the phone back on the hook, but the line remained busy during the ensuing events. Sandra reported that no one else was inside, that Fish had 18 rifles, and that he had been drinking.

At approximately 4:00 a.m., Jan Mal, a tactical negotiator, communicated with Fish. Fish informed Mal that he had a right to bear arms. He invited her into his apartment, but said he would shoot her if she did enter. Throughout the morning Fish repeatedly told the police to "go away, leave me alone, and don't bother me." He twice was seen pointing a rifle at the officers closest to his apartment. At around 7:00 a.m., the Mobile Emergency Response Team (MERT) replaced the officers who had first arrived. Because pointing a rifle at police officers was a criminal offense, MERT officers sought to force Fish out of his apartment to arrest him. They had Fish's power turned off at 8:48 a.m. Because the phone line remained busy, the officers broke the sliding glass doors and tossed a "throw phone" inside. (A "throw phone" is a phone encased in a box that also contains an open microphone.) At 10:50 a.m., the police set off a "flash-bang" device, designed to get Fish's attention and disorient him. Two hours later, the police threw CS gas canisters into the apartment. CS gas causes irritation and burning sensations. One of the CS canisters sent glass flying, cutting Fish's forehead.

At 2 p.m., the police finally contacted Fish via the throw phone. Fish offered to come out naked so that the police would not suspect him of carrying a weapon. When told that this was not necessary, Fish said that he would come out in boxers and socks, a plan the police approved. He emerged at 2:35 p.m., initially following instructions by walking in a designated direction and keeping his hands in the air. Soon, however, Fish stopped walking. An officer then shot him in the leg with a rubber bullet. When Fish dropped to the ground, the officers handcuffed him. At no point did they secure a warrant.

Did the officers' actions violate the Fourth Amendment?

4A–7: At some time during the week preceding June 24, 2010, during an encounter with Conan, Trooper Politano saw a state identification card indicating that Conan lived at an apartment at an address in Minster. Subsequently, Politano learned that Conan was the subject of two valid "motor vehicle" arrest warrants. He confirmed that the address on Conan's identification card matched the address listed on his driver's license. On June 24, at 9:30 a.m., the trooper, assisted by Detective Wolf and two Minster police officers, went to Conan's apartment. At the time, Politano had no specific information indicating that Conan was home and he did not know how many people resided in the apartment.

Trooper Politano and Detective Wolf knocked twice on the back door. When Maura came to the door, Politano told her that he was looking for Conan and had a warrant to arrest him. Daisy, Maura's teenage daughter, was standing beside her.

Maura appeared nervous and avoided making eye contact with Politano. She said, "He's not here," a couple of times, and looked toward a bedroom that was straight across from where Politano was standing. The bedroom door was "probably half to three-quarters open." Politano did not see anyone else in the apartment and did not ask Maura whether anyone other than she and her daughter were at home. While at the door, however, Politano heard "movement" indicating to him that "somebody else was present." He told Maura that he believed Conan was in the apartment, walked past her into the bedroom toward which she had looked, and found Conan inside. He also noticed the "butt end" of what appeared to be a rifle (but was actually an antique musket) sticking out from under the bed.

Trooper Politano handcuffed Conan and removed the musket from beneath the bed. In the process, he observed three firearm cases. Two contained shotguns and the third, labeled "Beretta," was empty. When Politano asked Conan about the firearms, he responded that they were not his and he did not know where they had come from. Conan then yelled that Politano was "illegally searching" his bedroom. Politano seized the musket, firearms, and firearm cases, and took them and Conan to the police station.

The firearms proved to be stolen. Conan was indicted for receiving stolen property. He moved to suppress the items taken from his bedroom, claiming violation of his Fourth Amendment rights. At the hearing on this suppression motion Trooper Politano testified as follows:

> Based on my training and experience, I have developed a sense of sincerity or credibility when executing arrest warrants, because I have often found that people will misrepresent . . . a person's presence in a dwelling. I have good judgment of whether people are telling the truth or lying, and the nervousness when someone's talking to you and they're not making eye contact. You're asking them questions and they're looking around, almost looking like someone's hiding as you're talking to them-type thing. Catch them in some lies.

How should the trial judge rule on the motion to suppress the evidence?

4A–8: In May, Curt made a false statement on a credit application he submitted to a high-end car dealership where he was attempting to purchase an Aston Martin. Specifically, Curt's credit application listed as his Social Security Number a number that actually belonged to a seven-year-old girl. An internal investigator at the dealership's bank alerted a joint anti-fraud task force to Curt's fraudulent activity. Vincent, a Secret Service special agent who was a member of the task force, took charge of the investigation into Curt. After verifying that the SSN on the application did not belong to Curt, Vincent subpoenaed Curt's bank records. Vincent's review of Curt's bank records led him to believe that Curt was masterminding a mortgage-fraud scheme.

In July 2007, Vincent and the task force obtained an arrest warrant on the state-law charge of making a false statement to obtain credit. The arrest warrant was not related to Curt's participation in the mortgage-fraud scheme. Vincent and several other task-force members executed the arrest warrant on Curt while he was driving. Curt was talking on his cell phone as he was pulled over. As the officers pulled Curt out of his car, he placed his cell phone on top of the car's center console. Vincent took the phone out of the car as Curt was being arrested and began looking through text messages on the phone. The officers then drove back to the Secret Service office, initiated prisoner processing, and attempted to interview Curt. While Curt was in the prisoner-processing area, Vincent resumed looking through the text messages on Curt's phone. He discovered two incoming texts that incriminated Curt in a criminal conspiracy. Curt has moved to exclude the text messages from his trial, claiming that they were found as a result of an unreasonable search.

Does Curt have a valid Fourth Amendment claim?

4A–9: Deputy Luz arrived at the Coins' home shortly before 6:30 p.m. to serve Mr. Coin with a "Temporary Injunction Against Repeat Violence." Mr. Coin's tenant had obtained the injunction six days earlier under a statutory provision that authorizes issuance against anyone who has committed two or more incidents of violence or stalking. The Coins' home faces the street and is in close proximity to the sidewalk. The attached garage, which also faces the street, was open when Luz arrived. The driveway leads directly from the street to the garage, and a pathway veers left from the driveway up to the front door. Between the front door and the garage, the house has a large front bay window.

Upon arriving, Luz approached the Coins' front door and rang the bell. Mrs. Coin answered the door, and Luz explained that he had papers to deliver to Mr. Coin. Mrs. Coin responded that Mr. Coin was in the bathroom and that Luz would have to wait. She then shut and locked the front door. Luz walked back down the pathway along the front bay window. Believing he had made eye contact with Mrs. Coin through the window, he waved the paperwork above his head to remind her that he was waiting. Under the impression that Mrs. Coin had seen him, Luz walked back up to the front door expecting her to open it. As he approached the front door, he overheard a man's voice asking, "What did he want?" Luz then rang the bell, but received no answer. He then walked into the planter and up to the front window to try to get the Coins' attention. An upset Mrs. Coin began shouting for Luz to get out of her bushes and off her property. She threatened to call the police. Luz walked to his patrol car to call for backup because he believed that the Coins were trying to avoid service and that there was a possibility of obstruction.

About five to eight minutes later, Deputy Brand arrived. Around the same time, Luz spotted a man resembling Mr. Coin at the front window. While Luz and Brand stood on the driveway, in front of the open garage door, Mrs. Coin opened the door from the kitchen to the garage, reached out and pushed the button to close the automatic garage door. Brand immediately walked into the open garage, tripping the electronic sensor and causing the garage door to retreat to an open position. Luz followed. Brand knocked on the interior door from the garage to the kitchen, whereupon Mrs. Coin came out into the garage and yelled at the deputies to get off her property. Brand informed Mrs. Coin that she was under arrest for obstructing service of process. A struggle ensued as the deputies attempted to handcuff her. At one point, Mr. Coin intervened in the struggle. Eventually, the deputies subdued and arrested both Coins. The Coins subsequently brought a civil suit for violation of their Fourth Amendment rights.

Did the deputies' conduct violate the Fourth Amendment?

4A–10: Late on the evening of August 6, Officers Donovan, Budryk, and Smythe arrived at the home of James and Joanne Joy, seeking to arrest their son Lance. Lance did not live with his parents, but the police had received a call earlier in the evening from Lance's ex-girlfriend informing them that he was at his parents' home. At the time, there was an outstanding arrest warrant for Lance for violating a domestic restraining order.

Lance answered the officers' knock at the Joys' side door. He opened the interior door, but kept the outer screen door closed. Budryk told Lance that the officers had a warrant for his arrest and asked him to step outside. Lance retorted, "Ya, right," and withdrew from the doorway, calling for his mother. The officers followed him inside.

Joanne Joy, who had been asleep, came downstairs to find her son and the police officers standing in her dining room. James entered the room minutes later. The Joys asked the officers what was going on and whether they had a warrant. The officers replied that they had come to arrest Lance, that a warrant for his arrest did exist, but that they did not have it with them. James and Officer Smythe left to call the police department to confirm the existence of the outstanding warrant.

In the interim, Joanne protested Lance's arrest and scuffled with Officers Donovan and Budryk. The events surrounding the scuffle are the subject of dispute. Joanne was charged with assault and battery, but was acquitted. James and Joanne then brought suit against the town, the chief of police, and the officers, claiming that the officers' actions violated the Fourth Amendment.

Is there merit to the Joys' claim? Would the answer be different if Lance lived with his parents?

Selected Bibliography

Surell Brady, *Arrests Without Prosecution and the Fourth Amendment*, 59 Md. L. Rev. 1 (2000)

Frank Rudy Cooper, *Post Racialism and Searches Incident to Arrest*, 44 Ariz. St. L. J. 113 (2012)

Geoffrey S. Corn, Arizona v. Gant: *The Good, the Bad, and the Meaning of "Reasonable Belief*," 45 Conn. L. Rev. 177 (2012)

George M. Dery III, *A Case of Doubtful Certainty: The Court Relapses Into Search Incident to Arrest Confusion in* Arizona v. Gant, 44 Ind. L. Rev. 395 (2011)

Jeffrey L. Evans, *Constitutional Restraints on Residential Warrantless Arrest Entries: More Protection for Privacy Interests in the Home*, 10 Am. J. Crim. L. 1 (1982)

Nancy Lesse Faust & Joseph D. Harbaugh, *"Knock on Any Door" — Home Arrests After* Payton *and* Steagald, 86 Dick. L. Rev. 191 (1982)

Adam M. Gershowitz, *The iPhone Meets the Fourth Amendment*, 56 UCLA L. Rev. 27 (2008)

Catherine Hancock, *State Court Activism and Searches Incident to Arrest*, 68 Va. L. Rev. 1085 (1982)

Wayne R. LaFave, *"Case-By-Case Adjudication" Versus "Standardized Procedures": The* Robinson *Dilemma*, 1974 Sup. Ct. Rev. 127 (1974)

Ric Simmons, *The Missed Opportunities of* Riley v. California, 12 Ohio St. J. Crim. L. 253 (2014)

James J. Tomkovicz, *Divining and Designing the Future of the Search Incident to Arrest Doctrine: Avoiding Instability, Irrationality, and Infidelity*, 2007 U. Ill. L. Rev. 1417

[B] Exigent Circumstances Searches

Warden, Maryland Penitentiary v. Hayden

United States Supreme Court

387 U.S. 294, 87 S. Ct. 1642, 18 L. Ed. 2d 782 (1967)

Mr. Justice Brennan delivered the opinion of the Court.

. . . .

I

About 8:00 a.m. on March 17, 1962, an armed robber entered the business premises of the Diamond Cab Company in Baltimore, Maryland. He took some $363 and ran. Two cab drivers in the vicinity, attracted by shouts of "Holdup," followed the man to 2111 Cocoa Lane. One driver notified the company dispatcher by radio that the man was a Negro about 5' 8" tall, wearing a light cap and dark jacket, and that he had entered the house on Cocoa Lane. The dispatcher relayed the information to police who were proceeding to the scene of the robbery. Within minutes, police arrived at the house in a number of patrol cars. An officer knocked and announced their presence. Mrs. Hayden answered, and the officers told her they believed that a robber had entered the house, and asked to search the house. She offered no objection.

The officers spread out through the first and second floors and the cellar in search of the robber. Hayden was found in an upstairs bedroom feigning sleep. He was arrested when the officers on the first floor and in the cellar reported that no other man was in the house. Meanwhile an officer was attracted to an adjoining bathroom by the noise of running water, and discovered a shotgun and a pistol in a flush tank; another officer who, according to the District Court, "was searching the cellar for a man or the money" found in a washing machine a jacket and trousers of the type the fleeing man was said to have worn. A clip of ammunition for the pistol and a cap were found under the mattress of Hayden's bed, and ammunition for the shotgun was found in a bureau drawer in Hayden's room. All these items of evidence were introduced against respondent at his trial.

II

We agree with the Court of Appeals that neither the entry without warrant to search for the robber, nor the search for him without warrant was invalid. Under the circumstances of this case, "the exigencies of the situation made that course imperative." *McDonald v. United States*, 335 U.S. 451, 456. The police were informed that an armed robbery had taken place, and that the suspect had entered 2111 Cocoa Lane less than five minutes before they reached it. They acted reasonably when they entered the house and began to search for a man of the description they had been given and for weapons which he had used in the robbery or might use against them. The Fourth Amendment does not require police officers to delay in the course of an investigation if to do so would gravely endanger their lives or the lives of others. Speed here was essential, and only a thorough search of the house for persons and weapons could have insured that Hayden was the only man present and that the police had control of all weapons which could be used against them or to effect an escape.

. . . The permissible scope of search must . . . at the least, be as broad as may reasonably be necessary to prevent the dangers that the suspect at large in the house may resist or escape.

It is argued that, while the weapons, ammunition, and cap may have been seized in the course of a search for weapons, the officer who seized the clothing was searching neither for the suspect nor for weapons when he looked into the washing machine in which he found the clothing. But even if we assume, although we do not decide, that the exigent circumstances in this case made lawful a search without warrant only for the suspect or his weapons, it cannot be said on this record that the officer who found the clothes in the washing machine was not searching for weapons. He testified that he was searching for the man or the money, but his failure to state explicitly that he was searching for weapons, in the absence of a specific question to that effect, can hardly be accorded controlling weight. He knew that the robber was armed and he did not know that some weapons had been found at the time he opened the machine. In these circumstances the inference that he was in fact also looking for weapons is fully justified.

. . . .

[The concurring opinion of Mr. Justice Fortas has been omitted.]

[The dissenting opinion of Mr. Justice Douglas has been omitted.]

Notes and Questions

(1) In general, what showing must the government make to justify a warrantless entry and search of a home under the exigent circumstances doctrine? How likely

must it be that the harm threatened by the "exigency" relied upon to justify a warrantless search will actually come to pass? In connection with this question, consider *Richards v. Wisconsin*, 520 U.S. 385, 117 S. Ct. 1416, 137 L. Ed. 2d 615 (1997) (concluding that an exception to the "knock and announce" requirement is justified by a "reasonable suspicion" that harm will occur if officers knock and announce their presence and identity). For a case setting out seven criteria for evaluating the presence of exigent circumstances, see *Dorman v. United States*, 435 F.2d 385 (D.C. Cir. 1970); *see also United States v. Harris*, 629 A.2d 481 (D.C. Ct. App. 1993).

For another case in which the Supreme Court held that the exigency created by "hot pursuit" of a suspect justified the warrantless entry of a dwelling, see *United States v. Santana*, 427 U.S. 38, 96 S. Ct. 2406, 49 L. Ed. 2d 300 (1976).

(2) Assuming that officers have properly entered a place based on exigent circumstances, what is the permissible scope of the warrantless search they are authorized to conduct? More specifically, what *areas* are subject to search? And *how long* does the authority to conduct a warrantless search last?

(3) In *Welsh v. Wisconsin*, 466 U.S. 740, 104 S. Ct. 2091, 80 L. Ed. 2d 732 (1984), the government relied on the exigent circumstances exception to justify a warrantless nighttime entry of a home to arrest a resident. In the course of rejecting the government's arguments, the Supreme Court imposed a significant restriction upon the application of the exigent circumstances exception to entries of homes.

Shortly before 9:00 p.m., Welsh was seen driving erratically. He swerved off the road and into an open field. By the time officers arrived at the scene to investigate, Welsh had departed on foot, abandoning his vehicle. A witness who had conversed with Welsh at the scene told an investigating officer that the driver of the vehicle was either inebriated or sick. Upon checking the vehicle's registration, the police learned that it was registered to Welsh. They noted that he lived within walking distance. Proceeding to his house without a warrant, they arrived at 9:00 p.m. They entered, found him lying naked in bed, and arrested him for driving a motor vehicle while under the influence of an intoxicant.

The Court observed that it had "recognized only a few ... emergency conditions" that justify dispensing with the warrant requirement. After first noting that the home has a special Fourth Amendment sanctity that militates against warrantless entries, the Court then placed heavy reliance upon the "relatively minor" nature of the offense involved in *Welsh*. The Court broadly asserted that "it is difficult to conceive of a warrantless home arrest that would not be unreasonable under the Fourth Amendment when the underlying offense is extremely minor," and that "application of the exigent-circumstances exception in the context of a home entry should rarely be sanctioned when there is probable cause to believe that only a minor offense ... has been committed."

The government asserted that three different exigencies justified the warrantless entry to arrest Welsh. First, officers were in "hot pursuit" of a criminal. Second, they needed to prevent the threat he posed to the public safety. Finally, they needed to preserve evidence of his blood alcohol level, which would dissipate over time. The Court rejected all three alleged bases for application of the exigent circumstances doctrine and held that the warrantless entry was unreasonable. The "hot pursuit" contention was unsuccessful because "there was no immediate and continuous pursuit of the petitioner from the scene of the crime." The public safety argument failed because the suspect had abandoned his car at the scene of the accident and, therefore, posed "little remaining threat to the public safety." The Court did not deny that the need to preserve dissipating evidence could create an exigency. However, because Wisconsin had chosen to classify first offense driving while intoxicated as a "non-criminal, civil forfeiture offense for which no imprisonment is possible," and had thereby indicated that it did not have a major interest in arresting such offenders, the Court concluded that an exigency based on the destruction of evidence could not justify the warrantless entry of Welsh's home.

(4) EMERGENCY ASSISTANCE AS EXIGENCY: (a) In *Brigham City, Utah v. Stuart*, 547 U.S. 398, 126 S. Ct. 1943, 164 L. Ed. 2d 650 (2006), officers entered a home without a warrant after witnessing an altercation in the kitchen that involved four adults and one juvenile. A unanimous Court sustained the warrantless entry under the exigent circumstances exception. According to the Court, "[o]ne exigency obviating the requirement of a warrant is the need to assist persons who are seriously injured or threatened with such injury." It is reasonable for an officer to "enter a home without a warrant to render emergency assistance to an injured occupant or to protect an occupant from imminent injury." The defendants had argued that the entry in this case, however, was unreasonable because "the officers were more interested in making arrests than quelling violence." In addition, they contended that "their conduct was not serious enough to justify the officers' intrusion into the home."

In response to the first argument, the Court opined that an "officer's subjective motivation is irrelevant." An entry is valid if the objective circumstances establish sufficient need to assist or protect an occupant. Consequently, it did "not matter . . . whether the officers entered the kitchen to arrest [the defendants] and gather evidence against them or to assist the injured and prevent further violence."

The Court also rejected the second argument, distinguishing *Welsh v. Wisconsin* as a case that "involved a warrantless entry . . . to arrest a suspect for driving while intoxicated." The " 'only potential emergency' " therein "was the need to preserve evidence — an exigency that we held insufficient under the circumstances to justify entry into the suspect's home." In contrast, in *Stuart*, "the officers were confronted with *ongoing* violence occurring *within* the home." Their entry "was plainly reasonable under the circumstances." The officers "were responding, at 3 o'clock in the morning, to complaints about a loud party," and "could hear from within [the house] 'an altercation occurring, some kind of fight.' " Moreover, after they proceeded to the rear of the house, the officers

> could see that a fracas was taking place inside the kitchen. A juvenile, fists clenched, was being held back by several adults. As the officers watch, he

breaks free and strikes one of the adults in the face, sending the adult to the sink spitting blood. In these circumstances, the officers had an objectively reasonable basis for believing both that the injured adult might need help and that the violence in the kitchen was just beginning .... The role of a peace officer includes preventing violence and restoring order, not simply rendering first aid to casualties; an officer is not like a boxing (or hockey) referee, poised to stop a bout only if it becomes too one-sided.

(b) In *Michigan v. Fisher*, 558 U.S. 45, 130 S. Ct. 546, 175 L. Ed. 2d 410 (2009), officers who were responding "to a complaint of a disturbance" were directed "to a residence where a man was 'going crazy.'" They "found a household in considerable chaos." A pickup truck, fenceposts, and windows were damaged, and there was blood on the truck, on one of the doors to the house, and on clothing inside the house. Officers could see "Fisher, inside the house, screaming and throwing things." He did not respond to their knock. Upon seeing a cut on his hand, they asked if "he needed medical attention," but he "ignored these questions and demanded, with accompanying profanity, that the officers go to get a search warrant." One officer "pushed the front door partway open and ventured" inside. When he could see "Fisher pointing a long gun at him," he retreated.

The Supreme Court reversed a state court ruling that the home entry violated the Fourth Amendment, deeming it "contrary to" *Brigham City, Utah v. Stuart*. According to the Court, *Brigham City* had held that "'the need to assist persons who are seriously injured or threatened with such injury'" was an "exigency" that justified a warrantless home entry. Officers may enter a home to provide assistance to an occupant who is injured or to prevent an imminent injury, and their authority "does not depend on [their] subjective intent or the seriousness of any crime" being investigated. It exists when there is "'an objectively reasonable basis for believing,' that 'a person within [the house] is in need of immediate aid.'" Officers do "not need ironclad proof of 'a likely serious, life-threatening' injury." The reasonableness of an entry depends on an "objective inquiry into appearances," and not upon a "hindsight determination" of whether "there was in fact [an] emergency." In this case, officers could enter under the "emergency aid exception" because "it was reasonable to believe that Fisher had hurt himself (albeit nonfatally) and needed treatment that in his rage he was unable to provide, or that Fisher was about to hurt, or had already hurt, someone else."

Kentucky v. King

563 U.S. 452, 131 S. Ct. 1849, 179 L. Ed 2d 865 (2011)

JUSTICE ALITO delivered the opinion of the Court.

. . . .

I

A

This case concerns the search of an apartment in Lexington, Kentucky. Police officers set up a controlled buy of crack cocaine outside an apartment complex. Undercover Officer Gibbons watched the deal take place from an unmarked car in a nearby parking lot. After the deal occurred, Gibbons radioed uniformed officers to move in on the suspect. He told the officers that the suspect was moving quickly toward the breezeway of an apartment building, and he urged them to "hurry up and get there" before the suspect entered an apartment.

In response to the radio alert, the uniformed officers drove into the nearby parking lot, left their vehicles, and ran to the breezeway. Just as they entered the breezeway, they heard a door shut and detected a very strong odor of burnt marijuana. At the end of the breezeway, the officers saw two apartments, one on the left and one on the right, and they did not know which apartment the suspect had entered. Gibbons had radioed that the suspect was running into the apartment on the right, but the officers did not hear this statement because they had already left their vehicles. Because they smelled marijuana smoke emanating from the apartment on the left, they approached the door of that apartment.

Officer Steven Cobb, one of the uniformed officers who approached the door, testified that the officers banged on the left apartment door "as loud as [they] could" and announced, "'This is the police'" or "'Police, police, police.'" Cobb said that "[a]s soon as [the officers] started banging on the door," they "could hear people inside moving," and "[i]t sounded as [though] things were being moved inside the apartment." These noises, Cobb testified, led the officers to believe that drug-related evidence was about to be destroyed.

At that point, the officers announced that they "were going to make entry inside the apartment." Cobb then kicked in the door, the officers entered the apartment, and they found three people in the front room: respondent Hollis King, respondent's girlfriend, and a guest who was smoking marijuana. The officers performed a protective sweep of the apartment during which they saw marijuana and powder cocaine in plain view. In a subsequent search, they also discovered crack cocaine, cash, and drug paraphernalia.

Police eventually entered the apartment on the right. Inside, they found the suspected drug dealer who was the initial target of their investigation.

B

In the Fayette County Circuit Court, a grand jury charged respondent with trafficking in marijuana, first-degree trafficking in a controlled substance, and second-degree persistent felony offender status. Respondent filed a motion to suppress the evidence from the warrantless search, but the Circuit Court denied the motion. The Circuit Court concluded that . . . [e]xigent circumstances justified the warrantless entry . . . . Respondent then entered a conditional guilty plea, reserving his right to appeal the denial of his suppression motion. . . .

The Kentucky Court of Appeals affirmed. It held that exigent circumstances justified the warrantless entry because the police reasonably believed that evidence would be destroyed. . . .

The Supreme Court of Kentucky reversed. . . . [T]he court . . . "assume[d] for the purpose of argument that exigent circumstances existed" . . . [but] held that [the] exigent circumstances could not justify the search because it was reasonably foreseeable that the occupants would destroy evidence when the police knocked on the door and announced their presence.

. . . .

II
A

. . . .

Although the text of the Fourth Amendment does not specify when a search warrant must be obtained, this Court has inferred that a warrant must generally be secured. "It is a 'basic principle of Fourth Amendment law,'" we have often said, "'that searches and seizures inside a home without a warrant are presumptively unreasonable.'" *Brigham City v. Stuart,* 547 U.S. 398, 403, 126 S. Ct. 1943, 164 L. Ed.2d 650 (2006) (quoting *Groh v. Ramirez,* 540 U.S. 551, 559, 124 S. Ct. 1284, 157 L. Ed.2d 1068 (2004)). But we have also recognized that this presumption may be overcome in some circumstances because "[t]he ultimate touchstone of the Fourth Amendment is 'reasonableness.'" *Brigham City, supra,* at 403, 126 S. Ct. 1943. Accordingly, the warrant requirement is subject to certain reasonable exceptions.

One well-recognized exception applies when "'the exigencies of the situation' make the needs of law enforcement so compelling that [a] warrantless search is objectively reasonable under the Fourth Amendment." *Mincey v. Arizona,* 437 U.S. 385, 394, 98 S. Ct. 2408, 57 L. Ed.2d 290 (1978).

This Court has identified several exigencies that may justify a warrantless search of a home. See *Brigham City,* 547 U.S., at 403, 126 S. Ct. 1943. Under the "emergency aid" exception, for example, "officers may enter a home without a warrant to render emergency assistance to an injured occupant or to protect an occupant from imminent injury." *Ibid.* Police officers may enter premises without a warrant when they are in hot pursuit of a fleeing suspect. See *United States v. Santana,* 427 U.S. 38, 42–43, 96 S. Ct. 2406, 49 L. Ed.2d 300 (1976). And — what is relevant here — the need "to prevent the imminent destruction of evidence" has long been recognized as a sufficient justification for a warrantless search. *Brigham City, supra,* at 403, 126 S. Ct. 1943.

B

Over the years, lower courts have developed an exception to the exigent circumstances rule, the so-called "police-created exigency" doctrine. Under this doctrine, police may not rely on the need to prevent destruction of evidence when that exigency was "created" or "manufactured" by the conduct of the police.

. . . .

. . . [T]he lower courts have held that the police-created exigency doctrine requires more than simple causation [of the exigency by the police], but the lower courts have not agreed on the test to be applied. . . .

III
A

Despite the welter of tests devised by the lower courts, the answer to the question presented in this case follows directly and clearly from the principle that permits warrantless searches in the first place. As previously noted, warrantless searches are allowed when the circumstances make it reasonable, within the meaning of the Fourth Amendment, to dispense with the warrant requirement. Therefore, the answer to the question before us is that the exigent circumstances rule justifies a warrantless search when the conduct of the police preceding the exigency is reasonable in the same sense. Where, as here, the police did not create the exigency by engaging or threatening to engage in conduct that violates the Fourth Amendment, warrantless entry to prevent the destruction of evidence is reasonable and thus allowed.[1]

. . . .

B

. . . .

Bad faith. Some courts . . . ask whether law enforcement officers "'deliberately created the exigent circumstances with the bad faith intent to avoid the warrant requirement.'" 302 S.W.3d, at 656.

This approach is fundamentally inconsistent with our Fourth Amendment jurisprudence. "Our cases have repeatedly rejected" a subjective approach, asking only whether "the circumstances, viewed *objectively,* justify the action." *Brigham City,* 547 U.S., at 404, 126 S. Ct. 1943 (alteration and internal quotation marks omitted). . . .

The reasons for looking to objective factors, rather than subjective intent, are clear. Legal tests based on reasonableness are generally objective, and this Court has long taken the view that "evenhanded law enforcement is best achieved by the application of objective standards of conduct, rather than standards that depend upon the subjective state of mind of the officer." *Horton, supra,* at 138, 110 S. Ct. 2301.

Reasonable foreseeability. Some courts . . . hold that police may not rely on an exigency if "'it was reasonably foreseeable that the investigative tactics employed by the police would create the exigent circumstances.'" 302 S.W.3d, at 656.

. . . .

Adoption of a reasonable foreseeability test would . . . introduce an unacceptable degree of unpredictability. For example, whenever law enforcement officers knock on the door of premises occupied by a person who may be involved in the drug trade,

---

1. There is a strong argument to be made that, at least in most circumstances, the exigent circumstances rule should not apply where the police, without a warrant or any legally sound basis for a warrantless entry, threaten that they will enter without permission unless admitted. In this case, however, no such actual threat was made, and therefore we have no need to reach that question.

there is *some* possibility that the occupants may possess drugs and may seek to destroy them. Under a reasonable foreseeability test, it would be necessary to quantify the degree of predictability that must be reached before the police-created exigency doctrine comes into play.

. . . .

. . . The reasonable foreseeability test would create unacceptable and unwarranted difficulties for law enforcement officers who must make quick decisions in the field, as well as for judges who would be required to determine after the fact whether the destruction of evidence in response to a knock on the door was reasonably foreseeable based on what the officers knew at the time.

Probable cause and time to secure a warrant. Some courts, in applying the police-created exigency doctrine, fault law enforcement officers if, after acquiring evidence that is sufficient to establish probable cause to search particular premises, the officers do not seek a warrant but instead knock on the door and seek either to speak with an occupant or to obtain consent to search.

This approach unjustifiably interferes with legitimate law enforcement strategies. There are many entirely proper reasons why police may not want to seek a search warrant as soon as the bare minimum of evidence needed to establish probable cause is acquired. Without attempting to provide a comprehensive list of these reasons, we note a few. [The Court proceeded to describe five reasons why officers might not seek a warrant immediately upon gaining probable cause to search.]

. . . .

. . . Faulting the police for failing to apply for a search warrant at the earliest possible time after obtaining probable cause imposes a duty that is nowhere to be found in the Constitution.

Standard or good investigative tactics. Finally, some lower court cases suggest that law enforcement officers may be found to have created or manufactured an exigency if the court concludes that the course of their investigation was "contrary to standard or good law enforcement practices (or to the policies or practices of their jurisdictions)." *Gould,* 364 F.3d, at 591. This approach fails to provide clear guidance for law enforcement officers and authorizes courts to make judgments on matters that are the province of those who are responsible for federal and state law enforcement agencies.

C

. . . Respondent contends that law enforcement officers impermissibly create an exigency when they "engage in conduct that would cause a reasonable person to believe that entry is imminent and inevitable." In respondent's view, relevant factors include the officers' tone of voice in announcing their presence and the forcefulness of their knocks. But the ability of law enforcement officers to respond to an exigency cannot turn on such subtleties.

. . . .

If respondent's test were adopted, it would be extremely difficult for police officers to know how loudly they may announce their presence or how forcefully they may knock on a door without running afoul of the police-created exigency rule. And in most cases, it would be nearly impossible for a court to determine whether that threshold had been passed. The Fourth Amendment does not require the nebulous and impractical test that respondent proposes.

D

For these reasons, we conclude that the exigent circumstances rule applies when the police do not gain entry to premises by means of an actual or threatened violation of the Fourth Amendment. This holding provides ample protection for the privacy rights that the Amendment protects.

When law enforcement officers who are not armed with a warrant knock on a door, they do no more than any private citizen might do. . . . [T]he occupant has no obligation to open the door or to speak. . . . And even if an occupant chooses to open the door and speak with the officers, the occupant need not allow the officers to enter the premises and may refuse to answer any questions at any time.

Occupants who choose not to stand on their constitutional rights but instead elect to attempt to destroy evidence have only themselves to blame for the warrantless exigent-circumstances search that may ensue.

IV

We now apply our interpretation of the police-created exigency doctrine to the facts of this case.

A

We need not decide whether exigent circumstances existed in this case. . . . The Kentucky Supreme Court "assum[ed] for the purpose of argument that exigent circumstances existed," and it held that the police had impermissibly manufactured the exigency.

We, too, assume for purposes of argument that an exigency existed. . . . Any question about whether an exigency actually existed is better addressed by the Kentucky Supreme Court on remand.

B

In this case, we see no evidence that the officers either violated the Fourth Amendment or threatened to do so prior to the point when they entered the apartment. . . .

. . . .

Like the court below, we assume for purposes of argument that an exigency existed. Because the officers in this case did not violate or threaten to violate the Fourth Amendment prior to the exigency, we hold that the exigency justified the warrantless search of the apartment.

The judgment of the Kentucky Supreme Court is reversed, and the case is remanded for further proceedings not inconsistent with this opinion.

It is so ordered.

JUSTICE GINSBURG, dissenting.

The Court today arms the police with a way routinely to dishonor the Fourth Amendment's warrant requirement in drug cases. In lieu of presenting their evidence to a neutral magistrate, police officers may now knock, listen, then break the door down, nevermind that they had ample time to obtain a warrant. I dissent from the Court's reduction of the Fourth Amendment's force.

. . . .

I . . . would not allow an expedient knock to override the warrant requirement. Instead, I would accord that core requirement of the Fourth Amendment full respect. When possible, "a warrant must generally be secured," the Court acknowledges. There is every reason to conclude that securing a warrant was entirely feasible in this case, and no reason to contract the Fourth Amendment's dominion.

Notes and Questions

(1) How does the Court's opinion in *King* limit the scope of the exigent circumstances exception to the search warrant rule? More specifically, when does the fact that an officer's conduct caused a need to act quickly to prevent harm preclude reliance on that exception?

(2) In *Vale v. Louisiana*, 399 U.S. 30, 90 S. Ct. 1696, 26 L. Ed. 2d 409 (1970), officers saw Vale engage in an apparent drug transaction in the street in front of the home where he lived with his mother and brother. As the officers approached him, Vale recognized them, "turned around, [and] walk[ed] quickly toward [his] house." The officers called to him as he reached the front steps, then arrested him outside his home. Based on what they had seen, the officers had probable cause to believe that illegal narcotics were in Vale's home. Shortly after the officers had ascertained that no one was inside the home, Vale's mother and brother arrived, were informed of his arrest, and were told that their home would be searched. A search led to the discovery of "a quantity of narcotics."

Louisiana concluded that the search was "supportable because it involved narcotics, which are easily removed, hidden, or destroyed." A majority of the Supreme Court held that the warrantless search was unreasonable, rejecting the contention that the potential removal, concealment, or destruction of the narcotics gave rise to an exigency that justified the failure to secure judicial approval. The majority stressed that warrantless searches of dwellings are constitutional "only in 'a few specifically established and well-delineated' situations . . . even though the authorities have probable cause" to search. In *Vale*, the State had not carried its "burden" of showing "the existence of . . . an exceptional situation" that justified a search without prior judicial approval. The Justices "decline[d] to hold that an arrest on the

4 · REASONABLE SEARCHES WITHOUT WARRANTS   267

street can provide its own 'exigent circumstance' so as to justify a warrantless search of the arrestee's house."

The narcotics transaction, arrest of Vale, and presence of interested family members surely gave rise to a risk that the narcotics would disappear by the time officers returned with a search warrant. If the government's interest in seizing the contraband in the home might have been defeated by the delay involved in the warrant application process, why did the Court reject the exigency claim? Apparently, the majority believed that the facts relied upon as a basis for concluding that the evidence was at risk of being concealed or destroyed did not generate sufficient likelihood of concealment or destruction to outweigh the threat to home privacy inherent in an officer's determination of probable cause. The *Vale* decision highlights a question that has never been addressed by the Justices: How probable must it be that the harm that allegedly justifies an immediate search will come to pass if officers delay the search in order to seek a warrant? Is a "fair probability" of evidence loss necessary, or does a lesser likelihood suffice? This unresolved issue is inherent in every situation in which the government relies on the exigent circumstances exception to justify a warrantless search.

The dissenting Justices in *Vale* opined that the facts did give rise to a sufficient need to act. They pointedly asked "how . . . a policeman" in a situation like *Vale* was supposed to "protect evidence necessary" for prosecution "if he [had to] leave the premises to get a warrant." One possibility is for officers to remain on the premises, applying for and securing a warrant by telephone or other expedited means. The case described in the next note suggests another course of action that might be constitutional when an immediate warrantless search is not.

(3) In *Illinois v. McArthur*, 531 U.S. 326, 121 S. Ct. 946, 148 L. Ed. 2d 838 (2001), the defendant's wife "asked two police officers to accompany her to the trailer where she lived with her husband" to "keep the peace while she removed her belongings." The officers remained outside the trailer. When Ms. McArthur exited the trailer, she told the officers that her husband had "dope" in the trailer and stated that she had seen him "slid[e] some dope underneath the couch." One officer knocked on the door and asked for permission to search the trailer, but the defendant refused to permit entry. After the other officer left with Ms. McArthur to apply for a search warrant, the officer who remained informed the defendant — who now stood on the porch — that "he could not reenter the trailer unless a police officer accompanied him." Less than two hours later, officers returned to the trailer with a search warrant, searched the trailer, and found a marijuana pipe, a box for marijuana, and a small amount of marijuana. The defendant was arrested and charged with two misdemeanors — "unlawfully possessing drug paraphernalia and marijuana." The trial judge granted his motion to suppress the evidence found in the trailer, and the ruling was affirmed on appeal.

The question before the Supreme Court was whether officers who "had probable cause to believe that [the defendant] had marijuana in his home" acted in violation of the Fourth Amendment when they "prevented [him] from entering the home for about two hours while they obtained a search warrant." The Court acknowledged that warrants are sometimes required to render seizures reasonable. It concluded, however, that the "warrantless seizure" of the premises in this case "was [not] *per se* unreasonable" because it "involve[d] a plausible claim of specially pressing or urgent law enforcement need, i.e., 'exigent circumstances'" and "the restraint at issue was tailored to that need, being limited in time and scope." Upon balancing "the privacy-related and law enforcement-related concerns," the Court concluded "that the restriction at issue was reasonable."

The Court's conclusion was based on a "combination" of circumstances. "[T]he police had probable cause to believe that [the] trailer home contained evidence of a crime and contraband"; they "had good reason to fear that, unless restrained, [the defendant] would destroy the drugs before they could return with a warrant"; they "made reasonable efforts to reconcile their law enforcement needs with the demands of personal privacy" because they did not search the trailer or arrest the defendant, but "imposed a significantly less restrictive restraint"; and they "imposed the restraint for a limited period of time, namely, two hours." In the Court's view, "[g]iven the nature of the intrusion and the law enforcement interest at stake, this brief seizure of the premises was permissible."

The Court disagreed with the Illinois appellate court's conclusion that the Fourth Amendment forbade the officers' conduct because the porch was part of the defendant's home and the order not to enter "'amounted to a constructive eviction.'" In the first place, "a person standing in the doorway of a house is 'in a "public" place.'" (Quoting *United States v. Santana*, 427 U.S. 38, 42 (1976).) Even if that were not the case, the distinction on which the appellate court relied — "porch versus, *e.g.*, front walk — could [not] make a significant difference here as to the reasonableness of the police restraint." The Court rejected the defendant's reliance on *Welsh v. Wisconsin*, 466 U.S. 740 (1984), because there were two "significant distinctions" between that case and this one. First, the "evidence at issue here was of crimes that were 'jailable,' not 'nonjailable.'" Second, "the restriction at issue here [was] less serious" than the intrusion into the home in *Welsh*. The Court made it clear that it was not deciding "whether the circumstances [of *McArthur*] would have justified a greater restriction for this type of offense or the same restriction were only a 'nonjailable' offense at issue."

"In sum," the officers did not violate the Fourth Amendment because they "had probable cause to believe that a home contained contraband," they "reasonably believed that the home's resident, if left free of any restraint, would destroy that evidence," and they "imposed a restraint that was both limited and tailored reasonably to secure law enforcement needs while protecting privacy interests."

Justice Stevens dissented, "believ[ing] that the majority [got] the balance wrong." In his view, "the governmental interest implicated by the particular criminal prohibition at issue" was "slight" and interest of the ordinary citizen in "the sanctity" of his "home" merited "the most serious constitutional protection."

(4) The Court provided further insights into the nature and operation of the exigent circumstances exception in *Missouri v. McNeely*, 569 U.S. ____, 133 S. Ct. 1552, 185 L. Ed. 2d 696 (2013). After arresting McNeely for driving under the influence, an officer, without obtaining a search warrant, took him to a hospital where his blood was drawn. Subsequent laboratory testing established that his blood-alcohol content "was well above the legal limit." Lower courts had split over "the question whether the natural dissipation of alcohol in the bloodstream establishes a *per se* exigency that suffices on its own to justify an exception to the warrant requirement for nonconsensual blood testing in drunk-driving investigations." The Supreme Court rejected a categorical rule that there was sufficient exigency to justify warrantless blood draws in every drunk-driving case.

The Justices acknowledged that one type of exigency was the need "to prevent the imminent destruction of evidence." In that situation, as in other varieties of exigent circumstances, a warrantless search "is potentially reasonable because" of a "'compelling need for official action and no time to secure a warrant.'" In general, the determination of "whether a law enforcement officer faced an emergency that justified acting without a warrant" must be based on "the totality of circumstances." Without the "established justification" provided by a warrant, the Fourth Amendment reasonableness requirement "demands" evaluation of "each case of alleged exigency based 'on its own facts and circumstances.'" Put simply, the "general exigency exception . . . naturally calls for a case-specific inquiry."

The State conceded that a case-specific, totality approach was ordinarily required, but argued that the "inherently evanescent" nature of blood-alcohol content evidence justified "a *per se* rule for blood testing in drunk-driving cases." The contention was that "so long as the officer has probable cause and the blood test is conducted in a reasonable manner, it is categorically reasonable . . . to obtain [a] blood sample without a warrant." The Court was unpersuaded, opining that in cases "where police officers can reasonably obtain a warrant before a blood sample can be drawn without significantly undermining the efficacy of the search, the Fourth Amendment mandates that they do so." The categorical rule proposed entailed "'considerable overgeneralization.'" Moreover, this context was "different in [two] critical respects from other destruction-of-evidence cases." First, unlike other evidence destruction scenarios that involve a "suspect [with] control over easily disposable evidence," blood-alcohol evidence destruction is the result of "natural[] dissipat[ion] over time in a gradual and relatively predictable manner." In addition, because an officer "must typically transport . . . a suspect to a medical facility and obtain assistance" from a medically trained person, "some delay . . . is inevitable regardless of whether . . . officers are required to obtain a warrant." Consequently, there are "situation[s] in which the warrant process will not significantly increase the delay before the blood test is conducted because an officer can . . . secure a warrant while the suspect is being transported to a medical facility by another officer." In such situations, there is "no plausible justification for an exception to the warrant requirement."

"In short, while the natural dissipation of alcohol in the blood may support a finding of exigency in a specific case, . . . it does not do so categorically. Whether a warrantless blood test of a drunk-driving suspect is reasonable must be determined case by case based on the totality of circumstances."

In a separate opinion, Chief Justice Roberts, Justice Breyer, and Justice Alito agreed that a categorical approach was unacceptable. However, to provide more guidance for officers, they proposed a more "straightforward [approach]: If there is time to secure a warrant *before blood can be drawn* the police must seek one. If an officer could reasonably conclude that there is not sufficient time to seek and receive a warrant, or he applies for one but does not receive a response *before blood can be drawn*, a warrantless blood draw may ensue." (Emphasis added.)

Justice Thomas alone agreed that a *per se* rule of exigency justified warrantless blood draws in all drunk-driving investigations.

Exigent Circumstances Problems

4B–1: On May 1, Heidi Lund was doing yard work at the home that she shared with her mother. Sparky, a pit bull mix that was one of several dogs owned by Edgar, her next door neighbor, wandered onto the Lund property and began sniffing and running around the yard. Edgar followed Sparky into the yard and apparently was exasperated that the animal would not come to him. After Edgar made what Heidi considered to be a threat against the dog, she became concerned that he was about to harm it and said, "Please don't kill him. It's not his fault." According to Heidi, Edgar reiterated that "a dog that doesn't listen is no good to me." He then returned to his property. Although Sparky had a somewhat checkered behavioral past, on the date in question, he did not bark, growl, show his teeth, or display any signs of aggressive behavior.

Shortly thereafter, Heidi heard the sound of an engine starting up and then a gunshot. Alarmed, she dashed into the family home. Her mother, Sari, upon seeing her frightened daughter, and also having heard the gunshot, immediately called 911. Officer Kevin, a 34 year veteran of the police department, was dispatched to Edgar's home based on "a woman's complaint that her neighbor was shooting at his dog." When he arrived at Edgar's property, Kevin got out of his car and approached Edgar, who was standing in the driveway. Kevin told Edgar that he was investigating a complaint from neighbors that "someone was shooting at a dog." Edgar responded, "They should mind their own business." Kevin then asked Edgar "if he shot at his dog." Edgar said that "he had a lot of dogs and a lot of guns." Kevin then asked Edgar "if he killed his dog," and Edgar said "Yes." When Kevin asked, "Where is the dog now?" Edgar replied, "It's gone," and then grinned and said "You'll never find it." Kevin handcuffed Edgar and secured him in the back of his patrol car. He then went next door and spoke with the Lunds, who informed him that Edgar had been "chasing his dog in his yard with a firearm and said if he caught it he would kill it and that it was a dog that didn't obey, so it shouldn't live." The Lunds also reported they had heard a gunshot and had heard Edgar's "backhoe start up."

After Kevin observed "a fresh excavation" on Edgar's property, he performed a "cursory walk" around the property. During the walk he spotted a dog collar on top of the freshly dug earth and a .22-caliber rifle in a shed. Based on all of this information, Officer Kevin applied for and obtained a warrant to search Edgar's property. During a search pursuant to the warrant, officers unearthed Sparky's corpse from a shallow grave located next to a small backhoe excavator and found an illegal, sawed-off shotgun. The state charged Edgar with "maliciously killing a domestic canine" and with "possession of an illegal firearm." Edgar claims that the warrantless entry of his property was unreasonable.

How should the prosecutor respond? How should the judge rule?

4B–2: Late on Christmas Day a woman was robbed and raped by a man who said he had a gun. The victim walked home and immediately called the police. Investigators escorted her back to the scene, where they found two sets of footprints in the fresh snow. The officers concluded that one set belonged to the victim and that the other was made by a person wearing footwear with a distinctive zigzag pattern.

An officer began following these footprints, which, at some points, indicated that the person was traveling at a run. At other places, the person doubled back over his own prints or walked in vehicle tracks. The footprints eventually led to Room 11 of the Alpine Motel, several blocks from the crime scene.

The lights were on in Room 11, and noise from a television or radio could be heard. After radioing for backup and ascertaining that one male was registered in Room 11, the officer knocked on the door. Dow, clad only in his underwear, opened the door.

Dow's appearance matched the victim's description of her assailant. The officer identified himself and entered the room. Dow's boots were drying on the radiator. The pattern on the soles matched the zigzag in the tracks the officer had been following. Dow was then arrested.

Was the entry of Room 11 justified by an exigency?

4B–3: When a dispatcher at the County Emergency Communication Center received a 911 call from Joseph's residence, she heard only static on the line. The dispatcher disconnected the call and placed a return call to the residence, but there was no answer and she again heard only static. The dispatcher contacted the police department. Sergeant Roberts and Deputy Nathan of the County Sheriff's Office were assigned to investigate. Roberts was aware that line problems or bad weather sometimes caused static-only telephone calls. Approximately half of the open-line or hangup 911 calls to which Roberts had responded had involved actual emergencies. The officers did not consider this a "priority call" — a call involving indications of immediate danger to life — so they did not activate their lights or sirens while en route.

Roberts and Nathan arrived at Joseph's residence approximately 26 minutes after the 911 call was received. Joseph's two-story house, which is in a rural area, sits on a secluded lot. The gate to the property was closed. The officers walked through an opening next to the gate and repeatedly knocked on the front door, announcing their presence. They received no response. They then inspected the perimeter of the house, looking into the windows. They saw no signs of forced entry and neither saw nor heard anyone inside. They ascended an exterior staircase which led to a second-floor balcony where they found a closed but unlocked sliding glass door. Through the glass, they saw electronics boxes near the door and noticed that the house looked "disheveled." The officers opened the sliding glass door, again announced their presence, but again received no response. They entered the house through the unlocked door and conducted a "sweep to ensure no one was injured, unconscious, or deceased." During the sweep, they saw drugs and drug paraphernalia in plain view, as well as pornography that appeared to depict minors. Once the officers ensured that no one inside the residence needed emergency assistance, they exited. They had spent approximately five minutes inside.

Roberts and Nathan obtained a search warrant for Joseph's residence based on an affidavit that included information learned during the warrantless entry and additional facts. During a search pursuant to the warrant, they seized evidence that the prosecution intends to use in prosecuting Joseph for possession of drugs and possession of child pornography.

Did the officers violate Joseph's Fourth Amendment rights?

4B–4: While on bicycle patrol, three uniformed police officers smelled a heavy and extremely strong odor of "burning marijuana" coming from the window of an apartment where Tevin and his mother lived. The officers knocked on the apartment door three times. Each time, Tevin's mother answered. The first time she came to the door, the officers asked "questions about someone smoking" and told her that they smelled a "heavy odor of marijuana." The second time she responded to the officers' knocks, Tevin's mother, who appeared to be "shaking" and "nervous," exclaimed, "Ain't nobody smoking weed in here." She then "slammed" the door in the "face" of one of the officers. During this brief encounter, the officers smelled the odor of marijuana "like a gust of wind" coming from inside the apartment.

When the officers knocked on the door the third time, they "announced out loud that it was the police." No one responded to the knocks for approximately five minutes. During this period, the officers heard unspecified movement inside the apartment. After Tevin's mother opened the door, she quickly tried to close it again. Another strong marijuana odor wafted through the doorway. One of the officers put his hand on the door to prevent it from closing, telling Tevin's mother that they were coming inside to investigate. The officers then entered the apartment and saw "a burnt marijuana blunt" and marijuana residue. When the officers asked her if there was any marijuana in the apartment, Tevin's mother admitted, "My son was smoking a blunt," and stated, "I'll get it for you."

Shortly thereafter, the officers asked for and received written consent from Tevin to search the apartment. During the search, the officers found cocaine, morphine, a loaded Glock handgun previously reported as stolen, a loaded Taurus handgun, three boxes containing a total of 119 rounds of ammunition, and a revolver in a container along with six rounds of ammunition. They also discovered plastic sandwich bags and more than $1,000 in cash.

Prior to trial for a number of offenses, Tevin moved to suppress the incriminating evidence found in the apartment, claiming that the consented-to search was the product of an illegal warrantless entry. The government asserted that the exigent circumstances exception justified the entry.

How should the trial court rule?

4B–5: On July 3, at 8:00 p.m., Sergeant Brian Hitch began surveillance of the How home in Marblehead. Pauline How lived in the home with her two sons, Alex and Will, both of whom were under 21 years of age. Based on numerous complaints from neighbors over the past several years concerning noise, traffic, and possible illegal activity at the home — including one as recently as a few days earlier — Hitch suspected that an underage drinking party would be taking place at the home that night. The neighbors had said that Ms. How frequently left her sons alone, and that the boys, while unsupervised, threw wild parties. In addition, Bill How, the boys' father and Pauline's ex-husband, had told Hitch that he believed that drinking and drug abuse were occurring regularly at the home. Hitch was also aware that Alex had been arrested a year before for purchasing marijuana. Moreover, based on a recent conversation he had had with Pauline How, Hitch was concerned that she was using narcotics.

From the time he arrived on July 3, Hitch observed a large number of teenagers pulling up in cars and entering or exiting the home carrying bottles and cans of beer. He also saw cases of beer being taken to the garage. He watched for two and a half hours. At 10:30, Hitch met briefly in a nearby parking lot with three other Marblehead officers, Lapham, Decker, and McLellan. Hitch told them that an underage drinking party was underway at the home and indicated that he expected to make some arrests. The officers drove back to the How residence and parked out of sight of the occupants.

Lapham and Hitch went to the back of the house. Hitch stationed himself on the rear deck, inside the fenced-in backyard. Decker and McLellan went to the front of the home. Decker knocked on the door to ascertain "the extent of the underage drinking seen by" Hitch and to determine "whether an adult was present." When Darryl, a minor, answered the door, Decker could see a number of teenagers drinking alcohol and milling about in the living room. He asked to speak to the owner. Darryl shut the door and went to get Alex and Will How. Moments later, the two boys appeared at the door. Decker said he thought that teenagers were drinking inside. He asked Alex and Will if their parents were home. The boys replied that their parents were not home and reported that there was no one there who was 21 years of age. Decker said he wanted to enter, but the boys refused permission. He entered anyway.

Meanwhile, at the back of the home, Officer Lapham heard the bedroom window open and saw teenagers attempting to climb out. He told them to stay inside. From his place on the deck, Hitch could see through the kitchen window. He observed a number of people running through the house and downstairs. Hitch decided to enter through the back door. Under the applicable law, it is a misdemeanor for "a person under 21 and not accompanied by a parent or legal guardian knowingly to possess, transport, or carry on his person any alcohol or alcoholic beverages." Once they were inside the house, the officers arrested 19 teenagers for violating this provision.

Pauline How sued Officer Hitch and the town of Marblehead, claiming that the warrantless entries of her home violated her Fourth Amendment rights.

Were the officers' entries of the home without a warrant justified?

4B–6: In the early morning hours of May 22, Officers Clark and Tucker received a complaint of loud noise coming from Donald's residence. When the officers were within a block of the home, they heard loud music. Shortly after they arrived, several pajama-clad neighbors emerged from their homes to complain of the noise. Using his flashlight, Clark banged repeatedly on the front door, but got no response. The officers then walked around the outside of the two-story home, all the while tapping on the windows. They saw two stereo speakers in the first-floor living room and another pair in an upstairs room.

The back door of the house was open. Only an unlocked screen door prevented access. The two officers knocked and hollered to announce their presence, but received no answer. They opened the screen door and entered the kitchen. The music was so loud that the officers had to raise their voices to communicate.

The officers noticed a light coming from the basement doorway. Hoping to find an occupant who could turn down the music, they went into the basement where they found "wall-to-wall marijuana plants." They returned to the first floor, then went upstairs, announcing their presence all along the way. At the top of the stairs, the officers saw Donald sleeping on the floor of a bedroom that contained the stereo that was the source of the loud music. As Clark roused Donald, Tucker turned down the stereo.

Before leaving Donald's home, the officers searched the basement, seizing approximately 150 marijuana plants, processed marijuana, and two firearms. They also issued Donald a citation for violating a noise ordinance that prohibited the operation of "any noise-making device" in such a manner that "the peace and good order of a neighborhood is disturbed." This offense was a "minor misdemeanor" punishable by a maximum fine of $100. Later, Donald was charged with possession of marijuana with intent to distribute and possession of an unregistered shotgun. He claimed that the officers had searched his home in violation of the Fourth Amendment.

Is Donald's claim valid?

4B–7: Late in the morning of June 8, Deputy John Mayer received an anonymous telephone call reporting that marijuana plants could be seen in a window of a white, single-story house located across from "Tuck Excavating" on Flat Iron Road. The location was about fifteen minutes from the county courthouse. At 1:00 p.m., Mayer and Detective Lay, in plain clothes and an unmarked car, drove to the location. From the driveway of the excavating business, they observed what they believed to be marijuana in a birdcage in a side window of the house. Lay knocked on the front door of the house. When there was no answer, he and Mayer drove one-eighth of a mile to a parking lot. They could still see the house. The officers called for back-up units to "sit on the residence and see if somebody returned." At 2:00 p.m., Trooper Guy arrived in a marked car.

Shortly thereafter, Frances Nuck arrived and went inside the house. Ten minutes later, a pick-up truck drove into the driveway next door. According to Deputy Mayer, "the driver looked at us really suspiciously." Three minutes after the truck arrived, Lay and Guy approached the house. Deputy Mayer was stationed at the window where the birdcage containing the marijuana could be seen. Lay knocked on the door. Nuck opened the blinds and asked, "Who is it?" Lay replied, "County Drug Task Force. We need to come in." Soon after Nuck asked the officers to "hold on a minute," Mayer yelled that the plants were moving. Officer Lay began to kick the door. According to Nuck, the officers gained entry to her home by kicking the door open. To the contrary, the officers assert that they entered after Nuck opened the door. Nuck was naked at the time. She explained that she had asked the officers to "hold on" so that she could put on some clothing.

Detective Lay told Nuck that the officers could get a warrant or "you could consent to a search." Deputy Mayer informed her that the officers would "seize" the house so that "nobody can go in" during the time needed to secure a search warrant. He stated that "it would be a lot faster" if Nuck consented to a search. Nuck signed a consent to search form. A search led to the seizure of the marijuana plants and paraphernalia used to grow them.

Prior to trial for possession of marijuana, Nuck moved to suppress the evidence, claiming that the officers' warrantless entry violated her Fourth Amendment rights. The government asserted that the entry was justified by exigent circumstances.

Does the exigent circumstances doctrine justify the warrantless entry?

4B–8: On April 4, the police received a phone call from a resident of an apartment complex about a yelling male and female. Officers Kori and Michaels responded to the call. Upon arriving at the apartment, the officers stood outside and overheard a man and woman talking with raised voices. They overheard the man say that he wanted to be left alone and needed his space. Kori knocked on the apartment door and Patricia, who appeared agitated and flustered, answered. When Kori asked Patricia where the male occupant of the apartment was, Patricia denied that anyone else was there. When Kori told Patricia that she had heard a male voice in the apartment, Patricia called for Sam, who emerged from a nearby bedroom. Patricia then stepped back, opening the door wider. Officers Kori and Michaels entered the apartment.

The officers separated Patricia and Sam. Kori spoke to Patricia inside the apartment, while Michaels went outside with Sam. Upon noticing that Patricia's neck was red and blotchy, Kori asked whether anything physical had happened during the argument. Patricia reported that nothing physical had occurred, stating that her neck reddens when she becomes upset. She also explained that the argument started because she wanted Sam to change the locks on the door, but Sam just sat on the couch. According to Kori, during the conversation Patricia acted "fidgety" and kept picking things up. Meanwhile, Sam told Officer Michaels that there had been no physical violence and that the argument had been about his failure to change the locks on the apartment door. The discussion outside took between five and ten minutes, whereupon Sam and Michaels returned inside to confer with Kori.

Inside the apartment, Patricia continuously picked things up off a table near where she stood. When Officer Michaels noticed a handgun and a marijuana pipe resting on that table, he secured the weapon and unloaded it. He then asked Patricia who the pipe belonged to, and she said it belonged to her son who lived in another state. Michaels asked Patricia if he could search the apartment for more narcotics, and Patricia consented. At that point, Patricia stood up and began picking things up off the table once again. Kori handcuffed Patricia to prevent her from grabbing anything but told Patricia that she was not under arrest. Patricia then revoked her consent. Officer Michaels sought and received a search warrant by telephone. The officers searched the apartment, discovering methamphetamine. Patricia was charged with possession of methamphetamine.

Was the entry of the apartment reasonable?

4B–9: In New York City, shortly after midnight on January 1, Police Officer Kevin and another officer entered an apartment building after hearing gunshots and observing muzzle fire from the building's roof. As the officers ascended the stairwell, they heard a gunshot directly above them. When the officers reached the eighth floor, they heard voices from the adjoining hallway. They entered the hallway where Officer Kevin observed Benjamin and another man. Benjamin was holding a firearm. Benjamin and the other man ran into an apartment upon seeing the officers. The officers sought to enter the apartment, but found the door locked. When no one responded to their knocks, they used a sledgehammer to break down the door. Upon entering the apartment the officers observed two women in the living room. One was in a wheelchair. The women denied that anyone had entered the apartment.

The officers searched the apartment, locating Benjamin and his cohort hiding under a bed in one of the bedrooms. The officers removed the men from the room, frisked them, placed them in handcuffs, and took them to the living room to join the two women. By this time, there were several additional officers in the apartment. Officer Kevin returned to the bedroom where he had found Benjamin "in order to search for the gun." When he did not find it, he entered an adjoining bedroom, where he found "a 12-inch-by-12-inch silver box on the floor." He picked up the box, shook it, and, upon hearing a sound, opened it. The gun was inside. Officer Kevin took possession of the gun and returned to the living room, where he placed Benjamin under arrest. Benjamin was indicted for illegal possession of a firearm. He moved to suppress the gun from trial, claiming that Officer Kevin had conducted an unreasonable search in violation of his Fourth Amendment rights.

Were the searches reasonable under the exigent circumstances exception to the warrant requirement?

4B–10: At 1:45 a.m., Captain Greg received a dispatch concerning an accident on Milligan Highway. He arrived within five minutes and found a "horrific" accident and an accident scene that was "a mess." A BMW was "intertwined with a metal pole which intruded into the rear right passenger seat." The car's engine had been thrown approximately 40 feet away. Debris "was everywhere." Micah, a 19-year-old college student, who was lying outside the driver's door, had an open fracture of his leg and was "obviously in pain" and "confused." An unconscious young man was in the front passenger seat. When asked by Greg, Micah could recall neither how many occupants had been in his car nor the identity of the young man in the passenger seat. Greg smelled an "odor of alcohol, but could not determine whether or not it was coming from Micah or the vehicle." He observed Micah for approximately 45 seconds to one minute while at the scene.

An ambulance transported Micah to the City Medical Center ("CMC") for treatment of his injuries. Captain Greg suspected that Micah was under the influence of alcohol and thought that it was "necessary to draw his blood as soon as he got to the hospital." Greg believed that surgery for internal injuries was likely and was concerned that the drugs that would be introduced into Micah's bloodstream could compromise the results of toxicological analysis. Greg directed two officers to follow the ambulance and obtain a blood sample from Micah. When the officers arrived at the CMC, they instructed a nurse to collect a sample of Micah's blood. Micah's blood was drawn at 2:30 a.m. At 7:00 a.m., Micah was taken into surgery. Later analysis of his blood sample provided evidence that Micah was heavily under the influence of intoxicants. The front seat passenger in his BMW, who was later identified as Tanner, died at the scene of the crash from injuries he had sustained.

Micah was charged with "vehicular homicide by intoxication." He moved to suppress the evidence obtained from the warrantless blood draw. At a hearing on this motion, Captain Greg testified that he had investigated three prior blood draw cases and had not sought a search warrant in any of them. He had applied for approximately 40 search warrants during his career and had taken 20 to 25 of those applications to a nearby judge's house "at all hours of the night." He stated that at least four of the eleven officers who had responded to the accident scene did have experience drafting search warrant applications. When asked, he acknowledged that two judges who lived within a few miles of the accident scene were willing to review warrant applications at any hour of the night, that the police department has "search warrant application templates," and that officers sometimes draft applications based on information they receive from other officers. Greg, who had access to both a cell phone and a radio on the night on of the accident, stated that no officers were on duty at the police station at the time of the accident. According to Captain Greg, to secure a search warrant to draw Micah's blood, an officer would have had to return to the police station, draft an application, contact the district attorney for review, and then contact a judge to issue the warrant. He claimed that every officer who had responded to the accident dispatch was needed to process the accident scene — which included gathering evidence, diverting traffic, and clearing the area.

The trial court denied Micah's motion, finding that exigency justified the failure to secure a search warrant. Micah was convicted and has appealed the trial judge's ruling.

How should the court of appeals rule?

Selected Bibliography

John F. Decker, *Emergency Circumstances, Police Responses, and Fourth Amendment Restrictions*, 89 J. Crim. L. & Criminology 433 (1999)

George Dery, *Expedient Knocks and Cowering Citizens: The Supreme Court Enables Police to Manufacture Exigencies by Pounding on Doors at Will in* Kentucky v. King, 17 Berkeley J. Crim. L. 225 (2012)

William C. Donnino & Anthony J. Girese, *Exigent Circumstances for a Warrantless Home Arrest*, 45 Alb. L. Rev. 90 (1980)

Edward G. Mascolo, *Emergency Arrest in the Home*, 3 W. New Eng. L. Rev. 387 (1981)

Barbara C. Salken, *Balancing Exigency and Privacy in Warrantless Searches to Prevent Destruction of Evidence: The Need for a Rule*, 39 Hastings L.J. 283 (1988)

William A. Schroeder, *Factoring the Seriousness of the Offense Into Fourth Amendment Equations — Warrantless Entries Into Premises: The Legacy of* Welsh v. Wisconsin, 38 U. Kan. L. Rev. 439 (1990)

[C] Vehicle and Container Searches

Chambers v. Maroney

United States Supreme Court

399 U.S. 42, 90 S. Ct. 1975, 26 L. Ed. 2d 419 (1970)

Mr. Justice White delivered the opinion of the Court.

. . . .

I

During the night of May 20, 1963, a Gulf service station in North Braddock, Pennsylvania, was robbed by two men, each of whom carried and displayed a gun. The robbers took the currency from the cash register; the service station attendant, one Stephen Kovacich, was directed to place the coins in his right-hand glove, which was then taken by the robbers. Two teen-agers, who had earlier noticed a blue compact station wagon circling the block in the vicinity of the Gulf station, then saw the station wagon speed away from a parking lot close to the Gulf station. About the same time, they learned that the Gulf station had been robbed. They reported to police, who arrived immediately, that four men were in the station wagon and one was wearing a green sweater. Kovacich told the police that one of the men who robbed him was wearing a green sweater and the other was wearing a trench coat. A description of the car and the two robbers was broadcast over the police radio. Within an hour, a light blue compact station wagon answering the description and carrying four men was stopped by the police about two miles from the Gulf station. Petitioner was one of the men in the station wagon. He was wearing a green sweater and there was a trench coat in the car. The occupants were arrested and the car was driven to the police station. In the course of a thorough search of the car at the station, the police found concealed in a compartment under the dashboard two .38-caliber revolvers (one loaded with dumdum bullets), a right-hand glove containing small change, and certain cards bearing the name of Raymond Havicon, the attendant at a Boron service station in McKeesport, Pennsylvania, who had been robbed at gunpoint on May 13, 1963. In the course of a warrant-authorized search of petitioner's home the day after petitioner's arrest, police found and seized certain .38-caliber ammunition, including some dumdum bullets similar to those found in one of the guns taken from the station wagon.

Petitioner was indicted for both robberies. His first trial ended in a mistrial but he was convicted of both robberies at the second trial. Both Kovacich and Havicon identified petitioner as one of the robbers. The materials taken from the station wagon were introduced into evidence, Kovacich identifying his glove and Havicon the cards taken in the May 13 robbery . . . .

II

. . . .

Here . . . the police had probable cause to believe that the robbers, carrying guns and the fruits of the crime, had fled the scene in a light blue compact station wagon which would be carrying four men, one wearing a green sweater and another wearing a trench coat. As the state courts correctly held, there was probable cause to arrest the occupants of the station wagon that the officers stopped; just as obviously was there probable cause to search the car for guns and stolen money.

In terms of the circumstances justifying a warrantless search, the Court has long distinguished between an automobile and a home or office. In *Carroll v. United States*, 267 U.S. 132, 45 S. Ct. 280, 69 L. Ed. 543 (1925), the issue was the admissibility in evidence of contraband liquor seized in a warrantless search of a car on the highway. After surveying the law from the time of the adoption of the Fourth Amendment onward, the Court held that automobiles and other conveyances may be searched without a warrant in circumstances that would not justify the search without a warrant of a house or an office, provided that there is probable cause to believe that the car contains articles that the officers are entitled to seize. The Court expressed its holding as follows:

> "We have made a somewhat extended reference to these statutes to show that the guaranty of freedom from unreasonable searches and seizures by the Fourth Amendment has been construed, practically since the beginning of the Government, as recognizing a necessary difference between a search of a store, dwelling house, or other structure in respect of which a proper official warrant readily may be obtained, and a search of a ship, motor boat, wagon, or automobile, for contraband goods, where it is not practicable to secure a warrant because the vehicle can be quickly moved out of the locality or jurisdiction in which the warrant must be sought.

> "Having thus established that contraband goods concealed and illegally transported in an automobile or other vehicle may be searched for without a warrant, we come now to consider under what circumstances such search may be made . . . . Those lawfully within the country, entitled to use the public highways, have a right to free passage without interruption or search unless there is known to a competent official authorized to search, probable cause for believing that their vehicles are carrying contraband or illegal merchandise . . . .

> . . . .

> "The right to search and the validity of the seizure are not dependent on the right to arrest. They are dependent on the reasonable cause the seizing officer has for belief that the contents of the automobile offend against the law." 267 U.S., at 158–159, 45 S. Ct. at 287.

> . . . .

Neither *Carroll* nor other cases in this Court require or suggest that in every conceivable circumstance the search of an auto even with probable cause may be made without the extra protection for privacy that a warrant affords. But the circumstances that furnish probable cause to search a particular auto for particular articles are most often unforeseeable; moreover, the opportunity to search is fleeting since a car is readily movable. Where this is true, as in *Carroll* and the case before us now, if an effective search is to be made at any time, either the search must be made immediately without a warrant or the car itself must be seized and held without a warrant for whatever period is necessary to obtain a warrant for the search.[9]

---

9. Following the car until a warrant can be obtained seems an impractical alternative since, among other things, the car may be taken out of the jurisdiction. Tracing the car and searching it

. . . *Carroll* holds a search warrant unnecessary where there is probable cause to search an automobile stopped on the highway; the car is movable, the occupants are alerted, and the car's contents may never be found again if a warrant must be obtained. Hence an immediate search is constitutionally permissible.

Arguably, because of the preference for a magistrate's judgment, only the immobilization of the car should be permitted until a search warrant is obtained; arguably, only the "lesser" intrusion is permissible until the magistrate authorizes the "greater." But which is the "greater" and which the "lesser" intrusion is itself a debatable question and the answer may depend on a variety of circumstances. For constitutional purposes, we see no difference between on the one hand seizing and holding a car before presenting the probable cause issue to a magistrate and on the other hand carrying out an immediate search without a warrant. Given probable cause to search, either course is reasonable under the Fourth Amendment.

On the facts before us, the blue station wagon could have been searched on the spot when it was stopped since there was probable cause to search and it was a fleeting target for a search. The probable-cause factor still obtained at the station house and so did the mobility of the car unless the Fourth Amendment permits a warrantless seizure of the car and the denial of its use to anyone until a warrant is secured. In that event there is little to choose in terms of practical consequences between an immediate search without a warrant and the car's immobilization until a warrant is obtained.[10] The same consequences may not follow where there is unforeseeable cause to search a house. Compare *Vale v. Louisiana, ante,* 399 U.S. 30, 90 S. Ct. 1969, 26 L. Ed. 2d 409. But as *Carroll, supra,* held, for the purposes of the Fourth Amendment there is a constitutional difference between houses and cars.

Affirmed.

MR. JUSTICE BLACKMUN took no part in the consideration or decision of this case.

[The concurring opinion of MR. JUSTICE STEWART has been omitted.]

MR. JUSTICE HARLAN, concurring in part and dissenting in part.

. . . .

I

. . . .

II

In sustaining the search of the automobile I believe the Court ignores the framework of our past decisions circumscribing the scope of permissible search without a warrant.

---

hours or days later would of course permit instruments or fruits of crime to be removed from the car before the search.

10. It was not unreasonable in this case to take the car to the station house. All occupants in the car were arrested in a dark parking lot in the middle of the night. A careful search at that point was impractical and perhaps not safe for the officers, and it would serve the owner's convenience and the safety of his car to have the vehicle and the keys together at the station house.

. . . .

Where officers have probable cause to search a vehicle on a public way, a further limited exception to the warrant requirement is reasonable because "the vehicle can be quickly moved out of the locality or jurisdiction in which the warrant must be sought." *Carroll v. United States*, 267 U.S. 132, 153, 45 S. Ct. 280, 285, 69 L. Ed. 543 (1925). Because the officers might be deprived of valuable evidence if required to obtain a warrant before effecting any search or seizure, I agree with the Court that they should be permitted to take the steps necessary to preserve evidence and to make a search possible. *Cf.* ALI, Model Code of Pre-Arraignment Procedure § 6.03 (Tent. Draft No. 3, 1970). The Court holds that those steps include making a warrantless search of the entire vehicle on the highway—a conclusion reached by the Court in *Carroll* without discussion—and indeed appears to go further and to condone the removal of the car to the police station for a warrantless search there at the convenience of the police. I cannot agree that this result is consistent with our insistence in other areas that departures from the warrant requirement strictly conform to the exigency presented.

The Court concedes that the police could prevent removal of the evidence by temporarily seizing the car for the time necessary to obtain a warrant. It does not dispute that such a course would fully protect the interests of effective law enforcement; rather it states that whether temporary seizure is a "lesser" intrusion than warrantless search "is itself a debatable question and the answer may depend on a variety of circumstances."[8] I believe it clear that a warrantless search involves the greater sacrifice of Fourth Amendment values.

The Fourth Amendment proscribes, to be sure, unreasonable "seizures" as well as "searches." However, in the circumstances in which this problem is likely to occur, the lesser intrusion will almost always be the simple seizure of the car for the period—perhaps a day—necessary to enable the officers to obtain a search warrant. In the first place, as this case shows, the very facts establishing probable cause to search will often also justify arrest of the occupants of the vehicle. Since the occupants themselves are to be taken into custody, they will suffer minimal further inconvenience from the temporary immobilization of their vehicle. Even where no arrests are made, persons who wish to avoid a search—either to protect their privacy or to conceal incriminating evidence—will almost certainly prefer a brief loss of the use of the vehicle in exchange for the opportunity to have a magistrate pass upon the justification for the search. To be sure, one can conceive of instances in which the occupant, having nothing to hide and lacking concern for the privacy of the automobile, would be more

---

8. The Court, unable to decide whether search or temporary seizure is the "lesser" intrusion, in this case authorizes both. The Court concludes that it was reasonable for the police to take the car to the station, where they searched it once to no avail. The searching officers then entered the station, interrogated petitioner and the car's owner, and returned later for another search of the car—this one successful. At all times the car and its contents were secure against removal or destruction. Nevertheless the Court approves the searches without even an inquiry into the officers' ability promptly to take their case before a magistrate.

deeply offended by a temporary immobilization of his vehicle than by a prompt search of it. However, such a person always remains free to consent to an immediate search, thus avoiding any delay. Where consent is not forthcoming, the occupants of the car have an interest in privacy that is protected by the Fourth Amendment even where the circumstances justify a temporary seizure. The Court's endorsement of a warrantless invasion of that privacy where another course would suffice is simply inconsistent with our repeated stress on the Fourth Amendment's mandate of "adherence to judicial processes." *E.g., Katz v. United States*, 389 U.S., at 357.[9]

Notes and Questions

(1) *Chambers* was the first in a series of significant Supreme Court decisions during the 1970s and 1980s involving the "automobile exception" to the search warrant requirement.

(a) What specific circumstances must be established to trigger the exception found applicable in *Chambers*? Why is an exception justified in those circumstances?

(b) Under *Chambers*, may "automobile exception" searches always be delayed until after the vehicle has been seized and removed to the police station? Why?

(c) What considerations could lead a court to reject the doctrine of *Chambers*? *See State v. Sterndale*, 656 A.2d 409 (N.H. 1995); *State v. Miller*, 29 Conn. App. 207, 614 A.2d 1229 (1992).

(2) One question not clearly answered by *Chambers* was whether the exception to the warrant requirement recognized there extends to vehicles that have not been stopped while in transit but, instead, are parked when found. In two cases decided after *Chambers*, the Court struggled with that question. In each case, the answers provided could only garner plurality support.

Coolidge v. New Hampshire, 403 U.S. 443, 91 S. Ct. 2022, 29 L. Ed. 2d 564 (1971), involved searches of an automobile that was parked on an arrestee's driveway at the time he was arrested in his home. The car was towed to the police station and searched immediately. It was searched twice more, 11 months and 14 months later. Although a search warrant had been issued, it was declared invalid because it had been issued by the Attorney General, who did not qualify as a "neutral and detached magistrate." Consequently, the Court had to determine whether a warrantless search was justified. A majority held that the *Chambers* doctrine did not justify the searches of the car.

---

9. Circumstances might arise in which it would be impracticable to immobilize the car for the time required to obtain a warrant—for example, where a single police officer must take arrested suspects to the station, and has no way of protecting the suspects' car during his absence. In such situations it might be wholly reasonable to perform an on-the-spot search based on probable cause. However, where nothing in the situation makes impracticable the obtaining of a warrant, I cannot join the Court in shunting aside that vital Fourth Amendment safeguard.

Four Justices indicated that the exception recognized by *Chambers* was *limited to* situations in which there is probable cause to search a vehicle that has been "'*stopped on the highway*'" because in that case "the car is 'movable, the occupants are alerted, and the car's contents may never be found again if a warrant must be obtained.'" (quoting *Chambers*). In their opinion, "[t]he word 'automobile' is not a talisman in whose presence the Fourth Amendment fades away and disappears." The warrant requirement is dispensed with for automobile searches *only* in cases where the surrounding circumstances give rise to a sufficient need to act to prevent escape of the automobile's contents. The mere mobility of the automobile, in their view, does not give rise to a sufficient need to act immediately. In *Coolidge*, the vehicle was parked on private property when it was seized. Moreover, the owner and his wife had no access to the car and there was no other specific reason to believe that the car and its contents would disappear if a warrant were sought. "[B]y no possible stretch of the legal imagination" could the situation qualify as one in which "'it [was] not practicable to secure a warrant.'" (Quoting *Carroll v. United States*). Consequently, "the 'automobile exception,' despite its label, [was] simply irrelevant."

The plurality believed that when the *Chambers* exception does apply to a vehicle, it authorizes a warrantless search either at the place where the vehicle is found or after the vehicle has been impounded and taken to the police station. In their view, the search at the station is permissible because "there is little difference between a search on the open highway and a later search at the station." In this case, however, because a warrantless search of the car parked in Coolidge's driveway was not justified initially, a later warrantless search at the station was also impermissible.

Justice Harlan agreed that the warrantless searches of Coolidge's car were unreasonable because of his fear that a contrary conclusion would undermine the warrant requirement, but he refused to join the plurality's reasoning regarding *Chambers*'s inapplicability to this situation. Justice White disagreed with the plurality's analysis of and confinement of *Chambers*, asserting that the doctrine of that case was applicable "whether [a] car is at rest or in motion when it is discovered." He believed that "the difference between a moving and a movable vehicle is tenuous at best" and that it is "a metaphysical distinction without roots" in the Fourth Amendment. In his view, therefore, the initial search of the car was valid under *Chambers*. The two subsequent warrantless searches were unreasonable, but "only because of the long detention of the car" that preceded those searches.

Three years later, a plurality read *Coolidge* very narrowly. In *Cardwell v. Lewis*, 417 U.S. 583, 94 S. Ct. 2464, 41 L. Ed. 2d 325 (1974), a warrantless search of a vehicle that had been found parked "in a public commercial parking lot" was at issue. Four Justices asserted that the determinative fact in *Coolidge* was that the automobile had been parked on *private* property when officers came upon it. In their opinion, the search in *Cardwell* was constitutional because a vehicle parked on *public* property is subject to a warrantless search under the *Chambers* exception. Justice Powell concurred in the result, but did not join the plurality's reasoning. Four Justices dissented, disagreeing with the plurality's limiting interpretation of *Coolidge*. In *California v. Carney*, 471 U.S. 386, 105 S. Ct. 2066, 85 L. Ed. 2d 406 (1985), *infra*, a majority resolved this disagreement over the scope of the "automobile exception."

(3) In *Texas v. White*, 423 U.S. 67, 96 S. Ct. 304, 46 L. Ed. 2d 209 (1975), in a per curiam opinion, the Court upheld the warrantless search of a car after it had been towed to the police station even though there was no reason that it was unsafe or impractical to conduct that search at the place where it was found. The opinion asserted that *Chambers* had "held that police officers with probable cause to search an automobile at the scene where it was stopped could constitutionally do so later at the station house without first obtaining a warrant." In dissent, Justices Marshall and Brennan contended that the Court had misread *Chambers*. In their view, "*Chambers* simply held that" a warrantless automobile search may be carried out later at the police station "when it is reasonable to take the car to the station house in the first place." When it is neither "impractical [n]or unsafe" to search a vehicle at the scene where it is found, officers must either search the car on the spot or seize it and apply for a search warrant.

(4) In *United States v. Johns*, 469 U.S. 478, 105 S. Ct. 881, 83 L. Ed. 2d 890 (1985), the Court focused on an issue raised by Justice White in *Coolidge:* How long may officers delay before conducting the warrantless search authorized by the "automobile exception"? The *Johns* Court refused to specify any presumptively unreasonable or excessive time period. It stated, however, that police officers may not "indefinitely" delay a warrantless vehicle search. In addition, the Court held open the possibility that an aggrieved person "might attempt to prove that the delay in the completion of a vehicle search was unreasonable because it adversely affected a privacy or possessory interest." Because the aggrieved parties in *Johns* had neither alleged nor proven such an adverse effect, the Court concluded that the three-day delay prior to the warrantless search in that case was constitutionally acceptable.

California v. Carney

United States Supreme Court

471 U.S. 386, 105 S. Ct. 2066, 85 L. Ed. 2d 406 (1985)

CHIEF JUSTICE BURGER delivered the opinion of the Court.

We granted certiorari to decide whether law enforcement agents violated the Fourth Amendment when they conducted a warrantless search, based on probable cause, of a fully mobile "motor home" located in a public place.

I

On May 31, 1979, Drug Enforcement Agency Agent Robert Williams watched respondent, Charles Carney, approach a youth in downtown San Diego. The youth accompanied Carney to a Dodge Mini Motor Home parked in a nearby lot. Carney and the youth closed the window shades in the motor home, including one across the front window. Agent Williams had previously received uncorroborated information that the same motor home was used by another person who was exchanging marihuana for sex. Williams, with assistance from other agents, kept the motor home under surveillance for the entire one and one-quarter hours that Carney and the youth remained inside. When the youth left the motor home, the agents followed and stopped him. The youth told the agents that he had received marihuana in return for allowing Carney sexual contacts.

At the agents' request, the youth returned to the motor home and knocked on its door; Carney stepped out. The agents identified themselves as law enforcement officers. Without a warrant or consent, one agent entered the motor home and observed marihuana, plastic bags, and a scale of the kind used in weighing drugs on a table. Agent Williams took Carney into custody and took possession of the motor home. A subsequent search of the motor home at the police station revealed additional marihuana in the cupboards and refrigerator.

Respondent was charged with possession of marihuana for sale. At a preliminary hearing, he moved to suppress the evidence discovered in the motor home. The Magistrate denied the motion . . . .

. . . Respondent . . . pleaded *nolo contendere* to the charges against him, and was placed on probation for three years.

. . . .

II

. . . .

[O]ur cases have consistently recognized ready mobility as one of the principal bases of the automobile exception . . . . The mobility of automobiles, we have observed, "creates circumstances of such exigency that, as a practical necessity, rigorous enforcement of the warrant requirement is impossible." *South Dakota v. Opperman*, 428 U.S., at 367.

However, although ready mobility alone was perhaps the original justification for the vehicle exception, our later cases have made clear that ready mobility is not the only basis for the exception. The reasons for the vehicle exception, we have said, are twofold. 428 U.S., at 367, 96 S. Ct., at 3096. "Besides the element of mobility, less rigorous warrant requirements govern because the expectation of privacy with respect to one's automobile is significantly less than that relating to one's home or office." *Id.*

. . . .

These reduced expectations of privacy derive not from the fact that the area to be searched is in plain view, but from the pervasive regulation of vehicles capable of traveling on the public highways . . . .

The public is fully aware that it is accorded less privacy in its automobiles because of this compelling governmental need for regulation . . . .

When a vehicle is being used on the highways, or if it is readily capable of such use and is found stationary in a place not regularly used for residential purposes — temporary or otherwise — the two justifications for the vehicle exception come into play. First, the vehicle is obviously readily mobile by the turn of a switch key, if not actually moving. Second, there is a reduced expectation of privacy stemming from its use as a licensed motor vehicle subject to a range of police regulation inapplicable to a fixed dwelling. At least in these circumstances, the overriding societal interests in effective law enforcement justify an immediate search before the vehicle and its occupants become unavailable.

While it is true that respondent's vehicle possessed some, if not many of the attributes of a home, it is equally clear that the vehicle falls clearly within the scope of the exception laid down in *Carroll* and applied in succeeding cases . . . . And the vehicle was so situated that an objective observer would conclude that it was being used not as a residence, but as a vehicle.

Respondent urges us to distinguish his vehicle from other vehicles within the exception because it was capable of functioning as a home. In our increasingly mobile society, many vehicles used for transportation can be and are being used not only for transportation but for shelter, *i.e.*, as a "home" or "residence." To distinguish between respondent's motor home and an ordinary sedan for purposes of the vehicle exception would require that we apply the exception depending upon the size of the vehicle and the quality of its appointments. Moreover, to fail to apply the exception to vehicles such as a motor home ignores the fact that a motor home lends itself easily to use as an instrument of illicit drug traffic and other illegal activity. In *United States v. Ross*, 456 U.S., at 822, we declined to distinguish between "worthy" and "unworthy" containers, noting that "the central purpose of the Fourth Amendment forecloses such a distinction." We decline today to distinguish between "worthy" and "unworthy" vehicles which are either on the public roads and highways, or situated such that it is reasonable to conclude that the vehicle is not being used as a residence.

Our application of the vehicle exception has never turned on the other uses to which a vehicle might be put. The exception has historically turned on the ready mobility of the vehicle, and on the presence of the vehicle in a setting that objectively indicates that the vehicle is being used for transportation.[3] . . .

III

The question remains whether, apart from the lack of a warrant, this search was unreasonable . . . .

---

3. We need not pass on the application of the vehicle exception to a motor home that is situated in a way or place that objectively indicates that it is being used as a residence. Among the factors that might be relevant in determining whether a warrant would be required in such a circumstance is its location, whether the vehicle is readily mobile or instead, for instance, elevated on blocks, whether the vehicle is licensed, whether it is connected to utilities, and whether it has convenient access to a public road.

This search was not unreasonable; it was plainly one that the magistrate could authorize if presented with these facts . . . .

The judgment of the California Supreme Court is reversed, and the case is remanded for further proceedings not inconsistent with this opinion.

It is so ordered.

JUSTICE STEVENS with whom JUSTICE BRENNAN and JUSTICE MARSHALL join, dissenting.

. . . .

I

. . . .

II

. . . .

In *United States v. Ross*, [456 U.S. 798, 102 S. Ct. 2157, 72 L. Ed. 2d 572 (1982)], the Court reaffirmed the primary importance of the general rule condemning warrantless searches, and emphasized that the exception permitting the search of automobiles without a warrant is a narrow one.

. . . .

If the motor home were parked in the exact middle of the intersection between the general rule and the exception for automobiles, priority should be given to the rule rather than the exception.

III

The motor home, however, was not parked in the middle of that intersection. Our prior cases teach us that inherent mobility is not a sufficient justification for the fashioning of an exception to the warrant requirement, especially in the face of heightened expectations of privacy in the location searched. Motor homes, by their common use and construction, afford their owners a substantial and legitimate expectation of privacy when they dwell within. When a motor home is parked in a location that is removed from the public highway, I believe that society is prepared to recognize that the expectations of privacy within it are not unlike the expectations one has in a fixed dwelling. As a general rule, such places may only be searched with a warrant based upon probable cause. Warrantless searches of motor homes are only reasonable when the motor home is traveling on the public streets or highways, or when exigent circumstances otherwise require an immediate search without the expenditure of time necessary to obtain a warrant.

. . . .

In this case, the motor home was parked in an off-the-street lot only a few blocks from the courthouse in downtown San Diego where dozens of magistrates were available to entertain a warrant application. The officers clearly had the element of surprise with them, and with curtains covering the windshield, the motor home offered no indication of any imminent departure. The officers plainly had probable cause to arrest the petitioner and search the motor home, and on this record, it is inexplicable why they eschewed the safe harbor of a warrant.

In the absence of any evidence of exigency in the circumstances of this case, the Court relies on the inherent mobility of the motor home to create a conclusive presumption of exigency. This Court, however, has squarely held that mobility of the place to be searched is not a sufficient justification for abandoning the warrant requirement.

. . . .

It is perfectly obvious that the citizen has a much greater expectation of privacy concerning the interior of a mobile home than of a piece of luggage such as a footlocker. If "inherent mobility" does not justify warrantless searches of containers, it cannot rationally provide a sufficient justification for the search of a person's dwelling place.

Unlike a brick bungalow or a frame Victorian, a motor home seldom serves as a permanent lifetime abode. The motor home in this case, however, was designed to accommodate a breadth of ordinary everyday living . . . . Moreover, curtains and large opaque walls inhibit viewing the activities inside from the exterior of the vehicle. The interior configuration of the motor home establishes that the vehicle's size, shape, and mode of construction should have indicated to the officers that it was a vehicle containing mobile living quarters.

. . . .

In my opinion, searches of places that regularly accommodate a wide range of private human activity are fundamentally different from searches of automobiles which primarily serve a public transportation function. Although it may not be a castle, a motor home is usually the functional equivalent of a hotel room, a vacation and retirement home, or a hunting and fishing cabin. These places may be as Spartan as a humble cottage when compared to the most majestic mansion, . . . but the highest and most legitimate expectations of privacy associated with these temporary abodes should command the respect of this Court. In my opinion, a warrantless search of living quarters in a motor home is "presumptively unreasonable absent exigent circumstances."

I respectfully dissent.

Notes and Questions

(1) After *Carney*, what must the government show to bring a warrantless search within the terms of the "automobile exception"?

(2) In *Pennsylvania v. Labron* and *Pennsylvania v. Kilgore*, 518 U.S. 938, 116 S. Ct. 2485, 135 L. Ed. 2d 1031 (1996), the Supreme Court once again explored the premises and scope of the "automobile exception to the Fourth Amendment's warrant requirement."

In *Labron*, police observed a series of drug transactions on a street in Philadelphia. They arrested the participants and searched the trunk of a car from which the drugs had been produced, finding bags containing cocaine. The Pennsylvania Supreme Court concluded that the warrantless search of the stationary vehicle was unconstitutional. According to the court, the automobile exception requires both probable cause and exigent circumstances, and the police had time to secure a warrant in *Labron*.

In *Kilgore*, officers developed probable cause to believe that narcotics would be found in a pickup truck owned by Kilgore. The truck was parked on the driveway of a farmhouse that belonged to another individual. Without obtaining a warrant, police officers searched the pickup, finding cocaine on its floor. The Supreme Court of Pennsylvania, citing *Labron*, held that even though there was probable cause for the search, the search violated the Fourth Amendment because no exigent circumstances justified the failure to obtain a warrant.

In a brief, *per curiam* opinion, the Supreme Court reversed the holdings in both cases, declaring that the Pennsylvania Supreme Court's conclusion that "the Fourth Amendment . . . requires police to obtain a warrant before searching an automobile unless exigent circumstances are present . . . rest[ed] on an incorrect reading of the automobile exception." According to the Court:

> Our first cases establishing the automobile exception to the Fourth Amendment's warrant requirement were based on the automobile's "ready mobility," an exigency sufficient to excuse failure to obtain a search warrant once probable cause to conduct the search is clear. *California v. Carney*, 471 U.S. 386, 390–391, 105 S. Ct. 2066, 2068–2069, 85 L. Ed. 2d 406 (1985) (tracing the history of the exception); *Carroll v. United States*, 267 U.S. 132, 45 S. Ct. 280, 69 L. Ed. 543 (1925). More recent cases provide a further justification: the individual's reduced expectation of privacy in an automobile, owing to its pervasive regulation. *Carney, supra,* at 391–392, 105 S. Ct., at 2069–2070. If a car is readily mobile and probable cause exists to believe it contains contraband, the Fourth Amendment thus permits police to search the vehicle without more. *Carney, supra,* at 393, 105 S. Ct. at 2070. As the state courts found, there was probable cause in both of these cases: Police had seen respondent Labron put drugs in the trunk of the car they searched, and had seen respondent Kilgore act in ways that suggested he had drugs in his truck. We conclude the searches of the automobiles in these cases did not violate the Fourth Amendment.

After *Carney*, *Labron*, and *Kilgore*, what vehicles, if any, are protected by the warrant rule? Why?

(3) In *Florida v. White*, 526 U.S. 559, 119 S. Ct. 1555, 143 L. Ed. 2d 748 (1999), police officers saw the defendant use his car to deliver cocaine, thereby developing probable cause to believe that the car was subject to forfeiture under the Florida Contraband Forfeiture Act (the Act). Months later, after arresting the defendant

on unrelated charges, the police seized his car from his employer's parking lot without obtaining a warrant to do so. An inventory search of the car led to the discovery of contraband in an ashtray. The trial court and Florida Court of Appeal rejected the defendant's claim that the warrantless seizure of his car had violated the Fourth Amendment. The Florida Supreme Court, however, concluded that probable cause to believe that a vehicle is subject to forfeiture under the Act cannot ordinarily justify a seizure. Unless there are exigent circumstances, officers must obtain a warrant before seizing a vehicle that has been used in violation of the Act.

The Supreme Court reversed. According to a majority of the Court, the "principles underlying" the *Carroll-Chambers* automobile doctrine "fully support" the warrantless seizure of a vehicle when there is probable cause to believe it is subject to forfeiture as "contraband." The automobile doctrine allows officers to search a vehicle without a warrant whenever there is probable cause to believe it *contains* contraband because there is a "need to seize readily movable contraband before it is spirited away." According to the Court, the need to act without a warrant "is equally weighty when the *automobile*, as opposed to its contents, is the contraband that the police seek to secure." In addition, a warrantless action is permissible because the seizure of a vehicle "from a public area" does "not involve any invasion of . . . privacy." Under *United States v. Watson*, officers with probable cause to believe that a person has committed a felony may arrest that person in a public place without an arrest warrant. The "principle" underlying that conclusion "extends to the seizure" of a vehicle in a public place when there is probable cause to believe the vehicle is forfeitable contraband.

United States v. Chadwick

United States Supreme Court

433 U.S. 1, 97 S. Ct. 2476, 53 L. Ed. 2d 538 (1977)

Mr. Chief Justice Burger delivered the opinion of the Court.

. . . .

(1)

On May 8, 1973, Amtrak railroad officials in San Diego observed respondents Gregory Machado and Bridget Leary load a brown footlocker onto a train bound for Boston. Their suspicions were aroused when they noticed that the trunk was unusually heavy for its size, and that it was leaking talcum powder, a substance often used to mask the odor of marihuana or hashish. Because Machado matched a profile used to spot drug traffickers, the railroad officials reported these circumstances to federal agents in San Diego, who in turn relayed the information, together with detailed descriptions of Machado and the footlocker, to their counterparts in Boston.

When the train arrived in Boston two days later, federal narcotics agents were on hand. Though the officers had not obtained an arrest or search warrant, they had with them a police dog trained to detect marihuana. The agents identified Machado and Leary and kept them under surveillance as they claimed their suitcases and the footlocker, which had been transported by baggage cart from the train to the departure area. Machado and Leary lifted the footlocker from the baggage cart, placed it on the floor and sat down on it.

The agents then released the dog near the footlocker. Without alerting respondents, the dog signaled the presence of a controlled substance inside. Respondent Chadwick then joined Machado and Leary, and they engaged an attendant to move the footlocker outside to Chadwick's waiting automobile. Machado, Chadwick, and the attendant together lifted the 200-pound footlocker into the trunk of the car, while Leary waited in the front seat. At that point, while the trunk of the car was still open and before the car engine had been started, the officers arrested all three. A search disclosed no weapons, but the keys to the footlocker were apparently taken from Machado.

Respondents were taken to the Federal Building in Boston; the agents followed with Chadwick's car and the footlocker. As the Government concedes, from the moment of respondents' arrests at about 9 p.m., the footlocker remained under the exclusive control of law enforcement officers at all times. The footlocker and luggage were placed in the Federal Building, where, as one of the agents later testified, "there was no risk that whatever was contained in the footlocker trunk would be removed by the defendants or their associates." The agents had no reason to believe that the footlocker contained explosives or other inherently dangerous items, or that it contained evidence which would lose its value unless the footlocker were opened at once. Facilities were readily available in which the footlocker could have been stored securely; it is not contended that there was any exigency calling for an immediate search.

At the Federal Building an hour and a half after the arrests, the agents opened the footlocker and luggage. They did not obtain respondents' consent; they did not secure a search warrant. The footlocker was locked with a padlock and a regular trunk lock. It is unclear whether it was opened with the keys taken from respondent Machado, or by other means. Large amounts of marihuana were found in the footlocker.

Respondents were indicted for possession of marihuana with intent to distribute it . . . .

. . . .

(2)

In this Court the Government . . . contends that the Fourth Amendment Warrant Clause protects only interests traditionally identified with the home. Recalling the colonial writs of assistance, which were often executed in searches of private dwellings, the Government claims that the Warrant Clause was adopted primarily, if not exclusively, in response to unjustified intrusions into private homes on the authority of general warrants. The Government argues there is no evidence that the Framers of the Fourth Amendment intended to disturb the established practice of permitting warrantless searches outside the home, or to modify the initial clause of the Fourth Amendment by making warrantless searches supported by probable cause *per se* unreasonable.

Drawing on its reading of history, the Government argues that only homes, offices, and private communications implicate interests which lie at the core of the Fourth Amendment. Accordingly, it is only in these contexts that the determination whether a search or seizure is reasonable should turn on whether a warrant has been obtained. In all other situations, the Government contends, less significant privacy values are at stake, and the reasonableness of a government intrusion should depend solely on whether there is probable cause to believe evidence of criminal conduct is present. Where personal effects are lawfully seized outside the home on probable cause, the Government would thus regard searches without a warrant as not "unreasonable."

. . . .

(3)

. . . .

Although the searches and seizures which deeply concerned the colonists, and which were foremost in the minds of the Framers, were those involving invasions of the home, it would be a mistake to conclude, as the Government contends, that the Warrant Clause was therefore intended to guard only against intrusions into the home. First, the Warrant Clause does not in terms distinguish between searches conducted in private homes and other searches. There is also a strong historical connection between the Warrant Clause and the initial clause of the Fourth Amendment, which draws no distinctions among "persons, houses, papers, and effects" in safeguarding against unreasonable searches and seizures. *See United States v. Rabinowitz*, 339 U.S. 56, 68, 70 S. Ct. 430, 445, 94 L. Ed. 653 (1950) (Frankfurter, J., dissenting).

Moreover, if there is little evidence that the Framers intended the Warrant Clause to operate outside the home, there is no evidence at all that they intended to exclude from protection of the Clause all searches occurring outside the home. The absence of a contemporary outcry against warrantless searches in public places was because, aside from searches incident to arrest, such warrantless searches were not a large issue in colonial America. Thus, silence in the historical record tells us little about the Framers' attitude toward application of the Warrant Clause to the search of respondents' footlocker. What we do know is that the Framers were men who focused on the wrongs of that day but who intended the Fourth Amendment to safeguard fundamental values which would far outlast the specific abuses which gave it birth.

. . . .

Just as the Fourth Amendment "protects people, not places," the protections a judicial warrant offers against erroneous governmental intrusions are effective whether applied in or out of the home. Accordingly, we have held warrantless searches unreasonable, and therefore unconstitutional, in a variety of settings.

294 REASONABLE SEARCHES WITHOUT WARRANTS

. . . .

... [Our] cases illustrate the applicability of the Warrant Clause beyond the narrow limits suggested by the Government. They also reflect the settled constitutional principle, discussed earlier, that a fundamental purpose of the Fourth Amendment is to safeguard individuals from unreasonable government invasions of legitimate privacy interests, and not simply those interests found inside the four walls of the home. *Wolf v. Colorado*, 338 U.S. 25, 27, 69 S. Ct. 1359, 1361, 93 L. Ed. 1782 (1949).

In this case, important Fourth Amendment privacy interests were at stake. By placing personal effects inside a double-locked footlocker, respondents manifested an expectation that the contents would remain free from public examination. No less than one who locks the doors of his home against intruders, one who safeguards his personal possessions in this manner is due the protection of the Fourth Amendment Warrant Clause. There being no exigency, it was unreasonable for the Government to conduct this search without the safeguards a judicial warrant provides.

(4)

The Government does not contend that the footlocker's brief contact with Chadwick's car makes this an automobile search, but it is argued that the rationale of our automobile search cases demonstrates the reasonableness of permitting warrantless searches of luggage; the Government views such luggage as analogous to motor vehicles for Fourth Amendment purposes . . . .

Our treatment of automobiles has been based in part on their inherent mobility, which often makes obtaining a judicial warrant impracticable. Nevertheless, we have also sustained "warrantless searches of vehicles . . . in cases in which the possibilities of the vehicle's being removed or evidence in it destroyed were remote, if not nonexistent." *Cady v. Dombrowski*, 413 U.S. 433, 441–442, 93 S. Ct. 2523, 2528, 37 L. Ed. 2d 706 (1973).

The answer lies in the diminished expectation of privacy which surrounds the automobile:

> One has a lesser expectation of privacy in a motor vehicle because its function is transportation and it seldom serves as one's residence or as the repository of personal effects . . . . It travels public thoroughfares where both its occupants and its contents are in plain view.

Cardwell v. Lewis, 417 U.S. 583, 590, 94 S. Ct. 2464, 2469, 41 L. Ed. 2d 325 (1974) (plurality opinion).

Other factors reduce automobile privacy. "All States require vehicles to be registered and operators to be licensed. States and localities have enacted extensive and detailed codes regulating the condition and manner in which motor vehicles may be operated on public streets and highways." *Cady v. Dombrowski, supra*, 413 U.S., at 441, 93 S. Ct., at 2528. Automobiles periodically undergo official inspection, and they are often taken into police custody in the interests of public safety. *South Dakota v. Opperman, supra*, 428 U.S., at 368, 96 S. Ct., at 3096.

The factors which diminish the privacy aspects of an automobile do not apply to respondents' footlocker. Luggage contents are not open to public view, except as a condition to a border entry or common carrier travel, nor is luggage subject to regular inspections and official scrutiny on a continuing basis. Unlike an automobile, whose primary function is transportation, luggage is intended as a repository of personal effects. In sum, a person's expectations of privacy in personal luggage are substantially greater than in an automobile.

[margin note: unlike motor vehicle]

[margin note: ⚹ substantially greater]

Nor does the footlocker's mobility justify dispensing with the added protections of the Warrant Clause. Once the federal agents had seized it at the railroad station and had safely transferred it to the Boston Federal Building under their exclusive control, there was not the slightest danger that the footlocker or its contents could have been removed before a valid search warrant could be obtained.[7] The initial seizure and detention of the footlocker, the validity of which respondents do not contest, were sufficient to guard against any risk that evidence might be lost. With the footlocker safely immobilized, it was unreasonable to undertake the additional and greater intrusion of a search without a warrant.[8]

[margin note: "step 1"]

[margin note: → unreasonable search b/c the FL was immobilized!]

Finally, the Government urges that the Constitution permits the warrantless search of any property in the possession of a person arrested in public, so long as there is probable cause to believe that the property contains contraband or evidence of crime. Although recognizing that the footlocker was not within respondents' immediate control, the Government insists that the search was reasonable because the footlocker was seized contemporaneously with respondents' arrests and was searched as soon thereafter as was practicable. The reasons justifying search in a custodial arrest are quite different . . . .

[margin note: GOV'T ARG FOR REASONABLE (ITS WRONG)]

Such searches may be conducted without a warrant, and they may also be made whether or not there is probable cause to believe that the person arrested may have a weapon or is about to destroy evidence. The potential dangers lurking in all custodial arrests make warrantless searches of items within the "immediate control" area reasonable without requiring the arresting officer to calculate the probability that weapons or destructible evidence may be involved. However, warrantless searches of luggage or other property seized at the time of an arrest cannot be justified as incident

---

7. This may often not be the case when automobiles are seized. Absolutely secure storage facilities may not be available, *see South Dakota v. Opperman*, 428 U.S. 364, 96 S. Ct. 3092, 49 L. Ed. 2d 1000 (1976); *Cady v. Dombrowski*, 413 U.S. 433, 93 S. Ct. 2523, 37 L. Ed. 2d 706 (1973), and the size and inherent mobility of a vehicle make it susceptible to theft or intrusion by vandals.

8. Respondents' principal privacy interest in the footlocker was, of course, not in the container itself, which was exposed to public view, but in its contents. A search of the interior was therefore a far greater intrusion into Fourth Amendment values than the impoundment of the footlocker. Though surely a substantial infringement of respondents' use and possession, the seizure did not diminish respondents' legitimate expectation that the footlocker's contents would remain private. It was the greatly reduced expectation of privacy in the automobile, coupled with the transportation function of the vehicle, which made the Court in *Chambers* unwilling to decide whether an immediate search of an automobile, or its seizure and indefinite immobilization, constituted a greater interference with the rights of the owner. This is clearly not the case with locked luggage.

[margin note: Happened here b/c the Δ's were so where near the footlocker]

to that arrest either if the "search is remote in time or place from the arrest," *Preston v. United States*, 376 U.S., at 367, 84 S. Ct., at 883, or no exigency exists. Once law enforcement officers have reduced luggage or other personal property not immediately associated with the person of the arrestee to their exclusive control, and there is no longer any danger that the arrestee might gain access to the property to seize a weapon or destroy evidence, a search of that property is no longer an incident of the arrest.[9]

Here the search was conducted more than an hour after federal agents had gained exclusive control of the footlocker and long after respondents were securely in custody; the search therefore cannot be viewed as incidental to the arrest or as justified by any other exigency. Even though on this record the issuance of a warrant by a judicial officer was reasonably predictable, a line must be drawn. In our view, when no exigency is shown to support the need for an immediate search, the Warrant Clause places the line at the point where the property to be searched comes under the exclusive dominion of police authority. Respondents were therefore entitled to the protection of the Warrant Clause with the evaluation of a neutral magistrate, before their privacy interests in the contents of the footlocker were invaded.[10]

[margin note: The "line" drawn here → Holding]

Accordingly, the judgment is

Affirmed.

Mr. Justice Brennan, concurring.

I fully join The Chief Justice's thorough opinion for the Court. I write only to comment upon two points made by my Brother Blackmun's dissent.

. . . .

. . . [I]t should be noted that while . . . the dissent suggests a number of possible alternative courses of action that the agents could have followed without violating the Constitution, no decision of this Court is cited to support the constitutionality of these courses, but only some decisions of Courts of Appeals. In my view, it is not at all obvious that the agents could legally have searched the footlocker had they seized it after Machado and Leary had driven away with it in their car[1] or "at the time and place of the arrests."[2]

---

9. Of course, there may be other justifications for a warrantless search of luggage taken from a suspect at the time of his arrest; for example, if officers have reason to believe that luggage contains some immediately dangerous instrumentality, such as explosives, it would be foolhardy to transport it to the station house without opening the luggage and disarming the weapon. *See e.g., United States v. Johnson*, 467 F.2d 630, 639 (2d Cir. 1972).

10. Unlike searches of the person, *United States v. Robinson*, 414 U.S. 218, 94 S. Ct. 467, 38 L. Ed. 2d 427 (1973); *United States v. Edwards*, 415 U.S. 800, 94 S. Ct. 1234, 39 L. Ed. 2d 77 (1974), searches of possessions within an arrestee's immediate control cannot be justified by any reduced expectations of privacy caused by the arrest. Respondents' privacy interest in the contents of the footlocker was not eliminated simply because they were under arrest.

1. While the contents of the car could have been searched pursuant to the automobile exception, it is by no means clear that the contents of locked containers found inside a car are subject to search under this exception, any more than they would be if the police found them in any other place.

2. When Machado and Leary were "standing next to [the] open automobile trunk containing the footlocker," and even when they "were seated on it," it is not obvious to me that the contents of

Mr. Justice Blackmun, with whom Mr. Justice Rehnquist joins, dissenting.

I think it somewhat unfortunate that the Government sought a reversal in this case primarily to vindicate an extreme view of the Fourth Amendment that would restrict the protection of the Warrant Clause to private dwellings and a few other "high privacy" areas. I reject this argument for the reasons stated in Parts (2) and (3) of the Court's opinion, with which I am in general agreement. The overbroad nature of the Government's principal argument, however, has served to distract the Court from the more important task of defining the proper scope of a search incident to an arrest. . . . .

I

. . . .

I would . . . hold generally that a warrant is not required to seize and search any movable property in the possession of a person properly arrested in a public place. A person arrested in a public place is likely to have various kinds of property with him: items inside his clothing, a briefcase or suitcase, packages, or a vehicle. In such instances the police cannot very well leave the property on the sidewalk or street while they go to get a warrant. The items may be stolen by a passer-by or removed by the suspect's confederates. Rather than requiring the police to "post a guard" over such property, I think it is surely reasonable for the police to take the items along to the station with the arrested person.

. . . .

As the Court in *Robinson* recognized, custodial arrest is such a serious deprivation that various lesser invasions of privacy may be fairly regarded as incidental. An arrested person, of course, has an additional privacy interest in the objects in his possession at the time of arrest. To be sure, allowing impoundment of those objects pursuant to arrest, but requiring a warrant for examination of their contents, would protect that incremental privacy interest in cases where the police assessment of probable cause is subsequently rejected by a magistrate. But a countervailing consideration is that a warrant would be routinely forthcoming in the vast majority of situations where the property has been seized in conjunction with the valid arrest of a person in a public place. I therefore doubt that requiring the authorities to go through the formality of obtaining a warrant in this situation would have much practical effect in protecting Fourth Amendment values.[1]

---

the heavy, securely locked footlocker were within the area of their "immediate control" for purposes of the search-incident-to-arrest doctrine, the justification for which is the possibility that the arrested person might have immediate access to weapons that might endanger the officer's safety or assist in his escape, or to items of evidence that he might conceal or destroy. I would think that the footlocker in this case hardly was "'within [respondents'] immediate control' — construing that phrase to mean the area from within which [they] might gain possession of a weapon or destructible evidence." *Chimel v. California*, 395 U.S. 752, 763, 89 S. Ct. 2034, 2040, 23 L. Ed. 2d 685 (1969).

1. A search warrant serves additional functions where an arrest takes place in a home or office. The warrant assures the occupants that the officers have legal authority to conduct the search and defines the area to be searched and the objects to be seized. *See Camara v. Municipal Court*, 387 U.S.

. . . .

II

The approach taken by the Court has the perverse result of allowing fortuitous circumstances to control the outcome of the present case. The agents probably could have avoided having the footlocker search held unconstitutional either by delaying the arrest for a few minutes or by conducting the search on the spot rather than back at their office. Probable cause for the arrest was present from the time respondents Machado and Leary were seated on the footlocker inside Boston's South Station and the agents' dog signaled the presence of marihuana. Rather than make an arrest at this moment, the agents commendably sought to determine the possible involvement of others in the illegal scheme. They waited a short time until respondent Chadwick arrived and the footlocker had been loaded into the trunk of his car, and then made the arrest. But if the agents had postponed the arrest just a few minutes longer until the respondents started to drive away, then the car could have been seized, taken to the agents' office, and all its contents — including the footlocker — searched without a warrant.[4]

PC Existed

Alternatively, the agents could have made a search of the footlocker at the time and place of the arrests. Machado and Leary were standing next to an open automobile trunk containing the footlocker, and thus it was within the area of their "immediate control." And certainly the footlocker would have been properly subject to search at the time if the arrest had occurred a few minutes earlier while Machado and Leary were seated on it.

In many cases, of course, small variations in the facts are determinative of the legal outcome. Criminal law necessarily involves some line drawing. But I see no way that these alternative courses of conduct, which likely would have been held constitutional under the Fourth Amendment, would have been any more solicitous of the privacy or well-being of the respondents . . . .

Notes and Questions

(1) Under the holding of *Chadwick*, the Fourth Amendment clearly extends greater protection to nonvehicular containers than it does to vehicles. Why should

523, 532, 87 S. Ct. 1727, 1732, 18 L. Ed. 2d 930 (1967). But a warrant would serve none of these functions where the arrest takes place in a public area and the authorities are admittedly empowered to seize the objects in question. *Cf. United States v. Watson*, 423 U.S. 411, 414–424, 96 S. Ct. 820, 823–828, 46 L. Ed. 2d 598 (1976) (warrant not required for arrest, based on probable cause, in public place).

4. The scope of the "automobile search" exception to the warrant requirement extends to the contents of locked compartments, including glove compartments and trunks. The Courts of Appeals have construed this doctrine to include briefcases, suitcases, and footlockers inside automobiles. *United States v. Tramunti*, 513 F.2d 1087, 1104–1105 (CA2 1975); *United States v. Issod*, 508 F.2d 990, 993 (7th Cir. 1974), *cert. denied*, 421 U.S. 916, 95 S. Ct. 1578, 43 L. Ed. 2d 783 (1975); *United States v. Soriano*, 497 F.2d 147 (5th Cir. 1974) (*en banc*), convictions summarily *aff'd sub nom. United States v. Aviles*, 535 F.2d 658 (1976), *cert. pending*, Nos. 76–5132 and 76–5143; *United States v. Evans*, 481 F.2d 990, 993–994 (9th Cir. 1973).

an officer's authority to conduct warrantless searches of vehicles be greater than his authority to conduct similar searches of other "movable containers"?

(2) Justice Blackmun asserted that officers could have conducted a legitimate warrantless search of the footlocker in *Chadwick* if they had waited "until the respondents had started to drive away," or, alternatively, if they had "made a search of [it] at the time and place of the arrests." Is he correct? Why?

In *Arkansas v. Sanders*, 442 U.S. 753, 99 S. Ct. 2586, 61 L. Ed. 2d 235 (1979), the Court dealt with the first of Justice Blackmun's two alternatives. Therein, police officers developed probable cause to believe that a green suitcase contained marihuana. They watched as the defendant and a cohort loaded the suitcase into the trunk of a taxicab. When the taxicab drove away, the officers pursued and stopped it. They opened the trunk and then opened the suitcase without a warrant. The Court observed first that it was "presented with the task of determining whether the warrantless search of [the] suitcase [fell] on the *Chadwick* or the *Carroll/Chambers* side of the Fourth Amendment line." A majority concluded that there was "no justification for the extension" of the automobile doctrine "to the warrantless search of one's personal luggage merely because it was located in an automobile." Consequently, they held "that the warrant requirement of the Fourth Amendment applies to personal luggage taken from an automobile to the same degree as it applies to such luggage in other locations."

In a significant concurrence, Chief Justice Burger asserted that the "automobile exception" was inapplicable to the facts of *Sanders* because the officers "had probable cause to believe that . . . [the] suitcase contained marihuana before it was placed in the . . . taxicab." In his view, *Chadwick* clearly controlled such a situation, and the majority's opinion was "unnecessarily broad" and incorrect to suggest that the "automobile exception" was implicated. The Chief Justice contended that *Sanders* did not "present the question of whether a warrant is required before opening luggage when the police have probable cause to believe contraband is located *somewhere* in the vehicle, but when they do *not* know whether, for example, it is inside a piece of luggage in the trunk, in the glove compartment, or concealed in some part of the car's structure."

(3) In *Robbins v. California*, 453 U.S. 420, 101 S. Ct. 2841, 69 L. Ed. 2d 744 (1981), the Court again considered the applicability of the warrant requirement to containers discovered inside a vehicle. A four-member plurality endorsed the *Sanders* rule and rejected the government's argument that distinctions should be made among different kinds of containers. The plurality opined that the *Sanders* warrant requirement governed every container "unless the container is such that its contents may be said to be in plain view." Justice Powell concurred in the judgment, agreeing that the warrantless searches of the containers in *Robbins* were impermissible. He disagreed with the plurality's analysis, however, because he thought that distinctions should be made among containers found in automobiles. According to Justice Powell, only containers that evidence a sufficient "expectation of privacy in [their] contents"

should be protected by the warrant requirement. Significantly, Justice Powell also expressed sympathy with the dissenters' view that the automobile exception should be expanded to cover the containers searched in *Robbins*. Such an approach was attractive to him "not so much for its logical virtue, but because it [could] provide ground for agreement by a majority of the presently fractured Court." He refrained from endorsing the dissenters' position, however, because it had not been argued by the parties. At the same time, he hoped for a "future case affording an opportunity for more thorough consideration of the basic principles," a case that would "offer some better, if more radical, solution to the confusion that infects this benighted area of the law."

(4) Just one term later, Justice Powell's hope became a reality. In *United States v. Ross*, 456 U.S. 798, 102 S. Ct. 2157, 72 L. Ed. 2d 572 (1982), a majority of the Court coalesced around an opinion that swept away much of the confusion engendered by the short-lived *Robbins* decision.

Ross involved the scenario described by Chief Justice Burger's concurrence in *Arkansas v. Sanders*. With probable cause to believe that an automobile contained narcotics, officers pulled it over. A search of the trunk revealed a closed paper bag. Upon opening the bag, officers discovered "glassine bags containing white powder" that later laboratory analysis proved to be heroin. Justice Stevens, for the majority, concluded that the warrantless search of the paper bag was reasonable because it fell within the ambit of the "automobile doctrine." The Court distinguished *Sanders*, in which officers had *probable cause to search the container in the vehicle*, from *Ross*, in which the container turned up during a search of a vehicle based on *probable cause to search the vehicle.* Justice Stevens's reasoning was that the scope of a warrantless vehicle search should be the same as the scope of a vehicle search made pursuant to a search warrant. If the officers had possessed a search warrant for Ross's car, they would have been allowed to search a bag found in the car. Therefore, officers conducting a warrantless search of the car should also be permitted to search a bag found inside. Wait, what?

Justice Marshall, joined by Justice Brennan, dissented. Adhering to the broadest assertions in *Sanders*, they would have ruled that a container found within the confines of a vehicle should not be exempt from the protection of the warrant requirement.

Nearly a decade later, in *California v. Acevedo*, the next main case in this section, the Court revisited—and revamped—the *Ross-Sanders* dichotomy.

California v. Acevedo

United States Supreme Court

500 U.S. 565, 111 S. Ct. 1982, 114 L. Ed. 2d 619 (1991)

JUSTICE BLACKMUN delivered the opinion of the Court.

This case requires us once again to consider the so-called "automobile exception" to the warrant requirement of the Fourth Amendment and its application to the search of a closed container in the trunk of a car.

I

On October 28, 1987, Officer Coleman of the Santa Ana, Cal., Police Department received a telephone call from a federal drug enforcement agent in Hawaii. The agent informed Coleman that he had seized a package containing marijuana which was to have been delivered to the Federal Express Office in Santa Ana and which was addressed to J.R. Daza at 805 West Stevens Avenue in that city. The agent arranged to send the package to Coleman instead. Coleman then was to take the package to the Federal Express office and arrest the person who arrived to claim it.

Coleman received the package on October 29, verified its contents, and took it to the Senior Operations Manager at the Federal Express office. At about 10:30 a.m. on October 30, a man, who identified himself as Jamie Daza, arrived to claim the package. He accepted it and drove to his apartment on West Stevens. He carried the package into the apartment. *-*

At 11:45 a.m., officers observed Daza leave the apartment and drop the box and paper that had contained the marijuana into a trash bin. <u>Coleman at that point left the scene to get a search warrant.</u> About 12:05 p.m., the officers saw Richard St. George leave the apartment carrying a blue knapsack which appeared to be half full. The officers stopped him as he was driving off, searched the knapsack, and found 1 1/2 pounds of marijuana.

At 12:30 p.m., respondent Charles Steven Acevedo arrived. He entered Daza's apartment, stayed for about 10 minutes, and reappeared carrying a brown paper bag that looked full. The officers noticed that the bag was the size of one of the wrapped marijuana packages sent from Hawaii. Acevedo walked to a silver Honda in the parking lot. He placed the bag in the trunk of the car and started to drive away. Fearing the loss of evidence, officers in a marked police car stopped him. <u>They opened the trunk and the bag, and found marijuana.</u> *-*

Respondent was charged in state court with possession of marijuana for sale, in violation of Cal. Health & Safety Code Ann. § 11359 (Supp. 1987). He moved to suppress the marijuana found in the car. The motion was denied. He then pleaded guilty but appealed the denial of the suppression motion.

The California Court of Appeal, Fourth District, concluded that the marijuana found in the paper bag in the car's trunk should have been suppressed. *People v. Acevedo*, 216 Cal. App. 3d 586, 265 Cal. Rptr. 23 (1990) . . . .   *Appeal reversed*

The Supreme Court of California denied the State's petition for review . . . .   → *S.C Denied*

We granted certiorari, 498 U.S. 807 (1990), to reexamine the law applicable to a → *certiorari granted*
closed container in an automobile, a subject that has troubled courts and law enforcement officers since it was first considered in *Chadwick*.

II

The Fourth Amendment protects the "right of the people to be secure in their persons, houses, papers, and effects, against unreasonable searches and seizures." Contemporaneously with the adoption of the Fourth Amendment, the First Congress, and, later, the Second and Fourth Congresses, distinguished between the need for a warrant to search for contraband concealed in "a dwelling house or similar place" and the need for a warrant to search for contraband concealed in a movable vessel. *See Carroll v. United States*, 267 U.S. 132, 151 (1925). In *Carroll*, this Court established an exception to the warrant requirement for moving vehicles, for it recognized

> "a necessary difference between a search of a store, dwelling house or other structure in respect of which a proper official warrant readily may be obtained, and a search of a ship, motor boat, wagon or automobile, for contraband goods, where it is not practicable to secure a warrant because the vehicle can be quickly moved out of the locality or jurisdiction in which the warrant must be sought." 267 U.S., at 153.

Carroll's Reasoning

It therefore held that a warrantless search of an automobile based upon probable cause to believe that the vehicle contained evidence of crime in the light of an exigency arising out of the likely disappearance of the vehicle did not contravene the Warrant Clause of the Fourth Amendment. *See id.*, at 158–159.

The Court refined the exigency requirement in *Chambers v. Maroney*, 399 U.S. 42 (1970), when it held that the existence of exigent circumstances was to be determined at the time the automobile is seized . . . . Following *Chambers*, if the police have probable cause to justify a warrantless seizure of an automobile on a public roadway, they may conduct either an immediate or a delayed search of the vehicle.

In *United States v. Ross*, 456 U.S. 798, decided in 1982, we held that a warrantless search of an automobile under the *Carroll* doctrine could include a search of a container or package found inside the car when such a search was supported by probable cause. The warrantless search of Ross' car occurred after an informant told the police that he had seen Ross complete a drug transaction using drugs stored in the trunk of his car. The police stopped the car, searched it, and discovered in the trunk a brown paper bag containing drugs. We decided that the search of Ross' car was not unreasonable under the Fourth Amendment: "The scope of a warrantless search based on probable cause is no narrower — and no broader — than the scope of a search authorized by a warrant supported by probable cause." *Id.*, at 823. Thus, "[i]f probable cause justifies the search of a lawfully stopped vehicle, it justifies the search of every part of the vehicle and its contents that may conceal the object of the search." *Id.*, at 825. In *Ross*, therefore, we clarified the scope of the *Carroll* doctrine as properly including a "probing search" of compartments and containers within the automobile so long as the search is supported by probable cause. *Id.*, at 800.

Ross

In addition to this clarification, *Ross* distinguished the *Carroll* doctrine from the separate rule that governed the search of closed containers. *See* 456 U.S., at 817. The Court had announced this separate rule, unique to luggage and other closed packages, bags, and containers, in *United States v. Chadwick*, 433 U.S. 1 (1977). In *Chad-*

wick, . . . the United States urged that the search of movable luggage could be considered analogous to the search of an automobile. 433 U.S., at 11–12.

The Court rejected this argument because, it reasoned, a person expects more privacy in his luggage and personal effects than he does in his automobile. *Id.*, at 13. Moreover, it concluded that as "may often not be the case when automobiles are seized," secure storage facilities are usually available when the police seize luggage. *Id.*, at 13, n. 7.

In *Arkansas v. Sanders*, 442 U.S. 753 (1979), the Court extended *Chadwick*'s rule to apply to a suitcase actually being transported in the trunk of a car. In *Sanders*, the police had probable cause to believe a suitcase contained marijuana. They watched as the defendant placed the suitcase in the trunk of a taxi and was driven away. The police pursued the taxi for several blocks, stopped it, found the suitcase in the trunk, and searched it. Although the Court had applied the *Carroll* doctrine to searches of integral parts of the automobile itself, (indeed, in *Carroll*, contraband whiskey was in the upholstery of the seats, *see* 267 U.S., at 136), it did not extend the doctrine to the warrantless search of personal luggage "merely because it was located in an automobile lawfully stopped by the police." 442 U.S., at 765. Again, the *Sanders* majority stressed the heightened privacy expectation in personal luggage and concluded that the presence of luggage in an automobile did not diminish the owner's expectation of privacy in his personal items. *Id.*, at 764–765.

In *Ross*, the Court endeavored to distinguish between *Carroll*, which governed the *Ross* automobile search, and *Chadwick*, which governed the *Sanders* automobile search. It held that the *Carroll* doctrine covered searches of automobiles when the police had probable cause to search an entire vehicle but that the *Chadwick* doctrine governed searches of luggage when the officers had probable cause to search only a container within the vehicle. Thus, in a *Ross* situation, the police could conduct a reasonable search under the Fourth Amendment without obtaining a warrant, whereas in a *Sanders* situation, the police had to obtain a warrant before they searched.

The dissent is correct, of course, that *Ross* involved the scope of an automobile search. *Ross* held that closed containers encountered by the police during a warrantless search of a car pursuant to the automobile exception could also be searched. Thus, this Court in *Ross* took the critical step of saying that closed containers in cars could be searched without a warrant because of their presence within the automobile. Despite the protection that *Sanders* purported to extend to closed containers, the privacy interest in those closed containers yielded to the broad scope of an automobile search.

III

The facts in this case closely resemble the facts in *Ross*. In *Ross*, the police had probable cause to believe that drugs were stored in the trunk of a particular car. *See* 456 U.S., at 800. Here, the California Court of Appeal concluded that the police had probable cause to believe that respondent was carrying marijuana in a bag in his car's trunk. Furthermore, for what it is worth, in *Ross*, as here, the drugs in the trunk were contained in a brown paper bag.

This Court in *Ross* rejected *Chadwick*'s distinction between containers and cars. It concluded that the expectation of privacy in one's vehicle is equal to one's expectation of privacy in the container, and noted that "the privacy interests in a car's trunk or glove compartment may be no less than those in a movable container." 456 U.S., at 823. It also recognized that it was arguable that the same exigent circumstances that permit a warrantless search of an automobile would justify the warrantless search of a movable container. *Id.*, at 809. In deference to the rule of *Chadwick* and *Sanders*, however, the Court put that question to one side. *Id.*, at 809–810. It concluded that the time and expense of the warrant process would be misdirected if the police could search every cubic inch of an automobile until they discovered a paper sack, at which point the Fourth Amendment required them to take the sack to a magistrate for permission to look inside. We now must decide the question deferred in *Ross*: whether the Fourth Amendment requires the police to obtain a warrant to open the sack in a movable vehicle simply because they lack probable cause to search the entire car. We conclude that it does not.

[margin annotation: question + Answer]

IV

. . . [W]e see no principled distinction in terms of either the privacy expectation or the exigent circumstances between the paper bag found by the police in *Ross* and the paper bag found by the police here. Furthermore, by attempting to distinguish between a container for which the police are specifically searching and a container which they come across in a car, we have provided only minimal protection for privacy and have impeded effective law enforcement.

The line between probable cause to search a vehicle and probable cause to search a package in that vehicle is not always clear, and separate rules that govern the two objects to be searched may enable the police to broaden their power to make warrantless searches and disserve privacy interests. We noted this in *Ross* in the context of a search of an entire vehicle. Recognizing that under *Carroll*, the "entire vehicle itself . . . could be searched without a warrant," we concluded that "prohibiting police from opening immediately a container in which the object of the search is most likely to be found and instead forcing them first to comb the entire vehicle would actually exacerbate the intrusion on privacy interests." 456 U.S., at 821, n. 28. At the moment when officers stop an automobile, it may be less than clear whether they suspect with a high degree of certainty that the vehicle contains drugs in a bag or simply contains drugs. If the police know that they may open a bag only if they are actually searching the entire car, they may search more extensively than they otherwise would in order to establish the general probable cause required by *Ross*.

. . . .

To the extent that the *Chadwick-Sanders* rule protects privacy, its protection is minimal. Law enforcement officers may seize a container and hold it until they obtain a search warrant. *Chadwick*, 433 U.S., at 13. "Since the police, by hypothesis, have probable cause to seize the property, we can assume that a warrant will be routinely forthcoming in the overwhelming majority of cases." *Sanders*, 442 U.S., at 770 (dissenting opinion). And the police often will be able to search containers without a warrant, despite the *Chadwick-Sanders* rule, as a search incident to a lawful arrest . . . .

. . . .

V

The *Chadwick-Sanders* rule not only has failed to protect privacy but it has also confused courts and police officers and impeded effective law enforcement . . . .

. . . .

Although we have recognized firmly that the doctrine of *stare decisis* serves profoundly important purposes in our legal system, this Court has overruled a prior case on the comparatively rare occasion when it has bred confusion or been a derelict or led to anomalous results. *See e.g., Complete Auto Transit, Inc. v. Brady*, 430 U.S. 274, 288–289 (1977). *Sanders* was explicitly undermined in *Ross*, 456 U.S., at 824, and the existence of the dual regimes for automobile searches that uncover containers has proved as confusing as the *Chadwick* and *Sanders* dissenters predicted. We conclude that it is better to adopt one clear-cut rule to govern automobile searches and eliminate the warrant requirement for closed containers set forth in *Sanders*.

VI

The interpretation of the *Carroll* doctrine set forth in *Ross* now applies to all searches of containers found in an automobile. In other words, the police may search without a warrant if their search is supported by probable cause. The Court in *Ross* put it this way:

> "The scope of a warrantless search of an automobile . . . is not defined by the nature of the container in which the contraband is secreted. Rather, it is defined by the object of the search and the places in which there is probable cause to believe that it may be found." 456 U.S., at 824.

It went on to note: "Probable cause to believe that a container placed in the trunk of a taxi contains contraband or evidence does not justify a search of the entire cab." *Id*. We reaffirm that principle. In the case before us, the police had probable cause to believe that the paper bag in the automobile's trunk contained marijuana. That probable cause now allows a warrantless search of the paper bag. The facts in the record reveal that the police did not have probable cause to believe that contraband was hidden in any other part of the automobile and a search of the entire vehicle would have been without probable cause and unreasonable under the Fourth Amendment.

. . . .

Until today, this Court has drawn a curious line between the search of an automobile that coincidentally turns up a container and the search of a container that coincidentally turns up in an automobile. The protections of the Fourth Amendment must not turn on such coincidences. We therefore interpret *Carroll* as providing one rule to govern all automobile searches. The police may search an automobile and the containers within it where they have probable cause to believe contraband or evidence is contained.

[handwritten margin note: ONE RULE FOR containers PC & AUTO]

The judgment of the California Court of Appeal is reversed and the case is remanded to that court for further proceedings not inconsistent with this opinion.

It is so ordered.

JUSTICE SCALIA, concurring in the judgment.

. . . .

Although the Fourth Amendment does not explicitly impose the requirement of a warrant, it is of course textually possible to consider that implicit within the requirement of reasonableness. For some years after the (still continuing) explosion in Fourth Amendment litigation that followed our announcement of the exclusionary rule in *Weeks v. United States*, 232 U.S. 383 (1914), our jurisprudence lurched back and forth between imposing a categorical warrant requirement and looking to reasonableness alone. (The opinions preferring a warrant involved searches of structures.) *See generally Chimel v. California*, 395 U.S. 752 (1969). By the late 1960's, the preference for a warrant had won out, at least rhetorically. *See Chimel; Coolidge v. New Hampshire*, 403 U.S. 443 (1971).

The victory was illusory. Even before today's decision, the "warrant requirement" had become so riddled with exceptions that it was basically unrecognizable . . . .

Unlike the dissent, therefore, I do not regard today's holding as some momentous departure, but rather as merely the continuation of an inconsistent jurisprudence that has been with us for years . . . .

In my view, the path out of this confusion should be sought by returning to the first principle that the "reasonableness" requirement of the Fourth Amendment affords the protection that the common law afforded. I have no difficulty with the proposition that that includes the requirement of a warrant, where the common law required a warrant; and it may even be that changes in the surrounding legal rules . . . may make a warrant indispensable to reasonableness where it once was not. But the supposed "general rule" that a warrant is always required does not appear to have any basis in the common law, and confuses rather than facilitates any attempt to develop rules of reasonableness in light of changed legal circumstances, as the anomaly eliminated and the anomaly created by today's holding both demonstrate.

. . . .

I would reverse the judgment in the present case, not because a closed container carried inside a car becomes subject to the "automobile" exception to the general warrant requirement, but because the search of a closed container, outside a privately owned building, with probable cause to believe that the container contains contraband, and when it in fact does contain contraband, is not one of those searches whose

Fourth Amendment reasonableness depends upon a warrant. For that reason I concur in the judgment of the Court.

JUSTICE WHITE, dissenting.

Agreeing as I do with most of JUSTICE STEVENS' opinion and with the result he reaches, I dissent and would affirm the judgment below.

JUSTICE STEVENS, with whom JUSTICE MARSHALL joins, dissenting.

. . . .

I

The Fourth Amendment is a restraint on Executive power. The Amendment constitutes the Framers' direct constitutional response to the unreasonable law enforcement practices employed by agents of the British Crown . . . .

This history is, however, only part of the explanation for the warrant requirement. The requirement also reflects the sound policy judgment that, absent exceptional circumstances, the decision to invade the privacy of an individual's personal effects should be made by a neutral magistrate rather than an agent of the Executive . . . .

Our decisions have always acknowledged that the warrant requirement imposes a burden on law enforcement. And our cases have not questioned that trained professionals normally make reliable assessments of the existence of probable cause to conduct a search. We have repeatedly held, however, that these factors are outweighed by the individual interest in privacy that is protected by advance judicial approval. The Fourth Amendment dictates that the privacy interest is paramount, no matter how marginal the risk of error might be if the legality of warrantless searches were judged only after the fact.

. . . .

[In *Chadwick*, w]e concluded that neither of the justifications for the automobile exception could support a similar exception for luggage. We first held that the privacy interest in luggage is "substantially greater than in an automobile." *Id.*, at 13 . . . .

We then held that the mobility of luggage did not justify creating an additional exception to the Warrant Clause. Unlike an automobile, luggage can easily be seized and detained pending judicial approval of a search . . . .

Two Terms after *Chadwick*, we decided a case in which the relevant facts were identical to those before the Court today. In *Arkansas v. Sanders*, 442 U.S. 753 (1979), the police had probable cause to search a green suitcase that had been placed in the trunk of a taxicab at the Little Rock Airport. Several blocks from the airport, they stopped the cab, arrested the passengers, seized the suitcase and, without obtaining a warrant, opened and searched it.

. . . In his opinion for the Court, JUSTICE POWELL noted that the seizure of the green suitcase was entirely proper, but that the State nevertheless had the burden of justifying the warrantless search, and that it had "failed to carry its burden of demonstrating the need for warrantless searches of luggage properly taken from automobiles." 442 U.S., at 763.

. . . .

We held in *Ross* that "the scope of the warrantless search authorized by [the automobile] exception is no broader and no narrower than a magistrate could legitimately authorize by warrant." *See id.*, at 825. The inherent mobility of the vehicle justified the immediate search without a warrant, but did not affect the scope of the search. *See id.*, at 822. Thus, the search could encompass containers, which might or might not conceal the object of the search, as well as the remainder of the vehicle. *See id.*, at 821.

Our conclusion was supported not only by prior cases defining the proper scope of searches authorized by warrant, as well as cases involving the automobile exception, but also by practical considerations that apply to searches in which the police have only generalized probable cause to believe that contraband is somewhere in a vehicle. We explained that, in such instances, "prohibiting police from opening immediately a container in which the object of the search is most likely to be found and instead forcing them first to comb the entire vehicle would actually exacerbate the intrusion on privacy interests." *Id.*, at 821, n. 28. Indeed, because "the police could never be certain that the contraband was not secreted in a yet undiscovered portion of the vehicle," the most likely result would be that "the vehicle would need to be secured while a warrant was obtained." *Id.*

These concerns that justified our holding in *Ross* are not implicated in cases like *Chadwick* and *Sanders* in which the police have probable cause to search a *particular* container rather than the *entire* vehicle. Because the police can seize the container which is the object of their search, they have no need either to search or to seize the entire vehicle. Indeed, as even the Court today recognizes, they have no authority to do so.

In reaching our conclusion in *Ross*, we therefore did not retreat at all from the holding in either *Chadwick* or *Sanders* . . . .

Thus, we recognized in *Ross* that *Chadwick* and *Sanders* had not created a special rule for container searches, but rather had merely applied the cardinal principle that warrantless searches are *per se* unreasonable unless justified by an exception to the general rule. *Ross* dealt with the scope of the automobile exception; *Chadwick* and *Sanders* were cases in which the exception simply did not apply.

II

In its opinion today, the Court recognizes that the police did not have probable cause to search respondent's vehicle and that a search of anything but the paper bag that respondent had carried from Daza's apartment and placed in the trunk of his car would have been unconstitutional. Moreover, as I read the opinion, the Court assumes that the police could not have made a warrantless inspection of the bag before it was placed in the car. Finally, the Court also does not question the fact that, under our prior cases, it would have been lawful for the police to seize the container and detain it (and respondent) until they obtained a search warrant. Thus, all of the relevant facts that governed our decisions in *Chadwick* and *Sanders* are present here whereas the relevant fact that justified the vehicle search in *Ross* is not present.

The Court does not attempt to identify any exigent circumstances that would justify its refusal to apply the general rule against warrantless searches. Instead, it advances these three arguments: First, the rules identified in the foregoing cases are confusing and anomalous. Second, the rules do not protect any significant interest in privacy. And, third, the rules impede effective law enforcement. None of these arguments withstands scrutiny.

The "Confusion"

In the nine years since *Ross* was decided, the Court has considered three cases in which the police had probable cause to search a particular container and one in which they had probable cause to search two vehicles. The decisions in all four of those cases were perfectly straightforward and provide no evidence of confusion in the state or lower federal courts.

. . . .

To the extent there was any "anomaly" in our prior jurisprudence, the Court has "cured" it at the expense of creating a more serious paradox. For surely it is anomalous to prohibit a search of a briefcase while the owner is carrying it exposed on a public street yet to permit a search once the owner has placed the briefcase in the locked trunk of his car. One's privacy interest in one's luggage can certainly not be diminished by one's removing it from a public thoroughfare and placing it — out of sight — in a privately owned vehicle. Nor is the danger that evidence will escape increased if the luggage is in a car rather than on the street . . . .

The Privacy Argument

The Court's statement that *Chadwick* and *Sanders* provide only "minimal protection to privacy" is also unpersuasive. Every citizen clearly has an interest in the privacy of the contents of his or her luggage, briefcase, handbag or any other container that conceals private papers and effects from public scrutiny. That privacy interest has been recognized repeatedly in cases spanning more than a century.

Under the Court's holding today, the privacy interest that protects the contents of a suitcase or a briefcase from a warrantless search when it is in public view simply vanishes when its owner climbs into a taxicab. Unquestionably the rejection of the *Sanders* line of cases by today's decision will result in a significant loss of individual privacy.

. . . .

The Burden on Law Enforcement

The Court's suggestion that *Chadwick* and *Sanders* have created a significant burden on effective law enforcement is unsupported, inaccurate, and, in any event, an insufficient reason for creating a new exception to the warrant requirement.

Despite repeated claims that *Chadwick* and *Sanders* have "impeded effective law enforcement," the Court cites no authority for its contentions . . . .

. . . .

Even if the warrant requirement does inconvenience the police to some extent, that fact does not distinguish this constitutional requirement from any other procedural protection secured by the Bill of Rights. It is merely a part of the price that our society must pay in order to preserve its freedom . . . .

It is too early to know how much freedom America has lost today. The magnitude of the loss is, however, not nearly as significant as the Court's willingness to inflict it without even a colorable basis for its rejection of prior law.

I respectfully dissent.

Notes and Questions

(1) Justice Stevens, author of the opinion upholding the warrantless search of the paper bag inside the car in *Ross*, dissented in *Acevedo*. He contended that the paper bag inside the car in that case should have been protected by the warrant requirement.

(a) What critical difference did he discern between the two paper bags in *Ross* and *Acevedo*? In his view, why should searches like the one in *Acevedo* be constrained by the warrant process?

(b) Why did the majority reject Justice Stevens's distinction and hold, instead, that the search of the paper bag in *Acevedo* was not governed by the warrant rule? After *Ross* and *Acevedo*, which containers in vehicles are protected by the warrant requirement and which are subject to warrantless search under the automobile doctrine exception?

(2) Is the majority's opinion and conclusion in *Acevedo* consistent with the reasoning and holding of *Chadwick*? For purposes of the Fourth Amendment warrant rule and the policies it serves, how is a container found outside a vehicle distinguishable, in any material way, from a container that is placed inside a vehicle?

If the Court decided to overrule *Chadwick* in a future case, a result suggested by Justice Scalia's concurring opinion, what would be the scope of the remaining warrant rule? Would such a rule be defensible in terms of Fourth Amendment logic and purposes?

(3) In *Wyoming v. Houghton*, 526 U.S. 295, 119 S. Ct. 1297, 143 L. Ed. 2d 408 (1999), the Court held that when there is probable cause to search a vehicle, the automobile exception permits the warrantless search of a *passenger's* personal belongings. The Court rejected Wyoming's conclusion that a container falls "'outside the scope of the'" exception when an "'officer knows or should know that [it] is the personal effect of a passenger who is not suspected of criminal activity.'"

The majority first observed that the Court had already "read the historical evidence to show that the Framers would have regarded as reasonable (if there was probable cause) the warrantless search of containers *within* an automobile." Neither history nor precedent suggests that it makes a difference that the container searched belongs to a passenger. Moreover, "[e]ven if the historical evidence" was "equivocal," extension of the automobile doctrine to a passenger's belongings reflects a proper "balancing of the relative interests."

On the one hand, passengers, like "drivers, possess a reduced expectation of privacy with regard to" property transported in cars which travel public roads, seldom serve as personal repositories, and may be involved in accidents that expose their contents. On the other hand, the "governmental interests at stake are substantial." The inability to search a passenger's belongings would impair effective law enforcement when there is reason to believe contraband or evidence is in a vehicle. The mobility of a vehicle "creates a risk" that such items will be "permanently lost" while a warrant is sought. Criminals would be able to hide contraband in passenger's belongings and thereby thwart law enforcement. The requirement of a specific reason to believe that the object of a search was in a passenger's belongings "would dramatically reduce the ability to find and seize contraband and evidence." Passengers who are in fact confederates in crime might well claim all property as theirs in order to defeat law enforcement. And the practical impact could be a "bog of litigation" over questions of what an officer knew or should have known about the ownership of an item. Consequently, the balance of interests "militate[s] in favor of the needs of law enforcement, and against a personal-privacy interest that is ordinarily weak."

The *Houghton* majority's historical and logical analyses led it to the "sensible rule . . . that . . . a package may be searched, whether or not its owner is present as a passenger or otherwise, because it may contain the contraband that [an] officer has reason to believe is in [a] car." In the process of arriving at this conclusion, the majority did reaffirm the earlier holding in *United States v. Di Re*, 332 U.S. 581, 68 S. Ct. 222, 92 L. Ed. 210 (1948), "that probable cause to search a car [does] not justify a body search of a passenger." According to the Court, the distinction between a passenger's belongings and his or her person turns "on the unique, significantly heightened protection afforded against searches of one's person." Those searches intrude more severely on "personal privacy and . . . personal dignity," effecting "traumatic consequences [that] are not to be expected when the police examine an item of personal property." What remains somewhat unclear is whether all items attached to or carried on or by a person are governed by the holding of *Di Re*. In *Houghton*, the container searched was a purse that belonged to a passenger who was sitting in the front seat of the car. The purse was found on the back seat. Concurring Justice Breyer observed that the search of a passenger's purse that is "attached to her person" might not fall within the automobile doctrine, but might instead be entitled to the "increased protection" afforded by *Di Re*.

Three dissenting Justices would have affirmed the result reached by Wyoming, preferring "a rule requiring a warrant or individualized probable cause to search belongings that are . . . obviously owned by and in the custody of a passenger" because it "is every bit as simple as the Court's rule" and "it simply protects more privacy."

Vehicle and Container Problems

4C–1: On March 27, Officers Jennings and Forbeck were patrolling an area of town where narcotics were frequently used and sold at all times of day or night. On two previous occasions when they were on patrol in the area, the officers had stopped Al, who lived 58 blocks away. Both times Al had been on his bicycle. The first time, around mid-March, the officers had confiscated from Al food stamps that belonged to another person. Officer Jennings had witnessed instances in the neighborhood when food stamps had been illicitly traded for narcotics, alcohol, and other items. After the mid-March stop, Jennings had released Al, but had arrested his companion for possession of narcotics. Around March 20, the officers stopped Al a second time because he had ridden his bicycle through a stop sign without stopping.

On March 27, around 6:45 p.m., Jennings and Forbeck noticed Al once again riding his bike through the area. Forbeck was aware that Al had a history of arrests for narcotics-related offenses. Al once again rode his bicycle through a stop sign without stopping. The officers pulled up next to him and ordered him to stop, but Al continued to ride. As he did so, Al moved his right hand to the right handlebar and used his thumb to push something inside. After traveling another 25 feet, at a spot about 100 feet from the point where he had been told to stop, Al stopped his bicycle.

Forbeck then patted Al down, finding a knife and seizing it. Al became nervous as Jennings began to look closely at his bicycle. Jennings decided to search the bicycle's handlebar by turning the bicycle upside down and tapping on it. Three small rocks of cocaine dropped out. Al was then arrested for possession of narcotics.

Prior to his trial, Al objected to the warrantless search of his bicycle.

Was it reasonable to search the bicycle without a warrant?

4C–2: Leich left Fort Lauderdale on a train bound for New York City. An Amtrak officer grew suspicious of him for various reasons, including the fact that he purchased his ticket with cash just minutes before departure. When the train stopped at Union Station in Washington, D.C., for a 20-minute layover, the sleeper car in which Leich was riding was boarded by two Amtrak officers, a drug-detection dog, and the dog's handler, a D.C. police detective. The dog showed interest but did not "alert" while "sweeping" the corridor. The detective and dog then left the train.

An Amtrak officer initiated contact with Leich, who refused to allow a search of his luggage and compartment but agreed to a dog sniff of his luggage. The dog and detective returned and the luggage was placed in the corridor. The dog alerted to two of the three bags. Leich again denied permission to open the bags, whereupon he was arrested, handcuffed, and removed from the train along with his luggage.

The officers waited on the platform until they could obtain help in moving the luggage to a security office. Leich was handcuffed to a chair. The luggage was placed in the same room, but was clearly put beyond his reach. The officers had planned to secure a warrant. After a federal prosecutor told them that no warrant was needed, however, they conducted a warrantless search of the luggage. They found cash and other incriminating items.

Was the advice of the prosecutor constitutionally sound?

4C–3: On September 9, Wartz was driving in Madison County when he lost control of his vehicle and struck a utility pole. Wartz was severely injured, and his passenger, Megan Solin, died at the scene of the accident as a result of injuries she sustained. Law enforcement officers found a Garmin GPS device somewhere near Wartz's wrecked vehicle. Wartz personally owned the device and kept it inside his vehicle at all times. The device includes preloaded street maps and has the ability to store hundreds of waypoints and locations. The device is also compatible with microSD cards, which are routinely able to store from 16 to 128 gigabytes (GB) of data. In addition, Wartz's device is designed to automatically record and store information such as location, past routes traveled, and speed.

Approximately one week after the accident, law enforcement officers visited Wartz at the hospital and requested consent to examine the content saved in the GPS unit. Wartz, who was under the influence of heavy doses of painkillers, signed a written consent form. The GPS required a pin code to gain access to the information inside the device. Captain Rick Gatt contacted Garmin International, the company that produces the GPS device, and secured the pin code for Wartz's device. He then accessed and collected information from the GPS device, including the route Wartz had traveled and his speed at the time of the accident.

The State charged Wartz with reckless homicide, a Class C felony, and Wartz filed a motion to suppress evidence obtained through the warrantless search of his GPS device. Although the trial judge found that Wartz's condition at the time of the written consent — specifically, the influence of the painkillers on his mind — rendered his consent invalid, he ruled that the search was nonetheless reasonable. Wartz has filed an interlocutory appeal challenging that ruling.

Was the search of the GPS device valid under the "automobile exception" to the search warrant rule?

4C–4: At approximately 2:30 a.m. on October 9, Kelly Conn called the County Sheriff to report that her husband, Kevin Conn, was in her house in violation of a no-contact order. The Sheriff's Office confirmed the existence of the no-contact order and dispatched Sergeant Greg Giverin, Deputy David Mar and Deputy Gary Cura to Kelly's house to arrest Kevin. While the officers were on their way to Kelly's house, she called back and told the Sheriff's Office that Kevin had left her house in a blue Ford Escort and was likely headed to his parents' house at 1199 Grove Road. Giverin and Cura, driving separate vehicles, switched routes and went to 1199 Grove Road to arrest Kevin. At approximately 2:45 a.m., Giverin and Cura arrived at a farm located at 1199 Grove Road. They entered the property on a gravel lane.

Giverin and Cura traveled eastward on the gravel lane for approximately one-quarter mile, until they reached a circular drive. There was a farmhouse on the drive. The officers drove past the house, continuing their search for the Escort. Giverin and Cura drove around on various gravel and dirt pathways that connected the buildings on the farm and eventually found the Escort east of the house and east of a number of outbuildings. The Escort was parked next to a field in some tall weeds, approximately 100 yards away from the house. It was not visible from either a public road or from the circular drive next to the farmhouse. A 4.5 foot high barbed-wire fence surrounded the entire compound, i.e., the house and the outbuildings. The Escort was located inside the fence. A gray conversion van was parked approximately five to six feet away from the Escort, in one-to-two-feet-tall weeds. The van's front tires were flat and the front of it was badly damaged, it did not have license plates, and it was not registered. A month and a half before the date in question, the van had been "totaled" in an accident, and had been towed to the farm.

After first checking the Escort, Giverin looked into the front passenger compartment of the van, but did not find Kevin. The van was completely silent and dark. Giverin opened one of the van's doors and saw a plugged-in cell phone cord. When Giverin called out Kevin's name, Kevin answered. Giverin then drew his weapon, ordered Kevin out of the van, and handcuffed and arrested him. Kevin was dressed in boxer shorts, a t-shirt, and socks. Giverin searched the van, finding a loaded Remington 20-gauge shotgun, three cases of empty beer cans, and a case of full beer cans. It was apparent to Giverin that someone had been living in or was at least sleeping in the van. There were a lot of blankets inside and the back seat was folded down to make a bed. Kevin told Cura that he had gone to the van to sleep.

Was the warrantless search of the van reasonable under the automobile doctrine?

4C–5: At 11:00 p.m., Tony Cado had his malfunctioning minivan towed to a 24-hour tow shop. He inquired about having it towed to Denver, Colorado, a distance of 320 miles. The owner informed Cado that the price for towing the vehicle to Denver would be $750. Cado indicated that he could not pay the price. He made a series of phone calls, then reported that his brother would pay for the towing when the van arrived in Denver. The owner replied that he needed payment up front. Highway Patrolman Bush, who was not in uniform, was in the tow shop at the time. Upon overhearing Cado's discussion with the shop owner, he became suspicious that Cado was engaged in illegal activity. When Bush asked why Cado was in such a hurry, Cado answered that he had "to get back to work." In response to further questions, Cado was unable to tell who he worked for or where he worked.

The owner explained that he would not be able to tow the van that night even if Cado had the money to pay. He indicated that he would prefer to determine if he could repair the van for less than the cost of towing. Cado agreed to that plan. He accompanied the owner to his van while Officer Bush followed. When the owner asked Cado to open the hood, Cado unlocked and opened the door, got inside, closed the door, unlatched the hood, got back out, and relocked the door. Later in the inspection, Cado left the van's door slightly ajar. Officer Bush approached the van to see how Cado would react, whereupon Cado quickly jumped in front of the officer and slammed the door shut. The owner ascertained that the van had minor problems and probably just needed an alternator and a belt. He stated that the cost would be "only a couple hundred dollars." Cado agreed to have the van repaired, offering to bring the keys back in the morning. When the owner responded that he could have the van fixed by morning, Cado handed over the keys and went to find a motel.

Shortly after Cado left, Officer Bush observed through the window of the van that it had been altered to create a three or four-inch space between the ceiling and the shell. He obtained the keys from the owner, opened the van, and immediately smelled marijuana. Bush searched the altered ceiling space and other areas in the van, finding 86 packages of marijuana and three packages of methamphetamine. He then tracked Cado to a motel and arrested him. Cado was charged with possession of narcotics with intent to distribute them.

Was the officer's warrantless search of the minivan reasonable?

4C–6: Officers Real and Herman were conducting surveillance of a residence for suspected drug activity. A week earlier, they had arrested Betty Marco, the woman who lived in the house, for possession of cocaine. They had also arrested a man who was visiting her. At 1:30 a.m., a vehicle that had been parked in front of the residence drove away and made a turn without signaling. The officers stopped the vehicle. Officer Real asked the driver, Rich Lass, for his license and proof of insurance. At the same time, Officer Herman approached the other side of the vehicle and obtained identification from the passenger, Tracy Boysen. After removing her identification from her purse, Boysen placed her purse back on the floorboard of the vehicle.

Because Lass appeared a lot more nervous than most drivers, Real asked him to get out of his vehicle. In response to questions from Real, Lass reported that he and Boysen were coming from visiting Betty Marco. When Officer Real asked Lass if he had any illegal substances on him, Lass responded negatively. He consented to a search of his person, and no illegal substances were found. Real asked Lass if the vehicle was his and, if so, whether he could search it. Lass responded affirmatively to both questions.

When Real informed Herman that Lass had consented to a search of the vehicle, Herman asked Boysen to get out. Boysen reached for her purse to take it with her, but Herman told her to leave it inside the vehicle. Boysen put her purse down and stepped out. Officer Real, who was now inside the passenger compartment, asked Boysen if the purse belonged to her and if he could search it. She replied that her purse was a personal belonging and that she did not want him to search it. Officer Real searched the passenger compartment, finding a crack pipe in the center console ashtray. He then decided to search Boysen's purse, which was sitting on the floorboard in front of the center console. Inside, he found a plastic bag containing off-white nuggets, which were later confirmed to be crack cocaine. Boysen was arrested and charged with possession of cocaine.

Was the search of Boysen's purse reasonable under the "automobile doctrine"?

4C–7: Police Officer Scarlet was on patrol at approximately 1:27 a.m. on July 26 near Frontier Drive when she observed a camper sitting in a commercial parking lot. The front door was wide open, the "landing gear" was down, power cords from the camper were plugged in, and no vehicle was hooked up to it. ("Landing gear" consists of two jacks that are coupled together and motor driven. These jacks lift the front of the trailer so that a vehicle can be backed under the front of and hitched to the camper. Once a vehicle is hitched to the camper, the landing gear jacks are raised to a stowed position for traveling.) Scarlet saw a light flashing around the camper, "like some type of flashlight," so she stopped her vehicle in the middle of the street, turned off the headlights, and watched.

After she saw the door to the camper "shut several times, but keep swinging open," she called for backup. When backup arrived, Scarlet and another officer approached the camper. They could smell a strong odor of marijuana coming from the camper. As the officers approached, Loretta came out of the camper and informed the officers that she was there to check on and secure the camper for her stepfather, Otto. Loretta said that no one else was in the camper, but the officers could hear someone moving around inside. As they again began to approach the camper, the front door slammed shut. Loretta volunteered that Mark was inside the camper. When Loretta, at the officers' request, asked the occupant to "come outside," Otto emerged. The officers arrested him based on an outstanding arrest warrant.

Sergeant Jesse then arrived at the scene. Jesse and Scarlet entered the camper to make sure no one else was inside. According to the officers, they were concerned for their safety. Jesse and Scarlet observed a large shoe box full of marijuana and two zip-lock baggies containing a white substance they believed to be methamphetamine. They seized those items.

The State charged Otto with three drug-related offenses. He moved to suppress the drugs found during the officers' entry. The government claimed that both the exigent circumstances exception and the automobile doctrine justified the warrantless entry.

How should the trial court rule?

4C–8: In February 2003, at 2:49 in the morning, an officer with the Twin Falls Sheriff's Office observed a vehicle traveling approximately 33 mph on the right shoulder of the road. The officer watched as the vehicle stopped and the driver and passenger switched places. The officer activated his overhead lights and called for backup. When the officer made contact with the vehicle, he identified Gibby as the occupant who had moved to the driver's seat. The other occupant, who had been operating the vehicle when the officer first observed it, was a 14-year-old boy. A second officer arrived on the scene with a certified drug dog. The dog was walked around the outside of the vehicle while Gibby and the passenger were still inside. The dog alerted on the passenger-side door.

Following the dog's indication that it detected the odor of controlled substances, the officers removed Gibby and the boy from the vehicle and patted them both down for weapons. Gibby appeared agitated and excited. The officers removed several items from Gibby's jacket, including his wallet, and placed them in a paper bag. They searched the vehicle, but did not discover any drugs. The officers then searched Gibby's wallet and discovered a small baggie containing methamphetamine. They arrested Gibby and charged him with possession of a controlled substance. Prior to trial, he moved to suppress the methamphetamine, claiming that it was the product of an illegal search of his wallet. The trial court ruled that the methamphetamine was found during a warrantless search that fell within the "automobile exception." Gibby has appealed that ruling.

Did the trial court rule correctly? Is there any other basis on which the warrantless search of the wallet might be justified?

4C–9: Officer Burns saw a car driven by Timothy pull away from a residence that was "fairly well known for drug activity." When Burns noticed that the car had no license plates, he pulled it over. Burns knew that in the past individuals who had left the residence were stopped and found to be in possession of drugs. He noticed two young female passengers in Timothy's car, one in the front seat and one in the back seat. Timothy did not have a license with him, but provided a Social Security card and told Burns that he had just purchased the car and had not had a chance to license it. In a computer check, Burns discovered that Timothy had a valid driver's license and that the car had a valid title in a neighboring state. Burns then noticed that the pupils of the two female passengers were quite dilated. From his training as a "Drug Recognition Expert," he concluded that the girls could well be under the influence of narcotics.

Officers Burns summoned a "K-9 unit" to the location. He informed Timothy that he was free to leave, but that his car would have to remain at the scene because it lacked a license. Burns asked if he could search the car, but Timothy refused to give consent. Burns then told him that a drug-sniffing canine was on the way to the scene to check the vehicle for illegal substances. When Timothy got out of the car, Officer Burns noticed a contact lens case protruding from his pocket and asked Timothy "what the case was for." Timothy replied that it was for his "contacts." Burns asked if he could look inside the case, and Timothy handed it to him. Inside, Burns noticed a liquid material with a "white blob" of substance in the center. When Burns tested the substance with a field kit, the result was positive for methamphetamine. He arrested Timothy, placed him in his patrol vehicle, and then removed the passengers from Timothy's car.

The K-9 unit arrived 20 minutes later. The dog alerted to both the driver's seat and dash panel area. Officer Burns then began to search the vehicle. He found no contraband in the areas of the driver's seat or the dash panel, but did discover a purse on the floor of the front passenger side. Inside the purse, he found a glass pipe of the type used to smoke illegal substances and a cell phone. Burns searched through the text messages and contact list in the phone, "looking for drug information such as contacts, different texts back and forth to different people." In past searches of cars for illegal drugs, Burns had found evidence in cell phones. In the phone taken from the purse, Burns found a text message with an attached photograph of Timothy and the front seat passenger having sexual relations. Further examination of the phone's contents revealed additional pictures of the two engaged in sex. Burns also found a digital camera on the back seat floorboard. Inside the camera were more images of Timothy and the young girl having sex and pictures of the girl naked. Timothy was 33 years old; the girl was 15. Burns informed Timothy that he was also under arrest for statutory rape and possession of child pornography.

Did the searches of the car and contents violate the Fourth Amendment?

4C–10: BASE jumping involves parachuting from a fixed object. BASE jumping in a national recreation area is a federal offense. National Park Service rangers discovered Mark Labers and several of his friends in a rented houseboat floating on Lake Powell in Arizona. Ranger Chris Cessna had seen Labers's boat below a cliff known for BASE jumping. Earlier in the day, he had received a report that BASE jumping was occurring in that area. In addition, damp BASE jumping equipment could be seen on the deck of Labers's boat, and the men on the boat seemed nervous and refused to answer the questions Cessna asked when he first approached the boat. Because the rangers suspected that the men were BASE jumping by parachuting from the canyon walls into Lake Powell, they decided to search Labers's houseboat.

During the search, the rangers spotted a video camera. They also found videotapes labeled "Throw Mama from the Plane," "BASE Jump Copy," and "Bungi BASE Jump." According to Cessna, BASE jumpers often videotape their illegal activities. The rangers also discovered and seized undeveloped film, parachutes, helmets, and other equipment. At the end of their search, the rangers arrested all of the men for BASE jumping in violation of federal law. The videotapes and the undeveloped film were taken to headquarters and were viewed seven to 10 days later. They contained additional evidence that Labers and his friends had been involved in illegal BASE jumping.

Prior to their trials, the men moved to suppress the evidence found on the houseboat, claiming that the rangers had violated their Fourth Amendment rights.

How should the trial court rule?

Selected Bibliography

Carol A. Chase, *Cars, Cops, and Crooks: A Reexamination of* Belton *and* Carroll *With an Eye Toward Restoring Fourth Amendment Privacy Protection to Automobiles,* 85 Or. L. Rev. 913 (2006)

Steven G. Davison, *Warrantless Investigative Seizures and Searches of Automobiles and Their Contents and Occupants,* 6 Geo. Mason L. Rev. 1 (1983)

George M. Dery III, *Improbable Cause: The Court's Purposeful Evasion of a Traditional Fourth Amendment Protection in* Wyoming v. Houghton, 50 Case W. Res. L. Rev. 547 (2000)

George M. Dery III, *Missing the Big Picture: The Supreme Court's Willful Blindness to Fourth Amendment Fundamentals in* Florida v. White, 28 Fla. St. U. L. Rev. 71 (2001)

Martin R. Gardner, *Searches and Seizures of Automobiles and Their Contents: Fourth Amendment Considerations in a Post-*Ross *World*, 62 Neb. L. Rev. 1 (1983)

Joseph D. Grano, *Rethinking the Fourth Amendment Warrant Requirement*, 19 Am. Crim. L. Rev. 603 (1982)

Lewis R. Katz, United States v. Ross: *Evolving Standards for Warrantless Searches*, 74 J. Crim. L. & Criminology 172 (1983)

Lewis R. Katz, *The Automobile Exception Transformed: The Rise of a Public Place Exemption to the Warrant Requirement*, 36 Case W. Res. L. Rev. 375 (1985–86)

David E. Steinberg, *The Drive Toward Warrantless Auto Searches: Suggestions From a Back Seat Driver*, 80 B.U. L. Rev. 545 (2000)

James J. Tomkovicz, California v. Acevedo: *The Walls Close in on the Warrant Requirement*, 29 Am. Crim. L. Rev. 1103 (1992)

Eldon D. Wedlock, Jr., *Car 54—How Dare You!: Toward a Unified Theory of Warrantless Automobile Searches*, 75 Marq. L. Rev. 79 (1991)

[D] Inventory Searches

South Dakota v. Opperman

United States Supreme Court

428 U.S. 364, 96 S. Ct. 3092, 49 L. Ed. 2d 1000 (1976)

MR. CHIEF JUSTICE BURGER delivered the opinion of the Court.

. . . .

(1)

Local ordinances prohibit parking in certain areas of downtown Vermillion, S.D., between the hours of 2 a.m. and 6 a.m. During the early morning hours of December 10, 1973, a Vermillion police officer observed respondent's unoccupied vehicle illegally parked in the restricted zone. At approximately 3 a.m., the officer issued an overtime parking ticket and placed it on the car's windshield. The citation warned:

"Vehicles in violation of any parking ordinance may be towed from the area."

At approximately 10 o'clock on the same morning, another officer issued a second ticket for an overtime parking violation. These circumstances were routinely reported to police headquarters, and after the vehicle was inspected, the car was towed to the city impound lot.

From outside the car at the impound lot, a police officer observed a watch on the dashboard and other items of personal property located on the back seat and back floorboard. At the officer's direction, the car door was then unlocked and, using a standard inventory form pursuant to standard police procedures, the officer inventoried the contents of the car, including the contents of the glove compartment which was unlocked. There he found marihuana contained in a plastic bag. All items, including the contraband, were removed to the police department for safekeeping.[1] During the late afternoon of December 10, respondent appeared at the police department to claim his property. The marihuana was retained by police.

Respondent was subsequently arrested on charges of possession of marihuana. His motion to suppress the evidence yielded by the inventory search was denied; he was convicted after a jury trial and sentenced to a fine of $100 and 14 days' incarceration in the county jail . . . .

(2)

This Court has traditionally drawn a distinction between automobiles and homes or offices in relation to the Fourth Amendment . . . .

The reason for this well-settled distinction is twofold. First, the inherent mobility of automobiles creates circumstances of such exigency that, as a practical necessity, rigorous enforcement of the warrant requirement is impossible. But the Court has also upheld warrantless searches where no immediate danger was presented that the car would be removed from the jurisdiction. Besides the element of mobility, less rigorous warrant requirements govern because the expectation of privacy with respect to one's automobile is significantly less than that relating to one's home or office. In discharging their varied responsibilities for ensuring the public safety, law enforcement officials are necessarily brought into frequent contact with automobiles. Most of this contact is distinctly noncriminal in nature. Automobiles, unlike homes, are subjected to pervasive and continuing governmental regulation and controls, including periodic inspection and licensing requirements . . . .

The expectation of privacy as to automobiles is further diminished by the obviously public nature of automobile travel . . . .

In the interests of public safety and as part of what the Court has called "community caretaking functions," *Cady v. Dombrowski*, [413 U.S. 433, 441, 93 S. Ct. 2523,

---

1. At respondent's trial, the officer who conducted the inventory testified as follows:

> "Q. And why did you inventory this car?
> "A. Mainly for safekeeping, because we have had a lot of trouble in the past of people getting into the impound lot and breaking into cars and stealing stuff out of them.
> "Q. Do you know whether the vehicles that were broken into . . . were locked or unlocked?
> "A. Both of them were locked, they would be locked."

In describing the impound lot, the officer stated:

> "A. It's the old county highway yard. It has a wooden fence partially around part of it, and kind of a dilapidated wire fence, a makeshift fence."

2528, 37 L. Ed. 2d 706 (1973)], automobiles are frequently taken into police custody. Vehicle accidents present one such occasion. To permit the uninterrupted flow of traffic and in some circumstances to preserve evidence, disabled or damaged vehicles will often be removed from the highways or streets at the behest of police engaged solely in caretaking and traffic-control activities. Police will also frequently remove and impound automobiles which violate parking ordinances and which thereby jeopardize both the public safety and the efficient movement of vehicular traffic. The authority of police to seize and remove from the streets vehicles impeding traffic or threatening public safety and convenience is beyond challenge.

When vehicles are impounded, local police departments generally follow a routine practice of securing and inventorying the automobiles' contents. These procedures developed in response to three distinct needs: the protection of the owner's property while it remains in police custody; the protection of the police against claims or disputes over lost or stolen property; and the protection of the police from potential danger. The practice has been viewed as essential to respond to incidents of theft or vandalism. In addition, police frequently attempt to determine whether a vehicle has been stolen and thereafter abandoned.

... Applying the Fourth Amendment standard of "reasonableness,"[5] the state courts have overwhelmingly concluded that, even if an inventory is characterized as a "search," the intrusion is constitutionally permissible . . . .

The majority of the Federal Courts of Appeals have likewise sustained inventory procedures as reasonable police intrusions.

. . . .

(3)

. . . .

In applying the reasonableness standard adopted by the Framers, this Court has consistently sustained police intrusions into automobiles impounded or otherwise

---

5. In analyzing the issue of reasonableness *vel non*, the courts have not sought to determine whether a protective inventory was justified by "probable cause." The standard of probable cause is peculiarly related to criminal investigations, not routine, noncriminal procedures. *See generally* Note, *Warrantless Searches and Seizures of Automobiles*, 87 Harv. L. Rev. 835, 850–851 (1974). The probable-cause approach is unhelpful when analysis centers upon the reasonableness of routine administrative caretaking functions, particularly when no claim is made that the protective procedures are a subterfuge for criminal investigations. In view of the noncriminal context of inventory searches, and the inapplicability in such a setting of the requirement of probable cause, courts have held — and quite correctly — that search warrants are not required, linked as the warrant requirement textually is to the probable-cause concept. We have frequently observed that the warrant requirement assures that legal inferences and conclusions as to probable cause will be drawn by a neutral magistrate unrelated to the criminal investigative-enforcement process. With respect to noninvestigative police inventories of automobiles lawfully within governmental custody, however, the policies underlying the warrant requirement, to which Mr. Justice Powell refers, are inapplicable.

in lawful police custody where the process is aimed at securing or protecting the car and its contents. In *Cooper v. California*, [386 U.S. 58, 87 S. Ct. 788, 17 L. Ed. 2d 730 (1967)], the Court upheld the inventory of a car impounded under the authority of a state forfeiture statute. Even though the inventory was conducted in a distinctly criminal setting[7] and carried out a week after the car had been impounded, the Court nonetheless found that the car search, including examination of the glove compartment where contraband was found, was reasonable under the circumstances. This conclusion was reached despite the fact that no warrant had issued and probable cause to search for the contraband in the vehicle had not been established. The Court said in language explicitly applicable here:

> It would be unreasonable to hold that the police, having to retain the car in their custody for such a length of time, had no right, even for their own protection, to search it.

386 U.S., at 61–62, 87 S. Ct. at 791.[8]

In the following Term, the Court in *Harris v. United States*, 390 U.S. 234, 88 S. Ct. 992, 19 L. Ed. 2d 1067 (1968), upheld the introduction of evidence, seized by an officer who, after conducting an inventory search of a car and while taking means to safeguard it, observed a car registration card lying on the metal stripping of the car door. Rejecting the argument that a warrant was necessary, the Court held that the intrusion was justifiable since it was "taken to protect the car while it was in police custody." *Id.*, at 236.

Finally, in *Cady v. Dombrowski, supra*, the Court upheld a warrantless search of an automobile towed to a private garage even though no probable cause existed to believe that the vehicle contained fruits of a crime. The sole justification for the warrantless incursion was that it was incident to the caretaking function of the local police to protect the community's safety. Indeed, the protective search was instituted solely because the local police "were under the impression" that the incapacitated driver, a Chicago police officer, was required to carry his service revolver at all times; the police had reasonable grounds to believe a weapon might be in the car, and thus available to vandals. 413 U.S., at 436, 93 S. Ct. at 2525. The Court carefully noted that the protective search was carried out in accordance with *standard procedures* in the local police department, *ibid.*, a factor tending to ensure that the intrusion would be limited in scope to the extent necessary to carry out the caretaking function.

---

7. In *Cooper*, the owner had been arrested on narcotics charges, and the car was taken into custody pursuant to the state forfeiture statute. The search was conducted several months before the forfeiture proceedings were actually instituted.

8. There was, of course, no certainty at the time of the search that forfeiture proceedings would ever be held. Accordingly, there was no reason for the police to assume automatically that the automobile would eventually be forfeited to the State. Indeed, as the California Court of Appeal stated, "[T]he instant record nowhere discloses that forfeiture proceedings were instituted in respect to defendant's car . . . ." *People v. Cooper*, 234 Cal. App. 2d 587, 596, 44 Cal. Rptr. 483, 489 (1965). No reason would therefore appear to limit *Cooper* to an impoundment pursuant to a forfeiture statute.

. . . .

The Vermillion police were indisputably engaged in a caretaking search of a lawfully impounded automobile. The inventory was conducted only after the car had been impounded for multiple parking violations. The owner, having left his car illegally parked for an extended period, and thus subject to impoundment, was not present to make other arrangements for the safekeeping of his belongings. The inventory itself was prompted by the presence in plain view of a number of valuables inside the car. As in *Cady*, there is no suggestion whatever that this standard procedure, essentially like that followed throughout the country, was a pretext concealing an investigatory police motive.[10]

On this record we conclude that in following standard police procedures, prevailing throughout the country and approved by the overwhelming majority of courts, the conduct of the police was not "unreasonable" under the Fourth Amendment.

The judgment of the South Dakota Supreme Court is therefore reversed, and the case is remanded for further proceedings not inconsistent with this opinion.

Reversed and remanded.

MR. JUSTICE POWELL, concurring.

. . . .

I

. . . .

Except in rare cases, there is little danger associated with impounding unsearched automobiles. But the occasional danger that may exist cannot be discounted entirely. The harmful consequences in those rare cases may be great, and there does not appear to be any effective way of identifying in advance those circumstances or classes of automobile impoundments which represent a greater risk. Society also has an important interest in minimizing the number of false claims filed against police since they may diminish the community's respect for law enforcement generally and lower department morale, thereby impairing the effectiveness of the police.[3] It is not

---

10. The inventory was not unreasonable in scope. Respondent's motion to suppress in state court challenged the inventory only as to items inside the car not in plain view. But once the policeman was lawfully inside the car to secure the personal property in plain view, it was not unreasonable to open the unlocked glove compartment, to which vandals would have had ready and unobstructed access once inside the car. The "consent" theory advanced by the dissent rests on the assumption that the inventory is exclusively for the protection of the car owner. It is not. The protection of the municipality and public officers from claims of lost or stolen property and the protection of the public from vandals who might find a firearm, *Cady v. Dombrowski*, or as here, contraband drugs, are also crucial.

3. The interest in protecting the police from liability for lost or stolen property is not relevant in this case. Respondent's motion to suppress was limited to items inside the automobile not in plain view. And, the Supreme Court of South Dakota here held that the removal of objects in plain view, and the closing of windows and locking of doors, satisfied any duty the police department owed the automobile's owner to protect property in police possession. S.D., 228 N.W.2d 152, 159 (1975).

clear, however, that inventories are a completely effective means of discouraging false claims, since there remains the possibility of accompanying such claims with an assertion that an item was stolen prior to the inventory or was intentionally omitted from the police records.

The protection of the owner's property is a significant interest for both the policeman and the citizen. It is argued that an inventory is not necessary since locked doors and rolled-up windows afford the same protection that the contents of a parked automobile normally enjoy. But many owners might leave valuables in their automobile temporarily that they would not leave there unattended for the several days that police custody may last. There is thus a substantial gain in security if automobiles are inventoried and valuable items removed for storage. And, while the same security could be attained by posting a guard at the storage lot, that alternative may be prohibitively expensive, especially for smaller jurisdictions.

Against these interests must be weighed the citizen's interest in the privacy of the contents of his automobile. Although the expectation of privacy in an automobile is significantly less than the traditional expectation of privacy associated with the home, the unrestrained search of an automobile and its contents would constitute a serious intrusion upon the privacy of the individual in many circumstances. But such a search is not at issue in this case. As the Court's opinion emphasizes, the search here was limited to an inventory of the unoccupied automobile and was conducted strictly in accord with the regulations of the Vermillion Police Department. Upholding searches of this type provides no general license for the police to examine all the contents of such automobiles.

I agree with the Court that the Constitution permits routine inventory searches, and turn next to the question whether they must be conducted pursuant to a warrant.

II

. . . .

The routine inventory search under consideration in this case does not fall within any of the established exceptions to the warrant requirement. But examination of the interests which are protected when searches are conditioned on warrants issued by a judicial officer reveals that none of these is implicated here. A warrant may issue only upon "probable cause." In the criminal context the requirement of a warrant protects the individual's legitimate expectation of privacy against the overzealous police officer . . . .

A related purpose of the warrant requirement is to prevent hindsight from affecting the evaluation of the reasonableness of a search. In the case of an inventory search conducted in accordance with standard police department procedures, there is no significant danger of hindsight justification. The absence of a warrant will not impair the effectiveness of post-search review of the reasonableness of a particular inventory search.

. . . .

In sum, I agree with the Court that the routine inventory search in this case is constitutional.

Mr. Justice Marshall, with whom Mr. Justice Brennan and Mr. Justice Stewart join, dissenting.

. . . .

To begin with, the Court appears to suggest by reference to a "diminished" expectation of privacy that a person's constitutional interest in protecting the integrity of closed compartments of his locked automobile may routinely be sacrificed to governmental interests requiring interference with that privacy that are less compelling than would be necessary to justify a search of similar scope of the person's home or office. This has never been the law . . . .

The Court's opinion appears to suggest that its result may in any event be justified because the inventory search procedure is a "reasonable" response to

> three distinct needs: the protection of the owner's property while it remains in police custody . . . ; the protection of the police against claims or disputes over lost or stolen property . . . ; and the protection of the police from potential danger.

This suggestion is flagrantly misleading, however, because the record of this case explicitly belies any relevance of the last two concerns. In any event it is my view that none of these "needs," separately or together, can suffice to justify the inventory search procedure approved by the Court.

First, this search cannot be justified in any way as a safety measure, for — though the Court ignores it — the sole purpose given by the State for the Vermillion police's inventory procedure was to secure *valuables*. Nor is there any indication that the officer's search in this case was tailored in any way to safety concerns, or that ordinarily it is so circumscribed. Even aside from the actual basis for the police practice in this case, however, I do not believe that any blanket safety argument could justify a program of routine searches of the scope permitted here. As Mr. Justice Powell recognizes, ordinarily "there is little danger associated with impounding unsearched automobiles."[8] Thus, while the safety rationale may not be entirely discounted when it is actually relied upon, it surely cannot justify the search of every car upon the basis of

---

8. The very premise of the State's chief argument, that the cars must be searched in order to protect valuables because no guard is posted around the vehicles, itself belies the argument that they must be searched at the city lot in order to protect the police there. These circumstances alone suffice to distinguish the dicta from *Cooper v. California*, 386 U.S., at 61–62, 87 S. Ct. at 791, recited by the Court. The Court suggests a further "crucial" justification for the search in this case: "protection of the *public* from vandals who might find a firearm, *Cady v. Dombrowski*, [413 U.S. 433, 93 S. Ct. 2523, 37 L. Ed. 2d 706 (1973)], or as here, contraband drugs" (emphasis added). This rationale, too, is absolutely without support in this record. There is simply no indication the police were looking for dangerous items. Indeed, even though the police found shotgun shells in the interior of

undifferentiated possibility of harm; on the contrary, such an intrusion could ordinarily be justified only in those individual cases where the officer's inspection was prompted by specific circumstances indicating the possibility of a particular danger.

Second, the Court suggests that the search for valuables in the closed glove compartment might be justified as a measure to protect the police against lost property claims. Again, this suggestion is belied by the record, since — although the Court declines to discuss it — the South Dakota Supreme Court's interpretation of state law explicitly absolves the police, as "gratuitous depositors," from any obligation beyond inventorying objects in plain view and locking the car. 228 N.W.2d 152, 159 (1975). Moreover, as MR. JUSTICE POWELL notes, it may well be doubted that an inventory procedure would in any event work significantly to minimize the frustrations of false claims.

Finally, the Court suggests that the public interest in protecting valuables that may be found inside a closed compartment of an impounded car may justify the inventory procedure. I recognize the genuineness of this governmental interest in protecting property from pilferage. But even if I assume that the posting of a guard would be fiscally impossible as an alternative means to the same protective end, I cannot agree with the Court's conclusion. The Court's result authorizes — indeed it appears to require — the routine search of nearly every[12] car impounded. In my view, the Constitution does not permit such searches as a matter of routine; absent specific consent, such a search is permissible only in exceptional circumstances of particular necessity.

It is at least clear that any owner might prohibit the police from executing a protective search of his impounded car, since by hypothesis the inventory is conducted for the owner's benefit. Moreover, it is obvious that not everyone whose car is impounded would want it to be searched. Respondent himself proves this; but one need not carry contraband to prefer that the police not examine one's private possessions. Indeed, that preference is the premise of the Fourth Amendment. Nevertheless, according to the Court's result the law may presume that each owner in respondent's

---

the car, they never opened the trunk to determine whether it might contain a shotgun. Aside from this, the suggestion is simply untenable as a matter of law. If this asserted rationale justifies search of all impounded automobiles, it must logically also justify the search of *all* automobiles, whether impounded or not, located in a similar area, for the argument is not based upon the custodial role of the police. But this Court has never permitted the search of any car or home on the mere undifferentiated assumption that it might be vandalized and the vandals might find dangerous weapons or substances. Certainly *Cady v. Dombrowski*, permitting a limited search of a wrecked automobile where, *inter alia*, the police had a reasonable belief that the car contained a specific firearm, does not so hold.

12. The Court makes clear that the police may not proceed to search an impounded car if the owner is able to make other arrangements for the safekeeping of his belongings. Additionally, while the Court does not require consent before a search, it does not hold that the police may proceed with such a search in the face of the owner's denial of permission. In my view, if the owner of the vehicle is in police custody or otherwise in communication with the police, his consent to the inventory is prerequisite to an inventory search.

position consents to the search. I cannot agree. In my view, the Court's approach is squarely contrary to the law of consent; it ignores the duty, in the absence of consent, to analyze in each individual case whether there is a need to search a particular car for the protection of its owner which is sufficient to outweigh the particular invasion. It is clear to me under established principles that in order to override the absence of explicit consent, such a search must at least be conditioned upon the fulfillment of two requirements. First, there must be specific cause to believe that a search of the scope to be undertaken is necessary in order to preserve the integrity of particular valuable property threatened by the impoundment . . . . Second, even where a search might be appropriate, such an intrusion may only follow the exhaustion and failure of reasonable efforts under the circumstances to identify and reach the owner of the property in order to facilitate alternative means of security or to obtain his consent to the search, for in this context the right to refuse the search remains with the owner.[16]

Because the record in this case shows that the procedures followed by the Vermillion police in searching respondent's car fall far short of these standards, in my view the search was impermissible and its fruits must be suppressed . . . .

The Court's result in this case elevates the conservation of property interests — indeed mere possibilities of property interests — above the privacy and security interests protected by the Fourth Amendment. For this reason I dissent . . . .

Statement of Mr. Justice White.

Although I do not subscribe to all of my Brother Marshall's dissenting opinion, particularly some aspects of his discussion concerning the necessity for obtaining the consent of the car owner, I agree with most of his analysis and conclusions and consequently dissent from the judgment of the Court.

Notes and Questions

(1) The majority opinion in *Opperman* intimates that "inventories" might not be "searches" at all. Indeed, some lower courts have concluded that they are not. *See, e.g., People v. Sullivan*, 29 N.Y.2d 69, 272 N.E.2d 464 (1971); *People v. Willis*, 46 Mich. App. 436, 208 N.W.2d 204 (1973). What reasoning would suggest that inventories are not searches subject to Fourth Amendment regulation? What Fourth Amendment principles suggest the contrary?

(2) The majority assumes that inventories are searches and then declares that such searches can be reasonable, despite the absence of both probable cause and a search

---

16. Additionally, although not relevant on this record, since the inventory procedure is premised upon benefit to the owner, it cannot be executed in any case in which there is reason to believe the owner would prefer to forgo it. This principle, which is fully consistent with the Court's result today, requires, for example, that when the police harbor suspicions (amounting to less than probable cause) that evidence or contraband may be found inside the automobile, they may not inventory it, for they must presume that the owner would refuse to permit the search.

warrant. What showing is necessary to justify an inventory search of a vehicle? Why does that showing render the search reasonable under the Fourth Amendment?

(3) Assuming that officers may inventory a vehicle, what are the limits upon the breadth of their inventory? For example, may they look under seats? In a locked glove compartment? In the trunk? Behind door panels and within the interior lining of the roof?

(4) If it is lawful to inventory every automobile taken into custody in certain circumstances, is it equally lawful to inventory two out of every three? Every fifth vehicle? Every vehicle that the impounding officer has time to inventory?

(5) On remand, the South Dakota Supreme Court held that the inventory in *Opperman* was impermissible under the state's constitutional counterpart of the Fourth Amendment. *State v. Opperman*, 247 N.W.2d 673 (S.D. 1976). Despite the fact that the language of the state provision was "almost identical to that found in the Fourth Amendment," the South Dakota Court concluded that the state guarantee requires noninvestigative inventories to be "restricted to safeguarding those articles which are within plain view of the officer's vision." *Id.* at 674–75.

Illinois v. Lafayette
United States Supreme Court
462 U.S. 640, 103 S. Ct. 2605, 77 L. Ed. 2d 65 (1983)

CHIEF JUSTICE BURGER delivered the opinion of the Court.

. . . .

I

On September 1, 1980, at about 10 p.m., Officer Maurice Mietzner of the Kankakee City Police arrived at the Town Cinema in Kankakee, Illinois, in response to a call about a disturbance. There he found respondent involved in an altercation with the theatre manager. He arrested respondent for disturbing the peace, handcuffed him, and took him to the police station. Respondent carried a purse-type shoulder bag on the trip to the station.

At the police station respondent was taken to the booking room; there, Officer Mietzner removed the handcuffs from respondent and ordered him to empty his pockets and place the contents on the counter. After doing so, respondent took a package of cigarettes from his shoulder bag and placed the bag on the counter. Mietzner then removed the contents of the bag, and found ten amphetamine pills inside a cigarette case package.

Respondent was subsequently charged with violating . . . the Illinois Controlled Substances Act on the basis of the controlled substances found in his shoulder bag.

. . . .

II

The question here is whether, consistent with the Fourth Amendment, it is reasonable for police to search the personal effects of a person under lawful arrest as part of the routine administrative procedure at a police stationhouse incident to booking and jailing the suspect. The justification for such searches does not rest on probable cause, and hence the absence of a warrant is immaterial to the reasonableness of the search . . . .

A so-called inventory search is not an independent legal concept but rather an incidental administrative step following arrest and preceding incarceration. To determine whether the search of respondent's shoulder bag was unreasonable we must "balanc[e] its intrusion on the individual's Fourth Amendment interests against its promotion of legitimate governmental interests." *Delaware v. Prouse*, 440 U.S. 648, 654, 99 S. Ct. 1391, 1396, 59 L. Ed. 2d 660 (1979).

In order to see an inventory search in proper perspective, it is necessary to study the evolution of interests along the continuum from arrest to incarceration. We have held that immediately upon arrest an officer may lawfully search the person of an arrestee, *United States v. Robinson*, 414 U.S. 218, 94 S. Ct. 467, 38 L. Ed. 2d 427 (1973); he may also search the area within the arrestee's immediate control, *Chimel v. California*, 395 U.S. 752, 89 S. Ct. 2034, 23 L. Ed. 2d 685 (1969) . . . .

An arrested person is not invariably taken to a police station or confined; if an arrestee is taken to the police station, that is no more than a continuation of the custody inherent in the arrest status. Nonetheless, the factors justifying a search of the person and personal effects of an arrestee upon reaching a police station but prior to being placed in confinement are somewhat different from the factors justifying an immediate search at the time and place of arrest.

The governmental interests underlying a stationhouse search of the arrestee's person and possessions may in some circumstances be even greater than those supporting a search immediately following arrest. Consequently, the scope of a stationhouse search will often vary from that made at the time of arrest. Police conduct that would be impractical or unreasonable—or embarrassingly intrusive—on the street can more readily—and privately—be performed at the station. For example, the interests supporting a search incident to arrest would hardly justify disrobing an arrestee on the street, but the practical necessities of routine jail administration may even justify taking a prisoner's clothes before confining him, although that step would be rare . . . .

At the stationhouse, it is entirely proper for police to remove and list or inventory property found on the person or in the possession of an arrested person who is to be jailed. A range of governmental interests support an inventory process. It is not unheard of for persons employed in police activities to steal property taken from arrested persons; similarly, arrested persons have been known to make false claims regarding what was taken from their possession at the stationhouse. A standardized procedure for making a list or inventory as soon as reasonable after reaching the stationhouse not only deters false claims but also inhibits theft or careless handling of articles taken from the arrested person. Arrested persons have also been known to injure themselves — or others — with belts, knives, drugs or other items on their person while being detained. Dangerous instrumentalities — such as razor blades, bombs, or weapons — can be concealed in innocent-looking articles taken from the arrestee's possession. The bare recital of these mundane realities justifies reasonable measures by police to limit these risks — either while the items are in police possession or at the time they are returned to the arrestee upon his release. Examining all the items removed from the arrestee's person or possession and listing or inventorying them is an entirely reasonable administrative procedure. It is immaterial whether the police actually fear any particular package or container; the need to protect against such risks arises independent of a particular officer's subjective concerns. *See United States v. Robinson, supra*, 414 U.S., at 235, 94 S. Ct., at 476–477. Finally, inspection of an arrestee's personal property may assist the police in ascertaining or verifying his identity. *See* 2 W. LaFave, Search and Seizure § 5.3, at 306–307 (1978). In short, every consideration of orderly police administration benefiting both police and the public points toward the appropriateness of the examination of respondent's shoulder bag prior to his incarceration.

. . . .

The Illinois court held that the search of respondent's shoulder bag was unreasonable because "preservation of the defendant's property and protection of police from claims of lost or stolen property, 'could have been achieved in a less intrusive manner.' For example, . . . the defendant's shoulder bag could easily have been secured by sealing it within a plastic bag or box and placing it in a secured locker." 99 Ill. App. 3d, at 835, 55 Ill. Dec., at 213, 425 N.E.2d, at 1386 (citation omitted). Perhaps so, but the real question is not what "could have been achieved," but whether the Fourth Amendment requires such steps; it is not our function to write a manual on administering routine, neutral procedures of the stationhouse. Our role is to assure against violations of the Constitution.

The reasonableness of any particular governmental activity does not necessarily or invariably turn on the existence of alternative "less intrusive" means . . . . We are hardly in a position to second-guess police departments as to what practical administrative method will best deter theft by and false claims against its employees and preserve the security of the stationhouse. It is evident that a stationhouse search of every item carried on or by a person who has lawfully been taken into custody by the police will amply serve the important and legitimate governmental interests involved.

Even if less intrusive means existed of protecting some particular types of property, it would be unreasonable to expect police officers in the everyday course of business to make fine and subtle distinctions in deciding which containers or items may be searched and which must be sealed as a unit . . . .

Applying these principles, we hold that it is not "unreasonable" for police, as part of the routine procedure incident to incarcerating an arrested person, to search any container or article in his possession, in accordance with established inventory procedures.[3]

The judgment of the Illinois Appellate Court is reversed and the case is remanded for proceedings not inconsistent with this opinion.

It is so ordered.

Justice Marshall, with whom Justice Brennan joins, concurring in the judgment.

I agree that the police do not need a warrant or probable cause to conduct an inventory search prior to incarcerating a suspect, and I therefore concur in the judgment. The practical necessities of securing persons and property in a jailhouse setting justify an inventory search as part of the standard procedure incident to incarceration.

A very different case would be presented if the State had relied solely on the fact of arrest to justify the search of respondent's shoulder bag. A warrantless search incident to arrest must be justified by a need to remove weapons or prevent the destruction of evidence . . . .

Notes and Questions

(1) Unlike *Opperman*, *Lafayette* dealt with an "inventory" of a person who had been arrested and taken to the police station. What showing is essential for a lawful inventory of an arrestee? Upon making such a showing, what areas may an officer search? How is that search distinguishable from a lawful search incident to an arrest under the *Chimel-Robinson* doctrine?

(2) Lafayette claimed that the government should be required to secure an arrestee's belongings without looking inside of them. What constitutional bases supported that claim? Why did the Court reject the contention? For an opinion concluding that a state constitutional guarantee against unreasonable searches and seizures places greater restrictions upon inventories of arrestees' belongings, see *State v. Perham*, 814 P.2d 914 (Haw. 1991).

(3) Two relatively recent, and highly controversial, Supreme Court rulings highlight additional intrusions upon privacy that, in some circumstances, are constitutionally reasonable following arrests. Like inventories, these intrusions are permissible without search warrants, without probable cause to search, and, indeed, without any individualized, articulable suspicion that they will serve government interests. The aggregate interests served by allowing all detainees or arrestees to be searched have been deemed sufficient to justify the privacy invasions.

(a) In *Florence v. Board of Chosen Freeholders of County of Burlington*, 566 U.S. ____, 132 S. Ct. 1510, 182 L. Ed. 2d 566 (2012), the issue was whether the Fourth Amendment allows prison authorities to require individuals arrested and detained

---

3. The record is unclear as to whether respondent was to have been incarcerated after being booked for disturbing the peace. That is an appropriate inquiry on remand.

for minor offenses "to remove their clothing and expose the most private areas of their bodies to close visual inspection as a routine part of the [jail] intake process." In a civil suit challenging this practice, the petitioner claimed that "officials could conduct this kind of search only if they had reason to suspect a particular inmate of concealing . . . contraband." A five-Justice majority upheld the routine searches, rejecting the contention that individualized suspicion was necessary.

In an opinion authored by Justice Kennedy, the majority stressed "the importance of deference to correctional officials" who are charged with maintaining the safety and security of their facilities. Courts should intervene only when there is "'substantial evidence'" indicating that "'officials have exaggerated their response'" to the "undoubted security imperatives involved in jail supervision"—in particular, the interest in detecting and deterring the introduction of contraband into jail facilities. According to the majority, close visual inspections of the naked bodies of all inmates are reasonable because "[t]here is a substantial interest in preventing any new inmate, either of his own will or as a result of coercion, from putting all who live or work at [correctional] institutions at . . . risk when he is admitted to the general population." Moreover, for every detainee admitted into the general population, routine visual inspections of areas beneath male genitals (accomplished by having the inmate lift his genitals) and of body cavities are also permissible. The Court deemed it "reasonable . . . for correctional officials to conclude" that a standard exempting "a new detainee who has not been arrested for a serious crime or for any offense involving a weapon or drugs" from such "invasive steps" would not be workable. First, "the seriousness of an offense is a poor predictor of who has contraband." In addition, such a case-by-case standard would undermine the "'essential interest in readily administrable rules'" because "it would be difficult in practice to determine whether individual detainees fall within" such an "exemption."

The majority highlighted the limits of its ruling and the questions not being resolved in *Florence*. The holding did not encompass searches of detainees who were held "without assignment to the general jail population and without substantial contact with other detainees." Moreover, there was no need "to consider" whether there should be "a narrow exception . . . which might restrict whether an arrestee whose detention has not yet been reviewed by a . . . judicial officer, and who can be held in available facilities removed from the general population, may be subjected to the types of searches" approved in *Florence*. Finally, the case did not address "intentional humiliation or other abusive practices" by officers or "searches that involve the touching of detainees."

Justice Breyer's dissent, joined by Justices Ginsburg, Sotomayor, and Kagan, asserted that an intrusive strip search of the sort involved in the case is unreasonable if "an individual" has been "arrested for a minor offense that does not involve drugs or violence . . . unless prison authorities have reasonable suspicion to believe that the individual possesses drugs or other contraband."

(b) One year after *Florence*, in *Maryland v. King*, 569 U.S. _____, 133 S. Ct. 1958, 186 L. Ed. 2d 1 (2013), another five-Justice majority held that "[w]hen officers make an arrest supported by probable cause to hold for a serious offense and they bring the suspect to the station to be detained in custody, taking and analyzing a cheek swab of the arrestee's DNA is, like fingerprinting and photographing, a legitimate police booking procedure that is reasonable under the Fourth Amendment." The procedure was deemed a reasonable search in the absence of either a warrant or any individualized suspicion about the person tested.

The majority reached this conclusion by balancing the intrusiveness of the testing procedure against the interests it served. The search of the human body involved in a "buccal swab" of the arrestee's cheek to obtain a DNA sample was characterized as "negligible," "minimal," and "brief." Moreover, the privacy intrusion occasioned by the analysis of the sample was limited by the fact that the analysis conducted could not reveal genetic information and that the relevant statute allowed the collection and storage only of records relating to identifying individuals. The majority asserted that DNA testing of this sort serves "significant state interests" — "identifying [the arrestee] not only so that the proper name can be attached to his charges but also so that the criminal justice system can make informed decisions concerning pretrial custody." According to the majority, "the interest served by the Maryland DNA Collection Act" was "well established: the need for law enforcement officers in a safe and accurate way to process and identify the persons and possessions they must take into custody." It was "beyond dispute that 'probable cause provides legal justification'" not only to arrest a person, but also "'for a brief period of detention to take the administrative steps incident to arrest.'" When officers have probable cause "to remove an individual from the normal channels of society and hold him in legal custody, DNA identification plays a critical role in serving . . . interests" that are sufficiently weighty to render the limited intrusion occasioned by DNA testing reasonable.

It bears mention that the Court's holding was limited to DNA testing of individuals arrested and held for *serious* offenses. At one point in his reasoning, Justice Kennedy stressed the significance of the fact that an arrestee subjected to the procedure was "already in valid police custody for a serious offense supported by probable cause." The majority, however, did not specify what constituted a serious offense. Maryland authorized the DNA testing only for those arrested for the commission or attempted commission of crimes of violence — "murder, rape, first-degree assault, kidnapping, arson, sexual assault, and a variety of other serious crimes" — or for burglaries or attempted burglaries.

In a dissent joined by three other Justices, Justice Scalia pointedly challenged the majority's conclusion that the DNA testing at issue promoted "identification" of arrestees. In the dissent's view, the searches involved clearly served "'crime detection'" purposes, not "'special needs.'" Because the Fourth Amendment does not allow suspicionless searches that serve such investigatory purposes, the suspicionless DNA testing in *King* was constitutionally forbidden.

Colorado v. Bertine

United States Supreme Court

479 U.S. 367, 107 S. Ct. 738, 93 L. Ed. 2d 739 (1987)

CHIEF JUSTICE REHNQUIST delivered the opinion of the Court.

On February 10, 1984, a police officer in Boulder, Colorado arrested respondent Steven Lee Bertine for driving while under the influence of alcohol. After Bertine was taken into custody and before the arrival of a tow truck to take Bertine's van to an impoundment lot, a backup officer inventoried the contents of the van. The officer opened a closed backpack in which he found controlled substances, cocaine paraphernalia, and a large amount of cash. Bertine was subsequently charged with driving while under the influence of alcohol, unlawful possession of cocaine with intent to dispense, sell, and distribute, and unlawful possession of methaqualone. We are asked to decide whether the Fourth Amendment prohibits the State from proving these charges with the evidence discovered during the inventory of Bertine's van. We hold that it does not.

The backup officer inventoried the van in accordance with local police procedures, which require a detailed inspection and inventory of impounded vehicles. He found the backpack directly behind the front seat of the van. Inside the pack, the officer observed a nylon bag containing metal canisters. Opening the canisters, the officer discovered that they contained cocaine, methaqualone tablets, cocaine paraphernalia, and $700 in cash. In an outside zippered pouch of the backpack, he also found $210 in cash in a sealed envelope. After completing the inventory of the van, the officer had the van towed to an impound lot and brought the backpack, money, and contraband to the police station.

. . . .

In *Opperman*, this Court assessed the reasonableness of an inventory search of the glove compartment in an abandoned automobile impounded by the police. We found that inventory procedures serve to protect an owner's property while it is in the custody of the police, to insure against claims of lost, stolen, or vandalized property, and to guard the police from danger. In light of these strong governmental interests and the diminished expectation of privacy in an automobile, we upheld the search . . . .

In our more recent decision, *Lafayette*, a police officer conducted an inventory search of the contents of a shoulder bag in the possession of an individual being taken into custody. In deciding whether this search was reasonable, we recognized that the search served legitimate governmental interests similar to those identified in *Opperman* . . . .

In the present case, as in *Opperman* and *Lafayette*, there was no showing that the police, who were following standardized procedures, acted in bad faith or for the sole purpose of investigation. In addition, the governmental interests justifying the inventory searches in *Opperman* and *Lafayette* are nearly the same as those which obtain here. In each case, the police were potentially responsible for the property taken into their custody. By securing the property, the police protected the property from unauthorized interference. Knowledge of the precise nature of the property helped guard against claims of theft, vandalism, or negligence. Such knowledge also helped to avert any danger to police or others that may have been posed by the property.

The Supreme Court of Colorado opined that *Lafayette* was not controlling here because there was no danger of introducing contraband or weapons into a jail facility. Our opinion in *Lafayette*, however, did not suggest that the stationhouse setting of the inventory search was critical to our holding in that case. Both in the present case and in *Lafayette*, the common governmental interests described above were served by the inventory searches.

The Supreme Court of Colorado also expressed the view that the search in this case was unreasonable because Bertine's van was towed to a secure, lighted facility and because Bertine himself could have been offered the opportunity to make other arrangements for the safekeeping of his property. But the security of the storage facility does not completely eliminate the need for inventorying; the police may still wish to protect themselves or the owners of the lot against false claims of theft or dangerous instrumentalities. And while giving Bertine an opportunity to make alternate arrangements would undoubtedly have been possible, we said in *Lafayette*:

> "[t]he real question is not what 'could have been achieved,' but whether the Fourth Amendment *requires* such steps . . . . The reasonableness of any particular governmental activity does not necessarily or invariably turn on the existence of alternative 'less intrusive' means." *Lafayette*, 462 U.S., at 647, 103 S. Ct., at 2610 (emphasis in original).

We conclude that here, as in *Lafayette*, reasonable police regulations relating to inventory procedures administered in good faith satisfy the Fourth Amendment, even though courts might as a matter of hindsight be able to devise equally reasonable rules requiring a different procedure.

The Supreme Court of Colorado also thought it necessary to require that police, before inventorying a container, weigh the strength of the individual's privacy interest in the container against the possibility that the container might serve as a repository for dangerous or valuable items. We think that such a requirement is contrary to our decisions in *Opperman* and *Lafayette*, and by analogy to our decision in *United States v. Ross*, 456 U.S. 798, 102 S. Ct. 2157, 72 L. Ed. 2d 572 (1982) . . . .

" '[A] . . . single familiar standard is essential to guide police officers, who have only limited time and expertise to reflect on and balance the social and individual interests involved in the specific circumstances they confront.' " *Lafayette, supra*, 462 U.S., at 648, 103 S. Ct., at 2610 (quoting *New York v. Belton*, 453 U.S. 454, 458, 101 S. Ct. 2860, 2863, 69 L. Ed. 2d 768 (1981)).

Bertine finally argues that the inventory search of his van was unconstitutional because departmental regulations gave the police officers discretion to choose between impounding his van and parking and locking it in a public parking place. The Supreme Court of Colorado did not rely on this argument in reaching its conclusion, and we reject it. Nothing in *Opperman* or *Lafayette* prohibits the exercise of police discretion so long as that discretion is exercised according to standard criteria and on the basis of something other than suspicion of evidence of criminal activity. Here, the discretion afforded the Boulder police was exercised in light of standardized criteria, related to the feasibility and appropriateness of parking and locking a vehicle rather than impounding it.[7] There was no showing that the police chose to impound Bertine's van in order to investigate suspected criminal activity.

While both *Opperman* and *Lafayette* are distinguishable from the present case on their facts, we think that the principles enunciated in those cases govern the present one. The judgment of the Supreme Court of Colorado is therefore.

Reversed.

Justice Blackmun, with whom Justice Powell and Justice O'Connor join, concurring.

... I join the Court's opinion, but write separately to underscore the importance of having such inventories conducted only pursuant to standardized police procedures .... [I]t is permissible for police officers to open closed containers in an inventory search only if they are following standard police procedures that mandate the opening of such containers in every impounded vehicle. As the Court emphasizes, the trial court in this case found that the police department's standard procedures did mandate the opening of closed containers and the listing of their contents.

Justice Marshall, with whom Justice Brennan joins, dissenting.

... This search — it cannot legitimately be labeled an inventory — was unreasonable and violated the Fourth Amendment ....

I

As the Court acknowledges, inventory searches are reasonable only if conducted according to standardized procedures ....

The Court today attempts to evade these clear prohibitions on unfettered police discretion by declaring that "the discretion afforded the Boulder police was exercised in light of standardized criteria, related to the feasibility and appropriateness of parking and locking a vehicle rather than impounding it." This vital assertion is flatly contradicted by the record in this case ....

Indeed, the record indicates that no standardized criteria limit a Boulder police officer's discretion. According to a departmental directive, after placing a driver under arrest, an officer has three options for disposing of the vehicle. First, he can

---

7. In arguing that the Boulder Police Department procedures set forth no standardized criteria guiding an officer's decision to impound a vehicle, the dissent selectively quotes from the police directive concerning the care and security of vehicles taken into police custody. The dissent fails to mention that the directive establishes several conditions that must be met before an officer may pursue the park and lock alternative. For example, police may not park and lock the vehicle where there is reasonable risk of damage or vandalism to the vehicle or where the approval of the arrestee cannot be obtained. Not only do such conditions circumscribe the discretion of individual officers, but they also protect the vehicle and its contents and minimize claims of property loss.

allow a third party to take custody. Second, the officer or the driver (depending on the nature of the arrest) may take the car to the nearest public parking facility, lock it, and take the keys. Finally, the officer can do what was done in this case: impound the vehicle, and search and inventory its contents, including closed containers.

. . . .

Once a Boulder police officer has made this initial completely discretionary decision to impound a vehicle, he is given little guidance as to which areas to search and what sort of items to inventory . . . . In application, these so-called procedures left the breadth of the "inventory" to the whim of the individual police officer . . . .

. . . Standardized procedures are necessary to ensure that this narrow exception is not improperly used to justify, after the fact, a warrantless investigative foray. Accordingly, to invalidate a search that is conducted without established procedures, it is not necessary to establish that the police actually acted in bad faith, or that the inventory was in fact a "pretext." By allowing the police unfettered discretion, Boulder's discretionary scheme, like the random spot checks in *Delaware v. Prouse*, is unreasonable because of the "'grave danger' of abuse of discretion." 440 U.S., at 662, 99 S. Ct., at 1400.

II

. . . .

A

The Court greatly overstates the justifications for the inventory exception to the Fourth Amendment . . . .

The protection-against-claims interest did not justify the inventory search either in *Opperman, see* 428 U.S., at 378, n. 3, 96 S. Ct., at n. 3 (POWELL, J., concurring), or in this case. As the majority apparently concedes, the use of secure impoundment facilities effectively eliminates this concern. As to false claims, "inventories are [not] a completely effective means of discouraging false claims, since there remains the possibility of accompanying such claims with an assertion that an item was stolen prior to the inventory or was intentionally omitted from the police records." 428 U.S., at 378–379, 96 S. Ct., at 3101–3102 (Powell, J., concurring).

. . . .

The third interest — protecting the police from potential danger — failed to receive the endorsement of a majority of the Court in *Opperman* . . . . Not only is protecting the police from dangerous instrumentalities an attenuated justification for most automobile inventory searches, but opening closed containers to inventory the contents can only increase the risk . . . .

Thus, only the government's interest in protecting the owner's property actually justifies an inventory search of an impounded vehicle. *See* 428 U.S., at 379, 96 S. Ct., at 3102 (Powell, J., concurring); *id.*, at 391, 96 S. Ct., at 3108 (Marshall, J., dissenting). While I continue to believe that preservation of property does not outweigh the privacy and security interests protected by the Fourth Amendment, I fail to see how preservation can even be asserted as a justification for the search in this case . . . . In this case . . . the owner was "present to make other arrangements for the safekeeping of his belongings," *Opperman*, 428 U.S., at 375, 96 S. Ct., at 3100, yet the police made no attempt to ascertain whether in fact he wanted them to "safeguard" his property . . . .

Thus, the government's interests in this case are weaker than in *Opperman*, but the search here is much more intrusive . . . .

In *Lafayette*, we upheld a stationhouse inventory search of an arrestee's shoulder bag. Notwithstanding the Court's assertions to the contrary, the inventory in that case was justified primarily by compelling governmental interests unique to the stationhouse, preincarceration context. There is a powerful interest in preventing the introduction of contraband or weapons into a jail . . . . Although *Lafayette* also involved the property justifications relied on in *Opperman*, I do not believe it can fairly be read to expand the scope of inventory searches where the pressing security concerns of the stationhouse are absent.

B

Not only are the government's interests weaker here than in *Opperman* and *Lafayette*, but respondent's privacy interest is greater . . . .

. . . Thus, even if the governmental interests in this case were the same as those in *Opperman*, they would nonetheless be outweighed by respondent's comparatively greater expectation of privacy in his luggage.

. . . .

Accordingly, I dissent.

Notes and Questions

(1) The *Bertine* Court states that the police are not required to extend to the owner of a vehicle an opportunity "to make alternate arrangements" for "safekeeping of his property." Suppose an owner affirmatively expresses a desire to make alternative arrangements. Must an officer acquiesce? In all circumstances?

(2) The Court held that containers in vehicles are subject to warrantless inventory searches to the same extent as the vehicles themselves. In the inventory context, are there plausible grounds for a distinction between vehicles and the containers found inside them? Between containers found in impounded vehicles and containers found on the persons of arrestees?

(3) The Court indicated that police may exercise discretion in deciding whether or not to impound an automobile and its contents "so long as that discretion is exercised according to standard criteria and on the basis of something other than suspicion of criminal activity." What is meant by "standard" criteria? Why are standard criteria a Fourth Amendment prerequisite? Should officers be permitted to exercise

similar discretion in deciding which impounded vehicles they should inventory? In deciding which areas within a vehicle they should inspect? Why?

In *Florida v. Wells*, 495 U.S. 1, 110 S. Ct. 1632, 109 L. Ed. 2d 1 (1990), a unanimous Court concluded that an inventory search of a locked suitcase found in the trunk of an impounded vehicle violated the Fourth Amendment because "the Florida Highway Patrol had no policy whatever with respect to the opening of closed containers encountered during an inventory search." Five members of the Court, however, rejected the Florida Supreme Court's conclusion that, to pass constitutional muster under *Bertine*, an inventory policy must mandate either that all containers or no containers will be opened. They concluded that "in forbidding uncanalized discretion to police officers conducting inventory searches, there is no reason to insist that they be conducted in a totally mechanical 'all or nothing' fashion. . . . [Instead,] a police officer may be allowed sufficient latitude to determine whether a particular container should or should not be opened in light of the nature of the search and the characteristics of the container itself. Thus, while policies of opening all containers or of opening no containers are unquestionably permissible, it would be equally permissible, for example, to allow the opening of closed containers whose contents officers determine they are unable to ascertain from examining the containers' exteriors. The allowance of the exercise of judgment based on concerns related to the purposes of an inventory search does not violate the Fourth Amendment."

For a variety of reasons, four members concurred in the judgment. They refused to join the majority's dictum regarding the permissible extent of discretion to select the containers to be inventoried.

(4) Suppose that an officer properly inventories a vehicle or an arrestee's belongings according to standard departmental procedures and finds a large stash of narcotics. She later admits that she had no actual interest in promoting the interests justifying an inventory search, but, instead, hoped she might find contraband during the course of the inventory. Should a court uphold a claim that the inventory was invalid and the search unreasonable? In connection with this question, consider *Whren v. United States*, 517 U.S. 806, 116 S. Ct. 1769, 135 L. Ed. 2d 89 (1996).

Inventory Search Problems

4D–1: State Trooper Grace was on a routine patrol when he encountered what appeared to be a one-car accident. The car had come to rest in a ditch after crossing an embankment, crashing through a fence, and breaking off a utility pole. Grace called to have the car towed and impounded. The driver of the car, Jack Hund, was not present.

Grace used a mechanical device to open the car's locked door in order to shift the transmission into neutral for towing. He then conducted an inventory prior to the removal of the car to an unguarded storage facility. He found a closed, snap-top cigarette case and opened it because in his experience women often put their driver's licenses and money in such containers. Inside was a snorting tube containing cocaine.

Grace prepared an inventory listing according to a state police policy found in General Order 13-4(a)(2) of the Illinois State Police. That Order provides that: "An examination and inventory of the contents of all vehicles/boats towed or held by authority of Division personnel shall be made by the officer who completes the Tow-In Recovery Report. This examination and inventory shall be restricted to those areas where an owner or operator would ordinarily place or store property or equipment in the vehicle/boat; and would normally include front and rear seat areas, glove compartments, sun visors, and trunk and engine compartments."

Upon being charged with possession of a controlled substance, Hund moved to suppress the cocaine found by Trooper Grace, alleging that the inventory was unconstitutional.

Should Hund's motion to suppress be granted? Why?

4D–2: On January 6, City Police Department (CPD) Detective Giles and her partner responded to a request by a fellow officer to follow a green 1500 Chevrolet truck and initiate a traffic stop if the driver, later identified as Christopher, committed a traffic violation. Officer Giles was informed that Christopher was suspected of involvement in a narcotics transaction and that the narcotics were believed to be in his vehicle. When Officer Giles observed Christopher fail to signal before changing lanes, she initiated a traffic stop. After Christopher could not produce a valid insurance card, Giles arrested him.

CPD towing policy dictates that when an individual is arrested for a traffic violation, the officer should give the individual the option to release the vehicle to another driver, allow the vehicle to be left at the scene, or drive the vehicle to the police station. Officer Giles did not provide Christopher with these options, however, because of another CPD policy requiring the impoundment of a vehicle "when the vehicle is known or believed to have been used in the commission of a crime and has evidentiary value." Based on this policy, Officer Giles decided to tow and search the vehicle.

When a vehicle is impounded, CPD policy requires officers to complete a tow-in report. The tow-in report must include a "content inventory," which is a "detailed inventory and listing of items located inside of the vehicle being towed." When a towed vehicle contains "valuable property in large quantities," officers must nevertheless generate a detailed inventory, using an additional form if more space is needed to list the contents of the vehicle. In a search of Christopher's vehicle, Officer Giles discovered, among other items, two toolboxes that each contained over one hundred items (including pliers, wrenches, screwdrivers, and drill bits), two additional toolboxes, several chains, a hydraulic jack, a crate, lug wrenches, a paint roller, a flashlight, a shingle remover, a band clamp, an electric chainsaw, and an electric circular saw. Giles also discovered a plastic bag containing approximately 74 grams of powder cocaine, clothing, toiletries, and paper. In completing the tow-in report, Officer

Giles did not itemize or list the hundreds of tools, but simply wrote "misc. tools" in the relevant section of the form.

After Christopher was charged with possession of the cocaine, he moved to suppress the contraband found in his vehicle, arguing that the search violated the Fourth Amendment. The Government contended that the search was valid under the inventory search exception to the Fourth Amendment warrant requirement.

How should the judge rule?

4D–3: Detective Todd and a team of narcotics officers were conducting surveillance of a suspected narcotics stash house. Around 1:20 p.m., Todd observed an unidentified male enter the house. A few minutes later, the unidentified male left the house with a large white box and placed it inside his truck. He drove to a nearby street, pulled over to the curb, got out of his truck, walked over to a GMC Envoy, and handed the white box to Jesus. After Todd saw Jesus engage in certain driving maneuvers, he concluded that Jesus was using a "counter-surveillance" technique indicative of narcotics trafficking. Todd believed that Jesus "had a large quantity of narcotics in his possession," but did not attempt to stop his vehicle.

At approximately 2:00 p.m., Jesus arrived at a residence on Polk Street and parked on the street. Jesus remained inside the Envoy for approximately five minutes, got out empty handed, and went inside a residence. At 5:30 p.m., Jesus and an unknown male left the residence on Polk Street in a BMW, but returned 45 minutes later. An hour later, Jesus came out of the house, raised the rear hatch area of his vehicle, closed it, then drove away. At this point, Todd asked a marked police unit to develop a lawful reason for a traffic stop.

Officers Sancho and Colly saw Jesus's Envoy fail to come to a complete stop behind the limit line at an intersection. They signaled for him to stop. Jesus cleared the intersection and then pulled to the curb. Although the stop occurred on a "major four-lane thoroughfare," it was lawful to park along the curb at all hours and for an unlimited period. Sancho and Colly asked Jesus for his license, registration, and proof of insurance. Jesus was unable to locate any of the documents. Colly asked Jesus to step out of the car and performed a pat down search for weapons. Jesus told Officer Sancho that he had been arrested previously for driving under the influence, that his license had been taken away, and that he was currently attending classes. After finding no record of a driver's license under the name Jesus provided, the officers concluded that he was driving without a license. Both the state vehicle code and police department policy authorize officers to impound vehicles when they arrest drivers. The officers decided to impound and search Jesus's Envoy.

During the inventory search of the vehicle, Officer Colly located the white cardboard box on the rear passenger seat. It contained approximately two kilograms of cocaine. The officers then arrested Jesus for unlawfully transporting narcotics. Jesus moved to suppress the cocaine from his trial, arguing that the officers searched his vehicle in violation of the Fourth Amendment.

342 · 4 · REASONABLE SEARCHES WITHOUT WARRANTS

Did the officers violate the Fourth Amendment?

4D–4: At approximately 12:30 a.m., Arkansas State Trooper Karl Byrd stopped Brett's automobile for weaving. Brett, who was heading back to Washington, D.C., after visiting his daughter in Texas, was driving a Ford Taurus that had been rented from Budget Car Rental at Washington Dulles Airport. Brett's friend, Susan Thom, had rented the car. Trooper Byrd started to issue a warning ticket for improper lane usage. At the same time, he initiated a license check on Brett. The check showed that Brett's license had been suspended for failure to appear in court for a traffic violation. Byrd wrote Brett a ticket for driving with a suspended license and informed him that because he was not a licensed driver, the Taurus would have to be towed.

At this point, Trooper Byrd conducted an inventory search of the car. In order to protect the government and the wrecker service from false claims against them, Byrd examined the Taurus for damage. While performing the inventory, Byrd discovered that the right front window would only roll down part of the way and that the back windows would not roll down at all. He shined his flashlight into the right front window slot to see if there was an obstruction inside, and saw what appeared to be a bundle of marijuana inside the door. Byrd then pulled the inside door panel away from the right front door and was able to confirm that there was marijuana inside the door. The State Trooper inventory policy provided that an inventory could extend to the contents of an automobile, and that opaque containers could be opened. The policy did not specifically authorize officers to look inside door panels.

Byrd then arrested Brett and ordered that his car be towed to the Arkansas State Police Headquarters. While completing the inventory search at Headquarters, officers discovered a total of 19 bundles of marijuana inside the vehicle.

Was the inventory search reasonable?

4D–5: On August 30, the body of Harty, the owner of a saloon in Athens, Georgia, was discovered slumped over a desk in his home. He had been shot once in the head. Shortly thereafter, Elmo Florence admitted that he had been hired to kill Harty by the appellant.

On October 7, Cobb County police discovered the appellant in a parking lot of an apartment building where he was standing with Rick Newman, a former college roommate. Appellant was in transit to his home in Georgia, and had arrived at Newman's apartment with his luggage. The two men had placed appellant's luggage temporarily in Newman's Datsun in the parking lot while they went for a drink. Armed with a warrant for his arrest, the officers arrested and led the appellant away. At the time of the arrest the two men were 75 or 100 yards away from the Datsun. Appellant asked permission to have a relative come by to pick up his luggage, but the officers ignored the request.

After appellant was gone, Lt. Moss informed Newman of the penalties for harboring and aiding a fugitive. Newman stated that he did not want to be involved. Lt.

Moss asked Newman where the appellant's luggage was. Newman said that it was in the Datsun and opened the car door. He and the officer then removed the items. Lt. Moss told Newman that if he did not want any further involvement, police would just take appellant's things and send them on to jail to be with the appellant. Appellant's "luggage," consisting of a pair of boots, a black leather suitcase, and a green shopping bag, was placed in a police vehicle.

Following his arrest, appellant was taken to the Cobb County jail. When his possessions arrived, Deputy Cantrell began to inventory them for weapons and contraband, which is a standard procedure to protect the police. Past experience had turned up drugs and razor blades hidden in folded paper, so inventorying officers normally unfolded papers and checked to see if there was anything in them.

In the plastic shopping bag, which was open at the top, the officer found and unfolded some pieces of paper. Out of curiosity he began to read them. He saw the word "death" along with other incriminating statements. Certain statements in the notes were introduced into evidence by the State at appellant's murder trial.

Did the inventory of appellant's shopping bag comply with Fourth Amendment requirements?

4D–6: Defendant and his girlfriend, Sherry Lynn Riser, had a fight in defendant's car. Blows were struck by each. Officer Brewer, on routine traffic patrol, observed the altercation. After summoning a backup officer, he approached the automobile. Neither defendant nor Riser would answer Brewer's questions about the incident. Brewer arrested them for violating a city ordinance against "fighting." He took them, along with a briefcase located on the backseat of defendant's car, to the city jail.

In connection with all arrests, it was standard procedure to inventory all personal property brought to the jail with arrestees. These inventories were conducted for the protection of both the arrestees and the police. Upon their arrival at the jail, defendant and Riser were subjected to standard booking procedures and the items of property on their persons were inventoried. The briefcase that had been in the back of the car was locked. The inventorying officer requested the combination to the lock, but the defendant refused to give it to him.

The customary practice on an ordinance violation arrest of this type was to book the defendant, take information pertaining to the arrest, fill out the city complaint, write a report, and then usually release the defendant on $50 bond. Defendant, however, was not released on bond, but, instead, was placed in a jail cell. A police officer told the defendant that he was being put in the cell because he had refused to turn over the combination to his locked briefcase.

A short time later, the officers broke open the briefcase. Inside, they discovered $800 in cash, personal papers and effects, and a loaded .38 caliber revolver. Defendant was charged with a misdemeanor weapons offense.

Was the search of the briefcase a legitimate inventory?

4D–7: On May 10, at 12:45 p.m., Agent Glen Anderson of the Bureau of Alcohol, Tobacco, and Firearms (ATF) received a call from a confidential informant (CI) who had provided reliable information in the past. The CI told Anderson that Lump would be driving westbound in Tennessee on Interstate 440 toward Interstate 65 in a turquoise Mercury Tracer with Tennessee license number 862 XBX. The informant described Lump, stated that he would have a white female passenger with him, and alleged that he would be in possession of one or two pounds of methamphetamine.

At approximately 1:00 p.m., the same day, Anderson relayed this information to Officer Donegan of the Nashville Police Department's Narcotics Section. Donegan contacted several other officers, asking them for assistance, and began to drive in a direction calculated to intercept Lump's vehicle. Soon thereafter, Donegan saw the turquoise Tracer traveling west on I-440 toward I-65. The vehicle had the license plate and occupants described by the CI. Donegan asked Officer Lynn Hampton to stop the Tracer on the pretense that it fit the description of a vehicle that had driven away from a gasoline pump without paying. Hampton complied with the request. Six minutes later, Donegan arrived at the place where Hampton had stopped the Tracer. Lump was sitting in the back of Hampton's marked police car. The female occupant of Lump's car — Dusty Thompson — was standing outside.

Officer Burrow, who was also at the scene, asked Thompson whether she had drugs or firearms in the car. Thompson replied that there was a pistol in her purse. Burrow found the purse on the passenger floorboard, and removed a loaded .38 caliber Derringer. Based on the information from the CI, the facts that had been corroborated, the loaded gun, a slight conflict between Lump's and Thompson's stories about where they were going, and Lump's statement that there was approximately $20,000 in the trunk, Donegan believed that he had probable cause to search the Tracer. After removing the money from the trunk and finding nothing in the car's interior, he raised the hood. Lying against the car battery was a cylindrical roll wrapped with brown tape. The roll contained white powder that had a slight odor that Donegan believed was the odor of methamphetamine. At this point, Lump and Thompson were arrested for possession of a controlled substance for resale.

While still at the scene of the stop, Thompson told officers that she and Lump had driven to Tennessee from Oklahoma. She said that she didn't understand why they had rented a car in Nashville when the red and white pickup truck they had arrived in was parked at the Opryland Complex in Nashville. After taking the keys to this pickup from Thompson's purse, Donegan and Burrow went to the Opryland Complex to seize the truck. They transported the truck to the police impound lot and inventoried its contents. Another tape-wrapped cylinder containing approximately one pound of methamphetamine was found in the engine compartment of the truck.

Was the inventory search of the pickup truck constitutional?

4D–8: On February 17 and 24, government agents made two controlled purchases of crack cocaine from Elmer. At the time of the second purchase, the agents provided Elmer with $500 in marked bills, which Elmer then took to Peter's apartment at the Terrace Apartments. At 8:30 a.m. Elmer returned to the agents with 2.2 grams of crack cocaine. After Elmer was arrested, he agreed to cooperate with the government. That same morning, the agents fitted Elmer with a listening device and instructed him to return to Peter's apartment. A few minutes later, Elmer returned to the agents and told them that Peter had discussed doing a drug transaction later that day, around 3:00 p.m. Elmer also told them that Peter had sent him out to "fetch a soda" and that Peter had said that he would give him "a line" when he returned.

The agents faced a dilemma. On the one hand, they were unwilling to allow Elmer to use drugs while cooperating with the government. On the other hand, Elmer said that if he did not return with the soda within a few minutes, Peter would be suspicious. After considering their options, the agents decided to secure Peter's apartment immediately. Around noon, they knocked on the door and announced their presence. Peter opened the door, wearing a tee-shirt and boxer shorts. One agent grabbed him to make sure that he was unarmed. In the commotion Peter and the agent tripped and fell backwards into the apartment. Peter was then handcuffed. Because his underpants were "soiled," the agents retrieved a pair of pants off the floor and helped Peter put them on. It is uncertain whether the pants were put on at the suggestion of Peter or at the insistence of the agents.

Peter's girlfriend gave consent to search the apartment. In the search that ensued, the agents discovered a quantity of drugs and a large amount of U.S. currency. Peter was arrested and brought to the Marshal's office, where, following standard procedures, he was strip-searched before being put in a holding cell. In his pants pocket, the marshals discovered $380 of the marked $500 that the agents had used to purchase drugs from Elmer.

Was the search of Elmer at the station reasonable?

4D–9: On September 6, Officer Ortiz encountered Noelle at her work place, the Red Cove Bar, where she was a bartender. Ortiz observed that Noelle had dilated pupils, a rapid pulse rate, a nervous attitude and rapid speech. Because he suspected that she was under the influence of cocaine or methamphetamine, misdemeanor drug offenses, he arrested her. The time was 2:10 a.m. Ortiz took Noelle to the County's pretrial detention facility for booking. The booking policy of the County provided for a "visual body cavity search of all persons arrested on fresh misdemeanor drug charges." The search must be performed by a deputy of the same sex as the detainee, and it involves no touching. The person arrested must be searched immediately upon booking, without a waiting period for posting bail.

Officer Henson obtained her supervisor's approval to perform a body cavity search upon Noelle. The search, which involved a visual inspection of Noelle's unclothed body cavities, took place in a private room with only Henson present. Henson directed Noelle to remove all her clothing. She then directed Noelle to remove her tampon and to tear it and discard it in a wastebasket. Pursuant to the search policy,

Noelle was required to "bend forward, spread the buttocks, and cough to allow for a visual inspection of the anal area" as well as to "spread her labia at the same time to allow a check of the vaginal area." The search yielded no contraband, weapons or drugs.

The booking process lasted 25 minutes, from 3:10 a.m. to 3:35 a.m. Within 20 minutes after the completion of the body cavity search, Noelle was informed of the amount of her bail. She was then placed in a holding cell with five or six other women and was allowed to make phone calls. She remained in the holding cell for several hours. She then posted bail and was released without entering the jail's general population.

Noelle filed a civil rights action against the County, Henson, and Henson's supervisor, alleging a violation of her Fourth Amendment rights. The defendants replied that they had conducted a permissible inventory.

Did the search of Noelle violate her fourth amendment rights?

4D–10: One afternoon, several officers of a state-federal task force were conducting surveillance of Javier, a suspected narcotics trafficker, at a mall in Houston. Javier was accompanied by Susana and an unidentified Hispanic male. The officers saw Susana and the Hispanic man leave the mall in a grey van. Susana got out at a K-Mart, while the man drove on to a known stash house. After a while, he returned to K-Mart and retrieved Susana. Along the way, the man had made several evasive maneuvers that appeared to be designed to lose anyone who might be following him. The two then went to a local motel, where they were joined by Edgar and Muriel.

From the motel, Edgar drove a blue Suburban to the mall. Susana and Muriel followed in two separate cars. After they spent 15 minutes in the mall, the trio departed in the Suburban. They traveled north on Highway 59. Edgar was driving, Muriel was in the front seat, and Susana was in the rear. Task force members followed Edgar, Muriel, and Susana for 115 miles, through four counties, before contacting Lieutenant Mike Nettles of the County Sheriff's Department. They provided Nettles with a description of the vehicle and reported that it was involved in a narcotics investigation. They told Nettles that he would have to "develop [his] own probable cause" for stopping the car. Nettles, whose patrol car was positioned in the median of Highway 59, watched as the Suburban passed by. He noticed that Edgar was not wearing his seatbelt and seemed to be exceeding the speed limit. He followed the Suburban for several miles, clocking it at 67 m.p.h. in a 55 m.p.h. zone. Nettles also noticed that Muriel was not wearing her seatbelt and that the vehicle appeared to have a heavy rear load which caused it to sway slightly.

Nettles stopped the Suburban for speeding and for seatbelt violations. Upon approaching the car, he noted again that neither Edgar nor Muriel was wearing a seatbelt. Edgar produced a valid driver's license and explained that all three of the occupants were from out of state. Nettles ran a check on Edgar's license, finding no outstanding warrants. Based on conflicting statements from Edgar and his passengers and on their nervous demeanor, Nettles arrested Edgar and Muriel for seatbelt violations. After Edgar denied a request by Nettles for consent to a search of the vehicle, Nettles took Edgar and Muriel into custody and impounded the Suburban.

At the sheriff's department, officers conducted an inventory search of the Suburban. They found almost 900 pounds of powder cocaine, packaged in two-kilogram bricks inside large trash bags. Prior to his trial for possession of cocaine with intent to distribute it, Edgar moved to suppress the contraband, challenging the legality of the inventory.

Should the trial judge conclude that the inventory was legitimate?

Selected Bibliography

George M. Dery III, Florence *and the Machine: The Supreme Court Upholds Suspicionless Strip Searches Resulting from Computer Error*, 40 Am. J. Crim. L. 173 (2013)

David H. Kaye, *Why So Contrived? Fourth Amendment Balancing, Per Se Rules, and DNA Databases After* Maryland v. King, 104 J. Crim. L. & Criminology 535 (2014)

Wayne A. Logan, Florence v. Board of Chosen Freeholders: *Police Power Takes a More Intrusive Turn*, 46 Akron L. Rev. 413 (2013)

Charles E. Moylan, *The Inventory Search of an Automobile: A Willing Suspension of Disbelief*, 5 U. Balt. L. Rev. 203 (1976)

Gerald S. Reamey, *Reevaluating the Vehicle Inventory*, 19 Crim. L. Bull. 325 (1983)

Andrea Roth, Maryland v. King *and the Wonderful, Horrible DNA Revolution in Law Enforcement*, 11 Ohio St. J. Crim. L. 295 (2013)

[E] Consent Searches

Schneckloth v. Bustamonte

United States Supreme Court

412 U.S. 218, 93 S. Ct. 2041, 36 L. Ed. 2d 854 (1973)

Mr. Justice Stewart delivered the opinion of the Court.

. . . .

I

. . . .

While on routine patrol in Sunnyvale, California, at approximately 2:40 in the morning, Police Officer James Rand stopped an automobile when he observed that one headlight and its license plate light were burned out. Six men were in the vehicle. Joe Alcala and the respondent, Robert Bustamonte, were in the front seat with Joe Gonzales, the driver. Three older men were seated in the rear. When, in response to the policeman's question, Gonzales could not produce a driver's license, Officer Rand asked if any of the other five had any evidence of identification. Only Alcala produced a license, and he explained that the car was his brother's. After the six occupants had stepped out of the car at the officer's request and after two additional policemen had arrived, Officer Rand asked Alcala if he could search the car. Alcala replied, "Sure, go ahead." Prior to the search no one was threatened with arrest and, according to Officer Rand's uncontradicted testimony, it "was all very congenial at this time." Gonzales testified that Alcala actually helped in the search of the car, by opening the trunk and glove compartment. In Gonzales' words: "[T]he police officer asked Joe [Alcala], he goes, 'Does the trunk open?' And Joe said, 'Yes.' He went to the car and got the keys and opened up the trunk." Wadded up under the left rear seat, the police officers found three checks that had previously been stolen from a car wash.

The trial judge denied the motion to suppress, and the checks in question were admitted in evidence at Bustamonte's trial. On the basis of this and other evidence he was convicted . . . .

. . . .

II

It is important to make it clear at the outset what is not involved in this case. The respondent concedes that a search conducted pursuant to a valid consent is constitutionally permissible . . . .

The precise question in this case, then, is what must the prosecution prove to demonstrate that a consent was "voluntarily" given. And upon that question there is a square conflict of views between the state and federal courts that have reviewed the search involved in the case before us. The Court of Appeals for the Ninth Circuit concluded that it is an essential part of the State's initial burden to prove that a person knows he has a right to refuse consent. The California courts have followed the rule that voluntariness is a question of fact to be determined from the totality of all the circumstances, and that the state of a defendant's knowledge is only one factor to be taken into account in assessing the voluntariness of a consent.

A

The most extensive judicial exposition of the meaning of "voluntariness" has been developed in those cases in which the Court has had to determine the "voluntariness" of a defendant's confession for purposes of the Fourteenth Amendment . . . . It is to that body of case law to [sic] which we turn for initial guidance on the meaning of "voluntariness" in the present context.

Those cases yield no talismanic definition of "voluntariness," mechanically applicable to the host of situations where the question has arisen . . . .

Rather, "voluntariness" has reflected an accommodation of the complex of values implicated in police questioning of a suspect.

. . . .

In determining whether a defendant's will was overborne in a particular case, the Court has assessed the totality of all the surrounding circumstances — both the characteristics of the accused and the details of the interrogation.

. . . .

B

. . . As with police questioning, two competing concerns must be accommodated in determining the meaning of a "voluntary" consent — the legitimate need for such searches and the equally important requirement of assuring the absence of coercion.

In situations where the police have some evidence of illicit activity, but lack probable cause to arrest or search, a search authorized by a valid consent may be the only means of obtaining important and reliable evidence. In the present case for example, while the police had reason to stop the car for traffic violations, the State does not contend that there was probable cause to search the vehicle or that the search was incident to a valid arrest of any of the occupants. Yet, the search yielded tangible evidence that served as a basis for a prosecution, and provided some assurance that others, wholly innocent of the crime, were not mistakenly brought to trial. And in those cases where there is probable cause to arrest or search, but where the police lack a warrant, a consent search may still be valuable. If the search is conducted and proves fruitless, that in itself may convince the police that an arrest with its possible stigma and embarrassment is unnecessary, or that a far more extensive search pursuant to a warrant is not justified. In short, a search pursuant to consent may result in considerably less inconvenience for the subject of the search, and, properly conducted, is a constitutionally permissible and wholly legitimate aspect of effective police activity.

But the Fourth and Fourteenth Amendments require that a consent not be coerced, by explicit or implicit means, by implied threat or covert force. For, no matter how subtly the coercion was applied, the resulting "consent" would be no more than a pretext for the unjustified police intrusion against which the Fourth Amendment is directed . . . .

. . . Just as was true with confessions, the requirement of a "voluntary" consent reflects a fair accommodation of the constitutional requirements involved. In examining all the surrounding circumstances to determine if in fact the consent to search was coerced, account must be taken of subtly coercive police questions, as well as the possibly vulnerable subjective state of the person who consents. Those searches that are the product of police coercion can thus be filtered out without undermining the continuing validity of consent searches. In sum, there is no reason for us to depart in the area of consent searches, from the traditional definition of "voluntariness."

The approach of the Court of Appeals for the Ninth Circuit finds no support in any of our decisions that have attempted to define the meaning of "voluntariness." Its ruling, that the State must affirmatively prove that the subject of the search knew that he had a right to refuse consent, would, in practice, create serious doubt whether consent searches could continue to be conducted. There might be rare cases where it could be proved from the record that a person in fact affirmatively knew of his right to refuse — such as a case where he announced to the police that if he didn't sign the consent form, "you [police] are going to get a search warrant"; or a case where by prior experience and training a person had clearly and convincingly demonstrated such knowledge. But more commonly where there was no evidence of any coercion, explicit or implicit, the prosecution would nevertheless be unable to demonstrate that the subject of the search in fact had known of his right to refuse consent.

The very object of the inquiry — the nature of a person's subjective understanding — underlines the difficulty of the prosecution's burden under the rule applied by the Court of Appeals in this case. Any defendant who was the subject of a search authorized solely by his consent could effectively frustrate the introduction into evidence of the fruits of that search by simply failing to testify that he in fact knew he could refuse to consent. And the near impossibility of meeting this prosecutorial burden suggests why this Court has never accepted any such litmus-paper test of voluntariness . . . .

One alternative that would go far toward proving that the subject of a search did know he had a right to refuse consent would be to advise him of that right before eliciting his consent. That, however, is a suggestion that has been almost universally repudiated by both federal and state courts, and, we think, rightly so. For it would be thoroughly impractical to impose on the normal consent search the detailed requirements of an effective warning. Consent searches are part of the standard investigatory techniques of law enforcement agencies. They normally occur on the highway, or in a person's home or office, and under informal and unstructured conditions. The circumstances that prompt the initial request to search may develop quickly or be a logical extension of investigative police questioning. The police may seek to investigate further suspicious circumstances or to follow up leads developed in questioning persons at the scene of a crime. These situations are a far cry from the structured atmosphere of a trial where, assisted by counsel if he chooses, a defendant is informed of his trial rights. And, while surely a closer question, these situations are still immeasurably far removed from "custodial interrogation" where, in *Miranda v. Arizona*, 384 U.S. 436, we found that the Constitution required certain now familiar warnings as a prerequisite to police interrogation.

. . . .

In short, neither this Court's prior cases, nor the traditional definition of "voluntariness" requires proof of knowledge of a right to refuse as the *sine qua non* of an effective consent to a search.

C

It is said, however, that a "consent" is a "waiver" of a person's rights under the Fourth and Fourteenth Amendments. The argument is that by allowing the police to conduct a search, a person "waives" whatever right he had to prevent the police from searching. It is argued that under the doctrine of *Johnson v. Zerbst*, 304 U.S. 458, 464, 58 S. Ct. 1019, 1023, 82 L. Ed. 1461, to establish such a "waiver" the State must demonstrate "an intentional relinquishment or abandonment of a known right or privilege."

But these standards were enunciated in *Johnson* in the context of the safeguards of a fair criminal trial. Our cases do not reflect an uncritical demand for a knowing and intelligent waiver in every situation where a person has failed to invoke a constitutional protection . . . .

The requirement of a "knowing" and "intelligent" waiver was articulated in a case involving the validity of a defendant's decision to forgo a right constitutionally guaranteed to protect a fair trial and the reliability of the truth-determining process. *Johnson v. Zerbst* dealt with the denial of counsel in a federal criminal trial . . . .

Almost without exception, the requirement of a knowing and intelligent waiver has been applied only to those rights which the Constitution guarantees to a criminal defendant in order to preserve a fair trial . . . .

The guarantees afforded a criminal defendant at trial also protect him at certain stages before the actual trial, and any alleged waiver must meet the strict standard of an intentional relinquishment of a "known" right. But the "trial" guarantees that have been applied to the "pretrial" stage of the criminal process are similarly designed to protect the fairness of the trial itself.

        . . . .

There is a vast difference between those rights that protect a fair criminal trial and the rights guaranteed under the Fourth Amendment. Nothing, either in the purposes behind requiring a "knowing" and "intelligent" waiver of trial rights, or in the practical application of such a requirement suggests that it ought to be extended to the constitutional guarantee against unreasonable searches and seizures.

A strict standard of waiver has been applied to those rights guaranteed to a criminal defendant to insure that he will be accorded the greatest possible opportunity to utilize every facet of the constitutional model of a fair criminal trial. Any trial conducted in derogation of that model leaves open the possibility that the trial reached an unfair result precisely because all the protections specified in the Constitution were not provided. A prime example is the right to counsel . . . .

The protections of the Fourth Amendment are of a wholly different order, and have nothing whatever to do with promoting the fair ascertainment of truth at a criminal trial . . . . The Fourth Amendment "is not an adjunct to the ascertainment of truth." The guarantees of the Fourth Amendment stand "as a protection of quite different constitutional values — values reflecting the concern of our society for the right of each individual to be let alone. To recognize this is no more than to accord those values undiluted respect." *Tehan v. United States ex rel. Shott*, 382 U.S. 406, 416, 86 S. Ct. 459, 465, 15 L. Ed. 2d 453.

Nor can it even be said that a search, as opposed to an eventual trial, is somehow "unfair" if a person consents to a search. While the Fourth and Fourteenth Amendments limit the circumstances under which the police can conduct a search, there is nothing constitutionally suspect in a person's voluntarily allowing a search. The actual conduct of the search may be precisely the same as if the police had obtained a warrant. And, unlike those constitutional guarantees that protect a defendant at trial, it cannot be said every reasonable presumption ought to be indulged against voluntary relinquishment. We have only recently stated: "[I]t is no part of the policy underlying the Fourth and Fourteenth Amendments to discourage citizens from aiding to the utmost of their ability in the apprehension of criminals." *Coolidge v. New Hampshire*, 403 U.S., at 488, 91 S. Ct., at 2049. Rather, the community has a real interest in encouraging consent, for the resulting search may yield necessary evidence for the solution and prosecution of crime, evidence that may insure that a wholly innocent person is not wrongly charged with a criminal offense.

Those cases that have dealt with the application of the *Johnson v. Zerbst* rule make clear that it would be next to impossible to apply to a consent search the standard of "an intentional relinquishment or abandonment of a known right or privilege." To be true to *Johnson* and its progeny, there must be examination into the knowing and understanding nature of the waiver, an examination that was designed for a trial judge in the structured atmosphere of a courtroom . . . . It would be unrealistic to expect that in the informal, unstructured context of a consent search, a policeman, upon pain of tainting the evidence obtained, could make the detailed type of examination demanded by *Johnson*. And, if for this reason a diluted form of "waiver" were found acceptable, that would itself be ample recognition of the fact that there is no universal standard that must be applied in every situation where a person forgoes a constitutional right.

Similarly, a "waiver" approach to consent searches would be thoroughly inconsistent with our decisions that have approved "third party consents." . . . [I]t is inconceivable that the Constitution could countenance the waiver of a defendant's right to counsel by a third party, or that a waiver could be found because a trial judge reasonably, though mistakenly, believed a defendant had waived his right to plead not guilty.

In short, there is nothing in the purposes or application of the waiver requirements of *Johnson v. Zerbst* that justifies, much less compels, the easy equation of a knowing waiver with a consent search . . . .

D

Much of what has already been said disposes of the argument that the Court's decision in the *Miranda* case requires the conclusion that knowledge of a right to refuse is an indispensable element of a valid consent. The considerations that informed the Court's holding in *Miranda* are simply inapplicable in the present case . . . .

In this case, there is no evidence of any inherently coercive tactics — either from the nature of the police questioning or the environment in which it took place. Indeed, since consent searches will normally occur on a person's own familiar territory, the specter of incommunicado police interrogation in some remote station house is simply inapposite. There is no reason to believe, under circumstances such as are present here, that the response to a policeman's question is presumptively coerced; and there is, therefore, no reason to reject the traditional test for determining the voluntariness of a person's response . . . .

It is also argued that the failure to require the Government to establish knowledge as a prerequisite to a valid consent, will relegate the Fourth Amendment to the
special province of "the sophisticated, the knowledgeable and the privileged." We
cannot agree. The traditional definition of voluntariness we accept today has always
taken into account evidence of minimal schooling, low intelligence, and the lack of
any effective warnings to a person of his rights; and the voluntariness of any statement taken under those conditions has been carefully scrutinized to determine
whether it was in fact voluntarily given.

E

Our decision today is a narrow one. We hold only that when the subject of a search
is not in custody and the State attempts to justify a search on the basis of his consent, the Fourth and Fourteenth Amendments require that it demonstrate that the
consent was in fact voluntarily given, and not the result of duress or coercion, express or implied. Voluntariness is a question of fact to be determined from all the
circumstances, and while the subject's knowledge of a right to refuse is a factor to be
taken into account, the prosecution is not required to demonstrate such knowledge
as a prerequisite to establishing a voluntary consent. Because the California court
followed these principles in affirming the respondent's conviction, and because the
Court of Appeals for the Ninth Circuit in remanding for an evidentiary hearing required more, its judgment must be reversed.

It is so ordered.

[The concurring opinion of MR. JUSTICE BLACKMUN has been omitted.]

[The concurring opinion of MR. JUSTICE POWELL has been omitted.]

[The dissenting opinion of MR. JUSTICE DOUGLAS has been omitted.]

MR. JUSTICE BRENNAN, dissenting.

The Fourth Amendment specifically guarantees "[t]he right of the people to be
secure in their persons, houses, papers, and effects, against unreasonable searches
and seizures . . . ." We have consistently held that governmental searches conducted
pursuant to a validly obtained warrant or reasonably incident to a valid arrest do not
violate this guarantee. Here, however, as the Court itself recognizes, no search warrant was obtained and the State does not even suggest "that there was probable cause
to search the vehicle or that the search was incident to a valid arrest of any of the
occupants." As a result, the search of the vehicle can be justified solely on the ground
that the owner's brother gave his consent — that is, that he waived his Fourth Amendment right "to be secure" against an otherwise "unreasonable" search. The Court
holds today that an individual can effectively waive this right even though he is totally ignorant of the fact that, in the absence of his consent, such invasions of his
privacy would be constitutionally prohibited. It wholly escapes me how our citizens
can meaningfully be said to have waived something as precious as a constitutional
guarantee without ever being aware of its existence. In my view, the Court's conclu-

sion is supported neither by "linguistics," nor by "epistemology," nor, indeed, by "common sense." I respectfully dissent.

MR. JUSTICE MARSHALL, dissenting.

    . . . .

I

I believe that the Court misstates the true issue in this case. That issue is not, as the Court suggests, whether the police overbore Alcala's will in eliciting his consent, but rather, whether a simple statement of assent to search, without more, should be sufficient to permit the police to search and thus act as a relinquishment of Alcala's constitutional right to exclude the police.

    . . . .

A

The Court assumes that the issue in this case is: what are the standards by which courts are to determine that consent is voluntarily given? It then imports into the law of search and seizure standards developed to decide entirely different questions about coerced confessions.

The Fifth Amendment, in terms, provides that no person "shall be compelled in any criminal case to be a witness against himself." Nor is the interest protected by the Due Process Clause of the Fourteenth Amendment any different. The inquiry in a case where a confession is challenged as having been elicited in an unconstitutional manner is, therefore, whether the behavior of the police amounted to compulsion of the defendant. Because of the nature of the right to be free of compulsion, it would be pointless to ask whether a defendant knew of it before he made a statement; no sane person would knowingly relinquish a right to be free of compulsion. Thus, the questions of compulsion and of violation of the right itself are inextricably intertwined. The cases involving coerced confessions, therefore, pass over the question of knowledge of that right as irrelevant, and turn directly to the question of compulsion.

    . . . .

B

In contrast, this case deals not with "coercion," but with "consent," a subtly different concept to which different standards have been applied in the past. Freedom from coercion is a substantive right, guaranteed by the Fifth and Fourteenth Amendments. Consent, however, is a mechanism by which substantive requirements, otherwise applicable, are avoided. In the context of the Fourth Amendment, the relevant substantive requirements are that searches be conducted only after evidence justifying them has been submitted to an impartial magistrate for a determination of probable cause. There are, of course, exceptions to these requirements based on a variety of exigent circumstances that make it impractical to invalidate a search simply because the police failed to get a warrant. But none of the exceptions relating to the overriding needs of law enforcement are applicable when a search is justified solely by consent. On the contrary, the needs of law enforcement are significantly more attenuated, for probable cause to search may be lacking but a search permitted if the subject's consent has been obtained. Thus, consent searches are permitted, not because such an exception to the requirements of probable cause and warrant is essential to proper law enforcement, but because we permit our citizens to choose whether or not they wish to exercise their constitutional rights. Our prior decisions simply do not support the view that a meaningful choice has been made solely because no coercion was brought to bear on the subject.

. . . .

II

My approach to the case is straightforward and, to me, obviously required by the notion of consent as a relinquishment of Fourth Amendment rights. I am at a loss to understand why consent "cannot be taken literally to mean a 'knowing' choice." In fact, I have difficulty in comprehending how a decision made without knowledge of available alternatives can be treated as a choice at all.

If consent to search means that a person has chosen to forgo his right to exclude the police from the place they seek to search, it follows that his consent cannot be considered a meaningful choice unless he knew that he could in fact exclude the police. The Court appears, however, to reject even the modest proposition that, if the subject of a search convinces the trier of fact that he did not know of his right to refuse assent to a police request for permission to search, the search must be held unconstitutional. For it says only that "knowledge of the right to refuse consent is one factor to be taken into account." I find this incomprehensible. I can think of no other situation in which we would say that a person agreed to some course of action if he convinced us that he did not know that there was some other course he might have pursued. I would therefore hold, at a minimum, that the prosecution may not rely on a purported consent to search if the subject of the search did not know that he could refuse to give consent . . . .

If one accepts this view, the question then is a simple one: must the Government show that the subject knew of his rights, or must the subject show that he lacked such knowledge?

I think that any fair allocation of the burden would require that it be placed on the prosecution . . . .

If the burden is placed on the defendant, all the subject can do is to testify that he did not know of his rights. And I doubt that many trial judges will find for the defendant simply on the basis of that testimony. Precisely because the evidence is very hard to come by, courts have traditionally been reluctant to require a party to prove negatives such as the lack of knowledge.

In contrast, there are several ways by which the subject's knowledge of his rights may be shown. The subject may affirmatively demonstrate such knowledge by his responses at the time the search took place . . . . Denials of knowledge may be disproved by establishing that the subject had, in the recent past, demonstrated his knowledge of his rights, for example, by refusing entry when it was requested by the police. The prior experience or training of the subject might in some cases support an inference that he knew of his right to exclude the police.

The burden on the prosecutor would disappear, of course, if the police, at the time they requested consent to search, also told the subject that he had a right to refuse consent and that his decision to refuse would be respected. The Court's assertions to the contrary notwithstanding, there is nothing impractical about this method of satisfying the prosecution's burden of proof. It must be emphasized that the decision about informing the subject of his rights would lie with the officers seeking consent. If they believed that providing such information would impede their investigation, they might simply ask for consent, taking the risk that at some later date the prosecutor would be unable to prove that the subject knew of his rights or that some other basis for the search existed.

The Court contends that if an officer paused to inform the subject of his rights, the informality of the exchange would be destroyed. I doubt that a simple statement by an officer of an individual's right to refuse consent would do much to alter the informality of the exchange, except to alert the subject to a fact that he surely is entitled to know. It is not without significance that for many years the agents of the Federal Bureau of Investigation have routinely informed subjects of their right to refuse consent, when they request consent to search . . . . What evidence there is, then, rather strongly suggests that nothing disastrous would happen if the police, before requesting consent, informed the subject that he had a right to refuse consent and that his refusal would be respected.

I must conclude with some reluctance that when the Court speaks of practicality, what it really is talking of is the continued ability of the police to capitalize on the ignorance of citizens so as to accomplish by subterfuge what they could not achieve by relying only on the knowing relinquishment of constitutional rights. Of course it would be "practical" for the police to ignore the commands of the Fourth Amendment, if by practicality we mean that more criminals will be apprehended, even though the constitutional rights of innocent people also go by the board. But such a practical advantage is achieved only at the cost of permitting the police to disregard the limitations that the Constitution places on their behavior, a cost that a constitutional democracy cannot long absorb.

. . . .

III

The proper resolution of this case turns, I believe, on a realistic assessment of the nature of the interchange between citizens and the police, and of the practical import of allocating the burden of proof in one way rather than another. The Court seeks to escape such assessments by escalating its rhetoric to unwarranted heights, but no matter how forceful the adjectives the Court uses, it cannot avoid being judged by how well its image of these interchanges accords with reality. Although the Court says without real elaboration that it "cannot agree," the holding today confines the protection of the Fourth Amendment against searches conducted without probable cause to the sophisticated, the knowledgeable, and, I might add, the few.

. . . .

I respectfully dissent.

Notes and Questions

(1) Why are searches conducted pursuant to consent acceptable under the Fourth Amendment? Is it because, as Justice Marshall suggests, citizens should be free to surrender their constitutional rights? If so, is it logical to accept as valid a surrender of Fourth Amendment rights by a person who is unaware of his or her right to refuse to surrender them?

(2) What is necessary to establish a valid consent under the Court's holding? What evidence is relevant to the consent inquiry? Suppose an individual with a mental disorder that deprives her of the power to resist requests by authority figures gives permission to a police officer to search because she feels compelled to do so. Is the consent invalid? For a decision dealing with an analogous issue, see *Colorado v. Connelly*, 479 U.S. 157, 107 S. Ct. 515, 93 L. Ed. 2d 473 (1986).

(3) The majority in *Schneckloth* specifically noted that the individual who consented was not in police custody at the time of the consent. In *United States v. Watson*, 423 U.S. 411, 96 S. Ct. 820, 46 L. Ed. 2d 598 (1976), the Court rejected the contention that in order to establish a valid consent the government must prove that an individual in custody was informed of or otherwise aware of the right to refuse consent. "[U]nder *Schneckloth*," the Court stated, "the absence of proof that Watson knew he could withhold his consent, though it may be a factor in the overall judgment, is not to be given controlling significance." *See also Gentile v. United States*, 419 U.S. 979, 95 S. Ct. 241, 42 L. Ed. 2d 191 (1974) (Douglas, J., dissenting from denial of certiorari).

(4) *Ohio v. Robinette*, 519 U.S. 33, 117 S. Ct. 417, 136 L. Ed. 2d 347 (1996), involved a similar question and provided a similar answer. As framed by the Court, the narrow question was "whether the Fourth Amendment requires that a *lawfully seized* defendant must be advised that he is 'free to go' before consent to search will be recognized as *voluntary*." (Emphasis added). As in *Bustamonte* and *Watson*, the Court rejected the proposed "*per se* rule" and held that the voluntariness of consent is a question of fact to be determined based on the totality of facts. Advice that one is free to go, like advice that one has a right to refuse, is a relevant fact, but is not essential to voluntariness.

A premise of the Court's holding and ruling in *Robinette* was that the officer who had pulled the defendant over for speeding was "objectively justified" in detaining him at the time he gave consent to search his vehicle. It seems clear, however, that even if a lawful detention has ended, advice that a suspect is free to go is *not* a prerequisite for a *voluntary* consent to search. The Court observed that it had "consistently eschewed [such] bright-line rules" in this area and proved that it would continue to do so. If an officer continues to detain an individual after he no longer has objective reasons to do so, the individual might successfully claim that a consent to search, even though voluntary, was the fruit of an unlawful seizure. Evidence found would be subject to suppression not because the consented to search was unreasonable, but, rather, because the search was the product of an unreasonable seizure. Whether a person who has been detained has been informed that he is "free to go" is highly relevant to the question of whether there was a continuing, potentially illegal seizure.

United States v. Matlock

United States Supreme Court

415 U.S. 164, 94 S. Ct. 988, 39 L. Ed. 2d 242 (1974)

MR. JUSTICE WHITE delivered the opinion of the Court.

. . . .

I

Respondent Matlock was indicted in February 1971 for the robbery of a federally insured bank in Wisconsin, in violation of 18 U.S.C. § 2113 . . . . As found by the District Court, the facts were that respondent was arrested in the yard in front of the Pardeeville home on November 12, 1970. The home was leased from the owner by Mr. and Mrs. Marshall. Living in the home were Mrs. Marshall, several of her children, including her daughter Mrs. Gayle Graff, Gayle's three-year-old son, and respondent. Although the officers were aware at the time of the arrest that respondent lived in the house, they did not ask him which room he occupied or whether he would consent to a search. Three of the arresting officers went to the door of the house and were admitted by Mrs. Graff, who was dressed in a robe and was holding her son in her arms. The officers told her they were looking for money and a gun and asked if they could search the house. Although denied by Mrs. Graff at the suppression hearings, it was found that she consented voluntarily to the search of the house, including the east bedroom on the second floor which she said was jointly occupied by Matlock and herself. The east bedroom was searched and the evidence at issue here, $4,995 in cash, was found in a diaper bag in the only closet in the room . . . .

The District Court ruled that before the seized evidence could be admitted at trial, the Government had to prove, first, that it reasonably appeared to the searching officers "just prior to the search, that facts exist which will render the consenter's consent binding on the putative defendant," and, second that "just prior to the search, facts do exist which render the consenter's consent binding on the putative defendant." . . . The first requirement was held satisfied because of respondent's presence in the yard of the house at the time of his arrest, because of Gayle Graff's residence in the house for some time and her presence in the house just prior to the search, and because of her statement to the officers that she and the respondent occupied the east bedroom.

The District Court concluded, however, that the Government had failed to satisfy the second requirement and had not satisfactorily proved Mrs. Graff's actual authority to consent to the search. To arrive at this result, the District Court held that although Gayle Graff's statements to the officers that she and the respondent occupied the east bedroom were admissible to prove the good-faith belief of the officers, they were nevertheless extrajudicial statements inadmissible to prove the truth of the facts therein averred.... There was also testimony that both Gayle Graff and respondent, at various times and places and to various persons, had made statements that they were wife and husband. These statements were deemed inadmissible to prove that respondent and Gayle Graff were married, which they were not, or that they were sleeping together as a husband and wife might be expected to do. Having excluded these declarations, the District Court then concluded that the remaining evidence was insufficient to prove "to a reasonable certainty, by the greater weight of the credible evidence, that at the time of the search, and for some period of reasonable length theretofore, Gayle Graff and the defendant were living together in the east bedroom."... The District Court also rejected the Government's claim that it was required to prove only that at the time of the search the officers could reasonably have concluded that Gayle Graff's relationship to the east bedroom was sufficient to make her consent binding on respondent.

The Court of Appeals affirmed the judgment of the District Court in all respects....

II

It has been assumed by the parties and the courts below that the voluntary consent of any joint occupant of a residence to search the premises jointly occupied is valid against the co-occupant, permitting evidence discovered in the search to be used against him at a criminal trial.... [Decisions of this Court] at least make clear that when the prosecution seeks to justify a warrantless search by proof of voluntary consent, it is not limited to proof that consent was given by the defendant, but may show that permission to search was obtained from a third party who possessed common authority over or other sufficient relationship to the premises or effects sought to be inspected.[7] The issue now before us is whether the Government made the requisite showing in this case.

III

The District Court excluded from evidence at the suppression hearings, as inadmissible hearsay, the out-of-court statements of Mrs. Graff with respect to her and

---

7. Common authority is, of course, not to be implied from the mere property interest a third party has in the property. The authority which justifies the third-party consent does not rest upon the law of property, with its attendant historical and legal refinements, *see Chapman v. United States*, 365 U.S. 610, 81 S. Ct. 776, 5 L. Ed. 2d 828 (1961) (landlord could not validly consent to the

respondent's joint occupancy and use of the east bedroom, as well as the evidence that both respondent and Mrs. Graff at various times and to various persons had represented themselves as husband and wife. The Court of Appeals affirmed the ruling. Both courts were in error.

. . . .

IV

It appears to us, given the admissibility of Mrs. Graff's and respondent's out-of-court statements, that the Government sustained its burden of proving by the preponderance of the evidence that Mrs. Graff's voluntary consent to search the east bedroom was legally sufficient to warrant admitting into evidence the $4,995 found in the diaper bag.[14] But we prefer that the District Court first reconsider the sufficiency of the evidence in the light of this decision and opinion. The judgment of the Court of Appeals is reversed and the case is remanded to the Court of Appeals with directions to remand the case to the District Court for further proceedings consistent with this opinion.

So ordered.

Reversed and remanded.

MR. JUSTICE DOUGLAS, dissenting.

. . . Because I believe that the absence of a search warrant in this case, where the authorities had opportunity to obtain one, is fatal, I dissent from that disposition of this case.

. . . .

We have . . . held that only the gravest of circumstances could excuse the failure to secure a properly issued search warrant.

Up to now, a police officer had a duty to secure a warrant when he had the opportunity to do so, even if substantial probable cause existed to justify a search.

. . . .

. . . [I]ndeed, the provisions of the Fourth Amendment carefully and explicitly restricting the circumstances in which warrants can issue and the breadth of searches have become "empty phrases," when the Court sanctions this search conducted without any effort by the police to secure a valid search warrant. This was not a case

---

search of a house he had rented to another), *Stoner v. California*, 376 U.S. 483, 84 S. Ct. 889, 11 L. Ed. 2d 856 (1964) (night hotel clerk could not validly consent to search of customer's room), but rests rather on mutual use of the property by persons generally having joint access or control for most purposes, so that it is reasonable to recognize that any of the co-inhabitants has the right to permit the inspection in his own right and that the others have assumed the risk that one of their number might permit the common area to be searched.

14. Accordingly, we do not reach another major contention of the United States in bringing this case here: that the Government in any event had only to satisfy the District Court that the searching officers reasonably believed that Mrs. Graff had sufficient authority over the premises to consent to the search . . . .

where a grave emergency, such as the imminent loss of evidence or danger to human life, might excuse the failure to secure a warrant. Mrs. Graff's permission to the police to invade the house, simultaneously violating the privacy of Matlock and the Marshalls, provides a sorry and wholly inadequate substitute for the protections which inhere in a judicially granted warrant. It is inconceivable that a search conducted without a warrant can give more authority than a search conducted with a warrant. *See United States v. Lefkowitz*, 285 U.S. 452, 464, 52 S. Ct. 420, 423, 76 L. Ed. 877. But here the police procured without a warrant all the authority which they had under the feared general warrants, hatred of which led to the passage of the Fourth Amendment. Government agents are now free to rummage about the house, unconstrained by anything except their own desires .... Since the Framers of the Amendment did not abolish the hated general warrants only to impose another oppressive regime on the people, I dissent.

Mr. Justice Brennan, with whom Mr. Justice Marshall joins, dissenting.

I would not limit the remand to the determination whether Mrs. Graff was in fact a joint occupant of the bedroom with sufficient authority to consent to the search. In my view the determination is also required that Mrs. Graff consented knowing that she was not required to consent ....

Notes and Questions

If a person with authority to consent voluntarily gives officers permission to search, what is the permissible *scope* of the search they are constitutionally authorized to perform? If a person expressly specifies the breadth of the search he or she intends to permit, officers may search only as far as the person has specified. But what about situations in which a general consent of unspecified scope is given? Will the scope be dictated by what the person later asserts to have been his or her intent at the time of the search?

In *Florida v. Jimeno*, 500 U.S. 248, 111 S. Ct. 1801, 114 L. Ed. 2d 297 (1991), the Supreme Court held that the scope of a consent search is governed by a standard of "objective reasonableness." The dispositive question is "what would [a] reasonable person have understood by the exchange between the officer and the suspect?" If it is objectively reasonable to understand a person to be giving consent to search her entire home, the entire home may be searched. If there are objective indicia that would indicate to a reasonable person that the person was only permitting the search of one floor or one room in the home, the scope of the consent is limited to that floor or room. In *Jimeno*, the Court applied this "objective" standard to a situation in which a man had given general consent to search his automobile to officers who had made it evident that they were looking for narcotics. The Court concluded that when a person gives officers general, unrestricted consent to search for narcotics in his vehicle, it is reasonable to understand that consent to extend to the vehicle itself and to any unlocked containers that are within the vehicle and could contain the contraband that is the object of the search.

Georgia v. Randolph

United States Supreme Court

547 U.S. 103, 126 S. Ct. 1515, 164 L. Ed. 2d 208 (2006)

JUSTICE SOUTER delivered the opinion of the Court.

. . . .

I

Respondent Scott Randolph and his wife, Janet, separated in late May 2001, when she left the marital residence in Americus, Georgia, and went to stay with her parents in Canada, taking their son and some belongings. In July, she returned to the Americus house with the child, though the record does not reveal whether her object was reconciliation or retrieval of remaining possessions.

On the morning of July 6, she complained to the police that after a domestic dispute her husband took their son away, and when officers reached the house she told them that her husband was a cocaine user whose habit had caused financial troubles. She mentioned the marital problems and said that she and their son had only recently returned after a stay of several weeks with her parents. Shortly after the police arrived, Scott Randolph returned and explained that he had removed the child to a neighbor's house out of concern that his wife might take the boy out of the country again; he denied cocaine use, and countered that it was in fact his wife who abused drugs and alcohol.

One of the officers, Sergeant Murray, went with Janet Randolph to reclaim the child, and when they returned she not only renewed her complaints about her husband's drug use, but also volunteered that there were "'items of drug evidence'" in the house. Sergeant Murray asked Scott Randolph for permission to search the house, which he unequivocally refused.

The sergeant turned to Janet Randolph for consent to search, which she readily gave. She led the officer upstairs to a bedroom that she identified as Scott's, where the sergeant noticed a section of a drinking straw with a powdery residue he suspected was cocaine. He then left the house to get an evidence bag from his car and to call the district attorney's office, which instructed him to stop the search and apply for a warrant. When Sergeant Murray returned to the house, Janet Randolph withdrew her consent. The police took the straw to the police station, along with the Randolphs. After getting a search warrant, they returned to the house and seized further evidence of drug use, on the basis of which Scott Randolph was indicted for possession of cocaine.

He moved to suppress the evidence, as products of a warrantless search of his house unauthorized by his wife's consent over his express refusal. The trial court denied the motion, ruling that Janet Randolph had common authority to consent to the search.

The Court of Appeals of Georgia reversed, 264 Ga. App. 396, 590 S.E.2d 834 (2003), and was itself sustained by the State Supreme Court, principally on the ground that "the consent to conduct a warrantless search of a residence given by one occupant is not valid in the face of the refusal of another occupant who is physically present at the scene to permit a warrantless search." 278 Ga. 614, 604 S.E.2d 835, 836 (2004) . . . .

We granted certiorari to resolve a split of authority on whether one occupant may give law enforcement effective consent to search shared premises, as against a co-tenant who is present and states a refusal to permit the search. We now affirm.

II

To the Fourth Amendment rule ordinarily prohibiting the warrantless entry of a person's house as unreasonable *per se*, one "jealously and carefully drawn" exception, *Jones v. United States*, 357 U.S. 493, 499, 78 S. Ct. 1253, 2 L. Ed. 2d 1514 (1958), recognizes the validity of searches with the voluntary consent of an individual possessing authority, *Rodriguez*, 497 U.S., at 181, 110 S. Ct. 2793. That person might be the householder against whom evidence is sought, *Schneckloth v. Bustamonte*, 412 U.S. 218, 222, 93 S. Ct. 2041, 36 L. Ed. 2d 854 (1973), or a fellow occupant who shares common authority over property, when the suspect is absent, *Matlock, supra*, at 170, 94 S. Ct. 988, and the exception for consent extends even to entries and searches with the permission of a co-occupant whom the police reasonably, but erroneously, believe to possess shared authority as an occupant, *Rodriguez, supra*, at 186, 110 S. Ct. 2793. None of our co-occupant consent-to-search cases, however, has presented the further fact of a second occupant physically present and refusing permission to search, and later moving to suppress evidence so obtained. The significance of such a refusal turns on the underpinnings of the co-occupant consent rule, as recognized since *Matlock*.

A

The defendant in that case was arrested in the yard of a house where he lived with a Mrs. Graff and several of her relatives, and was detained in a squad car parked nearby. When the police went to the door, Mrs. Graff admitted them and consented to a search of the house. 415 U.S., at 166, 94 S. Ct. 988. In resolving the defendant's objection to use of the evidence taken in the warrantless search, we said that "the consent of one who possesses common authority over premises or effects is valid as against the absent, nonconsenting person with whom that authority is shared." *Id.*, at 170, 94 S. Ct. 988 . . . . [W]e explained that the third party's "common authority" is not synonymous with a technical property interest:

> "The authority which justifies the third-party consent does not rest upon the law of property, with its attendant historical and legal refinement, but rests rather on mutual use of the property by persons generally having joint access or control for most purposes, so that it is reasonable to recognize that any of the co-inhabitants has the right to permit the inspection in his own right and that the others have assumed the risk that one of their number might permit the common area to be searched." 415 U.S., at 171, n. 7, 94 S. Ct. 988 (citations omitted).

The common authority that counts under the Fourth Amendment may thus be broader than the rights accorded by property law, although its limits, too, reflect specialized tenancy arrangements apparent to the police, *see Chapman v. United States*, 365 U.S. 610, 81 S. Ct. 776, 5 L. Ed. 2d 828 (1961) (landlord could not consent to search of tenant's home).

The constant element in assessing Fourth Amendment reasonableness in the consent cases, then, is the great significance given to widely shared social expectations, which are naturally enough influenced by the law of property, but not controlled by its rules. *Matlock* accordingly not only holds that a solitary co-inhabitant may sometimes consent to a search of shared premises, but stands for the proposition that the reasonableness of such a search is in significant part a function of commonly held understanding about the authority that co-inhabitants may exercise in ways that affect each other's interests.

B

Matlock's example of common understanding is readily apparent. When someone comes to the door of a domestic dwelling with a baby at her hip, as Mrs. Graff did, she shows that she belongs there, and that fact standing alone is enough to tell a law enforcement officer or any other visitor that if she occupies the place along with others, she probably lives there subject to the assumption tenants usually make about their common authority when they share quarters. They understand that any one of them may admit visitors, with the consequence that a guest obnoxious to one may nevertheless be admitted in his absence by another. As *Matlock* put it, shared tenancy is understood to include an "assumption of risk," on which police officers are entitled to rely, and although some group living together might make an exceptional arrangement that no one could admit a guest without the agreement of all, the chance of such an eccentric scheme is too remote to expect visitors to investigate a particular household's rules before accepting an invitation to come in. So, *Matlock* relied on what was usual and placed no burden on the police to eliminate the possibility of atypical arrangements, in the absence of reason to doubt that the regular scheme was in place.

It is also easy to imagine different facts on which, if known, no common authority could sensibly be suspected. A person on the scene who identifies himself, say, as a landlord or a hotel manager calls up no customary understanding of authority to admit guests without the consent of the current occupant. See *Chapman v. United States, supra* (landlord); *Stoner v. California*, 376 U.S. 483, 84 S. Ct. 889, 11 L. Ed. 2d 856 (1964) (hotel manager). A tenant in the ordinary course does not take rented premises subject to any formal or informal agreement that the landlord may let visitors into the dwelling, *Chapman, supra*, at 617, 81 S. Ct. 776, and a hotel guest customarily has no reason to expect the manager to allow anyone but his own employees into his room, *see Stoner, supra*, at 489, 84 S. Ct. 889. In these circumstances, neither state-law property rights, nor common contractual arrangements, nor any other source points to a common understanding of authority to admit third parties generally without the consent of a person occupying the premises. And when it comes to searching through bureau drawers, there will be instances in which even a person clearly belonging on premises as an occupant may lack any perceived authority to consent; "a child of eight might well be considered to have the power to consent to the police crossing the threshold into that part of the house where any caller, such as a pollster or salesman, might well be admitted," 4 LaFave 8.4(c), at 207 (4th ed. 2004), but no one would reasonably expect such a child to be in a position to authorize anyone to rummage through his parents' bedroom.

C

. . . .

To begin with, it is fair to say that a caller standing at the door of shared premises would have no confidence that one occupant's invitation was a sufficiently good reason to enter when a fellow tenant stood there saying, "stay out." Without some very good reason, no sensible person would go inside under those conditions. Fear for the safety of the occupant issuing the invitation, or of someone else inside, would be thought to justify entry, but the justification then would be the personal risk, the threats to life or limb, not the disputed invitation.

The visitor's reticence without some such good reason would show not timidity but a realization that when people living together disagree over the use of their common quarters, a resolution must come through voluntary accommodation, not by appeals to authority. Unless the people living together fall within some recognized hierarchy, like a household of parent and child or barracks housing military personnel of different grades, there is no societal understanding of superior and inferior . . . . In sum, there is no common understanding that one co-tenant generally has a right or authority to prevail over the express wishes of another, whether the issue is the color of the curtains or invitations to outsiders.

D

Since the co-tenant wishing to open the door to a third party has no recognized authority in law or social practice to prevail over a present and objecting co-tenant, his disputed invitation, without more, gives a police officer no better claim to reasonableness in entering than the officer would have in the absence of any consent at all. Accordingly, in the balancing of competing individual and governmental interests entailed by the bar to unreasonable searches, the cooperative occupant's invitation adds nothing to the government's side to counter the force of an objecting individual's claim to security against the government's intrusion into his dwelling place. Since we hold to the "centuries-old principle of respect for the privacy of the home," *Wilson v. Layne*, 526 U.S. 603, 610, 119 S. Ct. 1692, 143 L. Ed. 2d 818 (1999), "it is beyond dispute that the home is entitled to special protection as the center of the private lives of our people," *Minnesota v. Carter*, 525 U.S. 83, 99, 119 S. Ct. 469, 142 L. Ed. 2d 373 (1998) (Kennedy, J., concurring). We have, after all, lived our whole national history with an understanding of "the ancient adage that a man's home is his castle [to the point that t]he poorest man may in his cottage bid defiance to all the forces of the Crown," *Miller v. United States*, 357 U.S. 301, 307, 78 S. Ct. 1190, 2 L. Ed. 2d 1332 (1958) (internal quotation marks omitted).[4]

Disputed permission is thus no match for this central value of the Fourth Amendment, and the State's other countervailing claims do not add up to outweigh it. Yes, we recognize the consenting tenant's interest as a citizen in bringing criminal activity to light. And we understand a co-tenant's legitimate self-interest in siding with the police to deflect suspicion raised by sharing quarters with a criminal.

But society can often have the benefit of these interests without relying on a theory of consent that ignores an inhabitant's refusal to allow a warrantless search. The co-tenant acting on his own initiative may be able to deliver evidence to the police and can tell the police what he knows, for use before a magistrate in getting a warrant.[6] The reliance on a co-tenant's information instead of disputed consent accords with the law's general partiality toward "police action taken under a warrant [as against] searches and seizures without one," *United States v. Ventresca*, 380 U.S. 102, 107, 85 S. Ct. 741, 13 L. Ed. 2d 684 (1965); "the informed and deliberate determinations of magistrates empowered to issue warrants as to what searches and seizures are permissible under the Constitution are to be preferred over the hurried action of officers," *United States v. Lefkowitz*, 285 U.S. 452, 464, 52 S. Ct. 420, 76 L. Ed. 877 (1932).

Nor should this established policy of Fourth Amendment law be undermined by the principal dissent's claim that it shields spousal abusers and other violent co-tenants who will refuse to allow the police to enter a dwelling when their victims ask the police for help. It is not that the dissent exaggerates violence in the home; we recognize that domestic abuse is a serious problem in the United States.

But this case has no bearing on the capacity of the police to protect domestic victims. The dissent's argument rests on the failure to distinguish two different issues:

---

4. In the principal dissent's view, the centuries of special protection for the privacy of the home are over. The dissent equates inviting the police into a co-tenant's home over his contemporaneous objection with reporting a secret, *post*, 126 S. Ct. at 1537–1538 (opinion of Roberts, C.J.), and the emphasis it places on the false equation suggests a deliberate intent to devalue the importance of the privacy of a dwelling place. The same attitude that privacy of a dwelling is not special underlies the dissent's easy assumption that privacy shared with another individual is privacy waived for all purposes including warrantless searches by the police. *Post*, 126 S. Ct. at 1533.

6. Sometimes, of course, the very exchange of information like this in front of the objecting inhabitant may render consent irrelevant by creating an exigency that justifies immediate action on the police's part; if the objecting tenant cannot be incapacitated from destroying easily disposable evidence during the time required to get a warrant, *see Illinois v. McArthur*, 531 U.S. 326, 331–332, 121 S. Ct. 946, 148 L. Ed. 2d 838 (2001) (denying suspect access to his trailer home while police applied for a search warrant), a fairly perceived need to act on the spot to preserve evidence may justify entry and search under the exigent circumstances exception to the warrant requirement, *cf. Schmerber v. California*, 384 U.S. 757, 770–771, 86 S. Ct. 1826, 16 L. Ed. 2d 908 (1966) (warrantless search permitted when "the delay necessary to obtain a warrant . . . threatened the destruction of evidence" (internal quotation marks omitted)).

Additional exigent circumstances might justify warrantless searches.

when the police may enter without committing a trespass, and when the police may enter to search for evidence. No question has been raised, or reasonably could be, about the authority of the police to enter a dwelling to protect a resident from domestic violence; so long as they have good reason to believe such a threat exists, it would be silly to suggest that the police would commit a tort by entering, say, to give a complaining tenant the opportunity to collect belongings and get out safely, or to determine whether violence (or threat of violence) has just occurred or is about to (or soon will) occur, however much a spouse or other co-tenant objected. (And since the police would then be lawfully in the premises, there is no question that they could seize any evidence in plain view or take further action supported by any consequent probable cause, *see Texas v. Brown*, 460 U.S. 730, 737–739, 103 S. Ct. 1535, 75 L. Ed. 2d 502 (1983) (plurality opinion).) Thus, the question whether the police might lawfully enter over objection in order to provide any protection that might be reasonable is easily answered yes. The undoubted right of the police to enter in order to protect a victim, however, has nothing to do with the question in this case, whether a search with the consent of one co-tenant is good against another, standing at the door and expressly refusing consent.[7]

None of the cases cited by the dissent support its improbable view that recognizing limits on merely evidentiary searches would compromise the capacity to protect a fearful occupant. In the circumstances of those cases, there is no danger that the fearful occupant will be kept behind the closed door of the house simply because the abusive tenant refuses to consent to a search.

The dissent's red herring aside, we know, of course, that alternatives to disputed consent will not always open the door to search for evidence that the police suspect is inside. The consenting tenant may simply not disclose enough information, or information factual enough, to add up to a showing of probable cause, and there may be no exigency to justify fast action. But nothing in social custom or its reflection in private law argues for placing a higher value on delving into private premises to search for evidence in the face of disputed consent, than on requiring clear justification before the government searches private living quarters over a resident's objection. We therefore hold that a warrantless search of a shared dwelling for evidence over the express refusal of consent by a physically present resident cannot be justified as reasonable as to him on the basis of consent given to the police by another resident.

E

There are two loose ends, the first being the explanation given in *Matlock* for the constitutional sufficiency of a co-tenant's consent to enter and search: it "rests . . . on

---

7. We understand the possibility that a battered individual will be afraid to express fear candidly, but this does not seem to be a reason to think such a person would invite the police into the dwelling to search for evidence against another. Hence, if a rule crediting consent over denial of consent were built on hoping to protect household victims, it would distort the Fourth Amendment with little, if any, constructive effect on domestic abuse investigations.

mutual use of the property by persons generally having joint access or control for most purposes, so that it is reasonable to recognize that any of the co-inhabitants has the right to permit the inspection in his own right . . . ." 415 U.S., at 171, n. 7, 94 S. Ct. 988. If *Matlock*'s co-tenant is giving permission "in his own right," how can his "own right" be eliminated by another tenant's objection? The answer appears in the very footnote from which the quoted statement is taken: the "right" to admit the police to which *Matlock* refers is not an enduring and enforceable ownership right as understood by the private law of property, but is instead the authority recognized by customary social usage as having a substantial bearing on Fourth Amendment reasonableness in specific circumstances. Thus, to ask whether the consenting tenant has the right to admit the police when a physically present fellow tenant objects is not to question whether some property right may be divested by the mere objection of another. It is, rather, the question whether customary social understanding accords the consenting tenant authority powerful enough to prevail over the co-tenant's objection. The *Matlock* Court did not purport to answer this question, a point made clear by another statement (which the dissent does not quote): the Court described the co-tenant's consent as good against "the absent, nonconsenting resident." *Id.*, at 170, 94 S. Ct. 988.

The second loose end is the significance of *Matlock* and *Rodriguez* after today's decision . . . . If those cases are not to be undercut by today's holding, we have to admit that we are drawing a fine line; if a potential defendant with self-interest in objecting is in fact at the door and objects, the co-tenant's permission does not suffice for a reasonable search, whereas the potential objector, nearby but not invited to take part in the threshold colloquy, loses out.

This is the line we draw, and we think the formalism is justified. So long as there is no evidence that the police have removed the potentially objecting tenant from the entrance for the sake of avoiding a possible objection, there is practical value in the simple clarity of complementary rules, one recognizing the co-tenant's permission when there is no fellow occupant on hand, the other according dispositive weight to the fellow occupant's contrary indication when he expresses it. For the very reason that *Rodriguez* held it would be unjustifiably impractical to require the police to take affirmative steps to confirm the actual authority of a consenting individual whose authority was apparent, we think it would needlessly limit the capacity of the police to respond to ostensibly legitimate opportunities in the field if we were to hold that reasonableness required the police to take affirmative steps to find a potentially objecting co-tenant before acting on the permission they had already received. There is no ready reason to believe that efforts to invite a refusal would make a difference in many cases, whereas every co-tenant consent case would turn into a test about the adequacy of the police's efforts to consult with a potential objector. Better to accept the formalism of distinguishing *Matlock* from this case than to impose a requirement, time-consuming in the field and in the courtroom, with no apparent systemic justification. The pragmatic decision to accept the simplicity of this line is, moreover, supported by the substantial number of instances in which suspects who are asked for permission to search actually consent, albeit imprudently, a fact that undercuts any argument that the police should try to locate a suspected inhabitant because his denial of consent would be a foregone conclusion.

III

This case invites a straightforward application of the rule that a physically present inhabitant's express refusal of consent to a police search is dispositive as to him, regardless of the consent of a fellow occupant. Scott Randolph's refusal is clear, and nothing in the record justifies the search on grounds independent of Janet Randolph's consent. The State does not argue that she gave any indication to the police of a need for protection inside the house that might have justified entry into the portion of the premises where the police found the powdery straw (which, if lawfully seized, could have been used when attempting to establish probable cause for the warrant issued later). Nor does the State claim that the entry and search should be upheld under the rubric of exigent circumstances, owing to some apprehension by the police officers that Scott Randolph would destroy evidence of drug use before any warrant could be obtained.

The judgment of the Supreme Court of Georgia is therefore affirmed.

It is so ordered.

JUSTICE ALITO took no part in the consideration or decision of this case.

[The concurring opinion of JUSTICE STEVENS has been omitted.]

[The concurring opinion of JUSTICE BREYER has been omitted.]

CHIEF JUSTICE ROBERTS, with whom JUSTICE SCALIA joins, dissenting.

. . . .

The correct approach to the question presented is clearly mapped out in our precedents: The Fourth Amendment protects privacy. If an individual shares information, papers, *or places* with another, he assumes the risk that the other person will in turn share access to that information or those papers *or places* with the government. And just as an individual who has shared illegal plans or incriminating documents with another cannot interpose an objection when that other person turns the information over to the government, just because the individual happens to be present at the time, so too someone who shares a place with another cannot interpose an objection when that person decides to grant access to the police, simply because the objecting individual happens to be present.

A warrantless search is reasonable if police obtain the voluntary consent of a person authorized to give it. Co-occupants have "assumed the risk that one of their number might permit [a] common area to be searched." *United States v. Matlock*, 415 U.S. 164, 171, n. 7, 94 S. Ct. 988, 39 L. Ed. 2d 242 (1974). Just as Mrs. Randolph could walk upstairs, come down, and turn her husband's cocaine straw over to the police, she can consent to police entry and search of what is, after all, her home, too.

I

... Today's opinion creates an exception to [an] otherwise clear rule: A third-party consent search is unreasonable, and therefore constitutionally impermissible, if the co-occupant against whom evidence is obtained was present and objected to the entry and search.

This exception is based on what the majority describes as "widely shared social expectations" that "when people living together disagree over the use of their common quarters, a resolution must come through voluntary accommodation." *Ante*, 126 S. Ct. at 1521, 1523. But this fundamental predicate to the majority's analysis gets us nowhere: Does the objecting cotenant accede to the consenting cotenant's wishes, or the other way around? ...

Nevertheless, the majority is confident in assuming ... that an invited social guest who arrives at the door of a shared residence, and is greeted by a disagreeable co-occupant shouting "'stay out,'" would simply go away. *Ante*, 126 S. Ct. at 1523. The Court observes that "no sensible person would go inside under those conditions," *ibid.*, and concludes from this that the inviting co-occupant has no "authority" to insist on getting her way over the wishes of her co-occupant, *ibid.* But it seems equally accurate to say — based on the majority's conclusion that one does not have a right to prevail over the express wishes of his co-occupant — that the objector has no "authority" to insist on getting *his* way over his co-occupant's wish that her guest be admitted.

The fact is that a wide variety of differing social situations can readily be imagined, giving rise to quite different social expectations. A relative or good friend of one of two feuding roommates might well enter the apartment over the objection of the other roommate. The reason the invitee appeared at the door also affects expectations: A guest who came to celebrate an occupant's birthday, or one who had traveled some distance for a particular reason, might not readily turn away simply because of a roommate's objection. The nature of the place itself is also pertinent: Invitees may react one way if the feuding roommates share one room, differently if there are common areas from which the objecting roommate could readily be expected to absent himself. Altering the numbers might well change the social expectations: Invitees might enter if two of three co-occupants encourage them to do so, over one dissenter.

The possible scenarios are limitless, and slight variations in the fact pattern yield vastly different expectations about whether the invitee might be expected to enter or to go away. Such shifting expectations are not a promising foundation on which to ground a constitutional rule, particularly because the majority has no support for its basic assumption — that an invited guest encountering two disagreeing co-occupants would flee — beyond a hunch about how people would typically act in an atypical situation.

And in fact the Court has not looked to such expectations to decide questions of consent under the Fourth Amendment, but only to determine when a search has occurred and whether a particular person has standing to object to a search. For these latter inquiries, we ask whether a person has a subjective expectation of privacy in a particular place, and whether "the expectation [is] one that society is prepared to recognize as 'reasonable.'" *Katz v. United States*, 389 U.S. 347, 361, 88 S. Ct. 507, 19 L. Ed. 2d 576 (1967) (Harlan, J., concurring); *see Minnesota v. Olson*, 495 U.S. 91, 95–96, 100, 110 S. Ct. 1684, 109 L. Ed. 2d 85 (1990) (extending *Katz* test to standing inquiry). But the social expectations concept has not been applied to all questions arising under the Fourth Amendment, least of all issues of consent. A criminal might have a strong expectation that his longtime confidant will not allow the government to listen to their private conversations, but however profound his shock might be upon betrayal, government monitoring with the confidant's consent is reasonable under the Fourth Amendment. *See United States v. White*, 401 U.S. 745, 752, 91 S. Ct. 1122, 28 L. Ed. 2d 453 (1971).

The majority suggests that "widely shared social expectations" are a "constant element in assessing Fourth Amendment reasonableness," *ante*, 126 S. Ct. at 1521 (citing *Rakas v. Illinois*, 439 U.S. 128, 144, n. 12, 99 S. Ct. 421, 58 L. Ed. 2d 387 (1978)), but that is not the case; the Fourth Amendment precedents the majority cites refer instead to a "legitimate expectation of *privacy*." *Ibid.* (emphasis added; internal quotation marks omitted). Whatever social expectation the majority seeks to protect, it is not one of privacy. The very predicate giving rise to the question in cases of shared information, papers, containers, or places is that privacy has been shared with another. Our common social expectations may well be that the other person will not, in turn, share what we have shared with them with another — including the police — but that is the risk we take in sharing. If two friends share a locker and one keeps contraband inside, he might trust that his friend will not let others look inside. But by sharing private space, privacy has "already been frustrated" with respect to the lockermate. *United States v. Jacobsen*, 466 U.S. 109, 117, 104 S. Ct. 1652, 80 L. Ed. 2d 85 (1984). If two roommates share a computer and one keeps pirated software on a shared drive, he might assume that his roommate will not inform the government. But that person has given up his privacy with respect to his roommate by saving the software on their shared computer.

A wide variety of often subtle social conventions may shape expectations about how we act when another shares with us what is otherwise private, and those conventions go by a variety of labels — courtesy, good manners, custom, protocol, even honor among thieves. The Constitution, however, protects not these but privacy, and once privacy has been shared, the shared information, documents, or places remain private only at the discretion of the confidant.

II

Our cases reflect this understanding. In *United States v. White*, we held that one party to a conversation can consent to government eavesdropping, and statements made by the other party will be admissible at trial. 401 U.S., at 752, 91 S. Ct. 1122. This rule is based on privacy: "Inescapably, one contemplating illegal activities must realize and risk that his companions may be reporting to the police . . . . [I]f he has no doubts, or allays them, or risks what doubt he has, the risk is his." *Ibid.*

The Court has applied this same analysis to objects and places as well. In *Frazier v. Cupp*, 394 U.S. 731, 89 S. Ct. 1420, 22 L. Ed. 2d 684 (1969), a duffel bag "was being used jointly" by two cousins. *Id.*, at 740, 89 S. Ct. 1420. The Court held that the consent of one was effective to result in the seizure of evidence used against both: "[I]n allowing [his cousin] to use the bag and in leaving it in his house, [the defendant] must be taken to have assumed the risk that [his cousin] would allow someone else to look inside." *Ibid.*

. . . .

The common thread in our decisions upholding searches conducted pursuant to third-party consent is an understanding that a person "assume[s] the risk" that those who have access to and control over his shared property might consent to a search. *Matlock*, 415 U.S., at 171, n. 7, 94 S. Ct. 988. In *Matlock*, we explained that this assumption of risk is derived from a third party's "joint access or control for most purposes" of shared property. *Ibid.* And we concluded that shared use of property makes it "reasonable to recognize that any of the co-inhabitants has the right to permit the inspection in his own right." *Ibid.*

In this sense, the risk assumed by a joint occupant is comparable to the risk assumed by one who reveals private information to another. If a person has incriminating information, he can keep it private in the face of a request from police to share it, because he has that right under the Fifth Amendment. If a person occupies a house with incriminating information in it, he can keep that information private in the face of a request from police to search the house, because he has that right under the Fourth Amendment. But if he shares the information — or the house — with another, that other can grant access to the police in each instance.[1]

---

1. The majority considers this comparison to be a "false equation," and even discerns "a deliberate intent to devalue the importance of the privacy of a dwelling place." *Ante*, at 115 n.4, 126 S. Ct. at 1524 n. 4. But the differences between the majority and this dissent reduce to this: Under the majority's view, police may not enter and search when an objecting co-occupant is *present at the door*, but they *may* do so when he is asleep in the next room; under our view, the co-occupant's consent is effective in both cases. It seems a bit overwrought to characterize the former approach as affording great protection to a man in his castle, the latter as signaling that "the centuries of special protection for the privacy of the home are over." *Ibid.* The Court in *United States v. Matlock*, 415 U.S. 164, 94 S. Ct. 988, 39 L. Ed. 2d 242 (1974), drew the same comparison the majority faults today, *see id.*, at 171, n. 7, 94 S. Ct. 988, and the "deliberate intent" the majority ascribes to this dissent is apparently shared by all Courts of Appeals and the great majority of State Supreme Courts to have considered the question, *see ante*, at 1520 n.1. The majority also mischaracterizes this dissent as assuming that "privacy shared with another individual is privacy waived for all purposes including warrantless searches by the police." *Ante*, at __ n. 4, 126 S. Ct. at 1524 n.4. The point, of course, is not that a person waives his privacy by sharing space with others such that police may enter at will, but that sharing space necessarily entails a limited yielding of privacy *to the person with whom the space is shared*, such that the other person shares authority to consent to a search of the shared space.

To the extent a person wants to ensure that his possessions will be subject to a consent search only due to his *own* consent, he is free to place these items in an area over which others do *not* share access and control, be it a private room or a locked suitcase under a bed . . . .

. . . .

The law acknowledges that although we might not expect our friends and family to admit the government into common areas, sharing space entails risk. A person assumes the risk that his co-occupants — just as they might report his illegal activity or deliver his contraband to the government — might consent to a search of areas over which they have access and control.

III

. . . .

Just as the source of the majority's rule is not privacy, so too the interest it protects cannot reasonably be described as such. That interest is not protected if a co-owner happens to be absent when the police arrive, in the backyard gardening, asleep in the next room, or listening to music through earphones so that only his co-occupant hears the knock on the door. That the rule is so random in its application confirms that it bears no real relation to the privacy protected by the Fourth Amendment. What the majority's rule protects is not so much privacy as the good luck of a co-owner who just happens to be present at the door when the police arrive . . . . We should not embrace a rule at the outset that its *sponsors* appreciate will result in drawing fine, formalistic lines.

. . . .

The scope of the majority's rule is not only arbitrary but obscure as well. The majority repeats several times that a present co-occupant's refusal to permit entry renders the search unreasonable and invalid "as to him." *Ante*, 126 S. Ct. at 1519, 1526, 1528. This implies entry and search would be reasonable "as to" someone else, presumably the consenting co-occupant and any other absent co-occupants . . . .

While the majority's rule protects something random, its consequences are particularly severe. The question presented often arises when innocent cotenants seek to disassociate or protect themselves from ongoing criminal activity. Under the majority's rule, there will be many cases in which a consenting co-occupant's wish to have the police enter is overridden by an objection from another present co-occupant. What does the majority imagine will happen, in a case in which the consenting co-occupant is concerned about the other's criminal activity, once the door clicks shut? The objecting co-occupant may pause briefly to decide whether to destroy any evidence of wrongdoing or to inflict retribution on the consenting co-occupant first, but there can be little doubt that he will attend to both in short order. It is no answer to say that the consenting co-occupant can depart with the police; remember that it is her home, too, and the other co-occupant's very presence, which allowed him to object, may also prevent the consenting co-occupant from doing more than urging the police to enter.

Perhaps the most serious consequence of the majority's rule is its operation in domestic abuse situations, a context in which the present question often arises. While people living together might typically be accommodating to the wishes of their cotenants, requests for police assistance may well come from co-inhabitants who are having a disagreement. The Court concludes that because "no sensible person would go inside" in the face of disputed consent, *ante*, 126 S. Ct. at 1523, and the consenting cotenant thus has "no recognized authority" to insist on the guest's admission, *ante*, 126 S. Ct. at 1523, a "police officer [has] no better claim to reasonableness in entering than the officer would have in the absence of any consent at all," *ibid*. But the police officer's superior claim to enter is obvious: Mrs. Randolph did not invite the police to join her for dessert and coffee; the officer's precise purpose in knocking on the door was to assist with a dispute between the Randolphs — one in which Mrs. Randolph felt the need for the protective presence of the police. The majority's rule apparently forbids police from entering to assist with a domestic dispute if the abuser whose behavior prompted the request for police assistance objects.[2]

. . . .

. . . In response to the concern that police might be turned away under its rule before entry can be justified based on exigency, the majority creates a new rule: A "good reason" to enter, coupled with one occupant's consent, will ensure that a police officer is "lawfully in the premises." *Ante*, 126 S. Ct. at 1525 . . . . For the sake of defending what it concedes are fine, formalistic lines, the majority spins out an entirely new framework for analyzing exigent circumstances. Police may now enter with a "good reason" to believe that "violence (or threat of violence) has just occurred or is about to (or soon will) occur." *Ante*, 126 S. Ct. at 1525. And apparently a key factor allowing entry with a "good reason" short of exigency is the very consent of one co-occupant the majority finds so inadequate in the first place.

The majority's analysis alters a great deal of established Fourth Amendment law. The majority imports the concept of "social expectations," previously used only to determine when a search has occurred and whether a particular person has standing to object to a search, into questions of consent. *Ante*, 126 S. Ct. at 1521, 1522. To

---

2. In response to this concern, the majority asserts that its rule applies "merely [to] evidentiary searches." *Ante*, at 1526. But the fundamental premise of the majority's argument is that an inviting co-occupant has "no recognized authority" to "open the door" over a co-occupant's objection. *Ante*, at 1523; *see also ante*, at 1519 ("[A] physically present co-occupant's stated refusal to permit *entry* prevails, rendering the warrantless search unreasonable and invalid as to him" (emphasis added)); *ante*, at 1522–1523 ("[A] caller standing at the door of shared premises would have no confidence . . . to *enter* when a fellow tenant stood there saying 'stay out'" (emphasis added)); *ante*, at 1523 ("[A] disputed invitation, without more, gives a police officer no . . . claim to reasonableness in *entering*" (emphasis added)). The point is that the majority's rule transforms what may have begun as a request for consent to conduct an evidentiary search into something else altogether, by giving veto power over the consenting co-occupant's wishes to an occupant who would exclude the police from *entry*. The majority would afford the now quite vulnerable consenting co-occupant sufficient time to gather her belongings and leave, *see ante*, at 1525, apparently putting to one side the fact that it is her castle, too.

determine whether entry and search are reasonable, the majority considers a police officer's subjective motive in asking for consent, which we have otherwise refrained from doing in assessing Fourth Amendment questions. *Ante*, 126 S. Ct. at 1525–1526. And the majority creates a new exception to the warrant requirement to justify warrantless entry short of exigency in potential domestic abuse situations.

Considering the majority's rule is solely concerned with protecting a person who happens to be present at the door when a police officer asks his co-occupant for consent to search, but not one who is asleep in the next room or in the backyard gardening, the majority has taken a great deal of pain in altering Fourth Amendment doctrine, for precious little (if any) gain in privacy . . . .

. . . .

I respectfully dissent.

[The dissenting opinion of JUSTICE SCALIA has been omitted.]

[The dissenting opinion of JUSTICE THOMAS has been omitted.]

Notes and Questions

(1) According to the *Randolph* majority, under what circumstances is a search unreasonable even though officers have obtained consent from a person with common authority? Why is such a search unreasonable? Whose Fourth Amendment rights are violated by such a search?

(2) Justice Souter conceded that the majority was "drawing a fine line." Chief Justice Roberts alleged that the line drawn is "formalistic," that it produces "random" results, and that it protects "good luck," not privacy. Is the line drawn in *Randolph* between searches that are validated by third-party consent and searches that are invalid despite third-party consent a sensible interpretation of the Fourth Amendment or an arbitrary explanation of that guarantee? If the latter, what alternative line seems preferable? Why?

(3) In which of the following situations would a search by officers violate the Fourth Amendment rights of the nonconsenting co-tenant?

(a) A seventeen-year-old high school senior objects to officers' entry of the family home and search of her bedroom pursuant to her father's consent.

(b) A woman who is driving home from work and will arrive in under five minutes informs the police, by cell phone, that she opposes a search of her home consented to by her husband or her 18-year-old son.

(c) A young man who shares an apartment with his brother has expressly refused to allow the police to search, but the brother consents to a search when the police return shortly after the young man leaves for school.

(d) Suspecting a woman of selling contraband and believing that she will not permit a search of her duplex, officers wait until she goes to visit her mother then secure consent to search from her teenage daughter or her husband.

(e) In the prior situation, the woman has not left to visit her mother, but, instead, has gone for a swim in her backyard swimming pool at the time the officers secure consent to search.

(f) Believing that a man will probably not allow them to enter his home to search for child pornography, officers recruit an informant to befriend the man and invite him to a football game and then secure consent to search his condominium from the woman with whom he lives.

(g) After police officers have entered an elderly man's home pursuant to the consent of his adult daughter, who lives with and takes care of him, the man returns home from a walk and orders the police to leave the home immediately.

(h) A passenger, who jointly owns and uses a car with a driver, gives an officer consent to search the glove compartment and trunk shortly after the driver has refused to consent.

(4) Chief Justice Roberts suggests, in dissent, that the majority's rule may well have "serious consequence[s] . . . in domestic abuse situations." The majority refers to the dissent's "claim that [its rule will] shield[] spousal abusers" as a "red herring," and asserts that "this case has no bearing on the capacity of the police to protect domestic victims." Does the holding of *Randolph* increase the risk that the police will be unable to protect victims of domestic violence? If so, is that a reason to reject that holding?

(5) The majority opinion in *Fernandez v. California*, 571 U.S. ____, 134 S. Ct. 1126, 188 L. Ed. 2d 25 (2014), evidences a determination to ensure that the qualification upon third-party consent authority announced in *Randolph* is kept exceedingly narrow.

Fernandez, who was physically present in his apartment, objected to a police entry. Based on suspicion that he had assaulted a woman who also lived in the apartment, officers arrested Fernandez and took him to the police station for booking. Approximately one hour after the arrest, one officer returned to the apartment, informed the woman of Fernandez's arrest, and obtained her consent to search the apartment. During the search, the officer found evidence that incriminated Fernandez. California courts rejected Fernandez's contention that the search had violated his Fourth Amendment rights. A six-Justice majority agreed, holding that despite Fernandez's objection to a search of the apartment and his removal by the police, the consent given by the woman — a third party with authority to consent — rendered the search reasonable.

According to the majority, "consent by one resident of jointly occupied premises is generally sufficient to justify a warrantless search." In *Randolph*, the Court did "recognize[] a narrow exception to this rule," holding "that '*a physically present inhabitant's* express refusal of consent to a police search [of his home] is dispositive as to him, regardless of the consent of a fellow occupant.' (emphasis added)." The *Randolph* opinion, however, "went to great lengths to make clear that its holding was limited to situations in which the objecting occupant is present."

Although Fernandez "was not present when [his co-occupant] consented," he offered two reasons why *Randolph* controlled in his case. He first claimed "that his absence should not matter since he was absent only because the police had taken him away." He also argued that "it was sufficient that he [had] objected to the search while he was still present." According to the majority, "[n]either of these arguments [was] sound."

Randolph did "suggest[] in dictum that consent by one occupant might not be sufficient if 'there is evidence that the police have removed the potentially objecting tenant from the entrance for the sake of avoiding a possible objection.'" The Court did "not believe that th[is] statement should be read to suggest that improper motive may invalidate objectively justified removal." It was "best understood not to require an inquiry into the subjective intent of officers who detain or arrest a potential objector but instead to refer to situations in which the removal of a potential objector is not objectively reasonable." Under the "test . . . of objective reasonableness," Fernandez's "argument collapse[d]" because he did "not contest . . . that the police had reasonable grounds for removing him from the apartment" or "the existence of probable cause" for his arrest. The majority held "that an occupant who is absent due to a lawful detention or arrest stands in the same shoes as an occupant who is absent for any other reason."

According to the Court, Fernandez's second contention — "that his objection . . . remained effective until he changed his mind and withdrew his objection" — was "inconsistent with *Randolph*'s reasoning in at least two important ways." It could not "be squared with the 'widely shared social expectations' or 'customary social usage' upon which the *Randolph* holding was based." In addition, the proposed principle "would create the very sort of practical complications that *Randolph* sought to avoid. The *Randolph* Court" adopted "a 'formalis[tic]' rule . . . in the interests of 'simple clarity' and administrability." Fernandez's suggested rule "would produce a plethora of practical problems." If an objection "last[ed] until it is withdrawn by the objector," it could unreasonably bar one co-occupant from consenting to a home search for years. If the putative bar that arose instead "last[ed] for a 'reasonable' time," the question of "what interval of time would be reasonable in this context" would arise. Moreover, "the procedure needed to register a continuing objection" would have to be specified. Finally, there would be "the question of the particular law enforcement officers who would be bound by an objection." By taking *Randolph* "at its word — that it applies only when the objector is standing in the door saying 'stay out' when officers propose to make a consent search — all of these problems disappear."

In the majority's view, in situations other than those governed by the *Randolph* exception, "the lawful occupant of a house . . . should have the right to invite police to enter the dwelling and conduct a search. Any other rule would trample on the rights of the occupant who is willing to consent" and "would . . . show disrespect for [the] independence" of the consenting occupant.

A dissent authored by Justice Ginsburg, and joined by Justices Sotomayor and Kagan, asserted that the ruling in *Randolph* dictated a conclusion that Fernandez's objection rendered the third-party consent search unreasonable as to him. The dissent accused the majority of "shrink[ing] to petite size our holding in" *Randolph* and of demonstrating "disregard for the warrant requirement."

Students should reconsider the hypothetical situations in Question (3), *supra*, in light of the ruling in *Fernandez*.

Illinois v. Rodriguez

United States Supreme Court

497 U.S. 177, 110 S. Ct. 2793, 111 L. Ed. 2d 148 (1990)

JUSTICE SCALIA delivered the opinion of the Court.

. . . .

I

. . . .

On July 26, 1985, police were summoned to the residence of Dorothy Jackson on South Wolcott in Chicago. They were met by Ms. Jackson's daughter, Gail Fischer, who showed signs of a severe beating. She told the officers that she had been assaulted by respondent Edward Rodriguez earlier that day in an apartment on South California. Fischer stated that Rodriguez was then asleep in the apartment, and she consented to travel there with the police in order to unlock the door with her key so that the officers could enter and arrest him. During this conversation, Fischer several times referred to the apartment on South California as "our" apartment, and said that she had clothes and furniture there. It is unclear whether she indicated that she currently lived at the apartment, or only that she used to live there.

The police officers drove to the apartment on South California, accompanied by Fischer. They did not obtain an arrest warrant for Rodriguez, nor did they seek a search warrant for the apartment. At the apartment, Fischer unlocked the door with her key and gave the officers permission to enter. They moved through the door into the living room, where they observed in plain view drug paraphernalia and containers filled with white powder that they believed (correctly, as later analysis showed) to be cocaine. They proceeded to the bedroom, where they found Rodriguez asleep and discovered additional containers of white powder in two open attaché cases. The officers arrested Rodriguez and seized the drugs and related paraphernalia.

Rodriguez was charged with possession of a controlled substance with intent to deliver. He moved to suppress all evidence seized at the time of his arrest, claiming that Fischer had vacated the apartment several weeks earlier and had no authority to consent to the entry. The Cook County Circuit Court granted the motion, holding that at the time she consented to the entry Fischer did not have common authority over the apartment. The Court concluded that Fischer was not a "usual resident" but rather an "infrequent visitor" at the apartment on South California, based upon its

(1)

findings that Fischer's name was not on the lease, that she did not contribute to the rent, that she was not allowed to invite others to the apartment on her own, that she did not have access to the apartment when respondent was away, and that she had moved some of her possessions from the apartment. The Circuit Court also rejected the State's contention that, even if Fischer did not possess common authority over the premises, there was no Fourth Amendment violation if the police reasonably believed at the time of their entry that Fischer possessed the authority to consent.

The Appellate Court of Illinois affirmed the Circuit Court in all respects. The Illinois Supreme Court denied the State's Petition for Leave to Appeal, 125 Ill. 2d 572, 537 N.E.2d 816 (1989), and we granted certiorari. 493 U.S. 932 (1989).

II

. . . .

As we stated in [*United States v.*] *Matlock*, 415 U.S. [164,] 171, n. 7 [(1974)], "common authority" rests "on mutual use of the property by persons generally having joint access or control for most purposes . . . ." The burden of establishing that common authority rests upon the State. On the basis of this record, it is clear that burden was not sustained. The evidence showed that although Fischer, with her two small children, had lived with Rodriguez beginning in December 1984, she had moved out on July 1, 1985, almost a month before the search at issue here, and had gone to live with her mother. She took her and her children's clothing with her, though leaving behind some furniture and household effects. During the period after July 1 she sometimes spent the night at Rodriguez's apartment, but never invited her friends there, and never went there herself when he was not home. Her name was not on the lease nor did she contribute to the rent. She had a key to the apartment, which she said at trial she had taken without Rodriguez's knowledge (though she testified at the preliminary hearing that Rodriguez had given her the key). On these facts the State has not established that, with respect to the South California apartment, Fischer had "joint access or control for most purposes." To the contrary, the Appellate Court's determination of no common authority over the apartment was obviously correct.

III

A

The State contends that, even if Fischer did not in fact have authority to give consent, it suffices to validate the entry that the law enforcement officers reasonably believed she did . . . .

. . . .

B

. . . [R]espondent asserts that permitting a reasonable belief of common authority to validate an entry would cause a defendant's Fourth Amendment rights to be "vicariously waived." We disagree.

We have been unyielding in our insistence that a defendant's waiver of his trial rights cannot be given effect unless it is "knowing" and "intelligent." *Colorado v. Spring*, 479 U.S. 564, 574–575 (1987); *Johnson v. Zerbst*, 304 U.S. 458 (1938). We would assuredly not permit, therefore, evidence seized in violation of the Fourth Amendment to be introduced on the basis of a trial court's mere "reasonable belief" — derived from statements by unauthorized persons — that the defendant has waived his objection. But one must make a distinction between, on the one hand, trial rights that derive from the violation of constitutional guarantees and, on the other hand, the nature of those constitutional guarantees themselves. As we said in *Schneckloth:* "There is a vast difference between those rights that protect a fair criminal trial and the rights guaranteed under the Fourth Amendment. Nothing, either in the purposes behind requiring a 'knowing' and 'intelligent' waiver of trial rights, or in the practical application of such a requirement suggests that it ought to be extended to the constitutional guarantee against unreasonable searches and seizures." 412 U.S., at 241.

What Rodriguez is assured by the trial right of the exclusionary rule, where it applies, is that no evidence seized in violation of the Fourth Amendment will be introduced at his trial unless he consents. What he is assured by the Fourth Amendment itself, however, is not that no government search of his house will occur unless he consents; but that no such search will occur that is "unreasonable." U.S. Const., Amdt. 4. There are various elements, of course, that can make a search of a person's house "reasonable" — one of which is the consent of the person or his cotenant. The essence of respondent's argument is that we should impose upon this element a requirement that we have not imposed upon other elements that regularly compel government officers to exercise judgment regarding the facts: namely, the requirement that their judgment be not only responsible but correct.

The fundamental objective that alone validates all unconsented government searches is, of course, the seizure of persons who have committed or are about to commit crimes, or of evidence related to crimes. But "reasonableness," with respect to this necessary element, does not demand that the government be factually correct in its assessment that that is what a search will produce. Warrants need only be supported by "probable cause," which demands no more than a proper "assessment of probabilities in particular factual contexts . . . ." *Illinois v. Gates*, 462 U.S. 213, 232 (1983). If a magistrate, based upon seemingly reliable but factually incorrect information, issues a warrant for the search of a house in which the sought-after felon is not present, has never been present, and was never likely to have been present, the owner of that house suffers one of the inconveniences we all expose ourselves to as the cost of living in a safe society; he does not suffer a violation of the Fourth Amendment.

Another element often, though not invariably, required in order to render an unconsented search "reasonable" is, of course, that the officer be authorized by a valid warrant. Here also we have not held that "reasonableness" precludes error with respect to those factual judgments that law enforcement officials are expected to make. In *Maryland v. Garrison*, 480 U.S. 79 (1987), a warrant supported by probable cause with respect to one apartment was erroneously issued for an entire floor that was divided (though not clearly) into two apartments. We upheld the search of the apartment not properly covered by the warrant. We said:

> The validity of the search of respondent's apartment pursuant to a warrant authorizing the search of the entire third floor depends on whether the officers' failure to realize the overbreadth of the warrant was objectively understandable and reasonable. Here it unquestionably was. The objective facts available to the officers at the time suggested no distinction between [the suspect's] apartment and the third-floor premises.

Id., at 88.

The ordinary requirement of a warrant is sometimes supplanted by other elements that render the unconsented search "reasonable." Here also we have not held that the Fourth Amendment requires factual accuracy. A warrant is not needed, for example, where the search is incident to an arrest. In *Hill v. California*, 401 U.S. 797 (1971), we upheld a search incident to an arrest, even though the arrest was made of the wrong person . . . .

It would be superfluous to multiply these examples. It is apparent that in order to satisfy the "reasonableness" requirement of the Fourth Amendment, what is generally demanded of the many factual determinations that must regularly be made by agents of the government — whether the magistrate issuing a warrant, the police officer executing a warrant, or the police officer conducting a search or seizure under one of the exceptions to the warrant requirement — is not that they always be correct, but that they always be reasonable. As we put it in *Brinegar v. United States*, 338 U.S. 160, 176 (1949): "Because many situations which confront officers in the course of executing their duties are more or less ambiguous, room must be allowed for some mistakes on their part. But the mistakes must be those of reasonable men, acting on facts leading sensibly to their conclusions of probability."

We see no reason to depart from this general rule with respect to facts bearing upon the authority to consent to a search. Whether the basis for such authority exists is the sort of recurring factual question to which law enforcement officials must be expected to apply their judgment; and all the Fourth Amendment requires is that they answer it reasonably. The Constitution is no more violated when officers enter without a warrant because they reasonably (though erroneously) believe that the person who has consented to their entry is a resident of the premises, than it is violated when they enter without a warrant because they reasonably (though erroneously) believe they are in pursuit of a violent felon who is about to escape.*

   . . . .

---

* Justice Marshall's dissent rests upon a rejection of the proposition that searches pursuant to valid third-party consent are "generally reasonable." Only a warrant or exigent circumstances, he contends, can produce "reasonableness"; consent validates the search only because the object of the search thereby "limit[s] his expectation of privacy," so that the search becomes not really a search at all.

... [W]hat we hold today does not suggest that law enforcement officers may always accept a person's invitation to enter premises. Even when the invitation is accompanied by an explicit assertion that the person lives there, the surrounding circumstances could conceivably be such that a reasonable person would doubt its truth and not act upon it without further inquiry. As with other factual determinations bearing upon search and seizure, determination of consent to enter must "be judged against an objective standard: would the facts available to the officer at the moment . . . 'warrant a man of reasonable caution in the belief'" that the consenting party had authority over the premises? *Terry v. Ohio*, 392 U.S. 1, 21–22 (1968). If not, then warrantless entry without further inquiry is unlawful unless authority actually exists. But if so, the search is valid.

In the present case, the Appellate Court found it unnecessary to determine whether the officers reasonably believed that Fischer had the authority to consent, because it ruled as a matter of law that a reasonable belief could not validate the entry. Since we find that ruling to be in error, we remand for consideration of that question. The judgment of the Illinois Appellate Court is reversed and remanded for further proceedings not inconsistent with this opinion.

So ordered.

JUSTICE MARSHALL, with whom JUSTICE BRENNAN and JUSTICE STEVENS join, dissenting.

. . . .

... The Court holds that the warrantless entry into Rodriguez's home was nonetheless valid if the officers reasonably believed that Fischer had authority to consent. The majority's defense of this position rests on a misconception of the basis for third-party consent searches. That such searches do not give rise to claims of constitutional violations rests not on the premise that they are "reasonable" under the Fourth Amendment, but on the premise that a person may voluntarily limit his expectation of privacy by allowing others to exercise authority over his possessions. Thus, an individual's decision to permit another "joint access [to] or control [over the property] for most purposes," *United States v. Matlock*, 415 U.S. 164, 171, n. 7 (1974), limits that individual's reasonable expectation of privacy and to that extent limits his Fourth Amendment protections. If an individual has not so limited his expectation of privacy, the police may not dispense with the safeguards established by the Fourth Amendment.

We see no basis for making such an artificial distinction. To describe a consented search as a non-invasion of privacy and thus a non-search is strange in the extreme. And while it must be admitted that this ingenious device can explain why consented searches are lawful, it cannot explain why seemingly consented searches are "unreasonable," which is all that the Constitution forbids. The only basis for contending that the constitutional standard could not possibly have been met here is the argument that reasonableness must be judged by the facts as they were, rather than by the facts as they were known. As we have discussed in text, that argument has long since been rejected.

The baseline for the reasonableness of a search or seizure in the home is the presence of a warrant. Indeed, "searches and seizures inside a home without a warrant are presumptively unreasonable." *Payton v. New York*, 445 U.S. 573, 586 (1980). Exceptions to the warrant requirement must therefore serve "compelling" law enforcement goals. *Mincey v. Arizona*, 437 U.S. 385, 394 (1978). Because the sole law enforcement purpose underlying third-party consent searches is avoiding the inconvenience of securing a warrant, a departure from the warrant requirement is not justified simply because an officer reasonably believes a third party has consented to a search of the defendant's home. In holding otherwise, the majority ignores our long-standing view that "the informed and deliberate determinations of magistrates . . . as to what searches and seizures are permissible under the Constitution are to be preferred over the hurried action of officers and others who may happen to make arrests." *United States v. Lefkowitz*, 285 U.S. 452, 464 (1932).

I

. . . .

. . . The Court has often heard, and steadfastly rejected, the invitation to carve out further exceptions to the warrant requirement for searches of the home because of the burdens on police investigation and prosecution of crime. Our rejection of such claims is not due to a lack of appreciation of the difficulty and importance of effective law enforcement, but rather to our firm commitment to "the view of those who wrote the Bill of Rights that the privacy of a person's home and property may not be totally sacrificed in the name of maximum simplicity in enforcement of the criminal law." *Mincey, supra*, at 393 (citing *United States v. Chadwick*, 433 U.S. 1, 6–11 (1977)).

In the absence of an exigency, then, warrantless home searches and seizures are unreasonable under the Fourth Amendment. The weighty constitutional interest in preventing unauthorized intrusions into the home overrides any law enforcement interest in relying on the reasonable but potentially mistaken belief that a third party has authority to consent to such a search or seizure. Indeed, as the present case illustrates, only the minimal interest in avoiding the inconvenience of obtaining a warrant weighs in on the law enforcement side.

Against this law enforcement interest in expediting arrests is "the right of a man to retreat into his own home and there be free from unreasonable governmental intrusion." *Silverman v. United States*, 365 U.S. 505, 511 (1961). To be sure, in some cases in which police officers reasonably rely on a third party's consent, the consent will prove valid, no intrusion will result, and the police will have been spared the inconvenience of securing a warrant. But in other cases, such as this one, the authority claimed by the third party will be false. The reasonableness of police conduct must be measured in light of the possibility that the target has not consented. Where "no reason is offered for not obtaining a search warrant except the inconvenience to the officers and some slight delay necessary to prepare and present the evidence to a magistrate," the Constitution demands that the warrant procedure be observed.

Johnson v. United States, 333 U.S. 10, 15 (1948). The concerns of expediting police work and avoiding paperwork "are never very convincing reasons and, in these circumstances, certainly are not enough to by-pass the constitutional requirement." *Id.* In this case, as in *Johnson*, "no suspect was fleeing or likely to take flight. The search was of permanent premises, not of a movable vehicle. No evidence or contraband was threatened with removal or destruction . . . . If the officers in this case were excused from their constitutional duty of presenting their evidence to a magistrate, it is difficult to think of a case in which it should be required." *Id.*

Unlike searches conducted pursuant to the recognized exceptions to the warrant requirement, third-party consent searches are not based on an exigency and therefore serve no compelling social goal. Police officers, when faced with the choice of relying on consent by a third party or securing a warrant, should secure a warrant and must therefore accept the risk of error should they instead choose to rely on consent.

II

Our prior cases discussing searches based on third-party consent have never suggested that such searches are "reasonable." In *United States v. Matlock*, this Court upheld a warrantless search conducted pursuant to the consent of a third party who was living with the defendant. The Court rejected the defendant's challenge to the search, stating that a person who permits others to have "joint access or control for most purposes . . . assume[s] the risk that [such persons] might permit the common area to be searched." 415 U.S., at 171, n. 7. As the Court's assumption-of-risk analysis makes clear, third-party consent limits a person's ability to challenge the reasonableness of the search only because that person voluntarily has relinquished some of his expectation of privacy by sharing access or control over his property with another person.

A search conducted pursuant to an officer's reasonable but mistaken belief that a third party had authority to consent is thus on an entirely different constitutional footing from one based on the consent of a third party who in fact has such authority. Even if the officers reasonably believed that Fischer had authority to consent, she did not, and Rodriguez's expectation of privacy was therefore undiminished. Rodriguez accordingly can challenge the warrantless intrusion into his home as a violation of the Fourth Amendment . . . .

III

Acknowledging that the third party in this case lacked authority to consent, the majority seeks to rely on cases suggesting that reasonable but mistaken factual judgments by police will not invalidate otherwise reasonable searches. The majority reads these cases as establishing a "general rule" that "what is generally demanded of the many factual determinations that must regularly be made by agents of the government — whether the magistrate issuing a warrant, the police officer executing a warrant, or the police officer conducting a search or seizure under one of the exceptions to the warrant requirement — is not that they always be correct, but that they always be reasonable."

The majority's assertion, however, is premised on the erroneous assumption that third-party consent searches are generally reasonable. The cases the majority cites thus provide no support for its holding . . . . Because reasonable factual errors by law enforcement officers will not validate unreasonable searches, the reasonableness of the officer's mistaken belief that the third party had authority to consent is irrelevant.

. . . .

IV

Our cases demonstrate that third-party consent searches are free from constitutional challenge only to the extent that they rest on consent by a party empowered to do so. The majority's conclusion to the contrary ignores the legitimate expectations of privacy on which individuals are entitled to rely. That a person who allows another joint access over his property thereby limits his expectation of privacy does not justify trampling the rights of a person who has not similarly relinquished any of his privacy expectation.

Instead of judging the validity of consent searches, as we have in the past, based on whether a defendant has in fact limited his expectation of privacy, the Court today carves out an additional exception to the warrant requirement for third-party consent searches without pausing to consider whether "'the exigencies of the situation' make the needs of law enforcement so compelling that the warrantless search is objectively reasonable under the Fourth Amendment," *Mincey*, 437 U.S., 394 (citations omitted). Where this free-floating creation of "reasonable" exceptions to the warrant requirement will end, now that the Court has departed from the balancing approach that has long been part of our Fourth Amendment jurisprudence, is unclear. But by allowing a person to be subjected to a warrantless search in his home without his consent and without exigency, the majority has taken away some of the liberty that the Fourth Amendment was designed to protect.

Notes and Questions

(1) The *Rodriguez* majority had no difficulty reconciling its analysis and conclusion with the reasoning and holding of *Matlock*. The dissent, however, maintained that the searches authorized in *Rodriguez* and *Matlock* rest "on . . . entirely different constitutional footing[s]." Are the logical underpinnings of the holdings in the two cases different? If so, are they inconsistent?

(2) Suppose that an officer enters a private area based on a reasonable belief that an individual's consent to search that area is voluntary. The particular characteristics of the individual that were neither evident nor known to the officer render the consent involuntary in fact under the totality-of-the-circumstances test of *Bustamonte*. After *Rodriguez*, will the officer's search nonetheless be reasonable? Should it be?

Consent Search Problems

4E–1: Drug interdiction officers were conducting surveillance at a bus station in Washington, D.C. At about 2:30 a.m., a southbound bus arrived from New York. After the driver announced a 10-minute rest stop, Detective Zattau and two other officers, all dressed in civilian clothes, boarded the bus. Zattau took the intercom and announced that the officers belonged to a drug-interdiction unit and would interview passengers arriving from New York because it was a drug source city.

After questioning several passengers, Zattau approached 14-year-old J.T., who was seated about three-quarters of the way to the rear. He asked where J.T. had boarded and where he was going, and asked to see his ticket. Zattau then asked J.T. if he was carrying drugs or weapons. J.T. said no. The detective asked to search his bag, and J.T. agreed. Nothing was found. Zattau then asked if he could pat J.T. down. J.T. raised his arms. The detective felt a large lump next to J.T.'s ribs, lifted his shirt, and found a plastic bag containing 110 grams of crack cocaine. J.T. was then arrested.

Was the discovery of the cocaine constitutional?

4E–2: The police department received a call reporting an altercation in MacDougald Terrace. The caller stated that three African-American males in white t-shirts were chasing an individual who had a firearm. Officer Doug drove to the area in his patrol car. After arriving, he approached a group of people who were standing near where the foot chase was reported to have occurred. The group, which had not been involved in the chase, could not furnish any useful information.

Officer Doug started to walk back to his patrol car when he noticed a group of six or seven individuals in a sheltered bus stop. Three of the individuals were African-American males wearing white shirts. Jamaal was in the bus shelter but was wearing a dark shirt. Officer Doug approached the bus stop shelter to investigate. By the time he arrived, three or four other police officers had already converged on the scene in their patrol cars. Because the other officers were "dealing with the other subjects at the bus shelter," Officer Doug decided to focus on Jamaal, who was still sitting in the shelter with his back against the rear wall. Doug stopped about four yards in front of Jamaal. Jamaal was blocked on three sides by the walls of the shelter and was facing Officer Doug who stood directly in front of him. Another three or four police officers who were nearby were "dealing with" all of the other individuals at the bus stop.

Doug first asked Jamaal whether he had anything illegal on him. Jamaal did not respond. Doug then waved Jamaal forward and simultaneously asked if he could search his person. In response to Officer Doug's hand gesture, Jamaal stood up, walked two yards towards Officer Doug, turned around, and raised his hands. During the search, Officer Doug recovered a firearm from Jamaal.

After being indicted for illegal possession of a firearm, Jamaal moved to suppress all evidence seized during the search, claiming that the officer had violated his Fourth Amendment rights.

Does Jamaal's claim have merit?

4E–3: One evening, Border Patrol Agent Sorto and his partner were patrolling an area of southern California near the Mexican border that was known for the smuggling of undocumented individuals. The agents began surveillance of Cruz because he was driving a car that they did not recognize as belonging to any of the residents of the nearby small town, and because he was "brake tapping" — behavior that was consistent with people being "guided in to pick up somebody or something." When Cruz pulled over to the shoulder of the road to make a U-turn, the agents stopped their unmarked SUV behind him and activated the lights.

After approaching the car, Agent Sorto asked Cruz where he was going and what he was doing. Cruz said he was going to pick up a friend, Border Patrol Agent Wandy, at a nearby casino. He also told Sorto that the car that he was driving belonged to a friend. Agent Sorto did not ask Cruz who the friend was. Sorto noticed two cell phones in the car's center console and asked Cruz whether the phones were his. Cruz replied that the phones, like the car, belonged to a friend. Sorto then asked, "Can I look in the phones? Can I search the phones?" Cruz replied, "Yes." Sorto took the phones behind the car, out of Cruz's presence where he could not "see or hear what I was doing with the phones."

Within about a minute, one of the phones rang. Without asking Cruz's permission, Sorto answered the call and initiated a conversation with the caller. The caller asked, "How many did you pick up?" The agent responded, "None," and the caller hung up. The phone rang again less than two minutes later. The agent answered again and a different caller asked, "How did it go?" The agent replied in Spanish, "I didn't pick up anybody. There were too many Border Patrol in the area." The caller told him to return to San Diego. Shortly thereafter, the caller phoned again. Believing that she was speaking with Cruz, she stated that there were two people next to a house where there was a lot of lighting. She told him to "drive there, flash your high beams, and the two people will come out."

The agents arrested Cruz and followed the caller's instructions. They picked up two undocumented Mexicans citizens at the location indicated by the caller. After being charged with conspiracy to transport illegal aliens, Cruz moved to suppress the evidence gained from answering the cell phone.

Did the officer violate Cruz's Fourth Amendment rights?

4E–4: ATF Agents Stephens and Darrell received information that Harry owed a thousand dollars to a suspected firearms trafficker and was selling drugs out of his apartment. They watched Harry's apartment for several months but saw no indications of drug trafficking. Because they did not have probable cause for a warrant, Stephens and Darrell decided to attempt to gain consent to search the apartment. The Agents were dressed in plain clothes with their badges around their necks. They were armed, but their firearms were not visible. They went to Harry's apartment and knocked on the door. Harry responded from inside the apartment, "Who is it?" Stephens replied, "Steve." Two or three minutes passed before Harry opened the door.

During this time, Stephens knocked periodically. When Harry opened the door, the Agents identified themselves as law enforcement officers and asked if they could come inside to talk. Harry introduced himself and agreed to talk.

Agent Stephens told Harry that he had "received an anonymous phone call claiming that there were drugs and bombs in this apartment." He asked if Harry "would mind if we look around." Stephens had no reason to believe there were bombs in the apartment but made the assertion "in an effort to gain Harry's consent." Harry replied that there were no bombs in the apartment. Stephens then stated, "Well, you know, any time we get a phone call like this, you know, our boss makes us come out and investigate it further and see if there's any threat or danger to the community." Harry said that he did not know if he could give permission because it was his girlfriend's apartment. Stephens informed him that he could consent because he lived there and had control. Agent Darrell then assured him, "We're not here to bust you on a small bag of weed. We have bigger fish to fry." Harry then gave the Agents permission to search the apartment. Stephens found a loaded handgun that was hidden in a hole in the drywall underneath a sink.

Was the warrantless search reasonable under the Fourth Amendment?

4E–5: K.A., a 12-year-old girl, reported to the police that she had been sexually assaulted. When officers arrived at her home at approximately 3:30 a.m., she identified her attackers as her next-door neighbors, Tommy and Donald. Officer Benfield went to Tommy's home and knocked on the back door.

A young boy, later identified as Tommy's 15-year-old son, answered the door. According to Benfield, he identified himself and told the boy that he needed to speak to an adult. The boy then gave him permission to enter the home. Officer Benfield entered the home and walked past the boy to a nearby bedroom where he arrested Donald. Two other officers entered the home and arrested Tommy in an adjacent bedroom. They also found evidence relevant to the sexual assault. The officers placed Donald and Tommy in the back of their police car. K.A. identified them as her attackers.

Was the entry of Tommy's home reasonable?

4E–6: On July 10, Detective Renee Payne received the following voicemail message:

> *A very light complected male is standing on the front walk in the area of 320 West Grace Street. He is dealing narcotics, and keeps the money in his left pocket. The drugs are kept in his underwear area. He is wearing a white shirt, blue jeans, and has very pretty hair.*

Acting on this information within 10 minutes of receiving it, Payne and two other uniformed officers arrived at the intersection of Grace Street and Madison Avenue. They saw Hugh standing in the area indicated by the caller. The officers determined that Hugh, a very light complected male with dark wavy hair, a white shirt, and blue jeans, was the individual described in the voicemail tip.

Payne approached Hugh and advised him that she had received information that a person of his description was dealing narcotics. Hugh denied possessing drugs or weapons and consented to a patdown search. After discovering money in Hugh's left pocket during the patdown, Payne declared, "Well, if the money is in your left pocket, then the drugs should be in your underwear." Hugh agreed to allow Payne to "check further."

To ensure Hugh's privacy, Officer Rogers escorted him to the front hallway of a nearby apartment building. Hugh disrobed, whereupon Rogers checked his underwear. Upon finding nothing there, Rogers said, "Well, if it's not in your underwear, it's got to be behind you. You don't mind going ahead and bending over then, right?" Without replying, Hugh bent over. Rogers, who was standing behind Hugh, told him to cough. When Hugh did so, Rogers was able to see part of a plastic bag protruding from his anus. Using gloves, Officer Rogers removed the bag from Hugh's anal cavity. The bag contained cocaine.

Prior to trial, Hugh moved to suppress the cocaine. The trial court denied the motion, holding that the narcotics were discovered during a valid consent search. Hugh was convicted of possession of cocaine with intent to distribute it. He has appealed the trial court's denial of his suppression motion.

Should the court of appeals reverse the trial court ruling?

4E–7: Delores was a passenger in the front seat of an automobile driven by Ruth Boolman. Officers stopped the vehicle to investigate a possible vehicle license violation. After ascertaining that there was no problem with the license, one officer stated that the area was a high drug-traffic area and that the officers were checking vehicles. Boolman, outside of Delores's presence and without her awareness, gave consent to a search of her car for drugs.

Officers removed Delores and three other passengers. Delores left her purse on the front seat. During the search of the car, officers opened the purse and found a pipe and a substance that they thought was cocaine. They seized the items. After ascertaining that the purse belonged to Delores, the officers arrested her. Later, she was charged with possession of narcotics.

What claim should Delores raise? Should it be successful?

4E–8: A special team of agents was assigned to execute a search warrant at Handi-Pak Services, Inc. The object of the search was evidence of excessive sales of pseudoephedrine. Agent Coop, the supervisor of the team executing the warrant, assumed responsibility for searching the office of Roy Hud, CEO of Handi-Pak. Coop noticed a computer and compact disks (CDs) on Hud's desk. He selected a homemade CD with a handwritten label and opened a folder containing thumbnail images of graphics files. Several images contained obvious child pornography.

Coop informed Agent Nash about his discovery. When Nash asked Hud about the images Coop had discovered, Hud replied that he knew there was "guy stuff" on the computer and CDs, but did not know that it was illegal. He disclosed that he had downloaded Internet images onto his office computer, and had then burned the images onto CDs. Hud refused to say whether he had downloaded similar images on his home computer. He also refused Nash's request for permission to search his home computer. Nash then had Hud arrested and transported to the county jail.

Nash believed that Hud's home computer also contained child pornography. Along with three other officers, he went to the Hud home. Hud's wife, Georgia, was at home with the couple's children. Nash introduced himself, showed Mrs. Hud his identification, and identified the men with him as law enforcement officers. None of the officers were in uniform or carrying weapons. Mrs. Hud sent the children to a back bedroom and permitted the officers to enter.

Nash then informed Mrs. Hud that they had arrested her husband after finding child pornography on his office computer. Nash explained his concern that the home computer contained similar images. He did not tell Mrs. Hud that her husband had refused to consent to a search of the home computer. Nash asked for permission to search the residence, but Mrs. Hud refused. Nash then requested permission to take and search the computer in the garage. Mrs. Hud said she did not know what to do and asked Nash what would happen if she did not consent. Nash told Mrs. Hud he would leave an armed uniformed officer at the home to prevent destruction of the computer and other evidence while he applied for a search warrant. Mrs. Hud said she wanted to make a phone call, went into the kitchen, and tried unsuccessfully to contact her attorney. After a few minutes, she returned and gave officers permission to take and search the computer. Nash saw homemade CDs next to the computer similar to the ones found at Handi-Pak and asked Mrs. Hud if he could take and examine the CDs. She said, "Yes." The entire visit lasted approximately 30 minutes.

Officers looked at the contents of the disks seized from the home, finding images of child pornography that Hud had downloaded. Similar images were found on the computer's hard drive. The investigators also found movie files of Hud's stepdaughter appearing nude and in various stages of undress. Hud had surreptitiously recorded her by using a computer web camera.

Did the search of the computer and disks found in Hud's garage violate Hud's Fourth Amendment rights?

4E–9: Mark James was arrested in Illinois on a Missouri warrant alleging sexual misconduct with a child. He was held in the county jail awaiting extradition to Missouri. While detained, James attempted to smuggle a letter out of the jail. He gave the letter to another inmate, instructing him to deliver it to his friends, Mike and Carrie Finn. The inmate gave the letter to his lawyer to mail. The lawyer read the letter, then turned it over to Illinois authorities. They forwarded it to Henry Post, the Missouri prosecutor responsible for the sexual misconduct charges against James. The letter instructed the Finns to:

> *CALL Michael Schober at 636-296-2295 for me. Ask Schober to forward my mail to you and also tell him to destroy and scratch ALL backup CD discs he has in the BROWN envelope I just left with him. These are old and useless and one CD has a virus. Tell him to be sure to cut it up too.*

Schober and James had known each other since they were children. At a time when he was a functioning clergyman, James had presided over Schober's marriage. Prosecutor Post showed the letter to two detectives and asked them to investigate the matter. The detectives went to Schober's home. Schober informed them that two weeks earlier James had delivered some computer discs for storage as back-ups. According to Schober, James frequently brought him computer discs to store because of concern that his PC would crash or be destroyed. James wanted to ensure the safety of back-up discs by storing them offsite. When the detectives inquired about the discs that James had recently delivered, Schober retrieved the brown envelope that James had delivered. It was addressed to James and sealed with tape. Schober said that he believed the discs contained church and financial records because previously delivered discs had been so labeled.

When the detectives asked if he knew how many discs were in the envelope, Schober offered to open the envelope and look. The detectives asked if it would be all right if they opened the envelope instead. When Schober said, "Sure, go ahead," one of the detectives opened the envelope with a pocket knife. Inside were 10 discs stacked on top of each other and held together with blue tape. The top disc had a note attached which read: "CD VIRUS DANGER, CONFIDENTIAL CLASSIFIED, VIRUS RESEARCH PROJECT CONTAMINATED CD—DANGER PERSONAL PRIVATE." Schober agreed that the detectives could take the discs with them.

Assisted by another officer with computer expertise, the detectives were able to open the "VIRUS" disc. They found digital images of child pornography. James was charged in federal court with possession of child pornography. Before trial, he moved to suppress the discs and the information gained from viewing them, arguing that the detectives had violated the Fourth Amendment.

Should the trial court grant James's motion?

4E–10: After a computer check of a license plate on a blue and white Oldsmobile revealed that the plate was actually registered to a yellow Oldsmobile, Police Sergeant Henson pulled the car over. Steve Martin was driving. Smitty was a passenger in the front seat. Henson asked Martin for his license and registration. Soon thereafter, Troopers Sunier and Spellman arrived. They asked Martin and Smitty to exit the vehicle, separated the two men, and questioned them in an effort to determine whether the car was stolen. The troopers ascertained that the car belonged to Smitty, and that it had been painted recently.

During the investigation, Trooper Wild arrived. He asked Smitty if he and Trooper Spellman could search the car for guns, drugs, money, or illegal contraband. Smitty consented to the search. No guns, drugs, money, or contraband were found in the car, but two cellular phones were retrieved from the front seat of the car—one from the passenger's side and one from the driver's side. When asked, Smitty claimed that the phone found on his seat belonged to his girlfriend. He could not recall the name of her service provider.

Trooper Wild took both telephones back to his police car. He removed the batteries and performed a "short-out technique" on each of the phones. The results of this "field test" revealed that the phones' internal "ESNs" did not match their external "ESNs." This indicated that the phones had been illegally cloned or had been reprogrammed so that any charges incurred would be billed to someone else's phone number. Wild then called a law enforcement hotline and discovered that the internal ESN of the phone that Smitty had claimed belonged to his girlfriend in fact belonged to GTE Mobilnet and was assigned to one of its legitimate customers, Technology Marketing Corporation. In response to further questioning, Smitty admitted that he had purchased the phone on the street from an acquaintance and that he knew it was a clone.

Based on the phone calls he had made from the cloned phone, the State charged Smitty with theft from GTE Mobilnet. Smitty challenged the admission of the evidence that had been obtained as a result of the searches, alleging violation of his Fourth Amendment rights.

Should the court sustain Smitty's challenge to the evidence?

4E–11: On October 30, four law enforcement officers conducted a "knock and talk" at 220 Bonfield Avenue ("the residence"). They went to the residence to investigate a tip that they received from an anonymous caller indicating that residents at the address possessed marijuana and a firearm. At the time of the knock and talk, the home was owned by Angela, who is Lanner's mother-in-law. Angela lived in the home with her mother, Maudie, and her daughter, Karen (Lanner's wife), along with several children. Although Lanner and Karen had been separated for some time, he had been staying with her intermittently at the residence since May.

When the officers knocked, Maudie answered the door. The officers explained the purpose of their visit and told her that they would like to search the house. When they asked who else was home, Maudie said that Karen was in the back bedroom with her husband (Lanner) and that Angela was sick in her bed. Karen and Lanner emerged from the bedroom and came into the living room. The police asked who lived at the residence, and Maudie and Karen indicated that they lived there. Lanner's response is disputed. According to Lanner, he told the police that he, too, lived at the residence. He further claims that he expressly objected to a search. The police officers assert that Lanner stated that he did *not* live at the residence, but that he "came and went" freely to visit his children. They further stated that he did not object to a search.

Two of the officers took Maudie and Karen outside and obtained formal consent forms from them authorizing a search of the home. According to Lanner, he again objected to the search when everyone came back inside. The police maintain that he never objected. Before the police started their search, Karen voluntarily turned over a small amount of marijuana from her dresser drawer. Detective Braver then began to search the bedroom that Karen shared with Lanner. In the bedroom, Braver found a handgun, counterfeit money, 100 grams of marijuana, digital scales, computer equipment, and some media storage devices, all of which belonged to Lanner.

Did the search violate Lanner's rights?

4E-12: Deputy Jesse of the Victory County Sheriff's Office was observing a house known for illegal narcotics activity. He saw a sport utility vehicle ("SUV") approach the house and observed a passenger, Shirley, get out of the SUV, leave the deputy's sight, and quickly return to the SUV. After the SUV left the house, the deputy stopped the driver of the SUV for a traffic violation.

Suspecting possible narcotics activity, the deputy asked the driver, Wayne, for consent to search the SUV. Wayne agreed, but Shirley objected to the search and refused to give consent. She asserted that she was a co-owner of the SUV—even though she was not listed as the owner on the vehicle registration. Shirley and Wayne informed Jesse that they were married under common law. Although Shirley continued to refuse consent, after Wayne consented to the search a second time, Deputy Jesse searched the SUV.

He found two white pills, later identified as Tramadol, in the middle console. Shirley claimed that she was holding the pills for a friend. Jesse arrested her and charged her with possession of a dangerous drug. Shirley filed a motion to suppress the pills from her trial, contending that the deputy violated her Fourth Amendment rights.

Does Shirley have a meritorious claim?

Selected Bibliography

Thomas Y. Davies, *Denying a Right by Disregarding Doctrine: How* Illinois v. Rodriguez *Demeans Consent, Trivializes Fourth Amendment Reasonableness, and Exaggerates the Excusability of Police Error,* 59 Tenn. L. Rev. 1 (1991)

John F. Decker and Kathryn A. Idzik, *Distinguishing a New Exception to the Warrant Requirement: An Examination of the Consent-Once-Removed Doctrine and Its Hollow Justifications,* 61 Drake L. Rev. 127 (2012)

George M. Dery III, *Creating the Right to Deny Yourself Privacy: The Supreme Court Broadens Police Search Powers in Consent Cases in* Fernandez v. California, 2014 Mich. St. L. Rev. 1129 (2014)

Peter Goldberger, *Consent, Expectations of Privacy, and the Meaning of "Searches" in the Fourth Amendment,* 75 J. Crim. L. & Criminology 319 (1984)

Christo Lassiter, *Consent to Search by Ignorant People,* 39 Tex. Tech L. Rev. 1171 (2007)

Arnold H. Loewy, *Knowing "Consent" Means "Knowing Consent": The Underappreciated Wisdom of Justice Marshall's* Schneckloth v. Bustamonte *Dissent,* 79 Miss. L.J. 97 (2009)

Tracey Maclin, *The Good and Bad News About Consent Searches in the Supreme Court,* 39 McGeorge L. Rev. 27 (2008)

Daniel L. Rotenberg, *An Essay on Consent(less) Searches,* 69 Wash. U. L.Q. 175 (1991)

Robert V. Ward, *Consenting to a Search and Seizure in Poor and Minority Neighborhoods: No Place for a "Reasonable Person,"* 36 How. L.J. 239 (1993)

Russell L. Weaver, *The Myth of "Consent,"* 39 Tex. Tech L. Rev. 1195 (2007)

John B. Wefing and John G. Miles, *Consent Searches and the Fourth Amendment: Voluntariness and Third Party Problems,* 5 Seton Hall L. Rev. 211 (1974)

James B. White, *The Fourth Amendment as a Way of Talking About People: A Study of* Robinson *and* Matlock, 1974 Sup. Ct. Rev. 165 (1974)

[F] The "Plain View" Doctrine

Horton v. California

United States Supreme Court

496 U.S. 128, 110 S. Ct. 2301, 110 L. Ed. 2d 112 (1990)

JUSTICE STEVENS delivered the opinion of the Court.

In this case we revisit an issue that was considered, but not conclusively resolved, in *Coolidge v. New Hampshire*, 403 U.S. 443 (1971): Whether the warrantless seizure of evidence of crime in plain view is prohibited by the Fourth Amendment if the discovery of the evidence was not inadvertent. We conclude that even though inadvertence is a characteristic of most legitimate "plain view" seizures, it is not a necessary condition.

I

Petitioner was convicted of the armed robbery of Erwin Wallaker, the treasurer of the San Jose Coin Club. When Wallaker returned to his home after the Club's annual show, he entered his garage and was accosted by two masked men, one armed with a machine gun and the other with an electrical shocking device, sometimes referred to as a "stun gun." The two men shocked Wallaker, bound and handcuffed him, and robbed him of jewelry and cash. During the encounter sufficient conversation took place to enable Wallaker subsequently to identify petitioner's distinctive voice. His identification was partially corroborated by a witness who saw the robbers leaving the scene, and by evidence that petitioner had attended the coin shows.

Sergeant LaRault, an experienced police officer, investigated the crime and determined that there was probable cause to search petitioner's home for the proceeds of the robbery and for the weapons used by the robbers. His affidavit for a search warrant referred to police reports that described the weapons as well as the proceeds, but the warrant issued by the Magistrate only authorized a search for the proceeds, including three specifically described rings.

Pursuant to the warrant, LaRault searched petitioner's residence, but he did not find the stolen property. During the course of the search, however, he discovered the weapons in plain view and seized them. Specifically, he seized an Uzi machine gun, a .38 caliber revolver, two stun guns, a handcuff key, a San Jose Coin Club advertising brochure, and a few items of clothing identified by the victim. LaRault testified that while he was searching for the rings, he also was interested in finding other evidence connecting petitioner to the robbery. Thus, the seized evidence was not discovered "inadvertently."

The trial court refused to suppress the evidence found in petitioner's home and, after a jury trial, petitioner was found guilty and sentenced to prison. The California Court of Appeal affirmed . . . . The California Supreme Court denied petitioner's request for review.

Because the California courts' interpretation of the "plain view" doctrine conflicts with the view of other courts, and because the unresolved issue is important, we granted certiorari, 493 U.S. 889 (1989).

II

. . . .

The right to security in person and property protected by the Fourth Amendment may be invaded in quite different ways by searches and seizures. A search compromises the individual interest in privacy; a seizure deprives the individual of dominion over his or her person or property. The "plain view" doctrine is often considered an exception to the general rule that warrantless searches are presumptively unreasonable, but this characterization overlooks the important difference between searches and seizures. If an article is already in plain view, neither its observation nor its seizure would involve any invasion of privacy. A seizure of the article, however, would obviously invade the owner's possessory interest. If "plain view" justifies an exception from an otherwise applicable warrant requirement, therefore, it must be an exception that is addressed to the concerns that are implicated by seizures rather than by searches.

The criteria that generally guide "plain view" seizures were set forth in *Coolidge v. New Hampshire*, 403 U.S. 443 (1971). The Court held that the seizure of two automobiles parked in plain view on the defendant's driveway in the course of arresting the defendant violated the Fourth Amendment. Accordingly, particles of gun powder that had been subsequently found in vacuum sweepings from one of the cars could not be introduced in evidence against the defendant. The State endeavored to justify the seizure of the automobiles, and their subsequent search at the police station, on four different grounds, including the "plain view" doctrine. The scope of that doctrine as it had developed in earlier cases was fairly summarized in these three paragraphs from Justice Stewart's opinion:

> It is well established that under certain circumstances the police may seize evidence in plain view without a warrant. But it is important to keep in mind that, in the vast majority of cases, any evidence seized by the police will be in plain view, at least at the moment of seizure. The problem with the "plain view" doctrine has been to identify the circumstances in which plain view has legal significance rather than being simply the normal concomitant of any search, legal or illegal.

> An example of the applicability of the "plain view" doctrine is the situation in which the police have a warrant to search a given area for specified ob-

jects, and in the course of the search come across some other article of in-criminating character. Where the initial intrusion that brings the police within plain view of such an article is supported, not by a warrant, but by one of the recognized exceptions to the warrant requirement, the seizure is also legitimate. Thus the police may inadvertently come across evidence while in "hot pursuit" of a fleeing suspect. And an object that comes into view during a search incident to arrest that is appropriately limited in scope under existing law may be seized without a warrant. Finally, the "plain view" doctrine has been applied where a police officer is not searching for evidence against the accused, but nonetheless inadvertently comes across an incrim-inating object.

What the "plain view" cases have in common is that the police officer in each of them had a prior justification for an intrusion in the course of which he came inadvertently across a piece of evidence incriminating the accused. The doctrine serves to supplement the prior justification — whether it be a warrant for another object, hot pursuit, search incident to lawful arrest, or some other legitimate reason for being present unconnected with a search directed against the accused — and permits the warrantless seizure. Of course, the extension of the original justification is legitimate only where it is immediately apparent to the police that they have evidence before them; the "plain view" doctrine may not be used to extend a general exploratory search from one object to another until something incriminating at last emerges.

Id., at 465–466 (footnote omitted).

Justice Stewart then described the two limitations on the doctrine that he found implicit in its rationale: First, "that plain view alone is never enough to justify the war-rantless seizure of evidence," *id.*, at 468; and second, "that the discovery of evidence in plain view must be inadvertent." *Id.*, at 469.

Justice Stewart's analysis of the "plain view" doctrine did not command a major-ity and a plurality of the court has since made clear that the discussion is "not a bind-ing precedent." *Texas v. Brown*, 460 U.S., at 737 (opinion of Rehnquist, J.). Justice Harlan, who concurred in the Court's judgment and in its response to the dissent-ing opinions, 403 U.S., at 473–484, 490–493, did not join the plurality's discussion of the "plain view" doctrine. *See id.*, at 464–473. The decision nonetheless is a bind-ing precedent. Before discussing the second limitation, which is implicated in this case, it is therefore necessary to explain why the first adequately supports the Court's judgment.

It is, of course, an essential predicate to any valid warrantless seizure of incrimi-nating evidence that the officer did not violate the Fourth Amendment in arriving at the place from which the evidence could be plainly viewed. There are, moreover, two additional conditions that must be satisfied to justify the warrantless seizure. First, not only must the item be in plain view, its incriminating character must also be "immediately apparent." *Id.*, at 466; *see also Arizona v. Hicks*, 480 U.S., at 326–327. Thus, in *Coolidge*, the cars were obviously in plain view, but their probative value remained uncertain until after the interiors were swept and examined microscopically. Second, not only must the officer be lawfully located in a place from which the object can be plainly seen, but he or she must also have a lawful right of access to the object itself.[7] As the Solicitor General has suggested, Justice Harlan's vote in *Coolidge* may have rested on the fact that the seizure of the cars was accomplished by means of a warrantless trespass on the defendant's property. In all events, we are satisfied that the absence of inadvertence was not essential to the Court's rejection of the State's "plain view" argument in *Coolidge*.

III

Justice Stewart concluded that the inadvertence requirement was necessary to avoid a violation of the express constitutional requirement that a valid warrant must particularly describe the things to be seized. He explained:

> The rationale of the exception to the warrant requirement, as just stated, is that a plain-view seizure will not turn an initially valid (and therefore limited) search into a "general" one, while the inconvenience of procuring a warrant to cover an inadvertent discovery is great. But where the discovery is anticipated, where the police know in advance the location of the evidence and intend to seize it, the situation is altogether different. The requirement of a warrant to seize imposes no inconvenience whatever, or at least none which is constitutionally cognizable in a legal system that regards warrantless searches as "*per se* unreasonable" in the absence of "exigent circumstances."

> If the initial intrusion is bottomed upon a warrant that fails to mention a particular object, though the police know its location and intend to seize it, then there is a violation of the express constitutional requirement of "Warrants . . . particularly describing . . . [the] things to be seized."

403 U.S., at 469–471.

We find two flaws in this reasoning. First, evenhanded law enforcement is best achieved by the application of objective standards of conduct, rather than standards that depend upon the subjective state of mind of the officer. The fact that an officer is interested in an item of evidence and fully expects to find it in the course of a

---

7. "This is simply a corollary of the familiar principle discussed above, that no amount of probable cause can justify a warrantless search or seizure absent 'exigent circumstances.' Incontrovertible testimony of the senses that an incriminating object is on premises belonging to a criminal suspect may establish the fullest possible measure of probable cause. But even where the object is contraband, this Court has repeatedly stated and enforced the basic rule that the police may not enter and make a warrantless seizure. [Citations omitted.]" *Coolidge*, 403 U.S., at 468. We have since applied the same rule to the arrest of a person in his home. *See Minnesota v. Olson*, 495 U.S. 91 (1990); *Payton v. New York*, 445 U.S. 573 (1980).

search should not invalidate its seizure if the search is confined in area and duration by the terms of a warrant or a valid exception to the warrant requirement. If the officer has knowledge approaching certainty that the item will be found, we see no reason why he or she would deliberately omit a particular description of the item to be seized from the application for a search warrant.[9] Specification of the additional item could only permit the officer to expand the scope of the search. On the other hand, if he or she has a valid warrant to search for one item and merely a suspicion concerning the second, whether or not it amounts to probable cause, we fail to see why that suspicion should immunize the second item from seizure if it is found during a lawful search for the first. The hypothetical case put by Justice White in his dissenting opinion in *Coolidge* is instructive:

> Let us suppose officers secure a warrant to search a house for a rifle. While staying well within the range of a rifle search, they discover two photographs of the murder victim, both in plain sight in the bedroom. Assume also that the discovery of the one photograph was inadvertent but finding the other was anticipated. The Court would permit the seizure of only one of the photographs. But in terms of the "minor" peril to Fourth Amendment values there is surely no difference between these two photographs: the interference with possession is the same in each case and the officers' appraisal of the photograph they expected to see is no less reliable than their judgment about the other. And in both situations the actual inconvenience and danger to evidence remain identical if the officers must depart and secure a warrant.

Id., at 516.

Second, the suggestion that the inadvertence requirement is necessary to prevent the police from conducting general searches, or from converting specific warrants into general warrants, is not persuasive because that interest is already served by the requirements that no warrant issue unless it "particularly describ[es] the place to be searched and the persons or things to be seized," and that a warrantless search be circumscribed by the exigencies which justify its initiation. Scrupulous adherence to these requirements serves the interests in limiting the area and duration of the search that the inadvertence requirement inadequately protects. Once those commands have been satisfied and the officer has a lawful right of access, however, no additional Fourth Amendment interest is furthered by requiring that the discovery of evidence be inadvertent. If the scope of the search exceeds that permitted by the terms of a validly issued warrant or the character of the relevant exception from the warrant requirement, the subsequent seizure is unconstitutional without more. Thus, in the

---

9. "If the police have probable cause to search for a photograph as well as a rifle and they proceed to seek a warrant, they could have no possible motive for deliberately including the rifle but omitting the photograph. Quite the contrary is true. Only oversight or careless mistake would explain the omission in the warrant application if the police were convinced they had probable cause to search for the photograph." *Coolidge*, 403 U.S., at 517 (White, J., dissenting).

case of a search incident to a lawful arrest, "[i]f the police stray outside the scope of an authorized *Chimel* search they are already in violation of the Fourth Amendment, and evidence so seized will be excluded; adding a second reason for excluding evidence hardly seems worth the candle." *Coolidge*, 403 U.S., at 517 [(White, J., dissenting)] . . . .

In this case, the scope of the search was not enlarged in the slightest by the omission of any reference to the weapons in the warrant. Indeed, if the three rings and other items named in the warrant had been found at the outset — or petitioner had them in his possession and had responded to the warrant by producing them immediately — no search for weapons could have taken place. Again, Justice White's dissenting opinion in *Coolidge* is instructive:

> Police with a warrant for a rifle may search only places where rifles might be and must terminate the search once the rifle is found; the inadvertence rule will in no way reduce the number of places into which they may lawfully look.

403 U.S., at 517.

As we have already suggested, by hypothesis the seizure of an object in plain view does not involve an intrusion on privacy. If the interest in privacy has been invaded, the violation must have occurred before the object came into plain view and there is no need for an inadvertence limitation on seizures to condemn it. The prohibition against general searches and general warrants serves primarily as a protection against unjustified intrusions on privacy. But reliance on privacy concerns that support that prohibition is misplaced when the inquiry concerns the scope of an exception that merely authorizes an officer with a lawful right of access to an item to seize it without a warrant.

In this case the items seized from petitioner's home were discovered during a lawful search authorized by a valid warrant. When they were discovered, it was immediately apparent to the officer that they constituted incriminating evidence. He had probable cause, not only to obtain a warrant to search for the stolen property, but also to believe that the weapons and handguns had been used in the crime he was investigating. The search was authorized by the warrant, the seizure was authorized by the "plain view" doctrine. The judgment is affirmed.

It is so ordered.

JUSTICE BRENNAN, with whom JUSTICE MARSHALL joins, dissenting.

I remain convinced that Justice Stewart correctly articulated the plain view doctrine in *Coolidge v. New Hampshire*, 403 U.S. 443 (1971). The Fourth Amendment permits law enforcement officers to seize items for which they do not have a warrant when those items are found in plain view and (1) the officers are lawfully in a position to observe the items, (2) the discovery of the items is "inadvertent," and (3) it is immediately apparent to the officers that the items are evidence of a crime, contraband, or otherwise subject to seizure. In eschewing the inadvertent discovery requirement, the majority ignores the Fourth Amendment's express command that warrants particularly describe not only the places to be searched, but also the things to be seized. I respectfully dissent from this rewriting of the Fourth Amendment.

I

... The Fourth Amendment, by its terms, declares the privacy and possessory interests [that it protects] to be equally important. As this Court recently stated, "Although the interest protected by the Fourth Amendment injunction against unreasonable searches is quite different from that protected by its injunction against unreasonable seizures, neither the one nor the other is of inferior worth or necessarily requires only lesser protection." *Arizona v. Hicks*, 480 U.S. 321, 328 (1987) (citation omitted).

The Amendment protects these equally important interests in precisely the same manner: by requiring a neutral and detached magistrate to evaluate, before the search or seizure, the government's showing of probable cause and its particular description of the place to be searched and the items to be seized. Accordingly, just as a warrantless search is *per se* unreasonable absent exigent circumstances, so too a seizure of personal property is "*per se* unreasonable within the meaning of the Fourth Amendment unless it is accomplished pursuant to a judicial warrant issued upon probable cause and particularly describing the items to be seized." *United States v. Place*, 462 U.S. 696, 701 (1983) (footnote omitted) (citing *Marron v. United States*, 275 U.S. 192, 196, Treas. Dec. 42528 (1927)). "Prior review by a neutral and detached magistrate is the time-tested means of effectuating Fourth Amendment rights." *United States v. United States District Court*, 407 U.S. 297, 318 (1972). A decision to invade a possessory interest in property is too important to be left to the discretion of zealous officers "engaged in the often competitive enterprise of ferreting out crime." *Johnson v. United States*, 333 U.S. 10, 14 (1948). "The requirement that warrants shall particularly describe the things to be seized makes general searches under them impossible and prevents the seizure of one thing under a warrant describing another. As to what is to be taken, nothing is left to the discretion of the officer executing the warrant." *Marron, supra*, at 196.

The plain view doctrine is an exception to the general rule that a seizure of personal property must be authorized by a warrant. As Justice Stewart explained in *Coolidge*, 403 U.S., at 470, we accept a warrantless seizure when an officer is lawfully in a location and inadvertently sees evidence of a crime because of "the inconvenience of procuring a warrant" to seize this newly discovered piece of evidence. But "where the discovery is anticipated, where the police know in advance the location of the evidence and intend to seize it," the argument that procuring a warrant would be "inconvenient" loses much, if not all, of its force. *Id.* Barring an exigency, there is no reason why the police officers could not have obtained a warrant to seize this evidence before entering the premises. The rationale behind the inadvertent discovery requirement is simply that we will not excuse officers from the general requirement of a warrant to seize if the officers know the location of evidence, have probable cause to seize it, intend to seize it, and yet do not bother to obtain a warrant particularly

describing that evidence. To do so would violate "the express constitutional requirement of 'Warrants . . . particularly describing . . . [the] things to be seized,'" and
would "fly in the face of the basic rule that no amount of probable cause can justify
a warrantless seizure." *Id.*, at 471.

. . . .

The Court posits two "flaws" in Justice Stewart's reasoning that it believes demonstrate the inappropriateness of the inadvertent discovery requirement. But these
flaws are illusory. First, the majority explains that it can see no reason why an officer
who "has knowledge approaching certainty" that an item will be found in a particular location "would deliberately omit a particular description of the item to be seized
from the application for a search warrant." But to the individual whose possessory
interest has been invaded, it matters not why the police officer decided to omit a particular item from his application for a search warrant. When an officer with probable cause to seize an item fails to mention that item in his application for a search
warrant — for whatever reason — and then seizes the item anyway, his conduct is *per
se* unreasonable. Suppression of the evidence so seized will encourage officers to be
more precise and complete in future warrant applications.

Furthermore, there are a number of instances in which a law enforcement officer
might deliberately choose to omit certain items from a warrant application even
though he has probable cause to seize them, knows they are on the premises, and
intends to seize them when they are discovered in plain view. For example, the warrant application process can often be time-consuming, especially when the police
attempt to seize a large number of items. An officer interested in conducting a search
as soon as possible might decide to save time by listing only one or two hard-to-find
items, such as the stolen rings in this case, confident that he will find in plain view
all of the other evidence he is looking for before he discovers the listed items. Because
rings could be located almost anywhere inside or outside a house, it is unlikely that
a warrant to search for and seize the rings would restrict the scope of the search. An
officer might rationally find the risk of immediately discovering the items listed in
the warrant — thereby forcing him to conclude the search immediately — outweighed
by the time saved in the application process.

. . . It is true that the inadvertent discovery requirement furthers no privacy interests. The requirement in no way reduces the scope of a search or the number of
places into which officers may look. But it does protect possessory interests. The inadvertent discovery requirement is essential if we are to take seriously the Fourth
Amendment's protection of possessory interests as well as privacy interests. The
Court today eliminates a rule designed to further possessory interests on the ground
that it fails to further privacy interests. I cannot countenance such constitutional
legerdemain.

II

. . . .

I respectfully dissent.

Notes and Questions

(1) Both the majority and dissenters in *Horton* agree that the "plain view" doctrine is *not* an exception to the rule that warrantless *searches* are *per se* unreasonable. Justice Brennan maintains that it is an exception to a parallel and equally important rule — that warrantless *seizures* are *per se* unreasonable. Does the majority's analysis and formulation of the "plain view" doctrine recognize such a rule? After *Horton*, is it ever the case that officers must obtain a warrant in order to seize property? When?

(2) The majority asserts that the "unresolved issue" of whether "inadvertence" is an essential element of the "plain view" doctrine "is important." Why is the issue "important"? Would an inadvertence requirement pose a significant impediment to law enforcement? Would it provide substantial protection for weighty constitutional interests?

Arizona v. Hicks

United States Supreme Court

480 U.S. 321, 107 S. Ct. 1149, 94 L. Ed. 2d 347 (1987)

JUSTICE SCALIA delivered the opinion of the Court.

. . . .

I

On April 18, 1984, a bullet was fired through the floor of respondent's apartment, striking and injuring a man in the apartment below. Police officers arrived and entered respondent's apartment to search for the shooter, for other victims, and for weapons. They found and seized three weapons, including a sawed-off rifle, and in the course of their search also discovered a stocking-cap mask.

One of the policemen, Officer Nelson, noticed two sets of expensive stereo components, which seemed out of place in the squalid and otherwise ill-appointed four-room apartment. Suspecting that they were stolen, he read and recorded their serial numbers — moving some of the components, including a Bang and Olufsen turntable, in order to do so — which he then reported by phone to his headquarters. On being advised that the turntable had been taken in an armed robbery, he seized it immediately. It was later determined that some of the other serial numbers matched those on other stereo equipment taken in the same armed robbery, and a warrant was obtained and executed to seize that equipment as well. Respondent was subsequently indicted for the robbery.

. . . .

II

As an initial matter, the State argues that Officer Nelson's actions constituted neither a "search" nor a "seizure" within the meaning of the Fourth Amendment. We agree that the mere recording of the serial numbers did not constitute a seizure. To be sure, that was the first step in a process by which respondent was eventually deprived of the stereo equipment. In and of itself, however, it did not "meaningfully interfere" with respondent's possessory interest in either the serial numbers or the equipment, and therefore did not amount to a seizure.

Officer Nelson's moving of the equipment, however, did constitute a "search" separate and apart from the search for the shooter, victims, and weapons that was the lawful objective of his entry into the apartment. Merely inspecting those parts of the turntable that came into view during the latter search would not have constituted an independent search, because it would have produced no additional invasion of respondent's privacy interest. But taking action, unrelated to the objectives of the authorized intrusion, which exposed to view concealed portions of the apartment or its contents, did produce a new invasion of respondent's privacy unjustified by the exigent circumstance that validated the entry . . . . It matters not that the search uncovered nothing of any great personal value to the respondent—serial numbers rather than (what might conceivably have been hidden behind or under the equipment) letters or photographs. A search is a search, even if it happens to disclose nothing but the bottom of a turntable.

III

The remaining question is whether the search was "reasonable" under the Fourth Amendment.

. . . .

"It is well established that under certain circumstances the police may *seize* evidence in plain view without a warrant," *Coolidge v. New Hampshire*, 403 U.S., at 465, 91 S. Ct. at 2037 (plurality opinion) (emphasis added) . . . . It would be absurd to say that an object could lawfully be seized and taken from the premises, but could not be moved for closer examination. It is clear, therefore, that the search here was valid if the "plain view" doctrine would have sustained a seizure of the equipment.

There is no doubt it would have done so if Officer Nelson had probable cause to believe that the equipment was stolen. The State has conceded, however, that he had only a "reasonable suspicion," by which it means something less than probable cause . . . .

We now hold that probable cause is required. To say otherwise would be to cut the "plain view" doctrine loose from its theoretical and practical moorings. The theory of that doctrine consists of extending to nonpublic places such as the home, where searches and seizures without a warrant are presumptively unreasonable, the police's longstanding authority to make warrantless seizures in public places of such objects as weapons and contraband. And the practical justification for that extension is the desirability of sparing police, whose viewing of the object in the course of a lawful search is as legitimate as it would have been in a public place, the inconvenience and the risk—to themselves or to preservation of the evidence—of going to obtain a warrant. Dispensing with the need for a warrant is worlds apart from permitting a lesser standard of cause for the seizure than a warrant would require, *i.e.*, the standard of probable cause. No reason is apparent why an object should routinely be seizable on lesser grounds, during an unrelated search and seizure, than would have been needed to obtain a warrant for that same object if it had been known to be on the premises.

We do not say, of course, that a seizure can never be justified on less than probable cause. We have held that it can — where, for example, the seizure is minimally intrusive and operational necessities render it the only practicable means of detecting certain types of crime. No special operational necessities are relied on here, however — but rather the mere fact that the items in question came lawfully within the officer's plain view. That alone cannot supplant the requirement of probable cause.

The same considerations preclude us from holding that, even though probable cause would have been necessary for a seizure, the search of objects in plain view that occurred here could be sustained on lesser grounds. A dwelling-place search, no less than a dwelling-place seizure, requires probable cause, and there is no reason in theory or practicality why application of the "plain view" doctrine would supplant that requirement. Although the interest protected by the Fourth Amendment injunction against unreasonable searches is quite different from that protected by its injunction against unreasonable seizures, neither the one nor the other is of inferior worth or necessarily requires only lesser protection. We have not elsewhere drawn a categorical distinction between the two insofar as concerns the degree of justification needed to establish the reasonableness of police action, and we see no reason for a distinction in the particular circumstances before us here. Indeed, to treat searches more liberally would especially erode the plurality's warning in *Coolidge* that "the 'plain view' doctrine may not be used to extend a general exploratory search from one object to another until something incriminating at last emerges." 403 U.S., at 466, 91 S. Ct. at 2038. In short, whether legal authority to move the equipment could be found only as an inevitable concomitant of the authority to seize it, or also as a consequence of some independent power to search certain objects in plain view, probable cause to believe the equipment was stolen was required.

JUSTICE O'CONNOR's dissent suggests that we uphold the action here on the ground that it was a "cursory inspection" rather than a "full-blown search," and could therefore be justified by reasonable suspicion instead of probable cause. As already noted, a truly cursory inspection — one that involves merely looking at what is already exposed to view, without disturbing it — is not a "search" for Fourth Amendment purposes, and therefore does not even require reasonable suspicion. We are unwilling to send police and judges into a new thicket of Fourth Amendment law, to seek a creature of uncertain description that is neither a "plain view" inspection nor yet a "full-blown search." . . .

JUSTICE POWELL's dissent reasonably asks what it is we would have had Officer Nelson do in these circumstances. The answer depends, of course, upon whether he had probable cause to conduct a search, a question that was not preserved in this case. If he had, then he should have done precisely what he did. If not, then he should have followed up his suspicions, if possible, by means other than a search — just as he would have had to do if, while walking along the street, he had noticed the same suspicious stereo equipment sitting inside a house a few feet away from him, beneath an open window. It may well be that, in such circumstances, no effective means short of a search exist. But there is nothing new in the realization that the Constitution sometimes insulates the criminality of a few in order to protect the privacy of us all. Our disagreement with the dissenters pertains to where the proper balance should be struck; we choose to adhere to the textual and traditional standard of probable cause.

. . . .

For the reasons stated, the judgment of the Court of Appeals of Arizona is

Affirmed.

[The concurring opinion of JUSTICE WHITE has been omitted.]

JUSTICE POWELL, with whom THE CHIEF JUSTICE and JUSTICE O'CONNOR join, dissenting.

. . . .

Today the Court holds for the first time that the requirement of probable cause operates as a separate limitation on the application of the plain-view doctrine . . . . All the pertinent objects were in plain view and could be identified as objects frequently stolen. There was no looking into closets, opening of drawers or trunks, or other "rummaging around." . . .

The officers' suspicion that the stereo components at issue were stolen was both reasonable and based on specific, articulable facts . . . .

It is fair to ask what Officer Nelson should have done in these circumstances . . . .

The Court holds that there was an unlawful search of the turntable. It agrees that the "mere recording of the serial numbers did not constitute a seizure." Thus, if the computer had identified as stolen property a component with a visible serial number, the evidence would have been admissible. But the Court further holds that "Officer Nelson's moving of the equipment . . . did constitute a 'search' . . . ." It perceives a constitutional distinction between reading a serial number on an object and moving or picking up an identical object to see its serial number . . . . With all respect, this distinction between "looking" at a suspicious object in plain view and "moving" it even a few inches trivializes the Fourth Amendment.[4] The Court's new rule will cause uncertainty, and could deter conscientious police officers from lawfully obtaining evidence necessary to convict guilty persons. Apart from the importance of rationality in the interpretation of the Fourth Amend-

---

4. Numerous articles that frequently are stolen have identifying numbers, including expensive watches and cameras, and also credit cards. Assume for example that an officer reasonably suspects that two identical watches, both in plain view, have been stolen. Under the Court's decision, if one

ment, today's decision may handicap law enforcement without enhancing privacy interests. Accordingly, I dissent.

Justice O'Connor, with whom The Chief Justice and Justice Powell join, dissenting.

The Court today gives the right answer to the wrong question. The Court asks whether the police must have probable cause before either seizing an object in plain view or conducting a full-blown search of that object, and concludes that they must. I agree. In my view, however, this case presents a different question: whether police must have probable cause before conducting a cursory inspection of an item in plain view. Because I conclude that such an inspection is reasonable if the police are aware of facts or circumstances that justify a reasonable suspicion that the item is evidence of a crime, I would reverse the judgment of the Arizona Court of Appeals, and therefore dissent.

. . . The officers were lawfully in the apartment pursuant to exigent circumstances, and the discovery of the stereo was inadvertent — the officers did not "'know in advance the location of [certain] evidence and intend to seize it,' relying on the plain-view doctrine only as a pretext." [*Texas v. Brown*, 460 U.S. 730, 737, 103 S. Ct. 1535, 1540–1541, 75 L. Ed. 2d 502 (1983)] (quoting *Coolidge v. New Hampshire, supra*, at 470, 91 S. Ct. at 2040). Instead, the dispute in this case focuses on the application of the "immediately apparent" requirement; at issue is whether a police officer's reasonable suspicion is adequate to justify a cursory examination of an item in plain view.

The purpose of the "immediately apparent" requirement is to prevent "general, exploratory rummaging in a person's belongings." *Coolidge v. New Hampshire*, 403 U.S., at 467, 91 S. Ct. at 2038. If an officer could indiscriminately search every item in plain view, a search justified by a limited purpose — such as exigent circumstances — could be used to eviscerate the protections of the Fourth Amendment. In order to prevent such a general search, therefore, we require that the relevance of the item be "immediately apparent." . . .

Thus, I agree with the Court that even under the plain view doctrine, probable cause is required before the police seize an item, or conduct a full-blown search of evidence in plain view. Such a requirement of probable cause will prevent the plain view doctrine from authorizing general searches. This is not to say, however, that even a mere inspection of a suspicious item must be supported by probable cause. When a police officer makes a cursory inspection of a suspicious item in plain view in order to determine whether it is indeed evidence of a crime, there is no "exploratory rummaging." Only those items that the police officer

---

watch is lying face up and the other lying face down, reading the serial number on one of the watches would not be a search. But turning over the other watch to read its serial number would be a search. Moreover, the officer's ability to read a serial number may depend on its location in a room and light conditions at a particular time. Would there be a constitutional difference if an officer, on the basis of a reasonable suspicion, used a pocket flashlight or turned on a light to read a number rather than moving the object to a point where a serial number was clearly visible?

"reasonably suspects" as evidence of a crime may be inspected, and perhaps more importantly, the scope of such an inspection is quite limited. In short, if police officers have a reasonable, articulable suspicion that an object they come across during the course of a lawful search is evidence of crime, in my view they may make a cursory examination of the object to verify their suspicion. If the officers wish to go beyond such a cursory examination of the object, however, they must have probable cause.

. . . .

We have long recognized that searches can vary in intrusiveness, and that some brief searches "may be so minimally intrusive of Fourth Amendment interests that strong countervailing governmental interests will justify a [search] based only on specific articulable facts" that the item in question is contraband or evidence of a crime. *United States v. Place*, 462 U.S. 696, 706, 103 S. Ct. 2637, 2644, 77 L. Ed. 2d 110 (1983) . . . .

In my view, the balance of the governmental and privacy interests strongly supports a reasonable suspicion standard for the cursory examination of items in plain view.

. . . .

I respectfully dissent.

Notes and Questions

(1) In footnote 4, Justice Powell hypothesizes a scenario involving two watches, one lying face down and the other face up. He concludes that under the majority's approach reading the serial number on the first watch would not be governed by the Fourth Amendment. Turning the second watch over to read the serial number, however, would be regulated by the Fourth Amendment. Are these conclusions correct? If so, does the different treatment of the two situations "trivialize the Fourth Amendment"?

(2) One requirement of the plain view doctrine defined by *Coolidge* and *Horton* is that the incriminating nature of an item be "immediately apparent" to an officer. Lower courts have struggled with interpretation of that requirement. What is the meaning of the "immediately apparent" demand? Why is it constitutionally required?

(3) Justice O'Connor suggests that the Court's analysis and outcome are inconsistent with a "balancing" approach taken in another line of Fourth Amendment cases. That line of cases is considered in Chapter Five. After reading the authorities alluded to by Justice O'Connor, students should consider whether the *Hicks* opinion is consistent with or analytically unfaithful to them.

Plain View Problems

4F–1: In the course of executing a valid search warrant for narcotics at 168 Sharry Road, Matthew's home, police officers came upon two sets of golf clubs out in the middle of the floor of one of the bedrooms. The clubs looked brand new. In a closet of the same room, the officers discovered brand new golf shirts with a Los Dios Country Club logo embroidered on them. The officers believed that these items were "suspicious." The officers contacted the police department dispatcher to inquire whether there had been any reports of recent burglaries, especially of a country club. They were informed by a burglary detective that the Los Dios Country Club had reported the theft of golf merchandise. The officers then made contact with the country club to confirm the report and obtain a description of the stolen property. The officers then seized the golf clubs and the golf shirts. Matthew was charged with theft. He challenged the officers' actions in his home.

What arguments should Matthew make in support of his challenge? Did the officers' actions violate the Fourth Amendment?

4F–2: Police responded to a disturbance call at an apartment complex and were advised by the manager that a fight was in progress in one of the units. The officers observed two men exiting the apartment in question, their voices raised and blood on their clothing. The door to the apartment was open. Both men were stopped, asked for identification, and questioned. The manager walked into the open apartment, then called to the officers to examine the damage resulting from the fight between the two men. Two officers entered and observed property strewn about the floor, but neither officer saw any "damage."

During the inspection, one officer looked around the apartment and noticed that there was a large amount of "female" jewelry strewn about one area of the floor and several stereos and other items of personal property also scattered about the apartment. The officer took the serial number from the back of one stereo without moving the piece of equipment and also copied a name and address that was written on a backpack found on the floor. The officer called the police station to check on the items. He learned that the items were not reported as stolen. The officer then left the apartment, walked upstairs to the manager's apartment, phoned the records and identification section of the police department and gave them the name found on the backpack to check for filed complaints. He was advised that the individual had filed a burglary complaint. The officer requested that the incident report be read to him over the telephone. He copied down a list of the property stolen along with the complainant's telephone number. A telephone call to the complainant confirmed that several items seen in the apartment had been stolen from her residence two days earlier. At this point, the tenants were arrested and the contents of the apartment were seized.

Did the government obtain the stolen items in compliance with the Fourth Amendment?

4F–3: On July 17, Provo City police officers went to Lego's home in Provo to execute a search warrant. The warrant ordered seizure of "all controlled substances and stolen property." An affidavit in support of issuance of the warrant stated that an "informant did see within the last 48 hours at least one pound of marijuana and several items purported by Lego to be stolen . . . (lawn chairs, electrical wiring, and a child's swing) at Lego's home."

While searching the home, Officer Craig Geslison noticed a VCR attached to a television set and two videotapes close by. He asked Lego about them, and Lego remarked that he had rented them from "Norton's" supermarket. Geslison called Norton's. Based on the fact that there was no rental contract on file under the name of Lego or his girlfriend, the assistant manager advised him that Norton's had not rented the VCR. This inquiry took from 10 to 15 minutes. After receiving this information, Geslison examined the VCR. The serial number was missing. When the defendant and his girlfriend were unable to produce a rental receipt for the VCR, Geslison seized the VCR and the tapes.

Eventually, ownership of the VCR and tapes was traced to Sounds Easy, an audio-video store, which had reported them stolen. Prior to trial, the defendant filed a motion to suppress evidence of the discovery of the VCR and the tapes in his home.

What arguments should be made in support of and against the motion? How should the trial court rule?

4F–4: The body of a prostitute, Shirley Ellis, was discovered on November 29, 1987. The Medical Examiner determined that death was caused by strangulation and blunt force head trauma. On June 29, 1988, the body of Catherine DiMauro, another prostitute, was found at a construction site. Numerous blue fibers were collected from her body and two red fibers were removed from her face. The injuries were similar to those suffered by Ellis, and the causes of death were determined to be identical.

The police commenced an investigatory decoy operation along a highway corridor that the victims had frequented. Female officers, wearing hidden microphones and dressed as prostitutes, engaged in conversations with men who stopped for them. On August 22, 1988, Margaret Finner, another prostitute, was reported missing. She was last seen entering a blue van described as having no side window and rounded headlights. Finner was later found murdered.

On September 14, 1988, Officer Renee Lano was working as a decoy on the highway when she saw a blue van cruise past seven times. She called in the plate number and learned that it was registered to Penn. Lano moved to a darker area of the highway, whereupon the van stopped for her. She approached, but did not enter the van. She spoke with the driver, later identified as Penn. During the conversation, Lano became suspicious. She noticed that the interior of the van was covered with blue carpeting. Aware that blue fibers had been found on DiMauro's body, Lano surreptitiously removed some fibers from the door jamb of Penn's van during her conversation with him. Those fibers later proved useful in the prosecution of Penn for the three murders.

Did Lano lawfully acquire the fibers?

4F–5: On May 27, Akron police executed a valid search warrant at the Hells Angels' Motorcycle Club headquarters. The objects of the search warrant were items of bedroom furniture suspected of being stolen property. The police found a dresser listed in the search warrant in Bell's apartment which was located on the second floor of the establishment. Because the search warrant authorized seizure of the dresser, but not its contents, police officer John Williams began removing personal effects and clothing, one at a time. While doing so, he came upon two items which appeared to be fountain pens. Williams noted that they were "extremely heavy" and therefore were "suspicious." He showed them to F.B.I. Agent Thornton, who was executing a federal search warrant in an adjoining room. Thornton in turn asked Agent Baraducci to look at the pens. Baraducci told Williams and Thornton that he thought the pens were actually guns and that their possession would be illegal under federal law. The pens were seized.

Later lab analysis confirmed that the "pens" could expel .22 caliber projectiles. Bell was indicted on one count of possessing unregistered firearms and one count of possessing firearms not identified by serial numbers. Bell moved to suppress the "pens" at trial.

Should Bell succeed on his motion to suppress the "pens" on Fourth Amendment grounds?

4F–6: In November, the police received an anonymous report of an abandoned minor at a specified home. Officer Darryl and two other officers responded. Upon arriving at the home in question, Darryl knocked on the front door. After receiving no response, Darryl peered in a front window and saw someone asleep on the couch. Darryl again knocked on the door, and Dedra's adolescent son responded.

When the front door was opened, Darryl observed a pipe sitting on a table in the front room. The pipe, which was ceramic, had a stem two to four inches long and had a large bowl bearing a skull on the front of it. Darryl asked Dedra's son if he could come in and was given permission to enter. Darryl picked up the pipe and, by smelling it, detected an odor of marijuana.

Dedra returned home just as the officers were preparing to leave. When asked, she admitted that she owned the pipe, claiming that it was for her personal use. She was arrested and charged with possession of drug paraphernalia. Prior to trial, Dedra moved to suppress the pipe on the grounds that it had been obtained in violation of her Fourth Amendment rights. The trial judge denied the motion, ruling that the officer's conduct fit within the "plain view" doctrine.

Did the trial judge rule correctly?

4F–7: On January 6, the Oakwood Police Department took a complaint from a woman who resides in Oakwood. According to the complaint, after the woman exited the shower and started dressing, she observed a silver object that appeared to be a camera sitting on her outside bedroom window ledge. She decided to shut her bedroom blinds completely. By the time she got to the window, the silver object was gone.

On January 15, Officer Bell of the Dayton Police Department went to a residence on Firewood Drive to investigate a possible "Peeping Tom." Upon arriving, Bell observed Darren Cake holding a video camera and looking into a window. Cake began to run from the scene. Officer Bell pursued Cake, took him into custody, and took a camcorder away from him. When Officer Bell viewed the videotape found inside the camcorder, it was apparent that Cake had been surreptitiously taping women through the windows of their residences.

On January 25, Detective Jeff Count of the Oakwood Police Department went to the Dayton Police Department to view the videotape. His objective was to determine whether the Oakwood victim appeared on the tape. After viewing the tape, Officer Count decided to show it to the victim to see if she could identify herself. Upon seeing the tape, the victim immediately identified herself.

Cake was charged with "voyeurism," a third degree misdemeanor. After his motion to suppress the videotape evidence was overruled, Cake entered a "no contest" plea. The trial court found him guilty and imposed a 60-day jail sentence, 50 days of which were suspended, a $500 fine, $350 of which was suspended, and a two-year probationary term. Cake has appealed the trial court's ruling on his motion to suppress.

How should the appellate court rule?

4F–8: On June 4, Pat Rowans, a realtor, was showing a house in Wabash to prospective buyer Sam Hips and his fiancee. Hips was a probationary police officer who had not yet attended the police academy. While inspecting the home, Hips saw what he believed to be marijuana on a nightstand in an upstairs bedroom. He also saw seeds, stems, rolling papers, and scales. According to Rowans, Hips said that he was going to confiscate the marijuana, but changed his mind after she told him that he could not. Hips tried to radio other officers from inside the house, but was unsuccessful. He left the house and radioed for assistance from his police vehicle which was parked nearby. Rowans and Hips's fiancee came out of the house a minute or two after Hips had exited. Rowans locked the front door, but left the back door unlocked as it had been when they had arrived.

Several officers arrived within two or three minutes. After discussing the matter, they decided to enter the home. Rowans requested that they not enter. After further discussion, the officers went into the home through the unlocked back door. They seized the items seen earlier by Hips. At the time, Rowans was in her car telephoning the owner of her realty company.

Eighteen-year-old Matt Middle, the occupant of the upstairs bedroom, was subsequently charged with possession of marijuana and drug paraphernalia. He moved to suppress the evidence obtained during the warrantless search of his home. The trial court denied the motion, relying on the plain view doctrine.

Was the trial court's decision correct?

4F–9: Officer Darren Burns went to Simon's motel room to investigate the harboring of a runaway. Simon allowed him to enter. Burns immediately noticed an open pocketknife on a white-surfaced drafting table. For his safety, Burns picked up the knife, closed it, and laid it back down on the table. When he laid the knife down, he noticed a picture on plain white paper that was face-down right next to the knife. It appeared to be an image of a young child, partially nude, in a sexual pose. Burns, who was about two feet away from the picture, moved a step closer and looked at it again from directly overhead. From this angle, he confirmed his suspicion that the picture was child pornography.

Officer Burns turned the picture over and asked Simon about it. Simon told him that someone had sent it to him by e-mail and that he did not have any others like it. Burns asked for and received Simon's permission to search the room. He soon found other pictures containing child pornography. Simon then turned over some computer diskettes containing child pornography and a white, three-ring binder that contained additional child pornography.

Simon was charged with possession of child pornography. He moved to suppress the evidence, contending that Officer Burns's actions had violated the Fourth Amendment. At a hearing on Simon's motion, on cross-examination of Officer Burns, the following exchange took place:

Q. Officer Burns, you testified that the photograph on the drafting table was face-down?

A. That is correct.

Q. After you moved closer and looked at that photograph from directly overhead, did you, at that time, intend to ask Simon if he knew anything about the photograph?

A. Not at that time, no, sir.

Q. Why not?

A. Because I hadn't flipped it over and hadn't seen for sure that it was, in fact, child pornography. I believed it to be child pornography, but I wasn't yet sure if it was child pornography.

Does the plain view doctrine justify Officer Burns's conduct?

4F–10: Gregory is the owner of property located at 2420 Highway 66. The property is in a rural area on the west side of the highway. There are no other houses in the vicinity. The property is bounded on the east by Highway 66. On the north, south, and west barbed wire fencing separates the property from surrounding pasture. The house is approximately 25 yards west of the highway. Its front porch and door face south. A barn is located 50 to 60 yards west of the house near the barbed wire fence. A shed sits equidistant between the house and the barn. From Highway 66, a driveway runs from east to west on the south of the house, curving to the north and ending in a turn-around near the center of the area bounded by the three buildings. The only apparent walkway or sidewalk leads directly south from the front door of the house to the driveway. Several large trees surround the house inside of the driveway.

In late August, Deputy Paul told Detective Shane that a concerned citizen had noticed a strong, peculiar odor emanating from trash being burned on Gregory's property and had also observed numerous cars stopping there for short intervals of time. A week earlier, another concerned citizen had seen a woman drive a van to a shed located on the property. She had unloaded boxes from the van and had then placed other boxes in the van before driving off. At 1:00 a.m., on the day after he received this report from Deputy Paul, Shane drove to the vicinity of Gregory's property. While standing in a grass field to the west of the property, approximately 30 yards west of the barn, Shane noticed a strong odor of ether. He suspected that methamphetamine was being manufactured.

Later that morning, Shane returned to the area twice more. From a position near Highway 66 about 50 yards south of Gregory's driveway, and not on Gregory's property, Detective Shane saw a burn barrel and a white translucent plastic trash bag sitting near the barn. Using binoculars, he determined that the bag contained yellow containers of what he believed to be "Heet." ("Heet" is a substance used in the manufacture of methamphetamine.) Shane then walked to the field north of Gregory's property, where he again smelled ether. He got into his patrol car, pulled it into the driveway, went to the front door, and knocked several times. After no one responded, he got back into his vehicle and drove by the rear of Gregory's home on the circle driveway. While passing the white trash bag he had seen, Shane spotted several pseudoephedrine blister packs and a number of "Heet" bottles. He stopped his car, got out, and "collected the trash bag."

Shane took the bag to the sheriff's department for examination. In addition to the "Heet" bottles and eight to 10 packs of ephedrine, the bag contained plastic gloves, coffee filters with a pinkish powder residue, and documents with Gregory's name on them. Based on this evidence and the other facts he had, Shane applied for and secured a search warrant for Gregory's property. A search of the buildings on the property yielded a considerable amount of additional evidence. Gregory was charged with manufacturing methamphetamine and related narcotics offenses.

Did Detective Shane violate the Fourth Amendment before he secured the search warrant?

Selected Bibliography

Jacob W. Landynski, *The Supreme Court's Search for Fourth Amendment Standards: The Extraordinary Case of* Coolidge v. New Hampshire, 45 Conn. B.J. 330 (1972)

Charles E. Moylan, Jr., *The Plain View Doctrine: Unexpected Child of the Great "Search Incident" Geography Battle*, 26 Mercer L. Rev. 1047 (1975)

Diane Eyre Scott, *"Plain View" — Anything But Plain:* Coolidge *Divides the Lower Courts*, 7 Loy. L.A. L. Rev. 489 (1974)

Chapter 5

The Balancing Approach to Fourth Amendment Reasonableness

Introductory Note

The cases in this chapter involve situations in which either the government or the individual is claiming that the probable cause and warrant norms are not appropriate measures of the reasonableness of the government conduct at issue. Each of these claims is rooted in an effort to "balance" society's interests against those of the individual. In most of the cases, the government contends that the balance justifies *diminution* of the normal standards of reasonableness. In a few, however, individuals contend that balancing analysis should lead to *elevation* of the normal standards.

Chapter Five consists of three subsections. Subsection A is further organized into four subparts. The first of those subparts includes *Terry v. Ohio*, 392 U.S. 1, 88 S. Ct. 1868, 20 L. Ed. 2d 889 (1968), the landmark Warren Court decision that is the foundation for the subsection. In *Terry*, the Supreme Court addressed the constitutionality of law enforcement authority to stop individuals on the street and to frisk them for weapons. Stop and frisk authority was controversial at the time of *Terry* and remains controversial today. *Terry* and the notes that follow provide an introduction to the basic Fourth Amendment doctrine governing stop and frisk authority and furnish the opportunity to explore the constitutional reasoning underlying that doctrine.

The remaining subparts are devoted to *Terry*'s progeny. In each, a distinct issue raised by the *Terry* doctrine is considered. Subpart 2 discusses the standards for determining when a person has been "seized." Subpart 3 explores the showing that is necessary to justify a "stop" and a "frisk." And subpart 4 considers the permissible scope of the seizures and the searches that are authorized. In the cases in these subparts, the Court has been asked to define, explain, and often to expand the original authority recognized by the Warren Court. The balancing analysis employed in *Terry* lies at the core of each. As will be seen, the Court's willingness to use that analysis has resulted in an expansive interpretation of *Terry* and a substantial growth of official authority to search and seize without probable cause.

Students should pay close attention to the reasoning of *Terry* and to the precise limits that the Warren Court imposed on the law enforcement activity it sanctioned. *Terry* is the source of all that follows. With respect to the subsequent decisions, students should consider the extent to which each is consistent or inconsistent with *Terry* and with the values that underlie the Fourth Amendment. One of the most general and important questions raised by this line of authority is whether the sphere of official activities that need not be based on a warrant or probable cause has been kept within appropriate bounds.

Subsection B is divided into five subparts, each of which is devoted to a discrete variety of search or seizure. The topics include searches of students by school officials, checkpoint seizures of motorists, drug test searches, DNA testing, and border searches. The most intriguing and controversial subjects are suspicionless stops of vehicles at checkpoints, random drug testing of blood, urine, and/or breath samples taken from individuals, and suspicionless taking and testing of DNA from certain arrestees for purposes of "identification." In *Sitz* and *Lidster* the Justices found checkpoint stops to be constitutional, but in *Edmond* the Court concluded that law enforcement officials exceeded their constitutional authority. Students should try to identify the constitutional criteria that dictate whether suspicionless checkpoint seizures are constitutionally acceptable. Similarly, in *Skinner*, the Justices found random drug testing to be reasonable, but in *Chandler* they deemed random drug tests unconstitutional. Based on these opinions and the notes describing other decisions in which the Court has sustained or invalidated random drug testing programs, students should do their best to identify the factors that determine whether such drug testing is consistent with the Fourth Amendment. In *Maryland v. King*, a bare majority of Justices upheld the authority of officers, without individualized suspicion, to take DNA samples from those arrested for "serious" crimes and to test those samples in order to "identify" the arrestees as perpetrators of unsolved crimes. Students should carefully examine the balance struck by the majority and should analyze whether there is merit to the dissenters' critiques of the majority's balance. All told, this subsection includes seven main cases in which the government claimed that the balance of relevant interests dictates less demanding standards of reasonableness. In five of them, the Court agreed with the government's contention; in the other two, the Court rejected it. After reading all of the opinions in this subsection, students should consider whether there is a principled basis for deciding whether and when it is constitutionally appropriate to suspend the basic Fourth Amendment norms.

The final subsection illustrates that the balancing approach can lead not only to less demanding, but also to more demanding Fourth Amendment standards. The two situations in which the Court has been willing to elevate the constitutional demands are seizures by means of "deadly force," and searches that intrude inside human bodies. Each of the cases included in this subsection involves a contention that heightened Fourth Amendment requirements are essential because of the special character of the search or seizure at issue. In each situation, students should question whether and why the Fourth Amendment ought to demand more than the normal justification required to search and seize and whether the justifications adopted by the Court are well-conceived. Students should also identify the specifics of the heightened standards that govern in certain, limited contexts.

Overall, this final Fourth Amendment Chapter raises fundamental questions about the scope and importance of the warrant and probable cause requirements considered in Chapters Two, Three, and Four. After considering all of the material in this Chapter, students should reflect upon the constitutional legitimacy of interest balancing, the fairness of the balances struck by the Court, and the advisability of the resultant variable standards for judging the reasonableness of searches and seizures.

[A] Stops, Frisks, and the Right to Be Secure in One's Person, House, and Effects

[1] The Constitutional Doctrine and Its Theoretical Underpinnings

Terry v. Ohio

United States Supreme Court

392 U.S. 1, 88 S. Ct. 1868, 20 L. Ed. 2d 889 (1968)

MR. CHIEF JUSTICE WARREN delivered the opinion of the Court.

. . . .

Petitioner Terry was convicted of carrying a concealed weapon and sentenced to the statutorily prescribed term of one to three years in the penitentiary . . . . Officer McFadden testified that while he was patrolling in plain clothes in downtown Cleveland at approximately 2:30 in the afternoon of October 31, 1963, his attention was attracted by two men, Chilton and Terry, standing on the corner of Huron Road and Euclid Avenue. He had never seen the two men before, and he was unable to say precisely what first drew his eye to them. However, he testified that he had been a policeman for 39 years and a detective for 35 and that he had been assigned to patrol this vicinity of downtown Cleveland for shoplifters and pickpockets for 30 years. He explained that he had developed routine habits of observation over the years and that he would "stand and watch people or walk and watch people at many intervals of the day." He added: "Now, in this case when I looked over they didn't look right to me at the time."

His interest aroused, Officer McFadden took up a post of observation in the entrance to a store 300 to 400 feet away from the two men. "I get more purpose to watch them when I seen [sic] their movements," he testified. He saw one of the men leave the other one and walk southwest on Huron Road, past some stores. The man paused for a moment and looked in a store window, then walked on a short distance, turned around and walked back toward the corner, pausing once again to look in the same store window. He rejoined his companion at the corner, and the two conferred briefly.

Then the second man went through the same series of motions, strolling down Huron Road, looking in the same window, walking on a short distance, turning back, peering in the store window again, and returning to confer with the first man at the corner. The two men repeated this ritual alternately between five and six times apiece — in all, roughly a dozen trips. At one point, while the two were standing together on the corner, a third man approached them and engaged them briefly in conversation. This man then left the two others and walked west on Euclid Avenue. Chilton and Terry resumed their measured pacing, peering, and conferring. After this had gone on for 10 to 12 minutes, the two men walked off together, heading west on Euclid Avenue, following the path taken earlier by the third man.

By this time Officer McFadden had become thoroughly suspicious. He testified that after observing their elaborately casual and oft-repeated reconnaissance of the store window on Huron Road, he suspected the two men of "casing a job, a stick-up," and that he considered it his duty as a police officer to investigate further. He added that he feared "they may have a gun." Thus, Officer McFadden followed Chilton and Terry and saw them stop in front of Zucker's store to talk to the same man who had conferred with them earlier on the street corner. Deciding that the situation was ripe for direct action, Officer McFadden approached the three men, identified himself as a police officer and asked for their names. At this point his knowledge was confined to what he had observed. He was not acquainted with any of the three men by name or by sight, and he had received no information concerning them from any other source. When the men "mumbled something" in response to his inquiries, Officer McFadden grabbed petitioner Terry, spun him around so that they were facing the other two, with Terry between McFadden and the others, and patted down the outside of his clothing. In the left breast pocket of Terry's overcoat Officer McFadden felt a pistol. He reached inside the overcoat pocket, but was unable to remove the gun. At this point, keeping Terry between himself and the others, the officer ordered all three men to enter Zucker's store. As they went in, he removed Terry's overcoat completely, removed a .38-caliber revolver from the pocket and ordered all three men to face the wall with their hands raised. Officer McFadden proceeded to pat down the outer clothing of Chilton and the third man, Katz. He discovered another revolver in the outer pocket of Chilton's overcoat, but no weapons were found on Katz. The officer testified that he only patted the men down to see whether they had weapons, and that he did not put his hands beneath the outer garments of either Terry or Chilton until he felt their guns . . . . Officer McFadden seized Chilton's gun, asked the proprietor of the store to call a police wagon, and took all three men to the station, where Chilton and Terry were formally charged with carrying concealed weapons.

. . . .

I

. . . .

Unquestionably petitioner was entitled to the protection of the Fourth Amendment as he walked down the street in Cleveland. The question is whether in all the circumstances of this on-the-street encounter, his right to personal security was violated by an unreasonable search and seizure.

We would be less than candid if we did not acknowledge that this question thrusts to the fore difficult and troublesome issues regarding a sensitive area of police activity — issues which have never before been squarely presented to this Court. Reflective of the tensions involved are the practical and constitutional arguments pressed with great vigor on both sides of the public debate over the power of the police to "stop and frisk" — as it is sometimes euphemistically termed — suspicious persons.

On the one hand, it is frequently argued that in dealing with the rapidly unfolding and often dangerous situations on city streets the police are in need of an escalating set of flexible responses, graduated in relation to the amount of information they possess. For this purpose it is urged that distinctions should be made between a "stop" and an "arrest" (or a "seizure" of a person), and between a "frisk" and a "search." Thus, it is argued, the police should be allowed to "stop" a person and detain him briefly for questioning upon suspicion that he may be connected with criminal activity. Upon suspicion that the person may be armed, the police should have the power to "frisk" him for weapons. If the "stop" and the "frisk" give rise to probable cause to believe that the suspect has committed a crime, then the police should be empowered to make a formal "arrest," and a full incident "search" of the person. This scheme is justified in part upon the notion that a "stop" and a "frisk" amount to a mere "minor inconvenience and petty indignity," which can properly be imposed upon the citizen in the interest of effective law enforcement on the basis of a police officer's suspicion.

On the other side the argument is made that the authority of the police must be strictly circumscribed by the law of arrest and search as it has developed to date in the traditional jurisprudence of the Fourth Amendment. It is contended with some force that there is not — and cannot be — a variety of police activity which does not depend solely upon the voluntary cooperation of the citizen and yet which stops short of an arrest based upon probable cause to make such an arrest. The heart of the Fourth Amendment, the argument runs, is a severe requirement of specific justification for any intrusion upon protected personal security, coupled with a highly developed system of judicial controls to enforce upon the agents of the State the commands of the Constitution. . . .

In this context we approach the issues in this case mindful of the limitations of the judicial function in controlling the myriad daily situations in which policemen and citizens confront each other on the street. The State has characterized the issue here as "the right of a police officer . . . to make an on-the-street stop, interrogate and pat down for weapons (known in street vernacular as 'stop and frisk')." But this is only partly accurate. For the issue is not the abstract propriety of the police conduct, but the admissibility against petitioner of the evidence uncovered by the search and seizure. Ever since its inception, the rule excluding evidence seized in violation of the Fourth Amendment has been recognized as a principal mode of discouraging lawless police conduct. Thus its major thrust is a deterrent one, *see Linkletter v. Walker*, 381 U.S. 618, 629–635, 85 S. Ct. 1731, 1741, 14 L. Ed. 2d 601 (1965), and experience has taught that it is the only effective deterrent to police misconduct in the criminal context, and that without it the constitutional guarantee against unreasonable searches and seizures would be a mere "form of words." *Mapp v. Ohio*, 367 U.S. 643, 655, 81 S. Ct. 1684, 1692, 6 L. Ed. 2d 1081 (1961). The rule also serves another vital function — "the imperative of judicial integrity." *Elkins v. United States*, 364 U.S. 206, 222, 80 S. Ct. 1437, 1447, 4 L. Ed. 2d 1669 (1960). Courts which sit under our Constitution cannot and will not be made party to lawless invasions of the constitutional rights of citizens by permitting unhindered governmental use of the fruits of such invasions. Thus in our system evidentiary rulings provide the context in which the judicial process of inclusion and exclusion approves some conduct as comporting with constitutional guarantees and disapproves other actions by state agents. A ruling admitting evidence in a criminal trial, we recognize, has the necessary effect of legitimizing the conduct which produced the evidence, while an application of the exclusionary rule withholds the constitutional imprimatur.

The exclusionary rule has its limitations, however, as a tool of judicial control. It cannot properly be invoked to exclude the products of legitimate police investigative techniques on the ground that much conduct which is closely similar involves unwarranted intrusions upon constitutional protections. Moreover, in some contexts the rule is ineffective as a deterrent. Street encounters between citizens and police officers are incredibly rich in diversity. They range from wholly friendly exchanges of pleasantries or mutually useful information to hostile confrontations of armed men involving arrests, or injuries, or loss of life. Moreover, hostile confrontations are not all of a piece. Some of them begin in a friendly enough manner, only to take a different turn upon the injection of some unexpected element into the conversation. Encounters are initiated by the police for a wide variety of purposes, some of which are wholly unrelated to a desire to prosecute for crime. Doubtless some police "field interrogation" conduct violates the Fourth Amendment. But a stern refusal by this Court to condone such activity does not necessarily render it responsive to the exclusionary rule. Regardless of how effective the rule may be where obtaining convictions is an important objective of the police, it is powerless to deter invasions of constitutionally guaranteed rights where the police either have no interest in prosecuting or are willing to forgo successful prosecution in the interest of serving some other goal.

Proper adjudication of cases in which the exclusionary rule is invoked demands a constant awareness of these limitations. The wholesale harassment by certain elements of the police community, of which minority groups, particularly Negroes, frequently complain, will not be stopped by the exclusion of any evidence from any criminal trial. Yet a rigid and unthinking application of the exclusionary rule, in futile protest against practices which it can never be used effectively to control, may exact a high toll in human injury and frustration of efforts to prevent crime. No judicial opinion can comprehend the protean variety of the street encounter, and we can only judge the facts of the case before us. Nothing we say today is to be taken as indicating approval of police conduct outside the legitimate investigative sphere. Under our decision, courts still retain their traditional responsibility to guard against police conduct which is over-bearing or harassing, or which trenches upon personal security without the objective evidentiary justification which the Constitution requires. When such conduct is identified, it must be condemned by the judiciary and its fruits must be excluded from evidence in criminal trials. And, of course, our approval of legitimate and restrained investigative conduct undertaken on the basis of ample factual justification should in no way discourage the employment of other remedies than the exclusionary rule to curtail abuses for which that sanction may prove inappropriate.

Having thus roughly sketched the perimeters of the constitutional debate over the limits on police investigative conduct in general and the background against which this case presents itself, we turn our attention to the quite narrow question posed by the facts before us: whether it is always unreasonable for a policeman to seize a person and subject him to a limited search for weapons unless there is probable cause for an arrest. Given the narrowness of this question, we have no occasion to canvass in detail the constitutional limitations upon the scope of a policeman's power when he confronts a citizen without probable cause to arrest him.

II

Our first task is to establish at what point in this encounter the Fourth Amendment becomes relevant. That is, we must decide whether and when Officer McFadden "seized" Terry and whether and when he conducted a "search." There is some suggestion in the use of such terms as "stop" and "frisk" that such police conduct is outside the purview of the Fourth Amendment because neither action rises to the level of a "search" or "seizure" within the meaning of the Constitution. We emphatically reject this notion. It is quite plain that the Fourth Amendment governs "seizures" of the person which do not eventuate in a trip to the station house and prosecution for crime — "arrests" in traditional terminology. It must be recognized that whenever a police officer accosts an individual and restrains his freedom to walk away, he has "seized" that person. And it is nothing less than sheer torture of the English language to suggest that a careful exploration of the outer surfaces of a person's clothing all over his or her body in an attempt to find weapons is not a "search." Moreover, it is simply fantastic to urge that such a procedure performed in public by a policeman while the citizen stands helpless, perhaps facing a wall with his hands raised, is a "petty indignity."[13] It is a serious intrusion upon the sanctity of the person, which may inflict great indignity and arouse strong resentment, and it is not to be undertaken lightly.

---

13. Consider the following apt description: "The officer must feel with sensitive fingers every portion of the prisoner's body. A thorough search must be made of the prisoner's arms and armpits, waistline and back, the groin and area about the testicles, and entire surface of the legs down to the feet." Priar & Martin, *Searching and Disarming Criminals*, 45 J. Crim. L.C. & P.S. 481 (1954).

The danger in the logic which proceeds upon distinctions between a "stop" and an "arrest," or "seizure" of the person, and between a "frisk" and a "search" is twofold. It seeks to isolate from constitutional scrutiny the initial stages of the contact between the policeman and the citizen. And by suggesting a rigid all-or-nothing model of justification and regulation under the Amendment, it obscures the utility of limitations upon the scope, as well as the initiation, of police action as a means of constitutional regulation. This Court has held in the past that a search which is reasonable at its inception may violate the Fourth Amendment by virtue of its intolerable intensity and scope. The scope of the search must be "strictly tied to and justified by" the circumstances which rendered its initiation permissible.

The distinctions of classical "stop-and-frisk" theory thus serve to divert attention from the central inquiry under the Fourth Amendment — the reasonableness in all the circumstances of the particular governmental invasion of a citizen's personal security. "Search" and "seizure" are not talismans. We therefore reject the notions that the Fourth Amendment does not come into play at all as a limitation upon police conduct if the officers stop short of something called a "technical arrest" or a "full-blown search."

In this case there can be no question, then, that Officer McFadden "seized" petitioner and subjected him to a "search" when he took hold of him and patted down the outer surfaces of his clothing. We must decide whether at that point it was reasonable for Officer McFadden to have interfered with petitioner's personal security as he did.[16] And in determining whether the seizure and search were "unreasonable" our inquiry is a dual one — whether the officer's action was justified at its inception, and whether it was reasonably related in scope to the circumstances which justified the interference in the first place.

III

If this case involved police conduct subject to the Warrant Clause of the Fourth Amendment, we would have to ascertain whether "probable cause" existed to justify the search and seizure which took place. However, that is not the case. We do not retreat from our holdings that the police must, whenever practicable, obtain advance judicial approval of searches and seizures through the warrant procedure, or that in most instances failure to comply with the warrant requirement can only be excused by exigent circumstances. But we deal here with an entire rubric of police conduct — necessarily swift action predicated upon the on-the-spot observations of the officer on the beat — which historically has not been, and as a practical matter could not be,

---

16. We thus decide nothing today concerning the constitutional propriety of an investigative "seizure" upon less than probable cause for purposes of "detention" and/or interrogation. Obviously, not all personal intercourse between policemen and citizens involves "seizures" of persons. Only when the officer, by means of physical force or show of authority, has in some way restrained the liberty of a citizen may we conclude that a "seizure" has occurred. We cannot tell with any certainty upon this record whether any such "seizure" took place here prior to Officer McFadden's initiation of physical contact for purposes of searching Terry for weapons, and we thus may assume that up to that point no intrusion upon constitutionally protected rights had occurred.

subjected to the warrant procedure. Instead, the conduct involved in this case must be tested by the Fourth Amendment's general proscription against unreasonable searches and seizures.

Nonetheless, the notions which underlie both the warrant procedure and the requirement of probable cause remain fully relevant in this context. In order to assess the reasonableness of Officer McFadden's conduct as a general proposition, it is necessary "first to focus upon the governmental interest which allegedly justifies official intrusion upon the constitutionally protected interests of the private citizen," for there is "no ready test for determining reasonableness other than by balancing the need to search [or seize] against the invasion which the search [or seizure] entails." *Camara v. Municipal Court*, 387 U.S. 523, 534–535, 536–537, 87 S. Ct. 1727, 1735, 18 L. Ed. 2d 930 (1967). And in justifying the particular intrusion the police officer must be able to point to specific and articulable facts which, taken together with rational inferences from those facts, reasonably warrant that intrusion. The scheme of the Fourth Amendment becomes meaningful only when it is assured that at some point the conduct of those charged with enforcing the laws can be subjected to the more detached, neutral scrutiny of a judge who must evaluate the reasonableness of a particular search or seizure in light of the particular circumstances. And in making that assessment it is imperative that the facts be judged against an objective standard: would the facts available to the officer at the moment of the seizure or the search "warrant a man of reasonable caution in the belief" that the action taken was appropriate? Anything less would invite intrusions upon constitutionally guaranteed rights based on nothing more substantial than inarticulate hunches, a result this Court has consistently refused to sanction. . . .

Applying these principles to this case, we consider first the nature and extent of the governmental interests involved. One general interest is of course that of effective crime prevention and detection; it is this interest which underlies the recognition that a police officer may in appropriate circumstances and in an appropriate manner approach a person for purposes of investigating possibly criminal behavior even though there is no probable cause to make an arrest. It was this legitimate investigative function Officer McFadden was discharging when he decided to approach petitioner and his companions. He had observed Terry, Chilton, and Katz go through a series of acts, each of them perhaps innocent in itself, but which taken together warranted further investigation. There is nothing unusual in two men standing together on a street corner, perhaps waiting for someone. Nor is there anything suspicious about people in such circumstances strolling up and down the street, singly or in pairs. Store windows, moreover, are made to be looked in. But the story is quite different where, as here, two men hover about a street corner for an extended period of time, at the end of which it becomes apparent that they are not waiting for anyone or anything; where these men pace alternately along an identical route, pausing to stare in the same store window roughly 24 times; where each completion of this route is followed immediately by a conference between the two men on the corner; where they are joined in one of these conferences by a third man who leaves swiftly; and where the two men finally follow the third and rejoin him a couple of blocks away. It would have been poor police work indeed for an officer of 30 years' experience in the detection of thievery from stores in this same neighborhood to have failed to investigate this behavior further.

The crux of this case, however, is not the propriety of Officer McFadden's taking steps to investigate petitioner's suspicious behavior, but rather, whether there was justification for McFadden's invasion of Terry's personal security by searching him for weapons in the course of that investigation. We are now concerned with more than the governmental interest in investigating crime; in addition, there is the more immediate interest of the police officer in taking steps to assure himself that the person with whom he is dealing is not armed with a weapon that could unexpectedly and fatally be used against him. Certainly it would be unreasonable to require that police officers take unnecessary risks in the performance of their duties. American criminals have a long tradition of armed violence, and every year in this country many law enforcement officers are killed in the line of duty, and thousands more are wounded. Virtually all of these deaths and a substantial portion of the injuries are inflicted with guns and knives.

In view of these facts, we cannot blind ourselves to the need for law enforcement officers to protect themselves and other prospective victims of violence in situations where they may lack probable cause for an arrest. When an officer is justified in believing that the individual whose suspicious behavior he is investigating at close range is armed and presently dangerous to the officer or to others, it would appear to be clearly unreasonable to deny the officer the power to take necessary measures to determine whether the person is in fact carrying a weapon and to neutralize the threat of physical harm.

. . . .

Petitioner does not argue that a police officer should refrain from making any investigation of suspicious circumstances until such time as he has probable cause to make an arrest; nor does he deny that police officers in properly discharging their investigative function may find themselves confronting persons who might well be armed and dangerous. Moreover, he does not say that an officer is always unjustified in searching a suspect to discover weapons. Rather, he says it is unreasonable for the policeman to take that step until such time as the situation evolves to a point where there is probable cause to make an arrest. When that point has been reached, petitioner would concede the officer's right to conduct a search of the suspect for weapons, fruits or instrumentalities of the crime, or "mere" evidence, incident to the arrest.

There are two weaknesses in this line of reasoning, however. First, it fails to take account of traditional limitations upon the scope of searches, and thus recognizes no distinction in purpose, character, and extent between a search incident to an arrest and a limited search for weapons. The former, although justified in part by the acknowledged necessity to protect the arresting officer from assault with a concealed weapon, is also justified on other grounds, and can therefore involve a relatively extensive exploration of the person. A search for weapons in the absence of probable cause to arrest, however, must, like any other search, be strictly circumscribed by the exigencies which justify its initiation. Thus it must be limited to that which is necessary for the discovery of weapons which might be used to harm the officer or others nearby, and may realistically be characterized as something less than a "full" search, even though it remains a serious intrusion.

A second, and related, objection to petitioner's argument is that it assumes that the law of arrest has already worked out the balance between the particular interests involved here — the neutralization of danger to the policeman in the investigative circumstance and the sanctity of the individual. But this is not so. An arrest is a wholly different kind of intrusion upon individual freedom from a limited search for weapons, and the interests each is designed to serve are likewise quite different. An arrest is the initial stage of a criminal prosecution. It is intended to vindicate society's interest in having its laws obeyed, and it is inevitably accompanied by future interference with the individual's freedom of movement, whether or not trial or conviction ultimately follows. The protective search for weapons, on the other hand, constitutes a brief, though far from inconsiderable, intrusion upon the sanctity of the person. It does not follow that because an officer may lawfully arrest a person only when he is apprised of facts sufficient to warrant a belief that the person has committed or is committing a crime, the officer is equally unjustified, absent that kind of evidence, in making any intrusions short of an arrest. Moreover, a perfectly reasonable apprehension of danger may arise long before the officer is possessed of adequate information to justify taking a person into custody for the purpose of prosecuting him for a crime. Petitioner's reliance on cases which have worked out standards of reasonableness with regard to "seizures" constituting arrests and searches incident thereto is thus misplaced. It assumes that the interests sought to be vindicated and the invasions of personal security may be equated in the two cases, and thereby ignores a vital aspect of the analysis of the reasonableness of particular types of conduct under the Fourth Amendment.

Our evaluation of the proper balance that has to be struck in this type of case leads us to conclude that there must be a narrowly drawn authority to permit a reasonable search for weapons for the protection of the police officer, where he has reason to believe that he is dealing with an armed and dangerous individual, regardless of whether he has probable cause to arrest the individual for a crime. The officer need not be absolutely certain that the individual is armed; the issue is whether a reasonably prudent man in the circumstances would be warranted in the belief that his safety or that of others was in danger. And in determining whether the officer acted reasonably in such circumstances, due weight must be given, not to his inchoate and unparticularized suspicion or "hunch," but to the specific reasonable inferences which he is entitled to draw from the facts in light of his experience.

IV

... We think on the facts and circumstances Officer McFadden detailed before the trial judge a reasonably prudent man would have been warranted in believing petitioner was armed and thus presented a threat to the officer's safety while he was investigating his suspicious behavior. The actions of Terry and Chilton were consistent with McFadden's hypothesis that these men were contemplating a daylight robbery—which, it is reasonable to assume, would be likely to involve the use of weapons—and nothing in their conduct from the time he first noticed them until the time he confronted them and identified himself as a police officer gave him sufficient reason to negate that hypothesis. Although the trio had departed the original scene, there was nothing to indicate abandonment of an intent to commit a robbery at some point. Thus, when Officer McFadden approached the three men gathered before the display window at Zucker's store he had observed enough to make it quite reasonable to fear that they were armed; and nothing in their response to his hailing them, identifying himself as a police officer, and asking their names served to dispel that reasonable belief. ...

The manner in which the seizure and search were conducted is, of course, as vital a part of the inquiry as whether they were warranted at all. The Fourth Amendment proceeds as much by limitations upon the scope of governmental action as by imposing preconditions upon its initiation. ...

We need not develop at length in this case, however, the limitations which the Fourth Amendment places upon a protective seizure and search for weapons. These limitations will have to be developed in the concrete factual circumstances of individual cases. *See Sibron v. New York*, 392 U.S. 40, 88 S. Ct. 1889, 1912, 20 L. Ed. 2d 917 decided today. Suffice it to note that such a search, unlike a search without a warrant incident to a lawful arrest, is not justified by any need to prevent the disappearance or destruction of evidence of crime. The sole justification of the search in the present situation is the protection of the police officer and others nearby, and it must therefore be confined in scope to an intrusion reasonably designed to discover guns, knives, clubs, or other hidden instruments for the assault of the police officer.

The scope of the search in this case presents no serious problem in light of these standards. Officer McFadden patted down the outer clothing of petitioner and his two companions. He did not place his hands in their pockets or under the outer surface of their garments until he had felt weapons, and then he merely reached for and removed the guns. He never did invade Katz' person beyond the outer surfaces of his clothes, since he discovered nothing in his patdown which might have been a weapon. Officer McFadden confined his search strictly to what was minimally necessary to learn whether the men were armed and to disarm them once he discovered the weapons. He did not conduct a general exploratory search for whatever evidence of criminal activity he might find.

V

We conclude that the revolver seized from Terry was properly admitted in evidence against him. At the time he seized petitioner and searched him for weapons, Officer McFadden had reasonable grounds to believe that petitioner was armed and dangerous, and it was necessary for the protection of himself and others to take swift measures to discover the true facts and neutralize the threat of harm if it materialized. The policeman carefully restricted his search to what was appropriate to the discovery of the particular items which he sought. Each case of this sort will, of course, have to be decided on its own facts. We merely hold today that where a police officer observes unusual conduct which leads him reasonably to conclude in light of his experience that criminal activity may be afoot and that the persons with whom he is dealing may be armed and presently dangerous, where in the course of investigating this behavior he identifies himself as a policeman and makes reasonable inquiries, and where nothing in the initial stages of the encounter serves to dispel his reasonable fear for his own or others' safety, he is entitled for the protection of himself and others in the area to conduct a carefully limited search of the outer clothing of such persons in an attempt to discover weapons which might be used to assault him. Such a search is a reasonable search under the Fourth Amendment, and any weapons seized may properly be introduced in evidence against the person from whom they were taken.

Affirmed.

Mr. Justice Black concurs in the judgment and the opinion except where the opinion quotes from and relies upon this Court's opinion in *Katz v. United States* and the concurring opinion in *Warden v. Hayden.*

Mr. Justice Harlan, concurring.

While I unreservedly agree with the Court's ultimate holding in this case, I am constrained to fill in a few gaps, as I see them, in its opinion. I do this because what is said by this Court today will serve as initial guidelines for law enforcement authorities and courts throughout the land as this important new field of law develops.

. . . .

The state courts held . . . that when an officer is lawfully confronting a possibly hostile person in the line of duty he has a right, springing only from the necessity of the situation and not from any broader right to disarm, to frisk for his own protection. This holding, with which I agree and with which I think the Court agrees, offers the only satisfactory basis I can think of for affirming this conviction. The holding has, however, two logical corollaries that I do not think the Court has fully expressed.

In the first place, if the frisk is justified in order to protect the officer during an encounter with a citizen, the officer must first have constitutional grounds to insist on an encounter, to make a *forcible* stop. Any person, including a policeman, is at liberty to avoid a person he considers dangerous. If and when a policeman has a right instead to disarm such a person for his own protection, he must first have a right not to avoid him but to be in his presence. That right must be more than the liberty (again, possessed by every citizen) to address questions to other persons, for ordinarily the person addressed has an equal right to ignore his interrogator and walk away; he certainly need not submit to a frisk for the questioner's protection. I would make it perfectly clear that the right to frisk in this case depends upon the reasonableness of a forcible stop to investigate a suspected crime.

Where such a stop is reasonable, however, the right to frisk must be immediate and automatic if the reason for the stop is, as here, an articulable suspicion of a crime of violence. Just as a full search incident to a lawful arrest requires no additional justification, a limited frisk incident to a lawful stop must often be rapid and routine. There is no reason why an officer, rightfully but forcibly confronting a person suspected of a serious crime, should have to ask one question and take the risk that the answer might be a bullet.

. . . .

I would affirm this conviction for what I believe to be the same reasons the Court relies on. I would, however, make explicit what I think is implicit in affirmance on the present facts. Officer McFadden's right to interrupt Terry's freedom of movement and invade his privacy arose only because circumstances warranted forcing an encounter with Terry in an effort to prevent or investigate a crime. Once that forced encounter was justified, however, the officer's right to take suitable measures for his own safety followed automatically.

Upon the foregoing premises, I join the opinion of the Court.

Mr. Justice White, concurring.

. . . .

There is nothing in the Constitution which prevents a policeman from addressing questions to anyone on the streets. Absent special circumstances, the person approached may not be detained or frisked but may refuse to cooperate and go on his way. However, given the proper circumstances, such as those in this case, it seems to me the person may be briefly detained against his will while pertinent questions are directed to him. Of course, the person stopped is not obliged to answer, answers may not be compelled, and refusal to answer furnishes no basis for an arrest, although it may alert the officer to the need for continued observation. In my view, it is temporary detention, warranted by the circumstances, which chiefly justifies the protective frisk for weapons. Perhaps the frisk itself, where proper, will have beneficial results whether questions are asked or not. If weapons are found, an arrest will follow. If none are found, the frisk may nevertheless serve preventive ends because of its unmistakable message that suspicion has been aroused. But if the investigative stop is sustainable at all, constitutional rights are not necessarily violated if pertinent questions are asked and the person is restrained briefly in the process.

Mr. Justice Douglas, dissenting.

I agree that petitioner was "seized" within the meaning of the Fourth Amendment. I also agree that frisking petitioner and his companions for guns was a "search." But it is a mystery how that "search" and that "seizure" can be constitutional by Fourth Amendment standards, unless there was "probable cause" to believe that (1) a crime had been committed or (2) a crime was in the process of being committed or (3) a crime was about to be committed.

The opinion of the Court disclaims the existence of "probable cause." ... Had a warrant been sought, a magistrate would, therefore, have been unauthorized to issue one, for he can act only if there is a showing of "probable cause." We hold today that the police have greater authority to make a "seizure" and conduct a "search" than a judge has to authorize such action. We have said precisely the opposite over and over again.

In other words, police officers up to today have been permitted to effect arrests or searches without warrants only when the facts within their personal knowledge would satisfy the constitutional standard of probable cause. At the time of their "seizure" without a warrant they must possess facts concerning the person arrested that would have satisfied a magistrate that "probable cause" was indeed present. The term "probable cause" rings a bell of certainty that is not sounded by phrases such as "reasonable suspicion." Moreover, the meaning of "probable cause" is deeply imbedded in our constitutional history. ...

The infringement on personal liberty of any "seizure" of a person can only be "reasonable" under the Fourth Amendment if we require the police to possess "probable cause" before they seize him. Only that line draws a meaningful distinction between an officer's mere inkling and the presence of facts within the officer's personal knowledge which would convince a reasonable man that the person seized has committed, is committing, or is about to commit a particular crime.

. . . .

There have been powerful hydraulic pressures throughout our history that bear heavily on the Court to water down constitutional guarantees and give the police the upper hand. That hydraulic pressure has probably never been greater than it is today.

Yet if the individual is no longer to be sovereign, if the police can pick him up whenever they do not like the cut of his jib, if they can "seize" and "search" him in their discretion, we enter a new regime. The decision to enter it should be made only after a full debate by the people of this country.

Notes and Questions

(1) What official conduct did the *Terry* Court validate? What showing is necessary to render that conduct reasonable? Chief Justice Warren's opinion makes it clear that the actions *Terry* authorized are "searches" and "seizures," and, therefore, that they are regulated by the Fourth Amendment. Why then aren't probable cause and a warrant necessary to make them reasonable?

(2) If an officer has a "hunch" — an objectively unsupported belief — that an individual is preparing to engage in criminal activity, what actions does the Constitution allow him to take?

(3) In *Sibron v. New York*, 392 U.S. 40, 88 S. Ct. 1889, 20 L. Ed. 2d 917 (1968), a companion case decided with *Terry*, the Court shed additional light upon the meaning of its landmark decision. In *Sibron*, an officer watched a man converse with

several known narcotics addicts over the course of the eight-hour period between 4:00 p.m. and midnight. Late in the evening, the man entered a restaurant and ordered pie and coffee, whereupon the officer approached him and told him to come outside. When they were outside, the officer said, "You know what I am after." When the man mumbled and reached into his pocket, the officer thrust his hand into the pocket and extracted packets of heroin.

The Court concluded that the officer did not have "reasonable grounds to believe that Sibron was armed and dangerous." In the Court's view, mere association with known narcotics addicts did not give rise to "a reasonable fear of life or limb." As a result, the Court held that it was unconstitutional for the officer to stop and frisk Sibron. Moreover, the Court noted that even if there had been adequate grounds for a detention and frisk, the search conducted by the officer had exceeded the limited bounds of the patdown authorized by *Terry*.

(4) Justice Harlan agreed with the Court's outcome in *Sibron*. In his concurrence, however, he suggested that the authority granted by *Terry* is limited to necessitous situations. Harlan expressed the view that a *Terry* stop and frisk can only be justified by a showing that there is a "need for immediate action" to prevent a violent crime or some other imminent harm. In *Adams v. Williams*, 407 U.S. 143, 92 S. Ct. 1921, 32 L. Ed. 2d 612 (1972), the Court cast doubt on the Harlan view. The Court held that it was permissible under *Terry* to stop and frisk an individual suspected of possessing narcotics and a concealed weapon. Are there legitimate reasons for confining the constitutional authority recognized by the Warren Court to imminent, potentially violent offenses such as the daytime robbery in *Terry* itself?

(5) In *Dunaway v. New York*, 442 U.S. 200, 99 S. Ct. 2248, 60 L. Ed. 2d 824 (1979), after a pizza parlor proprietor "was killed during an attempted robbery," detectives learned information implicating the defendant. They found him at a neighbor's home and took him "into custody." Even though the detectives did not tell him that "he was under arrest, he would have been physically restrained if he had attempted to leave." The detectives drove the defendant "to police headquarters in a police car, . . . placed him in an interrogation room," and questioned him. He incriminated himself.

The defendant claimed that he had been unreasonably seized. The government conceded that the detectives had lacked probable cause to arrest the defendant, but argued that no arrest had occurred and that the seizure was reasonable because the officers had a "reasonable suspicion" that he "possessed 'intimate knowledge about a serious and unsolved crime.'" In essence, the government contended that the seizure of the defendant on less than probable cause was reasonable under *Terry v. Ohio*.

The Court rejected that contention, concluding that the seizure exceeded the scope of those *Terry* had authorized on less than probable cause. Specifically, "[i]n contrast to the brief and narrowly circumscribed intrusions involved in" *Terry* and subsequent decisions, "the detention of [the defendant] was in important respects indistinguishable from a traditional arrest." He had been "taken from a neighbor's home to a police car, transported to a police station, and placed in an interrogation room, . . .

was never informed he was 'free to go,' [and] . . . would have been physically re-strained if he had refused to accompany the officers or had tried to escape." For these reasons, the "seizure" was not "even roughly analogous to the narrowly defined intrusions involved in *Terry* and its progeny." Probable cause was necessary to ren-der it reasonable.

The majority opinion in *Dunaway* raised (and arguably suggested answers to) sig-nificant questions about the scope of *Terry* authority and the utility of the "balanc-ing" process relied upon by the *Terry* Court. The majority stressed that the "exception to the general rule requiring probable cause" had a "narrow scope," that only "brief and narrowly circumscribed intrusions" were permissible, and that the "special cat-egory of Fourth Amendment 'seizures'" that could be effected on less than probable cause were "substantially less intrusive than arrests" and were "narrowly defined." Moreover, such seizures were allowed, "only for the purpose of a pat-down for weap-ons." The *Dunaway* majority seemed determined to confine the seizures and searches *Terry* had authorized on less than probable cause within exceedingly tight, "narrow" bounds. In addition, the Court intimated that employment of "the balancing test" to dilute Fourth Amendment norms was quite exceptional, that it was rarely appropri-ate for the Justices to do what they had done in *Terry*—to depart from the traditional and "familiar threshold standard of probable cause for Fourth Amendment seizures." The Court rejected the government's argument that "all seizures that do not amount to technical arrests" should be governed by a "multifactor balancing test of 'reason-able police conduct'" because, under such an approach "the protections intended by the Framers could all too easily disappear." In sum, the message of *Dunaway* seemed to be that *Terry* must not be read expansively, that the judicial interest balancing that had led to a lowering of the constitutional norm in *Terry* was generally forbidden, and that the probable cause norm governed the vast majority of searches and sei-zures. The Court declared that "[f]or all but th[e] narrowly defined intrusions" en-tailed in a *Terry* stop and frisk, "the requisite 'balancing' has been performed in centuries of precedent and is embodied in the principle that seizures are 'reasonable' only if supported by probable cause."

In a concurring opinion, Justice White agreed that the seizure in *Dunaway* was unreasonable on less than probable cause. He was concerned, however, that the ma-jority's opinion "might be read to indicate that *Terry* . . . is an almost unique excep-tion to the hard-and-fast standard of probable cause." In his view, "the key principle of the Fourth Amendment is reasonableness—the balancing of competing interests." He believed that the door should be left open to "the recognition in particular cases of extraordinary private or public interests" and to "the generic recognition of certain exceptions to the normal rule of probable cause where more flexibility is essential." Clearly, Justice White believed that it was appropriate for the Justices to employ the balancing process to identify other types of exceptional Fourth Amendment intru-sion that were not subject to the probable cause demand.

The tension between the majority's and Justice White's attitudes toward the use of interest balancing to modify constitutional norms is evident and significant. The general question raised is whether the balancing process is the general rule, a rare exception, or something between those two extremes. Students should keep this question in mind — and should consider which attitude toward balancing has prevailed — while analyzing the opinions in Subsections 5[A] and 5[B].

[2] "Seizures" of Persons

Notes on *United States v. Mendenhall*

In *United States v. Mendenhall*, 446 U.S. 544, 100 S. Ct. 1870, 64 L. Ed. 2d 497 (1980), a splintered Supreme Court reversed a Court of Appeals conclusion that Drug Enforcement Administration agents had violated a woman's Fourth Amendment rights when they approached her in an airport concourse, escorted her to a DEA office in the airport, and found narcotics in her undergarments during a search of her person. Although four Justices disagreed, a five-Justice majority held that the record provided adequate evidentiary support for the trial court's conclusions that she had voluntarily consented to accompany the agents to the DEA office and had voluntarily consented to the search of her person.

The Justices divided into three camps, however, in evaluating the constitutionality of the initial encounter in the airport. Two Justices concluded that Ms. Mendenhall was not seized when the agents approached her, asked to see her identification and ticket, and posed a few questions. Three other Justices described the question of whether she was seized as "extremely close." They assumed that a seizure had occurred, but concluded that the encounter was constitutional because the officers "had reasonable suspicion that [Ms. Mendenhall] was engaging in criminal activity" — in particular, that she was transporting narcotics. Thus, for two entirely distinct reasons, a majority found that the encounter in the concourse did not violate her Fourth Amendment right against unreasonable seizures. The four dissenting Justices found a Fourth Amendment violation because they assumed that Ms. Mendenhall was seized and concluded that the agents lacked "reasonable grounds for suspecting her of criminal activity at the time of the stop."

The *Terry* Court had deemed it "[o]bvious[]" that the Fourth Amendment does not govern "all personal intercourse between policemen and citizens." According to Chief Justice Warren, a seizure occurs "[o]nly when the officer, by means of physical force or show of authority, . . . in some way restrain[s] the liberty of a citizen." The primary constitutional significance of the *Mendenhall* case lies in Justice Stewart's effort to furnish a governing doctrinal standard for the important issue of when a person is "seized" under the Fourth Amendment. In his lead opinion in *Mendenhall*, Justice Stewart "conclude[d] that a person has been 'seized' within the meaning of the Fourth Amendment only if, in view of all the circumstances surrounding the incident, *a reasonable person would have believed that he was not free to leave.*" (Emphasis added). The seven Justices who assumed that a seizure had occurred neither endorsed nor rejected this proposed standard. Later, however, a majority of the Court endorsed this standard, deeming it an appropriate means of assessing whether the Fourth Amendment applies to an encounter between an officer and an individual. *See Michigan v. Chesternut*, 486 U.S. 567, 573, 108 S. Ct. 1975, 100 L. Ed. 2d 565 (1988); *INS v. Delgado*, 466 U.S. 210, 215, 104 S. Ct. 1758, 80 L. Ed. 2d 247 (1984).

(1) As noted, in *Mendenhall* there was no resolution of whether the defendant was seized when officers approached her in the airport concourse. Should a court conclude that officers seize a person if they approach her in a public place, ask her a few questions, request to see her identification, and seek permission to search her belongings? Would a reasonable person believe she was free to leave in those circumstances? What are the constitutional consequences of concluding that this law enforcement conduct does not constitute a seizure?

(2) After the decision in *Mendenhall*, and before the next two main cases, the Court addressed other situations raising the threshold "seizure" issue:

(a) In *Florida v. Royer*, 460 U.S. 491, 103 S. Ct. 1319, 75 L. Ed. 2d 229 (1983), a plurality of the Court concluded that no seizure occurred when officers approached a suspect in an airport concourse and asked for and examined his airline ticket and driver's license. The suspect was seized, however, when the officers subsequently identified themselves as narcotics agents, told him he was suspected of narcotics transportation, and asked him to accompany them to a police room, while retaining his ticket and license and not indicating that he was free to leave.

(b) In *Michigan v. Chesternut*, 486 U.S. 567, 108 S. Ct. 1975, 100 L. Ed. 2d 565 (1988), a man standing on a corner turned and ran as a marked police car approached. The car turned the corner and followed, accelerating to catch up and driving alongside the suspect for a short distance. The Court held that the mere following of the suspect in a marked police car did not amount to a seizure. It was important that the police had not used sirens or flashers, had not commanded the suspect to stop, had not displayed weapons, and had not used the car to block or control the suspect's movements.

Florida v. Bostick

United States Supreme Court

501 U.S. 429, 111 S. Ct. 2382, 115 L. Ed. 2d 389 (1991)

JUSTICE O'CONNOR delivered the opinion of the Court.

We have held that the Fourth Amendment permits police officers to approach individuals at random in airport lobbies and other public places to ask them questions and to request consent to search their luggage, so long as a reasonable person would understand that he or she could refuse to cooperate. This case requires us to determine whether the same rule applies to police encounters that take place on a bus.

I

Drug interdiction efforts have led to the use of police surveillance at airports, train stations, and bus depots. Law enforcement officers stationed at such locations routinely approach individuals, either randomly or because they suspect in some vague way that the individuals may be engaged in criminal activity, and ask them potentially incriminating questions. Broward County has adopted such a program. County Sheriff's Department officers routinely board buses at scheduled stops and ask passengers for permission to search their luggage.

In this case, two officers discovered cocaine when they searched a suitcase belonging to Terrance Bostick. The underlying facts of the search are in dispute, but the Florida Supreme Court, whose decision we review here, stated explicitly the factual premise for its decision:

> "Two officers, complete with badges, insignia and one of them holding a recognizable zipper pouch, containing a pistol, boarded a bus bound from Miami to Atlanta during a stopover in Fort Lauderdale. Eyeing the passengers, the officers, admittedly without articulable suspicion, picked out the defendant passenger and asked to inspect his ticket and identification. The ticket, from Miami to Atlanta, matched the defendant's identification and both were immediately returned to him as unremarkable. However, the two police officers persisted and explained their presence as narcotics agents on the lookout for illegal drugs. In pursuit of that aim, they then requested the defendant's consent to search his luggage. Needless to say, there is a conflict in the evidence about whether the defendant consented to the search of the second bag in which the contraband was found and as to whether he was informed of his right to refuse consent. However, any conflict must be resolved in favor of the state, it being a question of fact decided by the trial judge." 554 So. 2d 1153, 1154–1155 (1989), quoting 510 So. 2d 321, 322 (Fla. Dist. Ct. App. 1987) (Letts, J., dissenting in part).

Two facts are particularly worth noting. First, the police specifically advised Bostick that he had the right to refuse consent. Bostick appears to have disputed the point, but, as the Florida Supreme Court noted explicitly, the trial court resolved this evidentiary conflict in the State's favor. Second, at no time did the officers threaten Bostick with a gun. The Florida Supreme Court indicated that one officer carried a zipper pouch containing a pistol — the equivalent of carrying a gun in a holster — but the court did not suggest that the gun was ever removed from its pouch, pointed at Bostick, or otherwise used in a threatening manner. The dissent's characterization of the officers as "gun — wielding inquisitor[s]," is colorful, but lacks any basis in fact.

Bostick was arrested and charged with trafficking in cocaine. He moved to suppress the cocaine on the grounds that it had been seized in violation of his Fourth Amendment rights. The trial court denied the motion but made no factual findings. Bostick subsequently entered a plea of guilty, but reserved the right to appeal the denial of the motion to suppress.

The Florida District Court of Appeal affirmed, but considered the issue sufficiently important that it certified a question to the Florida Supreme Court. The Supreme Court reasoned that Bostick had been seized because a reasonable passenger in his situation would not have felt free to leave the bus to avoid questioning by the police. It rephrased and answered the certified question so as to make the bus setting dispositive in every case. It ruled categorically that "'an impermissible seizure result[s] when police mount a drug search on buses during scheduled stops and question boarded passengers without articulable reasons for doing so, thereby obtaining consent to search the passengers' luggage.'" The Florida Supreme Court thus adopted a *per se* rule that the Broward County Sheriff's practice of "working the buses" is unconstitutional. The result of this decision is that police in Florida, as elsewhere, may approach persons at random in most public places, ask them questions and seek consent to a search; but they may not engage in the same behavior on a bus. We granted certiorari to determine whether the Florida Supreme Court's *per se* rule is consistent with our Fourth Amendment jurisprudence.

II

The sole issue presented for our review is whether a police encounter on a bus of the type described above necessarily constitutes a "seizure" within the meaning of the Fourth Amendment. . . .

Our cases make it clear that a seizure does not occur simply because a police officer approaches an individual and asks a few questions. So long as a reasonable person would feel free "to disregard the police and go about his business," *California v. Hodari D.*, 499 U.S. 621, 627 (1991), the encounter is consensual and no reasonable suspicion is required. . . .

. . . .

There is no doubt that if this same encounter had taken place before Bostick boarded the bus or in the lobby of the bus terminal, it would not rise to the level of a seizure. The Court has dealt with similar encounters in airports and has found them to be "the sort of consensual encounter[s] that implicat[e] no Fourth Amendment interest." *Florida v. Rodriguez*, 469 U.S. 1, 5–6 (1984). We have stated that even when officers have no basis for suspecting a particular individual, they may generally ask questions of that individual, see *INS v. Delgado*, 466 U.S. 210, 216 (1984); *Rodriguez, supra*, at 5–6; ask to examine the individual's identification, see *Delgado, supra*, at 216; [*Florida v.*] *Royer*, [460 U.S. 491, 501 (1983)] (plurality opinion); *United States v. Mendenhall*, 446 U.S. 544, 557–558 (1980); and request consent to search his or her luggage, see *Royer, supra*, at 501 (plurality opinion) — as long as the police do not convey a message that compliance with their requests is required.

Bostick insists that this case is different because it took place in the cramped confines of a bus. A police encounter is much more intimidating in this setting, he argues, because police tower over a seated passenger and there is little room to move around. Bostick claims to find support in language from *Michigan v. Chesternut*, 486 U.S. 567, 573 (1988), and other cases, indicating that a seizure occurs when a reasonable person would believe that he or she is not "free to leave." Bostick maintains that a reasonable bus passenger would not have felt free to leave under the circumstances of this case because there is nowhere to go on a bus. Also, the bus was about to depart. Had Bostick disembarked, he would have risked being stranded and losing whatever baggage he had locked away in the luggage compartment.

The Florida Supreme Court found this argument persuasive, so much so that it adopted a *per se* rule prohibiting the police from randomly boarding buses as a means of drug interdiction. The state court erred, however, in focusing on whether Bostick was "free to leave" rather than on the principle that those words were intended to capture. When police attempt to question a person who is walking down the street or through an airport lobby, it makes sense to inquire whether a reasonable person would feel free to continue walking. But when the person is seated on a bus and has no desire to leave, the degree to which a reasonable person would feel that he or she could leave is not an accurate measure of the coercive effect of the encounter.

Here, for example, the mere fact that Bostick did not feel free to leave the bus does not mean that the police seized him. Bostick was a passenger on a bus that was scheduled to depart. He would not have felt free to leave the bus even if the police had not been present. Bostick's movements were "confined" in a sense, but this was the natural result of his decision to take the bus; it says nothing about whether or not the police conduct at issue was coercive.

In this respect, the Court's decision in *INS v. Delgado, supra,* is dispositive. At issue there was the INS' practice of visiting factories at random and questioning employees to determine whether any were illegal aliens. Several INS agents would stand near the building's exits, while other agents walked through the factory questioning workers. The Court acknowledged that the workers may not have been free to leave their worksite, but explained that this was not the result of police activity: "Ordinarily, when people are at work their freedom to move about has been meaningfully restricted, not by the actions of law enforcement officials, but by the workers' voluntary obligations to their employers." *Id.*, at 218. We concluded that there was no seizure because, even though the workers were not free to leave the building without being questioned, the agents' conduct should have given employees "no reason to believe that they would be detained if they gave truthful answers to the questions put to them or if they simply refused to answer." *Id.*

The present case is analytically indistinguishable from *Delgado.* Like the workers in that case, Bostick's freedom of movement was restricted by a factor independent of police conduct — i.e., by his being a passenger on a bus. Accordingly, the "free to leave" analysis on which Bostick relies is inapplicable. In such a situation, the appropriate inquiry is whether a reasonable person would feel free to decline the officers' requests or otherwise terminate the encounter. This formulation follows logically from prior cases and breaks no new ground. We have said before that the crucial test is whether, taking into account all of the circumstances surrounding the encounter, the police conduct would "have communicated to a reasonable person that he was not at liberty to ignore the police presence and go about his business." *Chesternut, supra*, at 569. *See also Hodari D., infra*, at 628. Where the encounter takes place is one factor, but it is not the only one. And, as the Solicitor General correctly observes, an individual may decline an officer's request without fearing prosecution. See Brief for the United States as *Amicus Curiae* 25. We have consistently held that a refusal to cooperate, without more, does not furnish the minimal level of objective justification needed for a detention or seizure. *See Delgado*, 466 U.S., at 216–217; *Royer*, 460 U.S., at 498 (plurality opinion); *Brown v. Texas*, 443 U.S. 47, 52–53 (1979).

The facts of this case, as described by the Florida Supreme Court, leave some doubt whether a seizure occurred. Two officers walked up to Bostick on the bus, asked him a few questions, and asked if they could search his bags. As we have explained, no seizure occurs when police ask questions of an individual, ask to examine the individual's identification, and request consent to search his or her luggage — so long as the officers do not convey a message that compliance with their requests is required. Here, the facts recited by the Florida Supreme Court indicate that the officers did not point guns at Bostick or otherwise threaten him and that they specifically advised Bostick that he could refuse consent.

Nevertheless, we refrain from deciding whether or not a seizure occurred in this case. The trial court made no express findings of fact, and the Florida Supreme Court rested its decision on a single fact — that the encounter took place on a bus — rather than on the totality of the circumstances. We remand so that the Florida courts may evaluate the seizure question under the correct legal standard. We do reject, however, Bostick's argument that he must have been seized because no reasonable person would freely consent to a search of luggage that he or she knows contains drugs. This argument cannot prevail because the "reasonable person" test presupposes an *innocent* person.

. . . .

The dissent . . . attempts to characterize our decision as applying a lesser degree of constitutional protection to those individuals who travel by bus, rather than by other forms of transportation. This, too, is an erroneous characterization. Our Fourth Amendment inquiry in this case — whether a reasonable person would have felt free to decline the officers' requests or otherwise terminate the encounter — applies equally to police encounters that take place on trains, planes, and city streets. It is the dissent that would single out this particular mode of travel for differential treatment by adopting a *per se* rule that random bus searches are unconstitutional.

The dissent reserves its strongest criticism for the proposition that police officers can approach individuals as to whom they have no reasonable suspicion and ask them potentially incriminating questions. But this proposition is by no means novel; it has been endorsed by the Court any number of times. . . .

This Court, as the dissent correctly observes, is not empowered to suspend constitutional guarantees so that the Government may more effectively wage a "war on drugs." If that war is to be fought, those who fight it must respect the rights of individuals, whether or not those individuals are suspected of having committed a crime. By the same token, this Court is not empowered to forbid law enforcement practices simply because it considers them distasteful. The Fourth Amendment proscribes unreasonable searches and seizures; it does not proscribe voluntary cooperation. The cramped confines of a bus are one relevant factor that should be considered in evaluating whether a passenger's consent is voluntary. We cannot agree, however, with the Florida Supreme Court that this single factor will be dispositive in every case.

We adhere to the rule that, in order to determine whether a particular encounter constitutes a seizure, a court must consider all the circumstances surrounding the encounter to determine whether the police conduct would have communicated to a reasonable person that the person was not free to decline the officers' requests or otherwise terminate the encounter. That rule applies to encounters that take place on a city street or in an airport lobby, and it applies equally to encounters on a bus. The Florida Supreme Court erred in adopting a *per se* rule.

The judgment of the Florida Supreme Court is reversed, and the case remanded for further proceedings not inconsistent with this opinion.

It is so ordered.

JUSTICE MARSHALL, with whom JUSTICE BLACKMUN and JUSTICE STEVENS join, dissenting.

. . . .

I

At issue in this case is a "new and increasingly common tactic in the war on drugs": the suspicionless police sweep of buses in interstate or intrastate travel. *United States v. Lewis*, 921 F.2d 1294, 1295, 287 U.S. App. D.C. 306, 307 (1990). Typically under this technique, a group of state or federal officers will board a bus while it is stopped at an intermediate point on its route. Often displaying badges, weapons or other indicia of authority, the officers identify themselves and announce their purpose to intercept drug traffickers. They proceed to approach individual passengers, requesting them to show identification, produce their tickets, and explain the purpose of their travels. Never do the officers advise the passengers that they are free not to speak with the officers. An "interview" of this type ordinarily culminates in a request for consent to search the passenger's luggage.

These sweeps are conducted in "dragnet" style. The police admittedly act without an "articulable suspicion" in deciding which buses to board and which passengers to approach for interviewing.[1] By proceeding systematically in this fashion, the police are able to engage in a tremendously high volume of searches. *See e.g., Florida v. Kerwick*, 512 So. 2d 347, 348–349 (Fla. Dist. Ct. App. 1987) (single officer employing sweep technique able to search over 3,000 bags in nine-month period). The percentage of successful drug interdictions is low. *See United States v. Flowers, supra*, at 710 (sweep of 100 buses resulted in seven arrests).

To put it mildly, these sweeps "are inconvenient, intrusive, and intimidating." *United States v. Chandler*, 744 F. Supp., at 335. They occur within cramped confines, with officers typically placing themselves in between the passenger selected for an interview and the exit of the bus. Because the bus is only temporarily stationed at a point short of its destination, the passengers are in no position to leave as a means of evading the officers' questioning. Undoubtedly, such a sweep holds up the progress of the bus. *See United States v. Fields*, 909 F.2d 470, 474 n. 2 (CA11 1990). Thus, this "new and increasingly common tactic," *United States v. Lewis, supra*, at 307, 921 F.2d, at 1295, burdens the experience of traveling by bus with a degree of governmental interference to which, until now, our society has been proudly unaccustomed.

. . . .

The question for this Court, then, is whether the suspicionless, dragnet-style sweep of buses in intrastate and interstate travel is consistent with the Fourth Amendment. The majority suggests that this latest tactic in the drug war is perfectly compatible with the Constitution. I disagree.

II

I have no objection to the manner in which the majority frames the test for determining whether a suspicionless bus sweep amounts to a Fourth Amendment "seizure." I agree that the appropriate question is whether a passenger who is approached during such a sweep "would feel free to decline the officers' requests or otherwise terminate the encounter." What I cannot understand is how the majority can possibly suggest an affirmative answer to this question.

The majority reverses what it characterizes as the Florida Supreme Court's "*per se* rule" against suspicionless encounters between the police and bus passengers, suggesting only in dictum its "doubt" that a seizure occurred on the facts of this case.

---

1. That is to say, the police who conduct these sweeps decline to offer a reasonable, articulable suspicion of criminal wrongdoing sufficient to justify a warrantless "stop" or "seizure" of the confronted passenger. It does not follow, however, that the approach of passengers during a sweep is completely random. Indeed, at least one officer who routinely confronts interstate travelers candidly admitted that *race* is a factor influencing his decision whom to approach. *See United States v. Williams*, No. 1:89CR0135 (N.D. Ohio, June 13, 1989), p. 3 ("Detective Zaller testified that the factors initiating the focus upon the three young black males in this case included: (1) that they were young and black . . . ."), *aff'd*, No. 89–4083 (6th Cir., Oct. 19, 1990), p. 7 (the officers "knew that the couriers, more often than not, were young black males"), vacated and remanded, 500 U.S. 901 (1991). Thus, the basis of the decision to single out particular passengers during a suspicionless sweep is less likely to be *inarticulable* than *unspeakable*.

However, the notion that the Florida Supreme Court decided this case on the basis of any *"per se* rule" *independent* of the facts of this case is wholly a product of the majority's imagination. As the majority acknowledges, the Florida Supreme Court "stated explicitly the factual premise for its decision." This factual premise contained *all* of the details of the encounter between respondent and the police. The lower court's analysis of whether respondent was seized drew heavily on these facts, and the court repeatedly emphasized that its conclusion was based on *"all the circumstances"* of this case. (emphasis added).

. . . .

These facts exhibit all of the elements of coercion associated with a typical bus sweep. Two officers boarded the Greyhound bus on which respondent was a passenger while the bus, en route from Miami to Atlanta, was on a brief stop to pick up passengers in Fort Lauderdale. The officers made a visible display of their badges and wore bright green "raid" jackets bearing the insignia of the Broward County Sheriff's Department; one held a gun in a recognizable weapons pouch. These facts alone constitute an intimidating "show of authority." Once on board, the officers approached respondent, who was sitting in the back of the bus, identified themselves as narcotics officers and began to question him. One officer stood in front of respondent's seat, partially blocking the narrow aisle through which respondent would have been required to pass to reach the exit of the bus.

As far as is revealed by facts on which the Florida Supreme Court premised its decision, the officers did not advise respondent that he was free to break off this "interview." Inexplicably, the majority repeatedly stresses the trial court's implicit finding that the police officers advised respondent that he was free to refuse permission to search his travel bag. This aspect of the exchange between respondent and the police is completely irrelevant to the issue before us. For as the State concedes, and as the majority purports to "accept," *if* respondent was unlawfully seized when the officers approached him and initiated questioning, the resulting search was likewise unlawful no matter how well advised respondent was of his right to refuse it. Consequently, the issue is not whether a passenger in respondent's position would have felt free to deny consent to the search of his bag, but whether such a passenger — without being apprised of his rights — would have felt free to terminate the antecedent encounter with the police.

Unlike the majority, I have no doubt that the answer to this question is no. Apart from trying to accommodate the officers, respondent had only two options. First, he could have remained seated while obstinately refusing to respond to the officers' questioning. But in light of the intimidating show of authority that the officers made upon boarding the bus, respondent reasonably could have believed that such behavior would only arouse the officers' suspicions and intensify their interrogation. . . .

Second, respondent could have tried to escape the officers' presence by leaving the bus altogether. But because doing so would have required respondent to squeeze past the gunwielding inquisitor who was blocking the aisle of the bus, this hardly seems like a course that respondent reasonably would have viewed as available to him. The majority lamely protests that nothing in the stipulated facts shows that the questioning officer "*point[ed]* [his] gu[n] at [respondent] or otherwise *threaten[ed]* him" with the weapon. (emphasis added). Our decisions recognize the obvious point, however, that the choice of the police to "display" their weapons during an encounter exerts significant coercive pressure on the confronted citizen. We have never suggested that the police must go so far as to put a citizen in immediate apprehension of *being shot* before a court can take account of the intimidating effect of being questioned by an officer with weapon in hand.

Even if respondent had perceived that the officers would *let* him leave the bus, moreover, he could not reasonably have been expected to resort to this means of evading their intrusive questioning. For so far as respondent knew, the bus' departure from the terminal was imminent. Unlike a person approached by the police on the street, or at a bus or airport terminal after reaching his destination, a passenger approached by the police at an intermediate point in a long bus journey cannot simply leave the scene and repair to a safe haven to avoid unwanted probing by law enforcement officials. The vulnerability that an intrastate or interstate traveler experiences when confronted by the police outside of his "own familiar territory" surely aggravates the coercive quality of such an encounter. *See Schneckloth v. Bustamonte,* 412 U.S. 218, 247 (1973).

. . . .

Rather than requiring the police to justify the coercive tactics employed here, the majority blames respondent for his own sensation of constraint. The majority concedes that respondent "did not feel free to leave the bus" as a means of breaking off the interrogation by the Broward County officers. But this experience of confinement, the majority explains, "was the natural result of *his* decision to take the bus." *Id.* (emphasis added). Thus, in the majority's view, because respondent's "freedom of movement was restricted by a factor independent of police conduct — *i.e.*, by his being a passenger on a bus," respondent was not seized for purposes of the Fourth Amendment.

This reasoning borders on sophism and trivializes the values that underlie the Fourth Amendment. Obviously, a person's "voluntary decision" to place himself in a room with only one exit does not authorize the police to force an encounter upon him by placing themselves in front of the exit. It is no more acceptable for the police to force an encounter on a person by exploiting his "voluntary decision" to expose himself to perfectly legitimate personal or social constraints. By consciously deciding to single out persons who have undertaken interstate or intrastate travel, officers who conduct suspicionless, dragnet-style sweeps put passengers to the choice of cooperating or of exiting their buses and possibly being stranded in unfamiliar locations. It is exactly because this "choice" is no "choice" at all that police engage [in] this technique.

. . . .

III

The majority attempts to gloss over the violence that today's decision does to the Fourth Amendment with empty admonitions. "If th[e] [war on drugs] is to be fought," the majority intones, "those who fight it must respect the rights of individuals, whether or not those individuals are suspected of having committed a crime." The majority's actions, however, speak louder than its words.

I dissent.

Notes and Questions

(1) Which encounters between bus passengers and law enforcement officers are governed by the Fourth Amendment? Which are not? Why shouldn't any official encounter with a person seated on a bus in transit be considered a seizure *per se*?

(2) Does the Court's refinement of the doctrine for determining whether a person has been seized seem like a fair translation of the constitutional commands of the Fourth Amendment? Are the dissenters correct to assert that the Court's decision will allow officers to exploit the vulnerabilities of bus passengers? Are they correct to suggest that the decision will free officers to engage in invidious discrimination by using inappropriate selection criteria such as race? Should either of these concerns bear upon Fourth Amendment interpretation? Why?

(3) The Court reaffirmed the lessons of *Florida v. Bostick* and clarified a few additional matters in *United States v. Drayton*, 536 U.S. 194, 122 S. Ct. 2105, 153 L. Ed. 2d 242 (2002). When the bus on which respondents Drayton and Brown were traveling made a scheduled stop in Tallahassee, Florida, the driver allowed three police officers to board the bus "as part of a routine drug and weapons interdiction effort." One officer knelt on the driver's seat, facing the rear. The other two went to the rear of the bus, where one remained stationed while the other worked his way forward. The latter, who stood next to or just behind each passenger while speaking to them, approached Drayton and Brown, who were seated next to each other. He leaned over Drayton's shoulder, held up his badge, stated that he was an investigator with the police department "conducting bus interdiction [sic], attempting to deter drugs and illegal weapons being transported on the bus" and asked "Do you have any bags on the bus?" Both men pointed to a green bag on the overhead rack and Brown gave the officer permission to search it. No contraband was found.

The officer noticed that the two men "were wearing heavy jackets and baggy pants despite the warm weather. In [his] experience, drug traffickers often use baggy clothing to conceal weapons or narcotics." He asked Brown, "Do you mind if I check your person?" Brown answered "'Sure,' and cooperated" with a patdown search of his person. The officer detected "hard objects similar to drug packages detected on other occasions," whereupon he "arrested and handcuffed Brown" and removed him from the bus. He then asked Drayton "'Mind if I check you?'" Drayton responded by lifting "his hands about eight inches from his legs." During a patdown, the officer detected similar hard objects and arrested Drayton. Further searches of both men led to the discovery of substantial amounts of cocaine in "duct-taped plastic bundles . . . between several pairs of their boxer shorts."

The district court denied motions to suppress the narcotics, but the Eleventh Circuit reversed based on two prior decisions in which it "had held that bus passengers do not feel free to disregard police officers' requests to search absent 'some positive indication that consent could have been refused.'" The Supreme Court reversed, holding that Drayton and Brown "were not seized and their consent to the search[es] was voluntary."

According to the Court, *Bostick* made it clear that "for the most part *per se* rules are inappropriate in the Fourth Amendment context" and that "a consideration of 'all the circumstances surrounding the encounter'" is necessary to determine whether a bus passenger has been seized. In remanding *Bostick*, the Court had "identified two factors 'particularly worth noting'"—that the officer "did not remove [his] gun from its pouch or use it in a threatening way" and that he had "advised the passenger that he could refuse consent to the search." The Eleventh Circuit had erred by relying upon the latter factor to adopt "in effect a *per se* rule that" officers must "advise[] passengers of their right not to cooperate and to refuse consent."

No seizure had occurred in *Drayton* because the "officers gave the passengers no reason to believe that they were required to answer the officers' questions." The questioning officer "did not brandish a weapon or make any intimidating movements[,] . . . left the aisle free so that respondents could exit[,] . . . spoke to passengers one by one and in a polite, quiet voice[,]" and said nothing that "would suggest to a reasonable person that he or she was barred from leaving the bus or otherwise terminating the encounter." In bus settings, "because many fellow passengers are present to witness officers' conduct, a reasonable person *may feel even more secure in his or her decision not to cooperate with police on a bus than in other circumstances.*" (Emphasis added.)

In general, the presence or absence of uniforms and the display of badges "should have little weight in the analysis" because officers "are often required to wear uniforms and in many circumstances this is cause for assurance, not discomfort. Much the same can be said for wearing sidearms. That most . . . officers are armed is . . . well known to the public. The presence of a holstered firearm thus is unlikely to contribute to the coerciveness of the encounter absent active brandishing of the weapon."

One officer's presence at the front of the bus did "not tip the scale" because he "did nothing to intimidate passengers, and said nothing to suggest that people could not exit and indeed he left the aisle clear. . . . [Moreover], the fact that in [the officer's] experience only a few passengers ha[d] refused to cooperate [did] not suggest that a reasonable person would not feel free to terminate the bus encounter." Passengers commonly left for a cigarette or snack while the questioning of others was conducted and, "of more importance," bus passengers answer officers' questions and otherwise cooperate not because of coercion, "but because the passengers know that their participation enhances their own safety and the safety of those around them."

In addition, Brown's arrest did not turn the encounter with Drayton into a seizure because the "arrest of one person does not mean that everyone around him has been seized by the police. If anything, Brown's arrest should have put Drayton on notice of the consequences of continuing the encounter by answering the officer's questions."

The searches were reasonable because the consents were "voluntary." By asking for permission to search the bag and asking if the men objected to searches of their persons, the officer provided indications "to a reasonable person that he . . . was free to refuse." Knowledge of the right to refuse is only a factor in the voluntariness inquiry and no "presumption of invalidity" arises from the lack of "explicit notification" that an individual is "free to refuse to cooperate." "Police officers act in full accord with the law when they ask citizens for consent. It reinforces the rule of law for the citizen to advise the police of his or her wishes and for the police to act in reliance on that understanding. When this exchange takes place, it dispels inferences of coercion."

Dissenting Justices Souter, Stevens, and Ginsburg objected that there was "an air of unreality about the Court's explanation that bus passengers consent to searches . . . to 'enhanc[e] their own safety and the safety of those around them.'" In their view, "when the attention of several officers is brought to bear on one civilian the imbalance of immediate power is unmistakable." The "display of power" can rise to a "'threatening' level [that] may overbear a normal person's ability to act freely, even in the absence of explicit commands or the formalities of detention."

In this case, the "officers took control of the entire passenger compartment." One "officer accosted each passenger [in] . . . extremely close and . . . cramped" quarters. "None was asked whether he was willing to converse . . . or take part." "The reasonable inference" from the officer's words "was that the 'interdiction' was not a consensual exercise, but one the police would carry out whatever the circumstances; that they would prefer 'cooperation' but would not let the lack of it stand in their way. . . . The scene was set and an atmosphere of obligatory participation was established by [the officer's] introduction." In these circumstances, "[n]o reasonable passenger could have believed" that he stood to lose nothing if he refused cooperation or that he had "any free choice to ignore the police altogether." Although some bus encounters might "pass the *Bostick* test without a warning that passengers are free to say no," the encounter in *Drayton* did not.

California v. Hodari D.

United States Supreme Court

499 U.S. 621, 111 S. Ct. 1547, 113 L. Ed. 2d 690 (1991)

JUSTICE SCALIA delivered the opinion of the Court.

Late one evening in April 1988, Officers Brian McColgin and Jerry Pertoso were on patrol in a high-crime area of Oakland, California. They were dressed in street clothes but wearing jackets with "Police" embossed on both front and back. Their unmarked car proceeded west on Foothill Boulevard, and turned south onto 63rd

Avenue. As they rounded the corner, they saw four or five youths huddled around a small red car parked at the curb. When the youths saw the officers' car approaching they apparently panicked, and took flight. The respondent here, Hodari D., and one companion ran west through an alley; the others fled south. The red car also headed south, at a high rate of speed.

The officers were suspicious and gave chase. McColgin remained in the car and continued south on 63rd Avenue; Pertoso left the car, ran back north along 63rd, then west on Foothill Boulevard, and turned south on 62nd Avenue. Hodari, meanwhile, emerged from the alley onto 62nd and ran north. Looking behind as he ran, he did not turn and see Pertoso until the officer was almost upon him, whereupon he tossed away what appeared to be a small rock. A moment later, Pertoso tackled Hodari, handcuffed him, and radioed for assistance. Hodari was found to be carrying $130 in cash and a pager; and the rock he had discarded was found to be crack cocaine.

In the juvenile proceeding brought against him, Hodari moved to suppress the evidence relating to the cocaine. The court denied the motion without opinion. The California Court of Appeal reversed . . . . The California Supreme Court denied the State's application for review. We granted certiorari. 498 U.S. 807 (1990).

As this case comes to us, the only issue presented is whether, at the time he dropped the drugs, Hodari had been "seized" within the meaning of the Fourth Amendment.[1] If so, respondent argues, the drugs were the fruit of that seizure and the evidence concerning them was properly excluded. If not, the drugs were abandoned by Hodari and lawfully recovered by the police, and the evidence should have been admitted. (In addition, of course, Pertoso's seeing the rock of cocaine, at least if he recognized it as such, would provide reasonable suspicion for the unquestioned seizure that occurred when he tackled Hodari. *Cf. Rios v. United States*, 364 U.S. 253 (1960).)

We have long understood that the Fourth Amendment's protection against "unreasonable . . . seizures" includes seizure of the person, see *Henry v. United States*, 361 U.S. 98, 100 (1959). From the time of the founding to the present, the word "seizure" has meant a "taking possession," 2 N. Webster, AN AMERICAN DICTIONARY OF THE ENGLISH LANGUAGE 67 (1828); 2 J. Bouvier, A LAW DICTIONARY 510 (6th ed. 1856); WEBSTER'S THIRD NEW INTERNATIONAL DICTIONARY 2057 (1981). For most purposes at common law, the word connoted not merely grasping, or applying physical force to, the animate or inanimate object in question, but actually bringing it

---

1. California conceded below that Officer Pertoso did not have the "reasonable suspicion" required to justify stopping Hodari, *see Terry v. Ohio*, 392 U.S. 1 (1968). That it would be unreasonable to stop, for brief inquiry, young men who scatter in panic upon the mere sighting of the police is not self-evident, and arguably contradicts proverbial common sense. See Proverbs 28:1 ("The wicked flee when no man pursueth"). We do not decide that point here, but rely entirely upon the State's concession.

✶NICE✶

[margin note, left: A Actually bringin' w/I physical control.]

within physical control. A ship still fleeing, even though under attack, would not be considered to have been seized as a war prize. A *res* capable of manual delivery was not seized until "tak[en] into custody." *Pelham v. Rose*, 9 Wall. 103, 106 (1870). To constitute an arrest, however — the quintessential "seizure of the person" under our Fourth Amendment jurisprudence — the mere grasping or application of physical force with lawful authority, whether or not it succeeded in subduing the arrestee, was sufficient. As one commentator has described it:

> "There can be constructive detention, which will constitute an arrest, although the party is never actually brought within the physical control of the party making an arrest. This is accomplished by merely touching, however slightly, the body of the accused, by the party making the arrest and for that purpose, although he does not succeed in stopping or holding him even for an instant; as where the bailiff had tried to arrest one who fought him off by the fork, the court said, 'If the bailiff had touched him, that had been an arrest . . . .'" A. Cornelius, SEARCH AND SEIZURE 163–164 (2d ed. 1930) (footnote omitted).

[margin note, left: ✶ Touch ✶]

To say that an arrest is effected by the slightest application of physical force, despite the arrestee's escape, is not to say that for Fourth Amendment purposes there is a *continuing* arrest during the period of fugitivity. If, for example, Pertoso had laid his hands upon Hodari to arrest him, but Hodari had broken away and had *then* cast away the cocaine, it would hardly be realistic to say that that disclosure had been made during the course of an arrest. The present case, however, is even one step further removed. It does not involve the application of any physical force; Hodari was untouched by Officer Pertoso at the time he discarded the cocaine. His defense relies instead upon the proposition that a seizure occurs "when the officer, by means of physical force *or show of authority,* has in some way restrained the liberty of a citizen." *Terry v. Ohio*, 392 U.S. 1, 19, n. 16 (1968) (emphasis added). Hodari contends (and we accept as true for purposes of this decision) that Pertoso's pursuit qualified as a "show of authority" calling upon Hodari to halt. The narrow question before us is whether, with respect to a show of authority as with respect to application of physical force, a seizure occurs even though the subject does not yield. We hold that it does not.

[margin note, left: w/ Respect to show of Authority as w/ Respect to App of phys. Force → Does A seizure occur even though subject does not yield? [ret seizure DN occur] HA!]

The language of the Fourth Amendment, of course, cannot sustain respondent's contention. The word "seizure" readily bears the meaning of a laying on of hands or application of physical force to restrain movement, even when it is ultimately unsuccessful. ("She seized the purse-snatcher, but he broke out of her grasp.") It does not remotely apply, however, to the prospect of a policeman yelling "Stop, in the name of the law!" at a fleeing form that continues to flee. That is no seizure. Nor can the result respondent wishes to achieve be produced — indirectly, as it were — by suggesting that Pertoso's uncomplied-with show of authority was a common-law arrest, and then appealing to the principle that all common-law arrests are seizures. An arrest requires *either* physical force (as described above) *or,* where that is absent, *submission* to the assertion of authority. . . .

[margin note, bottom left: ① pF If ① ABSENT THEN Submission to A of Authority]

. . . .

Respondent contends that his position is sustained by the so-called *Mendenhall* test, formulated by Justice Stewart's opinion in *United States v. Mendenhall*, 446 U.S. 544, 554 (1980), and adopted by the Court in later cases, *see Michigan v. Chesternut*, 486 U.S. 567, 573 (1988); *INS v. Delgado*, 466 U.S. 210, 215 (1984): "A person has been 'seized' within the meaning of the Fourth Amendment only if, in view of all the circumstances surrounding the incident, a reasonable person would have believed that he was not free to leave." 446 U.S., at 554. In seeking to rely upon that test here, respondent fails to read it carefully. It says that a person has been seized "only if," not that he has been seized "whenever"; it states a *necessary*, but not a *sufficient* condition for seizure — or, more precisely, for seizure effected through a "show of authority." *Mendenhall* establishes that the test for existence of a "show of authority" is an objective one: not whether the citizen perceived that he was being ordered to restrict his movement, but whether the officer's words and actions would have conveyed that to a reasonable person. Application of this objective test was the basis for our decision in the other case principally relied upon by respondent, *Chesternut, supra,* where we concluded that the police cruiser's slow following of the defendant did not convey the message that he was not free to disregard the police and go about his business. We did not address in *Chesternut*, however, the question whether, if the *Mendenhall* test was met — if the message that the defendant was not free to leave *had* been conveyed — a Fourth Amendment seizure would have occurred.

. . . .

In sum, assuming that Pertoso's pursuit in the present case constituted a "show of authority" enjoining Hodari to halt, since Hodari did not comply with that injunction he was not seized until he was tackled. The cocaine abandoned while he was running was in this case not the fruit of a seizure, and his motion to exclude evidence of it was properly denied. We reverse the decision of the California Court of Appeal, and remand for further proceedings not inconsistent with this opinion.

It is so ordered.

JUSTICE STEVENS, with whom JUSTICE MARSHALL joins, dissenting.

. . . .

I

The Court today takes a narrow view of "seizure," which is at odds with the broader view adopted by this Court almost 25 years ago. In *Katz v. United States*, 389 U.S. 347 (1967), the Court considered whether electronic surveillance conducted "without any trespass and without the seizure of any material object fell outside the ambit of the Constitution." *Id.*, at 353. Over Justice Black's powerful dissent, we rejected that "narrow view" of the Fourth Amendment and held that electronic eavesdropping is a "search and seizure" within the meaning of the Amendment. *Id.*, at 353–354. We thus endorsed the position expounded by two of the dissenting Justices in *Olmstead v. United States*, 277 U.S. 438 (1928):

"Time and again, this Court in giving effect to the principle underlying the Fourth Amendment, has refused to place an unduly literal construction upon it." *Id.*, at 476 (Brandeis, J., dissenting).

"The direct operation or literal meaning of the words used do not measure the purpose or scope of its provisions. Under the principles established and applied by this Court, the Fourth Amendment safeguards against all evils that are like and equivalent to those embraced within the ordinary meaning of its words." *Id.*, at 488 (Butler, J., dissenting).

. . . .

Significantly, in the *Katz* opinion, the Court repeatedly used the word "seizure" to describe the process of recording sounds that could not possibly have been the subject of a common-law seizure. *See id.*, at 356, 357.

Justice Black's reasoning, which was rejected by the Court in 1967, is remarkably similar to the reasoning adopted by the Court today. . . .

The expansive construction of the word "seizure" in the *Katz* case provided an appropriate predicate for the Court's holding in *Terry v. Ohio*, 392 U.S. 1 (1968), the following year. Prior to *Terry* the Fourth Amendment proscribed any seizure of the person that was not supported by the same probable cause showing that would justify a custodial arrest. Given the fact that street encounters between citizens and police officers "are incredibly rich in diversity," *Terry*, 392 U.S., at 13, the Court recognized the need for flexibility and held that "reasonable" suspicion — a quantum of proof less demanding than probable cause — was adequate to justify a stop for investigatory purposes. *Id.*, at 21–22. As a corollary to the lesser justification for the stop, the Court necessarily concluded that the word "seizure" in the Fourth Amendment encompasses official restraints on individual freedom that fall short of a common-law arrest. Thus, *Terry* broadened the range of encounters between the police and the citizen encompassed within the term "seizure," while at the same time, lowering the standard of proof necessary to justify a "stop" in the newly expanded category of seizures now covered by the Fourth Amendment. . . .

The decisions in *Katz* and *Terry* unequivocally reject the notion that the common law of arrest defines the limits of the term "seizure" in the Fourth Amendment. In *Katz*, the Court abandoned the narrow view that would have limited a seizure to a material object, and instead, held that the Fourth Amendment extended to the recording of oral statements. And in *Terry*, the Court abandoned its traditional view that a seizure under the Fourth Amendment required probable cause, and instead, expanded the definition of a seizure to include an investigative stop made on less than probable cause. Thus, the major premise underpinning the majority's entire analysis today — that the common law of arrest should define the term "seizure" for Fourth Amendment purposes — is seriously flawed. The Court mistakenly hearkens back to common law, while ignoring the expansive approach that the Court has taken in Fourth Amendment analysis since *Katz* and *Terry*.

II

The Court fares no better when it tries to explain why the proper definition of the term "seizure" has been an open question until today. In *Terry*, in addition to stating that a seizure occurs "whenever a police officer accosts an individual and restrains his freedom to walk away," 392 U.S., at 16, the Court noted that a seizure occurs "when the officer, by means of physical force or show of authority, has in some way restrained the liberty of a citizen . . . ." *Id.*, at 19, n. 16. The touchstone of a seizure is the restraint of an individual's personal liberty "*in some way.*" *Id.* (emphasis added). Today the Court's reaction to respondent's reliance on *Terry* is to demonstrate that in "show of force" cases no common-law arrest occurs unless the arrestee submits. That answer, however, is plainly insufficient given the holding in *Terry* that the Fourth Amendment applies to stops that need not be justified by probable cause in the absence of a full-blown arrest.

[handwritten margin note: "plainly insufficient"]

In *United States v. Mendenhall*, 446 U.S. 544 (1980), the Court "adhere[d] to the view that a person is 'seized' only when, by means of physical force or a show of authority, his freedom of movement is restrained." *Id.*, at 553. The Court looked to whether the citizen who is questioned "remains free to disregard the questions and walk away," and if she is able to do so, then "there has been no intrusion upon that person's liberty or privacy" that would require some "particularized and objective justification" under the Constitution. *Id.*, at 554. The test for a "seizure," as formulated by the Court in *Mendenhall*, was whether, "in view of all of the circumstances surrounding the incident, a reasonable person would have believed that he was not free to leave." *Id.* . . .

The Court today draws the novel conclusion that even though no seizure can occur *unless* the *Mendenhall* reasonable person standard is met, the fact that the standard has been met does not necessarily mean that a seizure has occurred. . . .

[handwritten margin note: Dissent says ✷ this is the majority conclusion]

. . . .

Even though momentary, a seizure occurs whenever an objective evaluation of a police officer's show of force conveys the message that the citizen is not entirely free to leave — in other words, that his or her liberty is being restrained in a significant way. . . .

. . . .

Whatever else one may think of today's decision, it unquestionably represents a departure from earlier Fourth Amendment case law. The notion that our prior cases contemplated a distinction between seizures effected by a touching on the one hand, and those effected by a show of force on the other hand, and that all of our repeated descriptions of the *Mendenhall* test stated only a necessary, but not a sufficient, condition for finding seizures in the latter category, is nothing if not creative lawmaking. Moreover, by narrowing the definition of the term seizure, instead of enlarging the scope of reasonable justifications for seizures, the Court has significantly limited the protection provided to the ordinary citizen by the Fourth Amendment. As we explained in *Terry*:

> "The danger in the logic which proceeds upon distinctions between a 'stop' and an 'arrest,' or 'seizure' of the person, and between a 'frisk' and a 'search' is twofold. It seeks to isolate from constitutional scrutiny the initial stages of the contact between the policeman and the citizen. And by suggesting a rigid all-or-nothing model of justification and regulation under the Amendment, it obscures the utility of limitations upon the scope, as well as the initiation, of police action as a means of constitutional regulation." *Terry v. Ohio*, 392 U.S., at 17.

III

In this case the officer's show of force — taking the form of a head-on chase — adequately conveyed the message that respondent was not free to leave. Whereas in *Mendenhall*, there was "nothing in the record [to] sugges[t] that the respondent had any objective reason to believe that she was not free to end the conversation in the concourse and proceed on her way," 446 U.S., at 555, here, respondent attempted to end "the conversation" before it began and soon found himself literally "not free to leave" when confronted by an officer running toward him head-on who eventually tackled him to the ground. There was an interval of time between the moment that respondent saw the officer fast approaching and the moment when he was tackled, and thus brought under the control of the officer. The question is whether the Fourth Amendment was implicated at the earlier or the later moment.

Because the facts of this case are somewhat unusual, it is appropriate to note that the same issue would arise if the show of force took the form of a command to "freeze," a warning shot, or the sound of sirens accompanied by a patrol car's flashing lights. In any of these situations, there may be a significant time interval between the initiation of the officer's show of force and the complete submission by the citizen. At least on the facts of this case, the Court concludes that the timing of the seizure is governed by the citizen's reaction, rather than by the officer's conduct. One consequence of this conclusion is that the point at which the interaction between citizen and police officer becomes a seizure occurs, not when a reasonable citizen believes he or she is no longer free to go, but rather only after the officer exercises control over the citizen.

In my view, our interests in effective law enforcement and in personal liberty would be better served by adhering to a standard that "allows the police to determine in advance whether the conduct contemplated will implicate the Fourth Amendment." *Chesternut*, 486 U.S., at 574. The range of possible responses to a police show of force, and the multitude of problems that may arise in determining whether, and at which moment, there has been "submission," can only create uncertainty and generate litigation.

. . . .

If an officer effects an arrest by touching a citizen, apparently the Court would accept the fact that a seizure occurred, even if the arrestee should thereafter break loose and flee. In such a case, the constitutionality of the seizure would be evaluated as of the time the officer acted. That category of seizures would then be analyzed in the same way as searches, namely, was the police action justified when it took place? It is anomalous, at best, to fashion a different rule for the subcategory of "show of force" arrests.

. . . .

It is too early to know the consequences of the Court's holding. If carried to its logical conclusion, it will encourage unlawful displays of force that will frighten countless innocent citizens into surrendering whatever privacy rights they may still have . . . . The Court today defines a seizure as commencing, not with egregious police conduct, but rather, with submission by the citizen. Thus, it both delays the point at which "the Fourth Amendment becomes relevant"[19] to an encounter and limits the range of encounters that will come under the heading of "seizure." Today's qualification of the Fourth Amendment means that innocent citizens may remain "secure in their persons . . . against unreasonable searches and seizures" only at the discretion of the police.

Some sacrifice of freedom always accompanies an expansion in the executive's unreviewable law enforcement powers. A court more sensitive to the purposes of the Fourth Amendment would insist on greater rewards to society before decreeing the sacrifice it makes today . . . . The Court's immediate concern with containing criminal activity poses a substantial, though unintended, threat to values that are fundamental and enduring.

I respectfully dissent.

Notes and Questions

(1) Why did the Court conclude that Officer Pertoso did not "seize" Hodari D. prior to the time he discarded the narcotics he sought to suppress? Should the criterion that dictated that conclusion be used to determine whether an individual has been "seized"? Why? Some state courts have rejected the *Hodari* standard as a matter of state constitutional law. They prefer to employ the *Mendenhall* "reasonable person" standard as the sole relevant inquiry. *See, e.g., State v. Oquendo*, 223 Conn. 635, 613 A.2d 1300 (1992); *State v. Quino*, 840 P.2d 358 (Hawaii 1992); *Commonwealth v. Stoute*, 422 Mass. 782, 665 N.Ed.2d 93 (1996); *In the Matter of the Welfare of E.D.J.*, 502 N.W.2d 779 (Minn. 1993); *Commonwealth v. Matos*, 543 Pa. 449, 672 A.2d 769 (1996); *State v. Young*, 135 Wn.2d 498, 957 P.2d 681 (1998).

(2) Is the majority's reasoning inconsistent with the *Katz* approach to the threshold "search" question, as Justice Stevens suggests? Is the dissent's suggestion that the

---

19. *Terry v. Ohio*, 392 U.S., at 16.

Court's decision "poses a substantial . . . threat to values that are fundamental and enduring" supportable? In what ways might the law enforcement conduct approved by the majority jeopardize protected liberties?

(3) With regard to the standard for judging whether a seizure has occurred, see also *Brower v. County of Inyo*, 489 U.S. 593, 109 S. Ct. 1378, 103 L. Ed. 2d 628 (1989), in which a majority observed that a Fourth Amendment seizure occurs "only when there is a governmental termination of freedom of movement *through means intentionally applied*." *Id.* at 597, 109 S. Ct. at 1381, 103 L. Ed. 2d at 635 (emphasis in original).

(4) In *Brendlin v. California*, 551 U.S. 249, 127 S. Ct. 2400, 168 L. Ed. 2d 132 (2007), a unanimous Supreme Court rejected the California Supreme Court's conclusion that a passenger was not "seized" when the car in which he was riding was stopped to verify that its temporary operating permit was valid. The Court reasoned that the standards announced in *Mendenhall, Bostick*, and *Hodari D.* govern the determination of whether a passenger has been subjected to a Fourth Amendment seizure when an officer pulls over a vehicle in which he is riding.

The first question was whether "a reasonable" passenger in a stopped car would "believe[] himself free to 'terminate the encounter' between the police and himself." (Quoting *Bostick*.) In the Court's view, in the typical situation where a vehicle is pulled over for a traffic infraction or on suspicion of some other criminal activity, "any reasonable passenger would [understand] the police . . . to be exercising control to the point that no one in the car [is] free to depart without police permission." The Court did not suggest that it was impossible for an officer to convey a message that would lead to a contrary understanding by a reasonable passenger, but made it clear that ordinarily a "traffic stop necessarily curtails the travel a passenger has chosen just as much as it halts the driver." As for the *Hodari D.* demand for "submission," the Court asserted that "what may amount to submission depends on what a person was doing before [an officer's] show of authority . . . . [O]ne sitting in a chair may submit to authority by not getting up to run away." Although a passenger has "no effective way to signal submission while [a] car [is] still moving on the roadway," once the car has stopped, he can and does "submit [merely] by staying inside."

In support of its holding, the *Brendlin* Court expressed concern that a rule that a "passenger in a private car is not (without more) seized in a traffic stop would invite police officers to stop cars with passengers" whether or not they had adequate reason to do so. "The fact that evidence uncovered as a result of an arbitrary traffic stop would still be admissible against any passengers," because those passengers' rights would not be violated by the stop, "would be a powerful incentive to run the kind of 'roving patrols' that would still violate the driver's Fourth Amendment right." The Court reserved the question of whether a passenger in a bus or cab is seized during a typical traffic stop, observing only that "the relationship between the driver and passenger is not the same in a common carrier as it is in a private vehicle," and that "the crucial question would be whether a reasonable" passenger in a stopped common carrier "would feel free to take steps to terminate the encounter."

"Seizure" Problems

5A–1: On June 6, Officers Michaels and Flanny were on bicycle patrol in uniform in downtown Milwaukee. Around 10 p.m., the officers heard three to four gunshots fired north of their location. They rode their bicycles to 2600 North 15th Street, where a witness reported hearing gunshots west of his location. The officers rode one block west, then turned north on North 16th Street toward Center Street. In this residential area, they saw Dontray, a resident of the area, crossing North 16th Street. He had just exited an alley on the east side of the street and was heading in the direction of an alley on the west side. He was not running or engaging in any suspicious behavior, nor was he coming from the direction where the shots were reportedly fired.

The officers rode ahead of Dontray into the alley. When they were roughly 20 feet in front of him (and all were in the alley), the officers made a U-turn to face Dontray and began closing the distance. They stopped approximately five feet in front of Dontray, positioning their bicycles at a 45-degree angle to face him. Neither Michaels nor Flanny identified himself as an officer, said hello, or asked Dontray for identifying information. Michaels got off his bicycle, approached Dontray with his hand on his gun, and asked, "Are you in possession of any guns, knives, weapons, or anything illegal?"

Dontray nodded toward his right side and said, "Yes, I have a gun." Officer Flanny got off his bicycle and asked Dontray if he had a concealed weapon permit. When he responded "No," the officers handcuffed him and searched his front pocket, where they found a gun. After seizing the gun, the officers obtained Dontray's identification. Dontray was later indicted for being a felon in possession of a firearm. He moved to suppress the gun, claiming it was the product of a violation of his Fourth Amendment rights.

Did the officers seize Dontray prior to discovering the gun?

5A–2: On May 11, at about 12:13 p.m., County Sheriff's Deputy Walters was on routine patrol in the City of Rancho Moonbeam when he saw Hoory in the middle of Kirkwood Avenue "just south" of its intersection with Meadow Street, in a residential area. Hoory was walking in the street. For safety reasons, Deputy Walters, who was driving "less than five miles per hour at the time," activated his patrol vehicle overhead lights, stopped his vehicle in the middle of the street, and made contact with Hoory "to avoid hitting" him. According to Walters, Hoory "stopped in the middle of the street when he saw my patrol vehicle." According to a witness on the scene, Hoory was crossing the street to visit the witness's home.

454 5 · THE BALANCING APPROACH TO 4TH AMENDMENT REASONABLENESS

Deputy Walters asked Hoory "to move to the sidewalk for his safety and mine as well." Hoory complied. Walters got out of his patrol car, identified himself to Hoory, and told Hoory that the reason he had initiated the contact "was for your own safety because you were in the middle of the street." As he was speaking with Hoory, Walters detected an "extremely strong" odor of marijuana emanating from Hoory's person and, in particular, from a backpack on his shoulder. Walters asked Hoory if he had anything illegal on his person or in his backpack. Hoory replied that he did not and stated that he had "magazines in my backpack." The deputy then asked Hoory if he could look inside Hoory's backpack to determine if he had anything illegal inside. Hoory handed the deputy the backpack and said, "Go ahead." As soon as the deputy opened the backpack, he saw a large amount of marijuana packaged in a plastic bag.

Did the officer seize Hoory prior to the search of the backpack?

5A–3: On September 17, Jesus was traveling by bus from Calexico to Newark. In Tulsa, all 25 passengers left the bus for a scheduled 90-minute stop. Officer Pat Dunn had a canine sniff the bus's cargo bays. The dog alerted to a blue suitcase, which was locked and bore a tag containing the name "Jesus R." Typically, passengers re-board the bus 15 minutes prior to departure. In this case, however, Dunn directed the bus driver to recall the passengers 10 minutes earlier, i.e., 25 minutes prior to departure, in order to determine which passenger owned the blue suitcase. After the passengers re-boarded the bus, Dunn, posing as a bus company employee and wearing a company shirt and hat, informed them that the bus had mechanical problems. He directed the passengers to leave the bus, claim their luggage and await the arrival of another bus. Dunn then began removing luggage from the cargo bays. While doing so, he observed Jesus walk up to the blue suitcase, look down at it, stand it on end, and examine its tag.

Officer Dunn approached Jesus, identified himself as a police officer, and received Jesus's permission to speak with him. Dunn asked Jesus for his bus ticket; the name on the ticket matched the name on the blue suitcase's tag. He then requested identification. Jesus provided Dunn with his passport and United States visa. Next, Dunn asked Jesus why a drug dog had alerted to his suitcase. Jesus responded, "I don't speak English." Dunn asked Jesus if the bag belonged to him. Jesus replied in English, "That's not my bag." Finally, Dunn asked Jesus to accompany him to the parcel storage area of the bus station. Jesus agreed, picked up the suitcase and followed Dunn into the parcel storage room. The other passengers re-boarded the bus, which then departed on time.

In the parcel storage room, Dunn asked Jesus if he could search the suitcase. Jesus again replied in English, "That's not my bag." Another officer then broke the lock on the suitcase, searched it and discovered approximately 12 pounds of heroin. Dunn then arrested Jesus and read him his rights in English and Spanish. Jesus admitted that the heroin was his. Subsequently, Jesus was indicted for possession with intent to distribute heroin.

At what point during this encounter was Jesus first seized? What if Officer Dunn had not posed as a bus company employee, but had announced he was a police officer before directing the passengers to get off the bus and claim their luggage?

5A–4: DEA Agent Small and a fellow member of an anti-drug task force, dressed in plain clothes, boarded a train while it was stopped briefly in Albuquerque en route from Los Angeles to Chicago. They walked through a coach car in which 45 to 55 people were riding. Zap, his common-law wife, and their young son were among the passengers. Small decided to question Zap. He knelt down in the aisle, showed Zap his DEA badge, and asked him a series of questions. Small asked about Zap's itinerary, where he lived, how long he had lived there, where his luggage was, whether there were drugs in it, and whether he would voluntarily consent to a search of the luggage. Zap stood up, removed two duffel bags from an overhead rack, and opened them. Inside the bags Agent Small found several kilograms of cocaine.

Zap moved to suppress the narcotics. At a hearing, it was established that Zap was never told he could refuse to answer the questions or could otherwise refuse to comply with Small's request. It was also shown that Zap was foreign-born, and that Zap's upbringing in his native culture led him to believe that he had to comply with all police requests because failure to do so could result in dire consequences, including physical harm.

Does Zap have a valid claim of violation of his Fourth Amendment rights?

5A–5: Officer Birney was patrolling the area of East Main and Center Streets in a marked cruiser at 1:00 a.m. He was wearing a uniform and a badge and was armed with a nightstick and firearm. There had been a recent string of burglaries in the area.

While driving east on Center, Birney saw a man and woman walking toward him. It was a very warm night, yet both wore heavy jackets. The man carried a gym-type duffel bag. Birney had recently arrested the woman, Nannette, on larceny and burglary charges. He had a "hunch" that the two had committed or were about to commit a burglary.

Birney turned the cruiser around and drove back in the couple's direction. From about seven yards away, he asked Nannette what she and her companion were doing. She replied that they were coming from the Junction Cafe. Birney knew that they were in fact walking toward the cafe and that it had closed two hours earlier. When Birney asked, the man identified himself as "Freddy." Birney then asked him to approach the cruiser. The man handed his bag to Nannette and stepped forward. Birney told him to bring the bag with him.

At that point, Freddy grabbed the bag, gave a quick look up and down, and ran away. Birney yelled to him to stop and pursued him on foot through a yard and into a wooded area. As he entered the wooded area, Freddy threw the bag down. Birney retrieved it and found two plastic bags of cocaine inside.

A police search of the wooded area the next day yielded a wallet containing an identification card bearing the name "Rafael Torrance." The narcotics and the identification card were introduced into evidence at Torrance's trial.

Were the contraband and evidence legally discovered?

5A–6: On September 19, Carl Steps was traveling by Greyhound bus from Los Angeles to Seattle. The bus stopped for servicing at the station in Sacramento where the passengers were required to disembark. The stop lasted roughly one hour.

The Sacramento Transportation Interdiction Narcotic Group ("STING") routinely inspects busses at the Greyhound station for drugs and weapons. Two STING officers, Risley and Villon, observed Steps while he was waiting in line to reboard the bus. They noticed that he carried a gym bag which appeared heavy and bulging. The officers did not approach Steps, but continued to observe him as he boarded the bus and placed his bag in the overhead compartment above his seat.

At the time scheduled for departure, Villon, Risley, and a third officer boarded the bus. The officers were not wearing uniforms or displaying badges and their weapons were concealed. They positioned themselves at the back, middle, and front of the bus. Because the aisle was very narrow, it would have been very difficult, though not impossible, for a person to exit the bus.

The officer at the front of the bus, using the Greyhound company's public address system to speak to the passengers, made the following announcement:

> *Good morning, ladies and gentlemen. We're police officers from various agencies. We're conducting a routine narcotics and weapons investigation on this bus. No one is under arrest, and you are free to leave. However, we would like to talk to you. Thank you.*

The other two officers began to question the passengers immediately. Officer Risley approached Steps first, asking him whether he had any carry-on baggage. Steps said that he did not. Risley then repeated the question, this time pointing to the overhead compartment. Steps again replied that he did not. After the officers interviewed other passengers, Risley took the bag he had observed Steps carrying, went to the front of the bus, and asked if anyone claimed the bag. When none of the passengers claimed it, Risley took the bag off of the bus where additional narcotics officers and a narcotics detection dog were waiting. The dog alerted to the bag. The officers opened it and found a substance that later proved to be cocaine. Steps was arrested. Ten to fifteen minutes had elapsed from the time the officers had initially boarded the bus.

Steps was charged with possession with intent to distribute cocaine. He moved to suppress the narcotics found in his bag, contending it was the product of an unlawful seizure.

Was Steps seized by the officers prior to his arrest?

5A–7: On the morning of July 5, Joanne left film at CVS Pharmacy (hereinafter "CVS") for development. A CVS employee noticed it contained several images of two adolescent minors posing with various weaponry, including several guns and a crossbow, and, in accord with policy, phoned the police. An officer requested that CVS notify him when someone came to retrieve the photographs. Later that day, Joanne returned to CVS to pick up the pictures. The photo development counter employee notified the police. Patrolman Harry Strom was dispatched. When he arrived at CVS, an employee handed Strom the pictures. In the state, it is illegal for unsupervised minors to possess loaded firearms and it is illegal for anyone to have a crossbow without a permit.

Strom asked Joanne whether she had seen the photographs. Joanne responded she had not and that she could not wait to view them. After looking at them, Joanne asserted that she had not taken the pictures and that the guns were not real, but rather were her son's paintball and BB guns. (This later proved to be a mistaken belief. The firearms were real.) To indicate that he thought the guns were real, Strom remarked, "I'd shoot him if he pulled that gun on me." The discussion then focused on a picture of Joanne's son holding a crossbow. Strom remarked that possession of a crossbow is illegal under state law. Joanne replied that her husband had a permit. Strom reiterated that crossbows are illegal. A hostile Joanne then exclaimed, "This is ridiculous!" Strom replied, "It's ridiculous that you have this going on." Joanne responded that her "husband shoots guns all the time." Strom asked "Is this proper behavior?" and Joanne replied "They are taking pictures of each other. What's the big deal?" As the hostility grew, Joanne exclaimed, "You are ridiculous!" and told Strom to "step away from me." When asked, Joanne refused to provide her name. Strom then stated he would call the Division of Youth and Family Services (DYFS).

Joanne backed away from Strom in an effort to gain some "personal space," walking several feet to the photo checkout counter where she stopped. At the counter, Strom requested identification, but Joanne refused, indicating it was not in her possession. Strom then requested her name again. Following another refusal to disclose her name, Strom informed Joanne she was under arrest for "obstructing the administration of law." Joanne has filed a civil claim for violation of her Fourth Amendment rights.

Did the officer seize Joanne prior to the arrest?

5A–8: On December 6, the police received an anonymous telephone tip that an intoxicated driver was slumped over the steering wheel of a purple pickup truck that was parked, with its motor running, outside the Fifties Tavern. Officers Gram and Tico were dispatched to investigate. When the officers arrived at the location they saw a truck matching the description given. A man was in the car, and the engine was running. Officer Gram parked his police cruiser behind the truck and activated his overhead emergency lights. When he approached the driver's door, he noticed that the man in the driver's seat, John Yatt, was slumped forward over the steering wheel. Even though the windows were rolled up, Officer Gram detected an odor of alcohol coming from inside the truck. He knocked on the driver's window. Yatt, who was either asleep or unconscious, did not respond. When Gram opened the driver's door, he detected a very strong odor of alcohol coming from inside the vehicle. At this point, Yatt awoke and stared at him.

Officer Gram asked Yatt for his driver's license. Yatt did not respond, but, instead, continued to stare at the officer. Gram noticed that Yatt had vomited on himself and on the inside of the truck. Gram then asked Yatt a second time for his driver's license. Yatt slowly got his wallet out and held it in his lap without removing his license. When Officer Gram reached for Yatt's wallet to get his driver's license, Yatt pulled away and moved to the passenger side of the truck. Officer Gram then informed Yatt that he was under arrest for driving under the influence. Yatt struggled, attempting to get away, but was eventually subdued with pepper spray. At the police station, Yatt submitted to a breath test that produced a reading of 0.225 blood alcohol level.

Yatt was charged with driving under the influence of alcohol and resisting arrest. He filed a motion to suppress evidence of the offenses, arguing that the anonymous telephone tip was insufficiently reliable to justify an investigative stop.

Does Yatt have a valid Fourth Amendment claim?

5A–9: On April 20, Officer More was patrolling Interstate 25. He observed two motorcycles on the road a short distance ahead. One of the motorcycles was red. The driver of the red motorcycle, a blond man, 18 to 25 years of age, was swerving in and out of traffic and "popping wheelies." More activated his overhead lights and siren. The motorcycles did not stop, but rapidly accelerated instead. The officer lost sight of the motorcycles when his car developed engine trouble.

More recorded the license plate number of the red motorcycle. When he looked up the plate number later, he learned that it corresponded to a motorcycle registered in William's name. The address on the registration was William's home. If More had been confident that the registered owner was the driver he had observed, he could have mailed William a summons to appear in court on the charges. However, he was uncertain whether the driver and the motorcycle's registered owner were the same person. Because More did not want to inconvenience William if William was the owner of the motorcycle, but not the driver he had seen, he decided to contact William personally.

More worked the "graveyard" shift and did not report for duty again until about 10:00 p.m. on April 22. A little more than two hours after reporting for duty, More went to William's address "in hopes of making contact with the owner or driver or at least observing a motorcycle there." More believed that the danger of the violation he had observed outweighed any inconvenience occasioned by the late hour. He believed that if William was not the driver he had observed, as owner of the motorcycle he would "want to know how recklessly his motorcycle was being operated."

Dressed in uniform and driving a police car, More arrived at William's home at 12:21 a.m., on April 23. When William's roommate responded to his knock on the front door, More said that he was conducting an investigation and wanted to speak with William if he was home. The roommate reported that William was in the back of the house and would need to be awakened. He then went to get him. When William came to the door, More informed him that he was investigating a traffic violation and asked him to step outside. As soon as William exited More recognized him as the driver of the red motorcycle. He then advised William that he was conducting a criminal investigation. In the course of the ensuing conversation, William admitted that he was the driver More had observed. More issued a citation for reckless driving.

Did Officer More intrude upon William's Fourth Amendment interests during the visit to his home?

5A–10: At about 3:00 a.m. on Friday, September 21, Wichita police officers received word from Wick County 911 that two black males were handling a gun while sitting in a black Ford Focus parked in a Denny's parking lot. The 911 caller had identified himself as Brandon Johnson. He admitted that he himself had not seen the gun. Rather, another anonymous person had told Brandon about the gun.

Two officers initially responded to the call. They pulled into a shopping center next to the Denny's. Only one black Ford Focus was in the Denny's parking lot. The officers sneaked up on the car from the front passenger's side with their weapons drawn. When the officers were 25 to 30 feet from the car, they could see two black males inside. The officers then approached the car. One crossed in front of the car from the passenger's side over to the driver's side, and the other remained on the passenger's side.

With their weapons raised, the officers surprised the occupants, shouting, "Hands up, hands up, get your hands up." The driver put his hands up immediately, but the passenger, Lamar, hesitated briefly and appeared momentarily disoriented. He then quickly began making furtive motions with his right shoulder and arm that officers believed were consistent with trying to either hide or retrieve a weapon. In response, one of the officers began yelling louder and kicking the driver's door to shock Lamar into heeding the order to put his hands up. After ignoring repeated commands to put his hands up, Lamar eventually raised them. One of the officers re-holstered his weapon, opened the passenger side door, and ordered Lamar to exit. Lamar did not immediately respond so the officer pulled him from the car, put him on the ground face-down, and handcuffed him before taking him into custody. Because he believed that Lamar had stashed a gun under the seat, one of the officers reached beneath the seat. He found a black nine-millimeter handgun there.

At what point did the officers seize Lamar?

[3] The Showing Needed to "Stop" and "Frisk"

Illinois v. Wardlow

Unites States Supreme Court

528 U.S. 119, 120 S. Ct. 673, 145 L. Ed. 2d 570 (2000)

CHIEF JUSTICE REHNQUIST delivered the opinion of the Court.

. . . .

On September 9, 1995, Officers Nolan and Harvey were working as uniformed officers in the special operations section of the Chicago Police Department. The officers were driving the last car of a four car caravan converging on an area known for heavy narcotics trafficking in order to investigate drug transactions. The officers were traveling together because they expected to find a crowd of people in the area, including lookouts and customers.

As the caravan passed 4035 West Van Buren, Officer Nolan observed respondent Wardlow standing next to the building holding an opaque bag. Respondent looked in the direction of the officers and fled. Nolan and Harvey turned their car southbound, watched him as he ran through the gangway and an alley, and eventually cornered him on the street. Nolan then exited his car and stopped respondent. He immediately conducted a protective pat-down search for weapons because in his experience it was common for there to be weapons in the near vicinity of narcotics transactions. During the frisk, Officer Nolan squeezed the bag respondent was carrying and felt a heavy, hard object similar to the shape of a gun. The officer then opened the bag and discovered a .38-caliber handgun with five live rounds of ammunition. The officers arrested Wardlow.

The Illinois trial court denied respondent's motion to suppress, finding the gun was recovered during a lawful stop and frisk. Following a stipulated bench trial, Wardlow was convicted of unlawful use of a weapon by a felon. The Illinois Appellate Court reversed Wardlow's conviction, concluding that the gun should have been suppressed because Officer Nolan did not have reasonable suspicion sufficient to justify an investigative stop pursuant to *Terry v. Ohio*, 392 U.S. 1, 88 S. Ct. 1868, 20 L. Ed. 2d 889 (1968).

The Illinois Supreme Court agreed. While rejecting the Appellate Court's conclusion that Wardlow was not in a high crime area, the Illinois Supreme Court determined that sudden flight in such an area does not create a reasonable suspicion justifying a *Terry* stop. Relying on *Florida v. Royer*, 460 U.S. 491, 103 S. Ct. 1319, 75 L. Ed. 2d 229 (1983), the court explained that although police have the right to approach individuals and ask questions, the individual has no obligation to respond. The person may decline to answer and simply go on his or her way, and the refusal to respond, alone, does not provide a legitimate basis for an investigative stop. The court then determined that flight may simply be an exercise of this right to "go on one's way," and, thus, could not constitute reasonable suspicion justifying a *Terry* stop.

The Illinois Supreme Court also rejected the argument that flight combined with the fact that it occurred in a high crime area supported a finding of reasonable suspicion because the "high crime area" factor was not sufficient standing alone to justify a *Terry* stop. Finding no independently suspicious circumstances to support an investigatory detention, the court held that the stop and subsequent arrest violated the Fourth Amendment. We granted certiorari, and now reverse.

This case, involving a brief encounter between a citizen and a police officer on a public street, is governed by the analysis we first applied in *Terry*. In *Terry*, we held that an officer may, consistent with the Fourth Amendment, conduct a brief, investigatory stop when the officer has a reasonable, articulable suspicion that criminal activity is afoot. *Terry, supra*, at 30, 88 S. Ct. 1868. While "reasonable suspicion" is a less demanding standard than probable cause and requires a showing considerably less than preponderance of the evidence, the Fourth Amendment requires at least a minimal level of objective justification for making the stop. *United States v. Sokolow*, 490 U.S. 1, 7, 109 S. Ct. 1581, 104 L. Ed. 2d 1 (1989). The officer must be able to articulate more than an "inchoate and unparticularized suspicion or 'hunch'" of criminal activity. *Terry, supra*, at 27, 88 S. Ct. 1868.

[margin note: → Requires min level of objective justifn]

Nolan and Harvey were among eight officers in a four car caravan that was converging on an area known for heavy narcotics trafficking, and the officers anticipated encountering a large number of people in the area, including drug customers and individuals serving as lookouts. It was in this context that Officer Nolan decided to investigate Wardlow after observing him flee. An individual's presence in an area of expected criminal activity, standing alone, is not enough to support a reasonable, particularized suspicion that the person is committing a crime. *Brown v. Texas*, 443 U.S. 47, 99 S. Ct. 2637, 61 L. Ed. 2d 357 (1979). But officers are not required to ignore the relevant characteristics of a location in determining whether the circumstances are sufficiently suspicious to warrant further investigation. Accordingly, we have previously noted the fact that the stop occurred in a "high crime area" among the relevant contextual considerations in a *Terry* analysis. *Adams v. Williams*, 407 U.S. 143, 144 and 147–148, 92 S. Ct. 1921, 32 L. Ed. 2d 612 (1972).

[margin note: "Hunting"]

In this case, moreover, it was not merely respondent's presence in an area of heavy narcotics trafficking that aroused the officers' suspicion but his unprovoked flight upon noticing the police. Our cases have also recognized that nervous, evasive behavior is a pertinent factor in determining reasonable suspicion. *United States v. Brignoni-Ponce*, 422 U.S. 873, 885, 95 S. Ct. 2574, 45 L. Ed. 2d 607 (1975); *Florida v. Rodriguez*, 469 U.S. 1, 6, 105 S. Ct. 308, 83 L. Ed. 2d 165 (1984) (*per curiam*); *United States v. Sokolow, supra*, at 8–9, 109 S. Ct. 1581. Headlong flight—wherever it occurs—is the consummate act of evasion: it is not necessarily indicative of wrongdoing, but it is certainly suggestive of such. In reviewing the propriety of an officer's conduct, courts do not have available empirical studies dealing with inferences drawn from suspicious behavior, and we cannot reasonably demand scientific certainty from judges or law enforcement officers where none exists. Thus, the determination of reasonable suspicion must be based on commonsense judgments and inferences about human behavior. We conclude Officer Nolan was justified in suspecting that Wardlow was involved in criminal activity, and, therefore, in investigating further.

[margin note: sugg. NOT Determinative]

[margin note: Justified in suspicion & further investigation]

Such a holding is entirely consistent with our decision in *Florida v. Royer*, 460 U.S. 491, 103 S. Ct. 1319, 75 L. Ed. 2d 229 (1983), where we held that when an officer, without reasonable suspicion or probable cause, approaches an individual, the individual has a right to ignore the police and go about his business. *Id.*, at 498, 103 S. Ct. 1319. And any "refusal to cooperate, without more, does not furnish the minimal level of objective justification needed for a detention or seizure." *Florida v. Bostick*, 501 U.S.

462 5 · THE BALANCING APPROACH TO 4TH AMENDMENT REASONABLENESS

429, 437, 111 S. Ct. 2382, 115 L. Ed. 2d 389 (1991). But unprovoked flight is simply not a mere refusal to cooperate. Flight, by its very nature, is not "going about one's business"; in fact, it is just the opposite. Allowing officers confronted with such flight to stop the fugitive and investigate further is quite consistent with the individual's right to go about his business or to stay put and remain silent in the face of police questioning.

Respondent and *amici* also argue that there are innocent reasons for flight from police and that, therefore, flight is not necessarily indicative of ongoing criminal activity. This fact is undoubtedly true, but does not establish a violation of the Fourth Amendment. Even in *Terry*, the conduct justifying the stop was ambiguous and susceptible of an innocent explanation. The officer observed two individuals pacing back and forth in front of a store, peering into the window and periodically conferring. *Terry*, 392 U.S., at 5–6, 88 S. Ct. 1868. All of this conduct was by itself lawful, but it also suggested that the individuals were casing the store for a planned robbery. *Terry* recognized that the officers could detain the individuals to resolve the ambiguity. *Id.*, at 30, 88 S. Ct. 1868.

In allowing such detentions, *Terry* accepts the risk that officers may stop innocent people. Indeed, the Fourth Amendment accepts that risk in connection with more drastic police action; persons arrested and detained on probable cause to believe they have committed a crime may turn out to be innocent. The *Terry* stop is a far more minimal intrusion, simply allowing the officer to briefly investigate further. If the officer does not learn facts rising to the level of probable cause, the individual must be allowed to go on his way. But in this case the officers found respondent in possession of a handgun, and arrested him for violation of an Illinois firearms statute. No question of the propriety of the arrest itself is before us.

The judgment of the Supreme Court of Illinois is reversed, and the cause is remanded for further proceedings not inconsistent with this opinion.

It is so ordered.

JUSTICE STEVENS, with whom JUSTICE SOUTER, JUSTICE GINSBURG, and JUSTICE BREYER join, concurring in part and dissenting in part.

The State of Illinois asks this Court to announce a "bright-line rule" authorizing the temporary detention of anyone who flees at the mere sight of a police officer. Respondent counters by asking us to adopt the opposite *per se* rule — that the fact that a person flees upon seeing the police can never, by itself, be sufficient to justify a temporary investigative stop of the kind authorized by *Terry v. Ohio*, 392 U.S. 1, 88 S. Ct. 1868, 20 L. Ed. 2d 889 (1968).

The Court today wisely endorses neither *per se* rule. Instead, it rejects the proposition that "flight is . . . necessarily indicative of ongoing criminal activity," adhering to the view that "[t]he concept of reasonable suspicion . . . is not readily, or even usefully, reduced to a neat set of legal rules," but must be determined by looking to "the totality of the circumstances — the whole picture." *United States v. Sokolow*, 490 U.S.

1, 7–8, 109 S. Ct. 1581, 104 L. Ed. 2d 1 (1989) (internal quotation marks and citation omitted). Abiding by this framework, the Court concludes that "Officer Nolan was justified in suspecting that Wardlow was involved in criminal activity."

Although I agree with the Court's rejection of the *per se* rules proffered by the parties, unlike the Court, I am persuaded that in this case the brief testimony of the officer who seized respondent does not justify the conclusion that he had reasonable suspicion to make the stop. . . .

I

. . . .

The question in this case concerns "the degree of suspicion that attaches to" a person's flight — or, more precisely, what "commonsense conclusions" can be drawn respecting the motives behind that flight. A pedestrian may break into a run for a variety of reasons — to catch up with a friend a block or two away, to seek shelter from an impending storm, to arrive at a bus stop before the bus leaves, to get home in time for dinner, to resume jogging after a pause for rest, to avoid contact with a bore or a bully, or simply to answer the call of nature — any of which might coincide with the arrival of an officer in the vicinity. A pedestrian might also run because he or she has just sighted one or more police officers. In the latter instance, the State properly points out "that the fleeing person may be, *inter alia*, (1) an escapee from jail; (2) wanted on a warrant; (3) in possession of contraband, (*i.e.* drugs, weapons, stolen goods, etc.); or (4) someone who has just committed another type of crime." In short, there are unquestionably circumstances in which a person's flight is suspicious, and undeniably instances in which a person runs for entirely innocent reasons.[3]

Given the diversity and frequency of possible motivations for flight, it would be profoundly unwise to endorse either *per se* rule. The inference we can reasonably draw about the motivation for a person's flight, rather, will depend on a number of different circumstances. Factors such as the time of day, the number of people in the area, the character of the neighborhood, whether the officer was in uniform, the way the runner was dressed, the direction and speed of the flight, and whether the person's behavior was otherwise unusual might be relevant in specific cases. This number of variables is surely sufficient to preclude either a bright-line rule that always justi-

---

3. Compare, *e.g.*, Proverbs 28:1 ("The wicked flee when no man pursueth: but the righteous are as bold as a lion") with Proverbs 22:3 ("A shrewd man sees trouble coming and lies low; the simple walk into it and pay the penalty"). I have rejected reliance on the former proverb in the past, because its "ivory-towered analysis of the real world" fails to account for the experiences of many citizens of this country, particularly those who are minorities. *See California v. Hodari D.*, 499 U.S. 621, 630, n. 4, 111 S. Ct. 1547, 113 L. Ed. 2d 690 (1991) (Stevens, J., dissenting). That this pithy expression fails to capture the total reality of our world, however, does not mean it is inaccurate in all instances.

fies, or that never justifies, an investigative stop based on the sole fact that flight began after a police officer appeared nearby.[4]

Still, Illinois presses for a *per se* rule regarding "unprovoked flight upon seeing a clearly identifiable police officer." [*United States v. Sokolow*, 490 U.S.], at 7, 109 S. Ct. 1581. The phrase "upon seeing," as used by Illinois, apparently assumes that the flight is motivated by the presence of the police officer.[5] Illinois contends that unprovoked flight is "an extreme reaction," *id.*, at 8, 109 S. Ct. 1581, because innocent people simply do not "flee at the mere sight of the police," *id.*, at 24, 109 S. Ct. 1581. To be sure, Illinois concedes, an innocent person — even one distrustful of the police — might "avoid eye contact or even sneer at the sight of an officer," and that would not justify a *Terry* stop or any sort of *per se* inference. *Id.*, at 8–9, 109 S. Ct. 1581. But, Illinois insists, unprovoked flight is altogether different. Such behavior is so "aberrant" and "abnormal" that a *per se* inference is justified. *Id.*, at 8–9, and n. 4, 109 S. Ct. 1581.

Even assuming we know that a person runs because he sees the police, the inference to be drawn may still vary from case to case. Flight to escape police detection, we have said, may have an entirely innocent motivation:

> "[I]t is a matter of common knowledge that men who are entirely innocent do sometimes fly from the scene of a crime through fear of being apprehended as the guilty parties, or from an unwillingness to appear as witnesses. Nor is it true as an accepted axiom of criminal law that 'the wicked flee when no man pursueth, but the righteous are as bold as a lion.' Innocent men sometimes hesitate to confront a jury — not necessarily because they fear that the jury will not protect them, but because they do not wish their names to appear in connection with criminal acts, are humiliated at

---

4. Of course, *Terry* itself recognized that sometimes behavior giving rise to reasonable suspicion is entirely innocent, but it accepted the risk that officers may stop innocent people. 392 U.S., at 30, 88 S. Ct. 1868. And as the Court correctly observes, it is "undoubtedly true" that innocent explanations for flight exist, but they do not "establish a violation of the Fourth Amendment." It is equally true, however, that the innocent explanations make the single act of flight sufficiently ambiguous to preclude the adoption of a *per se* rule. In *Terry*, furthermore, reasonable suspicion was supported by a concatenation of acts, each innocent when viewed in isolation, that when considered collectively amounted to extremely suspicious behavior. *See* 392 U.S., at 5–7, 22–23, 88 S. Ct. 1868. Flight alone, however, is not at all like a "series of acts, each of them perhaps innocent in itself, but which taken together warran[t] further investigation." *Id.*, at 22, 88 S. Ct. 1868. Nor is flight similar to evidence which in the aggregate provides "fact on fact and clue on clue afford[ing] a basis for the deductions and inferences," supporting reasonable suspicion. *United States v. Cortez*, 449 U.S. 411, 419, 101 S. Ct. 690, 66 L. Ed. 2d 621 (1981).

5. Nowhere in Illinois' briefs does it specify what it means by "unprovoked." At oral argument, Illinois explained that if officers precipitate a flight by threats of violence, that flight is "provoked." But if police officers in a patrol car — with lights flashing and siren sounding — descend upon an individual for the sole purpose of seeing if he or she will run, the ensuing flight is "unprovoked."

being obliged to incur the popular odium of an arrest and trial, or because they do not wish to be put to the annoyance or expense of defending themselves." *Alberty v. United States*, 162 U.S. 499, 511, 16 S. Ct. 864, 40 L. Ed. 1051 (1896).

In addition to these concerns, a reasonable person may conclude that an officer's sudden appearance indicates nearby criminal activity. And where there is criminal activity there is also a substantial element of danger — either from the criminal or from a confrontation between the criminal and the police. These considerations can lead to an innocent and understandable desire to quit the vicinity with all speed. YEAH, OOHKAY.

Among some citizens, particularly minorities and those residing in high crime areas, there is also the possibility that the fleeing person is entirely innocent, but, with or without justification, believes that contact with the police can itself be dangerous, apart from any criminal activity associated with the officer's sudden presence.[7] For such a person, unprovoked flight is neither "aberrant" nor "abnormal."[8]

---

7. *See* Johnson, *Americans' Views on Crime and Law Enforcement: Survey Findings*, National Institute of Justice Journal 13 (Sept. 1997) (reporting study by the Joint Center for Political and Economic Studies in April 1996, which found that 43% of African-Americans consider "police brutality and harassment of African-Americans a serious problem" in their own community); President's Comm'n on Law Enforcement and Administration of Justice, Task Force Report: The Police 183–184 (1967) (documenting the belief, held by many minorities, that field interrogations are conducted "indiscriminately" and "in an abusive . . . manner," and labeling this phenomenon a "principal problem" causing "friction" between minorities and the police) (cited in *Terry*, 392 U.S., at 14, n. 11, 88 S. Ct. 1868); *see also* Casimir, *Minority Men: We Are Frisk Targets*, N.Y. Daily News, Mar. 26, 1999, p. 34 (informal survey of 100 young black and Hispanic men living in New York City; 81 reported having been stopped and frisked by police at least once; none of the 81 stops resulted in arrests); Brief for NAACP Legal Defense & Educational Fund as *Amicus Curiae* 17–19 (reporting figures on disproportionate street stops of minority residents in Pittsburgh and Philadelphia, Pennsylvania, and St. Petersburg, Florida); U.S. Dept. of Justice, Bureau of Justice Statistics, S. Smith, Criminal Victimization and Perceptions of Community Safety in 12 Cities 25 (June 1998) (African-American residents in 12 cities are more than twice as likely to be dissatisfied with police practices than white residents in same community).

8. *See, e.g.*, Kotlowitz, *Hidden Casualties: Drug War's Emphasis on Law Enforcement Takes a Toll on Police*, Wall Street Journal, Jan. 11, 1991, p. A2, col. 1 ("Black leaders complained that innocent people were picked up in the drug sweeps. . . . Some teen-agers were so scared of the task force they ran even if they weren't selling drugs"). Many stops never lead to an arrest, which further exacerbates the perceptions of discrimination felt by racial minorities and people living in high crime areas. *See* Goldberg, *The Color of Suspicion*, N.Y. Times Magazine, June 20, 1999, p. 85 (reporting that in 2-year period, New York City Police Department Street Crimes Unit made 45,000 stops, only 9,500, or 20%, of which resulted in arrest); Casimir, *supra*, n. 7 (reporting that in 1997, New York City's Street Crimes Unit conducted 27,061 stop-and-frisks, only 4,647 of which, 17%, resulted in arrest). Even if these data were race neutral, they would still indicate that society as a whole is paying a significant cost in infringement on liberty by these virtually random stops.

Moreover, these concerns and fears are known to the police officers themselves,[9] and are validated by law enforcement investigations into their own practices.[10] Accordingly, the evidence supporting the reasonableness of these beliefs is too pervasive to be dismissed as random or rare, and too persuasive to be disparaged as inconclusive or insufficient.[11] In any event, just as we do not require "scientific certainty" for our

---

9. The Chief of the Washington, D.C., Metropolitan Police Department, for example, confirmed that "sizeable percentages of Americans today — especially Americans of color — still view policing in the United States to be discriminatory, if not by policy and definition, certainly in its day-to-day application." P. Verniero, Attorney General of New Jersey, Interim Report of the State Police Review Team Regarding Allegations of Racial Profiling 46 (Apr. 20, 1999) (hereinafter Interim Report). And a recent survey of 650 Los Angeles Police Department officers found that 25% felt that "'racial bias (prejudice) on the part of officers toward minority citizens currently exists and contributes to a negative interaction between police and the community.'" Report of the Independent Comm'n on the Los Angeles Police Department 69 (1991); *see also* 5 United States Comm'n on Civil Rights, *Racial and Ethnic Tensions in American Communities: Poverty, Inequality and Discrimination*, The Los Angeles Report 26 (June 1999).

10. New Jersey's Attorney General, in a recent investigation into allegations of racial profiling on the New Jersey Turnpike, concluded that "minority motorists have been treated differently [by New Jersey State Troopers] than non-minority motorists during the course of traffic stops on the New Jersey Turnpike." "[T]he problem of disparate treatment is real — not imagined," declared the Attorney General. Not surprisingly, the report concluded that this disparate treatment "engender[s] feelings of fear, resentment, hostility, and mistrust by minority citizens." See Interim Report 4, 7. Recently, the United States Department of Justice, citing this very evidence, announced that it would appoint an outside monitor to oversee the actions of the New Jersey State Police and ensure that it enacts policy changes advocated by the Interim Report, and keeps records on racial statistics and traffic stops. *See* Kocieniewski, *U.S. Will Monitor New Jersey Police on Race Profiling*, N.Y. Times, Dec. 23, 1999, p. A1, col. 6. Likewise, the Massachusetts Attorney General investigated similar allegations of egregious police conduct toward minorities. The report stated:

> "We conclude that Boston police officers engaged in improper, and unconstitutional, conduct in the 1989–90 period with respect to stops and searches of minority individuals.... Although we cannot say with precision how widespread this illegal conduct was, we believe that it was sufficiently common to justify changes in certain Department practices.

> "Perhaps the most disturbing evidence was that the *scope* of a number of *Terry* searches went far beyond anything authorized by that case and indeed, beyond anything that we believe would be acceptable under the federal and state constitutions even where probable cause existed to conduct a full search incident to an arrest. Forcing young men to lower their trousers, or otherwise searching inside their underwear, on public streets or in public hallways, is so demeaning and invasive of fundamental precepts of privacy that it can only be condemned in the strongest terms. The fact that not only the young men themselves, but independent witnesses complained of strip searches, should be deeply alarming to all members of this community." J. Shannon, Attorney General of Massachusetts, Report of the Attorney General's Civil Rights Division on Boston Police Department Practices 60–61 (Dec. 18, 1990).

11. Taking into account these and other innocent motivations for unprovoked flight leads me to reject Illinois' requested *per se* rule in favor of adhering to a totality-of-the-circumstances test. This conclusion does not, as Illinois suggests, "establish a separate *Terry* analysis based on the individual characteristics of the person seized." My rejection of a *per se* rule, of course, applies to members of all races. It is true, as Illinois points out, that *Terry* approved of the stop and frisk procedure notwithstanding "[t]he wholesale harassment by certain elements of the police community, of which

commonsense conclusion that unprovoked flight can sometimes indicate suspicious motives, neither do we require scientific certainty to conclude that unprovoked flight can occur for other, innocent reasons.

The probative force of the inferences to be drawn from flight is a function of the varied circumstances in which it occurs. Sometimes those inferences are entirely consistent with the presumption of innocence, sometimes they justify further investigation, and sometimes they justify an immediate stop and search for weapons. These considerations have led us to avoid categorical rules concerning a person's flight and the presumptions to be drawn therefrom. . . .

"Unprovoked flight," in short, describes a category of activity too broad and varied to permit a *per se* reasonable inference regarding the motivation for the activity. While the innocent explanations surely do not establish that the Fourth Amendment is always violated whenever someone is stopped solely on the basis of an unprovoked flight, neither do the suspicious motivations establish that the Fourth Amendment is never violated when a *Terry* stop is predicated on that fact alone. For these reasons, the Court is surely correct in refusing to embrace either *per se* rule advocated by the parties. The totality of the circumstances, as always, must dictate the result.

II

. . . .

Respondent Wardlow was arrested a few minutes after noon on September 9, 1995. Nolan was part of an eight-officer, four-car caravan patrol team. The officers were headed for "one of the areas in the 11th District [of Chicago] that's high [in] narcotics traffic." The reason why four cars were in the caravan was that "[n]ormally in these different areas there's an enormous amount of people, sometimes lookouts, customers." Officer Nolan testified that he was in uniform on that day, but he did not recall whether he was driving a marked or an unmarked car.

Officer Nolan and his partner were in the last of the four patrol cars that "were all caravaning eastbound down Van Buren." Nolan first observed respondent "in front of 4035 West Van Buren." Wardlow "looked in our direction and began fleeing." Nolan then "began driving southbound down the street observing [respondent] running through the gangway and the alley southbound," and observed that Wardlow was carrying a white, opaque bag under his arm. After the car turned south and intercepted respondent as he "ran right towards us," Officer Nolan stopped him and conducted a "protective search," which revealed that the bag under respondent's arm contained a loaded handgun.

---

minority groups, particularly Negroes, frequently complain." 392 U.S., at 14, 88 S. Ct. 1868. But in this passage, *Terry* simply held that such concerns would not preclude the use of the stop and frisk procedure altogether. *See id.*, at 17, n. 14, 88 S. Ct. 1868. Nowhere did *Terry* suggest that such concerns cannot inform a court's assessment of whether reasonable suspicion sufficient to justify a particular stop existed.

This terse testimony is most noticeable for what it fails to reveal. Though asked whether he was in a marked or unmarked car, Officer Nolan could not recall the answer. He was not asked whether any of the other three cars in the caravan were marked, or whether any of the other seven officers were in uniform. Though he explained that the size of the caravan was because "[n]ormally in these different areas there's an enormous amount of people, sometimes lookouts, customers," Officer Nolan did not testify as to whether *anyone* besides Wardlow was nearby 4035 West Van Buren. Nor is it clear that that address was the intended destination of the caravan. As the Appellate Court of Illinois interpreted the record, "it appears that the officers were simply driving by, on their way to some unidentified location, when they noticed defendant standing at 4035 West Van Buren." Officer Nolan's testimony also does not reveal how fast the officers were driving. It does not indicate whether he saw respondent notice the other patrol cars. And it does not say whether the caravan, or any part of it, had already passed Wardlow by before he began to run.

Indeed, the Appellate Court thought the record was even "too vague to support the inference that . . . defendant's flight was related to his expectation of police focus on him." Presumably, respondent did not react to the first three cars, and we cannot even be sure that he recognized the occupants of the fourth as police officers. The adverse inference is based entirely on the officer's statement: "He looked in our direction and began fleeing."

No other factors sufficiently support a finding of reasonable suspicion. Though respondent was carrying a white, opaque bag under his arm, there is nothing at all suspicious about that. Certainly the time of day — shortly after noon — does not support Illinois' argument. Nor were the officers "responding to any call or report of suspicious activity in the area." Officer Nolan did testify that he expected to find "an enormous amount of people," including drug customers or lookouts, and the Court points out that "[i]t was in this context that Officer Nolan decided to investigate Wardlow after observing him flee." This observation, in my view, lends insufficient weight to the reasonable suspicion analysis; indeed, in light of the absence of testimony that anyone else was nearby when respondent began to run, this observation points in the opposite direction.

The State, along with the majority of the Court, relies as well on the assumption that this flight occurred in a high crime area. Even if that assumption is accurate, it is insufficient because even in a high crime neighborhood unprovoked flight does not invariably lead to reasonable suspicion. On the contrary, because many factors providing innocent motivations for unprovoked flight are concentrated in high crime areas, the character of the neighborhood arguably makes an inference of guilt less appropriate, rather than more so. Like unprovoked flight itself, presence in a high crime neighborhood is a fact too generic and susceptible to innocent explanation to satisfy the reasonable suspicion inquiry.

It is the State's burden to articulate facts sufficient to support reasonable suspicion. In my judgment, Illinois has failed to discharge that burden. I am not persuaded that the mere fact that someone standing on a sidewalk looked in the direction of a pass-ing car before starting to run is sufficient to justify a forcible stop and frisk.

I therefore respectfully dissent from the Court's judgment to reverse the court below.

Notes and Questions

(1) How does an officer or judge determine the relevance and weight of "unpro-voked flight" in making a reasonable suspicion determination? Is "unprovoked flight" from a police officer alone ever a sufficient basis for finding a reasonable suspicion of criminal activity? Why?

(2) The *Wardlow* majority observed that the fact that an individual is present in a "high crime area" is not by itself sufficient to justify a stop. On the other hand, "the fact that [a] stop occur[s] in a 'high crime area' [is] among the relevant contextual considerations" in reasonable suspicion determinations. How much should a "high crime" location count in assessing the reasonableness of a forcible stop? What are the dangers of relying on that factor?

(3) The *Wardlow* Court rejected the state's proposed *per se* rule that "unpro-voked flight" always provides the reasonable suspicion needed to justify an investi-gatory detention. Does the Court's conclusion that the officers had grounds for detaining Wardlow, however, constitute an implicit adoption of an alternative *per se* rule that "unprovoked flight in a high crime area" always gives rise to a reasonable suspicion? If not, why not?

(4) Like the officer in *Terry*, the officer in *Wardlow* immediately conducted a protective frisk of the suspect. The Court did not address the question of whether that frisk was justifiable. Did the facts support a reasonable suspicion that Mr. Ward-low was armed and dangerous?

(5) Justice Stevens maintains that the fact that members of minority groups suffer "harassment" by law enforcement officers should be taken into account in deciding whether flight in a high crime area gives rise to a reasonable suspicion. In the *Ward-low* majority's view, is this a relevant consideration? Should it be? How would a judge factor this concern into the reasonable suspicion analysis in any particular case?

Alabama v. White

United States Supreme Court

496 U.S. 325, 110 S. Ct. 2412, 110 L. Ed. 2d 301 (1990)

JUSTICE WHITE delivered the opinion of the Court.

. . . .

On April 22, 1987, at approximately 3 p.m., Corporal B. H. Davis of the Mont-gomery Police Department received a telephone call from an anonymous person, stating that Vanessa White would be leaving 235-C Lynwood Terrace Apartments at a particular time in a brown Plymouth station wagon with the right taillight lens broken, that she would be going to Dobey's Motel, and that she would be in possession of about an ounce of cocaine inside a brown attaché case. Corporal Davis and his partner, Corporal P. A. Reynolds, proceeded to the Lynwood Terrace Apartments. The officers saw a brown Plymouth station wagon with a broken right taillight in the parking lot in front of the 235 building. The officers observed respondent leave the 235 building, carrying nothing in her hands, and enter the station wagon. They followed the vehicle as it drove the most direct route to Dobey's Motel. When the vehicle reached the Mobile Highway, on which Dobey's Motel is located, Corporal Reynolds requested a patrol unit to stop the vehicle. The vehicle was stopped at approximately 4:18 p.m., just short of Dobey's Motel. Corporal Davis asked respondent to step to the rear of her car, where he informed her that she had been suspected of carrying cocaine in the vehicle. He asked if they could look for cocaine and respondent said they could look. The officers found a locked brown attaché case in the car and, upon request, respondent provided the combination to the lock. The officers found marijuana in the attaché case and placed respondent under arrest. During processing at the station, the officers found three milligrams of cocaine in respondent's purse.

Respondent was charged in Montgomery County court with possession of marijuana and possession of cocaine. The trial court denied respondent's motion to suppress and she pleaded guilty to the charges, reserving the right to appeal the denial of her suppression motion. The Court of Criminal Appeals of Alabama held that the officers did not have the reasonable suspicion necessary under *Terry v. Ohio*, 392 U.S. 1 (1968), to justify the investigatory stop of respondent's car, and that the marijuana and cocaine were fruits of respondent's unconstitutional detention. The court concluded that respondent's motion to dismiss should have been granted and reversed her conviction. 550 So. 2d 1074 (1989). The Supreme Court of Alabama denied the State's petition for writ of certiorari, two justices dissenting. 550 So. 2d 1081 (1989). Because of differing views in the state and federal courts over whether an anonymous tip may furnish reasonable suspicion for a stop, we granted the State's petition for certiorari, 493 U.S. 1042 (1990). We now reverse. It was not a terry step (it actually was according to SC) that

. . . .

Illinois v. Gates, 462 U.S. 213 (1983), dealt with an anonymous tip in the probable cause context. The Court there abandoned the "two-pronged test" of *Aguilar v. Texas*, 378 U.S. 108 (1964), and *Spinelli v. United States*, 393 U.S. 410 (1969), in favor of a "totality of the circumstances" approach to determining whether an informant's tip establishes probable cause. *Gates* made clear, however, that those factors that had been considered critical under *Aguilar* and *Spinelli* — an informant's "veracity," "reliability," and "basis of knowledge" — remain "highly relevant in determining the value of his report." 462 U.S., at 230. These factors are also relevant in the reasonable suspicion context, although allowance must be made in applying them for the lesser showing required to meet that standard.

The opinion in *Gates* recognized that an anonymous tip alone seldom demonstrates the informant's basis of knowledge or veracity inasmuch as ordinary citizens generally do not provide extensive recitations of the basis of their everyday observations and given that the veracity of persons supplying anonymous tips is "by hypothesis largely unknown, and unknowable." *Id.*, at 237. This is not to say that an anonymous caller could never provide the reasonable suspicion necessary for a *Terry* stop. But the tip in *Gates* was not an exception to the general rule, and the anonymous tip in this case is like the one in *Gates*: "[it] provides virtually nothing from which one might conclude that [the caller] is either honest or his information reliable; likewise, the [tip] gives absolutely no indication of the basis for the [caller's] predictions regarding [Vanessa White's] criminal activities." 462 U.S., at 227. By requiring "[s]omething more," as *Gates* did, *ibid.*, we merely apply what we said in *Adams [v. Williams*, 407 U.S. 143 (1972)]: "Some tips, completely lacking in indicia of reliability, would either warrant no police response or require further investigation before a forcible stop of a suspect would be authorized," 407 U.S., at 147. Simply put, a tip such as this one, standing alone, would not "'warrant a man of reasonable caution in the belief' that [a stop] was appropriate." *Terry, supra*, at 22, quoting *Carroll v. United States*, 267 U.S. 132, 162 (1925).

As there was in *Gates*, however, in this case there is more than the tip itself. The tip was not as detailed, and the corroboration was not as complete, as in *Gates*, but the required degree of suspicion was likewise not as high. We discussed the difference in the two standards last Term in *United States v. Sokolow*, 490 U.S. 1, 7 (1989):

> The officer [making a *Terry* stop] . . . must be able to articulate something more than an "inchoate and unparticularized suspicion or 'hunch.'" [*Terry*, 392 U.S.,] at 27. The Fourth Amendment requires "some minimal level of objective justification" for making the stop. *INS v. Delgado*, 466 U.S. 210, 217 (1984). That level of suspicion is considerably less than proof of wrongdoing by a preponderance of the evidence. We have held that probable cause means "a fair probability that contraband or evidence of a crime will be found," [*Gates*, 462 U.S., at 238], and the level of suspicion required for a *Terry* stop is obviously less demanding than for probable cause.

Reasonable suspicion is a less demanding standard than probable cause not only in the sense that reasonable suspicion can be established with information that is different in quantity or content than that required to establish probable cause, but also in the sense that reasonable suspicion can arise from information that is less reliable than that required to show probable cause. *Adams v. Williams, supra*, demonstrates as much. We there assumed that the unverified tip from the known informant might not have been reliable enough to establish probable cause, but nevertheless found it sufficiently reliable to justify a *Terry* stop. 407 U.S. at 147. Reasonable suspicion, like probable cause, is dependent upon both the content of information possessed by police and its degree of reliability. Both factors — quantity and quality — are considered in the "totality of the circumstances—the whole picture," *United States v. Cortez*, 449 U.S. 411, 417 (1981), that must be taken into account when evaluating whether there is reasonable suspicion. Thus, if a tip has a relatively low degree of reliability, more information will be required to establish the requisite quantum of suspicion than would be required if the tip were more reliable. The *Gates* Court applied its totality of the circumstances approach in this manner, taking into account the facts known to the officers from personal observation, and giving the anonymous tip the weight it deserved in light of its indicia of reliability as established through independent police work. The same approach applies in the reasonable suspicion context, the only difference being the level of suspicion that must be established. Contrary to the court below, we conclude that when the officers stopped respondent, the anonymous tip had been sufficiently corroborated to furnish reasonable suspicion that respondent was engaged in criminal activity and that the investigative stop therefore did not violate the Fourth Amendment.

It is true that not every detail mentioned by the tipster was verified, such as the name of the woman leaving the building or the precise apartment from which she left; but the officers did corroborate that a woman left the 235 building and got into the particular vehicle that was described by the caller. With respect to the time of departure predicted by the informant, Corporal Davis testified that the caller gave a particular time when the woman would be leaving, but he did not state what that time was. He did testify that, after the call, he and his partner proceeded to the Lynwood Terrace Apartments to put the 235 building under surveillance. Given the fact that the officers proceeded to the indicated address immediately after the call and that respondent emerged not too long thereafter, it appears from the record before us that respondent's departure from the building was within the timeframe predicted by the caller. As for the caller's prediction of respondent's destination, it is true that the officers stopped her just short of Dobey's Motel and did not know whether she would have pulled in or continued on past it. But given that the four-mile route driven by respondent was the most direct route possible to Dobey's Motel, but nevertheless involved several turns, we think respondent's destination was significantly corroborated. *Hotel ✓, car, ✓, name ✗, Building, ✓/✗*

The Court's opinion in *Gates* gave credit to the proposition that because an informant is shown to be right about some things, he is probably right about other facts that he has alleged, including the claim that the object of the tip is engaged in criminal activity. 462 U.S., at 244. Thus, it is not unreasonable to conclude in this case that the independent corroboration by the police of significant aspects of the informer's predictions imparted some degree of reliability to the other allegations made by the caller.

We think it also important that, as in *Gates*, "the anonymous [tip] contained a range of details relating not just to easily obtained facts and conditions existing at the time of the tip, but to future actions of third parties ordinarily not easily predicted." *Gates*, 462 U.S., at 245. The fact that the officers found a car precisely matching the caller's description in front of the 235 building is an example of the former. Anyone could have "predicted" that fact because it was a condition presumably existing at the time of the call. What was important was the caller's ability to predict respondent's future behavior, because it demonstrated inside information — a special familiarity with respondent's affairs. The general public would have had no way of knowing that respondent would shortly leave the building, get in the described car, and drive the most direct route to Dobey's Motel. Because only a small number of people are generally privy to an individual's itinerary, it is reasonable for police to believe that a person with access to such information is likely to also have access to reliable information about that individual's illegal activities. *See Gates, supra,* at 245. When significant aspects of the caller's predictions were verified, there was reason to believe not only that the caller was honest but also that he was well informed, at least well enough to justify the stop.

Although it is a close case, we conclude that under the totality of the circumstances the anonymous tip, as corroborated, exhibited sufficient indicia of reliability to justify the investigatory stop of respondent's car. We therefore reverse the judgment of the Court of Criminal Appeals of Alabama and remand for further proceedings not inconsistent with this opinion.   ↓APP said no reason 5w5
US says Hell ya.

So ordered.

JUSTICE STEVENS, with whom JUSTICE BRENNAN and JUSTICE MARSHALL join, dissenting.

Millions of people leave their apartments at about the same time every day carrying an attaché case and heading for a destination known to their neighbors. Usually, however, the neighbors do not know what the briefcase contains. An anonymous neighbor's prediction about somebody's time of departure and probable destination is anything but a reliable basis for assuming that the commuter is in possession of an illegal substance — particularly when the person is not even carrying the attaché case described by the tipster.

The record in this case does not tell us how often respondent drove from the Lynwood Terrace Apartments to Dobey's Motel; for all we know, she may have been a room clerk or telephone operator working the evening shift. It does not tell us whether Officer Davis made any effort to ascertain the informer's identity, his reason for calling, or the basis of his prediction about respondent's destination. Indeed, for all that this record tells us, the tipster may well have been another police officer who had a "hunch" that respondent might have cocaine in her attaché case.

Anybody with enough knowledge about a given person to make her the target of a prank, or to harbor a grudge against her, will certainly be able to formulate a tip about her like the one predicting Vanessa White's excursion. In addition, under the Court's holding, every citizen is subject to being seized and questioned by any officer who is prepared to testify that the warrantless stop was based on an anonymous tip predicting whatever conduct the officer just observed. Fortunately, the vast majority of those in our law enforcement community would not adopt such a practice. But the Fourth Amendment was intended to protect the citizen from the overzealous and unscrupulous officer as well as from those who are conscientious and truthful. This decision makes a mockery of that protection.

I respectfully dissent.

Florida v. J.L.

United States Supreme Court

529 U.S. 266, 120 S. Ct. 1375, 146 L. Ed. 2d 254 (2000)

JUSTICE GINSBURG delivered the opinion of the Court.

. . . .

I

On October 13, 1995, an anonymous caller reported to the Miami-Dade Police that a young black male standing at a particular bus stop and wearing a plaid shirt was carrying a gun. So far as the record reveals, there is no audio recording of the tip, and nothing is known about the informant. Sometime after the police received the tip — the record does not say how long — two officers were instructed to respond. They arrived at the bus stop about six minutes later and saw three black males "just hanging out [there]." One of the three, respondent J.L., was wearing a plaid shirt. Apart from the tip, the officers had no reason to suspect any of the three of illegal conduct. The officers did not see a firearm, and J.L. made no threatening or otherwise unusual movements. One of the officers approached J.L., told him to put his hands up on the bus stop, frisked him, and seized a gun from J.L.'s pocket. The second officer frisked the other two individuals, against whom no allegations had been made, and found nothing.

J.L., who was at the time of the frisk "10 days shy of his 16th birth[day]," was charged under state law with carrying a concealed firearm without a license and possessing a firearm while under the age of 18. He moved to suppress the gun as the fruit of an unlawful search, and the trial court granted his motion. The intermediate appellate court reversed, but the Supreme Court of Florida quashed that decision and held the search invalid under the Fourth Amendment.

. . . .

Seeking review in this Court, the State of Florida noted that the decision of the State's Supreme Court conflicts with decisions of other courts declaring similar searches compatible with the Fourth Amendment. We granted certiorari, and now affirm the judgment of the Florida Supreme Court.

II

Our "stop and frisk" decisions begin with *Terry v. Ohio*, 392 U.S. 1, 88 S. Ct. 1868, 20 L. Ed. 2d 889 (1968). This Court held in *Terry*

> "[W]here a police officer observes unusual conduct which leads him reasonably to conclude in light of his experience that criminal activity may be afoot and that the persons with whom he is dealing may be armed and presently dangerous, where in the course of investigating this behavior he identifies himself as a policeman and makes reasonable inquiries, and where nothing in the initial stages of the encounter serves to dispel his reasonable fear for his own or others' safety, he is entitled for the protection of himself and

others in the area to conduct a carefully limited search of the outer clothing of such persons in an attempt to discover weapons which might be used to assault him." *Id.*, at 30, 88 S. Ct. 1868.

In the instant case, the officers' suspicion that J.L. was carrying a weapon arose not from any observations of their own but solely from a call made from an unknown location by an unknown caller. Unlike a tip from a known informant whose reputation can be assessed and who can be held responsible if her allegations turn out to be fabricated, *see Adams v. Williams*, 407 U.S. 143, 146–147, 92 S. Ct. 1921, 32 L. Ed. 2d 612 (1972), "an anonymous tip alone seldom demonstrates the informant's basis of knowledge or veracity," *Alabama v. White*, 496 U.S., at 329, 110 S. Ct. 2412. As we have recognized, however, there are situations in which an anonymous tip, suitably corroborated, exhibits "sufficient indicia of reliability to provide reasonable suspicion to make the investigatory stop." *Id.*, at 327, 110 S. Ct. 2412. The question we here confront is whether the tip pointing to J.L. had those indicia of reliability.

In *White*, the police received an anonymous tip asserting that a woman was carrying cocaine and predicting that she would leave an apartment building at a specified time, get into a car matching a particular description, and drive to a named motel. *Ibid.* Standing alone, the tip would not have justified a *Terry* stop. *Id.*, at 329, 110 S. Ct. 2412. Only after police observation showed that the informant had accurately predicted the woman's movements, we explained, did it become reasonable to think the tipster had inside knowledge about the suspect and therefore to credit his assertion about the cocaine. *Id.*, at 332, 110 S. Ct. 2412. Although the Court held that the suspicion in *White* became reasonable after police surveillance, we regarded the case as borderline. Knowledge about a person's future movements indicates some familiarity with that person's affairs, but having such knowledge does not necessarily imply that the informant knows, in particular, whether that person is carrying hidden contraband. We accordingly classified *White* as a "close case." *Ibid.*

The tip in the instant case lacked the moderate indicia of reliability present in *White* and essential to the Court's decision in that case. The anonymous call concerning J.L. provided no predictive information and therefore left the police without means to test the informant's knowledge or credibility. That the allegation about the gun turned out to be correct does not suggest that the officers, prior to the frisks, had a reasonable basis for suspecting J.L. of engaging in unlawful conduct: The reasonableness of official suspicion must be measured by what the officers knew before they conducted their search. All the police had to go on in this case was the bare report of an unknown, unaccountable informant who neither explained how he knew about the gun nor supplied any basis for believing he had inside information about J.L. If *White* was a close case on the reliability of anonymous tips, this one surely falls on the other side of the line.

Florida contends that the tip was reliable because its description of the suspect's visible attributes proved accurate: There really was a young black male wearing a plaid shirt at the bus stop. The United States as *amicus curiae* makes a similar argument, proposing that a stop and frisk should be permitted "when (1) an anonymous tip provides a description of a particular person at a particular location illegally carrying a concealed firearm, (2) police promptly verify the pertinent details of the tip except the existence of the firearm, and (3) there are no factors that cast doubt on the reliability of the tip . . . ." These contentions misapprehend the reliability needed for a tip to justify a *Terry* stop.

An accurate description of a subject's readily observable location and appearance is of course reliable in this limited sense: It will help the police correctly identify the person whom the tipster means to accuse. Such a tip, however, does not show that the tipster has knowledge of concealed criminal activity. The reasonable suspicion here at issue requires that a tip be reliable in its assertion of illegality, not just in its tendency to identify a determinate person.

A second major argument advanced by Florida and the United States as *amicus* is, in essence, that the standard *Terry* analysis should be modified to license a "firearm exception." Under such an exception, a tip alleging an illegal gun would justify a stop and frisk even if the accusation would fail standard pre-search reliability testing. We decline to adopt this position.

Firearms are dangerous, and extraordinary dangers sometimes justify unusual precautions. Our decisions recognize the serious threat that armed criminals pose to public safety; *Terry's* rule, which permits protective police searches on the basis of reasonable suspicion rather than demanding that officers meet the higher standard of probable cause, responds to this very concern. But an automatic firearm exception to our established reliability analysis would rove too far. Such an exception would enable any person seeking to harass another to set in motion an intrusive, embarrassing police search of the targeted person simply by placing an anonymous call falsely reporting the target's unlawful carriage of a gun. Nor could one securely confine such an exception to allegations involving firearms. Several Courts of Appeals have held it *per se* foreseeable for people carrying significant amounts of illegal drugs to be carrying guns as well. If police officers may properly conduct *Terry* frisks on the basis of bare-boned tips about guns, it would be reasonable to maintain under the above-cited decisions that the police should similarly have discretion to frisk based on bare-boned tips about narcotics. As we clarified when we made indicia of reliability critical in *Adams* and *White*, the Fourth Amendment is not so easily satisfied. *Cf. Richards v. Wisconsin*, 520 U.S. 385, 393–394, 117 S. Ct. 1416, 137 L. Ed. 2d 615 (1997) (rejecting a *per se* exception to the "knock and announce" rule for narcotics cases partly because "the reasons for creating an exception in one category [of Fourth Amendment cases] can, relatively easily, be applied to others," thus allowing the exception to swallow the rule).*

---

* At oral argument, petitioner also advanced the position that J.L.'s youth made the stop and frisk valid, because it is a crime in Florida for persons under the age of 21 to carry concealed firearms. *See* Fla. Stat. § 790.01 (1997) (carrying a concealed weapon without a license is a misdemeanor), § 790.06(2)(b) (only persons aged 21 or older may be licensed to carry concealed weapons). This contention misses the mark. Even assuming that the arresting officers could be sure

The facts of this case do not require us to speculate about the circumstances under which the danger alleged in an anonymous tip might be so great as to justify a search even without a showing of reliability. We do not say, for example, that a report of a person carrying a bomb need bear the indicia of reliability we demand for a report of a person carrying a firearm before the police can constitutionally conduct a frisk. Nor do we hold that public safety officials in quarters where the reasonable expectation of Fourth Amendment privacy is diminished, such as airports, *see Florida v. Rodriguez,* 469 U.S. 1, 105 S. Ct. 308, 83 L. Ed. 2d 165 (1984) (*per curiam*), and schools, *see New Jersey v. T.L.O.,* 469 U.S. 325, 105 S. Ct. 733, 83 L. Ed. 2d 720 (1985), cannot conduct protective searches on the basis of information insufficient to justify searches elsewhere.

Finally, the requirement that an anonymous tip bear standard indicia of reliability in order to justify a stop in no way diminishes a police officer's prerogative, in accord with *Terry*, to conduct a protective search of a person who has already been legitimately stopped. We speak in today's decision only of cases in which the officer's authority to make the initial stop is at issue. In that context, we hold that an anonymous tip lacking indicia of reliability of the kind contemplated in *Adams* and *White* does not justify a stop and frisk whenever and however it alleges the illegal possession of a firearm.

The judgment of the Florida Supreme Court is affirmed.

It is so ordered.

[The concurring opinion of JUSTICE KENNEDY, joined by THE CHIEF JUSTICE, has been omitted.]

Notes and Questions

(1) After reading *Alabama v. White* and *Florida v. J.L.*, how would you explain to a police officer the differences between probable cause and a reasonable suspicion? Between a reasonable suspicion and a mere hunch?

(2) In *White*, an anonymous tip, plus official corroboration of certain facts, justified the forcible detention of the defendant. That detention led to the discovery that the tipster had been correct in reporting that the defendant would be in possession of contraband. In *J.L.*, an anonymous tip, plus official corroboration, did not support an investigatory stop that similarly confirmed the validity of the tipster's report that the defendant was in possession of a firearm.

(a) What critical distinctions were there between the justification for the detention in *White* and the justification for the detention in *J.L.*? Which anonymous tips justify investigatory detentions? Which do not?

---

that J.L. was under 21, they would have had reasonable suspicion that J.L. was engaged in criminal activity only if they could be confident that he was carrying a gun in the first place. The mere fact that a tip, if true, would describe illegal activity does not mean that the police may make a *Terry* stop without meeting the reliability requirement, and the fact that J.L. was under 21 in no way made the gun tip more reliable than if he had been an adult.

CART B/4 HORSE guys

(b) Should judges be more inclined to find reasonable suspicion when a tipster's identity is known to law enforcement officers? If the tipster in *J.L.* had provided his or her identity, would the outcome of the case have been different?

(3) In *Navarette v. California*, 572 U.S. ____, 134 S. Ct. 1683, 188 L. Ed. 2d 680 (2014), an anonymous 911 caller reported that she had been run off the road by a pickup truck. The caller specified the area where the event occurred and the color, model, and license plate number of the truck. Soon thereafter, an officer spotted the truck. After following the truck for five minutes and witnessing no traffic violations or suspicious driving, the officer pulled the truck over. As he approached, he smelled marijuana. A subsequent search of the truck bed led to the discovery of 30 pounds of marijuana.

In an opinion authored by Justice Thomas, a five-Justice majority acknowledged that "an anonymous tip *alone* seldom demonstrates the informant's basis of knowledge or veracity[,]" but observed that "under appropriate circumstances, an anonymous tip can demonstrate 'sufficient indicia of reliability to provide reasonable suspicion.'" The majority concluded that in this case "the stop complied with the Fourth Amendment because, under the totality of the circumstances, the officer had reasonable suspicion that the driver was intoxicated."

The first question was "whether the 911 call was sufficiently reliable to credit the allegation that [the] truck 'ran the [caller] off the roadway.'" The Court concluded that the call did bear "adequate indicia of reliability for the officer to credit the caller's account." First, by reporting being "run off the road by a specific vehicle . . . the caller necessarily claimed eyewitness knowledge of the alleged dangerous driving. That basis of knowledge len[t] significant support to the tip's reliability." The necessary implication was "that the informant [knew] the other car was driven dangerously."

In addition, there was "reason to think that the 911 caller . . . was telling the truth." The caller apparently made the call "soon after she was run off the road." Both the fact that the report was "contemporaneous" with the caller's observations and the fact that it pertained to a "startling event" and was made while "under the stress of excitement" were "considerations" that the law of evidence recognizes as supportive "of the caller's veracity." Moreover, "the caller's use of the 911 emergency system" was an "indicator of veracity." The 911 system's "features that allow for identifying and tracing callers . . . provide . . . safeguards against making false reports with immunity." As a result, "a reasonable officer could conclude that a false tipster would think twice before using [the 911] system." NO HEARSAY! 803(2)

The Court noted that, to justify a stop, "[e]ven a reliable tip" must "create[] reasonable suspicion that 'criminal activity may be afoot.'" Consequently, the second question was "whether the 911 caller's report . . . created reasonable suspicion of an ongoing crime." In this case, "the behavior alleged," from the viewpoint of a reasonable officer, gave rise to a "'reasonable suspicion' of drunk driving." The anonymous "911 caller . . . reported more than a minor traffic infraction and more than a conclusory allegation of drunk or reckless driving. Instead, she alleged a specific and dangerous result of the driver's conduct: running another car off the highway." This was "conduct" indicative of "drunk driving" and not simply "isolated . . . reckless-ness" because it suggested "lane-positioning problems, decreased vigilance, impaired judgment, or some combination of those recognized drunk driving cues." In sum, the "alleged conduct was a significant indicator of drunk driving."

The fact that the officer did not observe "additional suspicious conduct" did not "dispel the reasonable suspicion." It was not "surprising that . . . a marked police car would inspire more careful driving for a time." Although "[e]xtended observation . . . might eventually dispel a reasonable suspicion of intoxication, . . . the 5-minute" ob-servation here did not. In addition, once the officer had a reasonable suspicion, he was not obligated to take the "less intrusive" step of following the truck for a longer time. Such a requirement here would be "particularly inappropriate . . . because al-lowing a drunk driver a second chance for dangerous conduct could have disastrous consequences."

The majority conceded that, like *Alabama v. White*, the facts of *Navarette* pre-sented "a 'close case.'" Nonetheless, the indicia of reliability were "stronger than those in *J.L.*" and were "sufficient to provide the officer with reasonable suspicion" that the truck's driver "had run another vehicle off the road." For this reason, it was "reasonable . . . to execute a traffic stop."

Justice Scalia wrote a blistering dissent that was joined by Justices Ginsburg, Sotomayor, and Kagan. He predicted that law enforcers would realize the implica-tions of the majority opinion — that "[s]o long as [a] caller identifies where [a] car is, anonymous claims of a single instance of possibly careless or reckless driving, called in to 911, will support a traffic stop." This did not comport with his "concept . . . of a people secure from unreasonable searches and seizures."

According to Justice Scalia, the police here "knew nothing about the tipster" and "had no reason to credit [her] charge," but had "many reasons to doubt it." It did not matter that the caller "'claimed eyewitness knowledge'" because "[t]he issue [was] not how she claimed to know, but whether what she claimed to know was true." In his view, it was "unlikely that the law of evidence would deem the mystery caller in this case 'especially trustworthy.'" Moreover, the caller's use of the 911 system did not support her veracity, because "[t]here is no reason to believe that [an] average anonymous 911 tipster is aware that 911 callers are readily identifiable."

Additionally, the caller's report "neither assert[ed] that the driver was drunk nor even raise[d] the *likelihood* that the driver was drunk." A "reasonable suspicion of a discrete instance of irregular or hazardous driving" did not "generate[] a reasonable suspicion of ongoing intoxicated driving." The majority "ha[d] no grounds for its un-supported assertion that the tipster's report in this case gave rise to a *reasonable sus-picion* of drunken driving." To stop the truck, "the officer[] . . . not only had to assume without basis the accuracy of the anonymous accusation but also had to posit an unlikely reason (drunkenness) for the accused behavior."

Moreover, at the time of the stop, the officer "had very good reason . . . to know that" the driver "was not" drunk. After he followed the truck for five minutes and saw no traffic offense or other indication of drunk driving, any suggestion of drunk driving "was affirmatively undermined." What he saw "strongly suggest[ed] that the suspected crime was *not* occurring." The majority's belief that a drunk driver can determine whether he "drives drunkenly" was not consistent with Justice Scalia's "understand[ing of] the influence of alcohol."

The dissenters accused the majority of "serv[ing] up a freedom-destroying cocktail consisting of two parts patent falsity: (1) that anonymous 911 reports of traffic violations are reliable so long as they correctly identify a car and its location, and (2) that a single instance of careless or reckless driving necessarily supports a reasonable suspicion of drunkenness." In their view, the ruling in *Navarette* meant that "all of us on the road, and not just drug dealers, are at risk of having our freedom of movement curtailed on suspicion of drunkenness, based upon a phone tip, true or false, of a single instance of careless driving."

(4) The relatively brief opinion in *White* is the Court's most direct and significant effort to address and explain the meaning and substance of the reasonable suspicion standard. Since *White*, the opinions in *Wardlow* and *J.L.* have furnished additional insight into that concept.

(a) In *United States v. Mendenhall*, discussed in subsection [A][2], seven Justices discussed whether there was "reasonable suspicion" to suspect a woman of transporting narcotics. Three Justices concluded that the following facts did support a reasonable suspicion:

> The two officers . . . were federal agents assigned to the Drug Enforcement Administration. Agent Anderson, who initiated the stop and questioned [Mendenhall], had 10 years of experience and special training in drug enforcement. He had been assigned to the Detroit Airport, known to be a crossroads for illicit narcotics traffic, for over a year and he had been involved in approximately 100 drug-related arrests. The agents observed [Mendenhall] as she arrived in Detroit from Los Angeles. [She] . . . appeared very nervous, [and] engaged in behavior that the agents believed was designed to evade detection. She deplaned only after all other passengers had left the aircraft. Agent Anderson testified that drug couriers often disembark last in order to have a clear view of the terminal so that they more easily can detect government agents. Once inside the terminal, [Mendenhall] scanned the entire gate area and walked "very, very slowly" toward the baggage area. When she arrived there, she claimed no baggage. Instead, she asked a skycap for directions to the Eastern Airlines ticket counter . . . . Although she carried an American Airlines ticket for a flight from Detroit to Pittsburgh, she asked for an Eastern Airlines ticket. An airline employee gave her an Eastern Airlines boarding pass. Agent Anderson testified that drug couriers frequently travel without baggage and change flights en route to avoid surveillance.

The four dissenting Justices disagreed, asserting that the stop had been "based solely on . . . brief observations of [Mendenhall's] conduct at the airport" and that the conduct the federal agents "observed . . . was not 'unusual,'" but "could reasonably be expected of anyone changing planes in an airport terminal." In their view, "[n]one of the aspects of Ms. Mendenhall's conduct, either alone or in combination, were sufficient to provide reasonable suspicion that she was engaged in criminal activity. The fact that [she] was the last person to alight from a flight originating in Los Angeles was plainly insufficient." The fact she had traveled "from a 'major source city'" for narcotics, was also insufficient because "mere proximity of a person to areas with a high incidence of drug activity or to persons known to be drug addicts, does not provide the necessary reasonable suspicion for an investigatory stop." Moreover, Ms. Mendenhall's failure to claim luggage and change of airlines "were also insufficient" in this case because an agent "heard the [Eastern Airlines] ticket agent tell [her] that her ticket to Pittsburgh already was in order and that all she needed was a boarding pass for the flight." Consequently, it should have been apparent that she had not made a suspicious decision to change flights and that there was no reason for her to claim her luggage at that point in her travels.

In three airport cases following *Mendenhall* and preceding *White*, the Court had already shed a limited amount of light on the constitutional justification required for an investigative detention. Those cases merit study by anyone seeking a more complete understanding of the notion of "reasonable suspicion":

(b) In *Reid v. Georgia*, 448 U.S. 438, 100 S. Ct. 2752, 65 L. Ed. 2d 890 (1980), the Court held that officers "could not, as a matter of law, have reasonably suspected [an individual] of criminal activity on the basis of" the facts that: (1) he had arrived on a flight from Fort Lauderdale, Florida (alleged by the narcotics agent to be a principal place of origin of cocaine sold in the United States); (2) he had arrived in the early morning, when law enforcement activity is diminished; and (3) he and his companion appeared to be trying to conceal the fact that they were traveling together and had no luggage other than their shoulder bags. In a terse *per curiam* opinion, the Court observed that all but one of the circumstances described "a very large category of presumably innocent travelers, who would be subject to virtually random seizures were [we] to conclude that as little foundation as there was in this case could justify a seizure."

(c) In *Florida v. Royer*, 460 U.S. 491, 103 S. Ct. 1319, 75 L. Ed. 2d 229 (1983), the plurality concluded that a *Terry* seizure was justified under the following circumstances: Officers observed that the suspect was young, casually dressed, pale and nervous. He had been looking around at other persons in the airport, had paid cash for a one-way ticket, and had checked his suitcases by placing on each an identification tag bearing only a false name and the name of the airport to which he was travelling. In addition, when the officers approached the suspect and asked him for identification, they discovered that he was travelling under an assumed name.

(d) Finally, in *United States v. Sokolow*, 490 U.S. 1, 109 S. Ct. 1581, 104 L. Ed. 2d 1 (1989), the Court confronted a case in which agents stopped a suspect after becoming aware that: (1) he had paid $2100 for two round-trip tickets from a roll of $20 bills; (2) he was travelling under a name that did not match the name under which his telephone number was listed; (3) his original destination was Miami, a source city for drugs; (4) he had stayed in Miami only 48 hours, even though a round-trip from his point of origin, Honolulu, to Miami takes 20 hours; (5) he appeared nervous during his trip; and (6) he checked none of his luggage. The lower court had held that a reasonable suspicion could not be based solely on factors describing "personal characteristics" of drug couriers, but, instead, required at least one factor describing "ongoing criminal activity."

The Supreme Court rejected that premise and held that the facts of *Sokolow* did give rise to a reasonable suspicion of narcotics transportation.

(5) In *United States v. Arvizu*, 534 U.S. 266, 122 S. Ct. 744, 151 L. Ed. 2d 740 (2002), a unanimous Court concluded that the analysis employed by a court of appeals was inconsistent with the "teachings" of the reasonable suspicion precedents in two respects. The court had evaluated relevant factors "in isolation from each other" and had deemed it necessary to "'clearly delimit' an officer's consideration of certain factors." The Supreme Court reemphasized the importance of considering the "'totality of the circumstances' of each case" in making reasonable suspicion determinations. In addition, the Court stressed that facts that are innocent when viewed in isolation may well be suspicious when viewed together and observed that officers may "draw on their own experience and specialized training to make inferences" that "'might well elude an untrained person.'"

(6) *Wardlow* discussed the relationship between flight and reasonable suspicion. *White* and *J.L.* addressed the relationship between anonymous tips and reasonable suspicion. The Court's airport cases—*Mendenhall, Reid, Royer*, and *Sokolow* (see Note (4), *supra*)—all involved official reliance, at least in part, upon "drug courier profiles"—compilations of the characteristics of drug traffickers developed by law enforcement agencies. These cases all raise the question of the relationship between such profiles and reasonable suspicion.

The Court has not provided a comprehensive picture of the role of profiles in reasonable suspicion inquiries. Nevertheless, certain aspects of the role of profiles are clear. The Court has indicated, for example, that judges must make independent evaluations of reasonable suspicion showings. They should not simply defer to an officer's reliance on a "drug courier profile" or some combination of factors set forth in a profile. *See United States v. Sokolow*, 490 U.S. at 10, 109 S. Ct. at 1587, 104 L. Ed. 2d at 12 (observing that a "court sitting to determine the existence of reasonable suspicion must require the agent to articulate the factors leading to that conclusion"); *see also Reid v. Georgia*, 448 U.S. 438, 100 S. Ct. 2752, 65 L. Ed. 2d 890 (1980) (concluding that no reasonable suspicion was established despite the presence of three profile factors). On the other hand, "the fact that . . . factors may be set forth in [a drug courier] 'profile' does not," according to the Court, "somehow detract from their evidentiary significance as seen by a trained agent." *Sokolow*, 490 U.S. at 10, 109 S. Ct. at 1587, 104 L. Ed. 2d at 12. In other words, the factors found in a profile might well provide a judge with objective bases for finding reasonable suspicion.

For a critique of drug courier profiles, see Charles L. Becton, *The Drug Courier Profile: "All Seems Infected That Th' Infected Spy, As All Looks Yellow to the Jaundiced Eye,"* 65 N.C. L. Rev. 417 (1987).

(7) In *Heien v. North Carolina*, 574 U.S. ____, 135 S. Ct. 530, 190 L. Ed. 2d 475 (2014), the Justices considered "whether reasonable suspicion can rest on a mistaken understanding of the scope of a legal prohibition." An officer had stopped a vehicle that had only one functioning brake light because he believed this was a violation of the law. In a search of the vehicle that was consented to, the officer found cocaine. The North Carolina Court of Appeals interpreted the state vehicle code to require only one working brake light. Consequently, the operation of Heien's vehicle "with only one working brake light was not actually a violation of North Carolina law." The North Carolina Supreme Court did not disagree with this interpretation of the code or with the conclusion that Heien was not violating the law, but decided that because the officer's "mistaken understanding of the vehicle code was reasonable, the stop was valid."

In an opinion authored by Chief Justice Roberts, an eight-Justice majority sustained that ruling. According to the majority, "the Fourth Amendment allows for some mistakes" by "government officials" because that provision only requires reasonableness and "[t]o be reasonable is not to be perfect." The Court had already "recognized that searches and seizures based on mistakes of fact can be reasonable." The Justices believed that reasonable mistakes of law were "no less compatible with the concept of reasonable suspicion" than equivalent mistakes of fact. When it turns out that the facts are not what they were thought to be or the law is not as it was thought to be, "the result is the same: the facts are outside the scope of the law. There is no reason . . . why this same result should be acceptable when reached by way of a reasonable mistake of fact, but not when reached by way of a similarly reasonable mistake of law." The majority stressed that "[t]he Fourth Amendment tolerates only *reasonable* mistakes, and [that] those mistakes — whether of fact or of law — must be *objectively* reasonable." For that reason, the Court's decision would "not discourage officers from learning the law."

In *Heien*, ambiguities in the state's vehicle code meant that it was, in fact, "objectively reasonable for an officer in . . . [the] position" of the officer who stopped Heien's vehicle "to think that Heien's faulty . . . brake light was a violation of . . . law. And because the mistake of law was reasonable, there was reasonable suspicion justifying the stop."

Justice Sotomayor alone dissented. In her view, "determining whether a search or seizure is reasonable requires evaluating an officer's understanding of the facts against the actual state of the law." Consequently, the Court should "hold that an officer's mistake of law, no matter how reasonable, cannot support the individualized suspicion necessary to justify a seizure under the Fourth Amendment."

(8) In *United States v. Hensley*, 469 U.S. 221, 105 S. Ct. 675, 83 L. Ed. 2d 604 (1985), the question was whether *Terry* detentions are permissible to investigate "completed" criminal activity, as opposed to criminal activity that is imminent or ongoing. The Court held that such detentions are constitutional if based upon a reasonable suspicion "that a person . . . was involved in or is wanted in connection with a completed felony." It specifically reserved the question of whether such detentions are permissible for "all past crimes, however serious."

(9) Suppose that the police receive an anonymous telephone tip informing them that a young woman uses her van to transport illegal firearms. Knowing that they do not have grounds to stop her vehicle to investigate the tip, officers follow the woman until she exceeds the speed limit by three miles per hour. They then stop her van, look through the windows, and request consent to search it. Is their conduct constitutional?

Suppose the officers do not witness a traffic violation. Instead, their investigation of the woman leads to a reasonable suspicion that she sold cocaine to an acquaintance several months earlier. Based on that suspicion, they stop her van with the hope of seeing firearms inside or securing her consent to search. Is their conduct constitutional? In connection with both of these situations, consider the implications of *Whren v. United States*, 517 U.S. 806, 116 S. Ct. 1769, 135 L. Ed. 2d 89 (1996), *supra*, Chapter 2.

"Showing" Problems

5A–11: On the evening of December 18, Police Officer R.B. Tinn was on routine patrol in his police car. Around 7:30 p.m., his route took him to the intersection of 27th Street and Chestnut Avenue, the location of a small shopping plaza occupied mainly by a local convenience store. In Officer Tinn's experience, the shopping plaza was a "high-drug" and "high-crime" area where "multiple shootings" and "many drug arrests" had taken place. Officer Tinn considered it to be one of the worst crime spots in the city—an assessment that specifically included the convenience store's parking lot. The convenience store had a history of trespassing problems that had prompted the store's owner to post "no trespassing" signs around the store and to file a written request for the police to "enforce criminal violations" on the premises.

As he approached the shopping plaza, Officer Tinn noticed two men standing next to a pair of garbage dumpsters "toward the back" of the convenience store's side parking lot, off to the north side of the building. The place where the men were standing was "not even close" to the convenience store's front entrance, which was located on the west side of the building. There was no indication that the men had shopping bags or any other items suggestive of recent purchases from the store.

Officer Tinn observed the two men standing by the dumpsters for five to ten seconds as he approached the parking lot. Once he pulled his car into the lot, the men saw him "almost immediately" and began to walk away from the area "at a fast pace." They walked past the convenience store's entrance, but neither man made an attempt

What arguments should Rod make in support of his motion? How should the government respond?

5A–15: The Highway Patrol (HP) set up a drug interdiction checkpoint at the end of the Sugar Road exit ramp from eastbound Highway 44 ("I-44"). It was a "ruse checkpoint." Approximately one-quarter mile west of the Sugar Road exit, signs were placed along the road, stating: "Drug Enforcement Checkpoint 1/4 Mile Ahead." Approximately 100 yards west of the exit, another sign stated: "Drug Dogs in Use Ahead." In fact, the checkpoint was located on the Sugar Road exit ramp. This exit was chosen because officers believed that I-44 was commonly used for transporting drugs, there was little use of the exit for commercial or local traffic, and the end of the ramp was not visible from the highway.

Operation of the checkpoint was governed by procedures issued by the HP. When a vehicle arrived at the checkpoint, a uniformed officer would ask the driver for his or her license, registration, and proof of insurance, would record the license plate number of the vehicle, and would ask the driver if he or she saw the signs and why he or she exited the highway. If there were any indications of illegal activity, the officer would question the driver further. If there were any reason to believe that the vehicle contained contraband, the officer would ask for consent to search it. If consent were denied, but the officer still had a suspicion, the officer would ask the occupants to step out and would have a drug detection dog sniff the exterior.

Shortly before 3:00 p.m., Patrolman Senby observed Osift's SUV turn onto the Sugar Road exit ramp. Senby was standing with other officers at the top of the ramp. A sign indicating the presence of a police checkpoint was visible as the vehicle approached the end of the ramp. When Osift's vehicle slowed to a near stop halfway up the ramp, Senby directed it to come forward. After Osift stopped at the checkpoint, Senby approached and asked Osift for his driver's license, registration, and proof of insurance. Osift produced a license and a rental agreement. His hands were shaking, and he nearly dropped his license. When Senby asked why Osift had exited, his wife, a passenger in the vehicle, volunteered that their dog had needed to relieve itself.

Osift consented to a search of his vehicle. Senby opened the back, finding six large suitcases containing bundles of what appeared to be marijuana. He placed Osift and his wife under arrest. They were charged with possession with intent to distribute more than 100 kilograms of marijuana. After an appellate court ruled that suspicionless stops at "drug interdiction" checkpoints violate the Fourth Amendment, Osift moved to suppress the marijuana.

Should the trial judge grant the motion to suppress?

5A–16: At approximately 12:30 p.m., Officer Price was in a marked squad car on Highway 20 when he saw a blue Ford Taurus traveling westbound. The car had an air freshener suspended from the rearview mirror and a GPS unit was visible through the front windshield. Price activated his emergency lights and pulled the Taurus over. Rick Hough, an out-of-state resident, was driving. While Price was asking Hough for identification, he smelled the odor of marijuana coming from the car. Price searched the car, finding two partially smoked marijuana cigarettes, rolling papers, a digital scale, a 150-count package of sandwich bags, and some sandwich bags containing marijuana. The state charged Hough with possession with intent to deliver marijuana. Prior to trial, Hough filed a motion to suppress the evidence, claiming that the stop of his car was unreasonable.

The state code contains the following provisions:

> (3)(a) No person shall drive any motor vehicle with any sign, poster or other nontransparent material upon the front windshield, front side wings, side windows in the driver's compartment or rear window of such vehicle other than a certificate or other sticker issued by order of a governmental agency.

> (b) No person shall drive any motor vehicle upon a highway with any object so placed or suspended in or upon the vehicle so as to obstruct the driver's clear view through the front windshield.

The State contends that these provisions mean that a driver may have *nothing* attached to or suspended from the front windshield, including the rearview mirror (except certain items specifically exempted and not relevant in this case). The State's interpretation would include oil change stickers and rosaries as well as standard pine-tree-shaped air fresheners. Hough claims that the provisions do not create an absolute prohibition on any items being attached to or suspended from a vehicle's front windshield or rearview mirror. More specifically, Hough contends that the first provision bars only "the attachment to the windshield of signs, posters, and other items of a similar nature," and that the second provision, by use of the term "obstruct" requires that an item have more than a minor effect on a driver's vision. Instead, it must have a "material effect" to be considered "obstruction." Under Hough's interpretations, the items in his car were not prohibited by the state code provisions, which have not yet been interpreted by the courts of the state.

Did Officer Price's stop of Hough's vehicle violate the Fourth Amendment?

5A–17: Early one Saturday morning, the 911 system in South Forks received this call from a pay telephone: "I would like to report a black male with a silver hand gun. He was arguing with his, ah, girlfriend, or whatever . . . . They were walking toward the 7-Eleven on Mimi Street. He's tall. He's wearing a black jacket and blue jean pants. He has the gun on a holster. And I seen him pull it out."

Police quickly spotted a couple in the area where they were reported to be. The man and woman were not arguing, but, instead, were eating snack food. Believing that an armed domestic quarrel could break out at any time, Officer Gary stopped the pair. He immediately patted down Woody, the male, and found a gun, just as the caller had described it. The safety was off; the serial number had been obliterated.

When it was discovered that Woody had a felony conviction, the government charged him with being a convicted felon in possession of a firearm. He was charged with a second count alleging possession of a firearm with a missing serial number. Woody contends that the evidence found in the patdown should be suppressed as the product of an unreasonable stop and frisk. The government contends that the officer's actions were in compliance with the Fourth Amendment.

How should the trial court rule?

5A–18: At around 1:30 a.m., on January 24, York City police officers received a radio call of "shots fired" in the 700 block of West King Street. The area was known as a "very high crime area." Shortly thereafter, a second radio transmission reported that two victims of the shooting had been taken away in a private vehicle. Officer Kolt, a uniformed policeman in a marked car, responded immediately. As he approached the area, he saw five African-American men walking approximately one block from the reported crime scene. Except for these men, the streets were deserted. Kolt stopped his car and asked the men to "hold up." Two of the men stopped. They were frisked, questioned and released. Three of the men, however, continued to walk. Kolt radioed a description of the three men, stating that one of the men was wearing a black leather jacket and bright white knit cap.

Uniformed officer Ross was on patrol in a marked car. As he was responding to the "shots fired" call, he heard Kolt radio that three potential suspects were walking east along West Princess Street. Within seconds, Ross saw a man wearing a black leather jacket and a bright white knit cap on West Princess Street, near the crime scene. When Ross stopped his car, the man turned and ran into an alley. Ross reported this information by radio. Shortly thereafter, Kolt radioed that he had just seen the man in the black jacket and white cap enter Gus's Bar. Ross went into the bar and saw a white knit cap next to a man wearing a black leather jacket. The man, Mr. Row, stated that the cap was his. Kolt entered the bar and identified Row as one of the men who had walked away from him earlier in the evening. The officers then frisked Row and found an unloaded, sawed-off .22-caliber rifle. They arrested him. Row was subsequently charged with two counts of illegal firearm possession.

Did the officers have justification for the actions that led to the discovery of the rifle?

5A–19: A Sheriff's Department dispatcher, took a 911 call at 10:23 p.m. from a man who did not give his name. The caller said that a man named "Conrado" had come to the caller's house and had stated he was going to shoot his (Conrado's) wife. The caller said Conrado had a "steel colored" revolver and that it was "strapped to his back." He described Conrado as about 40, thin, Hispanic, and wearing a white shirt and dark pants. The caller, who was calling from his car, indicated that he had been following Conrado's truck, but could no longer see it. He described the truck as a full-size white Ford with a green stripe and a long bed and "the letters GTO painted on the side." He furnished Conrado's wife's address and claimed that Conrado was driving toward her street. He also gave the wife's name, described her as Hispanic and in her forties, and stated that she was then at home with her daughters. The caller's wife had just called Conrado's wife to warn her. The dispatcher asked whether Conrado and his wife were "going through a divorce or something." The caller replied that "apparently they were split up," but he did not "know the whole details

490 5 · THE BALANCING APPROACH TO 4TH AMENDMENT REASONABLENESS

about it." When the dispatcher asked for the caller's name, he declined to give it and said, "I just don't want her hurt and I don't want to get involved."

The contents of the call were relayed to the Highway Patrol (HP). Shortly after the information was dispatched, HP officers located and stopped Conrado's truck. The officers ordered Conrado and his two passengers, Debra and Felix, to get out of the truck. The officers then saw the butt of a .22 caliber handgun protruding from a bag inside the car. They also found 10 rounds of .22 caliber ammunition in Conrado's pocket. Subsequently, it was determined that this ammunition fit the gun found in the truck.

Conrado was charged with one count of possession of a firearm by a person with prior offenses. Conrado filed a motion to suppress all the fruits of the stop, arguing that the stop was unreasonable under the Fourth Amendment.

Was the stop unreasonable?

5A–20: Officer Johnson was on patrol when he stopped a vehicle with a broken taillight. Zach Hen was the driver. His brother, Jeremy Hen, was a passenger in the vehicle. Officer Johnson conversed with Zach about the taillight. Sergeant Baker, who arrived shortly after the initial stop, approached Jeremy while he was still in the vehicle. Baker told Jeremy that he was not under arrest and was free to go, but that he (Baker) wanted to talk to him "about some things." Jeremy was "nervous, but real cooperative and polite." He agreed to answer Baker's questions.

Jeremy got out of the vehicle and Baker asked if he could search the vehicle. Jeremy declined, stating that the vehicle belonged to his father. Baker then asked Jeremy if he had any contraband on his person and Jeremy responded that he had a knife. Baker proceeded to perform a pat down search of Jeremy, finding and removing the knife. Baker then continued to pat Jeremy down. He felt a large hard object in one of Jeremy's cargo pockets. When asked what the object was, Jeremy replied that he did not know. Baker reached into the pocket and removed a glass pipe and a cigar tube. Baker opened the cigar tube and found a white rock later identified as methamphetamine.

Jeremy was subsequently cited for possession of a controlled substance and drug paraphernalia. He moved to suppress the contraband, contending that Sergeant Baker had violated the Fourth Amendment. When the district court denied the motion to suppress, Jeremy entered a guilty plea. However, he reserved the right to appeal the denial of his motion to suppress.

Should an appellate court reverse the denial of the motion to suppress?

5A–21: City Police Department ("CPD") Officers Toff and Wiles were on patrol near downtown in a marked police car. Several times during their patrol, they passed by a shopping center located in an area from which the police department received many complaints pertaining to robberies, thefts, drug activity, and loitering. The officers noticed a distinct group of people in the parking lot — people who were not going in or out of the stores, but were "simply gathered in the lot." They also saw a man on a bicycle riding back and forth across the lot. Because the people remained in the lot for an extended time, the officers decided to address what they considered to be a "loitering problem."

Sometime before the officers took action, Peter, an African-American man, arrived at the shopping center on his bicycle. He was not a member of the group suspected of loitering. Peter entered a grocery store and purchased a snack and a bottled water. He stopped for three or four minutes in the lot to consume the snack and water. At about the same time, Officers Toff and Wiles summoned two other police cars and a CPD helicopter to the area. The officers assembled down the street to discuss a "strategy" to deal with the loiterers. Their plan was to "bum rush" the lot with several ground units and a helicopter in order to round up the group suspected of loitering. The officers in the cars planned to position themselves to prevent any member of the group in the lot from fleeing on foot, while officers in the helicopter intended to hover overhead to watch in case anyone did flee.

As Toff and Wiles approached the shopping center, they saw an African-American male on a bicycle. They thought it was the same man they had seen riding back and forth in the lot earlier. In fact, it was Peter. He was "pedaling normally" toward an exit. Wiles rolled down his car window and "asked to speak with Peter." Peter did not respond, but "began to wander away on his bike." Toff pulled the police car onto a grassy area in the lot, effectively blocking Peter from exiting into the street. When Peter stopped, the officers got out, intending "to talk to him." Peter looked at them, dropped his bike, and started running. As he ran, he "clutched the right front pocket of his shorts." The officers chased him into an alley and caught him. Upon searching his person, they discovered a .22 caliber handgun in the right front pocket of his shorts. They transported Peter to the police station and, subsequently, charged him with being a felon in possession of a firearm. Before trial, Peter moved to suppress the gun, claiming that he was unreasonably seized.

How should the court rule on Peter's claim?

[4] The Permissible Scope of "Stops," "Frisks," and "Sweeps"

Hayes v. Florida

United States Supreme Court

470 U.S. 811, 105 S. Ct. 1643, 84 L. Ed. 2d 705 (1985)

Justice White delivered the opinion of the Court.

. . . .

A series of burglary-rapes occurred in Punta Gorda, Florida, in 1980. Police found latent fingerprints on the doorknob of the bedroom of one of the victims, fingerprints they believed belonged to the assailant. The police also found a herringbone pattern tennis shoe print near the victim's front porch. Although they had little specific information to tie petitioner Hayes to the crime, after police interviewed him along with 30

492 5 · THE BALANCING APPROACH TO 4TH AMENDMENT REASONABLENESS

to 40 other men who generally fit the description of the assailant, the investigators came to consider petitioner a principal suspect. They decided to visit petitioner's home to obtain his fingerprints or, if he was uncooperative, to arrest him. They did not seek a warrant authorizing this procedure.

Arriving at petitioner's house, the officers spoke to petitioner on his front porch. When he expressed reluctance voluntarily to accompany them to the station for fingerprinting, one of the investigators explained that they would therefore arrest him. Petitioner, in the words of the investigator, then "blurted out" that he would rather go with the officers to the station than be arrested. While the officers were on the front porch, they also seized a pair of herringbone pattern tennis shoes in plain view.

Petitioner was then taken to the station house, where he was fingerprinted. When police determined that his prints matched those left at the scene of the crime, petitioner was placed under formal arrest. Before trial, petitioner moved to suppress the fingerprint evidence, claiming it was the fruit of an illegal detention. The trial court denied the motion and admitted the evidence without expressing a reason. Petitioner was convicted of the burglary and sexual battery committed at the scene where the latent fingerprints were found.

. . . .

We agree with petitioner that *Davis v. Mississippi*, 394 U.S. 721, 89 S. Ct. 1394, 22 L. Ed. 2d 676 (1969), requires reversal of the judgment below. In *Davis*, in the course of investigating a rape, police officers brought petitioner Davis to police headquarters on December 3, 1965. He was fingerprinted and briefly questioned before being released. He was later charged and convicted of the rape. An issue there was whether the fingerprints taken on December 3 were the inadmissible fruits of an illegal detention. Concededly, the police at that time were without probable cause for an arrest, there was no warrant, and Davis had not consented to being taken to the station house. The State nevertheless contended that the Fourth Amendment did not forbid an investigative detention for the purpose of a fingerprinting, even in the absence of probable cause or a warrant. We rejected that submission, holding that Davis's detention for the purpose of fingerprinting was subject to the constraints of the Fourth Amendment and exceeded the permissible limits of those temporary seizures authorized by *Terry v. Ohio* . . . . The Court indicated that perhaps under narrowly confined circumstances, a detention for fingerprinting on less than probable cause might comply with the Fourth Amendment, but found it unnecessary to decide that question since no effort was made to employ the procedures necessary to satisfy the Fourth Amendment. Rather, Davis had been detained at police headquarters without probable cause to arrest and without authorization by a judicial officer.

. . . .

None of our later cases have undercut the holding in *Davis* that transportation to and investigative detention at the station house without probable cause or judicial authorization together violate the Fourth Amendment. Indeed, some 10 years later, in *Dunaway v. New York*, 442 U.S. 200, 99 S. Ct. 2248, 60 L. Ed. 2d 824 (1979), we refused to extend *Terry v. Ohio* to authorize investigative interrogations at police stations on less than probable cause . . . . Since that time, we have several times revisited and explored the reach of *Terry v. Ohio* . . . . But none of these cases has sustained against Fourth Amendment challenge the involuntary removal of a suspect from his home to a police station and his detention there for investigative purposes, whether for interrogation or fingerprinting, absent probable cause or judicial authorization.

Nor are we inclined to forswear *Davis*. There is no doubt that at some point in the investigative process, police procedures can qualitatively and quantitatively be so intrusive with respect to a suspect's freedom of movement and privacy interests as to trigger the full protection of the Fourth and Fourteenth Amendments. *Dunaway*, 442 U.S., at 212, 99 S. Ct., at 2256; *Florida v. Royer*, 460 U.S. 491, 499, 103 S. Ct. 1319, 1325, 75 L. Ed. 2d 229 (1983) (plurality opinion). And our view continues to be that the line is crossed when the police, without probable cause or a warrant, forcibly remove a person from his home or other place in which he is entitled to be and transport him to the police station, where he is detained, although briefly, for investigative purposes. We adhere to the view that such seizures, at least where not under judicial supervision, are sufficiently like arrests to invoke the traditional rule that arrests may constitutionally be made only on probable cause.

None of the foregoing implies that a brief detention in the field for the purpose of fingerprinting, where there is only reasonable suspicion not amounting to probable cause, is necessarily impermissible under the Fourth Amendment . . . . There is . . . support in our cases for the view that the Fourth Amendment would permit seizures for the purpose of fingerprinting, if there is reasonable suspicion that the suspect has committed a criminal act, if there is a reasonable basis for believing that fingerprinting will establish or negate the suspect's connection with that crime, and if the procedure is carried out with dispatch. Of course, neither reasonable suspicion nor probable cause would suffice to permit the officers to make a warrantless entry into a person's house for the purpose of obtaining fingerprint identification. *Payton v. New York*, 445 U.S. 573, 100 S. Ct. 1371, 63 L. Ed. 2d 639 (1980).

We also do not abandon the suggestion in *Davis* and *Dunaway* that under circumscribed procedures, the Fourth Amendment might permit the judiciary to authorize the seizure of a person on less than probable cause and his removal to the police station for the purpose of fingerprinting. We do not, of course, have such a case before us.[3] We do note, however, that some States, in reliance on the suggestion in *Davis*, have enacted procedures for judicially authorized seizures for the purpose of fingerprinting. . . .

---

3. Nor is there any suggestion in this case that there were any exigent circumstances making necessary the removal of Hayes to the station house for the purpose of fingerprinting.

As we have said, absent probable cause and a warrant, *Davis v. Mississippi*, 394 U.S. 721, 89 S. Ct. 1394, 22 L. Ed. 2d 676 (1969), requires the reversal of the judgment of the Florida Court of Appeal.

So ordered.

JUSTICE BLACKMUN concurs in the judgment.

JUSTICE POWELL took no part in the consideration or decision in this case.

MR. JUSTICE BRENNAN, with whom MR. JUSTICE MARSHALL joins, concurring in the judgment.

. . . .

Unlike the Court in *Davis*, . . . the Court today—after tidily disposing of the case before it—returns to its regrettable assault on the Fourth Amendment by reaching beyond any issue properly before us virtually to hold that on-site fingerprinting without probable cause or a warrant is constitutionally reasonable . . . . The validity of on-site fingerprinting is no more implicated by the facts of this case than it was by *Davis*. Consequently I disagree with the Court's strained effort to reach the question today.

If the police wanted to detain an individual for on-site fingerprinting, the intrusion would have to be measured by the standards of *Terry v. Ohio*, 392 U.S. 1, 88 S. Ct. 1868, 20 L. Ed. 2d 889 (1968), and our other Fourth Amendment cases. Yet the record here contains no information useful in applying *Terry* to this hypothetical police practice. It would seem that on-site fingerprinting (apparently undertaken in full view of any passerby) would involve a singular intrusion on the suspect's privacy, an intrusion that would not be justifiable (as was the patdown in *Terry*) as necessary for the officer's protection. How much time would elapse before the individual would be free to go? Could the police hold the individual until the fingerprints could be compared with others? . . .

. . . I disagree with the Court's apparent attempt to render an advisory opinion concerning the Fourth Amendment implications of a police practice that, as far as we know, has never been attempted by the police in this or any other case.

Notes and Questions

In *Hayes*, the police clearly had a factual basis for suspecting that the defendant had been involved in the burglary-rapes.

(1) Why wasn't the method chosen to secure his fingerprints reasonable? If officers had been able to complete the transportation of the defendant and the fingerprinting within five minutes, would it have been permissible?

(2) Assuming that the officers could not discover any additional facts indicative of defendant's involvement in the crimes, would any of the following methods of securing his fingerprints have been constitutional?

(a) Asking the defendant if he would agree to accompany the officers to the station for fingerprinting, and taking him there after he agreed.

(b) Taking the defendant to the police station on the basis of a court order issued by a magistrate authorizing the officers to do so.

(c) Detaining the defendant on the street briefly and taking his fingerprints at the site of the detention.

(d) Detaining the defendant on the street for 90 minutes, the time it takes for other officers to respond to a request to bring fingerprinting equipment to the site of the detention.

(e) Taking the defendant to a printing shop three blocks from the original site of his detention, and "informally" taking his fingerprints with an ink pad borrowed from the proprietor.

(3) The question addressed in *Hayes* and in *Davis* and *Dunaway*, the two prior decisions that involved forcible transportation of a suspect to a police station, was whether a seizure was sufficiently intrusive to constitute a *de facto* arrest. This issue is raised whenever an individual claims that an officer exceeded the scope of the liberty deprivation that is permissible during a *Terry* detention. Once a seizure crosses the line that separates limited "stops" from full "arrests," probable cause is necessary to render it reasonable.

In the opinions in subsection 5[A][2], the Justices announced a general standard for determining whether officers have seized an individual at all. In no Fourth Amendment case, however, has the Court announced a general standard for deciding whether an infringement upon freedom is sufficiently limited to fall within the *Terry* detention category or, instead, crosses the line and, in substance, constitutes an arrest. *Miranda* doctrine decisions, however, do provide a standard that surely governs in the Fourth Amendment arena. Under *Miranda*, custody is a key concept. The Justices have equated custody with arrest, holding that a person is in custody when officers subject him or her to either a "formal arrest" or "the functional equivalent of formal arrest." *Berkemer v. McCarty*, 468 U.S. 420, 104 S. Ct. 3138, 82 L. Ed. 2d 317 (1984). Restrictions on liberty are the functional equivalent of a formal arrest when "a reasonable [person] in the suspect's position" would believe that his or her "freedom of action [has been] curtailed to a 'degree associated with a formal arrest.'" *Id.* Put otherwise, a *de facto* arrest occurs when a reasonable person would conclude that he or she has been "subjected to restraints comparable to those associated with a formal arrest." *Id.*

United States v. Sharpe

United States Supreme Court

470 U.S. 675, 105 S. Ct. 1568, 84 L. Ed. 2d 605 (1985)

CHIEF JUSTICE BURGER delivered the opinion of the Court.

. . . .

I

A

496 5 · THE BALANCING APPROACH TO 4TH AMENDMENT REASONABLENESS

On the morning of June 9, 1978, Agent Cooke of the Drug Enforcement Administration (DEA) was on patrol in an unmarked vehicle on a coastal road near Sunset Beach, North Carolina, an area under surveillance for suspected drug trafficking. At approximately 6:30 a.m., Cooke noticed a blue pickup truck with an attached camper shell traveling on the highway in tandem with a blue Pontiac Bonneville. Respondent Savage was driving the pickup, and respondent Sharpe was driving the Pontiac. The Pontiac also carried a passenger, Davis, the charges against whom were later dropped. Observing that the truck was riding low in the rear and that the camper did not bounce or sway appreciably when the truck drove over bumps or around curves, Agent Cooke concluded that it was heavily loaded. A quilted material covered the rear and side windows of the camper.

Cooke's suspicions were sufficiently aroused to follow the two vehicles for approximately 20 miles as they proceeded south into South Carolina. He then decided to make an "investigative stop" and radioed the State Highway Patrol for assistance. Officer Thrasher, driving a marked patrol car, responded to the call. Almost immediately after Thrasher caught up with the procession, the Pontiac and the pickup turned off the highway and onto a campground road. Cooke and Thrasher followed the two vehicles as the latter drove along the road at 55 to 60 miles an hour, exceeding the speed limit of 35 miles an hour. The road eventually looped back to the highway, onto which Savage and Sharpe turned and continued to drive south.

At this point, all four vehicles were in the middle lane of the three right-hand lanes of the highway. Agent Cooke asked Officer Thrasher to signal both vehicles to stop. Thrasher pulled alongside the Pontiac, which was in the lead, turned on his flashing light, and motioned for the driver of the Pontiac to stop. As Sharpe moved the Pontiac into the right lane, the pickup truck cut between the Pontiac and Thrasher's patrol car, nearly hitting the patrol car, and continued down the highway. Thrasher pursued the truck while Cooke pulled up behind the Pontiac.

Cooke approached the Pontiac and identified himself. He requested identification, and Sharpe produced a Georgia driver's license bearing the name of Raymond J. Pavlovich. Cooke then attempted to radio Thrasher to determine whether he had been successful in stopping the pickup truck, but he was unable to make contact for several minutes, apparently because Thrasher was not in his patrol car. Cooke radioed the local police for assistance, and two officers from the Myrtle Beach Police Department arrived about 10 minutes later. Asking the two officers to "maintain the situation," Cooke left to join Thrasher.

In the meantime, Thrasher had stopped the pickup truck about one-half mile down the road. After stopping the truck, Thrasher had approached it with his revolver drawn, ordered the driver, Savage, to get out and assume a "spread eagled" position against the side of the truck, and patted him down. Thrasher then holstered his gun and asked Savage for his driver's license and the truck's vehicle registration. Savage produced his own Florida driver's license and a bill of sale for the truck bearing the name of Pavlovich. In response to questions from Thrasher concerning the ownership of the truck, Savage said that the truck belonged to a friend and that he was taking it to have its shock absorbers repaired. When Thrasher told Savage that he would be held until the arrival of Cooke, whom Thrasher identified as a DEA agent, Savage became nervous, said that he wanted to leave, and requested the return of his driver's license. Thrasher replied that Savage was not free to leave at that time.

Agent Cooke arrived at the scene approximately 15 minutes after the truck had been stopped. Thrasher handed Cooke Savage's license and the bill of sale for the truck; Cooke noted that the bill of sale bore the same name as Sharpe's license. Cooke identified himself to Savage as a DEA agent and said that he thought the truck was loaded with marihuana. Cooke twice sought permission to search the camper, but Savage declined to give it, explaining that he was not the owner of the truck. Cooke then stepped on the rear of the truck and, observing that it did not sink any lower, confirmed his suspicion that it was probably overloaded. He put his nose against the rear window, which was covered from the inside, and reported that he could smell marihuana. Without seeking Savage's permission, Cooke removed the keys from the ignition, opened the rear of the camper, and observed a large number of burlap-wrapped bales resembling bales of marihuana that Cooke had seen in previous investigations. Agent Cooke then placed Savage under arrest and left him with Thrasher.

Cooke returned to the Pontiac and arrested Sharpe and Davis. Approximately 30 to 40 minutes had elapsed between the time Cooke stopped the Pontiac and the time he returned to arrest Sharpe and Davis. Cooke assembled the various parties and vehicles and led them to the Myrtle Beach police station. That evening, DEA agents took the truck to the Federal Building in Charleston, South Carolina. Several days later, Cooke supervised the unloading of the truck, which contained 43 bales weighing a total of 2,629 pounds. Acting without a search warrant, Cooke had eight randomly selected bales opened and sampled. Chemical tests showed that the samples were marihuana.

B

Sharpe and Savage were charged with possession of a controlled substance with intent to distribute it . . . . The United States District Court for the District of South Carolina denied respondents' motion to suppress the contraband, and respondents were convicted.

A divided panel of the Court of Appeals for the Fourth Circuit reversed the convictions.

. . . .

II

A

. . . In *Terry v. Ohio*, 392 U.S. 1, 88 S. Ct. 1868, 20 L. Ed. 2d 889 (1968), we adopted a dual inquiry for evaluating the reasonableness of an investigative stop. Under this approach, we examine whether the officer's action was justified at its inception, and whether it was reasonably related in scope to the circumstances which justified the interference in the first place.

Id., at 20, 88 S. Ct., at 1879.

As to the first part of this inquiry, the Court of Appeals assumed that the police had an articulable and reasonable suspicion that Sharpe and Savage were engaged in marihuana trafficking, given the setting and all the circumstances when the police attempted to stop the Pontiac and the pickup. That assumption is abundantly supported by the record. As to the second part of the inquiry, however, the court concluded that the 30- to 40-minute detention of Sharpe and the 20-minute detention of Savage "failed to meet the [Fourth Amendment's] requirement of brevity."

. . . .

It is not necessary for us to decide whether the length of Sharpe's detention was unreasonable, because that detention bears no causal relation to Agent Cooke's discovery of the marihuana . . . . The only issue in this case, then, is whether it was reasonable under the circumstances facing Agent Cooke and Officer Thrasher to detain Savage, whose vehicle contained the challenged evidence, for approximately 20 minutes. . . .

The Court of Appeals did not question the reasonableness of Officer Thrasher's or Agent Cooke's conduct during their detention of Savage. Rather, the court concluded that the length of the detention alone transformed it from a *Terry* stop into a *de facto* arrest. Counsel for respondents, as *amicus curiae*, assert that conclusion as their principal argument before this Court, relying particularly upon our decisions in *Dunaway v. New York*, 442 U.S. 200, 99 S. Ct. 2248, 60 L. Ed. 2d 824 (1979); *Florida v. Royer*, 460 U.S. 491, 103 S. Ct. 1319, 75 L. Ed. 2d 229 (1983); and *United States v. Place*, 462 U.S. 696, 103 S. Ct. 2637, 77 L. Ed. 2d 110 (1983). That reliance is misplaced.

. . . *Dunaway* is simply inapposite here: the Court was not concerned with the length of the defendant's detention, but with events occurring during the detention.

In *Royer*, . . . the focus was primarily on facts other than the duration of the defendant's detention — particularly the fact that the police confined the defendant in a small airport room for questioning.

The plurality in *Royer* did note that "an investigative detention must be temporary and last no longer than is necessary to effectuate the purpose of the stop." 460 U.S., at 500, 103 S. Ct., at 1325. The Court followed a similar approach in *Place*. . . . We decided that an investigative seizure of personal property could be justified under the *Terry* doctrine, but that "[t]he length of the detention of respondent's luggage alone precludes the conclusion that the seizure was reasonable in the absence of probable cause." 462 U.S., at 709, 103 S. Ct., at 2645. However, the rationale underlying that conclusion was premised on the fact that the police knew of respondent's arrival time for several hours beforehand, and the Court assumed that the police could have arranged for a trained narcotics dog in advance and thus avoided the necessity of holding respondent's luggage for 90 minutes. "[I]n assessing the effect of the length of the detention, we take into account whether the police diligently pursue their investigation." *Id.; see also Royer*, 460 U.S., at 500, 103 S. Ct., at 1325.

Here, the Court of Appeals did not conclude that the police acted less than diligently, or that they *unnecessarily* prolonged Savage's detention. *Place* and *Royer* thus provide no support for the Court of Appeals' analysis.

Admittedly, *Terry, Dunaway, Royer*, and *Place*, considered together, may in some instances create difficult line-drawing problems in distinguishing an investigative stop from a *de facto* arrest. Obviously, if an investigative stop continues indefinitely, at some point it can no longer be justified as an investigative stop. But our cases impose no rigid time limitation on *Terry* stops. While it is clear that "the brevity of the invasion of the individual's Fourth Amendment interests is an important factor in determining whether the seizure is so minimally intrusive as to be justifiable on reasonable suspicion," *United States v. Place*, 462 U.S., at 709, 103 S. Ct., at 2645, we have emphasized the need to consider the law enforcement purposes to be served by the stop as well as the time reasonably needed to effectuate those purposes. Much as a "bright line" rule would be desirable, in evaluating whether an investigative detention is unreasonable, common sense and ordinary human experience must govern over rigid criteria.

. . . .

The Court of Appeals' decision would effectively establish a *per se* rule that a 20-minute detention is too long to be justified under the *Terry* doctrine. Such a result is clearly and fundamentally at odds with our approach in this area.

B

In assessing whether a detention is too long in duration to be justified as an investigative stop, we consider it appropriate to examine whether the police diligently pursued a means of investigation that was likely to confirm or dispel their suspicions quickly, during which time it was necessary to detain the defendant . . . . The question is not simply whether some other alternative was available, but whether the police acted unreasonably in failing to recognize or to pursue it.

We readily conclude that, given the circumstances facing him, Agent Cooke pursued his investigation in a diligent and reasonable manner. During most of Savage's 20-minute detention, Cooke was attempting to contact Thrasher and enlisting the help of the local police who remained with Sharpe while Cooke left to pursue Officer Thrasher and the pickup. Once Cooke reached Officer Thrasher and Savage,[5] he

---

5. It was appropriate for Officer Thrasher to hold Savage for the brief period pending Cooke's arrival. Thrasher could not be certain that he was aware of all of the facts that had aroused Cooke's suspicions; and, as a highway patrolman, he lacked Cooke's training and experience in dealing with narcotics investigations. In this situation, it cannot realistically be said that Thrasher, a state patrolman called in to assist a federal agent in making a stop, acted unreasonably because he did not release Savage based solely on his own limited investigation of the situation and without the consent of Agent Cooke.

proceeded expeditiously: within the space of a few minutes, he examined Savage's driver's license and the truck's bill of sale, requested (and was denied) permission to search the truck, stepped on the rear bumper and noted that the truck did not move, confirming his suspicion that it was probably overloaded. He then detected the odor of marihuana.

Clearly this case does not involve any delay unnecessary to the legitimate investigation of the law enforcement officers. Respondents presented no evidence that the officers were dilatory in their investigation. The delay in this case was attributable almost entirely to the evasive actions of Savage, who sought to elude the police as Sharpe moved his Pontiac to the side of the road. Except for Savage's maneuvers, only a short and certainly permissible pre-arrest detention would likely have taken place. The somewhat longer detention was simply the result of a "graduate[d] . . . respons[e] to the demands of [the] particular situation," *Place*, 462 U.S., at 709, n. 10, 103 S. Ct., at 2646, n. 10.

We reject the contention that a 20-minute stop is unreasonable when the police have acted diligently and a suspect's actions contribute to the added delay about which he complains. The judgment of the Court of Appeals is reversed, and the case is remanded for further proceedings consistent with this opinion.

Reversed and remanded.

JUSTICE MARSHALL, concurring in the judgment.

. . . .

I join the result in this case because only the evasive actions of the defendants here turned what otherwise would have been a permissibly brief *Terry* stop into the prolonged encounter now at issue. I write separately, however, because in my view the Court understates the importance of *Terry*'s brevity requirement to the constitutionality of *Terry* stops.

I

. . . .

Terry must be justified, not because it makes law enforcement easier, but because a *Terry* stop does not constitute the sort of arrest that the Constitution requires be made only upon probable cause.

For this reason, in reviewing any *Terry* stop, the "critical threshold issue is the intrusiveness of the seizure." *Place v. United States*, 462 U.S. 696, 722, 103 S. Ct. 2637, 2653, 77 L. Ed. 2d 110 (1983) (Blackmun, J., concurring). Regardless how efficient it may be for law enforcement officials to engage in prolonged questioning to investigate a crime, or how reasonable in light of law enforcement objectives it may be to detain a suspect until various inquiries can be made and answered, a seizure that in duration, scope, or means goes beyond the bounds of *Terry* cannot be reconciled with the Fourth Amendment in the absence of probable cause. *See Dunaway, supra*. Legitimate law enforcement interests that do not rise to the level of probable cause simply cannot turn an overly intrusive seizure into a constitutionally permissible one.

In my view, the length of the stop in and of itself may make the stop sufficiently intrusive to be unjustifiable in the absence of probable cause to arrest. *Terry* "stops" are justified, in part, because they are stops, rather than prolonged seizures. . . .

Consistent with the rationales that make *Terry* stops legitimate, we have recognized several times that the requirement that *Terry* stops be brief imposes an independent and *per se* limitation on the extent to which officials may seize an individual on less than probable cause. The Court explicitly so held in *Place*, where we invalidated a search that was the product of a lengthy detention; as the Court said: "The length of the detention . . . alone precludes the conclusion that the seizure was reasonable in the absence of probable cause . . . . [T]he 90-minute detention . . . is sufficient to render the seizure unreasonable . . . ."[3]

. . . .

The requirement that *Terry* stops be brief no matter what the needs of law enforcement in the particular case is buttressed by several sound pragmatic considerations. First, if the police know they must structure their *Terry* encounters so as to confirm or dispel the officer's reasonable suspicion in a brief time, police practices will adapt to minimize the intrusions worked by these encounters. . . .

Second, a *per se* ban on stops that are not brief yields the sort of objective standards mandated by our Fourth Amendment precedents, standards that would avoid placing courts in the awkward position of second-guessing police as to what constitutes reasonable police practice . . . . Whether the police have acted with due diligence is a function not just of how quickly they completed their investigation, but of an almost limitless set of alternative ways in which the investigation *might* have been completed. . . .

. . . The better and judicially more manageable rule would be a *per se* requirement that *Terry* stops be brief, for that rule would avoid the Court's measuring police conduct according to a virtually standardless yardstick.

Finally, dissolving the brevity requirement into the general standard that the seizure simply be reasonable will "inevitably produce friction and resentment [among the police], for there are bound to be inconsistent and confusing decisions." Schwartz, *Stop and Frisk*, 58 J. Crim. L.C. & P.S. 449 (1967) . . . . A brevity requirement makes clear that the Constitution imposes certain limitations on police powers no matter how reasonably those powers have been exercised . . . . *Terry*'s brevity requirement will instead breed respect for the law among both police and citizens.

For these reasons, fidelity to the rationales that justify *Terry* stops requires that the intrusiveness of the stop be measured independently of law enforcement needs.

---

3. The majority suggests that the 90-minute detention in *Place* was held too long only because the police had not acted diligently enough. In my view, the statements quoted in text adequately demonstrate that the length of the detention "alone" was "sufficient" to invalidate the seizure.

A stop must first be found not unduly intrusive, particularly in its length, before it is proper to consider whether law enforcement aims warrant limited investigation.

II

We have had little occasion to specify the length to which a stop can be extended before it can no longer be justified on less than probable cause. . . .

. . . While a *Terry* stop must be brief no matter what the needs of the authorities, I agree that *Terry*'s brevity requirement is not to be judged by a stopwatch but rather by the facts of particular stops. At the same time, the time it takes to "briefly stop [the] person, ask questions, or check identification," *United States v. Hensley*, and, if warranted, to conduct a brief pat-down for weapons, is typically just a few minutes. In my view, anything beyond this short period is presumptively a *de facto* arrest. That presumption can be overcome by showing that a lengthier detention was not unduly intrusive for some reason; as in this case, for example, the suspects, rather than the police, may have prolonged the stop. It cannot, however, be overcome simply by showing that police needs required a more intrusive stop. For that reason, I regard [a] suggested maximum of 20 minutes as too long; "any suggestion that the *Terry* reasonable suspicion standard justifies anything but the briefest of detentions or the most limited of searches finds no support in the *Terry* line of cases." *Royer, supra* (Brennan, J., concurring).

. . . [T]he very least that ought to be true of *Terry*'s brevity requirement is that, if the initial encounter provides no greater grounds for suspicion than existed before the stop, the individual must be free to leave after the few minutes permitted for the initial encounter. . . .

III

In light of these principles, I cannot join the Court's opinion. The Court offers a hodgepodge of reasons to explain why the 20-minute stop at issue here was permissible. At points we are told that the stop was no longer than "necessary" and that the police acted "diligently" in pursuing their investigation, all of which seems to suggest that, as long as a stop is no longer than necessary to the "legitimate investigation of the law enforcement officers," the stop is perfectly lawful. As I have just argued, such reasoning puts the horse before the cart by failing to focus on the critical threshold question of the intrusiveness of the stop, particularly its length. . . .

Fortunately, it is unnecessary to try to sort all of this out, for another rationale offered by the Court adequately disposes of this case. As the Court recognizes: "The delay in this case was attributable almost entirely to the evasive actions of Savage, who sought to elude the police as Sharpe moved his Pontiac to the side of the road. Except for Savage's maneuvers, only a short and certainly permissible pre-arrest detention would likely have taken place." With that holding I agree . . . . While a 20-minute stop would, under most circumstances, be longer than the limited intrusion entailed by the brief stop that *Terry* allows, I believe such a stop is permissible when a suspect's own actions are the primary cause for prolonging an encounter beyond the bounds to which *Terry*'s brevity requirement ordinarily limits such stops. Nothing more is necessary to decide this case, and any further suggestions in the Court's opinion I find unwarranted, confusing, and potentially corrosive of the principles upon which *Terry* is grounded.

. . . .

V

In my view, the record demonstrates that the lengthy stop at issue in this case would have been permissibly brief but for the respondents' efforts to evade law enforcement officials. Accordingly, I agree with the Court's judgment. But because there is no way to fathom the extent to which the majority's holding rests on this basis, and because the majority acts with unseemly haste to decide other issues not presented, I join only its judgment.

JUSTICE BRENNAN, dissenting.

I dissent. I have previously expressed my views on the permissible scope and duration of *Terry* stops, and need not recount those views in detail today.

. . . .

II

The Court's opinion is flawed in [a] critical respect: its discussion of Savage's purported attempt "to elude the police" amounts to nothing more than a *de novo* factual finding made on a record that is, at best, hopelessly ambiguous. . . .

. . . Neither Cooke nor Thrasher ever testified that Savage "sought to elude" them, and there is nothing here that is necessarily inconsistent with the actions of any motorist who happens to be behind a vehicle that is being pulled over to the side of the road.

. . . .

Today's opinion unfortunately is representative of a growing number of instances in which the Court is willing to make *de novo* factual findings in criminal cases where convenient to support its decisions. . . .

III
A

Because it has not been shown that Savage "sought to elude" the police, I agree with the Court that the constitutional propriety of these detentions is governed by *Terry* and its progeny. These precedents lead inexorably to the conclusion that the investigative actions at issue here violated the Fourth Amendment. As the Fourth Circuit emphasized, the lengthy detentions of Sharpe and Savage did not accord with *Terry*'s threshold brevity requirement. But even if the length of these detentions did not *alone* compel affirmance of the Fourth Circuit's judgment, the Court today has evaded a further requirement of our *Terry* precedents: that "the investigative methods employed should be the least intrusive means reasonably available to verify or dispel the officer's suspicion in a short period of time," and that the Government bears the burden of demonstrating that it was objectively infeasible to investigate "in a more expeditious way." *Florida v. Royer*, 460 U.S., at 500, 505, 103 S. Ct., at 1325, 1328 (opinion of White, J.).[11] The record before us demonstrates that, for at least four reasons, the Government has not carried this burden.

First. Assuming that Savage did not break away from the officers by taking "evasive actions" to "elude" them — in which instance this is not a *Terry* case at all — the Government has not demonstrated why two trained law enforcement officers driving in separate vehicles, both equipped with flashing lights, could not have carried out a stop of a Pontiac and a pickup truck in such a manner as to ensure that both vehicles would be stopped together. . . .

Second. If the officers believed that the suspected marihuana was in Savage's pickup truck, and if only Cooke was capable of investigating for the presence of marihuana, I am at a loss why Cooke did not follow the truck and leave Thrasher with the Pontiac, rather than vice versa.

Third. The Government has offered no plausible explanation why Thrasher, a trained South Carolina highway patrolman, could not have carried out the limited *Terry* investigation of Savage and the pickup truck.

. . . .

Finally. The record strongly suggests that the delay may have been attributable in large measure to the poor investigative coordination and botched communications on the part of the DEA. . . .

Far from demonstrating that these investigative stops were carried out in the most "expeditious way" using all "reasonably available" investigative methods, *Florida v. Royer*, 460 U.S., at 500, 505, 103 S. Ct., at 1325, 1328 (opinion of White, J.), the record in this case therefore strongly suggests custodial detentions more accurately characterized as resulting from hopelessly bungled communications and from Thrasher's unwillingness to tread on Cooke's investigative turf. . . .

B

. . . .

Terry's brevity requirement . . . functions as an important constitutional safeguard that prevents an investigative stop from being transformed into a custodial detention merely because "the law enforcement purposes to be served by the stop" are considered important. Absent a rigorously enforced brevity requirement, the *Terry* rationale "would threaten to swallow the general rule that Fourth Amendment seizures are "reasonable' only if based on probable cause." *Dunaway v. New York*, 442 U.S., at 212–213, 99 S. Ct., at 2256–2257 . . . . And while it may be tempting to relax these requirements when a defendant is believed to be guilty, the standards we

---

11. As I have previously argued, I do not believe that "the absence of a less intrusive means can make an otherwise unreasonable stop reasonable." *Florida v. Royer*, 460 U.S., at 511, n. *, 103 S. Ct., at 1331 n. * (concurring in result).

prescribe for the guilty define the authority of the police in detaining the innocent as well.

. . . .

IV

Justice Douglas, the lone dissenter in *Terry*, warned that "[t]here have been powerful hydraulic pressures throughout our history that bear heavily on the Court to water down constitutional guarantees and give the police the upper hand." 392 U.S., at 39, 88 S. Ct., at 1889. Those hydraulic pressures are readily apparent in the outcome of this case . . . . I dissent.

[The dissenting opinion of JUSTICE STEVENS has been omitted.]

Notes and Questions

(1) After *Sharpe*, is there any time limit on the length of a *Terry* detention? If so, what is that limit?

The Court's decision in *United States v. Montoya de Hernandez*, 473 U.S. 531, 105 S. Ct. 3304, 87 L. Ed. 2d 381 (1985), sheds additional light on this question. In that case, the defendant arrived at Los Angeles International Airport on a direct flight from Bogota, Colombia. Customs agents' inquiries and investigation led to a reasonable suspicion that she was concealing narcotics-filled balloons in her alimentary canal in order to smuggle them into the United States. Defendant's refusal to consent to an X-ray resulted in an approximately 16-hour detention during which the customs agents awaited a bowel movement. Ultimately, the suspect excreted 88 balloons filled with narcotics.

The Court observed that the "length of time undoubtedly exceed[ed] any other detention we have approved under reasonable suspicion." Nevertheless, the Court concluded that "the detention in this case was not unreasonably long." The Court relied on the facts: (1) that the detention had occurred at the international border, where the Fourth Amendment's demands are considerably less stringent; (2) that alimentary canal smuggling, by its nature, "cannot be detected in the amount of time in which other illegal activity may be investigated through brief *Terry*-type stops"; (3) that, because the defendant refused to submit to an X-ray, the only alternatives were a lengthy detention or the release of a person reasonably suspected of narcotics smuggling; and (4) that defendant's own "heroic" efforts to resist a bowel movement extended the period of the detention. According to the majority, in these circumstances the exceptionally lengthy detention was "necessary to either verify or dispel the [agents' reasonable] suspicion."

(2) A related issue that the Court has adverted to on more than one occasion is whether officers must, during a *Terry* detention, use the "least intrusive means" available to conduct their investigation. In *Florida v. Royer*, 460 U.S. 491, 103 S. Ct. 1319, 75 L. Ed. 2d 229 (1983), the plurality opinion suggested such a requirement. Speaking for four members of the Court, Justice White observed that in a *Terry* detention

"the investigative methods employed should be the least intrusive means reasonably available to verify or dispel the officer's suspicion in a short period of time." Although he did not join the plurality opinion, Justice Brennan agreed that "the availability of a less intrusive means may make an otherwise reasonable stop unreasonable."

Despite this apparent acceptance of a "least intrusive alternative" requirement, in *United States v. Sokolow*, 490 U.S. 1, 109 S. Ct. 1581, 104 L. Ed. 2d 1 (1989), the majority concluded that the "reasonableness of [an] officer's *decision to stop a suspect* does not turn on the availability of less intrusive investigatory techniques. Such a rule would unduly hamper the police's ability to make swift on-the-spot decisions . . . and it would require courts to 'indulge in "unrealistic second-guessing."'" (Emphasis added; citation omitted.) The majority asserted that the above-quoted statement from the *Royer* plurality opinion "was directed at the *length* of the investigative stop, not at whether the police had a less intrusive means to verify their suspicions *before stopping*" the suspect. (Emphasis added.)

(3) *Hiibel v. Sixth Judicial District Court of Nevada, Humboldt County*, 542 U.S. 177, 124 S. Ct. 2451, 159 L. Ed. 2d 292 (2004), resolved a longstanding issue concerning the permissible scope of an investigative detention. By a 5-4 vote, the Court held that it was not unreasonable for officers to require a suspect who is being lawfully detained to identify himself. Like the law of many states, Nevada law includes a "stop and identify" provision. According to the statute, a person properly detained for investigation "shall identify himself, but may not be compelled to answer any other inquiry." When Hiibel, who was under investigation for a suspected assault, refused to respond to an officer's request for identification, the officer arrested him. Based on his refusal to identify himself, Hiibel was charged with and convicted of "willfully resist[ing], delay[ing], or obstruct[ing] a public officer in discharging or attempting to discharge [a] legal duty." He challenged the conviction, contending that the statutory mandate that he identify himself violated both the Fourth and Fifth Amendments.

The Court first noted that Hiibel's detention "was based on reasonable suspicion." It then suggested that Nevada's "stop and identify" statute was sufficiently "narrow[]" and "precise" to avoid invalidation on "vagueness" grounds because it required "only that a suspect disclose his name" — i.e. that he either "state[] his name or communicate[] it to the officer by other means." Responding to Hiibel's Fourth Amendment challenge, the majority observed that "questions concerning a suspect's identity are a routine and accepted part of many *Terry* stops" and that "[o]btaining a suspect's name . . . serves important government interests." It then concluded that the "principles of *Terry* permit a State to require a suspect to disclose his name in the course of a *Terry* stop." According to the majority, the

> reasonableness of a seizure . . . is determined "by balancing the intrusion on . . . Fourth Amendment interests against its promotion of legitimate government interests." *Delaware v. Prouse*, 440 U.S. 648, 654 (1979). The Nevada statute satisfies that standard. The request for identity has an immediate relation to the purpose, rationale, and practical demands of a *Terry*

stop. The threat of criminal sanction helps ensure that the request for identity does not become a legal nullity. On the other hand, the Nevada statute does not alter the nature of the stop itself: it does not change its duration or its location. A state law requiring a suspect to disclose his name in the course of a valid *Terry* stop is consistent with Fourth Amendment prohibitions against unreasonable searches and seizures.

Hiibel argued that the statute "circumvents the probable cause requirement, in effect allowing an officer to arrest a person for being suspicious" and "creates a risk of arbitrary police conduct" unpermitted by the Fourth Amendment. The majority was unpersuaded, reasoning that these "concerns are met by the requirement that a *Terry* stop must be justified at its inception and 'reasonably related in scope to the circumstances which justified' the initial stop. Under these principles, an officer may not arrest a suspect for failure to identify himself if the request for identification is not reasonably related to the circumstances justifying the stop."

The majority rejected the claim that the statutory identification requirement transgressed Hiibel's Fifth Amendment privilege against self-incrimination because "in this case disclosure of [Hiibel's] name presented no reasonable danger of incrimination." The Court asserted that "[a]nswering a request to disclose a name is likely to be so insignificant in the scheme of things as to be incriminating only in unusual circumstances" and left unresolved the Fifth Amendment questions that would arise in such circumstances.

Four dissenters found merit in Hiibel's constitutional challenge.

(4) In *Rodriguez v. United States*, 575 U.S. ___, 135 S. Ct. 1609, 191 L. Ed. 2d 492 (2015), a six-Justice majority held "that a police stop exceeding the time needed to handle the matter for which the stop was made violated the Constitution's shield against unreasonable seizures." More specifically, the Court ruled that a "seizure justified only by a police-observed traffic violation . . . 'become[s] unlawful if it is prolonged beyond the time reasonably required to complete th[e] mission' of issuing a ticket for the violation." (Quoting *Illinois v. Caballes*, 543 U.S. 405, 407 (2005)).

An officer stopped a car driven by Rodriguez after seeing it "veer slowly onto the shoulder of" the highway for "seconds and then jerk back onto the road." After Rodriguez said "that he had swerved to avoid a pothole," the officer took his "license, registration, and proof of insurance," ran "a records check on" him, then asked the passenger in the car for his license, ran a records check on him as well, "and called for a second officer." He then began to write "a warning ticket for Rodriguez for driving on the shoulder," and returned to the vehicle to issue the ticket and return the mens' documents. After he completed the traffic stop's objectives, the officer "asked for permission to walk his dog around Rodriguez's vehicle. Rodriguez said no." The officer told him to turn the car off, get out, and stand in front of the patrol car to await the second officer's arrival. Minutes later, the second officer arrived. The first officer "retrieved his dog and led him twice" around the vehicle. The "dog alerted to the presence of drugs" during the second time around — "seven or eight minutes" after issuance of the warning ticket. "A search of the vehicle revealed a large bag of methamphetamine." The trial court denied Rodriguez's motion to suppress the drugs, and the court of appeals affirmed.

In an opinion authored by Justice Ginsburg and joined by Chief Justice Roberts and Justices Scalia, Breyer, Sotomayor, and Kagan, the majority reasoned that, "[l]ike a *Terry* stop, the tolerable duration of police inquiries in the traffic-stop context is determined by the seizure's 'mission' — to address the traffic violation . . . , and attend to related safety concerns." The stop may "last no longer than is necessary to effectuate th[at] purpose," and "[a]uthority for the seizure . . . ends when tasks tied to the traffic infraction are — or reasonably should have been — completed." The Court acknowledged that "unrelated investigations" are tolerable when they do "not lengthen the roadside detention," but noted that an officer may not conduct "unrelated checks . . . in a way that prolongs the stop, absent the reasonable suspicion ordinarily demanded" for a detention.

The mission of a traffic stop includes "determining whether to issue a traffic ticket" and "ordinary inquiries incident to" the stop. Those inquiries "[t]ypically . . . involve checking the driver's license, determining whether there are outstanding warrants against the driver, and inspecting the automobile's registration and proof of insurance" — all of which serve to "ensur[e] that vehicles on the road are operated safely and responsibly." In contrast, a "dog sniff" is "aimed at 'detect[ing] evidence of ordinary criminal wrongdoing'" and lacks a "close connection to roadway safety." For that reason, it "is not fairly characterized as part of the officer's traffic mission."

In response to one of the dissents, the majority pointedly observed that "[t]he critical question . . . is not whether the dog sniff occurs before or after the officer issues a ticket . . . but whether conducting the sniff 'prolongs' — *i.e.*, adds time to — 'the stop.'" Because the dog sniff in this case did prolong the traffic stop, if "reasonable suspicion of criminal activity [did not] justif[y] detaining Rodriguez beyond completion of the traffic stop infraction investigation" — a question that was "open for . . . consideration on remand" — that detention was unreasonable.

Justices Kennedy, Thomas, and Alito dissented.

The Court has made it clear that an officer who has properly detained a suspect for a traffic stop does not need additional justification to ask questions about an unrelated topic as long as those questions do not increase the length of the justified detention beyond what is justified by the traffic infraction. According to the Court, "[a]n officer's inquiries into matters unrelated to the justification for the traffic stop . . . do not convert the encounter into something other than a lawful seizure, so long as those inquiries do not measurably extend the duration of the stop." *Arizona v. Johnson*, 555 U.S. 323, 129 S. Ct. 781, 172 L. Ed. 2d 694 (2009). Unrelated questioning alone does not increase the intrusion upon a motorist's Fourth Amendment interests in any way that requires justification. The same principle surely allows officers to ask unrelated questions during investigatory *Terry* detentions based upon reasonable suspicion of criminal activity.

United States v. Place

United States Supreme Court

462 U.S. 696, 103 S. Ct. 2637, 77 L. Ed. 2d 110 (1983)

JUSTICE O'CONNOR delivered the opinion of the Court.

. . . .

I

Respondent Raymond J. Place's behavior aroused the suspicions of law enforcement officers as he waited in line at the Miami International Airport to purchase a ticket to New York's LaGuardia Airport. As Place proceeded to the gate for his flight, the agents approached him and requested his airline ticket and some identification. Place complied with the request and consented to a search of the two suitcases he had checked. Because his flight was about to depart, however, the agents decided not to search the luggage.

Prompted by Place's parting remark that he had recognized that they were police, the agents inspected the address tags on the checked luggage and noted discrepancies in the two street addresses. Further investigation revealed that neither address existed and that the telephone number Place had given the airline belonged to a third address on the same street. On the basis of their encounter with Place and this information, the Miami agents called Drug Enforcement Administration (DEA) authorities in New York to relay their information about Place.

Two DEA agents waited for Place at the arrival gate at LaGuardia Airport in New York. There again, his behavior aroused the suspicion of the agents. After he had claimed his two bags and called a limousine, the agents decided to approach him. They identified themselves as federal narcotics agents, to which Place responded that he knew they were "cops" and had spotted them as soon as he had deplaned. One of the agents informed Place that, based on their own observations and information obtained from the Miami authorities, they believed that he might be carrying narcotics. After identifying the bags as belonging to him, Place stated that a number of police at the Miami Airport had surrounded him and searched his baggage. The agents responded that their information was to the contrary. The agents requested and received identification from Place — a New Jersey driver's license, on which the agents later ran a computer check that disclosed no offenses, and his airline ticket receipt. When Place refused to consent to a search of his luggage, one of the agents told him that they were going to take the luggage to a federal judge to try to obtain a search warrant and that Place was free to accompany them. Place declined, but obtained from one of the agents telephone numbers at which the agents could be reached.

The agents then took the bags to Kennedy Airport, where they subjected the bags to a "sniff test" by a trained narcotics detection dog. The dog reacted positively to the smaller of the two bags but ambiguously to the larger bag. Approximately 90 minutes had elapsed since the seizure of respondent's luggage. Because it was late on a

Friday afternoon, the agents retained the luggage until Monday morning, when they secured a search warrant from a magistrate for the smaller bag. Upon opening that bag, the agents discovered 1,125 grams of cocaine.

Place was indicted for possession of cocaine with intent to distribute. . . .

. . . .

II

The Fourth Amendment protects the "right of the people to be secure in their persons, houses, papers, *and effects*, against unreasonable searches and seizures." (Emphasis added.) Although in the context of personal property, and particularly containers, the Fourth Amendment challenge is typically to the subsequent search of the container rather than to its initial seizure by the authorities, our cases reveal some general principles regarding seizures. In the ordinary case, the Court has viewed a seizure of personal property as *per se* unreasonable within the meaning of the Fourth Amendment unless it is accomplished pursuant to a judicial warrant issued upon probable cause and particularly describing the items to be seized. Where law enforcement authorities have probable cause to believe that a container holds contraband or evidence of a crime, but have not secured a warrant, the Court has interpreted the Amendment to permit seizure of the property, pending issuance of a warrant to examine its contents, if the exigencies of the circumstances demand it or some other recognized exception to the warrant requirement is present. For example, "objects such as weapons or contraband found in a public place may be seized by the police without a warrant," *Payton v. New York*, 445 U.S. 573, 587, 100 S. Ct. 1371, 1380, 63 L. Ed. 2d 639 (1980), because, under these circumstances, the risk of the item's disappearance or use for its intended purpose before a warrant may be obtained outweighs the interest in possession.

In this case, the Government asks us to recognize the reasonableness under the Fourth Amendment of warrantless seizures of personal luggage from the custody of the owner on the basis of less than probable cause, for the purpose of pursuing a limited course of investigation, short of opening the luggage, that would quickly confirm or dispel the authorities' suspicion.

. . . .

We examine first the governmental interest offered as a justification for a brief seizure of luggage from the suspect's custody for the purpose of pursuing a limited course of investigation. The Government contends that, where the authorities possess specific and articulable facts warranting a reasonable belief that a traveler's luggage contains narcotics, the governmental interest in seizing the luggage briefly to pursue further investigation is substantial. We agree. As observed in *United States v. Mendenhall*, "[t]he public has a compelling interest in detecting those who would traffic in deadly drugs for personal profit." 446 U.S. 544, 561, 100 S. Ct. 1870, 1880, 64 L. Ed. 2d 497 (1980) (opinion of Powell, J.).

. . . Because of the inherently transient nature of drug courier activity at airports, allowing police to make brief investigative stops of persons at airports on reasonable suspicion of drug-trafficking substantially enhances the likelihood that police will be able to prevent the flow of narcotics into distribution channels.

Against this strong governmental interest, we must weigh the nature and extent of the intrusion upon the individual's Fourth Amendment rights when the police briefly detain luggage for limited investigative purposes. . . .

. . . The intrusion on possessory interests occasioned by a seizure of one's personal effects can vary both in its nature and extent. The seizure may be made after the owner has relinquished control of the property to a third party or, as here, from the immediate custody and control of the owner. Moreover, the police may confine their investigation to an on-the-spot inquiry—for example, immediate exposure of the luggage to a trained narcotics detection dog—or transport the property to another location. Given the fact that seizures of property can vary in intrusiveness, some brief detentions of personal effects may be so minimally intrusive of Fourth Amendment interests that strong countervailing governmental interests will justify a seizure based only on specific articulable facts that the property contains contraband or evidence of a crime.

In sum, we conclude that when an officer's observations lead him reasonably to believe that a traveler is carrying luggage that contains narcotics, the principles of *Terry* and its progeny would permit the officer to detain the luggage briefly to investigate the circumstances that aroused his suspicion, provided that the investigative detention is properly limited in scope.

The purpose for which respondent's luggage was seized, of course, was to arrange its exposure to a narcotics detection dog. Obviously, if this investigative procedure is itself a search requiring probable cause, the initial seizure of respondent's luggage for the purpose of subjecting it to the sniff test—no matter how brief—could not be justified on less than probable cause.

. . . A "canine sniff" by a well-trained narcotics detection dog . . . does not require opening the luggage. It does not expose noncontraband items that otherwise would remain hidden from public view, as does, for example, an officer's rummaging through the contents of the luggage. Thus, the manner in which information is obtained through this investigative technique is much less intrusive than a typical search. Moreover, the sniff discloses only the presence or absence of narcotics, a contraband item. Thus, despite the fact that the sniff tells the authorities something about the contents of the luggage, the information obtained is limited. This limited disclosure also ensures that the owner of the property is not subjected to the embarrassment and inconvenience entailed in less discriminate and more intrusive investigative methods.

In these respects, the canine sniff is *sui generis*. We are aware of no other investigative procedure that is so limited both in the manner in which the information is obtained and in the content of the information revealed by the procedure. Therefore, we conclude that the particular course of investigation that the agents intended to pursue here — exposure of respondent's luggage, which was located in a public place, to a trained canine — did not constitute a "search" within the meaning of the Fourth Amendment.

III

. . . .

At the outset, we must reject the Government's suggestion that the point at which probable cause for seizure of luggage from the person's presence becomes necessary is more distant than in the case of a *Terry* stop of the person himself. The premise of the Government's argument is that seizures of property are generally less intrusive than seizures of the person. While true in some circumstances, that premise is faulty on the facts we address in this case. The precise type of detention we confront here is seizure of personal luggage from the immediate possession of the suspect for the purpose of arranging exposure to a narcotics detection dog. Particularly in the case of detention of luggage within the traveler's immediate possession, the police conduct intrudes on both the suspect's possessory interest in his luggage as well as his liberty interest in proceeding with his itinerary. The person whose luggage is detained is technically still free to continue his travels or carry out other personal activities pending release of the luggage. Moreover, he is not subjected to the coercive atmosphere of a custodial confinement or to the public indignity of being personally detained. Nevertheless, such a seizure can effectively restrain the person since he is subjected to the possible disruption of his travel plans in order to remain with his luggage or to arrange for its return. Therefore, when the police seize luggage from the suspect's custody, we think the limitations applicable to investigative detentions of the person should define the permissible scope of an investigative detention of the person's luggage on less than probable cause. Under this standard, it is clear that the police conduct here exceeded the permissible limits of a *Terry*-type investigative stop.

The length of the detention of respondent's luggage alone precludes the conclusion that the seizure was reasonable in the absence of probable cause . . . . Moreover, in assessing the effect of the length of the detention, we take into account whether the police diligently pursue their investigation. We note that here the New York agents knew the time of Place's scheduled arrival at LaGuardia, had ample time to arrange for their additional investigation at that location, and thereby could have minimized the intrusion on respondent's Fourth Amendment interests. Thus, although we decline to adopt any outside time limitation for a permissible *Terry* stop, we have never approved a seizure of the person for the prolonged 90-minute period involved here and cannot do so on the facts presented by this case.

Although the 90-minute detention of respondent's luggage is sufficient to render the seizure unreasonable, the violation was exacerbated by the failure of the agents to accurately inform respondent of the place to which they were transporting his luggage, of the length of time he might be dispossessed, and of what arrangements would be made for return of the luggage if the investigation dispelled the suspicion.

In short, we hold that the detention of respondent's luggage in this case went beyond the narrow authority possessed by police to detain briefly luggage reasonably suspected to contain narcotics.

IV

We conclude that, under all of the circumstances of this case, the seizure of respondent's luggage was unreasonable under the Fourth Amendment. Consequently, the evidence obtained from the subsequent search of his luggage was inadmissible, and Place's conviction must be reversed. The judgment of the Court of Appeals, accordingly, is affirmed.

It is so ordered.

JUSTICE BRENNAN, with whom JUSTICE MARSHALL joins, concurring in the result.

. . . .

Because the Court reaches issues unnecessary to its judgment and because I cannot subscribe to the Court's analysis of those issues, I concur only in the result.

. . . .

II

. . . .

It is true that *Terry* stops may involve seizures of personal effects incidental to the seizure of the person involved. Obviously, an officer cannot seize a person without also seizing the personal effects that the individual has in his possession at the time. But there is a difference between incidental seizures of personal effects and seizures of property independent of the seizure of the person.

. . . .

In this case, the officers' seizure of respondent and their later independent seizure of his luggage implicated separate Fourth Amendment interests. First, respondent had a protected interest in maintaining his personal security and privacy. *Terry* allows this interest to be overcome, and authorizes a limited intrusion, if the officers have reason to suspect that criminal activity is afoot. Second, respondent had a protected interest in retaining possession of his personal effects. While *Terry* may authorize seizures of personal effects incident to a lawful seizure of the person, nothing in the *Terry* line of cases authorizes the police to seize personal property, such as luggage, independent of the seizure of the person. Such seizures significantly expand the scope of a *Terry* stop and may not be effected on less than probable cause. Obviously, they also significantly expand the scope of the intrusion.

. . . .

In my view, as soon as the officers seized respondent's luggage, independent of their seizure of him, they exceeded the scope of a permissible *Terry* stop and violated respondent's Fourth Amendment rights. In addition, the officers' seizure of respondent's luggage violated the established rule that seizures of personal effects must be based on probable cause. Their actions, therefore, should not be upheld.

The Court acknowledges that seizures of personal property must be based on probable cause. Despite this recognition, the Court employs a balancing test drawn from *Terry* to conclude that personal effects may be seized based on reasonable suspicion . . . . [T]he use of a balancing test in this case is inappropriate. First, the intrusion involved in this case is no longer the "narrow" one contemplated by the *Terry* line of cases. In addition, the intrusion involved in this case involves not only the seizure of a person, but also the seizure of property. As noted, *Terry* and its progeny did not address seizures of property. Those cases left unchanged the rule that seizures of property must be based on probable cause. The *Terry* balancing test should not be wrenched from its factual and conceptual moorings.

. . . .

III

The Court also suggests today, in a discussion unnecessary to the judgment, that exposure of respondent's luggage to a narcotics detection dog "did not constitute a 'search' within the meaning of the Fourth Amendment." In the District Court, respondent did "not contest the validity of sniff searches *per se*. . . ." *United States v. Place*, 498 F. Supp. 1217, 1228 (E.D.N.Y. 1980). The Court of Appeals did not reach or discuss the issue. It was not briefed or argued in this Court. In short, I agree with Justice Blackmun that the Court should not address the issue.

. . . .

Justice Blackmun, with whom Justice Marshall joins, concurring in the judgment.

. . . .

I

In providing guidance to other courts, we often include in our opinions material that, technically, constitutes dictum. I cannot fault the Court's desire to set guidelines for *Terry* seizures of luggage based on reasonable suspicion. I am concerned, however, with what appears to me to be an emerging tendency on the part of the Court to convert the *Terry* decision into a general statement that the Fourth Amendment requires only that any seizure be reasonable.

. . . While the Fourth Amendment speaks in terms of freedom from unreasonable seizures, the Amendment does not leave the reasonableness of most seizures to the judgment of courts or government officers: the Framers of the Amendment balanced the interests involved and decided that a seizure is reasonable only if supported by a judicial warrant based on probable cause.

Terry v. Ohio, however, teaches that in some circumstances a limited seizure that is less restrictive than a formal arrest may constitutionally occur upon mere reasonable suspicion, if "supported by a special law enforcement need for greater flexibility." *Florida v. Royer*, 460 U.S., at 514, 103 S. Ct., at 1333 (dissenting opinion). . . .

Because I agree with the Court that there is a significant law enforcement interest in interdicting illegal drug traffic in the Nation's airports, a limited intrusion caused by a temporary seizure of luggage for investigative purposes could fall within the *Terry* exception. The critical threshold issue is the intrusiveness of the seizure. In this case, the seizure went well beyond a minimal intrusion and therefore cannot fall within the *Terry* exception.

II

. . . .

For the foregoing reasons, I concur only in the judgment of the Court.

Notes and Questions

(1) Why was the investigatory detention in *Place* not justifiable under the *Terry* doctrine? If Place had shipped a locked suitcase to New York one week prior to his own trip, and officers had the same level of suspicion about its contents as in *Place*, would a seizure of the suitcase and a subsequent dog sniff have been constitutional? If so, how long could the officers have held the suitcase pending the sniff?

(2) Justice Brennan suggests that the seizure of an inanimate object not only falls outside the scope of the intrusion authorized by *Terry*, but that the balancing analysis underlying the *Terry* doctrine cannot justify such a seizure. The suggestion that a limited detention of an inanimate object requires probable cause while an equally limited detention of a human being can be justified by a reasonable suspicion seems counterintuitive. What constitutional reasoning could support such a conclusion?

(3) The conclusion in *Place* that the dog sniff of the luggage was not a Fourth Amendment "search" was dictum. In *City of Indianapolis v. Edmond*, an opinion included later in this chapter, *see infra* subsection 5[B][2], a majority, again in dictum, relied on *Place* to conclude that a dog sniff of the exterior of a stopped vehicle was not a search. In *Illinois v. Caballes*, 543 U.S. 405, 125 S. Ct. 834, 160 L. Ed. 2d 842 (2005), the Court finally addressed the constitutional status of a dog sniff in a case where the issue was determinative of the defendant's claim. Not surprisingly, a seven-Justice majority turned the powerful dicta in *Place* and *Edmond* into holding.

In *Caballes*, the defendant was lawfully stopped for speeding. While one officer wrote him a warning ticket, another officer walked a trained canine around his vehicle. When the dog alerted to the trunk, the officers conducted a search, found marijuana, and arrested Caballes. The Illinois Supreme Court decided that a suspicionless dog sniff during a routine traffic stop impermissibly enlarged the scope of the stop. The Supreme Court overturned that ruling, concluding that officers do not need reasonable suspicion to conduct canine sniffs of lawfully stopped vehicles.

The Court acknowledged that a vehicle seizure that is lawful at its inception can become unconstitutional "if it is prolonged beyond the time reasonably required to complete [the officer's] mission." The stop in *Caballes*, however, was not excessive in duration. According to the Court, the question of whether a dog sniff "change[s] the character of a traffic stop that is lawful at its inception and otherwise executed in a reasonable manner" depends solely upon whether a "dog sniff itself infringe[s a] constitutionally protected interest in privacy." Justice Stevens observed that the Court had already "held that any interest in possessing contraband cannot be deemed 'legitimate,'" and that "governmental conduct that *only* reveals the possession of contraband 'compromises no legitimate privacy interest.'" *Place* and *Edmond* both recognized that canine sniffs are unique insofar as they reveal *only* whether contraband is or is not present.

The defendant argued that the number of false positives by trained canines undermines the premise that they alert *only* to contraband. The Court was not persuaded. First, "the record contain[ed] no evidence or findings" supporting this argument. More significantly, the Court observed that the defendant had not suggested "that an erroneous alert, in and of itself, reveals any legitimate private information." According to the majority, "the use of a well-trained narcotics-detection dog—one that 'does not expose noncontraband items that otherwise would remain hidden from public view,' *Place*, 462 U.S., at 707—generally does not implicate legitimate privacy interests." The "intrusion" upon "privacy expectations" effected by dog sniffs simply "does not rise to the level of a constitutionally cognizable infringement." Moreover, this holding was "entirely consistent" with the conclusion that the use of a thermal imager on a home *is* a search. *See Kyllo v. United States, supra* Chapter One. "Critical to that decision was the fact that the device was capable of detecting lawful activity," including "intimate details" such as the hour at which an occupant "'takes her daily sauna and bath.'" In contrast, a "dog sniff conducted during a . . . lawful traffic stop that reveals no information other than the location of a substance that no individual has any right to possess does not violate the Fourth Amendment."

Michigan v. Long

United States Supreme Court

463 U.S. 1032, 103 S. Ct. 3469, 77 L. Ed. 2d 1201 (1983)

Justice O'Connor delivered the opinion of the Court.

. . . .

I

Deputies Howell and Lewis were on patrol in a rural area one evening when, shortly after midnight, they observed a car traveling erratically and at excessive speed. The officers observed the car turning down a side road, where it swerved off into a shallow ditch. The officers stopped to investigate. Long, the only occupant of the automobile, met the deputies at the rear of the car, which was protruding from the ditch onto the road. The door on the driver's side of the vehicle was left open.

Deputy Howell requested Long to produce his operator's license, but he did not respond. After the request was repeated, Long produced his license. Long again failed to respond when Howell requested him to produce the vehicle registration. After another repeated request, Long, whom Howell thought "appeared to be under the influence of something," 413 Mich. 461, 469, 320 N.W.2d 866, 868 (1982), turned from the officers and began walking toward the open door of the vehicle. The officers followed Long and both observed a large hunting knife on the floorboard of the driver's side of the car. The officers then stopped Long's progress and subjected him to a *Terry* protective pat-down, which revealed no weapons.

Long and Deputy Lewis then stood by the rear of the vehicle while Deputy Howell shined his flashlight into the interior of the vehicle, but did not actually enter it. The purpose of Howell's action was "to search for other weapons." *Id.*, 413 Mich. at 469, 320 N.W.2d, at 868. The officer noticed that something was protruding from under the armrest on the front seat. He knelt in the vehicle and lifted the armrest. He saw an open pouch on the front seat, and upon flashing his light on the pouch, determined that it contained what appeared to be marijuana. After Deputy Howell showed the pouch and its contents to Deputy Lewis, Long was arrested for possession of marijuana. A further search of the interior of the vehicle, including the glovebox, revealed neither more contraband nor the vehicle registration. The officers decided to impound the vehicle. Deputy Howell opened the trunk, which did not have a lock, and discovered inside it approximately 75 pounds of marijuana.

. . . .

III

. . . .

In *Terry*, the Court examined the validity of a "stop and frisk" in the absence of probable cause and a warrant. . . .

Examining the reasonableness of the officer's conduct in *Terry*, we held that there is "'no ready test for determining reasonableness other than by balancing the need to search [or seize] against the invasion which the search [or seizure] entails.'" 392 U.S., at 21, 88 S. Ct., at 1879 (quoting *Camara v. Municipal Court*, 387 U.S. 523, 536–537, 87 S. Ct. 1727, 1734–1735, 18 L. Ed. 2d 930 (1967)). . . .

Although *Terry* itself involved the stop and subsequent pat-down search of a person, we were careful to note that "[w]e need not develop at length in this case, however, the limitations which the Fourth Amendment places upon a protective search and seizure for weapons. These limitations will have to be developed in the concrete factual circumstances of individual cases." *Id.*, at 29, 88 S. Ct., at 1884. Contrary to Long's view, *Terry* need not be read as restricting the preventative search to the person of the detained suspect.

In two cases in which we applied *Terry* to specific factual situations, we recognized that investigative detentions involving suspects in vehicles are especially fraught with danger to police officers. In *Pennsylvania v. Mimms*, 434 U.S. 106, 98 S. Ct. 330, 54 L. Ed. 2d 331 (1977), we held that police may order persons out of an automobile during a stop for a traffic violation, and may frisk those persons for weapons if there is a reasonable belief that they are armed and dangerous. Our decision rested in part on the "inordinate risk confronting an officer as he approaches a person seated in an automobile." *Id.*, at 110, 98 S. Ct., at 333. In *Adams v. Williams*, 407 U.S. 143, 92 S. Ct. 1921, 32 L. Ed. 2d 612 (1972), we held that the police, acting on an informant's tip, may reach into the passenger compartment of an automobile to remove a gun from a driver's waistband even where the gun was not apparent to police from outside the car and the police knew of its existence only because of the tip. Again, our decision rested in part on our view of the danger presented to police officers in "traffic stop" and automobile situations.

Finally, we have also expressly recognized that suspects may injure police officers and others by virtue of their access to weapons, even though they may not themselves be armed. In the Term following *Terry*, we decided *Chimel v. California*, 395 U.S. 752, 89 S. Ct. 2034, 23 L. Ed. 2d 685 (1969), which involved the limitations imposed on police authority to conduct a search incident to a valid arrest . . . . We reasoned that "[a] gun on a table or in a drawer in front of one who is arrested can be as dangerous to the arresting officer as one concealed in the clothing of the person arrested." *Id.* In *New York v. Belton*, 453 U.S. 454, 101 S. Ct. 2860, 69 L. Ed. 2d 768 (1981), we determined that the lower courts "have found no workable definition of 'the area within the immediate control of the arrestee' when that area arguably includes the interior of an automobile and the arrestee is its recent occupant." *Id.*, at 460, 101 S. Ct., at 2864. In order to provide a "workable rule," *ibid.*, we held that "articles inside the relatively narrow compass of the passenger compartment of an automobile are in fact generally, even if not inevitably, within 'the area into which an arrestee might reach in order to grab a weapon' . . . ." *Id.* (quoting *Chimel, supra*, 395 U.S., at 763, 89 S. Ct., at 2040). We also held that the police may examine the contents of any open or closed container found within the passenger compartment, "for if the passenger compartment is within the reach of the arrestee, so will containers in it be within his reach." 453 U.S., at 460, 101 S. Ct., at 2864 (footnote omitted).

Our past cases indicate then that protection of police and others can justify protective searches when police have a reasonable belief that the suspect poses a danger, that roadside encounters between police and suspects are especially hazardous, and that danger may arise from the possible presence of weapons in the area surrounding a suspect. These principles compel our conclusion that the search of the passenger compartment of an automobile, limited to those areas in which a weapon may be placed or hidden, is permissible if the police officer possesses a reasonable belief based on "specific and articulable facts which, taken together with the rational inferences from those facts, reasonably warrant" the officers in believing that the suspect is dangerous and the suspect may gain immediate control of weapons.[14] *See*

---

14. We stress that our decision does not mean that the police may conduct automobile searches whenever they conduct an investigative stop, although the "bright line" that we drew in *Belton* clearly authorizes such a search whenever officers effect a custodial arrest. An additional interest exists in the arrest context, *i.e.*, preservation of evidence, and this justifies an "automatic" search. However, that additional interest does not exist in the *Terry* context. A *Terry* search, "unlike a search without a warrant incident to a lawful arrest, is not justified by any need to prevent the

Terry, 392 U.S., at 21, 88 S. Ct., at 1880. "[T]he issue is whether a reasonably prudent man in the circumstances would be warranted in the belief that his safety or that of others was in danger." *Id.*, at 27, 88 S. Ct., at 1883. If a suspect is "dangerous," he is no less dangerous simply because he is not arrested. If, while conducting a legitimate *Terry* search of the interior of the automobile, the officer should, as here, discover contraband other than weapons, he clearly cannot be required to ignore the contraband, and the Fourth Amendment does not require its suppression in such circumstances.

The circumstances of this case clearly justified Deputies Howell and Lewis in their reasonable belief that Long posed a danger if he were permitted to reenter his vehicle. The hour was late and the area rural. Long was driving his automobile at excessive speed, and his car swerved into a ditch. The officers had to repeat their questions to Long, who appeared to be "under the influence" of some intoxicant. Long was not frisked until the officers observed that there was a large knife in the interior of the car into which Long was about to reenter. The subsequent search of the car was restricted to those areas to which Long would generally have immediate control, and that could contain a weapon. The trial court determined that the leather pouch containing marijuana could have contained a weapon. It is clear that the intrusion was "strictly circumscribed by the exigencies which justifi[ed] its initiation." *Terry, supra*, 392 U.S., at 26, 88 S. Ct., at 1882.

. . . In this case, the officers did not act unreasonably in taking preventive measures to ensure that there were no other weapons within Long's immediate grasp before permitting him to reenter his automobile. Therefore, the balancing required by *Terry* clearly weighs in favor of allowing the police to conduct an area search of the passenger compartment to uncover weapons, as long as they possess an articulable and objectively reasonable belief that the suspect is potentially dangerous.

. . . Just as a *Terry* suspect on the street may, despite being under the brief control of a police officer, reach into his clothing and retrieve a weapon, so might a *Terry* suspect in Long's position break away from police control and retrieve a weapon from his automobile. In addition, if the suspect is not placed under arrest, he will be permitted to reenter his automobile, and he will then have access to any weapons inside. Or, as here, the suspect may be permitted to reenter the vehicle before the *Terry* investigation is over, and again, may have access to weapons. In any event, we stress

---

disappearance or destruction of evidence of crime . . . . The sole justification of the search . . . is the protection of police officers and others nearby . . . ." 392 U.S., at 29, 88 S. Ct., at 1884. What we borrow now from *Chimel v. California*, 395 U.S. 752, 89 S. Ct. 2034, 23 L. Ed. 2d 685 (1969) and *Belton* is merely the recognition that part of the reason to allow area searches incident to an arrest is that the arrestee, who may not himself be armed, may be able to gain access to weapons to injure officers or others nearby, or otherwise to hinder legitimate police activity. This recognition applies as well in the *Terry* context. However, because the interest in collecting and preserving evidence is not present in the *Terry* context, we require that officers who conduct area searches during investigative detentions must do so only when they have the level of suspicion identified in *Terry*.

that a *Terry* investigation, such as the one that occurred here, involves a police investigation "at close range," *Terry, supra,* 392 U.S., at 24, 88 S. Ct., at 1881, when the officer remains particularly vulnerable in part because a full custodial arrest has not been effected, and the officer must make a "quick decision as to how to protect himself and others from possible danger . . . ." *Id.,* at 28, 88 S. Ct., at 1883. In such circumstances, we have not required that officers adopt alternate means to ensure their safety in order to avoid the intrusion involved in a *Terry* encounter.

IV

The trial court and the court of appeals upheld the search of the trunk as a valid inventory search under this Court's decision in *South Dakota v. Opperman,* 428 U.S. 364, 96 S. Ct. 3092, 49 L. Ed. 2d 1000 (1976). The Michigan Supreme Court did not address this holding, and instead suppressed the marijuana taken from the trunk as a fruit of the illegal search of the interior of the automobile. Our holding that the initial search was justified under *Terry* makes it necessary to determine whether the trunk search was permissible under the Fourth Amendment. However, we decline to address this question because it was not passed upon by the Michigan Supreme Court, whose decision we review in this case. We remand this issue to the court below, to enable it to determine whether the trunk search was permissible under *Opperman, supra,* or other decisions of this Court. *See e.g., United States v. Ross,* 456 U.S. 798, 102 S. Ct. 2157, 72 L. Ed. 2d 572 (1982).

V

The decision of the Michigan Supreme Court is reversed, and the case is remanded for further proceedings not inconsistent with this opinion.

It is so ordered.

[The concurring opinion of JUSTICE BLACKMUN has been omitted.]

JUSTICE BRENNAN, with whom JUSTICE MARSHALL joins, dissenting.

. . . .

It is clear that *Terry* authorized only limited searches of the person for weapons. In light of what *Terry* said, relevant portions of which the Court neglects to quote, the Court's suggestion that "*Terry* need not be read as restricting the preventive search to the person of the detained suspect," can only be described as disingenuous. Nothing in *Terry* authorized police officers to search a suspect's car based on reasonable suspicion. The Court confirmed this this very Term in *United States v. Place, supra,* where it described the search authorized by *Terry* as a "limited search for weapons, or 'frisk' . . . ." 462 U.S., at 702, 103 S. Ct., at 2642. The search at issue in this case is a far cry from a "frisk" and certainly was not "limited."

. . . .

The critical distinction between this case and *Terry* on the one hand, and *Chimel* and *Belton* on the other, is that the latter two cases arose within the context of lawful custodial arrests supported by probable cause. The Court in *Terry* expressly recognized the difference between a search incident to arrest and the "limited search for weapons," 392 U.S., at 25, 88 S. Ct., at 1882, involved in that case.

. . . .

. . . [T]he scope of a search is determined not only by reference to its purpose, but also by reference to its intrusiveness. Yet the Court today holds that a search of a car (and the containers within it) that is not even occupied by the suspect is only as intrusive as, or perhaps less intrusive than, thrusting a hand into a pocket after an initial patdown has suggested the presence of concealed objects that might be used as weapons.

The Court suggests no limit on the "area search" it now authorizes. The Court states that a "search of the passenger compartment of an automobile, limited to those areas in which a weapon may be placed or hidden, is permissible if the police officer possesses a reasonable belief based on 'specific and articulable facts which, taken together with the rational inferences from those facts, reasonably warrant' the officers to believe that the suspect is dangerous and the suspect may gain immediate control of weapons." Presumably a weapon "may be placed or hidden" anywhere in a car. A weapon also might be hidden in a container in the car. In this case, the Court upholds the officer's search of a leather pouch because it "could have contained a weapon." In addition, the Court's requirement that an officer have a reasonable suspicion that a suspect is armed and dangerous does little to check the initiation of an area search. In this case, the officers saw a hunting knife in the car, but the Court does not base its holding that the subsequent search was permissible on the ground that possession of the knife may have been illegal under state law. An individual can lawfully possess many things that can be used as weapons. A hammer, or a baseball bat, can be used as a very effective weapon. . . . . . Even assuming that the facts in this case justified the officers' initial "frisk" of respondent, they hardly provide adequate justification for a search of a suspect's car and the containers within it. This represents an intrusion not just different in degree, but in kind, from the intrusion sanctioned by *Terry*. In short, the implications of the Court's decision are frightening.

The Court also rejects the Michigan Supreme Court's view that it "was not reasonable for the officers to fear that [respondent] could injure them, because he was effectively under their control during the investigative stop and could not get access to any weapons that might have been located in the automobile . . . ." Putting aside the fact that the search at issue here involved a far more serious intrusion than that "involved in a *Terry* encounter," and as such might suggest the need for resort to "alternate means," the Court's reasoning is perverse. The Court's argument in essence is that the *absence* of probable cause to arrest compels the conclusion that a broad search, traditionally associated in scope with a search incident to arrest, must be permitted based on reasonable suspicion. But *United States v. Robinson, supra,* stated: "It is scarcely open to doubt that the danger to an officer is far greater in the case of the extended exposure which follows the taking of a suspect into custody and transporting him to the police station than in the case of the relatively fleeting contact resulting from the typical *Terry*-type stop." 414 U.S., at 234–235, 94 S. Ct., at 476–477. . . . .

Moreover, the Court's reliance on a "balancing" of the relevant interests to justify its decision is certainly inappropriate. . . . . The intrusion involved in this case is precisely "the kind of intrusion associated with an arrest." *Id.* There is no justification, therefore, for "balancing" the relevant interests.

In sum, today's decision reflects once again the threat to Fourth Amendment values posed by "balancing."

. . . .

. . . Of course, police should not be exposed to unnecessary danger in the performance of their duties. But a search of a car and the containers within it based on nothing more than reasonable suspicion, even under the circumstances present here, cannot be sustained without doing violence to the requirements of the Fourth Amendment. There is no reason in this case why the officers could not have pursued less intrusive, but equally effective, means of insuring their safety. The Court takes a long step today toward "balancing" into oblivion the protections the Fourth Amendment affords. I dissent. . . .

[The dissenting opinion of Justice Stevens has been omitted.]

Notes and Questions

(1) How is the authority to search defined by *Long* different from the authority to conduct a warrantless search incident to arrest defined by *Chimel* and *Belton*? Could a suitcase carried by a suspect be searched under *Terry* or *Long*? If a suspect has just exited his home prior to an official detention, does the rationale of *Long* permit an officer to enter the home?

(2) *Long* voluntarily got out of his vehicle before the officers approached it. In an earlier case, *Pennsylvania v. Mimms*, 434 U.S. 106, 98 S. Ct. 330, 54 L. Ed. 2d 331 (1977), the Court was confronted with the question of whether it is permissible for an officer routinely to require a driver to get out of a vehicle during a lawful stop for a traffic infraction. Describing the interest in officer safety promoted by this practice as "legitimate and weighty" and the incremental intrusion on a lawfully stopped driver as "*de minimis*" and a "mere inconvenience," the Court concluded that the balance of interests dictated the conclusion that it is reasonable for officers to routinely order drivers to get out of their vehicles.

In *Maryland v. Wilson*, 519 U.S. 408, 117 S. Ct. 882, 137 L. Ed. 2d 41 (1997), the Supreme Court extended the *Mimms* doctrine to passengers. According to the majority, "[o]n the public interest side of the balance, the same weighty interest in officer safety is present regardless of whether the occupant of the stopped vehicle is a driver or passenger." In fact, the "danger to an officer from a traffic stop is likely to be greater when there are passengers in addition to the driver in the stopped car."

The majority conceded that "[o]n the personal liberty side of the balance, the case for passengers is in one sense stronger than that for the driver" because the passenger has not committed an offense. It nonetheless concluded that the intrusion on passengers is limited by the fact that they "are already stopped by virtue of the stop of the vehicle. The only change in their circumstances that will result from ordering them out of the car is that they will be outside of, rather than inside of, the stopped car." This "additional intrusion is minimal." Based on this assessment of the interests in the balance, the Court held "that an officer making a traffic stop may order passengers to get out of the car pending completion of the stop." The Court expressly reserved the question of whether "an officer may forcibly detain a passenger for the entire duration of the stop."

Justices Stevens and Kennedy dissented, expressing the view that a passenger may be ordered out of a lawfully stopped vehicle only "if a police officer conducting a traffic stop has an articulable suspicion of possible danger." According to them, "the Fourth Amendment prohibits [the] routine and arbitrary seizures of innocent citizens" authorized by the majority opinion in *Wilson*.

(3) In *Arizona v. Johnson*, 555 U.S. 323, 129 S. Ct. 781, 172 L. Ed. 2d 694 (2009), officers stopped a car because the vehicle registration had been suspended, a civil infraction that justified a citation. Johnson was a passenger in the rear seat. An officer asked him to get out of the car after observing suspicious behavior and receiving suspicious responses to her inquiries. Because the officer believed that Johnson might have a weapon, she patted him down and found a gun. The Arizona Court of Appeals deemed the patdown unlawful because the encounter had become "consensual," and an officer may not perform a weapons frisk during a consensual encounter even if she has reason to suspect the individual is armed and dangerous.

The Supreme Court disagreed. The Court observed that when an officer stops a vehicle for a traffic infraction, he seizes the vehicle and all of the occupants. The seizure of a passenger is lawful even though there is no additional reason to believe that he or she is "involved in criminal activity," and, because traffic stops are particularly dangerous encounters, officers may automatically remove both drivers and passengers from stopped vehicles. "To justify a patdown of [either a] driver or a passenger during a traffic stop, however, just as in the case of a pedestrian reasonably suspected of criminal activity, the police must harbor reasonable suspicion that the person subjected to the frisk is armed and dangerous."

After officers stop a vehicle to investigate a traffic violation, "[t]he temporary seizure of driver and passengers ordinarily continues, and remains reasonable, for the duration of the stop. Normally, the stop ends when the police have no further need to control the scene, and inform the driver and passengers they are free to leave."

The encounter with Johnson had *not* become consensual because "[n]othing . . . would have conveyed to [him] that, prior to the frisk, the traffic stop had ended or that he was otherwise free" to leave. The lower court assumed that the officer "had reasonable suspicion that Johnson was armed and dangerous." In these circumstances, the officer "surely was not constitutionally required to give Johnson an opportunity to depart the scene after he exited the vehicle without first ensuring that, in so doing, she was not permitting a dangerous person to get behind her." In sum, if it was based on a reasonable suspicion that Johnson was armed and dangerous, the frisk was constitutionally valid.

Minnesota v. Dickerson

United States Supreme Court

508 U.S. 366, 113 S. Ct. 2130, 124 L. Ed. 2d 334 (1993)

JUSTICE WHITE delivered the opinion of the Court.

In this case, we consider whether the Fourth Amendment permits the seizure of contraband detected through a police officer's sense of touch during a protective pat-down search.

I

On the evening of November 9, 1989, two Minneapolis police officers were patrolling an area on the city's north side in a marked squad car. At about 8:15 p.m., one of the officers observed respondent leaving a 12-unit apartment building on Morgan Avenue North. The officer, having previously responded to complaints of drug sales in the building's hallways and having executed several search warrants on the premises, considered the building to be a notorious "crack house." According to testimony credited by the trial court, respondent began walking toward the police but, upon spotting the squad car and making eye contact with one of the officers, abruptly halted and began walking in the opposite direction. His suspicion aroused, this officer watched as respondent turned and entered an alley on the other side of the apartment building. Based upon respondent's seemingly evasive actions and the fact that he had just left a building known for cocaine traffic, the officers decided to stop respondent and investigate further.

The officers pulled their squad car into the alley and ordered respondent to stop and submit to a patdown search. The search revealed no weapons, but the officer conducting the search did take an interest in a small lump in respondent's nylon jacket. The officer later testified:

> As I pat-searched the front of his body, I felt a lump, a small lump, in the front pocket. I examined it with my fingers and it slid and it felt to be a lump of crack cocaine in cellophane.

The officer then reached into respondent's pocket and retrieved a small plastic bag containing one fifth of one gram of crack cocaine. Respondent was arrested and charged in Hennepin County District Court with possession of a controlled substance.

Before trial, respondent moved to suppress the cocaine. The trial court first concluded that the officers were justified under *Terry v. Ohio*, 392 U.S. 1, 88 S. Ct. 1868, 20 L. Ed. 2d 889 (1968), in stopping respondent to investigate whether he might be engaged in criminal activity. The court further found that the officers were justified in frisking respondent to ensure that he was not carrying a weapon. Finally, analogizing to the "plain-view" doctrine, under which officers may make a warrantless seizure of contraband found in plain view during a lawful search for other items, the trial court ruled that the officers' seizure of the cocaine did not violate the Fourth Amendment . . . . His suppression motion having failed, respondent proceeded to trial and was found guilty.

On appeal, the Minnesota Court of Appeals reversed. . . .

The Minnesota Supreme Court affirmed. Like the Court of Appeals, the State Supreme Court held that both the stop and the frisk of respondent were valid under *Terry*, but found the seizure of the cocaine to be unconstitutional. . . . The court . . . appeared to adopt a categorical rule barring the seizure of any contraband detected by an officer through the sense of touch during a patdown search for weapons. . . .

We granted certiorari, 506 U.S. 814 (1992), to resolve a conflict among the state and federal courts over whether contraband detected through the sense of touch during a patdown search may be admitted into evidence. We now affirm.

II

A

. . . .

Terry . . . held that "when an officer is justified in believing that the individual whose suspicious behavior he is investigating at close range is armed and presently dangerous to the officer or to others," the officer may conduct a patdown search "to determine whether the person is in fact carrying a weapon." 392 U.S., at 24. "The purpose of this limited search is not to discover evidence of crime, but to allow the officer to pursue his investigation without fear of violence . . . ." [*Adams v. Williams*, 407 U.S. 143, 146, 92 S. Ct. 1921, 32 L. Ed. 2d 612 (1972)]. Rather, a protective search — permitted without a warrant and on the basis of reasonable suspicion less than probable cause — must be strictly "limited to that which is necessary for the discovery of weapons which might be used to harm the officer or others nearby." *Terry, supra*, at 26; *see also Michigan v. Long*, 463 U.S. 1032, 1049, and 1052, n. 16, 103 S. Ct. 3469, 77 L. Ed. 2d 1201 (1983); *Ybarra v. Illinois*, 444 U.S. 85, 93–94, 100 S. Ct. 338, 62 L. Ed. 2d 238 (1979). If the protective search goes beyond what is necessary to determine if the suspect is armed, it is no longer valid under *Terry* and its fruits will be suppressed. *Sibron v. New York*, 392 U.S. 40, 65–66, 88 S. Ct. 1889, 20 L. Ed. 2d 917 (1968).

These principles were settled 25 years ago when, on the same day, the Court announced its decisions in *Terry* and *Sibron*. The question presented today is whether police officers may seize nonthreatening contraband detected during a protective patdown search of the sort permitted by *Terry*. We think the answer is clearly that they may, so long as the officer's search stays within the bounds marked by *Terry*.

B

We have already held that police officers, at least under certain circumstances, may seize contraband detected during the lawful execution of a *Terry* search. In *Michigan v. Long, supra,* for example, police approached a man who had driven his car into a ditch and who appeared to be under the influence of some intoxicant. As the man moved to reenter the car from the roadside, police spotted a knife on the floorboard. The officers stopped the man, subjected him to a patdown search, and then inspected the interior of the vehicle for other weapons. During the search of the passenger compartment, the police discovered an open pouch containing marijuana and seized it. This Court upheld the validity of the search and seizure under *Terry.* The Court held first that, in the context of a roadside encounter, where police have reasonable suspicion based on specific and articulable facts to believe that a driver may be armed and dangerous, they may conduct a protective search for weapons not only of the driver's person but also of the passenger compartment of the automobile. 463 U.S., at 1049. Of course, the protective search of the vehicle, being justified solely by the danger that weapons stored there could be used against the officers or bystanders, must be "limited to those areas in which a weapon may be placed or hidden." *Id.* The Court then held: "If, while conducting a legitimate *Terry* search of the interior of the automobile, the officer should, as here, discover contraband other than weapons, he clearly cannot be required to ignore the contraband, and the Fourth Amendment does not require its suppression in such circumstances." *Id.*, at 1050; *accord, Sibron,* 392 U.S., at 69–70 (White, J., concurring); *id.*, at 79 (Harlan, J., concurring in result).

The Court in *Long* justified this latter holding by reference to our cases under the "plain-view" doctrine. *See Long, supra,* at 1050. Under that doctrine, if police are lawfully in a position from which they view an object, if its incriminating character is immediately apparent, and if the officers have a lawful right of access to the object, they may seize it without a warrant. *See Horton v. California,* 496 U.S. 128, 136–137, 110 S. Ct. 2301, 110 L. Ed. 2d 112 (1990); *Texas v. Brown,* 460 U.S. 730, 739, 103 S. Ct. 1535, 75 L. Ed. 2d 502 (1983) (plurality opinion). If, however, the police lack probable cause to believe that an object in plain view is contraband without conducting some further search of the object — *i.e.*, if "its incriminating character [is not] 'immediately apparent,'" *Horton, supra,* at 136 — the plain-view doctrine cannot justify its seizure. *Arizona v. Hicks,* 480 U.S. 321, 107 S. Ct. 1149, 94 L. Ed. 2d 347 (1987).

We think that this doctrine has an obvious application by analogy to cases in which an officer discovers contraband through the sense of touch during an otherwise lawful search. The rationale of the plain view doctrine is that if contraband is left in open view and is observed by a police officer from a lawful vantage point, there has been no invasion of a legitimate expectation of privacy and thus no "search" within the meaning of the Fourth Amendment — or at least no search independent of the initial intrusion that gave the officers their vantage point. The warrantless seizure of contraband that presents itself in this manner is deemed justified by the realization that resort to a neutral magistrate under such circumstances would often be impracticable and would do little to promote the objectives of the Fourth Amendment. The same can be said of tactile discoveries of contraband. If a police officer lawfully pats down a suspect's outer clothing and feels an object whose contour or mass makes its identity immediately apparent, there has been no invasion of the suspect's privacy beyond that already authorized by the officer's search for weapons; if the object is contraband, its warrantless seizure would be justified by the same practical considerations that inhere in the plain view context.

The Minnesota Supreme Court rejected an analogy to the plain-view doctrine on two grounds: first, its belief that "the sense of touch is inherently less immediate and less reliable than the sense of sight," and second, that "the sense of touch is far more intrusive into the personal privacy that is at the core of the Fourth Amendment." 481 N.W.2d, at 845. We have a somewhat different view. First, *Terry* itself demonstrates that the sense of touch is capable of revealing the nature of an object with sufficient reliability to support a seizure. The very premise of *Terry*, after all, is that officers will be able to detect the presence of weapons through the sense of touch and *Terry* upheld precisely such a seizure. Even if it were true that the sense of touch is generally less reliable than the sense of sight, that only suggests that officers will less often be able to justify seizures of unseen contraband. Regardless of whether the officer detects the contraband by sight or by touch, however, the Fourth Amendment's requirement that the officer have probable cause to believe that the item is contraband before seizing it ensures against excessively speculative seizures. The court's second concern — that touch is more intrusive into privacy than is sight — is inapposite in light of the fact that the intrusion the court fears has already been authorized by the lawful search for weapons. The seizure of an item whose identity is already known occasions no further invasion of privacy. Accordingly, the suspect's privacy interests are not advanced by a categorical rule barring the seizure of contraband plainly detected through the sense of touch.

III

It remains to apply these principles to the facts of this case. Respondent has not challenged the finding made by the trial court and affirmed by both the Court of Appeals and the State Supreme Court that the police were justified under *Terry* in stopping him and frisking him for weapons. Thus, the dispositive question before this Court is whether the officer who conducted the search was acting within the lawful bounds marked by *Terry* at the time he gained probable cause to believe that the lump in respondent's jacket was contraband. The State District Court did not make precise findings on this point. . . . The Minnesota Supreme Court, after "a close examination of the record," held that the officer's own testimony "belies any notion that he 'immediately'" recognized the lump as crack cocaine. *See* 481 N.W.2d, at 844. Rather, the court concluded, the officer determined that the lump was contraband only after "squeezing, sliding and otherwise manipulating the contents of the defendant's pocket" — a pocket which the officer already knew contained no weapon. *Id.*

Under the State Supreme Court's interpretation of the record before it, it is clear that the court was correct in holding that the police officer in this case overstepped the bounds of the "strictly circumscribed" search for weapons allowed under *Terry*. See *Terry*, 392 U.S., at 26. Where, as here, "an officer who is executing a valid search for one item seizes a different item," this Court rightly "has been sensitive to the danger . . . that officers will enlarge a specific authorization, furnished by a warrant or an exigency, into the equivalent of a general warrant to rummage and seize at will." *Texas v. Brown*, 460 U.S., at 748 (Stevens, J., concurring in judgment). Here, the officer's continued exploration of respondent's pocket after having concluded that it contained no weapon was unrelated to "[t]he sole justification of the search [under *Terry*:] . . . the protection of the police officer and others nearby." 392 U.S., at 29. It therefore amounted to the sort of evidentiary search that *Terry* expressly refused to authorize, *see id.*, at 26, and that we have condemned in subsequent cases. See *Michigan v. Long*, 463 U.S., at 1049, n. 14; *Sibron*, 392 U.S., at 65–66.

. . . Although the officer was lawfully in a position to feel the lump in respondent's pocket, because *Terry* entitled him to place his hands upon respondent's jacket, the court below determined that the incriminating character of the object was not immediately apparent to him. Rather, the officer determined that the item was contraband only after conducting a further search, one not authorized by *Terry* or by any other exception to the warrant requirement. Because this further search of respondent's pocket was constitutionally invalid, the seizure of the cocaine that followed is likewise unconstitutional.

IV

For these reasons, the judgment of the Minnesota Supreme Court is

Affirmed.

JUSTICE SCALIA, concurring.

I take it to be a fundamental principle of constitutional adjudication that the terms in the Constitution must be given the meaning ascribed to them at the time of their ratification. Thus, when the Fourth Amendment provides that "the right of the people to be secure in their persons, houses, papers, and effects, against *unreasonable searches and seizures*, shall not be violated" (emphasis added), it "is to be construed in the light of what was deemed an unreasonable search and seizure when it was adopted," *Carroll v. United States*, 267 U.S. 132, 149, 45 S. Ct. 280, 69 L. Ed. 543 (1925); see also *California v. Acevedo*, 500 U.S. 565, 583–584 (1991) (Scalia, J., concurring in judgment). The purpose of the provision, in other words, is to preserve that degree of respect for the privacy of persons and the inviolability of their property that existed when the provision was adopted — even if a later, less virtuous age should become accustomed to considering all sorts of intrusion "reasonable."

My problem with the present case is that I am not entirely sure that the physical search — the "frisk" — that produced the evidence at issue here complied with that constitutional standard. The decision of ours that gave approval to such searches, *Terry v. Ohio*, 392 U.S. 1, 88 S. Ct. 1868, 20 L. Ed. 2d 889 (1968), made no serious attempt to determine compliance with traditional standards, but rather, according to the style of this Court at the time, simply adjudged that such a search was "reasonable" by current estimations. *Id.*, at 22–27.

There is good evidence, I think, that the "stop" portion of the *Terry* "stop-and-frisk" holding accords with the common law — that it had long been considered reasonable to detain suspicious persons for the purpose of demanding that they give an account of themselves. . . . .

I am unaware, however, of any precedent for a physical search of a person thus temporarily detained for questioning. . . . When . . . the detention did not rise to the level of a full-blown arrest (and was not supported by the degree of cause needful for that purpose), there appears to be no clear support at common law for physically searching the suspect.

. . . On the other hand, even if a "frisk" prior to arrest would have been considered impermissible in 1791, perhaps it was considered permissible by 1868, when the Fourteenth Amendment (the basis for applying the Fourth Amendment to the States) was adopted. Or perhaps it is only since that time that concealed weapons capable of harming the interrogator quickly and from beyond arm's reach have become common — which might alter the judgment of what is "reasonable" under the original standard. But technological changes were no more discussed in *Terry* than was the original state of the law.

. . . .

. . . . [T]hough I do not favor the mode of analysis in *Terry*, I cannot say that its result was wrong. Constitutionality of the "frisk" in the present case was neither challenged nor argued. Assuming, therefore, that the search was lawful, I agree with the Court's premise that any evidence incidentally discovered in the course of it would be admissible, and join the Court's opinion in its entirety.

CHIEF JUSTICE REHNQUIST, with whom JUSTICE BLACKMUN and JUSTICE THOMAS join, concurring in part and dissenting in part.

I join Parts I and II of the Court's opinion. Unlike the Court, however, I would vacate the judgment of the Supreme Court of Minnesota and remand the case to that court for further proceedings.

Notes and Questions

(1) Although the Court did not consider the question, what grounds did the officers have for stopping Dickerson in the first place? Were they constitutionally adequate?

(2) What showing is required for a frisk of a person? What showing is necessary to "manipulate" an object felt during such a frisk in order to ascertain its identity? To reach beneath the outer clothing of a suspect? Why?

(3) The majority concluded that adequate cause to seize an object other than a weapon can be developed from the sense of touch employed during a weapons frisk.

It further opined that the removal of such an item from the person of a suspect is constitutionally justified because the "seizure of an item whose identity is already known occasions no further invasion of privacy." Is that reasoning correct? May an officer reach beneath a suspect's clothing to remove such an object because his or her action does not infringe on the privacy interests of the suspect? Or is such an action allowable because it is a justifiable privacy invasion?

(4) The opinion in *Dickerson* seems atypical in one significant respect. The Court was unwilling to conclude that a balancing of the respective interests — the degree of intrusion involved in tactile manipulation and the government interest in eradicating illegal narcotics — led to the conclusion that the intrusion in *Dickerson* was justifiable. The Court's prior recognition of the difficulty of detecting narcotics trafficking and the resultant need to equip officers with effective methods of doing so makes the Court's unwillingness all the more noteworthy. Can the analysis in *Dickerson* be reconciled with the reasoning underlying the majority opinions in *Sharpe*, *Place*, and *Long*, for example?

Maryland v. Buie

United States Supreme Court

494 U.S. 325, 110 S. Ct. 1093, 108 L. Ed. 2d 276 (1990)

JUSTICE WHITE delivered the opinion of the court.

A "protective sweep" is a quick and limited search of a premises, incident to an arrest and conducted to protect the safety of police officers or others. It is narrowly confined to a cursory visual inspection of those places in which a person might be hiding. In this case we must decide what level of justification is required by the Fourth and Fourteenth Amendments before police officers, while effecting the arrest of a suspect in his home pursuant to an arrest warrant, may conduct a warrantless protective sweep of all or part of the premises. . . .

I

On February 3, 1986, two men committed an armed robbery of a Godfather's Pizza restaurant in Prince George's County, Maryland. One of the robbers was wearing a red running suit. That same day, Prince George's County police obtained arrest warrants for respondent Jerome Edward Buie and his suspected accomplice in the robbery, Lloyd Allen. Buie's house was placed under police surveillance.

On February 5, the police executed the arrest warrant for Buie. They first had a police department secretary telephone Buie's house to verify that he was home. The secretary spoke to a female first, then to Buie himself. Six or seven officers proceeded to Buie's house. Once inside, the officers fanned out through the first and second floors. Corporal James Rozar announced that he would "freeze" the basement so that no one could come up and surprise the officers. With his service revolver drawn, Rozar twice shouted into the basement, ordering anyone down there to come out. When a voice asked who was calling, Rozar announced three times: "this is the police, show me your hands." Eventually a pair of hands appeared around the bottom of the stairwell and Buie emerged from the basement. He was arrested, searched, and handcuffed by Rozar. Thereafter, Detective Joseph Frolich entered the basement "in case there was someone else" down there. He noticed a running suit lying in plain view on a stack of clothing and seized it.

The trial court denied Buie's motion to suppress the running suit. . . .

The Court of Appeals of Maryland reversed by a 4 to 3 vote.

. . . .

II

It is not disputed that until the point of Buie's arrest the police had the right, based on the authority of the arrest warrant, to search anywhere in the house that Buie might have been found, including the basement. "If there is sufficient evidence of a citizen's participation in a felony to persuade a judicial officer that his arrest is justified, it is constitutionally reasonable to require him to open his doors to the officers of the law." *Payton v. New York*, 445 U.S. 573, 602–03 (1980). There is also no dispute that if Detective Frolich's entry into the basement was lawful, the seizure of the red running suit, which was in plain view and which the officer had probable cause to believe was evidence of a crime, was also lawful under the Fourth Amendment. The issue in this case is what level of justification the Fourth Amendment required before Detective Frolich could legally enter the basement to see if someone else was there.

. . . .

III

It goes without saying that the Fourth Amendment bars only unreasonable searches and seizures. Our cases show that in determining reasonableness, we have balanced the intrusion on the individual's Fourth Amendment interests against its promotion of legitimate governmental interests. Under this test, a search of the house or office is generally not reasonable without a warrant issued on probable cause. There are other contexts, however, where the public interest is such that neither a warrant nor probable cause is required.

The *Terry* case is most instructive for present purposes. There we held that an on-the-street "frisk" for weapons must be tested by the Fourth Amendment's general proscription against unreasonable searches because such a frisk involves "an entire rubric of police conduct — necessarily swift action predicated upon the on-the-spot observations of the officer on the beat — which historically has not been, and as a practical matter could not be, subjected to the warrant procedure." [392 U.S. at 20.] We stated that there is " 'no ready test for determining reasonableness other than by balancing the need to search . . . against the invasion which the search . . . entails.' " *Id.*, at 21 (quoting *Camara v. Municipal Court*, 387 U.S. 523, 536–537 [1967]). Applying that balancing test, it was held that although a frisk for weapons "constitutes a severe, though brief, intrusion upon cherished personal security," 392 U.S., at 24–25, such a frisk is reasonable when weighed against the "need for law enforcement officers to protect themselves and other prospective victims of violence in situations where they may lack probable cause for an arrest." *Id.*, at 24. We therefore authorized a limited pat-down for weapons where a reasonably prudent officer would be warranted in the belief, based on "specific and articulable facts," *id.*, at 21, and not on a mere "inchoate and unparticularized suspicion or 'hunch,'" *id.*, at 27, "that he is dealing with an armed and dangerous individual." *Id.*

In *Michigan v. Long*, 463 U.S. 1032 (1983), the principles of *Terry* were applied in the context of a roadside encounter: "The search of the passenger compartment of an automobile, limited to those areas in which a weapon may be placed or hidden, is permissible if the police officer possesses a reasonable belief based on 'specific and articulable facts which, taken together with the rational inferences from those facts, reasonably warrant' the officer in believing that the suspect is dangerous and the suspect may gain immediate control of weapons." *Id.*, at 1049–50 (quoting *Terry, supra*, at 21). The *Long* Court expressly rejected the contention that *Terry* restricted preventative searches to the person of a detained suspect. 463 U.S., at 1047. In a sense, *Long* authorized a "frisk" of an automobile for weapons.

The ingredients to apply the balance struck in *Terry* and *Long* are present in this case. Possessing an arrest warrant and probable cause to believe Buie was in his home, the officers were entitled to enter and to search anywhere in the house in which Buie might be found. Once he was found, however, the search for him was over, and there was no longer that particular justification for entering any rooms that had not yet been searched.

That Buie had an expectation of privacy in those remaining areas of his house, however, does not mean such rooms were immune from entry. In *Terry* and *Long* we were concerned with the immediate interest of the police officers in taking steps to assure themselves that the persons with whom they were dealing were not armed with or able to gain immediate control of a weapon that could unexpectedly and fatally be used against them. In the instant case, there is an analogous interest of the officers in taking steps to assure themselves that the house in which a suspect is being or had just been arrested is not harboring other persons who are dangerous and could unexpectedly launch an attack. The risk of danger in the context of an arrest in the home is as great as, if not greater than, it is in an on-the-street or roadside investigatory encounter. A *Terry* or *Long* frisk occurs before a police-citizen confrontation has escalated to the point of arrest. A protective sweep, in contrast, occurs as an adjunct to the serious step of taking a person into custody for the purpose of prosecuting him for a crime. Moreover, unlike an encounter on the street or along a highway, an in-home arrest puts the officer at the disadvantage of being on his adversary's "turf." An ambush in a confined setting of unknown configuration is more to be feared than it is in open, more familiar surroundings.

We recognized in *Terry* that "[e]ven a limited search of the outer clothing for weapons constitutes a severe, though brief, intrusion upon cherished personal security, and it must surely be an annoying, frightening, and perhaps humiliating experience." *Terry, supra,* at 24–25. But we permitted the intrusion, which was no more than necessary to protect the officer from harm. Nor do we here suggest, as the State does, that entering rooms not examined prior to the arrest is a *de minimis* intrusion that may be disregarded. We are quite sure, however, that the arresting officers are permitted in such circumstances to take reasonable steps to ensure their safety after, and while making, the arrest. That interest is sufficient to outweigh the intrusion such procedures may entail.

We agree with the State, as did the court below, that a warrant was not required.[1] We also hold that as an incident to the arrest the officers could, as a precautionary matter and without probable cause or reasonable suspicion, look in closets and other spaces immediately adjoining the place of arrest from which an attack could be immediately launched. Beyond that, however, we hold that there must be articulable facts which, taken together with the rational inferences from those facts, would warrant a reasonably prudent officer in believing that the area to be swept harbors an individual posing a danger to those on the arrest scene. This is no more and no less than was required in *Terry* and *Long*, and as in those cases, we think this balance is the proper one.

We reject the State's attempts to analogize this case to *Pennsylvania v. Mimms*, 434 U.S. 106 (1977) (*per curiam*), and *Michigan v. Summers*, 452 U.S. 692 (1981). The intrusion in *Mimms*—requiring the driver of a lawfully stopped vehicle to exit the car—was "*de minimis*," 434 U.S., at 111. *Summers* held that a search warrant for a house carries with it the authority to detain its occupants until the search is completed. The State contends that this case is the "mirror image" of *Summers* and that the arrest warrant carried with it the authority to search for persons who could interfere with the arrest. In that case, however, the search warrant implied a judicial determination that police had probable cause to believe that someone in the home was committing a crime. Here, the existence of the arrest warrant implies nothing about whether dangerous third parties will be found in the arrestee's house. Moreover, the intrusion in *Summers* was less severe and much less susceptible to exploitation than a protective sweep. A more analogous case is *Ybarra v. Illinois*, 444 U.S. 85 (1979), in which we held that, although armed with a warrant to search a bar and bartender, the police could not frisk the bar's patrons absent individualized, reasonable suspicion that the person to be frisked was armed and presently dangerous. Here, too, the reasonable suspicion standard—"one of the relatively simple concepts embodied in the Fourth Amendment," *United States v. Sokolow*, 490 U.S. 1 (1989)—strikes the proper balance between officer safety and citizen privacy.

We should emphasize that such a protective sweep, aimed at protecting the arresting officers, if justified by the circumstances, is nevertheless not a full search of the

---

1. *Buie* suggests that because the police could have sought a warrant to search for dangerous persons in the house, they were constitutionally required to do so. But the arrest warrant gave the police every right to enter the home to search for *Buie*. Once inside, the potential for danger justified a standard of less than probable cause for conducting a limited protective sweep.

premises, but may extend only to a cursory inspection of those spaces where a person may be found. The sweep lasts no longer than is necessary to dispel the reasonable suspicion of danger and in any event no longer than it takes to complete the arrest and depart the premises.

IV

Affirmance is not required by *Chimel v. California*, 395 U.S. 752 (1969), where it was held that in the absence of a search warrant, the justifiable search incident to an in-home arrest could not extend beyond the arrestee's person and the area from within which the arrestee might have obtained a weapon. First, *Chimel* was concerned with a full-blown search of the entire house for evidence of the crime for which the arrest was made, *see id.*, at 754, 763, not the more limited intrusion contemplated by a protective sweep. Second, the justification for the search incident to an arrest considered in *Chimel* was the threat posed by the arrestee, not the safety threat posed by the house, or more properly by unseen third parties in the house. To reach our conclusion today, therefore, we need not disagree with the Court's statement in *Chimel*, *id.*, at 766–67, n. 12, that "the invasion of privacy that results from a top-to-bottom search of a man's house [cannot be characterized] as 'minor,'" nor hold that "simply because some interference with an individual's privacy and freedom of movement has lawfully taken place, further intrusions should automatically be allowed despite the absence of a warrant that the Fourth Amendment would otherwise require." *Id.* The type of search we authorize today is far removed from the "top-to-bottom" search involved in *Chimel*; moreover, it is decidedly not "automatic," but may be conducted only when justified by a reasonable, articulable suspicion that the house is harboring a person posing a danger to those on the arrest scene.

V

We conclude that by requiring a protective sweep to be justified by probable cause to believe that a serious and demonstrable potentiality for danger existed, the Court of Appeals of Maryland applied an unnecessarily strict Fourth Amendment standard. The Fourth Amendment permits a properly limited protective sweep in conjunction with an in-home arrest when the searching officer possesses a reasonable belief based on specific and articulable facts that the area to be swept harbors an individual posing a danger to those on the arrest scene. We therefore vacate the judgment below and remand this case to the Court of Appeals of Maryland for further proceedings not inconsistent with this opinion.

It is so ordered.

[The concurring opinions of JUSTICES STEVENS and KENNEDY have been omitted.]

JUSTICE BRENNAN, with whom JUSTICE MARSHALL joins, dissenting.

. . . .

The Court today holds that *Terry*'s "reasonable suspicion" standard "strikes the proper balance between officer safety and citizen privacy" for protective sweeps in private dwellings. I agree with the majority that officers executing an arrest warrant within a private dwelling have an interest in protecting themselves against potential ambush by third parties, but the majority offers no support for its assumption that the danger of ambush during planned home arrests approaches the danger of unavoidable "on-the-beat" confrontations in "the myriad daily situations in which policemen and citizens confront each other on the street." *Terry, supra*, at 12.[2] In any event, the Court's implicit judgment that a protective sweep constitutes a "minimally intrusive" search akin to that involved in *Terry* markedly undervalues the nature and scope of the privacy interests involved.

While the Fourth Amendment protects a person's privacy interests in a variety of settings, "physical entry of the home is the chief evil against which the wording of the Fourth Amendment is directed." *United States v. United States District Court*, 407 U.S. 297, 313 (1972). The Court discounts the nature of the intrusion because it believes that the scope of the intrusion is limited.

The Court explains that a protective sweep's scope is "narrowly confined to a cursory visual inspection of those places in which a person might be hiding," and confined in duration to a period "no longer than is necessary to dispel the reasonable suspicion of danger and in any event no longer than it takes to complete the arrest and depart the premises." But these spatial and temporal restrictions are not particularly limiting. A protective sweep would bring within police purview virtually all personal possessions within the house not hidden from view in a small enclosed space. Police officers searching for potential ambushers might enter every room including basements and attics; open up closets, lockers, chests, wardrobes, and cars; and peer under beds and behind furniture. The officers will view letters, documents, and personal effects that are on tables or desks or are visible inside open drawers; books, records, tapes, and pictures on shelves; and clothing, medicines, toiletries and other paraphernalia not carefully stored in dresser drawers or bathroom cupboards. While perhaps not a "full-blown" or "top-to-bottom" search, a protective sweep is much closer to it than to a "limited patdown for weapons" or a "'frisk' of an automobile." Because the nature and scope of the intrusion sanctioned here are far greater than those upheld in *Terry* and *Long*, the Court's conclusion that "[t]he ingredients to apply the balance struck in *Terry* and *Long* are present in this case," is unwarranted. The "ingredient" of a minimally intrusive search is absent, and the Court's holding today therefore unpalatably deviates from *Terry* and its progeny.[6]

---

2. Individual police officers necessarily initiate street encounters without advance planning "for a wide variety of purposes." *Terry v. Ohio*, 392 U.S., at 13. But officers choosing to execute an arrest warrant in the suspect's house may minimize any risk of ambush by, for example, a show of force; in this case, at least six armed officers secured the premises. And, of course, officers could select a safer venue for making their arrest.

6. The Court's decision also to expand the "search incident to arrest" exception previously recognized in *Chimel v. California, supra*, allowing police officers without any requisite level of suspicion to look into "closets and other spaces immediately adjoining the place of arrest from which an attack could be immediately launched," is equally disquieting. *Chimel* established that police officers may presume as a matter of law, without need for factual support in a particular case, that arrestees might

In light of the special sanctity of a private residence and the highly intrusive nature of a protective sweep, I firmly believe that police officers must have probable cause to fear that their personal safety is threatened by a hidden confederate of an arrestee before they may sweep through the entire home . . . . I respectfully dissent.

Notes and Questions

(1) Should officers have a similar authority to "sweep" premises following an arrest if they have reason to believe that an individual is destroying or will destroy contraband connected to the arrest? Why?

(2) In *Buie*, Justice White briefly discussed two important prior decisions. He rejected the State's contention that *Michigan v. Summers*, 452 U.S. 692, 101 S. Ct. 2587, 69 L. Ed. 2d 340 (1981), supported suspicionless protective sweeps of homes, deeming *Ybarra v. Illinois*, 444 U.S. 85, 100 S. Ct. 338, 62 L. Ed. 2d 238 (1979), "more analogous." In *Ybarra*, the Court had held that it was unreasonable for officers to frisk patrons who were present in a bar during the execution of a valid warrant to search the bar for narcotics. The patrons could not be frisked merely because they were present in the place the warrant authorized the officers to search. Instead, officers needed the individualized reasonable suspicion ordinarily required to justify a *Terry* frisk.

Summers, on the other hand, had concluded that officers could reasonably *detain* an occupant of a home during the execution of a valid search warrant for narcotics even in the absence of additional, individualized suspicion pertaining to the occupant. Interests in the safety of the searching officers, in facilitating the efficient completion of the search of the home, and in preventing flight by the occupant justified a detention during the time the search was being conducted. In *Bailey v. United States*, 568 U.S. ____, 133 S. Ct. 1031, 185 L. Ed. 2d 19 (2013), the Court concluded that these interests did not apply "with the same or similar force to the detention of recent occupants beyond the immediate vicinity of the premises to be searched." Consequently, the Court overturned a lower court ruling that officers could detain an occupant who was beyond the immediate vicinity of the searched premises if he was seen leaving the premises shortly before the search and the detention was "'effected *as soon as reasonably practicable*.'" According to the *Bailey* majority, to detain an occupant who was beyond the immediate vicinity of the home to be searched, officers need individualized reasonable suspicion of criminal activity. The Court declined to specify the area that constitutes "the immediate vicinity" of premises, observing that in making that determination courts should consider "the lawful limits

---

take advantage of weapons or destroy evidence in the area "within [their] immediate control"; therefore, a protective search of that area is *per se* reasonable under the Fourth Amendment. *Chimel, supra*, at 763. I find much less plausible the Court's implicit assumption today that arrestees are likely to sprinkle hidden allies throughout the rooms in which they might be arrested. Hence there is no comparable justification for permitting arresting officers to presume as a matter of law that they are threatened by ambush from "immediately adjoining" spaces.

of the premises, whether the occupant was within the line of sight of his dwelling, the ease of reentry from the occupant's location, and other relevant factors."

(3) *Buie* is the last of the *Terry* cases in this subchapter. In light of the entire line of preceding authority, is it fair to suggest, as Justice Brennan did in his *Michigan v. Long* dissent, that the Court has engaged in a process of "balancing into oblivion the protections [of] the Fourth Amendment"?

"Scope" Problems

5A–22: On July 6, around 1:45 p.m., two men wearing plastic Halloween masks robbed a bank in Franklin. One held a shotgun and stood in the lobby issuing commands. The other, carrying a semiautomatic pistol, vaulted the counter and collected the money. The men fled in a light-blue GMC Jimmy truck. A short time later, the State Police located the truck abandoned less than a mile from the bank. Witnesses reported that a red Pontiac Sunbird with Rhode Island plates had been parked near that spot.

About 2:30 p.m., Officer Arthur spotted a red Sunbird with Rhode Island plates at a gas station not far from Franklin. He stopped the car as it was preparing to enter the interstate highway and ordered the driver, a white male, out of the car. After patting him down, Arthur directed him to take a seat in the back of his police cruiser. The cruiser's internal rear door handles were not functional and a plastic spit guard and wire cage separated the front and rear seats.

The driver identified himself as Jeff Hunt. Arthur ran a check on the car and learned it was registered to a rental agency at a Rhode Island airport. Hunt said a friend had rented the car for him, but would not identify the friend. Within minutes, several other officers arrived. Trooper Jerry, who spoke to Hunt through the open rear door of Arthur's cruiser, detected alcohol on his breath. At Jerry's request, Hunt took a sobriety test, which he passed.

Around 2:43 p.m., Jerry advised Hunt of his rights, adding that although he was not under arrest, he was being detained for investigative purposes. Hunt waived his rights, but declined to say where he had been since 1:00 p.m., stating only that he had been with a "Born-Again-Christian" friend. Jerry explained that they were detaining him because the Sunbird matched a vehicle involved in a bank robbery. Jerry then questioned Hunt intermittently for 45 minutes and took three Polaroid photographs of him.

Meanwhile, Trooper Eller discovered that the Sunbird had been rented to Lance, a black male, and that he had listed Hunt as a co-driver. Around 3:45 p.m., Eller approached Arthur's cruiser and asked Hunt where he had been prior to the stop. Hunt said he had not been near Franklin, but had spent the day at a friend's place in the woods. He claimed not to remember his friend's name nor the location of the place where he stayed. Eller asked Hunt if his friend was black, whereupon Hunt became agitated, swore at Eller, gestured in a general direction and told him to find out for himself.

Eller knew the area well. He drove to the home of the only black male living in the direction Hunt had gestured and inquired whether Hunt had visited earlier that day. James, the man who lived there, said that Hunt had been there with a man named John. James also said that Hunt and John had borrowed his truck earlier in the day and had later returned to his house to change their clothes. At 4:43 p.m., after finishing the interview of James, Eller returned to Arthur's cruiser and released Hunt.

What arguments should Hunt make in support of a claim that the officers violated his Fourth Amendment rights?

5A–23: David King, a drug interdiction officer in San Diego, received a telephone tip from an unidentified airline employee. According to the tip, a man named Raoul would be arriving in Philadelphia at 3:24 p.m. in seat 38C on a Delta flight from Atlanta. The flight originated in San Juan, Puerto Rico. The informer reported that he or she had learned from a centralized computer system that Raoul had purchased a one-way ticket in cash on the day of the flight, had not checked any bags, and had given a "call-back number" to the purchasing agent.

King suspected that Raoul was a drug courier. He telephoned the Philadelphia Police Department and spoke to Detective Kosmalski. King reported what he knew, adding that there was a drug organization in Puerto Rico that had been transporting drugs from San Juan to cities on the eastern seaboard. He also told Kosmalski, who had no airport drug interdiction experience, that couriers often carry contraband in body packs.

Kosmalski arranged with Delta for a stewardess to point out the passenger in 38C as he exited flight 904. He made plans to have a patrol car waiting at the gate to drive Raoul to the police station at the airport. Kosmalski then proceeded to the gate to meet Raoul's plane. He was joined by two officers who had parked their patrol car at the foot of the stairs from the jetway to the tarmac.

When the stewardess pointed out the man who had occupied seat 38C, Kosmalski and his colleagues approached, flashed their badges, and asked if the man was Raoul. He answered "yes." Kosmalski told him he was "under investigation." He then set Raoul's duffel bags to one side, and asked him to put his hands on the jetway wall. A patdown revealed no weapons or contraband. Kosmalski then handcuffed Raoul and the three officers took him down the stairs to the waiting patrol car and drove him a short distance from the terminal to the airport police station.

At the station, Kosmalski removed the handcuffs. Raoul then admitted that his real name was Joe Zitro. A security check revealed that he was the subject of three outstanding warrants for drug offenses. Kosmalski placed Zitro under arrest and summoned a drug-sniffing dog. Upon smelling Zitro's bags, the dog reacted strongly to one of them, seizing it and shaking it violently, and causing one of the zippers to come part way open. Inside, Kosmalski could see white brick-shaped objects wrapped in pink cellophane. He opened the bag and found 14 kilo-sized bricks of narcotics.

Did the officers comply with the Fourth Amendment prior to the discovery of the narcotics?

5A–24: Steppes, who was traveling in a pickup truck on Highway 66, was pulled over by Officer Peace for going 47 mph in a 35 mph speed zone. Steppes exited his vehicle with driver's license and proof of insurance in hand. As he stood by his truck, Officer Peace approached and asked, "Do you have a gun in the car?" Steppes hesitated and then said, "No. Why do you ask?" Officer Peace again asked, "Do you have a gun in this vehicle?" Steppes said "No," but then told Peace that he had mace on his key chain. Steppes took his keys from the ignition, showed Peace the mace, and asked Peace if he considered mace a weapon. Peace said "No," and again asked if Steppes had a gun in the vehicle. Steppes said he did not have a gun and asked again why he had been stopped.

At that point, Officer Peace asked for Steppes's license, told Steppes to stay in the vehicle, and called for backup. Officer Quinn soon arrived. Peace told Quinn that he felt there was a weapon in the vehicle. He told Quinn that Steppes had denied having a pistol, but that something made him nervous. Officer Peace then summoned Steppes from his vehicle, informing him that he had been stopped for speeding. While Steppes signed a speeding citation, Officer Quinn began to search his vehicle. Steppes protested that the search was a violation of his constitutional rights. Under the backseat of the truck, Quinn found a case that contained a pistol.

Officer Peace arrested Steppes and took him to his police car. In Steppes's presence, Peace admitted to Quinn that an "NRA" sticker on Steppes's truck had made him suspect the presence of a weapon. After charges for wrongfully possessing a firearm were dismissed, Steppes filed a civil suit against Officers Peace and Quinn, alleging that the search of his truck was in violation of his Fourth Amendment rights. At the trial, Officer Peace testified that he had feared danger not only because of the NRA sticker, but also because the truck contained camouflage material and hunting equipment, because Steppes had waved the mace at him, and because Steppes had claimed his constitutional rights were being violated. Steppes testified that he did not have hunting equipment in the truck, that he merely showed Officer Peace the can of mace, and that he did not complain that his constitutional rights were being violated until the search of his vehicle began.

Does Steppes have a valid claim?

5A–25: At 10:36 p.m., an automobile with Ohio license places was traveling on I-95 southbound. The vehicle was going 34 miles per hour, 21 miles per hour under the speed limit. The driver was making erratic movements back and forth over the lane divider line. A trooper pulled the car over on the left shoulder. Dion was driving and Dick was sitting in the front passenger seat. According to the trooper, both men were "extremely nervous." Dion produced his license, but could not find the registration or insurance card. Although his hands were shaking and his eyes bloodshot and red, a field sobriety test proved negative. Meanwhile, Dick moved about in the car and repeatedly turned around.

The trooper ordered both men out of the car. Dick began to pace, wave his hands, and make some "laughing-coughing" noises. When asked about ownership of the vehicle, he stated that "Leo" owned the car, but claimed he did not know his last name or address. He first referred to Leo as a "cousin," but later said he was "like a nephew." When the trooper asked why Dion was so nervous, he replied "Nothing is in the ride. I'm not nervous." When the trooper asked him why he had said that "nothing is in the ride," Dion stated that nothing was in the trunk or car. The two men gave somewhat inconsistent stories regarding their whereabouts earlier in the day. Neither would sign a "Consent to Search" form.

The trooper ran a stolen car check and was informed that there was no report that the car was stolen. He then asked the two men to accompany him to the State Trooper Barracks, and they complied with the request. Both men were handcuffed during the trip and, according to the trooper, were not free to leave until the investigation was completed.

The trooper was able to find the name and address of the owner of the car, but was unsuccessful in his attempt to contact the man. Because he suspected that there were drugs in the car, the trooper had called from the scene of the stop for the assistance of a K-9 officer. Sometime between 1:00 and 2:00 a.m., about two hours after the group's arrival at the barracks, the K-9 officer and his dog arrived at the barracks. The car had already been towed to the barracks. While examining the exterior, the dog scratched at the trunk, indicating the presence of contraband there. In the presence of Dion and Dick, the K-9 officer initiated an application for a search warrant, whereupon both Dion and Dick said that they had "nothing to hide" and agreed to sign a consent form. The K-9 officer opened the trunk and found a bag containing two kilograms of cocaine. Dick and Dion were placed under arrest.

Did any of the trooper's actions violate the Fourth Amendment?

5A–26: Officers Reed and Vickers received a call from an informant who told them that a tall, black male was armed and selling drugs at a particular location in the city. The officers went to the location where they found a group of four men standing near a black Honda. David, who appeared to match the description provided by the informant, was one of the four. As the officers, wearing badges and guns, approached, David first moved to conceal the right side of his body from the officers, then broke into a run. As he ran, the officers noticed that his gym shorts "contained a heavy object that made a sort of swinging motion consistent with possession of a handgun." The officers called out to David to stop. When he did not, Officer Reed fired two stainless steel darts from his Taser. The darts, which lodged in David's back, remained connected to Reed's Taser by insulated wires. Upon striking David, the Taser darts delivered "a 1200-volt, low ampere electrical charge into his muscles, overriding his central nervous system, paralyzing his muscles throughout his body," and causing him to "go limp." The darts could be removed only by a medical technician or other medical personnel. Officer Vickers approached and asked David if he had anything illegal on him. David replied that there was a gun in his pocket. Vickers reached into the pocket and removed the gun, possession of which was illegal. David was convicted after a trial judge denied his motion to suppress his admission and the gun. He has appealed, contending that the officers seized him in violation of his Fourth Amendment rights.

How should the appellate court resolve David's contention?

5A–27: After receiving informants' reports and conducting an investigation, Detective Blaine suspected that James regularly traveled from Nevada to California to pick up several pounds of methamphetamine. One evening, after learning that James was at a motel in California, he contacted Deputy Zucker, who worked with Thor, a drug detection dog. Blaine told Zucker of his investigation, providing a description of James's Chevrolet and his license plate number. Blaine asked Zucker to wait on the interstate, just over the Nevada line and to "develop probable cause" to pull James over. Zucker parked on the highway, watched James drive past, and followed him for a mile. At 7:09 p.m., Zucker stopped James for "making unsafe lane changes and following another vehicle too closely."

Zucker asked James for his license and registration. He thought he detected an odor that might be "methamphetamine" coming from inside the vehicle. He asked James to get out, told him he had made an unsafe lane change, and asked "where he was coming from." James replied that he had been visiting friends in California. Zucker asked James to wait by the patrol car while he "checked some numbers" on James's vehicle. After obtaining the Chevrolet's vehicle identification number, Zucker noticed that April, James's passenger, "appeared to be feigning sleep." Her "hands were shaking, and the pulse in her carotid artery seemed to be racing." When asked, April also said that they had stayed in California with James's friends.

At 7:13, Zucker told James, who was still standing by his patrol car, that he would not issue a traffic ticket, but needed "to run a check for outstanding warrants before letting him go." While Zucker ran a check to determine whether James's driver's license was valid and whether there were any outstanding arrest warrants, James reported that he "had had trouble with his license and child support, but had straightened things out." James admitted that he had been arrested before. Around 7:20, a dispatch operator informed Zucker that the records checks on both James and April were "clean." Zucker then requested an "ex-felon registration check" on James because a check of records from his patrol car computer had indicated that James had a felony arrest record. The check was designed to ascertain James's criminal history and to determine whether he was properly registered at the address he had provided. While awaiting the results, Zucker asked James why April had stated that they had stayed at a motel (although April had, in fact, said they had stayed with friends). James responded that they had stayed at a motel the night before arriving at his friends' home. Zucker told James that if the ex-felon registration check showed he was properly registered he would be free to leave.

At 7:26 p.m., the dispatch operator told Zucker that she was still on the phone with the records department. Two minutes later, she informed him that James had two drug-related convictions and that he was properly registered. Zucker gave James a warning, returned his license and registration, shook his hand, and said, "You're good to go." As James began to walk away, Zucker asked if he would "answer a few more questions." When James returned to his car, Zucker asked if he had drugs in his car. James said that he did not, but refused to consent to a search of his car. Zucker then took three minutes to "prepare" Thor, and proceeded to walk the canine around the Chevrolet. At 7:33, Thor alerted to the passenger door. Upon searching the car, Zucker found methamphetamine, marijuana, and crack cocaine. He arrested James and April.

Did Officer Zucker violate the Fourth Amendment?

5A–28: Around 9:10 p.m., Officer Jim was conducting surveillance of a "known drug house" located on Fatt Street. Jim, who lived in the area, had been told by numerous neighbors that the occupants dealt drugs at the house and that there was an extremely high amount of foot, bicycle, and car traffic coming to the house. The visitors would stay for two or three minutes, then leave. Jim was aware that officers had previously arrested the occupants for dealing drugs. Jim saw a car pull up to the house with three persons inside. Renson, the sole backseat passenger, got out and went inside the house, remaining there for about three minutes before returning to the car. Suspecting that a drug transaction had taken place, Officer Jim followed the car.

After the driver failed to signal for a left turn, Jim stopped the car. He felt "uneasy" about the stop because of the location, because the road was dark, and because there were three persons in the car. Moreover, in his experience, persons involved in drugs are known to carry weapons. According to Jim, "officers die all the time in similar situations." As Jim approached, the driver produced his license and proof of insurance. When Jim asked if he had "any weapons, drugs, or needles," the driver consented to a pat-down search. Nothing was found.

Jim then turned toward Renson who was on his side of the car and would have been the "quickest threat" to him. Jim asked Renson if he had "any weapons, drugs, needles or anything that could hurt" the officer. Renson responded that he did not. Jim then frisked Renson. Renson's boots — steel-toed hiking boots that came above his ankles — were unlaced. Jim believed, based on experience, that there was "a very strong possibility that a weapon could have been located in them. Knives, razors and small caliber handguns fit inside such boots." Jim asked Renson to remove the boots and kick them to the side. When Renson complied, Jim observed a white, rock-like substance in one of the boots. The substance proved to be cocaine. Prior to trial for possession of narcotics, the trial judge denied Renson's motion to suppress the cocaine. After conviction, Renson appealed the ruling.

How should the court of appeals rule?

5A–29: At about 11 p.m., a Police Department radio broadcast reported an armed robbery near 9th and G Streets. The report described the suspect as male, six feet tall, and wearing a blue hooded sweatshirt and blue jeans. Officer Tony Bow heard the dispatch and began canvassing the area near the robbery scene. Within minutes, Bow saw Paul Skew walking near 9th Street and Independence Avenue. Noticing that Skew had a mustache and "vaguely matched" the robber's description, Bow asked the dispatcher whether the alleged robber had a mustache and the dispatcher replied that a mustache was part of the description. Meanwhile, upon seeing a police car following him, Skew had turned and walked in a different direction.

After calling in his location to other officers, Officer Bow parked, got out, and stopped Skew. He requested identification, then instructed Skew to keep his hands on top of his head, not in his pockets. Skew complied. Bow then told Skew that he had been stopped because he matched the description of an armed robbery suspect. He noticed that Skew was wearing two jackets, a navy blue outer jacket with a darker blue fleece type jacket underneath.

Officer Wills soon arrived at the scene. For safety purposes, he patted down Skew's outer clothing, but did not feel a weapon. Officer Kean then arrived with the robbery victim in the back of his car. His intent was to conduct a "show-up" — an identification procedure that involves presenting a single suspect to an eyewitness. While the victim remained inside Kean's car, Officer Wills walked Skew toward the car. Wills recalled that the robbery suspect had been described as wearing a "blue hooded sweatshirt." Because he wanted the victim to see what Skew had on and wanted to make sure that Skew wasn't using the outer jacket to cover up what he had been wearing, Wills began to unzip Skew's outer jacket. The zipper stopped and would not go down further when it hit a hard, solid object. At this point, Skew then knocked Wills's hand away from his zipper.

At the same time, the show-up ended, and Officer Kean drove away with the victim. Officer Wills did not know whether the victim had identified Skew as the robber. Less than a minute later, Wills walked Skew backwards, seating him upright on the hood of a police car. Wills fully unzipped Skew's outer jacket, revealing that he was wearing a black pouch beneath the jacket. Protruding from the partially open pouch was a silver object which Wills recognized as a gun. He arrested Skew for carrying a firearm without a license. Sometime during this period, the victim had informed Officer Kean that Skew was not the robber. Officer Wills was not made aware of this fact until after he had arrested Skew.

Was the police conduct prior to discovery of the gun authorized by the *Terry* doctrine?

5A–30: While investigating drug trafficking in a Midwestern state, Agent Jose Rubias of Homeland Security received a report from a confidential informant that Cristo had entered the United States illegally, was involved in methamphetamine trafficking, and might have purchased a firearm. Agent Rubias and another agent approached the apartment where they believed Cristo resided. When they knocked on the door, Ray, the boyfriend and roommate of one of the lessees, opened the door. When Agent Rubias asked if they could "come in and speak with you," Ray stepped aside and allowed the agents to enter. Upon entering, the agents noticed a baby and a woman, later identified as Cristo's girlfriend, Juliet, in the kitchen. Rubias asked if anyone else was in the home. Neither Ray nor Juliet responded. When Rubias repeated the question, Ray "paused and turned his head slightly towards the hallway."

Rubias concluded that the hesitance and slight head turn indicated that other people were in the house. Both agents drew their guns and informed Ray that they were going to check the apartment for other people. While walking down the hall, the agents yelled "Police! Police!" in Spanish. Cristo emerged from a bedroom with his hands up. Rubias handcuffed him and took him to the living room. The agents then questioned all of the occupants, asking for their names and inquiring about their immigration statuses. Cristo admitted he was in the country illegally. He also consented to a search of the apartment, which led to the discovery of drugs. The agents arrested Cristo. He was subsequently charged with re-entering the U.S. illegally and possession of narcotics. Cristo sought to suppress the evidence against him, contending that the agents exceeded the scope of the consent to enter the apartment, thereby conducting an unreasonable search. The government did not claim that the consent validated the agents' actions, but argued that the search for other persons was a legitimate "protective sweep" of the premises.

Is the government's argument valid?

5A–31: At 10:00 a.m., Officer Perry was on routine patrol near the intersection of Master and Myrtle Streets, a high drug-crime area in which he had made several drug-related arrests. As he stopped his marked police car at the intersection and looked down the 1400 Block of Myrtle, Perry observed C.B., a young man, standing approximately 70 feet away on the sidewalk. Perry watched C.B. remove a clear plastic sandwich bag that "had an orange tint to it" from the waistband of his pants and show it to a woman companion. The orange tint came from the small packets inside the bag. From his experience, Perry suspected that the baggie tucked into C.B.'s waistband contained narcotics.

Perry drove around the block and approached C.B. He patted C.B. down for weapons. When he reached the front area of C.B.'s waistband, Perry felt the bulge of a plastic baggie. He removed the baggie, which contained 33 orange-tinted packets of crack cocaine, and arrested C.B. Later, at a hearing on C.B.'s motion to suppress the crack, Perry testified as follows:

Q.: Would you describe how you conduct a patdown such as the one in this case?

A.: When I feel something during a patdown I give a slight squeeze. When I pat somebody down, when I reach their pockets I squeeze. When I felt the baggie with the packets in there, it was like — just like a small bulge in there, which I'd felt several hundred times. So from my experience I knew what it was.

Q.: When you patted C.B. down you could feel the baggie through his pants, but you had to take your fingers and play with it a little so you knew it was a baggie?

A.: I didn't play with it. I came up to him. I patted him down. As soon as I squeezed it, I knew what it was. I reached in and pulled it out.

After hearing this testimony, the trial court denied C.B.'s motion to suppress. C.B. was adjudicated a delinquent based on his possession of contraband, and has appealed the denial of his motion.

Should the trial court's ruling on the motion to suppress be reversed?

5A–32: As part of a homicide investigation in which Bert was a suspect, a task force consisting of state and federal officers was conducting surveillance outside an apartment where Bert was staying. The apartment was leased by Andrea, Bert's girlfriend. The officers had a warrant for Bert's arrest on other charges. Although the task force members were able to surround the apartment and trace Bert's movements effectively, they could not see the front door of the apartment and, consequently, could not see whether any of the foot traffic in the area went into or came out of the apartment.

At 12:30 p.m., three hours after the surveillance began, Bert left the apartment and walked to his car. The vehicle was parked 40 to 50 feet away from the entrance of the apartment. Eight or nine members of the task force, brandishing weapons, closed in at this point. They arrested and handcuffed Bert as he stood next to the driver's door of his car.

A few moments later, Andrea ran out of the apartment. She was "very irate," "very agitated, screaming and yelling," and in a "hostile rage." The officers detained, but did not search her. Special Agent Thomas immediately went to the front door of the apartment because he was "concerned that somebody might still be in there." The entrance was barred by a screen door, which Thomas opened. He yelled "Police!" into the apartment, but received no answer. He saw a shotgun leaning against a wall. He then conducted a protective sweep of the apartment during the course of which he saw a revolver and scales. Officers then secured the apartment for four hours, pending issuance of a search warrant. A warranted search yielded a small amount of cocaine, the shotgun, revolver, ammunition, scales, and some personal papers.

Prior to trial for possession with intent to distribute cocaine, Bert moved to suppress the evidence, claiming that Agent Thomas had violated the Fourth Amendment.

How should the trial court rule?

5A–33: At 12:53 a.m., a police department 911 operator was told by a caller from 501 Berks Avenue that someone was attempting to break into his residence. The caller said that more than one person was trying to enter the house and that some of the perpetrators had gone around to the back of the house. A dispatcher sent a radio message to patrol cars in the area. Officers Lace and Hite were in a car less than two blocks from 501 Berks when they received the radio transmission. They proceeded eastbound on Berks. As they came to the intersection of Berks and Suffolk, the officers saw Cargo crossing Berks and continuing to walk north on the east side of Suffolk. The residence at 501 Berks is located on the south side of Berks, approximately 200 feet to the east of the intersection. As Cargo was walking north he was staring intently to his right at another patrol car that had already arrived at 501 Berks. He apparently did not notice Lace and Hite's car approaching.

Officers Lace and Hite turned left onto Suffolk, drew alongside Cargo, and ordered him to stop. They intended to place Cargo in the back of their vehicle and take him back to 501 Berks for possible identification by the victim. Both officers got out of the car. Officer Lace proceeded to conduct a patdown of Cargo. For safety purposes, it was departmental policy to pat down all persons before placing them in the back of a police car.

While patting down Cargo, Lace felt a gun in his waistband. Cargo jumped away from Lace. The gun became lodged in Cargo's sweatshirt before eventually falling to the ground. The officers placed Cargo under arrest and took him to police headquarters. A total of two minutes and 38 seconds elapsed between the time the officers advised dispatch that they were proceeding to the scene and the time of the arrest. Less than six minutes elapsed between the time of the 911 call and the time of Cargo's arrest. A grand jury indicted Cargo for the possession of a firearm by a convicted felon.

Were the actions that led to the discovery of the gun consistent with the dictates of the Fourth Amendment?

Selected Bibliography

Jeffrey Bellin, *The Inverse Relationship between the Constitutionality and Effectiveness of New York City "Stop and Frisk,"* 94 B.U.L. Rev. 1495 (2014)

Paul Butler, *"A Long Step Down the Totalitarian Path": Justice Douglas's Great Dissent in* Terry v. Ohio, 79 Miss. L.J. 9 (2009)

Devon W. Carbado, *(E)racing the Fourth Amendment*, 100 Mich. L. Rev. 946 (2002)

Thomas K. Clancy, *The Future of Fourth Amendment Seizure Analysis after* Hodari D. *and* Bostick, 28 Am. Crim. L. Rev. 799 (1991)

Frank Rudy Cooper, *The Un-Balanced Fourth Amendment: A Cultural Study of the Drug War, Racial Profiling, and* Arvizu, 47 Vill. L. Rev. 851 (2002)

David A. Harris, *Across the Hudson: Taking the Stop and Frisk Debate Beyond New York City*, 16 N.Y.U. J. Legis. & Pub. Pol'y 1495 (2014)

David A. Harris, *Using Race or Ethnicity as a Factor in Assessing the Reasonableness of Fourth Amendment Activity: Description, Yes; Prediction, No*, 73 Miss. L.J. 423 (2003)

Stephen E. Henderson, *"Move On" Orders as Fourth Amendment Seizures*, 2008 B.Y.U. L. Rev. 1 (2008)

Lewis R. Katz & Aaron P. Golembiewski, *Curbing the Dog: Extending the Protection of the Fourth Amendment to Police Drug Dogs*, 85 Neb. L. Rev. 735 (2007)

Lewis R. Katz, Terry v. Ohio *at Thirty-Five: A Revisionist View*, 74 Miss. L.J. 423 (2004)

Edward J. Loya, Jr., *Sweeping Away the Fourth Amendment*, 1 Stan. J. Civ. Rts. & Civ. Liberties 457 (2005)

Tracey Maclin, *The Decline of the Right of Locomotion: The Fourth Amendment on the Streets*, 75 Cornell L. Rev. 1258 (1990)

Tracey Maclin, *"Voluntary" Interviews and Airport Searches of Middle Eastern Men: The Fourth Amendment in a Time of Terror*, 73 Miss. L.J. 471 (2003)

Anne Bowen Poulin, *The Plain Feel Doctrine and the Evolution of the Fourth Amendment*, 42 Vill. L. Rev. 741 (1997)

Amy D. Ronner, *Fleeing While Black: The Fourth Amendment Apartheid*, 32 Colum. Hum. Rts. L. Rev. 383 (2001)

Lawrence Rosenthal, *Pragmatism, Originalism, Race, and the Case Against* Terry v. Ohio, 43 Tex. Tech L. Rev. 299 (2010)

Kami Chavis Simmons, *The Legacy of Stop and Frisk: Addressing the Vestiges of a Violent Police Culture*, 49 Wake Forest L. Rev. 849 (2014)

Brando Simeo Starkey, *A Failure of the Fourth Amendment & Equal Protection's Promise: How the Equal Protection Clause Can Change Discriminatory Stop and Frisk Policies*, 18 Mich. J. Race & L. 131 (2012)

Daniel J. Steinbock, *The Wrong Line Between Freedom and Restraint: The Unreality, Obscurity, and Incivility of the Fourth Amendment Consensual Encounter Doctrine*, 38 San Diego L. Rev. 507 (2001)

Carol S. Steiker, Terry *Unbound*, 82 Miss. L.J. 329 (2013)

Scott E. Sundby, *A Return to Fourth Amendment Basics: Undoing the Mischief of* Camara *and* Terry, 72 Minn. L. Rev. 383 (1988)

Terry v. Ohio *30 Years Later: A Symposium on the Fourth Amendment, Law Enforcement and Police-Citizen Encounters*, 72 St. John's L. Rev. 721–1382 (1998)

[B] Special Balancing Contexts

[1] School Searches

New Jersey v. T.L.O.
United States Supreme Court
469 U.S. 325, 105 S. Ct. 733, 83 L. Ed. 2d 720 (1985)

JUSTICE WHITE delivered the opinion of the Court.

. . . .

I

On March 7, 1980, a teacher at Piscataway High School in Middlesex County, N.J., discovered two girls smoking in a lavatory. One of the two girls was the respondent T.L.O., who at that time was a 14-year-old high school freshman. Because smoking in the lavatory was a violation of a school rule, the teacher took the two girls to the Principal's office, where they met with Assistant Vice Principal Theodore Choplick. In response to questioning by Mr. Choplick, T.L.O.'s companion admitted that she had violated the rule. T.L.O., however, denied that she had been smoking in the lavatory and claimed that she did not smoke at all.

Mr. Choplick asked T.L.O. to come into his private office and demanded to see her purse. Opening the purse, he found a pack of cigarettes, which he removed from the purse and held before T.L.O. as he accused her of having lied to him. As he reached into the purse for the cigarettes, Mr. Choplick also noticed a package of cigarette rolling papers. In his experience, possession of rolling papers by high school students was closely associated with the use of marihuana. Suspecting that a closer examination of the purse might yield further evidence of drug use, Mr. Choplick proceeded to search the purse thoroughly. The search revealed a small amount of marihuana, a pipe, a number of empty plastic bags, a substantial quantity of money in one-dollar bills, an index card that appeared to be a list of students who owed T.L.O. money, and two letters that implicated T.L.O. in marihuana dealing.

Mr. Choplick notified T.L.O.'s mother and the police, and turned the evidence of drug dealing over to the police. At the request of the police, T.L.O.'s mother took her daughter to police headquarters, where T.L.O. confessed that she had been selling marihuana at the high school. On the basis of the confession and the evidence seized by Mr. Choplick, the State brought delinquency charges against T.L.O. in the Juvenile and Domestic Relations Court of Middlesex County. Contending that Mr. Choplick's search of her purse violated the Fourth Amendment, T.L.O. moved to suppress the evidence found in her purse as well as her confession, which, she argued, was tainted by the allegedly unlawful search. . . .

. . . Having denied the motion to suppress, the court . . . found T.L.O. to be a delinquent and . . . sentenced her to a year's probation.

. . . T.L.O. appealed the Fourth Amendment ruling, and the Supreme Court of New Jersey reversed the judgment of the Appellate Division and ordered the suppression of the evidence found in T.L.O.'s purse.

. . . .

Having heard argument on the legality of the search of T.L.O.'s purse, we are satisfied that the search did not violate the Fourth Amendment.[3]

II

In determining whether the search at issue in this case violated the Fourth Amendment, we are faced initially with the question whether that Amendment's

---

3. In holding that the search of T.L.O.'s purse did not violate the Fourth Amendment, we do not implicitly determine that the exclusionary rule applies to the fruits of unlawful searches conducted by school authorities. The question whether evidence should be excluded from a criminal proceeding involves two discrete inquiries: whether the evidence was seized in violation of the Fourth Amendment, and whether the exclusionary rule is the appropriate remedy for the violation. Neither question is logically antecedent to the other, for a negative answer to either question is sufficient to dispose of the case. Thus, our determination that the search at issue in this case did not violate the Fourth Amendment implies no particular resolution of the question of the applicability of the exclusionary rule.

prohibition on unreasonable searches and seizures applies to searches conducted by public school officials. We hold that it does.

It is now beyond dispute that "the Federal Constitution, by virtue of the Fourteenth Amendment, prohibits unreasonable searches and seizures by state officers." *Elkins v. United States*, 364 U.S. 206, 80 S. Ct. 1437, 1442, 4 L. Ed. 2d 1669 (1960). Equally indisputable is the proposition that the Fourteenth Amendment protects the rights of students against encroachment by public school officials. . . .

. . . [T]he State of New Jersey has argued that the history of the Fourteenth Amendment indicates that the Amendment was intended to regulate only searches and seizures carried out by law enforcement officers; accordingly, although public school officials are concededly state agents for purposes of the Fourteenth Amendment, the Fourth Amendment creates no rights enforceable against them.

It may well be true that the evil toward which the Fourth Amendment was primarily directed was the resurrection of the pre-Revolutionary practice of using general warrants or "writs of assistance" to authorize searches for contraband by officers of the Crown. But this Court has never limited the Amendment's prohibition on unreasonable searches and seizures to operations conducted by the police. Rather, the Court has long spoken of the Fourth Amendment's strictures as restraints imposed upon "governmental action" — that is, "upon the activities of sovereign authority." *Burdeau v. McDowell*, 256 U.S. 465, 41 S. Ct. 574, 65 L. Ed. 1048 (1921). . . .

Notwithstanding the general applicability of the Fourth Amendment to the activities of civil authorities, a few courts have concluded that school officials are exempt from the dictates of the Fourth Amendment by virtue of the special nature of their authority over schoolchildren. Teachers and school administrators, it is said, act *in loco parentis* in their dealings with students: their authority is that of the parent, not the State, and is therefore not subject to the limits of the Fourth Amendment.

Such reasoning is in tension with contemporary reality and the teachings of this Court. We have held school officials subject to the commands of the First Amendment, *see Tinker v. Des Moines Independent Community School District*, 393 U.S. 503, 89 S. Ct. 733, 21 L. Ed. 2d 731 (1969), and the Due Process Clause of the Fourteenth Amendment, *see Goss v. Lopez*, 419 U.S. 565, 95 S. Ct. 729, 42 L. Ed. 2d 725 (1975). If school authorities are state actors for purposes of the constitutional guarantees of freedom of expression and due process, it is difficult to understand why they should be deemed to be exercising parental rather than public authority when conducting searches of their students . . . . In carrying out searches and other disciplinary functions pursuant to such policies, school officials act as representatives of the State, not merely as surrogates for the parents, and they cannot claim the parents' immunity from the strictures of the Fourth Amendment.

III

To hold that the Fourth Amendment applies to searches conducted by school authorities is only to begin the inquiry into the standards governing such searches. Although the underlying command of the Fourth Amendment is always that searches and seizures be reasonable, what is reasonable depends on the context within which a search takes place. The determination of the standard of reasonableness governing any specific class of searches requires "balancing the need to search against the invasion which the search entails." *Camara v. Municipal Court, supra*, 387 U.S., at 536–37, 87 S. Ct., at 1735. On one side of the balance are arrayed the individual's legitimate expectations of privacy and personal security; on the other, the government's need for effective methods to deal with breaches of public order.

We have recognized that even a limited search of the person is a substantial invasion of privacy. *Terry v. Ohio*, 392 U.S. 1, 24–25, 88 S. Ct. 1868, 1881–1882, 20 L. Ed. 2d 889 (1967). We have also recognized that searches of closed items of personal luggage are intrusions on protected privacy interests, for "the Fourth Amendment provides protection to the owner of every container that conceals its contents from plain view." *United States v. Ross*, 456 U.S. 798, 822–823, 102 S. Ct. 2157, 2171, 72 L. Ed. 2d 572 (1982). A search of a child's person or of a closed purse or other bag carried on her person,[5] no less than a similar search carried out on an adult, is undoubtedly a severe violation of subjective expectations of privacy.

Of course, the Fourth Amendment does not protect subjective expectations of privacy that are unreasonable or otherwise "illegitimate."

. . . .

. . . [But] the State's suggestion that children have no legitimate need to bring personal property into the schools [does not] seem well-anchored in reality . . . . [S]choolchildren may find it necessary to carry with them a variety of legitimate, noncontraband items, and there is no reason to conclude that they have necessarily waived all rights to privacy in such items merely by bringing them onto school grounds.

Against the child's interest in privacy must be set the substantial interest of teachers and administrators in maintaining discipline in the classrooom and on school grounds. Maintaining order in the classroom has never been easy, but in recent years, school disorder has often taken particularly ugly forms: drug use and violent crime in the schools have become major social problems. Even in schools that have been spared the most severe disciplinary problems, the preservation of order and a proper educational environment requires close supervision of schoolchildren, as well as the

---

5. We do not address the question, not presented by this case, whether a schoolchild has a legitimate expectation of privacy in lockers, desks, or other school property provided for the storage of school supplies. Nor do we express any opinion on the standards (if any) governing searches of such areas by school officials or by other public authorities acting at the request of school officials . . . .

enforcement of rules against conduct that would be perfectly permissible if undertaken by an adult. . . .

. . . It is evident that the school setting requires some easing of the restrictions to
which searches by public authorities are ordinarily subject. The warrant requirement,
in particular, is unsuited to the school environment: requiring a teacher to obtain a
warrant before searching a child suspected of an infraction of school rules (or of the
criminal law) would unduly interfere with the maintenance of the swift and informal disciplinary procedures needed in the schools. . . .

The school setting also requires some modification of the level of suspicion of
illicit activity needed to justify a search. . . .

We join the majority of courts that have examined this issue in concluding that
the accommodation of the privacy interests of schoolchildren with the substantial
need of teachers and administrators for freedom to maintain order in the schools
does not require strict adherence to the requirement that searches be based on probable cause to believe that the subject of the search has violated or is violating the law.
Rather, the legality of the search of a student should depend simply on the reasonableness, under all the circumstances, of the search . . . . Under ordinary circumstances, a search of a student by a teacher or other school official[7] will be "justified at
its inception" when there are reasonable grounds for suspecting that the search will
turn up evidence that the student has violated or is violating either the law or the
rules of the school.[8] Such a search will be permissible in its scope when the measures
adopted are reasonably related to the objectives of the search and not excessively intrusive in light of the age and sex of the student and the nature of the infraction.[9]

---

7. We here consider only searches carried out by school authorities acting alone and on their
own authority. This case does not present the question of the appropriate standard for assessing the
legality of searches conducted by school officials in conjunction with or at the behest of law enforcement agencies, and we express no opinion on that question.

8. We do not decide whether individualized suspicion is an essential element of the reasonableness standard we adopt for searches by school authorities. In other contexts, however, we have held
that although "some quantum of individualized suspicion is usually a prerequisite to a constitutional search or seizure[,] . . . the Fourth Amendment imposes no irreducible requirement of such
suspicion." *United States v. Martinez-Fuerte*, 428 U.S. 543, 560–561, 96 S. Ct. 3074, 3084, 49 L. Ed. 2d
1116 (1976). *See also Camara v. Municipal Court*, 387 U.S. 523, 87 S. Ct. 1727, 18 L. Ed. 2d 930 (1967).
Exceptions to the requirement of individualized suspicion are generally appropriate only where the
privacy interests implicated by a search are minimal and where "other safeguards" are available "to
assure that the individual's reasonable expectation of privacy is not 'subject to the discretion of the
official in the field.'" *Delaware v. Prouse*, 440 U.S. 648, 654–655, 99 S. Ct. 1391, 1396–1397, 59 L. Ed.
2d 660 (1979) (citation omitted). Because the search of T.L.O.'s purse was based upon an individualized suspicion that she had violated school rules, we need not consider the circumstances that might
justify school authorities in conducting searches unsupported by individualized suspicion.

9. Our reference to the nature of the infraction is not intended as an endorsement of JUSTICE
STEVENS' suggestion that some rules regarding student conduct are by nature too "trivial" to justify
a search based upon reasonable suspicion. We are unwilling to adopt a standard under which the
legality of a search is dependent upon a judge's evaluation of the relative importance of various

This standard will, we trust, neither unduly burden the efforts of school authorities to maintain order in their schools nor authorize unrestrained intrusions upon the privacy of schoolchildren. By focusing attention on the question of reasonableness, the standard will spare teachers and school administrators the necessity of schooling themselves in the niceties of probable cause and permit them to regulate their conduct according to the dictates of reason and common sense. At the same time, the reasonableness standard should ensure that the interests of students will be invaded no more than is necessary to achieve the legitimate end of preserving order in the schools.

IV

. . . .

The incident that gave rise to this case actually involved two separate searches, with the first — the search for cigarettes — providing the suspicion that gave rise to the second — the search for marihuana. Although it is the fruits of the second search that are at issue here, the validity of the search for marihuana must depend on the reasonableness of the initial search for cigarettes, as there would have been no reason to suspect that T.L.O. possessed marihuana had the first search not taken place. Accordingly, it is to the search for cigarettes that we first turn our attention.

. . . .

T.L.O. had been accused of smoking, and had denied the accusation in the strongest possible terms when she stated that she did not smoke at all. Surely it cannot be said that, under these circumstances, T.L.O.'s possession of cigarettes would be irrelevant to the charges against her or to her response to those charges. T.L.O.'s possession of cigarettes, once it was discovered, would both corroborate the report that she had been smoking and undermine the credibility of her defense to the charge of smoking. To be sure, the discovery of the cigarettes would not prove that T.L.O. had been smoking in the lavatory; nor would it, strictly speaking, necessarily be inconsistent with her claim that she did not smoke at all. But it is universally recognized that evidence, to be relevant to an inquiry, need not conclusively prove the ultimate fact in issue, but only have "any tendency to make the existence of any fact that is of consequence to the determination of the action more probable or less probable than it would be without the evidence." Fed. Rule Evid. 401 . . . . Thus, if Mr. Choplick in

---

school rules. The maintenance of discipline in the schools requires not only that students be restrained from assaulting one another, abusing drugs and alcohol, and committing other crimes, but also that students conform themselves to the standards of conduct prescribed by school authorities. We have "repeatedly emphasized the need for affirming the comprehensive authority of the States and of school officials, consistent with fundamental constitutional safeguards, to prescribe and control conduct in the schools." *Tinker v. Des Moines Independent Community School Dist.*, 393 U.S. 503, 507, 89 S. Ct. 733, 737, 21 L. Ed. 2d 731, (1969). The promulgation of a rule forbidding specified conduct presumably reflects a judgment on the part of school officials that such conduct is destructive of school order or of a proper educational environment. Absent any suggestion that the rule violates some substantive constitutional guarantee, the courts should, as a general matter, defer to that judgment and refrain from attempting to distinguish between rules that are important to the preservation of order in the schools and the rules that are not.

fact had a reasonable suspicion that T.L.O. had cigarettes in her purse, the search was justified despite the fact that the cigarettes, if found, would constitute "mere evidence" of a violation.

. . . A teacher had reported that T.L.O. was smoking in the lavatory. Certainly this report gave Mr. Choplick reason to suspect that T.L.O. was carrying cigarettes with her; and if she did have cigarettes, her purse was the obvious place in which to find them. Mr. Choplick's suspicion that there were cigarettes in the purse was not an "inchoate and unparticularized suspicion or 'hunch,'" *Terry v. Ohio*, 392 U.S., at 27, 88 S. Ct., at 1883; rather, it was the sort of "common-sense conclusio[n] about human behavior" upon which "practical people" — including government officials — are entitled to rely. *United States v. Cortez*, 449 U.S. 411, 418, 101 S. Ct. 690, 695, 66 L. Ed. 2d 621 (1981) . . . . Accordingly, it cannot be said that Mr. Choplick acted unreasonably when he examined T.L.O.'s purse to see if it contained cigarettes.[12]

Our conclusion that Mr. Choplick's decision to open T.L.O.'s purse was reasonable brings us to the question of the further search for marihuana once the pack of cigarettes was located. The suspicion upon which the search for marihuana was founded was provided when Mr. Choplick observed a package of rolling papers in the purse as he removed the pack of cigarettes. Although T.L.O. does not dispute the reasonableness of Mr. Choplick's belief that the rolling papers indicated the presence of marihuana, she does contend that the scope of the search Mr. Choplick conducted exceeded permissible bounds when he seized and read certain letters that implicated T.L.O. in drug dealing. This argument, too, is unpersuasive. The discovery of the rolling papers concededly gave rise to a reasonable suspicion that T.L.O. was carrying marihuana as well as cigarettes in her purse. This suspicion justified further exploration of T.L.O.'s purse, which turned up more evidence of drug-related activities: a pipe, a number of plastic bags of the type commonly used to store marihuana, a small quantity of marihuana, and a fairly substantial amount of money. Under these circumstances, it was not unreasonable to extend the search to a separate zippered compartment of the purse; and when a search of that compartment revealed an index card containing a list of "people who owe me money" as well as two

---

12. T.L.O. contends that even if it was reasonable for Mr. Choplick to open her purse to look for cigarettes, it was not reasonable for him to reach in and take the cigarettes out of her purse once he found them. Had he not removed the cigarettes from the purse, she asserts, he would not have observed the rolling papers that suggested the presence of marihuana, and the search for marihuana could not have taken place. T.L.O.'s argument is based on the fact that the cigarettes were not "contraband," as no school rule forbade her to have them. Thus, according to T.L.O., the cigarettes were not subject to seizure or confiscation by school authorities, and Mr. Choplick was not entitled to take them out of T.L.O.'s purse regardless of whether he was entitled to peer into the purse to see if they were there. Such hairsplitting argumentation has no place in an inquiry addressed to the issue of reasonableness. If Mr. Choplick could permissibly search T.L.O.'s purse for cigarettes, it hardly seems reasonable to suggest that his natural reaction to finding them — picking them up — could be a constitutional violation. We find that neither in opening the purse nor in reaching into it to remove the cigarettes did Mr. Choplick violate the Fourth Amendment.

letters, the inference that T.L.O. was involved in marihuana trafficking was substantial enough to justify Mr. Choplick in examining the letters to determine whether they contained any further evidence. In short, we cannot conclude that the search for marihuana was unreasonable in any respect.

Because the search resulting in the discovery of the evidence of marihuana dealing by T.L.O. was reasonable, the New Jersey Supreme Court's decision to exclude that evidence from T.L.O.'s delinquency proceedings on Fourth Amendment grounds was erroneous. Accordingly, the judgment of the Supreme Court of New Jersey is

Reversed.

JUSTICE POWELL, with whom JUSTICE O'CONNOR joins, concurring.

I agree with the Court's decision, and generally with its opinion. I would place greater emphasis, however, on the special characteristics of elementary and secondary schools that make it unnecessary to afford students the same constitutional protections granted adults and juveniles in a nonschool setting.

In any realistic sense, students within the school environment have a lesser expectation of privacy than members of the population generally. They spend the school hours in close association with each other, both in the classroom and during recreation periods. The students in a particular class often know each other and their teachers quite well. Of necessity, teachers have a degree of familiarity with, and authority over, their students that is unparalleled except perhaps in the relationship between parent and child. It is simply unrealistic to think that students have the same subjective expectation of privacy as the population generally. But for purposes of deciding this case, I can assume that children in school — no less than adults — have privacy interests that society is prepared to recognize as legitimate.

. . . .

The special relationship between teacher and student also distinguishes the setting within which schoolchildren operate. Law enforcement officers function as adversaries of criminal suspects. These officers have the responsibility to investigate criminal activity, to locate and arrest those who violate our laws, and to facilitate the charging and bringing of such persons to trial. Rarely does this type of adversarial relationship exist between school authorities and pupils.[1] Instead, there is a commonality of interests between teachers and their pupils. The attitude of the typical teacher is one of personal responsibility for the student's welfare as well as for his education.

The primary duty of school officials and teachers, as the Court states, is the education and training of young people. A state has a compelling interest in assuring

---

1. Unlike police officers, school authorities have no law enforcement responsibility or indeed any obligation to be familiar with the criminal laws. Of course, as illustrated by this case, school authorities have a layman's familiarity with the types of crimes that occur frequently in our schools: the distribution and use of drugs, theft, and even violence against teachers as well as fellow students.

that the schools meet this responsibility. Without first establishing discipline and maintaining order, teachers cannot begin to educate their students. And apart from education, the school has the obligation to protect pupils from mistreatment by other children, and also to protect teachers themselves from violence by the few students whose conduct in recent years has prompted national concern. For me, it would be unreasonable and at odds with history to argue that the full panoply of constitutional rules applies with the same force and effect in the schoolhouse as it does in the enforcement of criminal laws.

In sum, although I join the Court's opinion and its holding,[3] my emphasis is somewhat different.

JUSTICE BLACKMUN, concurring in the judgment.

I join the judgment of the Court and agree with much that is said in its opinion. I write separately, however, because I believe the Court omits a crucial step in its analysis of whether a school search must be based upon probable cause . . . . I believe that we have used . . . a balancing test, rather than strictly applying the Fourth Amendment's Warrant and Probable Cause Clause, only when we were confronted with "a special law enforcement need for greater flexibility." *Florida v. Royer*, 460 U.S. 491, 103 S. Ct. 1319, 1333, 75 L. Ed. 2d 229 (1983) (Blackmun, J., dissenting) . . . . Only in those exceptional circumstances in which special needs, beyond the normal need for law enforcement, make the warrant and probable cause requirement impracticable, is a court entitled to substitute its balancing of interests for that of the Framers.

. . . .

The Court's implication that the balancing test is the rule rather than the exception is troubling for me because it is unnecessary in this case . . . . A single teacher often must watch over a large number of students, and, as any parent knows, children at certain ages are inclined to test the outer boundaries of acceptable conduct and to imitate the misbehavior of a peer if that misbehavior is not dealt with quickly. Every adult remembers from his own schooldays the havoc a water pistol or pea-shooter can wreak until it is taken away . . . . Indeed, because drug use and possession of weapons have become increasingly common among young people, an immediate response frequently is required not just to maintain an environment conducive to learning but to protect the very safety of students and school personnel.

Such immediate action obviously would not be possible if a teacher were required to secure a warrant before searching a student. Nor would it be possible if a teacher could not conduct a necessary search until the teacher thought there was probable cause for the search . . . . A teacher's focus is, and should be, on teaching and helping students, rather than on developing evidence against a particular troublemaker.

---

3. The Court's holding is that "when there are reasonable grounds for suspecting that [a] search will turn up evidence that the student has violated or is violating either the law or the rules of the school," a search of the student's person or belongings is justified. This is in accord with the Court's summary of the views of a majority of state and federal courts that have addressed this issue.

. . . The special need for an immediate response to behavior that threatens either the safety of schoolchildren and teachers or the educational process itself justifies the Court in excepting school searches from the warrant and probable cause requirement, and in applying a standard determined by balancing the relevant interests. I agree with the standard the Court has announced, and with its application of the standard to the facts of this case. I therefore concur in its judgment.

Justice Brennan, with whom Justice Marshall joins, concurring in part and dissenting in part.

I fully agree with Part II of the Court's opinion. Teachers, like all other government officials, must conform their conduct to the Fourth Amendment's protections of personal privacy and personal security. . . .

I do not, however, otherwise join the Court's opinion. Today's decision sanctions school officials to conduct full-scale searches on a "reasonableness" standard whose only definite content is that it is not the same test as the "probable cause" standard found in the text of the Fourth Amendment.

I

. . . .

Vice Principal Choplick's thorough excavation of T.L.O.'s purse was undoubtedly a serious intrusion on her privacy. Unlike the searches in *Terry v. Ohio*, 407 U.S. 143, 92 S. Ct. 1921, 32 L. Ed. 2d 612 (1972), the search at issue here encompassed a detailed and minute examination of respondent's pocketbook, in which the contents of private papers and letters were thoroughly scrutinized.[1] Wisely, neither petitioner nor the Court today attempts to justify the search of T.L.O.'s pocketbook as a minimally intrusive search in the *Terry* line. To be faithful to the Court's settled doctrine, the inquiry therefore must focus on the warrant and probable-cause requirements.

A

I agree that schoolteachers or principals, when not acting as agents of law enforcement authorities, generally may conduct a search of their students' belongings without first obtaining a warrant . . . . The undifferentiated governmental interest in law enforcement is insufficient to justify an exception to the warrant requirement. Rather, some *special* governmental interest beyond the need merely to apprehend lawbreakers is necessary to justify a categorical exception to the warrant requirement. For the most part, special governmental needs sufficient to override the warrant requirement flow from "exigency" — that is, from the press of time that makes obtaining a warrant either impossible or hopelessly infeasible.

. . . .

---

1. A purse typically contains items of a highly personal nature. Especially for shy or sensitive adolescents, it could prove extremely embarrassing for a teacher or principal to rummage through its contents, which could include notes from friends, fragments of love poems, caricatures of school authorities, and items of personal hygiene.

In this case, such extraordinary governmental interests do exist and are sufficient to justify an exception to the warrant requirement. Students are necessarily confined for most of the school day in close proximity to each other and to the school staff. I agree with the Court that we can take judicial notice of the serious problems of drugs and violence that plague our schools . . . . A teacher or principal could neither carry out essential teaching functions nor adequately protect students' safety if required to wait for a warrant before conducting a necessary search.

B

I emphatically disagree with the Court's decision to cast aside the constitutional probable-cause standard when assessing the constitutional validity of a schoolhouse search. The Court's decision jettisons the probable-cause standard — the only standard that finds support in the text of the Fourth Amendment — on the basis of its Rohrschach-like "balancing test." Use of such a "balancing test" to determine the standard for evaluating the validity of a full-scale search represents a sizable innovation in Fourth Amendment analysis . . . . Moreover, even if this Court's historic understanding of the Fourth Amendment were mistaken and a balancing test of some kind were appropriate, any such test that gave adequate weight to the privacy and security interests protected by the Fourth Amendment would not reach the preordained result the Court's conclusory analysis reaches today. . . .

1

An unbroken line of cases in this Court have held that probable cause is a requisite for a full-scale search.

. . . .

I . . . fully agree with the Court that "the underlying command of the Fourth Amendment is always that searches and seizures be reasonable." But this "underlying command" is not directly interpreted in each category of cases by some amorphous "balancing test." Rather, the provisions of the warrant clause — a warrant and probable cause — provide the yardstick against which official searches and seizures are to be measured. The Fourth Amendment neither requires nor authorizes the conceptual free-for-all that ensues when an unguided balancing test is used to assess specific categories of searches. If the search in question is more than a minimally intrusive *Terry*-stop, the constitutional probable-cause standard determines its validity.

. . . .

. . . I cannot agree with the Court's assertions today that a "balancing test" can replace the constitutional threshold with one that is more convenient for those enforcing the laws but less protective of the citizens' liberty; the Fourth Amendment's protections should not be defaced by "a balancing process that overwhelms the individual's protection against unwarranted official intrusion by a governmental interest said to justify the search and seizure." *United States v. Martinez-Fuerte*, 428 U.S., at 570, 96 S. Ct., at 3088 (Brennan, J., dissenting).

2

... But even if I believed that a "balancing test" appropriately replaces the judgment of the Framers of the Fourth Amendment, I would nonetheless object to the cursory and shortsighted "test" that the Court employs to justify its predictable weakening of the Fourth Amendment protections....

The Court begins to articulate its "balancing test" by observing that "the government's need for effective methods to deal with breaches of public order" is to be weighed on one side of the balance. Of course, this is not correct .... Rather, it is the cost of applying probable cause as opposed to applying some lesser standard that should be weighed on the government's side.[5]

In order to tote up the costs of applying the probable-cause standard, it is thus necessary first to take into account the nature and content of that standard, and the likelihood that it would hamper achievement of the goal — vital not just to "teachers and administrators" — of maintaining an effective educational setting in the public schools....

Two terms ago, in *Illinois v. Gates*, 462 U.S. 213, 103 S. Ct. 2317, 76 L. Ed. 2d 527 (1983), this Court expounded at some length its view of the probable-cause standard....

Ignoring what *Gates* took some pains to emphasize, the Court today holds that a new "reasonableness" standard is appropriate because it "will spare teachers and school administrators the necessity of schooling themselves in the niceties of probable cause and permit them to regulate their conduct according to the dictates of reason and common sense." I had never thought that our pre-*Gates* understanding of probable cause defied either reason or common sense. But after *Gates*, I would have thought that there could be no doubt that this "nontechnical," "practical," and "easily applied" concept was eminently serviceable in a context like a school, where teachers require the flexibility to respond quickly and decisively to emergencies.

. . . .

As compared with the relative ease with which teachers can apply the probable-cause standard, the amorphous "reasonableness under all the circumstances" standard freshly coined by the Court today will likely spawn increased litigation and greater uncertainty among teachers and administrators.

. . . .

---

5. I speak of the "government's side" only because it is the terminology used by the Court. In my view, this terminology itself is seriously misleading. The government is charged with protecting the privacy and security of the citizen, just as it is charged with apprehending those who violate the criminal law. Consequently, the government has no legitimate interest in conducting a search that unduly intrudes on the privacy and security of the citizen. The balance is not between the rights of the government and the rights of the citizen, but between opposing conceptions of the constitutionally legitimate means of carrying out the government's varied responsibilities.

A legitimate balancing test whose function was something more substantial than reaching a predetermined conclusion acceptable to this Court's impressions of what authority teachers need would therefore reach rather a different result than that reached by the Court today. On one side of the balance would be the costs of applying traditional Fourth Amendment standards — the "practical" and "flexible" probable-cause standard where a full-scale intrusion is sought, a lesser standard in situations where the intrusion is much less severe and the need for greater authority compelling. Whatever costs were toted up on this side would have to be discounted by the costs of applying an unprecedented and ill-defined "reasonableness under all the circumstances" test that will leave teachers and administrators uncertain as to their authority and will encourage excessive fact-based litigation.

On the other side of the balance would be the serious privacy interests of the student, interests that the Court admirably articulates in its opinion, but which the Court's new ambiguous standard places in serious jeopardy. I have no doubt that a fair assessment of the two sides of the balance would necessarily reach the same conclusion that, as I have argued above, the Fourth Amendment's language compels — that school searches like that conducted in this case are valid only if supported by probable cause.

II

Applying the constitutional probable-cause standard to the facts of this case, I would find that Mr. Choplick's search violated T.L.O.'s Fourth Amendment rights.

. . . .

On my view of the case, we need not decide whether the initial search conducted by Mr. Choplick — the search for evidence of the smoking violation that was completed when Mr. Choplick found the cigarettes — was valid. For Mr. Choplick at that point did not have probable cause to continue to rummage through T.L.O.'s purse. Mr. Choplick's suspicion of marihuana possession at this time was based solely on the presence of the package of cigarette papers. The mere presence without more of such a staple item of commerce is insufficient to warrant a person of reasonable caution in inferring both that T.L.O. had violated the law by possessing marihuana and that evidence of that violation would be found in her purse. Just as a police officer could not obtain a warrant to search a home based solely on his claim that he had seen a package of cigarette papers in that home, Mr. Choplick was not entitled to search possibly the most private possessions of T.L.O. based on the mere presence of a package of cigarette papers. Therefore, the fruits of this illegal search must be excluded and the judgment of the New Jersey Supreme Court affirmed.

III

In the past several Terms, this Court has produced a succession of Fourth Amendment opinions in which "balancing tests" have been applied to resolve various questions concerning the proper scope of official searches. . . .

All of these "balancing tests" amount to brief nods by the Court in the direction of a neutral utilitarian calculus while the Court in fact engages in an unanalyzed exercise of judicial will. Perhaps this doctrinally destructive nihilism is merely a convenient umbrella under which a majority that cannot agree on a genuine rationale can conceal its differences. . . .

On my view, the presence of the word "unreasonable" in the text of the Fourth Amendment does not grant a shifting majority of the Court the authority to answer all Fourth Amendment questions by consulting its momentary vision of the social good. Full-scale searches unaccompanied by probable cause violate the Fourth Amendment. I do not pretend that our traditional Fourth Amendment doctrine automatically answers all of the difficult legal questions that occasionally arise. I do contend, however, that this Court has an obligation to provide some coherent framework to resolve such questions on the basis of more than a conclusory recitation of the results of a "balancing test." The Fourth Amendment itself supplies that framework and, because the Court today fails to heed its message, I must respectfully dissent.

Justice Stevens, with whom Justice Marshall joins, and with whom Justice Brennan joins as to Part I, concurring in part and dissenting in part.

. . . .

II

The search of a young woman's purse by a school administrator is a serious invasion of her legitimate expectations of privacy. . . .

. . . When viewed from the institutional perspective, "the substantial need of teachers and administrators for freedom to maintain order in the schools," is no less acute. Violent, unlawful, or seriously disruptive conduct is fundamentally inconsistent with the principal function of teaching institutions which is to educate young people and prepare them for citizenship. When such conduct occurs amidst a sizeable group of impressionable young people, it creates an explosive atmosphere that requires a prompt and effective response.

Thus, warrantless searches of students by school administrators are reasonable when undertaken for those purposes. But the majority's statement of the standard for evaluating the reasonableness of such searches is not suitably adapted to that end. The majority holds that "a search of a student by a teacher or other school official will be 'justified at its inception' when there are reasonable grounds for suspecting *that the search will turn up evidence that the student has violated or is violating either the law or the rules of the school.*" This standard will permit teachers and school administrators to search students when they suspect that the search will reveal evidence of even the most trivial school regulation or precatory guideline for student behavior. The Court's standard for deciding whether a search is justified "at its inception" treats all violations of the rules of the school as though they were fungible. For the Court, a search for curlers and sunglasses in order to enforce the school dress code is apparently just as important as a search for evidence of heroin addiction or violent gang activity.

. . . In arguing that teachers and school administrators need the power to search students based on a lessened standard, the United States as *amicus curiae* relies heavily on empirical evidence of a contemporary crisis of violence and unlawful behavior that is seriously undermining the process of education in American schools. A standard better attuned to this concern would permit teachers and school administrators to search a student when they have reason to believe that the search will uncover evidence that the student is violating the law or engaging in conduct that is seriously disruptive of school order, or the educational process.

. . . .

The logic of distinguishing between minor and serious offenses in evaluating the reasonableness of school searches is almost too clear for argument. In order to justify the serious intrusion on the persons and privacy of young people that New Jersey asks this Court to approve, the State must identify "some real immediate and serious consequences." *McDonald v. United States*, 335 U.S. 451, 460, 69 S. Ct. 191, 93 L. Ed. 153 (1948) (Jackson, J., concurring, joined by Frankfurter, J.).

. . . .

Unlike the Court, I believe the nature of the suspected infraction is a matter of first importance in deciding whether any invasion of privacy is permissible.

III

. . . .

I would view this case differently if the Assistant Principal had reason to believe T.L.O.'s purse contained evidence of criminal activity, or of an activity that would seriously disrupt school discipline. There was, however, absolutely no basis for any such assumption — not even a "hunch."

In this case, Mr. Choplick overreacted to what appeared to be nothing more than a minor infraction — a rule prohibiting smoking in the bathroom of the freshmen's and sophomores' building. It is, of course, true that he actually found evidence of serious wrongdoing by T.L.O., but no one claims that the prior search may be justified by his unexpected discovery. As far as the smoking infraction is concerned, the search for cigarettes merely tended to corroborate a teacher's eyewitness account of T.L.O.'s violation of a minor regulation designed to channel student smoking behavior into designated locations. Because this conduct was neither unlawful nor significantly disruptive of school order or the educational process, the invasion of privacy associated with the forcible opening of T.L.O.'s purse was entirely unjustified at its inception.

A review of the sampling of school search cases relied on by the Court demonstrates how different this case is from those in which there was indeed a valid justification for intruding on a student's privacy. In most of them the student was suspected of a criminal violation; in the remainder either violence or substantial disruption of school order or the integrity of the academic process was at stake. Few involved matters as trivial as the no-smoking rule violated by T.L.O. The rule the

Court adopts today is so open-ended that it may make the Fourth Amendment virtually meaningless in the school context. Although I agree that school administrators must have broad latitude to maintain order and discipline in our classrooms, that authority is not unlimited.

IV

The schoolroom is the first opportunity most citizens have to experience the power of government. Through it passes every citizen and public official, from schoolteachers to policemen and prison guards. The values they learn there, they take with them in life. One of our most cherished ideals is the one contained in the Fourth Amendment: that the Government may not intrude on the personal privacy of its citizens without a warrant or compelling circumstance. The Court's decision today is a curious moral for the Nation's youth. . . .

I respectfully dissent.

Notes and Questions

(1) Every member of the Court agreed that an exception to the search warrant requirement in the context of *T.L.O.* is justified. Members of the Court did dispute, however, the propriety of excepting school searches from the probable cause requirement. Why shouldn't probable cause be required to conduct warrantless school searches?

(2) Who may conduct school searches? Where may they be conducted? What persons and areas are properly subject to these searches?

(3) In *Safford Unified School District #1 v. Redding*, 557 U.S. 364, 129 S. Ct. 2633, 174 L. Ed. 2d 354 (2009), the Court held that a strip search of a 13-year-old student by school officials looking for "forbidden prescription and over-the-counter drugs" violated the Fourth Amendment "[b]ecause there were no reasons to suspect the drugs presented a danger or were concealed in [the student's] underwear." A school rule prohibited the "nonmedical use, possession, or sale" of "'"prescription or over-the-counter drug[s]. "'" Under *T.L.O.*, a "reasonable suspicion" that a student has violated such a rule justifies a school search. Reasonable suspicion, a "lesser standard" than probable cause, can "be described as a moderate chance of finding evidence of wrongdoing." In addition, *T.L.O.* declared it necessary that "'the search as actually conducted [be] reasonably related in scope to the circumstances which justified the interference in the first place.' The scope will be permissible . . . when it is 'not excessively intrusive in light of the age and sex of the student and the nature of the infraction.'"

The facts justified "a search of [the student's] backpack and outer clothing," and these searches were "not excessively intrusive." While "[t]he exact label for" the further search of the student's person was "not important," it was fair to describe it as a "strip search." The fact that the women conducting the search "did not see anything" was irrelevant. The "very fact" that the student, in accord with their instructions, "pull[ed] her underwear away from her body in the presence of the two officials who were able to see her necessarily her exposed breasts and pelvic area to some degree, and both subjective and reasonable societal expectations of personal privacy support the treatment of such a search as categorically distinct, requiring distinct elements of justification on the part of school authorities for going beyond a search of outer clothing and belongings."

For this search, "the content of the suspicion failed to match the degree of intrusion." The pills sought were "prescription-strength ibuprofen and over-the-counter naproxen, common pain relievers" that posed a "limited threat." There was "no reason to suspect that large amounts" that might be dangerous were being distributed. Nor was there a specific reason for suspecting the student of "hiding common painkillers in her underwear." The "categorically extreme intrusiveness" of this type of search "requires some justification in suspected facts." According to the Court, "what was missing . . . was any indication of danger to the students from the power of the drugs or their quantity, and any reason to suppose that [the searched student] was carrying pills in her underwear . . . . [T]he combination of these deficiencies was fatal to finding the search reasonable."

The concern with limiting "a school search to reasonable scope requires the support of reasonable suspicion of danger or of resort to underwear for hiding evidence of wrongdoing before a search can reasonably make the quantum leap from outer clothes and backpacks to exposure of intimate parts. The meaning of such a search, and the degradation its subject may reasonably feel, place a search that intrusive in a category of its own demanding its own specific suspicions."

[2] Checkpoints

Michigan Department of State Police v. Sitz

United States Supreme Court

496 U.S. 444, 110 S. Ct. 2481, 110 L. Ed. 2d 412 (1990)

CHIEF JUSTICE REHNQUIST delivered the opinion of the Court.

This case poses the question whether a State's use of highway sobriety checkpoints violates the Fourth and Fourteenth Amendments to the United States Constitution. We hold that it does not and therefore reverse the contrary holding of the Court of Appeals of Michigan.

Petitioners, the Michigan Department of State Police and its Director, established a sobriety checkpoint pilot program in early 1986. The Director appointed a Sobriety Checkpoint Advisory Committee comprising representatives of the State Police force, local police forces, state prosecutors, and the University of Michigan Transportation Research Institute. Pursuant to its charge, the Advisory Committee created guidelines setting forth procedures governing checkpoint operations, site selection, and publicity.

Under the guidelines, checkpoints would be set up at selected sites along state roads. All vehicles passing through a checkpoint would be stopped and their drivers briefly examined for signs of intoxication. In cases where a checkpoint officer detected signs of intoxication, the motorist would be directed to a location out of the traffic flow where an officer would check the motorist's driver's license and car registration and, if warranted, conduct further sobriety tests. Should the field tests and the officer's observations suggest that the driver was intoxicated, an arrest would be made. All other drivers would be permitted to resume their journey immediately.

The first — and to date the only — sobriety checkpoint operated under the program was conducted in Saginaw County with the assistance of the Saginaw County Sheriff's Department. During the hour-and-15-minute duration of the checkpoint's operation, 126 vehicles passed through the checkpoint. The average delay for each vehicle was approximately 25 seconds. Two drivers were detained for field sobriety testing, and one of the two was arrested for driving under the influence of alcohol. A third driver who drove through without stopping was pulled over by an officer in an observation vehicle and arrested for driving under the influence.

On the day before the operation of the Saginaw County checkpoint, respondents filed a complaint in the Circuit Court of Wayne County seeking declaratory and injunctive relief from potential subjection to the checkpoints. Each of the respondents "is a licensed driver in the State of Michigan . . . who regularly travels throughout the State in his automobile." *See* Complaint, App. 3a–4a. During pretrial proceedings, petitioners agreed to delay further implementation of the checkpoint program pending the outcome of this litigation.

After the trial, at which the court heard extensive testimony concerning, *inter alia*, the "effectiveness" of highway sobriety checkpoint programs, the court ruled that the Michigan program violated the Fourth Amendment and Art. 1, § 11, of the Michigan Constitution. On appeal, the Michigan Court of Appeals affirmed the holding that the program violated the Fourth Amendment and, for that reason, did not consider whether the program violated the Michigan Constitution. After the Michigan Supreme Court denied petitioners' application for leave to appeal, we granted certiorari. 493 U.S. 806 (1989).

. . . .

Petitioners concede, correctly in our view, that a Fourth Amendment "seizure" occurs when a vehicle is stopped at a checkpoint. The question thus becomes whether such seizures are "reasonable" under the Fourth Amendment.

It is important to recognize what our inquiry is not about. No allegations are before us of unreasonable treatment of any person after an actual detention at a particular checkpoint. As pursued in the lower courts, the instant action challenges only the use of sobriety checkpoints generally. We address only the initial stop of each motorist passing through a checkpoint and the associated preliminary questioning and observation by checkpoint officers. Detention of particular motorists for more extensive field sobriety testing may require satisfaction of an individualized suspicion standard.

No one can seriously dispute the magnitude of the drunken driving problem or the States' interest in eradicating it. Media reports of alcohol-related death and mutilation on the Nation's roads are legion. The anecdotal is confirmed by the statistical. "Drunk drivers cause an annual death toll of over 25,000* and in the same time span cause nearly one million personal injuries and more than five billion dollars in property damage." 4 W. LaFave, SEARCH AND SEIZURE: A TREATISE ON THE FOURTH AMENDMENT § 10.8(d), p. 71 (2d ed. 1987). For decades, this Court has "repeatedly lamented the tragedy." *South Dakota v. Neville*, 459 U.S. 553, 558 (1983); *see Breithaupt v. Abram*, 352 U.S. 432, 439 (1957) ("The increasing slaughter on our highways . . . now reaches the astounding figures only heard of on the battlefield").

Conversely, the weight bearing on the other scale — the measure of the intrusion on motorists stopped briefly at sobriety checkpoints — is slight. We reached a similar conclusion as to the intrusion on motorists subjected to a brief stop at a highway checkpoint for detecting illegal aliens. *See [United States v.] Martinez-Fuerte,* [428 U.S. 543,] 558 [(1976)]. We see virtually no difference between the levels of intrusion on law-abiding motorists from the brief stops necessary to the effectuation of these two types of checkpoints, which to the average motorist would seem identical save for the nature of the questions the checkpoint officers might ask. The trial court and the Court of Appeals, thus, accurately gauged the "objective" intrusion, measured by the duration of the seizure and the intensity of the investigation, as minimal.

With respect to what it perceived to be the "subjective" intrusion on motorists, however, the Court of Appeals found such intrusion substantial. The court first affirmed the trial court's finding that the guidelines governing checkpoint operation minimize the discretion of the officers on the scene. But the court also agreed with the trial court's conclusion that the checkpoints have the potential to generate fear and surprise in motorists. This was so because the record failed to demonstrate that approaching motorists would be aware of their option to make U-turns or turnoffs to avoid the checkpoints. On that basis, the court deemed the subjective intrusion from the checkpoints unreasonable.

We believe the Michigan courts misread our cases concerning the degree of "subjective intrusion" and the potential for generating fear and surprise. The "fear and surprise" to be considered are not the natural fear of one who has been drinking over

---

* Statistical evidence incorporated in the dissent suggests that this figure declined between 1982 and 1988. It was during this same period that police departments experimented with sobriety checkpoint systems. Petitioners, for instance, operated their checkpoint in May 1986, and the Maryland State Police checkpoint program, about which much testimony was given before the trial court, began in December 1982. Indeed, it is quite possible that jurisdictions which have recently decided to implement sobriety checkpoint systems have relied on such data from the 1980s in assessing the likely utility of such checkpoints.

the prospect of being stopped at a sobriety checkout but, rather, the fear and surprise engendered in law-abiding motorists by the nature of the stop. This was made clear in *Martinez-Fuerte*. Comparing checkpoint stops to roving patrol stops considered in prior cases, we said, "we view checkpoint stops in a different light because the subjective intrusion — the generating of concern or even fright on the part of lawful travelers — is appreciably less in the case of a checkpoint stop. In [*United States v.*] *Ortiz*, [422 U.S. 891 (1975),] we noted: '[T]he circumstances surrounding a checkpoint stop and search are far less intrusive than those attending a roving-patrol stop. Roving patrols often operate at night on seldom-traveled roads, and their approach may frighten motorists. At traffic checkpoints the motorist can see that other vehicles are being stopped, he can see visible signs of the officers' authority, and he is much less likely to be frightened or annoyed by the intrusion.' 422 U.S., at 894–895." *Martinez-Fuerte*, 428 U.S., at 558. *See also id.*, at 559. Here, checkpoints are selected pursuant to the guidelines, and uniformed police officers stop every approaching vehicle. The intrusion resulting from the brief stop at the sobriety checkpoint is for constitutional purposes indistinguishable from the checkpoint stops we upheld in *Martinez-Fuerte*.

The Court of Appeals went on to consider as part of the balancing analysis the "effectiveness" of the proposed checkpoint program. Based on extensive testimony in the trial record, the court concluded that the checkpoint program failed the "effectiveness" part of the test, and that this failure materially discounted petitioners' strong interest in implementing the program. We think the Court of Appeals was wrong on this point as well.

The actual language from *Brown v. Texas*, upon which the Michigan courts based their evaluation of "effectiveness," describes the balancing factor as "the degree to which the seizure advances the public interest." 443 U.S., at 51. This passage from *Brown* was not meant to transfer from politically accountable officials to the courts the decision as to which among reasonable alternative law enforcement techniques should be employed to deal with a serious public danger. Experts in police science might disagree over which of several methods of apprehending drunken drivers is preferable as ideal. But for purposes of Fourth Amendment analysis, the choice among such reasonable alternatives remains with the governmental officials who have a unique understanding of, and a responsibility for, limited public resources, including a finite number of police officers. . . .

. . . .

. . . [T]his case involves neither a complete absence of empirical data nor a challenge to random highway stops. During the operation of the Saginaw County checkpoint, the detention of each of the 126 vehicles that entered the checkpoint resulted in the arrest of two drunken drivers. Stated as a percentage, approximately 1.5 percent of the drivers passing through the checkpoint were arrested for alcohol impairment. In addition, an expert witness testified at the trial that experience in other States demonstrated that, on the whole, sobriety checkpoints resulted in drunken driving arrests of around 1 percent of all motorists stopped. 170 Mich. App., at 441, 429 N.W.2d, at 183. By way of comparison, the record from one of the consolidated cases in *Martinez-Fuerte* showed that in the associated checkpoint, illegal aliens were found in only 0.12 percent of the vehicles passing through the checkpoint. *See* 428 U.S., at 554. The ratio of illegal aliens detected to vehicles stopped (considering that on occasion two or more illegal aliens were found in a single vehicle) was approximately 0.5 percent. *See Id.* We concluded that this "record . . . provides a rather complete picture of the effectiveness of the San Clemente checkpoint," *ibid.*, and we sustained its constitutionality. We see no justification for a different conclusion here.

In sum, the balance of the State's interest in preventing drunken driving, the extent to which this system can reasonably be said to advance that interest, and the degree of intrusion upon individual motorists who are briefly stopped, weighs in favor of the state program. We therefore hold that it is consistent with the Fourth Amendment. The judgment of the Michigan Court of Appeals is accordingly reversed, and the cause is remanded for further proceedings not inconsistent with this opinion.

Reversed.

[JUSTICE BLACKMUN's concurrence in the judgment has been omitted.]

JUSTICE BRENNAN, with whom JUSTICE MARSHALL joins, dissenting.

. . . .

. . . I agree with the Court that the initial stop of a car at a roadblock under the Michigan State Police sobriety checkpoint policy is sufficiently less intrusive than an arrest so that the reasonableness of the seizure may be judged, not by the presence of probable cause, but by balancing "the gravity of the public concerns served by the seizure, the degree to which the seizure advances the public interest, and the severity of the interference with individual liberty." *Brown v Texas*, 443 U.S. 47, 51 (1979). But one searches the majority opinion in vain for any acknowledgement that the reason for employing the balancing test is that the seizure is minimally intrusive.

Indeed, the opinion reads as if the minimal nature of the seizure ends rather than begins the inquiry into reasonableness. Once the Court establishes that the seizure is "slight," it asserts without explanation that the balance "weighs in favor of the state program." The Court ignores the fact that in this class of minimally intrusive searches, we have generally required the Government to prove that it had reasonable suspicion for a minimally intrusive seizure to be considered reasonable. Some level of individualized suspicion is a core component of the protection the Fourth Amendment provides against arbitrary government action. By holding that no level of suspicion is necessary before the police may stop a car for the purpose of preventing drunken driving, the Court potentially subjects the general public to arbitrary or harassing conduct by the police. I would have hoped that before taking such a step, the Court would carefully explain how such a plan fits within our constitutional framework.

. . . .

I do not dispute the immense social cost caused by drunken drivers, nor do I slight the government's efforts to prevent such tragic losses. Indeed, I would hazard a guess that today's opinion will be received favorably by a majority of our society, who would willingly suffer the minimal intrusion of a sobriety checkpoint stop in order to prevent drunken driving. But consensus that a particular law enforcement technique serves a laudable purpose has never been the touchstone of constitutional analysis . . . . I respectfully dissent.

JUSTICE STEVENS, with whom JUSTICE BRENNAN and JUSTICE MARSHALL join as to Parts I and II, dissenting.

. . . .

The Court overvalues the law enforcement interest in using sobriety checkpoints, undervalues the citizen's interest in freedom from random, unannounced investigatory seizures, and mistakenly assumes that there is "virtually no difference" between a routine stop at a permanent, fixed checkpoint and a surprise stop at a sobriety checkpoint. I believe this case is controlled by our several precedents condemning suspicionless random stops of motorists for investigatory purposes. *Delaware v. Prouse*, 440 U.S. 648 (1979); *United States v. Brignoni-Ponce*, 422 U.S. 873 (1975); *United States v. Ortiz*, 422 U.S. 891 (1975); *Almeida-Sanchez v. United States*, 413 U.S. 266 (1973); *cf. Carroll v. United States*, 267 U.S. 132, 153–154 (1925).

I

There is a critical difference between a seizure that is preceded by fair notice and one that is effected by surprise. That is one reason why a border search, or indeed any search at a permanent and fixed checkpoint, is much less intrusive than a random stop. A motorist with advance notice of the location of a permanent checkpoint has an opportunity to avoid the search entirely, or at least to prepare for, and limit, the intrusion on her privacy.

No such opportunity is available in the case of a random stop or a temporary checkpoint, which both depend for their effectiveness on the element of surprise. A driver who discovers an unexpected checkpoint on a familiar local road will be startled and distressed. She may infer, correctly, that the checkpoint is not simply "business as usual," and may likewise infer, again correctly, that the police have made a discretionary decision to focus their law enforcement efforts upon her and others who pass the chosen point.

This element of surprise is the most obvious distinction between the sobriety checkpoints permitted by today's majority and the interior border checkpoints approved by this Court in *Martinez-Fuerte*. The distinction casts immediate doubt upon the majority's argument, for *Martinez-Fuerte* is the only case in which we have upheld suspicionless seizures of motorists. But the difference between notice and surprise is only one of the important reasons for distinguishing between permanent and mobile checkpoints. With respect to the former, there is no room for discretion in either the timing or the location of the stop — it is a permanent part of the land-scape. In the latter case, however, although the checkpoint is most frequently em-ployed during the hours of darkness on weekends (because that is when drivers with alcohol in their blood are most apt to be found on the road), the police have extremely broad discretion in determining the exact timing and placement of the roadblock.

There is also a significant difference between the kind of discretion that the offi-cer exercises after the stop is made. A check for a driver's license, or for identifica-tion papers at an immigration checkpoint, is far more easily standardized than is a search for evidence of intoxication. A Michigan officer who questions a motorist at a sobriety checkpoint has virtually unlimited discretion to detain the driver on the basis of the slightest suspicion. A ruddy complexion, an unbuttoned shirt, bloodshot eyes or a speech impediment may suffice to prolong the detention. Any driver who had just consumed a glass of beer, or even a sip of wine, would almost certainly have the burden of demonstrating to the officer that her driving ability was not impaired.

Finally, it is significant that many of the stops at permanent checkpoints occur during daylight hours, whereas the sobriety checkpoints are almost invariably oper-ated at night. A seizure followed by interrogation and even a cursory search at night is surely more offensive than a daytime stop that is almost as routine as going through a toll gate. Thus we thought it important to point out that the random stops at issue in *Ortiz* frequently occurred at night. 422 U.S., at 894.

These fears are not, as the Court would have it, solely the lot of the guilty. To be law-abiding is not necessarily to be spotless, and even the most virtuous can be un-lucky. Unwanted attention from the local police need not be less discomforting sim-ply because one's secrets are not the stuff of criminal prosecutions. Moreover, those who have found — by reason of prejudice or misfortune — that encounters with the police may become adversarial or unpleasant without good cause will have grounds for worrying at any stop designed to elicit signs of suspicious behavior. Being stopped by the police is distressing even when it should not be terrifying, and what begins mildly may by happenstance turn severe.

For all these reasons, I do not believe that this case is analogous to *Martinez-Fuerte.* In my opinion, the sobriety checkpoints are instead similar to — and in some respects more intrusive than — the random investigative stops that the Court held unconstitutional in *Brignoni-Ponce* and *Prouse.* . . .

II

The Court, unable to draw any persuasive analogy to *Martinez-Fuerte,* rests its decision today on application of a more general balancing test taken from *Brown v. Texas,* 443 U.S. 47 (1979) . . . . In [*Brown*], we stated: "Consideration of the constitu-tionality of such seizures involves a weighing of the gravity of the public concerns served by the seizure, the degree to which the seizure advances the public interest, and the severity of the interference with individual liberty." *Id.,* at 50–51.

The gravity of the public concern with highway safety that is implicated by this case is, of course, undisputed. Yet, that same grave concern was implicated in

Delaware v. Prouse. Moreover, I do not understand the Court to have placed any lesser value on the importance of the drug problem implicated in *Texas v. Brown*, or on the need to control the illegal border crossings that were at stake in *Almeida-Sanchez* and its progeny. A different result in this case must be justified by the other two factors in the *Brown* formulation.

As I have already explained, I believe the Court is quite wrong in blithely asserting that a sobriety checkpoint is no more intrusive than a permanent checkpoint. In my opinion, unannounced investigatory seizures are, particularly when they take place at night, the hallmark of regimes far different from ours; the surprise intrusion upon individual liberty is not minimal. On that issue, my difference with the Court may amount to nothing less than a difference in our respective evaluations of the importance of individual liberty, a serious albeit inevitable source of constitutional disagreement. On the degree to which the sobriety checkpoint seizures advance the public interest, however, the Court's position is wholly indefensible.

The Court's analysis of this issue resembles a business decision that measures profits by counting gross receipts and ignoring expenses. The evidence in this case indicates that sobriety checkpoints result in the arrest of a fraction of one percent of the drivers who are stopped, but there is absolutely no evidence that this figure represents an increase over the number of arrests that would have been made by using the same law enforcement resources in conventional patrols. Thus, although the gross number of arrests is more than zero, there is a complete failure of proof on the question whether the wholesale seizures have produced any net advance in the public interest in arresting intoxicated drivers.

. . . .

The Court's sparse analysis of this issue differs markedly from Justice Powell's opinion for the Court in *Martinez-Fuerte*. He did not merely count the 17,000 arrests made at the San Clemente checkpoint in 1973; he also carefully explained why those arrests represented a net benefit to the law enforcement interest at stake. Common sense, moreover, suggests that immigration checkpoints are more necessary than sobriety checkpoints: there is no reason why smuggling illegal aliens should impair a motorist's driving ability, but if intoxication did not noticeably affect driving ability it would not be unlawful. Drunk driving, unlike smuggling, may thus be detected absent any checkpoints. A program that produces thousands of otherwise impossible arrests is not a relevant precedent for a program that produces only a handful of arrests which would be more easily obtained without resort to suspicionless seizures of hundreds of innocent citizens.

III

. . . .

This is a case that is driven by nothing more than symbolic state action — an insufficient justification for an otherwise unreasonable program of random seizures. Unfortunately, the Court is transfixed by the wrong symbol — the illusory prospect of punishing countless intoxicated motorists — when it should keep its eyes on the road plainly marked by the Constitution.

I respectfully dissent.

Notes and Questions

(1) Upon remand, the Michigan Supreme Court concluded that the roadblock conducted in *Sitz* violated the Michigan Constitution's provision regulating searches and seizures. *See Sitz v. Michigan Department of State Police*, 443 Mich. 744, 506 N.W.2d 209 (1993).

(2) The Supreme Court upheld the sobriety checkpoint in *Sitz*. What circumstances would justify the conclusion that a sobriety checkpoint is sufficiently distinguishable from the one sustained in *Sitz* to render it unreasonable under the Fourth Amendment?

(3) Which motorists initially stopped at a valid sobriety checkpoint may be singled out and detained for more extensive investigation? What investigatory steps are permissible during such a "secondary" detention?

City of Indianapolis v. Edmond

United States Supreme Court

531 U.S. 32, 121 S. Ct. 447, 148 L. Ed. 2d 333 (2000)

JUSTICE O'CONNOR delivered the opinion of the Court.

. . . .

I

In August 1998, the city of Indianapolis began to operate vehicle checkpoints on Indianapolis roads in an effort to interdict unlawful drugs. The city conducted six such roadblocks between August and November that year, stopping 1,161 vehicles and arresting 104 motorists. Fifty-five arrests were for drug-related crimes, while 49 were for offenses unrelated to drugs. *Edmond v. Goldsmith*, 183 F.3d 659, 661 (7th Cir. 1999). The overall "hit rate" of the program was thus approximately nine percent.

The parties stipulated to the facts concerning the operation of the checkpoints by the Indianapolis Police Department (IPD) for purposes of the preliminary injunction proceedings instituted below. At each checkpoint location, the police stop a predetermined number of vehicles. Approximately 30 officers are stationed at the checkpoint. Pursuant to written directives issued by the chief of police, at least one officer approaches the vehicle, advises the driver that he or she is being stopped briefly at a drug checkpoint, and asks the driver to produce a license and registration. The officer also looks for signs of impairment and conducts an open-view examination of the vehicle from the outside. A narcotics-detection dog walks around the outside of each stopped vehicle.

The directives instruct the officers that they may conduct a search only by consent or based on the appropriate quantum of particularized suspicion. The officers must conduct each stop in the same manner until particularized suspicion develops, and the officers have no discretion to stop any vehicle out of sequence. The city agreed in the stipulation to operate the checkpoints in such a way as to ensure that the total duration of each stop, absent reasonable suspicion or probable cause, would be five minutes or less.

The affidavit of Indianapolis Police Sergeant Marshall DePew, although it is technically outside the parties' stipulation, provides further insight concerning the operation of the checkpoints. According to Sergeant DePew, checkpoint locations are selected weeks in advance based on such considerations as area crime statistics and traffic flow. The checkpoints are generally operated during daylight hours and are identified with lighted signs reading, "NARCOTICS CHECKPOINT ___ MILE AHEAD, NARCOTICS K-9 IN USE, BE PREPARED TO STOP." App. to Pet. for Cert. 57a. Once a group of cars has been stopped, other traffic proceeds without interruption until all the stopped cars have been processed or diverted for further processing. Sergeant DePew also stated that the average stop for a vehicle not subject to further processing lasts two to three minutes or less.

Respondents James Edmond and Joell Palmer were each stopped at a narcotics checkpoint in late September 1998. Respondents then filed a lawsuit on behalf of themselves and the class of all motorists who had been stopped or were subject to being stopped in the future at the Indianapolis drug checkpoints. Respondents claimed that the roadblocks violated the Fourth Amendment of the United States Constitution and the search and seizure provision of the Indiana Constitution. Respondents requested declaratory and injunctive relief for the class, as well as damages and attorney's fees for themselves.

Respondents then moved for a preliminary injunction. Although respondents alleged that the officers who stopped them did not follow the written directives, they agreed to the stipulation concerning the operation of the checkpoints for purposes of the preliminary injunction proceedings. The parties also stipulated to certification of the plaintiff class. The United States District Court for the Southern District of Indiana agreed to class certification and denied the motion for a preliminary injunction, holding that the checkpoint program did not violate the Fourth Amendment. *Edmond v. Goldsmith*, 38 F. Supp. 2d 1016 (1998). A divided panel of the United States Court of Appeals for the Seventh Circuit reversed, holding that the checkpoints contravened the Fourth Amendment. 183 F.3d 659 (1999). The panel denied rehearing. We granted certiorari, 528 U.S. 1153 (2000), and now affirm.

II

The Fourth Amendment requires that searches and seizures be reasonable. A search or seizure is ordinarily unreasonable in the absence of individualized suspicion of wrongdoing. While such suspicion is not an "irreducible" component of reasonableness, *Martinez-Fuerte*, 428 U.S., at 561, we have recognized only limited circumstances in which the usual rule does not apply. For example, we have upheld certain regimes of suspicionless searches where the program was designed to serve "special needs, beyond the normal need for law enforcement." *See, e.g., Vernonia School Dist. 47J v. Acton*, 515 U.S. 646 (1995) (random drug testing of student-athletes); *Treasury Employees v. Von Raab*, 489 U.S. 656 (1989) (drug tests for United States Customs Service employees seeking transfer or promotion to certain positions); *Skinner v. Railway Labor Executives' Assn.*, 489 U.S. 602 (1989) (drug and alcohol tests for railway employees involved in train accidents or found to be in violation of particular safety regulations). We have also allowed searches for certain administrative purposes without particularized suspicion of misconduct, provided that those searches are appropriately limited. *See, e.g., New York v. Burger*, 482 U.S. 691, 702–704 (1987) (warrantless administrative inspection of premises of "closely regulated" business); *Michigan v. Tyler*, 436 U.S. 499, 507–509, 511–512 (1978) (administrative inspection of fire-damaged premises to determine cause of blaze); *Camara v. Municipal Court of City and County of San Francisco*, 387 U.S. 523, 534–539 (1967) (administrative inspection to ensure compliance with city housing code).

We have also upheld brief, suspicionless seizures of motorists at a fixed Border Patrol checkpoint designed to intercept illegal aliens, *Martinez-Fuerte, supra*, and at a sobriety checkpoint aimed at removing drunk drivers from the road, *Michigan Dept. of State Police v. Sitz*, 496 U.S. 444 (1990). In addition, in *Delaware v. Prouse*, 440 U.S. 648, 663 (1979), we suggested that a similar type of roadblock with the purpose of verifying drivers' licenses and vehicle registrations would be permissible. In none of these cases, however, did we indicate approval of a checkpoint program whose primary purpose was to detect evidence of ordinary criminal wrongdoing.

In *Martinez-Fuerte*, we entertained Fourth Amendment challenges to stops at two permanent immigration checkpoints located on major United States highways less than 100 miles from the Mexican border. We noted at the outset the particular context in which the constitutional question arose, describing in some detail the "formidable law enforcement problems" posed by the northbound tide of illegal entrants into the United States. *Martinez-Fuerte, supra*, at 551–554. . . . In *Martinez-Fuerte*, we found that the balance tipped in favor of the Government's interests in policing the Nation's borders. 428 U.S., at 561–564. In so finding, we emphasized the difficulty of effectively containing illegal immigration at the border itself. *Id.*, at 556. We also stressed the impracticality of the particularized study of a given car to discern whether it was transporting illegal aliens, as well as the relatively modest degree of intrusion entailed by the stops. *Id.*, at 556–564.

Our subsequent cases have confirmed that considerations specifically related to the need to police the border were a significant factor in our *Martinez-Fuerte* decision. . . .

In *Sitz*, we evaluated the constitutionality of a Michigan highway sobriety checkpoint program. The *Sitz* checkpoint involved brief suspicionless stops of motorists so that police officers could detect signs of intoxication and remove impaired drivers from the road. 496 U.S., at 447–448. . . . This checkpoint program was clearly aimed at reducing the immediate hazard posed by the presence of drunk drivers on the highways, and there was an obvious connection between the imperative of highway safety and the law enforcement practice at issue. The gravity of the drunk driving problem and the magnitude of the State's interest in getting drunk drivers off the road weighed heavily in our determination that the program was constitutional. *See id.*, at 451.

In *Prouse*, we invalidated a discretionary, suspicionless stop for a spot check of a motorist's driver's license and vehicle registration. The officer's conduct in that case was unconstitutional primarily on account of his exercise of "standardless and unconstrained discretion." 440 U.S., at 661. We nonetheless acknowledged the States' "vital interest in ensuring that only those qualified to do so are permitted to operate motor vehicles, that these vehicles are fit for safe operation, and hence that licensing, registration, and vehicle inspection requirements are being observed." *Id.*, at 658. Accordingly, we suggested that "[q]uestioning of all oncoming traffic at roadblock-type stops" would be a lawful means of serving this interest in highway safety. *Id.*, at 663.

We further indicated in *Prouse* that we considered the purposes of such a hypothetical roadblock to be distinct from a general purpose of investigating crime. . . .

III

It is well established that a vehicle stop at a highway checkpoint effectuates a seizure within the meaning of the Fourth Amendment. The fact that officers walk a narcotics-detection dog around the exterior of each car at the Indianapolis checkpoints does not transform the seizure into a search. *See United States v. Place*, 462 U.S. 696, 707 (1983). Just as in *Place*, an exterior sniff of an automobile does not require entry into the car and is not designed to disclose any information other than the presence or absence of narcotics. See *ibid.* Like the dog sniff in *Place*, a sniff by a dog that simply walks around a car is "much less intrusive than a typical search." *Ibid.* Rather, what principally distinguishes these checkpoints from those we have previously approved is their primary purpose.

As petitioners concede, the Indianapolis checkpoint program unquestionably has the primary purpose of interdicting illegal narcotics. In their stipulation of facts, the parties repeatedly refer to the checkpoints as "drug checkpoints" and describe them as "being operated by the City of Indianapolis in an effort to interdict unlawful drugs in Indianapolis." App. to Pet. for Cert. 51a-52a. In addition, the first document attached to the parties' stipulation is entitled "DRUG CHECKPOINT CONTACT OFFICER DIRECTIVES BY ORDER OF THE CHIEF OF POLICE." *Id.*, at 53a. These directives instruct officers to "[a]dvise the citizen that they are being stopped briefly at a drug checkpoint." *Ibid.* The second document attached to the stipulation is entitled "1998 Drug Road Blocks" and contains a statistical breakdown of information relating to the checkpoints conducted. *Id.*, at 55a. Further, according to Sergeant DePew, the checkpoints are identified with lighted signs reading, "NARCOTICS CHECKPOINT ___ MILE AHEAD, NARCOTICS K-9 IN USE, BE PREPARED TO

STOP." *Id.*, at 57a. Finally, both the District Court and the Court of Appeals recognized that the primary purpose of the roadblocks is the interdiction of narcotics.

We have never approved a checkpoint program whose primary purpose was to detect evidence of ordinary criminal wrongdoing. Rather, our checkpoint cases have recognized only limited exceptions to the general rule that a seizure must be accompanied by some measure of individualized suspicion. We suggested in *Prouse* that we would not credit the "general interest in crime control" as justification for a regime of suspicionless stops. 440 U.S., at 659, n. 18. Consistent with this suggestion, each of the checkpoint programs that we have approved was designed primarily to serve purposes closely related to the problems of policing the border or the necessity of ensuring roadway safety. Because the primary purpose of the Indianapolis narcotics checkpoint program is to uncover evidence of ordinary criminal wrongdoing, the program contravenes the Fourth Amendment.

Petitioners propose several ways in which the narcotics-detection purpose of the instant checkpoint program may instead resemble the primary purposes of the checkpoints in *Sitz* and *Martinez-Fuerte*. Petitioners state that the checkpoints in those cases had the same ultimate purpose of arresting those suspected of committing crimes. Securing the border and apprehending drunk drivers are, of course, law enforcement activities, and law enforcement officers employ arrests and criminal prosecutions in pursuit of these goals. If we were to rest the case at this high level of generality, there would be little check on the ability of the authorities to construct roadblocks for almost any conceivable law enforcement purpose. Without drawing the line at roadblocks designed primarily to serve the general interest in crime control, the Fourth Amendment would do little to prevent such intrusions from becoming a routine part of American life.

Petitioners also emphasize the severe and intractable nature of the drug problem as justification for the checkpoint program. There is no doubt that traffic in illegal narcotics creates social harms of the first magnitude. The law enforcement problems that the drug trade creates likewise remain daunting and complex, particularly in light of the myriad forms of spin-off crime that it spawns. The same can be said of various other illegal activities, if only to a lesser degree. But the gravity of the threat alone cannot be dispositive of questions concerning what means law enforcement officers may employ to pursue a given purpose. Rather, in determining whether individualized suspicion is required, we must consider the nature of the interests threatened and their connection to the particular law enforcement practices at issue. We are particularly reluctant to recognize exceptions to the general rule of individualized suspicion where governmental authorities primarily pursue their general crime control ends.

Nor can the narcotics-interdiction purpose of the checkpoints be rationalized in terms of a highway safety concern similar to that present in *Sitz*. The detection and punishment of almost any criminal offense serves broadly the safety of the community, and our streets would no doubt be safer but for the scourge of illegal drugs. Only with respect to a smaller class of offenses, however, is society confronted with the type of immediate, vehicle-bound threat to life and limb that the sobriety checkpoint in *Sitz* was designed to eliminate.

Petitioners also liken the anticontraband agenda of the Indianapolis checkpoints to the antismuggling purpose of the checkpoints in *Martinez-Fuerte*. Petitioners cite this Court's conclusion in *Martinez-Fuerte* that the flow of traffic was too heavy to permit "particularized study of a given car that would enable it to be identified as a possible carrier of illegal aliens," *Martinez-Fuerte, supra,* at 557, and claim that this logic has even more force here. The problem with this argument is that the same logic prevails any time a vehicle is employed to conceal contraband or other evidence of a crime. This type of connection to the roadway is very different from the close connection to roadway safety that was present in *Sitz* and *Prouse*. Further, the Indianapolis checkpoints are far removed from the border context that was crucial in *Martinez- Fuerte*. While the difficulty of examining each passing car was an important factor in validating the law enforcement technique employed in *Martinez-Fuerte*, this factor alone cannot justify a regime of suspicionless searches or seizures. Rather, we must look more closely at the nature of the public interests that such a regime is designed principally to serve.

The primary purpose of the Indianapolis narcotics checkpoints is in the end to advance "the general interest in crime control," *Prouse*, 440 U.S., at 659, n. 18. We decline to suspend the usual requirement of individualized suspicion where the police seek to employ a checkpoint primarily for the ordinary enterprise of investigating crimes. We cannot sanction stops justified only by the generalized and ever-present possibility that interrogation and inspection may reveal that any given motorist has committed some crime.

Of course, there are circumstances that may justify a law enforcement checkpoint where the primary purpose would otherwise, but for some emergency, relate to ordinary crime control. For example, as the Court of Appeals noted, the Fourth Amendment would almost certainly permit an appropriately tailored roadblock set up to thwart an imminent terrorist attack or to catch a dangerous criminal who is likely to flee by way of a particular route. *See* 183 F.3d at 662–663. The exigencies created by these scenarios are far removed from the circumstances under which authorities might simply stop cars as a matter of course to see if there just happens to be a felon leaving the jurisdiction. While we do not limit the purposes that may justify a checkpoint program to any rigid set of categories, we decline to approve a program whose primary purpose is ultimately indistinguishable from the general interest in crime control.[1]

---

1. THE CHIEF JUSTICE's dissent erroneously characterizes our opinion as resting on the application of a "non-law-enforcement primary purpose test." *Post*, at 53. Our opinion nowhere describes the purposes of the *Sitz* and *Martinez-Fuerte* checkpoints as being "not primarily related to criminal law enforcement." *Post*, at 50. Rather, our judgment turns on the fact that the primary purpose of the Indianapolis checkpoints is to advance the general interest in crime control. THE CHIEF JUSTICE's dissent also erroneously characterizes our opinion as holding that the "use of a drug-sniffing dog . . . annuls what is otherwise plainly constitutional under our Fourth Amendment jurisprudence." *Post*, at 48. Again, the constitutional defect of the program is that its primary purpose is to advance the general interest in crime control.

Petitioners argue that our prior cases preclude an inquiry into the purposes of the checkpoint program. For example, they cite *Whren v. United States*, 517 U.S. 806 (1996) . . . to support the proposition that "where the government articulates and pursues a legitimate interest for a suspicionless stop, courts should not look behind that interest to determine whether the government's 'primary purpose' is valid." Brief for Petitioners 34; *see also id.*, at 9. . . . .

In *Whren*, we held that an individual officer's subjective intentions are irrelevant to the Fourth Amendment validity of a traffic stop that is justified objectively by probable cause to believe that a traffic violation has occurred. 517 U.S., at 810–813. We observed that our prior cases "foreclose any argument that the constitutional reasonableness of traffic stops depends on the actual motivations of the individual officers involved." *Id.*, at 813. In so holding, we expressly distinguished cases where we had addressed the validity of searches conducted in the absence of probable cause.

Whren therefore reinforces the principle that, while "[s]ubjective intentions play no role in ordinary, probable-cause Fourth Amendment analysis," 517 U.S., at 813, programmatic purposes may be relevant to the validity of Fourth Amendment intrusions undertaken pursuant to a general scheme without individualized suspicion. Accordingly, *Whren* does not preclude an inquiry into programmatic purpose in such contexts. It likewise does not preclude an inquiry into programmatic purpose here.

. . . .

Petitioners argue that the Indianapolis checkpoint program is justified by its lawful secondary purposes of keeping impaired motorists off the road and verifying licenses and registrations. If this were the case, however, law enforcement authorities would be able to establish checkpoints for virtually any purpose so long as they also included a license or sobriety check. For this reason, we examine the available evidence to determine the primary purpose of the checkpoint program. While we recognize the challenges inherent in a purpose inquiry, courts routinely engage in this enterprise in many areas of constitutional jurisprudence as a means of sifting abusive governmental conduct from that which is lawful. As a result, a program driven by an impermissible purpose may be proscribed while a program impelled by licit purposes is permitted, even though the challenged conduct may be outwardly similar. While reasonableness under the Fourth Amendment is predominantly an objective inquiry, our special needs and administrative search cases demonstrate that purpose is often relevant when suspicionless intrusions pursuant to a general scheme are at issue.[2]

---

2. Because petitioners concede that the primary purpose of the Indianapolis checkpoints is narcotics detection, we need not decide whether the State may establish a checkpoint program with the primary purpose of checking licenses or driver sobriety and a secondary purpose of interdicting narcotics. Specifically, we express no view on the question whether police may expand the scope of a license or sobriety checkpoint seizure in order to detect the presence of drugs in a stopped car. *Cf. New Jersey v. T.L.O.*, 469 U.S. 325, 341 (1985) (search must be "'reasonably related in scope to the circumstance which justified the interference in the first place'" (quoting *Terry v. Ohio*, 392 U.S. 1, 20 (1968))); *Michigan v. Clifford*, 464 U.S. 287, 294–295 (1984) (plurality opinion).

It goes without saying that our holding today does nothing to alter the constitutional status of the sobriety and border checkpoints that we approved in *Sitz* and *Martinez-Fuerte*, or of the type of traffic checkpoint that we suggested would be lawful in *Prouse*. The constitutionality of such checkpoint programs still depends on a balancing of the competing interests at stake and the effectiveness of the program. *See Sitz*, 496 U.S., at 450–455; *Martinez-Fuerte*, 428 U.S., at 556–564. When law enforcement authorities pursue primarily general crime control purposes at checkpoints such as here, however, stops can only be justified by some quantum of individualized suspicion.

Our holding also does not affect the validity of border searches or searches at places like airports and government buildings, where the need for such measures to ensure public safety can be particularly acute. Nor does our opinion speak to other intrusions aimed primarily at purposes beyond the general interest in crime control. Our holding also does not impair the ability of police officers to act appropriately upon information that they properly learn during a checkpoint stop justified by a lawful primary purpose, even where such action may result in the arrest of a motorist for an offense unrelated to that purpose. Finally, we caution that the purpose inquiry in this context is to be conducted only at the programmatic level and is not an invitation to probe the minds of individual officers acting at the scene.

Because the primary purpose of the Indianapolis checkpoint program is ultimately indistinguishable from the general interest in crime control, the checkpoints violate the Fourth Amendment. The judgment of the Court of Appeals is accordingly affirmed.

It is so ordered.

Chief Justice Rehnquist, with whom Justice Thomas joins, and with whom Justice Scalia joins as to Part I, dissenting.

The State's use of a drug-sniffing dog, according to the Court's holding, annuls what is otherwise plainly constitutional under our Fourth Amendment jurisprudence: brief, standardized, discretionless, roadblock seizures of automobiles, seizures which effectively serve a weighty state interest with only minimal intrusion on the privacy of their occupants. Because these seizures serve the State's accepted and significant interests of preventing drunken driving and checking for driver's licenses and vehicle registrations, and because there is nothing in the record to indicate that the addition of the dog sniff lengthens these otherwise legitimate seizures, I dissent.

I

As it is nowhere to be found in the Court's opinion, I begin with blackletter roadblock seizure law. "The principal protection of Fourth Amendment rights at checkpoints lies in appropriate limitations on the scope of the stop." *United States v. Martinez-Fuerte*, 428 U.S. 543, 566–567 (1976). Roadblock seizures are consistent with the Fourth Amendment if they are "carried out pursuant to a plan embodying explicit, neutral limitations on the conduct of individual officers." *Brown v. Texas*, 443 U.S. 47, 51 (1979). Specifically, the constitutionality of a seizure turns upon "a weighing of the gravity of the public concerns served by the seizure, the degree to which the seizure advances the public interest, and the severity of the interference with individual liberty." *Id.*, at 50–51.

We first applied these principles in *Martinez-Fuerte, supra*, which approved highway checkpoints for detecting illegal aliens. In *Martinez-Fuerte*, we balanced the United States' formidable interest in checking the flow of illegal immigrants against the limited "objective" and "subjective" intrusion on the motorists. . . . And although the decision in *Martinez-Fuerte* did not turn on the checkpoints' effectiveness, the record in one of the consolidated cases demonstrated that illegal aliens were found in 0.12 percent of the stopped vehicles.

In *Michigan Dept. of State Police v. Sitz*, 496 U.S. 444 (1990), we upheld the State's use of a highway sobriety checkpoint after applying the framework set out in *Martinez-Fuerte, supra*, and *Brown v. Texas, supra*. . . .

This case follows naturally from *Martinez-Fuerte* and *Sitz*. Petitioners acknowledge that the "primary purpose" of these roadblocks is to interdict illegal drugs, but this fact should not be controlling. Even accepting the Court's conclusion that the checkpoints at issue in *Martinez-Fuerte* and *Sitz* were not primarily related to criminal law enforcement, the question whether a law enforcement purpose could support a roadblock seizure is not presented in this case. The District Court found that another "purpose of the checkpoints is to check driver's licenses and vehicle registrations," App. to Pet. for Cert. 44a, and the written directives state that the police officers are to "[l]ook for signs of impairment." *Id.*, at 53a. The use of roadblocks to look for signs of impairment was validated by *Sitz*, and the use of roadblocks to check for driver's licenses and vehicle registrations was expressly recognized in *Delaware v. Prouse*, 440 U.S. 648, 663 (1979). That the roadblocks serve these legitimate state interests cannot be seriously disputed, as the 49 people arrested for offenses unrelated to drugs can attest. *Edmond v. Goldsmith*, 183 F.3d 659, 661 (7th Cir. 1999). And it would be speculative to conclude — given the District Court's findings, the written directives, and the actual arrests — that petitioners would not have operated these roadblocks but for the State's interest in interdicting drugs.

Because of the valid reasons for conducting these roadblock seizures, it is constitutionally irrelevant that petitioners also hoped to interdict drugs. In *Whren v. United States*, 517 U.S. 806 (1996), we held that an officer's subjective intent would not invalidate an otherwise objectively justifiable stop of an automobile. The reasonableness of an officer's discretionary decision to stop an automobile, at issue in *Whren*, turns on whether there is probable cause to believe that a traffic violation has occurred. The reasonableness of highway checkpoints, at issue here, turns on whether they effectively serve a significant state interest with minimal intrusion on motorists. The stop in *Whren* was objectively reasonable because the police officers had witnessed traffic violations; so too the roadblocks here are objectively reasonable because they serve the substantial interests of preventing drunken driving and checking for driver's licenses and vehicle registrations with minimal intrusion on motorists.

Once the constitutional requirements for a particular seizure are satisfied, the subjective expectations of those responsible for it, be it police officers or members of a city council, are irrelevant. . . .

With these checkpoints serving two important state interests, the remaining prongs of the *Brown v. Texas* balancing test are easily met. The seizure is objectively reasonable as it lasts, on average, two to three minutes and does not involve a search. The subjective intrusion is likewise limited as the checkpoints are clearly marked and operated by uniformed officers who are directed to stop every vehicle in the same manner. The only difference between this case and *Sitz* is the presence of the dog. . . . Finally, the checkpoints' success rate — 49 arrests for offenses unrelated to drugs — only confirms the State's legitimate interests in preventing drunken driving and ensuring the proper licensing of drivers and registration of their vehicles.

These stops effectively serve the State's legitimate interests; they are executed in a regularized and neutral manner; and they only minimally intrude upon the privacy of the motorists. They should therefore be constitutional.

II

The Court, unwilling to adopt the straightforward analysis that these precedents dictate, adds a new non-law-enforcement primary purpose test lifted from a distinct area of Fourth Amendment jurisprudence relating to the *searches* of homes and businesses. As discussed above, the question that the Court answers is not even posed in this case given the accepted reasons for the seizures. But more fundamentally, whatever sense a non-law-enforcement primary purpose test may make in the search setting, it is ill suited to brief roadblock seizures, where we have consistently looked at "the scope of the stop" in assessing a program's constitutionality. *Martinez-Fuerte*, 428 U.S., at 567.

We have already rejected an invitation to apply the non-law-enforcement primary purpose test that the Court now finds so indispensable. . . .

Considerations of *stare decisis* aside, the "perfectly plain" reason for not incorporating the "special needs" test in our roadblock seizure cases is that seizures of automobiles "deal neither with searches nor with the sanctity of private dwellings, ordinarily afforded the most stringent Fourth Amendment protection." *Martinez-Fuerte, supra*, at 561.

The "special needs" doctrine, which has been used to uphold certain suspicionless searches performed for reasons unrelated to law enforcement, is an exception to the general rule that a search must be based on individualized suspicion of wrongdoing. *See, e.g., Skinner v. Railway Labor Executives' Assn.*, 489 U.S. 602 (1989) (drug test search); *Camara v. Municipal Court of City and County of San Francisco*, 387 U.S. 523 (1967) (home administrative search). The doctrine permits intrusions into a person's body and home, areas afforded the greatest Fourth Amendment protection. But there were no such intrusions here.

"One's expectation of privacy in an automobile and of freedom in its operation are significantly different from the traditional expectation of privacy and freedom in one's residence." *Martinez-Fuerte, supra*, at 561. . . . The lowered expectation of privacy in one's automobile is coupled with the limited nature of the intrusion: a brief, standardized, nonintrusive seizure. The brief seizure of an automobile can hardly be compared to the intrusive search of the body or the home. Thus, just as the "special needs" inquiry serves to both define and limit the permissible scope of those searches, the *Brown v. Texas* balancing test serves to define and limit the permissible scope of automobile seizures.

Because of these extrinsic limitations upon roadblock seizures, the Court's new-found non-law-enforcement primary purpose test is both unnecessary to secure Fourth Amendment rights and bound to produce wide-ranging litigation over the "purpose" of any given seizure. Police designing highway roadblocks can never be sure of their validity, since a jury might later determine that a forbidden purpose exists. Roadblock stops identical to the one that we upheld in *Sitz* 10 years ago, or to the one that we upheld 24 years ago in *Martinez-Fuerte*, may now be challenged on the grounds that they have some concealed forbidden purpose.

Efforts to enforce the law on public highways used by millions of motorists are obviously necessary to our society. The Court's opinion today casts a shadow over what had been assumed, on the basis of *stare decisis*, to be a perfectly lawful activity. Conversely, if the Indianapolis police had assigned a different purpose to their activity here, but in no way changed what was done on the ground to individual motorists, it might well be valid. The Court's non-law-enforcement primary purpose test simply does not serve as a proxy for anything that the Fourth Amendment is, or should be, concerned about in the automobile seizure context.

Petitioners' program complies with our decisions regarding roadblock seizures of automobiles, and the addition of a dog sniff does not add to the length or the intrusion of the stop. Because such stops are consistent with the Fourth Amendment, I would reverse the decision of the Court of Appeals.

JUSTICE THOMAS, dissenting.

Taken together, our decisions in *Michigan Dept. of State Police v. Sitz*, 496 U.S. 444 (1990), and *United States v. Martinez-Fuerte*, 428 U.S. 543 (1976), stand for the proposition that suspicionless roadblock seizures are constitutionally permissible if conducted according to a plan that limits the discretion of the officers conducting the stops. I am not convinced that *Sitz* and *Martinez-Fuerte* were correctly decided. Indeed, I rather doubt that the Framers of the Fourth Amendment would have considered "reasonable" a program of indiscriminate stops of individuals not suspected of wrongdoing.

Respondents did not, however, advocate the overruling of *Sitz* and *Martinez-Fuerte*, and I am reluctant to consider such a step without the benefit of briefing and argument. For the reasons given by THE CHIEF JUSTICE, I believe that those cases compel upholding the program at issue here. I, therefore, join his opinion.

Notes and Questions

(1) The sobriety checkpoint in *Sitz* qualified as one of the "limited exceptions to the general rule that a seizure must be accompanied by some measure of individualized suspicion." The drug interdiction checkpoint in *Edmond* did not. What is the critical distinction between checkpoint stops that may be permissible without individualized suspicion and those that cannot be constitutional without such suspicion? Why should this distinction make a difference?

(2) How can a court ascertain the primary "programmatic purpose" of a checkpoint? Must a judge accept the assertions of those responsible for the program? If not, what other indicia are relevant?

(3) Suppose that a city designs a suspicionless checkpoint program to check drivers' licenses and vehicle registrations. Soon after the program is implemented, vice officers seek and obtain permission to have drug-sniffing dogs examine vehicles while they are stopped. The dog sniffs do not extend the length of the initial stops, but positive responses by the dogs lead to further detentions and inquiries. Would a constitutional challenge to the checkpoint stops have merit?

Illinois v. Lidster

United States Supreme Court

540 U.S. 419, 124 S. Ct. 885, 157 L. Ed. 2d 843 (2004)

JUSTICE BREYER delivered the opinion of the Court.

This Fourth Amendment case focuses upon a highway checkpoint where police stopped motorists to ask them for information about a recent hit-and-run accident. We hold that the police stops were reasonable, hence, constitutional.

I

The relevant background is as follows: On Saturday, August 23, 1997, just after midnight, an unknown motorist traveling eastbound on a highway in Lombard, Illinois, struck and killed a 70-year-old bicyclist. The motorist drove off without identifying himself. About one week later at about the same time of night and at about the same place, local police set up a highway checkpoint designed to obtain more information about the accident from the motoring public.

Police cars with flashing lights partially blocked the eastbound lanes of the highway. The blockage forced traffic to slow down, leading to lines of up to 15 cars in each lane. As each vehicle drew up to the checkpoint, an officer would stop it for 10 to 15 seconds, ask the occupants whether they had seen anything happen there the previous weekend, and hand each driver a flyer. The flyer said "ALERT . . . FATAL HIT & RUN ACCIDENT" and requested "ASSISTANCE IN IDENTIFYING THE VEHICLE AND DRIVER IN THIS ACCIDENT WHICH KILLED A 70 YEAR OLD BICYCLIST."

Robert Lidster, the respondent, drove a minivan toward the checkpoint. As he approached the checkpoint, his van swerved, nearly hitting one of the officers. The officer smelled alcohol on Lidster's breath. He directed Lidster to a side street where another officer administered a sobriety test and then arrested Lidster. Lidster was tried and convicted in Illinois state court of driving under the influence of alcohol.

Lidster challenged the lawfulness of his arrest and conviction on the ground that the government had obtained much of the relevant evidence through use of a checkpoint stop that violated the Fourth Amendment. The trial court rejected that challenge. But an Illinois appellate court reached the opposite conclusion. The Illinois Supreme Court . . . held (by a vote of 4 to 3) that our decision in *Indianapolis v. Edmond*, 531 U.S. 32, 121 S. Ct. 447, 148 L. Ed. 2d 333 (2000), required it to find the stop unconstitutional.

. . . .

II

. . . *Edmond* involved a checkpoint at which police stopped vehicles to look for evidence of drug crimes committed by occupants of those vehicles. . . . We found that police had set up this checkpoint primarily for general "crime control" purposes, *i.e.*, "to detect evidence of ordinary criminal wrongdoing." *Id.*, at 41, 121 S. Ct. 447. We noted that the stop was made without individualized suspicion. And we held that the Fourth Amendment forbids such a stop, in the absence of special circumstances. *Id.*, at 44, 121 S. Ct. 447.

The checkpoint stop here differs significantly from that in *Edmond*. The stop's primary law enforcement purpose was *not* to determine whether a vehicle's occupants were committing a crime, but to ask vehicle occupants, as members of the public, for their help in providing information about a crime in all likelihood committed by others. The police expected the information elicited to help them apprehend, not the vehicle's occupants, but other individuals.

. . . *Edmond* refers to the subject matter of its holding as "stops justified only by the generalized and ever-present possibility that interrogation and inspection may reveal that *any given motorist has committed some crime*." *Ibid.* (emphasis added). We concede that *Edmond* describes the law enforcement objective there in question as a "general interest in crime control," but it specifies that the phrase "general interest in crime control" does not refer to every "law enforcement" objective. *Id.*, at 44, n. 1, 121 S. Ct. 447. . . .

Neither do we believe, *Edmond* aside, that the Fourth Amendment would have us apply an *Edmond*-type rule of automatic unconstitutionality to brief, information-seeking highway stops of the kind now before us. For one thing, the fact that such stops normally lack individualized suspicion cannot by itself determine the constitutional outcome. As in *Edmond*, the stop here at issue involves a motorist. The Fourth Amendment does not treat a motorist's car as his castle. And special law enforcement concerns will sometimes justify highway stops without individualized suspicion. *See Michigan Dept. of State Police v. Sitz*, 496 U.S. 444, 110 S. Ct. 2481, 110 L. Ed. 2d 412 (1990) (sobriety checkpoint); *United States v. Martinez-Fuerte*, 428 U.S. 543, 561, 96 S. Ct. 3074, 49 L. Ed. 2d 1116 (1976) (Border Patrol checkpoint). Moreover, unlike *Edmond*, the context here (seeking information from the public) is one in which, by definition, the concept of individualized suspicion has little role to play. Like certain other forms of police activity, say, crowd control or public safety, an information-seeking stop is not the kind of event that involves suspicion, or lack of suspicion, of the relevant individual.

For another thing, information-seeking highway stops are less likely to provoke anxiety or to prove intrusive. The stops are likely brief. The police are not likely to ask questions designed to elicit self-incriminating information. And citizens will often react positively when police simply ask for their help as "responsible citizen[s]" to "give whatever information they may have to aid in law enforcement." *Miranda v. Arizona*, 384 U.S. 436, 477–478, 86 S. Ct. 1602, 16 L. Ed. 2d 694 (1966).

Further, the law ordinarily permits police to seek the voluntary cooperation of members of the public in the investigation of a crime. "[L]aw enforcement officers do not violate the Fourth Amendment by merely approaching an individual on the street or in another public place, by asking him if he is willing to answer some questions, [or] by putting questions to him if the person is willing to listen." *Florida v. Royer*, 460 U.S. 491, 497, 103 S. Ct. 1319, 75 L. Ed. 2d 229 (1983). That, in part, is because voluntary requests play a vital role in police investigatory work.

The importance of soliciting the public's assistance is offset to some degree by the need to stop a motorist to obtain that help — a need less likely present where a pedestrian, not a motorist, is involved. The difference is significant in light of our determinations that such an involuntary stop amounts to a "seizure" in Fourth Amendment terms. That difference, however, is not important enough to justify an *Edmond*-type rule here. After all, as we have said, the motorist stop will likely be brief. Any accompanying traffic delay should prove no more onerous than many that typically accompany normal traffic congestion. And the resulting voluntary questioning of a motorist is as likely to prove important for police investigation as is the questioning of a pedestrian. Given these considerations, it would seem anomalous were the law (1) ordinarily to allow police freely to seek the voluntary cooperation of pedestrians but (2) ordinarily to forbid police to seek similar voluntary cooperation from motorists.

Finally, we do not believe that an *Edmond*-type rule is needed to prevent an unreasonable proliferation of police checkpoints. Practical considerations — namely, limited police resources and community hostility to related traffic tie-up — seem likely to inhibit any such proliferation. And, of course, the Fourth Amendment's normal insistence that the stop be reasonable in context will still provide an important legal limitation on police use of this kind of information-seeking checkpoint.

These considerations, taken together, convince us that an *Edmond*-type presumptive rule of unconstitutionality does not apply here. That does not mean the stop is automatically, or even presumptively, constitutional. It simply means that we must judge its reasonableness, hence, its constitutionality, on the basis of the individual circumstances. And as this Court said in *Brown v. Texas*, 443 U.S. 47, 51, 99 S. Ct. 2637, 61 L. Ed. 2d 357 (1979), in judging reasonableness, we look to "the gravity of the public concerns served by the seizure, the degree to which the seizure advances the public interest, and the severity of the interference with individual liberty." *See also Sitz, supra*, at 450–455, 110 S. Ct. 2481 (balancing these factors in determining reasonableness of a checkpoint stop); *Martinez-Fuerte, supra*, at 556–564, 96 S. Ct. 3074 (same).

III

We now consider the reasonableness of the checkpoint stop before us in light of the factors just mentioned. . . .

The relevant public concern was grave. Police were investigating a crime that had resulted in a human death. No one denies the police's need to obtain more information at that time. And the stop's objective was to help find the perpetrator of a specific and known crime, not of unknown crimes of a general sort. *Cf. Edmond, supra*, at 44, 121 S. Ct. 447.

The stop advanced this grave public concern to a significant degree. The police appropriately tailored their checkpoint stops to fit important criminal investigatory needs. The stops took place about one week after the hit-and-run accident, on the same highway near the location of the accident, and at about the same time of night. And police used the stops to obtain information from drivers, some of whom might well have been in the vicinity of the crime at the time it occurred. *See* App. 28–29 (describing police belief that motorists routinely leaving work after night shifts at nearby industrial complexes might have seen something relevant).

Most importantly, the stops interfered only minimally with liberty of the sort the Fourth Amendment seeks to protect. Viewed objectively, each stop required only a brief wait in line—a very few minutes at most. Contact with the police lasted only a few seconds. *Cf. Martinez-Fuerte*, 428 U.S., at 547, 96 S. Ct. 3074 (upholding stops of three-to-five minutes); *Sitz*, 496 U.S., at 448, 110 S. Ct. 2481 (upholding delays of 25 seconds). Police contact consisted simply of a request for information and the distribution of a flyer. *Cf. Martinez-Fuerte, supra*, at 546, 96 S. Ct. 3074 (upholding inquiry as to motorists' citizenship and immigration status); *Sitz, supra*, at 447, 110 S. Ct. 2481 (upholding examination of all drivers for signs of intoxication). Viewed subjectively, the contact provided little reason for anxiety or alarm. The police stopped all vehicles systematically. *Cf. Martinez-Fuerte, supra*, at 558, 96 S. Ct. 3074; *Sitz, supra*, at 452–453, 110 S. Ct. 2481. And there is no allegation here that the police acted in a discriminatory or otherwise unlawful manner while questioning motorists during stops.

For these reasons we conclude that the checkpoint stop was constitutional.

The judgment of the Illinois Supreme Court is

Reversed.

JUSTICE STEVENS, with whom JUSTICE SOUTER and JUSTICE GINSBURG join, concurring in part and dissenting in part.

There is a valid and important distinction between seizing a person to determine whether she has committed a crime and seizing a person to ask whether she has any information about an unknown person who committed a crime a week earlier. I therefore join Parts I and II of the Court's opinion explaining why our decision in *Indianapolis v. Edmond*, 531 U.S. 32, 121 S. Ct. 447, 148 L. Ed. 2d 333 (2000), is not controlling in this case. However, I find the issue discussed in Part III of the opinion closer than the Court does and believe it would be wise to remand the case to the Illinois state courts to address that issue in the first instance.

In contrast to pedestrians, who are free to keep walking when they encounter police officers handing out flyers or seeking information, motorists who confront a roadblock are required to stop, and to remain stopped for as long as the officers choose to detain them. Such a seizure may seem relatively innocuous to some, but annoying to others who are forced to wait for several minutes when the line of cars is lengthened — for example, by a surge of vehicles leaving a factory at the end of a shift. Still other drivers may find an unpublicized roadblock at midnight on a Saturday somewhat alarming.

On the other side of the equation, the likelihood that questioning a random sample of drivers will yield useful information about a hit-and-run accident that occurred a week earlier is speculative at best. To be sure, the sample in this case was not entirely random: The record reveals that the police knew that the victim had finished work at the Post Office shortly before the fatal accident, and hoped that other employees of the Post Office or the nearby industrial park might work on similar schedules and, thus, have been driving the same route at the same time the previous week. That is a plausible theory, but there is no evidence in the record that the police did anything to confirm that the nearby businesses in fact had shift changes at or near midnight on Saturdays, or that they had reason to believe that a roadblock would be more effective than, say, placing flyers on the employees' cars.

In short, the outcome of the multifactor test prescribed in *Brown v. Texas*, 443 U.S. 47, 99 S. Ct. 2637, 61 L. Ed. 2d 357 (1979), is by no means clear on the facts of this case. . . . We should be especially reluctant to abandon our role as a court of review in a case in which the constitutional inquiry requires analysis of local conditions and practices more familiar to judges closer to the scene. . . .

Notes and Questions

(1) What are the majority's reasons for treating the checkpoint in *Lidster* differently from the checkpoint in *Edmond*? Does the Court provide adequate support for a different Fourth Amendment conclusion?

(2) The Court observes that "the Fourth Amendment's normal insistence that [a] stop be reasonable in context will still provide an important legal limitation on po-

lice use of [the] kind of information-seeking checkpoint" employed in *Lidster* and that the "reasonableness" of a stop at such a checkpoint must be judged "on the basis of the individual circumstances." What specific limitations are imposed by the Fourth Amendment? When should a stop at an "information-seeking checkpoint" be deemed unreasonable?

(3) In the final line of the majority opinion, Justice Breyer observes that "there is no allegation here that the police acted in a discriminatory . . . manner while questioning motorists during stops." If the facts had shown discriminatory treatment, would the Court have reached a different Fourth Amendment conclusion? Would such a conclusion be consistent with the Court's reasoning and holding in *Whren v. United States, supra*, Chapter 2?

[3] *Drug Testing*

Skinner v. Railway Labor Executives' Association

United States Supreme Court

489 U.S. 602, 109 S. Ct. 1402, 103 L. Ed. 2d 639 (1989)

JUSTICE KENNEDY delivered the opinion of the Court.

. . . .

I

A

The problem of alcohol use on American railroads is as old as the industry itself, and efforts to deter it by carrier rules began at least a century ago. For many years, railroads have prohibited operating employees from possessing alcohol or being intoxicated while on duty and from consuming alcoholic beverages while subject to being called for duty. More recently, these proscriptions have been expanded to forbid possession or use of certain drugs. These restrictions are embodied in "Rule G," an industry-wide operating rule promulgated by the Association of American Railroads, and are enforced, in various formulations, by virtually every railroad in the country. The customary sanction for Rule G violations is dismissal.

In July 1983, the [Federal Railroad Administration (FRA)] expressed concern that these industry efforts were not adequate to curb alcohol and drug abuse by railroad employees. The FRA pointed to evidence indicating that on-the-job intoxication was a significant problem in the railroad industry. The FRA also found, after a review of accident investigation reports, that from 1972 to 1983 "the nation's railroads experienced at least 21 significant train accidents involving alcohol or drug use as a probable cause or contributing factor," and that these accidents "resulted in 25 fatalities, 61 non-fatal injuries, and property damage estimated at $19 million (approximately $27 million in 1982 dollars)." 48 Fed. Reg. 30726 (1983). The FRA further identified "an additional 17 fatalities to operating employees working on or around rail rolling stock that involved alcohol or drugs as a contributing factor." *Ibid.* In light of these problems, the FRA solicited comments from interested parties on various regulatory approaches to the problems of alcohol and drug abuse throughout the Nation's railroad system.

Comments submitted in response to this request indicated that railroads were able to detect a relatively small number of Rule G violations, owing, primarily, to their practice of relying on observation by supervisors and co-workers to enforce the rule. 49 Fed. Reg. 24266–24267 (1984). At the same time, "industry participants . . . confirmed that alcohol and drug use [did] occur on the railroads with unacceptable frequency," and available information from all sources "suggest[ed] that the problem includ[ed] 'pockets' of drinking and drug use involving multiple crew members (before and during work), sporadic cases of individuals reporting to work impaired, and repeated drinking and drug use by individual employees who are chemically or psychologically dependent on those substances." *Id.*, at 24253–24254. "Even without the benefit of regular post-accident testing," the FRA "identified 34 fatalities, 66 injuries and over $28 million in property damage (in 1983 dollars) that resulted from the errors of alcohol and drug-impaired employees in 45 train accidents and train incidents during the period 1975 through 1983." *Id.*, at 24254. Some of these accidents resulted in the release of hazardous materials and, in one case, the ensuing pollution required the evacuation of an entire Louisiana community. *Id.*, at 24254, 24259. In view of the obvious safety hazards of drug and alcohol use by railroad employees, the FRA announced in June 1984 its intention to promulgate federal regulations on the subject.

B

After reviewing further comments from representatives of the railroad industry, labor groups, and the general public, the FRA, in 1985, promulgated regulations addressing the problem of alcohol and drugs on the railroads. The final regulations apply to employees assigned to perform service subject to the Hours of Service Act, ch. 2939, 34 Stat. 1415, as amended, 45 U.S.C. § 61 *et seq.* The regulations prohibit covered employees from using or possessing alcohol or any controlled substance. 49 CFR § 219.101(a)(1) (1987). The regulations further prohibit those employees from reporting for covered service while under the influence of, or impaired by, alcohol, while having a blood alcohol concentration of 0.04 or more, or while under the influence of, or impaired by, any controlled substance. § 219.101(a)(2). The regulations do not restrict, however, a railroad's authority to impose an absolute prohibition on the presence of alcohol or any drug in the body fluids of persons in its employ, § 219.101(c), and, accordingly, they do not "replace Rule G or render it unenforceable." 50 Fed. Reg. 31538 (1985).

To the extent pertinent here, two subparts of the regulations relate to testing. Subpart C, which is entitled "Post-Accident Toxicological Testing," is mandatory. It provides that railroads "shall take all practicable steps to assure that all covered employees of the railroad directly involved . . . provide blood and urine samples for toxicological testing by FRA," § 219.203(a), upon the occurrence of certain specified events. Toxicological testing is required following a "major train accident," which is defined as any train accident that involves (i) a fatality, (ii) the release of hazardous material accompanied by an evacuation or a reportable injury, or (iii) damage to railroad property of $500,000 or more. § 219.201(a)(1). The railroad has the further duty of collecting blood and urine samples for testing after an "impact accident," which is defined as a collision that results in a reportable injury, or in damage to railroad property of $50,000 or more. § 219.201(a)(2). Finally, the railroad is also obligated to test after "[a]ny train incident that involves a fatality to any on-duty railroad employee." § 219.201(a)(3).

After occurrence of an event which activates its duty to test, the railroad must transport all crew members and other covered employees directly involved in the accident or incident to an independent medical facility, where both blood and urine samples must be obtained from each employee. After the samples have been collected, the railroad is required to ship them by prepaid air freight to the FRA laboratory for analysis. § 219.205(d). There, the samples are analyzed using "state-of-the-art equipment and techniques" to detect and measure alcohol and drugs. The FRA proposes to place primary reliance on analysis of blood samples, as blood is "the only available body fluid . . . that can provide a clear indication not only of the presence of alcohol and drugs but also their current impairment effects." 49 Fed. Reg. 24291 (1984). Urine samples are also necessary, however, because drug traces remain in the urine longer than in blood, and in some cases it will not be possible to transport employees to a medical facility before the time it takes for certain drugs to be eliminated from the bloodstream. In those instances, a "positive urine test, taken with specific information on the pattern of elimination for the particular drug and other information on the behavior of the employee and the circumstances of the accident, may be crucial to the determination of" the cause of an accident. *Ibid.*

The regulations require that the FRA notify employees of the results of the tests and afford them an opportunity to respond in writing before preparation of any final investigative report. *See* 219.211(a)(2). Employees who refuse to provide required blood or urine samples may not perform covered service for nine months, but they are entitled to a hearing concerning their refusal to take the test. 219.213.

Subpart D of the regulations, which is entitled "Authorization to Test for Cause," is permissive. It authorizes railroads to require covered employees to submit to breath or urine tests in certain circumstances not addressed by Subpart C. Breath or urine tests, or both, may be ordered (1) after a reportable accident or incident, where a supervisor has a "reasonable suspicion" that an employee's acts or omissions contributed to the occurrence or severity of the accident or incident, 219.301(b)(2); or (2) in the event of certain specific rule violations, including noncompliance with a signal and excessive speeding, 219.301(b)(3). A railroad also may require breath tests where a supervisor has a "reasonable suspicion" that an employee is under the influence of alcohol, based upon specific, personal observations concerning the appearance, behavior, speech, or body odors of the employee. 219.301(b)(1). Where impairment is suspected, a railroad, in addition, may require urine tests, but only if two supervisors make the appropriate determination, 219.301(c)(2)(i), and, where the supervisors suspect impairment due to a substance other than alcohol, at least one of those supervisors must have received specialized training in detecting the signs of drug intoxication, 219.301(c)(2)(ii).

Subpart D further provides that whenever the results of either breath or urine tests are intended for use in a disciplinary proceeding, the employee must be given the opportunity to provide a blood sample for analysis at an independent medical facility. 219.303(c). If an employee declines to give a blood sample, the railroad may presume impairment, absent persuasive evidence to the contrary, from a positive showing of controlled substance residues in the urine. The railroad must, however, provide detailed notice of this presumption to its employees, and advise them of their right to provide a contemporaneous blood sample. As in the case of samples procured under Subpart C, the regulations set forth procedures for the collection of samples, and require that samples "be analyzed by a method that is reliable within known tolerances." 219.307(b).

C

Respondents, the Railway Labor Executives' Association and various of its member labor organizations, brought the instant suit in the United States District Court for the Northern District of California, seeking to enjoin the FRA's regulations on various statutory and constitutional grounds. In a ruling from the bench, the District Court granted summary judgment in petitioners' favor. . . .

A divided panel of the Court of Appeals for the Ninth Circuit reversed. . . .

. . . .

We granted the federal parties' petition for a writ of certiorari, 486 U.S. 1042 (1988), to consider whether the regulations invalidated by the Court of Appeals violate the Fourth Amendment. We now reverse.

II

[In Part A, the majority concluded that none of the drug testing authorized by the FRA regulations qualifies as *private party* action. Instead, all of the drug tests performed by railroads pursuant to the FRA regulations are sufficiently *governmental* in character to trigger Fourth Amendment control.]

B

. . . .

We have long recognized that a "compelled intrusio[n] into the body for blood to be analyzed for alcohol content" must be deemed a Fourth Amendment search. *See Schmerber v. California*, 384 U.S. 757, 767–768 (1966). *See also Winston v. Lee*, 470 U.S. 753, 760 (1985). In light of our society's concern for the security of one's person, it is obvious that this physical intrusion, penetrating beneath the skin, infringes an expectation of privacy that society is prepared to recognize as reasonable. The ensuing chemical analysis of the sample to obtain physiological data is a further invasion of the tested employee's privacy interests. Much the same is true of the breath-testing procedures required under Subpart D of the regulations. Subjecting a person to a breathalyzer test, which generally requires the production of alveolar or "deep lung" breath for chemical analysis, implicates similar concerns about bodily integrity and, like the blood-alcohol test we considered in *Schmerber*, should also be deemed a search.

Unlike the blood-testing procedure at issue in *Schmerber*, the procedures prescribed by the FRA regulations for collecting and testing urine samples do not entail a surgical intrusion into the body. It is not disputed, however, that chemical analysis of urine, like that of blood, can reveal a host of private medical facts about an employee, including whether he or she is epileptic, pregnant, or diabetic. Nor can it be disputed that the process of collecting the sample to be tested, which may in some cases involve visual or aural monitoring of the act of urination, itself implicates privacy interests. . . . Because it is clear that the collection and testing of urine intrudes upon expectations of privacy that society has long recognized as reasonable, the Federal Courts of Appeals have concluded unanimously, and we agree, that these intrusions must be deemed searches under the Fourth Amendment.

. . . .

III

A

To hold that the Fourth Amendment is applicable to the drug and alcohol testing prescribed by the FRA regulations is only to begin the inquiry into the standards governing such intrusions. For the Fourth Amendment does not proscribe all searches and seizures, but only those that are unreasonable. What is reasonable, of course, "depends on all of the circumstances surrounding the search or seizure and the nature of the search or seizure itself." *United States v. Montoya de Hernandez*, 473 U.S. 531, 537 (1985). Thus, the permissibility of a particular practice "is judged by balancing its intrusion on the individual's Fourth Amendment interests against its promotion of legitimate governmental interests." *Delaware v. Prouse*, 440 U.S., at 654; *United States v. Martinez-Fuerte*, 428 U.S. 543 (1976).

In most criminal cases, we strike this balance in favor of the procedures described by the Warrant Clause of the Fourth Amendment. Except in certain well-defined circumstances, a search or seizure in such a case is not reasonable unless it is accomplished pursuant to a judicial warrant issued upon probable cause. We have recognized exceptions to this rule, however, "when 'special needs, beyond the normal need for law enforcement, make the warrant and probable-cause requirement impracticable.'" *Griffin v. Wisconsin*, 483 U.S. 868, 873 (1987), quoting *New Jersey v. T.L.O.*, [469 U.S. 325, 351 (1985)] (BLACKMUN, J., concurring in judgment). When faced with such special needs, we have not hesitated to balance the governmental and privacy interests to assess the practicality of the warrant and probable-cause requirements in the particular context.

The Government's interest in regulating the conduct of railroad employees to ensure safety . . . "presents 'special needs' beyond normal law enforcement that may justify departures from the usual warrant and probable-cause requirements." *Griffin v. Wisconsin, supra,* at 873–874. The hours of service employees covered by the FRA regulations include persons engaged in handling orders concerning train movements, operating crews, and those engaged in the maintenance and repair of signal systems. 50 Fed. Reg. 31511 (1985). It is undisputed that these and other covered employees are engaged in safety-sensitive tasks. . . .

The FRA has prescribed toxicological tests, not to assist in the prosecution of employees, but rather "to prevent accidents and casualties in railroad operations that result from impairment of employees by alcohol or drugs." 49 CFR § 219.1(a) (1987).[5] This governmental interest in ensuring the safety of the traveling public and of the employees themselves plainly justifies prohibiting covered employees from using alcohol or drugs on duty, or while subject to being called for duty. This interest also "require[s] and justif[ies] the exercise of supervision to assure that the restrictions are in fact observed." *Griffin v. Wisconsin, supra,* at 875. The question that remains, then, is whether the Government's need to monitor compliance with these restrictions justifies the privacy intrusions at issue absent a warrant or individualized suspicion.

B

An essential purpose of a warrant requirement is to protect privacy interests by assuring citizens subject to a search or seizure that such intrusions are not the random or arbitrary acts of government agents. A warrant assures the citizen that the intrusion is authorized by law, and that it is narrowly limited in its objectives and scope. A warrant also provides the detached scrutiny of a neutral magistrate, and thus ensures an objective determination whether an intrusion is justified in any given case. In the present context, however, a warrant would do little to further these aims. Both the circumstances justifying toxicological testing and the permissible limits of such intrusions are defined narrowly and specifically in the regulations that authorize them, and doubtless are well known to covered employees. Indeed, in light of the standardized nature of the tests and the minimal discretion vested in those charged with administering the program, there are virtually no facts for a neutral magistrate to evaluate.

---

5. [W]hile respondents aver generally that test results might be made available to law enforcement authorities, they do not seriously contend that this provision, or any other part of the administrative scheme, was designed as "a 'pretext' to enable law enforcement authorities to gather evidence of penal law violations." *New York v. Burger,* 482 U.S. 691, 716–717, n.27 (1987). Absent a persuasive showing that the FRA's testing program is pretextual, we assess the FRA's scheme in light of its obvious administrative purpose. We leave for another day the question whether routine use in criminal prosecutions of evidence obtained pursuant to the administrative scheme would give rise to an inference of pretext, or otherwise impugn the administrative nature of the FRA's program.

We have recognized, moreover, that the government's interest in dispensing with the warrant requirement is at its strongest when, as here, "the burden of obtaining a warrant is likely to frustrate the governmental purpose behind the search." *Camara v. Municipal Court of San Francisco,* [387 U.S. 523, 533 (1967)]. As the FRA recognized, alcohol and other drugs are eliminated from the bloodstream at a constant rate, *see* 49 Fed. Reg. 24291 (1984), and blood and breath samples taken to measure whether these substances were in the bloodstream when a triggering event occurred must be obtained as soon as possible. Although the metabolites of some drugs remain in the urine for longer periods of time and may enable the FRA to estimate whether the employee was impaired by those drugs at the time of a covered accident, incident, or rule violation, 49 Fed. Reg. 24291 (1984), the delay necessary to procure a warrant nevertheless may result in the destruction of valuable evidence.

The Government's need to rely on private railroads to set the testing process in motion also indicates that insistence on a warrant requirement would impede the achievement of the Government's objective. Railroad supervisors, like school officials, *see New Jersey v. T.L.O., supra,* at 339–340, and hospital administrators, *see O'Connor v. Ortega,* 480 U.S., at 722, are not in the business of investigating violations of the criminal laws or enforcing administrative codes, and otherwise have little occasion to become familiar with the intricacies of this Court's Fourth Amendment jurisprudence. . . .

In sum, imposing a warrant requirement in the present context would add little to the assurances of certainty and regularity already afforded by the regulations, while significantly hindering, and in many cases frustrating, the objectives of the Government's testing program. We do not believe that a warrant is essential to render the intrusions here at issue reasonable under the Fourth Amendment.

C

Our cases indicate that even a search that may be performed without a warrant must be based, as a general matter, on probable cause to believe that the person to be searched has violated the law. When the balance of interests precludes insistence on a showing of probable cause, we have usually required "some quantum of individualized suspicion" before concluding that a search is reasonable. We made it clear, however, that a showing of individualized suspicion is not a constitutional floor, below which a search must be presumed unreasonable. In limited circumstances, where the privacy interests implicated by the search are minimal, and where an important governmental interest furthered by the intrusion would be placed in jeopardy by a requirement of individualized suspicion, a search may be reasonable despite the absence of such suspicion. We believe this is true of the intrusions in question here.

By and large, intrusions on privacy under the FRA regulations are limited. To the extent transportation and like restrictions are necessary to procure the requisite blood, breath, and urine samples for testing, this interference alone is minimal given the employment context in which it takes place. Ordinarily, an employee consents to significant restrictions in his freedom of movement where necessary for his employment, and few are free to come and go as they please during working hours. Any additional interference with a railroad employee's freedom of movement that occurs in the time it takes to procure a blood, breath, or urine sample for testing cannot, by itself, be said to infringe significant privacy interests.

Our decision in *Schmerber v. California, supra,* indicates that the same is true of the blood tests required by the FRA regulations. In that case, we held that a State could direct that a blood sample be withdrawn from a motorist suspected of driving while intoxicated, despite his refusal to consent to the intrusion. We noted that the test was performed in a reasonable manner, as the motorist's "blood was taken by a physician in a hospital environment according to accepted medical practices." *Id.*, at 771. We said also that the intrusion occasioned by a blood test is not significant, since such "tests are a commonplace in these days of periodic physical examinations and experience with them teaches that the quantity of blood extracted is minimal, and that for most people the procedure involves virtually no risk, trauma, or pain." *Ibid. Schmerber* thus confirmed "society's judgment that blood tests do not constitute an unduly extensive imposition on an individual's privacy and bodily integrity." *Winston v. Lee*, 470 U.S., at 762.

The breath tests authorized by Subpart D of the regulations are even less intrusive than the blood tests prescribed by Subpart C. Unlike blood tests, breath tests do not require piercing the skin and may be conducted safely outside a hospital environment and with a minimum of inconvenience or embarrassment. Further, breath tests reveal the level of alcohol in the employee's bloodstream and nothing more. Like the blood-testing procedures mandated by Subpart C, which can be used only to ascertain the presence of alcohol or controlled substances in the bloodstream, breath tests reveal no other facts in which the employee has a substantial privacy interest. In all the circumstances, we cannot conclude that the administration of a breath test implicates significant privacy concerns.

A more difficult question is presented by urine tests. Like breath tests, urine tests are not invasive of the body and, under the regulations, may not be used as an occasion for inquiring into private facts unrelated to alcohol or drug use. We recognize, however, that the procedures for collecting the necessary samples, which require employees to perform an excretory function traditionally shielded by great privacy, raise concerns not implicated by blood or breath tests. While we would not characterize these additional privacy concerns as minimal in most contexts, we note that the regulations endeavor to reduce the intrusiveness of the collection process. The regulations do not require that samples be furnished under the direct observation of a monitor, despite the desirability of such a procedure to ensure the integrity of the sample. The sample is also collected in a medical environment, by personnel unrelated to the railroad employer, and is thus not unlike similar procedures encountered often in the context of a regular physical examination.

More importantly, the expectations of privacy of covered employees are diminished by reason of their participation in an industry that is regulated pervasively to ensure safety, a goal dependent, in substantial part, on the health and fitness of covered employees. . . .

We do not suggest, of course, that the interest in bodily security enjoyed by those employed in a regulated industry must always be considered minimal. Here, however, the covered employees have long been a principal focus of regulatory concern . . . . Though some of the privacy interests implicated by the toxicological testing at issue reasonably might be viewed as significant in other contexts, logic and history show that a diminished expectation of privacy attaches to information relating to the physical condition of covered employees and to this reasonable means of procuring such information. We conclude, therefore, that the testing procedures contemplated by Subparts C and D pose only limited threats to the justifiable expectations of privacy of covered employees.

By contrast, the Government interest in testing without a showing of individualized suspicion is compelling. Employees subject to the tests discharge duties fraught with such risks of injury to others that even a momentary lapse of attention can have disastrous consequences . . . . [E]mployees who are subject to testing under the FRA regulations can cause great human loss before any signs of impairment become noticeable to supervisors or others. An impaired employee, the FRA found, will seldom display any outward "signs detectable by the lay person or, in many cases, even the physician." 50 Fed. Reg. 31526 (1985) . . . . Indeed, while respondents posit that impaired employees might be detected without alcohol or drug testing,[9] the premise of respondents' lawsuit is that even the occurrence of a major calamity will not give rise to a suspicion of impairment with respect to any particular employee.

While no procedure can identify all impaired employees with ease and perfect accuracy, the FRA regulations supply an effective means of deterring employees engaged in safety-sensitive tasks from using controlled substances or alcohol in the first place. 50 Fed. Reg. 31541 (1985). The railroad industry's experience with Rule G persuasively shows, and common sense confirms, that the customary dismissal sanction that threatens employees who use drugs or alcohol while on duty cannot serve as an effective deterrent unless violators know that they are likely to be discovered. By ensuring that employees in safety-sensitive positions know they will be tested upon the occurrence of a triggering event, the timing of which no employee can pre-

---

9. Respondents offer a list of "less drastic and equally effective means" of addressing the Government's concerns, including reliance on the private proscriptions already in force, and training supervisory personnel "to effectively detect employees who are impaired by drug or alcohol use without resort to such intrusive procedures as blood and urine tests." Brief for Respondents 40–43. We have repeatedly stated, however that "[t]he reasonableness of any particular government activity does not necessarily or invariably turn on the existence of alternative 'less intrusive' means." *Illinois v. Lafayette*, 462 U.S. 640, 647 (1983) . . . . Here, the FRA expressly considered various alternatives to its drug-screening program and reasonably found them wanting. At bottom, respondents' insistence on less drastic alternatives would require us to second-guess the reasonable conclusions drawn by the FRA after years of investigation and study. This we decline to do.

596   5 · THE BALANCING APPROACH TO 4TH AMENDMENT REASONABLENESS

dict with certainty, the regulations significantly increase the deterrent effect of the administrative penalties associated with the prohibited conduct, concomitantly increasing the likelihood that employees will forgo using drugs or alcohol while subject to being called for duty.

The testing procedures contemplated by Subpart C also help railroads obtain invaluable information about the causes of major accidents and to take appropriate measures to safeguard the general public. Positive test results would point toward drug or alcohol impairment on the part of members of the crew as a possible cause of an accident, and may help to establish whether a particular accident, otherwise not drug related, was made worse by the inability of impaired employees to respond appropriately. Negative test results would likewise furnish invaluable clues, for eliminating drug impairment as a potential cause or contributing factor would help establish the significance of equipment failure, inadequate training, or other potential causes, and suggest a more thorough examination of these alternatives. . . .

A requirement of particularized suspicion of drug or alcohol use would seriously impede an employer's ability to obtain this information, despite its obvious importance. Experience confirms the FRA's judgment that the scene of a serious rail accident is chaotic . . . . Indeed, any attempt to gather evidence relating to the possible impairment of particular employees likely would result in the loss or deterioration of the evidence furnished by the tests. It would be unrealistic, and inimical to the Government's goal of ensuring safety in rail transportation, to require a showing of individualized suspicion in these circumstances.

 . . . .

 . . . Because the record indicates that blood and urine tests, taken together, are highly effective means of ascertaining on-the-job impairment and of deterring the use of drugs by railroad employees, we believe the Court of Appeals erred in concluding that the postaccident testing regulations are not reasonably related to the Government objectives that support them.

We conclude that the compelling Government interests served by the FRA's regulations would be significantly hindered if railroads were required to point to specific facts giving rise to a reasonable suspicion of impairment before testing a given employee. In view of our conclusion that, on the present record, the toxicological testing contemplated by the regulations is not an undue infringement on the justifiable expectations of privacy of covered employees, the Government's compelling interests outweigh privacy concerns.

IV

The possession of unlawful drugs is a criminal offense that the Government may punish, but it is a separate and far more dangerous wrong to perform certain sensitive tasks while under the influence of those substances. Performing those tasks while impaired by alcohol is, of course, equally dangerous, though consumption of alcohol is legal in most other contexts. . . .

... In light of the limited discretion exercised by the railroad employers under the regulations, the surpassing safety interests served by toxicological tests in this context, and the diminished expectation of privacy that attaches to information pertaining to the fitness of covered employees, we believe that it is reasonable to conduct such tests in the absence of a warrant or reasonable suspicion that any particular employee may be impaired. We hold that the alcohol and drug tests contemplated by Subparts C and D of the FRA's regulations are reasonable within the meaning of the Fourth Amendment. The judgment of the Court of Appeals is accordingly reversed.

It is so ordered.

[The opinion of JUSTICE STEVENS, concurring in part and concurring in the judgment, has been omitted.]

JUSTICE MARSHALL, with whom JUSTICE BRENNAN joins, dissenting.

. . . .

In permitting the Government to force entire railroad crews to submit to invasive blood and urine tests, even when it lacks any evidence of drug or alcohol use or other wrongdoing, the majority today joins those shortsighted courts which have allowed basic constitutional rights to fall prey to momentary emergencies. . . .

. . . .

I

The Court today takes its longest step yet toward reading the probable-cause requirement out of the Fourth Amendment. . . .

. . . As this Court has long recognized, the Framers intended the provisions of th[e Warrant] Clause — a warrant and probable cause — to "provide the yardstick against which official searches and seizures are to be measured." *T.L.O., supra,* at 359–360 (opinion of Brennan, J.). Without the content which those provisions give to the Fourth Amendment's overarching command that searches and seizures be "reasonable," the Amendment lies virtually devoid of meaning, subject to whatever content shifting judicial majorities, concerned about the problems of the day, choose to give to that supple term. Constitutional requirements like probable cause are not fairweather friends, present when advantageous, conveniently absent when "special needs" make them seem not.

Until recently, an unbroken line of cases had recognized probable cause as an indispensable prerequisite for a full-scale search, regardless of whether such a search was conducted pursuant to a warrant or under one of the recognized exceptions to the warrant requirement. *T.L.O., supra,* at 358 and 359, n. 3 (opinion of BRENNAN, J.); *see also Chambers v. Maroney,* 99 U.S. 42, 51 (1970). Only where the government action in question had a "substantially less intrusive" impact on privacy, *Dunaway,* 442 U.S., at 210, and thus clearly fell short of a full-scale search, did we relax the probable-cause standard. *Id.,* at 214. Even in this class of cases, we almost always required the government to show some individualized suspicion to justify the search. . . .

. . . .

. . . After determining that the Fourth Amendment applies to the FRA's testing regime, the majority embarks on an extended inquiry into whether that regime is "reasonable," an inquiry in which it balances "'all of the circumstances surrounding the search or seizure and the nature of the search or seizure itself.'" *Ante*, at 619, quoting *United States v. Montoya de Hernandez*, 473 U.S. 531, 537 (1985). The result is "special needs" balancing analysis' deepest incursion yet into the core protections of the Fourth Amendment. . . .

. . . .

. . . Because abandoning the explicit protections of the Fourth Amendment seriously imperils "the right to be let alone — the most comprehensive of rights and the right most valued by civilized men," *Olmstead v. United States*, 277 U.S. 438, 478 (1928) (Brandeis, J., dissenting) — I reject the majority's "special needs" rationale as unprincipled and dangerous.

II

. . . .

The majority's threshold determination that "covered" railroad employees have been searched under the FRA's testing program is certainly correct. . . .

. . . By any measure, the FRA's highly intrusive collection and testing procedures qualify as full-scale personal searches. Under our precedents, a showing of probable cause is therefore clearly required. But even if these searches were viewed as entailing only minimal intrusions on the order, say, of a police stop-and-frisk, the FRA's program would still fail to pass constitutional muster, for we have, without exception, demanded that even minimally intrusive searches of the person be founded on individualized suspicion. . . .

Compelling a person to submit to the piercing of his skin by a hypodermic needle so that his blood may be extracted significantly intrudes on the "personal privacy and dignity against unwarranted intrusion by the State" against which the Fourth Amendment protects. *Schmerber, supra*, at 767. As we emphasized in *Terry v. Ohio*, 392 U.S. 1, 24–25 (1968), "Even a limited search of the outer clothing . . . constitutes a severe, though brief, intrusion upon cherished personal security, and it must surely be an annoying, frightening, and perhaps humiliating experience." We have similarly described the taking of a suspect's fingernail scrapings as a "'severe, though brief, intrusion upon cherished personal security.'" *Cupp v. Murphy*, 412 U.S. 291, 295 (1973) (quoting *Terry, supra*, at 24–25, and upholding this procedure upon a showing of probable cause). The government-compelled withdrawal of blood, involving as it does the added aspect of physical invasion, is surely no less an intrusion. The surrender of blood on demand is, furthermore, hardly a quotidian occurrence.

In recognition of the intrusiveness of this procedure, we specifically required in *Schmerber* that police have evidence of a drunken-driving suspect's impairment before forcing him to endure a blood test . . . . Exactly why a blood test which, if conducted on one person, requires a showing of at least individualized suspicion may, if conducted on many persons, be based on no showing whatsoever, the majority does not — and cannot — explain.

Compelling a person to produce a urine sample on demand also intrudes deeply on privacy and bodily integrity. Urination is among the most private of activities. It is generally forbidden in public, eschewed as a matter of conversation, and performed in places designed to preserve this tradition of personal seclusion. . . .

The majority's characterization of the privacy interests implicated by urine collection as "minimal" is nothing short of startling. . . .

Finally, the chemical analysis the FRA performs upon the blood and urine samples implicates strong privacy interests apart from those intruded upon by the collection of bodily fluids. Technological advances have made it possible to uncover, through analysis of chemical compounds in these fluids, not only drug or alcohol use, but also medical disorders such as epilepsy, diabetes, and clinical depression. The FRA's requirement that workers disclose the medications they have taken during the 30 days prior to chemical testing further impinges upon the confidentiality customarily attending personal health secrets.

By any reading of our precedents, the intrusiveness of these three searches demands that they — like other full-scale searches — be justified by probable cause. It is no answer to suggest, as does the majority, that railroad workers have relinquished the protection afforded them by this Fourth Amendment requirement, either by "participat[ing] in an industry that is regulated pervasively to ensure safety" or by undergoing periodic fitness tests pursuant to state law or to collective-bargaining agreements. *Ante*, at 627.

Our decisions in the regulatory search area refute the suggestion that the heavy regulation of the railroad industry eclipses workers' rights under the Fourth Amendment to insist upon a showing of probable cause when their bodily fluids are being extracted. This line of cases has exclusively involved searches of *employer* property, with respect to which "[c]ertain industries have such a history of government oversight that no reasonable expectation of privacy could exist for a *proprietor* over the *stock* of such an enterprise." *Marshall v. Barlow's, Inc.*, 436 U.S. 307, 313 (1978) (emphasis added; citation omitted), quoted in *New York v. Burger*, 482 U.S. 691, 700 (1987). Never have we intimated that regulatory searches reduce employees' rights of privacy in their *persons*. These rights mean little indeed if, having passed through these portals, an individual may remain subject to a suspicionless search of his person justified solely on the grounds that the government already is permitted to conduct a search of the inanimate contents of the surrounding area. In holding that searches of persons may fall within the category of regulatory searches permitted in the absence of probable cause or even individualized suspicion, the majority sets a dangerous and ill-conceived precedent.

The majority's suggestion that railroad workers' privacy is only minimally invaded by the collection and testing of their bodily fluids because they undergo periodic fitness tests is equally baseless. . . .

I recognize that invalidating the full-scale searches involved in the FRA's testing regime for failure to comport with the Fourth Amendment's command of probable cause may hinder the Government's attempts to make rail transit as safe as humanly possible. But constitutional rights have their consequences, and one is that efforts to maximize the public welfare, no matter how well intentioned, must always be pursued within constitutional boundaries. Were the police freed from the constraints of the Fourth Amendment for just one day to seek out evidence of criminal wrongdoing, the resulting convictions and incarcerations would probably prevent thousands of fatalities. Our refusal to tolerate this specter reflects our shared belief that even beneficent governmental power — whether exercised to save money, save lives, or make the trains run on time — must always yield to "a resolute loyalty to constitutional safeguards." *Almeida-Sanchez v. United States*, 413 U.S. 266, 273 (1973). The Constitution demands no less loyalty here.

III

Even accepting the majority's view that the FRA's collection and testing program is appropriately analyzed under a multifactor balancing test, and not under the literal terms of the Fourth Amendment, I would still find the program invalid. The benefits of suspicionless blood and urine testing are far outstripped by the costs imposed on personal liberty by such sweeping searches. Only by erroneously deriding as "minimal" the privacy and dignity interests at stake, and by uncritically inflating the likely efficacy of the FRA's testing program, does the majority strike a different balance.

For the reasons stated above, I find nothing minimal about the intrusion on individual liberty that occurs whenever the Government forcibly draws and analyzes a person's blood and urine. . . .

   . . . .

The majority's trivialization of the intrusions on worker privacy posed by the FRA's testing program is matched at the other extreme by its blind acceptance of the Government's assertion that testing will "dete[r] employees engaged in safety-sensitive tasks from using controlled substances or alcohol," and "help railroads obtain invaluable information about the causes of major accidents." *Ante*, at 629, 630. With respect, first, to deterrence, it is simply implausible that testing employees after major accidents occur, 49 CFR § 219.201(a)(1) (1987), will appreciably discourage them from using drugs or alcohol. As JUSTICE STEVENS observes in his concurring opinion:

> "Most people — and I would think most railroad employees as well — do not go to work with the expectation that they may be involved in a major accident, particularly one causing such catastrophic results as loss of life or the release of hazardous material requiring an evacuation. Moreover, even if

they are conscious of the possibilities that such an accident might occur and that alcohol or drug use might be a contributing factor, if the risk of serious personal injury does not deter their use of these substances, it seems highly unlikely that the additional threat of loss of employment would have any effect on their behavior." *Ante*, at 634.

Under the majority's deterrence rationale, people who skip school or work to spend a sunny day at the zoo will not taunt the lions because their truancy or absenteeism might be discovered in the event they are mauled. It is, of course, the fear of the accident, not the fear of a postaccident revelation, that deters. . . .

The poverty of the majority's deterrence rationale leaves the Government's interest in diagnosing the causes of major accidents as the sole remaining justification for the FRA's testing program. I do not denigrate this interest, but it seems a slender thread from which to hang such an intrusive program, particularly given that the knowledge that one or more workers were impaired at the time of an accident falls far short of proving that substance abuse caused or exacerbated that accident. Some corroborative evidence is needed . . . . Furthermore, reliance on the importance of diagnosing the causes of an accident as a critical basis for upholding the FRA's testing plan is especially hard to square with our frequent admonition that the interest in ascertaining the causes of a criminal episode does not justify departure from the Fourth Amendment's requirements. "[T]his Court has never sustained a search upon the sole ground that officers reasonably expected to find evidence of a particular crime . . . ." *Katz*, 389 U.S. at 356. Nor should it here.

IV

. . . .

A majority of this Court, swept away by society's obsession with stopping the scourge of illegal drugs, today succumbs to . . . popular pressures . . . . I believe the Framers would be appalled by the vision of mass governmental intrusions upon the integrity of the human body that the majority allows to become reality. The immediate victims of the majority's constitutional timorousness will be those railroad workers whose bodily fluids the Government may now forcibly collect and analyze. But ultimately, today's decision will reduce the privacy all citizens may enjoy, for . . . principles of law, once bent, do not snap back easily. I dissent.

Notes and Questions

(1) According to the *Skinner* majority, blood, urine, and breath tests for drugs clearly qualify as Fourth Amendment "searches." Those searches, however, can be "reasonable" despite the lack of any particularized showing that the individual being tested has taken narcotics. What reasoning supports the conclusion that "random, suspicionless" drug testing can satisfy Fourth Amendment requirements? In what circumstances is random testing unconstitutional?

(2) In *National Treasury Employees Union v. Von Raab*, 489 U.S. 656 (1989), a companion case to *Skinner*, the Court also upheld a United States Customs Service

drug testing program. Under the Customs Service testing scheme, employees who sought transfer or promotion to positions involving drug interdiction, to positions requiring the carrying of a firearm, or to positions requiring the handling of classified material were required to submit to urinalysis as a condition of such transfer or promotion. According to the Court, the purposes of the program were to prevent and deter drug use among those eligible for promotion to certain sensitive positions. Those who sought transfers or promotions knew of the automatic, nondiscretionary drug test condition.

The Court concluded that "the Government has . . . compelling interests in safeguarding our borders and the public safety [that] outweigh the privacy expectations of employees who seek to be promoted to positions that directly involve the interdiction of illegal drugs or that require the incumbent to carry a firearm." As a result, it held that the urinalysis searches without warrants and without individualized suspicion were reasonable. The Court also concluded that the government's interest in protecting "classified" information was compelling. However, because it had doubt about whether the category of employees subject to testing for that reason was overbroad, the Court remanded the case to the lower court for clarification of the scope of that category.

Justice Scalia, who had joined the majority in *Skinner*, dissented in *Von Raab*. He expressed concern about the complete lack of evidence of a drug abuse problem among Customs Service employees and criticized the Court's broad approval of drug testing of those who carry firearms or handle sensitive information. In his opinion, the effect of that approval is the exposure of "vast numbers of public employees" and the potential exposure of even "private citizens" to "needless indignity." Justice Scalia concluded that the Customs Service program approved by five members of the Court was "a kind of immolation of privacy and human dignity in symbolic opposition to drug use."

(3) Six years later, in *Vernonia School District 47J v. Acton*, 515 U.S. 646, 115 S. Ct. 2386, 132 L. Ed. 2d 564 (1995), the Court addressed the constitutionality of a school board policy that required high school and grade school students who wished to participate in interscholastic athletics to consent to random urinalysis drug testing. The expressed purposes of the policy were "to prevent student athletes from using drugs, to protect their health and safety, and to provide drug users with assistance programs."

The case arose when James Acton, a seventh-grader, was denied the opportunity to participate in football because his parents had refused to sign the testing consent forms. The Actons sought declaratory and injunctive relief against the program, claiming that it violated the Fourth Amendment. After the trial court denied relief, the Ninth Circuit reversed, sustaining the Actons' constitutional claim. The Supreme Court reversed the Ninth Circuit, holding that the policy was constitutional.

Invoking the "balancing" analysis employed in *Skinner* and *Von Raab*, the majority first turned to "the nature of the privacy interest" intruded upon by the testing in

Vernonia. It concluded that students' constitutional privacy interests are diminished by the fact that they are in the custody of and under the supervision and control of school officials. Moreover, student athletes' interests are further diminished by the nonprivate nature of locker room facilities and by their voluntary choice to subject themselves to an even higher degree of regulation than other students — regulation that includes a physical examination and compliance with rules established by coaches and athletic directors.

The majority then assessed "the character of the intrusion" that occurs. Because the monitoring of the students' urination was "nearly identical to [the conditions] encountered in public restrooms," the infringement of privacy interests occasioned by the process of obtaining urine samples was deemed "negligible." In addition, because the urinalysis performed looked only for drugs, not for other private information, because the drugs for which samples were screened were standard, and because the results of the tests were disclosed only to a limited class of school personnel and were not turned over to law enforcement or used for internal disciplinary functions, the Court concluded that the invasions of privacy that occurred were "not significant."

Next, the majority considered "the nature and immediacy of the governmental concern at issue" and "the efficacy of [the means used] for meeting it." The Court pointedly observed that interests furthered by random drug testing do not have to be "compelling," but only have to be "*important enough* to justify the particular search at hand." The interest in *Vernonia* — deterring drug use by schoolchildren — was sufficiently important because the effects of drugs are "most severe" during school years, the educational process can be disrupted by student drug use, and the risk of "immediate physical harm" to drug-using athletes and their fellow competitors "is particularly high." In addition, the district court's conclusion that students, particularly athletes, were in a "state of rebellion" that was "fueled by alcohol and drug abuse" confirmed the "immediacy" of the school district's concerns. Finally, the Court found it "self-evident" that the drug problem documented in the findings below was "effectively addressed by making sure that athletes do not use drugs." It rejected the argument that the availability of a "less intrusive alternative" — drug testing on suspicion of drug use — rendered the random testing program unreasonable. Suspicion-based testing was deemed "impracticable" because the same parents who opposed random testing might not accept "accusatory" testing based on individualized suspicion, because teachers might well impose suspicion-based testing "arbitrarily on troublesome but not drug-likely students," and because a requirement of individualized suspicion would impose on schoolteachers "the new function of spotting and bringing to account drug abuse, a task for which they are ill prepared, and which is not readily compatible with their vocation."

In conclusion, the Court "caution[ed] against the assumption that suspicionless drug testing will readily pass constitutional muster in other contexts," noting that the "most significant element in this case" was that "the [p]olicy was undertaken in furtherance of the government's responsibilities . . . as guardian and tutor of children entrusted to its care."

Justice O'Connor, joined by Justice Stevens and Justice Souter, dissented. In their view, the majority had "misconstrued the fundamental role of the individualized suspicion requirement in Fourth Amendment analysis" and had "never seriously engage[d] the practicality of such a requirement in the instant case." Because the dissenters believed that a suspicion-based scheme would have been sufficiently effective to combat drug use by student athletes, they did not think that an exemption from the individualized suspicion requirement was justified in the situation at issue in *Vernonia*. They would have declared the random drug testing program unreasonable.

(4) Most recently, in *Board of Education of Independent School District No. 92 of Pottawatomie County v. Earls*, 536 U.S. 822, 122 S. Ct. 2559, 153 L. Ed. 2d 735 (2002), the Court addressed the constitutionality of a "Student Activities Drug Testing Policy," which required middle and high school students to consent to urinalysis drug testing as a condition for participation in any extracurricular activities. The policy had been applied to students involved in "the Academic Team, Future Farmers of America, Future Homemakers of America, band, choir, pom pon, cheerleading, and athletics." It required students to undergo drug testing *before* participation in an extracurricular activity, submit to random drug testing *while* participating in the activity, and agree to be tested at any time upon reasonable suspicion. The tests were designed to detect *only* illegal drugs, not medical conditions or authorized prescription drugs. Two students and their parents filed a civil suit, claiming that the policy violated the Fourth Amendment.

By a 5-4 vote, the Court declared the policy constitutional. The majority observed "that 'special needs' inhere in the public school context," citing *Vernonia* and *T.L.O.* It then turned to the interests at stake, concluding first that the students affected had "a limited expectation of privacy" because of the "public school environment where the State is responsible for maintaining discipline, health, and safety." The fact that the athletes in *Vernonia* were "subject to regular physicals and communal undress" was deemed "supplemental" and "not essential to [the Court's] decision" in that case. Moreover, students in other extracurricular activities "subject themselves to many of the same intrusions on their privacy as do athletes." The "regulation of extracurricular activities" that occurs "further diminishes the expectation of privacy among schoolchildren."

As for the "character of the intrusion" on privacy, the method of collecting urine was "virtually identical" to the method deemed " 'negligible' " in *Vernonia*. Moreover, the policy required "that the test results be kept in confidential files" and "released to school personnel only on a 'need to know' basis" and those results were "not turned over to any law enforcement authority." In addition, the "only consequence of a failed test was limitation of the privilege to participate." Consequently, "the invasion of students' privacy [was] not significant."

With regard to "the nature and immediacy of the government's concerns and the efficacy of the policy in meeting them," the Court noted that it had "already articulated in detail the importance of the governmental concern in preventing drug use by schoolchildren," that drug abuse "ha[d] only grown worse" since *Vernonia* was decided, that "the health and safety risks identified in *Vernonia* appl[ied] with equal force" to the students in *Earls*, and that "the nationwide drug epidemic [made] the war against drugs a pressing concern in every school." Although there was "specific evidence of drug use" in the schools in this district, the Court stressed that such evidence was not necessary because "the need to prevent and deter the substantial harm of childhood drug use provides the necessary immediacy for a school testing policy." The majority rejected the contention that safety concerns were not at stake for nonathletes, asserting that "the safety interest furthered by drug testing is undoubtedly substantial for all children" because "drug use carries a variety of health risks for children, including death from overdose."

For reasons similar to those found persuasive in *Vernonia*, the Court rejected an "individualized suspicion" requirement. It then concluded that testing the students who participate "in extracurricular activities is a reasonably effective means of addressing the School District's legitimate concerns in preventing, deterring, and detecting drug use."

Justices Ginsburg, Stevens, O'Connor, and Souter dissented. In their view, the drug testing program involved in *Earls* was "not reasonable, it [was] capricious, even perverse" because it "target[ed] for testing a student population least likely to be at risk from illicit drugs and their damaging effects." Distinctions from the program upheld in *Vernonia* led the dissenters to conclude that the "sweeping" program in *Earls* had an "unreasonable reach [that] render[ed] it impermissible under the Fourth Amendment."

Chandler v. Miller

United States Supreme Court

520 U.S. 305, 117 S. Ct. 1295, 137 L. Ed. 2d 513 (1997)

JUSTICE GINSBURG delivered the opinion of the Court.

. . . .

Georgia requires candidates for designated state offices to certify that they have taken a drug test and that the test result was negative. Ga. Code Ann. § 21-2-140 (1993) (hereinafter § 21-2-140). We confront in this case the question whether that requirement ranks among the limited circumstances in which suspicionless searches are warranted. Relying on this Court's precedents sustaining drug-testing programs for student athletes, customs employees, and railway employees, *see Vernonia School Dist. 47J v. Acton*, 515 U.S. 646, 650, 665–666 (1995) (random drug testing of students who participate in interscholastic sports); [*National Treasury Employees Union v.*] *Von Raab*, 489 U.S. at 659 (drug tests for United States Customs Service employees who seek transfer or promotion to certain positions); *Skinner v. Railway Labor Executives' Assn.*, 489 U.S. 602, 608–613, 103 L. Ed. 2d 639, 109 S. Ct. 1402 (1989) (drug and alcohol tests for railway employees involved in train accidents and for those who violate particular safety rules), the United States Court of Appeals for the Eleventh Circuit judged Georgia's law constitutional. We reverse that judgment.

Georgia's requirement that candidates for state office pass a drug test, we hold, does not fit within the closely guarded category of constitutionally permissible suspicion-less searches.

I

The prescription at issue, approved by the Georgia Legislature in 1990, orders that "[e]ach candidate seeking to qualify for nomination or election to a state office shall as a condition of such qualification be required to certify that such candidate has tested negative for illegal drugs." § 21-2-140(b). Georgia was the first, and apparently remains the only, State to condition candidacy for state office on a drug test.

Under the Georgia statute, to qualify for a place on the ballot, a candidate must present a certificate from a state-approved laboratory, in a form approved by the Secretary of State, reporting that the candidate submitted to a urinalysis drug test within 30 days prior to qualifying for nomination or election and that the results were negative. § 21-2-140(c). The statute lists as "[i]llegal drug[s]": marijuana, cocaine, opiates, amphetamines, and phencyclidines. § 21-2-140(a)(3). The designated state offices are: "the Governor, Lieutenant Governor, Secretary of State, Attorney General, State School Superintendent, Commissioner of Insurance, Commissioner of Agriculture, Commissioner of Labor, Justices of the Supreme Court, Judges of the Court of Appeals, judges of the superior courts, district attorneys, members of the General Assembly, and members of the Public Service Commission." § 21-2-140(a)(4).

Candidate drug tests are to be administered in a manner consistent with the United States Department of Health and Human Services Guidelines, 53 Fed. Reg. 11979–11989 (1988), or other professionally valid procedures approved by Georgia's Commissioner of Human Resources. *See* § 21-2-140(a)(2). A candidate may provide the test specimen at a laboratory approved by the State, or at the office of the candidate's personal physician. Once a urine sample is obtained, an approved laboratory determines whether any of the five specified illegal drugs are present, *id.*, at 5; § 21-2-140(c), and prepares a certificate reporting the test results to the candidate.

Petitioners were Libertarian Party nominees in 1994 for state offices subject to the requirements of § 21-2-140. The Party nominated Walker L. Chandler for the office of Lieutenant Governor, Sharon T. Harris for the office of Commissioner of Agriculture, and James D. Walker for the office of member of the General Assembly. In May 1994, about one month before the deadline for submission of the certificates required by § 21-2-140, petitioners Chandler, Harris, and Walker filed this action in the United States District Court for the Northern District of Georgia. They asserted, *inter alia*, that the drug tests required by § 21-2-140 violated their rights under the First, Fourth, and Fourteenth Amendments to the United States Constitution. Naming as defendants Governor Zell D. Miller and two other state officials involved in the administration of § 21-2-140, petitioners requested declaratory and injunctive relief barring enforcement of the statute.

In June 1994, the District Court denied petitioners' motion for a preliminary injunction. Stressing the importance of the state offices sought and the relative unintrusiveness of the testing procedure, the court found it unlikely that petitioners would prevail on the merits of their claims. App. to Pet. for Cert. 5B. Petitioners apparently submitted to the drug tests, obtained the certificates required by § 21-2-140, and appeared on the ballot. After the 1994 election, the parties jointly moved for the entry of final judgment on stipulated facts. In January 1995, the District Court entered final judgment for respondents.

A divided Eleventh Circuit panel affirmed. . . .

. . . .

II

We begin our discussion of this case with an uncontested point: Georgia's drug-testing requirement, imposed by law and enforced by state officials, effects a search within the meaning of the Fourth and Fourteenth Amendments . . . . Because "these intrusions [are] searches under the Fourth Amendment," [*Skinner v. Railway Labor Executives' Assn.*], we focus on the question: Are the searches reasonable?

To be reasonable under the Fourth Amendment, a search ordinarily must be based on individualized suspicion of wrongdoing. *See Vernonia*, 515 U.S. at 652–653. But particularized exceptions to the main rule are sometimes warranted based on "special needs, beyond the normal need for law enforcement." *Skinner*, 489 U.S. at 619. When such "special needs" — concerns other than crime detection — are alleged in justification of a Fourth Amendment intrusion, courts must undertake a context-specific inquiry, examining closely the competing private and public interests advanced by the parties. *See Von Raab*, 489 U.S. at 665–666; *see also id.*, at 668. As *Skinner* stated: "In limited circumstances, where the privacy interests implicated by the search are minimal, and where an important governmental interest furthered by the intrusion would be placed in jeopardy by a requirement of individualized suspicion, a search may be reasonable despite the absence of such suspicion." 489 U.S. at 624.

. . . .

A

Skinner concerned Federal Railroad Administration (FRA) regulations that required blood and urine tests of rail employees involved in train accidents; the regulations also authorized railroads to administer breath and urine tests to employees who violated certain safety rules. 489 U.S. at 608–612. The FRA adopted the drug-testing program in response to evidence of drug and alcohol abuse by some railroad employees, the obvious safety hazards posed by such abuse, and the documented link between drug- and alcohol-impaired employees and the incidence of train accidents. *Id.*, at 607–608. Recognizing that the urinalysis tests, most conspicuously, raised evident privacy concerns, the Court noted two offsetting considerations: First, the regulations reduced the intrusiveness of the collection process, *id.*, at 626; and, more important, railway employees, "by reason of their participation in an industry that is regulated pervasively to ensure safety," had diminished expectations of privacy, *id.*, at 627.

"[S]urpassing safety interests," the Court concluded, warranted the FRA testing program. *Id.*, at 634. The drug tests could deter illegal drug use by railroad employees, workers positioned to "cause great human loss before any signs of impairment become noticeable to supervisors." *Id.*, at 628. The program also helped railroads to obtain invaluable information about the causes of major train accidents. *See id.*, at 630. Testing without a showing of individualized suspicion was essential, the Court explained, if these vital interests were to be served. *See id.*, at 628. Employees could not forecast the timing of an accident or a safety violation, events that would trigger testing. The employee's inability to avoid detection simply by staying drug-free at a prescribed test time significantly enhanced the deterrent effect of the program. *See ibid.* Furthermore, imposing an individualized suspicion requirement for a drug test in the chaotic aftermath of a train accident would seriously impede an employer's ability to discern the cause of the accident; indeed, waiting until suspect individuals could be identified "likely would result in the loss or deterioration of the evidence furnished by the tests." *Id.*, at 631.

In *Von Raab*, the Court sustained a United States Customs Service program that made drug tests a condition of promotion or transfer to positions directly involving drug interdiction or requiring the employee to carry a firearm. 489 U.S. at 660–661, 667–677. While the Service's regime was not prompted by a demonstrated drug abuse problem, *id.*, at 660, it was developed for an agency with an "almost unique mission," *id.*, at 674, as the "first line of defense" against the smuggling of illicit drugs into the United States, *id.* at 668. Work directly involving drug interdiction and posts that require the employee to carry a firearm pose grave safety threats to employees who hold those positions, and also expose them to large amounts of illegal narcotics and to persons engaged in crime; illicit drug users in such high-risk positions might be unsympathetic to the Service's mission, tempted by bribes, or even threatened with blackmail. *See id.*, at 668–671. The Court held that the government had a "compelling" interest in assuring that employees placed in these positions would not include drug users. *See id.*, at 670–671. Individualized suspicion would not work in this setting, the Court determined, because it was "not feasible to subject [these] employees and their work product to the kind of day-to-day scrutiny that is the norm in more traditional office environments." *Id.*, at 674.

Finally, in *Vernonia*, the Court sustained a random drug-testing program for high school students engaged in interscholastic athletic competitions. The program's context was critical, for local governments bear large "responsibilities, under a public school system, as guardian and tutor of children entrusted to its care." 515 U.S. at 665. An "immediate crisis," *id.*, at 663, caused by "a sharp increase in drug use" in the school district, *id.*, at 648, sparked installation of the program. District Court findings established that student athletes were not only "among the drug users," they were "leaders of the drug culture." *Id.*, at 649. Our decision noted that "'students within the school environment have a lesser expectation of privacy than members of the population generally.'" *Id.*, at 657 (quoting *New Jersey v. T.L.O.*, 469 U.S. 325, 348, 105 S. Ct. 733, 83 L. Ed. 2d 720 (1985) (Powell, J., concurring)). We emphasized the importance of deterring drug use by schoolchildren and the risk of injury a drug-using student athlete cast on himself and those engaged with him on the playing field. *See Vernonia*, 515 U.S. at 662.

B

. . . .

[W]e note, first, that the testing method the Georgia statute describes is relatively noninvasive; therefore, if the "special need" showing had been made, the State could not be faulted for excessive intrusion. Georgia's statute invokes the drug-testing guidelines applicable to the federal programs upheld in *Skinner* and *Von Raab*. The State permits a candidate to provide the urine specimen in the office of his or her private physician; and the results of the test are given first to the candidate, who controls further dissemination of the report. Because the State has effectively limited the invasiveness of the testing procedure, we concentrate on the core issue: Is the certification requirement warranted by a special need?

Our precedents establish that the proffered special need for drug testing must be substantial — important enough to override the individual's acknowledged privacy interest, sufficiently vital to suppress the Fourth Amendment's normal requirement of individualized suspicion. *See supra*, at 7–11. Georgia has failed to show, in justification of § 21-2-140, a special need of that kind.

Respondents' defense of the statute rests primarily on the incompatibility of unlawful drug use with holding high state office. The statute is justified, respondents contend, because the use of illegal drugs draws into question an official's judgment and integrity; jeopardizes the discharge of public functions, including antidrug law enforcement efforts; and undermines public confidence and trust in elected officials. The statute, according to respondents, serves to deter unlawful drug users from becoming candidates and thus stops them from attaining high state office. Notably lacking in respondents' presentation is any indication of a concrete danger demanding departure from the Fourth Amendment's main rule.

Nothing in the record hints that the hazards respondents broadly describe are real and not simply hypothetical for Georgia's polity. The statute was not enacted, as counsel for respondents readily acknowledged at oral argument, in response to any fear or suspicion of drug use by state officials:

> "QUESTION: Is there any indication anywhere in this record that Georgia has a particular problem here with State officeholders being drug abusers?
>
> "[COUNSEL FOR RESPONDENTS]: No, there is no such evidence. . . . and to be frank, there is no such problem as we sit here today." Tr. of Oral Arg. 32.

A demonstrated problem of drug abuse, while not in all cases necessary to the validity of a testing regime, *see Von Raab*, 489 U.S. at 673–675, would shore up an assertion of special need for a suspicionless general search program. Proof of unlawful drug use may help to clarify — and to substantiate — the precise hazards posed by such use. . . .

In contrast to the effective testing regimes upheld in *Skinner, Von Raab*, and *Vernonia*, Georgia's certification requirement is not well designed to identify candidates who violate antidrug laws. Nor is the scheme a credible means to deter illicit drug users from seeking election to state office. The test date — to be scheduled by the candidate anytime within 30 days prior to qualifying for a place on the ballot — is no secret. As counsel for respondents acknowledged at oral argument, users of illegal drugs, save for those prohibitively addicted, could abstain for a pretest period sufficient to avoid detection. Even if we indulged respondents' argument that one purpose of § 21-2-140 might be to detect those unable so to abstain, respondents have not shown or argued that such persons are likely to be candidates for public office in Georgia. Moreover, respondents have offered no reason why ordinary law enforcement methods would not suffice to apprehend such addicted individuals, should they appear in the limelight of a public stage. Section 21-2-140, in short, is not needed and cannot work to ferret out lawbreakers, and respondents barely attempt to support the statute on that ground.

Respondents and the United States as *amicus curiae* rely most heavily on our decision in *Von Raab*, which sustained a drug-testing program for Customs Service officers prior to promotion or transfer to certain high-risk positions, despite the absence of any documented drug abuse problem among Service employees. The posts in question in *Von Raab* directly involved drug interdiction or otherwise required the Service member to carry a firearm.

Hardly a decision opening broad vistas for suspicionless searches, *Von Raab* must be read in its unique context. As the Customs Service reported in announcing the testing program, "[Customs employees], more than any other Federal workers, are routinely exposed to the vast network of organized crime that is inextricably tied to illegal drug use." *National Treasury Employees Union v. Von Raab*, 816 F.2d 170, 173 (5th Cir. 1987) (internal quotation marks omitted), *aff'd in part, vacated in part*, 489 U.S. 656 (1989). We stressed that "[d]rug interdiction ha[d] become the agency's primary enforcement mission," *id.*, at 660, and that the employees in question would have "access to vast sources of valuable contraband," *id.*, at 669. Furthermore, Customs officers "ha[d] been the targets of bribery by drug smugglers on numerous occasions," and several had succumbed to the temptation. *Ibid.*

Respondents overlook a telling difference between *Von Raab* and Georgia's candidate drug-testing program. In *Von Raab* it was "not feasible to subject employees [required to carry firearms or concerned with interdiction of controlled substances] and their work product to the kind of day-to-day scrutiny that is the norm in more traditional office environments." *Id.*, at 674. Candidates for public office, in contrast, are subject to relentless scrutiny — by their peers, the public, and the press. Their day-to-day conduct attracts attention notably beyond the norm in ordinary work environments.

What is left, after close review of Georgia's scheme, is the image the State seeks to project. By requiring candidates for public office to submit to drug testing, Georgia displays its commitment to the struggle against drug abuse. The suspicionless tests, according to respondents, signify that candidates, if elected, will be fit to serve their constituents free from the influence of illegal drugs. But Georgia asserts no evidence of a drug problem among the State's elected officials, those officials typically do not perform high-risk, safety-sensitive tasks, and the required certification immediately aids no interdiction effort. The need revealed, in short, is symbolic, not "special," as that term draws meaning from our case law.

. . . .

. . . However well-meant, the candidate drug test Georgia has devised diminishes personal privacy for a symbol's sake. The Fourth Amendment shields society against that state action.

III

. . . .

We reiterate . . . that where the risk to public safety is substantial and real, blanket suspicionless searches calibrated to the risk may rank as "reasonable" — for example, searches now routine at airports and at entrances to courts and other official buildings. *See Von Raab*, 489 U.S. at 674–676, and n. 3. But where, as in this case, public safety is not genuinely in jeopardy, the Fourth Amendment precludes the suspicionless search, no matter how conveniently arranged.

. . . .

For the reasons stated, the judgment of the Court of Appeals for the Eleventh Circuit is

Reversed.

[The dissenting opinion of CHIEF JUSTICE REHNQUIST has been omitted.]

Notes and Questions

(1) The drug testing program in *Chandler* was the first to be declared unconstitutional by the Supreme Court. In *Ferguson v. City of Charleston*, 532 U.S. 67, 121 S. Ct. 1281, 149 L. Ed. 2d 205 (2001), the Court found another suspicionless drug testing program to be violative of the Fourth Amendment. In *Ferguson*, a task force formed by the Charleston Solicitor developed a policy for testing pregnant women. The policy provided for both "education and referral to a substance abuse clinic" and "added the threat of law enforcement intervention" that was "essential to . . . success in getting women into treatment and keeping them there." The policy stated that: (1) if drug use *after labor* was detected, "the police were to be notified without delay and the patient promptly arrested"; and (2) if a patient tested positive *during pregnancy or labor*, "the police were to be notified (and the patient arrested) only if the patient tested positive . . . a second time or . . . missed an appointment with a substance abuse counselor." The various criminal offenses that could be charged were specified.

Ten women who were arrested after positive tests challenged the policy. A six-Justice majority concluded that the "invasion of privacy in this case [was] far more substantial" than in prior cases before the Court which had involved programs with "protections against dissemination of [test] results to third parties." The "critical difference," however, was that the "'special need'" that justified the programs in prior cases was "divorced from the . . . general interest in law enforcement," whereas in *Ferguson* "the central and indispensable feature of the policy from its inception was the use of law enforcement to coerce the patients into substance abuse treatment."

The state claimed that the policy's "ultimate purpose" was to protect the health of mother and child. The Court responded that "the purpose actually served" by the drug testing policy was "'ultimately indistinguishable from the general interest in crime control.'" Although the "ultimate goal of th[e] program may well have been to get the women" into treatment and off of drugs, the "immediate objective" of the drug testing "was to generate evidence *for law enforcement purposes.*" It was "critical" that "the direct and primary purpose of [the] policy was to ensure" that the threat of law enforcement was used as a "means" to the ultimate end. Because the "primary purpose of the . . . program was to use the threat of arrest and prosecution in order to force women into treatment" and because of the "extensive involvement of law enforcement officials at every stage of the policy, th[e] case simply [did] not fit within the closely guarded category of 'special needs.'"

Justice Scalia, along with Chief Justice Rehnquist and Justice Thomas, dissented, concluding that "the 'special needs' doctrine validated the program" implemented in *Ferguson*.

(2) Of the six random drug testing programs to reach the Supreme Court, four have been found reasonable — those in *Skinner, Von Raab, Vernonia,* and *Earls* — while two have been deemed unreasonable — those in *Chandler* and *Ferguson*. Are the distinctions that the Court has discerned between those programs that are reasonable and those that are unreasonable persuasive bases for reaching dramatically different constitutional conclusions? Why?

(3) The majority opinion in *Skinner* relied upon a number of Supreme Court precedents that are often categorized as "administrative" or "regulatory" search and seizure cases. The reason for that description is that the ostensible primary goal of the searches or seizures involved is improving society through the implementation and enforcement of a regulatory scheme. The Supreme Court has consistently concluded that administrative or regulatory searches and seizures are governed by the Fourth Amendment. Nonetheless, a balancing analysis like that employed in *Skinner* has led to modifications and dilutions of Fourth Amendment norms in a variety of contexts. *See Griffin v. Wisconsin*, 483 U.S. 868, 107 S. Ct. 3164, 97 L. Ed. 2d 709 (1987) (probation officer searches of probationers' homes); *New York v. Burger*, 482 U.S. 691, 107 S. Ct. 2636, 96 L. Ed. 2d 601 (1987) (inspections of automobile junkyards); *O'Connor v. Ortega*, 480 U.S. 709, 107 S. Ct. 1492, 94 L. Ed. 2d 714 (1987) (work-related searches of desk and file cabinets of a publicly-employed doctor by

hospital supervisors); *United States v. Villamonte-Marquez*, 462 U.S. 579, 103 S. Ct. 2573, 77 L. Ed. 2d 22 (1983) (Coast Guard stops of vessels on high seas and U.S. waters to inspect required documentation and safety equipment); *Donovan v. Dewey*, 452 U.S. 594, 101 S. Ct. 2534, 69 L. Ed. 2d 262 (1981) (statutorily authorized inspections of mines); *Bell v. Wolfish*, 441 U.S. 520, 99 S. Ct. 1861, 60 L. Ed. 2d 447 (1979) (visual body cavity inspections of pretrial detainees); *Marshall v. Barlow's, Inc.*, 436 U.S. 307, 98 S. Ct. 1816, 56 L. Ed. 2d 305 (1978) (federal OSHA enforcement inspections of business premises); *United States v. Ramsey*, 431 U.S. 606, 97 S. Ct. 1972, 52 L. Ed. 2d 617 (1977) (search of incoming international mail); *United States v. Martinez-Fuerte*, 428 U.S. 543, 96 S. Ct. 3074, 49 L. Ed. 2d 1116 (1976) (vehicle stops at fixed checkpoints near U.S. borders); *United States v. Biswell*, 406 U.S. 311, 92 S. Ct. 1593, 32 L. Ed. 2d 87 (1972) (inspection of firearm dealer's premises to examine required records, firearms, ammunition); *See v. City of Seattle*, 387 U.S. 541, 87 S. Ct. 1737, 18 L. Ed. 2d 943 (1967) (inspection of business premises for fire code compliance); *Camara v. Municipal Court*, 387 U.S. 523, 87 S. Ct. 1727, 18 L. Ed. 2d 930 (1967) (inspection of private residences for fire, health, housing code compliance).

[4] DNA Testing

Maryland v. King

United States Supreme Court

569 U.S. ____, 133 S. Ct. 1958, 186 L. Ed. 2d 1 (2013)

JUSTICE KENNEDY delivered the opinion of the Court.

. . . .

I

When [Alonzo] King was arrested on April 10, 2009, for menacing a group of people with a shotgun and charged in state court with both first- and second-degree assault, he was processed for detention in custody at the Wicomico County Central Booking facility. Booking personnel used a cheek swab to take [a] DNA sample from him pursuant to provisions of the Maryland DNA Collection Act (or Act).

On July 13, 2009, King's DNA record was uploaded to the Maryland DNA database, and three weeks later, on August 4, 2009, his DNA profile was matched to the DNA sample collected in the unsolved 2003 rape case. Once the DNA was matched to King, detectives presented the forensic evidence to a grand jury, which indicted him for the rape. Detectives obtained a search warrant and took a second sample of DNA from King, which again matched the evidence from the rape. He moved to suppress the DNA match on the grounds that Maryland's DNA collection law violated the Fourth Amendment. The Circuit Court Judge upheld the statute as constitutional. King pleaded not guilty to the rape charges but was convicted and sentenced to life in prison without the possibility of parole.

In a divided opinion, the Maryland Court of Appeals struck down the portions of the Act authorizing collection of DNA from felony arrestees as unconstitutional. The majority concluded that a DNA swab was an unreasonable search in violation of the Fourth Amendment. . . .

Both federal and state courts have reached differing conclusions as to whether the Fourth Amendment prohibits the collection and analysis of a DNA sample from persons arrested, but not yet convicted, on felony charges. . . .

II

The advent of DNA technology is one of the most significant scientific advancements of our era. The full potential for use of genetic markers in medicine and science is still being explored, but the utility of DNA identification in the criminal justice system is already undisputed. Since the first use of forensic DNA analysis to catch a rapist and murderer in England in 1986, see J. Butler, Fundamentals of Forensic DNA Typing 5 (2009) (hereinafter Butler), law enforcement, the defense bar, and the courts have acknowledged DNA testing's "unparalleled ability both to exonerate the wrongly convicted and to identify the guilty. It has the potential to significantly improve both the criminal justice system and police investigative practices." *District Attorney's Office for Third Judicial Dist. v. Osborne*, 557 U.S. 52, 55, 129 S. Ct. 2308, 174 L. Ed. 2d 38 (2009).

A

The current standard for forensic DNA testing relies on an analysis of the chromosomes located within the nucleus of all human cells. "The DNA material in chromosomes is composed of 'coding' and 'noncoding' regions. The coding regions are known as *genes* and contain the information necessary for a cell to make proteins. . . . Non-protein-coding regions . . . are not related directly to making proteins, [and] have been referred to as 'junk' DNA." Butler 25. The adjective "junk" may mislead the layperson, for in fact this is the DNA region used with near certainty to identify a person. The term apparently is intended to indicate that this particular noncoding region, while useful and even dispositive for purposes like identity, does not show more far-reaching and complex characteristics like genetic traits.

Many of the patterns found in DNA are shared among all people, so forensic analysis focuses on "repeated DNA sequences scattered throughout the human genome," known as "short tandem repeats" (STRs). *Id.*, at 147–148. The alternative possibilities for the size and frequency of these STRs at any given point along a strand of DNA are known as "alleles," *id.*, at 25; and multiple alleles are analyzed in order to ensure that a DNA profile matches only one individual. Future refinements may improve present technology, but even now STR analysis makes it "possible to determine whether a biological tissue matches a suspect with near certainty." *Osborne, supra*, at 62, 129 S. Ct. 2308, 174 L. Ed. 2d 38.

The Act authorizes Maryland law enforcement authorities to collect DNA samples from "an individual who is charged with . . . a crime of violence or an attempt

to commit a crime of violence; or . . . burglary or an attempt to commit burglary."
Md. Pub. Saf. Code Ann. § 2–504(a)(3)(I) (Lexis 2011). Maryland law defines a
crime of violence to include murder, rape, first-degree assault, kidnaping, arson,
sexual assault, and a variety of other serious crimes. Md. Crim. Law Code Ann.
§ 14–101 (Lexis 2012). Once taken, a DNA sample may not be processed or placed
in a database before the individual is arraigned (unless the individual consents).
Md. Pub. Saf. Code Ann. § 2–504(d)(1) (Lexis 2011). It is at this point that a judicial
officer ensures that there is probable cause to detain the arrestee on a qualifying
serious offense. If "all qualifying criminal charges are determined to be unsupported by probable cause . . . the DNA sample shall be immediately destroyed."
§ 2–504(d)(2)(I). DNA samples are also destroyed if "a criminal action begun against
the individual . . . does not result in a conviction," "the conviction is finally reversed or vacated and no new trial is permitted," or "the individual is granted an
unconditional pardon." § 2–511(a)(1).

The Act also limits the information added to a DNA database and how it may be
used. Specifically, "[o]nly DNA records that directly relate to the identification of
individuals shall be collected and stored." § 2–505(b)(1). No purpose other than
identification is permissible: "A person may not willfully test a DNA sample for
information that does not relate to the identification of individuals as specified in
this subtitle." § 2–512(c). Tests for familial matches are also prohibited. See § 2–506(d).
The officers involved in taking and analyzing respondent's DNA sample complied
with the Act in all respects.

Respondent's DNA was collected in this case using a common procedure known
as a "buccal swab." "Buccal cell collection involves wiping a small piece of filter
paper or a cotton swab similar to a Q-tip against the inside cheek of an individual's
mouth to collect some skin cells." Butler 86. The procedure is quick and pain-
less. . . . .

B

Respondent's identification as the rapist resulted in part through the operation of
a national project to standardize collection and storage of DNA profiles. Authorized
by Congress and supervised by the Federal Bureau of Investigation, the Combined
DNA Index System (CODIS) connects DNA laboratories at the local, state, and national level. Since its authorization in 1994, the CODIS system has grown to include
all 50 States and a number of federal agencies. CODIS collects DNA profiles provided
by local laboratories taken from arrestees, convicted offenders, and forensic evidence
found at crime scenes. To participate in CODIS, a local laboratory must sign a memorandum of understanding agreeing to adhere to quality standards and submit to
audits to evaluate compliance with the federal standards for scientifically rigorous
DNA testing. Butler 270.

One of the most significant aspects of CODIS is the standardization of the points
of comparison in DNA analysis. The CODIS database is based on 13 loci at which
the STR alleles are noted and compared. These loci make possible extreme accuracy

in matching individual samples, with a "random match probability of approximately 1 in 100 trillion (assuming unrelated individuals)." *Ibid.* The CODIS loci are from the non-protein coding junk regions of DNA, and "are not known to have any association with a genetic disease or any other genetic predisposition. Thus, the information in the database is only useful for human identity testing." *Id.,* at 279. STR information is recorded only as a "string of numbers"; and the DNA identification is accompanied only by information denoting the laboratory and the analyst responsible for the submission. *Id.,* at 270. In short, CODIS sets uniform national standards for DNA matching and then facilitates connections between local law enforcement agencies who can share more specific information about matched STR profiles.

All 50 States require the collection of DNA from felony convicts, and respondent does not dispute the validity of that practice. Twenty-eight States and the Federal Government have adopted laws similar to the Maryland Act authorizing the collection of DNA from some or all arrestees. Although those statutes vary in their particulars, such as what charges require a DNA sample, their similarity means that this case implicates more than the specific Maryland law. At issue is a standard, expanding technology already in widespread use throughout the Nation.

III

A

. . . . [U]sing a buccal swab on the inner tissues of a person's cheek in order to obtain DNA samples is a search. Virtually any "intrusio[n] into the human body," *Schmerber v. California,* 384 U.S. 757, 770, 86 S. Ct. 1826, 16 L. Ed. 2d 908 (1966), will work an invasion of "'cherished personal security' that is subject to constitutional scrutiny," *Cupp v. Murphy,* 412 U.S. 291, 295, 93 S. Ct. 2000, 36 L. Ed. 2d 900 (1973) (quoting *Terry v. Ohio,* 392 U.S. 1, 24–25, 88 S. Ct. 1868, 20 L. Ed. 2d 889 (1968)). . . .

A buccal swab is a far more gentle process than a venipuncture to draw blood. It involves but a light touch on the inside of the cheek; and although it can be deemed a search within the body of the arrestee, it requires no "surgical intrusions beneath the skin." *Winston [v. Lee],* 470 U.S. [753], 760, 105 S. Ct. 1611 [(1985)]. The fact that an intrusion is negligible is of central relevance to determining reasonableness, although it is still a search as the law defines that term.

B

. . . In giving content to the inquiry whether an intrusion is reasonable, the Court has preferred "some quantum of individualized suspicion . . . [as] a prerequisite to a constitutional search or seizure. But the Fourth Amendment imposes no irreducible requirement of such suspicion." *United States v. Martinez-Fuerte,* 428 U.S. 543, 560–561, 96 S. Ct. 3074, 49 L. Ed. 2d 1116 (1976) (citation and footnote omitted).

In some circumstances, such as "[w]hen faced with special law enforcement needs, diminished expectations of privacy, minimal intrusions, or the like, the Court has found that certain general, or individual, circumstances may render a warrantless search or seizure reasonable." *Illinois v. McArthur,* 531 U.S. 326, 330, 121 S. Ct. 946,

148 L. Ed. 2d 838 (2001). . . . The need for a warrant is perhaps least when the search involves no discretion that could properly be limited by the "interpo[lation of] a neutral magistrate between the citizen and the law enforcement officer." *Treasury Employees v. Von Raab,* 489 U.S. 656, 667, 109 S. Ct. 1384, 103 L. Ed. 2d 685 (1989).

. . . The Maryland DNA Collection Act provides that, in order to obtain a DNA sample, all arrestees charged with serious crimes must furnish the sample on a buccal swab applied, as noted, to the inside of the cheeks. The arrestee is already in valid police custody for a serious offense supported by probable cause. The DNA collection is not subject to the judgment of officers whose perspective might be "colored by their primary involvement in 'the often competitive enterprise of ferreting out crime.'" *Terry, supra,* at 12, 88 S. Ct. 1868 (quoting *Johnson v. United States,* 333 U.S. 10, 14, 68 S. Ct. 367, 92 L. Ed. 436 (1948)). . . . Here, the search effected by the buccal swab of respondent falls within the category of cases this Court has analyzed by reference to the proposition that the "touchstone of the Fourth Amendment is reasonableness, not individualized suspicion." *Samson* [*v. California,* 547 U.S. 843], 855, n. 4, 126 S. Ct. 2193 [(2006)].

. . . To say that no warrant is required is merely to acknowledge that "rather than employing a *per se* rule of unreasonableness, we balance the privacy-related and law enforcement-related concerns to determine if the intrusion was reasonable." *McArthur, supra,* at 331, 121 S. Ct. 946. This application of "traditional standards of reasonableness" requires a court to weigh "the promotion of legitimate governmental interests" against "the degree to which [the search] intrudes upon an individual's privacy." *Wyoming v. Houghton,* 526 U.S. 295, 300, 119 S. Ct. 1297, 143 L. Ed. 2d 408 (1999). . . .

IV

A

The legitimate government interest served by the Maryland DNA Collection Act is one that is well established: the need for law enforcement officers in a safe and accurate way to process and identify the persons and possessions they must take into custody. It is beyond dispute that "probable cause provides legal justification for arresting a person suspected of crime, and for a brief period of detention to take the administrative steps incident to arrest." *Gerstein v. Pugh,* 420 U.S. 103, 113–114, 95 S. Ct. 854, 43 L. Ed. 2d 54 (1975). Also uncontested is the "right on the part of the Government, always recognized under English and American law, to search the person of the accused when legally arrested." *Weeks v. United States,* 232 U.S. 383, 392, 34 S. Ct. 341, 58 L. Ed. 652 (1914). . . . [I]ndividual suspicion is not necessary, because "[t]he constitutionality of a search incident to an arrest does not depend on whether there is any indication that the person arrested possesses weapons or evidence. The fact of a lawful arrest, standing alone, authorizes a search." *Michigan v. DeFillippo,* 443 U.S. 31, 35, 99 S. Ct. 2627, 61 L. Ed. 2d 343 (1979).

The "routine administrative procedure[s] at a police station house incident to booking and jailing the suspect" derive from different origins and have different constitutional justifications than, say, the search of a place, *Illinois v. Lafayette,* 462 U.S. 640, 643, 103 S. Ct. 2605, 77 L. Ed. 2d 65 (1983); for the search of a place not incident to an arrest depends on the "fair probability that contraband or evidence of a crime will be found in a particular place," *Illinois v. Gates,* 462 U.S. 213, 238, 103 S. Ct. 2317, 76 L. Ed. 2d 527 (1983). The interests are further different when an individual is formally processed into police custody. Then "the law is in the act of subjecting the body of the accused to its physical dominion." *People v. Chiagles,* 237 N.Y. 193, 197, 142 N. E. 583, 584 (1923) (Cardozo, J.). When probable cause exists to remove an individual from the normal channels of society and hold him in legal custody, DNA identification plays a critical role in serving those interests.

First, "[i]n every criminal case, it is known and must be known who has been arrested and who is being tried." *Hiibel v. Sixth Judicial Dist. Court of Nev., Humboldt Cty.,* 542 U.S. 177, 191, 124 S. Ct. 2451, 159 L. Ed. 2d 292 (2004). An individual's identity is more than just his name or Social Security number, and the government's interest in identification goes beyond ensuring that the proper name is typed on the indictment. Identity has never been considered limited to the name on the arrestee's birth certificate. In fact, a name is of little value compared to the real interest in identification at stake when an individual is brought into custody. . . .

A suspect's criminal history is a critical part of his identity that officers should know when processing him for detention. It is a common occurrence that "[p]eople detained for minor offenses can turn out to be the most devious and dangerous criminals. Hours after the Oklahoma City bombing, Timothy McVeigh was stopped by a state trooper who noticed he was driving without a license plate. Police stopped serial killer Joel Rifkin for the same reason. One of the terrorists involved in the September 11 attacks was stopped and ticketed for speeding just two days before hijacking Flight 93." [*Florence v. Board of Chosen Freeholders of County of Burlington,* 566 U.S.], at ____, 132 S. Ct., at 1520 (citations omitted). Police already seek this crucial identifying information. They use routine and accepted means as varied as comparing the suspect's booking photograph to sketch artists' depictions of persons of interest, showing his mugshot to potential witnesses, and of course making a computerized comparison of the arrestee's fingerprints against electronic databases of known criminals and unsolved crimes. In this respect the only difference between DNA analysis and the accepted use of fingerprint databases is the unparalleled accuracy DNA provides.

The task of identification necessarily entails searching public and police records based on the identifying information provided by the arrestee to see what is already known about him. The DNA collected from arrestees is an irrefutable identification of the person from whom it was taken. Like a fingerprint, the 13 CODIS loci are not themselves evidence of any particular crime, in the way that a drug test can by itself be evidence of illegal narcotics use. A DNA profile is useful to the police because it gives them a form of identification to search the records already in their valid possession. . . . DNA is another metric of identification used to connect the arrestee with his or her public persona, as reflected in records of his or her actions that are available to the police. . . . Finding occurrences of the arrestee's CODIS profile in outstanding cases is consistent with . . . common practice. It uses a different form of identification than a name or fingerprint, but its function is the same.

Second, law enforcement officers bear a responsibility for ensuring that the custody of an arrestee does not create inordinate "risks for facility staff, for the existing detainee population, and for a new detainee." *Florence* [*v. Board of Chosen Freeholders of County of Burlington*, 566 U.S.] ____, 132 S. Ct., at 1518 [(2012)]. DNA identification can provide untainted information to those charged with detaining suspects and detaining the property of any felon. For these purposes officers must know the type of person whom they are detaining, and DNA allows them to make critical choices about how to proceed. . . .

Third, looking forward to future stages of criminal prosecution, "the Government has a substantial interest in ensuring that persons accused of crimes are available for trials." *Bell v. Wolfish*, 441 U.S. 520, 534, 99 S. Ct. 1861, 60 L. Ed. 2d 447 (1979). A person who is arrested for one offense but knows that he has yet to answer for some past crime may be more inclined to flee the instant charges, lest continued contact with the criminal justice system expose one or more other serious offenses. For example, a defendant who had committed a prior sexual assault might be inclined to flee on a burglary charge, knowing that in every State a DNA sample would be taken from him after his conviction on the burglary charge that would tie him to the more serious charge of rape. In addition to subverting the administration of justice with respect to the crime of arrest, this ties back to the interest in safety; for a detainee who absconds from custody presents a risk to law enforcement officers, other detainees, victims of previous crimes, witnesses, and society at large.

Fourth, an arrestee's past conduct is essential to an assessment of the danger he poses to the public, and this will inform a court's determination whether the individual should be released on bail. "The government's interest in preventing crime by arrestees is both legitimate and compelling." *United States v. Salerno*, 481 U.S. 739, 749, 107 S. Ct. 2095, 95 L. Ed. 2d 697 (1987). DNA identification of a suspect in a violent crime provides critical information to the police and judicial officials in making a determination of the arrestee's future dangerousness. . . .

This interest is not speculative. In considering laws to require collecting DNA from arrestees, government agencies around the Nation found evidence of numerous cases in which felony arrestees would have been identified as violent through DNA identification matching them to previous crimes but who later committed additional crimes because such identification was not used to detain them.

Present capabilities make it possible to complete a DNA identification that provides information essential to determining whether a detained suspect can be released pending trial. . . .

. . . .

Finally, in the interests of justice, the identification of an arrestee as the perpetrator of some heinous crime may have the salutary effect of freeing a person wrongfully imprisoned for the same offense. "[P]rompt [DNA] testing . . . would speed up apprehension of criminals before they commit additional crimes, and prevent the grotesque detention of . . . innocent people." J. Dwyer, P. Neufeld, & B. Scheck, Actual Innocence 245 (2000).

Because proper processing of arrestees is so important and has consequences for every stage of the criminal process, the Court has recognized that the "governmental interests underlying a station-house search of the arrestee's person and possessions may in some circumstances be even greater than those supporting a search immediately following arrest." *Lafayette,* 462 U.S., at 645, 103 S. Ct. 2605. Thus, the Court has been reluctant to circumscribe the authority of the police to conduct reasonable booking searches. . . .

B

DNA identification represents an important advance in the techniques used by law enforcement to serve legitimate police concerns for as long as there have been arrests, concerns the courts have acknowledged and approved for more than a century. Law enforcement agencies routinely have used scientific advancements in their standard procedures for the identification of arrestees. . . .

    . . . .

Perhaps the most direct historical analogue to the DNA technology used to identify respondent is the familiar practice of fingerprinting arrestees. From the advent of this technique, courts had no trouble determining that fingerprinting was a natural part of "the administrative steps incident to arrest." *County of Riverside v. McLaughlin,* 500 U.S. 44, 58, 111 S. Ct. 1661, 114 L. Ed. 2d 49 (1991). . . .

DNA identification is an advanced technique superior to fingerprinting in many ways, so much so that to insist on fingerprints as the norm would make little sense to either the forensic expert or a layperson. The additional intrusion upon the arrestee's privacy beyond that associated with fingerprinting is not significant, see Part V, *infra,* and DNA is a markedly more accurate form of identifying arrestees. A suspect who has changed his facial features to evade photographic identification or even one who has undertaken the more arduous task of altering his fingerprints cannot escape the revealing power of his DNA.

The respondent's primary objection to this analogy is that DNA identification is not as fast as fingerprinting, and so it should not be considered to be the 21st-century equivalent. But rapid analysis of fingerprints is itself of recent vintage. . . . The question of how long it takes to process identifying information obtained from a valid search goes only to the efficacy of the search for its purpose of prompt identification, not the constitutionality of the search. Given the importance of DNA in the identification of police records pertaining to arrestees and the need to refine and confirm that identity for its important bearing on the decision to continue release on bail or to impose new conditions, DNA serves an essential purpose despite the existence of delays such as the one that occurred in this case. Even so, the delay in processing DNA from arrestees is being reduced to a substantial degree by rapid technical advances. . . . By identifying not only who the arrestee is but also what other available records disclose about his past to show who he is, the police can ensure that they have the proper person under arrest and that they have made the necessary arrangements for his custody; and, just as important, they can also prevent suspicion against or prosecution of the innocent.

In sum, there can be little reason to question "the legitimate interest of the government in knowing for an absolute certainty the identity of the person arrested, in knowing whether he is wanted elsewhere, and in ensuring his identification in the event he flees prosecution." 3 W. LaFave, Search and Seizure § 5.3(c), p. 216 (5th ed. 2012). To that end, courts have confirmed that the Fourth Amendment allows police to take certain routine "administrative steps incident to arrest — *i.e.,* . . . book[ing], photograph[ing], and fingerprint[ing]." *McLaughlin,* 500 U.S., at 58, 111 S. Ct. 1661. DNA identification of arrestees, of the type approved by the Maryland statute here at issue, is "no more than an extension of methods of identification long used in dealing with persons under arrest." *Kelly,* 55 F.2d, at 69. In the balance of reasonableness required by the Fourth Amendment, therefore, the Court must give great weight both to the significant government interest at stake in the identification of arrestees and to the unmatched potential of DNA identification to serve that interest.

V
A

By comparison to this substantial government interest and the unique effectiveness of DNA identification, the intrusion of a cheek swab to obtain a DNA sample is a minimal one. True, a significant government interest does not alone suffice to justify a search. The government interest must outweigh the degree to which the search invades an individual's legitimate expectations of privacy. In considering those expectations in this case, however, the necessary predicate of a valid arrest for a serious offense is fundamental. . . . "[T]he legitimacy of certain privacy expectations vis-á-vis the State may depend upon the individual's legal relationship with the State." *Vernonia School Dist. 47J,* 515 U.S., at 654, 115 S. Ct. 2386.

. . . .

The expectations of privacy of an individual taken into police custody "necessarily [are] of a diminished scope." *Bell,* 441 U.S., at 557, 99 S. Ct. 1861. "[B]oth the person and the property in his immediate possession may be searched at the station house." *United States v. Edwards,* 415 U.S. 800, 803, 94 S. Ct. 1234, 39 L. Ed. 2d 771 (1974). A search of the detainee's person when he is booked into custody may "'involve a relatively extensive exploration,'" *Robinson,* 414 U.S., at 227, 94 S. Ct. 467, including "requir[ing] at least some detainees to lift their genitals or cough in a squatting position," *Florence,* 566 U.S., at ____, 132 S. Ct., at 1520.

In this critical respect, the search here at issue differs from the sort of programmatic searches of either the public at large or a particular class of regulated but otherwise law-abiding citizens that the Court has previously labeled as "'special needs'" searches. *Chandler v. Miller,* 520 U.S. 305, 314, 117 S. Ct. 1295, 137 L. Ed. 2d 513 (1997). . . . Once an individual has been arrested on probable cause for a dangerous offense that may require detention before trial . . . his or her expectations of privacy and freedom from police scrutiny are reduced. DNA identification like that at issue here thus does not require consideration of any unique needs that would be required to justify searching the average citizen. The special needs cases, though in full accord with the result reached here, do not have a direct bearing on the issues presented in this case, because unlike the search of a citizen who has not been suspected of a wrong, a detainee has a reduced expectation of privacy.

The reasonableness inquiry here considers two other circumstances in which the Court has held that particularized suspicion is not categorically required: "diminished expectations of privacy [and] minimal intrusions." *McArthur,* 531 U.S., at 330, 121 S. Ct. 946. This is not to suggest that any search is acceptable solely because a person is in custody. . . .

Here, by contrast to the approved standard procedures incident to any arrest detailed above, a buccal swab involves an even more brief and still minimal intrusion. A gentle rub along the inside of the cheek does not break the skin, and it "involves virtually no risk, trauma, or pain." *Schmerber,* 384 U.S., at 771, 86 S. Ct. 1826. "A crucial factor in analyzing the magnitude of the intrusion . . . is the extent to which the procedure may threaten the safety or health of the individual," *Winston, supra,* at 761, 105 S. Ct. 1611, and nothing suggests that a buccal swab poses any physical danger whatsoever. A brief intrusion of an arrestee's person is subject to the Fourth Amendment, but a swab of this nature does not increase the indignity already attendant to normal incidents of arrest.

B

In addition the processing of respondent's DNA sample's 13 CODIS loci did not intrude on respondent's privacy in a way that would make his DNA identification unconstitutional.

First, as already noted, the CODIS loci come from noncoding parts of the DNA that do not reveal the genetic traits of the arrestee. . . .

And even if non-coding alleles could provide some information, they are not in fact tested for that end. It is undisputed that law enforcement officers analyze DNA for the sole purpose of generating a unique identifying number against which future samples may be matched. . . .

Finally, the Act provides statutory protections that guard against further invasion of privacy. As noted above, the Act requires that "[o]nly DNA records that directly relate to the identification of individuals shall be collected and stored." Md. Pub. Saf. Code Ann. § 2–505(b)(1). . . . In light of the scientific and statutory safeguards, once respondent's DNA was lawfully collected the STR analysis of respondent's DNA pursuant to CODIS procedures did not amount to a significant invasion of privacy that would render the DNA identification impermissible under the Fourth Amendment.

* * *

In light of the context of a valid arrest supported by probable cause respondent's expectations of privacy were not offended by the minor intrusion of a brief swab of his cheeks. By contrast, that same context of arrest gives rise to significant state interests in identifying respondent not only so that the proper name can be attached to his charges but also so that the criminal justice system can make informed decisions concerning pretrial custody. Upon these considerations the Court concludes that DNA identification of arrestees is a reasonable search that can be considered part of a routine booking procedure. When officers make an arrest supported by probable cause to hold for a serious offense and they bring the suspect to the station to be detained in custody, taking and analyzing a cheek swab of the arrestee's DNA is, like fingerprinting and photographing, a legitimate police booking procedure that is reasonable under the Fourth Amendment.

The judgment of the Court of Appeals of Maryland is reversed.

It is so ordered.

JUSTICE SCALIA, with whom JUSTICE GINSBURG, JUSTICE SOTOMAYOR, and JUSTICE KAGAN join, dissenting.

The Fourth Amendment forbids searching a person for evidence of a crime when there is no basis for believing the person is guilty of the crime or is in possession of incriminating evidence. That prohibition is categorical and without exception; it lies at the very heart of the Fourth Amendment. Whenever this Court has allowed a suspicionless search, it has insisted upon a justifying motive apart from the investigation of crime.

It is obvious that no such noninvestigative motive exists in this case. The Court's assertion that DNA is being taken, not to solve crimes, but to *identify* those in the State's custody, taxes the credulity of the credulous. And the Court's comparison of Maryland's DNA searches to other techniques, such as fingerprinting, can seem apt only to those who know no more than today's opinion has chosen to tell them about how those DNA searches actually work.

I

A

At the time of the Founding, Americans despised the British use of so-called "general warrants" — warrants not grounded upon a sworn oath of a specific infraction by a particular individual, and thus not limited in scope and application. . . . .

. . . .

. . . . [T]he Fourth Amendment's Warrant Clause forbids a warrant to "issue" except "upon probable cause," and requires that it be "particula[r]" (which is to say, *individualized*) to "the place to be searched, and the persons or things to be seized." And we have held that, even when a warrant is not constitutionally necessary, the Fourth Amendment's general prohibition of "unreasonable" searches imports the same requirement of individualized suspicion. See *Chandler v. Miller,* 520 U.S. 305, 308, 117 S. Ct. 1295, 137 L. Ed. 2d 513 (1997).

Although there is a "closely guarded category of constitutionally permissible suspicionless searches," *id.,* at 309, 117 S. Ct. 1295, that has never included searches designed to serve "the normal need for law enforcement," *Skinner v. Railway Labor Executives' Assn.,* 489 U.S. 602, 619, 109 S. Ct. 1402, 103 L. Ed. 2d 639 (1989) (internal quotation marks omitted). Even the common name for suspicionless searches — "special needs" searches — itself reflects that they must be justified, *always,* by concerns "other than crime detection." *Chandler, supra,* at 313–314, 117 S. Ct. 1295. . . .

So while the Court is correct to note that there are instances in which we have permitted searches without individualized suspicion, "[i]n none of these cases . . . did we indicate approval of a [search] whose primary purpose was to detect evidence of ordinary criminal wrongdoing." *Indianapolis v. Edmond,* 531 U.S. 32, 38, 121 S. Ct. 447, 148 L. Ed. 2d 333 (2000). That limitation is crucial. It is only when a governmental purpose aside from crime-solving is at stake that we engage in the free-form "reasonableness" inquiry that the Court indulges at length today. To put it another way, both the legitimacy of the Court's method and the correctness of its outcome hinge entirely on the truth of a single proposition: that the primary purpose of these DNA searches is something other than simply discovering evidence of criminal wrongdoing. As I detail below, that proposition is wrong.

B

The Court alludes at several points to the fact that King was an arrestee, and arrestees may be validly searched incident to their arrest. But the Court does not really *rest* on this principle, and for good reason: The objects of a search incident to arrest must be either (1) weapons or evidence that might easily be destroyed, or (2) evidence relevant to the crime of arrest. See *Arizona v. Gant,* 556 U.S. 332, 343–344, 129 S. Ct. 1710, 173 L. Ed. 2d 485 (2009); *Thornton v. United States,* 541 U.S. 615, 632, 124 S. Ct. 2127, 158 L. Ed. 2d 905 (2004) (SCALIA, J., concurring in judgment). Neither is the object of the search at issue here.

. . . .

. . . . No matter the degree of invasiveness, suspicionless searches are *never* allowed if their principal end is ordinary crime-solving. A search incident to arrest either serves other ends (such as officer safety, in a search for weapons) or is not suspicionless (as when there is reason to believe the arrestee possesses evidence relevant to the crime of arrest).

Sensing (correctly) that it needs more, the Court elaborates at length the ways that the search here served the special purpose of "identifying" King.[1] But that seems to

---

1. The Court's insistence that our special-needs cases "do not have a direct bearing on the issues presented in this case" is perplexing. Why spill so much ink on the special need of identification if a special need is not required? Why not just come out and say that any suspicionless search of an arrestee is allowed if it will be useful to solve crimes? The Court does not say that because most Members of the Court do not believe it. So whatever the Court's major premise — the opinion does not really contain what you would call a rule of decision — the *minor* premise is "this search was

me quite wrong — unless what one means by "identifying" someone is "searching for evidence that he has committed crimes unrelated to the crime of his arrest." At points the Court does appear to use "identifying" in that peculiar sense — claiming, for example, that knowing "an arrestee's past conduct is essential to an assessment of the danger he poses." *Ante,* at ____, 186 L. Ed. 2d, at 24. If identifying someone means finding out what unsolved crimes he has committed, then identification is indistinguishable from the ordinary law-enforcement aims that have never been thought to justify a suspicionless search. . . . I will therefore assume that the Court means that the DNA search at issue here was useful to "identify" King in the normal sense of that word — in the sense that would identify the author of Introduction to the Principles of Morals and Legislation as Jeremy Bentham.

1

The portion of the Court's opinion that explains the identification rationale is strangely silent on the actual workings of the DNA search at issue here. To know those facts is to be instantly disabused of the notion that what happened had anything to do with identifying King.

King was arrested on April 10, 2009, on charges unrelated to the case before us. That same day, April 10, the police searched him and seized the DNA evidence at issue here. What happened next? Reading the Court's opinion, particularly its insistence that the search was necessary to know "who [had] been arrested," *ante,* at ____, 186 L. Ed. 2d, at 22, one might guess that King's DNA was swiftly processed and his identity thereby confirmed — perhaps against some master database of known DNA profiles, as is done for fingerprints. After all, was not the suspicionless search here crucial to avoid "inordinate risks for facility staff" or to "existing detainee population," *ante,* at ____, 186 L. Ed. 2d at 23? Surely, then — *surely* — the State of Maryland got cracking on those grave risks immediately, by rushing to identify King with his DNA as soon as possible.

Nothing could be further from the truth. Maryland officials did not even begin the process of testing King's DNA that day. Or, actually, the next day. Or the day after that. And that was for a simple reason: Maryland law forbids them to do so. A "DNA sample collected from an individual charged with a crime . . . *may not* be tested or placed in the statewide DNA data base system prior to the first scheduled arraignment date." Md. Pub. Saf. Code Ann. § 2–504(d)(1) (Lexis 2011) (emphasis added). And King's first appearance in court was not until three days after his arrest. . . .

This places in a rather different light the Court's solemn declaration that the search here was necessary so that King could be identified at "every stage of the criminal process." *Ante,* at ____, 186 L. Ed. 2d, at 26 . . . . The truth, known to Maryland and increasingly to the reader: this search had nothing to do with establishing King's identity.

---

used to identify King." The incorrectness of that minor premise will therefore suffice to demonstrate the error in the Court's result.

It gets worse. King's DNA sample was not received by the Maryland State Police's Forensic Sciences Division until April 23, 2009 — two weeks after his arrest. It sat in that office, ripening in a storage area, until the custodians got around to mailing it to a lab for testing on June 25, 2009 — two months after it was received, and nearly *three* since King's arrest. After it was mailed, the data from the lab tests were not available for several more weeks, until July 13, 2009, which is when the test results were entered into Maryland's DNA database, *together with information identifying the person from whom the sample was taken.* Meanwhile, bail had been set, King had engaged in discovery, and he had requested a speedy trial — presumably not a trial of John Doe. It was not until August 4, 2009 — four months after King's arrest — that the forwarded sample transmitted (*without* identifying information) from the Maryland DNA database to the Federal Bureau of Investigation's national database was matched with a sample taken from the scene of an unrelated crime years earlier.

A more specific description of exactly what happened at this point illustrates why, by definition, King could not have been *identified* by this match. The FBI's DNA database (known as CODIS) consists of two distinct collections. FBI, CODIS and NDIS Fact Sheet, http://www.fbi.gov/about-us/lab/codis/codis-and-ndis-fact-sheet (all Internet materials as visited May 31, 2013, and available in Clerk of Court's case file). One of them, the one to which King's DNA was submitted, consists of DNA samples taken from known convicts or arrestees. I will refer to this as the "Convict and Arrestee Collection." The other collection consists of samples taken from crime scenes; I will refer to this as the "Unsolved Crimes Collection." The Convict and Arrestee Collection stores "no names or other personal identifiers of the offenders, arrestees, or detainees." *Ibid.* Rather, it contains only the DNA profile itself, the name of the agency that submitted it, the laboratory personnel who analyzed it, and an identification number for the specimen. *Ibid.* This is because the submitting state laboratories are expected *already* to know the identities of the convicts and arrestees from whom samples are taken. (And, of course, they do.)

Moreover, the CODIS system works by checking to see whether any of the samples in the Unsolved Crimes Collection match any of the samples in the Convict and Arrestee Collection. *Ibid.* That is sensible, if what one wants to do is solve those cold cases, but note what it requires: that the identity of the people whose DNA has been entered in the Convict and Arrestee Collection *already be known.*[2] If one wanted to identify someone in custody using his DNA, the logical thing to do would be to compare that DNA against the Convict and Arrestee Collection: to search, in other words, the collection that could be used (by checking back with the submitting state agency) to identify people, rather than the collection of evidence from unsolved

---

2. By the way, this procedure has nothing to do with exonerating the wrongfully convicted, as the Court soothingly promises. See *ante,* at ___, 186 L. Ed. 2d, at 25. The FBI CODIS database includes DNA from *unsolved* crimes. I know of no indication (and the Court cites none) that it also includes DNA from all — or even any — crimes whose perpetrators have already been convicted.

crimes, whose perpetrators are by definition unknown. But that is not what was done. And that is because this search had nothing to do with identification.

In fact, if anything was "identified" at the moment that the DNA database returned a match, it was not King — his identity was already known. . . . King was not identified by his association with the sample; rather, the sample was identified by its association with King. . . . . King was who he was, and volumes of his biography could not make him any more or any less King. No minimally competent speaker of English would say, upon noticing a known arrestee's similarity "to a wanted poster of a previously unidentified suspect," *ante,* at ____, 186 L. Ed. 2d, at 23, that the *arrestee* had thereby been identified. It was the previously unidentified suspect who had been identified — just as, here, it was the previously unidentified rapist.

2

That taking DNA samples from arrestees has nothing to do with identifying them is confirmed not just by actual practice (which the Court ignores) but by the enabling statute itself (which the Court also ignores). The Maryland Act . . . lists five purposes for which DNA samples may be tested. By this point, it will not surprise the reader to learn that the Court's imagined purpose is not among them.

Instead, the law provides that DNA samples are collected and tested, as a matter of Maryland law, "as part of an official investigation into a crime." § 2–505(a)(2). . . . .

. . . .

So, to review: DNA testing does not even begin until after arraignment and bail decisions are already made. The samples sit in storage for months, and take weeks to test. When they are tested, they are checked against the Unsolved Crimes Collection — rather than the Convict and Arrestee Collection, which could be used to identify them. The Act forbids the Court's purpose (identification), but prescribes as its purpose what our suspicionless-search cases forbid ("official investigation into a crime"). Against all of that, it is safe to say that if the Court's identification theory is not wrong, there is no such thing as error.

II

The Court also attempts to bolster its identification theory with a series of inapposite analogies.

. . . .

It is on the fingerprinting of arrestees . . . that the Court relies most heavily. *Ante,* at ____, 186 L. Ed. 2d, at 27–29. The Court does not actually say whether it believes that taking a person's fingerprints is a Fourth Amendment search, and our cases provide no ready answer to that question. Even assuming so, however, law enforcement's post-arrest use of fingerprints could not be more different from its post-arrest use of DNA. Fingerprints of arrestees are taken primarily to identify them (though that process sometimes solves crimes); the DNA of arrestees is taken to solve crimes (and nothing else). . . .

The Court asserts that the taking of fingerprints was "constitutional for genera-tions prior to the introduction" of the FBI's rapid computer-matching system. *Ante,* at ____, 186 L. Ed. 2d, at 28. This bold statement is bereft of citation to authority because there is none for it. The "great expansion in fingerprinting came before the modern era of Fourth Amendment jurisprudence," and so we were never asked to decide the legitimacy of the practice. *United States v. Kincade,* 379 F.3d 813, 874 (C.A.9 2004) (Kozinski, J., dissenting). As fingerprint databases expanded from con-victed criminals, to arrestees, to civil servants, to immigrants, to everyone with a driver's license, Americans simply "became accustomed to having our fingerprints on file in some government database." *Ibid.* But it is wrong to suggest that this was uncontroversial at the time, or that this Court blessed universal fingerprinting for "generations" before it was possible to use it effectively for identification.

. . . .

The Court also accepts uncritically the Government's representation at oral argu-ment that it is developing devices that will be able to test DNA in mere minutes. At most, this demonstrates that it may one day be possible to design a program that uses DNA for a purpose other than crime-solving—not that Maryland has in fact designed such a program today. And that is the main point, which the Court's discussion of the brave new world of instant DNA analysis should not obscure. The issue before us is not whether DNA can *some day* be used for identification; nor even whether it can *today* be used for identification; but whether it *was used for identification here.*

Today, it can fairly be said that fingerprints really are used to identify people—so well, in fact, that there would be no need for the expense of a separate, wholly redundant DNA confirmation of the same information. What DNA adds—what makes it a valuable weapon in the law-enforcement arsenal—is the ability to solve unsolved crimes, by matching old crime-scene evidence against the profiles of people whose identities are already known. That is what was going on when King's DNA was taken, and we should not disguise the fact. Solving unsolved crimes is a noble objective, but it occupies a lower place in the American pantheon of noble objectives than the protection of our people from suspicionless law-enforcement searches. The Fourth Amendment must prevail.

* * *

The Court disguises the vast (and scary) scope of its holding by promising a limi-tation it cannot deliver. The Court repeatedly says that DNA testing, and entry into a national DNA registry, will not befall thee and me, dear reader, but only those ar-rested for "serious offense[s]." *Ante,* at ____; see also *ante,* at ____ (repeatedly limit-ing the analysis to "serious offenses"). I cannot imagine what principle could possibly justify this limitation, and the Court does not attempt to suggest any. If one believes that DNA will "identify" someone arrested for assault, he must believe that it will "identify" someone arrested for a traffic offense. This Court does not base its judgments on senseless distinctions. At the end of the day, *logic will out.* When there comes before us the taking of DNA from an arrestee for a traffic violation, the Court will predictably (and quite rightly) say, "We can find no significant difference between this case and *King*." Make no mistake about it: As an entirely predictable consequence of today's decision, your DNA can be taken and entered into a national DNA database if you are ever arrested, rightly or wrongly, and for whatever reason.

The most regrettable aspect of the suspicionless search that occurred here is that it proved to be quite unnecessary. All parties concede that it would have been entirely permissible, as far as the Fourth Amendment is concerned, for Maryland to take a sample of King's DNA as a consequence of his conviction for second-degree assault. So the ironic result of the Court's error is this: The only arrestees to whom the outcome here will ever make a difference are those who *have been acquitted* of the crime of arrest (so that their DNA could not have been taken upon conviction). In other words, this Act manages to burden uniquely the sole group for whom the Fourth Amendment's protections ought to be most jealously guarded: people who are innocent of the State's accusations.

Today's judgment will, to be sure, have the beneficial effect of solving more crimes; then again, so would the taking of DNA samples from anyone who flies on an airplane (surely the Transportation Security Administration needs to know the "identity" of the flying public), applies for a driver's license, or attends a public school. Perhaps the construction of such a genetic panopticon is wise. But I doubt that the proud men who wrote the charter of our liberties would have been so eager to open their mouths for royal inspection.

I therefore dissent, and hope that today's incursion upon the Fourth Amendment . . . will some day be repudiated.

[5] Border Searches

United States v. Flores-Montano

United States Supreme Court

541 U.S. 149, 124 S. Ct. 1582, 158 L. Ed. 2d 311 (2004)

CHIEF JUSTICE REHNQUIST delivered the opinion of the Court.

. . . .

Respondent, driving a 1987 Ford Taurus station wagon, attempted to enter the United States at the Otay Mesa Port of Entry in southern California. A customs inspector conducted an inspection of the station wagon, and requested respondent to leave the vehicle. The vehicle was then taken to a secondary inspection station.

At the secondary station, a second customs inspector inspected the gas tank by tapping it, and noted that the tank sounded solid. Subsequently, the inspector requested a mechanic under contract with Customs to come to the border station to remove the tank. Within 20 to 30 minutes, the mechanic arrived. He raised the car on a hydraulic lift, loosened the straps and unscrewed the bolts holding the gas tank to the undercarriage of the vehicle, and then disconnected some hoses and electrical connections. After the gas tank was removed, the inspector hammered off bondo (a putty-like hardening substance that is used to seal openings) from the top of the gas tank. The inspector opened an access plate underneath the bondo and found 37 kilograms of marijuana bricks. The process took 15 to 25 minutes.

A grand jury for the Southern District of California indicted respondent on one count of unlawfully importing marijuana, in violation of 21 U.S.C. § 952, and one count of possession of marijuana with intent to distribute, in violation of § 841(a)(1). [R]espondent filed a motion to suppress the marijuana recovered from the gas tank. . . .

The Government advised the District Court that it was not relying on reasonable suspicion as a basis for denying respondent's suppression motion. . . . The District Court . . . held that reasonable suspicion was required to justify the search and, accordingly, granted respondent's motion to suppress. The Court of Appeals, citing [*United States v. Molina-Tarazon*, 279 F.3d 709 (2002)], summarily affirmed the District Court's judgment. We granted certiorari, 540 U.S. 945 (2003), and now reverse.

In *Molina-Tarazon*, the Court of Appeals decided a case presenting similar facts to the one at bar. It asked "whether [the removal and dismantling of the defendant's fuel tank] is a 'routine' border search for which no suspicion whatsoever is required." 279 F.3d, at 711. The Court of Appeals stated that "[i]n order to conduct a search that goes beyond the routine, an inspector must have reasonable suspicion," and the "critical factor" in determining whether a search is "routine" is the "degree of intrusiveness." *Id.*, at 712–713.

The Court of Appeals seized on language from our opinion in *United States v. Montoya de Hernandez*, 473 U.S. 531, 105 S. Ct. 3304, 87 L. Ed. 2d 381 (1985), in which we used the word "routine" as a descriptive term in discussing border searches. *Id.*, at 538 ("Routine searches of the persons and effects of entrants are not subject to any requirement of reasonable suspicion, probable cause, or warrant"); *id.*, at 541, n. 4 ("Because the issues are not presented today we suggest no view on what level of suspicion, if any, is required for nonroutine border searches such as strip, body-cavity, or involuntary x-ray searches"). The Court of Appeals took the term "routine," fashioned a new balancing test, and extended it to searches of vehicles. But the reasons that might support a requirement of some level of suspicion in the case of highly intrusive searches of the person — dignity and privacy interests of the person being searched — simply do not carry over to vehicles. Complex balancing tests to determine what is a "routine" search of a vehicle, as opposed to a more "intrusive" search of a person, have no place in border searches of vehicles.

The Government's interest in preventing the entry of unwanted persons and effects is at its zenith at the international border. Time and again, we have stated that "searches made at the border, pursuant to the longstanding right of the sovereign to protect itself by stopping and examining persons and property crossing into this

country, are reasonable simply by virtue of the fact that they occur at the border."
United States v. Ramsey, 431 U.S. 606, 616, 97 S. Ct. 1972, 52 L. Ed. 2d 617 (1977).
Congress, since the beginning of our Government, "has granted the Executive ple-
nary authority to conduct routine searches and seizures at the border, without probable cause or a warrant, in order to regulate the collection of duties and to prevent
the introduction of contraband into this country." *Montoya de Hernandez, supra*, at
537 (citing *Ramsey, supra*, at 616–617 (citing Act of July 31, 1789, ch. 5, 1 Stat. 29)).
The modern statute that authorized the search in this case, 46 Stat. 747, 19 U.S.C.
§ 1581(a),[26] derived from a statute passed by the First Congress, the Act of Aug. 4,
1790, ch. 35, § 31, 1 Stat. 164, *see United States v. Villamonte-Marquez*, 462 U.S.
579, 584, 103 S. Ct. 2573, 77 L. Ed. 2d 22 (1983), and reflects the "impressive historical pedigree" of the Government's power and interest, *id.*, at 585. It is axiomatic that
the United States, as sovereign, has the inherent authority to protect, and a paramount interest in protecting, its territorial integrity.

That interest in protecting the borders is illustrated in this case by the evidence
that smugglers frequently attempt to penetrate our borders with contraband secreted
in their automobiles' fuel tank. Over the past 5 1/2 fiscal years, there have been 18,788
vehicle drug seizures at the southern California ports of entry. Of those 18,788, gas
tank drug seizures have accounted for 4,619 of the vehicle drug seizures, or approximately 25%. *Ibid*. In addition, instances of persons smuggled in and around gas tank
compartments are discovered at the ports of entry of San Ysidro and Otay Mesa at a
rate averaging 1 approximately every 10 days.

Respondent asserts two main arguments with respect to his Fourth Amendment
interests. First, he urges that he has a privacy interest in his fuel tank, and that the
suspicionless disassembly of his tank is an invasion of his privacy. But on many occasions, we have noted that the expectation of privacy is less at the border than it is
in the interior. We have long recognized that automobiles seeking entry into this
country may be searched. It is difficult to imagine how the search of a gas tank, which
should be solely a repository for fuel, could be more of an invasion of privacy than
the search of the automobile's passenger compartment.

Second, respondent argues that the Fourth Amendment "protects property as
well as privacy," *Soldal v. Cook County*, 506 U.S. 56, 62, 113 S. Ct. 538, 121 L. Ed. 2d
450 (1992), and that the disassembly and reassembly of his gas tank is a significant
deprivation of his property interest because it may damage the vehicle. He does not,
and on the record cannot, truly contend that the procedure of removal, disassembly,

---

26. Section 1581(a) provides: "Any officer of the customs may at any time go on board of any vessel or vehicle at any place in the United States or within the customs waters or, as he may be authorized, within a customs-enforcement area established under the Anti-Smuggling Act, or at any other
authorized place, without as well as within his district, and examine the manifest and other documents and papers and examine, inspect, and search the vessel or vehicle and every part thereof and
any person, trunk, package, or cargo on board, and to this end may hail and stop such vessel or
vehicle, and use all necessary force to compel compliance."

and reassembly of the fuel tank in this case or any other has resulted in serious damage to, or destruction of, the property.[27] According to the Government, for example, in fiscal year 2003, 348 gas tank searches conducted along the southern border were negative (*i.e.*, no contraband was found), the gas tanks were reassembled, and the vehicles continued their entry into the United States without incident.

Respondent cites not a single accident involving the vehicle or motorist in the many thousands of gas tank disassemblies that have occurred at the border. A gas tank search involves a brief procedure that can be reversed without damaging the safety or operation of the vehicle. If damage to a vehicle were to occur, the motorist might be entitled to recovery. *See, e.g.*, 31 U.S.C. § 3723; 19 U.S.C. § 1630. While the interference with a motorist's possessory interest is not insignificant when the Government removes, disassembles, and reassembles his gas tank, it nevertheless is justified by the Government's paramount interest in protecting the border.

For the reasons stated, we conclude that the Government's authority to conduct suspicionless inspections at the border includes the authority to remove, disassemble, and reassemble a vehicle's fuel tank. While it may be true that some searches of property are so destructive as to require a different result, this was not one of them. The judgment of the United States Court of Appeals for the Ninth Circuit is therefore reversed, and the case is remanded for further proceedings consistent with this opinion.

It is so ordered.

[The concurring opinion of JUSTICE BREYER has been omitted.]

Notes and Questions

(1) Why are "routine" searches at the border reasonable under the Fourth Amendment in the absence of any particularized suspicion? What areas and objects are subject to suspicionless searches at the border?

(2) What types of border searches might be sufficiently "nonroutine" to be considered unreasonable in the absence of particularized suspicion? Why should those border searches be treated differently?

---

27. Respondent's reliance on cases involving exploratory drilling searches is misplaced. *See United States v. Rivas*, 157 F.3d 364 (5th Cir. 1998) (drilling into body of trailer required reasonable suspicion); *United States v. Robles*, 45 F.3d 1 (1st Cir. 1995) (drilling into machine part required reasonable suspicion); *United States v. Carreon*, 872 F.2d 1436 (10th Cir. 1989) (drilling into camper required reasonable suspicion). We have no reason at this time to pass on the reasonableness of drilling, but simply note the obvious factual difference that this case involves the procedure of removal, disassembly, and reassembly of a fuel tank, rather than potentially destructive drilling. We again leave open the question "whether, and under what circumstances, a border search might be deemed 'unreasonable' because of the particularly offensive manner it is carried out." *United States v. Ramsey*, 431 U.S. 606, 618, n. 13, 97 S. Ct. 1972, 52 L. Ed. 2d 617 (1977).

"Special Balancing" Problems

5B–1: On December 20, teachers and administrators at Musko High School attempted to complete an annual pre-winter break "cleanout" of the students' lockers. Three days before the cleanout, the students were asked to report to their lockers at an assigned time to open it so that a faculty member could observe the contents. Because the general purpose was to ensure the health and safety of the students and staff and to help maintain the school's supplies, faculty assigned to examine the lockers kept an eye out for overdue library books, excessive trash, and misplaced food items. They also watched for weapons and controlled substances.

A sizeable minority of students — including Marzel — did not report for the cleanout at the designated time. The next day, pursuant to rules and regulations adopted by the school board, two building aides inspected each locker that had not been checked the day before. One of the lockers that was opened contained only one item — a blue, nylon coat that was hanging on a hook inside the locker. Curious about its ownership and concerned that it might hold trash, supplies, or contraband, one of the aides manipulated the coat, discovering a small bag of what appeared to be marijuana in an outside pocket. The aides returned the coat to the locker and contacted the principal.

From administrative records, the principal determined that the locker belonged to Marzel. He went to Marzel's classroom, escorted him to his locker, and asked him to open it. After Marzel did so, the principal asked if anything in the locker "would cause any educational or legal difficulties for him." Marzel said, "No." When the principal removed the coat from the locker, Marzel grabbed it, struck the principal across the arms, broke free from him, and ran away. The principal pursued and captured Marzel, holding him until the police arrived. The police retrieved the bag from the coat and determined that it contained marijuana. Marzel was charged with possession of a controlled substance.

Was the search of Marzel's locker reasonable?

5B–2: On June 7, the seniors at Plainville High School were scheduled to attend their class picnic at an off-campus location. Prior to departure, school officials performed a pre-announced search of all bags for security purposes. This search revealed a package of cigarettes in Kelly's purse. School regulations prohibited the possession of cigarettes by students on school grounds.

A student named Michele reported to Cindy Bird, a physical education teacher, that Kelly told her and other students that she had marijuana and that she planned to hide it "down her pants" during the mandatory bag check. Bird reported this information to the principal, Marie Priano. Priano considered Michele's report reliable because Michele at some point worked closely with the school's staff as an office aid. Priano boarded the bus on which Kelly sat, and asked her to disembark. Priano and Bird led Kelly to the nurse's office, explaining to her that a fellow classmate had informed them that she had marijuana. Kelly denied the allegation, but both Priano and Bird believed she was lying. Kelly had a history of disciplinary problems, though none involved drug possession.

At the nurse's office, Priano instructed the substitute nurse, Dorene Raikin, to "open up and check" Kelly's underpants. When Raikin expressed apprehension about conducting that search herself, Raikin and Priano called Kelly's mother, Lisa, and asked her to come to the school to conduct the search. While waiting for Lisa to arrive, Priano searched Kelly's purse, and found cigarettes and a lighter.

When Lisa arrived she expressed objections to the search but was told that if she refused to participate, school officials would call the police. At that point Lisa, Raikin, and Kelly went into a small room within the nurse's office. Lisa searched her daughter, while Raikin stood behind her. A closed curtain separated the room from the common area of the nurse's office. Kelly first raised her shirt and pulled down her bra to show that nothing was concealed there. Kelly then dropped her skirt to the floor, around her ankles. When Lisa asked Raikin if this was enough, Raikin answered that it was not. Kelly then pulled her underpants away from her body and turned around so that her mother could view her buttocks. Raikin claims that her back was turned during the entire search, but Kelly asserts that Raikin watched. According to Kelly, "I felt extremely upset and anxious before, during and after the search, to the point of being hysterical." No marijuana was found. Priano then gave Kelly a ride to the picnic.

Kelly filed a civil suit, alleging that her Fourth Amendment rights were violated by school officials. The school officials moved for summary judgment on the grounds that the search was reasonable. The district court agreed that the search was reasonable and granted summary judgment. Kelly has appealed the ruling.

Did the search of Kelly violate her Fourth Amendment rights?

5B–3: Julia Webb and other members of the Hixson High School Band travelled from Chattanooga to Hawaii for a band competition. While in Hawaii, they were housed in a hotel. Webb shared a room with three other girls. One afternoon, Principal Thomas McCull was informed by one of the chaperones that on the previous night some students had used an unoccupied room that was adjacent to and shared a partitioned balcony with Webb's room. McCull asked a hotel security guard to open the adjacent room. McCull entered the unoccupied room and discovered alcohol on the balcony. He then entered Webb's room and discovered Webb and a teenage boy drinking alcohol. Subsequently, he suspended Webb for possession of alcohol and for having a male in her room.

Should Webb's claim that Principal McCull violated her Fourth Amendment rights be successful?

5B–4: C.G. enrolled as an out-of-district student in the Owens Creek Public School District (OCPSD). OCPSD has a reciprocal agreement with the district where C.G.'s parents reside. Continued enrollment of out-of-district students is "subject to the recommendation of the school Principal and the approval of the Superintendent." During his freshman year at Owens Creek High, C.G. began to have disciplinary problems. He was warned for using profanity in class and for excessive tardiness, and he was disciplined for fighting in the boys' locker room. He informed school officials that he used drugs, that he was disposed to anger and depression, that he had girl-friend problems and felt pressure due to football, and that he had thought about sui-cide. Assistant Principal Smitty suggested that he be evaluated for mental health issues. His parents took him to a treatment center.

One day, C.G. walked out of a meeting with the school's "prevention coordina-tor." He was later found in the parking lot and escorted to Smitty's office. He again indicated the he was thinking about suicide. Subsequently, school officials convened a hearing with C.G. and his parents. He was placed on probation and given a four-day in-school suspension. Following additional incidents, Superintendent Vickson rejected a recommendation by Principal Burnham that C.G.'s enrollment be revoked. Instead, Vickson met with C.G.'s parents, informing them that if there were further disciplinary infractions, his permission to attend Owens Creek High would be re-voked immediately.

The following academic year, well over a year after C.G. had last spoken about having drug problems and suicidal thoughts, he violated the school's cell-phone policy by texting during class. C.G.'s teacher confiscated his cell phone, and took it to Assistant Principal Smitty, who then read four text messages on the phone "to see if there was an issue with which I could help him so that he would not do some-thing harmful to himself or someone else." Smitty was "concerned how C.G. would further react to his phone being taken away and that he might hurt himself or someone else."

After this incident, Principal Burnham recommended to Superintendent Vickson that C.G.'s out-of-district privilege be revoked, and Vickson revoked C.G.'s privi-lege. C.G. contends that his Fourth Amendment rights were violated.

Does C.G. have a valid Fourth Amendment claim?

5B–5: On February 8, around 7:00 p.m., the Newark Police Department set up a roadblock in the area of Clinton Avenue and 18th Street. It was staffed by 10 to 12 uniformed officers in marked police cars, was preceded by signs, cones, and flares, and was lit by portable lights and the headlights of the police cars. Uniformed officers in marked vehicles were also stationed at Hopkins and 18th Street and at Clinton Avenue and 17th Street "to prevent anyone from trying to evade the roadblock." Around 9:00 p.m., the two officers at Hopkins and 18th, Officers Falu and Cone, ob-served a burgundy Cavalier proceeding south on 18th Street (a one-way street) toward Clinton. The driver, Nolan Lowers, stopped the Cavalier before it reached the roadblock and backed up to a point that was approximately 50–100 yards past the officers. He then turned the wrong way into another one-way street. The officers ac-tivated their lights and siren and pursued the vehicle.

Lowers parked his car after traveling about 150 yards down the street, got out, and began to walk away. As he was doing so, he reached into his waistband and dropped a clear, plastic bag to the ground. He then started to run. Officer Cone picked up the plastic bag and informed Officer Falu that it contained numerous vials of what looked like cocaine. When Lowers ignored Officer Falu's order to stop, Falu chased and apprehended him. A search of Lowers' pockets led to the discovery of $708. Lowers was charged with several narcotics crimes. He moved to suppress the drugs and money from his trial.

At the suppression hearing, Lieutenant Poll, the "Quality of Life Supervisor" for Newark, testified. As part of his duties, Poll was required to address citizen complaints about the quality of life in the city. According to Lieutenant Poll, he had been in charge of establishing and supervising the operation of the February 8 roadblock. The roadblock's purpose had been to "detect stolen cars." Officers had stopped every third or fourth vehicle that had approached the roadblock and had asked the drivers to produce driving credentials. If everything checked out, the vehicles were allowed to proceed. If motor vehicle violations were detected, the drivers were directed to the side of the road. Summons were issued and, when necessary, vehicles were towed. According to Lieutenant Poll, one or two roadblocks had been conducted each week in different parts of Newark. Several of these roadblocks had been set up within a one or two block radius of the February 8 roadblock because of an acute stolen car problem in that area. Poll reported that the police department had received a number of citizen complaints concerning vehicle thefts in the vicinity. In fact, the City of Newark has an exceptionally high rate of automobile theft.

What arguments should Lowers make in support of his motion to suppress? What arguments should the government make against suppression? How should the trial judge rule?

5B–6: The Dayton Police Department estimates that one out every eight drivers in Dayton is unlicensed. Thirty percent of the traffic citations issued by Dayton officers are for license violations. In response to this situation, Deputy Chief Compston directed Lieutenant Bard to investigate the development of a driver's license checkpoint program. Bard did not uncover any empirical evidence of a correlation between licensing and the safe operation of a motor vehicle. Nonetheless, after he had researched license checkpoint programs in other states and consulted with legal counsel for the city of Dayton, Lieutenant Bard developed guidelines for a checkpoint program and was appointed commanding officer of the program. The primary functions of checkpoints operated pursuant to the guidelines were to detect motorists who were driving without a valid license and to deter others from doing so.

Locations for checkpoints were selected after input was received from a variety of commanding officers and from the Assistant Police Chief. Among the criteria considered in selecting sites were safety and traffic volume. "Target enforcement areas" were selected on the basis of traffic and crime problems. The Dayton Police Department has five districts. In each of these districts, except District Four, two or three checkpoints were conducted. Approximately 100 yards before each checkpoint, officers set up reflective signs that warned drivers of the upcoming checkpoint. At some of them, motorists could make legal turns to avoid the checkpoint; at others, there was no such opportunity. Each of the checkpoints was staffed by Lieutenant Bard, a supervisor, and nine or 10 officers, and was conducted between 6:00 p.m. and 2:00 a.m. Ordinarily, every car was stopped at a checkpoint unless traffic flow made it unsafe to do so. When that was the case, Bard would instruct officers to route every third, fourth, or fifth car into the checkpoint, and to wave the rest through. The average length of detention for a motorist with a valid license was 45 seconds. When a motorist was not in possession of his or her license, officers ran a computer check to determine whether he or she had a valid license. Such a check took about two minutes. If the computer showed proper licensing and if there was no other reason to detain the motorist, he or she was given a pamphlet explaining the license checkpoint program and was allowed to proceed. Drivers who did not have valid driver's licenses were cited.

Magnus was stopped at a checkpoint operated on June 16. He was cited for driving without being properly licensed. On June 18, Kevin was driving westbound on Corn Street when he noticed signs warning of a driver's license checkpoint. Kevin stopped his car, backed up eastbound in a westbound lane for 100–200 feet, then turned around in a driveway and headed eastbound on Corn Street. One of the officers at the checkpoint, Officer Zimmer, followed Kevin to his home and cited him for driving without being properly licensed and for two other traffic offenses. During the operation of all of the driver's license checkpoints, 2,100 cars were stopped, 224 traffic citations were issued (some motorists received more than one), and 159 people were arrested. It is unclear how many of the citations and/or arrests were for violations related to driver's licenses.

Both Magnus and Kevin challenged the constitutionality of the checkpoints.

Should their claims be sustained?

5B–7: At 3:40 a.m., Lieutenant Arthur received a radio report of multiple gunshots and numerous 911 calls in the Nut Circle area. Nut Circle is a residential cul-de-sac running off of Nut Street. Nut Street is accessed from Main Street, the main thoroughfare in town. Between Nut Circle and Main Street, a number of streets intersect with Nut Street. Arthur proceeded to the area. When traveling west down Nut Street toward Nut Circle, he noticed several vehicles heading east at a high rate of speed. The occupant of one waved Arthur to stop, exclaiming, "They're shooting up the place!"

The scene at the end of Nut Circle was chaotic. At least 50 people were standing around. Arthur had no idea who was involved in the shooting, whether anyone was injured, or whether the shooters were escaping. In front of a house at the center of the disturbance, Arthur saw several empty shell casings. He radioed for backup, advising officers to use extreme caution because firearms were involved. He also ordered officers to stop all vehicles leaving the scene and to question the occupants, because he was concerned that someone had been shot and that the shooters might be fleeing the scene by car.

Officer Tut also responded to the 3:40 a.m. radio dispatch. In the heavy traffic near the intersection of Main and Nut, he narrowly avoided a collision with a sport utility vehicle that failed to stop at a red light. Tut pursued and stopped the vehicle. After observing other cars speeding and failing to stop for the red light, Tut positioned his cruiser across the eastbound lane of Nut Street, close to the intersection of Main Street and one-half mile from Nut Circle, in an attempt to stop traffic and prevent an accident.

Before exiting from his cruiser, Tut heard Arthur's radio broadcast ordering that "everyone leaving the scene be questioned." Although the police knew there had been a shooting, they did not know whether those involved in the shooting were on foot or in a car. Because he was concerned that one or more of the vehicle occupants could have been involved, Tut began questioning the occupants of the 10 to 15 vehicles that had been stopped. After questioning the occupants of the first two cars and allowing them to go on their way, Tut approached the third car, which contained four male occupants, two in the front and two in the rear. Believing his own safety could best be preserved by questioning the occupants separately, Tut asked the driver to get out and questioned him. Tut next asked the front seat passenger to exit. As he did, Tut noticed the butt end of a firearm beneath the front passenger seat. Because he now had increased concern for safety, he ordered the two rear seat occupants to get out of the vehicle. The four men were then patted down, handcuffed, and arrested. A semi-automatic pistol with a defaced serial number was seized from the vehicle.

Was the stop of the vehicles constitutional?

5B–8: The state vehicle code provides that "Any person who drives or is in actual control of a motor vehicle upon the public highways of this State shall be deemed to have given consent to a breath test . . . or to a chemical test or tests of blood, breath, or urine for the purpose of determining the alcohol or other drug content of such person's blood if there is probable cause to believe that such person was the driver at fault, in whole or in part, for a motor vehicle accident which resulted in the death or personal injury of any person." The code provision does not require any cause to believe that the person was under the influence of drugs or alcohol.

The results of a test may be used in any civil or criminal proceeding. In addition, refusal to submit to the required test results in the suspension of one's driver's license, and such refusal is admissible as evidence in a civil or criminal proceeding related to the individual's operation of a motor vehicle.

Allen was involved in a car accident that involved a personal injury. The police officer at the scene concluded that there was probable cause to believe that Allen was at fault, at least partially, for the accident. He requested Allen to submit to a breath test. Allen refused and later challenged the constitutionality of the code provision.

How should the court rule on Allen's challenge?

5B–9: Juvenile "A," a 14-year-old male, was found to have committed "indecent liberties" by holding a younger boy down and sodomizing him. Juvenile "B," a 14-year-old boy, pleaded guilty to "child molestation," a charge that entailed kissing a 4-year-old girl, laying on top of her, removing her pants, and licking her vaginal area. Juvenile "C," a 15-year-old girl, pleaded guilty to one of three "child molestation" charges, admitting that she "let a 5-year-old boy lay on top of me, touch my breast, look inside my underwear, and kiss my mouth." It was alleged that she had also touched the boy's penis on several occasions. Juvenile "D," a 16-year-old male, pleaded guilty to "indecent liberties" based on an incident in which he kissed an 11-year-old girl, took off her shirt, unbuttoned her pants, and touched her breast and crotch. It was alleged that he had also removed his own clothes and rubbed his hands and genitals against the girl's genitals. Juvenile "E," a 15-year-old boy, pleaded guilty to "sexual contact" with a 7-year-old boy he was babysitting based on allegations that he had placed his mouth on the boy's penis three times.

A provision of the state health code provides for mandatory AIDS testing of convicted sex offenders. In passing the provision, the legislature declared that "sexually transmitted diseases constitute a serious and sometimes fatal threat to the public and individual health and welfare of the people of the state." Further, it found "that the incidence of sexually transmitted diseases is rising at an alarming rate and that these diseases result in significant social, health, and economic costs, including infant and maternal mortality, temporary and lifelong disability, and premature death." The mandatory testing statute was intended "to reduce the incidence of sexually transmitted diseases."

The State sought orders that the five juveniles submit to blood tests for HIV. The juveniles opposed the testing on constitutional grounds, but the juvenile court rejected their contentions and directed that testing go forward.

Are the mandatory blood tests constitutional?

5B–10: After Craig was hired as a City firefighter, the City implemented a Substance Abuse Program for the Fire Department. The Program requires testing of firefighters: (1) if the Department has reasonable suspicion to believe an individual firefighter has abused drugs or alcohol; (2) after a firefighter is involved in an accident on the job; (3) following a firefighter's return to duty or as a follow-up to "a determination that a covered member is in need of assistance"; and (4) "on an unannounced and random basis spread reasonably throughout the calendar year."

The primary purpose of the random testing provision "is to deter controlled substance use and to detect controlled substance use for the purpose of removing identified users from the safety-sensitive work force." This advances the City's goal of "a work environment that is totally free of the harmful effects of drugs and the misuse of alcohol." Under the random testing provision, a computer program selects firefighters to be tested. The Department notifies firefighters of their selection immediately before, during, or after work. The firefighters are supposed to be tested within 30 minutes of notification, with allowance for travel time to a laboratory. At the laboratory, firefighters may use private bathroom stalls to provide urine samples. The samples are inspected by a monitor for the proper color and temperature.

The lab tests each sample for marijuana, cocaine, opiates, amphetamines, and phencyclidine. The lab initially uses an immunoassay test, then confirms all positive results using a gas chromatography/mass spectrometry technique. It reports positive results to a Medical Review Officer (MRO), who has "detailed knowledge of possible alternate medical explanations." The MRO reviews the results before giving the information to the Department's administrative official. Only confirmed tests are reported to the Department as positive for a specific drug. Before verifying a positive result, however, the MRO must contact and inform the firefighter confidentially.

The Department does not release information in a firefighter's drug testing record outside the Department without the firefighter's consent. A firefighter who tests positive for any of several specified drugs is removed from all covered positions and is evaluated by a substance abuse professional. The Department may discipline or terminate the employment of a firefighter who tests positive a second time or who refuses to submit to a required test.

Craig filed a complaint seeking declaratory and injunctive relief, alleging that the random testing component of the Program violated the Fourth Amendment.

Is there merit in Craig's complaint?

5B–11: Harry Potterman was driving home to the United States from a vacation in Mexico with his wife when he approached the Lucasville Port of Entry. During primary inspection by a border agent, the Treasury Enforcement Communication System ("TECS") returned a hit for Potterman, indicating he was a sex offender — he had a 1992 conviction for two counts of use of a minor in sexual conduct and three counts of child molestation — and that he was potentially involved in child sex tourism and child pornography. Potterman and his wife were referred to secondary inspection, where they were instructed to exit their vehicle. Border agents searched the vehicle and retrieved two laptop computers and a digital camera. Officer Antonio inspected the devices and found family and other personal photos, along with several password-protected files.

Antonio contacted Supervisor Craig and informed him about Potterman's entry and the fact that he was a sex offender potentially involved in child sex tourism. Craig told Antonio that the alert on Potterman was part of Operation Angel Watch, which was aimed at combating child sex tourism by identifying sex offenders, particularly those who travel frequently outside the United States. Antonio was instructed to review any media equipment, such as computers, cameras, or other electronic devices, for potential evidence of child pornography. Alvarado reported that he had been able to review some of the photographs on Potterman's computers, but had encountered password-protected files that he was unable to access.

Agent Craig and Lucy then traveled to Lucasville. During an interview, Potterman offered to help them access his computer. They declined the offer out of concern that Potterman might be able to delete files surreptitiously or that the laptop might be "booby trapped." The agents allowed the Pottermans to leave the border crossing, but retained the laptops and camera. Agent Craig delivered both laptops and the camera to Forensic Examiner Johns at a location 170 miles from Lucasville. Agent Johns used a program to copy the hard drives of the devices. He determined that the digital camera did not contain any contraband and released the camera that day to Potterman. He then used software that often must run for several hours to examine copies of the laptop hard drives. That evening, Johns found 75 images of child pornography within the unallocated space of Potterman's laptop.

Agent Johns contacted Potterman, saying that he needed help accessing password-protected files on the laptop. Potterman agreed to help the following day, but never showed up. Instead, he flew to Mexico, then continued on to Australia. Two days later, Johns was able to open 23 password-protected files on the laptop and found 378 images of child pornography.

Potterman was apprehended and indicted for multiple child pornography offenses. He moved to suppress the evidence found on his laptop.

Did the searches of Potterman's devices violate the Fourth Amendment?

5B–12: The New York City (NYC) subway system is America's largest and busiest. Terrorists view the subway as a prime target. In 1997 and again in 2004, police uncovered plots to bomb two very busy NYC subway stations, one in Brooklyn and one in Manhattan. Also in 2004, terrorists killed over 240 people by using concealed explosives to bomb commuter trains in Madrid and Moscow. In 2005, terrorists with explosives killed more than 56 people and wounded another 700 individuals by launching a coordinated series of attacks on the London subway and bus systems.

The day of the London attack, the New York City Police Department ("NYPD") announced the Container Inspection Program (the "Program"), which was designed chiefly to deter terrorists from carrying concealed explosives onto the subway and, to a lesser extent, to uncover any attempt. The NYPD establishes daily inspection checkpoints at selected subway facilities. A group of uniformed police officers stand at a folding table near the turnstiles that lead onto the train platform. Officers search the bags of a portion of subway riders entering the station.

To enhance the deterrent effect, the NYPD selects the checkpoint locations "in a deliberative manner, but aims to have them appear to be random." The NYPD switches checkpoint locations and varies their number, staffing, and scheduling. Deployment patterns are constantly shifting. Although it strives for the appearance of random deployment, the NYPD bases its decisions on fluctuations in passenger volume and threat level, overlapping coverage provided by its other counter-terrorism initiatives, and available manpower.

Officers give notice of the searches and make clear that they are voluntary. They display a large poster notifying passengers that "Backpacks and Other Containers Are Subject to Inspection," and similar audio announcements are made in subway stations and on trains. A supervisor at each checkpoint announces through a bullhorn that all persons wishing to enter are subject to a container search and that those wishing to avoid the search must leave the station. Officers exercise virtually no discretion in determining whom to search. The supervisor establishes a selection rate, such as every fifth or tenth person, based upon the number of officers and passenger volume at the checkpoint. Officers search individuals according to the established rate and search only those containers large enough to carry an explosive. Thus, they may not inspect wallets and small purses. Further, they must limit their inspection "to what is minimally necessary to ensure that the item does not contain an explosive device," which they have been trained to recognize. They may not intentionally look for other contraband, although if they incidentally discover it, they may arrest the individual carrying it. Officers may not attempt to read any written or printed material and may not request or record a passenger's personal information.

The preferred inspection method is to ask the passenger to open his bag and manipulate his possessions himself so that an officer may visually determine if the bag contains an explosive. If necessary, the officer may open the container and manipulate its contents himself. Because officers must conduct the inspection for no "longer than necessary to ensure that the individual is not carrying an explosive device," a typical inspection lasts for a matter of seconds. Two weeks after the Program started, a group consisting of individuals who had encountered subway checkpoints sued to halt the Program, claiming that it violates the Fourth Amendment.

Do the plaintiffs have a valid constitutional claim?

Selected Bibliography

Ricardo J. Bascuas, *Fourth Amendment Lessons from the Highway and the Subway: A Principled Approach to Suspicionless Searches,* 38 Rutgers L.J. 719 (2007)

Edwin J. Butterfoss, *A Suspicionless Search and Seizure Quagmire: The Supreme Court Revives the Pretext Doctrine and Creates Another Fine Fourth Amendment Mess,* 40 Creighton L. Rev. 419 (2007)

George M. Dery, *Are Politicians More Deserving of Privacy Than Schoolchildren? How* Chandler v. Miller *Exposed the Absurdities of Fourth Amendment "Special Needs" Balancing,* 40 Ariz. L. Rev. 73 (1998)

Barry C. Feld, T.L.O. *and* Redding's *Unanswered (Misanswered) Fourth Amendment Questions: Few Rights and Fewer Remedies,* 80 Miss. L.J. 847 (2011)

James Felman & Christopher J. Petrini, *Drug Testing and Public Employment: Toward a Rational Application of the Fourth Amendment,* 51 Law & Contemp. Probs. 253 (1988)

Martin R. Gardner, *Strip Searching Students: The Supreme Court's Latest Failure to Articulate a "Sufficiently Clear" Statement of Fourth Amendment Law,* 80 Miss. L.J. 955 (2011)

Bernhard E. Harcourt & Tracey L. Meares, *Randomization and the Fourth Amendment,* 78 U. CHI. L. REV. 809 (2011)

Mary Graw Leary, *Reasonable Expectations of Privacy for Youth in a Digital Age,* 80 Miss. L.J. 1035 (2011)

Laura A. Lundquist, *Weighing the Factors of Drug Testing for Fourth Amendment Balancing,* 60 Geo. Wash. L. Rev. 1151 (1992)

Kenneth Nuger, *The Special Needs Rationale: Creating a Chasm in Fourth Amendment Analysis,* 32 Santa Clara L. Rev. 89 (1992)

Michael Pinard, *From the Classroom to the Courtroom: Reassessing Fourth Amendment Standards in Public School Searches Involving Law Enforcement Authorities*, 45 Ariz. L. Rev. 1067 (2003)

Gerald S. Reamey, *When "Special Needs" Meet Probable Cause: Denying the Devil Benefit of Law*, 19 Hastings Const. L.Q. 295 (1992)

David E. Steinberg, *High School Drug Testing and the Original Understanding of the Fourth Amendment*, 30 Hastings Const. L.Q. 263 (2003)

Nadine Strossen, Michigan Department of State Police v. Sitz: *A Roadblock to Meaningful Judicial Enforcement of Constitutional Rights*, 42 Hastings L.J. 285 (1991)

Scott E. Sundby, *Protecting the Citizen "Whilst He Is Quiet": Suspicionless Searches, "Special Needs" and General Warrants*, 74 Miss. L.J. 501 (2004)

Brenda J. Walts, New Jersey v. T.L.O.: *The Questions the Court Did Not Answer About School Searches*, 14 J.L. & Educ. 421 (1985)

Silas J. Wasserstrom, *The Court's Turn Toward a General Reasonableness Interpretation of the Fourth Amendment*, 27 Am. Crim. L. Rev. 119 (1989)

Phoebe Weaver Williams, *Governmental Drug Testing: Critique and Analysis of Fourth Amendment Jurisprudence*, 8 Hofstra Lab. L.J. 1 (1990)

[C] Higher Than Usual Standards of Reasonableness

Tennessee v. Garner

United States Supreme Court

471 U.S. 1, 105 S. Ct. 1694, 85 L. Ed. 2d 1 (1985)

Justice White delivered the opinion of the Court.

. . . .

I

At about 10:45 p.m. on October 3, 1974, Memphis Police Officers Elton Hymon and Leslie Wright were dispatched to answer a "prowler inside call." Upon arriving at the scene they saw a woman standing on her porch and gesturing toward the adjacent house. She told them she had heard glass breaking and that "they" or "someone" was breaking in next door. While Wright radioed the dispatcher to say that they were on the scene, Hymon went behind the house. He heard a door slam and saw someone run across the backyard. The fleeing suspect, who was appellee-respondent's decedent, Edward Garner, stopped at a 6-feet-high chain link fence at the edge of the yard. With the aid of a flashlight, Hymon was able to see Garner's face and hands. He saw no sign of a weapon, and, though not certain, was "reasonably sure" and "figured" that Garner was unarmed. He thought Garner was 17 or 18 years old and about 5′5″ or 5′7″ tall. While Garner was crouched at the base of the fence, Hymon called out "police, halt" and took a few steps toward him. Garner then began to climb over the fence. Convinced that if Garner made it over the fence he would elude capture, Hymon shot him. The bullet hit Garner in the back of the head. Garner was taken by ambulance to a hospital, where he died on the operating table. Ten dollars and a purse taken from the house were found on his body.

In using deadly force to prevent the escape, Hymon was acting under the authority of a Tennessee statute and pursuant to Police Department policy. The statute provides that "[i]f, after notice of the intention to arrest the defendant, he either flee [sic] or forcibly resist [sic], the officer may use all the necessary means to effect the arrest." Tenn. Code Ann. § 40-7-108 (1982). The Department policy was slightly more restrictive than the statute, but still allowed the use of deadly force in cases of burglary. . . .

Garner's father then brought this action in the Federal District Court for the Western District of Tennessee, seeking damages under 42 U.S.C. § 1983 for asserted violations of Garner's constitutional rights. The complaint alleged that the shooting violated the Fourth, Fifth, Sixth, Eighth, and Fourteenth Amendments of the United States Constitution . . . . [The District Court] concluded that Hymon's actions were authorized by the Tennessee statute, which in turn was constitutional. Hymon had employed the only reasonable and practicable means of preventing Garner's escape. Garner had "recklessly and heedlessly attempted to vault over the fence to escape, thereby assuming the risk of being fired upon."

. . . .

The Court of Appeals reversed and remanded. 710 F.2d 240 (6th Cir. 1983). It reasoned that the killing of a fleeing suspect is a "seizure" under the Fourth Amendment, and is therefore constitutional only if "reasonable." The Tennessee statute failed as applied to this case because it did not adequately limit the use of deadly force by distinguishing between felonies of different magnitudes — "the facts, as found, did not justify the use of deadly force under the Fourth Amendment." *Id.*, at 246.

. . . .

II

. . . .

A

A police officer may arrest a person if he has probable cause to believe that person committed a crime. *E.g., United States v. Watson*, 423 U.S. 411, 96 S. Ct. 820, 46 L. Ed. 2d 598 (1976). Petitioners and appellant argue that if this requirement is satisfied the Fourth Amendment has nothing to say about how that seizure is made. This submission ignores the many cases in which this Court, by balancing the extent of the intrusion against the need for it, has examined the reasonableness of the manner in which a search or seizure is conducted. To determine the constitutionality of a seizure "[w]e must balance the nature and quality of the intrusion on the individual's Fourth Amendment interests against the importance of the governmental interests alleged to justify the intrusion." *United States v. Place*, 462 U.S. 696, 703, 103 S. Ct. 2637, 2642, 77 L. Ed. 2d 110 (1983)[.]

. . . .

B

The same balancing process ... demonstrates that, notwithstanding probable cause to seize a suspect, an officer may not always do so by killing him. The intrusiveness of a seizure by means of deadly force is unmatched. The suspect's fundamental interest in his own life need not be elaborated upon. The use of deadly force also frustrates the interest of the individual, and of society, in judicial determination of guilt and punishment. Against these interests are ranged governmental interests in effective law enforcement. It is argued that overall violence will be reduced by encouraging the peaceful submission of suspects who know that they may be shot if they flee. Effectiveness in making arrests requires the resort to deadly force, or at least the meaningful threat thereof. "Being able to arrest such individuals is a condition precedent to the state's entire system of law enforcement." Brief for Petitioners 14.

Without in any way disparaging the importance of these goals, we are not convinced that the use of deadly force is a sufficiently productive means of accomplishing them to justify the killing of nonviolent suspects. The use of deadly force is a self-defeating way of apprehending a suspect and so setting the criminal justice mechanism in motion. If successful, it guarantees that that mechanism will not be set in motion. And while the meaningful threat of deadly force might be thought to lead to the arrest of more live suspects by discouraging escape attempts, the presently available evidence does not support this thesis. The fact is that a majority of police departments in this country have forbidden the use of deadly force against nonviolent suspects. If those charged with the enforcement of the criminal law have abjured the use of deadly force in arresting nondangerous felons, there is a substantial basis for doubting that the use of such force is an essential attribute of the arrest power in all felony cases. Petitioners and appellant have not persuaded us that shooting nondangerous fleeing suspects is so vital as to outweigh the suspect's interest in his own life.

The use of deadly force to prevent the escape of all felony suspects, whatever the circumstances, is constitutionally unreasonable. It is not better that all felony suspects die than that they escape. Where the suspect poses no immediate threat to the officer and no threat to others, the harm resulting from failing to apprehend him does not justify the use of deadly force to do so. It is no doubt unfortunate when a suspect who is in sight escapes, but the fact that the police arrive a little late or are a little slower afoot does not always justify killing the suspect. A police officer may not seize an unarmed, nondangerous suspect by shooting him dead. The Tennessee statute is unconstitutional insofar as it authorizes the use of deadly force against such fleeing suspects.

It is not, however, unconstitutional on its face. Where the officer has probable cause to believe that the suspect poses a threat of serious physical harm, either to the officer or to others, it is not constitutionally unreasonable to prevent escape by using deadly force. Thus, if the suspect threatens the officer with a weapon or there is probable cause to believe that he has committed a crime involving the infliction or threatened infliction of serious physical harm, deadly force may be used if necessary to prevent escape, and if, where feasible, some warning has been given. As applied in such circumstances, the Tennessee statute would pass constitutional muster.

III
A

It is insisted that the Fourth Amendment must be construed in light of the common-law rule, which allowed the use of whatever force was necessary to effect the arrest of a fleeing felon, though not a misdemeanant.

. . . .

It is true that this Court has often looked to the common law in evaluating the reasonableness, for Fourth Amendment purposes, of police activity. On the other hand, it "has not simply frozen into constitutional law those law enforcement practices that existed at the time of the Fourth Amendment's passage." *Payton v. New York*, 445 U.S. 573, 591, n. 33, 100 S. Ct. 1371, 1382, n. 33, 63 L. Ed. 2d 639 (1980). Because of sweeping change in the legal and technological context, reliance on the common-law rule in this case would be a mistaken literalism that ignores the purposes of a historical inquiry.

B

It has been pointed out many times that the common-law rule is best understood in light of the fact that it arose at a time when virtually all felonies were punishable by death . . . . Courts have also justified the common-law rule by emphasizing the relative dangerousness of felons.

Neither of these justifications makes sense today. Almost all crimes formerly punishable by death no longer are or can be. And while in earlier times "the gulf between the felonies and the minor offences was broad and deep," 2 Pollock & Maitland 467, n. 3; *Carroll v. United States*, 267 U.S. 132, 158, 45 S. Ct. 280, 287, 69 L. Ed. 543 (1925), today the distinction is minor and often arbitrary. Many crimes classified as misdemeanors, or nonexistent, at common law are now felonies. These changes have undermined the concept, which was questionable to begin with, that use of deadly force against a fleeing felon is merely a speedier execution of someone who has already forfeited his life. They have also made the assumption that a "felon" is more dangerous than a misdemeanant untenable. Indeed, numerous misdemeanors involve conduct more dangerous than many felonies.

There is an additional reason why the common-law rule cannot be directly translated to the present day. The common-law rule developed at a time when weapons were rudimentary. Deadly force could be inflicted almost solely in a hand-to-hand struggle during which, necessarily, the safety of the arresting officer was at risk. Handguns were not carried by police officers until the latter half of the last century. Only then did it become possible to use deadly force from a distance as a means of apprehension. As a practical matter, the use of deadly force under the standard articulation of the common-law rule has an altogether different meaning — and harsher consequences — now than in past centuries.

. . . .

In short, though the common law pedigree of Tennessee's rule is pure on its face, changes in the legal and technological context mean the rule is distorted almost beyond recognition when literally applied.

C

In evaluating the reasonableness of police procedures under the Fourth Amendment, we have also looked to prevailing rules in individual jurisdictions. The rules in the States are varied. . . .

It cannot be said that there is a constant or overwhelming trend away from the common-law rule. In recent years, some States have reviewed their laws and expressly rejected abandonment of the common-law rule. Nonetheless, the long-term movement has been away from the rule that deadly force may be used against any fleeing felon, and that remains the rule in less than half the States.

This trend is more evident and impressive when viewed in light of the policies adopted by the police departments themselves. Overwhelmingly, these are more restrictive than the common-law rule . . . . In light of the rules adopted by those who must actually administer them, the older and fading common-law view is a dubious indicium of the constitutionality of the Tennessee statute now before us.

D

Actual departmental policies are important for an additional reason. We would hesitate to declare a police practice of long standing "unreasonable" if doing so would severely hamper effective law enforcement. But the indications are to the contrary. There has been no suggestion that crime has worsened in any way in jurisdictions that have adopted, by legislation or departmental policy, rules similar to that announced today. *Amici* noted that "[a]fter extensive research and consideration, [they] have concluded that laws permitting police officers to use deadly force to apprehend unarmed, non-violent fleeing felony suspects actually do not protect citizens or law enforcement officers, do not deter crime or alleviate problems caused by crime, and do not improve the crime-fighting ability of law enforcement agencies." Brief for Police Foundation et al. as *Amici Curiae* 11. The submission is that the obvious state interests in apprehension are not sufficiently served to warrant the use of lethal weapons against all fleeing felons.

Nor do we agree with petitioners and appellant that the rule we have adopted requires the police to make impossible, split-second evaluations of unknowable facts. We do not deny the practical difficulties of attempting to assess the suspect's dangerousness. However, similarly difficult judgments must be made by the police in equally uncertain circumstances. *See e.g., Terry v. Ohio,* 392 U.S., at 20, 27, 88 S. Ct., at 1879, 1883. Nor is there any indication that in States that allow the use of deadly force only against dangerous suspects, the standard has been difficult to apply or has led to a rash of litigation involving inappropriate second-guessing of police officers' split-second decisions. Moreover, the highly technical felony/misdemeanor distinction is equally, if not more, difficult to apply in the field. An officer is in no position to know, for example, the precise value of property stolen, or whether the crime was a first or second offense. Finally, as noted above, this claim must be viewed with suspicion in light of the similar self-imposed limitations of so many police departments.

IV

The District Court concluded that Hymon was justified in shooting Garner because state law allows, and the Federal Constitution does not forbid, the use of deadly force to prevent the escape of a fleeing felony suspect if no alternative means of apprehension is available. This conclusion made a determination of Garner's apparent dangerousness unnecessary. The court did find, however, that Garner appeared to be unarmed, though Hymon could not be certain that was the case. Restated in Fourth Amendment terms, this means Hymon had no articulable basis to think Garner was armed.

In reversing, the Court of Appeals accepted the District Court's factual conclusions and held that "the facts, as found, did not justify the use of deadly force." 710 F.2d, at 246. We agree. Officer Hymon could not reasonably have believed that Garner — young, slight, and unarmed — posed any threat . . . . Hymon did not have probable cause to believe that Garner, whom he correctly believed to be unarmed, posed any physical danger to himself or others.

The dissent argues that the shooting was justified by the fact that Officer Hymon had probable cause to believe that Garner had committed a nighttime burglary. While we agree that burglary is a serious crime, we cannot agree that it is so dangerous as automatically to justify the use of deadly force . . . . In fact, the available statistics demonstrate that burglaries only rarely involve physical violence. During the 10-year period from 1973–1982, only 3.8% of all burglaries involved violent crime. Bureau of Justice Statistics, Household Burglary, p. 4 (1985).[23]

V

. . . We hold that the statute is invalid insofar as it purported to give Hymon the authority to act as he did. As for the policy of the Police Department, the absence of

---

23. The dissent points out that three-fifths of all rapes in the home, three-fifths of all home robberies, and about a third of home assaults are committed by burglars. These figures mean only that if one knows that a suspect committed a rape in the home, there is a good chance that the suspect is also a burglar. That has nothing to do with the question here, which is whether the fact that someone has committed a burglary indicates that he has committed, or might commit, a violent crime. The dissent also points out that this 3.8% adds up to 2.8 million violent crimes over a 10-year period, as if to imply that today's holding will let loose 2.8 million violent burglars. The relevant universe is, of course, far smaller. At issue is only that tiny fraction of cases where violence has taken place and an officer who has no other means of apprehending the suspect is unaware of its occurrence.

any discussion of this issue by the courts below, and the uncertain state of the record, preclude any consideration of its validity.

The judgment of the Court of Appeals is affirmed, and the case is remanded for further proceedings consistent with this opinion.

So ordered.

JUSTICE O'CONNOR, with whom THE CHIEF JUSTICE and JUSTICE REHNQUIST join, dissenting.

. . . .

II

For purposes of Fourth Amendment analysis, I agree with the Court that Officer Hymon "seized" Garner by shooting him. Whether that seizure was reasonable and therefore permitted by the Fourth Amendment requires a careful balancing of the important public interest in crime prevention and detection and the nature and quality of the intrusion upon legitimate interests of the individual. In striking this balance here, it is crucial to acknowledge that police use of deadly force to apprehend a fleeing criminal suspect falls within the "rubric of police conduct . . . necessarily [involving] swift action predicated upon the on-the-spot observations of the officer on the beat." *Terry v. Ohio*, 392 U.S. 1, 20, 88 S. Ct. 1868, 1879, 20 L. Ed. 2d 889 (1968). The clarity of hindsight cannot provide the standard for judging the reasonableness of police decisions made in uncertain and often dangerous circumstances. Moreover, I am far more reluctant than is the Court to conclude that the Fourth Amendment proscribes a police practice that was accepted at the time of the adoption of the Bill of Rights and has continued to receive the support of many state legislatures. . . .

The public interest involved in the use of deadly force as a last resort to apprehend a fleeing burglary suspect relates primarily to the serious nature of the crime. Household burglaries represent not only the illegal entry into a person's home, but also "pos[e] real risk of serious harm to others." *Solem v. Helm*, 463 U.S. 277, 315–316, 103 S. Ct. 3001, 3023, 77 L. Ed. 2d 637 (1983) (Burger, C.J., dissenting). According to recent Department of Justice statistics, "[t]hree-fifths of all rapes in the home, three-fifths of all home robberies, and about a third of home aggravated and simple assaults are committed by burglars." Bureau of Justice Statistics Bulletin, Household Burglary 1 (January 1985). During the period 1973–1982, 2.8 million such violent crimes were committed in the course of burglaries. *Id.* Victims of a forcible intrusion into their home by a nighttime prowler will find little consolation in the majority's confident assertion that "burglaries only rarely involve physical violence." Moreover, even if a particular burglary, when viewed in retrospect, does not involve physical harm to others, the "harsh potentialities for violence" inherent in the forced entry into a home preclude characterization of the crime as "innocuous, inconsequential, minor, or 'nonviolent.'" *Solem v. Helm, supra,* at 316, 103 S. Ct., at 3023 (Burger, C.J., dissenting).

Because burglary is a serious and dangerous felony, the public interest in the prevention and detection of the crime is of compelling importance. Where a police officer has probable cause to arrest a suspected burglar, the use of deadly force as a last resort might well be the only means of apprehending the suspect. With respect to a particular burglary, subsequent investigation simply cannot represent a substitute for immediate apprehension of the criminal suspect at the scene . . . . [Statutes such as Tennessee's] assist the police in apprehending suspected perpetrators of serious crimes and provide notice that a lawful police order to stop and submit to arrest may not be ignored with impunity.

. . . There is no question that the effectiveness of police use of deadly force is arguable and that many States or individual police departments have decided not to authorize it in circumstances similar to those presented here. But it should go without saying that the effectiveness or popularity of a particular police practice does not determine its constitutionality. . . .

Against the strong public interests justifying the conduct at issue here must be weighed the individual interests implicated in the use of deadly force by police officers. The majority declares that "[t]he suspect's fundamental interest in his own life need not be elaborated upon." This blithe assertion hardly provides an adequate substitute for the majority's failure to acknowledge the distinctive manner in which the suspect's interest in his life is even exposed to risk. For purposes of this case, we must recall that the police officer, in the course of investigating a nighttime burglary, had reasonable cause to arrest the suspect and ordered him to halt. The officer's use of force resulted because the suspected burglar refused to heed this command and the officer reasonably believed that there was no means short of firing his weapon to apprehend the suspect. Without questioning the importance of a person's interest in his life, I do not think this interest encompasses a right to flee unimpeded from the scene of a burglary. *Cf. Payton v. New York*, 445 U.S. 573, 617, n. 14, 100 S. Ct. 1371, 1395, n. 14, 63 L. Ed. 2d 639 (1980) (White, J., dissenting) ("[T]he policeman's hands should not be tied merely because of the possibility that the suspect will fail to cooperate with legitimate actions by law enforcement personnel"). The legitimate interests of the suspect in these circumstances are adequately accommodated by the Tennessee statute: to avoid the use of deadly force and the consequent risk to his life, the suspect need merely obey the valid order to halt.

A proper balancing of the interests involved suggests that use of deadly force as a last resort to apprehend a criminal suspect fleeing from the scene of a nighttime burglary is not unreasonable within the meaning of the Fourth Amendment. Admittedly, the events giving rise to this case are in retrospect deeply regrettable. No one can view the death of an unarmed and apparently nonviolent 15-year-old without sorrow, much less disapproval. Nonetheless, the reasonableness of Officer Hymon's conduct for purposes of the Fourth Amendment cannot be evaluated by what later appears to have been a preferable course of police action. The officer pursued a suspect in the darkened backyard of a house that from all indications had just been burglarized. The police officer was not certain whether the suspect was alone or unarmed; nor did he know what had transpired inside the house. He ordered the suspect to halt, and when the suspect refused to obey and attempted to flee into the night, the officer fired his weapon to prevent escape. The reasonableness of this action for purposes of the Fourth Amendment is not determined by the unfortunate nature of this particular case; instead, the question is whether it is constitutionally impermissible for police officers, as a last resort, to shoot a burglary suspect fleeing the scene of the crime.

. . . .

III

. . . .

The Court's silence on critical factors in the decision to use deadly force simply invites second-guessing of difficult police decisions that must be made quickly in the most trying of circumstances. Police are given no guidance for determining which objects, among an array of potentially lethal weapons ranging from guns to knives to baseball bats to rope, will justify the use of deadly force. The Court also declines to outline the additional factors necessary to provide "probable cause" for believing that a suspect "poses a significant threat of death or serious physical injury," when the officer has probable cause to arrest and the suspect refuses to obey an order to halt. . . .

IV

The Court's opinion sweeps broadly to adopt an entirely new standard for the constitutionality of the use of deadly force to apprehend fleeing felons . . . . I cannot accept the majority's creation of a constitutional right to flight for burglary suspects seeking to avoid capture at the scene of the crime. Whatever the constitutional limits on police use of deadly force in order to apprehend a fleeing felon, I do not believe they are exceeded in a case in which a police officer has probable cause to arrest a suspect at the scene of a residential burglary, orders the suspect to halt, and then fires his weapon as a last resort to prevent the suspect's escape into the night. I respectfully dissent.

Notes and Questions

(1) Assume there is probable cause to believe that each of the following fleeing felons committed the crime specified and that it is necessary to use deadly force to prevent each from escaping. Which of them may an officer, after issuing a warning, apprehend by means of deadly force?

(a) The head of a large-scale, national cocaine and heroin distribution conspiracy;

(b) The largest producer and distributor of child pornography in the United States;

(c) A bank robber who verbally threatened the life of a teller, but never displayed a weapon and kept his hand in his coat pocket during the entire robbery;

(d) An accomplice who drove the getaway car for the bank robber in situation (c).

In light of your responses to the preceding situations, what are the arguable problems with the *Garner* majority's standard for the use of deadly force? On balance, is the standard satisfactory?

(2) *Scott v. Harris*, 550 U.S. 372, 127 S. Ct. 1769, 167 L. Ed. 2d 686 (2007), involved a very different situation in which an officer used deadly force to seize a suspect. The Supreme Court concluded that *Garner* did not prescribe a standard designed to govern *all* official uses of deadly force.

When a county deputy attempted to pull Harris over for speeding, he "sped away, initiating a chase . . . at speeds exceeding 85 miles per hour." Upon hearing a radio report, Deputy Scott "joined the pursuit along with other officers." At one point, Harris entered a parking lot and "was nearly boxed in by . . . police vehicles." He "evaded the trap by making a sharp turn, colliding with Scott's police car, . . . and speeding off once again." Thereafter, Deputy "Scott took over as the lead pursuit vehicle. Six minutes and nearly 10 miles after the chase had begun," Scott "applied his push bumper to the rear of [Harris's] vehicle" in an effort to end the chase. This caused Harris to lose control of and crash his vehicle. Harris "was badly injured and rendered a quadriplegic."

Harris sued Deputy Scott and others, alleging that he had been unreasonably seized in violation of his Fourth Amendment rights. Scott moved for summary judgment. The District Court denied the motion and the Court of Appeals affirmed, concluding that the seizure could have been found unreasonable. The Supreme Court granted certiorari and reversed.

The Court acknowledged that on a motion for summary judgment, the "plaintiff's version of the facts" ordinarily must be adopted, but observed that the existence of a videotape of the chase showed Harris's version to be "visible fiction" that was "so utterly discredited by the record that no reasonable jury could have believed him." Consequently, the Court had to "view[] the facts in the light depicted by the videotape."

Deputy Scott did not contest that he had seized Harris and both sides agreed that the "question . . . [was] whether Scott's actions were objectively reasonable." Harris claimed that the standards of *Tennessee v. Garner* governed and that under those standards "Scott's actions were *per se* unreasonable." The Court rejected this contention, observing that "*Garner* did not establish a magical on/off switch that triggers rigid preconditions whenever an officer's actions constitute 'deadly force.' [Instead,] *Garner* was simply an application of the Fourth Amendment's 'reasonableness' test . . . to the use of a particular type of force in a particular situation." According to the Court, the "factors" that the *Garner* Court said "*might have* justified shooting the suspect in that case . . . ha[d] scant applicability to" the "vastly different facts" of *Harris*. Moreover, there was no "easy-to-apply legal test" that governed situations like this. Instead, the Justices had to "slosh [their] way through the factbound morass of 'reasonableness.' Whether or not Scott's actions constituted application of 'deadly force,' all that matter[ed was] whether Scott's actions were reasonable."

To determine reasonableness the Court had to "'balance the nature and quality of the intrusion on the individual's Fourth Amendment interests against the importance of the governmental interests alleged to justify the intrusion.' *United States v. Place*, 462 U.S. 696, 703 (1983)." Specifically, it was necessary to "consider the risk of bodily harm that Scott's actions posed to [Harris] in light of the threat to the public that Scott was trying to eliminate." The videotape showed that Harris "posed an actual and imminent threat to the lives of any pedestrians who might have been present, to other civilian motorists, and to the officers involved." On the other hand, "Scott's actions posed a high likelihood of serious injury or death to" Harris — "though not the near *certainty* of death posed by" shooting a fleeing felon or motorist. In addition, in striking the balance it was "appropriate . . . to take into account not only the number of lives at risk, but also their relative culpability." Harris had "intentionally placed himself and the public in danger by" his unlawful flight "that ultimately produced the choice between two evils that Scott confronted." In contrast, the individuals "who might have been harmed" by Harris "were entirely innocent." In light of these competing interests, the Court had "little difficulty in concluding it was reasonable for Scott to take the action that he did."

The Court was unpersuaded by Harris's contention that the "innocent public" could "equally have been protected, and the tragic accident entirely avoided, if the police had simply ceased their pursuit." Ending the pursuit was not *certain* to eliminate the risk . . . posed to the public." Because the police had "no way to convey convincingly to [Harris] that the chase was off," he might well have "continu[ed] to drive recklessly." In addition, the Justices were "loath to lay down a rule requiring the police to allow fleeing suspects to get away whenever they drive *so recklessly* that they put other people's lives in danger." Such a rule would create "perverse incentives." Instead, the Court adopted "a more sensible rule: A police officer's attempt to terminate a dangerous high-speed car chase that threatens the lives of innocent bystanders does not violate the Fourth Amendment, even when it places the fleeing motorist at risk of serious injury or death." Because the chase "initiated" by Harris "posed a substantial and immediate risk of serious physical injury to others," Deputy "Scott's attempt to terminate [it] by forcing [him] off the road was reasonable." Consequently, summary judgment was appropriate.

Two concurring Justices qualified their agreement with the majority's "more sensible rule." Justice Ginsburg observed that she did "not read [the] decision as articulating a mechanical, *per se* rule," while Justice Breyer expressed "disagree[ment] with the Court insofar as it articulates a *per se* rule." According to him, the Court's "statement" of the governing rule was "too absolute" because the constitutionality of "a high-speed chase . . . may well depend upon more circumstances than the majority's rule reflects." Justice Stevens dissented, asserting that "[w]hether a person's actions" warrant "deadly force is a question of fact best reserved for the jury." In his view, "the Court ha[d] usurped the jury's factfinding function" in this case.

Schmerber v. California

United States Supreme Court

384 U.S. 757, 86 S. Ct. 1826, 16 L. Ed. 2d 908 (1966)

Mr. Justice Brennan delivered the opinion of the Court.

Petitioner was convicted in Los Angeles Municipal Court of the criminal offense of driving an automobile while under the influence of intoxicating liquor. He had been arrested at a hospital while receiving treatment for injuries suffered in an accident involving the automobile that he had apparently been driving. At the direction of a police officer, a blood sample was then withdrawn from petitioner's body by a physician at the hospital. The chemical analysis of this sample revealed a percent by weight of alcohol in his blood at the time of the offense which indicated intoxication, and the report of this analysis was admitted in evidence at the trial. Petitioner objected to receipt of this evidence of the analysis. . . .

. . . .

IV
THE SEARCH AND SEIZURE CLAIM

. . . .

The overriding function of the Fourth Amendment is to protect personal privacy and dignity against unwarranted intrusion by the State. . . .

The values protected by the Fourth Amendment thus substantially overlap those the Fifth Amendment helps to protect. History and precedent have required that we today reject the claim that the Self-Incrimination Clause of the Fifth Amendment requires the human body in all circumstances to be held inviolate against state expeditions seeking evidence of crime. But if compulsory administration of a blood test does not implicate the Fifth Amendment, it plainly involves the broadly conceived reach of a search and seizure under the Fourth Amendment. . . .

Because we are dealing with intrusions into the human body rather than with state interferences with property relationships or private papers — "houses, papers, and effects" — we write on a clean slate.

. . . .

While early cases suggest that there is an unrestricted "right on the part of the government, always recognized under English and American law, to search the person of the accused when legally arrested to discover and seize the fruits or evidences of crime," *Weeks v. United States*, 232 U.S. 383, 392, 34 S. Ct. 341, 344, 58 L. Ed. 2d 652; *People v. Chiagles*, 237 N.Y. 190, 142 N.E. 583 (1923) (Cardozo, J.), the mere fact of a lawful arrest does not end our inquiry. The suggestion of these cases apparently rests on two factors — first, there may be more immediate danger of concealed weapons or of destruction of evidence under the direct control of the accused; second, once a search of the arrested person for weapons is permitted, it would be both impractical and unnecessary to enforcement of the Fourth Amendment's purpose to attempt to confine the search to those objects alone. Whatever the validity of these considerations in general, they have little applicability with respect to searches involving intrusions beyond the body's surface. The interests in human dignity and privacy which the Fourth Amendment protects forbid any such intrusions on the mere chance that desired evidence might be obtained. In the absence of a clear indication that in fact such evidence will be found, these fundamental human interests require law officers to suffer the risk that such evidence may disappear unless there is an immediate search.

Although the facts which established probable cause to arrest in this case also suggested the required relevance and likely success of a test of petitioner's blood for alcohol, the question remains whether the arresting officer was permitted to draw these inferences himself, or was required instead to procure a warrant before proceeding with the test. Search warrants are ordinarily required for searches of dwellings, and, absent an emergency, no less could be required where intrusions into the human body are concerned. . . .

The officer in the present case, however, might reasonably have believed that he was confronted with an emergency, in which the delay necessary to obtain a warrant, under the circumstances, threatened "the destruction of evidence," *Preston v. United States*, 376 U.S. 364, 367, 84 S. Ct. 881, 883, 11 L. Ed. 2d 777. We are told that the percentage of alcohol in the blood begins to diminish shortly after drinking stops, as the body functions to eliminate it from the system. Particularly in a case such as this, where time had to be taken to bring the accused to a hospital and to investigate the scene of the accident, there was no time to seek out a magistrate and secure a warrant. Given these special facts, we conclude that the attempt to secure evidence of blood-alcohol content in this case was an appropriate incident to petitioner's arrest.

Similarly, we are satisfied that the test chosen to measure petitioner's blood-alcohol level was a reasonable one. Extraction of blood samples for testing is a highly effective means of determining the degree to which a person is under the influence of alcohol. Such tests are a commonplace in these days of periodic physical examination and experience with them teaches that the quantity of blood extracted is minimal, and that for most people the procedure involves virtually no risk, trauma, or pain. Petitioner is not one of the few who on grounds of fear, concern for health, or religious scruple might prefer some other means of testing, such as the "breathalyzer" test petitioner refused. We need not decide whether such wishes would have to be respected.

Finally, the record shows that the test was performed in a reasonable manner. Petitioner's blood was taken by a physician in a hospital environment according to accepted medical practices. We are thus not presented with the serious questions which would arise if a search involving use of a medical technique, even of the most rudimentary sort, were made by other than medical personnel or in other than a medical environment — for example, if it were administered by police in the privacy of the stationhouse. To tolerate searches under these conditions might be to invite an unjustified element of personal risk of infection and pain.

We thus conclude that the present record shows no violation of petitioner's right under the Fourth and Fourteenth Amendments to be free of unreasonable searches and seizures. It bears repeating, however, that we reach this judgment only on the facts of the present record. The integrity of an individual's person is a cherished value of our society. That we today hold that the Constitution does not forbid the States' minor intrusions into an individual's body under stringently limited conditions in no way indicates that it permits more substantial intrusions, or intrusions under other conditions.

Affirmed.

[The concurring opinion of MR. JUSTICE HARLAN has been omitted.]

[The dissenting opinion of MR. JUSTICE BLACK has been omitted.]

Notes and Questions

In *McNeely v. Missouri*, 569 U.S. ____, 133 S. Ct. 1552, 185 L. Ed. 2d 696 (2013), the Supreme Court addressed a lower court split in the interpretation of *Schmerber*. One view was that "the natural dissipation of alcohol in the bloodstream establishe[d] a *per se* exigency that suffice[d] on its own to justify an exception to the warrant requirement for nonconsensual blood testing in drunk-driving investigations." According to this understanding of *Schmerber*, officers could always rely on their own assessments of probable cause. There was never a need to secure a search warrant to draw blood in such circumstances. The contrasting understanding was that the search warrant rule presumptively governed drunk-driving investigations and that judges had to determine on a case-by-case basis whether the government had demonstrated a sufficient exigency to justify dispensing with a magistrate's predetermination of probable cause. In *McNeely*, the Justices acknowledged "that as a result of the human body's natural metabolic processes, the alcohol level in a person's blood begins to dissipate once the alcohol is fully absorbed and continues to decline until the alcohol is eliminated." They concluded, however, that this natural process of evidence destruction did not justify a categorical, *per se* exception to the search warrant requirement. Instead, a judge must determine whether the government has shown exigent circumstances in each particular case, based on the totality of relevant circumstances. More specifically, the *McNeely* majority held that officers must obtain a search warrant before a blood sample is drawn "[i]n those drunk-driving investigations where [they] can reasonably obtain a warrant . . . without significantly undermining the efficacy of the search" for evidence of drunk driving. What facts should a judge take into account in determining whether the process of securing a search warrant will "significantly undermin[e] the efficacy" of a blood draw?

Winston v. Lee

United States Supreme Court

470 U.S. 753, 105 S. Ct. 1611, 84 L. Ed. 2d 662 (1985)

JUSTICE BRENNAN delivered the opinion of the Court.

. . . .

I

A

At approximately 1 a.m. on July 18, 1982, Ralph E. Watkinson was closing his shop for the night. As he was locking the door, he observed someone armed with a gun coming toward him from across the street. Watkinson was also armed and when he drew his gun, the other person told him to freeze. Watkinson then fired at the other person, who returned his fire. Watkinson was hit in the legs, while the other individual, who appeared to be wounded in his left side, ran from the scene. The police arrived on the scene shortly thereafter, and Watkinson was taken by ambulance to the emergency room of the Medical College of Virginia (MCV) Hospital.

Approximately 20 minutes later, police officers responding to another call found respondent eight blocks from where the earlier shooting occurred. Respondent was suffering from a gunshot wound to his left chest area and told the police that he had been shot when two individuals attempted to rob him. An ambulance took respondent to the MCV Hospital. Watkinson was still in the MCV emergency room and, when respondent entered that room, said "[t]hat's the man that shot me." After an investigation, the police decided that respondent's story of having been himself the victim of a robbery was untrue and charged respondent with attempted robbery, malicious wounding, and two counts of using a firearm in the commission of a felony.

B

The Commonwealth shortly thereafter moved in state court for an order directing respondent to undergo surgery to remove an object thought to be a bullet lodged under his left collarbone. The court conducted several evidentiary hearings on the motion. At the first hearing, the Commonwealth's expert testified that the surgical procedure would take 45 minutes and would involve a three to four percent chance of temporary nerve damage, a one percent chance of permanent nerve damage, and a one-tenth of one percent chance of death. At the second hearing, the expert testified that on re-examination of respondent, he discovered that the bullet was not "back inside close to the nerves and arteries," as he originally had thought. Instead, he now believed the bullet to be located "just beneath the skin." He testified that the surgery would require an incision of only one and one-half centimeters (slightly more than one-half inch), could be performed under local anesthesia, and would result in "no danger on the basis that there's no general anesthesia employed."

The state trial judge granted the motion to compel surgery. Respondent petitioned the Virginia Supreme Court for a writ of prohibition and/or a writ of habeas corpus, both of which were denied. Respondent then brought an action in the United States District Court for the Eastern District of Virginia to enjoin the pending operation on Fourth Amendment grounds. The court refused to issue a preliminary injunction, holding that respondent's cause had little likelihood of success on the merits. 551 F. Supp. 247, 247–253 (1982).

On October 18, 1982, just before the surgery was scheduled, the surgeon ordered that X rays be taken of respondent's chest. The X rays revealed that the bullet was in fact lodged two and one-half to three centimeters (approximately one inch) deep in muscular tissue in respondent's chest, substantially deeper than had been thought when the state court granted the motion to compel surgery. The surgeon now believed that a general anesthetic would be desirable for medical reasons.

Respondent moved the state trial court for a rehearing based on the new evidence. After holding an evidentiary hearing, the state trial court denied the rehearing and the Virginia Supreme Court affirmed. Respondent then returned to federal court, where he moved to alter or amend the judgment previously entered against him. After an evidentiary hearing, the District Court enjoined the threatened surgery. 551 F. Supp., at 253–261 (supplemental opinion). A divided panel of the Court of Appeals for the Fourth Circuit affirmed. 717 F.2d 888 (1983). We granted certiorari, 466 U.S. 935, 104 S. Ct. 1906, 80 L. Ed. 2d 455 (1984), to consider whether a State may consistently with the Fourth Amendment compel a suspect to undergo surgery of this kind in a search for evidence of a crime.

II

. . . [T]he Fourth Amendment generally protects the "security" of "persons, houses, papers, and effects" against official intrusions up to the point where the community's need for evidence surmounts a specified standard, ordinarily "probable cause . . . ."

A compelled surgical intrusion into an individual's body for evidence, however, implicates expectations of privacy and security of such magnitude that the intrusion may be "unreasonable" even if likely to produce evidence of a crime.

. . . .

The Fourth Amendment neither forbids nor permits all such intrusions; rather, the Amendment's "proper function is to constrain, not against all intrusions as such, but against intrusions which are not justified in the circumstances, or which are made in an improper manner." [*Schmerber*, 384 U.S.] at 768, 86 S. Ct., at 1834.

The reasonableness of surgical intrusions beneath the skin depends on a case-by-case approach, in which the individual's interests in privacy and security are weighed against society's interests in conducting the procedure. In a given case, the question whether the community's need for evidence outweighs the substantial privacy interests at stake is a delicate one admitting of few categorical answers. We believe that *Schmerber*, however, provides the appropriate framework of analysis for such cases.

Schmerber recognized that the ordinary requirements of the Fourth Amendment would be the threshold requirements for conducting this kind of surgical search and seizure. We noted the importance of probable cause. *Id.*, at 768–769, 86 S. Ct., at 1834–1835. And we pointed out: "Search warrants are ordinarily required for searches of dwellings, and, absent an emergency, no less could be required where intrusions into the human body are concerned . . . . The importance of informed, detached and deliberate determinations of the issue whether or not to invade another's body in search of evidence of guilt is indisputable and great." *Id.*, at 770, 86 S. Ct., at 1835.

Beyond these standards, *Schmerber*'s inquiry considered a number of other factors in determining the "reasonableness" of the blood test. A crucial factor in analyzing the magnitude of the intrusion in *Schmerber* is the extent to which the procedure may threaten the safety or health of the individual. "[F]or most people [a blood test] involves virtually no risk, trauma, or pain." *Id.*, at 771, 86 S. Ct., at 1836. Moreover, all reasonable medical precautions were taken and no unusual or untested procedures were employed in *Schmerber;* the procedure was performed "by a physician in a hospital environment according to accepted medical practices." *Id.* Notwithstanding the existence of probable cause, a search for evidence of a crime may be unjustifiable if it endangers the life or health of the suspect.

Another factor is the extent of intrusion upon the individual's dignitary interests in personal privacy and bodily integrity . . . . In noting that a blood test was "a commonplace in these days of periodic physical examinations," 384 U.S., at 771, 86 S. Ct., at 1836, *Schmerber* recognized society's judgment that blood tests do not constitute an unduly extensive imposition on an individual's personal privacy and bodily integrity.

Weighed against these individual interests is the community's interest in fairly and accurately determining guilt or innocence . . . . In *Schmerber,* we concluded that this state interest was sufficient to justify the intrusion, and the compelled blood test was thus "reasonable" for Fourth Amendment purposes.

III

Applying the *Schmerber* balancing test in this case, we believe that the Court of Appeals reached the correct result. The Commonwealth plainly had probable cause to conduct the search. In addition, all parties apparently agree that respondent has had a full measure of procedural protections and has been able fully to litigate the difficult medical and legal questions necessarily involved in analyzing the reasonableness of a surgical incision of this magnitude. Our inquiry therefore must focus on the extent of the intrusion on respondent's privacy interests and on the State's need for the evidence.

The threats to the health or safety of respondent posed by the surgery are the subject of sharp dispute between the parties. . . .

. . . Moreover, there was conflict in the testimony concerning the nature and the scope of the operation. . . .

Both lower courts in this case believed that the proposed surgery, which for purely medical reasons required the use of a general anesthetic, would be an "extensive" intrusion on respondent's personal privacy and bodily integrity. When conducted with the consent of the patient, surgery requiring general anesthesia is not necessarily demeaning or intrusive. In such a case, the surgeon is carrying out the patient's own will concerning the patient's body and the patient's right to privacy is therefore preserved. In this case, however, the Court of Appeals noted that the Commonwealth proposes to take control of respondent's body, to "drug this citizen — not yet convicted of a criminal offense — with narcotics and barbiturates into a state of unconsciousness," and then to search beneath his skin for evidence of a crime. This kind of surgery involves a virtually total divestment of respondent's ordinary control over surgical probing beneath his skin.

The other part of the balance concerns the Commonwealth's need to intrude into respondent's body to retrieve the bullet. The Commonwealth claims to need the bullet to demonstrate that it was fired from Watkinson's gun, which in turn would show that respondent was the robber who confronted Watkinson. However, although we recognize the difficulty of making determinations in advance as to the strength of the case against respondent, petitioners' assertions of a compelling need for the bullet are hardly persuasive. The very circumstances relied on in this case to demonstrate probable cause to believe that evidence will be found tend to vitiate the Commonwealth's need to compel respondent to undergo surgery. The Commonwealth has available substantial additional evidence that respondent was the individual who accosted Watkinson on the night of the robbery. No party in this case suggests that Watkinson's entirely spontaneous identification of respondent at the hospital would be inadmissible. In addition, petitioners can no doubt prove that Watkinson was found a few blocks from Watkinson's store shortly after the incident took place. And petitioners can certainly show that the location of the bullet (under respondent's left collarbone) seems to correlate with Watkinson's report that the robber "jerked" to the left. The fact that the Commonwealth has available such substantial evidence of the origin of the bullet restricts the need for the Commonwealth to compel respondent to undergo the contemplated surgery.

In weighing the various factors in this case, we therefore reach the same conclusion as the courts below. The operation sought will intrude substantially on respondent's protected interests. The medical risks of the operation, although apparently not extremely severe, are a subject of considerable dispute; the very uncertainty militates against finding the operation to be "reasonable." In addition, the intrusion on respondent's privacy interests entailed by the operation can only be characterized as severe. On the other hand, although the bullet may turn out to be useful to the Commonwealth in prosecuting respondent, the Commonwealth has failed to demonstrate a compelling need for it. We believe that in these circumstances the Commonwealth has failed to demonstrate that it would be "reasonable" under the terms of the Fourth Amendment to search for evidence of this crime by means of the contemplated surgery.

IV

. . . Where the Court has found a lesser expectation of privacy, or where the search involves a minimal intrusion on privacy interests, the Court has held that the Fourth Amendment's protections are correspondingly less stringent. Conversely, however, the Fourth Amendment's command that searches be "reasonable" requires that when the State seeks to intrude upon an area in which our society recognizes a significantly heightened privacy interest, a more substantial justification is required to make the search "reasonable." Applying these principles, we hold that the proposed search in this case would be "unreasonable" under the Fourth Amendment.

Affirmed.

Justice Blackmun and Justice Rehnquist concur in the judgment.

[The concurring opinion of Chief Justice Burger has been omitted.]

Notes and Questions

(1) Under what circumstances, if any, would serious surgery of the sort contemplated in *Lee* be constitutional? Why?

(2) What showing is required for officers:

(a) to have medical personnel extract a sample of a suspect's semen to match it against that found at the scene of a sexual assault?

(b) to conduct a visual or manual search of a suspect's "body cavities"?

(3) In *Zurcher v. Stanford Daily*, 436 U.S. 457, 98 S. Ct. 1970, 56 L. Ed. 2d 525 (1978), a university newspaper challenged the search of its newsroom for photographic materials that could have provided evidence of the identities of the perpetrators of assaults upon police officers. The newspaper contended that there were two grounds for concluding that the normally required showings of probable cause and a search warrant were insufficient to protect their interests and, therefore, that Fourth Amendment standards had to be elevated. The first ground was the peril to First Amendment values engendered when law enforcement officers search a newsroom. The second ground was the arguably more serious threat to privacy inherent in the unannounced search of the premises of an "innocent third party" (one who is not suspected of involvement in the crime) for evidence of a crime.

A majority of the Court concluded that neither ground required that Fourth Amendment standards be heightened. It concluded that the norms of probable cause and a search warrant were fully adequate to protect the interests at stake when a newsroom or an innocent third party's premises are searched.

(4) It has also been suggested that probable cause and a search warrant are not enough to justify the search of a private dwelling during nighttime hours. What reasoning would support that contention? *See Gooding v. United States*, 416 U.S. 430, 461–62, 94 S. Ct. 1780, 1796, 40 L. Ed. 2d 250, 270 (1974) (Marshall, J., dissenting).

"Higher than Usual" Problems

5C–1: Detective Wycoff of the Greenwood police observed Garcon sitting in a stolen car. Based on information he had received, Wycoff had probable cause to arrest Garcon for auto theft and burglary. When Wycoff approached, Garcon fled. Following a 20-minute foot chase, Wycoff caught and apprehended Garcon. At the time, Garcon wore only tennis shorts and shoes. Wycoff handcuffed him and placed him in the back of his vehicle. Garcon complained that the handcuffs were cutting off his circulation, so the detective loosened them.

While Wycoff was transporting Garcon to the police station, he freed himself from the handcuffs. Garcon then escaped while the car was stopped at an intersection. As he crossed the intersection, he was struck by a car, but got up and continued his flight. Wycoff chased Garcon through several backyards, down an alley, and over fences. During the chase he fired two shots at Garcon. The second shot struck him on the left side, causing a superficial gunshot wound. Finally, Wycoff apprehended Garcon and took him to the hospital for treatment before transporting him to the police station.

Did Wycoff violate Garcon's constitutional rights?

5C–2: Damon stole a taxicab and drove it to a nearby Taco Bell. Three uniformed police officers quickly surrounded the cab and confronted Damon. Sergeant Eny ordered him out of the cab, but Damon locked all of the doors instead. He then put the car in reverse and slowly backed the cab into Eny's car. He drove forward and to the right, but his escape path was blocked by a utility pole. Standing behind the utility pole was Officer Black.

Damon reversed again, edging the rear of the cab to the left to improve the vehicle's angle with respect to the pole. At that point, the cab was approximately 10 feet from the utility pole. Damon put it into drive and floored the accelerator. The angle now permitted him to clear the pole and drive away.

Officer Black, who had remained behind the pole until Damon had already accelerated forward the second time, then moved out from behind the pole. He jumped into a position directly in front of the moving cab. All three officers opened fire on Damon, killing him. It is not clear how fast the car was moving at the time, but is known that Damon had come to a full stop, had floored the accelerator, and had traveled fewer than 10 feet before he was killed.

Should Damon's estate be awarded damages for violation of his constitutional rights?

5C–3: La Habra police officers received information from a reliable informant that Jagui had unpackaged heroin in the motel room where he lived. The informant stated that Jagui had the equivalent of 10 balloons of heroin. Officers immediately secured a search warrant for Jagui's room and for his person and proceeded to the motel. As they approached the room, Jagui emerged, saw the officers, and appeared to swallow hard. Based on previous experience, the officers were aware that dealers sometimes carried balloons of heroin in their mouths.

The officers searched Jagui's room and person. They discovered narcotics paraphernalia, including a syringe, and empty toy balloons in the room, but found no narcotics. The officers then arrested Jagui for unlawful possession of a syringe. They transported him to the police station.

After arriving at the station, one officer called the community hospital to solicit a doctor's advice concerning medical problems that could result from the presence of balloons of heroin in Jagui's stomach. The doctor suggested bringing Jagui to the hospital. At the hospital, Jagui refused to consent to treatment. He exhibited no symptoms of being under the influence of narcotics. At a physician's suggestion, Jagui's stomach was x-rayed without his consent. The x-ray seemed to show two balloons. The physician then recommended that Jagui be administered syrup of ipe-cac, an emetic solution that induces vomiting.

Officers applied for and obtained a search warrant authorizing the administra-tion of the ipecac. When confronted with the warrant, Jagui drank the syrup. He began regurgitating 20 minutes later, and five balloons of heroin were recovered.

Did the officers violate the Fourth Amendment at any point?

5C–4: After an informant told Detective Hank that Rodrick possessed and sold crack cocaine, officers pulled over Rodrick's vehicle. Sarah, a passenger, told the of-ficers that as they were approaching Rodrick threw a plastic bag containing what she believed to be crack cocaine at her and asked her to conceal it, but that she refused. The officers searched the car and Rodrick, but found nothing. A drug dog alerted on the center console of the car, but no drugs were found. A search of the area where the vehicle was stopped, a two-hour search of the vehicle at the station, and a strip search of Rodrick all yielded nothing.

Rodrick was strip-searched a second time at the station. He was instructed to squat, pull his buttocks apart, and cough, to dislodge anything that may be con-cealed in the anus. Rodrick seemed "evasive, bending only slightly and giving only a faint cough." Strip searches of all inmates in Rodrick's holding cell also turned up no contraband. At this point, Hank offered three options: Rodrick could undergo a third strip search, could be held in a cell with a waterless toilet, or could consent to a rectal x-ray. Rodrick did not consent to any of the options. Believing that the "only place" Rodrick could be concealing the crack was in his rectum, Hank informed Rodrick that he would seek a warrant. At 10:45 p.m., more than seven hours after Rodrick's arrest, a judge issued a search warrant.

The warrant ordered that Rodrick be presented to a "qualified medical technician to examine him for the concealment of controlled substances and to remove said controlled substances from his body in accordance with recognized accepted medi-cal procedure as described in the supporting affidavit." The affidavit stated that the police suspected Rodrick of concealing crack cocaine in his "anal cavity." At the hos-pital, a technician x-rayed Rodrick with a portable machine, but Rodrick's lack of cooperation prevented him from getting "a good picture." Eventually, using a sta-tionary machine, the technician obtained "a useable picture" which showed some-thing that could have been "either a gas pocket or a foreign object." A doctor performed a digital rectal exam on Rodrick, but was unable to determine if there was an object in his rectum.

The hospital's Trauma Medical Director, Dr. Flinn believed that the best next step was a proctoscopic examination, which involved insertion of a proctoscope, an il-luminated tube, into the rectum. The rectum is filled with air, which distends the rectum walls and permits more thorough evaluation of objects within the rectal vault. Two sedatives, Versed and Etomidate, were administered intravenously. Although the sedatives entail some risks of respiratory depression or arrest, the risks are low. Ordinarily, proctoscopic exams are not performed on uncooperative individuals. Other available means of recovering the drugs — a cathartic or an enema — would not have required sedation.

Dr. Flinn was unable to completely visualize the rectal vault due to a "substantial amount of fecal debris," but did see and feel something different from the other contents. He removed the scope, performed a second digital exam, removed a plastic bag from Rodrick's rectum, and gave it to a police officer. The bag contained 9.62 grams of cocaine base. The government indicted Rodrick for possession of crack cocaine with intent to distribute.

Did the searches violate Rodrick's Fourth Amendment rights?

5C–5: Brian Bar was marching in a gay pride parade when he was involved in a scuffle with police during which he bit two officers. Bar was taken into custody and charged with battery and obstructing an officer. Police took him to the hospital for treatment of injuries he sustained during the arrest. While at the hospital, he acknowledged to police that he was gay, but said that he did not have AIDS. The officers asked for permission to take his blood so they could test it for the disease. He refused to consent.

Officers then took him to the police department, where they took a blood sample without his consent. The sample was never tested.

Bar was acquitted of criminal charges. He then sued the police officers for violating his constitutional rights.

Does Bar have a valid claim that his Fourth Amendment rights were violated?

5C–6: Officers Britt and Hart arrested Jonna for DWI, took her to the police station, and informed her that they were going to draw blood. Jonna began to resist by kicking her feet and moving her arms. The officers restrained her feet and left arm with gauze. Britt held down her right arm while Hart drew blood from a vein in her right wrist. The State subsequently charged Jonna with DWI. She filed a pretrial motion to suppress the blood-test results, arguing that the blood draw violated her rights. At a hearing on the motion, Dr. Prince and Officers Hart and Britt testified.

According to Dr. Prince, he had developed a DWI blood-draw program for the Police Department to avoid long waits at the hospital to draw blood from DWI suspects. Officers complete a 14-hour classroom course and must perform a minimum of 50 "sticks" at the ER under the supervision of a blood technician or nurse. The training, which follows accepted medical practice, is equivalent to a hospital blood-draw technician's training. Officers are taught about how certain medications and medical conditions may increase the risks involved in blood draws and are instructed to inquire about medications and conditions. Upon completing the program, officers are certified to perform venipuncture blood draws. They take a bi-annual re-certification course. Dr. Prince established a blood-draw room at the police station — a room that is clean, but not sterile. According to Dr. Prince, a sterile environment is not necessary. Two blood-draw checklists ensure that officers follow the strict protocol. Dr. Prince testified that there is no policy for suspects who resist or fight officers, that a certified officer would be qualified to draw blood from a resistant suspect, and that forcibly taking blood from a suspect is "acceptable." He acknowledged the risks and dangers associated with venipuncture blood draws, noting that it is possible to puncture an artery (remedied by applying pressure until the blood clots), to stick a nerve (which can cause excruciating pain), or to inflict long-term nerve damage.

Officer Hart completed the course, receiving 90% or higher on his exams. He was exempted from doing the 50 sticks and from the re-certification course because of extensive experience as an EMT. At the time of the hearing, he had been an EMT for 16 years and a police officer for six years. Dr. Prince described Officer Hart as "exceptional" at performing venipuncture. Officer Hart testified that he had performed venipunctures as an EMT thousands of times. He asserted that he cleaned the blood-draw room at the start of his shift and again after each use of the room to draw blood. When he drew Jonna's blood, he had adhered to the practices he had learned. He explained his routine manner for drawing blood from suspects and stated that whether he inquires about medical history before drawing blood work "depends on the situation." He stated that he did not know whether Jonna was on blood thinners and admitted that she "may have had a medical condition that he did not know about that could have affected her health" when he drew her blood.

Officer Britt testified that he was also certified as an EMT and that he had completed Dr. Prince's course. He had performed approximately 125 to 130 blood draws and had observed around 150. He reported that the protocol when a suspect fights with an officer is to use as little force as possible to restrain the suspect. According to Officer Britt, jail personnel took a full medical history on Jonna before the blood draw, but he did not review it.

Should the judge grant Jonna's motion to suppress?

5C–7: On September 15, a fight occurred in Des Moines. Witnesses reported to officers that Jerry Song, a participant in the fight, was armed with a semi-automatic pistol. Later, when officers approached Song, he placed some small objects into his mouth and fled. When the officers gave chase and apprehended Song, he began to swallow the objects. The officers were able to see several small pieces of a rock-like substance in Song's mouth that appeared to them to be crack cocaine. The officers instructed Song to spit out the contents of his mouth, but Song refused and continued to try to swallow the objects. The officers again attempted to remove the objects from his mouth but were unsuccessful.

After he swallowed the objects, Song admitted to the officers that they had been crack cocaine. The officers then took him to Broadlawns Hospital and requested that medical personnel pump his stomach. The stomach pumping resulted in the recovery of crack.

Did any of the officers' actions violate the Fourth Amendment?

5C–8: At approximately 10:40 p.m., Officer Mills pulled Jamie over after seeing him drive at a high rate of speed and fail to stop at two stop signs. Mills detected an odor of alcohol and observed signs of intoxication—bloodshot eyes and slurred speech. He performed a series of field sobriety tests, which Jamie failed, and administered a portable breath test, which registered a reading of 0.07%. After Jamie refused Officer Mills's request to submit to a chemical test, Mills arrested Jamie and obtained a search warrant. The warrant provided: "You are hereby authorized and ordered with the necessary and proper assistance to obtain and remove a blood and urine sample from Jamie." Officer Mills had sought a warrant for both blood and urine samples because he was taught that in an OWI case the Department of Toxicology needed both specimens when completing toxicology kits. The Department does preliminary testing on the urine to have an idea of what to test for in the blood. This helps avoid using up the blood sample in the process of trying to figure out which substances might test positive.

Officer Mills drove Jamie to the county hospital at 12:34 a.m. He took Jamie to the registration desk and presented the search warrant to hospital personnel. At 1:05 a.m., Jamie voluntarily provided a blood sample. Around this time, Officer Lane arrived at the hospital to assist Officer Mills. Mills asked Jamie to provide a urine sample, but Jamie was either unable or unwilling to do so. According to Mills, Jamie responded "that he wasn't going to give a sample and that I could do what I had to do." Jamie claims that he "did not refuse. I just said that I didn't have to go right then. I told him several times I didn't have to go because he scared me."

Officer Mills instructed hospital personnel to take a urine sample from Jamie by catheterization. According to Nurse Walton, at that point she asked Jamie, "Why don't you just urinate?" and he replied, "Because I don't want to." At 1:35 a.m., Officers Mills and Lane took Jamie to bed number nine in the emergency room. Curtains were pulled around the bed to protect Jamie's privacy. Mills handcuffed Jamie to the bed, and the two officers grabbed his ankles to restrain him "so he wouldn't kick the nurses." Jamie resisted the procedure, telling Nurse Walton that he did not want to be catheterized.

Nurse Walton then pulled down Jamie's pants, exposing his genitals, put on sterile gloves and cleansed Jamie's penis. She prepared a straight size 16 Foley catheter by applying lubrication and attempted to insert it into Jamie's penis. Jamie informed Nurse Walton that he had an enlarged prostrate. For this reason and because of his failure to cooperate, Walton removed the catheter and prepared a Coude catheter, which is smaller and can pass through an enlarged prostrate. She completed the catheterization procedure, obtaining a urine specimen in roughly two minutes. Jamie claims that the procedure was painful, that it felt "as if somebody took a burning hot coal and stuck it up my penis." After the procedure, without further medical examination, Jamie was discharged from the hospital into police custody. He was subsequently charged with operating a motor vehicle under the influence.

Did the officers obtain Jamie's urine sample in violation of the Fourth Amendment?

5C–9: A man suspected that drug selling was taking place in his neighborhood. He called the police to report that every day, from 4:00 p.m. until 3:00 a.m., a black male parked a gray car in the driveway of 555 Fifth Street. While Officer Mine and three other officers were conducting surveillance at the location, the car drove away. They followed, but lost sight of the car. Soon after they returned to the site, the gray car again pulled into the driveway of 555 Fifth Street. A black male, Eunice Band, was in the driver's seat.

The officers approached the car. One of them recognized Band from a past incident involving a firearm. Band ignored repeated commands from the officers to "show your hands." Instead, he lowered his hands and placed them inside his underwear. He then lowered his head, raised his cupped hands to his lips, and appeared to place something in his mouth. When Band removed his hands from his face there was a very large lump in his left cheek. The officers took Band from his car, placed him on the ground, and handcuffed him. They instructed him to spit out the contents of his mouth. When Band refused, the officers arrested him for obstruction and resisting a police officer and took him to jail.

While one of the officers completed an application for a warrant to search Band's body, he was placed in a padded isolation cell. Before long, other officers saw Band start to sweat and twitch and saw his eyes begin to flutter and roll back. The bulge in his cheek had gotten smaller. Thinking that Band might be having a seizure, officers summoned an ambulance. During the trip to the hospital, Band displayed seizure-like symptoms.

At the hospital, after informing Band of the dangers presented by the foreign object in his mouth, Dr. Grave and others attempted to pry his mouth open with a ceramic spoon. This method failed and was abandoned for fear of damaging Band's teeth and gums. A judge had issued a search warrant approximately 10 minutes after Band had arrived at the hospital. Dr. Graves informed him of the warrant and told him that if he did not open his mouth drugs would be administered to render him unconscious. Band still did not open his mouth.

Dr. Grave then administered anesthesia to Band through an IV that had previously been inserted into his arm. When his mouth relaxed, the doctor opened it and removed 20 grams of crack cocaine in plastic baggies. As a result of the anesthesia, Band stopped breathing. Dr. Grave used a bag and mask to force breathing until he began breathing on his own. When Band recovered, he was taken back to jail. He was indicted for possession of crack cocaine with intent to distribute it.

Were Band's Fourth Amendment rights violated?

5C–10: Deputy Sheriff Rodney observed a motorcycle driven by Gerald crossing double yellow lines while passing a vehicle on a curve. Rodney activated his blue flashing lights and siren in an attempt to pull Gerald over, but Gerald did not stop. Instead, he went around a second curve — again in the opposite lane of traffic — running Dorothy White off the road. Deputy Rodney caught up with Gerald at an intersection. Gerald took off again, passing yet another vehicle by crossing over double yellow lines. He then turned left onto Farm Road. At that point, the motorcycle and Rodney's patrol car made brief contact. It is unclear who hit whom. One witness reported that when Gerald "made his left turn, he ran through a ditch . . . came back out toward the road and ran into the side of the cop car, knocking the mirror loose from the door." Other witnesses, however, asserted that Rodney intentionally struck the back of Gerald's motorcycle. After the collision, Gerald took off again, running a stop sign while swerving around a stopped van.

Deputy Jerry, who heard a radio report, joined the pursuit. In an effort to stop Gerald, Jerry parked his vehicle in the center of the two-lane road, directly in Gerald's path, and got out of his patrol car. Gerald swerved around Deputy Jerry and sped away. Gerald then turned onto Highway 64, running another stop sign, and causing several motorists to slow down quickly. The traffic on Highway 64 was fairly heavy. Neither Gerald nor Deputy Rodney exceeded the 55-mile-per-hour speed limit.

Gerald next made a right hand turn onto Shepherd Road and Deputy Rodney followed. A few seconds after the vehicles had turned, Rodney's car and Gerald's motorcycle collided for the second time. The motorcycle was knocked off the road and into an embankment where the patrol car ran over it. Gerald was pronounced dead on the scene. According to Deputy Rodney, the collision occurred when Gerald lost control of his motorcycle, went into a skid directly in front of him and decelerated rapidly. Rodney asserts that he slammed on his brakes and swerved to miss Gerald, but was unable to avoid a collision. There is some evidence, however, that Gerald never lost control until Deputy Rodney intentionally rammed the rear of his motorcycle.

Gerald's estate filed a civil suit against Deputy Rodney, claiming that he caused Gerald's death by conduct that violated the Fourth Amendment.

Does this claim have merit?

Selected Bibliography

Ronald J. Bacigal, *Dodging a Bullet, But Opening Old Wounds in Fourth Amendment Jurisprudence,* 16 Seton Hall L. Rev. 597 (1986)

George C. Edwards, *The Shot in the Back Case:* Tennessee v. Garner, 14 N.Y.U. Rev. L. & Soc. Change 733 (1986)

James J. Fyfe, Tennessee v. Garner: *The Issue Not Addressed,* 14 N.Y.U. Rev. L. & Soc. Change 721 (1986)

Michael R. Smith, *Police Use of Deadly Force: How Courts and Policy — Makers Have Misapplied* Tennessee v. Garner, 7 Kan. J.L. & Pub. Pol'y 100 (1998)

H. Richard Uviller, *Seizure by Gunshot: The Riddle of the Fleeing Felon*, 14 N.Y.U. Rev. L. & Soc. Change 705 (1986)

Silas J. Wasserstrom, *The Court's Turn Toward a General Reasonableness Interpretation of the Fourth Amendment*, 27 Am. Crim. L. Rev. 119 (1989)

Steven L. Winter, Tennessee v. Garner *and the Democratic Practice of Judicial Review*, 14 N.Y.U. Rev. L. & Soc. Change 679 (1986)

Part II
Entrapment

Chapter 6

Entrapment and Related Defenses

Introductory Note

The entrapment defense does not stem from the Federal Constitution. The Supreme Court first adopted the defense as a matter of federal law in *Sorrells v. United States*, 287 U.S. 435, 53 S. Ct. 210, 77 L. Ed. 413 (1932). The *Sorrells* Court's basis for recognizing the entrapment defense was its interpretation of Congressional policy. It concluded that the purposes of the criminal law required that federal criminal statutes be interpreted to allow this defense. Since *Sorrells*, some version of the entrapment defense has been created by legislation or judicial decision in all 50 states.

As the cases in this Chapter suggest, the *Sorrells* Court's view that the entrapment defense is required by statutory construction has been challenged. The major competing view is that the entrapment defense is based on a concern that government agents not engage in improper conduct. The content of the entrapment defense will naturally depend to some extent on the basis for accepting it. In reading the cases in this Chapter, students should form their own judgments concerning the appropriate justification.

Although the entrapment defense is not constitutionally based, related defenses have been derived from the Due Process Clauses of the Fifth and Fourteenth Amendments. In *Raley v. Ohio*, 360 U.S. 423, 79 S. Ct. 1257, 3 L. Ed. 2d 1344 (1959), and *Cox v. Louisiana*, 379 U.S. 559, 85 S. Ct. 476, 13 L. Ed. 2d 487 (1965), the Court reversed, on due process grounds, convictions of defendants who had been induced to commit criminal acts by representations from government officials that the acts were lawful. Lower courts have held that government agents' encouragement of or participation in criminal activity can also provide the basis for a due process defense in other situations. The Supreme Court's view of these due process defenses is presented in *United States v. Russell*, 411 U.S. 423, 93 S. Ct. 1637, 36 L. Ed. 2d 366 (1973), and *Hampton v. United States*, 425 U.S. 484, 96 S. Ct. 1646, 48 L. Ed. 2d 113 (1976). In evaluating these cases, students should consider what, if any, limits the Due Process Clause should impose on governmental efforts to induce defendants to commit crimes.

Sherman v. United States

United States Supreme Court

356 U.S. 369, 78 S. Ct. 819, 2 L. Ed. 2d 848 (1958)

MR. CHIEF JUSTICE WARREN delivered the opinion of the Court.

The issue before us is whether petitioner's conviction should be set aside on the ground that as a matter of law the defense of entrapment was established. Petitioner was convicted under an indictment charging three sales of narcotics in violation of 21 U.S.C. § 174. A previous conviction had been reversed on account of improper instructions as to the issue of entrapment. In the second trial, as in the first, petitioner's defense was a claim of entrapment: an agent of the Federal Government induced him to take part in illegal transactions when otherwise he would not have done so.

In late August 1951, Kalchinian, a government informer, first met petitioner at a doctor's office where apparently both were being treated to be cured of narcotics addiction. Several accidental meetings followed, either at the doctor's office or at the pharmacy where both filled their prescriptions from the doctor. From mere greetings, conversation progressed to a discussion of mutual experiences and problems, including their attempts to overcome addiction to narcotics. Finally Kalchinian asked petitioner if he knew of a good source of narcotics. He asked petitioner to supply him with a source because he was not responding to treatment. From the first, petitioner tried to avoid the issue. Not until after a number of repetitions of the request, predicated on Kalchinian's presumed suffering, did petitioner finally acquiesce. Several times thereafter he obtained a quantity of narcotics which he shared with Kalchinian. Each time petitioner told Kalchinian that the total cost of narcotics he obtained was twenty-five dollars and that Kalchinian owed him fifteen dollars. The informer thus bore the cost of his share of the narcotics plus the taxi and other expenses necessary to obtain the drug. After several such sales Kalchinian informed agents of the Bureau of Narcotics that he had another seller for them. On three occasions during November 1951, government agents observed petitioner give narcotics to Kalchinian in return for money supplied by the Government.

At the trial the factual issue was whether the informer had convinced an otherwise unwilling person to commit a criminal act or whether petitioner was already predisposed to commit the act and exhibited only the natural hesitancy of one acquainted with the narcotics trade. The issue of entrapment went to the jury, and a conviction resulted. Petitioner was sentenced to imprisonment for ten years. The Court of Appeals for the Second Circuit affirmed. We granted certiorari.

In *Sorrells v. United States*, 287 U.S. 435, 53 S. Ct. 210, 77 L. Ed. 413, this Court firmly recognized the defense of entrapment in the federal courts. The intervening years have in no way detracted from the principles underlying that decision. The function of law enforcement is the prevention of crime and the apprehension of criminals. Manifestly, that function does not include the manufacturing of crime. Criminal activity is such that stealth and strategy are necessary weapons in the arsenal of the police officer. However, "A different question is presented when the criminal design originates with the officials of the Government, and they implant in the mind of an innocent person the disposition to commit the alleged offense and induce its commission in order that they may prosecute." 287 U.S. at 442, 53 S. Ct. at 212–13. Then stealth and strategy become as objectionable police methods as the coerced confession and the unlawful search. Congress could not have intended that its statutes were to be enforced by tempting innocent persons into violations.

However, the fact that government agents "merely afford opportunities or facilities for the commission of the offense does not" constitute entrapment. Entrapment occurs only when the criminal conduct was "the product of the *creative* activity" of law-enforcement officials. (Emphasis supplied.) *See* 287 U.S. at 441, 451, 53 S. Ct. at 212, 216. To determine whether entrapment has been established, a line must be drawn between the trap for the unwary innocent and the trap for the unwary criminal. The principles by which the courts are to make this determination were outlined in *Sorrells.* On the one hand, at trial the accused may examine the conduct of the government agent; and on the other hand, the accused will be subjected to an "appropriate and searching inquiry into his own conduct and predisposition" as bearing on his claim of innocence. *See* 287 U.S. at 451, 53 S. Ct. at 216.

We conclude from the evidence that entrapment was established as a matter of law. In so holding, we are not choosing between conflicting witnesses, nor judging credibility. Aside from recalling Kalchinian, who was the Government's witness, the defense called no witnesses. We reach our conclusion from the undisputed testimony of the prosecution's witnesses.

It is patently clear that petitioner was induced by Kalchinian. The informer himself testified that, believing petitioner to be undergoing a cure for narcotics addiction, he nonetheless sought to persuade petitioner to obtain for him a source of narcotics. In Kalchinian's own words we are told of the accidental, yet recurring, meetings, the ensuing conversations concerning mutual experiences in regard to narcotics addiction, and then of Kalchinian's resort to sympathy. One request was not enough, for Kalchinian tells us that additional ones were necessary to overcome, first, petitioner's refusal, then his evasiveness, and then his hesitancy in order to achieve capitulation. Kalchinian not only procured a source of narcotics but apparently also induced petitioner to return to the habit. Finally, assured of a catch, Kalchinian informed the authorities so that they could close the net. The Government cannot disown Kalchinian and insist it is not responsible for his actions. Although he was not being paid, Kalchinian was an active government informer who had but recently been the instigator of at least two other prosecutions. Undoubtedly the impetus for such achievements was the fact that in 1951 Kalchinian was himself under criminal charges for illegally selling narcotics and had not yet been sentenced.[3] It makes no difference that the

---

3. Q. But you had made a promise, an agreement, though, to cooperate with the Federal Bureau of Narcotics before you received a suspended sentence from the court?

    A. [Kalchinian]. I had promised to cooperate in 1951.

sales for which petitioner was convicted occurred after a series of sales. They were not independent acts subsequent to the inducement but part of a course of conduct which was the product of the inducement. In his testimony the federal agent in charge of the case admitted that he never bothered to question Kalchinian about the way he had made contact with petitioner. The Government cannot make such use of an informer and then claim disassociation through ignorance.

The Government sought to overcome the defense of entrapment by claiming that petitioner evinced a "ready complaisance" to accede to Kalchinian's request. Aside from a record of past convictions, which we discuss in the following paragraph, the Government's case is unsupported. There is no evidence that petitioner himself was in the trade. When his apartment was searched after arrest, no narcotics were found. There is no significant evidence that petitioner even made a profit on any sale to Kalchinian. The Government's characterization of petitioner's hesitancy to Kalchinian's request as the natural wariness of the criminal cannot fill the evidentiary void.

The Government's additional evidence in the second trial to show that petitioner was ready and willing to sell narcotics should the opportunity present itself was petitioner's record of two past narcotics convictions. In 1942 petitioner was convicted of illegally selling narcotics; in 1946 he was convicted of illegally possessing them. However, a nine-year-old sales conviction and a five-year-old possession conviction are insufficient to prove petitioner had a readiness to sell narcotics at the time Kalchinian approached him, particularly when we must assume from the record he was trying to overcome the narcotics habit at the time.

The case at bar illustrates an evil which the defense of entrapment is designed to overcome. The government informer entices someone attempting to avoid narcotics not only into carrying out an illegal sale but also into returning to the habit of use. Selecting the proper time, the informer then tells the government agent. The set-up is accepted by the agent without even a question as to the manner in which the informer encountered the seller. Thus the Government plays on the weaknesses of an innocent party and beguiles him into committing crimes which he otherwise would not have attempted. Law enforcement does not require methods such as this.

It has been suggested that in overturning this conviction we should reassess the doctrine of entrapment according to principles announced in the separate opinion of Mr. Justice Roberts in *Sorrells v. United States*, 287 U.S. 435, 453, 53 S. Ct. 210, 217, 77 L. Ed. 413. To do so would be to decide the case on grounds rejected by the majority in *Sorrells* and, so far as the record shows, not raised here or below by the parties before us. We do not ordinarily decide issues not presented by the parties and there is good reason not to vary that practice in this case.

Q. And that was before your sentence?

A. Yes, that was before my sentence.

Kalchinian received a suspended sentence in 1952 after a statement by the United States Attorney to the Judge that he had been cooperative with the Government.

At least two important issues of law enforcement and trial procedure would have to be decided without the benefit of argument by the parties, one party being the Government. Mr. Justice Roberts asserted that although the defendant could claim that the Government had induced him to commit the crime, the Government could not reply by showing that the defendant's criminal conduct was due to his own readiness and not to the persuasion of government agents. The handicap thus placed on the prosecution is obvious. Furthermore, it was the position of Mr. Justice Roberts that the factual issue of entrapment — now limited to the question of what the government agents did — should be decided by the judge, not the jury. Not only was this rejected by the Court in *Sorrells*, but where the issue has been presented to them, the Courts of Appeals have since *Sorrells* unanimously concluded that unless it can be decided as a matter of law, the issue of whether a defendant has been entrapped is for the jury as part of its function of determining the guilt or innocence of the accused.

To dispose of this case on the ground suggested would entail both overruling a leading decision of this Court and brushing aside the possibility that we would be creating more problems than we would supposedly be solving.

The judgment of the Court of Appeals is reversed and the case is remanded to the District Court with instructions to dismiss the indictment.

Reversed and remanded.

Mr. Justice Frankfurter, whom Mr. Justice Douglas, Mr. Justice Harlan, and Mr. Justice Brennan join, concurring in the result.

Although agreeing with the Court that the undisputed facts show entrapment as a matter of law, I reach this result by a route different from the Court's.

. . . .

It is surely sheer fiction to suggest that a conviction cannot be had when a defendant has been entrapped by government officers or informers because "Congress could not have intended that its statutes were to be enforced by tempting innocent persons into violations." In these cases raising claims of entrapment, the only legislative intention that can with any show of reason be extracted from the statute is the intention to make criminal precisely the conduct in which the defendant has engaged. That conduct includes all the elements necessary to constitute criminality. Without compulsion and "knowingly," where that is requisite, the defendant has violated the statutory command. If he is to be relieved from the usual punitive consequences, it is on no account because he is innocent of the offense described. In these circumstances, conduct is not less criminal because the result of temptation, whether the tempter is a private person or government agent or informer.

The courts refuse to convict an entrapped defendant, not because his conduct falls outside the proscription of the statute, but because, even if his guilt be admitted, the methods employed on behalf of the Government to bring about conviction cannot be countenanced. As Mr. Justice Holmes said in *Olmstead v. United States*, 277 U.S. 438, 470, 48 S. Ct. 564, 569, 72 L. Ed. 944 (dissenting), in another connection, "It is desirable that criminals should be detected, and to that end that all available evidence should be used. It also is desirable that the government should not itself foster and pay for other crimes, when they are the means by which the evidence is to be obtained. . . . [F]or my part I think it a less [sic] evil that some criminals should escape than that the government should play an ignoble part." Insofar as they are used as instrumentalities in the administration of criminal justice, the federal courts have an obligation to set their face against enforcement of the law by lawless means or means that violate rationally vindicated standards of justice, and to refuse to sustain such methods by effectuating them. They do this in the exercise of a recognized jurisdiction to formulate and apply "proper standards for the enforcement of the federal criminal law in the federal courts," *McNabb v. United States*, 318 U.S. 332, 341, 63 S. Ct. 608, 613, 87 L. Ed. 819, an obligation that goes beyond the conviction of the particular defendant before the court. Public confidence in the fair and honorable administration of justice, upon which ultimately depends the rule of law, is the transcending value at stake.

The formulation of these standards does not in any way conflict with the statute the defendant has violated, or involve the initiation of a judicial policy disregarding or qualifying that framed by Congress. A false choice is put when it is said that either the defendant's conduct does not fall within the statute or he must be convicted. The statute is wholly directed to defining and prohibiting the substantive offense concerned and expresses no purpose, either permissive or prohibitory, regarding the police conduct that will be tolerated in the detection of crime. A statute prohibiting the sale of narcotics is as silent on the question of entrapment as it is on the admissibility of illegally obtained evidence. It is enacted, however, on the basis of certain presuppositions concerning the established legal order and the role of the courts within that system in formulating standards for the administration of criminal justice when Congress itself has not specifically legislated to that end. Specific statutes are to be fitted into an antecedent legal system.

It might be thought that it is largely an academic question whether the court's finding a bar to conviction derives from the statute or from a supervisory jurisdiction over the administration of criminal justice; under either theory substantially the same considerations will determine whether the defense of entrapment is sustained. But to look to a statute for guidance in the application of a policy not remotely within the contemplation of Congress at the time of its enactment is to distort analysis. It is to run the risk, furthermore, that the court will shirk the responsibility that is necessarily in its keeping, if Congress is truly silent, to accommodate the dangers of overzealous law enforcement and civilized methods adequate to counter the ingenuity of modern criminals. The reasons that actually underlie the defense of entrapment can too easily be lost sight of in the pursuit of a wholly fictitious congressional intent.

The crucial question, not easy to answer, to which the court must direct itself is whether the police conduct revealed in the particular case falls below standards, to which common feelings respond, for the proper use of governmental power. For answer it is wholly irrelevant to ask if the "intention" to commit the crime originated with the defendant or government officers, or if the criminal conduct was the product of "the creative activity" of law-enforcement officials. Yet in the present case the Court repeats and purports to apply these unrevealing tests. Of course in every case of this kind the intention that the particular crime be committed originates with the police, and without their inducement the crime would not have occurred. But it is perfectly clear from such decisions as the decoy letter cases in this Court, *e.g., Grimm v. United States*, 156 U.S. 604, 15 S. Ct. 470, 39 L. Ed. 550, where the police in effect simply furnished the opportunity for the commission of the crime, that this is not enough to enable the defendant to escape conviction.

The intention referred to, therefore, must be a general intention or predisposition to commit, whenever the opportunity should arise, crimes of the kind solicited, and in proof of such a predisposition evidence has often been admitted to show the defendant's reputation, criminal activities, and prior disposition. The danger of prejudice in such a situation, particularly if the issue of entrapment must be submitted to the jury and disposed of by a general verdict of guilty or innocent, is evident. The defendant must either forego the claim of entrapment or run the substantial risk that, in spite of instructions, the jury will allow a criminal record or bad reputation to weigh in its determination of guilt of the specific offense of which he stands charged. Furthermore, a test that looks to the character and predisposition of the defendant rather than the conduct of the police loses sight of the underlying reason for the defense of entrapment. No matter what the defendant's past record and present inclinations to criminality, or the depths to which he has sunk in the estimation of society, certain police conduct to ensnare him into further crime is not to be tolerated by an advanced society. And in the present case it is clear that the Court in fact reverses the conviction because of the conduct of the informer Kalchinian, and not because the Government has failed to draw a convincing picture of petitioner's past criminal conduct. Permissible police activity does not vary according to the particular defendant concerned; surely if two suspects have been solicited at the same time in the same manner, one should not go to jail simply because he has been convicted before and is said to have a criminal disposition. No more does it vary according to the suspicions, reasonable or unreasonable, of the police concerning the defendant's activities. Appeals to sympathy, friendship, the possibility of exorbitant gain, and so forth, can no more be tolerated when directed against a past offender than against an ordinary law-abiding citizen. A contrary view runs afoul of fundamental principles of equality under law, and would espouse the notion that when dealing with the criminal classes anything goes. The possibility that no matter what his past crimes and general disposition the defendant might not have committed the particular crime unless confronted with inordinate inducements, must not be ignored. Past crimes do not forever outlaw the criminal and open him to police practices, aimed at securing his repeated conviction, from which the ordinary citizen is protected. The whole ameliorative hopes of modern penology and prison administration strongly counsel against such a view.

This does not mean that the police may not act so as to detect those engaged in criminal conduct and ready and willing to commit further crimes should the occasion arise. Such indeed is their obligation. It does mean that in holding out inducements they should act in such a manner as is likely to induce to the commission of crime only these persons and not others who would normally avoid crime and through self-struggle resist ordinary temptations. This test shifts attention from the record and predisposition of the particular defendant to the conduct of the police and the likelihood, objectively considered, that it would entrap only those ready and willing to commit crime. It is as objective a test as the subject matter permits, and will give guidance in regulating police conduct that is lacking when the reasonableness of police suspicions must be judged or the criminal disposition of the defendant retrospectively appraised. It draws directly on the fundamental intuition that led in the first instance to the outlawing of "entrapment" as a prosecutorial instrument. The power of government is abused and directed to an end for which it was not constituted when employed to promote rather than detect crime and to bring about the downfall of those who, left to themselves, might well have obeyed the law. Human nature is weak enough and sufficiently beset by temptations without government adding to them and generating crime.

What police conduct is to be condemned, because likely to induce those not otherwise ready and willing to commit crime, must be picked out from case to case as new situations arise involving different crimes and new methods of detection. The *Sorrells* case involved persistent solicitation in the face of obvious reluctance, and appeals to sentiments aroused by reminiscences of experiences as companions in arms in the World War. Particularly reprehensible in the present case was the use of repeated requests to overcome petitioner's hesitancy, coupled with appeals to sympathy based on mutual experiences with narcotics addiction. Evidence of the setting in which the inducement took place is of course highly relevant in judging its likely effect, and the court should also consider the nature of the crime involved, its secrecy and difficulty of detection, and the manner in which the particular criminal business is usually carried on.

As Mr. Justice Roberts convincingly urged in the *Sorrells* case, such a judgment, aimed at blocking off areas of impermissible police conduct, is appropriate for the court and not the jury. "The protection of its own functions and the preservation of the purity of its own temple belongs only to the court. It is the province of the court and of the court alone to protect itself and the government from such prostitution of the criminal law. The violation of the principles of justice by the entrapment of the unwary into crime should be dealt with by the court no matter by whom or at what stage of the proceedings the facts are brought to its attention." Equally important is the consideration that a jury verdict, although it may settle the issue of entrapment in the particular case, cannot give significant guidance for official conduct for the future. Only the court, through the gradual evolution of explicit standards in accumulated precedents, can do this with the degree of certainty that the wise administration of criminal justice demands.

Notes and Questions

(1) The majority opinion asserts that "Congress could not have intended that its statutes were to be enforced by tempting innocent persons into violations." In what sense was Sherman an innocent person? If Kalchinian had not been a government agent, would Sherman have any defense to the charge of selling narcotics to Kalchinian?

(2) On what basis does the Court conclude that Kalchinian was a government agent? What should be the criteria for making this determination? Should Kalchinian be treated as a government agent even if he was not encouraged by any government official to become involved in drug transactions or to report them to the police? The Model Penal Code provisions provide that for purposes of the entrapment defense a government agent will include "[a] public law enforcement official or a person acting in cooperation with such an official." Model Penal Code § 2.13. The comments to this provision state that a person such as Kalchinian, who is cooperating with the government "in the hope that cooperation will lighten punishment," must be treated as a government agent. Is this proper?

(3) What is the underlying basis for the entrapment defense? Is it a concern for protecting "innocent" persons? A concern for controlling certain types of police conduct? A concern for protecting the integrity of the courts? Or some combination of these concerns? For commentators discussing this question, see Jonathan C. Carlson, *The Act Requirement and the Foundations of the Entrapment Defense*, 73 Va. L. Rev. 1011, 1023–52 (1987); Louis Michael Seidman, *The Supreme Court, Entrapment and Our Criminal Justice Dilemma*, 1981 Sup. Ct. Rev. 111, 127–46; Roger C. Park, *The Entrapment Controversy*, 60 Minn. L. Rev. 163, 240–43 (1976).

(4) The majority's test focuses on whether the defendant was predisposed to commit the crime. Judge Learned Hand, who wrote the opinion for the lower court in *Sherman*, had previously asserted that a defendant's predisposition to commit a crime may be shown by his "ready complaisance." Judge Hand had added, however, that he did "not wish to commit [the court] to the doctrine that mere readiness is enough" to establish predisposition. *United States v. Becker*, 62 F.2d 1007, 1008–09 (2d Cir. 1933). Should mere readiness to commit the crime ever be enough to establish predisposition? Assuming readiness to commit the crime sometimes is enough, why wasn't it enough in *Sherman*? In what other situations will the defendant be able to establish entrapment as a matter of law despite evidence that he voluntarily committed the crime charged?

(5) Justice Frankfurter's entrapment test has been called the "objective" or "hypothetical person" test. About 10 states and the Model Penal Code have adopted some variation of this test. How does this test differ from the one applied by the *Sherman* majority? How often will the two tests lead to different results? Which test is preferable? For discussions of these and related issues, see Seidman, *supra,* 1981 Sup. Ct. Rev. at 117–27; Park, *supra,* 60 Minn. L. Rev. at 171–84.

(6) In *Mathews v. United States*, 485 U.S. 58, 108 S. Ct. 883, 99 L. Ed. 2d 54 (1988), the Court held that "even if the defendant denies one or more elements of the crime, he is entitled to an entrapment instruction whenever there is sufficient evidence from which a reasonable jury could find entrapment." Is it inconsistent for a defendant to deny one or more elements of the crime and yet claim entrapment? In what types of cases would defendants be likely to take these seemingly contradictory positions?

United States v. Russell

United States Supreme Court

411 U.S. 423, 93 S. Ct. 1637, 36 L. Ed. 2d 366 (1973)

MR. JUSTICE REHNQUIST delivered the opinion of the Court.

Respondent Richard Russell was charged in three counts of a five-count indictment returned against him and codefendants John and Patrick Connolly. After a jury trial in the District Court, in which his sole defense was entrapment, respondent was convicted on all three counts of having unlawfully manufactured and processed methamphetamine ("speed") and of having unlawfully sold and delivered that drug in violation of 21 U.S.C. §§ 331(q)(1), (2), 360a(a), (b) (1964 ed., Supp. V). He was sentenced to concurrent terms of two years in prison for each offense, the terms to be suspended on the condition that he spend six months in prison and be placed on probation for the following three years. On appeal, the United States Court of Appeals for the Ninth Circuit, one judge dissenting, reversed the conviction solely for the reason that an undercover agent supplied an essential chemical for manufacturing the methamphetamine which formed the basis of respondent's conviction. The court concluded that as a matter of law "a defense to a criminal charge may be founded upon an intolerable degree of governmental participation in the criminal enterprise." 459 F.2d 671, 673 (1972). We granted certiorari, and now reverse that judgment.

There is little dispute concerning the essential facts in this case. On December 7, 1969, Joe Shapiro, an undercover agent for the Federal Bureau of Narcotics and Dangerous Drugs, went to respondent's home on Whidbey Island in the State of Washington where he met with respondent and his two codefendants, John and Patrick Connolly. Shapiro's assignment was to locate a laboratory where it was believed that methamphetamine was being manufactured illicitly. He told the respondent and the Connollys that he represented an organization in the Pacific Northwest that was interested in controlling the manufacture and distribution of methamphetamine. He then made an offer to supply the defendants with the chemical phenyl-2-propanone, an essential ingredient in the manufacture of methamphetamine, in return for one-half of the drug produced. This offer was made on the condition that Agent Shapiro be shown a sample of the drug which they were making and the laboratory where it was being produced.

During the conversation, Patrick Connolly revealed that he had been making the drug since May 1969 and since then had produced three pounds of it. John Connolly gave the agent a bag containing a quantity of methamphetamine that he represented as being from "the last batch that we made." Shortly thereafter, Shapiro and Patrick Connolly left respondent's house to view the laboratory which was located in the Connolly house on Whidbey Island. At the house, Shapiro observed an empty bottle bearing the chemical label phenyl-2-propanone.

By prearrangement, Shapiro returned to the Connolly house on December 9, 1969, to supply 100 grams of propanone and observe the manufacturing process. When he arrived he observed Patrick Connolly and the respondent cutting up pieces of aluminum foil and placing them in a large flask. There was testimony that some of the foil pieces accidentally fell on the floor and were picked up by the respondent and Shapiro and put into the flask.[3] Thereafter, Patrick Connolly added all of the necessary chemicals, including the propanone brought by Shapiro, to make two batches of methamphetamine. The manufacturing process having been completed the following morning, Shapiro was given one-half of the drug and respondent kept the remainder. Shapiro offered to buy, and the respondent agreed to sell, part of the remainder for $60.

About a month later, Shapiro returned to the Connolly house and met with Patrick Connolly to ask if he was still interested in their "business arrangement." Connolly replied that he was interested but that he had recently obtained two additional bottles of phenyl-2-propanone and would not be finished with them for a couple of days. He provided some additional methamphetamine to Shapiro at that time. Three days later Shapiro returned to the Connolly house with a search warrant and, among other items, seized an empty 500-gram bottle of propanone and a 100-gram bottle, not the one he had provided, that was partially filled with the chemical.

There was testimony at the trial of respondent and Patrick Connolly that phenyl-2-propanone was generally difficult to obtain. At the request of the Bureau of Narcotics and Dangerous Drugs, some chemical supply firms had voluntarily ceased selling the chemical.

At the close of the evidence, and after receiving the District Judge's standard entrapment instruction, the jury found the respondent guilty on all counts charged. On appeal, the respondent conceded that the jury could have found him predisposed to commit the offenses, but argued that on the facts presented there was entrapment as a matter of law. The Court of Appeals agreed, although it did not find the District Court had misconstrued or misapplied the traditional standards governing the entrapment defense. Rather, the court in effect expanded the traditional notion of entrapment, which focuses on the predisposition of the defendant, to mandate dismissal of a criminal prosecution whenever the court determines that there has been "an intolerable degree of governmental participation in the criminal enterprise." In this case the court decided that the conduct of the agent in supplying a scarce ingredient essential for the manufacture of a controlled substance established that defense.

---

3. Agent Shapiro did not otherwise participate in the manufacture of the drug or direct any of the work.

. . . .

In the instant case, respondent asks us to reconsider the theory of the entrapment defense as it is set forth in the majority opinions in *Sorrells* and *Sherman*. His principal contention is that the defense should rest on constitutional grounds. He argues that the level of Shapiro's involvement in the manufacture of the methamphetamine was so high that a criminal prosecution for the drug's manufacture violates the fundamental principles of due process. The respondent contends that the same factors that led this Court to apply the exclusionary rule to illegal searches and seizures and confessions should be considered here. But he would have the Court go further in deterring undesirable official conduct by requiring that any prosecution be barred absolutely because of the police involvement in criminal activity. The analogy is imperfect in any event, for the principal reason behind the adoption of the exclusionary rule was the Government's "failure to observe its own laws." *Mapp v. Ohio*, 367 U.S. 643, 659, 81 S. Ct. 1684, 1694, 61 L. Ed. 2d 1081 (1961). Unlike the situations giving rise to the holdings in *Mapp* and *Miranda*, the Government's conduct here violated no independent constitutional right of the respondent. Nor did Shapiro violate any federal statute or rule or commit any crime in infiltrating the respondent's drug enterprise.

Respondent would overcome this basic weakness in his analogy to the exclusionary rule cases by having the Court adopt a rigid constitutional rule that would preclude any prosecution when it is shown that the criminal conduct would not have been possible had not an undercover agent "supplied an indispensable means to the commission of the crime that could not have obtained otherwise, through legal or illegal channels." Even if we were to surmount the difficulties attending the notion that due process of law can be embodied in fixed rules, and those attending respondent's particular formulation, the rule he proposes would not appear to be of significant benefit to him. For, on the record presented, it appears that he cannot fit within the terms of the very rule he proposes.

The record discloses that although the propanone was difficult to obtain, it was by no means impossible. The defendants admitted making the drug both before and after those batches made with the propanone supplied by Shapiro. Shapiro testified that he saw an empty bottle labeled phenyl-2-propanone on his first visit to the laboratory on December 7, 1969. And when the laboratory was searched pursuant to a search warrant on January 10, 1970, two additional bottles labeled phenyl-2-propanone were seized. Thus, the facts in the record amply demonstrate that the propanone used in the illicit manufacture of methamphetamine not only *could have been obtained* without the intervention of Shapiro but was in fact obtained by these defendants.

While we may some day be presented with a situation in which the conduct of law enforcement agents is so outrageous that due process principles would absolutely bar the government from invoking judicial processes to obtain a conviction, *cf. Rochin v. California*, 342 U.S. 165, 72 S. Ct. 205, 96 L. Ed. 183 (1952), the instant case is distinctly not of that breed. Shapiro's contribution of propanone to the criminal enterprise already in process was scarcely objectionable. The chemical is by itself a harmless substance and its possession is legal. While the Government may have been seeking to make it more difficult for drug rings, such as that of which respondent was a member, to obtain the chemical, the evidence described above shows that it nonetheless was obtainable. The law enforcement conduct here stops far short of violating that "fundamental fairness, shocking to the universal sense of justice," mandated by the Due Process Clause of the Fifth Amendment. *Kinsella v. United States ex rel. Singleton*, 361 U.S. 234, 246, 80 S. Ct. 297, 304, 4 L. Ed. 2d 268 (1960).

The illicit manufacture of drugs is not a sporadic, isolated criminal incident, but a continuing, though illegal, business enterprise. In order to obtain convictions for illegally manufacturing drugs, the gathering of evidence of past unlawful conduct frequently proves to be an all but impossible task. Thus in drug-related offenses law enforcement personnel have turned to one of the only practicable means of detection: the infiltration of drug rings and a limited participation in their unlawful present practices. Such infiltration is a recognized and permissible means of investigation; if that be so, then the supply of some item of value that the drug ring requires must, as a general rule, also be permissible. For an agent will not be taken into the confidence of the illegal entrepreneurs unless he has something of value to offer them. Law enforcement tactics such as this can hardly be said to violate "fundamental fairness" or [be] "shocking to the universal sense of justice," *Kinsella, supra.*

Respondent also urges, as an alternative to his constitutional argument, that we broaden the nonconstitutional defense of entrapment in order to sustain the judgment of the Court of Appeals. This Court's opinions in *Sorrells v. United States, supra,* and *Sherman v. United States, supra,* held that the principal element in the defense of entrapment was the defendant's predisposition to commit the crime. Respondent conceded in the Court of Appeals, as well he might, "that he may have harbored a predisposition to commit the charged offenses." 459 F.2d, at 672. Yet he argues that the jury's refusal to find entrapment under the charge submitted to it by the trial court should be overturned and the views of Justices Roberts and Frankfurter, in *Sorrells* and *Sherman*, respectively, which make the essential element of the defense turn on the type and degree of governmental conduct, be adopted as the law.

We decline to overrule these cases. *Sorrells* is a precedent of long standing that has already been once reexamined in *Sherman* and implicitly there reaffirmed. Since the defense is not of a constitutional dimension, Congress may address itself to the question and adopt any substantive definition of the defense that it may find desirable.

. . . .

Several decisions of the United States district courts and courts of appeals have undoubtedly gone beyond this Court's opinions in *Sorrells* and *Sherman* in order to bar prosecutions because of what they thought to be, for want of a better term, "overzealous law enforcement." But the defense of entrapment enunciated in those opinions was not intended to give the federal judiciary a "chancellor's foot" veto over law enforcement practices of which it did not approve. The execution of the federal laws under our Constitution is confided primarily to the Executive Branch of the Government, subject to applicable constitutional and statutory limitations and to judicially fashioned rules to enforce those limitations. We think that the decision of the Court of Appeals in this case quite unnecessarily introduces an unmanageably subjective standard which is contrary to the holdings of this Court in *Sorrells* and *Sherman*.

Those cases establish that entrapment is a relatively limited defense. It is rooted, not in any authority of the Judicial Branch to dismiss prosecutions for what it feels to have been "overzealous law enforcement," but instead in the notion that Congress could not have intended criminal punishment for a defendant who has committed all the elements of a proscribed offense but was induced to commit them by the Government.

Sorrells and *Sherman* both recognize "that the fact that officers or employees of the Government merely afford opportunities or facilities for the commission of the offense does not defeat the prosecution," 287 U.S. at 441, 53 S. Ct. at 212, 356 U.S. at 372, 78 S. Ct. at 821. Nor will the mere fact of deceit defeat a prosecution, for there are circumstances when the use of deceit is the only practicable law enforcement technique available. It is only when the Government's deception actually implants the criminal design in the mind of the defendant that the defense of entrapment comes into play.

Respondent's concession in the Court of Appeals that the jury finding as to predisposition was supported by the evidence is, therefore, fatal to his claim of entrapment. He was an active participant in an illegal drug manufacturing enterprise which began before the Government agent appeared on the scene, and continued after the Government agent had left the scene. He was, in the words of *Sherman, supra,* not an "unwary innocent" but an "unwary criminal." The Court of Appeals was wrong, we believe, when it sought to broaden the principle laid down in *Sorrells* and *Sherman*. Its judgment is therefore reversed.

Reversed.

MR. JUSTICE DOUGLAS, with whom MR. JUSTICE BRENNAN concurs, dissenting.

A federal agent supplied the accused with one chemical ingredient of the drug known as methamphetamine ("speed") which the accused manufactured and for which act he was sentenced to prison. His defense was entrapment, which the Court of Appeals sustained and which the Court today disallows. Since I have an opposed view of entrapment, I dissent.

. . . .

In my view, the fact that the chemical ingredient supplied by the federal agent might have been obtained from other sources is quite irrelevant. Supplying the chemical ingredient used in the manufacture of this batch of "speed" made the United States an active participant in the unlawful activity. As stated by Mr. Justice Brandeis, dissenting in *Casey v. United States*, 276 U.S. 413, 423, 48 S. Ct. 373, 376, 72 L. Ed. 2d 632 (1928):

I am aware that courts — mistaking relative social values and forgetting that a desirable end cannot justify foul means — have, in their zeal to punish, sanctioned the use of evidence obtained through criminal violation of property and personal rights or by other practices of detectives even more revolting. But the objection here is of a different nature. It does not rest merely upon the character of the evidence or upon the fact that the evidence was illegally obtained. The obstacle to the prosecution lies in the fact that the alleged crime was instigated by officers of the Government; that the act for which the Government seeks to punish the defendant is the fruit of their criminal conspiracy to induce its commission. The Government may set decoys to entrap criminals. But it may not provoke or create a crime and then punish the criminal, its creature.

. . . .

Federal agents play a debased role when they become the instigators of the crime, or partners in its commission, or the creative brain behind the illegal scheme. That is what the federal agent did here when he furnished the accused with one of the chemical ingredients needed to manufacture the unlawful drug.

MR. JUSTICE STEWART, with whom MR. JUSTICE BRENNAN and MR. JUSTICE MARSHALL join, dissenting.

It is common ground that "[t]he conduct with which the defense of entrapment is concerned is the *manufacturing* of crime by law enforcement officials and their agents." *Lopez v. United States*, 373 U.S. 427, 434, 83 S. Ct. 1381, 1385, 10 L. Ed. 2d 462 (1963). For the Government cannot be permitted to instigate the commission of a criminal offense in order to prosecute someone for committing it. *Sherman v. United States*, 356 U.S. 369, 372, 78 S. Ct. 819, 820, 2 L. Ed. 2d 848 (1958). As Mr. Justice Brandeis put it, the Government "may not provoke or create a crime and then punish the criminal, its creature." *Casey v. United States*, 276 U.S. 413, 423, 48 S. Ct. 373, 376, 72 L. Ed. 632 (1928) (dissenting opinion). It is to prevent this situation from occurring in the administration of federal criminal justice that the defense of entrapment exists. *Sorrells v. United States*, 287 U.S. 435, 53 S. Ct. 210, 77 L. Ed. 413 (1932); *Sherman v. United States, supra*. But the Court has been sharply divided as to the proper basis, scope, and focus of the entrapment defense, and as to whether, in the absence of a conclusive showing, the issue of entrapment is for the judge or the jury to determine.

I

In *Sorrells v. United States, supra*, and *Sherman v. United States, supra*, the Court took what might be called a "subjective" approach to the defense of entrapment. In that view, the defense is predicated on an unexpressed intent of Congress to exclude from its criminal statutes the prosecution and conviction of persons, "otherwise innocent," who have been lured to the commission of the prohibited act through the Government's instigation. The key phrase in this formulation is "otherwise innocent," for the entrapment defense is available under this approach only to those who would not have committed the crime but for the Government's inducements. Thus, the subjective approach focuses on the conduct and propensities of the particular defendant in each individual case: if he is "otherwise innocent," he may avail himself of the defense; but if he had the "predisposition" to commit the crime, or if the "criminal design" originated with him, then — regardless of the nature and extent of the Government's participation — there has been no entrapment. And, in the absence of a conclusive showing one way or the other, the question of the defendant's "predisposition" to the crime is a question of fact for the jury. The Court today adheres to this approach.

The concurring opinion of Mr. Justice Roberts, joined by Justices Brandeis and Stone, in the *Sorrells* case, and that of Mr. Justice Frankfurter, joined by Justices Douglas, Harlan, and Brennan, in the *Sherman* case, took a different view of the entrapment defense. In their concept, the defense is not grounded on some unexpressed intent of Congress to exclude from punishment under its statutes those otherwise innocent persons tempted into crime by the Government, but rather on the belief that "the methods employed on behalf of the Government to bring about conviction cannot be countenanced." *Sherman v. United States, supra*, 356 U.S. at 380, 78 S. Ct. at 834. Thus, the focus of this approach is not on the propensities and predisposition of a specific defendant, but on "whether the police conduct revealed in the particular case falls below standards, to which common feelings respond, for the proper use of governmental power." *Id.* at 382, 78 S. Ct. at 825. Phrased another way, the question is whether — regardless of the predisposition to crime of the particular defendant involved — the governmental agents have acted in such a way as is likely to instigate or create a criminal offense. Under this approach, the determination of the lawfulness of the Government's conduct must be made — as it is on all questions involving the legality of law enforcement methods — by the trial judge, not the jury.

In my view, this objective approach to entrapment advanced by the Roberts opinion in *Sorrells* and the Frankfurter opinion in *Sherman* is the only one truly consistent with the underlying rationale of the defense. Indeed, the very basis of the entrapment defense itself demands adherence to an approach that focuses on the conduct of the governmental agents, rather than on whether the defendant was "predisposed" or "otherwise innocent." I find it impossible to believe that the purpose of the defense is to effectuate some unexpressed congressional intent to exclude from its criminal statutes persons who committed a prohibited act, but would not have done so except for the Government's inducements. For, as Mr. Justice Frankfurter put it, "the only legislative intention that can with any show of reason be extracted from the statute is the intention to make criminal precisely the conduct in which the defendant has engaged." *Sherman v. United States, supra*, at 379, 78 S. Ct. at 824. *See also Sorrells v. United States, supra*, 287 U.S. at 456, 53 S. Ct. at 218 (Roberts, J., concurring). Since, by definition, the entrapment defense cannot arise unless the defendant actually committed the proscribed act, that defendant is manifestly covered by the terms of the criminal statute involved.

Furthermore, to say that such a defendant is "otherwise innocent" or not "predisposed" to commit the crime is misleading, at best. The very fact that he has committed an act that Congress has determined to be illegal demonstrates conclusively that he is not innocent of the offense. He may not have originated the precise plan or the precise details, but he was "predisposed" in the sense that he has proved to be quite capable of committing the crime. That he was induced, provoked, or tempted to do so by government agents does not make him any more innocent or any less predisposed than he would be if he had been induced, provoked, or tempted by a private person — which, of course, would not entitle him to cry "entrapment." Since the only difference between these situations is the identity of the tempter, it follows that the significant focus must be on the conduct of the government agents, and not on the predisposition of the defendant.

. . . .

In my view, a person's alleged "predisposition" to crime should not expose him to government participation in the criminal transaction that would be otherwise unlawful.

This does not mean, of course, that the Government's use of undercover activity, strategy, or deception is necessarily unlawful. Indeed, many crimes, especially so-called victimless crimes, could not otherwise be detected. Thus, government agents may engage in conduct that is likely, when objectively considered, to afford a person ready and willing to commit the crime an opportunity to do so.

But when the agents' involvement in criminal activities goes beyond the mere offering of such an opportunity and when their conduct is of a kind that could induce or instigate the commission of a crime by one not ready and willing to commit it, then — regardless of the character or propensities of the particular person induced — I think entrapment has occurred. For in that situation, the Government has engaged in the impermissible manufacturing of crime, and the federal courts should bar the prosecution in order to preserve the institutional integrity of the system of federal criminal justice.

. . . .

I would affirm the judgment of the Court of Appeals.

Hampton v. United States

United States Supreme Court

425 U.S. 484, 96 S. Ct. 1646, 48 L. Ed. 2d 113 (1976)

MR. JUSTICE REHNQUIST announced the judgment of the Court in an opinion in which THE CHIEF JUSTICE and MR. JUSTICE WHITE join.

This case presents the question of whether a defendant may be convicted for the sale of contraband which he procured from a Government informant or agent. The Court of Appeals for the Eighth Circuit held he could be, and we agree.

I

Petitioner was convicted of two counts of distributing heroin in violation of 21 U.S.C. § 841(a)(1) in the United States District Court for the Eastern District of

Missouri and sentenced to concurrent terms of five years' imprisonment (suspended).[1] The case arose from two sales of heroin by petitioner to agents of the Federal Drug Enforcement Administration (DEA) in St. Louis on February 25 and 26, 1974. The sales were arranged by one Hutton, who was a pool-playing acquaintance of petitioner at the Pud Bar in St. Louis and also a DEA informant.

According to the Government's witnesses, in late February 1974, Hutton and petitioner were shooting pool at the Pud when petitioner, after observing "track" (needle) marks on Hutton's arms told Hutton that he needed money and knew where he could get some heroin. Hutton responded that he could find a buyer and petitioner suggested that he "get in touch with those people." Hutton then called DEA Agent Terry Sawyer and arranged a sale for 10 p.m. on February 25.

At the appointed time, Hutton and petitioner went to a prearranged meeting place and were met by Agent Sawyer and DEA Agent McDowell, posing as narcotics dealers. Petitioner produced a tinfoil packet from his cap and turned it over to the agents who tested it, pronounced it "okay," and negotiated a price of $145 which was paid to petitioner. Before they parted, petitioner told Sawyer that he could obtain larger quantities of heroin and gave Sawyer a phone number where he could be reached.

The next day Sawyer called petitioner and arranged for another "buy" that afternoon. Petitioner got Hutton to go along and they met the agents again near where they had been the previous night.

They all entered the agents' car, and petitioner again produced a tinfoil packet from his cap. The agents again field-tested it and pronounced it satisfactory. Petitioner then asked for $500 which Agent Sawyer said he would get from the trunk. Sawyer got out and opened the trunk which was a signal to other agents to move in and arrest petitioner, which they did.

Petitioner's version of events was quite different. According to him, in response to his statement that he was short of cash, Hutton said that he had a friend who was a pharmacist who could produce a non-narcotic counterfeit drug which would give the same reaction as heroin. Hutton proposed selling this drug to gullible acquaintances who would be led to believe they were buying heroin. Petitioner testified that they successfully duped one buyer with this fake drug and that the sales which led to the arrest were solicited by petitioner[3] in an effort to profit further from this ploy.

Petitioner contended that he neither intended to sell, nor knew that he was dealing in heroin and that all of the drugs he sold were supplied by Hutton. His account was at least partially disbelieved by the jury which was instructed that in order to convict petitioner they had to find that the Government proved "that the defendant knowingly did an act which the law forbids, purposely intending to violate the law."

---

1. Petitioner was placed on five years' probation which was to run concurrently with the remainder of a 28- to 30-year state armed robbery sentence from which petitioner had escaped.

3. On appeal, petitioner's counsel, who was also his counsel at trial, conceded that petitioner was predisposed to commit this offense.

Thus the guilty verdict necessarily implies that the jury rejected petitioner's claim that he did not know the substance was heroin, and petitioner himself admitted both soliciting and carrying out sales. The only relevance of his version of the facts, then, lies in his having requested an instruction embodying that version. He did not request a standard entrapment instruction but he did request the following:

> The defendant asserts that he was the victim of entrapment as to the crimes charged in the indictment.

> If you find that the defendant's sales of narcotics were sales of narcotics supplied to him by an informer in the employ of or acting on behalf of the government, then you must acquit the defendant because the law as a matter of policy forbids his conviction in such a case.

> Furthermore, under this particular defense, you need not consider the predisposition of the defendant to commit the offense charged, because if the governmental involvement through its informer reached the point that I have just defined in your own minds, then the predisposition of the defendant would not matter.

The trial court refused the instruction and petitioner was found guilty. He appealed to the United States Court of Appeals for the Eighth Circuit, claiming that if the jury had believed that the drug was supplied by Hutton he should have been acquitted. The Court of Appeals rejected this argument and affirmed the conviction, relying on our opinion in *United States v. Russell*, 411 U.S. 423, 93 S. Ct. 1637, 36 L. Ed. 2d 366 (1973).

II

In *Russell* we held that the statutory defense of entrapment was not available where it was conceded that a Government agent supplied a necessary ingredient in the manufacture of an illicit drug. . . .

In holding that "[i]t is only when the Government's deception actually implants the criminal design in the mind of the defendant that the defense of entrapment comes into play," 411 U.S. at 436, 93 S. Ct. at 1645, 36 L. Ed. 2d at 376, we, of course, rejected the contrary view of the dissents in that case and the concurrences in *Sorrells* and *Sherman*. In view of these holdings, petitioner correctly recognizes that his case does not qualify as one involving "entrapment" at all. He instead relies on the language in *Russell* that "we may some day be presented with a situation in which the conduct of law enforcement agents is so outrageous that due process principles would absolutely bar the government from invoking judicial processes to obtain a conviction, cf. *Rochin v. California*, 342 U.S. 165, 72 S. Ct. 205, 96 L. Ed. 183 (1952). . . ." 411 U.S. at 431–432, 93 S. Ct. at 1643, 36 L. Ed. 2d at 373.

In urging that this case involves a violation of his due process rights, petitioner misapprehends the meaning of the quoted language in *Russell, supra*. Admittedly petitioner's case is different from Russell's but the difference is one of degree, not of kind. In *Russell* the ingredient supplied by the Government agent was a legal drug which the defendants demonstrably could have obtained from other sources besides the Government. Here the drug which the Government informant allegedly supplied to petitioner both was illegal and constituted the *corpus delicti* for the sale of which the petitioner was convicted. The Government obviously played a more significant role in enabling petitioner to sell contraband in this case than it did in *Russell*.

But in each case the Government agents were acting in concert with the defendant, and in each case either the jury found or the defendant conceded that he was predisposed to commit the crime for which he was convicted. The remedy of the criminal defendant with respect to the acts of Government agents, which, far from being resisted, are encouraged by him, lies solely in the defense of entrapment. But, as noted, petitioner's conceded predisposition rendered this defense unavailable to him.

To sustain petitioner's contention here would run directly contrary to our statement in *Russell* that the defense of entrapment is not intended "to give the federal judiciary a 'chancellor's foot' veto over law enforcement practices of which it did not approve. The execution of the federal laws under our Constitution is confided primarily to the Executive Branch of the Government, subject to applicable constitutional and statutory limitations and to judicially fashioned rules to enforce those limitations." 411 U.S. at 435, 93 S. Ct. at 1644, 36 L. Ed. 2d at 375.

The limitations of the Due Process Clause of the Fifth Amendment come into play only when the Government activity in question violates some protected right of the *defendant*. Here, as we have noted, the police, the Government informant, and the defendant acted in concert with one another. If the result of the governmental activity is to "implant in the mind of an innocent person the disposition to commit the alleged offense and induce its commission . . . ," *Sorrells, supra*, 287 U.S. at 442, 53 S. Ct. at 212–213, 77 L. Ed. at 417, the defendant is protected by the defense of entrapment. If the police engage in illegal activity in concert with a defendant beyond the scope of their duties the remedy lies, not in freeing the equally culpable defendant, but in prosecuting the police under the applicable provisions of state or federal law. But the police conduct here no more deprived defendant of any right secured to him by the United States Constitution than did the police conduct in *Russell* deprive Russell of any rights.

Affirmed.

Mr. Justice Stevens took no part in the consideration or decision of this case.

Mr. Justice Powell, with whom Mr. Justice Blackmun joins, concurring in the judgment.

Petitioner, Charles Hampton, contends that the Government's supplying of contraband to one later prosecuted for trafficking in contraband constitutes a *per se* denial of due process. As I do not accept this proposition, I concur in the judgment of the Court and much of the plurality opinion directed specifically to Hampton's contention. I am not able to join the remainder of the plurality opinion, as it would unnecessarily reach and decide difficult questions not before us.

In *United States v. Russell*, 411 U.S. 423, 431, 93 S. Ct. 1637, 1642, 36 L. Ed. 2d 366, 373 (1973), we noted that significant "difficulties [attend] the notion that due process of law can be embodied in fixed rules." We also recognized that the practicalities of combating the narcotics traffic frequently require law enforcement officers legitimately to supply "some item of value that the drug ring requires." 411 U.S. at 432, 93 S. Ct. at 1643, 36 L. Ed. 2d at 374. Accordingly, we held that due process does not necessarily foreclose reliance on such investigative techniques. Hampton would distinguish *Russell* on the ground that here contraband itself was supplied by the Government, while the phenyl-2-propanone supplied in *Russell* was not contraband. Given the characteristics of phenyl-2-propanone,[1] this is a distinction without a difference and *Russell* disposes of this case.

But the plurality opinion today does not stop there. . . . [It] says that the concept of fundamental fairness inherent in the guarantee of due process would never prevent the conviction of a predisposed defendant, regardless of the outrageousness of police behavior in light of the surrounding circumstances.

I do not understand *Russell* or earlier cases delineating the predisposition-focused defense of entrapment to have gone so far, and there was no need for them to do so. In those cases the Court was confronted with specific claims of police "overinvolvement" in criminal activity involving contraband. Disposition of those claims did not require the Court to consider whether overinvolvement of Government agents in contraband offenses could ever reach such proportions as to bar conviction of a predisposed defendant as a matter of due process. Nor have we had occasion yet to confront Government overinvolvement in areas outside the realm of contraband offenses. In these circumstances, I am unwilling to conclude that an analysis other than one limited to predisposition would never be appropriate under due process principles.[4]

The plurality's use of the "chancellor's foot" passage from *Russell* may suggest that it also would foreclose reliance on our supervisory power to bar conviction of a predisposed defendant because of outrageous police conduct. Again, I do not understand *Russell* to have gone so far. There we indicated only that we should be extremely reluctant to invoke the supervisory power in cases of this kind because that power does not give the "federal judiciary a 'chancellor's foot' veto over law enforcement

---

1. Although phenyl-2-propanone is not contraband, it is useful only in the manufacture of methamphetamine ("speed"), the contraband involved in *Russell*. Further, it is an essential ingredient in that manufacturing process and is very difficult to obtain.

4. Judge Friendly recently expressed the view:

> "[T]here is certainly a [constitutional] limit to allowing governmental involvement in crime. It would be unthinkable, for example, to permit government agents to instigate robberies and beatings merely to gather evidence to convict other members of a gang of hoodlums. Governmental 'investigation' involving participation in activities that result in injury to the rights of its citizens is a course that courts should be extremely reluctant to sanction."

United States v. Archer, 486 F.2d at 676–677 (footnote omitted).

practices of which it [does] not approve." 411 U.S. at 435, 93 S. Ct. at 1644, 36 L. Ed. 2d at 375.

I am not unmindful of the doctrinal and practical difficulties of delineating limits to police involvement in crime that do not focus on predisposition, as Government participation ordinarily will be fully justified in society's "war with the criminal classes." *Sorrells v. United States*, 287 U.S. 435, 453, 53 S. Ct. 210, 217, 77 L. Ed. 413, 423 (1932) (opinion of Roberts, J.). This undoubtedly is the concern that prompts the plurality to embrace an absolute rule. But we left these questions open in *Russell*, and this case is controlled completely by *Russell*. I therefore am unwilling to join the plurality in concluding that, no matter what the circumstances, neither due process principles nor our supervisory power could support a bar to conviction in any case where the Government is able to prove predisposition.[7]

MR. JUSTICE BRENNAN, with whom MR. JUSTICE STEWART and MR. JUSTICE MARSHALL concur, dissenting.

. . . .

Two facts significantly distinguish this case from *Russell*. First, the chemical supplied in that case was not contraband. It is legal to possess and sell phenyl-2-propanone and, although the Government there supplied an ingredient that was essential to the manufacture of methamphetamine, it did not supply the contraband itself. In contrast, petitioner claims that the very narcotic he is accused of selling was supplied by an agent of the Government.

Second, the defendant in *Russell* "was an active participant in an illegal drug manufacturing enterprise which began before the Government agent appeared on the scene, and continued after the Government agent had left the scene." 411 U.S. at 436, 93 S. Ct. at 1645, 36 L. Ed. 2d at 376. Russell was charged with unlawfully manufacturing and processing methamphetamine, and his crime was participation in an ongoing operation. In contrast, the two sales for which petitioner was convicted were allegedly instigated by Government agents and completed by the Government's purchase. The beginning and end of this crime thus coincided exactly with the Government's entry into and withdrawal from the criminal activity involved in this case, while the Government was not similarly involved in Russell's crime.

Whether the differences from the *Russell* situation are of degree or of kind, I think they clearly require a different result. Where the Government's agent deliberately sets up the accused by supplying him with contraband and then bringing him to another agent as a potential purchaser, the Government's role has passed the point of toleration. The Government is doing nothing less than buying contraband from itself through an intermediary and jailing the intermediary. There is little, if any, law en-

---

7. I emphasize that the cases, if any, in which proof of predisposition is not dispositive will be rare. Police overinvolvement in crime would have to reach a demonstrable level of outrageousness before it could bar conviction. This would be especially difficult to show with respect to contraband offenses, which are so difficult to detect in the absence of undercover Government involvement. . . .

forcement interest promoted by such conduct; plainly it is not designed to discover ongoing drug traffic. Rather, such conduct deliberately entices an individual to commit a crime. That the accused is "predisposed" cannot possibly justify the action of government officials in purposefully creating the crime. No one would suggest that the police could round up and jail all "predisposed" individuals, yet that is precisely what set-ups like the instant one are intended to accomplish. Thus, this case is nothing less than an instance of "the Government . . . seeking to punish for an alleged offense which is the product of the creative activity of its own officials." *Sorrells v. United States*, 287 U.S. at 451, 53 S. Ct. at 216, 77 L. Ed. at 422.

. . . .

Notes and Questions

(1) In *Russell*, Justice Stewart echoed Justice Frankfurter in urging that the Court adopt the objective or hypothetical person test for entrapment. Would the Court's adoption of that test have benefited the defendant in *Russell*?

(2) What is the rationale for the due process defense? In *Hampton*, Justice Powell indicates that the defense should be available when the police conduct is outrageous. What criteria should be used to identify outrageous police conduct? Should the defendants in the case discussed by Justice Powell in footnote 4 of his opinion in *Hampton* have a due process defense?

Jacobson v. United States

United States Supreme Court

503 U.S. 540, 112 S. Ct. 1535, 118 L. Ed. 2d 174 (1992)

JUSTICE WHITE delivered the opinion of the Court.

. . . .

I

In February 1984, petitioner, a 56-year-old veteran-turned-farmer who supported his elderly father in Nebraska, ordered two magazines and a brochure from a California adult bookstore. The magazines, entitled Bare Boys I and Bare Boys II, contained photographs of nude preteen and teenage boys. The contents of the magazines startled petitioner, who testified that he had expected to receive photographs of "young men 18 years or older." On cross-examination, he explained his response to the magazines:

"[PROSECUTOR]: [Y]ou were shocked and surprised that there were pictures of very young boys without clothes on, is that correct?

"[JACOBSON]: Yes, I was.

"[PROSECUTOR]: Were you offended? . . .

"[JACOBSON]: I was not offended because I thought these were a nudist type publication. Many of the pictures were out in a rural or outdoor setting. There was — I didn't draw any sexual connotation or connection with that."

The young men depicted in the magazines were not engaged in sexual activity, and petitioner's receipt of the magazines was legal under both federal and Nebraska law. Within three months, the law with respect to child pornography changed; Congress passed the Act illegalizing the receipt through the mails of sexually explicit depictions of children. In the very month that the new provision became law, postal inspectors found petitioner's name on the mailing list of the California bookstore that had mailed him Bare Boys I and II. There followed over the next 2 1/2 years, repeated efforts by two Government agencies, through five fictitious organizations and a bogus pen pal, to explore petitioner's willingness to break the new law by ordering sexually explicit photographs of children through the mail.

The Government began its efforts in January 1985 when a postal inspector sent petitioner a letter supposedly from the American Hedonist Society, which in fact was a fictitious organization. The letter included a membership application and stated the Society's doctrine: that members had the "right to read what we desire, the right to discuss similar interests with those who share our philosophy, and finally that we have the right to seek pleasure without restrictions being placed on us by outdated puritan morality." Petitioner enrolled in the organization and returned a sexual attitude questionnaire that asked him to rank on a scale of one to four his enjoyment of various sexual materials, with one being "really enjoy," two being "enjoy," three being "somewhat enjoy," and four being "do not enjoy." Petitioner ranked the entry "[p]re-teen sex" as a two, but indicated that he was opposed to pedophilia.

For a time, the Government left petitioner alone. But then a new "prohibited mail specialist" in the Postal Service found petitioner's name in a file, and in May 1986, petitioner received a solicitation from a second fictitious consumer research company, "Midlands Data Research," seeking a response from those who "believe in the joys of sex and the complete awareness of those lusty and youthful lads and lasses of the neophite [sic] age." The letter never explained whether "neophite" referred to minors or young adults. Petitioner responded: "Please feel free to send me more information, I am interested in teenage sexuality. Please keep my name confidential."

Petitioner then heard from yet another Government creation, "Heartland Institute for a New Tomorrow" (HINT), which proclaimed that it was "an organization founded to protect and promote sexual freedom and freedom of choice. We believe that arbitrarily imposed legislative sanctions restricting your sexual freedom should be rescinded through the legislative process." The letter also enclosed a second survey. Petitioner indicated that his interest in "[p]reteen sex-homosexual" material was above average, but not high. In response to another question, petitioner wrote: "Not only sexual expression but freedom of the press is under attack. We must be ever vigilant to counter attack right wing fundamentalists who are determined to curtail our freedoms."

HINT replied, portraying itself as a lobbying organization seeking to repeal "all statutes which regulate sexual activities, except those laws which deal with violent behavior, such as rape. HINT is also lobbying to eliminate any legal definition of 'the age of consent.'" These lobbying efforts were to be funded by sales from a catalog to be published in the future "offering the sale of various items which we believe you will find to be both interesting and stimulating." HINT also provided computer matching of group members with similar survey responses; and, although petitioner was supplied with a list of potential "pen pals," he did not initiate any correspondence.

Nevertheless, the Government's "prohibited mail specialist" began writing to petitioner, using the pseudonym "Carl Long." The letters employed a tactic known as "mirroring," which the inspector described as "reflect[ing] whatever the interests are of the person we are writing to." Petitioner responded at first, indicating that his interest was primarily in "male-male items." Inspector "Long" wrote back:

> "My interests too are primarily male-male items. Are you satisfied with the type of VCR tapes available? Personally, I like the amateur stuff better if its [sic] well produced as it can get more kinky and also seems more real. I think the actors enjoy it more."

Petitioner responded:

> "As far as my likes are concerned, I like good looking young guys (in their late teens and early 20's) doing their thing together."

Petitioner's letters to "Long" made no reference to child pornography. After writing two letters, petitioner discontinued the correspondence.

By March 1987, 34 months had passed since the Government obtained petitioner's name from the mailing list of the California bookstore, and 26 months had passed since the Postal Service had commenced its mailings to petitioner. Although petitioner had responded to surveys and letters, the Government had no evidence that petitioner had ever intentionally possessed or been exposed to child pornography. The Postal Service had not checked petitioner's mail to determine whether he was receiving questionable mailings from persons — other than the Government — involved in the child pornography industry.

At this point, a second Government agency, the Customs Service, included petitioner in its own child pornography sting, "Operation Borderline," after receiving his name on lists submitted by the Postal Service. Using the name of a fictitious Canadian company called "Produit Outaouais," the Customs Service mailed petitioner a brochure advertising photographs of young boys engaging in sex. Petitioner placed an order that was never filled.

The Postal Service also continued its efforts in the Jacobson case, writing to petitioner as the "Far Eastern Trading Company Ltd." The letter began:

> As many of you know, much hysterical nonsense has appeared in the American media concerning "pornography" and what must be done to stop it from coming across your borders. This brief letter does not allow us to give much comments; however, why is your government spending millions of dollars to exercise international censorship while tons of drugs, which makes yours the world's most crime ridden country, are passed through easily.

The letter went on to say:

> [W]e have devised a method of getting these to you without prying eyes of U.S. Customs seizing your mail. . . . After consultations with American solicitors, we have been advised that once we have posted our material through your system, it cannot be opened for any inspection without authorization of a judge.

The letter invited petitioner to send for more information. It also asked petitioner to sign an affirmation that he was "not a law enforcement officer or agent of the U.S. Government acting in an undercover capacity for the purpose of entrapping Far Eastern Trading Company, its agents or customers." Petitioner responded. A catalogue was sent, and petitioner ordered Boys Who Love Boys, a pornographic magazine depicting young boys engaged in various sexual activities. Petitioner was arrested after a controlled delivery of a photocopy of the magazine.

When petitioner was asked at trial why he placed such an order, he explained that the Government had succeeded in piquing his curiosity:

> "Well, the statement was made of all the trouble and the hysteria over pornography and I wanted to see what the material was. It didn't describe the — I didn't know for sure what kind of sexual action they were referring to in the Canadian letter. . . ."

In petitioner's home, the Government found the Bare Boys magazines and materials that the Government had sent to him in the course of its protracted investigation, but no other materials that would indicate that petitioner collected, or was actively interested in, child pornography.

Petitioner was indicted for violating 18 U.S.C. § 2552(a)(2)(A). The trial court instructed the jury on the petitioner's entrapment defense, petitioner was convicted, and a divided Court of Appeals for the Eighth Circuit, sitting en banc, affirmed, concluding that "Jacobson was not entrapped as a matter of law." 916 F.2d 467, 470 (1990). We granted certiorari.

II

There can be no dispute about the evils of child pornography or the difficulties that laws and law enforcement have encountered in eliminating it. *See generally Osborne v. Ohio*, 495 U.S. 103, 110 (1990); *New York v. Ferber*, 458 U.S. 747, 759–760 (1982). Likewise, there can be no dispute that the Government may use undercover agents to enforce the law. . . .

In their zeal to enforce the law, however, Government agents may not originate a criminal design, implant in an innocent person's mind the disposition to commit a criminal act, and then induce commission of the crime so that the Government may prosecute. Where the Government has induced an individual to break the law and the defense of entrapment is at issue, as it was in this case, the prosecution must prove beyond reasonable doubt that the defendant was disposed to commit the criminal act prior to first being approached by Government agents. *United States v. Whoie*, 925 F.2d 1481, 1483-1484, 288 U.S. App. D.C. 261, 263–264 (1991).

Thus, an agent deployed to stop the traffic in illegal drugs may offer the opportunity to buy or sell drugs, and, if the offer is accepted, make an arrest on the spot or later. In such a typical case, or in a more elaborate "sting" operation involving government-sponsored fencing where the defendant is simply provided with the opportunity to commit a crime, the entrapment defense is of little use because the ready commission of the criminal act amply demonstrates the defendant's predisposition. Had the agents in this case simply offered petitioner the opportunity to order child pornography through the mails, and petitioner—who must be presumed to know the law—had promptly availed himself of this criminal opportunity, it is unlikely that his entrapment defense would have warranted a jury instruction.

But that is not what happened here. By the time petitioner finally placed his order, he had already been the target of 26 months of repeated mailings and communications from Government agents and fictitious organizations. Therefore, although he had become predisposed to break the law by May 1987, it is our view that the Government did not prove that this predisposition was independent and not the product of the attention that the Government had directed at petitioner since January 1985. *Sorrells v. United States*, 287 U.S. 435, 442 (1932); *Sherman v. United States*, 356 U.S. 369, 372 (1958).

The prosecution's evidence of predisposition falls into two categories: evidence developed prior to the Postal Service's mail campaign, and that developed during the course of the investigation. The sole piece of preinvestigation evidence is petitioner's 1984 order and receipt of the Bare Boys magazines. But this is scant if any proof of petitioner's predisposition to commit an illegal act, the criminal character of which a defendant is presumed to know. It may indicate a predisposition to view sexually-oriented photographs that are responsive to his sexual tastes; but evidence that merely indicates a generic inclination to act within a broad range, not all of which is criminal, is of little probative value in establishing predisposition.

Furthermore, petitioner was acting within the law at the time he received these magazines. Receipt through the mails of sexually explicit depictions of children for noncommercial use did not become illegal under federal law until May 1984, and Nebraska had no law that forbade petitioner's possession of such material until 1988. Evidence of predisposition to do what once was lawful is not, by itself, sufficient to show predisposition to do what is now illegal, for there is a common understanding that most people obey the law even when they disapprove of it. This obedience may reflect a generalized respect for legality or the fear of prosecution, but for whatever reason, the law's prohibitions are matters of consequence. Hence, the fact that petitioner legally ordered and received the Bare Boys magazines does little to further the Government's burden of proving that petitioner was predisposed to commit a criminal act. This is particularly true given petitioner's unchallenged testimony was that he did not know until they arrived that the magazines would depict minors.

The prosecution's evidence gathered during the investigation also fails to carry the Government's burden. Petitioner's responses to the many communications prior to the ultimate criminal act were at most indicative of certain personal inclinations, including a predisposition to view photographs of preteen sex and a willingness to promote a given agenda by supporting lobbying organizations. Even so, petitioner's responses hardly support an inference that he would commit the crime of receiving child pornography through the mails.[3] Furthermore, a person's inclinations and "fantasies . . . are his own and beyond the reach of government. . . ." *Paris Adult Theatre I v. Slaton*, 413 U.S. 49, 67 (1973); *Stanley v. Georgia*, 394 U.S. 557, 565–566 (1969).

On the other hand, the strong arguable inference is that, by waving the banner of individual rights and disparaging the legitimacy and constitutionality of efforts to restrict the availability of sexually explicit materials, the Government not only excited petitioner's interest in sexually explicit materials banned by law but also exerted substantial pressure on petitioner to obtain and read such material as part of a fight against censorship and the infringement of individual rights. For instance, HINT described itself as "an organization founded to protect and promote sexual freedom and freedom of choice" and stated that "the most appropriate means to accomplish [its] objectives is to promote honest dialogue among concerned individuals and to continue its lobbying efforts with State Legislators." These lobbying efforts were to be financed through catalog sales. Mailings from the equally fictitious American Hedonist Society and the correspondence from the nonexistent Carl Long endorsed these themes.

Similarly, the two solicitations in the spring of 1987 raised the spectre of censorship while suggesting that petitioner ought to be allowed to do what he had been solicited to do. The mailing from the Customs Service referred to "the worldwide ban and intense enforcement on this type of material," observed that "what was legal and commonplace is now an 'underground' and secretive service," and emphasized that "[t]his environment forces us to take extreme measures" to ensure delivery. The Postal Service solicitation described the concern about child pornography as "hysterical nonsense," decried "international censorship," and assured petitioner, based on consultation with "American solicitors," that an order that had been posted could not be opened for inspection without authorization of a judge. It further asked petitioner to affirm that he was not a Government agent attempting to entrap the mail order company or its customers. In these particulars, both Government solicitations suggested that receiving this material was something that petitioner ought to be allowed to do.

Petitioner's ready response to these solicitations cannot be enough to establish beyond reasonable doubt that he was predisposed, prior to the Government acts intended to create predisposition, to commit the crime of receiving child pornography through the mails. The evidence that petitioner was ready and willing to commit the offense came only after the Government had devoted 2 1/2 years to convincing him

---

3. We do not hold, as the dissent suggests, that the Government was required to prove that petitioner knowingly violated the law. We simply conclude that proof that petitioner engaged in legal conduct and possessed certain generalized personal inclinations is not sufficient evidence to prove beyond a reasonable doubt that he would have been predisposed to commit the crime charged independent of the Government's coaxing.

that he had or should have the right to engage in the very behavior proscribed by law. Rational jurors could not say beyond a reasonable doubt that petitioner possessed the requisite predisposition prior to the Government's investigation and that it existed independent of the Government's many and varied approaches to petitioner. As was explained in *Sherman*, where entrapment was found as a matter of law, "the Government [may not] pla[y] on the weaknesses of an innocent party and beguil[e] him into committing crimes which he otherwise would not have attempted." *Sherman*, 356 U.S. at 376.

Law enforcement officials go too far when they "implant in the mind of an innocent person the *disposition* to commit the alleged offense and induce its commission in order that they may prosecute." *Sorrells*, 287 U.S., at 442 (emphasis added). Like the *Sorrells* court, we are "unable to conclude that it was the intention of the Congress in enacting this statute that its processes of detection and enforcement should be abused by the instigation by government officials of an act on the part of persons otherwise innocent in order to lure them to its commission and to punish them." *Id.*, at 448. When the Government's quest for convictions leads to the apprehension of an otherwise law-abiding citizen who, if left to his own devices, likely would have never run afoul of the law, the courts should intervene.

Because we conclude that this is such a case and that the prosecution failed, as a matter of law, to adduce evidence to support the jury verdict that petitioner was predisposed, independent of the Government's acts and beyond a reasonable doubt, to violate the law by receiving child pornography through the mails, we reverse the Court of Appeals' judgment affirming the conviction of Keith Jacobson.

It is so ordered.

JUSTICE O'CONNOR, with whom THE CHIEF JUSTICE and JUSTICE KENNEDY join, and with whom JUSTICE SCALIA joins except as to Part II, dissenting.

Keith Jacobson was offered only two opportunities to buy child pornography through the mail. Both times, he ordered. Both times, he asked for opportunities to buy more. He needed no Government agent to coax, threaten, or persuade him; no one played on his sympathies, friendship, or suggested that his committing the crime would further a greater good. In fact, no Government agent even contacted him face-to-face. The Government contends that from the enthusiasm with which Mr. Jacobson responded to the chance to commit a crime, a reasonable jury could permissibly infer beyond a reasonable doubt that he was predisposed to commit the crime. I agree.

The first time the Government sent Mr. Jacobson a catalog of illegal materials, he ordered a set of photographs advertised as picturing "young boys in sex action fun." He enclosed the following note with his order: "I received your brochure and decided to place an order. If I like your product, I will order more later." For reasons undisclosed in the record, Mr. Jacobson's order was never delivered.

The second time the Government sent a catalog of illegal materials, Mr. Jacobson ordered a magazine called "Boys Who Love Boys," described as: "11 year old and 14 year old boys get it on in every way possible. Oral, anal sex and heavy masturbation. If you love boys, you will be delighted with this." Along with his order, Mr. Jacobson sent the following note: "Will order other items later. I want to be discreet in order to protect you and me."

Government agents admittedly did not offer Mr. Jacobson the chance to buy child pornography right away. Instead, they first sent questionnaires in order to make sure that he was generally interested in the subject matter. Indeed, a "cold call" in such a business would not only risk rebuff and suspicion, but might also shock and offend the uninitiated, or expose minors to suggestive materials. Mr. Jacobson's responses to the questionnaires gave the investigators reason to think he would be interested in photographs depicting preteen sex.

The Court, however, concludes that a reasonable jury could not have found Mr. Jacobson to be predisposed beyond a reasonable doubt on the basis of his responses to the Government's catalogs, even though it admits that, by that time, he was predisposed to commit the crime. The Government, the Court holds, failed to provide evidence that Mr. Jacobson's obvious predisposition at the time of the crime "was independent and not the product of the attention that the Government had directed at petitioner." In so holding, I believe the Court fails to acknowledge the reasonableness of the jury's inference from the evidence, redefines "predisposition," and introduces a new requirement that Government sting operations have a reasonable suspicion of illegal activity before contacting a suspect.

I

This Court has held previously that a defendant's predisposition is to be assessed as of the time the Government agent first suggested the crime, not when the Government agent first became involved. *Sherman v. United States*, 356 U.S. 369, 372–376 (1958). Until the Government actually makes a suggestion of criminal conduct, it could not be said to have "implant[ed] in the mind of an innocent person the disposition to commit the alleged offense and induce its commission. . . ." *Sorrells v. United States*, 287 U.S. 435, 442 (1932). Even in *Sherman v. United States, supra,* in which the Court held that the defendant had been entrapped as a matter of law, the Government agent had repeatedly and unsuccessfully coaxed the defendant to buy drugs, ultimately succeeding only by playing on the defendant's sympathy. The Court found lack of predisposition based on the Government's numerous unsuccessful attempts to induce the crime, not on the basis of preliminary contacts with the defendant.

Today, the Court holds that Government conduct may be considered to create a predisposition to commit a crime, even before any Government action to induce the commission of the crime. In my view, this holding changes entrapment doctrine. Generally, the inquiry is whether a suspect is predisposed before the Government induces the commission of the crime, not before the Government makes initial contact with him. There is no dispute here that the Government's questionnaires and letters were not sufficient to establish inducement; they did not even suggest that Mr. Jacobson should engage in any illegal activity. If all the Government had done was to send these materials, Mr. Jacobson's entrapment defense would fail. Yet the Court holds that the Government must prove not only that a suspect was predisposed to commit the crime before the opportunity to commit it arose, but also before the Government came on the scene.

The rule that preliminary Government contact can create a predisposition has the potential to be misread by lower courts as well as criminal investigators as requiring that the Government must have sufficient evidence of a defendant's predisposition *before it ever seeks to contact him.* Surely the Court cannot intend to impose such a requirement, for it would mean that the Government must have a reasonable suspicion of criminal activity before it begins an investigation, a condition that we have never before imposed. The Court denies that its new rule will affect run-of-the-mill sting operations, and one hopes that it means what it says. Nonetheless, after this case, every defendant will claim that something the Government agent did before soliciting the crime "created" a predisposition that was not there before.... No doubt the Court would protest that its opinion does not stand for so broad a proposition, but the apparent lack of a principled basis for distinguishing these scenarios exposes a flaw in the more limited rule the Court today adopts.

The Court's rule is all the more troubling because it does not distinguish between Government conduct that merely highlights the temptation of the crime itself, and Government conduct that threatens, coerces, or leads a suspect to commit a crime in order to fulfill some other obligation....

While the Court states that the Government "exerted substantial pressure on petitioner to obtain and read such material as part of a fight against censorship and the infringement of individual rights," one looks at the record in vain for evidence of such "substantial pressure." The most one finds is letters advocating legislative action to liberalize obscenity laws, letters which could easily be ignored or thrown away. Much later, the Government sent separate mailings of catalogs of illegal materials. Nowhere did the Government suggest that the proceeds of the sale of the illegal materials would be used to support legislative reforms. While one of the HINT letters suggested that lobbying efforts would be funded by sales from a catalog, the catalogs actually sent, nearly a year later, were from different fictitious entities (Produit Outaouais and Far Eastern Trading Company), and gave no suggestion that money would be used for any political purposes. Nor did the Government claim to be organizing a civil disobedience movement, which would protest the pornography laws by breaking them. Contrary to the gloss given the evidence by the Court, the Government's suggestions of illegality may also have made buyers beware, and increased the mystique of the materials offered: "[f]or those of you who have enjoyed youthful material ... we have devised a method of getting these to you without prying eyes of U.S. Customs seizing your mail." Mr. Jacobson's curiosity to see what "all the trouble and the hysteria" was about, is certainly susceptible of more than one interpretation. And it is the jury that is charged with the obligation of interpreting it. In sum, the Court fails to construe the evidence in the light most favorable to the Government, and fails to draw all reasonable inferences in the

Government's favor. It was surely reasonable for the jury to infer that Mr. Jacobson was predisposed beyond a reasonable doubt, even if other inferences from the evidence were also possible.

II

The second puzzling thing about the Court's opinion is its redefinition of predisposition. The Court acknowledges that "[p]etitioner's responses to the many communications prior to the ultimate criminal act were . . . indicative of certain personal inclinations, including a predisposition to view photographs of preteen sex. . . ." If true, this should have settled the matter; Mr. Jacobson was predisposed to engage in the illegal conduct. Yet, the Court concludes, "petitioner's responses hardly support an inference that he would commit the crime of receiving child pornography through the mails."

The Court seems to add something new to the burden of proving predisposition. Not only must the Government show that a defendant was predisposed to engage in the illegal conduct, here, receiving photographs of minors engaged in sex, but also that the defendant was predisposed to break the law knowingly in order to do so. The statute violated here, however, does not require proof of specific intent to break the law; it requires only knowing receipt of visual depictions produced by using minors engaged in sexually explicit conduct. *See* 18 U.S.C. § 2252(a)(2); *United States v. Moncini*, 882 F.2d 401, 404–406 (9th Cir. 1989). Under the Court's analysis, however, the Government must prove *more* to show predisposition than it need prove in order to convict.

The Court ignores the judgment of Congress that specific intent is not an element of the crime of receiving sexually explicit photographs of minors. The elements of predisposition should track the elements of the crime. The predisposition requirement is meant to eliminate the entrapment defense for those defendants who would have committed the crime anyway, even absent Government inducement. Because a defendant might very well be convicted of the crime here absent Government inducement even though he did not know his conduct was illegal, a specific intent requirement does little to distinguish between those who would commit the crime without the inducement and those who would not. In sum, although the fact that Mr. Jacobson's purchases of Bare Boys I and Bare Boys II were legal at the time may have some relevance to the question of predisposition, it is not, as the Court suggests, dispositive.

The crux of the Court's concern in this case is that the Government went too far and "abused" the "processes of detection and enforcement" by luring an innocent person to violate the law. Consequently, the Court holds that the Government failed to prove beyond a reasonable doubt that Mr. Jacobson was predisposed to commit the crime. It was, however, the jury's task, as the conscience of the community, to decide whether Mr. Jacobson was a willing participant in the criminal activity here or an innocent dupe. The jury is the traditional "defense against arbitrary law enforcement." *Duncan v. Louisiana*, 391 U.S. 145, 156 (1968). Indeed, in *Sorrells*, in which the Court was also concerned about overzealous law enforcement, the Court did not decide itself that the Government conduct constituted entrapment, but left the issue to the jury. *Sorrells, supra*, at 452. There is no dispute that the jury in this case was fully and accurately instructed on the law of entrapment, and nonetheless found Mr. Jacobson guilty. Because I believe there was sufficient evidence to uphold the jury's verdict, I respectfully dissent.

Notes and Questions

(1) In a normal "sting" operation, a government agent poses as a buyer of illicit goods and services. *Jacobson* involved a "reverse sting" operation in which a government agent sells illicit goods or services to a defendant. Should a "reverse sting" be treated differently from a "normal sting" for entrapment purposes? For a discussion of the special problems relating to entrapment that are likely to arise in "reverse sting" situations, see Damon D. Camp, *Out of the Quagmire After* Jacobson v. United States: *Towards a More Balanced Entrapment Standard*, 83 J. Crim. L. & Criminology 1055, 1073–78 (1993).

(2) What is the significance of the majority's conclusion that the government must show that the defendant's predisposition to commit the crime was "not the product of the attention that the government had directed at [him]" prior to the time they asked him to commit a crime? Is the dissent correct in concluding that the Court's opinion will be "misread . . . as requiring that the Government must have sufficient evidence of a defendant's predisposition *before it ever seeks to contact him*"? In what situations will the government be permitted to contact a suspect to set up a reverse sting operation without having prior information that the suspect is predisposed towards criminal activity?

Entrapment and Due Process Problems

6–1: Concerned about the illegal killing of eagles in South Dakota, the United States Fish and Wildlife Service (FWS) initiated an undercover operation known as "Operation Eagle." A Navajo medicine man in New Mexico gave FWS Agent Mauldin the names of five individuals who were shipping Indian crafts made with protected bird parts from South Dakota to New Mexico. Mauldin sent letters to these five individuals, advising them that he was "interested in obtaining Indian-made items for resale throughout the Southwest."

Subsequently, Mauldin met with several of these individuals, including Dwight Dion, and told them that his company, Night Hawk Trading Company (a fictitious company), would pay "top dollar" for Indian handcrafts made from eagle or other protected bird feathers or for eagle carcasses. Dion and others immediately agreed to do business with Mauldin.

Over the next two years, Mauldin and his associate Standish paid several thousands of dollars to Dion and other individuals for crafts made with protected eagle parts and eagle carcasses. During this period, word of these transactions spread throughout the Yankton reservation. This reservation is located in a remote and desolate area of South Dakota and is one of the most impoverished in the nation.

Two years after the commencement of Operation Eagle, Terry Fool Bull, an impoverished resident of the Yankton reservation, was told by his father-in-law that Mauldin would pay $750 for an eagle carcass. Fool Bull had a regular job and had never before dealt with protected birds in any way. Because he was attracted by the money, however, he killed an eagle and sold it to Mauldin for $750. Both Dion and Fool Bull were convicted under a federal statute prohibiting the selling of eagles and other migratory birds.

What arguments can each of these defendants raise on appeal? How should the appeals be decided?

6–2: The government operation, known as ABSCAM, began some time in 1978. The basic nature of ABSCAM was that FBI agents posed as employees of Abdul Enterprises, a fictional multinational corporation whose principal, Yassir Habib, a fictional Arab Sheik, was said to be interested in investing large amounts of money in this country and in emigrating here. Melvin Weinberg, a "career swindler" with a long criminal record, was utilized by the government to "spread the word" that the Sheik was interested in meeting public officials who could facilitate his planned investments.

The Philadelphia phase of ABSCAM began when Weinberg called Howard Criden, a Philadelphia attorney, and told him that the Sheik was "looking to build a hotel" in Philadelphia. Criden eventually arranged for a meeting between himself, City Councilman Schwartz and two FBI agents (Wald and Haridopolis) who were posing as representatives of the Arabs. One of the agents indicated that the people he represented were interested in building "a hotel facility in Philadelphia that may amount to some 30 or 40 million dollars." He went on to say that there might be zoning and variance problems and he wanted to take care of "any potential problems long before they exist."

Schwartz responded with a statement of his own political power and importance. The following exchange then took place:

Wald: Is it fair to say that by doing business with you, my zoning problems become. . . .

Criden: You don't have any.

Wald: Okay, there are 17 members here. Do we have a controlling vote?

Schwartz: Yes.

Wald: You can control them?

Schwartz: You tell me your birthdate. I'll give them to you for your birthday.

Later, Schwartz said he assumed the project was legitimate or he "wouldn't be here." Wald said the project was basically legitimate. He then asked Schwartz for assurances of his support if the project "violates some minor type statute or ordinance or something." Schwartz gave this support and later was paid $30,000.

Wald and Criden also met with Councilman Jannotti. Wald asked Jannotti if he could count on his vote if a problem arose. The following exchange took place:

> Jannotti: Why sure. First of all, you have a legitimate project. You're going to invest 36 million dollars in the City of Philadelphia, which is going to create a tax base and going to create employment.

> Wald: Right, but a lot of legitimate things get bogged down. We don't want to be bogged down.

> Jannotti: No, I can't see this being bogged down.

Later, Wald explained that the Arab mentality was to pay money in advance so that they would be sure to have a friend in case a problem came up. The conversation continued:

> Wald: I was sent to Philadelphia to pay for certain things because that is the psychology and that is the method of business that these people are used to, and that is how they conduct business.

> Jannotti: Well, just on the basis of what you want me to do, it's enough for me to get on the floor and argue. I don't have to even care what else they come up with. This has been our job to bring as much business and tax base and employment to the City of Philadelphia. If that's the way they want to do business, that's all right too.

Jannotti also said that he and Schwartz controlled the city council in the sense that over the last two years they had "never lost a vote on an issue they wanted passed." At the end of the meeting, Wald paid Jannotti $10,000.

Schwartz and Jannoti were found guilty of various federal offenses relating to accepting bribes.

On appeal, what entrapment or due process issues should defendants raise? How should the court rule on these claims?

6–3: After Federal Agents arrested Tracy for counterfeiting, Tracy agreed to provide them with information about Joost, his counterfeiting partner. Tracy introduced Joost to two Rhode Island detectives who pretended to be petty thieves. One of the detectives subsequently agreed to pay Joost 50 cents on the dollar for his counterfeit tokens. After getting to know the detectives, Joost talked to them about crimes, including ones he committed in the past and criminal activities planned for the future.

A month after meeting Joost, the detectives expressed interest in doing an armed robbery with him. Joost stated that he did not engage in armed robberies. Nevertheless, he exhibited considerable know-how, critiquing various plans the detectives brought forward and showing them how to use weapons during a robbery. According to Joost, he actually had no interest in participating in a robbery. He "talked tough" because he was dealing with "tough people." In addition, he wanted them to stay interested in him because they were providing him with income from his counterfeiting.

In one of his conversations with the detectives, Joost mentioned the possibility of robbing a particular warehouse. The detectives expressed interest and asked Joost to obtain a gun to use in the robbery. Joost said that he would, but failed to produce a gun for more than two months, despite repeated requests by the detectives. On some of the occasions when the detectives requested a gun, Joost asked them about their plans. When the detectives explained how the gun would be used to perpetrate a robbery, Joost criticized their plans, stating either that the plan would not work or that it would be better not to use a gun.

About four months after meeting Joost, the detectives again asked him to get a gun for use in a robbery. According to Joost, he was facing financial difficulties at this time and was worried that if he didn't get them a gun they would no longer buy his counterfeit coins. After the detectives explained the robbery they were going to commit, Joost speculated about what could go wrong. One of the detectives then said he wondered if Joost was "serious about it." In response, Joost replied, "I'll get you a piece."

Shortly after that, Joost obtained a gun from Tracy and gave it to the detectives. Joost was charged with the federal offense of "being a felon in possession of a firearm and ammunition." At trial, Joost requested that the judge submit an entrapment defense to the jury. The judge refused. Joost was convicted.

Did the judge err in refusing to submit Joost's entrapment defense to the jury?

6–4: Arthur Dawson arrived at the Miami International Airport with his girlfriend Kristin Spring. At the time of their arrival, airport police were conducting a decoy operation designed to catch luggage thieves. The operation was in response to an increasing number of thefts and tourist crimes at the airport.

The police had created a decoy bag — a black soft-sided camera case containing an Olympus 35mm camera and a Nikon 35mm camera. The two cameras were worth approximately $440. The camera bag had a name tag identifying the owner as J.A. Mendoza. The tag also included a fictitious address and phone number for Mendoza. The police placed the decoy bag on a pay telephone shelf in Concourse D and took up surveillance positions so that they could observe the decoy bag.

While Dawson and Spring were waiting to purchase air tickets to Barbados, Spring noticed that a man who had been using the telephone had walked away and appeared to have left a bag behind. When Spring approached the man about the bag, the man indicated that the bag did not belong to him. Dawson and Spring became concerned that the bag might contain a bomb. They waited 15 or 20 minutes, then went over to the telephone booth and looked inside the bag. Upon seeing the cameras, Dawson brought the bag and its contents back to his seat. Subsequently, Dawson and Spring rented a car and placed the decoy bag inside. At that point, the police approached and asked them about the bag. Dawson replied that he had found it abandoned in the airport and was taking it with him.

Dawson was charged with theft. He was gainfully employed and had no prior criminal record.

Was Dawson entrapped as a matter of law?

6–5: On June 6, 1991, Amy Lively sold a packet of cocaine to "Rick," an undercover detective, for $70. She was charged with selling cocaine. Amy's defenses were that she was entrapped and that the government's conduct was so outrageous that it violated due process.

Amy testified that at age 18 she realized she had a serious drinking problem. After attempting alcohol withdrawal on her own, she admitted herself into a detoxification program at St. Mary's Medical Center. Immediately following the program, she began attending Alcoholics Anonymous/Narcotics Anonymous (AA/NA) meetings. In March 1991, she had an alcoholic relapse and entered a 28-day inpatient detoxification program at Walla Walla General Hospital.

After her release from the hospital, Amy resumed attendance at AA/NA meetings. In April 1991, she met Desai, who was working as a police informant for the drug unit. Desai was attending AA/NA meetings in order to identify repeat drug addicts who were continuing to sell illegal drugs. According to Amy, two weeks after she met Desai, he asked her out on a date. Amy found Desai to be very supportive and responsive to her emotional needs. According to her, they began a sexual relationship in May 1991, and lived together for two months. Desai proposed marriage in late June 1991, and the two often talked of their plans to marry.

Amy also testified that, while they were living together, Desai repeatedly told her that he had a good friend named Rick who wanted to buy cocaine. After Desai asked her every day for two weeks to get drugs for Rick, she agreed to purchase cocaine. According to Amy, she did so only because she was emotionally dependent on Desai.

Desai testified on rebuttal and denied many of Amy's claims. Although he admitted that he and Amy had dates and that Amy moved in to his apartment during the summer of 1991, he denied that they ever had a sexual relationship. He testified that he and Amy slept in separate bedrooms and that Amy stayed at his apartment for only about three weeks. He admitted that marriage was discussed but testified that he never proposed to her, that she initiated the discussions, and that he thought she was joking when she talked about their marriage plans. According to Desai, Amy was the first to discuss drugs, mentioning that she had a connection and could get marihuana and cocaine. He admitted asking her to get cocaine for "Rick," but denied that he asked her repeatedly over a two-week period to do so.

At the conclusion of the evidence, the defense moved for a directed verdict on two grounds: (1) entrapment was established as a matter of law; (2) the government's conduct was so outrageous as to violate due process. The trial judge denied the motion. After proper jury instructions, the jury adjudicated Amy guilty of the sale of cocaine.

Should Amy's conviction be reversed on appeal? If so, on what ground?

6–6: Concerned about lax security at Miami International Airport, Federal Agents from United States Customs and the Drug Enforcement Agency (DEA) initiated "Operation Ramp Rat," a sting operation under which Federal Agents posed as drug dealers looking for drug couriers. The agents offered large amounts of cash to airport employees to unload cocaine from commercial flights and navigate it around security checkpoints and onto other planes. The employees, mainly baggage handlers and supervisors making $7 to $20 an hour, were offered amounts ranging from $500 to $17,500 to assist the smuggling operation.

Edwin Rodriguez was arrested along with 58 others in the sting operation. He was offered $15,000 to carry a bag containing 3 kilos of cocaine, hand grenades, and a pistol onto an American Airlines passenger airliner. Rodriguez claimed the informer pursued him for weeks and that, when they finally met, the undercover agent went out of his way to show him the contents of the bag. Rodriguez asserted that he took this gesture as an implied threat. Reluctantly, he agreed to carry the bag onto the plane in exchange for $15,000, $5000 to be paid in advance. Soon after receiving the bag and $5000, he was arrested by federal agents and charged with various offenses, including conspiracy to smuggle drugs.

Rodriguez worked 13 to 14 hours a day, and held down a second part-time job. He had passed a security check when he accepted the job, and had no prior record for drug offenses. He did, however, have a previous conviction for credit card fraud. At trial, Rodriguez asserted an entrapment defense.

Should his defense be accepted?

6–7: In August 1992, Mark Staufer was introduced to undercover DEA Agent Michael Daul. The meeting was initiated and arranged by Scott, an acquaintance of Staufer's who was working as a confidential informer for the DEA.

At the meeting, Daul asked Staufer, who was experiencing serious financial difficulties, to sell him 10,000 doses of LSD. Staufer expressed reluctance, stating that he would prefer to sell 5,000 doses of LSD. In response, Daul immediately raised the price he would pay for delivery of the 10,000 doses. Staufer eventually agreed to sell Daul 10,000 doses for $8,000.

Staufer was charged with possession with intent to distribute LSD. At his trial, he raised an entrapment defense. The jury found him guilty as charged. The sentencing judge found that prior to this case, Staufer had not engaged in any drug deals of similar magnitude. Based on the weight of the drugs and the paper on which the LSD had been placed, the judge set the offense level at 36 and reduced it two points on the basis of Staufer's clean prior record and his remorse. At sentencing, Staufer requested that the judge depart downwards from the sentencing guidelines based on sentencing entrapment. Believing he lacked the legal authority to depart downwards on this basis, the judge sentenced Staufer to 51 months in prison and five years' probation.

On appeal, Staufer is claiming that the sentencing judge should have departed downwards from the sentencing guidelines on the ground that, although predisposed to committing a lesser offense, Staufer was "entrapped into committing a greater offense subject to greater punishment."

How should the appellate court rule?

6–8: Poehlman, an Air Force veteran who happened to be a cross-dresser and a foot-fetishist, sought a female companion who would be accepting of his lifestyle and sexual interests. Poehlman discovered an internet ad placed by a "Sharon" who was looking for someone, preferably a serviceman, who would be understanding of her family's "unique needs." Poehlman sent Sharon an e-mail in response stating that he too had "unique needs" and that, if there was compatibility, he would ultimately be interested in marriage.

In subsequent correspondence, Sharon expressed support for Poehlman's alternative lifestyle and stated she needed a "special man teacher" for her three little girls. Sharon made it clear, however, that she herself did not want to have a relationship with Poehlman. Poehlman initially appeared uncertain as to what it meant to be a "special man teacher" for Sharon's girls. He assured Sharon that he would teach her children "proper morals." When Sharon hinted that she wanted a "sex instructor" for her children, however, Poehlman told her he could teach the children whatever she wanted him to. In the course of explaining the kind of instruction he could provide, he described performing anal and oral sex with Sharon's children.

Poehlman traveled from his home in Florida to California in order to meet Sharon in person at a hotel. Sharon greeted Poehlman with pornographic magazines, prompting Poehlman to volunteer that he "had always looked at little girls." Sharon then escorted Poehlman to an adjoining room where she told him he would meet her children and begin their lessons. Instead of meeting the children, however, Poehlman was greeted by federal and state agents who proceeded to arrest him for the federal crime of crossing state lines for the purpose of engaging in sexual acts with a minor.

At his trial, Poehlman claims that his correspondence with Sharon establishes that he was entrapped as a matter of law.

Should Poehlman's claim be accepted?

6–9: The FBI set up a reverse-sting operation where undercover agents, posing as drug dealers, asked San Antonio police officers to provide security for drug transactions in exchange for money. Pagan, an agent posing as a drug dealer, conducted several such transactions with Sergeant Fragozo. He then asked Fragozo for the names of other officers who might be interested in participating in the same illegal activity. Fragozo recommended Gutierrez, a lower-ranking officer on the force.

Pagan contacted Gutierrez and told him a businessman wanted someone to investigate his stripper girlfriend to determine whether she was cheating on him. When Gutierrez met with Pagan, however, Pagan told him that his job would actually be to provide security for illegal drug shipments. When Gutierrez expressed surprise at the change of the job offer, Pagan told him he should feel free to decline the job if he wanted to. Gutierrez, who knew that Fragozo had engaged in similar transactions, eventually agreed to participate. Subsequently, Gutierrez provided security for two drug shipping transactions. He was paid a total of $5,000.

The government charged Gutierrez with various federal drug distribution offenses. At his trial, Gutierrez sought to raise an entrapment defense. He claimed that he had participated in the illegal transactions because he was frightened of Fragozo who, as his superior, had access to his personal information and knew where he lived. The trial judge refused to instruct the jury on entrapment and the jury subsequently convicted Gutierrez of two charges.

Should the trial judge have instructed the jury on entrapment?

Selected Bibliography

John David Buretta, Note, *Reconfiguring the Entrapment and Outrageous Government Conduct Doctrines,* 84 Geo. L.J. 1945 (1996)

Damon D. Camp, *Criminal Law: Out of the Quagmire After* Jacobson v. United States: *Towards a More Balanced Entrapment Standard,* 83 J. Crim. L. & Criminology 1055 (1993)

Jonathan C. Carlson, *The Act Requirement and the Foundations of the Entrapment Defense,* 73 Va. L. Rev. 1011 (1987)

Joseph A. Colquitt, *Rethinking Entrapment,* 41 Am. Crim. L. Rev. 1389 (2004)

Anthony M. Dillof, *Unraveling Unlawful Entrapment,* 94 J. Crim. L. & Criminology 827 (2004)

Donald A. Dripps, *Fundamental Retribution Error: Criminal Justice and the Social Psychology of Blame,* 56 Vand. L. Rev. 1383 (2003)

Stephen A. Gardbaum, *"The Government Made Me Do It": A Proposed Approach to Entrapment Under* Jacobson v. United States, 79 Cornell L. Rev. 995 (1994)

Bennett L. Gershman, *Abscam, the Judiciary, and the Ethics of Entrapment,* 91 Yale L.J. 1565 (1982)

Bruce Hay, *Sting Operations, Undercover Agents, and Entrapment,* 70 Mo. L. Rev. 387 (2005)

Richard H. McAdams, *The Political Economy of Entrapment,* 96 J. Crim. L. & Criminology 107 (2005)

Roger C. Park, *The Entrapment Controversy,* 60 Minn. L. Rev. 163 (1976)

James F. Ponsoldt and Stephen Marsh, *Entrapment When the Spoken Word is the Crime,* 68 Fordham L. Rev. 1199 (2000)

Jessica A. Roth, *The Anomaly of Entrapment,* 91 Wash. U. L. Rev. 979 (2014)

Louis Michael Seidman, *The Supreme Court, Entrapment, and Our Criminal Justice Dilemma*, 1981 Sup. Ct. Rev. 111

Dru Stevenson, *Entrapment and the Problem of Deterring Police Misconduct*, 37 Conn. L. Rev. 67 (2004)

Maura F. J. Whelan, *Lead Us Not Into (Unwarranted) Temptation: A Proposal to Replace the Entrapment Defense with a Reasonable-Suspicion Requirement*, 133 U. Pa. L. Rev. 1193 (1985)

Part III
Confessions

Chapter 7

Due Process of Law and Confessions

Introductory Note

At common law, coerced confessions were excluded from evidence because of a fear that they would be untrustworthy. By the eighteenth century, it was established that "a confession forced from the mind by the flattery of hope, or the torture of fear, comes in so questionable a shape when it is to be considered as evidence of guilt, that no credit ought to be given to it; and therefore it is rejected." Otis H. Stephens, THE SUPREME COURT AND CONFESSIONS OF GUILT 20 (1973) (quoting *The King v. Warickshall*, 1 Leach 263–64, 168 Eng. Rep. 234–35 (K.B. 1783)).

In 1936, the Supreme Court for the first time considered a state case in which the constitutionality of a defendant's incriminating statement was at issue. In *Brown v. Mississippi*, 297 U.S. 278, 56 S. Ct. 461, 80 L. Ed. 682 (1936), the Court overturned convictions based on confessions obtained after the defendants had been whipped until they agreed to confess to such statements as the officers dictated. The convictions were held to be in violation of due process of law. This decision and some of those immediately following it seemed entirely consistent with the common law rule. Confessions obtained by the methods employed in *Brown* and some of the other early cases are obviously likely to be unreliable.

As the cases in this Chapter indicate, however, the Court's later decisions holding confessions in violation of the Due Process Clause could not be explained entirely on the basis of untrustworthiness. In considering the cases in Chapter Seven, students should try to identify the additional concerns that motivated the Court and assess the effect these concerns should have in determining whether an incriminating statement offends the Due Process Clause.

The due process confession cases are significant historically because they shed light on the Court's reasons for subsequently adopting additional constitutional approaches towards regulating the admissibility of confessions. During the 28 years between 1936 and 1964, the Due Process Clause was the only basis on which state defendants' incriminating statements were found to be unconstitutional. During the mid-1960s, however, the Court held that both the Fifth Amendment Privilege Against Self-Incrimination and the Sixth Amendment Right to Counsel also governed the constitutional admissibility of incriminating statements. In reading the first two cases in Chapter Seven, students should consider why the Court's experience with deciding confession cases under the due process test may have led it to turn to these additional guarantees in search of "some automatic device by which the potential evils of incommunicado interrogation [could] be controlled." Geoffrey R. Stone, *The Miranda Doctrine in the Burger Court*, 1977 Sup. Ct. Rev. 102–03 (quoting Walter V. Schaefer, The Suspect and Society 10 (1967)).

The due process cases are also important because they continue to play a significant role in determining the admissibility of confessions. The Court's Fifth and Sixth Amendment decisions regulating the admissibility of confessions did not completely displace the due process standard. The relationship between the due process test and the *Miranda* decision is particularly interesting. In some contexts, a defendant will be able to establish that an incriminating statement must be excluded on the basis of the due process cases even though it was not obtained in violation of *Miranda*. Moreover, even if it is established that a statement has been obtained in violation of *Miranda*, determining whether the statement would be admissible under the due process cases will often have important practical consequences. As will be seen in Chapter Thirteen, the exclusionary rule applied to a confession that is determined to be in violation of due process is much stricter than the one applied to a confession that is simply determined to be in violation of *Miranda*.

Ashcraft v. Tennessee

United States Supreme Court

322 U.S. 143, 64 S. Ct. 921, 88 L. Ed. 1192 (1944)

MR. JUSTICE BLACK delivered the opinion of the Court.

About three o'clock on the morning of Thursday, June 5, 1941, Mrs. Zelma Ida Ashcraft got in her automobile at her home in Memphis, Tennessee, and set out on a trip to visit her mother's home in Kentucky. Late in the afternoon of the same day, her car was observed a few miles out of Memphis, standing on the wrong side of a road which she would likely have taken on her journey. Just off the road, in a slough, her lifeless body was found. On her head were cut places inflicted by blows sufficient to have caused her death. Petitioner Ware, age 20, a Negro, was indicted in a state court and found guilty of her murder. Petitioner Ashcraft, age 45, a white man, husband of the deceased, charged with having hired Ware to commit the murder, was tried jointly with Ware and convicted as an accessory before the fact. Both were sentenced to ninety-nine years in the state penitentiary. The Supreme Court of Tennessee affirmed the convictions.

In applying to us for certiorari, Ware and Ashcraft urged that alleged confessions were used at their trial which had been extorted from them by state law enforcement officers in violation of the Fourteenth Amendment, and that "solely and alone" on the basis of these confessions they had been convicted.

. . . .

Ashcraft was born on an Arkansas farm. At the age of eleven he left the farm and became a farm hand working for others. Years later he gravitated into construction work, finally becoming a skilled dragline and steam shovel operator. Uncontradicted evidence in the record was that he had acquired for himself "an excellent reputation." In 1929 he married the deceased Zelma Ida Ashcraft. Childless, they accumulated, apparently through Ashcraft's earnings, a very modest amount of jointly held property including bank accounts and an equity in the home in which they lived. The Supreme Court of Tennessee found "nothing to show but what the home life of Ashcraft and the deceased was pleasant and happy." Several of Mrs. Ashcraft's friends who were guests at the Ashcraft home on the night before her tragic death testified that both husband and wife appeared to be in a happy frame of mind.

The officers first talked to Ashcraft about 6 p.m. on the day of his wife's murder as he was returning home from work. Informed by them of the tragedy, he was taken to an undertaking establishment to identify her body which previously had been identified only by a driver's license. From there he was taken to the county jail where he conferred with the officers until about 2 a.m. No clues of ultimate value came from this conference, though it did result in the officers' holding and interrogating the Ashcrafts' maid and several of her friends. During the following week the officers made extensive investigations in Ashcraft's neighborhood and elsewhere and further conferred with Ashcraft himself on several occasions, but none of these activities produced tangible evidence pointing to the identity of the murderer.

Then, early in the evening of Saturday, June 14, the officers came to Ashcraft's home and "took him into custody." In the words of the Tennessee Supreme Court,

> They took him to an office or room on the northwest corner of the fifth floor of the Shelby County jail. This office is equipped with all sorts of crime and detective devices such as a fingerprint outfit, cameras, high-powered lights, and such other devices as might be found in a homicide investigating office. . . . It appears that the officers placed Ashcraft at a table in this room on the fifth floor of the county jail with a light over his head and began to quiz him. They questioned him in relays until the following Monday morning, June 16, 1941, around nine-thirty or ten o'clock. It appears that Ashcraft from Saturday evening at seven o'clock until Monday morning at approximately nine-thirty never left this homicide room of the fifth floor.[4] Testimony of the officers shows that the reason they questioned Ashcraft "in relays" was that they became so tired they were compelled to rest. But

---

4. From the testimony it appears that Ashcraft was taken from the jail about 11 o'clock Sunday night for a period of approximately an hour to help the officers hunt the place where Ware lived. On his return Ashcraft was, for a short time, kept in a jail room different from that in which he was kept the rest of the time.

from 7:00 Saturday evening until 9:30 Monday morning Ashcraft had no rest. One officer did say that he gave the suspect a single five minutes' respite, but except for this five minutes the procedure consisted of one continuous stream of questions.

As to what happened in the fifth-floor jail room during this thirty-six hour secret examination the testimony follows the usual pattern and is in hopeless conflict. Ashcraft swears that the first thing said to him when he was taken into custody was, "Why in hell did you kill your wife?"; that during the course of the examination he was threatened and abused in various ways; and that as the hours passed his eyes became blinded by a powerful electric light, his body became weary, and the strain on his nerves became unbearable. The officers, on the other hand, swear that throughout the questioning they were kind and considerate. They say that they did not accuse Ashcraft of the murder until four hours after he was brought to the jail building, though they freely admit that from that time on their barrage of questions was constantly directed at him on the assumption that he was the murderer. Together with other persons whom they brought in on Monday morning to witness the culmination of the thirty-six hour ordeal the officers declare that at that time Ashcraft was "cool," "calm," "collected," "normal"; that his vision was unimpaired and his eyes not bloodshot; and that he showed no outward signs of being tired or sleepy.

As to whether Ashcraft actually confessed, there is a similar conflict of testimony. Ashcraft maintains that although the officers incessantly attempted by various tactics of intimidation to entrap him into a confession, not once did he admit knowledge concerning or participation in the crime. And he specifically denies the officers' statements that he accused Ware of the crime, insisting that in response to their questions he merely gave them the name of Ware as one of several men who occasionally had ridden with him to work. The officers' version of what happened, however, is that about 11 p.m. on Sunday night, after twenty-eight hours' constant questioning, Ashcraft made a statement that Ware had overpowered him at his home and abducted the deceased, and was probably the killer. About midnight the officers found Ware and took him into custody, and, according to their testimony, Ware made a self-incriminating statement as of early Monday morning, and at 5:40 a.m. signed by mark a written confession in which appeared the statement that Ashcraft had hired him to commit the murder. This alleged confession of Ware was read to Ashcraft about six o'clock Monday morning, whereupon Ashcraft is said substantially to have admitted its truth in a detailed statement taken down by a reporter. About 9:30 Monday morning a transcript of Ashcraft's purported statement was read to him. The State's position is that he affirmed its truth but refused to sign the transcript, saying that he first wanted to consult his lawyer. As to this latter 9:30 episode the officers' testimony is reinforced by testimony of the several persons whom they brought in to witness the end of the examination.

In reaching our conclusion as to the validity of Ashcraft's confession we do not resolve any of the disputed questions of fact relating to the details of what transpired within the confession chamber of the jail or whether Ashcraft actually did confess.

Such disputes, we may say, are an inescapable consequence of secret inquisitorial practices. And always evidence concerning the inner details of secret inquisitions is weighted against an accused, particularly where, as here, he is charged with a brutal crime, or where, as in many other cases, his supposed offense bears relation to an unpopular economic, political, or religious cause.

Our conclusion is that if Ashcraft made a confession it was not voluntary but compelled. We reach this conclusion from facts which are not in dispute at all. Ashcraft, a citizen of excellent reputation, was taken into custody by police officers. Ten days' examination of the Ashcrafts' maid, and of several others, in jail where they were held, had revealed nothing whatever against Ashcraft. Inquiries among his neighbors and business associates likewise had failed to unearth one single tangible clue pointing to his guilt. For thirty-six hours after Ashcraft's seizure during which period he was held incommunicado, without sleep or rest, relays of officers, experienced investigators, and highly trained lawyers questioned him without respite. From the beginning of the questioning at 7 o'clock on Saturday evening until 6 o'clock on Monday morning Ashcraft denied that he had anything to do with the murder of his wife. And at a hearing before a magistrate about 8:30 Monday morning Ashcraft pleaded not guilty to the charge of murder which the officers had sought to make him confess during the previous thirty-six hours.

We think a situation such as that here shown by uncontradicted evidence is so inherently coercive that its very existence is irreconcilable with the possession of mental freedom by a lone suspect against whom its full coercive force is brought to bear. It is inconceivable that any court of justice in the land, conducted as our courts are, open to the public, would permit prosecutors serving in relays to keep a defendant witness under continuous cross-examination for thirty-six hours without rest or sleep in an effort to extract a "voluntary" confession. Nor can we, consistently with Constitutional due process of law, hold voluntary a confession where prosecutors do the same thing away from the restraining influences of a public trial in an open court room.

The Constitution of the United States stands as a bar against the conviction of any individual in an American court by means of a coerced confession. There have been, and are now, certain foreign nations with governments dedicated to an opposite policy: governments which convict individuals with testimony obtained by police organizations possessed of an unrestrained power to seize persons suspected of crimes against the state, hold them in secret custody, and wring from them confessions by physical or mental torture. So long as the Constitution remains the basic law of our Republic, America will not have that kind of government.

. . . .

Mr. Justice Jackson, dissenting.

A sovereign State is now before us, summoned on the charge that it has obtained convictions by methods so unfair that a federal court must set aside what the state courts have done. Heretofore the State has had the benefit of a presumption of regularity and legality. A confession made by one in custody heretofore has been admissible in evidence unless it was proved and found that it was obtained by pressures so strong that it was *in fact* involuntarily made, that the individual will of the particular confessor had been overcome by torture, mob violence, fraud, trickery, threats, or promises. Even where there was excess and abuse of power on the part of officers, the State still was entitled to use the confession if upon examination of the whole evidence it was found to negative the view that the accused had "so lost his freedom of action that the statements made were not his but were the result of the deprivation of his free choice to admit, to deny, or to refuse to answer." *Lisenba v. California*, 314 U.S. 219, 241, 62 S. Ct. 280, 292, 86 L. Ed. 166.

In determining these issues of fact, respect for the sovereign character of the several States always has constrained this Court to give great weight to findings of fact of state courts. While we have sometimes gone back of state court determinations to make sure whether the guaranties of the Fourteenth Amendment have or have not been violated, in close cases the decisions of state courts have often been sufficient to tip the scales in favor of affirmance.

As we read the present decision the Court in effect declines to apply these well-established principles. Instead, it: (1) substitutes for determination on conflicting evidence the question whether this confession was actually produced by coercion, a presumption that it was, on a new doctrine that examination in custody of this duration is "inherently coercive"; (2) it makes that presumption irrebuttable — *i.e.*, a rule of law — because, while it goes back of the State decisions to find certain facts, it refuses to resolve conflicts in evidence to determine whether other of the State's proof is sufficient to overcome such presumption; and, in so doing, (3) it sets aside the findings by the courts of Tennessee that on all the facts this confession did not result from coercion, either giving those findings no weight or regarding them as immaterial.

We must bear in mind that this case does not come here from a lower federal court over whose conduct we may assert a general supervisory power. If it did, we should be at liberty to apply rules as to the admissibility of confessions, based on our own conception of permissible procedure, and in which we may embody restrictions even greater than those imposed upon the States by the Fourteenth Amendment. But we have no such supervisory power over state courts. We may not lay down rules of evidence for them nor revise their decisions merely because we feel more confidence in our own wisdom and rectitude. We have no power to discipline the police or law-enforcement officers of the State of Tennessee nor to reverse its convictions in retribution for conduct which we may personally disapprove.

The burden of protecting society from most crimes against persons and property falls upon the State. Different States have different crime problems and some freedom to vary procedures according to their own ideas. Here, a State was forced by an unwitnessed and baffling murder to vindicate its law and protect its society. To nullify its conviction in this particular case upon a consideration of all the facts would be a delicate exercise of federal judicial power. But to go beyond this, as the Court does today, and divine in the due process clause of the Fourteenth Amendment an exclusion of confessions on an irrebuttable presumption that custody and examination are "inherently coercive" if of some unspecified duration within thirty-six hours, requires us to make more than a passing expression of our doubts and disagreements.

I

The claim of a suspect to immunity from questioning creates one of the most vexing problems in criminal law — that branch of the law which does the courts and the legal profession least credit. The consequences upon society of limiting examination of persons out of court cannot fairly be appraised without recognition of the advantage criminals already enjoy in immunity from compulsory examination in court. Of this latter Mr. Justice Cardozo, for an all but unanimous Court, said: "This too might be lost, and justice still be done. Indeed, today as in the past there are students of our penal system who look upon the immunity as a mischief rather than a benefit, and who would limit its scope, or destroy it altogether. No doubt there would remain the need to give protection against torture, physical or mental." *Palko v. Connecticut*, 302 U.S. 319, 325–26, 58 S. Ct. 149, 151–52, 82 L. Ed. 288.

This Court never yet has held that the Constitution denies a State the right to use a confession just because the confessor was questioned in custody where it did not also find other circumstances that deprived him of a "free choice to admit, to deny, or to refuse to answer." *Lisenba v. California*, 314 U.S. 219, 241, 62 S. Ct. 280, 292, 86 L. Ed. 166. The Constitution requires that a conviction rest on a fair trial. Forced confessions are ruled out of a fair trial. They are ruled out because they have been wrung from a prisoner by measures which are offensive to concepts of fundamental fairness. Different courts have used different terms to express the test by which to judge the inadmissibility of a confession, such as "forced," "coerced," "involuntary," "extorted," "loss of freedom of will." But always where we have professed to speak with the voice of the due process clause, the test, in whatever words stated, has been applied to the particular confessor at the time of confession.

It is for this reason that American courts hold almost universally and very properly that a confession obtained during or shortly after the confessor has been subjected to brutality, torture, beating, starvation, or physical pain of any kind is *prima facie* "involuntary." The effect of threats alone may depend more on individual susceptibility to fear. But men are so constituted that many will risk the postponed consequences of yielding to a demand for a confession in order to be rid of present or imminent physical suffering. Actual or threatened violence have no place in eliciting truth and it is fair to assume that no officer of the law will resort to cruelty if truth is what he is seeking. We need not be too exacting about proof of the effects of such violence on the individual involved, for their effect on the human personality is invariably and seriously demoralizing.

When, however, we consider a confession obtained by questioning, even if persistent and prolonged, we are in a different field. Interrogation *per se* is not, while violence *per se* is, an outlaw. Questioning is an indispensable instrumentality of justice. It may be abused, of course, as cross-examination in court may be abused, but the principles by which we may adjudge when it passes constitutional limits are quite different from those that condemn police brutality, and are far more difficult to apply. And they call for a more responsible and cautious exercise of our office. For we may err on the side of hostility to violence without doing injury to legitimate prosecution of crime; we cannot read an undiscriminating hostility to mere interrogation into the Constitution without unduly fettering the States in protecting society from the criminal.

It probably is the normal instinct to deny and conceal any shameful or guilty act. Even a "voluntary confession" is not likely to be the product of the same motives with which one may volunteer information that does not incriminate or concern him. The term "voluntary" confession does not mean voluntary in the sense of a confession to a priest merely to rid one's soul of a sense of guilt. "Voluntary confessions" in criminal law are the product of calculations of a different order, and usually proceed from a belief that further denial is useless and perhaps prejudicial. To speak of any confessions of crime made after arrest as being "voluntary" or "uncoerced" is somewhat inaccurate, although traditional.

A confession is wholly and incontestably voluntary only if a guilty person gives himself up to the law and becomes his own accuser. The Court bases its decision on the premise that custody and examination of a prisoner for thirty six hours is "inherently coercive." Of course it is. And so is custody and examination for one hour. Arrest itself is inherently coercive, and so is detention. When not justified, infliction of such indignities upon the person is actionable as a tort. Of course such acts put pressure upon the prisoner to answer questions, to answer them truthfully, and to confess if guilty.

But does the Constitution prohibit use of all confessions made after arrest because questioning, while one is deprived of freedom, is "inherently coercive"? The Court does not quite say so, but it is moving far and fast in that direction. The step it now takes is to hold this confession inadmissible because of the time taken in getting it.

The duration and intensity of an examination or inquisition always have been regarded as one of the relevant and important considerations in estimating its effect on the will of the individual involved. Thirty-six hours is a long stretch of questioning. That the inquiry was prolonged and persistent is a factor that in any calculation of its effect on Ashcraft would count heavily against the confession. But some men would withstand for days pressures that would destroy the will of another in hours. Always heretofore the ultimate question has been whether the confessor was in possession of his own will and self-control at the time of confession. For its bearing on this question the Court always has considered the confessor's strength or weakness, whether he was educated or illiterate, intelligent or moronic, well or ill, Negro or white.

. . . .

If the constitutional admissibility of a confession is no longer to be measured by the mental state of the individual confessor but by a general doctrine dependent on the clock, it should be capable of statement in definite terms. If thirty-six hours is more than is permissible, what about 24? or 12? or 6? or 1? All are "inherently coercive." Of course questions of law like this often turn on matters of degree. But are not the States entitled to know, if this Court is able to state, what the considerations are which make any particular degree decisive? How else may state courts apply our tests?

. . . .

II

Apart from Ashcraft's uncorroborated testimony, which the Tennessee courts refused to believe, there is much evidence in this record from persons whom they did believe and were justified in believing. This evidence shows that despite the "inherent coerciveness" of the circumstances of his examination, the confession when made was deliberate, free, and voluntary in the sense in which that term is used in criminal law. This Court could not, in our opinion, hold this confession an involuntary one except by substituting its presumption in place of analysis of the evidence and refusing to weigh the evidence even in rebuttal of its presumption.

As in most such cases, we start with some admitted facts. In the early morning Mrs. Ashcraft left her home in an automobile to visit relatives. She was found murdered. She had not been robbed nor ravished, although an effort had been made to give the crime an appearance of robbery. The officers knew of no other motive for the killing and naturally turned to her husband for information.

On the afternoon of the crime, Thursday, June 5, 1941, they took Ashcraft to the morgue to identify the body, and to the county jail, where he was kept and interviewed until 2:00 a.m. He makes no complaint of his treatment at this time. In this and several later interviews he made a number of statements with reference to the condition of the car, and as to Mrs. Ashcraft's having taken a certain drug, and as to money which she was accustomed to carry on her person, which further investigation indicated to be untrue. Still Ashcraft was not arrested. He professed to be willing to assist in identifying the killer. At last, on Saturday evening, June 14, an officer brought Ashcraft to the jail for further questioning. He was taken to a room on the fifth floor and questioned intermittently by several officers over a period of about thirty-six hours.

There are two versions as to what happened during this period of questioning. According to the version of the officers, which was accepted by the court which saw the witnesses, what happened? On Saturday evening Ashcraft was taken to the jail, where he was questioned by Mr. Becker and Mr. Battle. Becker is in the Intelligence Service of the United States Army at the present time and before that was in charge of the Homicide Bureau of the Sheriff's office of Shelby County, Tennessee. Battle has for eight years been an Assistant Attorney General of the County. They began questioning Ashcraft about 7:00 p.m. They recounted various statements of his which had proved untrue. About 11:00 o'clock Ashcraft said he realized the circumstances all pointed to him and that he could not explain the circumstances. They then accused him of the murder, but he denied it. About 3:00 a.m. Becker and Battle retired and left Ashcraft in charge of Ezzell, a special investigator connected with the Attorney General's office. He questioned Ashcraft and discussed the crime with him until about 7:00 on Sunday morning. Becker and Battle then returned and interviewed him intermittently until about noon, when Ezzell returned and remained until about 5:00. Becker then returned, and about 11:00 o'clock Sunday night Ashcraft expressed a desire to talk with Ezzell. Ezzell was sent for and Ashcraft told him he wanted to tell him the truth. He said, "Mr. Ezzell, a Negro killed my wife." Ezzell asked the Negro's name, and Ashcraft said, "Tom Ware." Up to this time Ware had not been suspected, nor had his name been mentioned. Ashcraft explained that he did not tell the officers before because "I was scared; the Negro said he would burn my house down if I told the law."

Thereupon Becker, Battle, Ezzell, and Mr. Jayroe, connected with the Sheriff's office, took Ashcraft in a car and found Ware. When questioned at the jail, Ware turned to Ashcraft and said in substance that he had told Ashcraft when this thing happened that he did not intend to take the entire blame. The officers thereupon turned their attention to Ware. He promptly admitted the killing and said Ashcraft hired him to do it. Waldauer, the court reporter, was called to take down this confession, and completed his transcript at about 5:40 a.m. He read it to Ware and told him he did not have to sign it unless he so chose. Ware made his mark upon it and swore to it before Waldauer as a Notary Public. A copy was given to Ashcraft, and he then admitted that he had hired Ware to kill his wife. He was given breakfast and then in response to questions made a statement which was taken down by the court reporter, Waldauer. It was transcribed, but Ashcraft declined to sign it, saying that he wanted his lawyer to see it before he signed it. No effort was made to compel him to sign the confession. However, two businessmen of Memphis, Mr. Castle, vice president of a bank, and Mr. Pidgeon, president of the Coca-Cola Bottling Company were called in. Both testified that Ashcraft in their presence asserted that the transcript was correct but that he declined to sign it. The officers also called Dr. McQuiston to the jail to make a physical examination of both Ashcraft and Ware. He had practiced medicine in Memphis for twenty-eight years and both Mr. and Mrs. Ashcraft had been his patients for something like five years. In the presence of this friendly doctor Ashcraft might have complained of his treatment and avowed his innocence. The doctor testified, however, that Ashcraft said he had been treated all right, that he made no complaint about his eyes, and that they were not bloodshot. The doctor made a physical examination, and says Ashcraft appeared normal. He further testified as to Ashcraft, "Well, sir, he said he had not been able to get along with his wife for some time; that her health had been bad; that he had offered her a property settlement and that she might go her way and he his way; and he also stated that he offered this colored man, Ware, a sum of money to make away with his wife." The doctor says that that statement was entirely voluntary. No matter what pressure had been put on Ashcraft before, the courts below could reasonably believe that he made this statement voluntarily to a man of whom he had no fear and who knew his family relations.

Ashcraft's story of torture could only be accepted by disbelieving such credible and unimpeached contradiction. Ashcraft testified that he was refused food, was not allowed to go to the lavatory, and was denied even a drink of water. Other testimony is that on Saturday night he was brought a sandwich and coffee about midnight; that he drank the coffee but refused the sandwich; that on Sunday morning he was given a breakfast and was fed again about noon a plate lunch consisting of meat and vegetables and coffee. Both Waldauer, the Reporter, and Dr. McQuiston testified that they saw breakfast served to Ashcraft the next morning before the statement taken down by Waldauer. Ashcraft claims he was threatened and that a cigarette was slapped out of his mouth. This is all denied.

This Court rejects the testimony of the officers and disinterested witnesses in this case that the confession was voluntary not because it lacked probative value in itself nor because the witnesses were self-contradictory or were impeached. On the contrary, it is impugned only on grounds such as that such disputes "are an inescapable consequence of secret inquisitorial practices." We infer from this that since a prisoner's unsupported word often conflicts with that of the officers, the officer's testimony for constitutional purposes is always *prima facie* false. We know that police standards often leave much to be desired, but we are not ready to believe that the democratic process brings to office men generally less believable than the average of those accused of crime.

Reference also is made to the fact that when petitioner was questioned investigation had failed "to unearth one single tangible clue pointing to his guilt." We cannot see the relevance of such circumstances on the question of the voluntary or involuntary character of his statements to the officers. Is the suggestion that if they had probable clues to his guilt, their questioning of him would have been better justified?

This questioning is characterized as a "secret inquisition," invoking all of the horrendous historical associations of those words. Certainly the inquiry was participated in by a good many persons, and we do not see how it could have been much less "secret" unless the press should have been called in. Of course, any questioning may be characterized as an "inquisition," but the use of such characterizations is no substitute for the detached and judicial consideration that the court below gave to the case.

We conclude that even going behind the state court decisions into the facts, no independent judgment on the whole evidence that Ashcraft's confession was in fact coerced is possible. And against this background of facts the extreme character of the Court's ruling becomes apparent.

I am not sure whether the Court denies the State all right to arrest and question the husband of the slain woman. No investigation worthy of the name could fail to examine him. Of all persons he was most likely to know whether she had enemies or rivals. Would not the State have a constitutional right, whether he was accused or not, to arrest and detain him as a material witness? If it has the right to detain one as a witness, presumably it has the right to examine him.

Could the State not confront Ashcraft with his false statements and ask his explanation? He did not throw himself at any time on his rights, refuse to answer, and demand counsel, even according to his own testimony. The strategy of the officers evidently was to keep him talking, to give him plenty of rope and see if he would not hang himself. He does not claim to have made objection to this. Instead he relied on his wits. The time came when it dawned on him that his own story brought him under suspicion, and that he could not meet it. Must the officers stop at this point because he was coming to appreciate the uselessness of deception?

Then he became desperate and accused the Negro. Certainly from this point the State was justified in holding and questioning him as a witness, for he claimed to know the killer. That accusation backfired and only turned up a witness against him. He had run out of expedients and inventions; he knew he had lost the battle of wits. After all, honesty seemed to be the best, even if the last, policy. He confessed in detail.

At what point in all this investigation does the Court hold that the Constitution commands these officers to send Ashcraft on his way and give up the murder as insoluble? If the state is denied the right to apply any pressure to him which is "inherently coercive" it could hardly deprive him of his freedom at all. I, too, dislike to think of any man, under the disadvantages and indignities of detention being questioned about his personal life for thirty-six hours or for one hour. In fact, there is much in our whole system of penology that seems archaic and vindictive and badly managed. Every person in the community, no matter how inconvenient or embarrassing, no matter what retaliation it exposes him to, may be called upon to take the witness stand and tell all he knows about a crime — except the person who knows most about it. Efforts of prosecutors to compensate for this handicap by violent or brutal treatment or threats we condemn as passionately and sincerely as other members of the Court. But we are not ready to say that the pressure to disclose crime, involved in decent detention and lengthy examination, although we admit them to be "inherently coercive," are denied to a State by the Constitution, where they are not proved to have passed the individual's ability to resist and to admit, deny, or refuse to answer.

. . . .

Mr. Justice Roberts and Mr. Justice Frankfurter join in this opinion.

Notes and Questions

(1) The majority concludes that 36 hours of continuous custody and questioning is "inherently coercive." If 36 hours is impermissible, how about six hours? Or one hour? Why does Justice Jackson state that one hour is "inherently coercive" yet nev-

ertheless dissent from the majority's decision? For discussion of these issues, see Fred E. Inbau, *"The Importance of Being Guilty,"* 68 J. Crim. L. & Criminology 182, 184–87 (1977), *reprinted in* Yale Kamisar, POLICE INTERROGATION AND CONFESSIONS: ESSAYS IN LAW AND POLICY 97–102 (Univ. of Mich. 1980) [hereinafter "Kamisar, ESSAYS"].

(2) The federal government and many states have rules providing that people arrested must be arraigned before a magistrate "without unnecessary delay." *See e.g.,* Fed. R. Crim. P. 5(a); Tex. Code Crim. Proc. Ann. art. 15.17 (Vernon 2005); Wis. Stat. Ann. § 970.01(1) (1998). One approach to curbing prolonged interrogations of suspects in custody is to hold that confessions obtained during a period of unnecessary delay in bringing the arrested suspect to a magistrate are automatically inadmissible. *See, e.g., Mallory v. United States,* 354 U.S. 449, 77 S. Ct. 1356, 1 L. Ed. 2d 1479 (1957); *Commonwealth v. Davenport,* 471 Pa. 278, 370 A.2d 301 (1977). *See generally* Note, *The Ill-Advised State Court Revival of the* McNabb-Mallory *Rule,* 72 J. Crim. L. & Criminology 204 (1981). In *United States v. Alvarez-Sanchez,* 511 U.S. 350, 114 S. Ct. 1599, 128 L. Ed. 2d 319 (1994), the Court held that the federal statute governing the admissibility of statements given when there is a delay between arrest and arraignment does not apply to statements made by a person who is being held solely on state charges. Accordingly, a defendant's confession to United States Secret Service agents was held admissible even though the defendant gave the confession after being arrested and held in the custody of local law enforcement officers for nearly three days without being arraigned on either state or federal charges.

(3) In *Ashcraft,* the trial judge apparently submitted the defendants' confessions to the jury after determining that reasonable minds might differ as to whether the confessions were voluntary. The jury was then directed to consider each defendant's confession as evidence against that defendant if but only if it concluded the confession was voluntary. Prior to 1964, this procedure, known as the New York procedure, was followed in a large number of states. Does this procedure seem consistent with due process?

In *Jackson v. Denno,* 378 U.S. 368, 84 S. Ct. 1774, 12 L. Ed. 2d 908 (1964), the Court held that the New York procedure was in violation of due process. After *Jackson,* all states follow either the Massachusetts procedure or the "orthodox" procedure. Under the orthodox procedure, the judge resolves evidentiary conflicts and makes her own determination as to whether the confession is voluntary. If the judge determines the confession is voluntary, the confession is introduced into evidence and the jury is instructed to consider it along with the other evidence presented. The Massachusetts procedure is the same except that, if the judge admits the confession, the jury is instructed as to the definition of a voluntary confession and told to consider the confession as evidence only if it finds that it was a voluntary confession. In *Jackson,* the Supreme Court indicated that either of these procedures is constitutional. Which of the two is preferable?

Spano v. New York

United States Supreme Court

360 U.S. 315, 79 S. Ct. 1202, 3 L. Ed. 2d 1265 (1959)

Mr. Chief Justice Warren delivered the opinion of the Court.

This is another in the long line of cases presenting the question whether a confession was properly admitted into evidence under the Fourteenth Amendment. As in all such cases, we are forced to resolve a conflict between two fundamental interests of society; its interest in prompt and efficient law enforcement, and its interest in preventing the rights of its individual members from being abridged by unconstitutional methods of law enforcement. Because of the delicate nature of the constitutional determination which we must make, we cannot escape the responsibility of making our own examination of the record. *Norris v. Alabama*, 294 U.S. 587, 55 S. Ct. 579, 79 L. Ed. 1074.

The State's evidence reveals the following: Petitioner Vincent Joseph Spano is a derivative citizen of this country, having been born in Messina, Italy. He was 25 years old at the time of the shooting in question and had graduated from junior high school. He had a record of regular employment. The shooting took place on January 22, 1957.

On that day, petitioner was drinking in a bar. The decedent, a former professional boxer weighing almost 200 pounds who had fought in Madison Square Garden, took some of petitioner's money from the bar. Petitioner followed him out of the bar to recover it. A fight ensued, with the decedent knocking petitioner down and then kicking him in the head three or four times. Shock from the force of these blows caused petitioner to vomit. After the bartender applied some ice to his head, petitioner left the bar, walked to his apartment, secured a gun, and walked eight or nine blocks to a candy store where the decedent was frequently to be found. He entered the store in which decedent, three friends of decedent, at least two of whom were ex-convicts, and a boy who was supervising the store were present. He fired five shots, two of which entered the decedent's body, causing his death. The boy was the only eyewitness; the three friends of decedent did not see the person who fired the shot. Petitioner then disappeared for the next week or so.

On February 1, 1957, the Bronx County Grand Jury returned an indictment for first-degree murder against petitioner. Accordingly, a bench warrant was issued for his arrest, commanding that he be forthwith brought before the court to answer the indictment, or, if the court had adjourned for the term, that he be delivered into the custody of the Sheriff of Bronx County.

On February 3, 1957, petitioner called one Gaspar Bruno, a close friend of 8 or 10 years' standing who had attended school with him. Bruno was a fledgling police officer, having at that time not yet finished attending police academy. According to Bruno's testimony, petitioner told him "that he took a terrific beating, that the deceased hurt him real bad and he dropped him a couple of times and he was dazed;

he didn't know what he was doing and that he went and shot at him." Petitioner told Bruno that he intended to get a lawyer and give himself up. Bruno relayed this information to his superiors.

The following day, February 4, at 7:10 p.m., petitioner, accompanied by counsel, surrendered himself to the authorities in front of the Bronx County Building, where both the office of the Assistant District Attorney who ultimately prosecuted his case and the courtroom in which he was ultimately tried were located. His attorney had cautioned him to answer no questions, and left him in the custody of the officers. He was promptly taken to the office of the Assistant District Attorney and at 7:15 p.m. the questioning began, being conducted by Assistant District Attorney Goldsmith, Lt. Gannon, Detectives Farrell, Lehrer and Motta, and Sgt. Clarke. The record reveals that the questioning was both persistent and continuous. Petitioner, in accordance with his attorney's instructions, steadfastly refused to answer. Detective Motta testified: "He refused to talk to me." "He just looked up to the ceiling and refused to talk to me." Detective Farrell testified:

Q. And you started to interrogate him?

A. That is right.

. . . .

Q. What did he say?

A. He said "you would have to see my attorney. I tell you nothing but my name."

. . . .

Q. Did you continue to examine him?

A. Verbally, yes, sir.

He asked one officer, Detective Ciccone, if he could speak to his attorney, but that request was denied. Detective Ciccone testified that he could not find the attorney's name in the telephone book.[1] He was given two sandwiches, coffee and cake at 11 p.m.

At 12:15 a.m. on the morning of February 5, after five hours of questioning in which it became evident that petitioner was following his attorney's instructions, on the Assistant District Attorney's orders petitioner was transferred to the 46th Squad, Ryer Avenue Police Station. The Assistant District Attorney also went to the police station and to some extent continued to participate in the interrogation. Petitioner arrived at 12:30 and questioning was resumed at 12:40. The character of the questioning is revealed by the testimony of Detective Farrell:

---

1. How this could be so when the attorney's name, Tobias Russo, was concededly in the telephone book does not appear. The trial judge sustained objections by the Assistant District Attorney to questions designed to delve into this mystery.

Q. Who did you leave him in the room with?

A. With Detective Lehrer and Sergeant Clarke came in and Mr. Goldsmith came in or Inspector Halk came in. It was back and forth. People just came in, spoke a few words to the defendant or they listened a few minutes and they left.

But petitioner persisted in his refusal to answer, and again requested permission to see his attorney, this time from Detective Lehrer. His request was again denied.

It was then that those in charge of the investigation decided that petitioner's close friend, Bruno, could be of use. He had been called out on the case around 10 or 11 p.m., although he was not connected with the 46th Squad or Precinct in any way. Although, in fact, his job was in no way threatened, Bruno was told to tell petitioner that petitioner's telephone call had gotten him "in a lot of trouble," and that he should seek to extract sympathy from petitioner for Bruno's pregnant wife and three children. Bruno developed this theme with petitioner without success, and petitioner, also without success, again sought to see his attorney, a request which Bruno relayed unavailingly to his superiors. After this first session with petitioner, Bruno was again directed by Lt. Gannon to play on petitioner's sympathies, but again no confession was forthcoming. But the Lieutenant a third time ordered Bruno falsely to importune his friend to confess, but again petitioner clung to his attorney's advice. Inevitably, in the fourth such session directed by the Lieutenant, lasting a full hour, petitioner succumbed to his friend's prevarications and agreed to make a statement. Accordingly, at 3:25 a.m. the Assistant District Attorney, a stenographer, and several other law enforcement officials entered the room where petitioner was being questioned, and took his statement in question and answer form with the Assistant District Attorney asking the questions. The statement was completed at 4:05 a.m.

But this was not the end. At 4:30 a.m. three detectives took petitioner to Police Headquarters in Manhattan. On the way they attempted to find the bridge from which petitioner said he had thrown the murder weapon. They crossed the Triborough Bridge into Manhattan, arriving at Police Headquarters at 5 a.m., and left Manhattan for the Bronx at 5:40 a.m. via the Willis Avenue Bridge. When petitioner recognized neither bridge as the one from which he had thrown the weapon, they re-entered Manhattan via the Third Avenue Bridge, which petitioner stated was the right one, and then returned to the Bronx well after 6:00 a.m. During that trip the officers also elicited a statement from petitioner that the deceased was always "on [his] back," "always pushing" him and that he was "not sorry" he had shot the deceased. All three detectives testified to that statement at the trial.

Court opened at 10:00 a.m. that morning, and petitioner was arraigned at 10:15.

At the trial, the confession was introduced in evidence over appropriate objections. The jury was instructed that it could rely on it only if it was found to be voluntary. The jury returned a guilty verdict and petitioner was sentenced to death. The New York Court of Appeals affirmed the conviction over three dissents, and we granted certiorari to resolve the serious problem presented under the Fourteenth Amendment.

Petitioner's first contention is that his absolute right to counsel in a capital case, *Powell v. Alabama*, 287 U.S. 45, 53 S. Ct. 55, 77 L. Ed. 158, became operative on the return of an indictment against him, for at that time he was in every sense a defendant in a criminal case, the grand jury having found sufficient cause to believe that he had committed the crime. He argues accordingly that following indictment no confession obtained in the absence of counsel can be used without violating the Fourteenth Amendment. He seeks to distinguish *Crooker v. California*, 357 U.S. 433, 78 S. Ct. 1287, 2 L. Ed. 2d 1448, and *Cicenia v. Lagay*, 357 U.S. 504, 78 S. Ct. 1297, 2 L. Ed. 2d 1523, on the ground that in those cases no indictment had been returned. We find it unnecessary to reach that contention, for we find use of the confession obtained here inconsistent with the Fourteenth Amendment under traditional principles.

The abhorrence of society to the use of involuntary confessions does not turn alone on their inherent untrustworthiness. It also turns on the deep-rooted feeling that the police must obey the law while enforcing the law; that in the end life and liberty can be as much endangered from illegal methods used to convict those thought to be criminals as from the actual criminals themselves. . . . [I]n recent years law enforcement officials have become increasingly aware of the burden which they share, along with our courts, in protecting fundamental rights of our citizenry, including that portion of our citizenry suspected of crime. The facts of no case recently in this Court have quite approached the brutal beatings in *Brown v. Mississippi*, 297 U.S. 278, 56 S. Ct. 461, 80 L. Ed. 682 (1936), or the 36 consecutive hours of questioning present in *Ashcraft v. Tennessee*, 322 U.S. 143, 64 S. Ct. 921, 88 L. Ed. 1192 (1944). But as law enforcement officers become more responsible, and the methods used to extract confessions more sophisticated, our duty to enforce federal constitutional protections does not cease. It only becomes more difficult because of the more delicate judgments to be made. Our judgment here is that, on all the facts, this conviction cannot stand.

Petitioner was a foreign-born young man of 25 with no past history of law violation or of subjection to official interrogation, at least insofar as the record shows. He had progressed only one-half year into high school and the record indicates that he had a history of emotional instability.[3] He did not make a narrative statement, but was subject to the leading questions of a skillful prosecutor in a question and answer confession. He was subjected to questioning not by a few men, but by many. . . . All played some part, and the effect of such massive official interrogation must have been felt. Petitioner was questioned for virtually eight straight hours before he confessed, with his only respite being a transfer to an arena presumably considered more appropriate by the police for the task at hand. Nor was the questioning conducted

---

3. Medical reports from New York City's Fordham Hospital introduced by defendant showed that he had suffered a cerebral concussion in 1955. He was described by a private physician in 1951 as "an extremely nervous tense individual who is emotionally unstable and maladjusted," and was found unacceptable for military service in 1951, primarily because of "Psychiatric disorder." He failed the Army's AFQT-1 intelligence test. His mother had been in mental hospitals on three separate occasions.

during normal business hours, but began in early evening, continued into the night, and did not bear fruition until the not-too-early morning. The drama was not played out, with the final admissions obtained, until almost sunrise. In such circumstances slowly mounting fatigue does, and is calculated to, play its part. The questioners persisted in the face of his repeated refusals to answer on the advice of his attorney, and they ignored his reasonable requests to contact the local attorney whom he had already retained and who had personally delivered him into the custody of these officers in obedience to the bench warrant.

The use of Bruno, characterized in this Court by counsel for the State as a "childhood friend" of petitioner's, is another factor which deserves mention in the totality of the situation. Bruno's was the one face visible to petitioner in which he could put some trust. There was a bond of friendship between them going back a decade into adolescence. It was with this material that the officers felt that they could overcome petitioner's will. They instructed Bruno falsely to state that petitioner's telephone call had gotten him into trouble, that his job was in jeopardy, and that loss of his job would be disastrous to his three children, his wife and his unborn child. And Bruno played this part of a worried father, harried by his superiors, in not one, but four different acts, the final one lasting an hour. Petitioner was apparently unaware of John Gay's famous couplet: "An open foe may prove a curse, But a pretended friend is worse," and he yielded to his false friend's entreaties.

We conclude that petitioner's will was overborne by official pressure, fatigue and sympathy falsely aroused after considering all the facts in their post-indictment setting. Here a grand jury had already found sufficient cause to require petitioner to face trial on a charge of first-degree murder, and the police had an eyewitness to the shooting. The police were not therefore merely trying to solve a crime, or even to absolve a suspect. . . . They were rather concerned primarily with securing a statement from defendant on which they could convict him. The undeviating intent of the officers to extract a confession from petitioner is therefore patent. When such an intent is shown, this Court has held that the confession obtained must be examined with the most careful scrutiny, and has reversed a conviction on facts less compelling than these. *Malinski v. People of State of New York*, 324 U.S. 401, 65 S. Ct. 781, 89 L. Ed. 1029. Accordingly, we hold that petitioner's conviction cannot stand under the Fourteenth Amendment.

. . . .

Reversed.

Mr. Justice Douglas, with whom Mr. Justice Black and Mr. Justice Brennan join, concurring.

While I join the opinion of the Court, I add what for me is an even more important ground of decision.

We have often divided on whether state authorities may question a suspect for hours on end when he has no lawyer present and when he has demanded that he have the benefit of legal advice. *See Crooker v. California*, 357 U.S. 433, 78 S. Ct. 1287, 2 L.

Ed. 2d 1448, and cases cited. But here we deal not with a suspect but with a man who has been formally charged with a crime. The question is whether after the indictment and before the trial the Government can interrogate the accused *in secret* when he asked for his lawyer and when his request was denied. This is a capital case; and under the rule of *Powell v. Alabama*, 287 U.S. 45, 53 S. Ct. 55, 77 L. Ed. 158, the defendant was entitled to be represented by counsel. This representation by counsel is not restricted to the trial. As stated in *Powell v. Alabama, supra*, 287 U.S. at 57, 53 S. Ct. at 59:

> during perhaps the most critical period of the proceedings against these defendants, that is to say, from the time of their arraignment until the beginning of their trial, when consultation, thoroughgoing investigation and preparation were vitally important, the defendants did not have the aid of counsel in any real sense, although they were as much entitled to such aid during that period as at the trial itself.

Depriving a person, formally charged with a crime, of counsel during the period prior to trial may be more damaging than denial of counsel during the trial itself.

We do not have here mere suspects who are being secretly interrogated by the police as in *Crooker v. California, supra,* nor witnesses who are being questioned in secret administrative or judicial proceedings as in *In re Groban*, 352 U.S. 330, 77 S. Ct. 510, 1 L. Ed. 2d 376, and *Anonymous Nos. 6 & 7 v. Baker*, 360 U.S. 287, 79 S. Ct. 1157. This is a case of an accused, who is scheduled to be tried by a judge and jury, being tried in a preliminary way by the police. This is a kangaroo court procedure whereby the police produce the vital evidence in the form of a confession which is useful or necessary to obtain a conviction. They in effect deny him effective representation by counsel. This seems to me to be a flagrant violation of the principle announced in *Powell v. Alabama, supra*, that the right of counsel extends to the preparation for trial, as well as to the trial itself. As Professor Chafee once said, "A person accused of crime needs a lawyer right after his arrest probably more than at any other time." Chafee, DOCUMENTS ON FUNDAMENTAL HUMAN RIGHTS, Pamphlet 2 (1951–1952), p. 541. When he is deprived of that right after indictment and before trial, he may indeed be denied effective representation by counsel at the only stage when legal aid and advice would help him. This *secret inquisition* by the police when defendant asked for and was denied counsel was as serious an invasion of his constitutional rights as the denial of a continuance in order to employ counsel was held to be in *Chandler v. Fretag*, 348 U.S. 3, 10, 75 S. Ct. 1, 5, 99 L. Ed. 4. What we said in *Avery v. Alabama*, 308 U.S. 444, 446, 60 S. Ct. 321, 322, 84 L. Ed. 377, has relevance here:

> ... the denial of opportunity for appointed counsel to confer, to consult with the accused and to prepare his defense, could convert the appointment of counsel into a sham and nothing more than a formal compliance with the Constitution's requirement that an accused be given the assistance of counsel.

I join with Judges Desmond, Fuld, and Van Voorhis of the New York Court of Appeals (4 N.Y.2d 256, 266, 173 N.Y.S.2d 793, 801, 150 N.E.2d 226, 232–233), in asking, what use is a defendant's right to effective counsel at every stage of a criminal case if, while he is held awaiting trial, he can be questioned in the absence of counsel until he confesses? In that event the secret trial in the police precincts effectively supplants the public trial guaranteed by the Bill of Rights.

Mr. Justice Stewart, whom Mr. Justice Douglas and Mr. Justice Brennan join, concurring.

While I concur in the opinion of the Court, it is my view that the absence of counsel when this confession was elicited was alone enough to render it inadmissible under the Fourteenth Amendment.

Let it be emphasized at the outset that this is not a case where the police were questioning a suspect in the course of investigating an unsolved crime. When the petitioner surrendered to the New York authorities he was under indictment for first degree murder.

Under our system of justice an indictment is supposed to be followed by an arraignment and a trial. At every stage in those proceedings the accused has an absolute right to a lawyer's help if the case is one in which a death sentence may be imposed. *Powell v. Alabama*, 287 U.S. 45, 53 S. Ct. 55, 77 L. Ed. 158. Indeed the right to the assistance of counsel whom the accused has himself retained is absolute, whatever the offense for which he is on trial. *Chandler v. Fretag*, 348 U.S. 3, 75 S. Ct. 1, 99 L. Ed. 4.

What followed the petitioner's surrender in this case was not arraignment in a court of law, but an all-night inquisition in a prosecutor's office, a police station, and an automobile. Throughout the night the petitioner repeatedly asked to be allowed to send for his lawyer, and his requests were repeatedly denied. He finally was induced to make a confession. That confession was used to secure a verdict sending him to the electric chair.

Our Constitution guarantees the assistance of counsel to a man on trial for his life in an orderly courtroom, presided over by a judge, open to the public, and protected by all the procedural safeguards of the law. Surely a Constitution which promises that much can vouchsafe no less to the same man under midnight inquisition in the squad room of a police station.

Notes and Questions

(1) As the Court indicates, *Spano* was just one in a long line of cases in which the Court found that a confession was involuntary. For a later case in which the Court held a confession involuntary, see *Mincey v. Arizona*, 437 U.S. 385, 98 S. Ct. 2408, 57 L. Ed. 2d 290 (1978). In *Mincey*, the defendant was seriously wounded in a narcotics raid in which an officer was killed. Just a few hours later, a detective questioned him in the intensive care unit of a hospital. Lying on his back in a bed, encumbered by tubes, needles, and breathing apparatus, the defendant repeatedly expressed his wish not to be interrogated. The detective nevertheless continued to question him.

Unable to speak because of the tube in his mouth, the defendant responded to the questions by writing answers on pieces of paper provided by the hospital, at one point writing: "This is all I can say without a lawyer."

In an opinion by Justice Stewart, the Court held that the defendant's confession was inadmissible for all purposes because it was involuntary. It concluded that "the undisputed evidence makes clear that [the defendant] wanted *not* to answer [the detective]" but that, "weakened by pain and shock, isolated from family, friends and legal counsel, and barely conscious . . . his will was simply overborne." Justice Rehnquist dissented.

(2) After *Spano*, what does the Court mean when it refers to an "involuntary confession"? Is the focus solely on whether the defendant's "will was overborne by official pressure"? What other concerns are involved? For differing perspectives on the voluntariness test and the meaning of an involuntary confession, compare Yale Kamisar, *What is an "Involuntary" Confession?*, 17 Rutgers L. Rev. 728 (1963), *reprinted in* Kamisar, Essays at 1–25, with Joseph D. Grano, *Voluntariness, Free Will, and the Law of Confessions*, 65 Va. L. Rev. 859 (1979).

(3) The *Spano* Court seemed particularly concerned about the role played by Officer Bruno in inducing the confession. Should the use of police trickery to induce confessions ever in itself be a denial of due process? How about trickery that misrepresents the nature of the evidence against the suspect? Or trickery that deceives the suspect as to the nature of the interrogation? For general discussions of this subject, see Daniel W. Sasaki, Note, *Guarding the Guardians: Police Trickery and Confessions*, 40 Stan. L. Rev. 1593 (1988); Welsh S. White, *Police Trickery in Inducing Confessions*, 127 U. Pa. L. Rev. 581 (1979).

Colorado v. Connelly

United States Supreme Court

479 U.S. 157, 107 S. Ct. 515, 93 L. Ed. 2d 473 (1986)

CHIEF JUSTICE REHNQUIST delivered the opinion of the Court.

. . . .

I

On August 18, 1983, Officer Patrick Anderson of the Denver Police Department was in uniform, working in an off-duty capacity in downtown Denver. Respondent Francis Connelly approached Officer Anderson and, without any prompting, stated that he had murdered someone and wanted to talk about it. Anderson immediately advised respondent that he had the right to remain silent, that anything he said could be used against him in court, and that he had the right to an attorney prior to any police questioning. *See Miranda v. Arizona*, 384 U.S. 436, 86 S. Ct. 1602, 16 L. Ed. 2d 694 (1966). Respondent stated that he understood these rights but he still wanted to talk about the murder. Understandably bewildered by this confession, Officer Anderson asked respondent several questions. Connelly denied that he had been drinking, denied that he had been taking any drugs, and stated that, in the past, he had been a patient in several mental hospitals. Officer Anderson again told Connelly that he was under no obligation to say anything. Connelly replied that it was "all right," and that he would talk to Officer Anderson because his conscience had been bothering him. To Officer Anderson, respondent appeared to understand fully the nature of his acts.

Shortly thereafter, Homicide Detective Stephen Antuna arrived. Respondent was again advised of his rights, and Detective Antuna asked him "what he had on his mind." Respondent answered that he had come all the way from Boston to confess to the murder of Mary Ann Junta, a young girl whom he had killed in Denver sometime during November 1982. Respondent was taken to police headquarters, and a search of police records revealed that the body of an unidentified female had been found in April 1983. Respondent openly detailed his story to Detective Antuna and Sergeant Thomas Haney, and readily agreed to take the officers to the scene of the killing. Under Connelly's sole direction, the two officers and respondent proceeded in a police vehicle to the location of the crime. Respondent pointed out the exact location of the murder. Throughout this episode, Detective Antuna perceived no indication whatsoever that respondent was suffering from any kind of mental illness.

Respondent was held overnight. During an interview with the public defender's office the following morning, he became visibly disoriented. He began giving confused answers to questions, and for the first time, stated that "voices" had told him to come to Denver and that he had followed the directions of these voices in confessing. Respondent was sent to a state hospital for evaluation. He was initially found incompetent to assist in his own defense. By March 1984, however, the doctors evaluating respondent determined that he was competent to proceed to trial.

At a preliminary hearing, respondent moved to suppress all of his statements. Doctor Jeffrey Metzner, a psychiatrist employed by the state hospital, testified that respondent was suffering from chronic schizophrenia and was in a psychotic state at least as of August 17, 1983, the day before he confessed. Metzner's interviews with respondent revealed that respondent was following the "voice of God." This voice instructed respondent to withdraw money from the bank, to buy an airplane ticket, and to fly from Boston to Denver. When respondent arrived from Boston, God's voice became stronger and told respondent either to confess to the killing or to commit suicide. Reluctantly following the command of the voices, respondent approached Officer Anderson and confessed.

Dr. Metzner testified that, in his expert opinion, respondent was experiencing "command hallucinations." This condition interfered with respondent's "volitional abilities; that is, his ability to make free and rational choices." Dr. Metzner further testified that Connelly's illness did not significantly impair his cognitive abilities. Thus, respondent understood the rights he had when Officer Anderson and Detective Antuna advised him that he need not speak. Dr. Metzner admitted that the "voices" could in reality be Connelly's interpretation of his own guilt, but explained that in his opinion, Connelly's psychosis motivated his confession.

On the basis of this evidence the Colorado trial court decided that respondent's statements must be suppressed because they were "involuntary."

. . . .

The Colorado Supreme Court affirmed. . . .

II

The Due Process Clause of the Fourteenth Amendment provides that no State shall "deprive any person of life, liberty, or property, without due process of law." Just last Term, in *Miller v. Fenton*, 474 U.S. 104, 109, 106 S. Ct. 445, 449, 88 L. Ed. 2d 405 (1985), we held that by virtue of the Due Process Clause "certain interrogation techniques, either in isolation or as applied to the unique characteristics of a particular suspect, are so offensive to a civilized system of justice that they must be condemned."

Indeed, coercive government misconduct was the catalyst for this Court's seminal confession case, *Brown v. Mississippi*, 297 U.S. 278, 56 S. Ct. 461, 80 L. Ed. 682 (1936). In that case, police officers extracted confessions from the accused through brutal torture. The Court had little difficulty concluding that even though the Fifth Amendment did not at that time apply to the States, the actions of the police were "revolting to the sense of justice." *Id.* at 286, 56 S. Ct. at 465. . . .

Thus the cases considered by this Court over the 50 years since *Brown v. Mississippi* have focused upon the crucial element of *police overreaching*. While each confession case has turned on its own set of factors justifying the conclusion that police conduct was oppressive, all have contained a substantial element of coercive police conduct. Absent police conduct causally related to the confession, there is simply no basis for concluding that any state actor has deprived a criminal defendant of due process of law. Respondent correctly notes that as interrogators have turned to more subtle forms of psychological persuasion, courts have found the mental condition of the defendant a more significant factor in the "voluntariness" calculus. *See Spano v. New York*, 360 U.S. 315, 79 S. Ct. 1202, 3 L. Ed. 2d 1265 (1959). But this fact does not justify a conclusion that a defendant's mental condition, by itself and apart from its relation to official coercion, should ever dispose of the inquiry into constitutional "voluntariness."

Respondent relies on *Blackburn v. Alabama*, 361 U.S. 199, 80 S. Ct. 274, 4 L. Ed. 2d 242 (1960), and *Townsend v. Sain*, 372 U.S. 293, 83 S. Ct. 745, 9 L. Ed. 2d 770 (1963), for the proposition that the "deficient mental condition of the defendants in those cases was sufficient to render their confessions involuntary." But respondent's reading of *Blackburn* and *Townsend* ignores the integral element of police overreaching present in both cases. In *Blackburn*, the Court found that the petitioner was probably insane at the time of his confession and the police learned during the interrogation that Blackburn had a history of mental problems. The police exploited this weakness with coercive tactics: "the eight- to nine-hour sustained interrogation in a tiny room which was upon occasion literally filled with police officers; the absence of Blackburn's friends, relatives, or legal counsel; [and] the composition of the confession by the Deputy Sheriff rather than by Blackburn." These tactics supported a finding that the confession was involuntary. Indeed, the Court specifically condemned police activity that "wrings a confession out of an accused against his will." *Townsend* presented a similar instance of police wrongdoing. In that case, a police physician had given Townsend a drug with truth-serum properties. The subsequent confession, obtained by officers who knew that Townsend had been given drugs, was held involuntary. These two cases demonstrate that while mental condition is surely relevant to an individual's susceptibility to police coercion, mere examination of the confessant's state of mind can never conclude the due process inquiry.

Our "involuntary confession" jurisprudence is entirely consistent with the settled law requiring some sort of "state action" to support a claim of violation of the Due Process Clause of the Fourteenth Amendment. The Colorado trial court, of course, found that the police committed no wrongful acts, and that finding has been neither challenged by the respondent nor disturbed by the Supreme Court of Colorado. The latter court, however, concluded that sufficient state action was present by virtue of the admission of the confession into evidence in a court of the State.

The difficulty with the approach of the Supreme Court of Colorado is that it fails to recognize the essential link between coercive activity of the State, on the one hand, and a resulting confession by a defendant, on the other. The flaw in respondent's constitutional argument is that it would expand our previous line of "voluntariness" cases into a far-ranging requirement that courts must divine a defendant's motivation for speaking or acting as he did even though there be no claim that governmental conduct coerced his decision.

The most outrageous behavior by a private party seeking to secure evidence against a defendant does not make that evidence inadmissible under the Due Process Clause. *See Walter v. United States*, 447 U.S. 649, 656, 100 S. Ct. 2395, 2401, 65 L. Ed. 2d 410 (1980); *Coolidge v. New Hampshire*, 403 U.S. 443, 487–488, 91 S. Ct. 2022, 2048–49, 29 L. Ed. 2d 564 (1971); *Burdeau v. McDowell*, 256 U.S. 465, 476, 41 S. Ct. 574, 576, 65 L. Ed. 1048 (1921). We have also observed that "[j]urists and scholars uniformly have recognized that the exclusionary rule imposes a substantial cost on the societal interest in law enforcement by its proscription of what concededly is relevant evidence." *United States v. Janis*, 428 U.S. 433, 448–449, 96 S. Ct. 3021, 3029, 49 L. Ed. 2d 1046 (1976). Moreover, suppressing respondent's statements would serve absolutely no purpose in enforcing constitutional guarantees. The purpose of excluding evidence seized in violation of the Constitution is to substantially deter future violations of the Constitution. *See United States v. Leon*, 468 U.S. 897, 906–913, 104 S. Ct. 3405, 3412–3416, 82 L. Ed. 2d 677 (1984). Only if we were to establish a brand new constitutional right — the right of a criminal defendant to confess to his crime only when totally rational and properly motivated — could respondent's present claim be sustained.

We have previously cautioned against expanding "currently applicable exclusionary rules by erecting additional barriers to placing truthful and probative evidence before state juries. . . ." *Lego v. Twomey*, 404 U.S. 477, 488–489, 92 S. Ct. 619, 626,

30 L. Ed. 2d 618 (1972). We abide by that counsel now. "[T]he central purpose of a criminal trial is to decide the factual question of the defendant's guilt or innocence," *Delaware v. Van Arsdall*, 475 U.S. 673, 681, 106 S. Ct. 1431, 1436, 89 L. Ed. 2d 674 (1986), and while we have previously held that exclusion of evidence may be necessary to protect constitutional guarantees, both the necessity for the collateral inquiry and the exclusion of evidence deflect a criminal trial from its basic purpose. Respondent would now have us require sweeping inquiries into the state of mind of a criminal defendant who has confessed, inquiries quite divorced from any coercion brought to bear on the defendant by the State. We think the Constitution rightly leaves this sort of inquiry to be resolved by state laws governing the admission of evidence and erects no standard of its own in this area. (A statement rendered by one in the condition of respondent might be proved to be quite unreliable, but this is a matter to be governed by the evidentiary laws of the forum, *see, e.g.*, Fed. Rule Evid. 601, and not by the Due Process Clause of the Fourteenth Amendment.) "The aim of the requirement of due process is not to exclude presumptively false evidence, but to prevent fundamental unfairness in the use of evidence, whether true or false." *Lisenba v. California*, 314 U.S. 219, 236, 62 S. Ct. 280, 290, 86 L. Ed. 166 (1941).

We hold that coercive police activity is a necessary predicate to the finding that a confession is not "voluntary" within the meaning of the Due Process Clause of the Fourteenth Amendment. We also conclude that the taking of respondent's statements, and their admission into evidence, constitute no violation of that Clause.

. . . .

The judgment of the Supreme Court of Colorado is accordingly reversed, and the cause is remanded for further proceedings not inconsistent with this opinion.

[JUSTICE BLACKMUN's concurring opinion is omitted.]

[JUSTICE STEVENS's opinion, concurring in the judgment in part and dissenting in part, is omitted.]

JUSTICE BRENNAN, with whom JUSTICE MARSHALL joins, dissenting.

Today the Court denies Mr. Connelly his fundamental right to make a vital choice with a sane mind, involving a determination that could allow the State to deprive him of liberty or even life. This holding is unprecedented: "Surely in the present stage of our civilization a most basic sense of justice is affronted by the spectacle of incarcerating a human being upon the basis of a statement he made while insane. . . ." *Blackburn v. Alabama*, 361 U.S. 199, 207, 80 S. Ct. 274, 280, 4 L. Ed. 2d 242 (1960). Because I believe that the use of a mentally ill person's involuntary confession is antithetical to the notion of fundamental fairness embodied in the Due Process Clause, I dissent.

. . . .

The absence of police wrongdoing should not, by itself, determine the voluntariness of a confession by a mentally ill person. The requirement that a confession be voluntary reflects a recognition of the importance of free will and of reliability in determining the admissibility of a confession, and thus demands an inquiry into the totality of the circumstances surrounding the confession.

A

. . . .

The Court's failure to recognize all forms of involuntariness or coercion as antithetical to due process reflects a refusal to acknowledge free will as a value of constitutional consequence. But due process derives much of its meaning from a conception of fundamental fairness that emphasizes the right to make vital choices voluntarily: "The Fourteenth Amendment secures against state invasion . . . the right of a person to remain silent unless he chooses to speak in the unfettered exercise of his own will. . . ." *Malloy v. Hogan*, 378 U.S. 1, 8, 84 S. Ct. 1489, 1493, 12 L. Ed. 2d 653 (1964). This right requires vigilant protection if we are to safeguard the values of private conscience and human dignity.

. . . .

A true commitment to fundamental fairness requires that the inquiry be "not whether the conduct of state officers in obtaining the confession is shocking, but whether the confession was 'free and voluntary'. . . ." *Malloy v. Hogan, supra*, 378 U.S. at 7, 84 S. Ct. at 1493.

We have never confined our focus to police coercion, because the value of freedom of will has demanded a broader inquiry. *See Blackburn v. Alabama*, 361 U.S. at 206–207, 80 S. Ct. at 279–280. The confession cases decided by this Court over the 50 years since *Brown v. Mississippi*, 297 U.S. 278, 56 S. Ct. 461, 80 L. Ed. 682 (1936), have focused upon both police overreaching and free will. While it is true that police overreaching has been an element of every confession case to date, it is also true that in every case the Court has made clear that ensuring that a confession is a product of free will is an independent concern. The fact that involuntary confessions have always been excluded in part because of police overreaching, signifies only that this is a case of first impression. Until today, we have never upheld the admission of a confession that does not reflect the exercise of free will.

. . . .

B

Since the Court redefines voluntary confessions to include confessions by mentally ill individuals, the reliability of these confessions becomes a central concern. A concern for reliability is inherent in our criminal justice system, which relies upon accusatorial rather than inquisitorial practices. While an inquisitorial system prefers obtaining confessions from criminal defendants, an accusatorial system must place its faith in determinations of "guilt by evidence independently and freely secured." *Rogers v. Richmond*, 365 U.S. 534, 541, 81 S. Ct. 735, 739, 5 L. Ed. 2d 760 (1961).

. . . .

Our distrust for reliance on confessions is due, in part, to their decisive impact upon the adversarial process.... No other class of evidence is so profoundly prejudicial....

Because the admission of a confession so strongly tips the balance against the defendant in the adversarial process, we must be especially careful about a confession's reliability. We have to date not required a finding of reliability for involuntary confessions only because *all* such confessions have been excluded upon a finding of involuntariness, regardless of reliability. The Court's adoption today of a restrictive definition of an "involuntary" confession will require heightened scrutiny of a confession's reliability.

The instant case starkly highlights the danger of admitting a confession by a person with a severe mental illness. The trial court made no findings concerning the reliability of Mr. Connelly's involuntary confession, since it believed that the confession was excludable on the basis of involuntariness. However, the overwhelming evidence in the record points to the unreliability of Mr. Connelly's delusional mind....

Moreover, the record is barren of any corroboration of the mentally ill defendant's confession. No physical evidence links the defendant to the alleged crime. Police did not identify the alleged victim's body as the woman named by the defendant. Mr. Connelly identified the alleged scene of the crime, but it has not been verified that the unidentified body was found there or that a crime actually occurred there. There is not a shred of competent evidence in this record linking the defendant to the charged homicide. There is only Mr. Connelly's confession.

Minimum standards of due process should require that the trial court find substantial indicia of reliability, on the basis of evidence extrinsic to the confession itself, before admitting the confession of a mentally ill person into evidence.

. . . .

Notes and Questions

(1) Professor George Dix has observed that the most surprising aspect of *Connelly* is its "rejection of reliability as a relevant consideration" for determining the admissibility of a confession under federal constitutional law. *See* George E. Dix, *Federal Constitutional Confession Law: The 1986 and 1987 Supreme Court Terms*, 67 Tex. L. Rev. 231, 232 (1988). After *Connelly*, is reliability completely irrelevant to the admissibility of a confession under the due process test? If the police had obtained a confession from Connelly after interrogating him for an appreciable period, would the confession's potential untrustworthiness (because of Connelly's mental condition) be a factor to be weighed in determining whether admission of the confession would violate due process?

(2) In deciding whether police trickery renders a confession inadmissible under the due process test, some lower courts have drawn a distinction between trickery

that would be likely to induce a false confession and trickery that would have the effect of inducing a true confession. *See, e.g., State v. Kelekolio*, 849 P.2d 58 (Haw. 1993). *See generally* Fred E. Inbau, John E. Reid, & Joseph P. Buckley, Criminal Interrogation and Confessions 216 (3d ed. 1986). Do the *Connelly* majority's statements concerning the constitutional irrelevance of reliability cast doubt on these authorities?

(3) Since *Connelly*, considerable attention has been devoted to the question of whether standard interrogation methods precipitate false confessions. In particular, commentators have asserted that standard interrogation methods are likely to induce false confessions from mentally handicapped suspects. *See, e.g.*, Richard J. Ofshe & Richard A. Leo, *The Social Psychology of Police Interrogation: The Theory and Classification of True and False Confessions*, 16 Studies In Law, Politics and Society 189, 213–14 (1997); Welsh S. White, *Confessions in Capital Cases*, 2003 U. Ill. L. Rev. 979. Should evidence showing that standard interrogation methods tend to produce false or untrustworthy confessions from mentally handicapped suspects have any bearing on the test for determining whether a confession given by a mentally handicapped suspect is voluntary within the meaning of the due process test? In answering this question, should it matter whether the police knew or had reason to know of the suspect's mental infirmities at the time of the interrogation?

(4) What is the current status of confessions induced by government promises? During the eighteenth and nineteenth centuries, such confessions were excluded because of doubts about their reliability. In *Bram v. United States*, 168 U.S. 532, 542–43 (1897), the Court stated that in order to be constitutionally admissible "a confession . . . must not be . . . obtained by any direct or implied promises, however slight." *Bram*'s influence fluctuated over time, reaching its peak in the sixties but waning soon afterwards. In *Arizona v. Fulminante*, 499 U.S. 279, 285 (1991), the Court directly repudiated *Bram*, concluding that its prohibition on confessions induced by government promises "does not state the standard for determining the voluntariness of a confession."

Nevertheless, in *Fulminante* and other cases, the Court indicated that the effect of a government promise must be weighed in determining the voluntariness of a confession. In *Fulminante*, for example, it held that, under the circumstances presented in that case, a confession induced by an undercover government agent's promise of protection from other prison inmates was involuntary. (For a more detailed account of the *Fulminante* case, see Chapter 8, Part C, *infra*.) Moreover, the Court has indicated in dictum that even a "mild promise of leniency" may render a confession involuntary because of its potentially coercive effect. *See Brady v. United States*, 397 U.S. 742, 754 (1970). For a fuller discussion of the Court's treatment of confessions induced by government promises, see Welsh S. White, *Confessions Induced by Broken Government Promises*, 43 Duke L.J. 947, 952–55 (1994).

Involuntary Confession Problems

7–1: Around midnight, Tracy visited the home of Del, her former boyfriend and the father of her son. Del and Tracy talked in Del's driveway for 35–40 minutes. Tracy got into her car to leave when Kecia, Del's current girlfriend, came out of the house. As Kecia stood on Del's lawn, Tracy's car pulled forward and hit her. Kecia was trapped under the car and died. Police officers took Tracy to the police station around 1:30 a.m. They informed her of her *Miranda* rights, and she signed a waiver. Tracy said she had no medical problems, was not under the influence of alcohol or drugs, and understood English. Tracy was a 27-year-old high school graduate who had never been in jail.

Between 5:00 a.m. and 7:30 a.m., Detectives Palm and Shade interrogated Tracy. Tracy asserted that Kecia's death was an accident, stating that she was trying to back her car out of Del's driveway. She thought that she had put the car into reverse, but had accidentally put it into drive. When she pressed the gas pedal, the car lunged forward and hit Kecia. After 45 minutes of interrogation, the detectives gave Tracy a 20-minute coffee break. When the interrogation resumed, the detectives had Tracy repeat her story. They gave her several breaks during which she used the restroom and called her mother. The detectives had Tracy write down her version of what had happened. Her story did not change.

Detective Helga then took over the interrogation for approximately one and one-half hours during which time Tracy turned down food, coffee, and water. For the first 30 to 45 minutes, she continued to claim that the event was an accident. Helga then told Tracy that the officers did not believe her. He provided a "hook" — a question designed to get a suspect to admit to a crime while shifting the blame away. Specifically, he asked Tracy if she had merely tried to scare Kecia by driving towards her. According to Tracy, Helga told her that if she changed her story, the prosecutor might drop the charges and that she could go home if she said that she had intended to only scare Kecia. Helga concedes that he told Tracy that if she went to prison for first-degree murder, she would spend the rest of her life there and would not have contact with her family, including her children. According to Helga, Tracy, who had remained "quite unemotional" throughout the session, suddenly looked at him and said, "I did it. I drove my car towards her to scare her." Helga then reduced these admissions to written questions and answers. The interrogation ended at approximately 10:00 a.m.

Tracy was charged with first-degree murder. After Detective Palm, Detective Helga, and Tracy testified at a jury trial, the defense moved to suppress her confession on the ground that it was involuntary.

Does Tracy have a valid claim for suppression?

7–2: At approximately 4:30 a.m., Dalton was shot to death as he left a party at Valentina's home on an Indian Reservation. Two eyewitnesses identified 33-year-old Leland as the shooter. One told police that Leland knocked Dalton to the ground with the first shot and then walked over and shot him several more times before kicking him in the head. Police arrested Leland at approximately 12:30 p.m. that day and took him to the police station. At 1:30 p.m., Bureau of Indian Affairs ("BIA") Agent James and Federal Bureau of Investigation ("FBI") Agent Wall gave Leland *Miranda* warnings. After Leland agreed to talk, the agents interviewed him for one hour. He denied shooting Dalton, claiming that he had been at his mother's home asleep when the shooting occurred. He agreed to a gunshot residue test (GSR), which was conducted at this time. During this interview, Leland asked to talk to his mother, but was not permitted to do so.

After talking to witnesses, the agents conducted a second interview at 9:00 p.m. that day. Leland, who had slept, seemed more rested. However, he was in pain from a beating that he had received two days earlier — a beating which had apparently precipitated the shooting. Although officers had offered Leland food during the day, he could not eat solid food because his jaw had been broken. The agents again gave *Miranda* warnings, and Leland again agreed to talk. Initially, he repeated that he had been home asleep when the killing occurred. He suggested that two of his friends, Mondo and Corey, might have shot Dalton.

Although they had not received the test results, the agents insinuated that the GSR test had been positive. They told Leland that they had six witnesses who had identified him as the shooter, when in fact they had just two. The agents falsely told Leland that they had found his footprints at the crime scene. They had found footprints, but had not yet identified them. In addition, Agent James said that he would prove Leland's mother was a liar if she corroborated his alibi of being asleep at her house. Leland interpreted this to mean that if his mother testified, the Government "would make her a liar on the stand." Agent James took two pieces of paper and wrote the words "mistake" and "murder" on them. He asked Leland to make a choice — was the killing an accident or intentional murder. He took two more pieces of paper and wrote the numbers six and 60 on them, saying, "If you cooperate, you know, you could be looking at six years, but if you don't give us answers, you could be looking at 60 years." Agent James told Leland about a murder case in which the cooperative suspects had gotten less time than uncooperative suspects. According to the agent, the cooperative suspects were "treated leniently" because the crime had been a mistake.

At 10:18 p.m., a crying Leland told the agents that he shot Dalton by mistake. For two hours, Leland provided details of the shooting. All the while, he was "crying and going in and out of sobbing." This interview lasted almost four hours. According to Leland, he admitted shooting Dalton to avoid spending 60 years in jail and to prevent his mother from being prosecuted.

At noon the next day, after Leland had slept and had breakfast, Agent James and another officer interviewed him for a third time. This interview lasted 30 minutes. After he was warned again and agreed to talk, a crying Leland once again confessed, reiterating the story he had told the night before. At the end of this interview, Leland asked Agent James if he could have a hug, and Agent James hugged him.

Leland was charged with "murder within Indian country." On due process grounds, he moved to suppress the statements made in each of the three interviews. The trial judge refused to suppress Leland's statements from the first interview, but suppressed the confessions made during the second and third interviews. The Government has appealed the suppression of those confessions.

Should the appellate court reverse the suppression ruling?

7–3: Rama was arrested and taken to the police station in connection with a sexual assault. At 11:07, after he sat alone in an interview room for fifteen minutes, Detective Allon arrived. Allon told him that if he did not want to talk he was free to leave. Rama disclosed that he was 22 years old, that he was born in Iraq, where he had worked for the United States military, and that he had been brought to the U.S. by the military "for my safety." After *Miranda* warnings, Allon asked Rama what he knew about the assault. Rama said he had gotten drunk, passed out at his friends' apartment, then had awakened. When he went outside, he saw a woman lying on the ground, bleeding. He helped the woman to her apartment and asked a man inside the apartment to call the police.

Near 11:39, Allon told Rama that he had spent time in Iraq. Rama disclosed that the Iraqi military had killed his entire family. He said that his involvement with the United States military was well known. After both talked about the deaths of friends during the war, Allon asked about the assault again. Rama told the same story about finding the woman. At 11:49, Allon stated, "All I want is for you to be honest with me. . . . You've done some honorable stuff. . . . [T]he last thing I want to do is come here and ruin all of your hopes, whatever. . . . But I need you to be honest. . . . Because if you lie . . . and I find out later, I'll arrest you." Rama stuck to his story.

At 11:56, Allon asked Rama about injuries he sustained in Iraq. Allon talked about "being blown up and suffering my own injuries over there." Allon then told Rama that his friends had said he was at the scene of the assault and that he would give Rama "one more chance to be honest before I tell you what I know." He stated, "It is you, beyond a doubt it is you. All this stuff you want to do, being a police officer and going to college, it's all about to go away, right now." When Allon told Rama that he knew Rama was in the apartment with the victim and the other suspects, Rama admitted he was there, but said he could not remember what had happened because he was drunk. At 11:58, Allon raised the violent circumstances that had prompted the military to remove Rama from Iraq after his family was killed. He then accused Rama of raping the woman, implying that he would not be jailed if he revealed the details. Rama then began to change his story, stating that two other men had sexually assaulted the woman. He claimed he could not remember more.

At 12:01, Allon referred to the risk of violence and death Rama would face if deported to Iraq. Allon stated, "You need to tell me the truth. Because everything, even you being in this country, is in jeopardy." Rama responded, "I know that! My daughter, everything. But, I swear to you man, that's all I can remember." When Allon continued to question him, Rama made several statements that placed him in the apartment while the sexual assault occurred. He claimed he took the woman to her apartment at the behest of his friends. Allon repeatedly said that Rama would be jailed if he did not admit to sexually assaulting the woman. He had Rama handcuffed and taken to a detention cell. After twenty minutes in the cell, Rama asked to speak with Allon again. He then accused his two friends of drugging and raping the woman, but denied that he had touched her. When the assault ended, his friends told Rama to walk the woman back to her apartment. He did so to shield his friends from scrutiny. Rama was upset while describing the incident and cried when he talked about the possibility of being deported to Iraq. He said "I will be dead and my daughter will be without a father." The interrogation ended when Rama asked for a lawyer.

After being charged with sexual assault, Rama moved to suppress his incriminating statements. The trial court held that the statements made after 11:49 were inadmissible under the Due Process Clause. The prosecution has appealed.

How should the court of appeals rule?

7–4: Police arrested 18-year-old Arnold Rutter for robbery. A detective warned him of his *Miranda* rights and Arnold signed a waiver. While one of the detectives was questioning Arnold, Arnold's mother came to the police station and spoke to another detective. The detective told Mrs. Rutter that he believed her son was involved in two or three robberies but that because Mrs. Rutter was being "so cooperative," her son would only be charged with one robbery. After talking with the detective a little more, Mrs. Rutter asked to speak to her son. Up to this point, Arnold had denied any involvement in any robberies.

When Mrs. Rutter entered the interview room, she immediately got very angry at her son. She was angry both because he was involved in robberies and because she felt he was lying to the police. When her son continued to deny his involvement, Mrs. Rutter hit him across the side of the head and his nose started bleeding. She said to him, "You better tell these people what they want to know because you going to be in more trouble than you already is. The officer says you have two or three more robberies on you." As Mrs. Rutter continued to hit her son, one of the detectives told her to stop. He said, "We can't have child abuse at the police station." Mrs. Rutter then stopped hitting Arnold, but said to him, "You better start telling the truth." Arnold then told the detectives that he would make a statement but that "he would prefer that his mother not be in the room when he made the statement." Mrs. Rutter then left the interrogation room and Arnold made a statement confessing to the robbery.

Was Arnold's confession voluntary?

7–5: After being notified of a stolen Ford truck, Bob McCrary, a member of the Sheriff's Department, pursued the stolen truck. During the chase, the truck stopped and someone stabbed McCrary with a butcher knife. After another high speed chase, Kircher, who had been driving the stolen Ford truck, exited the truck and ran into a cotton field. While awaiting police in the field, Kircher stabbed himself several times with a butcher knife. By the time the police apprehended him, he had lost more than a quart of blood. The police rushed him to the hospital where he was given morphine while awaiting surgery.

After Kircher was treated and prepped for surgery, officers asked the emergency room physician if Kircher would be able to talk to them. The doctor gave them his permission, stating that he believed Kircher was stable, alert, and would be able to understand and respond to questions. Officers then gave Kircher his *Miranda* warnings. Kircher signed the card indicating that he understood and waived his rights. In response to the officers' questions, Kircher confessed to stealing the Ford truck and stabbing McCrary.

Shortly before this incident, Kircher had been voluntarily admitted to a drug and alcohol treatment center for drug addiction. The officers who questioned him at the hospital knew of his drug addiction but were not aware of the possible effect it would have on his condition at the time he was questioned. At Kircher's suppression hearing, a medical expert testified that due to his loss of blood, Kircher would have been in shock when he was questioned by the police. The expert further testified that, taking into account Kircher's blood loss, drug addiction, and morphine received at the hospital, he was certain that Kircher was intoxicated at the time he was questioned by the police.

Kircher claims that his confession to the police was involuntary.

Should Kircher's claim be accepted?

7–6: Patrick was the primary caretaker for his two children, K.M., an infant son who was two months old, and C.M., an older boy. Medical records and x-rays showed that K.M. had suffered at least 23 fractures that were in various stages of healing. Patrick was charged with "malicious punishment of a child causing substantial bodily harm." Based on the medical evidence and a statement he made to Detective Oldman, Patrick was convicted of the offense. On appeal, he argues that the trial judge should not have allowed the prosecution to use the statement.

At the time of his meeting with Detective Oldman, Patrick was 41 years old, college educated, and employed as a diving instructor. He was not placed under arrest, and he was advised that his participation in the interview was voluntary, that he did not have to speak with Oldman, and that he could leave. During an interview, Oldman told Patrick that unless someone confessed to injuring K.M., the infant would not be returning home. He also stated that C.M. would very likely be removed from Patrick's home and placed in foster care. Oldman suggested that the consequences of making a confession would be slight — that Patrick would have to spend a couple of weeks out of the home before the whole family could be reunited. The detective also said that he was "not interested in criminal prosecution" and would recommend that Patrick "not be charged criminally." Oldman indicated to Patrick that people "do not serve jail time" for this type of offense. Patrick steadfastly denied injuring K.M. throughout the interview.

The following day, Oldman made similar comments to Patrick's wife and urged her to encourage Patrick to confess to harming K.M. Patrick discussed the situation with his wife and with his mother — who is a social worker. He then sought out Detective Oldman and admitted that he "may" have "accidentally" inflicted the injuries that K.M. had suffered. This statement parroted the language suggested by Oldman during the interview on the prior day. It was introduced at Patrick's trial.

Did the introduction of Patrick's statement violate due process?

7–7: Timmy, an 18-year-old with an IQ of 65 and significant communication and comprehension problems, lived with his parents on the Navajo Nation. An eight-year-old boy who lived next door accused Timmy of sexual abuse. The boy's family called the police. When questioned the next day by Carl Monk, a forensic interviewer from the local medical center, the boy told a lengthy, fantastical, largely incomprehensible tale, but did assert that Timmy pulled his underwear down, "put his penis in my butt," and "put his mouth on my balls and my butt." He also stated that Timmy got "white stuff on my shirt." No semen was found on the boy's clothing and his body showed no signs of abuse.

A week later, FBI Agents Jameson and Gregg came to Timmy's home. They questioned Timmy outside his house, next to Jameson's vehicle for about 40 minutes. Early on, the agents became aware of Timmy's impairments. Timmy told them he was disabled and that he had not finished high school. The agents stated that they were investigating a "molestation" that took place "last Friday." Timmy truthfully said that he was not home that day, but the agents rejected his claim as untrue, falsely asserting that they had witnesses who had seen him at home. Timmy eventually conceded, falsely, that he was home on Friday. The agents told him about two types of sexual offenders — "cold-hearted predators, monsters who prey on children" and those who "just did a one-time thing," maybe because they were "curious" or "drunk." They repeatedly told Timmy that they wanted "to know what kind" he was, saying that the second type could "move on" if they told the truth. Their intended message was that an admission of guilt could minimize the consequences for Timmy and that he could get some sympathy if he was a one-time offender. When Gregg asked several times if Timmy had done "a one-time thing," Timmy gave confused, equivocal responses, including "I don't know, probably like that, one time, but I don't know. But I'm not, like, whatever you . . . guys are trying to think — I ain't like that."

The agents told Timmy that he was "not arrested" and "not in custody," but also indicated that he was free to stop talking to them only when they terminated the interview. They repeatedly said that Timmy had to tell them something or they would keep coming back until he did. More than 20 minutes into the questioning, after Timmy acquiesced in the false assertions that he was at home on Friday, Gregg and Jameson posed a series of questions that required choices between two incriminating alternatives. For example: "[I]s it because you wanted to have sex? . . . Or is it he's the one that came on to you?" "[I]s it something . . . where you forced the issue or is it something that he wanted?" "[D]id he pull away or did you pull out?" and "Did you . . . put your penis in all the way or just a little bit?" Each time, Timmy chose the less incriminating alternative.

Eventually, Timmy nodded when asked if he put his penis inside of the boy's "butt," stating that he did this for "five, six seconds" and that the boy then "walked out," said, "I'm going to tell on you," and "started crying." The agents twice misled Timmy about his statement's purpose, indicating that it would "stay in their file" and that it was "just an apology." Timmy said, "I'm sorry for what I did," but also stated, "You're just trying to accuse me of that shit. But I'm not like that."

Timmy's "confession" is a collection of details chosen by the agents and written out by Jameson. Many, including the facts that Timmy had "used a condom" and that he had "unzipped his pants," were details the agents had provided. After Jameson finished writing the statement, he had Timmy sign it. Timmy was charged with aggravated sexual abuse of a minor, an offense with a mandatory 30-year minimum sentence. Timmy moved to suppress his confession. The trial court denied the motion. Timmy has appealed the ruling.

Should the appellate court reverse the trial court's ruling?

7–8: The police had information that Maurice Johnson, who had a lengthy record of drug offenses, was dealing drugs from the house of Hennis Tracy, his half-sister. Police obtained a search warrant for Tracy's house and found nine grams of crack cocaine hidden in the headboard of her bed. Tracy claimed that she knew nothing about the drugs and blamed Johnson. The police, however, told her that she would be arrested unless Johnson turned himself in and accepted responsibility for the drugs.

Eventually, Tracy was able to track down Johnson, who came to her house. He asked one of the officers if it was true that his sister was going to be arrested if he didn't admit the drugs were his. The officer told him it was true. Johnson said, "That's not fair. You know she's never had anything to do with drugs." The officer replied, "Based on where the drugs were found, we have probable cause to arrest her for possession of cocaine. But we won't do it, if you accept responsibility."

Johnson then admitted that the drugs were his. The police arrested him and read him his *Miranda* rights. Later, he made a full confession. As a result, he was charged with possession with intent to distribute more than five grams of crack cocaine. Tracy was never charged with anything.

Was Johnson's confession involuntary?

7–9: On March 29, three days after her husband had been shot to death, Mrs. Whittington went to police headquarters for questioning. Detective Rhone, who met with Mrs. Whittington in a small interview room, began by asking her for biographical information. At 1:35 p.m., he warned her of her *Miranda* rights and she signed a form indicating she understood her rights and was waiving them. She then made an oral statement in which she denied shooting her husband.

At about 1:50 p.m., Detective Rhone gave Mrs. Whittington a pen to write her statement and then left the room. The Detective put powder on the pen that was invisible to the naked eye and would only show up under a neon or infrared light source. Detective Rhone returned to the room at about 2:30 p.m. Upon reading Mrs. Whittington's statement, he asked her a series of clarifying questions. He also asked her if she would consent to a test that would show whether she had "blow back" on her hands from recent handgun use. Mrs. Whittington consented.

At about 4:00 p.m., an evidence technician entered the room to examine Mrs. Whittington's hands under an infrared light. He showed her the orange "powder" on her hands, stating that it was residue from a gun. This statement was untrue. The powder came from the pen used by Mrs. Whittington to write her statement.

Over the next 12 hours, several other officers met with Mrs. Whittington and intermittently asked her questions. During this period, she was given food and water and was allowed to use the restroom whenever she requested to do so.

At 4:20 a.m., Detective Frankenfield met with Mrs. Whittington in the interview room. He observed that she was cooperative and did not appear fatigued. They talked about her marriage. She said she believed her husband had been "cheating" on her. She also stated that he had verbally and physically abused her. When Frankenfield asked her how she had responded, she said, "You're trying to break me, you're trying to break me." She then shook her head, said she was "so sorry," and confessed to shooting her husband.

At 7:00 a.m., Detective Frankenfield gave Mrs. Whittington some paper and asked her to write down her statement. While she was writing, they had a conversation about the "blow back" or residue evidence. She told the Detective she could not have any "blow back" on her hands because she had washed her hands with bleach after shooting her husband. By the time Mrs. Whittington signed her last statement, she had been at the police station for more than 18 hours.

Mrs. Whittington's attorney moved to suppress her confession on the ground that it was involuntary. After the trial judge ruled that it was voluntary, Mrs. Whittington was convicted of second-degree murder. On appeal, the defense claims that Mrs. Whittington's confession should have been excluded as involuntary.

How should the appellate court rule?

7–10: Accounting giant KMPG and many of its personnel were under criminal investigation for their role in allegedly abusive tax shelters. An indictment, regardless of whether KMPG was guilty of anything, almost certainly would have meant the demise of the firm — the fate met by its major competitor when it was indicted in the Enron scandal. KMPG long had paid legal fees for any of its employees who were sued or charged with crimes as a result of doing their jobs. During the course of the current investigation, the government had informed KMPG that it would consider such payments as a factor that weighed in favor of indicting the firm. The government had also warned KMPG that it would consider any failure by KMPG to induce its employees to make full disclosure to the government as a factor favoring indictment. Consequently, KMPG changed its practice regarding legal fees, informing its employees and partners that it would pay fees, up to $400,000, but *only* on the condition that they cooperated with the prosecutors. In essence, KMPG told its personnel that it would not pay the legal expenses of any employee who refused to talk to the government or who invoked his or her Fifth Amendment privilege against compulsory self-incrimination. Moreover, KMPG made it crystal clear that it would cut off any payments of legal fees to anyone who was indicted. According to KMPG's chief legal officer, "We decided to do everything we could to be able to say at the right time and with the right audience, that we had been fully responsive to the warnings issued to the firm by the government."

Following this policy change by KMPG, the government sought interviews with many KMPG employees and encouraged the firm to press the employees to cooperate. Government agents urged KMPG to tell employees to disclose any personal criminal wrongdoing. When any individual balked, the prosecutors informed KMPG, whereupon the firm would reiterate that it would stop payment of legal fees unless the government was satisfied with the individual's cooperation. In some cases, it told the employees to cooperate with prosecutors or be fired.

The government obtained statements from nine KMPG employees who were subsequently charged with accounting fraud. The nine employees have moved to have the statements they made excluded from the trial, contending that they were coerced.

What arguments should the defendants make in support of their motion? How should the prosecution respond? How should the trial judge rule?

Selected Bibliography

Laurence A. Benner, *Requiem for* Miranda: *The Rehnquist Court's Voluntariness Doctrine in Historical Perspective*, 67 Wash. U. L.Q. 59 (1989)

Geoffrey S. Corn & Kevin Cieply, *The Admissibility of Confessions Compelled by Foreign Coercion: A Compelling Question of Values in an Era of Increasing International Criminal Cooperation*, 42 Pepp. L. Rev. 467 (2015)

Steven A. Drizin & Marissa J. Reich, *Heeding the Lessons of History: The Need for Mandatory Recording of Police Interrogations to Accurately Assess the Reliability and Voluntariness of Confessions*, 52 Drake L. Rev. 619 (2004)

Brandon L. Garrett, *The Substance of False Confessions*, 62 Stan. L. Rev. 1051 (2010)

Brandon L. Garrett, *Contaminated Confessions Revisited*, 101 Va. L. Rev. 395 (2015)

Mark A. Godsey, *Rethinking the Involuntary Confession Rule: Toward a Workable Test for Identifying Compelled Self-Incrimination*, 93 Cal. L. Rev. 465 (2005)

Miriam S. Gohara, *A Lie for a Lie: False Confessions and the Case for Reconsidering the Legality of Deceptive Interrogation Techniques*, 33 Fordham Urb. L. J. 791 (2006)

Joseph D. Grano, Confessions, Truth, and the Law (1993)

Catherine Hancock, *Due Process Before* Miranda, 70 Tul. L. Rev. 2195 (1996)

Yale Kamisar, POLICE INTERROGATION AND CONFESSIONS: ESSAYS IN LAW AND POLICY (1980)

Richard A. Leo, Steven A. Drizin, Peter J. Neufeld, Bradley R. Hall & Amy Vatner, *Bringing Reliability Back In: False Confessions and Legal Safeguards in the Twenty-First Century*, 2006 Wis. L. Rev. 479 (2006)

Richard A. Leo, POLICE INTERROGATION AND AMERICAN JUSTICE (2008)

Laurie Magid, *Deceptive Police Interrogation Practices: How Far Is Too Far?* 99 Mich. L. Rev. 1168 (2001)

Paul Marcus, *It's Not Just About* Miranda: *Determining the Voluntariness of Confessions in Criminal Prosecutions*, 40 Val. U. L. Rev. 601 (2006)

Eugene R. Milhizer, *Confessions After* Connelly: *An Evidentiary Solution for Excluding Unreliable Confessions*, 81 Temp. L. Rev. 1 (2008)

Eve Brensike Primus, *The Future of Confession Law: Toward Rules for the Voluntariness Test*, 114 Mich. L. Rev. 1 (2015)

Daniel W. Sasaki, *Guarding the Guardians: Police Trickery and Confessions*, 40 Stan. L. Rev. 1593 (1988)

Otis H. Stephens, THE SUPREME COURT AND CONFESSIONS OF GUILT (1973)

George C. Thomas III & Richard A. Leo, CONFESSIONS OF GUILT: FROM TORTURE TO *MIRANDA* AND BEYOND (2012)

Welsh S. White, Miranda's *Failure to Restrain Pernicious Interrogation Practices*, 99 Mich. L. Rev. 1211 (2001)

Chapter 8

The Privilege Against Self-Incrimination and Confessions

Introductory Note

As noted in the introduction to the previous chapter, by the mid-1960s the Court was seeking new means of regulating police practices used to obtain incriminating statements from criminal suspects. The two constitutional provisions it turned to were the Fifth Amendment Privilege Against Self-Incrimination, the subject of this chapter, and the Sixth Amendment Right to the Assistance of Counsel, considered in Chapter Nine.

Miranda v. Arizona, 384 U.S. 436, 86 S. Ct. 1602, 16 L. Ed. 2d 694 (1966), the foundational opinion for this chapter, held that the Fifth Amendment Privilege provides specific protections for suspects subjected to custodial interrogation. Although the Supreme Court has refused to overrule *Miranda* despite considerable opposition, the Justices have dramatically modified the landmark ruling's constitutional rationale and logic. The Court, quite obviously, has a very different understanding of its premises and character than the one that originally animated the *Miranda* decision. Thus, in studying *Miranda*, it is desirable to consider both what the opinion meant when it was first promulgated and what it means today. Moreover, in evaluating the post-*Miranda* case law, it is important both to assess the current constitutional basis for *Miranda* and to determine how *Miranda* operates in specific contexts.

With these objectives in mind, Chapter Eight is divided into five sections, A through E. Section A includes the *Miranda* decision itself; *New York v. Quarles*, 467 U.S. 649, 104 S. Ct. 2626, 81 L. Ed. 2d 550 (1984), one of the opinions that explains the modification of *Miranda*'s underlying constitutional premises; and *Dickerson v. United States*, 530 U.S. 428, 120 S. Ct. 2326, 147 L. Ed. 2d 405 (2000), which reaffirmed *Miranda* when its constitutional legitimacy was challenged. In considering these opinions, students should focus on whether *Miranda* was a legitimate constitutional decision when it was rendered, and if so, whether it remains a legitimate constitutional decision in light of the Court's reinterpretation of its logical foundations.

The four remaining sections of the chapter address the specific doctrinal issues that arise under *Miranda*'s holding that the government may not introduce at trial a confession made by a suspect who is in custody and is subjected to official interrogation unless the police first issue warnings and also secure a waiver of the constitutional safeguards against such interrogation. The decision also provided that certain additional protections come into effect if a suspect invokes the right to remain silent or the right to the assistance of an attorney. When the Warren Court decided *Miranda* in 1966, it might have thought that the decision would eliminate much of the litigation surrounding the introduction of confessions in criminal cases. This has not proven to be the case. To the contrary, the decision has spawned extensive litigation and detailed doctrinal standards relating to the requirements for *Miranda*'s application, the constraints upon questioning of suspects when *Miranda* does apply, and the special safeguards that arise when suspects decide to exercise their rights. Sections B through E explore the post-*Miranda* opinions that address the issues of custody, interrogation, warnings, waiver, and invocation of the rights to silence and counsel. In reading these cases, students should consider whether the decisions following *Miranda* are consistent with the original ruling and whether they are consistent with the Fifth Amendment Privilege Against Compulsory Self-Incrimination, which is the sole basis for all *Miranda* law.

[A] The Constitutional Basis

Miranda v. Arizona

United States Supreme Court

384 U.S. 436, 86 S. Ct. 1602, 16 L. Ed. 2d 694 (1966)

Mr. Chief Justice Warren delivered the opinion of the Court.

The cases before us raise questions which go to the roots of our concepts of American criminal jurisprudence: the restraints society must observe consistent with the Federal Constitution in prosecuting individuals for crime. More specifically, we deal with the admissibility of statements obtained from an individual who is subjected to custodial police interrogation and the necessity for procedures which assure that the individual is accorded his privilege under the Fifth Amendment to the Constitution not to be compelled to incriminate himself.

. . . .

Our holding will be spelled out with some specificity in the pages which follow but briefly stated it is this: the prosecution may not use statements, whether exculpatory or inculpatory, stemming from custodial interrogation of the defendant unless it demonstrates the use of procedural safeguards effective to secure the privilege against self-incrimination. By custodial interrogation, we mean questioning initiated by law enforcement officers after a person has been taken into custody or otherwise deprived of his freedom of action in any significant way. As for the procedural safeguards to be employed, unless other fully effective means are devised to inform accused persons of their right of silence and to assure a continuous opportunity to exercise it, the following measures are required. Prior to any questioning, the person must be warned that he has a right to remain silent, that any statement he does make may be used as evidence against him, and that he has a right to the presence of an attorney, either retained or appointed. The defendant may waive effectuation of these rights, provided the waiver is made voluntarily, knowingly and intelligently. If, however, he indicates in any manner and at any stage of the process that he wishes to consult with an attorney before speaking there can be no questioning. Likewise, if the individual is alone and indicates in any manner that he does not wish to be interrogated, the police may not question him. The mere fact that he may have answered some questions or volunteered some statements on his own does not deprive him of the right to refrain from answering any further inquiries until he has consulted with an attorney and thereafter consents to be questioned.

I

The constitutional issue we decide in each of these cases is the admissibility of statements obtained from a defendant questioned while in custody or otherwise deprived of his freedom of action in any significant way. In each, the defendant was questioned by police officers, detectives, or a prosecuting attorney in a room in which he was cut off from the outside world. In none of these cases was the defendant given a full and effective warning of his rights at the outset of the interrogation process. In all the cases, the questioning elicited oral admissions, and in three of them, signed statements as well which were admitted at their trials. They all thus share salient features — incommunicado interrogation of individuals in a police-dominated atmosphere, resulting in self-incriminating statements without full warnings of constitutional rights.

An understanding of the nature and setting of this in-custody interrogation is essential to our decisions today. The difficulty in depicting what transpires at such interrogations stems from the fact that in this country they have largely taken place incommunicado. From extensive factual studies undertaken in the early 1930's, including the famous Wickersham Report to Congress by a Presidential Commission, it is clear that police violence and the "third degree" flourished at that time. In a series of cases decided by this Court long after these studies, the police resorted to physical brutality — beating, hanging, whipping — and to sustained and protracted questioning incommunicado in order to extort confessions. The Commission on Civil Rights in 1961 found much evidence to indicate that "some policemen still resort to physical force to obtain confessions," 1961 Comm'n on Civil Rights Rep., Justice, pt. 5, 17. The use of physical brutality and violence is not, unfortunately, relegated to the past or to any part of the country. Only recently in Kings County, New York, the police brutally beat, kicked and placed lighted cigarette butts on the back of a potential witness under interrogation for the purpose of securing a statement incriminating a third party. *People v. Portelli*, 15 N.Y.2d 235, 257 N.Y.S.2d 931, 205 N.E.2d 857 (1965).

The examples given above are undoubtedly the exception now, but they are sufficiently widespread to be the object of concern. Unless a proper limitation upon custodial interrogation is achieved — such as these decisions will advance — there can be no assurance that practices of this nature will be eradicated in the foreseeable future. . . .

Again we stress that the modern practice of in-custody interrogation is psychologically rather than physically oriented. As we have stated before, "Since *Chambers v. Florida*, 309 U.S. 227, 60 S. Ct. 472, 84 L. Ed. 716, this Court has recognized that coercion can be mental as well as physical, and that the blood of the accused is not the only hallmark of an unconstitutional inquisition." *Blackburn v. Alabama*, 361 U.S. 199, 206, 80 S. Ct. 274, 279, 4 L. Ed. 2d 242 (1960). Interrogation still takes place in privacy. Privacy results in secrecy and this in turn results in a gap in our knowledge as to what in fact goes on in the interrogation rooms. A valuable source of information about present police practices, however, may be found in various police manuals and texts which document procedures employed with success in the past, and which recommend various other effective tactics. These texts are used by law enforcement agencies themselves as guides.[9] It should be noted that these texts professedly present the most enlightened and effective means presently used to obtain statements through custodial interrogation. By considering these texts and other data, it is possible to describe procedures observed and noted around the country.

The officers are told by the manuals that the "principal psychological factor contributing to a successful interrogation is *privacy* — being alone with the person under interrogation."[10] The efficacy of this tactic has been explained as follows:

> If at all practicable, the interrogation should take place in the investigator's office or at least in a room of his own choice. The subject should be deprived of every psychological advantage. In his own home he may be confident, indignant, or recalcitrant. He is more keenly aware of his rights and more reluctant to tell of his indiscretions of criminal behavior within the walls of his home. Moreover his family and other friends are nearby, their presence lending moral support. In his office, the investigator possesses all the advantages. The atmosphere suggests the invincibility of the forces of the law.[11]

---

9. The methods described in Inbau & Reid, CRIMINAL INTERROGATION AND CONFESSIONS (1962), are a revision and enlargement of material presented in three prior editions of a predecessor text, LIE DETECTION AND CRIMINAL INTERROGATION (3d ed. 1953). The authors and their associates are officers of the Chicago Police Scientific Crime Detection Laboratory and have had extensive experience in writing, lecturing and speaking to law enforcement authorities over a 20-year period. They say that the techniques portrayed in their manuals reflect their experiences and are the most effective psychological stratagems to employ during interrogations. Similarly, the techniques described in O'Hara, FUNDAMENTALS OF CRIMINAL INVESTIGATION (1956), were gleaned from long service as observer, lecturer in police science, and work as a federal criminal investigator. All these texts have had rather extensive use among law enforcement agencies and among students of police science, with total sales and circulation of over 44,000.

10. Inbau & Reid, CRIMINAL INTERROGATION AND CONFESSIONS (1962), at 1.

11. O'Hara, *supra* at 99.

To highlight the isolation and unfamiliar surroundings, the manuals instruct the police to display an air of confidence in the suspect's guilt and from outward appearance to maintain only an interest in confirming certain details. The guilt of the subject is to be posited as a fact. The interrogator should direct his comments toward the reasons why the subject committed the act, rather than court failure by asking the subject whether he did it. Like other men, perhaps the subject has had a bad family life, had an unhappy childhood, had too much to drink, had an unrequited desire for women. The officers are instructed to minimize the moral seriousness of the offense, to cast blame on the victim or on society. These tactics are designed to put the subject in a psychological state where his story is but an elaboration of what the police purport to know already — that he is guilty. Explanations to the contrary are dismissed and discouraged.

The texts thus stress that the major qualities an interrogator should possess are patience and perseverance. One writer describes the efficacy of these characteristics in this manner:

> In the preceding paragraphs emphasis has been placed on kindness and stratagems. The investigator will, however, encounter many situations where the sheer weight of his personality will be the deciding factor. Where emotional appeals and tricks are employed to no avail, he must rely on an oppressive atmosphere of dogged persistence. He must interrogate steadily and without relent, leaving the subject no prospect of surcease. He must dominate his subject and overwhelm him with his inexorable will to obtain the truth. He should interrogate for a spell of several hours pausing only for the subject's necessities in acknowledgment of the need to avoid a charge of duress that can be technically substantiated. In a serious case, the interrogation may continue for days, with the required intervals for food and sleep, but with no respite from the atmosphere of domination. It is possible in this way to induce the subject to talk without resorting to duress or coercion. The method should be used only when the guilt of the subject appears highly probable.[14]

The manuals suggest that the suspect be offered legal excuses for his actions in order to obtain an initial admission of guilt. Where there is a suspected revenge-killing, for example, the interrogator may say:

> Joe, you probably didn't go out looking for this fellow with the purpose of shooting him. My guess is, however, that you expected something from him and that's why you carried a gun — for your own protection. You knew him for what he was, no good. Then when you met him he probably started using foul, abusive language and he gave some indication that he was about to pull a gun on you, and that's when you had to act to save your own life. That's about it, isn't it, Joe?[15]

---

14. O'Hara, *supra* at 112.
15. Inbau & Reid, *supra* at 40.

Having then obtained the admission of shooting, the interrogator is advised to refer to circumstantial evidence which negates the self-defense explanation. This should enable him to secure the entire story. One text notes that "Even if he fails to do so, the inconsistency between the subject's original denial of the shooting and his present admission of at least doing the shooting will serve to deprive him of a self-defense 'out' at the time of trial."[16]

When the techniques described above prove unavailing, the texts recommend they be alternated with a show of some hostility. One ploy often used has been termed the "friendly-unfriendly" or the "Mutt and Jeff" act:

> ... In this technique, two agents are employed. Mutt, the relentless investigator, who knows the subject is guilty and is not going to waste any time. He's sent a dozen men away for this crime and he's going to send the subject away for the full term. Jeff, on the other hand, is obviously a kindhearted man. He has a family himself. He has a brother who was involved in a little scrape like this. He disapproves of Mutt and his tactics and will arrange to get him off the case if the subject will cooperate. He can't hold Mutt off for very long. The subject would be wise to make a quick decision. The technique is applied by having both investigators present while Mutt acts out his role. Jeff may stand by quietly and demur at some of Mutt's tactics. When Jeff makes his plea for cooperation, Mutt is not present in the room.

The interrogators sometimes are instructed to induce a confession out of trickery. The technique here is quite effective in crimes which require identification or which run in series. In the identification situation, the interrogator may take a break in his questioning to place the subject among a group of men in a line-up. "The witness or complainant (previously coached, if necessary) studies the line-up and confidently points out the subject as the guilty party."[18] Then the questioning resumes "as though there were now no doubt about the guilt of the subject." A variation on this technique is called the "reverse line-up":

> The accused is placed in a line-up, but this time he is identified by several fictitious witnesses or victims who associated him with different offenses. It is expected that the subject will become desperate and confess to the offense under investigation in order to escape from the false accusations.

The manuals also contain instructions for police on how to handle the individual who refuses to discuss the matter entirely, or who asks for an attorney or relatives. The examiner is to concede him the right to remain silent. "This usually has a very undermining effect. First of all, he is disappointed in his expectation of an unfavorable reaction on the part of the interrogator. Secondly, a concession of this right to remain silent impresses the subject with the apparent fairness of his interrogator."[20]

---

16. *Id.*
18. O'Hara, *supra* at 105–106.
20. Inbau & Reid, *supra* at 111.

After this psychological conditioning, however, the officer is told to point out the incriminating significance of the suspect's refusal to talk:

> Joe, you have a right to remain silent. That's your privilege and I'm the last person in the world who'll try to take it away from you. If that's the way you want to leave this, O.K. But let me ask you this. Suppose you were in my shoes and I were in yours and you called me in to ask me about this and I told you, "I don't want to answer any of your questions." You'd think I had something to hide, and you'd probably be right in thinking that. That's exactly what I'll have to think about you, and so will everybody else. So let's sit here and talk this whole thing over.[21]

Few will persist in their initial refusal to talk, it is said, if this monologue is employed correctly.

In the event that the subject wishes to speak to a relative or an attorney, the following advice is tendered:

> The interrogator should respond by suggesting that the subject first tell the truth to the interrogator himself rather than get anyone else involved in the matter. If the request is for an attorney, the interrogator may suggest that the subject save himself or his family the expense of any such professional service, particularly if he is innocent of the offense under investigation. The interrogator may also add, "Joe, I'm only looking for the truth, and if you're telling the truth, that's it. You can handle this by yourself."[22]

From these representative samples of interrogation techniques, the setting prescribed by the manuals and observed in practice becomes clear. In essence, it is this: To be alone with the subject is essential to prevent distraction and to deprive him of any outside support. The aura of confidence in his guilt undermines his will to resist. He merely confirms the preconceived story the police seek to have him describe. Patience and persistence, at times relentless questioning, are employed. To obtain a confession, the interrogator must "patiently maneuver himself or his quarry into a position from which the desired objective may be attained."[23] When normal procedures fail to produce the needed result, the police may resort to deceptive stratagems such as giving false legal advice. It is important to keep the subject off balance, for example, by trading on his insecurity about himself or his surroundings. The police then persuade, trick, or cajole him out of exercising his constitutional rights.

Even without employing brutality, the "third degree" or the specific stratagems described above, the very fact of custodial interrogation exacts a heavy toll on individual liberty and trades on the weakness of individuals. . . .

---

21. *Id.*
22. Inbau & Reid, *supra* at 112.
23. Inbau & Reid, Lie Detection and Criminal Interrogation 185 (3d ed. 1953).

In the cases before us today, given this background, we concern ourselves primarily with this interrogation atmosphere and the evils it can bring. In No. 759, *Miranda v. Arizona*, the police arrested the defendant and took him to a special interrogation room where they secured a confession. In No. 760, *Vignera v. New York*, the defendant made oral admissions to the police after interrogation in the afternoon, and then signed an inculpatory statement upon being questioned by an assistant district attorney later the same evening. In No. 761, *Westover v. United States*, the defendant was handed over to the Federal Bureau of Investigation by local authorities after they had detained and interrogated him for a lengthy period, both at night and the following morning. After some two hours of questioning, the federal officers had obtained signed statements from the defendant. Lastly, in No. 584, *California v. Stewart*, the local police held the defendant five days in the station and interrogated him on nine separate occasions before they secured his inculpatory statement.

In these cases, we might not find the defendants' statements to have been involuntary in traditional terms. Our concern for adequate safeguards to protect precious Fifth Amendment rights is, of course, not lessened in the slightest. In each of the cases, the defendant was thrust into an unfamiliar atmosphere and run through menacing police interrogation procedures. The potentiality for compulsion is forcefully apparent, for example, in *Miranda*, where the indigent Mexican defendant was a seriously disturbed individual with pronounced sexual fantasies, and in *Stewart*, in which the defendant was an indigent Los Angeles Negro who had dropped out of school in the sixth grade. To be sure, the records do not evince overt physical coercion or patent psychological ploys. The fact remains that in none of these cases did the officers undertake to afford appropriate safeguards at the outset of the interrogation to insure that the statements were truly the product of free choice.

It is obvious that such an interrogation environment is created for no purpose other than to subjugate the individual to the will of his examiner. This atmosphere carries its own badge of intimidation. To be sure, this is not physical intimidation, but it is equally destructive of human dignity. The current practice of incommunicado interrogation is at odds with one of our Nation's most cherished principles — that the individual may not be compelled to incriminate himself. Unless adequate protective devices are employed to dispel the compulsion inherent in custodial surroundings, no statement obtained from the defendant can truly be the product of his free choice.

From the foregoing, we can readily perceive an intimate connection between the privilege against self-incrimination and police custodial questioning. It is fitting to turn to history and precedent underlying the Self-Incrimination Clause to determine its applicability in this situation.

II

We sometimes forget how long it has taken to establish the privilege against self-incrimination, the sources from which it came and the fervor with which it was defended. Its roots go back into ancient times. Perhaps the critical historical event shedding light on its origins and evolution was the trial of one John Lilburn, a vocal anti-Stuart Leveller, who was made to take the Star Chamber Oath in 1637. The oath would have bound him to answer to all questions posed to him on any subject. *The Trial of John Lilburn and John Wharton*, 3 How. St. Tr. 1315 (1637). He resisted the oath and declaimed the proceedings, stating:

> "Another fundamental right I then contended for, was, that no man's conscience ought to be racked by oaths imposed, to answer to questions concerning himself in matters criminal, or pretended to be so."

Haller & Davies, THE LEVELLER TRACTS 1647–1653, p. 454 (1944).

On account of the Lilburn Trial, Parliament abolished the inquisitorial Court of Star Chamber and went further in giving him generous reparation. The lofty principles to which Lilburn had appealed during his trial gained popular acceptance in England. These sentiments worked their way over to the Colonies and were implanted after great struggle into the Bill of Rights. Those who framed our Constitution and the Bill of Rights were ever aware of subtle encroachments on individual liberty. They knew that "illegitimate and unconstitutional practices get their first footing . . . by silent approaches and slight deviations from legal modes of procedure." *Boyd v. United States*, 116 U.S. 616, 635, 6 S. Ct. 524, 535, 29 L. Ed. 746 (1886). The privilege was elevated to constitutional status and has always been "as broad as the mischief against which it seeks to guard." *Counselman v. Hitchcock*, 142 U.S. 547, 562, 12 S. Ct. 195, 198, 35 L. Ed. 1110 (1892). We cannot depart from this noble heritage.

Thus we may view the historical development of the privilege as one which groped for the proper scope of governmental power over the citizen. As a "noble principle often transcends its origins," the privilege has come rightfully to be recognized in part as an individual's substantive right, a "right to a private enclave where he may lead a private life. That right is the hallmark of our democracy." *United States v. Grunewald*, 233 F.2d 556, 581–582 (Frank, J., dissenting), *rev'd*, 353 U.S. 391, 77 S. Ct. 963, 1 L. Ed. 2d 931 (1957). We have recently noted that the privilege against self-incrimination — the essential mainstay of our adversary system — is founded on a complex of values, *Murphy v. Waterfront Comm'n of New York Harbor*, 378 U.S. 52, 55–57, n.5, 84 S. Ct. 1594, 1596–1597, 12 L. Ed. 2d 678 (1964). All these policies point to one overriding thought: the constitutional foundation underlying the privilege is the respect a government — state or federal — must accord to the dignity and integrity of its citizens. To maintain a "fair state-individual balance," to require the government "to shoulder the entire load," 8 Wigmore, EVIDENCE 317 (McNaughton rev. 1961), to respect the inviolability of the human personality, our accusatory system of criminal justice demands that the government seeking to punish an individual produce the evidence against him by its own independent labors, rather than by the cruel, simple expedient of compelling it from his own mouth. In sum, the privilege is fulfilled only when the person is guaranteed the right "to remain silent unless he chooses to speak in the unfettered exercise of his own will." *Malloy v. Hogan*, 378 U.S. 1, 8, 84 S. Ct. 1489, 1493, 12 L. Ed. 2d 653 (1964).

The question in these cases is whether the privilege is fully applicable during a period of custodial interrogation. In this Court, the privilege has consistently been accorded a liberal construction. We are satisfied that all the principles embodied in the privilege apply to informal compulsion exerted by law-enforcement officers during in-custody questioning. An individual swept from familiar surroundings into police custody, surrounded by antagonistic forces, and subjected to the techniques of persuasion described above cannot be otherwise than under compulsion to speak.

. . . .

III

Today, then, there can be no doubt that the Fifth Amendment privilege is available outside of criminal court proceedings and serves to protect persons in all settings in which their freedom of action is curtailed in any significant way from being compelled to incriminate themselves. We have concluded that without proper safeguards the process of in-custody interrogation of persons suspected or accused of crime contains inherently compelling pressures which work to undermine the individual's will to resist and to compel him to speak where he would not otherwise do so freely. In order to combat these pressures and to permit a full opportunity to exercise the privilege against self-incrimination, the accused must be adequately and effectively apprised of his rights and the exercise of those rights must be fully honored.

It is impossible for us to foresee the potential alternatives for protecting the privilege which might be devised by Congress or the States in the exercise of their creative rule-making capacities. Therefore we cannot say that the Constitution necessarily requires adherence to any particular solution for the inherent compulsions of the interrogation process as it is presently conducted. Our decision in no way creates a constitutional straitjacket which will handicap sound efforts at reform, nor is it intended to have this effect. We encourage Congress and the States to continue their laudable search for increasingly effective ways of protecting the rights of the individual while promoting efficient enforcement of our criminal laws. However, unless we are shown other procedures which are at least as effective in apprising accused persons of their right of silence and in assuring a continuous opportunity to exercise it, the following safeguards must be observed.

At the outset, if a person in custody is to be subjected to interrogation, he must first be informed in clear and unequivocal terms that he has the right to remain silent. For those unaware of the privilege, the warning is needed simply to make them aware of it — the threshold requirement for an intelligent decision as to its exercise. More important, such a warning is an absolute prerequisite in overcoming the inherent pressures of the interrogation atmosphere. It is not just the subnormal or woefully ignorant who succumb to an interrogator's imprecations, whether implied or expressly stated, that the interrogation will continue until a confession is obtained or that silence in the face of accusation is itself damning and will bode ill when presented to a jury. Further, the warning will show the individual that his interrogators are prepared to recognize his privilege should he choose to exercise it.

The Fifth Amendment privilege is so fundamental to our system of constitutional rule and the expedient of giving an adequate warning as to the availability of the privilege so simple, we will not pause to inquire in individual cases whether the defendant was aware of his rights without a warning being given. Assessments of the knowledge the defendant possessed, based on information as to his age, education, intelligence, or prior contact with authorities, can never be more than speculation; a warning is a clear-cut fact. More important, whatever the background of the person interrogated, a warning at the time of the interrogation is indispensable to overcome its pressures and to insure that the individual knows he is free to exercise the privilege at that point in time.

The warning of the right to remain silent must be accompanied by the explanation that anything said can and will be used against the individual in court. This warning is needed in order to make him aware not only of the privilege, but also of the consequences of forgoing it. It is only through an awareness of these consequences that there can be any assurance of real understanding and intelligent exercise of the privilege. Moreover, this warning may serve to make the individual more acutely aware that he is faced with a phase of the adversary system — that he is not in the presence of persons acting solely in his interest.

The circumstances surrounding in-custody interrogation can operate very quickly to overbear the will of one merely made aware of his privilege by his interrogators. Therefore, the right to have counsel present at the interrogation is indispensable to the protection of the Fifth Amendment privilege under the system we delineate today. Our aim is to assure that the individual's right to choose between silence and speech remains unfettered throughout the interrogation process. A once-stated warning, delivered by those who will conduct the interrogation, cannot itself suffice to that end among those who most require knowledge of their rights. A mere warning given by the interrogators is not alone sufficient to accomplish that end. Prosecutors themselves claim that the admonishment of the right to remain silent without more "will benefit only the recidivist and the professional." Brief for the National District Attorneys Association as *amicus curiae*, p. 14. Even preliminary advice given to the accused by his own attorney can be swiftly overcome by the secret interrogation process. Thus, the need for counsel to protect the Fifth Amendment privilege comprehends not merely a right to consult with counsel prior to questioning, but also to have counsel present during any questioning if the defendant so desires.

The presence of counsel at the interrogation may serve several significant subsidiary functions as well. If the accused decides to talk to his interrogators, the assistance of counsel can mitigate the dangers of untrustworthiness. With a lawyer present the likelihood that the police will practice coercion is reduced, and if coercion is nevertheless exercised the lawyer can testify to it in court. The presence of a lawyer can also help to guarantee that the accused gives a fully accurate statement to the police and that the statement is rightly reported by the prosecution at trial.

An individual need not make a pre-interrogation request for a lawyer. While such request affirmatively secures his right to have one, his failure to ask for a lawyer does not constitute a waiver. No effective waiver of the right to counsel during interrogation can be recognized unless specifically made after the warnings we here delineate have been given. The accused who does not know his rights and therefore does not make a request may be the person who most needs counsel.

. . . .

Accordingly we hold that an individual held for interrogation must be clearly informed that he has the right to consult with a lawyer and to have the lawyer with him during interrogation under the system for protecting the privilege we delineate today. As with the warnings of the right to remain silent and that anything stated can be used in evidence against him, this warning is an absolute prerequisite to interrogation. No amount of circumstantial evidence that the person may have been aware of this right will suffice to stand in its stead. Only through such a warning is there ascertainable assurance that the accused was aware of this right.

If an individual indicates that he wishes the assistance of counsel before any interrogation occurs, the authorities cannot rationally ignore or deny his request on the basis that the individual does not have or cannot afford a retained attorney. The financial ability of the individual has no relationship to the scope of the rights involved here. The privilege against self-incrimination secured by the Constitution applies to all individuals. The need for counsel in order to protect the privilege exists for the indigent as well as the affluent. In fact, were we to limit these constitutional rights to those who can retain an attorney, our decisions today would be of little significance. The cases before us as well as the vast majority of confession cases with which we have dealt in the past involve those unable to retain counsel.

. . . .

In order fully to apprise a person interrogated of the extent of his rights under this system then, it is necessary to warn him not only that he has the right to consult with an attorney, but also that if he is indigent a lawyer will be appointed to represent him. Without this additional warning, the admonition of the right to consult with counsel would often be understood as meaning only that he can consult with a lawyer if he has one or has the funds to obtain one. The warning of a right to counsel would be hollow if not couched in terms that would convey to the indigent — the person most often subjected to interrogation — the knowledge that he too has a right to have counsel present. As with the warnings of the right to remain silent and of the general right to counsel, only by effective and express explanation to the indigent of this right can there be assurance that he was truly in a position to exercise it.

. . . .

Once warnings have been given, the subsequent procedure is clear. If the individual indicates in any manner, at any time prior to or during questioning, that he wishes to remain silent, the interrogation must cease. At this point he has shown that he intends to exercise his Fifth Amendment privilege; any statement taken after the person invokes his privilege cannot be other than the product of compulsion, subtle or otherwise. Without the right to cut off questioning, the setting of in-custody interrogation operates on the individual to overcome free choice in producing a statement after the privilege has been once invoked. If the individual states that he wants an attorney, the interrogation must cease until an attorney is present. At that time, the individual must have an opportunity to confer with the attorney and to have him present during any subsequent questioning. If the individual cannot obtain an attorney and he indicates that he wants one before speaking to police, they must respect his decision to remain silent.

This does not mean, as some have suggested, that each police station must have a "station house lawyer" present at all times to advise prisoners. It does mean, however, that if police propose to interrogate a person they must make known to him that he is entitled to a lawyer and that if he cannot afford one, a lawyer will be provided for him prior to any interrogation. If authorities conclude that they will not provide counsel during a reasonable period of time in which investigation in the field is carried out, they may refrain from doing so without violating the person's Fifth Amendment privilege so long as they do not question him during that time.

If the interrogation continues without the presence of an attorney and a statement is taken, a heavy burden rests on the government to demonstrate that the defendant knowingly and intelligently waived his privilege against self-incrimination and his right to retained or appointed counsel. This Court has always set high standards of proof for the waiver of constitutional rights, and we reassert these standards as applied to in-custody interrogation. Since the State is responsible for establishing the isolated circumstances under which the interrogation takes place and has the only means of making available corroborated evidence of warnings given during incommunicado interrogation, the burden is rightly on its shoulders.

An express statement that the individual is willing to make a statement and does not want an attorney followed closely by a statement could constitute a waiver. But a valid waiver will not be presumed simply from the silence of the accused after warnings are given or simply from the fact that a confession was in fact eventually obtained. A statement we made in *Carnley v. Cochran*, 369 U.S. 506, 516, 82 S. Ct. 884, 890, 8 L. Ed. 2d 70 (1962), is applicable here:

> Presuming waiver from a silent record is impermissible. The record must show, or there must be an allegation and evidence which show, that an accused was offered counsel but intelligently and understandingly rejected the offer. Anything less is not waiver.

Moreover, where in-custody interrogation is involved, there is no room for the contention that the privilege is waived if the individual answers some questions or gives some information on his own prior to invoking his right to remain silent when interrogated.

Whatever the testimony of the authorities as to waiver of rights by an accused, the fact of lengthy interrogation or incommunicado incarceration before a statement is made is strong evidence that the accused did not validly waive his rights. In these circumstances the fact that the individual eventually made a statement is consistent with the conclusion that the compelling influence of the interrogation finally forced him to do so. It is inconsistent with any notion of a voluntary relinquishment of the privilege. Moreover, any evidence that the accused was threatened, tricked, or cajoled into a waiver will, of course, show that the defendant did not voluntarily waive his privilege. The requirement of warnings and waiver of rights is a fundamental with respect to the Fifth Amendment privilege and not simply a preliminary ritual to existing methods of interrogation.

The warnings required and the waiver necessary in accordance with our opinion today are, in the absence of a fully effective equivalent, prerequisites to the admissibility of any statement made by a defendant. No distinction can be drawn between statements which are direct confessions and statements which amount to "admissions" of part or all of an offense. The privilege against self-incrimination protects the individual from being compelled to incriminate himself in any manner; it does not distinguish degrees of incrimination. Similarly, for precisely the same reason, no distinction may be drawn between inculpatory statements and statements alleged to be merely "exculpatory." If a statement made were in fact truly exculpatory it would, of course, never be used by the prosecution. In fact, statements merely intended to be exculpatory by the defendant are often used to impeach his testimony at trial or to demonstrate untruths in the statement given under interrogation and thus to prove guilt by implication. These statements are incriminating in any meaningful sense of the word and may not be used without the full warnings and effective waiver required for any other statement. In *Escobedo* itself, the defendant fully intended his accusation of another as the slayer to be exculpatory as to himself.

The principles announced today deal with the protection which must be given to the privilege against self-incrimination when the individual is first subjected to police interrogation while in custody at the station or otherwise deprived of his freedom of action in any significant way. It is at this point that our adversary system of criminal proceedings commences, distinguishing itself at the outset from the inquisitorial system recognized in some countries. Under the system of warnings we delineate today or under any other system which may be devised and found effective, the safeguards to be erected about the privilege must come into play at this point.

Our decision is not intended to hamper the traditional function of police officers in investigating crime. When an individual is in custody on probable cause, the police may, of course, seek out evidence in the field to be used at trial against him. Such investigation may include inquiry of persons not under restraint. General on-the-scene questioning as to facts surrounding a crime or other general questioning of citizens in the fact-finding process is not affected by our holding. It is an act of responsible citizenship for individuals to give whatever information they may have to aid in law enforcement. In such situations the compelling atmosphere inherent in the process of in-custody interrogation is not necessarily present.

. . . .

V

Because of the nature of the problem and because of its recurrent significance in numerous cases, we have to this point discussed the relationship of the Fifth Amendment privilege to police interrogation without specific concentration on the facts of the cases before us. We turn now to these facts to consider the application to these cases of the constitutional principles discussed above. In each instance, we have concluded that statements were obtained from the defendant under circumstances that did not meet constitutional standards for protection of the privilege.

No. 759. *Miranda v. Arizona.*

On March 13, 1963, petitioner, Ernesto Miranda, was arrested at his home and taken in custody to a Phoenix police station. He was there identified by the complaining witness. The police then took him to "Interrogation Room No. 2" of the detective bureau. There he was questioned by two police officers. The officers admitted at trial that Miranda was not advised that he had a right to have an attorney present. Two hours later, the officers emerged from the interrogation room with a written confession signed by Miranda. At the top of the statement was a typed paragraph stating that the confession was made voluntarily, without threats or promises of immunity and "with full knowledge of my legal rights, understanding any statement I make may be used against me."

At his trial before a jury, the written confession was admitted into evidence over the objection of defense counsel, and the officers testified to the prior oral confession made by Miranda during the interrogation. Miranda was found guilty of kidnapping and rape. . . .

We reverse.

From the testimony of the officers and by the admission of respondent, it is clear that Miranda was not in any way apprised of his right to consult with an attorney and to have one present during the interrogation, nor was his right not to be compelled to incriminate himself effectively protected in any other manner. Without these warnings the statements were inadmissible. The mere fact that he signed a statement which contained a typed-in clause stating that he had "full knowledge" of his "legal rights" does not approach the knowing and intelligent waiver required to relinquish constitutional rights.

. . . .

[The Court then discussed the three other cases before it, concluding that the confession in each case had to be excluded.]

[The concurring and dissenting opinion of Mr. Justice Clark has been omitted.]

MR. JUSTICE HARLAN, whom MR. JUSTICE STEWART and MR. JUSTICE WHITE join, dissenting.

. . . .

While the fine points of [the Court's] scheme are far less clear than the Court admits, the tenor is quite apparent. The new rules are not designed to guard against police brutality or other unmistakably banned forms of coercion. Those who use third-degree tactics and deny them in court are equally able and destined to lie as skillfully about warnings and waivers. Rather, the thrust of the new rules is to negate all pressures, to reinforce the nervous or ignorant suspect, and ultimately to discourage any confession at all. The aim in short is toward "voluntariness" in a utopian sense, or to view it from a different angle, voluntariness with a vengeance.

To incorporate this notion into the Constitution requires a strained reading of history and precedent and a disregard of the very pragmatic concerns that alone may on occasion justify such strains. I believe that reasoned examination will show that the Due Process Clauses provide an adequate tool for coping with confessions and that, even if the Fifth Amendment privilege against self-incrimination be invoked, its precedents taken as a whole do not sustain the present rules. . . .

. . . .

The Court's opinion in my view reveals no adequate basis for extending the Fifth Amendment's privilege against self-incrimination to the police station. Far more important, it fails to show that the Court's new rules are well supported, let alone compelled, by Fifth Amendment precedents. Instead, the new rules actually derive from quotation and analogy drawn from precedents under the Sixth Amendment, which should properly have no bearing on police interrogation.

The Court's opening contention, that the Fifth Amendment governs police station confessions, is perhaps not an impermissible extension of the law but it has little to commend itself in the present circumstances. Historically, the privilege against self-incrimination did not bear at all on the use of extra-legal confessions, for which distinct standards evolved; indeed, "the *history* of the two principles is wide apart, differing by one hundred years in origin, and derived through separate lines of precedents. . . ." 8 Wigmore, EVIDENCE § 2266, at 401 (McNaughton rev. 1961). Practice under the two doctrines has also differed in a number of important respects. Even those who would readily enlarge the privilege must concede some linguistic difficulties since the Fifth Amendment in terms proscribes only compelling any person "in any criminal case to be a witness against himself." *Cf.* Kamisar, *Equal Justice In the Gatehouses and Mansions of American Criminal Procedure*, in CRIMINAL JUSTICE IN OUR TIME 1, 25–26 (1965).

Though weighty, I do not say these points and similar ones are conclusive, for, as the Court reiterates, the privilege embodies basic principles always capable of expansion. Certainly the privilege does represent a protective concern for the accused and an emphasis upon accusatorial rather than inquisitorial values in law enforcement, although this is similarly true of other limitations such as the grand jury requirement and the reasonable doubt standard. Accusatorial values, however, have openly been absorbed into the due process standard governing confessions; this indeed is why at present "the kinship of the two rules [governing confessions and self-incrimination] is too apparent for denial." McCormick, EVIDENCE 155 (1954). Since extension of the general principle has already occurred, to insist that the privilege applies as such serves only to carry over inapposite historical details and engaging rhetoric and to obscure the policy choices to be made in regulating confessions.

Having decided that the Fifth Amendment privilege does apply in the police station, the Court reveals that the privilege imposes more exacting restrictions than does the Fourteenth Amendment's voluntariness test. It then emerges from a discussion of *Escobedo* that the Fifth Amendment requires for an admissible confession that it be given by one distinctly aware of his right not to speak and shielded from "the compelling atmosphere" of interrogation. From these key premises, the Court finally develops the safeguards of warning, counsel, and so forth. I do not believe these premises are sustained by precedents under the Fifth Amendment.

The more important premise is that pressure on the suspect must be eliminated though it be only the subtle influence of the atmosphere and surroundings. The Fifth Amendment, however, has never been thought to forbid *all* pressure to incriminate one's self in the situations covered by it. On the contrary, it has been held that failure to incriminate one's self can result in denial of removal of one's case from state to federal court, *Maryland v. Soper*, 270 U.S. 9, 46 S. Ct. 185, 70 L. Ed. 449; in refusal of a military commission, *Orloff v. Willoughby*, 345 U.S. 83, 73 S. Ct. 534, 97 L. Ed. 842; in denial of a discharge in bankruptcy, *Kaufman v. Hurwitz*, 176 F.2d 210 (4th Cir. 1949); and in numerous other adverse consequences. This is not to say that short of jail or torture any sanction is permissible in any case; policy and history alike may impose sharp limits. *See, e.g., Griffin v. California*, 380 U.S. 609, 85 S. Ct. 1229, 14 L. Ed. 2d 106. However, the Court's unspoken assumption that *any* pressure violates the privilege is not supported by the precedents and it has failed to show why the Fifth Amendment prohibits that relatively mild pressure the Due Process Clause permits.

The Court appears similarly wrong in thinking that precise knowledge of one's rights is a settled prerequisite under the Fifth Amendment to the loss of its protections. A number of lower federal court cases have held that grand jury witnesses need not always be warned of their privilege, *e.g., United States v. Scully*, 225 F.2d 113, 116 (2d Cir. 1955), and Wigmore states this to be the better rule for trial witnesses. *See* 8 Wigmore, EVIDENCE § 2269 (McNaughton rev. 1961). No Fifth Amendment precedent is cited for the Court's contrary view. There might of course be reasons apart from Fifth Amendment precedent for requiring warning or any other safeguard on questioning but that is a different matter entirely.

. . . .

III. Policy Considerations

Examined as an expression of public policy, the Court's new regime proves so dubious that there can be no due compensation for its weakness in constitutional law.

. . . .

Without at all subscribing to the generally black picture of police conduct painted by the Court, I think it must be frankly recognized at the outset that police questioning allowable under due process precedents may inherently entail some pressure on the suspect and may seek advantage in his ignorance or weaknesses. The atmosphere and questioning techniques, proper and fair though they be, can in themselves exert a tug on the suspect to confess, and in this light "[t]o speak of any confessions of crime made after arrest as being 'voluntary' or 'uncoerced' is somewhat inaccurate, although traditional. A confession is wholly and uncontestably voluntary only if a guilty person gives himself up to the law and becomes his own accuser." *Ashcraft v. Tennessee*, 322 U.S. 143, 161, 64 S. Ct. 921, 929, 88 L. Ed. 1192 (Jackson, J., dissenting). Until today, the role of the Constitution has been only to sift out *undue* pressure, not to assure spontaneous confessions.

The Court's new rules aim to offset these minor pressures and disadvantages intrinsic to any kind of police interrogation. The rules do not serve due process interests in preventing blatant coercion since, as I noted earlier, they do nothing to contain the policeman who is prepared to lie from the start. The rules work for reliability in confessions almost only in the Pickwickian sense that they can prevent some from being given at all. In short, the benefit of this new regime is simply to lessen or wipe out the inherent compulsion and inequities to which the Court devotes some nine pages of description.

What the Court largely ignores is that its rules impair, if they will not eventually serve wholly to frustrate, an instrument of law enforcement that has long and quite reasonably been thought worth the price paid for it. There can be little doubt that the Court's new code would markedly decrease the number of confessions. To warn the suspect that he may remain silent and remind him that his confession may be used in court are minor obstructions. To require also an express waiver by the suspect and an end to questioning whenever he demurs must heavily handicap questioning. And to suggest or provide counsel for the suspect simply invites the end of the interrogation.

How much harm this decision will inflict on law enforcement cannot fairly be predicted with accuracy. . . .

While passing over the costs and risks of its experiment, the Court portrays the evils of normal police questioning in terms which I think are exaggerated. Albeit stringently confined by the due process standards interrogation is no doubt often inconvenient and unpleasant for the suspect. However, it is no less so for a man to be arrested and jailed, to have his house searched, or to stand trial in court, yet all this may properly happen to the most innocent given probable cause, a warrant, or an indictment. Society has always paid a stiff price for law and order, and peaceful interrogation is not one of the dark moments of the law.

. . . .

[The dissenting opinion of MR. JUSTICE WHITE joined by MR. JUSTICE HARLAN and MR. JUSTICE STEWART has been omitted.]

Notes and Questions

(1) In his *Miranda* dissent, Justice White asserted that there was "every reason to believe that a good many criminal defendants who otherwise would have been convicted on what this Court has previously thought to be the most satisfactory kind of evidence will now, under this new version of the Fifth Amendment, either not be tried at all or will be acquitted if the State's evidence, minus the confession, is put to the test of litigation." 384 U.S. at 542, 86 S. Ct. at 1663, 16 L. Ed. 2d at 763. Is *Miranda*'s impact on law enforcement relevant to the question of whether *Miranda* is a proper interpretation of the Fifth Amendment Privilege?

(2) THE EMPIRICAL DEBATE. Numerous empirical studies have sought to examine *Miranda*'s impact on confessions and convictions. For a sampling of studies conducted within the first decade after *Miranda* was decided, see David W. Neubaner, *Confessions in Prairie City*, 65 J. Crim. L. & Criminology 103, 111 (1974) (1968 data from medium-sized Illinois city indicating that over 45% of the felony defendants made incriminating statements to the police); James W. Witt, *Non-Coercive Interrogation and the Administration of Criminal Justice*, 64 J. Crim. L. & Criminology 320, 325 (1973) (interrogations conducted in "Seaside City," a pseudonymous subdivision of the Los Angeles metropolitan area, were successful in 69% of pre-*Miranda* cases and 67% of post-*Miranda* cases); Evelle J. Younger, *Interrogation of Criminal Defendants — Some Views on* Miranda v. Arizona, 35 Fordham L. Rev. 255 (1966–67) (confession rate for a sample of Los Angeles County felony cases increased from 40% to 50% after *Miranda*); Richard H. Seeburger & R. Stanton Wettick, Miranda *in Pittsburgh — A Statistical Story*, 29 U. Pitt. L. Rev. 1 (1967) (confessions obtained by detective division dropped from 54.5% before *Miranda* to 37.5% after *Miranda* but conviction rate remained the same).

During the 1990s, the empirical debate relating to *Miranda*'s effect on law enforcement intensified. In *Miranda's Social Costs: An Empirical Reassessment*, 90 Nw. U. L. Rev. 387, 390 (1995), Professor Paul G. Cassell asserts that despite the "conventional academic wisdom" to the contrary, "*Miranda* has significantly harmed law enforcement efforts in this country." Specifically, Cassell claims that the existing empirical data support "the tentative estimate" that *Miranda* has led to "lost cases" against 3.8 percent of all criminal suspects, a figure that when "multiplied across the run of criminal cases reflects a large number of criminals." *Id.* at 438. After examining the same data as Cassell, Professor Stephen J. Schulhofer rejects his conclusions. Schulhofer concludes that "[f]or all practical purposes, *Miranda*'s empirically detectable net damage to law enforcement is zero." Stephen J. Schulhofer, Miranda's *Practical Effect: Substantial Benefits and Vanishingly Small Social Costs*, 90 Nw. U. L. Rev. 500, 547 (1996). For Professor Cassell's response to Professor Schulhofer, see Paul G. Cassell, Miranda's *"Negligible" Effect on Law Enforcement: Some Skeptical Observations*, 20 Harv. J.L. & Pub. Pol'y 327 (1997). For additional articles debating *Miranda*'s impact on the confession rate, see Paul G. Cassell & Bret S. Hayman, *Police Interrogation in the 1990s: An Empirical Study of the Effects of* Miranda, 43 UCLA L. Rev. 839 (1996); Richard A. Leo, *The Impact of* Miranda *Revisited*, 86 Crim. L. Rev. 621 (1996);

George C. Thomas III, *Plain Talk About the* Miranda *Empirical Debate, A "Steady-State" Theory of Confessions*, 43 UCLA L. Rev. 933 (1996).

(3) *MIRANDA* WAIVERS. Empirical studies indicate that the great majority of suspects waive their *Miranda* rights. *See* Richard A. Leo, *Inside the Interrogation Room*, 86 J. Crim. L. & Criminology 266 (1996) (finding, based on observation of 122 interrogations and examination of 60 videotapes of interrogations in police departments operating in three urban areas with populations ranging from about 116,000 to 372,000, that approximately 78% of suspects waived their *Miranda* rights); Paul G. Cassell & Bret S. Hayman, *Police Interrogation In the 1990s: An Empirical Study of the Effects of* Miranda, 43 UCLA L. Rev. 839, 860 (1996) (examination of 129 interrogations conducted within Salt Lake County, Utah, concluded that approximately 84% of suspects waived their *Miranda* rights).

Why do so many suspects waive their *Miranda* rights? Professor Schulhofer has suggested it is primarily because of suspects' "misplaced confidence in their own ability to talk their way out of trouble." Stephen J. Schulhofer, Miranda's *Practical Effect: Substantial Benefits and Vanishingly Small Social Costs*, 90 Nw. U. L. Rev. 500, 561 (1996). He thus concludes that "confessions are now mostly the result of persuasion and the suspect's overconfidence, not of pressure and fear. That difference in method is crucial." *Id.* at 562. Professor Peter Arenella challenges this conclusion, asserting that "when the efficacy of the police confidence game depends so heavily on police custodial control of the suspect in a very hostile, threatening environment," it may be impossible to "distinguish between persuasion and fear." Peter Arenella, Miranda *Stories*, 20 Harv. J.L. & Pub. Pol'y 375, 385–86 (1997).

New York v. Quarles
United States Supreme Court
467 U.S. 649, 104 S. Ct. 2626, 81 L. Ed. 2d 550 (1984)

JUSTICE REHNQUIST delivered the opinion of the Court.

. . . .

On September 11, 1980, at approximately 12:30 a.m., Officer Frank Kraft and Officer Sal Scarring were on road patrol in Queens, New York, when a young woman approached their car. She told them that she had just been raped by a black male, approximately six feet tall, who was wearing a black jacket with the name "Big Ben" printed in yellow letters on the back. She told the officers that the man had just entered an A & P supermarket located nearby and that the man was carrying a gun.

The officers drove the woman to the supermarket, and Officer Kraft entered the store while Officer Scarring radioed for assistance. Officer Kraft quickly spotted respondent, who matched the description given by the woman, approaching a checkout counter. Apparently upon seeing the officer, respondent turned and ran toward the rear of the store, and Officer Kraft pursued him with a drawn gun. When respondent turned the corner at the end of an aisle, Officer Kraft lost sight of him for several seconds, and upon regaining sight of respondent, ordered him to stop and put his hands over his head.

Although more than three other officers had arrived on the scene by that time, Officer Kraft was the first to reach respondent. He frisked him and discovered that he was wearing a shoulder holster which was then empty. After handcuffing him, Officer Kraft asked him where the gun was. Respondent nodded in the direction of some empty cartons and responded, "the gun is over there." Officer Kraft thereafter retrieved a loaded .38 caliber revolver from one of the cartons, formally placed respondent under arrest, and read him his *Miranda* rights from a printed card. Respondent indicated that he would be willing to answer questions without an attorney present. Officer Kraft then asked respondent if he owned the gun and where he had purchased it. Respondent answered that he did own it and that he had purchased it in Miami, Florida.

In the subsequent prosecution of respondent for criminal possession of a weapon,[2] the judge excluded the statement, "the gun is over there," and the gun because the officer had not given respondent the warnings required by our decision in *Miranda v. Arizona*, 384 U.S. 436, 86 S. Ct. 1602, 16 L. Ed. 2d 694 (1966), before asking him where the gun was located. The judge excluded the other statements about respondent's ownership of the gun and the place of purchase, as evidence tainted by the prior *Miranda* violation. The Appellate Division of the Supreme Court of New York affirmed without opinion.

The Court of Appeals granted leave to appeal and affirmed by a 4–3 vote. It concluded that respondent was in "custody" within the meaning of *Miranda* during all questioning and rejected the State's argument that the exigencies of the situation justified Officer Kraft's failure to read respondent his *Miranda* rights until after he had located the gun. The court declined to recognize an exigency exception to the usual requirements of *Miranda* because it found no indication from Officer Kraft's testimony at the suppression hearing that his subjective motivation in asking the question was to protect his own safety or the safety of the public. For the reasons which follow, we believe that this case presents a situation where concern for public safety must be paramount to adherence to the literal language of the prophylactic rules enunciated in *Miranda*.

The Fifth Amendment guarantees that "[n]o person . . . shall be compelled in any criminal case to be a witness against himself." In *Miranda* this Court for the first time extended the Fifth Amendment privilege against compulsory self-incrimination to individuals subjected to custodial interrogation by the police. The Fifth Amendment itself does not prohibit all incriminating admissions; "[a]bsent some officially *coerced* self-accusation, the Fifth Amendment privilege is not violated by even the most damning admissions." *United States v. Washington*, 431 U.S. 181, 187, 97 S. Ct. 1814, 1818, 52 L. Ed. 2d 238 (1977) (emphasis added). The *Miranda* Court,

---

2. The State originally charged respondent with rape, but the record provides no information as to why the State failed to pursue that charge.

however, presumed that interrogation in certain custodial circumstances is inherently coercive and held that statements made under those circumstances are inadmissible unless the suspect is specifically informed of his *Miranda* rights and freely decides to forgo those rights. The prophylactic *Miranda* warnings therefore are "not themselves rights protected by the Constitution but [are] instead measures to insure that the right against compulsory self-incrimination [is] protected." *Michigan v. Tucker*, 417 U.S. 433, 444, 94 S. Ct. 2357, 2364, 41 L. Ed. 2d 182 (1974). Requiring *Miranda* warnings before custodial interrogation provides "practical reinforcement" for the Fifth Amendment right. *Michigan v. Tucker, supra*, 417 U.S. at 444, 94 S. Ct. at 2364.

In this case we have before us no claim that respondent's statements were actually compelled by police conduct which overcame his will to resist. Thus the only issue before us is whether Officer Kraft was justified in failing to make available to respondent the procedural safeguards associated with the privilege against compulsory self-incrimination since *Miranda*.[5]

The New York Court of Appeals was undoubtedly correct in deciding that the facts of this case come within the ambit of the *Miranda* decision as we have subsequently interpreted it. We agree that respondent was in police custody because we have noted that "the ultimate inquiry is simply whether there is a " 'formal arrest or restraint on freedom of movement' of the degree associated with a formal arrest," *California v. Beheler*, 463 U.S. 1121, 1125, 103 S. Ct. 3517, 3519, 77 L. Ed. 2d 1275 (1983) *(per curiam)*, quoting *Oregon v. Mathiason*, 429 U.S. 492, 495, 97 S. Ct. 711, 714, 50 L. Ed. 2d 714 (1977) *(per curiam)*. Here Quarles was surrounded by at least four police officers and was handcuffed when the questioning at issue took place. As the New York Court of Appeals observed, there was nothing to suggest that any of the officers were any longer concerned for their own physical safety. The New York Court of Appeals' majority declined to express an opinion as to whether there might be an exception to the *Miranda* rule if the police had been acting to protect the public, because the lower courts in New York had made no factual determination that the police had acted with that motive.

We hold that on these facts there is a "public safety" exception to the requirement that *Miranda* warnings be given before a suspect's answers may be admitted into evidence, and that the availability of that exception does not depend upon the motivation of the individual officers involved. In a kaleidoscopic situation such as the one confronting these officers, where spontaneity rather than adherence to a police

---

5. The dissent curiously takes us to task for "endors[ing] the introduction of coerced self-incriminating statements in criminal prosecutions," and for "sanction[ing] *sub silentio* criminal prosecutions based on compelled self-incriminating statements." Of course our decision today does nothing of the kind. As the *Miranda* Court itself recognized, the failure to provide *Miranda* warnings in and of itself does not render a confession involuntary, and respondent is certainly free on remand to argue that his statement was coerced under traditional due process standards. Today we merely reject the only argument that respondent has raised to support the exclusion of his statement, that the statement must be *presumed* compelled because of Officer Kraft's failure to read him his *Miranda* warnings.

manual is necessarily the order of the day, the application of the exception which we recognize today should not be made to depend on *post hoc* findings at a suppression hearing concerning the subjective motivation of the arresting officer. Undoubtedly most police officers, if placed in Officer Kraft's position, would act out of a host of different, instinctive, and largely unverifiable motives — their own safety, the safety of others, and perhaps as well the desire to obtain incriminating evidence from the suspect.

Whatever the motivation of individual officers in such a situation, we do not believe that the doctrinal underpinnings of *Miranda* require that it be applied in all its rigor to a situation in which police officers ask questions reasonably prompted by a concern for the public safety. The *Miranda* decision was based in large part on this Court's view that the warnings which it required police to give to suspects in custody would reduce the likelihood that the suspects would fall victim to constitutionally impermissible practices of police interrogation in the presumptively coercive environment of the station house. The dissenters warned that the requirement of *Miranda* warnings would have the effect of decreasing the number of suspects who respond to police questioning. The *Miranda* majority, however, apparently felt that whatever the cost to society in terms of fewer convictions of guilty suspects, that cost would simply have to be borne in the interest of enlarged protection for the Fifth Amendment privilege.

The police in this case, in the very act of apprehending a suspect, were confronted with the immediate necessity of ascertaining the whereabouts of a gun which they had every reason to believe the suspect had just removed from his empty holster and discarded in the supermarket. So long as the gun was concealed somewhere in the supermarket, with its actual whereabouts unknown, it obviously posed more than one danger to the public safety: an accomplice might make use of it, a customer or employee might later come upon it.

In such a situation, if the police are required to recite the familiar *Miranda* warnings before asking the whereabouts of the gun, suspects in Quarles' position might well be deterred from responding. Procedural safeguards which deter a suspect from responding were deemed acceptable in *Miranda* in order to protect the Fifth Amendment privilege; when the primary social cost of those added protections is the possibility of fewer convictions, the *Miranda* majority was willing to bear that cost. Here, had *Miranda* warnings deterred Quarles from responding to Officer Kraft's question about the whereabouts of the gun, the cost would have been something more than merely the failure to obtain evidence useful in convicting Quarles. Officer Kraft needed an answer to his question not simply to make his case against Quarles but to insure that further danger to the public did not result from the concealment of the gun in a public area.

We conclude that the need for answers to questions in a situation posing a threat to the public safety outweighs the need for the prophylactic rule protecting the Fifth Amendment's privilege against self-incrimination. We decline to place officers such as Officer Kraft in the untenable position of having to consider, often in a matter of seconds, whether it best serves society for them to ask the necessary questions without the *Miranda* warnings and render whatever probative evidence they uncover inadmissible, or for them to give the warnings in order to preserve the admissibility of evidence they might uncover but possibly damage or destroy their ability to obtain that evidence and neutralize the volatile situation confronting them.[7]

In recognizing a narrow exception to the *Miranda* rule in this case, we acknowledge that to some degree we lessen the desirable clarity of that rule. At least in part in order to preserve its clarity, we have over the years refused to sanction attempts to expand our *Miranda* holding. As we have in other contexts, we recognize here the importance of a workable rule "to guide police officers, who have only limited time and expertise to reflect on and balance the social and individual interests involved in the specific circumstances they confront." *Dunaway v. New York*, 442 U.S. 200, 213–214, 99 S. Ct. 2248, 2257, 60 L. Ed. 2d 824 (1979). But as we have pointed out, we believe that the exception which we recognize today lessens the necessity of that on-the-scene balancing process. The exception will not be difficult for police officers to apply because in each case it will be circumscribed by the exigency which justifies it. We think police officers can and will distinguish almost instinctively between questions necessary to secure their own safety or the safety of the public and questions designed solely to elicit testimonial evidence from a suspect.

The facts of this case clearly demonstrate that distinction and an officer's ability to recognize it. Officer Kraft asked only the question necessary to locate the missing gun before advising respondent of his rights. It was only after securing the loaded revolver and giving the warnings that he continued with investigatory questions about the ownership and place of purchase of the gun. The exception which we recognize today, far from complicating the thought processes and the on-the-scene judgments of police officers, will simply free them to follow their legitimate instincts when confronting situations presenting a danger to the public safety.

We hold that the Court of Appeals in this case erred in excluding the statement, "the gun is over there," and the gun because of the officer's failure to read respondent his *Miranda* rights before attempting to locate the weapon. Accordingly we hold that it also erred in excluding the subsequent statements as illegal fruits of a *Miranda* violation. We therefore reverse and remand for further proceedings not inconsistent with this opinion.

It is so ordered.

JUSTICE O'CONNOR, concurring in part in the judgment and dissenting in part.

---

7. The dissent argues that a public safety exception to *Miranda* is unnecessary because in every case an officer can simply ask the necessary questions to protect himself or the public, and then the prosecution can decline to introduce any incriminating responses at a subsequent trial. But absent actual coercion by the officer, there is no constitutional imperative requiring the exclusion of the evidence that results from police inquiry of this kind; and we do not believe that the doctrinal underpinnings of *Miranda* require us to exclude the evidence, thus penalizing officers for asking the very questions which are the most crucial to their efforts to protect themselves and the public.

In *Miranda v. Arizona*, 384 U.S. 436, 86 S. Ct. 1602, 16 L. Ed. 2d 694 (1966), the Court held unconstitutional, because inherently compelled, the admission of statements derived from in-custody questioning not preceded by an explanation of the privilege against self-incrimination and the consequences of foregoing it. Today, the Court concludes that overriding considerations of public safety justify the admission of evidence — oral statements and a gun — secured without the benefit of such warnings. In so holding, the Court acknowledges that it is departing from prior precedent, and that it is "lessen[ing] the desirable clarity of [the *Miranda*] rule." Were the Court writing from a clean slate, I could agree with its holding. But *Miranda* is now the law and, in my view, the Court has not provided sufficient justification for departing from it or for blurring its now clear strictures. Accordingly, I would require suppression of the initial statement taken from respondent in this case.

. . . .

In my view, a "public safety" exception unnecessarily blurs the edges of the clear line heretofore established and makes *Miranda*'s requirements more difficult to understand. In some cases, police will benefit because a reviewing court will find that an exigency excused their failure to administer the required warnings. But in other cases, police will suffer because, though they thought an exigency excused their noncompliance, a reviewing court will view the "objective" circumstances differently and require exclusion of admissions thereby obtained. The end result will be a fine-spun new doctrine on public safety exigencies incident to custodial interrogation, complete with the hair-splitting distinctions that currently plague our Fourth Amendment jurisprudence. . . .

The justification the Court provides for upsetting the equilibrium that has finally been achieved — that police cannot and should not balance considerations of public safety against the individual's interest in avoiding compulsory testimonial self-incrimination — really misses the critical question to be decided. *Miranda* has never been read to prohibit the police from asking questions to secure the public safety. Rather, the critical question *Miranda* addresses is who shall bear the cost of securing the public safety when such questions are asked and answered: the defendant or the State. *Miranda*, for better or worse, found the resolution of that question implicit in the prohibition against compulsory self-incrimination and placed the burden on the State. When police ask custodial questions without administering the required warnings, *Miranda* quite clearly requires that the answers received be presumed compelled and that they be excluded from evidence at trial. *See Michigan v. Tucker, supra*, at 445, 447–448, 451, 452, and n. 26, 94 S. Ct. 2357, 41 L. Ed. 2d 182; *Orozco v. Texas, supra*, at 326.

The Court concedes, as it must, both that respondent was in "custody" and subject to "interrogation" and that his statement "the gun is over there" was compelled within the meaning of our precedent. In my view, since there is nothing about an exigency that makes custodial interrogation any less compelling, a principled application of *Miranda* requires that respondent's statement be suppressed.

. . . .

JUSTICE MARSHALL, with whom JUSTICE BRENNAN and JUSTICE STEVENS join, dissenting.

The police in this case arrested a man suspected of possessing a firearm in violation of New York law. Once the suspect was in custody and found to be unarmed, the arresting officer initiated an interrogation. Without being advised of his right not to respond, the suspect incriminated himself by locating the gun. The majority concludes that the State may rely on this incriminating statement to convict the suspect of possessing a weapon. I disagree. The arresting officers had no legitimate reason to interrogate the suspect without advising him of his rights to remain silent and to obtain assistance of counsel. By finding on these facts justification for unconsented interrogation, the majority abandons the clear guidelines enunciated in *Miranda v. Arizona*, 384 U.S. 436, 86 S. Ct. 1602, 16 L. Ed. 2d 694 (1966), and condemns the American judiciary to a new era of *post hoc* inquiry into the propriety of custodial interrogations. More significantly and in direct conflict with this Court's longstanding interpretation of the Fifth Amendment, the majority has endorsed the introduction of coerced self incriminating statements in criminal prosecutions. I dissent.

. . . .

III

Though unfortunate, the difficulty of administering the "public-safety" exception is not the most profound flaw in the majority's decision. The majority has lost sight of the fact that *Miranda v. Arizona* and our earlier custodial-interrogation cases all implemented a constitutional privilege against self-incrimination. The rules established in these cases were designed to protect criminal defendants against prosecutions based on coerced self-incriminating statements. The majority today turns its back on these constitutional considerations, and invites the government to prosecute through the use of what necessarily are coerced statements.

A

The majority's error stems from a serious misunderstanding of *Miranda v. Arizona* and of the Fifth Amendment upon which that decision was based. The majority implies that *Miranda* consisted of no more than a judicial balancing act in which the benefits of "enlarged protection for the Fifth Amendment privilege" were weighed against "the cost to society in terms of fewer convictions of guilty suspects." Supposedly because the scales tipped in favor of the privilege against self-incrimination, the *Miranda* Court erected a prophylactic barrier around statements made during custodial interrogations. The majority now proposes to return to the scales of social utility to calculate whether *Miranda*'s prophylactic rule remains cost-effective when threats to public's safety are added to the balance. The results of the majority's "test" are announced with pseudoscientific precision:

> We conclude that the need for answers to questions in a situation posing a threat to the public safety outweighs the need for the prophylactic rule protecting the Fifth Amendment's privilege against self-incrimination.

The majority misreads *Miranda*. Though the *Miranda* dissent prophesized dire consequences, the *Miranda* Court refused to allow such concerns to weaken the protections of the Constitution:

> A recurrent argument made in these cases is that society's need for interrogation outweighs the privilege. This argument is not unfamiliar to this Court. The whole thrust of our foregoing discussion demonstrates that the Constitution has prescribed the rights of the individual when confronted with the power of government when it provided in the Fifth Amendment that an individual cannot be compelled to be a witness against himself. That right cannot be abridged.

384 U.S. at 479, 86 S. Ct. at 1630 (citation omitted). Whether society would be better off if the police warned suspects of their rights before beginning an interrogation or whether the advantages of giving such warnings would outweigh their costs did not inform the *Miranda* decision. On the contrary, the *Miranda* Court was concerned with the proscriptions of the Fifth Amendment, and, in particular, whether the Self-Incrimination Clause permits the government to prosecute individuals based on statements made in the course of custodial interrogations.

Miranda v. Arizona was the culmination of a century-long inquiry into how this Court should deal with confessions made during custodial interrogations. Long before *Miranda*, the Court had recognized that the Federal Government was prohibited from introducing at criminal trials compelled confessions, including confessions compelled in the course of custodial interrogations. In 1924, Justice Brandeis was reciting settled law when he wrote: "[A] confession obtained by compulsion must be excluded whatever may have been the character of the compulsion, and whether the compulsion was applied in a judicial proceeding or otherwise." *Wan v. United States*, 266 U.S. 1, 14–15, 45 S. Ct. 1, 3–4, 69 L. Ed. 131 (citing *Bram v. United States*, 168 U.S. 532, 18 S. Ct. 183, 42 L. Ed. 568 (1897)).

. . . .

When *Miranda* reached this Court, it was undisputed that both the States and the Federal Government were constitutionally prohibited from prosecuting defendants with confessions coerced during custodial interrogations. As a theoretical matter, the law was clear. In practice, however, the courts found it exceedingly difficult to determine whether a given confession had been coerced. Difficulties of proof and subtleties of interrogation technique made it impossible in most cases for the judiciary to decide with confidence whether the defendant had voluntarily confessed his guilt or whether his testimony had been unconstitutionally compelled. Courts around the country were spending countless hours reviewing the facts of individual custodial interrogations. *See* Note, *Developments in the Law — Confessions*, 79 Harv. L. Rev. 935 (1966).

Miranda dealt with these practical problems. After a detailed examination of police practices and a review of its previous decisions in the area, the Court in *Miranda* determined that custodial interrogations are inherently coercive. The Court therefore created a constitutional presumption that statements made during custodial interrogations are compelled in violation of the Fifth Amendment and are thus inadmissible in criminal prosecutions. As a result of the Court's decision in *Miranda*, a statement made during a custodial interrogation may be introduced as proof of a defendant's guilt only if the prosecution demonstrates that the defendant knowingly and intelligently waived his constitutional rights before making the statement. The now-familiar *Miranda* warnings offer law-enforcement authorities a clear, easily administered device for ensuring that criminal suspects understand their constitutional rights well enough to waive them and to engage in consensual custodial interrogation.

In fashioning its "public-safety" exception to *Miranda*, the majority makes no attempt to deal with the constitutional presumption established by that case. The majority does not argue that police questioning about issues of public safety is any less coercive than custodial interrogations into other matters. The majority's only contention is that police officers could more easily protect the public if *Miranda* did not apply to custodial interrogations concerning the public's safety. But *Miranda* was not a decision about public safety; it was a decision about coerced confessions. Without establishing that interrogations concerning the public's safety are less likely to be coercive than other interrogations, the majority cannot endorse the "public-safety" exception and remain faithful to the logic of *Miranda v. Arizona*.

B

The majority's avoidance of the issue of coercion may not have been inadvertent. It would strain credulity to contend that Officer Kraft's questioning of respondent Quarles was not coercive.[8] In the middle of the night and in the back of an empty supermarket, Quarles was surrounded by four armed police officers. His hands were handcuffed behind his back. The first words out of the mouth of the arresting officer were: "Where is the gun?" In the majority's phrase, the situation was "kaleidoscopic." Police and suspect were acting on instinct. Officer Kraft's abrupt and pointed question pressured Quarles in precisely the way that the *Miranda* Court feared the custodial interrogations would coerce self-incriminating testimony.

That the application of the "public-safety" exception in this case entailed coercion is no happenstance. The majority's *ratio decidendi* is that interrogating suspects about matters of public safety *will* be coercive. In its cost-benefit analysis, the Court's strongest argument in favor of a "public-safety" exception to *Miranda* is that the police would be better able to protect the public's safety if they were not always required to give suspects their *Miranda* warnings. The crux of this argument is that, by deliberately withholding *Miranda* warnings, the police can get information out of suspects

---

8. The majority's reliance on respondent's failure to claim that his testimony was compelled by police conduct can only be disingenuous. Before today's opinion, respondent had no need to claim actual compulsion. Heretofore, it was sufficient to demonstrate that the police had conducted nonconsensual custodial interrogation. But now that the law has changed, it is only fair to examine the facts of the case to determine whether coercion probably was involved.

who would refuse to respond to police questioning were they advised of their constitutional rights. The "public-safety" exception is efficacious precisely because it permits police officers to coerce criminal defendants into making involuntary statements.

Indeed, in the efficacy of the "public-safety" exception lies a fundamental and constitutional defect. Until today, this Court could truthfully state that the Fifth Amendment is given "broad scope" "[w]here there has been genuine compulsion of testimony." *Michigan v. Tucker*, 417 U.S. 433, 440, 94 S. Ct. 2357, 2362, 41 L. Ed. 2d 182 (1974). Coerced confessions were simply inadmissible in criminal prosecutions. The "public-safety" exception departs from this principle by expressly inviting police officers to coerce defendants into making incriminating statements, and then permitting prosecutors to introduce those statements at trial. Though the majority's opinion is cloaked in the beguiling language of utilitarianism, the Court has sanctioned *sub silentio* criminal prosecutions based on compelled self-incriminating statements. I find this result in direct conflict with the Fifth Amendment's dictate that "[n]o person . . . shall be compelled in any criminal case to be a witness against himself."

The irony of the majority's decision is that the public's safety can be perfectly well protected without abridging the Fifth Amendment. If a bomb is about to explode or the public is otherwise imminently imperiled, the police are free to interrogate suspects without advising them of their constitutional rights. Such unconsented questioning may take place not only when police officers act on instinct but also when higher faculties lead them to believe that advising a suspect of his constitutional rights might decrease the likelihood that the suspect would reveal life-saving information. If trickery is necessary to protect the public, then the police may trick a suspect into confessing. While the Fourteenth Amendment sets limits on such behavior, nothing in the Fifth Amendment or our decision in *Miranda v. Arizona* proscribes this sort of emergency questioning. All the Fifth Amendment forbids is the introduction of coerced statements at trial.

. . . .

Notes and Questions

(1) In *Quarles*, Justice Rehnquist indicated that the *Miranda* warnings are prophylactic measures to protect the Fifth Amendment Privilege but that failure to give the warnings prior to custodial interrogation will not in itself lead to statements that are compelled within the meaning of the Privilege. Is the majority's interpretation of *Miranda* consistent with the original *Miranda* decision?

As explained by the *Quarles* majority, is *Miranda* a legitimate interpretation of the Fifth Amendment Privilege? For a negative answer, see Joseph D. Grano, *Prophylactic Rules in Criminal Procedure: A Question of Article III Legitimacy*, 80 Nw. U. L. Rev. 100 (1985). For a response to Professor Grano, see David A. Strauss, *The Ubiquity of Prophylactic Rules*, 55 U. Chi. L. Rev. 190 (1988). For other articles considering whether *Miranda* should be overruled, see, *e.g.*, Stephen J. Schulhofer, *Reconsidering*

Miranda, 54 U. Chi. L. Rev. 435 (1987) (opposing abolition of *Miranda*); Stephen J. Markman, *The Fifth Amendment and Custodial Questioning: A Response to "Reconsidering* Miranda," 54 U. Chi. L. Rev. 938 (1987) (favoring abolition of *Miranda*).

(2) *Quarles* is not the only case in which the Court has indicated that the *Miranda* decision imposes prophylactic safeguards rather than protections mandated by the Fifth Amendment privilege. For other decisions articulating this view, see, e.g., *Oregon v. Elstad*, 470 U.S. 298, 309, 105 S. Ct. 1285, 1293, 84 L. Ed. 2d 222, 232 (1985) ("prophylactic *Miranda* procedures"); *Michigan v. Tucker*, 417 U.S. 433, 446, 94 S. Ct. 2357, 2364, 41 L. Ed. 2d 182, 194 (1974) ("prophylactic standards").

(3) Suppose the police are trying to learn the location of a kidnap victim from a suspect. If the police believe that the victim's life may depend upon receiving immediate information from the suspect, may they use deception, promises, or threats to induce statements from the suspect? If they do, will the suspect's statements be admissible? For a discussion of these issues, see William T. Pizzi, *The Privilege Against Self-Incrimination in a Rescue Situation*, 76 J. Crim. L. & Criminology 567 (1985).

Dickerson v. United States

United States Supreme Court

530 U.S. 428, 120 S. Ct. 2326, 147 L. Ed. 2d 405 (2000)

Chief Justice Rehnquist delivered the opinion of the Court.

In *Miranda v. Arizona*, 384 U.S. 436, 86 S. Ct. 1602, 16 L. Ed. 2d 694 (1966), we held that certain warnings must be given before a suspect's statement made during custodial interrogation could be admitted in evidence. In the wake of that decision, Congress enacted 18 U.S.C. § 3501, which in essence laid down a rule that the admissibility of such statements should turn only on whether or not they were voluntarily made. We hold that *Miranda*, being a constitutional decision of this Court, may not be in effect overruled by an Act of Congress, and we decline to overrule *Miranda* ourselves. We therefore hold that *Miranda* and its progeny in this Court govern the admissibility of statements made during custodial interrogation in both state and federal courts.

Petitioner Dickerson was indicted for bank robbery, conspiracy to commit bank robbery, and using a firearm in the course of committing a crime of violence, all in violation of the applicable provisions of Title 18 of the United States Code. Before trial, Dickerson moved to suppress a statement he had made at a Federal Bureau of Investigation field office, on the grounds that he had not received "*Miranda* warnings" before being interrogated. The District Court granted his motion to suppress, and the Government took an interlocutory appeal to the United States Court of Appeals for the Fourth Circuit. That court, by a divided vote, reversed the District Court's suppression order. It agreed with the District Court's conclusion that petitioner had not received *Miranda* warnings before making his statement. But it went on to hold that § 3501, which in effect makes the admissibility of statements such as Dickerson's turn solely on whether they were made voluntarily, was satisfied in this case.

It then concluded that our decision in *Miranda* was not a constitutional holding, and that therefore Congress could by statute have the final say on the question of admissibility.

Because of the importance of the questions raised by the Court of Appeals' decision, we granted certiorari, and now reverse.

We begin with a brief historical account of the law governing the admission of confessions. Prior to *Miranda*, we evaluated the admissibility of a suspect's confession under a voluntariness test. The roots of this test developed in the common law, as the courts of England and then the United States recognized that coerced confessions are inherently untrustworthy. *See, e.g., King v. Rudd*, 1 Leach 115, 117–118, 122–123, 168 Eng. Rep. 160, 161, 164 (K.B. 1783) (Lord Mansfield, C.J.) (stating that the English courts excluded confessions obtained by threats and promises); *King v. Warickshall*, 1 Leach 262, 263–264, 168 Eng. Rep. 234, 235 (K.B. 1783) ("A free and voluntary confession is deserving of the highest credit, because it is presumed to flow from the strongest sense of guilt . . . but a confession forced from the mind by the flattery of hope, or by the torture of fear, comes in so questionable a shape . . . that no credit ought to be given to it; and therefore it is rejected"); *King v. Parratt*, 4 Car. & P. 570, 172 Eng. Rep. 829 (N.P. 1831); *Queen v. Garner*, 1 Den. 329, 169 Eng. Rep. 267 (Ct. Crim. App. 1848); *Queen v. Baldry*, 2 Den. 430, 169 Eng. Rep. 568 (Ct. Crim. App. 1852); *Hopt v. Territory of Utah*, 110 U.S. 574, 4 S. Ct. 202, 28 L. Ed. 262 (1884); *Pierce v. United States*, 160 U.S. 355, 357, 16 S. Ct. 321, 40 L. Ed. 454 (1896). Over time, our cases recognized two constitutional bases for the requirement that a confession be voluntary to be admitted into evidence: the Fifth Amendment right against self-incrimination and the Due Process Clause of the Fourteenth Amendment. *See, e.g., Bram v. United States*, 168 U.S. 532, 542, 18 S. Ct. 183, 42 L. Ed. 568 (1897) (stating that the voluntariness test "is controlled by that portion of the Fifth Amendment . . . commanding that no person shall be compelled in any criminal case to be a witness against himself"); *Brown v. Mississippi*, 297 U.S. 278, 56 S. Ct. 461, 80 L. Ed. 682 (1936) (reversing a criminal conviction under the Due Process Clause because it was based on a confession obtained by physical coercion).

While *Bram* was decided before *Brown* and its progeny, for the middle third of the 20th century our cases based the rule against admitting coerced confessions primarily, if not exclusively, on notions of due process. We applied the due process voluntariness test in "some 30 different cases decided during the era that intervened between *Brown* and *Escobedo v. Illinois*, 378 U.S. 478, 84 S. Ct. 1758, 12 L. Ed. 2d 977 [(1964)]." *Schneckloth v. Bustamonte*, 412 U.S. 218, 223, 93 S. Ct. 2041, 36 L. Ed. 2d 854 (1973). *See, e.g., Haynes v. Washington*, 373 U.S. 503, 83 S. Ct. 1336, 10 L. Ed. 2d 513 (1963); *Ashcraft v. Tennessee*, 322 U.S. 143, 64 S. Ct. 921, 88 L. Ed. 1192 (1944); *Chambers v. Florida*, 309 U.S. 227, 60 S. Ct. 472, 84 L. Ed. 716 (1940). Those cases refined the test into an inquiry that examines "whether a defendant's will was overborne" by the circumstances surrounding the giving of a confession. *Schneckloth*, 412 U.S. at 226. The due process test takes into consideration "the totality of all the surrounding circumstances — both the characteristics of the accused and the details of the interrogation." *Ibid. See also Haynes, supra,* at 513; *Gallegos v. Colorado,* 370 U.S. 49, 55, 82 S. Ct. 1209, 8 L. Ed. 2d 325 (1962); *Reck v. Pate,* 367 U.S. 433, 440, 81 S. Ct. 1541, 6 L. Ed. 2d 948 (1961) ("[A]ll the circumstances attendant upon the confession must be taken into account"); *Malinski v. New York,* 324 U.S. 401, 404, 65 S. Ct. 781, 89 L. Ed. 1029 (1945) ("If all the attendant circumstances indicate that the confession was coerced or compelled, it may not be used to convict a defendant"). The determination "depend[s] upon a weighing of the circumstances of pressure against the power of resistance of the person confessing." *Stein v. New York,* 346 U.S. 156, 185, 73 S. Ct. 1077, 97 L. Ed. 1522 (1953).

We have never abandoned this due process jurisprudence, and thus continue to exclude confessions that were obtained involuntarily. But our decisions in *Malloy v. Hogan,* 378 U.S. 1, 84 S. Ct. 1489, 12 L. Ed. 2d 653 (1964), and *Miranda* changed the focus of much of the inquiry in determining the admissibility of suspects' incriminating statements. In *Malloy,* we held that the Fifth Amendment's Self-Incrimination Clause is incorporated in the Due Process Clause of the Fourteenth Amendment and thus applies to the States. *Id.* at 6–11. We decided *Miranda* on the heels of *Malloy.*

In *Miranda,* we noted that the advent of modern custodial police interrogation brought with it an increased concern about confessions obtained by coercion. 384 U.S. at 445–458. Because custodial police interrogation, by its very nature, isolates and pressures the individual, we stated that "[e]ven without employing brutality, the 'third degree' or [other] specific stratagems, . . . custodial interrogation exacts a heavy toll on individual liberty and trades on the weakness of individuals." *Id.* at 455. We concluded that the coercion inherent in custodial interrogation blurs the line between voluntary and involuntary statements, and thus heightens the risk that an individual will not be "accorded his privilege under the Fifth Amendment . . . not to be compelled to incriminate himself." *Id.* at 439. Accordingly, we laid down "concrete constitutional guidelines for law enforcement agencies and courts to follow." *Id.* at 442. Those guidelines established that the admissibility in evidence of any statement given during custodial interrogation of a suspect would depend on whether the police provided the suspect with four warnings. These warnings (which have come to be known colloquially as "*Miranda* rights") are: a suspect "has the right to remain silent, that anything he says can be used against him in a court of law, that he has the right to the presence of an attorney, and that if he cannot afford an attorney one will be appointed for him prior to any questioning if he so desires." *Id.* at 479.

Two years after *Miranda* was decided, Congress enacted § 3501. That section provides, in relevant part:

> "(a) In any criminal prosecution brought by the United States or by the District of Columbia, a confession . . . shall be admissible in evidence if it is voluntarily given. Before such confession is received in evidence, the trial judge shall, out of the presence of the jury, determine any issue as to voluntariness. If the trial judge determines that the confession was voluntarily

made it shall be admitted in evidence and the trial judge shall permit the jury to hear relevant evidence on the issue of voluntariness and shall instruct the jury to give such weight to the confession as the jury feels it deserves under all the circumstances.

"(b) The trial judge in determining the issue of voluntariness shall take into consideration all the circumstances surrounding the giving of the confession, including (1) the time elapsing between arrest and arraignment of the defendant making the confession, if it was made after arrest and before arraignment, (2) whether such defendant knew the nature of the offense with which he was charged or of which he was suspected at the time of making the confession, (3) whether or not such defendant was advised or knew that he was not required to make any statement and that any such statement could be used against him, (4) whether or not such defendant had been advised prior to questioning of his right to the assistance of counsel; and (5) whether or not such defendant was without the assistance of counsel when questioned and when giving such confession.

"The presence or absence of any of the above-mentioned factors to be taken into consideration by the judge need not be conclusive on the issue of voluntariness of the confession."

Given § 3501's express designation of voluntariness as the touchstone of admissibility, its omission of any warning requirement, and the instruction for trial courts to consider a nonexclusive list of factors relevant to the circumstances of a confession, we agree with the Court of Appeals that Congress intended by its enactment to overrule *Miranda. See also Davis v. United States*, 512 U.S. 452, 464, 114 S. Ct. 2350, 129 L. Ed. 2d 362 (1994) (Scalia, J., concurring) (stating that, prior to *Miranda*, "voluntariness *vel non* was the touchstone of admissibility of confessions"). Because of the obvious conflict between our decision in *Miranda* and § 3501, we must address whether Congress has constitutional authority to thus supersede *Miranda*. If Congress has such authority, § 3501's totality-of-the-circumstances approach must prevail over *Miranda*'s requirement of warnings; if not, that section must yield to *Miranda*'s more specific requirements.

The law in this area is clear. This Court has supervisory authority over the federal courts, and we may use that authority to prescribe rules of evidence and procedure that are binding in those tribunals. . . . Congress retains the ultimate authority to modify or set aside any judicially created rules of evidence and procedure that are not required by the Constitution.

But Congress may not legislatively supersede our decisions interpreting and applying the Constitution. *See, e.g., City of Boerne v. Flores*, 521 U.S. 507, 517–521, 117 S. Ct. 2157, 138 L. Ed. 2d 624 (1997). This case therefore turns on whether the *Miranda* Court announced a constitutional rule or merely exercised its supervisory authority to regulate evidence in the absence of congressional direction. . . . Relying on the fact that we have created several exceptions to *Miranda*'s warnings requirement and that we have repeatedly referred to the *Miranda* warnings as "prophylactic," *New York v. Quarles,* 467 U.S. 649, 653, 104 S. Ct. 2626, 81 L. Ed. 2d 550 (1984), and "not themselves rights protected by the Constitution," *Michigan v. Tucker,* 417 U.S. 433, 444, 94 S. Ct. 2357, 41 L. Ed. 2d 182 (1974), the Court of Appeals concluded that the protections announced in *Miranda* are not constitutionally required.

We disagree with the Court of Appeals' conclusion, although we concede that there is language in some of our opinions that supports the view taken by that court. But first and foremost of the factors on the other side — that *Miranda* is a constitutional decision — is that both *Miranda* and two of its companion cases applied the rule to proceedings in state courts — to wit, Arizona, California, and New York. *See* 384 U.S. at 491–494, 497–499. Since that time, we have consistently applied *Miranda*'s rule to prosecutions arising in state courts. *See, e.g., Stansbury v. California,* 511 U.S. 318, 114 S. Ct. 1526, 128 L. Ed. 2d 293 (1994) (*per curiam*); *Minnick v. Mississippi,* 498 U.S. 146, 111 S. Ct. 486, 112 L. Ed. 2d 489 (1990); *Arizona v. Roberson,* 486 U.S. 675, 108 S. Ct. 2093, 100 L. Ed. 2d 704 (1988); *Edwards v. Arizona,* 451 U.S. 477, 481–482, 101 S. Ct. 1880, 68 L. Ed. 2d 378 (1981). It is beyond dispute that we do not hold a supervisory power over the courts of the several States. . . .

The *Miranda* opinion itself begins by stating that the Court granted certiorari "to explore some facets of the problems . . . of applying the privilege against self-incrimination to in-custody interrogation, *and to give concrete constitutional guidelines for law enforcement agencies and courts to follow.*" 384 U.S. at 441–442 (emphasis added). In fact, the majority opinion is replete with statements indicating that the majority thought it was announcing a constitutional rule. Indeed, the Court's ultimate conclusion was that the unwarned confessions obtained in the four cases before the Court in *Miranda* "were obtained from the defendant under circumstances that did not meet constitutional standards for protection of the privilege."[5] *Id.* at 491.

Additional support for our conclusion that *Miranda* is constitutionally based is found in the *Miranda* Court's invitation for legislative action to protect the constitutional right against coerced self-incrimination. After discussing the "compelling pressures" inherent in custodial police interrogation, the *Miranda* Court concluded that, "[i]n order to combat these pressures and to permit a full opportunity to exer-

---

5. Many of our subsequent cases have also referred to *Miranda*'s constitutional underpinnings. *See, e.g., Withrow,* 507 U.S., at 691 ("'Prophylactic' though it may be, in protecting a defendant's Fifth Amendment privilege against self-incrimination, *Miranda* safeguards a 'fundamental trial right'"); *Illinois v. Perkins,* 496 U.S. 292, 296, 110 S. Ct. 2394, 110, L. Ed. 2d 243 (1990) (describing *Miranda*'s warning requirement as resting on "the Fifth Amendment privilege against self-incrimination"); *Butler v. McKellar,* 494 U.S. 407, 411, 110 S. Ct. 1212, 108 L. Ed. 2d 347 (1990) ("[T]he Fifth Amendment bars police-initiated interrogation following a suspect's request for counsel in the context of a separate investigation"); *Michigan v. Jackson,* 475 U.S. 625, 629, 106 S. Ct. 1404, 89 L. Ed. 2d 631 (1986) ("The Fifth Amendment protection against compelled self-incrimination provides the right to counsel at custodial interrogations"); *Moran v. Burbine,* 475 U.S. 412, 427, 106 S. Ct. 1135, 89 L. Ed. 2d 410 (1986) (referring to *Miranda* as "our interpretation of the Federal Constitution"); *Edwards,* 451 U.S. at 481–82.

cise the privilege against self-incrimination, the accused must be adequately and effectively appraised of his rights and the exercise of those rights must be fully honored." *Id.* at 467. However, the Court emphasized that it could not foresee "the potential alternatives for protecting the privilege which might be devised by Congress or the States," and it accordingly opined that the Constitution would not preclude legislative solutions that differed from the prescribed *Miranda* warnings but which were "at least as effective in apprising accused persons of their right of silence and in assuring a continuous opportunity to exercise it."[6] *Ibid.*

The Court of Appeals also relied on the fact that we have, after our *Miranda* decision, made exceptions from its rule in cases such as *New York v. Quarles,* 467 U.S. 649, 104 S. Ct. 2626, 81 L. Ed. 2d 550 (1984), and *Harris v. New York,* 401 U.S. 222, 91 S. Ct. 643, 28 L. Ed. 2d 1 (1971). *See* 166 F.3d at 672, 689–691. But we have also broadened the application of the *Miranda* doctrine in cases such as *Doyle v. Ohio,* 426 U.S. 610, 96 S. Ct. 2240, 49 L. Ed. 2d 91 (1976), and *Arizona v. Roberson,* 486 U.S. 675, 108 S. Ct. 2093, 100 L. Ed. 2d 704 (1988). These decisions illustrate the principle — not that *Miranda* is not a constitutional rule — but that no constitutional rule is immutable. No court laying down a general rule can possibly foresee the various circumstances in which counsel will seek to apply it, and the sort of modifications represented by these cases are as much a normal part of constitutional law as the original decision.

. . . .

As an alternative argument for sustaining the Court of Appeals' decision, the court-invited *amicus curiae* contends that the section complies with the requirement that a legislative alternative to *Miranda* be equally as effective in preventing coerced confessions. We agree with the *amicus'* contention that there are more remedies available for abusive police conduct than there were at the time *Miranda* was decided, *see, e.g., Wilkins v. May,* 872 F.2d 190, 194 (7th Cir. 1989) (applying *Bivens v. Six Unknown Fed. Narcotics Agents,* 403 U.S. 388, 91 S. Ct. 1999, 29 L. Ed. 2d 619 (1971), to hold that a suspect may bring a federal cause of action under the Due Process Clause for police misconduct during custodial interrogation). But we do not agree that these additional measures supplement § 3501's protections sufficiently to meet the constitutional minimum. *Miranda* requires procedures that will warn a suspect in custody of his right to remain silent and which will assure the suspect that the exercise of that right will be honored. *See, e.g.,* 384 U.S. at 467. As discussed above, § 3501 explicitly eschews a requirement of pre-interrogation warnings in favor of an approach that looks to the administration of such warnings as only one factor in de-

---

6. The Court of Appeals relied in part on our statement that the *Miranda* decision in no way "creates a 'constitutional straightjacket.'" *See* 166 F.3d at 672 (quoting *Miranda,* 384 U.S. at 467). However, a review of our opinion in *Miranda* clarifies that this disclaimer was intended to indicate that the Constitution does not require police to administer the particular *Miranda* warnings, not that the Constitution does not require a procedure that is effective in securing Fifth Amendment rights.

termining the voluntariness of a suspect's confession. The additional remedies cited by *amicus* do not, in our view, render them, together with § 3501, an adequate substitute for the warnings required by *Miranda*.

The dissent argues that it is judicial overreaching for this Court to hold § 3501 unconstitutional unless we hold that the *Miranda* warnings are required by the Constitution, in the sense that nothing else will suffice to satisfy constitutional requirements. But we need not go farther than *Miranda* to decide this case. In *Miranda*, the Court noted that reliance on the traditional totality-of-the-circumstances test raised a risk of overlooking an involuntary custodial confession, 384 U.S. at 457, a risk that the Court found unacceptably great when the confession is offered in the case in chief to prove guilt. The Court therefore concluded that something more than the totality test was necessary. *See ibid.; see also id.* at 467, 490–491. As discussed above, § 3501 reinstates the totality test as sufficient. Section 3501 therefore cannot be sustained if *Miranda* is to remain the law.

Whether or not we would agree with *Miranda*'s reasoning and its resulting rule, were we addressing the issue in the first instance, the principles of *stare decisis* weigh heavily against overruling it now. . . .

. . . *Miranda* has become embedded in routine police practice to the point where the warnings have become part of our national culture. While we have overruled our precedents when subsequent cases have undermined their doctrinal underpinnings, *see, e.g., Patterson v. McLean Credit Union*, 491 U.S. 164, 173, 109 S. Ct. 2363, 105 L. Ed. 2d 132 (1989), we do not believe that this has happened to the *Miranda* decision. If anything, our subsequent cases have reduced the impact of the *Miranda* rule on legitimate law enforcement while reaffirming the decision's core ruling that unwarned statements may not be used as evidence in the prosecution's case in chief.

The disadvantage of the *Miranda* rule is that statements which may be by no means involuntary, made by a defendant who is aware of his "rights," may nonetheless be excluded and a guilty defendant go free as a result. But experience suggests that the totality-of-the-circumstances test which § 3501 seeks to revive is more difficult than *Miranda* for law enforcement officers to conform to, and for courts to apply in a consistent manner. The requirement that *Miranda* warnings be given does not, of course, dispense with the voluntariness inquiry. But as we said in *Berkemer v. McCarty*, 468 U.S. 420, 104 S. Ct. 3138, 82 L. Ed. 2d 317 (1984), "[c]ases in which a defendant can make a colorable argument that a self-incriminating statement was 'compelled' despite the fact that the law enforcement authorities adhered to the dictates of *Miranda* are rare." *Id.* at 433 n.20.

In sum, we conclude that *Miranda* announced a constitutional rule that Congress may not supersede legislatively. Following the rule of *stare decisis*, we decline to overrule *Miranda* ourselves. The judgment of the Court of Appeals is therefore

Reversed.

JUSTICE SCALIA, with whom JUSTICE THOMAS joins, dissenting.

Those to whom judicial decisions are an unconnected series of judgments that produce either favored or disfavored results will doubtless greet today's decision as a paragon of moderation, since it declines to overrule *Miranda v. Arizona*, 384 U.S. 436, 86 S. Ct. 1602, 16 L. Ed. 2d 694 (1966). Those who understand the judicial process will appreciate that today's decision is not a reaffirmation of *Miranda*, but a radical revision of the most significant element of *Miranda* (as of all cases): the rationale that gives it a permanent place in our jurisprudence.

... [T]o justify today's agreed-upon result, the Court must adopt a significant *new*, if not entirely comprehensible, principle of constitutional law. As the Court chooses to describe that principle, statutes of Congress can be disregarded, not only when what they prescribe violates the Constitution, but when what they prescribe contradicts a decision of this Court that "announced a constitutional rule." As I shall discuss in some detail, the only thing that can possibly mean in the context of this case is that this Court has the power, not merely to apply the Constitution, but to expand it, imposing what it regards as useful "prophylactic" restrictions upon Congress and the States. That is an immense, and frightening antidemocratic power, and it does not exist.

It takes only a small step to bring today's opinion out of the realm of power-judging and into the mainstream of legal reasoning: The Court need only go beyond its carefully couched iterations that "*Miranda* is a constitutional decision," that "*Miranda* is constitutionally based," that *Miranda* has "constitutional underpinnings," and come out and say quite clearly: "We reaffirm today that custodial interrogation that is not preceded by *Miranda* warnings or their equivalent violates the Constitution of the United States." It cannot say that, because a majority of the Court does not believe it. The Court therefore acts in plain violation of the Constitution when it denies effect to this Act of Congress.

I

Early in this Nation's history, this Court established the sound proposition that constitutional government in a system of separated powers requires judges to regard as inoperative any legislative act, even of Congress itself, that is "repugnant to the Constitution." ...

It was once possible to characterize the so-called *Miranda* rule as resting (however implausibly) upon the proposition that what the statute here before us permits — the admission at trial of un-*Mirandized* confessions — violates the Constitution. That is the fairest reading of the *Miranda* case itself. ...

. . . .

So understood, *Miranda* was objectionable for innumerable reasons, not least the fact that cases spanning more than 70 years had rejected its core premise that, absent the warnings and an effective waiver of the right to remain silent and of the (thitherto unknown) right to have an attorney present, a statement obtained pursuant to custodial interrogation was necessarily the product of compulsion. Moreover, history and precedent aside, the decision in *Miranda*, if read as an explication of what the Constitution *requires*, is preposterous. There is, for example, simply no basis in reason for concluding that a response to the very first question asked, by a suspect who already *knows* all of the rights described in the *Miranda* warning, is anything other than a volitional act. *See Miranda, supra* at 533–534 (White, J., dissenting). And even if one assumes that the elimination of compulsion absolutely requires informing even the most knowledgeable suspect of his right to remain silent, it cannot conceivably require the right to have *counsel* present. There is a world of difference, which the Court recognized under the traditional voluntariness test but ignored in *Miranda*, between compelling a suspect to incriminate himself and preventing him from foolishly doing so of his own accord. Only the latter (which is *not* required by the Constitution) could explain the Court's inclusion of a right to counsel and the requirement that it, too, be knowingly and intelligently waived. Counsel's presence is not required to tell the suspect that he *need* not speak; the interrogators can do that. The only good reason for having counsel there is that he can be counted on to advise the suspect that he *should* not speak.

. . . [W]hat is most remarkable about the *Miranda* decision and what made it unacceptable as a matter of straightforward constitutional interpretation in the *Marbury* tradition is its palpable hostility toward the act of confession *per se*, rather than toward what the Constitution abhors, *compelled* confession. The Constitution is not, unlike the *Miranda* majority, offended by a criminal's commendable qualm of conscience or fortunate fit of stupidity.

For these reasons, and others more than adequately developed in the *Miranda* dissents and in the subsequent works of the decision's many critics, any conclusion that a violation of the *Miranda* rules *necessarily* amounts to a violation of the privilege against compelled self-incrimination can claim no support in history, precedent, or common sense, and as a result would at least presumptively be worth reconsidering even at this late date. But that is unnecessary, since the Court has (thankfully) long since abandoned the notion that failure to comply with *Miranda*'s rules is itself a violation of the Constitution.

II

As the Court today acknowledges, since *Miranda* we have explicitly, and repeatedly, interpreted that decision as having announced, not the circumstances in which custodial interrogation runs afoul of the Fifth or Fourteenth Amendment, but rather only "prophylactic" rules that go beyond the right against compelled self-incrimination. Of course the seeds of this "prophylactic" interpretation of *Miranda* were present in the decision itself. *See Miranda, supra*, at 439 (discussing the "necessity for procedures which assure that the [suspect] is accorded his privilege"); *id.* at 447 ("[u]nless a proper limitation upon custodial interrogation is achieved — such as these decisions will advance — there can be no assurance that practices of this nature will be eradicated"); *id.* at 457 ("[i]n these cases, we might not find the defendants' statements to have been involuntary in traditional terms"); *ibid.* (noting "concern for adequate safeguards to protect precious Fifth Amendment rights" and the "potentiality for compulsion" in Ernesto Miranda's interrogation). In subsequent cases, the seeds have sprouted and borne fruit: The Court has squarely concluded that it is possible — indeed not uncommon — for the police to violate *Miranda* without also violating the Constitution.

. . . .

In light of these cases, and our statements to the same effect in others, it is simply no longer possible for the Court to conclude, even if it wanted to, that a violation of *Miranda*'s rules is a violation of the Constitution. But as I explained at the outset, that is what is required before the Court may disregard a law of Congress governing the admissibility of evidence in federal court. The Court today insists that the *decision* in *Miranda* is a "constitutional" one; that it has "constitutional underpinnings"; a "constitutional basis" and a "constitutional origin"; that it was "constitutionally based"; and that it announced a "constitutional rule." It is fine to play these word games; but what makes a decision "constitutional" in the only sense relevant here — in the sense that renders it impervious to supersession by congressional legislation such as § 3501 — is the determination that the Constitution *requires* the result that the decision announces and the statute ignores. By disregarding congressional action that concededly does not violate the Constitution, the Court flagrantly offends fundamental principles of separation of powers, and arrogates to itself prerogatives reserved to the representatives of the people.

The Court seeks to avoid this conclusion in two ways: First, by misdescribing these post-*Miranda* cases as mere dicta. The Court concedes only "that there is language in some of our opinions that supports the view" that *Miranda*'s protections are not "constitutionally required." It is not a matter of *language*; it is a matter of *holdings*. The proposition that failure to comply with *Miranda*'s rules does not establish a constitutional violation was central to the *holdings* of *Tucker, Hass, Quarles,* and *Elstad.*

The second way the Court seeks to avoid the impact of these cases is simply to disclaim responsibility for reasoned decisionmaking. It says:

> These decisions illustrate the principle — not that *Miranda* is not a constitutional rule — but that no constitutional rule is immutable. No court laying down a general rule can possibly foresee the various circumstances in which counsel will seek to apply it, and the sort of modifications represented by these cases are as much a normal part of constitutional law as the original decision.

The issue, however, is not whether court rules are "mutable"; they assuredly are. It is not whether, in the light of "various circumstances," they can be "modifi[ed]"; they assuredly can. The issue is whether, *as mutated and modified,* they must *make sense.* The requirement that they do so is the only thing that prevents this Court from being some sort of nine-headed Caesar, giving thumbs-up or thumbs-down to whatever outcome, case by case, suits or offends its collective fancy. And if confessions procured in violation of *Miranda* are confessions "compelled" in violation of the Constitution, the post-*Miranda* decisions I have discussed do not make sense. The only reasoned basis for their outcome was that a violation of *Miranda* is *not* a violation of the Constitution. . . .

Finally, the Court asserts that *Miranda* must be a "constitutional decision" announcing a "constitutional rule," and thus immune to congressional modification, because we have since its inception applied it to the States. If this argument is meant as an invocation of *stare decisis*, it fails because, though it is true that our cases applying *Miranda* against the States must be reconsidered if *Miranda* is not required by the Constitution, it is likewise true that our cases (discussed above) based on the principle that *Miranda* is *not* required by the Constitution will have to be reconsidered if it *is*. So the *stare decisis* argument is a wash. If, on the other hand, the argument is meant as an appeal to logic rather than *stare decisis*, it is a classic example of begging the question: Congress's attempt to set aside *Miranda*, since it represents an assertion that violation of *Miranda* is not a violation of the Constitution, *also* represents an assertion that the Court has no power to impose *Miranda* on the States. To answer this assertion — not by showing why violation of *Miranda* is a violation of the Constitution — but by asserting that *Miranda does* apply against the States, is to assume precisely the point at issue. In my view, our continued application of the *Miranda* code to the States despite our consistent statements that running afoul of its dictates does not necessarily — or even usually — result in an actual constitutional violation, represents not the source of *Miranda*'s salvation but rather evidence of its ultimate illegitimacy. *See generally* J. Grano, CONFESSIONS, TRUTH, AND THE LAW 173–198 (1993); Grano, *Prophylactic Rules in Criminal Procedure: A Question of Article III Legitimacy*, 80 Nw. U. L. Rev. 100 (1985).

. . . .

III

There was available to the Court a means of reconciling the established proposition that a violation of *Miranda* does not itself offend the Fifth Amendment with the Court's assertion of a right to ignore the present statute. That means of reconciliation was argued strenuously by both petitioner and the United States, who were evidently more concerned than the Court is with maintaining the coherence of our jurisprudence. It is not mentioned in the Court's opinion because, I assume, a majority of the Justices intent on reversing believes that incoherence is the lesser evil. They may be right.

Petitioner and the United States contend that there is nothing at all exceptional, much less unconstitutional, about the Court's adopting prophylactic rules to buttress constitutional rights, and enforcing them against Congress and the States. . . .

. . . .

. . . [W]hat the Court did in *Miranda* (assuming, as later cases hold, that *Miranda* went beyond what the Constitution actually requires) is in fact extraordinary. That the Court has, on rare and recent occasion, repeated the mistake does not transform error into truth, but illustrates the potential for future mischief that the error entails. Where the Constitution has wished to lodge in one of the branches of the Federal

Government some limited power to supplement its guarantees, it has said so. *See* Amdt. 14, § 5 ("The Congress shall have power to enforce, by appropriate legislation, the provisions of this article"). The power with which the Court would endow itself under a "prophylactic" justification for *Miranda* goes far beyond what it has permitted Congress to do under authority of that text. Whereas we have insisted that congressional action under § 5 of the Fourteenth Amendment must be "congruent" with, and "proportional" to, a *constitutional violation, see City of Boerne v. Flores*, 521 U.S. 507, 520, 117 S. Ct. 2157, 138 L. Ed. 2d 624 (1997), the *Miranda* nontextual power to embellish confers authority to prescribe preventive measures against not only constitutionally prohibited compelled confessions, but also (as discussed earlier) foolhardy ones.

I applaud, therefore, the refusal of the Justices in the majority to enunciate this boundless doctrine of judicial empowerment as a means of rendering today's decision rational. In nonetheless joining the Court's judgment, however, they overlook two truisms: that actions speak louder than silence, and that (in judge-made law at least) logic will out. Since there is in fact no other principle that can reconcile today's judgment with the post-*Miranda* cases that the Court refuses to abandon, what today's decision will stand for, whether the Justices can bring themselves to say it or not, is the power of the Supreme Court to write a prophylactic, extraconstitutional Constitution, binding on Congress and the States.

IV

Thus, while I agree with the Court that § 3501 cannot be upheld without also concluding that *Miranda* represents an illegitimate exercise of our authority to review state-court judgments, I do not share the Court's hesitation in reaching that conclusion. For while the Court is also correct that the doctrine of *stare decisis* demands some "special justification" for a departure from longstanding precedent — even precedent of the constitutional variety — that criterion is more than met here. . . . [L]ater cases . . . have "undermined [*Miranda's*] doctrinal underpinnings," denying constitutional violation and thus stripping the holding of its only constitutionally legitimate support. . . .

. . . .

Neither am I persuaded by the argument for retaining *Miranda* that touts its supposed workability as compared with the totality-of-the-circumstances test it purported to replace. *Miranda's* proponents cite *ad nauseam* the fact that the Court was called upon to make difficult and subtle distinctions in applying the "voluntariness" test in some 30-odd due process "coerced confessions" cases in the 30 years between *Brown v. Mississippi*, 297 U.S. 278, 56 S. Ct. 461, 80 L. Ed. 682 (1936), and *Miranda*. It is not immediately apparent, however, that the judicial burden has been eased by the "bright-line" rules adopted in *Miranda*. In fact, in the 34 years since *Miranda* was decided, this Court has been called upon to decide nearly 60 cases involving a host of *Miranda* issues, most of them predicted with remarkable prescience by Justice White in his *Miranda* dissent. 384 U.S. at 545.

Moreover, it is not clear why the Court thinks that the "totality-of-the-circumstances test . . . is more difficult than *Miranda* for law enforcement officers to conform to, and for courts to apply in a consistent manner." . . .

But even were I to agree that the old totality-of-the-circumstances test was more cumbersome, it is simply not true that *Miranda* has banished it from the law and replaced it with a new test. Under the current regime, which the Court today retains in its entirety, courts are frequently called upon to undertake *both* inquiries. That is because, as explained earlier, voluntariness remains the *constitutional* standard, and as such continues to govern the admissibility for impeachment purposes of statements taken in violation of *Miranda*, the admissibility of the "fruits" of such statements, and the admissibility of statements challenged as unconstitutionally obtained *despite* the interrogator's compliance with *Miranda, see, e.g., Colorado v. Connelly,* 479 U.S. 157, 107 S. Ct. 515, 93 L. Ed. 2d 473 (1986).

Finally, I am not convinced by petitioner's argument that *Miranda* should be preserved because the decision occupies a special place in the "public's consciousness." Brief for Petitioner 44. As far as I am aware, the public is not under the illusion that we are infallible. I see little harm in admitting that we made a mistake in taking away from the people the ability to decide for themselves what protections (beyond those required by the Constitution) are reasonably affordable in the criminal investigatory process. And I see much to be gained by reaffirming for the people the wonderful reality that they govern themselves — which means that "[t]he powers not delegated to the United States by the Constitution" that the people adopted, "nor prohibited . . . to the States" by that Constitution, "are reserved to the States respectively, or to the people," U.S. Const., Amdt. 10.

Today's judgment converts *Miranda* from a milestone of judicial overreaching into the very Cheops' Pyramid (or perhaps the Sphinx would be a better analogue) of judicial arrogance. In imposing its Court-made code upon the States, the original opinion at least *asserted* that it was demanded by the Constitution. Today's decision does not pretend that it is — and yet *still* asserts the right to impose it against the will of the people's representatives in Congress. Far from believing that *stare decisis* compels this result, I believe we cannot allow to remain on the books even a celebrated decision — *especially* a celebrated decision — that has come to stand for the proposition that the Supreme Court has power to impose extraconstitutional constraints upon Congress and the States. This is not the system that was established by the Framers, or that would be established by any sane supporter of government by the people.

I dissent from today's decision, and, until § 3501 is repealed, will continue to apply it in all cases where there has been a sustainable finding that the defendant's confession was voluntary.

Notes and Questions

(1) Is Justice Scalia correct to maintain that the *Dickerson* majority does not state or believe that "custodial interrogation that is not preceded by *Miranda* warnings or

their equivalent violates the Constitution"? If so, what is the *Dickerson* majority's basis for reaffirming *Miranda*?

(2) Does the *Dickerson* majority's assertion that *Miranda* "announced a constitutional rule" call into question *Quarles* and other decisions that seem to be based on the premise that *Miranda* merely prescribed prophylactic rules that provide suspects with more protection than that required by the Fifth Amendment privilege?

(3) In *Chavez v. Martinez*, 538 U.S. 760, 123 S. Ct. 1994, 155 L. Ed. 2d 984 (2003), Chavez, a patrol supervisor, interrogated Martinez in a hospital where he was being treated for gunshot wounds he received during an altercation with two police officers. Although Martinez had been arrested, the officers never gave him *Miranda* warnings. Chavez persisted in interrogating Martinez despite the fact that Martinez was obviously in great pain and repeatedly said that he did not want to answer questions until he been treated for his injuries. Martinez answered Chavez's questions with potentially incriminating admissions.

Martinez was never prosecuted for a crime. He brought a civil suit under 42 U.S.C. § 1983, claiming that Chavez's actions violated his Fifth Amendment privilege against compelled self-incrimination and his Fourteenth Amendment due process right to be free from coercive questioning.

A clear majority of the Court rejected Martinez's Fifth Amendment claim. Writing for a four-Justice plurality, Justice Thomas stated that violation of a person's Fifth Amendment privilege can only occur when compelled statements are introduced against a person in court. Although they did not endorse the plurality's reasoning, Justices Souter and Breyer agreed that, even though Chavez may have compelled Martinez to admit his guilt, Martinez could not recover damages based on the Fifth Amendment privilege. In their view, a civil damages remedy was not necessary to protect the "core" of the privilege against compulsory self-incrimination—i.e., an accused's right not to have his compelled statements used against him at trial. In an opinion by Justice Kennedy, three Justices dissented from this conclusion. In their view, the Fifth Amendment was violated by the coercive tactics Chavez employed to secure Martinez's statements, even though those statements were not used against him.

The plurality further stated that *Miranda* is a "judicially crafted prophylactic rule[]" designed to preserve "the core Fifth Amendment right from invasion by use of [the individual's] compelled testimony" in a criminal trial. A failure to comply with *Miranda* does not violate the individual's Fifth Amendment privilege and provides no basis for a damages claim. All nine Justices agreed that Martinez could not establish a Fifth Amendment violation simply by showing that his statements were obtained in violation of *Miranda*.

Justice Thomas's plurality opinion also concluded that Chavez's interrogation of Martinez did not violate Martinez's due process rights because Chavez's questioning of Martinez in the hospital was not "egregious" or "conscience shocking." The apparent basis for this conclusion was that the police had a justifiable interest in conducting a prompt investigation of the altercation (given the possibility that Martinez might die and thus be unavailable to answer questions at a later time) and there was no "evidence that Chavez acted with a purpose to harm Martinez by intentionally interfering with his medical treatment."

Five other Justices, however, concluded that Martinez's due process claim should be remanded to the lower courts. As to this issue, Justice Souter stated that the merits of Martinez's substantive due process claim would not depend upon his Fifth Amendment claim but rather "upon the particular charge of outrageous conduct by the police, extending from their initial encounter with Martinez through the questioning by Chavez."

Does the *Chavez* plurality's discussion of Fifth Amendment prophylactic rules provide insight into the constitutional status of the *Miranda* warnings or into the meaning of Fifth Amendment prophylactic rules? For an illuminating analysis of the issues raised by *Chavez*, see John T. Parry, *Constitutional Interpretation, Coercive Interrogation, and Civil Litigation After* Chavez v. Martinez, 39 Ga. L. Rev. 733 (2005).

Public Safety Problems

8A–1: After a disturbance in the prison yard at the state penitentiary, a corrections officer saw one of the inmates, Jamie, place something in his pants. The officer instructed a fellow officer to escort Jamie out of the yard and into a corridor. In the corridor, with several other corrections officers present, the officer who had escorted Jamie out of the yard instructed him to face the wall and asked him "if he had anything." According to the officer, it was his practice to ask inmates whether they "had anything on" them before any pat frisk so that he would not "get stuck or cut." In part, however, he asked Jamie the question in order to obtain information about a possible violation of inmate rules. Jamie responded that he had a weapon. A frisk revealed "a pick-type weapon" in Jamie's waistband. Prior to trial for possessing contraband in the prison, Jamie moved to suppress his response and the weapon, relying on *Miranda*.

How should the trial court rule on Jamie's motion?

8A–2: After receiving a complaint about an individual who was creating a disturbance in public, police went to a parking lot in a mall. They found Wallace, clad only in underwear, pacing erratically, mumbling to himself, and making jerky movements. After the police arrested Wallace, his condition appeared to worsen. This led an officer to ask Wallace, who had not yet been apprised of his *Miranda* rights, whether he had ingested heroin. Wallace gave an affirmative answer. The officer asked the question because he was concerned about Wallace's health and safety.

Will Wallace's admission to the officer be admissible?

8A–3: Earl Green was shot with a shotgun during a robbery attempt near his home. Green called 911 and identified his assailant as Raphael Trice. According to

Green, he recognized Trice because he had previously seen him in the neighborhood. Four days later, Detective Tugman went to Trice's house and arrested him. While in the house, Tugman saw Trice's mother and several small children. At the police station, Tugman advised Trice of his *Miranda* rights and asked him if he wanted to answer questions and if he was willing to answer questions without having an attorney present. Trice answered, "No," to both questions. For the next twenty minutes, the detective asked Trice for background information which Trice provided. The detective then said, "I'd like to know where the shotgun is. There are little kids in the house. I don't want anyone to get hurt." Trice replied, "It's okay. I gave it back to the person I borrowed it from." The detective asked no more questions.

Will Trice's incriminating statement be admissible?

8A–4: City Police Officers Anthony and Lenny were patrolling the city in an unmarked police car when they saw Herman pick up a red bag from beside a garbage can in an alley and then run north through the alley. When Herman emerged from the alley and turned left toward a nearby avenue, he saw the two officers. Realizing that he had been observed, Herman dropped the red bag on the ground beside him. As the officers approached him on foot, he volunteered, "I just have some dope." Herman then handed a key holder to Officer Anthony. Inside, Officer Anthony found five small bags of what appeared to be (and was later determined to be) heroin.

The officers arrested Herman. Officer Lenny asked him what was in the red bag that he had dropped on the ground. Herman replied that he had "ripped the guys around the corner for dope and a gun." After hearing that, Lenny opened the bag and found a loaded .38 caliber gun, 61 small bags of crack cocaine, and 55 small bags of marijuana. At that point, Lenny recited *Miranda* warnings, put Herman in the patrol car, and took him to the police station.

Prior to trial, Herman filed a motion to suppress his second statement, claiming it was inadmissible under *Miranda*. The prosecution responded that the public safety exception justified the use of that statement at trial.

Should the trial judge grant Herman's motion to suppress?

8A–5: At approximately 11:50 p.m., Officer Val heard a radio report that there were "shots fired" at 905 Baldwin Street and that "a black male in a red Cadillac" that left the scene was a possible suspect. When Val arrived at the location, he saw Bert lying on the ground, bleeding from gunshot wounds he had sustained. He called for an ambulance. He then observed a red Cadillac in an alley with its lights off. When the Cadillac pulled out of the alley, Val activated his lights and siren and called for backup. Val observed the driver stick his left arm out the driver's side window and throw something shiny over the top of the vehicle into the marsh-like parkway along the road in an unpopulated area. Val pulled the Cadillac over, ordered Dennis, the driver, to step out, then arrested and handcuffed him. Because Dennis was bleeding from the leg, Val summoned another ambulance. After ambulances arrived and took both Dennis and Bert to the hospital, Val and a number of other officers spent two hours searching the area for the object Dennis had thrown from his vehicle. They never located the object.

Detective Holm began to investigate the shooting shortly after midnight. He was aware that both Dennis and Bert had sustained gunshot wounds and were being transported to the hospital for treatment. Holm arrived at the hospital at 1:00 a.m. Dennis arrived at the emergency room at 1:30 a.m. As soon as the nurses left, Holm entered the curtained-off area where Dennis was lying. Dennis, who was "very calm and quiet," was clothed in only his underwear. He had what appeared to be a "through-and-through" bullet wound on his upper thigh. The injury was not bandaged, and he was still bleeding from the wound. Holm repeatedly asked Dennis if he knew the location of the gun used in the shooting. Dennis did not respond. Holm continued to ask Dennis "where the gun was," "what did he do with the gun," and "did he know what happened to the gun." Dennis responded, "I don't know where the gun is." Holm asked Dennis "several more times" about the location of the gun. Dennis then became visibly upset and began to cry. Holm asked Dennis "if he was okay, what was wrong." Dennis responded that Bert used to be his friend and that they had been coworkers. Dennis then told Holm that he had been to Bert's apartment earlier that evening. Dennis stated that Bert had "ruined his life, his soul, and his marriage," that Bert was sleeping with Dennis's wife, and that he was worried that he was going to lose his children. Holm asked Dennis once more about the location of the gun before a nurse told Holm to leave so that she could continue Dennis's treatment. At no time during the 10 minutes he was with Dennis did Holm deliver *Miranda* warnings.

Does the "public safety exception" support the admission of Dennis's statements?

8A–6: Snee was driving his vehicle late one night when his intoxicated passenger yanked the steering wheel and caused the vehicle to crash into a fence at a business facility. After the crash, the vehicle's engine would not start. Snee realized that his vehicle would have to be towed. He was afraid to leave a loaded gun in the vehicle's rear compartment, so he jumped out of the driver's seat and ran to the rear of the vehicle. He lifted the hatchback and grabbed his gun from behind the tire jack. He then ran down the street, threw the gun in some bushes, and returned to the vehicle to wait for the police.

When Officer Slow arrived at the scene, he saw track marks from Snee's vehicle leading up an embankment to a fence. He observed that the vehicle had rolled back down the embankment and had come to rest. At the scene, Officer Slow interviewed Doug, a worker at the business facility who had seen the crash. Doug said that he saw a man get out of the vehicle, run down the sidewalk toward some bushes, and then return to the vehicle. Fred, another witness, reported that he had seen a man get out of the crashed vehicle and throw an unknown object into some bushes down the street, about 100 yards south of the wreck.

Officer Slow was confused at first about who was responsible for the accident. After determining that Snee's passenger had grabbed the wheel while intoxicated, he arrested her for driving under the influence. Upon checking, Slow learned that Snee was the subject of two outstanding bench warrants. He arrested Snee, handcuffed him, and placed him in his cruiser.

Officer Slow then noticed an odor of alcohol. Believing that Snee might have tried to discard or hide alcohol in the bushes, Officer Slow asked him, "What did you toss into the bushes? Was it alcohol or was it a gun of any sort or any kind of weapon?" Snee replied, "Well, yeah, actually, it's a gun. I'll show you right where it is." Officer Slow then read Snee his *Miranda* rights.

Does Officer Slow's failure to warn Snee prior to his admission require that it be excluded from his trial?

8A-7: On Christmas Day, U.S. Customs and Border Protection officers in Detroit were advised of an incident on board international flight 253. They met the plane when it arrived at the gate at the Detroit airport. After determining that Umar's burns were too extensive to have been caused by firecrackers, the officers transported him to the University Hospital for treatment and informed the FBI's Joint Terrorism Task Force. Umar arrived at the hospital at about 12:25 p.m. He received treatment for his burns, including 50 micrograms of the painkiller fentanyl administered intravenously at 2:00 p.m. Umar was then transferred to the hospital's burn unit, where treatment was continued. Between 2:30 p.m. and 3:00 p.m., his primary care nurse, R.N. Julia, administered incremental intravenous doses of fentanyl — a total of 300 micrograms — to relieve pain while Umar's burns were scrubbed. According to Julia, his reaction to the painkiller was normal. Throughout his treatment, Umar remained lucid and alert. He gave appropriate responses to verbal commands and was "orientated times 3" — meaning that he knew who he was, where he was, and what time it was.

Around 3:35 p.m., after Umar was moved to a private room, FBI Special Agent Timothy questioned him in the presence of FBI Special Agent Pessing and U.S. Customs Officer Wald. Before the interview, Wald had informed Timothy of Umar's admissions that he had detonated an explosive device hidden in his underwear while on flight 253 and that he was acting on behalf of al-Qaeda. Timothy had learned from other federal agents that a similar explosive device had been used previously, although not on a plane. He knew that because the explosive device had no mechanical devices associated with it, it could defeat airport security. Knowing al-Qaeda's history, Timothy feared that there could be additional, imminent aircraft attacks. He questioned Umar for about 50 minutes without giving *Miranda* warnings.

During the questioning, Umar appeared alert and lucid. He told Timothy that he was not in pain, that he felt fine, and that he understood the need to ask him questions. Umar had no trouble understanding or speaking English. Agent Timothy asked Umar where he traveled, when he had traveled, how, and with whom; the details of the explosive device; the details regarding the bombmaker, including where Umar had received the bomb; his intentions in attacking flight 253; and who else might be planning an attack. Umar made many incriminating statements in response.

Are Umar's statements admissible at his trial for terrorism?

8A-8: On November 18, the United States Marshals Service learned that Mikos, a fugitive wanted for failure to appear on state sex offense charges, was staying in Elephant Bluff State Park. According to information received by the Marshals

Service, Mikos, a veteran who had worked in the federal prison system, had obtained weapons, ammunition, and a large amount of camping and survival equipment before traveling to the park.

The marshals devised a plan to arrest Mikos. After they met with a park ranger and confirmed that Mikos was staying in the park, they performed an initial sweep that identified his precise location. At 5:00 p.m., the marshals approached Mikos's campsite in three vehicles. They saw him standing near the door of his truck. The truck door was open and a gun was visible in the door pocket. Mikos had a yellow bag in his hands. Deputy Marshal Byron jumped out of the lead vehicle and ordered Mikos to get on the ground. Mikos complied and was handcuffed.

The marshals then secured the area. In a nearby trailer, they found an older man and ordered him to remain inside. They found no other persons in the shelter area or campsite where Mikos's tent had been pitched. Meanwhile, Marshal Heffman asked Mikos "if he had any other items in the truck, weapons, money, drugs, anything like that." Mikos stated that "he had weapons in the truck." When Heffman asked, "Do you mind if I go ahead and go inside and get those weapons?" Mikos said "No," then specified where the guns were located. The marshals seized seven guns and almost 1,000 rounds of ammunition. At no point did any of the marshals recite *Miranda* warnings.

Mikos was charged with possession of a firearm by a fugitive. He filed a motion to suppress his inculpatory statements. The trial judge denied the motion to suppress the statements about the weapons, holding them admissible under the public safety exception. Mikos pleaded guilty, but has now appealed the denial of his motion to suppress the statements.

Should the appellate court affirm or reverse the trial court's suppression ruling?

[B] Custody

Berkemer v. McCarty

United States Supreme Court

468 U.S. 420, 104 S. Ct. 3138, 82 L. Ed. 2d 317 (1984)

JUSTICE MARSHALL delivered the opinion of the Court.

This case presents two related questions: First, does our decision in *Miranda v. Arizona*, 384 U.S. 436, 86 S. Ct. 1602, 16 L. Ed. 2d 694 (1966), govern the admissibility of statements made during custodial interrogation by a suspect accused of a misdemeanor traffic offense? Second, does the roadside questioning of a motorist detained pursuant to a traffic stop constitute custodial interrogation for the purposes of the doctrine enunciated in *Miranda*?

I

A

The parties have stipulated to the essential facts. On the evening of March 31, 1980, Trooper Williams of the Ohio State Highway Patrol observed respondent's car weaving in and out of a lane on Interstate Highway 270. After following the car for two miles, Williams forced respondent to stop and asked him to get out of the vehicle. When respondent complied, Williams noticed that he was having difficulty standing. At that point, "Williams concluded that [respondent] would be charged with a traffic offense and, therefore, his freedom to leave the scene was terminated." However, respondent was not told that he would be taken into custody. Williams then asked respondent to perform a field sobriety test, commonly known as a "balancing test." Respondent could not do so without falling.

While still at the scene of the traffic stop, Williams asked respondent whether he had been using intoxicants. Respondent replied that "he had consumed two beers and had smoked several joints of marijuana a short time before." Respondent's speech was slurred, and Williams had difficulty understanding him. Williams thereupon formally placed respondent under arrest and transported him in the patrol car to the Franklin County Jail.

At the jail, respondent was given an Intoxilyzer test to determine the concentration of alcohol in his blood. The test did not detect any alcohol whatsoever in respondent's system. Williams then resumed questioning respondent in order to obtain information for inclusion in the State Highway Patrol Alcohol Influence Report. Respondent answered affirmatively a question whether he had been drinking. When then asked if he was under the influence of alcohol, he said, "I guess, barely." Williams next asked respondent to indicate on the form whether the marihuana he had smoked had been treated with any chemicals. In the section of the report headed "Remarks," respondent wrote, "No ang[el] dust or PCP in the pot. Rick McCarty."

At no point in this sequence of events did Williams or anyone else tell respondent that he had a right to remain silent, to consult with an attorney, and to have an attorney appointed for him if he could not afford one.

B

Respondent was charged with operating a motor vehicle while under the influence of alcohol and/or drugs in violation of Ohio Rev. Code Ann. § 4511.19 (Supp. 1983). Under Ohio law, that offense is a first-degree misdemeanor and is punishable by fine or imprisonment for up to six months. Incarceration for a minimum of three days is mandatory.

Respondent moved to exclude the various incriminating statements he had made to Patrolman Williams on the ground that introduction into evidence of those statements would violate the Fifth Amendment insofar as he had not been informed of his constitutional rights prior to his interrogation. When the trial court denied the motion, respondent pleaded "no contest" and was found guilty. He was sentenced to 90 days in jail, 80 of which were suspended, and was fined $300, $100 of which were suspended.

. . . .

II

The Fifth Amendment provides: "No person . . . shall be compelled in any criminal case to be a witness against himself. . . ." It is settled that this provision governs state as well as federal criminal proceedings.

In *Miranda v. Arizona*, 384 U.S. 436, 86 S. Ct. 1602, 16 L. Ed. 2d 694 (1966), the Court addressed the problem of how the privilege against compelled self-incrimination guaranteed by the Fifth Amendment could be protected from the coercive pressures that can be brought to bear upon a suspect in the context of custodial interrogation. The Court held:

> [T]he prosecution may not use statements, whether exculpatory or inculpatory, stemming from custodial interrogation of [a] defendant unless it demonstrates the use of procedural safeguards effective to secure the privilege against self-incrimination. By custodial interrogation, we mean questioning initiated by law enforcement officers after a person has been taken into custody or otherwise deprived of his freedom of action in any significant way. . . .

Id. at 444, 86 S. Ct. at 1612 (footnote omitted).

In the years since the decision in *Miranda*, we have frequently reaffirmed the central principle established by that case: if the police take a suspect into custody and then ask him questions without informing him of the rights enumerated above, his responses cannot be introduced into evidence to establish his guilt.

Petitioner asks us to carve an exception out of the foregoing principle. When the police arrest a person for allegedly committing a misdemeanor traffic offense and then ask him questions without telling him his constitutional rights, petitioner argues, his responses should be admissible against him. We cannot agree.

One of the principal advantages of the doctrine that suspects must be given warnings before being interrogated while in custody is the clarity of that rule.

. . . .

The exception to *Miranda* proposed by petitioner would substantially undermine this crucial advantage of the doctrine. The police often are unaware when they arrest a person whether he may have committed a misdemeanor or a felony. Consider, for example, the reasonably common situation in which the driver of a car involved in an accident is taken into custody. Under Ohio law, both driving while under the influence of intoxicants and negligent vehicular homicide are misdemeanors, while reckless vehicular homicide is a felony. When arresting a person for causing a collision, the police may not know which of these offenses he may have committed. Indeed, the nature of his offense may depend upon circumstances unknowable to the police, such as whether the suspect has previously committed a similar offense or has a criminal record of some other kind. It may even turn upon events yet to happen, such as whether a victim of the accident dies. It would be unreasonable to expect the police to make guesses as to the nature of the criminal conduct at issue before deciding how they may interrogate the suspect.

. . . .

We hold therefore that a person subjected to custodial interrogation is entitled to the benefit of the procedural safeguards enunciated in *Miranda*, regardless of the nature or severity of the offense of which he is suspected or for which he was arrested.

The implication of this holding is that the Court of Appeals was correct in ruling that the statements made by respondent at the County Jail were inadmissible. There can be no question that respondent was "in custody" at least as of the moment he was formally placed under arrest and instructed to get into the police car. Because he was not informed of his constitutional rights at that juncture, respondent's subsequent admissions should not have been used against him.

III

To assess the admissibility of the self-incriminating statements made by respondent prior to his formal arrest, we are obliged to address a second issue concerning the scope of our decision in *Miranda*: whether the roadside questioning of a motorist detained pursuant to a routine traffic stop should be considered "custodial interrogation." Respondent urges that it should, on the ground that *Miranda* by its terms applies whenever "a person has been taken into custody *or otherwise deprived of his freedom of action in any significant way*." 384 U.S. at 444, 86 S. Ct. at 1612 (emphasis added). Petitioner contends that a holding that every detained motorist must be advised of his rights before being questioned would constitute an unwarranted extension of the *Miranda* doctrine.

It must be acknowledged at the outset that a traffic stop significantly curtails the "freedom of action" of the driver and the passengers, if any, of the detained vehicle. Under the law of most States, it is a crime either to ignore a policeman's signal to stop one's car or, once having stopped, to drive away without permission. Certainly few motorists would feel free either to disobey a directive to pull over or to leave the scene of a traffic stop without being told they might do so. Partly for these reasons, we have long acknowledged that "stopping an automobile and detaining its occupants constitute a 'seizure' within the meaning of [the Fourth] Amendmen[t], even though the purpose of the stop is limited and the resulting detention quite brief." *Delaware v. Prouse*, 440 U.S. 648, 653, 99 S. Ct. 1391, 1396, 59 L. Ed. 2d 660 (1979) (citations omitted).

However, we decline to accord talismanic power to the phrase in the *Miranda* opinion emphasized by respondent. Fidelity to the doctrine announced in *Miranda* requires that it be enforced strictly, but only in those types of situations in which the concerns that powered the decision are implicated. Thus, we must decide whether a traffic stop exerts upon a detained person pressures that sufficiently impair his free exercise of his privilege against self-incrimination to require that he be warned of his constitutional rights.

Two features of an ordinary traffic stop mitigate the danger that a person questioned will be induced "to speak where he would not otherwise do so freely," *Miranda v. Arizona*, 384 U.S. at 467, 86 S. Ct. at 1624. First, detention of a motorist pursuant to a traffic stop is presumptively temporary and brief. The vast majority of roadside detentions last only a few minutes. A motorist's expectations, when he sees a policeman's light flashing behind him, are that he will be obliged to spend a short period of time answering questions and waiting while the officer checks his license and registration, that he may then be given a citation, but that in the end he most likely will be allowed to continue on his way. In this respect, questioning incident to an ordinary traffic stop is quite different from stationhouse interrogation, which frequently is prolonged, and in which the detainee often is aware that questioning will continue until he provides his interrogators the answers they seek.[27]

Second, circumstances associated with the typical traffic stop are not such that the motorist feels completely at the mercy of the police. To be sure, the aura of authority surrounding an armed, uniformed officer and the knowledge that the officer has some discretion in deciding whether to issue a citation, in combination, exert some pressure on the detainee to respond to questions. But other aspects of the situation substantially offset these forces. Perhaps most importantly, the typical traffic stop is public, at least to some degree. Passersby, on foot or in other cars, witness the interaction of officer and motorist. This exposure to public view both reduces the ability of an unscrupulous policeman to use illegitimate means to elicit self-incriminating statements and diminishes the motorist's fear that, if he does not cooperate, he will be subjected to abuse. The fact that the detained motorist typically is confronted by only one or at most two policemen further mutes his sense of vulnerability. In short, the atmosphere surrounding an ordinary traffic stop is substantially less "police dominated" than that surrounding the kinds of interrogation at issue in *Miranda* itself, *see* 384 U.S. at 445, 491–498, 86 S. Ct. at 1612, 1636–1640, and in the subsequent cases in which we have applied *Miranda*.[28]

In both of these respects, the usual traffic stop is more analogous to a so-called "*Terry* stop," *see Terry v. Ohio*, 392 U.S. 1, 88 S. Ct. 1868, 20 L. Ed. 2d 889 (1968), than to a formal arrest. Under the Fourth Amendment, we have held, a policeman who lacks probable cause but whose "observations lead him reasonably to suspect" that a

---

27. The brevity and spontaneity of an ordinary traffic stop also reduces the danger that the driver through subterfuge will be made to incriminate himself. One of the investigative techniques that *Miranda* was designed to guard against was the use by police of various kinds of trickery — such as "Mutt and Jeff" routines — to elicit confessions from suspects. A police officer who stops a suspect on the highway has little chance to develop or implement a plan of this sort. *Cf.* LaFave, "*Street Encounters" and the Constitution:* Terry, Sibron, Peters, *and Beyond*, 67 Mich. L. Rev. 39, 99 (1968).

28. *See Orozco v. Texas*, 394 U.S. 324, 325, 89 S. Ct. 1095, 1096, 22 L. Ed. 2d 311 (1969) (suspect arrested and questioned in his bedroom by four police officers); *Mathis v. United States*, 391 U.S. 1, 2–3, 88 S. Ct. 1503, 1503–1504, 20 L. Ed. 2d 381 (1968) (defendant questioned by a government agent while in jail).

particular person has committed, is committing, or is about to commit a crime, may detain that person briefly in order to "investigate the circumstances that provoke suspicion." *United States v. Brignoni-Ponce*, 422 U.S. 873, 881, 95 S. Ct. 2574, 2580, 45 L. Ed. 2d 607 (1975). "[T]he stop and inquiry must be 'reasonably related in scope to the justification for their initiation.'" *Id.* (quoting *Terry v. Ohio, supra*, 392 U.S. at 29, 88 S. Ct. at 1884.) Typically, this means that the officer may ask the detainee a moderate number of questions to determine his identity and to try to obtain information confirming or dispelling the officer's suspicions. But the detainee is not obliged to respond. And, unless the detainee's answers provide the officer with probable cause to arrest him, he must then be released. The comparatively nonthreatening character of detentions of this sort explains the absence of any suggestion in our opinions that *Terry* stops are subject to the dictates of *Miranda*. The similarly noncoercive aspect of ordinary traffic stops prompts us to hold that persons temporarily detained pursuant to such stops are not "in custody" for the purposes of *Miranda*.

Respondent contends that to "exempt" traffic stops from the coverage of *Miranda* will open the way to widespread abuse. Policemen will simply delay formally arresting detained motorists, and will subject them to sustained and intimidating interrogation at the scene of their initial detention. . . .

We are confident that the state of affairs projected by respondent will not come to pass. It is settled that the safeguards prescribed by *Miranda* become applicable as soon as a suspect's freedom of action is curtailed to a "degree associated with formal arrest." *California v. Beheler*, 463 U.S. 1121, 1125, 103 S. Ct. 3517, 3520, 77 L. Ed. 2d 1275 (1983) (*per curiam*). If a motorist who has been detained pursuant to a traffic stop thereafter is subjected to treatment that renders him "in custody" for practical purposes, he will be entitled to the full panoply of protections prescribed by *Miranda*.

Admittedly, our adherence to the doctrine just recounted will mean that the police and lower courts will continue occasionally to have difficulty deciding exactly when a suspect has been taken into custody. Either a rule that *Miranda* applies to all traffic stops or a rule that a suspect need not be advised of his rights until he is formally placed under arrest would provide a clearer, more easily administered line. However, each of these two alternatives has drawbacks that make it unacceptable. The first would substantially impede the enforcement of the Nation's traffic laws — by compelling the police either to take the time to warn all detained motorists of their constitutional rights or to forgo use of self-incriminating statements made by those motorists — while doing little to protect citizens' Fifth Amendment rights. The second would enable the police to circumvent the constraints on custodial interrogations established by *Miranda*.

Turning to the case before us, we find nothing in the record that indicates that respondent should have been given *Miranda* warnings at any point prior to the time Trooper Williams placed him under arrest. For the reasons indicated above, we reject the contention that the initial stop of respondent's car, by itself, rendered him "in custody." And respondent has failed to demonstrate that, at any time between the initial stop and the arrest, he was subjected to restraints comparable to those associated with a formal arrest. Only a short period of time elapsed between the stop and the arrest. At no point during that interval was respondent informed that his detention would not be temporary. Although Trooper Williams apparently decided as soon as respondent stepped out of his car that respondent would be taken into custody and charged with a traffic offense, Williams never communicated his intention to respondent. A policeman's unarticulated plan has no bearing on the question whether a suspect was "in custody" at a particular time; the only relevant inquiry is how a reasonable man in the suspect's position would have understood his situation. Nor do other aspects of the interaction of Williams and respondent support the contention that respondent was exposed to "custodial interrogation" at the scene of the stop. From aught that appears in the stipulation of facts, a single police officer asked respondent a modest number of questions and requested him to perform a simple balancing test at a location visible to passing motorists. Treatment of this sort cannot fairly be characterized as the functional equivalent of formal arrest.

We conclude, in short, that respondent was not taken into custody for the purposes of *Miranda* until Williams arrested him. Consequently, the statements respondent made prior to that point were admissible against him.

. . . .

Affirmed.

[JUSTICE STEVENS's concurring opinion has been omitted.]

Notes and Questions

(1) Is the interrogating officer's suspicion of the individual being questioned relevant to whether that individual is in custody within the meaning of *Berkemer*? In *Stansbury v. California*, 511 U.S. 318, 114 S. Ct. 1526, 128 L. Ed. 2d 293 (1994), police investigating the murder of 10-year-old Robyn Parks picked up Robert Stansbury for questioning because Parks was seen talking to Stansbury and another ice cream truck driver some hours before her disappearance. Initially, the police viewed the other driver as a suspect and Stansbury only as a material witness. They questioned Stansbury without giving him *Miranda* warnings. Stansbury made an incriminating admission and the police then gave him *Miranda* warnings. The lower courts held that *Miranda* warnings were not required prior to Stansbury's incriminating admission because the investigation had not focused on Stansbury until he made the admission. The Supreme Court reversed. In a *per curiam* opinion, the Court stated that "an officer's subjective and undisclosed view concerning whether the person being interrogated is a suspect is irrelevant to the assessment whether the person is in custody." The Court remanded the case to the lower courts for a determination of whether Stansbury's admission was made at a time when he was in custody under the test stated in *Berkemer*.

(2) Does the suspect's presence at the police station while being interrogated by the police tend to show that he is in custody within the meaning of *Berkemer*? In *Oregon v. Mathiason*, 429 U.S. 492, 97 S. Ct. 711, 50 L. Ed. 2d 714 (1977), the Court indicated that when a suspect comes voluntarily to the police station in response to an invitation by the police, he will not necessarily be in custody. In *Mathiason*, a police officer left his card at the defendant's apartment, asking him to call so that they could "discuss something." When the defendant called the officer, they agreed to meet at the state patrol office, which was located a few blocks from the defendant's apartment. When the officer met with the defendant, he told him he was not under arrest. Later, the officer falsely told the suspect his fingerprints had been found at the burglary scene; the defendant then confessed. In a per curiam opinion, the Court held that the defendant was not in custody. For a critical analysis of the *Mathiason* opinion, see Geoffrey Stone, *The Miranda Doctrine in the Burger Court*, 1977 Sup. Ct. Rev. 99, 150–54. In contrast to *Mathiason*, *Dunaway v. New York*, 442 U.S. 200, 99 S. Ct. 2248, 60 L. Ed. 2d 824 (1979), *supra*, and *Hayes v. Florida*, 470 U.S. 811, 105 S. Ct. 1643, 84 L. Ed. 2d 705 (1985), *supra*, suggest that if the suspect is brought to the station by police officers without his consent, he will be in custody within the meaning of *Berkemer*.

(3) The custody standard prescribed by the precedents is clearly objective. The custody determination depends on how a *reasonable* person in the suspect's situation would understand his or her situation. One question is whether specific characteristics of a suspect are ever relevant to determining whether he or she is in custody for purposes of *Miranda*. The Supreme Court addressed that question in the next case.

J. D. B. v. North Carolina

United States Supreme Court

564 U.S. 261, 131 S. Ct. 2394, 180 L. Ed. 2d 310 (2011)

JUSTICE SOTOMAYOR delivered the opinion of the Court.

. . . .

I

A

Petitioner J. D. B. was a 13-year-old, seventh-grade student attending class at Smith Middle School in Chapel Hill, North Carolina when he was removed from his classroom by a uniformed police officer, escorted to a closed-door conference room, and questioned by police for at least half an hour.

This was the second time that police questioned J. D. B. in the span of a week. Five days earlier, two home break-ins occurred, and various items were stolen. Police stopped and questioned J. D. B. after he was seen behind a residence in the neighborhood where the crimes occurred. That same day, police also spoke to J. D. B.'s grandmother — his legal guardian — as well as his aunt.

Police later learned that a digital camera matching the description of one of the stolen items had been found at J. D. B.'s middle school and seen in J. D. B.'s possession.

Investigator DiCostanzo, the juvenile investigator with the local police force who had been assigned to the case, went to the school to question J. D. B. Upon arrival, DiCostanzo informed the uniformed police officer on detail to the school (a so-called school resource officer), the assistant principal, and an administrative intern that he was there to question J. D. B. about the break-ins. Although DiCostanzo asked the school administrators to verify J. D. B.'s date of birth, address, and parent contact information from school records, neither the police officers nor the school administrators contacted J. D. B.'s grandmother.

The uniformed officer interrupted J. D. B.'s afternoon social studies class, removed J. D. B. from the classroom, and escorted him to a school conference room. There, J. D. B. was met by DiCostanzo, the assistant principal, and the administrative intern. The door to the conference room was closed. With the two police officers and the two administrators present, J. D. B. was questioned for the next 30 to 45 minutes. Prior to the commencement of questioning, J. D. B. was given neither *Miranda* warnings nor the opportunity to speak to his grandmother. Nor was he informed that he was free to leave the room.

Questioning began with small talk — discussion of sports and J. D. B.'s family life. DiCostanzo asked, and J. D. B. agreed, to discuss the events of the prior weekend. Denying any wrongdoing, J. D. B. explained that he had been in the neighborhood where the crimes occurred because he was seeking work mowing lawns. DiCostanzo pressed J. D. B. for additional detail about his efforts to obtain work; asked J. D. B. to explain a prior incident, when one of the victims returned home to find J. D. B. behind her house; and confronted J. D. B. with the stolen camera. The assistant principal urged J. D. B. to "do the right thing," warning J. D. B. that "the truth always comes out in the end."

Eventually, J. D. B. asked whether he would "still be in trouble" if he returned the "stuff." In response, DiCostanzo explained that return of the stolen items would be helpful, but "this thing is going to court" regardless. DiCostanzo then warned that he may need to seek a secure custody order if he believed that J. D. B. would continue to break into other homes. When J. D. B. asked what a secure custody order was, DiCostanzo explained that "it's where you get sent to juvenile detention before court."

After learning of the prospect of juvenile detention, J. D. B. confessed that he and a friend were responsible for the break-ins. DiCostanzo only then informed J. D. B. that he could refuse to answer the investigator's questions and that he was free to leave. Asked whether he understood, J. D. B. nodded and provided further detail, including information about the location of the stolen items. Eventually J. D. B. wrote a statement, at DiCostanzo's request. When the bell rang indicating the end of the school day, J. D. B. was allowed to leave to catch the bus home.

B

Two juvenile petitions were filed against J. D. B., each alleging one count of breaking and entering and one count of larceny. J. D. B.'s public defender moved to suppress his statements and the evidence derived therefrom, arguing that suppression was necessary because J. D. B. had been "interrogated by police in a custodial setting without being afforded *Miranda* warning[s]," and because his statements were involuntary under the totality of the circumstances test. After a suppression hearing at which DiCostanzo and J. D. B. testified, the trial court denied the motion, deciding that J. D. B. was not in custody at the time of the schoolhouse interrogation and that his statements were voluntary. As a result, J. D. B. entered a transcript of admission to all four counts, renewing his objection to the denial of his motion to suppress, and the court adjudicated J. D. B. delinquent.

A divided panel of the North Carolina Court of Appeals affirmed. *In re J. D. B.*, 196 N.C. App. 234, 674 S.E.2d 795 (2009). The North Carolina Supreme Court held, over two dissents, that J. D. B. was not in custody when he confessed, "declin[ing] to extend the test for custody to include consideration of the age . . . of an individual subjected to questioning by police." *In re J. D. B.*, 363 N.C. 664, 672, 686 S.E.2d 135, 140 (2009).

We granted certiorari to determine whether the *Miranda* custody analysis includes consideration of a juvenile suspect's age. 562 U.S. 1001, 131 S. Ct. 502, 178 L. Ed. 2d 368 (2010).

II

A

Any police interview of an individual suspected of a crime has "coercive aspects to it." *Oregon v. Mathiason*, 429 U.S. 492, 495, 97 S. Ct. 711, 50 L. Ed. 2d 714 (1977) (*per curiam*). Only those interrogations that occur while a suspect is in police custody, however, "heighte[n] the risk" that statements obtained are not the product of the suspect's free choice. *Dickerson v. United States*, 530 U.S. 428, 435, 120 S. Ct. 2326, 147 L. Ed. 2d 405 (2000).

By its very nature, custodial police interrogation entails "inherently compelling pressures." *Miranda*, 384 U.S., at 467, 86 S. Ct. 1602. Even for an adult, the physical and psychological isolation of custodial interrogation can "undermine the individual's will to resist and . . . compel him to speak where he would not otherwise do so freely." *Ibid.* Indeed, the pressure of custodial interrogation is so immense that it "can induce a frighteningly high percentage of people to confess to crimes they never committed." *Corley v. United States*, 556 U.S. 303, 321, 129 S. Ct. 1558, 1570, 173 L. Ed. 2d 443 (2009) (citing Drizin & Leo, The Problem of False Confessions in the Post — DNA World, 82 N. C. L. Rev. 891, 906–907 (2004)); see also *Miranda*, 384 U.S., at 455, n. 23, 86 S. Ct. 1602. That risk is all the more troubling — and recent studies suggest, all the more acute — when the subject of custodial interrogation is a juvenile.

Recognizing that the inherently coercive nature of custodial interrogation "blurs the line between voluntary and involuntary statements," *Dickerson*, 530 U.S., at 435, 120 S. Ct. 2326, this Court in *Miranda* adopted a set of prophylactic measures designed to safeguard the constitutional guarantee against self-incrimination.

[A suspect "'must be warned'" of his rights and the Government must "show" that he "waived his rights."] ...

Because these measures protect the individual against the coercive nature of custodial interrogation, they are required "'only where there has been such a restriction on a person's freedom as to render him "in custody."'" *Stansbury v. California*, 511 U.S. 318, 322, 114 S. Ct. 1526, 128 L. Ed. 2d 293 (1994) (*per curiam*) (quoting *Oregon v. Mathiason*, 429 U.S. 492, 495, 97 S. Ct. 711, 50 L. Ed. 2d 714 (1977) (*per curiam*)). As we have repeatedly emphasized, whether a suspect is "in custody" is an objective inquiry.

> "Two discrete inquiries are essential to the determination: first, what were the circumstances surrounding the interrogation; and second, given those circumstances, would a reasonable person have felt he or she was at liberty to terminate the interrogation and leave. Once the scene is set and the players' lines and actions are reconstructed, the court must apply an objective test to resolve the ultimate inquiry: was there a formal arrest or restraint on freedom of movement of the degree associated with formal arrest." *Thompson v. Keohane*, 516 U.S. 99, 112, 116 S. Ct. 457, 133 L. Ed. 2d 383 (1995) (internal quotation marks, alteration, and footnote omitted).

See also *Yarborough v. Alvarado*, 541 U.S. 652, 662–663, 124 S. Ct. 2140, 158 L. Ed. 2d 938 (2004); *Stansbury*, 511 U.S., at 323, 114 S. Ct. 1526; *Berkemer v. McCarty*, 468 U.S. 420, 442, and n. 35, 104 S. Ct. 3138, 82 L. Ed. 2d 317 (1984). Rather than demarcate a limited set of relevant circumstances, we have required police officers and courts to "examine all of the circumstances surrounding the interrogation," *Stansbury*, 511 U.S., at 322, 114 S. Ct. 1526, including any circumstance that "would have affected how a reasonable person" in the suspect's position "would perceive his or her freedom to leave," *id.*, at 325, 114 S. Ct. 1526. On the other hand, the "subjective views harbored by either the interrogating officers or the person being questioned" are irrelevant. *Id.*, at 323, 114 S. Ct. 1526. The test, in other words, involves no consideration of the "actual mindset" of the particular suspect subjected to police questioning. *Alvarado*, 541 U.S., at 667, 124 S. Ct. 2140; see also *California v. Beheler*, 463 U.S. 1121, 1125, n. 3, 103 S. Ct. 3517, 77 L. Ed. 2d 1275 (1983) (*per curiam*).

The benefit of the objective custody analysis is that it is "designed to give clear guidance to the police." *Alvarado*, 541 U.S., at 668, 124 S. Ct. 2140. Police must make in-the-moment judgments as to when to administer *Miranda* warnings. ... [T]he objective test avoids burdening police with the task of anticipating the idiosyncrasies of every individual suspect and divining how those particular traits affect each person's subjective state of mind.

B

The State and its *amici* contend that a child's age has no place in the custody analysis, no matter how young the child subjected to police questioning. We cannot agree. In some circumstances, a child's age "would have affected how a reasonable person" in the suspect's position "would perceive his or her freedom to leave." *Stansbury*, 511 U.S., at 325, 114 S. Ct. 1526. That is, a reasonable child subjected to police questioning will sometimes feel pressured to submit when a reasonable adult would feel free to go. We think it clear that courts can account for that reality without doing any damage to the objective nature of the custody analysis.

A child's age is far "more than a chronological fact." *Eddings v. Oklahoma*, 455 U.S. 104, 115, 102 S. Ct. 869, 71 L. Ed. 2d 1 (1982). It is a fact that "generates commonsense conclusions about behavior and perception." *Alvarado*, 541 U.S., at 674, 124 S. Ct. 2140 (Breyer, J., dissenting). Such conclusions apply broadly to children as a class. And, they are self-evident to anyone who was a child once himself, including any police officer or judge.

Time and again, this Court has drawn these commonsense conclusions for itself. We have observed that children "generally are less mature and responsible than adults," *Eddings*, 455 U.S., at 115–116, 102 S. Ct. 869; that they "often lack the experience, perspective, and judgment to recognize and avoid choices that could be detrimental to them," *Bellotti v. Baird*, 443 U.S. 622, 635, 99 S. Ct. 3035, 61 L. Ed. 2d 797 (1979) (plurality opinion); that they "are more vulnerable or susceptible to . . . outside pressures" than adults, *Roper* [*v. Simmons*], 543 U.S. [551,] 569, 125 S. Ct. 1183 [(2005)]; and so on. Addressing the specific context of police interrogation, we have observed that events that "would leave a man cold and unimpressed can overawe and overwhelm a lad in his early teens." *Haley v. Ohio*, 332 U.S. 596, 599, 68 S. Ct. 302, 92 L. Ed. 224 (1948) (plurality opinion). Describing no one child in particular, these observations restate what "any parent knows" — indeed, what any person knows — about children generally. *Roper*, 543 U.S., at 569, 125 S. Ct. 1183.[5]

. . . The law has historically reflected the . . . assumption that children characteristically lack the capacity to exercise mature judgment and possess only an incomplete ability to understand the world around them. Like this Court's own generalizations, the legal disqualifications placed on children as a class — *e.g.*, limitations on their ability to alienate property, enter a binding contract enforceable against them, and marry without parental consent — exhibit the settled understanding that the differentiating characteristics of youth are universal.

Indeed, even where a "reasonable person" standard otherwise applies, the common law has reflected the reality that children are not adults. In negligence suits, for instance, where liability turns on what an objectively reasonable person would do in the circumstances, "[a]ll American jurisdictions accept the idea that a person's childhood is a relevant circumstance" to be considered. Restatement (Third) of Torts § 10, Comment *b*, p. 117 (2005).

---

5. Although citation to social science and cognitive science authorities is unnecessary to establish these commonsense propositions, the literature confirms what experience bears out. See, *e.g.*, *Graham v. Florida*, 560 U.S. 48, 68, 130 S. Ct. 2011, 2026, 176 L. Ed. 2d 825 (2010) ("[D]evelopments in psychology and brain science continue to show fundamental differences between juvenile and adult minds[.]").

As this discussion establishes, "[o]ur history is replete with laws and judicial recognition" that children cannot be viewed simply as miniature adults. *Eddings*, 455 U.S., at 115–116, 102 S. Ct. 869. We see no justification for taking a different course here. So long as the child's age was known to the officer at the time of the interview, or would have been objectively apparent to any reasonable officer, including age as part of the custody analysis requires officers neither to consider circumstances "unknowable" to them, *Berkemer*, 468 U.S., at 430, 104 S. Ct. 3138, nor to "anticipat[e] the frailties or idiosyncrasies" of the particular suspect whom they question, *Alvarado*, 541 U.S., at 662, 124 S. Ct. 2140 (internal quotation marks omitted). The same "wide basis of community experience" that makes it possible, as an objective matter, "to determine what is to be expected" of children in other contexts, Restatement (Second) of Torts § 283A, at 15, likewise makes it possible to know what to expect of children subjected to police questioning.

In other words, a child's age differs from other personal characteristics that, even when known to police, have no objectively discernible relationship to a reasonable person's understanding of his freedom of action. *Alvarado*, holds, for instance, that a suspect's prior interrogation history with law enforcement has no role to play in the custody analysis because such experience could just as easily lead a reasonable person to feel free to walk away as to feel compelled to stay in place. 541 U.S., at 668, 124 S. Ct. 2140. Because the effect in any given case would be "contingent [on the] psycholog[y]" of the individual suspect, the Court explained, such experience cannot be considered without compromising the objective nature of the custody analysis. *Ibid.* A child's age, however, is different. Precisely because childhood yields objective conclusions like those we have drawn ourselves — among others, that children are "most susceptible to influence," *Eddings*, 455 U.S., at 115, 102 S. Ct. 869, and "outside pressures," *Roper*, 543 U.S., at 569, 125 S. Ct. 1183 — considering age in the custody analysis in no way involves a determination of how youth "subjectively affect[s] the mindset" of any particular child, Brief for Respondent 14.[7]

In fact, in many cases involving juvenile suspects, the custody analysis would be nonsensical absent some consideration of the suspect's age. This case is a prime example. Were the court precluded from taking J. D. B.'s youth into account, it would be forced to evaluate the circumstances present here through the eyes of a reasonable person of average years. In other words, how would a reasonable adult understand his situation, after being removed from a seventh-grade social studies class by a uniformed school resource officer; being encouraged by his assistant principal to "do the right thing"; and being warned by a police investigator of the prospect of juvenile detention and separation from his guardian and primary caretaker? To describe such an inquiry is to demonstrate its absurdity. Neither officers nor courts can

---

7. Thus, contrary to the dissent's protestations, today's holding neither invites consideration of whether a particular suspect is "unusually meek or compliant," *post*, at 2413 (opinion of ALITO, J.), nor "expan[ds]" the *Miranda* custody analysis, *post*, at 2412–2413, into a test that requires officers to anticipate and account for a suspect's every personal characteristic, see *post*, at 2414–2415.

reasonably evaluate the effect of objective circumstances that, by their nature, are specific to children without accounting for the age of the child subjected to those circumstances.

. . . [T]he effect of the schoolhouse setting cannot be disentangled from the identity of the person questioned. . . . Without asking whether the person "questioned in school" is a "minor," [*post* at 2417 (opinion of ALITO, J.)], the coercive effect of the schoolhouse setting is unknowable.

. . . .

. . . [W]e hold that so long as the child's age was known to the officer at the time of police questioning, or would have been objectively apparent to a reasonable officer, its inclusion in the custody analysis is consistent with the objective nature of that test.[8] This is not to say that a child's age will be a determinative, or even a significant, factor in every case. Cf. [*Alvarado*, 541 U.S., at 669, 124 S. Ct. 2140] (O'Connor, J., concurring) (explaining that a state-court decision omitting any mention of the defendant's age was not unreasonable under AEDPA's deferential standard of review where the defendant "was almost 18 years old at the time of his interview"); *post*, at 2417 (suggesting that "teenagers nearing the age of majority" are likely to react to an interrogation as would a "typical 18-year-old in similar circumstances"). It is, however, a reality that courts cannot simply ignore.

III

The State and its *amici* offer numerous reasons that courts must blind themselves to a juvenile defendant's age. None is persuasive.

. . . .

The State . . . argues that age is irrelevant to the custody analysis because it "go[es] to how a suspect may internalize and perceive the circumstances of an interrogation." Brief for Respondent 12. But the same can be said of every objective circumstance that the State agrees is relevant to the custody analysis: Each circumstance goes to how a reasonable person would "internalize and perceive" every other. See, e.g., *Stansbury*, 511 U.S., at 325, 114 S. Ct. 1526. Indeed, this is the very reason that we ask whether the objective circumstances "add up to custody," *Keohane*, 516 U.S., at 113, 116 S. Ct. 457, instead of evaluating the circumstances one by one.

---

8. This approach does not undermine the basic principle that an interrogating officer's unarticulated, internal thoughts are never — in and of themselves — objective circumstances of an interrogation. See *supra*, at 2402; *Stansbury v. California*, 511 U.S. 318, 323, 114 S. Ct. 1526, 128 L. Ed. 2d 293 (1994) (*per curiam*). Unlike a child's youth, an officer's purely internal thoughts have no conceivable effect on how a reasonable person in the suspect's position would understand his freedom of action. See *id.*, at 323–325, 114 S. Ct. 1526; *Berkemer v. McCarty*, 468 U.S. 420, 442, 104 S. Ct. 3138, 82 L. Ed. 2d 317 (1984). Rather than "overtur[n]" that settled principle, *post*, at 2415, the limitation that a child's age may inform the custody analysis only when known or knowable simply reflects our unwillingness to require officers to "make guesses" as to circumstances "unknowable" to them in deciding when to give *Miranda* warnings, *Berkemer*, 468 U.S., at 430–431, 104 S. Ct. 3138.

In the same vein, the State and its *amici* protest that the "effect of . . . age on [the] perception of custody is internal," Brief for Respondent 20, or "psychological," [Brief for United States as *Amicus Curiae* 21 (hereinafter U.S. Brief)]. But the whole point of the custody analysis is to determine whether, given the circumstances, "a reasonable person [would] have felt he or she was . . . at liberty to terminate the interrogation and leave." *Keohane*, 516 U.S., at 112, 116 S. Ct. 457. Because the *Miranda* custody inquiry turns on the mindset of a reasonable person in the suspect's position, it cannot be the case that a circumstance is subjective simply because it has an "internal" or "psychological" impact on perception. Were that so, there would be no objective circumstances to consider at all.

. . . [T]he State next argues that a child's age must be excluded from the analysis in order to preserve clarity. Similarly, the dissent insists that the clarity of the custody analysis will be destroyed unless a "one-size-fits-all reasonable-person test" applies. *Post*, at 2415. In reality, however, ignoring a juvenile defendant's age will often make the inquiry more artificial, and thus only add confusion. And in any event, a child's age, when known or apparent, is hardly an obscure factor to assess. Though the State and the dissent worry about gradations among children of different ages, that concern cannot justify ignoring a child's age altogether. Just as police officers are competent to account for other objective circumstances that are a matter of degree such as the length of questioning or the number of officers present, so too are they competent to evaluate the effect of relative age. . . . The same is true of judges, including those whose childhoods have long since passed. In short, officers and judges need no imaginative powers, knowledge of developmental psychology, training in cognitive science, or expertise in social and cultural anthropology to account for a child's age. They simply need the common sense to know that a 7-year-old is not a 13-year-old and neither is an adult.

There is, however, an even more fundamental flaw with the State's plea for clarity and the dissent's singular focus on simplifying the analysis: Not once have we excluded from the custody analysis a circumstance that we determined was relevant and objective, simply to make the fault line between custodial and noncustodial "brighter." Indeed, were the guiding concern clarity and nothing else, the custody test would presumably ask only whether the suspect had been placed under formal arrest. *Berkemer*, 468 U.S., at 441, 104 S. Ct. 3138; see *ibid.* (acknowledging the "occasiona[l] . . . difficulty" police officers confront in determining when a suspect has been taken into custody). But we have rejected that "more easily administered line," recognizing that it would simply "enable the police to circumvent the constraints on custodial interrogations established by *Miranda*." *Ibid.*; see also *ibid.*, n. 33.

Finally, the State and the dissent suggest that excluding age from the custody analysis comes at no cost to juveniles' constitutional rights because the due process voluntariness test independently accounts for a child's youth. To be sure, that test permits consideration of a child's age, and it erects its own barrier to admission of a defendant's inculpatory statements at trial. But *Miranda*'s procedural safeguards exist precisely because the voluntariness test is an inadequate barrier when custodial interrogation is at stake. To hold, as the State requests, that a child's age is never rel-evant to whether a suspect has been taken into custody — and thus to ignore the very real differences between children and adults — would be to deny children the full scope of the procedural safeguards that *Miranda* guarantees to adults.

The question remains whether J. D. B. was in custody when police interrogated him. We remand for the state courts to address that question, this time taking ac-count of all of the relevant circumstances of the interrogation, including J. D. B.'s age at the time. The judgment of the North Carolina Supreme Court is reversed, and the case is remanded for proceedings not inconsistent with this opinion.

It is so ordered.

JUSTICE ALITO, with whom THE CHIEF JUSTICE, JUSTICE SCALIA, and JUSTICE THOMAS join, dissenting.

The Court's decision in this case . . . is fundamentally inconsistent with one of the main justifications for the *Miranda* rule: the perceived need for a clear rule that can be easily applied in all cases. And today's holding is not needed to protect the consti-tutional rights of minors who are questioned by the police.

Miranda's prophylactic regime places a high value on clarity and certainty. Dis-satisfied with the highly fact-specific constitutional rule against the admission of in-voluntary confessions, the *Miranda* Court set down rigid standards that often require courts to ignore personal characteristics that may be highly relevant to a par-ticular suspect's actual susceptibility to police pressure. This rigidity, however, has brought with it one of *Miranda*'s principal strengths — "the ease and clarity of its application" by law enforcement officials and courts. See *Moran v. Burbine*, 475 U.S. 412, 425–426, 106 S. Ct. 1135, 89 L. Ed. 2d 410 (1986). A key contributor to this clarity, at least up until now, has been *Miranda*'s objective reasonable-person test for determining custody.

Miranda's custody requirement is based on the proposition that the risk of uncon-stitutional coercion is heightened when a suspect is placed under formal arrest or is subjected to some functionally equivalent limitation on freedom of movement. . . . [I]n the interest of simplicity, the custody analysis considers only whether, under the circumstances, a hypothetical reasonable person would consider himself to be con-fined.

Many suspects, of course, will differ from this hypothetical reasonable person. Some, including those who have been hardened by past interrogations, may have no need for *Miranda* warnings at all. And for other suspects — those who are unusually sensitive to the pressures of police questioning — *Miranda* warnings may come too late to be of any use. That is a necessary consequence of *Miranda*'s rigid standards, but it does not mean that the constitutional rights of these especially sensitive suspects are left unprotected. A vulnerable defendant can still turn to the constitutional rule against *actual* coercion and contend that his confession was extracted against his will.

Today's decision shifts the *Miranda* custody determination from a one-size-fits-all reasonable-person test into an inquiry that must account for at least one individualized characteristic — age — that is thought to correlate with susceptibility to coercive pressures. Age, however, is in no way the only personal characteristic that may correlate with pliability, and in future cases the Court will be forced to choose between two unpalatable alternatives. It may choose to limit today's decision by arbitrarily distinguishing a suspect's age from other personal characteristics — such as intelligence, education, occupation, or prior experience with law enforcement — that may also correlate with susceptibility to coercive pressures. Or, if the Court is unwilling to draw these arbitrary lines, it will be forced to effect a fundamental transformation of the *Miranda* custody test — from a clear, easily applied prophylactic rule into a highly fact-intensive standard resembling the voluntariness test that the *Miranda* Court found to be unsatisfactory.

. . . .

Safeguarding the constitutional rights of minors does not require the extreme makeover of *Miranda* that today's decision may portend.

I

. . . .

No less than other facets of *Miranda*, the threshold requirement that the suspect be in "custody" is "designed to give clear guidance to the police." *Yarborough v. Alvarado*, 541 U.S. 652, 668, 669, 124 S. Ct. 2140, 158 L. Ed. 2d 938 (2004). Custody under *Miranda* attaches where there is a "formal arrest" or a "restraint on freedom of movement" akin to formal arrest. *California v. Beheler*, 463 U.S. 1121, 1125, 103 S. Ct. 3517, 77 L. Ed. 2d 1275 (1983) (*per curiam*) (internal quotation marks omitted). This standard is "objective" and turns on how a hypothetical "reasonable person in the position of the individual being questioned would gauge the breadth of his or her freedom of action." *Stansbury v. California*, 511 U.S. 318, 322–323, 325, 114 S. Ct. 1526, 128 L. Ed. 2d 293 (1994) (*per curiam*) (internal quotation marks omitted).

Until today, the Court's cases applying this test have focused solely on the "objective circumstances of the interrogation," *id.*, at 323, 114 S. Ct. 1526, not the personal characteristics of the interrogated. *E.g., Berkemer, supra*, at 442, and n. 35, 104 S. Ct. 3138. Relevant factors have included such things as where the questioning occurred, how long it lasted, what was said, any physical restraints placed on the suspect's movement, and whether the suspect was allowed to leave when the questioning was through. The totality of *these* circumstances — the external circumstances, that is, of the interrogation itself — is what has mattered in this Court's cases. Personal characteristics of suspects have consistently been rejected or ignored as irrelevant under a one-size-fits-all reasonable-person standard.

. . . .

II

In light of this established practice, there is no denying that, by incorporating age into its analysis, the Court is embarking on a new expansion of the established custody standard. And since *Miranda* is this Court's rule, "not a constitutional command," it is up to the Court "to justify its expansion." Cf. *Arizona v. Roberson*, 486 U.S. 675, 688, 108 S. Ct. 2093, 100 L. Ed. 2d 704 (1988) (Kennedy, J., dissenting). This the Court fails to do.

In its present form, *Miranda*'s prophylactic regime already imposes "high cost[s]" by requiring suppression of confessions that are often "highly probative" and "voluntary" by any traditional standard. *Oregon v. Elstad*, 470 U.S. 298, 312, 105 S. Ct. 1285, 84 L. Ed. 2d 222 (1985). Nonetheless, a "core virtue" of *Miranda* has been the clarity and precision of its guidance to "police and courts." *Withrow v. Williams*, 507 U.S. 680, 694, 113 S. Ct. 1745, 123 L. Ed. 2d 407 (1993) (internal quotation marks omitted). This increased clarity "has been thought to outweigh the burdens" that *Miranda* imposes. *Fare [v. Michael C.]*, 442 U.S. [707,] 718, 99 S. Ct. 2560 [(1979)]. The Court has, however, repeatedly cautioned against upsetting the careful "balance" that *Miranda* struck, *Moran, supra*, at 424, 106 S. Ct. 1135, and it has "refused to sanction attempts to expand [the] *Miranda* holding" in ways that would reduce its "clarity." See [*New York v.*] *Quarles*, 467 U.S. [649,] 658, 104 S. Ct. 2626 [(1984)] (citing cases). Given this practice, there should be a "strong presumption" against the Court's new departure from the established custody test. In my judgment, that presumption cannot be overcome here.

A

. . . I do not dispute that many suspects who are under 18 will be more susceptible to police pressure than the average adult. . . . It is no less a "reality," however, that many persons *over* the age of 18 are also more susceptible to police pressure than the hypothetical reasonable person. Yet the *Miranda* custody standard has never accounted for the personal characteristics of these or any other individual defendants.

Indeed, it has always been the case under *Miranda* that the unusually meek or compliant are subject to the same fixed rules, including the same custody requirement, as those who are unusually resistant to police pressure. *Miranda*'s rigid standards are both overinclusive and underinclusive. They are overinclusive to the extent that they provide a windfall to the most hardened and savvy of suspects, who often have no need for *Miranda*'s protections. And *Miranda*'s requirements are underinclusive to the extent that they fail to account for "frailties," "idiosyncrasies," and other individualized considerations that might cause a person to bend more easily during a confrontation with the police. See *Alvarado*, 541 U.S., at 662, 124 S. Ct. 2140 (internal quotation marks omitted). Members of this Court have seen this rigidity as a major weakness in *Miranda*'s "code of rules for confessions." See 384 U.S., at 504, 86 S. Ct. 1602 (Harlan, J., dissenting). But if it is, then the weakness is an inescapable consequence of the *Miranda* Court's decision to supplement the more holistic voluntariness requirement with a one-size-fits-all prophylactic rule.

That is undoubtedly why this Court's *Miranda* cases have never before mentioned "the suspect's age" or any other individualized consideration in applying the custody standard. See *Alvarado, supra*, at 666, 124 S. Ct. 2140. And unless the *Miranda* custody rule is now to be radically transformed into one that takes into account the wide range of individual characteristics that are relevant in determining whether a confession is voluntary, the Court must shoulder the burden of explaining why age is different from these other personal characteristics.

Why, for example, is age different from intelligence? Suppose that an officer, upon going to a school to question a student, is told by the principal that the student has an I.Q. of 75 and is in a special-education class. Are those facts more or less important than the student's age in determining whether he or she "felt . . . at liberty to terminate the interrogation and leave"? See *Thompson v. Keohane*, 516 U.S. 99, 112, 116 S. Ct. 457, 133 L. Ed. 2d 383 (1995). An I.Q. score, like age, is more than just a number. *Ante*, at 2403 ("[A]ge is far 'more than a chronological fact'"). And an individual's intelligence can also yield "conclusions" similar to those "we have drawn ourselves" in cases far afield of *Miranda*. *Ante*, at 2404–2405.

How about the suspect's cultural background? Suppose the police learn (or should have learned, see *ante*, at 2404) that a suspect they wish to question is a recent immigrant from a country in which dire consequences often befall any person who dares to attempt to cut short any meeting with the police. Is this really less relevant than the fact that a suspect is a month or so away from his 18th birthday?

The defendant's education is another personal characteristic that may generate "conclusions about behavior and perception." *Ante*, at 2403 (internal quotation marks omitted). Under today's decision, why should police officers and courts "blind themselves," *ante*, at 2399, to the fact that a suspect has "only a fifth grade education"? Alternatively, what if the police know or should know that the suspect is "a college-educated man with law school training"? See *Crooker v. California*, 357 U.S. 433, 440, 78 S. Ct. 1287, 2 L. Ed. 2d 1448 (1958), overruled by *Miranda, supra*, at 479, and n. 48, 86 S. Ct. 1602. How are these individual considerations meaningfully different from age in their "relationship to a reasonable person's understanding of his freedom of action"? *Ante*, at 2404. The Court proclaims that "[a] child's age . . . is different," *ante*, at 2404, but the basis for this *ipse dixit* is dubious.

I have little doubt that today's decision will soon be cited by defendants — and perhaps by prosecutors as well — for the proposition that all manner of other individual characteristics should be treated like age and taken into account in the *Miranda* custody calculus. . . .

In time, the Court will have to confront these issues, and it will be faced with a difficult choice. It may choose to distinguish today's decision and adhere to the arbitrary proclamation that "age . . . is different." *Ante*, at 2404. Or it may choose to extend today's holding and, in doing so, further undermine the very rationale for the *Miranda* regime.

B

If the Court chooses the latter course, then a core virtue of *Miranda* — the "ease and clarity of its application" — will be lost. *Moran*, 475 U.S., at 425, 106 S. Ct. 1135. However, even today's more limited departure from *Miranda*'s one-size-fits-all reasonable-person test will produce the very consequences that prompted the *Miranda* Court to abandon exclusive reliance on the voluntariness test in the first place: The Court's test will be hard for the police to follow, and it will be hard for judges to apply.

The Court holds that age must be taken into account when it "was known to the officer at the time of the interview," or when it "would have been objectively apparent" to a reasonable officer. . . . In many cases, courts will presumably have to make findings as to whether a particular suspect had a sufficiently youthful look to alert a reasonable officer to the possibility that the suspect was under 18, or whether a reasonable officer would have recognized that a suspect's I.D. was a fake. The inquiry will be both "time-consuming and disruptive" for the police and the courts. See *Berkemer*, 468 U.S., at 432, 104 S. Ct. 3138 (refusing to modify the custody test based on similar considerations). It will also be made all the more complicated by the fact that a suspect's dress and manner will often be different when the issue is litigated in court than it was at the time of the interrogation.

Even after courts clear this initial hurdle, further problems will likely emerge as judges attempt to put themselves in the shoes of the average 16-year-old, or 15-year-old, or 13-year-old, as the case may be. Consider, for example, a 60-year-old judge attempting to make a custody determination through the eyes of a hypothetical, average 15-year-old. Forty-five years of personal experience and societal change separate this judge from the days when he or she was 15 years old. And this judge may or may not have been an average 15-year-old. . . .

Take a fairly typical case in which today's holding may make a difference. A 16½-year-old moves to suppress incriminating statements made prior to the administration of *Miranda* warnings. . . . [T]he judge will be required to determine whether the differences between a typical 16½-year-old and a typical 18-year-old with respect to susceptibility to the pressures of interrogation are sufficient to change the outcome of the custody determination. Today's opinion contains not a word of actual guidance as to how judges are supposed to go about making that determination.

C

Petitioner and the Court attempt to show that this task is not unmanageable by pointing out that age is taken into account in other legal contexts. . . . [N]egligence is generally a question for the jury, the members of which can draw on their varied experiences with persons of different ages. It also involves a *post hoc* determination, in the reflective atmosphere of a deliberation room, about whether the defendant conformed to a standard of care. The *Miranda* custody determination, by contrast, must be made in the first instance by police officers in the course of an investigation that may require quick decisionmaking.

Equally inapposite are the Eighth Amendment [cruel and unusual punishment] cases the Court cites in support of its new rule. Those decisions involve the "judicial exercise of independent judgment" about the constitutionality of certain punishments. *E.g.*, [*Graham v. Florida*, 560 U.S.], at 67, 130 S. Ct., at 2026. Like the negligence standard, they do not require on-the-spot judgments by the police.

. . . .

III

. . . [T]here are other, less disruptive tools available to ensure that minors are not coerced into confessing.

As an initial matter, the difficulties that the Court's standard introduces will likely yield little added protection for most juvenile defendants. Most juveniles who are subjected to police interrogation are teenagers nearing the age of majority. These defendants' reactions to police pressure are unlikely to be much different from the reaction of a typical 18-year-old in similar circumstances. A one-size-fits-all *Miranda* custody rule thus provides a roughly reasonable fit for these defendants.

In addition, many of the concerns that petitioner raises regarding the application of the *Miranda* custody rule to minors can be accommodated by considering the unique circumstances present when minors are questioned in school. The *Miranda* custody rule has always taken into account the setting in which questioning occurs, restrictions on a suspect's freedom of movement, and the presence of police officers or other authority figures. . . .[12]

Finally, in cases like the one now before us, where the suspect is much younger than the typical juvenile defendant, courts should be instructed to take particular care to ensure that incriminating statements were not obtained involuntarily. . . . If *Miranda*'s rigid, one-size-fits-all standards fail to account for the unique needs of juveniles, the response should be to rigorously apply the constitutional rule against coercion to ensure that the rights of minors are protected. There is no need to run *Miranda* off the rails.

The Court rests its decision to inject personal characteristics into the *Miranda* custody inquiry on the principle that judges applying *Miranda* cannot "blind themselves to . . . commonsense reality." But the Court's shift is fundamentally at odds with the clear prophylactic rules that *Miranda* has long enforced. *Miranda* frequently requires judges to blind themselves to the reality that many un-*Mirandized* custodial confessions are "by no means involuntary" or coerced. *Dickerson*, 530 U.S., at 444, 120 S. Ct. 2326. It also requires police to provide a rote recitation of *Miranda* warnings that many suspects already know and could likely recite from memory. Under today's new, "reality"-based approach to the doctrine, per-

---

12. The Court thinks it would be "absur[d]" to consider the school setting without accounting for age, *ante*, at 2406–2407, but the real absurdity is for the Court to require police officers to get inside the head of a reasonable minor while making the quick, on-the-spot determinations that *Miranda* demands.

haps these and other principles of our *Miranda* jurisprudence will, like the custody standard, now be ripe for modification. Then, bit by bit, *Miranda* will lose the clarity and ease of application that has long been viewed as one of its chief justifications.

I respectfully dissent.

Notes and Questions

(1) According to *Berkemer v. McCarty* and *J. D. B. v. North Carolina*, when is an officer's restraint on a suspect's freedom sufficient to constitute custody? Is it sufficient that a reasonable person in the suspect's position would not feel free to terminate the interrogation and leave? Should that be the standard that determines whether *Miranda*'s protective safeguards apply? Is the *J. D. B.* majority's conclusion that age is relevant to custody determinations consistent with the Court's prescription of an "objective" standard and *Miranda*'s goal of providing clear guidance for law enforcement officers and courts?

(2) Prior to *J. D. B.*, in *Yarborough v. Alvarado*, 541 U.S. 652, 124 S. Ct. 2140, 158 L. Ed. 2d 938 (2004), the Justices had discussed, but had not resolved, the issue of whether age should factor into custody assessments. In *Alvarado*, the Court did speak definitively about the relevance of "prior history with law enforcement" — more specifically, a suspect's lack of experience with the police and with interrogation — declaring it to be entirely irrelevant. In the first place, "police officers will not [usually] know a suspect's interrogation history." Moreover, the effect of "a suspect's past experiences" upon a reasonable person's feelings of restraint upon their freedom would "be speculative." According to the Court, police officers are not required to take into account such "contingent psychological factors" when deciding whether to advise suspects of their rights because those factors would make the "inquiry turn[] too much on the suspect's subjective state of mind and not enough on" objective criteria. In light of the conclusion that age matters, but lack of experience with law enforcement does not, what other individual characteristics should be taken into account in determining whether a particular suspect is in custody? Is gender a relevant consideration? In dissent, Justice Alito suggests that intelligence, cultural background, and education might affect suspects in ways similar to age. Should those personal characteristics count in the objective custody inquiry?

(3) PRISON INMATES AND CUSTODY: *Maryland v. Shatzer*, 559 U.S. 98, 130 S. Ct. 1213, 175 L. Ed. 2d 1045 (2010), indicated that an inmate is not in custody, for *Miranda* purposes, simply by virtue of his confinement in prison. (See subsection [E], *infra*.) The *Shatzer* Court, however, did not provide insights into when a prisoner is in custody. In *Howes v. Fields*, 565 U.S. ____, 132 S. Ct. 1181, 182 L. Ed. 2d 17 (2012), the Justices did address that issue.

While Fields was serving a jail sentence, a corrections officer escorted him "to a conference room where two sheriff's deputies questioned him about allegations" of "sexual conduct with a 12-year-old boy" prior to his confinement. The deputies did not recite *Miranda* warnings prior to the interrogation. After hours of questioning, Fields confessed. The Sixth Circuit affirmed a grant of habeas corpus relief, holding that an interrogation is *per se* custodial when an inmate is isolated "from the general prison population" and "question[ed] about conduct occurring outside the prison." A six-Justice majority deemed this "categorical rule ... simply wrong," declaring that the combination of "imprisonment, ... questioning in private, and ... questioning about events in the outside world ... [is] not necessarily enough to create a custodial situation."

According to the majority, to decide "whether a person is in custody ... , the initial step is to ascertain whether ... 'a reasonable person [would] have felt he or she was not at liberty to terminate the interrogation and leave.'" Because "[n]ot all restraints on freedom of movement amount to custody," however, a court must also determine "whether the relevant environment presents the same inherently coercive pressures as the type of station house questioning at issue in *Miranda*." The Court cited three reasons why "imprisonment alone is not enough to create a custodial situation." In the first place, "questioning a person ... serving a prison term does not generally involve the shock that very often accompanies arrest." The arrest of a person who is in his home or on the street "represents a sharp and ominous change, and the shock may give rise to coercive pressures," but the questioning of someone accustomed to "the ordinary restrictions of prison life" ordinarily does not involve "such change." In addition, "a prisoner ... is unlikely to be lured into speaking by a longing for prompt release" because he "knows that ... he will remain under confinement." Finally, a prisoner knows that the questioning officers "probably lack the authority to affect the duration of his sentence" and, thus, is not likely to fear reprisal or hope for leniency. "In short, standard conditions of confinement and associated restrictions on freedom will not necessarily implicate the same interests" protected by the "special safeguards" *Miranda* affords those "subjected to custodial interrogation."

When the "elements" of "questioning in private and questioning about events ... outside the prison" are added, the constraints on a prisoner are still "insufficient" to constitute custody. Escorting a prisoner to a private place for questioning "does not generally remove the prisoner from a supportive atmosphere." In fact, "[i]solation from the general prison population is often in the best interest of the interviewee and ... does not suggest on its own [an] atmosphere of coercion." The additional restrictions on "freedom of movement" that may be involved are "ordinary and familiar" to an inmate. Moreover, the fact that questioning concerns "criminal activity outside the prison" does not entail "a significantly greater potential for coercion." The location of the suspected conduct "neither mitigate[s] nor magnifie[s]" the peril to Fifth Amendment rights.

The majority instructed that a determination of whether a prisoner is in custody "should focus on all of the features of the interrogation," including "the language ... used" to summon the prisoner "and the manner" of conducting the interrogation. In *Fields*, a custody finding was unjustified. Some factors did support that conclusion — the defendant had not invited or consented to the interview; he was not advised the he was free to decline the interview; the interview lasted five-to-seven hours in the evening and "continued well past" the defendant's usual bedtime; the questioning deputies were armed; and one deputy "'[u]sed a very sharp tone,' and" once used "profanity." Offsetting these factors was the "important" fact that the defendant was "told at the outset," and "reminded again" later, "that he could leave and go back to his cell" at any time. In addition, he "was not physically restrained or threatened," the room was "well-lit" and "average-sized" and its "door . . . was sometimes left open," and the officers offered him "food and water." In these circumstances, "'a reasonable person would have felt free to terminate the interview and leave.'"

Justices Ginsburg, Breyer, and Sotomayor disagreed. They asserted that the "key questions" are whether an inmate has been "subjected to 'incommunicado interrogation . . . in a police-dominated atmosphere,'" whether he has been "placed, against his will, in an inherently stressful situation," and whether there has been significant curtailment of his "'freedom of action.'" Based on these inquiries, they would have held that Fields was in custody.

Custody Problems

8B–1: The Liberty Savings Bank was robbed on July 23, at approximately 9:20 a.m. The robber entered the bank, placed a gun on a teller's counter, and told her, "This is a robbery." The teller gave him all the money in her drawer. The man put the wad of bills in his pocket, then slowly backed away, and left through the front door. Officer Atkins responded to the report of the robbery. The teller informed him that the robber was a black male in his early to mid-20s, between 5 foot 7 inches and 5 foot 9 inches tall, wearing a gray hooded sweatshirt and blue jeans. Atkins decided to check out the area surrounding the bank. At the Lake George Recreational Area, about a half-mile away, he noticed a black male matching the height description, wearing a white tank top and blue pants and walking southbound very fast. The man, who was talking on his cell phone while walking, looked up at Atkins and quickly looked down again.

Atkins exited his car and told the man that he needed to talk with him. The man, Edwin Martin, cooperated, putting his hands behind his head. Atkins took the cell phone and laid it on the ground, grabbed Martin's hands, and told him that he was being detained because he matched the description of a bank robber. Atkins asked if Martin had any weapons, and Martin said that he possessed only a large sum of money. Atkins then performed a patdown for weapons because the robber had been armed. Atkins felt what he knew to be a wad of cash in Martin's pocket. He then placed handcuffs on Martin, and told him he would be further detained. Atkins pulled the wad of cash partly out of the pocket to confirm it was money, and then pushed it back into the pocket. When he asked Martin where he got the cash, Martin said that he had just been paid by his place of work. When Atkins expressed disbelief, Martin changed his story, saying he saw a man running in the park, and that he found the money.

Atkins placed Martin in the back of the police car, read him his *Miranda* rights, and took him to the bank for a showup identification. He placed Martin on the sidewalk in front of the bank toward the windows with his hands behind his back and cuffed. Upon seeing Martin, the teller, who was inside the bank, became physically shaken. When she identified Martin as the robber, he was arrested and taken to jail.

Should Officer Atkins have given Martin the *Miranda* warnings before he asked the questions?

8B–2: In January, police interviewed Edwin Farr's four-year-old daughter K.T. She told police that Farr had touched her vagina and had inserted a toy into her vagina. On February 21, Farr went to the police station in response to a police request to speak with him. He was accompanied by his mother. Two police officers escorted Farr to a room measuring approximately 8 feet x 11 feet. One of the officers informed Farr that he would be allowed to go home at the end of the interview. He then recited complete *Miranda* warnings to Farr, and Farr signed a waiver of rights.

The interview took approximately two hours. The officers did not record the entire session but began recording it after an hour and 15 minutes had already elapsed. In response to the officers' inquiries, Farr eventually admitted to touching his daughter's "pee-pee" and putting a toy inside her vagina. As promised, Farr was permitted to go home with his mother after the interview was completed.

On March 14, the state charged Farr with two counts of felony child molesting. In response to a request by Farr's attorney, he was evaluated by a psychiatrist and a psychologist, both of whom reported that he suffered from mental retardation. The psychologist found that Farr had a full-scale IQ of 52, which qualified him as moderately retarded. The normal IQ range is 84–116.

Farr's counsel has filed a motion to suppress the statement he gave to police, claiming that it is inadmissible under *Miranda*. The trial court held a hearing on the motion. The psychologist who examined him testified that Farr, who "has the approximate mental abilities of a second grader, would not have been able to understand the *Miranda* waiver of rights form that he signed." The officers who interviewed Farr testified that they were "unaware of his mental disability and that it was not evident in his demeanor or manner of speaking."

How should the judge rule on the motion to suppress the statement?

8B–3: Roger sold a personal computer and the buyer found on it what he correctly thought was child pornography. He notified the local police and turned over the computer. Because Roger was a non-commissioned Naval officer, the Naval Criminal Investigative Service (NCIS) was also notified. The local police obtained a warrant to search the small condominium that Roger occupied with his pregnant wife and small child. Officers made plans to conduct the search on a morning when Roger would be on duty. Two NCIS officers (one of whom was Heather) requested Roger's commanding officer to order him to report to them in the parking lot. The NCIS officers instructed Roger that he needed to go home but gave no further explanation beyond assuring him that his wife was all right.

When Roger arrived, an unmarked police cruiser with two officers was outside, along with an unmarked van used by the police computer crime unit. Inside the condominium were Van, a local police officer in plain clothes, and two state officers in battle dress with visible side arms. One of the state officers explained the circumstances to Roger when he entered the house, and Van then joined them in the living room, leaving one state officer with Roger's wife in the kitchen. The state officer told Roger that he was not about to be arrested. He suggested that the police were concerned not with the mere presence of child pornography on the computer but with its production. Roger denied that he had downloaded the material. Because of other activity in the room, Van suggested that they go elsewhere to talk. Roger chose the driveway, agreeing to speak further there.

While Van and Roger were standing on the driveway, NCIS officer Heather arrived. Van asked if Roger had anything further to tell him about the downloaded material, adding, "Today's the day mister, today is the day." In response to Van's questioning, Roger eventually admitted that he had downloaded the material. The interview inside the condominium and on the driveway had taken about 50 minutes.

At that point, Van asked if Roger would come to the police station for more formal questioning. Roger agreed to do so. Roger and his wife drove to the station house. Van reassured Roger that he would not be arrested, adding, "We're not forcing you to be right here. That door's unlocked and nobody's going to jump out and try to stop you." At the same time, Heather explained to him that he was free to go and that she was a civilian NCIS officer who did not work for Roger's commanding officer. After saying that he "just wanted to get this over with," Roger agreed to talk. He then answered additional questions, providing further details about his downloading of the child pornography. Approximately one hour after arriving at the police station, Roger and his wife left.

Roger was subsequently charged with unlawful possession of child pornography. He moved to suppress the statements made at his home and at the police station.

Was Roger in custody at any time?

8B–4: Police Officers Donte and Arthur went to an apartment building in response to a complaint about property destruction. The building manager told them that he had noticed a bullet hole while renovating apartment 11. When the officers went into that apartment, they saw a bullet hole in the wall between apartments 11 and 12. They concluded that the bullet had come from apartment 12, but did not know when the bullet hole had been made.

The officers knocked on the door of apartment 12. Shawn, who lived there, opened the door. After explaining the reason for their visit, the officers asked if they could "discuss the matter in private." Shawn allowed them to enter the apartment. Patrick, who was also in the apartment, informed the officers that he did not live there. Soon after entering, the officers saw a bullet hole in the wall. They immediately handcuffed Patrick and Shawn, telling them that they were "not under arrest but were being handcuffed for [the officers'] safety." When the officers said that they believed that there was a firearm in the apartment, both Patrick and Shawn denied knowledge of a firearm.

Moments later, Shawn's baby began to cry. The officers removed Shawn's handcuffs so she could attend to the child. The officers then announced that if there was a firearm inside the apartment, both Patrick and Shawn could be arrested, adding that if that happened the baby would be handed over to Family Services. According to Officer Donte, this statement was "not a threat" but, rather, was "advice about what would happen if they were not honest." Shawn started to cry. She pleaded with Patrick to tell the officers where the weapon was. At this point, about 10 minutes after the officers had entered, Patrick got up off the couch and motioned with his head toward the kitchen. With Officer Donte holding his arm, Patrick walked into the kitchen and motioned with his foot toward a kitchen cabinet. Officer Arthur opened the cabinet and found a firearm. Upon noticing that the firearm was empty, Arthur asked Patrick where the magazine was. Patrick said that it was in the bedroom. Shawn led Officer Arthur into the bedroom and pointed out the location of the magazine and additional ammunition.

The officers then advised Patrick that he was under arrest. Based on a distinctive aroma in the apartment, Officer Donte then asked Patrick "Where's your marijuana?" Patrick directed him to a bag of marijuana inside a kitchen cabinet. At no point did the officers recite the *Miranda* warnings. Prior to trial for possession of a firearm, ammunition, and marijuana, Patrick moved to suppress his indications of the location of the firearm and his statements regarding the locations of the magazine and the marijuana.

Does Patrick have a valid suppression claim under *Miranda*?

8B–5: Police Chief James Neill responded to a call asking for certain property to be removed from an apartment. When he arrived, Nicola escorted him to a bedroom and directed him to a dresser behind which he discovered a loaded .22 revolver and a holster. Nicola said that neither she nor her boyfriend, Johnny Lee, owned the gun. During that conversation, she also told Chief Neill that Lee was on parole. Upon returning to his office, Chief Neill telephoned Roy Klob, Lee's parole officer. In their conversation, Chief Neill stated that he wanted to talk with Lee concerning the handgun. Mr. Klob had a regularly scheduled meeting with Lee the following day. He told Chief Neill that he would order Lee to meet the chief at the police station.

The next day, following his parole meeting, Lee arrived at the police station. Chief Neill escorted him to an interview room. He did not recite *Miranda* warnings before beginning to interview Lee. In response to Chief Neill's questions, Lee twice said that he did not own or possess a gun. When the chief asked if Lee would continue to deny ownership if the police found fingerprints on the weapon that matched Lee's, Lee admitted that he had handled the gun. Chief Neill then asked Lee if he would be willing to give a written statement. He agreed, and Chief Neill then gave him *Miranda* warnings. Lee then completed a brief written statement, which indicated that he had received the gun in exchange for driving two people to a liquor store.

Before trial, Lee moved to suppress the oral and written statements that he made during his interview with Chief Neil, claiming that they were inadmissible under *Miranda*.

Did the officer fail to comply with *Miranda's* requirements?

8B–6: J.Y., a 14-year-old boy, moved to suppress oral and written statements he made to officers. Following an evidentiary hearing on the motion, the trial court made the following findings of fact:

> Two officers came to J.Y.'s residence and spoke to his aunt, who called him to the door. The officers told J.Y. they were there to interview him about an alleged sexual assault. They said they could interview him inside the house or inside their car, but preferred the car because juveniles can often speak more freely outside the hearing of an adult and their family. J.Y. agreed to be interviewed in the officers' SUV.

> J.Y. got into the front passenger seat. One of the officers sat in the driver's seat, while the other sat behind J.Y. The officers told J.Y. he did not have to answer questions, that he could open the car door from the inside and leave, and that he could stop the interview at any time. They added that he was not under arrest and would not be arrested at the end of the interview, and that they only wanted to hear the truth. The officers' weapons were not visible, although a rifle was hanging in the back of the SUV. At some point during the interview, J.Y.'s aunt came out of the house, got into her car and left for the post office.

> The officers asked J.Y. to tell his side of the story. After J.Y. did so, one officer said he didn't believe the boy. J.Y. then admitted that he had more to tell and the officer asked him to tell his story again. After he did so, the officer again said that he didn't believe it to be truthful. The officer discussed telling the truth, telling J.Y. that he was doing himself more harm by not telling the truth.

> At that point, J.Y. got out of the vehicle, leaving the door open, and went back to his house. He left the front door of the house open as well. One of the officers followed him to the threshold and yelled into the home, telling J.Y. that his story was inconsistent with medical evidence indicating that the alleged victim was involved in sexual activity and that it may not have been consensual. He again said that he thought that J.Y. was not being truthful.

> J.Y. came out of the house and got back into the SUV. During the ensuing interview he admitted having sexual intercourse with the alleged victim. The officers asked if they could write down J.Y.'s statement, and he said they could. Ultimately, J.Y. signed a two-page statement handwritten by one of

the officers. There was considerable evidence that J.Y. operates at a sixth- or seventh-grade level. There was also some evidence that he reads at the level of a second-grader.

Based on these findings, the district court denied the motion to suppress, concluding that J.Y. was not in custody at the time he made the oral and written statements.

Did the trial judge rule correctly?

8B–7: Craig, an inmate in the state prison, was involved in an altercation with two other inmates, Jason and Ronald. Two corrections officers, Stu and Will, had responded to a request for assistance, and upon arriving, found Sergeant Polka, another corrections officer, restraining Craig and Jason. Polka told Stu that the two men had been fighting.

Craig and Jason were then handcuffed and taken to separate rooms for "post-fight interviews." According to Officer Stu, this procedure was for administrative purposes, to secure the area, and to ensure the safe and orderly operation of the institution. He did not place Craig "under arrest" during the interview, but, rather, "restrained him for safety purposes." In fact, it was not common practice to arrest inmates for fights because fights happened every day. Nonetheless, Craig was not free to go while he was questioned about the incident during the "post-fight interview."

During the interview, Craig claimed that Jason had "disrespected him" by masturbating another inmate near Craig's bed. According to Craig, "I knocked the dude, and then stomped on him." Stu asked Craig to clarify whom he had "stomped on," and Craig responded: "I stomped on the other one." Craig then demonstrated what he had done by jumping up and down three times, with both feet coming off the floor. Prior to these admissions, Stu was not aware that anyone else had been involved. After Craig's admissions, Stu proceeded into the dorm, where he discovered Ronald lying on the floor. As a result of the severe injuries he suffered, Ronald was totally disabled. He is unable to stand up or walk, is unable to talk, and has to wear a diaper.

Craig was charged with attempted murder. Prior to his trial, he moved to suppress evidence of the statements he made, claiming that he was not given *Miranda* warnings. The trial court denied the motion, and Craig was convicted. Craig has appealed the denial of the motion to suppress.

How should the court of appeals rule?

8B–8: In January, Officer John Blackmon received information from a confidential informant that heroin was being sold from an apartment in a multifamily residence located on North Street. Officers then conducted surveillance of the apartment and used confidential informants to make controlled purchases of heroin from occupants. This led them to believe that "a Hispanic male named Bebos and a woman named Ada were selling heroin from the apartment." Officer Blackmon applied for and secured a valid search warrant for the apartment.

On February 5, Officer Blackmon, Officer Gerry Hix, and five other uniformed officers drove to the multifamily residence building. Officer Hix and two of the officers remained outside the building. Officer Blackmon and three other officers, equipped with handguns and wearing tactical vests, entered the building and proceeded to the apartment. Upon reaching the front door, Officer Blackmon knocked and advised the occupants of the search warrant. Ada answered the door and allowed the officers to enter. More than one of the officers entered with their weapons drawn. After entering the four-room dwelling, the officers first removed Ada's dog. They then guided Ada and her three daughters, who were 19, 16, and 13 years of age, into the living room area. The women were ordered to remain on the couch and were kept under direct observation for the duration of the ensuing search. None of the officers at any point informed the women of the reason for or likely duration of their detention. The officers did not mention whether Ada and her daughters were or were not under arrest.

After the apartment had been secured, Officer Hix and the two other officers who had waited outside proceeded to enter. Without reciting *Miranda* warnings, Hix asked Ada, "Are there any drugs or weapons in your apartment?" She answered, "Yes." She then told him, "There are drugs in the bedroom." Ada led Hix to her bedroom, pointed to a can of hairspray sitting on her dresser, and told him that it contained heroin. The officer removed a false bottom on the can and found 235 packets of heroin inside. He then placed Ada under arrest. Prior to trial for possession of heroin, Ada filed a motion to suppress her incriminating statements.

Was Ada in custody at the time she responded to Hix's question?

8B–9: Deputy Neikirk responded to a report that there had been a hit and run accident in the VFW parking lot. Deputy Neikirk went to the scene of the accident and spoke with several victims and witnesses. Some of the witnesses told Deputy Neikirk that Bond had struck some vehicles as he was driving his tractor-trailer out of the parking lot. Deputy Neikirk ran a driver's license check and obtained Bond's address, which was in a trailer park.

At about midnight, Deputy Neikirk and two other officers went to Bond's trailer home and knocked on the door. Bond's 11-year-old nephew answered the door. Deputy Neikirk asked if Bond was home; the 11-year-old responded that he was in the bedroom. Neikirk then asked if they could speak with Bond and the youth responded by letting the officers into the trailer and walking them to the bedroom.

When the officers entered the bedroom, Bond was in bed with his shirt off. Bond turned on a light and sat up in bed. Deputy Neikirk identified himself and stood inside the doorway of the bedroom at the foot of the bed. One of the other officers stood beside Deputy Neikirk and the other stood behind him.

Deputy Neikirk told Bond they were there "due to a hit and run accident that occurred at the VFW which [they were] advised that he was involved in." Bond at first denied any knowledge of the incident. The officers told him that witnesses at the scene of the accident had identified him as the driver. They also told him they had observed damage to his tractor-trailer. Eventually, Bond admitted he had been in the VFW parking lot that night and that he drove away through a side lot of the establishment.

Throughout most of the questioning, Bond remained in bed. At one point, however, he stood up to put on his shirt and a pair of pants. He then sat down again on the bed. While the officers never told Bond he was under arrest, they did not tell him he was free to leave or that he did not have to answer their questions. On the other hand, Bond never indicated that he wanted to leave or wished to terminate the interview. At the conclusion of the interview, Deputy Neikirk told Bond that although charges would be brought against him, he was not arresting him at that time.

Was Bond in custody when the police interrogated him in his bedroom?

8B–10: Police were investigating the firing of a gun in a train station. Because they suspected Coleman, a 19-year-old black youth, three officers went to the house of Coleman's aunt, where Coleman was living. After meeting with Coleman's aunt, they asked to speak to Coleman in a private place. Coleman's aunt directed them to a bedroom that measured 11 by 12 feet. Two of the officers remained standing, blocking the door to the bedroom. The other officer was seated on the bed next to Coleman. Gillespie, the officer in charge of the investigation, told Coleman that he was not under arrest and that he could leave the room if he wished.

Gillespie then told Coleman he had a theory about the case about which he was "confident": Coleman had fired a handgun in the station intending to scare members of the Columbia Point Dogs gang who were pursuing and threatening him. Gillespie added that he didn't believe Coleman intended to strike anyone. In support of his theory, Gillespie produced a fingerprint card and falsely told Coleman that the card showed his fingerprints had been found on the gun that had been fired in the station. Coleman then admitted "touching" the gun but denied firing it.

Gillespie told Coleman that he didn't believe his denial. He also told him that if he persisted in denying the shooting he could face more serious charges. Specifically, he told Coleman he was going to question Christopher Jaundoo, a member of the Columbia Point Dogs gang. He said that if Jaundoo said that Coleman had tried to shoot him, Coleman might have to face the more serious charge of assault with intent to murder. He added, however, that if Coleman admitted firing the gun, he would not have to worry about facing the more serious charge.

Although Gillespie reiterated that Coleman could leave the room if he wished, he continued to press him to confess: he told him that if he persisted in denials, he would be arrested and handcuffed in front of his aunt; on the other hand, if he confessed, he would not be arrested, but would rather be summoned into court "without handcuffs or shackles on him."

After about 30 minutes, Coleman began to weep and told a story in which he admitted firing the handgun. His story contributed to his conviction at trial.

Was Coleman in custody when he admitted touching the handgun? When he admitted firing it?

[C] Interrogation

Rhode Island v. Innis

United States Supreme Court

446 U.S. 291, 100 S. Ct. 1682, 64 L. Ed. 2d 297 (1980)

MR. JUSTICE STEWART delivered the opinion of the Court.

In *Miranda v. Arizona*, 384 U.S. 436, 474, 86 S. Ct. 1602, 1627, 16 L. Ed. 2d 694, the Court held that, once a defendant in custody asks to speak with a lawyer, all interrogation must cease until a lawyer is present. The issue in this case is whether the respondent was "interrogated" in violation of the standards promulgated in the *Miranda* opinion.

I

On the night of January 12, 1975, John Mulvaney, a Providence, R.I., taxicab driver, disappeared after being dispatched to pick up a customer. His body was discovered four days later buried in a shallow grave in Coventry, R.I. He had died from a shotgun blast aimed at the back of his head.

On January 17, 1975, shortly after midnight, the Providence police received a telephone call from Gerald Aubin, also a taxicab driver, who reported that he had just been robbed by a man wielding a sawed-off shotgun. Aubin further reported that he had dropped off his assailant near Rhode Island College in a section of Providence known as Mount Pleasant. While at the Providence police station waiting to give a statement, Aubin noticed a picture of his assailant on a bulletin board. Aubin so informed one of the police officers present. The officer prepared a photo array, and again Aubin identified a picture of the same person. That person was the respondent. Shortly thereafter, the Providence police began a search of the Mount Pleasant area.

At approximately 4:30 a.m. on the same date, Patrolman Lovell, while cruising the streets of Mount Pleasant in a patrol car, spotted the respondent standing in the street facing him. When Patrolman Lovell stopped his car, the respondent walked towards it. Patrolman Lovell then arrested the respondent, who was unarmed, and advised him of his so-called *Miranda* rights. While the two men waited in the patrol car for other police officers to arrive, Patrolman Lovell did not converse with the respondent other than to respond to the latter's request for a cigarette.

Within minutes, Sergeant Sears arrived at the scene of the arrest, and he also gave the respondent the *Miranda* warnings. Immediately thereafter, Captain Leyden and other police officers arrived. Captain Leyden advised the respondent of his *Miranda* rights. The respondent stated that he understood those rights and wanted to speak with a lawyer. Captain Leyden then directed that the respondent be placed in a "caged wagon," a four-door police car with a wire screen mesh between the front and rear seats, and be driven to the central police station. Three officers, Patrolmen Gleckman, Williams, and McKenna, were assigned to accompany the respondent to the central station. They placed the respondent in the vehicle and shut the doors. Captain Leyden then instructed the officers not to question the respondent or intimidate or coerce him in any way. The three officers then entered the vehicle, and it departed.

While en route to the central station, Patrolman Gleckman initiated a conversation with Patrolman McKenna concerning the missing shotgun.[1] As Patrolman Gleckman later testified:

> **A.** At this point, I was talking back and forth with Patrolman McKenna stating that I frequent this area while on patrol and [that because a school for handicapped children is located nearby,] there's a lot of handicapped children running around in this area, and God forbid one of them might find a weapon with shells and they might hurt themselves.

Patrolman McKenna apparently shared his fellow officer's concern:

> **A.** I more or less concurred with him [Gleckman] that it was a safety factor and that we should, you know, continue to search for the weapon and try to find it.

While Patrolman Williams said nothing, he overheard the conversation between the two officers:

> **A.** He [Gleckman] said it would be too bad if the little — I believe he said a girl — would pick up the gun, maybe kill herself.

The respondent then interrupted the conversation, stating that the officers should turn the car around so he could show them where the gun was located. At this point, Patrolman McKenna radioed back to Captain Leyden that they were returning to the scene of the arrest and that the respondent would inform them of the location of the gun. At the time the respondent indicated that the officers should turn back, they had traveled no more than a mile, a trip encompassing only a few minutes.

The police vehicle then returned to the scene of the arrest where a search for the shotgun was in progress. There, Captain Leyden again advised the respondent of his *Miranda* rights. The respondent replied that he understood those rights but that he "wanted to get the gun out of the way because of the kids in the area in the school." The respondent then led the police to a nearby field, where he pointed out the shotgun under some rocks by the side of the road.

On March 20, 1975, a grand jury returned an indictment charging the respondent with the kidnaping, robbery, and murder of John Mulvaney. Before trial, the respondent moved to suppress the shotgun and the statements he had made to the police regarding it. After an evidentiary hearing at which the respondent elected not to testify, the trial judge found that the respondent had been "repeatedly and completely advised of his *Miranda* rights." He further found that it was "entirely understandable that [the officers in the police vehicle] would voice their concern [for the safety of the handi-

---

1. Although there was conflicting testimony about the exact seating arrangements, it is clear that everyone in the vehicle heard the conversation.

capped children] to each other." The judge then concluded that the respondent's decision to inform the police of the location of the shotgun was "a waiver, clearly, and on the basis of the evidence that I have heard, and [sic] intelligent waiver, of his [Miranda] right to remain silent." Thus, without passing on whether the police officers had in fact "interrogated" the respondent, the trial court sustained the admissibility of the shotgun and testimony related to its discovery. That evidence was later introduced at the respondent's trial, and the jury returned a verdict of guilty on all counts.

On appeal, the Rhode Island Supreme Court, in a 3–2 decision, set aside the respondent's conviction. Relying at least in part on this Court's decision in *Brewer v. Williams*, 430 U.S. 387, 97 S. Ct. 1232, 51 L. Ed. 2d 424, the court concluded that the respondent had invoked his *Miranda* right to counsel and that, contrary to *Miranda*'s mandate that, in the absence of counsel, all custodial interrogation then cease, the police officers in the vehicle had "interrogated" the respondent without a valid waiver of his right to counsel. It was the view of the state appellate court that, even though the police officers may have been genuinely concerned about the public safety and even though the respondent had not been addressed personally by the police officers, the respondent nonetheless had been subjected to "subtle coercion" that was the equivalent of "interrogation" within the meaning of the *Miranda* opinion. Moreover, contrary to the holding of the trial court, the appellate court concluded that the evidence was insufficient to support a finding of waiver. Having concluded that both the shotgun and testimony relating to its discovery were obtained in violation of the *Miranda* standards and therefore should not have been admitted into evidence, the Rhode Island Supreme Court held that the respondent was entitled to a new trial.

We granted certiorari to address for the first time the meaning of "interrogation" under *Miranda v. Arizona*. 440 U.S. 934, 99 S. Ct. 1277, 59 L. Ed. 2d 492.

II

In its *Miranda* opinion, the Court concluded that in the context of "custodial interrogation" certain procedural safeguards are necessary to protect a defendant's Fifth and Fourteenth Amendment privilege against compulsory self-incrimination. More specifically, the Court held that "the prosecution may not use statements, whether exculpatory or inculpatory, stemming from custodial interrogation of the defendant unless it demonstrates the use of procedural safeguards effective to secure the privilege against self-incrimination." *Id.*, 384 U.S. at 444, 86 S. Ct. at 1612.

. . . .

In the present case, the parties are in agreement that the respondent was fully informed of his *Miranda* rights and that he invoked his *Miranda* right to counsel when he told Captain Leyden that he wished to consult with a lawyer. It is also uncontested that the respondent was "in custody" while being transported to the police station.

The issue, therefore, is whether the respondent was "interrogated" by the police officers in violation of the respondent's undisputed right under *Miranda* to remain silent until he had consulted with a lawyer.[2] In resolving this issue, we first define the term "interrogation" under *Miranda* before turning to a consideration of the facts of this case.

A

The starting point for defining "interrogation" in this context is, of course, the Court's *Miranda* opinion. There the Court observed that "[b]y custodial interrogation, we mean *questioning* initiated by law enforcement officers after a person has been taken into custody or otherwise deprived of his freedom of action in any significant way." *Id.* at 444, 86 S. Ct. at 1612 (emphasis added). This passage and other references throughout the opinion to "questioning" might suggest that the *Miranda* rules were to apply only to those police interrogation practices that involve express questioning of a defendant while in custody.

We do not, however, construe the *Miranda* opinion so narrowly. The concern of the Court in *Miranda* was that the "interrogation environment" created by the interplay of interrogation and custody would "subjugate the individual to the will of his examiner" and thereby undermine the privilege against compulsory self-incrimination. *Id.* at 457–458, 86 S. Ct. at 1619. The police practices that evoked this concern included several that did not involve express questioning. For example, one of the practices discussed in *Miranda* was the use of line-ups in which a coached witness would pick the defendant as the perpetrator. This was designed to establish that the defendant was in fact guilty as a predicate for further interrogation. A variation on this theme discussed in *Miranda* was the so-called "reverse line-up" in which a defendant would be identified by coached witnesses as the perpetrator of a fictitious crime, with the object of inducing him to confess to the actual crime of which he was suspected in order to escape the false prosecution. The Court in *Miranda* also included in its survey of interrogation practices the use of psychological ploys, such as to "posi[t]" "the guilt of the subject," to "minimize the moral seriousness of the offense," and "to cast blame on the victim or on society." *Id.* at 450, 86 S. Ct. at 1615. It is clear that these techniques of persuasion, no less than express questioning, were thought, in a custodial setting, to amount to interrogation.[3]

This is not to say, however, that all statements obtained by the police after a person has been taken into custody are to be considered the product of interrogation. As the Court in *Miranda* noted:

> Confessions remain a proper element in law enforcement. Any statement given freely and voluntarily without any compelling influences is, of course, admissible in evidence. *The fundamental import of the privilege while an individual is in custody is not whether he is allowed to talk to the police without*

---

2. Since we conclude that the respondent was not "interrogated" for *Miranda* purposes, we do not reach the question whether the respondent waived his right under *Miranda* to be free from interrogation until counsel was present.

3. To limit the ambit of *Miranda* to express questioning would "place a premium on the ingenuity of the police to devise methods of indirect interrogation, rather than to implement the plain mandate of *Miranda*." *Commonwealth v. Hamilton*, 445 Pa. 292, 297, 285 A.2d 172, 175.

the benefit of warnings and counsel, but whether he can be interrogated. . . . Volunteered statements of any kind are not barred by the Fifth Amendment and their admissibility is not affected by our holding today.

Id. at 478, 86 S. Ct. at 1630 (emphasis added). It is clear therefore that the special procedural safeguards outlined in *Miranda* are required not where a suspect is simply taken into custody, but rather where a suspect in custody is subjected to interrogation. "Interrogation," as conceptualized in the *Miranda* opinion, must reflect a measure of compulsion above and beyond that inherent in custody itself.[4]

We conclude that the *Miranda* safeguards come into play whenever a person in custody is subjected to either express questioning or its functional equivalent. That is to say, the term "interrogation" under *Miranda* refers not only to express questioning, but also to any words or actions on the part of the police (other than those normally attendant to arrest and custody) that the police should know are reasonably likely to elicit an incriminating response from the suspect.[6] The latter portion of this definition focuses primarily upon the perceptions of the suspect, rather than the intent of the police. This focus reflects the fact that the *Miranda* safeguards were designed to vest a suspect in custody with an added measure of protection against coercive police practices, without regard to objective proof of the underlying intent of the police. A practice that the police should know is reasonably likely to evoke an incriminating response from a suspect thus amounts to interrogation.[7] But, since the police surely cannot be held accountable for the unforeseeable results of their words or actions, the definition of interrogation can extend only to words or actions on the

---

4. There is language in the opinion of the Rhode Island Supreme Court in this case suggesting that the definition of "interrogation" under *Miranda* is informed by this Court's decision in *Brewer v. Williams*, 430 U.S. 387, 97 S. Ct. 1232, 51 L. Ed. 2d 424. R.I., 391 A.2d 1158, 1161–1162. This suggestion is erroneous. Our decision in *Brewer* rested solely on the Sixth and Fourteenth Amendment right to counsel. That right, as we held in *Massiah v. United States*, 377 U.S. 201, 206, 84 S. Ct. 1199, 1203, 12 L. Ed. 2d 246, prohibits law enforcement officers from "deliberately elicit[ing]" incriminating information from a defendant in the absence of counsel after a formal charge against the defendant has been filed. Custody in such a case is not controlling; indeed, the petitioner in *Massiah* was not in custody. By contrast, the right to counsel at issue in the present case is based not on the Sixth and Fourteenth Amendments, but rather on the Fifth and Fourteenth Amendments as interpreted in the *Miranda* opinion. The definitions of "interrogation" under the Fifth and Sixth Amendments, if indeed the term "interrogation" is even apt in the Sixth Amendment context, are not necessarily interchangeable, since the policies underlying the two constitutional protections are quite distinct. *See* Kamisar, Brewer v. Williams, Massiah *and* Miranda: *What is "Interrogation"? When Does it Matter?*, 67 Geo. L.J. 1, 41–55 (1978).

6. One of the dissenting opinions seems totally to misapprehend this definition in suggesting that it "will almost certainly exclude every statement [of the police] that is not punctuated with a question mark."

7. This is not to say that the intent of the police is irrelevant, for it may well have a bearing on whether the police should have known that their words or actions were reasonably likely to evoke an incriminating response. In particular, where a police practice is designed to elicit an incriminating response from the accused, it is unlikely that the practice will not also be one which the police should have known was reasonably likely to have that effect.

part of police officers that they *should have known* were reasonably likely to elicit an incriminating response.[8]

B

Turning to the facts of the present case, we conclude that the respondent was not "interrogated" within the meaning of *Miranda*. It is undisputed that the first prong of the definition of "interrogation" was not satisfied, for the conversation between Patrolmen Gleckman and McKenna included no express questioning of the respondent. Rather, that conversation was, at least in form, nothing more than a dialogue between the two officers to which no response from the respondent was invited.

Moreover, it cannot be fairly concluded that the respondent was subjected to the "functional equivalent" of questioning. It cannot be said, in short, that Patrolmen Gleckman and McKenna should have known that their conversation was reasonably likely to elicit an incriminating response from the respondent. There is nothing in the record to suggest that the officers were aware that the respondent was peculiarly susceptible to an appeal to his conscience concerning the safety of handicapped children. Nor is there anything in the record to suggest that the police knew that the respondent was unusually disoriented or upset at the time of his arrest.[9]

The case thus boils down to whether, in the context of a brief conversation, the officers should have known that the respondent would suddenly be moved to make a self-incriminating response. Given the fact that the entire conversation appears to have consisted of no more than a few offhand remarks, we cannot say that the officers should have known that it was reasonably likely that Innis would so respond. This is not a case where the police carried on a lengthy harangue in the presence of the suspect. Nor does the record support the respondent's contention that, under the circumstances, the officers' comments were particularly "evocative." It is our view, therefore, that the respondent was not subjected by the police to words or actions that the police should have known were reasonably likely to elicit an incriminating response from him.

The Rhode Island Supreme Court erred, in short, in equating "subtle compulsion" with interrogation. That the officers' comments struck a responsive chord is readily apparent. Thus, it may be said, as the Rhode Island Supreme Court did say, that the respondent was subjected to "subtle compulsion." But that is not the end of the inquiry. It must also be established that a suspect's incriminating response was the

---

8. Any knowledge the police may have had concerning the unusual susceptibility of a defendant to a particular form of persuasion might be an important factor in determining whether the police should have known that their words or actions were reasonably likely to elicit an incriminating response from the suspect.

9. The record in no way suggests that the officers' remarks were *designed* to elicit a response. It is significant that the trial judge, after hearing the officers' testimony, concluded that it was "entirely understandable that [the officers] would voice their concern [for the safety of the handicapped children] to each other."

product of words or actions on the part of the police that they should have known were reasonably likely to elicit an incriminating response.[10] This was not established in the present case.

For the reasons stated, the judgment of the Supreme Court of Rhode Island is vacated, and the case is remanded to that court for further proceedings not inconsistent with this opinion.

It is so ordered.

[Concurring opinions of MR. JUSTICE WHITE and MR. CHIEF JUSTICE BURGER have been omitted.]

MR. JUSTICE MARSHALL, with whom MR. JUSTICE BRENNAN joins, dissenting.

I am substantially in agreement with the Court's definition of "interrogation" within the meaning of *Miranda.* In my view, the *Miranda* safeguards apply whenever police conduct is intended or likely to produce a response from a suspect in custody. As I read the Court's opinion, its definition of "interrogation" for *Miranda* purposes is equivalent, for practical purposes, to my formulation, since it contemplates that "where a police practice is designed to elicit an incriminating response from the accused, it is unlikely that the practice will not also be one which the police should have known was reasonably likely to have that effect." Thus, the Court requires an objective inquiry into the likely effect of police conduct on a typical individual, taking into account any special susceptibility of the suspect to certain kinds of pressure of which the police know or have reason to know.

I am utterly at a loss, however, to understand how this objective standard as applied to the facts before us can rationally lead to the conclusion that there was no interrogation. Innis was arrested at 4:30 a.m., handcuffed, searched, advised of his rights, and placed in the back seat of a patrol car. Within a short time he had been twice more advised of his rights and driven away in a four-door sedan with three police officers. Two officers sat in the front seat and one sat beside Innis in the back seat. Since the car traveled no more than a mile before Innis agreed to point out the location of the murder weapon, Officer Gleckman must have begun almost immediately to talk about the search for the shotgun.

The Court attempts to characterize Gleckman's statements as "no more than a few offhand remarks" which could not reasonably have been expected to elicit a response. If the statements had been addressed to respondent, it would be impossible to draw such a conclusion. The simple message of the "talking back and forth" between

---

10. By way of example, if the police had done no more than to drive past the site of the concealed weapon while taking the most direct route to the police station, and if the respondent, upon noticing for the first time the proximity of the school for handicapped children, had blurted out that he would show the officers where the gun was located, it could not seriously be argued that this "subtle compulsion" would have constituted "interrogation" within the meaning of the *Miranda* opinion.

Gleckman and McKenna was that they had to find the shotgun to avert a child's death.

One can scarcely imagine a stronger appeal to the conscience of a suspect — *any* suspect — than the assertion that if the weapon is not found an innocent person will be hurt or killed. And not just any innocent person, but an innocent child — a little girl — a helpless, handicapped little girl on her way to school. The notion that such an appeal could not be expected to have any effect unless the suspect were known to have some special interest in handicapped children verges on the ludicrous. As a matter of fact, the appeal to a suspect to confess for the sake of others, to "display some evidence of decency and honor," is a classic interrogation technique. *See e.g.,* F. Inbau & J. Reid, CRIMINAL INTERROGATION AND CONFESSIONS 60–62 (2d ed. 1967).

Gleckman's remarks would obviously have constituted interrogation if they had been explicitly directed to respondent, and the result should not be different because they were nominally addressed to McKenna. This is not a case where police officers speaking among themselves are accidentally overheard by a suspect. These officers were "talking back and forth" in close quarters with the handcuffed suspect,* traveling past the very place where they believed the weapon was located. They knew respondent would hear and attend to their conversation, and they are chargeable with knowledge of and responsibility for the pressures to speak which they created.

I firmly believe that this case is simply an aberration, and that in future cases the Court will apply the standard adopted today in accordance with its plain meaning.

MR. JUSTICE STEVENS, dissenting.

. . . .

I

As the Court recognizes, *Miranda v. Arizona* makes it clear that, once respondent requested an attorney, he had an absolute right to have any type of interrogation cease until an attorney was present. As it also recognizes, *Miranda* requires that the term "interrogation" be broadly construed to include "either express questioning or its functional equivalent." In my view any statement that would normally be understood by the average listener as calling for a response is the functional equivalent of a direct question, whether or not it is punctuated by a question mark. The Court, however, takes a much narrower view. It holds that police conduct is not the "functional equivalent" of direct questioning unless the police should have known that what they were saying or doing was likely to elicit an incriminating response from the suspect. This holding represents a plain departure from the principles set forth in *Miranda*.

In *Miranda* the Court required the now-familiar warnings to be given to suspects prior to custodial interrogation in order to dispel the atmosphere of coercion that

---

* Gleckman may even have been sitting in the back seat beside respondent.

necessarily accompanies such interrogations. In order to perform that function effectively, the warnings must be viewed by both the police and the suspect as a correct and binding statement of their respective rights. Thus, if, after being told that he has a right to have an attorney present during interrogation, a suspect chooses to cut off questioning until counsel can be obtained, his choice must be "scrupulously honored" by the police. *See Michigan v. Mosley*, 423 U.S. 96, 104, 96 S. Ct. 321, 326, 46 L. Ed. 2d 313, *id.* at 110, 96 S. Ct. at 329, n.2 (White, J., concurring in result). At the least this must mean that the police are prohibited from making deliberate attempts to elicit statements from the suspect. Yet the Court is unwilling to characterize all such attempts as "interrogation," noting only that "where a police practice is designed to elicit an incriminating response from the accused, it is unlikely that the practice will not also be one which the police should have known was reasonably likely to have that effect."[8]

From the suspect's point of view, the effectiveness of the warnings depends on whether it appears that the police are scrupulously honoring his rights. Apparent attempts to elicit information from a suspect after he has invoked his right to cut off questioning necessarily demean that right and tend to reinstate the imbalance between police and suspect that the *Miranda* warnings are designed to correct.[9] Thus, if the rationale for requiring those warnings in the first place is to be respected, any police conduct or statements that would appear to a reasonable person in the suspect's position to call for a response must be considered "interrogation."[10]

In short, in order to give full protection to a suspect's right to be free from any interrogation at all, the definition of "interrogation" must include any police statement or conduct that has the same purpose or effect as a direct question. Statements that appear to call for a response from the suspect, as well as those that are designed to do so, should be considered interrogation. By prohibiting only those relatively few statements or actions that a police officer should know are likely to elicit an incriminating response, the Court today accords a suspect considerably less protection. Indeed, since I suppose most suspects are unlikely to incriminate themselves even when questioned directly, this new definition will almost certainly exclude every

---

8. This factual assumption is extremely dubious. I would assume that police often interrogate suspects without any reason to believe that their efforts are likely to be successful in the hope that a statement will nevertheless be forthcoming.

9. *See* White, *Police Trickery in Inducing Confessions*, 127 U. Pa. L. Rev. 581, 609–611 (1979). As Mr. Justice White pointed out in his opinion concurring in the result in *Michigan v. Mosley*, 423 U.S. 96, 96 S. Ct. 321, 46 L. Ed. 2d 313, when a suspect invokes his right to an attorney, he is expressing "his own view that he is not competent to deal with the authorities without legal advice." *Id.* at 110, n. 2, 96 S. Ct. at 329, n. 2. Under these circumstances, continued interrogation is likely to produce the same type of coercive atmosphere that the *Miranda* warnings are supposed to dispel.

10. I would use an objective standard both to avoid the difficulties of proof inherent in a subjective standard and to give police adequate guidance in their dealings with suspects who have requested counsel.

statement that is not punctuated with a question mark from the concept of "interrogation."[11]

The difference between the approach required by a faithful adherence to *Miranda* and the stinted test applied by the Court today can be illustrated by comparing three different ways in which Officer Gleckman could have communicated his fears about the possible dangers posed by the shotgun to handicapped children. He could have:

(1) directly asked Innis:

Will you please tell me where the shotgun is so we can protect handicapped school children from danger?

(2) announced to the other officers in the wagon:

If the man sitting in the back seat with me should decide to tell us where the gun is, we can protect handicapped children from danger.

or (3) stated to the other officers:

It would be too bad if a little handicapped girl would pick up the gun that this man left in the area and maybe kill herself.

In my opinion, all three of these statements should be considered interrogation because all three appear to be designed to elicit a response from anyone who in fact knew where the gun was located.[12] Under the Court's test, on the other hand, the form of the statements would be critical. The third statement would not be interrogation because in the Court's view there was no reason for Officer Gleckman to believe that Innis was susceptible to this type of an implied appeal; therefore, the statement would not be reasonably likely to elicit an incriminating response. Assuming that this is true, then it seems to me that the first two statements, which would be just as unlikely to elicit such a response, should also not be considered interrogation. But, because the first statement is clearly an express question, it *would* be considered interrogation under the Court's test. The second statement, although just as clearly a deliberate appeal to Innis to reveal the location of the gun, would presumably not be interrogation because (a) it was not in form a direct question and (b) it does not fit within the "reasonably likely to elicit an incriminating response" category that applies to indirect interrogation.

---

11. The Court's suggestion that I totally misapprehend the import of its definition is belied by its application of the new standard to the facts of this case.

12. *See* White, Rhode Island v. Innis: *The Significance of a Suspect's Assertion of His Right to Counsel*, 17 Am. Crim. L. Rev. 53, 68 (1979), where the author proposes the same test and applies it to the facts of this case, stating:

Under the proposed objective standard, the result is obvious. Since the conversation indicates a strong desire to know the location of the shotgun, any person with knowledge of the weapon's location would be likely to believe that the officers wanted him to disclose its location. Thus, a reasonable person in Innis's position would believe that the officers were seeking to solicit precisely the type of response that was given.

As this example illustrates, the Court's test creates an incentive for police to ignore a suspect's invocation of his rights in order to make continued attempts to extract information from him. If a suspect does not appear to be susceptible to a particular type of psychological pressure, the police are apparently free to exert that pressure on him despite his request for counsel, so long as they are careful not to punctuate their statements with question marks. And if, contrary to all reasonable expectations, the suspect makes an incriminating statement, that statement can be used against him at trial. The Court thus turns *Miranda*'s unequivocal rule against any interrogation at all into a trap in which unwary suspects may be caught by police deception.

. . . .

Notes and Questions

(1) How do the standards for interrogation proposed by Justice Marshall and Justice Stevens differ from the standard adopted by the majority? Which of these standards seems most consistent with *Miranda*'s objective of preventing the introduction of compelled, self-incriminating statements? Which best promotes *Miranda*'s clear guidance goal?

(2) Is age relevant to the interrogation determination? Are any other personal characteristics pertinent? A lack of prior experience with law enforcement or interrogation is irrelevant to custody assessments. Is it equally inapposite to interrogation assessments?

Illinois v. Perkins

United States Supreme Court

496 U.S. 292, 110 S. Ct. 2394, 110 L. Ed. 2d 243 (1990)

JUSTICE KENNEDY delivered the opinion of the Court.

. . . .

I

In November 1984, Richard Stephenson was murdered in a suburb of East St. Louis, Illinois. The murder remained unsolved until March 1986, when one Donald Charlton told police that he had learned about a homicide from a fellow inmate at the Graham Correctional Facility, where Charlton had been serving a sentence for burglary. The fellow inmate was Lloyd Perkins, who is the respondent here. Charlton told police that, while at Graham, he had befriended respondent, who told him in detail about a murder that respondent had committed in East St. Louis. On hearing Charlton's account, the police recognized details of the Stephenson murder that were not well known, and so they treated Charlton's story as a credible one.

By the time the police heard Charlton's account, respondent had been released from Graham, but police traced him to a jail in Montgomery County, Illinois, where he was being held pending trial on a charge of aggravated battery, unrelated to the

Stephenson murder. The police wanted to investigate further respondent's connection to the Stephenson murder, but feared that the use of an eavesdropping device would prove impracticable and unsafe. They decided instead to place an undercover agent in the cellblock with respondent and Charlton. The plan was for Charlton and undercover agent John Parisi to pose as escapees from a work release program who had been arrested in the course of a burglary. Parisi and Charlton were instructed to engage respondent in casual conversation and report anything he said about the Stephenson murder.

Parisi, using the alias "Vito Bianco," and Charlton, both clothed in jail garb, were placed in the cellblock with respondent at the Montgomery County jail. The cellblock consisted of 12 separate cells that opened onto a common room. Respondent greeted Charlton who, after a brief conversation with respondent, introduced Parisi by his alias. Parisi told respondent that he "wasn't going to do any more time," and suggested that the three of them escape. Respondent replied that the Montgomery County jail was "rinky-dink" and that they could "break out." The trio met in respondent's cell later that evening, after the other inmates were asleep, to refine their plan. Respondent said that his girlfriend could smuggle in a pistol. Charlton said: "Hey, I'm not a murderer, I'm a burglar. That's your guys' profession." After telling Charlton that he would be responsible for any murder that occurred, Parisi asked respondent if he had ever "done" anybody. Respondent said that he had, and proceeded to describe at length the events of the Stephenson murder. Parisi and respondent then engaged in some casual conversation before respondent went to sleep. Parisi did not give respondent *Miranda* warnings before the conversations.

Respondent was charged with the Stephenson murder. Before trial, he moved to suppress the statements made to Parisi in the jail. The trial court granted the motion to suppress, and the State appealed. The Appellate Court of Illinois affirmed, holding that *Miranda v. Arizona*, 384 U.S. 436 (1966), prohibits all undercover contacts with incarcerated suspects which are reasonably likely to elicit an incriminating response.

We granted certiorari, 493 U.S. 808 (1989), to decide whether an undercover law enforcement officer must give *Miranda* warnings to an incarcerated suspect before asking him questions that may elicit an incriminating response. We now reverse.

II

. . . .

Conversations between suspects and undercover agents do not implicate the concerns underlying *Miranda*. The essential ingredients of a "police-dominated atmosphere" and compulsion are not present when an incarcerated person speaks freely to someone that he believes to be a fellow inmate. Coercion is determined from the perspective of the suspect. *Rhode Island v. Innis*, 446 U.S. 291, 301 (1980); *Berkemer v. McCarty*, 468 U.S. 420, 442 (1984). When a suspect considers himself in the company of cellmates and not officers, the coercive atmosphere is lacking. *Miranda*, 384 U.S., at 449 ("[T]he 'principal psychological factor contributing to a successful interrogation is *privacy* — being alone with the person under interrogation'"). There is no empirical basis for the assumption that a suspect speaking to those whom he assumes are not officers will feel compelled to speak by the fear of reprisal for remaining silent or in the hope of more lenient treatment should he confess.

It is the premise of *Miranda* that the danger of coercion results from the interaction of custody and official interrogation. We reject the argument that *Miranda* warnings are required whenever a suspect is in custody in a technical sense and converses with someone who happens to be a government agent. Questioning by captors, who appear to control the suspect's fate, may create mutually reinforcing pressures that the Court has assumed will weaken the suspect's will, but where a suspect does not know that he is conversing with a government agent, these pressures do not exist. The state court here mistakenly assumed that because the suspect was in custody, no undercover questioning could take place. When the suspect has no reason to think that the listeners have official power over him, it should not be assumed that his words are motivated by the reaction he expects from his listeners. "[W]hen the agent carries neither badge nor gun and wears not 'police blue,' but the same prison gray" as the suspect, there is no "*interplay* between police interrogation and police custody." Kamisar, *Brewer v. Williams, Massiah and Miranda: What is "Interrogation"? When Does it Matter?*, 67 Geo. L.J. 1, 67, 63 (1978).

Miranda forbids coercion, not mere strategic deception by taking advantage of a suspect's misplaced trust in one he supposes to be a fellow prisoner. As we recognized in *Miranda*, "[c]onfessions remain a proper element in law enforcement. Any statement given freely and voluntarily without any compelling influences is, of course, admissible in evidence." 384 U.S., at 478. Ploys to mislead a suspect or lull him into a false sense of security that do not rise to the level of compulsion or coercion to speak are not within *Miranda*'s concerns.

Miranda was not meant to protect suspects from boasting about their criminal activities in front of persons whom they believe to be their cellmates. This case is illustrative. Respondent had no reason to feel that undercover agent Parisi had any legal authority to force him to answer questions or that Parisi could affect respondent's future treatment. Respondent viewed the cellmate-agent as an equal and showed no hint of being intimidated by the atmosphere of the jail. In recounting the details of the Stephenson murder, respondent was motivated solely by the desire to impress his fellow inmates. He spoke at his own peril.

The tactic employed here to elicit a voluntary confession from a suspect does not violate the Self-Incrimination Clause. We held in *Hoffa v. United States*, 385 U.S. 293 (1966), that placing an undercover agent near a suspect in order to gather incriminating information was permissible under the Fifth Amendment. In *Hoffa*, while petitioner Hoffa was on trial, he met often with one Partin, who, unbeknownst to Hoffa, was cooperating with law enforcement officials. Partin reported to officials that Hoffa had divulged his attempts to bribe jury members. We approved using Hoffa's statements at his subsequent trial for jury tampering, on the rationale that "no claim ha[d] been or could [have been] made that [Hoffa's] incriminating statements were the product of any sort of coercion, legal or factual." *Id.*, at 304. In addition, we found that the fact that Partin had fooled Hoffa into thinking that Partin was a sympathetic colleague did not affect the voluntariness of the statements. The only difference between this case and *Hoffa* is that the suspect here was incarcerated, but detention, whether or not for the crime in question, does not warrant a presumption that the use of an undercover agent to speak with an incarcerated suspect makes any confession thus obtained involuntary.

Our decision in *Mathis v. United States*, 391 U.S. 1 (1968), is distinguishable. In *Mathis*, an inmate in a state prison was interviewed by an Internal Revenue Service agent about possible tax violations. No *Miranda* warning was given before questioning. The Court held that the suspect's incriminating statements were not admissible at his subsequent trial on tax fraud charges. The suspect in *Mathis* was aware that the agent was a government official, investigating the possibility of non-compliance with the tax laws. The case before us now is different. Where the suspect does not know that he is speaking to a government agent there is no reason to assume the possibility that the suspect might feel coerced. (The bare fact of custody may not in every instance require a warning even when the suspect is aware that he is speaking to an official, but we do not have occasion to explore that issue here.)

This Court's Sixth Amendment decisions in *Massiah v. United States*, 377 U.S. 201 (1964), *United States v. Henry*, 447 U.S. 264 (1980), and *Maine v. Moulton*, 474 U.S. 159 (1985), also do not avail respondent. We held in those cases that the government may not use an undercover agent to circumvent the Sixth Amendment right to counsel once a suspect has been charged with the crime. After charges have been filed, the Sixth Amendment prevents the government from interfering with the accused's right to counsel. In the instant case no charges had been filed on the subject of the interrogation, and our Sixth Amendment precedents are not applicable.

Respondent can seek no help from his argument that a bright-line rule for the application of *Miranda* is desirable. Law enforcement officers will have little difficulty putting into practice our holding that undercover agents need not give *Miranda* warnings to incarcerated suspects. The use of undercover agents is a recognized law enforcement technique, often employed in the prison context to detect violence against correctional officials or inmates, as well as for the purposes served here. The interests protected by *Miranda* are not implicated in these cases, and the warnings are not required to safeguard the constitutional rights of inmates who make voluntary statements to undercover agents. We hold that an undercover law enforcement officer posing as a fellow inmate need not give *Miranda* warnings to an incarcerated suspect before asking questions that may elicit an incriminating response. The statements at issue in this case were voluntary, and there is no federal obstacle to their admissibility at trial. We now reverse and remand for proceedings not inconsistent with our opinion.

It is so ordered.

JUSTICE BRENNAN, concurring in the judgment.

The Court holds that *Miranda v. Arizona*, 384 U.S. 436 (1966), does not require suppression of a statement made by an incarcerated suspect to an undercover agent. Although I do not subscribe to the majority's characterization of *Miranda* in its entirety, I do agree that when a suspect does not know that his questioner is a police agent, such questioning does not amount to "interrogation" in an "inherently coercive" environment so as to require application of *Miranda*. Since the only issue raised at this stage of the litigation is the applicability of *Miranda*, I concur in the judgment of the Court.

This is not to say that I believe the Constitution condones the method by which the police extracted the confession in this case. To the contrary, the deception and manipulation practiced on respondent raise a substantial claim that the confession was obtained in violation of the Due Process Clause. As we recently stated in *Miller v. Fenton*, 474 U.S. 104, 109–110 (1985): "This Court has long held that certain interrogation techniques, either in isolation or as applied to the unique characteristics of a particular suspect, are so offensive to a civilized system of justice that they must be condemned under the Due Process Clause of the Fourteenth Amendment."

. . . .

The deliberate use of deception and manipulation by the police appears to be incompatible "with a system that presumes innocence and assures that a conviction will not be secured by inquisitorial means," *Miller, supra*, at 116, and raises serious concerns that respondent's will was overborne. It is open to the lower court on remand to determine whether, under the totality of the circumstances, respondent's confession was elicited in a manner that violated the Due Process Clause. That the confession was not elicited through means of physical torture or overt psychological pressure does not end the inquiry. "[A]s law enforcement officers become more responsible, and the methods used to extract confessions more sophisticated, [a court's] duty to enforce federal constitutional protections does not cease. It only becomes more difficult because of the more delicate judgments to be made." *Spano v. New York*, 360 U.S. 315, 321.

JUSTICE MARSHALL, dissenting.

This Court clearly and simply stated its holding in *Miranda v. Arizona*, 384 U.S. 436 (1966): "[T]he prosecution may not use statements, whether exculpatory or inculpatory, stemming from custodial interrogation of the defendant unless it demonstrates the use of procedural safeguards effective to secure the privilege against self-incrimination." *Id.*, at 444. The conditions that require the police to apprise a defendant of his constitutional rights — custodial interrogation conducted by an agent of the police — were present in this case. Because Lloyd Perkins received no *Miranda* warnings before he was subjected to custodial interrogation, his confession was not admissible. The Court reaches the contrary conclusion by fashioning an exception to the *Miranda* rule that applies whenever "an undercover law enforcement officer posing as a fellow inmate . . . ask[s] questions that may elicit an incriminating response" from an incarcerated suspect. This exception is inconsistent with the rationale supporting *Miranda* and allows police officers intentionally to take advantage of suspects unaware of their constitutional rights. I therefore dissent.

The Court does not dispute that the police officer here conducted a custodial interrogation of a criminal suspect. Perkins was incarcerated in county jail during the questioning at issue here; under these circumstances, he was in custody as that term is defined in *Miranda*. . . .

While Perkins was confined, an undercover police officer, with the help of a police informant, questioned him about a serious crime. Although the Court does not dispute that Perkins was interrogated, it downplays the nature of the 35-minute questioning by disingenuously referring to it as a "conversatio[n]." The officer's narration of the "conversation" at Perkins' trial, however, reveals that it clearly was an interrogation:

[Agent:] You ever do anyone?

Perkins: Yeah, once in East St. Louis, in a rich white neighborhood.

[Informant:] I didn't know they had any rich white neighborhoods in East St. Louis.

Perkins: It wasn't in East St. Louis, it was by a race track in Fairview Heights. . . .

[Agent:] You did a guy in Fairview Heights?

Perkins: Yeah in a rich white — where most of the houses look the same.

[Informant:] If all the houses look the same, how did you know you had the right house?

Perkins: Me and two guys cased the house for about a week. I knew exactly which house, the second house on the left from the corner.

[Agent:] How long ago did this happen?

Perkins: Approximately about two years ago. I got paid $5,000 for that job.

[Agent:] How did it go down?

Perkins: I walked up to . . . this guy['s] house with a sawed-off under my trench coat.

[Agent:] What type gun[?]

Perkins: A 12-gauge Remmington [*sic*] Automatic Model 1100 sawed-off.

App. 49–50.

The police officer continued the inquiry, asking a series of questions designed to elicit specific information about the victim, the crime scene, the weapon, Perkins' motive, and his actions during and after the shooting. *Id.*, at 50–52. This interaction was not a "conversation"; Perkins, the officer, and the informant were not equal participants in a free-ranging discussion, with each man offering his views on different topics. Rather, it was an interrogation: Perkins was subjected to express questioning likely to evoke an incriminating response. *Rhode Island v. Innis*, 446 U.S. 291, 300–301 (1980). Because Perkins was interrogated by police while he was in custody, *Miranda* required that the officer inform him of his rights. In rejecting that conclusion, the Court finds that "conversations" between undercover agents and suspects are devoid of the coercion inherent in stationhouse interrogations conducted by law enforcement officials who openly represent the State. *Miranda* was not, however, concerned solely with police *coercion*. It dealt with *any* police tactics that may operate to compel a suspect in custody to make incriminating statements without full awareness of his constitutional rights. Thus, when a law enforcement agent structures a custodial interrogation so that a suspect feels compelled to reveal incriminating information, he must inform the suspect of his constitutional rights and give him an opportunity to decide whether or not to talk.

The compulsion proscribed by *Miranda* includes deception by the police. *See Miranda, supra,* at 453 (indicting police tactics "to induce a confession out of trickery," such as using fictitious witnesses or false accusations). Although the Court did not find trickery by itself sufficient to constitute compulsion in *Hoffa v. United States*, 385 U.S. 293 (1966), the defendant in that case was not in custody. Perkins, however, was interrogated while incarcerated. . . .

Custody works to the State's advantage in obtaining incriminating information. The psychological pressures inherent in confinement increase the suspect's anxiety, making him likely to seek relief by talking with others. Dix, *Undercover Investigations and Police Rulemaking*, 53 Texas L. Rev. 203, 230 (1975). The inmate is thus more susceptible to efforts by undercover agents to elicit information from him. Similarly, where the suspect is incarcerated, the constant threat of physical danger peculiar to the prison environment may make him demonstrate his toughness to other inmates by recounting or inventing past violent acts. "Because the suspect's ability to select people with whom he can confide is completely within their control, the police have a unique opportunity to exploit the suspect's vulnerability. In short, the police can insure that if the pressures of confinement lead the suspect to confide in anyone, it will be a police agent." White, *Police Trickery in Inducing Confessions*, 127 U. Pa. L. Rev. 581, 605 (1979). In this case, the police deceptively took advantage of Perkins' psychological vulnerability by including him in a sham escape plot, a situation in which he would feel compelled to demonstrate his willingness to shoot a prison guard by revealing his past involvement in a murder.

Thus, the pressures unique to custody allow the police to use deceptive interrogation tactics to compel a suspect to make an incriminating statement. The compulsion is not eliminated by the suspect's ignorance of his interrogator's true identity. The Court therefore need not inquire past the bare facts of custody and interrogation to determine whether *Miranda* warnings are required.

. . . .

The Court's holding today complicates a previously clear and straightforward doctrine. The Court opines that "[l]aw enforcement officers will have little difficulty putting into practice our holding that undercover agents need not give *Miranda* warnings to incarcerated suspects." Perhaps this prediction is true with respect to fact patterns virtually identical to the one before the Court today. But the outer boundaries of the exception created by the Court are by no means clear. Would *Miranda* be violated, for instance, if an undercover police officer beat a confession out of a suspect, but the suspect thought the officer was another prisoner who wanted the information for his own purposes?

Even if *Miranda*, as interpreted by the Court, would not permit such obviously compelled confessions, the ramifications of today's opinion are still disturbing. The exception carved out of the *Miranda* doctrine today may well result in a proliferation of departmental policies to encourage police officers to conduct interrogations of confined suspects through undercover agents, thereby circumventing the need to administer *Miranda* warnings. Indeed, if *Miranda* now requires a police officer to issue warnings only in those situations in which the suspect might feel compelled "to speak by the fear of reprisal for remaining silent or in the hope of more lenient treatment should he confess," presumably it allows custodial interrogation by an undercover officer posing as a member of the clergy or a suspect's defense attorney. Although such abhorrent tricks would play on a suspect's need to confide in a trusted adviser, neither would cause the suspect to "think that the listeners have official power over him." The Court's adoption of the "undercover agent" exception to the *Miranda* rule thus is necessarily also the adoption of a substantial loophole in our jurisprudence protecting suspects' Fifth Amendment rights.

I dissent.

Notes and Questions

(1) By asking express questions about Perkins's crime, undercover agent Parisi clearly engaged in conduct that satisfied the *Innis* standard for interrogation. Why did a near-unanimous Court conclude, nonetheless, that it was not necessary to issue *Miranda* warnings? Is that conclusion consistent with *Miranda*'s Fifth Amendment goals?

(2) When an informer elicits incriminating statements from a suspect in prison, what is the constitutional standard for determining the admissibility of the suspect's admissions? If the government seeks to introduce the incriminating statements against the suspect to prove a crime with which he was already charged when the incriminating statements took place, the Sixth Amendment right to counsel and the Due Process Clause provide the governing standards. For the Sixth Amendment standard, see Chapter 9, *infra*. If, as in *Perkins*, the government seeks to introduce statements that relate to a crime with which the suspect has not yet been charged, the due process voluntariness test provides the sole constitutional constraint on admissibility. *See Arizona v. Fulminante*, 499 U.S. 279, 111 S. Ct. 1246, 113 L. Ed. 2d 302 (1991).

(3) In *Arizona v. Fulminante*, 499 U.S. 279, 111 S. Ct. 1246, 113 L. Ed. 2d 302 (1991), the defendant, an inmate in a federal penitentiary as a result of a weapons of-

fense, was suspected of murdering his 11-year-old stepdaughter. Because child killers are detested by the prison population, defendant had apparently been receiving
"rough treatment" from other prisoners. Sarivola, another inmate who was a government informer masquerading as an organized crime figure, told his superior in
the FBI that defendant was rumored to have killed his stepdaughter. The latter told
Sarivola "to find out more."

Sarivola had previously asked defendant about his stepdaughter's death, and defendant had denied any involvement. Sarivola now offered defendant "protection"
from the other inmates, but only if he would tell the truth about his stepdaughter's
death. Defendant then admitted to Sarivola that he had murdered his stepdaughter.
At defendant's murder trial, his confession to Sarivola was introduced into evidence.
The defendant was convicted and sentenced to death.

In a 5–4 decision, the Court agreed with the Arizona Supreme Court's conclusion
that defendant's confession had been coerced, and, therefore, that its admission into
evidence violated due process. Justice White's opinion for the majority determined
that the lower court finding that defendant's "will was overborne" was supportable
because defendant faced "a credible threat of physical violence" unless he confessed.
Justice Rehnquist's dissent emphasized that the defendant "offered no evidence that
he believed that his life was in danger or that he in fact confessed to Sarivola in order
to obtain the proffered protection." The dissent complained that the majority's conclusion was a misapplication of the "totality of the circumstances" test.

For consideration of some of the issues raised by the *Fulminante* case, see Welsh S.
White, *Regulating Prison Informers Under the Due Process Clause,* 1991 Sup. Ct.
Rev. 103.

Interrogation Problems

8C–1: Tigger returned from a short trip to Jamaica. As he was waiting to go
through customs at the airport, Inspector Joseph of U.S. Immigration and Customs Enforcement ("ICE") noticed that he was acting nervously. Joseph approached
and asked Tigger a few questions about his trip and his destination. Because Tigger's responses were contradictory and implausible, and because he was becoming
defensive, Joseph referred Tigger to a secondary processing area where he opened
Tigger's luggage and found three suspicious coffee bags. Opening one over Tigger's
protest, Joseph discovered a white powder that turned out to be cocaine. He arrested
Tigger.

Joseph took Tigger to a holding cell, handcuffed him to the bed, and read him his
Miranda rights. Tigger said he wanted to remain silent. Shortly thereafter, ICE Agent
Michael entered Tigger's cell, told him that testing had confirmed that the substance
in the coffee bag was cocaine, and suggested that he "could help himself out." Tigger
declined, and Michael left. Some time later, Michael reentered Tigger's cell and

apprised him that they had found cocaine in a rum bottle in his bag as well and that he had a "serious problem." Michael then left both the cell and the general area.

Approximately 10 minutes later, Tigger began shouting that he had never seen the coffee before. He then shouted that the coffee was already packaged when he took it off the shelf. Shortly thereafter, he shouted that he knew a lot about the smuggling trade. Agents responded that they could not discuss the subject.

Will Tigger's statements be subject to exclusion under *Miranda*?

8C–2: Kade was charged with first-degree felony murder, armed robbery, and possession of a firearm during the commission of a felony, arising from the shooting death of Willard. The prosecutor's theory was that Kade attempted to rob Willard at gunpoint, and when Willard resisted, Kade shot him. After Kade was arrested, he was given *Miranda* warnings and the following exchange occurred:

> DETECTIVE TILES: Okay. This is what they call the acknowledgment and waiver paragraph. I'm going to read this to you. If you wish to talk to me, I'm going to need you to sign and date the form. Even though you sign and date the form, you still have your rights to stop at any time you wish. Do you understand that?

> KADE: No. No thank you sir. I'm not going to sign it. I don't want to speak.

> DETECTIVE TILES: I understand. Okay then. The only thing I can tell you, is good luck man. Don't take this personal. It's not personal between me and you, I think I may have had one contact with you on the street. I've got to do my job. And I understand you've got to do what you've got to do to protect your best interests. The only thing that I can tell you is this, and I'm not asking you questions, I'm just telling you. I hope that the gun is in a place where nobody can get ahold of it and nobody else can get hurt by it, okay? All right?

> KADE: I didn't even mean for it to happen like that. It was a complete accident.

> DETECTIVE TILES: I understand. But like I said, you get your attorney, man. Hey, look dude, I don't think you're a monster, all right? I don't think that. You could have come down to me and turned yourself in and there ain't no damn way I'd beat you up. You all set, you straight with me? Who knows you're here? Who knows of your family? Because I know a lot of your family in town now.

> KADE: I didn't mean to do it. I guarantee that, I didn't mean to do it.

Are Kade's statements admissible under *Miranda*?

8C–3: The defendant flew from Colombia to Miami International Airport on January 27, 1976. Upon deplaning, she proceeded to Customs and presented herself and her luggage to Customs Inspector Rollins. Rollins noticed that she appeared very nervous and that her voice cracked. She was wearing tight-fitting clothes that revealed a bulge in her abdominal area. Further, the defendant was a young, single female traveling alone, and the duration of her stay in Colombia was short. Since these characteristics are traits that customs inspectors have found to be indicative of drug smugglers, Rollins believed a search was warranted. His supervisor, Inspector Korzeniowski, concurred.

The defendant was taken to the secondary search room where two female customs inspectors conducted a strip search. This search produced no incriminating evidence. Upon being informed of the unproductive search, Inspector Korzeniowski entered the secondary search room and handed the defendant a booklet made up of newspaper clippings reflecting a number of tragedies that had occurred when people had attempted to hide narcotics in their body cavities. Korzeniowski took the defendant into the supervisor's office and talked to her for seven or eight minutes as "a father might talk to a daughter." He told her that this was a very serious matter, that she could harm herself seriously, perhaps even cause her death, if she was carrying contraband in her body and if any of the containers ruptured and the narcotic came into immediate contact with her body or her internal organs. Following this, the defendant turned white, hung her head down and blurted out, "Yes, I do have narcotics in my body." The defendant was allowed to remove the narcotics from her body. She was then placed under arrest and advised of her rights.

Should Agent Korzeniowski have given the defendant *Miranda* warnings?

8C–4: Officers Robert and Earl received an anonymous tip that two men were selling drugs on the front steps of 1939 Hollins Street, the home of Damon Kim. The officers parked nearby and saw two men conduct an apparent drug transaction with the occupants of a vehicle. The officers approached and asked the men if they resided at 1939 Hollins, and the men replied that they were just visiting. Officer Robert knocked on the door of the house, and Ms. Kim, Damon's mother, came to the door. She insisted there were no drugs in her home and consented to an entry and search. Upon entering, the officers heard a disturbance in the basement. When they proceeded downstairs, they found Damon dividing cocaine with a razor blade. They arrested and handcuffed him.

While Earl took Damon upstairs, Robert called Ms. Kim down to the basement and showed her what they had found. Ms. Kim appeared shocked and surprised and asked to speak to her son. When Damon was brought downstairs, his mother asked him, "What is this?" and "Is there anything down here?" Officer Robert attempted to recite *Miranda* warnings from memory, but seriously misstated them. Damon agreed to speak without a lawyer present. Damon then responded to questions posed by his mother while looking at Robert. When Ms. Kim asked if there was anything else down in the basement, Damon replied that there was a gun under the cushion of the couch. Robert recovered the gun.

Prior to trial for drug and gun offenses, Damon moved to suppress all the statements made after his arrest. The government argued that *Miranda* was inapplicable because Ms. Kim asked the questions. The district court found that "official interrogation" had occurred, and granted the motion to suppress the statements he made in response to Ms. Kim's questions. The government has appealed.

How should the court of appeals rule?

8C–5: Charles and an 11-year-old boy were arrested for robbery and transported to the police station, where they were separated. Officer Pappo stayed with Charles in the main detectives' office, where he informed Charles of his *Miranda* rights. Charles informed Officer Pappo that he wanted to speak to an attorney. Meanwhile, the boy admitted to Detective Alton that he and Charles had robbed "a white lady." Detective Alton then joined Officer Pappo and Charles. Pappo informed Alton that Charles had asked for counsel, whereupon Alton stated, "[T]hat's fine if he doesn't want to talk to me. I wasn't the person that robbed a white lady and hit her in the head with a brick." Alton then stated either "If that's the story *you want* to tell the judge, that's fine," or "If that's the story *he wants* to tell the judge, that's fine."

When Charles said that he wanted to talk to the officers, Alton responded, "No, that's fine, you don't have to talk to me, I'm good." Charles again stated that he wanted to talk. Alton informed Charles that he must sign a waiver of rights form and that he must write on it that he wished to speak to the detectives. Charles signed the form. He wrote on the back that he had asked for an attorney but had changed his mind and wished to speak to Detective Alton. Charles subsequently admitted that he and the boy had decided to "rob a white lady," that he gave the boy a knife and armed himself with a brick wrapped in a shirt. He admitted that he hit the victim on the side of the head with the brick. When the victim resisted, Charles and the boy fled the scene.

Prior to trial, Charles moved to suppress his statements, relying on *Miranda*.

Does the *Miranda* doctrine bar the introduction of Charles's statements at trial?

8C–6: Lloyd C. Payne sold an ounce of cocaine to an undercover FBI agent on December 1, and again on December 9. Agents obtained a warrant for Payne's arrest and a search warrant for his residence.

Upon his arrest, Payne was warned of his *Miranda* rights and indicated his desire to consult with an attorney before speaking to the agents. Payne was then transported in a car with three FBI agents. Payne was seated in the rear of the car next to FBI Special Agent Deborah Martin. Sometime during the ride, Agent Martin received a call on the cellular car phone. During that conversation, another FBI agent informed her that a handgun had been found at Payne's residence during the execution of the search warrant. After the conversation, Agent Martin said to Payne, "They found a gun at your house." Payne responded, "I just had it for my protection." Based on the discovery of the gun, Payne was charged with a weapons offense.

Will Payne's statement to Agent Martin be admissible?

8C–7: DEA Agent Dunlap was involved in the investigation of a large scale cocaine smuggling operation. After Moreno was arrested for smuggling cocaine, Dunlap read him his *Miranda* warnings. Moreno immediately invoked his right to remain silent. Dunlap then said, "I want you to know that you are in serious trouble. You are facing a long prison sentence. After you have consulted with your attorney, I'd like to speak to you again. After you talk to your attorney, I hope you will be willing to talk to us about other individuals involved in cocaine distribution."

When Dunlap picked Moreno up to transport him to court the following morning, he asked Moreno how his night had been. Moreno responded, "Look, I was just doing this for $2500. I'm not a big guy in this thing." Dunlap reminded Moreno that he had invoked his right to remain silent, but Moreno continued, "Well, after you said it was cocaine last night, I wanted you to know that I thought it was just marihauna. And I wanted you to know that I'm not the big guy in this thing. I was just helping Pelayo."

Will Moreno's incriminating statements be admissible?

8C–8: Boggs, who was incarcerated awaiting trial on theft charges, asked another inmate, Daniel Krushinski, if he knew anyone who could murder the two witnesses who were scheduled to testify against him at his trial. Krushinski later informed Trooper Daniel Wertz of his conversation with Boggs. Wertz told Krushinski to tell Boggs that he would get someone to "take care of the problem." Krushinski then approached Boggs and told him that his cousin, who was an attorney, would come to the prison to discuss Boggs's "problem." Trooper Wertz then enlisted the aid of Corporal Craig Fenstermacher, who agreed to pose as Krushinski's cousin.

Posing as an attorney, Fenstermacher met with Boggs in a private room at the prison. Fenstermacher introduced himself as Chuck Fry. After some preliminary discussion, Boggs stated that he was having a legal problem with two witnesses and that he needed to get rid of the witnesses in order to get out of jail. Specifically, he said the witnesses needed to be "eliminated and unable to testify." Boggs gave Fenstermacher the names and addresses of the witnesses and told him that he would receive payment of $2500 from Boggs's girlfriend.

After Boggs's girlfriend paid $2500 to Trooper Wertz, Fenstermacher again met with Boggs at the prison. During this meeting, Boggs gave detailed descriptions of the witnesses, and said that "when this is done my attorney will have the charges against me dropped." The men then discussed the final payment arrangements and Fenstermacher said, "I will take care of it." Boggs replied, "It sounds good to me."

Based on his statements to Fenstermacher, Boggs was charged with attempted murder, criminal conspiracy to commit murder, and solicitation to commit murder. Prior to trial, Boggs moved to suppress his statements to Fenstermacher.

What arguments can Boggs assert in support of his motion? Should the motion be granted?

8C–9: Officer Brandon responded to a 911 dispatch concerning a stabbing. At the scene, Brandon found McKay, a man with blood on his shirt. McKay mentioned the name "Mike" and pointed to another man about 100 feet away who was wearing a dark shirt and carrying a dark-colored bag. Brandon radioed the description of this man to other officers. McKay subsequently died from the knife wounds he had sustained.

As Officer Aaron, who had responded to Brandon's radio report, neared the vicinity of the stabbing, he saw Michael Jay, a man who appeared to match the description provided by Brandon. Aaron approached Jay and yelled, "Hey." When Jay turned around, Aaron saw that he was bleeding from one eye. Aaron asked Jay what had happened to his eye, and Jay responded, "He threatened me so I stuck him." Aaron exited his cruiser, handcuffed Jay, and placed him in the back seat. While Aaron drove Jay to the scene of the stabbing, he heard Jay "make several statements to himself." Specifically, Jay said that "he stuck him once," that "he wanted to stick him again," and that "he wanted to kill him." Aaron did not ask any questions or engage Jay in conversation.

After informing the officers at the scene of the stabbing that he had detained Jay, Aaron drove Jay to the police station and took him to an interview room. Shortly thereafter, a detective came to the interview room. When he attempted to shake Jay's hand, Jay refused because his hands were "dirty." The following exchange then took place:

Detective: Okay, sir. I was speaking with the officer who brought you down here and he shared some information, so —

Jay: I told it to him 14 times.

Detective: Ok. Do you want to tell it to me?

Jay: The asshole's name was Jimmy McKay. He threatened to kill me. I took a knife, and I stuck him. I would have stuck him again, but he ran away. And after that I don't know what happened. I was a block away and he handcuffed me and wanted to know where the knife was. I don't even, after I stabbed that piece of shit, I don't remember anything. I'm guilty.

The detective then recited *Miranda* warnings.

Does *Miranda* require that any of Jay's incriminating statements be barred from his first-degree murder trial?

8C–10: Sergeant Johns and Lieutenant Leslie saw Oster and Wills conduct an apparent drug sale. A woman approached the two men and handed Oster what appeared to be money. In exchange, Wills retrieved a small object from the rear passenger side of a car parked nearby and handed it to the woman. As soon as the woman left the vicinity of the transaction, the officers stopped her and found a yellow ziplock bag containing cocaine base in her possession. The officers returned to the scene of the transaction and stopped Oster and Wills as they were beginning to drive away. With the two men detained on the sidewalk, Lieutenant Leslie retrieved a plastic bag containing roughly one gram of cocaine base from behind the fuel cap of their car. He also found $457 in small bills in the car's front console. Oster and Wills were then arrested and handcuffed.

Before advising the men of their *Miranda* rights, Sergeant Johns declared, "I can't believe with all the money and drugs we found we didn't find a handgun!" Oster replied, "If you want a gun I will get you a handgun." Johns announced that "It would take four handguns with whatever you have here," referring to the contraband that had been found. Oster replied, "I can get you one right now. I need to go in my car and go right around the corner and get you a nine millimeter." This exchange occurred against the backdrop of a well-known Police Department policy that may allow suspects to escape low-level drug charges if they turn guns over to the police.

Did Sergeant Johns interrogate Oster?

8C–11: Corporal Whaley went to the Hillside Market in response to a report of a break-in and theft at the market. The owner of the market told Whaley that he had found a tire iron behind the counter near the cash register. Upon investigating the break-in, Whaley concluded that the tire iron had probably been used to gain entry into the store.

Subsequently, Whaley arrested Drury and took him to the police station. Before advising Drury of his *Miranda* rights, Whaley showed Drury the tire iron and said to him, "They'll be checking this for fingerprints." Drury replied, "Well, my fingerprints could be on that because my prints are on hundreds of tire irons in this area." He then proceeded to make additional incriminating statements.

Did Corporal Whaley interrogate Drury?

[D] Warnings and Waiver

Notes on the Warnings Requirement

The *Miranda* Court specified warnings that were "absolute prerequisites" for the admission of incriminating statements made in response to custodial interrogation. The only time these prerequisites do not apply is when officers' questions fall within the "public safety exception" recognized in *New York v. Quarles*. One question that has arisen since *Miranda* is whether officers must use the precise language prescribed by the *Miranda* majority. The Court has addressed this issue on three occasions.

(1) In *California v. Prysock*, 453 U.S. 355, 101 S. Ct. 2806, 69 L. Ed. 2d 696 (1981), a minor was arrested for a murder and was given *Miranda* warnings. He declined to talk. After he met with his parents, however, he changed his mind. In the presence of his parents, an officer recited a second set of warnings which included the admonition "[y]ou have the right to talk to a lawyer before you are questioned, have him present with you while you are being questioned, and all during the questioning." After telling the minor that he had "the right to have your parents present," the officer stated, "you have the right to have a lawyer appointed to represent you at no cost to yourself." When the minor's mother asked whether her son "could still have an attorney at a later time if he gave a statement now without one," the officer responded that he "would have an attorney when he went to court and that 'he could have one at this time if he wished one.'" A state appellate court held that the warnings recited "were inadequate because [the minor] was not explicitly informed of his right to have an attorney appointed before further questioning."

In a 6-3 ruling, the Supreme Court held that the officer's statements to the minor and his parents were sufficient to convey the required *Miranda* warnings relating to the right to have an attorney present during interrogation and the right of an indigent to have such an attorney appointed at no cost to himself. The Court indicated that variations from the exact language of the warnings specified in *Miranda* are permissible as long as the warnings given "fully convey[]" the rights included in the original four warnings. According to the majority, the warnings in *Prysock* satisfied that standard.

(2) In *Duckworth v. Eagan*, 492 U.S. 195, 109 S. Ct. 2875, 106 L. Ed. 2d 166 (1989), a stationhouse officer delivered the four requisite warnings, specifically apprising the suspect that he had a right to speak with an attorney before and during questioning and that he had the "right to the advice and presence of a lawyer even if [he could not] afford to hire one." Reading from a form, the officer then added, "We have no way of giving you a lawyer, but one will be appointed for you, if you wish, if and when you go to court." In a habeas corpus proceeding, a federal court of appeals held that the addition of "the advice that counsel would be appointed 'if and when you go to court,' . . . was 'constitutionally defective because it denies an indigent a clear and unequivocal warning of the right to appointed counsel before any interrogation,' and 'link[s] an indigent's right to counsel before interrogation to a future event.'" According to the court of appeals, "as a result of [that] warning, [the defendant] arguably believed that he could not secure a lawyer during interrogation."

In a 5-4 decision, the Supreme Court reversed the ruling of the court of appeals, holding that the warnings given were sufficient to apprise the suspect of his entitlement to the assistance of counsel under *Miranda*. The majority first observed that the warnings given accurately describe Indiana's procedure. It then concluded that the procedure followed in Indiana was consistent with *Miranda* because "*Miranda* does not require that attorneys be producible on call, but only that the suspect be informed, as here, that he has the right to an attorney before and during questioning, and that an attorney would be appointed for him if he could not afford one." According to the majority, "[t]he inquiry is simply whether the warnings *reasonably 'convey[y]* to [a suspect] his rights as required by *Miranda*.'" (Emphasis added).

If a suspect has a "right to an [appointed] attorney before and during questioning," how can it be permissible for a state to follow a procedure under which a suspect who wishes to have the assistance of counsel during custodial interrogation will not have an opportunity to consult with a lawyer until he goes to court?

(3) In *Florida v. Powell*, 559 U.S. 50, 130 S. Ct. 1195, 175 L. Ed. 2d 1009 (2010), officers warned a suspect of the right to remain silent and that anything he said could be used in court, then told him, "'You have the right to talk to a lawyer before answering any of our questions.'" After apprising him of an indigent's entitlement to appointed counsel, they concluded by stating, "'You have the right to use any of these rights at any time you want during this interview.'" The Florida Supreme Court concluded that these warnings did not adequately inform the suspect of his entitlement to have counsel present *during* questioning. The Supreme Court disagreed, conclud-

ing by a 7-2 margin that the warnings recited "'satisfied'" *Miranda*'s "'absolute prerequisite to interrogation.'"

According to the majority, the "four warnings . . . require[d] are invariable." Nonetheless, the words used to communicate "the essential information" may vary, as long as they "'reasonably "conve[y] to [a suspect] his rights as required by *Miranda*."'" Powell was first informed that he "could consult with a lawyer before answering any particular question" and then was told "that he could exercise that right while the interrogation was underway. In combination, the two warnings reasonably conveyed [his] right to have an attorney present, not only at the outset of interrogation, but at all times." Upon hearing these warnings, a suspect was not likely to believe that he had "to exit and reenter the interrogation room" whenever he wished to consult with a lawyer about a question. "Instead, [he] would likely assume that he must stay put in the interrogation room and that his lawyer would be there with him the entire time." Consequently, "[a]lthough the warnings were not the *clearest possible* formulation of *Miranda*'s right-to-counsel advisement, they were sufficiently comprehensive and comprehensible when given a commonsense reading." (Emphasis in original).

Justice Stevens, joined by Justice Breyer, dissented, opining that the "more natural reading of the warning . . . given, which (1) contained a temporal limit and (2) failed to mention [the] right to the presence of counsel in the interrogation room, [was] that [the suspect] only had the right to consult with an attorney before the interrogation began." Because an "intelligent suspect could reasonably conclude that all he was provided was a one-time right to consult with an attorney, not a right to have an attorney present with him in the interrogation room at all times," the dissenters believed that "the warning at issue . . . did not reasonably convey" the prescribed content.

(4) In light of *Miranda*'s objectives, what arguments support the conclusion that officers should be required to recite warnings that are virtually identical to those set forth in *Miranda*? Why should officers be permitted to add additional warnings that might inject ambiguity? Why should it be sufficient to deliver warnings that "reasonably convey" the content of the original warnings? What does this doctrinal standard for assessing the adequacy of warnings mean?

Berghuis v. Thompkins

United States Supreme Court

560 U.S. 370, 130 S. Ct. 2250, 176 L. Ed. 2d 1098 (2010)

JUSTICE KENNEDY delivered the opinion of the Court.

. . . .

I

A

On January 10, 2000, a shooting occurred outside a mall in Southfield, Michigan. Among the victims was Samuel Morris, who died from multiple gunshot wounds. The other victim, Frederick France, recovered from his injuries and later testified.

Thompkins, who was a suspect, fled. About one year later he was found in Ohio and arrested there.

Two Southfield police officers traveled to Ohio to interrogate Thompkins, then awaiting transfer to Michigan. The interrogation began around 1:30 p.m. and lasted about three hours. The interrogation was conducted in a room that was 8 by 10 feet, and Thompkins sat in a chair that resembled a school desk (it had an arm on it that swings around to provide a surface to write on). At the beginning of the interrogation, one of the officers, Detective Helgert, presented Thompkins with a form derived from the *Miranda* rule. It stated [the four *Miranda* warnings, then added this fifth warning]:

> "5. You have the right to decide at any time before or during questioning to use your right to remain silent and your right to talk with a lawyer while you are being questioned." ([S]ome capitalization omitted).

Helgert asked Thompkins to read the fifth warning out loud. Thompkins complied. Helgert later said this was to ensure that Thompkins could read, and Helgert concluded that Thompkins understood English. Helgert then read the other four *Miranda* warnings out loud and asked Thompkins to sign the form to demonstrate that he understood his rights. Thompkins declined to sign the form. The record contains conflicting evidence about whether Thompkins then verbally confirmed that he understood the rights listed on the form.

Officers began an interrogation. At no point during the interrogation did Thompkins say that he wanted to remain silent, that he did not want to talk with the police, or that he wanted an attorney. Thompkins was "[l]argely" silent during the interrogation, which lasted about three hours. He did give a few limited verbal responses, however, such as "yeah," "no," or "I don't know." And on occasion he communicated by nodding his head. Thompkins also said that he "didn't want a peppermint" that was offered to him by the police and that the chair he was "sitting in was hard."

About 2 hours and 45 minutes into the interrogation, Helgert asked Thompkins, "Do you believe in God?" Thompkins made eye contact with Helgert and said "Yes," as his eyes "well[ed] up with tears." Helgert asked, "Do you pray to God?" Thompkins said "Yes." Helgert asked, "Do you pray to God to forgive you for shooting that boy down?" Thompkins answered "Yes" and looked away. Thompkins refused to make a written confession, and the interrogation ended about 15 minutes later.

Thompkins was charged with first-degree murder, assault with intent to commit murder, and certain firearms-related offenses. He moved to suppress the statements made during the interrogation. He argued . . . that he had not waived his right to remain silent, and that his inculpatory statements were involuntary. The trial court denied the motion.

[The Court then set forth the facts relevant to Thompkins's Sixth Amendment claim that his trial counsel had rendered ineffective assistance.]

. . . .

The jury found Thompkins guilty on all counts. He was sentenced to life in prison without parole.

B

[On appeal, the Michigan courts rejected all of Thompkins's claims. When Thompkins raised the claims in a petition for a writ of habeas corpus, a federal district court denied the petition.]

. . . .

The United States Court of Appeals for the Sixth Circuit reversed, ruling for Thompkins on . . . his *Miranda* . . . claim[]. 547 F.3d 572 (2008). . . .

. . . .

We granted certiorari.

. . . .

III

. . . .

All concede that the warning given in this case was in full compliance with [*Miranda*'s warning] requirements. The dispute centers on the response — or nonresponse — from the suspect.

A

[At this point, the Court discussed the claim that officers had not respected Thompkins's invocation of his right to remain silent.]

. . . .

B

We next consider whether Thompkins waived his right to remain silent. . . . [An] accused's statement during a custodial interrogation is inadmissible at trial unless the prosecution can establish that the accused "in fact knowingly and voluntarily waived [*Miranda*] rights" when making the statement. [*North Carolina v.*] *Butler*, 441 U.S. [369,] 373, 99 S. Ct. 1755[, 60 L. Ed. 2d 286 (1979)]. The waiver inquiry "has two distinct dimensions": waiver must be "voluntary in the sense that it was the product of a free and deliberate choice rather than intimidation, coercion, or deception," and "made with a full awareness of both the nature of the right being abandoned and the consequences of the decision to abandon it." [*Moran v.*] *Burbine*, [475 U.S.] 412, 106 S. Ct. 1135[, 89 L. Ed. 2d 410 (1986)].

Some language in *Miranda* could be read to indicate that waivers are difficult to establish absent an explicit written waiver or a formal, express oral statement. *Miranda* said "a valid waiver will not be presumed simply from the silence of the accused after warnings are given or simply from the fact that a confession was in fact eventually obtained." 384 U.S., at 475, 86 S. Ct. 1602; see *id.*, at 470, 86 S. Ct. 1602 ("No effective waiver . . . can be recognized unless specifically made after the [*Miranda*] warnings . . . have been given"). In addition, the *Miranda* Court stated that "a heavy burden rests on the government to demonstrate that the defendant know-ingly and intelligently waived his privilege against self-incrimination and his right to retained or appointed counsel." *Id.*, at 475, 86 S. Ct. 1602.

The course of decisions since *Miranda*, informed by the application of *Miranda* warnings in the whole course of law enforcement, demonstrates that waivers can be established even absent formal or express statements of waiver. . . . The main pur-pose of *Miranda* is to ensure that an accused is advised of and understands the right to remain silent and the right to counsel. . . .

One of the first cases to decide the meaning and import of *Miranda* with respect to the question of waiver was *North Carolina v. Butler.* . . . *Butler* interpreted the *Mi-randa* language concerning the "heavy burden" to show waiver, 384 U.S., at 475, 86 S. Ct. 1602, in accord with usual principles of determining waiver, which can in-clude waiver implied from all the circumstances. See *Butler, supra,* at 373, 376, 99 S. Ct. 1755. And in a later case, the Court stated that this "heavy burden" is not more than the burden to establish waiver by a preponderance of the evidence. *Colorado v. Connelly,* 479 U.S. 157, 168, 107 S. Ct. 515, 93 L. Ed. 2d 473 (1986).

The prosecution therefore does not need to show that a waiver of *Miranda* rights was express. An "implicit waiver" of the "right to remain silent" is sufficient to admit a suspect's statement into evidence. *Butler, supra,* at 376, 99 S. Ct. 1755. *Butler* made clear that a waiver of *Miranda* rights may be implied through "the defendant's si-lence, coupled with an understanding of his rights and a course of conduct indicat-ing waiver." 441 U.S., at 373, 99 S. Ct. 1755. The Court in *Butler* therefore "retreated" from the "language and tenor of the *Miranda* opinion," which "suggested that the Court would require that a waiver . . . be 'specifically made.'" *Connecticut v. Barrett,* 479 U.S. 523, 531–532, 107 S. Ct. 828, 93 L. Ed. 2d 920 (1987) (Brennan, J., concur-ring in judgment).

If the State establishes that a *Miranda* warning was given and the accused made an uncoerced statement, this showing, standing alone, is insufficient to demonstrate "a valid waiver" of *Miranda* rights. *Miranda, supra,* at 475, 86 S. Ct. 1602. The pros-ecution must make the additional showing that the accused understood these rights. See *Colorado v. Spring,* 479 U.S. 564, 573–575, 107 S. Ct. 851, 93 L. Ed. 2d 954 (1987); *Carnley v. Cochran,* 369 U.S. 506, 516, 82 S. Ct. 884, 8 L. Ed. 2d 70 (1962) (govern-ment could not show that accused "understandingly" waived his right to counsel in light of "silent record"). Where the prosecution shows that a *Miranda* warning was given and that it was understood by the accused, an accused's uncoerced statement establishes an implied waiver of the right to remain silent.

Although *Miranda* imposes on the police a rule that is both formalistic and prac-tical when it prevents them from interrogating suspects without first providing them with a *Miranda* warning, it does not impose a formalistic waiver procedure that a suspect must follow to relinquish those rights. As a general proposition, the law can presume that an individual who, with a full understanding of his or her rights, acts in a manner inconsistent with their exercise has made a deliberate choice to relinquish the protection those rights afford. See, *e.g., Butler, supra,* at 372–376, 99 S. Ct. 1755; *Connelly, supra,* at 169–170, 107 S. Ct. 515 ("There is obviously no reason to require more in the way of a 'voluntariness' inquiry in the *Miranda* waiver context than in the [due process] confession context"). The Court's cases have recognized that a waiver of *Miranda* rights need only meet the standard of *Johnson v. Zerbst,* 304 U.S. 458, 464, 58 S. Ct. 1019, 82 L. Ed. 1461 (1938). See *Butler, supra,* at 374–375, 99 S. Ct. 1755; *Miranda, supra,* at 475–476, 86 S. Ct. 1602 (applying *Zerbst* standard of intentional relinquishment of a known right). . . .

The record in this case shows that Thompkins waived his right to remain silent. There is no basis in this case to conclude that he did not understand his rights; and on these facts it follows that he chose not to invoke or rely on those rights when he did speak. First, there is no contention that Thompkins did not understand his rights; and from this it follows that he knew what he gave up when he spoke. There was more than enough evidence in the record to conclude that Thompkins understood his *Miranda* rights. Thompkins received a written copy of the *Miranda* warnings; Detective Helgert determined that Thompkins could read and understand English; and Thompkins was given time to read the warnings. Thompkins, furthermore, read aloud the fifth warning, which stated that "you have the right to decide at any time before or during questioning to use your right to remain silent and your right to talk with a lawyer while you are being questioned." He was thus aware that his right to remain silent would not dissipate after a certain amount of time and that police would have to honor his right to be silent and his right to counsel during the whole course of interrogation. Those rights, the warning made clear, could be asserted at any time. Helgert, moreover, read the warnings aloud.

Second, Thompkins's answer to Detective Helgert's question about whether Thompkins prayed to God for forgiveness for shooting the victim is a "course of conduct indicating waiver" of the right to remain silent. *Butler, supra,* at 373, 99 S. Ct. 1755. If Thompkins wanted to remain silent, he could have said nothing in response to Helgert's questions, or he could have unambiguously invoked his *Miranda* rights and ended the interrogation. The fact that Thompkins made a statement about three hours after receiving a *Miranda* warning does not overcome the fact that he engaged in a course of conduct indicating waiver. Police are not required to rewarn suspects from time to time. Thompkins's answer to Helgert's question about praying to God for forgiveness for shooting the victim was sufficient to show a course of conduct indicating waiver. This is confirmed by the fact that before then Thompkins had given sporadic answers to questions throughout the interrogation.

Third, there is no evidence that Thompkins's statement was coerced. Thompkins does not claim that police threatened or injured him during the interrogation or that he was in any way fearful. The interrogation was conducted in a standard-sized room in the middle of the afternoon. It is true that apparently he was in a straight-backed chair for three hours, but there is no authority for the proposition that an interrogation of this length is inherently coercive. Indeed, even where interrogations of greater duration were held to be improper, they were accompanied, as this one was not, by other facts indicating coercion, such as an incapacitated and sedated suspect, sleep and food deprivation, and threats. The fact that Helgert's question referred to Thompkins's religious beliefs also did not render Thompkins's statement involuntary. "[T]he Fifth Amendment privilege is not concerned 'with moral and psychological pressures to confess emanating from sources other than official coercion.'" [*Connelly*, 479 U.S.], at 170, 107 S. Ct. 515 (quoting *Oregon v. Elstad*, 470 U.S. 298, 305, 105 S. Ct. 1285, 84 L. Ed. 2d 222 (1985)). In these circumstances, Thompkins knowingly and voluntarily made a statement to police, so he waived his right to remain silent.

C

Thompkins next argues that, even if his answer to Detective Helgert could constitute a waiver of his right to remain silent, the police were not allowed to question him until they obtained a waiver first. *Butler* forecloses this argument. The *Butler* Court held that courts can infer a waiver of *Miranda* rights "from the actions and words of the person interrogated." 441 U.S., at 373, 99 S. Ct. 1755. This principle would be inconsistent with a rule that requires a waiver at the outset. . . . This holding also makes sense given that "the primary protection afforded suspects subject[ed] to custodial interrogation is the *Miranda* warnings themselves." *Davis*, 512 U.S., at 460, 114 S. Ct. 2350. The *Miranda* rule and its requirements are met if a suspect receives adequate *Miranda* warnings, understands them, and has an opportunity to invoke the rights before giving any answers or admissions. Any waiver, express or implied, may be contradicted by an invocation at any time. . . .

Interrogation provides the suspect with additional information that can put his or her decision to waive, or not to invoke, into perspective. As questioning commences and then continues, the suspect has the opportunity to consider the choices he or she faces and to make a more informed decision, either to insist on silence or to cooperate. When the suspect knows that *Miranda* rights can be invoked at any time, he or she has the opportunity to reassess his or her immediate and long-term interests. Cooperation with the police may result in more favorable treatment for the suspect; the apprehension of accomplices; the prevention of continuing injury and fear; beginning steps towards relief or solace for the victims; and the beginning of the suspect's own return to the law and the social order it seeks to protect.

In order for an accused's statement to be admissible at trial, police must have given the accused a *Miranda* warning. If that condition is established, the court can proceed to consider whether there has been an express or implied waiver of *Miranda* rights. In making its ruling on the admissibility of a statement made during custodial questioning, the trial court, of course, considers whether there is evidence to support the conclusion that, from the whole course of questioning, an express or implied waiver has been established. Thus, after giving a *Miranda* warning, police may interrogate a suspect who has neither invoked nor waived his or her *Miranda* rights. On these premises, it follows the police were not required to obtain a waiver of Thompkins's *Miranda* rights before commencing the interrogation.

D

In sum, a suspect who has received and understood the *Miranda* warnings, and has not invoked his *Miranda* rights, waives the right to remain silent by making an uncoerced statement to the police. Thompkins did not invoke his right to remain silent and stop the questioning. Understanding his rights in full, he waived his right to remain silent by making a voluntary statement to the police. The police, moreover, were not required to obtain a waiver of Thompkins's right to remain silent before interrogating him. The state court's decision rejecting Thompkins's *Miranda* claim was thus correct. . . .

. . . .

The judgment of the Court of Appeals is reversed, and the case is remanded with instructions to deny the petition.

It is so ordered.

JUSTICE SOTOMAYOR, with whom JUSTICE STEVENS, JUSTICE GINSBURG, and JUSTICE BREYER join, dissenting.

The Court concludes today that a criminal suspect waives his right to remain silent if, after sitting tacit and uncommunicative through nearly three hours of police interrogation, he utters a few one-word responses. . . . I respectfully dissent.

I

. . . .

The strength of Thompkins' *Miranda* claims depends in large part on the circumstances of the 3-hour interrogation, at the end of which he made inculpatory statements later introduced at trial. The Court's opinion downplays record evidence that Thompkins remained almost completely silent and unresponsive throughout that session. One of the interrogating officers, Detective Helgert, testified that although Thompkins was administered *Miranda* warnings, the last of which he read aloud, Thompkins expressly declined to sign a written acknowledgment that he had been advised of and understood his rights. There is conflicting evidence in the record about whether Thompkins ever verbally confirmed understanding his rights. The record contains no indication that the officers sought or obtained an express waiver.

. . . .

II

A

. . . .

Miranda's discussion of the prosecution's burden in proving waiver speaks with particular clarity to the facts of this case and therefore merits reproducing at length:

> "If [an] interrogation continues without the presence of an attorney and a statement is taken, a heavy burden rests on the government to demonstrate that the defendant knowingly and intelligently waived his privilege against self-incrimination and his right to retained or appointed counsel. . . . Since the State is responsible for establishing the isolated circumstances under

which [an] interrogation takes place and has the only means of making available corroborated evidence of warnings given during incommunicado interrogation, the burden is rightly on its shoulders.

"An express statement that the individual is willing to make a statement and does not want an attorney followed closely by a statement could constitute a waiver. But a valid waiver will not be presumed simply from the silence of the accused after warnings are given or simply from the fact that a confession was in fact eventually obtained." 384 U.S., at 475, 86 S. Ct. 1602.

Miranda went further in describing the facts likely to satisfy the prosecution's burden of establishing the admissibility of statements obtained after a lengthy interrogation:

"Whatever the testimony of the authorities as to waiver of rights by an accused, the fact of lengthy interrogation or incommunicado incarceration before a statement is made is strong evidence that the accused did not validly waive his rights. In these circumstances the fact that the individual eventually made a statement is consistent with the conclusion that the compelling influence of the interrogation finally forced him to do so. It is inconsistent with any notion of a voluntary relinquishment of the privilege." *Id.*, at 476, 86 S. Ct. 1602.

. . . .

Even in concluding that *Miranda* does not invariably require an express waiver of the right to silence or the right to counsel, this Court in *Butler* made clear that the prosecution bears a substantial burden in establishing an implied waiver. . . .

. . . While we stopped short in *Butler* of announcing a *per se* rule that "the defendant's silence, coupled with an understanding of his rights and a course of conduct indicating waiver, may never support a conclusion that a defendant has waived his rights," we reiterated that "courts must presume that a defendant did not waive his rights; the prosecution's burden is great." [*Butler*, 441 U.S., at 373, 99 S. Ct. 1755.]

. . . Together, *Miranda* and *Butler* establish that a court "must presume that a defendant did not waive his right[s]"; the prosecution bears a "heavy burden" in attempting to demonstrate waiver; the fact of a "lengthy interrogation" prior to obtaining statements is "strong evidence" against a finding of valid waiver; "mere silence" in response to questioning is "not enough"; and waiver may not be presumed "simply from the fact that a confession was in fact eventually obtained." *Miranda, supra*, at 475–476, 86 S. Ct. 1602; *Butler, supra*, at 372–373, 99 S. Ct. 1755.

It is undisputed here that Thompkins never expressly waived his right to remain silent. His refusal to sign even an acknowledgment that he understood his *Miranda* rights evinces, if anything, an intent not to waive those rights. That Thompkins did not make the inculpatory statements at issue until after approximately 2 hours and 45 minutes of interrogation serves as "strong evidence" against waiver. *Miranda* and

Butler expressly preclude the possibility that the inculpatory statements themselves are sufficient to establish waiver.

In these circumstances, Thompkins' "actions and words" preceding the inculpatory statements simply do not evidence a "course of conduct indicating waiver" sufficient to carry the prosecution's burden. . . . .

B

. . . .

The Court concludes that when *Miranda* warnings have been given and understood, "an accused's uncoerced statement establishes an implied waiver of the right to remain silent." More broadly still, the Court states that, "[a]s a general proposition, the law can presume that an individual who, with a full understanding of his or her rights, acts in a manner inconsistent with their exercise has made a deliberate choice to relinquish the protection those rights afford."

These principles flatly contradict our longstanding views that "a valid waiver will not be presumed . . . simply from the fact that a confession was in fact eventually obtained," *Miranda*, 384 U.S., at 475, 86 S. Ct. 1602, and that "[t]he courts must presume that a defendant did not waive his rights," *Butler*, 441 U.S., at 373, 99 S. Ct. 1755. . . . At best, the Court today creates an unworkable and conflicting set of presumptions that will undermine *Miranda*'s goal of providing "concrete constitutional guidelines for law enforcement agencies and courts to follow," 384 U.S., at 442, 86 S. Ct. 1602. At worst, it overrules *sub silentio* an essential aspect of the protections *Miranda* has long provided for the constitutional guarantee against self-incrimination.

The Court's conclusion that Thompkins' inculpatory statements were sufficient to establish an implied waiver finds no support in *Butler*. *Butler* itself distinguished between a sufficient "course of conduct" and inculpatory statements, reiterating *Miranda*'s admonition that "'a valid waiver will not be presumed simply from . . . the fact that a confession was in fact eventually obtained.'" *Butler, supra*, at 373, 99 S. Ct. 1755 (quoting *Miranda, supra*, at 475, 86 S. Ct. 1602). . . .

. . . .

Today's dilution of the prosecution's burden of proof to the bare fact that a suspect made inculpatory statements after *Miranda* warnings were given and understood takes an unprecedented step away from the "high standards of proof for the waiver of constitutional rights" this Court has long demanded. *Miranda, supra*, at 475, 86 S. Ct. 1602. When waiver is to be inferred during a custodial interrogation, there are sound reasons to require evidence beyond inculpatory statements themselves. *Miranda* and our subsequent cases are premised on the idea that custodial interrogation is inherently coercive. Requiring proof of a course of conduct beyond the inculpatory statements themselves is critical to ensuring that those statements are voluntary admissions and not the dubious product of an overborne will.

Today's decision thus ignores the important interests *Miranda* safeguards. . . . Today's decision bodes poorly for the fundamental principles that *Miranda* protects.

III

. . . .

Today's decision turns *Miranda* upside down. . . . [S]uspects will be legally presumed to have waived their rights even if they have given no clear expression of their intent to do so. . . . I respectfully dissent.

Notes and Questions

(1) WAIVER: As indicated in *Berghuis v. Thompkins*, a waiver of rights is "a deliberate choice to relinquish the protection those rights afford." In *North Carolina v. Butler*, 441 U.S. 369, 99 S. Ct. 1755, 60 L. Ed. 2d 286 (1979), which is relied upon by both the majority and dissent in *Thompkins*, the Court did reject the claim that *Miranda* waivers must be expressly made. The *Butler* Court observed that it had not been "offered any reason why . . . the absence of an *express* waiver" should preclude a finding that a suspect has intentionally relinquished his rights. (Emphasis in original.) What reasons would support the conclusion that a suspect must explicitly acknowledge that he understands and waives the protections afforded by *Miranda*? What reasons counsel against such categorical requirements?

The Court's opinion in *Berghuis v. Thompkins* confirms that "implicit waivers" are acceptable. The majority then prescribes what can constitute sufficient proof that a suspect has made an implicit choice to relinquish the "rights" described in the *Miranda* warnings. Is the majority's conclusion about what is adequate to carry the government's burden of proving a waiver of *Miranda* rights consistent with the language and objectives of the *Miranda* opinion? Are there good reasons to require more evidence that a suspect has made the "deliberate choice" necessary to waive rights?

(2) KNOWLEDGE: Waivers of constitutional rights must generally be knowing. As the *Thompkins* Court observes, a suspect must *understand* his rights in order to waive them. What exactly must be known and understood before a waiver is acceptable?

(a) In *Colorado v. Spring*, 479 U.S. 564, 107 S. Ct. 851, 93 L. Ed. 2d 954 (1987), the Court addressed this issue. In *Spring*, an informant told federal agents that the defendant "was engaged in the interstate transportation of stolen firearms" and also informed them that he "had discussed his participation in" a homicide in Colorado. The agents arranged for an undercover purchase of weapons from Spring, then arrested him and advised him of his *Miranda* rights. After a second set of warnings, he "signed a written form stating that he understood and waived his rights, and that he was willing to make a statement and answer questions." The agents first questioned Spring "about the firearms transactions that led to his arrest. They then asked Spring if he had a criminal record. He admitted to a juvenile record for shooting his aunt when he was 10 years old. The agents [then] asked if Spring had ever shot anyone else." He "mumbled, 'I shot another guy once.'" Subsequently, Colorado law enforcement officers came to question Spring about the homicide. After being warned, he signed another waiver and ultimately "confessed to the Colorado murder."

Spring was convicted of first-degree murder. The Colorado Court of Appeals reversed his conviction, concluding that he had not validly waived his rights before the first interrogation about the homicide by federal agents because they "'had a duty to inform [him] that he was a suspect, or to readvise him of his *Miranda* rights, before questioning him about the murder.'" The court further held that the state had not demonstrated that the confession given to the state officers during the second interrogation "was not the product of the prior illegal statement." The "question" before the Supreme Court was "whether [a] suspect's awareness of all the crimes about which he may be questioned is relevant to determining the validity of his decision to waive the Fifth Amendment privilege."

A seven-Justice majority concluded that awareness of the crimes that will be the subject of an interrogation is not necessary for a valid *Miranda* waiver. The Court first observed that there was "no doubt" about the voluntariness of Spring's waiver. He had not claimed that officers had employed any "coercion" in obtaining his waiver, and the circumstances provided no evidence that his "'will [was] overborne and his capacity for self-determination critically impaired' because of coercive police conduct." The Court then asserted that there was

> "no doubt that Spring's waiver . . . was knowingly and intelligently made: that is, that [he] understood that he had the right to remain silent and that anything he said could be used as evidence against him. The Constitution does not require that a criminal suspect know and understand every possible consequence of a waiver of the Fifth Amendment privilege. . . . The *Miranda* warnings protect th[e] privilege by ensuring that a suspect knows that he may choose not to talk to law enforcement officers, to talk only with counsel present, or to discontinue talking at any time."

The majority refused to hold that "mere silence by law enforcement officials as to the subject matter of an interrogation is 'trickery' sufficient to invalidate a suspect's waiver of *Miranda* rights." The Justices did not believe that silence was comparable to "affirmative misrepresentations by the police." If a suspect is adequately warned, "it is difficult to see how official silence could cause [him] to misunderstand the nature of his constitutional right" not to answer incriminating questions. "[A] valid waiver does not require that an individual be informed of all information 'useful' in making his decision or all information that 'might . . . affec[t] his decision to confess.' . . . Here, the additional information could [have] affect[ed] only the wisdom of a *Miranda* waiver, not its essentially voluntary and knowing nature." The failure to inform Spring about the "subject matter of the interrogation could not" have had a "constitutionally significant" effect on his waiver decision.

(b) In *Moran v. Burbine*, 475 U.S. 412, 106 S. Ct. 1135, 89 L. Ed. 2d 410 (1986), the defendant was in police custody following his arrest for murder. At the behest of the defendant's sister, an attorney called the police and said that she would act as defendant's counsel in the event the police intended to question him. The attorney received assurances that the defendant would not be questioned further until the next day. Later that same evening, however, the police gave the defendant *Miranda* warnings. In warning the defendant of his right to an attorney, the police did not inform him of the attorney's telephone call or say anything that would indicate an attorney was seeking to represent him. The defendant waived his rights without requesting an attorney and subsequently made incriminating statements. The lower court held that the police conduct fatally tainted defendant's "otherwise valid" waiver of his Fifth Amendment privilege. The court reasoned that by failing to inform defendant that an attorney had called and that she had been assured that no questioning would take place until the next day, the police had deprived defendant of information critical to his ability to waive his rights knowingly and intelligently. The court also characterized the police failure to tell the defendant of the attorney's call as "deliberate or reckless irresponsibility." It concluded that this "blameworthy action by the police," together with the defendant's ignorance of the attorney's phone call "vitiate[d] any claim that [the] waiver of counsel was knowing and voluntary."

The Supreme Court reversed. Justice O'Connor's opinion for a six-Justice majority concluded that the defendant's waiver was valid. Although the majority opinion expressed "distaste for the deliberate misleading of an officer of the court," it concluded that interactions between the officers and the attorney, which were unknown to the defendant, could have no impact on the validity of the defendant's waiver. As to the officers' failure to supply the defendant with information that might be relevant to his waiver decision, the majority admitted that "the additional information . . . might have affected [the defendant's] decision to confess." The majority concluded, however, that the police are not required to "supply a suspect with a flow of information to help him calibrate his self-interest in deciding whether to speak or stand by his rights. . . . Once it is determined that a suspect's decision not to rely on his rights was uncoerced, that he at all times knew he could stand mute and request a lawyer, and that he was aware of the State's intention to use his statements to secure a conviction, the analysis is complete and the waiver is valid as a matter of law."

(c) In *Connecticut v. Barrett*, 479 U.S. 523, 107 S. Ct. 828, 93 L. Ed. 2d 920 (1987), the defendant was advised of his *Miranda* rights three times. On each occasion, he indicated that he would not make a written statement but was willing to talk about the incident that led to his arrest. On the second and third occasion, he added that he would not make a written statement outside the presence of counsel and then orally admitted his involvement in the crime. The Court held that the defendant's waiver of his *Miranda* rights was valid because "*Miranda* gives the defendant a right to choose between speech and silence, and [defendant] chose to speak." The majority also rejected "the contention that the distinction drawn by [the defendant] between oral and written statements indicates an understanding of the consequences so incomplete that we should deem his limited invocation of the right to counsel effective for all purposes." Emphasizing that the lower court found that the defendant fully understood the *Miranda* warnings, the Court concluded that "[t]he fact that some might find Barrett's decision illogical is irrelevant, for we have never 'embraced the theory that a defendant's ignorance of the full consequences of his decisions vitiates their voluntariness.'" (quoting *Oregon v. Elstad*, 470 U.S. 298, 316, 105 S. Ct. 1285, 1297, 84 L. Ed. 2d 222 (1985)).

(3) VOLUNTARINESS: When is a *Miranda* waiver involuntary? In *Colorado v. Connelly*, 479 U.S. 157, 107 S. Ct. 515, 93 L. Ed. 2d 473 (1986), the Court held that a waiver of *Miranda* rights was valid despite the fact that at the time of the waiver the defendant was in a psychotic state that led him to believe that the voice of God had ordered him to either confess to the police or commit suicide. In response to the contention that the defendant's waiver of his Fifth Amendment Privilege was involuntary, the Court, in an opinion by Chief Justice Rehnquist, stated "[t]he voluntariness of a waiver of this privilege has always depended on the absence of police overreaching, not on 'free choice' in any broader sense of the word. . . . *Miranda* protects defendants against government coercion leading them to surrender rights protected by the Fifth Amendment; it goes no further than that. [Defendant's] perception of coercion flowing from the 'voice of God,' however important or significant such a perception may be in other disciplines, is a matter to which the United States Constitution does not speak." The voluntariness of a *Miranda* waiver, therefore, is analyzed identically to the voluntariness of a confession under the due process-coerced confession doctrine. An undefined amount of official coercion is essential to a finding of involuntariness. If sufficient official pressure is demonstrated, however, the characteristics of the suspect that bear upon the strength of her or his will are relevant to the voluntariness inquiry.

In fact, individual characteristics of a suspect are pertinent in determining both whether a waiver is sufficiently "knowing" — whether a particular suspect understood the *Miranda* warnings — and whether a suspect's relinquishment of "rights" is voluntary — whether coercion has overborne the particular suspect's will. As the Court observed in *Fare v. Michael C.*, 442 U.S. 707, 99 S. Ct. 2560, 61 L. Ed. 2d 197 (1979), the totality of circumstances approach governs waiver assessments and "mandates . . . inquiry into all the circumstances surrounding the interrogation" including "age, experience, education, background, . . . intelligence, and . . . capacity." An individual's weaknesses and vulnerabilities that impair understanding or diminish resistance must be factored into the assessment of whether his or her choice to relinquish the *Miranda* "rights" satisfies the criteria established for constitutionally acceptable waivers.

Warnings and Waiver Problems

8D–1: With grounds to believe that he had been involved in coercing and enticing a minor to travel across state lines for the purpose of engaging in sexual activity, officers arrested Max in a parking lot at gunpoint. They handcuffed him and transported him to the nearest police department substation. After he was booked,

Max was placed in an interview room. Shortly thereafter, Detective Nick came to the room, turned on video recording equipment, and recited the following admonitions:

> "You have the right to remain silent. Anything you say can and will be used against you in a court of law. You have the right to speak to an attorney. If you cannot afford one, one will be appointed to you. If you decide to stop answering questions once we have begun, all questioning will stop. You just say stop and we're done."

Nick then asked, "Do you understand your rights, Max?" and Max responded, "Yes." In response to Detective Nick's questioning, Max made statements that incriminated him in the offense for which he had been arrested. The prosecution plans to use those statements as part of its case-in-chief at Max's trial. Max has moved to suppress the statements, claiming that they are barred by *Miranda*.

Does Max have a valid *Miranda* claim?

8D–2: On August 10, nine victims, including six monks, were found face down inside a Buddhist temple, shot in the head. Temple living quarters had been ransacked. Police traced the rifle used to Carat, who denied involvement and reported that two minors, Andy and Alex, had borrowed his rifle shortly before the murders. On October 25, officers approached Andy at a high school football game. Andy, who was 17 years old, accompanied the officers to the station for questioning. Interrogation began at 9:25 p.m. The *Miranda* form used for juveniles is as follows: "(1) You have the right to remain silent. (This means that you do not have to talk to me or answer any questions about this offense. You can be quiet if you wish.); (2) Anything you say can and will be used against you in a court of law. (This means that anything you tell me, I can use later against you in court.); (3) You have the right to have an attorney present prior to and during questioning. (This means, if you want one, you are allowed to have a lawyer here before and during my questions to you.); (4) If you cannot afford an attorney, you have the right to have one appointed for you prior to questioning. (This means if you do not have the money to get a lawyer, if you wish, one will be given to you free of charge before you are questioned.)"

Before reading these admonitions to Andy, Riley stated, "What I'd like to do first, since we're in kind of a formal setting and because I'm a police officer and because some of the questions are a little bit sensitive, is read something to you so that you understand some of the protections and things that you have. It's not meant to scare you or anything like that. Don't take it out of context, okay? I'm sure you've heard this on t.v. What it's called is a *Miranda* warning. It's not necessarily something that is, like on t.v. where they portray it when somebody's guilty of doing something. We read these things to people on a regular basis, whether they're responsible for doing something or not, okay? So I don't want you to feel that because I'm reading this to you that we necessarily think that you're responsible for anything. It's for your benefit, it's for your protection and our protection, okay?"

While reciting the right to counsel warning, Detective Riley varied from the form, stating, "Okay, and the next one states that you have the right to have an attorney present prior to and during questioning, which means that if you want one, you're allowed to have a lawyer here before and during my questions to you, okay? An attorney is a lawyer who will speak for you and help you concerning the crime or any kind of offense that we might think that you or somebody else is involved in. Again, this does not necessarily mean that you are involved, but if you were, then that's when that would apply, okay?"

After some casual questions, Riley focused on the murders. One hour into the interrogation, he told Andy that it was important to tell the truth and asked whether Andy had ever borrowed Carat's rifle. Andy denied that he had, but stated that Alex might have borrowed it. Riley asked Andy where he was at the time of the murders and whether he knew anything about the murders. Andy denied knowing anything about the murders. Riley said he knew that Andy had borrowed the rifle and that Andy had to tell him about it. Andy then admitted that he and Alex had borrowed the rifle, but claimed that he had returned it to Carat before the murders.

After several more hours of interrogation, Andy admitted that Carat and Alex had approached him with a plan to conduct a war game with the goal of surrounding the temple without triggering the security system. He went to the temple with Carat and Alex but had no intention of entering. Once they had gotten past the security sensors, however, he followed them inside. Carat and Alex ransacked the temple's living quarters and gathered the victims into the main room. After one of the monks recognized Alex, Carat ordered Andy to go outside and confirm that the walls were sound-proof. Because the shootings occurred while he was outside, Andy did not know who fired the shots. The interrogation ended at 10:00 a.m. on October 26. The prosecution intends to use Andy's statements against him at his murder trial.

What claims should Andy raise?

8D–3: On April 23, at 12:40 p.m., a man entered a business that provides money-transfer and other services, pointed a gun at the cashier and demanded money. When the cashier dropped to the floor behind the counter and called 911, the would-be robber fled. Shortly thereafter, based on the cashier's description, police officers arrested Dunn.

The next day, at 12:03 p.m., while Dunn was awaiting arraignment, Sergeant Pinkman and Assistant District Attorney Griller took him to an interview room. A "Program" instituted by the District Attorney's Office prescribed a script of statements to be read to arrested individuals before they were arraigned or given *Miranda* warnings. Adhering to the script, Griller told Dunn, that "when [he went] to court," he would be charged with attempted robbery and criminal possession of a weapon based on the incident that had occurred the previous day. Pinkman informed Dunn that "in a few minutes" she would read him his *Miranda* rights, and that he would "be given an opportunity to explain what [he] did and what had happened on the previous day." She then stated:

- "If you have an alibi, give me as much information as you can, including the names of any people you were with."

- "If your version of what happened is different from what we've been told, this is your opportunity to tell us your story. If there is something you need us to investigate about this case you have to tell us now so we can look into it."

- "Even if you have already spoken to someone else you do not have to talk to us."

- "This will be your only opportunity to speak with us before you go to court on these charges."

Pinkman then recited the *Miranda* warnings, Dunn indicated his understanding, and Pinkman asked if he would answer questions. When Dunn said "Yes," Pinkman asked him about the attempted robbery. Dunn made some incriminating admissions. Twice, he interrupted the questioning to express confusion or concern about how the interview was helping him. Pinkman told him that the questioning was "beneficial to [him] if [he had] an alibi, [or] if there's something we need to investigate." She also explained that Dunn could tell them something that might benefit him, such as "it wasn't me, I wasn't there." When Dunn admitted that he could not truthfully say that it was not him, Pinkman immediately stated: "No, you can't say that because we have pictures of you and we have the gun." Griller and Pinkman both stated that it was their job to determine if there was anything Dunn needed them to investigate and to find out from him what his side of the story was. In response to further questions, Dunn made additional incriminating admissions.

Dunn was charged with attempted robbery and unlawful possession of a pistol. He moved to suppress his statements.

Does *Miranda* require the suppression of Dunn's admissions?

8D–4: Four young employees at a bowling alley were each shot in the head during a late-night burglary. A few weeks later, police stopped Farr for speeding, and arrested him after learning that the vehicle was stolen. The arresting officer recited the *Miranda* warnings to Farr. On the ride to the police station, Farr spontaneously told the arresting officer, "I'm not going to jail for some little motorcycle theft," and then hinted that he was involved in the bowling alley killings. The officer read the *Miranda* warnings to Farr once again. At the station, Officer Lawson was summoned to help interrogate Farr. Farr had previously worked as an informant for Lawson and considered him to be a friend. Before he began questioning Farr about the bowling alley killings, Lawson issued the *Miranda* warnings once again.

After briefly talking to Lawson, Farr was questioned by Detective Gill, who gave Farr yet another set of *Miranda* warnings before beginning his interrogation. Farr told him certain details of the crime that, according to Gill, "only the perpetrator would know." About 30 minutes later, Gill came out of the interrogation room and told Lawson that he had "hit a brick wall" with Farr. Lawson entered the room alone to speak with Farr. Farr asked Lawson whether he should talk to the police or obtain an attorney. Lawson responded, "If you were involved in the crime you should tell the detective you were involved. Otherwise, you should get a lawyer." Farr then asked how he could get a lawyer. Lawson asked him if he could afford a lawyer, knowing that he could not. Farr laughed, and asked how he could get a court-appointed attorney, and when he could get one. Lawson responded that he did not know the county's procedures, and guessed that it could take as little as one day or as long as a month. Lawson did know that the county had a 72-hour rule, which states that a suspect must be charged or released within that time period. He did not tell Farr about that rule. Farr then spat into a trash can, and said, "So you're telling me I'm on my own." Lawson said nothing. In response to questions from Lawson, Farr admitted that he was involved in the bowling alley murders, eventually signing three written confessions.

Did Farr validly waive his *Miranda* rights?

8D–5: On May 21, 1994, Daoud flagged down two officers who were on routine patrol in a marked police patrol car. He blurted out to them that he had just confessed to a 911 operator that he had killed his mother in 1985. In response to Daoud's roadside outburst, the two officers pulled their patrol car to the side of the road, approached Daoud, and read him his *Miranda* warnings. Daoud proceeded to waive his *Miranda* rights and to tell the officers how he had killed his mother in Troy, Michigan. The officers then drove Daoud to the Detroit Police Department's 9th Precinct where Daoud waived his *Miranda* rights a second time and then repeated what he had previously told the other officers.

After being notified of Daoud's statements, officers from the Troy Police Department met with Daoud at the Detroit Police Department on May 21. They warned Daoud of his *Miranda* rights and Daoud again waived his rights. In response to their questions, Daoud then gave a taped confession in which he explained that he repeatedly struck his mother in the head and choked her to get her to stop screaming.

At Daoud's motion to suppress his confession, three experts, who had previously examined him, testified as to his mental state at the time he waived his *Miranda* rights. One of the experts, Dr. Mogy, testified that in his opinion Daoud was delusional at the time he waived his rights. Daoud believed that God controlled the police and would set him free if he confessed. Dr. Mogy expressed the opinion that this delusion made Daoud unable to appreciate that the police would use his statements against him. Another expert agreed that Daoud had "delusions" and "preoccupations" which rendered him unable to use the information contained in the *Miranda* warnings.

Relying on these experts' testimony, the trial judge suppressed Daoud's statements on the ground that Daoud did not make a knowing and intelligent waiver of his *Miranda* rights. The judge ruled that the defendant's delusion that "God would be releasing him from jail as a reward for confessing to his mother's murder" prevented Daoud from having a "rational comprehension" of his *Miranda* rights. The prosecution appealed this ruling to an appellate court.

How should the appellate court rule?

8D–6: Mariano was arrested for possession with intent to distribute methamphetamine. He was questioned by Detective Madron. Madron first sought oral assurances that Mariano was not impaired by drugs, alcohol, or injury, and that he could understand what Madron was saying. Because Mariano's native language was Spanish, Madron then provided Mariano with a standard federal form containing a *Miranda* warning in Spanish. The form had two parts — a declaration of rights (entitled "Declaración de Derechos") and a waiver of those rights ("Renuncia a Los Derechos"). Mariano did not read the second part.

Madron first instructed Mariano to read aloud seven statements advising Mariano of his rights and, if Mariano understood the advisement, to place his initials beside the statement. Madron explained to Mariano that he should read and understand each advisement before placing his initials beside the statement, and Madron asked in Spanish no fewer than seven times — once after each advisement — whether Mariano understood the statement he had just read aloud. Each time, Mariano responded, "Yes." After reading that he had a right to an appointed attorney and being asked whether he understood that right, Mariano responded, "Yes . . . I don't have any . . . I don't have any money to pay a lawyer." In addition, after Mariano read the final advisement, the following exchange occurred:

[Madron]: Knowing your rights did I ask you some questions?

[Mariano]: Yes.

[Madron]: Ok. It is . . . it is. . . .

[Mariano]: I'm a little scared because of all this. It is ugly.

[Madron]: Put your name here and signature here please. I'm going to sign as a witness and then you want to talk to me? Now tell me what happened yesterday.

Mariano then related an incriminating account of the events leading to his arrest. Mariano had attended school for only three years.

Did the detective satisfy *Miranda's* requirements in obtaining Mariano's statements?

8D–7: On December 30, 2002, Jesus and an associate hijacked a rented helicopter and forced the pilot, at gunpoint and on threat of death, to fly them to the state penitentiary. Five inmates, including Jesus's brother, were waiting on the penitentiary's roof. Following a massive manhunt, Jesus and his brother were arrested. The police advised Jesus of his *Miranda* rights, then transported him to police headquarters. Several hours later, while police were asking routine booking questions, Jesus abruptly stated that he wanted to tell them about his participation in the hijacking. Although the police reminded him that he had the right to counsel and to remain silent, he proceeded to make a detailed inculpatory statement.

Jesus was indicted on one count of conspiring to commit aircraft piracy, armed aircraft piracy, and use of a semiautomatic weapon during or in relation to a crime of violence. Jesus filed a motion to suppress his post-arrest statement admitting participation in the hijacking. At the hearing on this motion, Jesus presented a written evaluation completed by the Federal Detention Center psychologist. The evaluation stated that Jesus "has a poor range of intellectual functioning, rating in the 3rd, 2nd, and 5th percentile in intellectual functioning tests performed on him," asserted that he has a low I.Q., and characterized his intellectual functioning as "borderline." The evaluation also stated that Jesus "is free of any debilitating mental illness, and has sufficient comprehension to render him competent to stand trial." Moreover, it concluded that Jesus "functions within the normal range in orientation, language comprehension, naming ability, memory, abstract reasoning, and judgment." The government introduced evidence that Jesus had an extensive criminal record that involved exposure to the *Miranda* warnings on more than one previous occasion.

What arguments should Jesus make in support of the motion to suppress his statement? How should the government respond? How should the trial judge rule?

[E] Invocation of Protections

Michigan v. Mosley
United States Supreme Court
423 U.S. 96, 96 S. Ct. 321, 46 L. Ed. 2d 313 (1975)

MR. JUSTICE STEWART delivered the opinion of the Court.

The respondent, Richard Bert Mosley, was arrested in Detroit, Mich., in the early afternoon of April 8, 1971, in connection with robberies that had recently occurred at the Blue Goose Bar and the White Tower Restaurant on that city's lower east side. The arresting officer, Detective James Cowie of the Armed Robbery Section of the Detroit Police Department, was acting on a tip implicating Mosley and three other men in the robberies. After effecting the arrest, Detective Cowie brought Mosley to the Robbery, Breaking and Entering Bureau of the Police Department, located on the fourth floor of the departmental headquarters building. The officer advised Mosley of his rights under this Court's decision in *Miranda v. Arizona*, 384 U.S. 436, 86 S. Ct. 1602, 16 L. Ed. 2d 694, and had him read and sign the department's constitutional rights notification certificate. After filling out the necessary arrest papers, Cowie began questioning Mosley about the robbery of the White Tower Restaurant. When Mosley said he did not want to answer any questions about the robberies, Cowie promptly ceased the interrogation. The completion of the arrest papers and the questioning of Mosley together took approximately 20 minutes. At no time during the questioning did Mosley indicate a desire to consult with a lawyer, and there is no claim that the procedures followed to this point did not fully comply with the strictures of the *Miranda* opinion. Mosley was then taken to a ninth-floor cell block.

Shortly after 6 p.m., Detective Hill of the Detroit Police Department Homicide Bureau brought Mosley from the cell block to the fifth-floor office of the Homicide Bureau for questioning about the fatal shooting of a man named Leroy Williams. Williams had been killed on January 9, 1971, during a holdup attempt outside the 101 Ranch Bar in Detroit. Mosley had not been arrested on this charge or interrogated about it by Detective Cowie.[2] Before questioning Mosley about this homicide, Detective Hill carefully advised him of his "*Miranda* rights." Mosley read the notification form both silently and aloud, and Detective Hill then read and explained the warnings to him and had him sign the form. Mosley at first denied any involvement in the Williams murder, but after the officer told him that Anthony Smith had confessed to participating in the slaying and had named him as the "shooter," Mosley made a statement implicating himself in the homicide.[3] The interrogation by Detective Hill lasted approximately 15 minutes, and at no time during its course did Mosley ask to consult with a lawyer or indicate that he did not want to discuss the homicide. In short, there is no claim that the procedures followed during Detective Hill's interrogation of Mosley, standing alone, did not fully comply with the strictures of the *Miranda* opinion.

Mosley was subsequently charged in a one-count information with first-degree murder. Before the trial he moved to suppress his incriminating statement on a number of grounds, among them the claim that under the doctrine of the *Miranda* case it was constitutionally impermissible for Detective Hill to question him about the Williams murder after he had told Detective Cowie that he did not want to answer any questions about the robberies. The trial court denied the motion to suppress after an evidentiary hearing, and the incriminating statement was subsequently introduced in evidence against Mosley at his trial. The jury convicted Mosley of first-degree murder, and the court imposed a mandatory sentence of life imprisonment.

On appeal to the Michigan Court of Appeals, Mosley renewed his previous objections to the use of his incriminating statement in evidence. The appellate court reversed the judgment of conviction, holding that Detective Hill's interrogation of Mosley had been a *per se* violation of the *Miranda* doctrine.

. . . .

Neither party in the present case challenges the continuing validity of the *Miranda* decision, or of any of the so-called guidelines it established to protect what the Court there said was a person's constitutional privilege against compulsory self-incrimination. The issue in this case, rather, is whether the conduct of the Detroit police that led to Mosley's incriminating statement did in fact violate the *Miranda* "guidelines," so as to render the statement inadmissible in evidence against Mosley at his trial. Resolution of the question turns almost entirely on the interpretation of

---

2. The original tip to Detective Cowie had, however, implicated Mosley in the Williams murder.

3. During cross-examination by Mosley's counsel at the evidentiary hearing, Detective Hill conceded that Smith in fact had not confessed but had "denied a physical participation in the robbery."

a single passage in the *Miranda* opinion, upon which the Michigan appellate court relied in finding a *per se* violation of *Miranda*:

> Once warnings have been given, the subsequent procedure is clear. If the individual indicates in any manner, at any time prior to or during questioning, that he wishes to remain silent, the interrogation must cease. At this point he has shown that he intends to exercise his Fifth Amendment privilege; any statement taken after the person invokes his privilege cannot be other than the product of compulsion, subtle or otherwise. Without the right to cut off questioning, the setting of in-custody interrogation operates on the individual to overcome free choice in producing a statement after the privilege has been once invoked.

384 U.S. at 473–474, 86 S. Ct. at 1627.

This passage states that "the interrogation must cease" when the person in custody indicates that "he wishes to remain silent." It does not state under what circumstances, if any, a resumption of questioning is permissible. The passage could be literally read to mean that a person who has invoked his "right to silence" can never again be subjected to custodial interrogation by any police officer at any time or place on any subject. Another possible construction of the passage would characterize "any statement taken after the person invokes his privilege" as "the product of compulsion" and would therefore mandate its exclusion from evidence, even if it were volunteered by the person in custody without any further interrogation whatever. Or the passage could be interpreted to require only the immediate cessation of questioning, and to permit a resumption of interrogation after a momentary respite.

It is evident that any of these possible literal interpretations would lead to absurd and unintended results. To permit the continuation of custodial interrogation after a momentary cessation would clearly frustrate the purposes of *Miranda* by allowing repeated rounds of questioning to undermine the will of the person being questioned. At the other extreme, a blanket prohibition against the taking of voluntary statements or a permanent immunity from further interrogation, regardless of the circumstances, would transform the *Miranda* safeguards into wholly irrational obstacles to legitimate police investigative activity, and deprive suspects of an opportunity to make informed and intelligent assessments of their interests. Clearly, therefore, neither this passage nor any other passage in the *Miranda* opinion can sensibly be read to create a *per se* proscription of indefinite duration upon any further questioning by any police officer on any subject, once the person in custody has indicated a desire to remain silent.

A reasonable and faithful interpretation of the *Miranda* opinion must rest on the intention of the Court in that case to adopt "fully effective means . . . to notify the person of his right of silence and to assure that the exercise of the right will be scrupulously honored. . . ." 384 U.S. at 479, 86 S. Ct. at 1630. The critical safeguard identified in the passage at issue is a person's "right to cut off questioning." *Id.* at 474, 86 S. Ct. at 1627. Through the exercise of his option to terminate questioning he can control the time at which questioning occurs, the subjects discussed, and the duration of the interrogation. The requirement that law enforcement authorities must respect a person's exercise of that option counteracts the coercive pressures of the custodial setting. We therefore conclude that the admissibility of statements obtained after the person in custody has decided to remain silent depends under *Miranda* on whether his "right to cut off questioning" was "scrupulously honored."[10]

A review of the circumstances leading to Mosley's confession reveals that his "right to cut off questioning" was fully respected in this case. Before his initial interrogation, Mosley was carefully advised that he was under no obligation to answer any questions and could remain silent if he wished. He orally acknowledged that he understood the *Miranda* warnings and then signed a printed notification-of-rights form. When Mosley stated that he did not want to discuss the robberies, Detective Cowie immediately ceased the interrogation and did not try either to resume the questioning or in any way to persuade Mosley to reconsider his position. After an interval of more than two hours, Mosley was questioned by another police officer at another location about an unrelated holdup murder. He was given full and complete *Miranda* warnings at the outset of the second interrogation. He was thus reminded again that he could remain silent and could consult with a lawyer, and was carefully given a full and fair opportunity to exercise these options. The subsequent questioning did not undercut Mosley's previous decision not to answer Detective Cowie's inquiries. Detective Hill did not resume the interrogation about the White Tower Restaurant robbery or inquire about the Blue Goose Bar robbery, but instead focused exclusively on the Leroy Williams homicide, a crime different in nature and in time and place of occurrence from the robberies for which Mosley had been arrested and interrogated by Detective Cowie. Although it is not clear from the record how much Detective Hill knew about the earlier interrogation, his questioning of Mosley about an unrelated homicide was quite consistent with a reasonable interpretation of Mosley's earlier refusal to answer any questions about the robberies.[11]

---

10. The dissenting opinion asserts that *Miranda* established a requirement that once a person has indicated a desire to remain silent, questioning may be resumed only when counsel is present. But clearly the Court in *Miranda* imposed no such requirement, for it distinguished between the procedural safeguards triggered by a request to remain silent and a request for an attorney and directed that "the interrogation must cease until an attorney is present" only "[i]f the individual states that he wants an attorney." 384 U.S. at 474, 86 S. Ct. at 1628.

11. Detective Cowie gave the only testimony at the suppression hearing concerning the scope of Mosley's earlier refusal to answer his questions:

A. I think at that time he declined to answer whether he had been involved.
Q. He declined to answer?
A. Yes. Anything about the robberies.

At the suppression hearing, Mosley did not in any way dispute Cowie's testimony. Not until trial, after the judge had denied the motion to suppress the incriminating statement, did Mosley offer a somewhat different version of his earlier refusal to answer Detective Cowie's questions. The briefs submitted by Mosley's counsel to the Michigan Court of Appeals and to this Court accepted Detective Cowie's account of the interrogation as correct, and the Michigan Court of Appeals decided the case on that factual premise. At oral argument before this Court, both counsel discussed the case solely in terms of Cowie's description of the events.

This is not a case, therefore, where the police failed to honor a decision of a person in custody to cut off questioning, either by refusing to discontinue the interrogation upon request or by persisting in repeated efforts to wear down his resistance and make him change his mind. In contrast to such practices, the police here immediately ceased the interrogation, resumed questioning only after the passage of a significant period of time and the provision of a fresh set of warnings, and restricted the second interrogation to a crime that had not been a subject of the earlier interrogation.

. . . .

For these reasons, we conclude that the admission in evidence of Mosley's incriminating statement did not violate the principles of *Miranda v. Arizona*. Accordingly, the judgment of the Michigan Court of Appeals is vacated, and the case is remanded to that court for further proceedings not inconsistent with this opinion.

It is so ordered.

Judgment vacated and case remanded.

Mr. Justice White, concurring in the result.

I concur in the result and in much of the majority's reasoning. However, it appears to me that in an effort to make only a limited holding in this case, the majority has implied that some custodial confessions will be suppressed even though they follow an informed and voluntary waiver of the defendant's rights. The majority seems to say that a statement obtained within some unspecified time after an assertion by an individual of his "right to silence" is always inadmissible, even if it was the result of an informed and voluntary decision — following, for example, a disclosure to such an individual of a piece of information bearing on his waiver decision which the police had failed to give him prior to his assertion of the privilege but which they gave him immediately thereafter. Indeed, the majority characterizes as "absurd" any contrary rule. I disagree. I do not think the majority's conclusion is compelled by *Miranda v. Arizona*, 384 U.S. 436, 86 S. Ct. 1602, 16 L. Ed. 2d 694 (1966), and I suspect that in the final analysis the majority will adopt voluntariness as the standard by which to judge the waiver of the right to silence by a properly informed defendant. I think the Court should say so now.

Miranda holds that custody creates an inherent compulsion on an individual to incriminate himself in response to questions, and that statements obtained under such circumstances are therefore obtained in violation of the Fifth Amendment privilege against compelled testimonial self-incrimination unless the privilege is "knowingly and intelligently waived." *Id.* at 471, 475, 86 S. Ct. at 1626, 1628. It also holds that an individual will not be deemed to have made a knowing and intelligent waiver of his "right to silence" unless the authorities have first informed him, *inter alia*, of that right — "the threshold requirement for an intelligent decision as to its exercise." *Id.* at 468, 86 S. Ct. at 1624. I am no more convinced that *Miranda* was required by the United States Constitution than I was when it was decided. However, there is at least some support in the law both before and after *Miranda* for the proposition that some rights will never be deemed waived unless the defendant is first expressly advised of their existence. *E.g., Carnley v. Cochran*, 369 U.S. 506, 82 S. Ct. 884, 8 L. Ed. 2d 70 (1962). There is little support in the law or in common sense for the proposition that an *informed* waiver of a right may be ineffective even where voluntarily made. Indeed, the law is exactly to the contrary, *e.g., Tollett v. Henderson*, 411 U.S. 258, 93 S. Ct. 1602, 36 L. Ed. 2d 235 (1973). Unless an individual is incompetent, we have in the past rejected any paternalistic rule protecting a defendant from his intelligent and voluntary decisions about his own criminal case. *Faretta v. California*, 422 U.S. 806, 95 S. Ct. 2525, 45 L. Ed. 2d 562 (1975). To do so would be to "imprison a man in his privileges,"[1] *Adams v. United States ex rel. McCann*, 317 U.S. 269, 280, 63 S. Ct. 236, 242, 87 L. Ed. 268 (1942), and to disregard "that respect for the individual which is the lifeblood of the law," *Faretta v. California, supra*, 422 U.S. at 834, 95 S. Ct. at 2541. I am very reluctant to conclude that *Miranda* stands for such a proposition.

The language of *Miranda* no more compels such a result than does its basic rationale. As the majority points out, the statement in *Miranda*, 384 U.S. at 474, 86 S. Ct. at 1627, requiring interrogation to *cease* after an assertion of the "right to silence" tells us nothing because it does not indicate how soon this interrogation may resume. The Court showed in the very next paragraph, moreover, that when it wanted to create a *per se* rule against further interrogation after assertion of a right, it knew how to do so. The Court there said "[i]f the individual states that he wants an attorney, the interrogation *must cease until an attorney is present.*" *Id.*[2] However, when the individual indicates that *he* will decide unaided by counsel whether or not to assert his "right to silence" the situation is different. In such a situation, the Court in *Miranda* simply said: "If the interrogation continues without the presence of an attorney and a statement is taken, a heavy burden rests on the government to demonstrate that

---

1. The majority's rule may cause an accused injury. Although a recently arrested individual may have indicated an initial desire not to answer questions, he would nonetheless want to know immediately — if it were true — that his ability to explain a particular incriminating fact or to supply an alibi for a particular time period would result in his immediate release. Similarly, he might wish to know — if it were true — that (1) the case against him was unusually strong and that (2) his immediate cooperation with the authorities in the apprehension and conviction of others or in the recovery of property would redound to his benefit in the form of a reduced charge. Certainly the individual's lawyer, if he had one, would be interested in such information, even if communication of such information followed closely on an assertion of the "right to silence." Where the individual has not requested counsel and has chosen instead to make his own decisions regarding his conversations with the authorities, he should not be deprived even temporarily of any information relevant to the decision.

2. The question of the proper procedure following expression by an individual of his desire to consult counsel is not presented in this case. It is sufficient to note that the reasons to keep the lines of communication between the authorities and the accused open when the accused has chosen to make his own decisions are not present when he indicates instead that he wishes legal advice with respect thereto. The authorities may then communicate with him through an attorney. More to the point, the accused having expressed his own view that he is not competent to deal with the authorities without legal advice, a later decision at the authorities' insistence to make a statement without counsel's presence may properly be viewed with skepticism.

the defendant knowingly and intelligently waived his privilege against self-incrimination and his right to retained or appointed counsel." *Id.* at 475, 86 S. Ct. at 1628.
Apparently, although placing a heavy burden on the government, *Miranda* intended
waiver of the "right to silence" to be tested by the normal standards. In any event,
insofar as the *Miranda* decision might be read to require interrogation to cease for
some magical and unspecified period of time following an assertion of the "right to
silence," and to reject voluntariness as the standard by which to judge informed waivers of that right, it should be disapproved as inconsistent with otherwise uniformly
applied legal principles.

In justifying the implication that questioning must inevitably cease for some unspecified period of time following an exercise of the "right to silence," the majority
says only that such a requirement would be necessary to avoid "undermining" "the
will of the person being questioned." Yet, surely a waiver of the "right to silence" obtained by "undermining the will" of the person being questioned would be considered an involuntary waiver. Thus, in order to achieve the majority's only stated
purpose, it is sufficient to exclude all confessions which are the result of involuntary
waivers. To exclude any others is to deprive the factfinding process of highly probative information for no reason at all. The "repeated rounds" of questioning following
an assertion of the privilege, which the majority is worried about, would, of course,
count heavily against the State in any determination of voluntariness — particularly
if no reason (such as new facts communicated to the accused or a new incident being
inquired about) appeared for repeated questioning. There is no reason, however, to
rob the accused of the choice to answer questions voluntarily for some unspecified
period of time following his own previous contrary decision. The Court should now
so state.

Mr. Justice Brennan, with whom Mr. Justice Marshall joins, dissenting.

. . . .

I agree that *Miranda* is not to be read, on the one hand, to impose an absolute ban
on resumption of questioning "at any time or place on any subject," or on the other
hand, "to permit a resumption of interrogation after a momentary respite." But this
surely cannot justify adoption of a vague and ineffective procedural standard that
falls somewhere between those absurd extremes, for *Miranda* in flat and unambiguous terms requires that questioning "cease" when a suspect exercises the right to remain silent. *Miranda*'s terms, however, are not so uncompromising as to preclude
the fashioning of guidelines to govern this case. Those guidelines must, of course,
necessarily be sensitive to the reality that "[a]s a practical matter, the compulsion
to speak in the isolated setting of the police station may well be greater than in
courts or other official investigations, where there are often impartial observers to
guard against intimidation or trickery." 384 U.S. at 461, 86 S. Ct. at 1621 (footnote
omitted).

The fashioning of guidelines for this case is an easy task. Adequate procedures
are readily available. Michigan law requires that the suspect be arraigned before a

judicial officer "without unnecessary delay," certainly not a burdensome requirement. Alternatively, a requirement that resumption of questioning should await appointment and arrival of counsel for the suspect would be an acceptable and readily
satisfied precondition to resumption.[3] *Miranda* expressly held that "[t]he presence
of counsel . . . would be the adequate protective device necessary to make the process of police interrogation conform to the dictates of the privilege [against self-
incrimination]." *Id.* at 466, 86 S. Ct. at 1623. The Court expediently bypasses this
alternative in its search for circumstances where renewed questioning would be permissible.[4]

Indeed, language in *Miranda* suggests that the presence of counsel is the only appropriate alternative. In categorical language we held in *Miranda:* "If the individual
indicates in any manner, at any time prior to or during questioning, that he wishes
to remain silent, the interrogation must cease." *Id.* at 473–474, 86 S. Ct. at 1627. We
then immediately observed:

> If an individual indicates his desire to remain silent, but has an attorney
> present, there *may* be some circumstances in which further questioning
> would be permissible. In the absence of evidence of overbearing, statements
> then made in the presence of counsel *might* be free of the compelling influ-
> ence of the interrogation process and *might* fairly be construed as a waiver
> of the privilege for purposes of these statements.

Id. at 474 n. 44, 86 S. Ct. at 1627 (emphasis added). This was the only circumstance
in which we at all suggested that questioning could be resumed, and even then, further questioning was not permissible in all such circumstances, for compulsion was
still the presumption not easily dissipated.

These procedures would be wholly consistent with the Court's rejection of a "*per
se* proscription of indefinite duration," a rejection to which I fully subscribe. Today's
decision, however, virtually empties *Miranda* of principle, for plainly the decision
encourages police asked to cease interrogation to continue the suspect's detention
until the police station's coercive atmosphere does its work and the suspect responds
to resumed questioning. Today's rejection of that reality of life contrasts sharply with
the Court's acceptance only two years ago that "[i]n *Miranda* the Court found that
the techniques of police questioning and the nature of custodial surroundings produce an inherently coercive situation." *Schneckloth v. Bustamonte,* 412 U.S. 218, 247,
93 S. Ct. 2041, 2058, 36 L. Ed. 2d 854 (1973). I can only conclude that today's decision signals rejection of *Miranda's* basic premise.

---

3. In addition, a break in custody for a substantial period of time would permit — indeed it
would require — law enforcement officers to give *Miranda* warnings a second time.

4. I do not mean to imply that counsel may be forced on a suspect who does not request an attorney. I suggest only that either arraignment or counsel must be provided before resumption of
questioning to eliminate the coercive atmosphere of in-custody interrogation. The Court itself apparently proscribes resuming questioning until counsel is present if an accused has exercised the
right to have an attorney present at questioning.

My concern with the Court's opinion does not end with its treatment of *Miranda*, but extends to its treatment of the facts in this case. The Court's effort to have the Williams homicide appear as "an unrelated holdup murder," is patently unsuccessful. The anonymous tip received by Detective Cowie, conceded by the Court to be the sole basis for Mosley's arrest, embraced both the robberies covered in Cowie's interrogation and the robbery-murder of Williams, about which Detective Hill questioned Mosley. Thus, when Mosley was apprehended, Cowie suspected him of being involved in the Williams robbery in addition to the robberies about which he tried to examine Mosley. On another matter, the Court treats the second interrogation as being "at another location." Yet the fact is that it was merely a different floor of the same building.

I also find troubling the Court's finding that Mosley never indicated that he did not want to discuss the robbery-murder. I cannot read Cowie's testimony as the Court does. Cowie testified that Mosley declined to answer "[a]nything about the robberies." That can be read only against the background of the anonymous tip that implicated Mosley in the Williams incident. Read in that light, it may reasonably be inferred that Cowie understood "[a]nything" to include the Williams episode, since the anonymous tip embraced that episode. More than this, the Court's reading of Cowie's testimony is not even faithful to the standard it articulates here today. "Anything about the robberies" may more than reasonably be interpreted as comprehending the Williams murder which occurred during a robbery. To interpret Mosley's alleged statement to the contrary, therefore, hardly honors "scrupulously" the suspect's rights.

. . . .

Notes and Questions

(1) *Miranda* stated that "questioning must cease" when a suspect indicates that he wishes to remain silent. What effect does a suspect's invocation of the "right to remain silent" have on officers' abilities to secure admissible confessions by means of custodial interrogation? When may an officer resume custodial interrogation of a suspect who has indicated that he does not want to talk? Is *Mosley*'s standard for resumption consistent with *Miranda*'s goals? Is there an alternative standard that better serves *Miranda*'s purposes without unduly interfering with legitimate efforts to secure admissions of guilt?

(2) In *Mosley*, the officer resumed interrogation about a "different crime." When a suspect informs officers that he does not want to talk to them about an offense, may they ever resume questioning about the very same offense?

(3) Suppose that officers believe that a suspect has information that will enable them to respond to a serious threat to the public safety. They ignore the suspect's invocation of the right to silence and immediately ask questions "reasonably prompted" by the public safety concern. Are the statements obtained admissible against the suspect at trial?

Edwards v. Arizona

United States Supreme Court

451 U.S. 477, 101 S. Ct. 1880, 68 L. Ed. 2d 378 (1981)

Justice White delivered the opinion of the Court.

We granted certiorari in this case, 446 U.S. 950, 100 S. Ct. 2915, 64 L. Ed. 2d 807 (1980), limited to Question 1 presented in the petition, which in relevant part was "whether the Fifth, Sixth, and Fourteenth Amendments require suppression of a post-arrest confession, which was obtained after Edwards had invoked his right to consult counsel before further interrogation. . . ."

I

On January 19, 1976, a sworn complaint was filed against Edwards in Arizona state court charging him with robbery, burglary, and first-degree murder. An arrest warrant was issued pursuant to the complaint, and Edwards was arrested at his home later that same day. At the police station, he was informed of his rights as required by *Miranda v. Arizona*, 384 U.S. 436, 86 S. Ct. 1602, 16 L. Ed. 2d 694 (1966). Petitioner stated that he understood his rights, and was willing to submit to questioning. After being told that another suspect already in custody had implicated him in the crime, Edwards denied involvement and gave a taped statement presenting an alibi defense. He then sought to "make a deal." The interrogating officer told him that he wanted a statement, but that he did not have the authority to negotiate a deal. The officer provided Edwards with the telephone number of a county attorney. Petitioner made the call, but hung up after a few moments. Edwards then said: "I want an attorney before making a deal." At that point, questioning ceased and Edwards was taken to county jail.

At 9:15 the next morning, two detectives, colleagues of the officer who had interrogated Edwards the previous night, came to the jail and asked to see Edwards. When the detention officer informed Edwards that the detectives wished to speak with him, he replied that he did not want to talk to anyone. The guard told him that "he had" to talk and then took him to meet with the detectives. The officers identified themselves, stated they wanted to talk to him, and informed him of his *Miranda* rights. Edwards was willing to talk, but he first wanted to hear the taped statement of the alleged accomplice who had implicated him.[2] After listening to the tape for several minutes, petitioner said that he would make a statement so long as it was not tape-recorded. The detectives informed him that the recording was irrelevant since they could testify in court concerning whatever he said. Edwards replied: "I'll tell you anything you want to know, but I don't want it on tape." He thereupon implicated himself in the crime.

Prior to trial, Edwards moved to suppress his confession on the ground that his *Miranda* rights had been violated when the officers returned to question him after

---

2. It appears from the record that the detectives had brought the tape-recording with them.

he had invoked his right to counsel. The trial court initially granted the motion to suppress,[3] but reversed its ruling when presented with a supposedly controlling decision of a higher Arizona court. The court stated without explanation that it found Edwards' statement to be voluntary. Edwards was tried twice and convicted.[5] Evidence concerning his confession was admitted at both trials.

On appeal, the Arizona Supreme Court held that Edwards had invoked both his right to remain silent and his right to counsel during the interrogation conducted on the night of January 19. The court then went on to determine, however, that Edwards had waived both rights during the January 20 meeting when he voluntarily gave his statement to the detectives after again being informed that he need not answer questions and that he need not answer without the advice of counsel: "The trial court's finding that the waiver and confession were voluntarily and knowingly made is upheld."

Because the use of Edwards' confession against him at his trial violated his rights under the Fifth and Fourteenth Amendments as construed in *Miranda v. Arizona, supra,* we reverse the judgment of the Arizona Supreme Court.

II

In *Miranda v. Arizona,* the Court determined that the Fifth and Fourteenth Amendments' prohibition against compelled self-incrimination required that custodial interrogation be preceded by advice to the putative defendant that he has the right to remain silent and also the right to the presence of an attorney. The Court also indicated the procedures to be followed subsequent to the warnings. If the accused indicates that he wishes to remain silent, "the interrogation must cease." If he requests counsel, "the interrogation must cease until an attorney is present." 384 U.S. at 474, 86 S. Ct. at 1627.

Miranda thus declared that an accused has a Fifth and Fourteenth Amendment right to have counsel present during custodial interrogation. Here, the critical facts as found by the Arizona Supreme Court are that Edwards asserted his right to counsel and his right to remain silent on January 19, but that the police, without furnishing him counsel, returned the next morning to confront him and as a result of the meeting secured incriminating oral admissions. Contrary to the holdings of the state courts, Edwards insists that having exercised his right on the 19th to have counsel present during interrogation, he did not validly waive that right on the 20th. For the following reasons, we agree.

First, the Arizona Supreme Court applied an erroneous standard for determining waiver where the accused has specifically invoked his right to counsel. It is reasonably clear under our cases that waivers of counsel must not only be voluntary, but

---

3. The trial judge emphasized that the detectives had met with Edwards on January 20, without being requested by Edwards to do so, and concluded that they had ignored his request for counsel made the previous evening.

5. The jury in the first trial was unable to reach a verdict.

must also constitute a knowing and intelligent relinquishment or abandonment of a known right or privilege, a matter which depends in each case "upon the particular facts and circumstances surrounding that case, including the background, experience, and conduct of the accused." *Johnson v. Zerbst*, 304 U.S. 458, 464, 58 S. Ct. 1019, 1023, 82 L. Ed. 1461 (1938).

Considering the proceedings in the state courts in the light of this standard, we note that in denying petitioner's motion to suppress, the trial court found the admission to have been "voluntary," without separately focusing on whether Edwards had knowingly and intelligently relinquished his right to counsel. The Arizona Supreme Court, in a section of its opinion entitled "Voluntariness of Waiver," stated that in Arizona, confessions are *prima facie* involuntary and that the State had the burden of showing by a preponderance of the evidence that the confession was freely and voluntarily made. The court stated that the issue of voluntariness should be determined based on the totality of the circumstances as it related to whether an accused's action was "knowing and intelligent and whether his will [was] overborne." 122 Ariz. 206, 212, 594 P.2d 72, 78. Once the trial court determines that "the confession is voluntary, the finding will not be upset on appeal absent clear and manifest error." *Id.* The court then upheld the trial court's finding that the "waiver and confession were voluntarily and knowingly made." *Id.*

In referring to the necessity to find Edwards' confession knowing and intelligent, the State Supreme Court cited *Schneckloth v. Bustamonte*, 412 U.S. 218, 226, 93 S. Ct. 2041, 2047, 36 L. Ed. 2d 854 (1973). Yet, it is clear that *Schneckloth* does not control the issue presented in this case. The issue in *Schneckloth* was under what conditions an individual could be found to have consented to a search and thereby waived his Fourth Amendment rights. The Court declined to impose the "intentional relinquishment or abandonment of a known right or privilege" standard and required only that the consent be voluntary under the totality of the circumstances. The Court specifically noted that the right to counsel was a prime example of those rights requiring the special protection of the knowing and intelligent waiver standard, *id.* at 241, 93 S. Ct. at 2055, but held that "[t]he considerations that informed the Court's holding in *Miranda* are simply inapplicable in the present case." *Id.* at 246, 93 S. Ct. at 2057. *Schneckloth* itself thus emphasized that the voluntariness of a consent or an admission on the one hand, and a knowing and intelligent waiver on the other, are discrete inquiries. Here, however sound the conclusion of the state courts as to the voluntariness of Edwards' admission may be, neither the trial court nor the Arizona Supreme Court undertook to focus on whether Edwards understood his right to counsel and intelligently and knowingly relinquished it. It is thus apparent that the decision below misunderstood the requirement for finding a valid waiver of the right to counsel, once invoked.

Second, although we have held that after initially being advised of his *Miranda* rights, the accused may himself validly waive his rights and respond to interrogation, *see North Carolina v. Butler, supra,* 441 U.S. at 372–376, 99 S. Ct. at 1757–1759, the Court has strongly indicated that additional safeguards are necessary when the accused asks for counsel; and we now hold that when an accused has invoked his right to have counsel present during custodial interrogation, a valid waiver of that right cannot be established by showing only that he responded to further police-initiated custodial interrogation even if he has been advised of his rights. We further hold that an accused, such as Edwards, having expressed his desire to deal with the police only through counsel, is not subject to further interrogation by the authorities until counsel has been made available to him, unless the accused himself initiates further communication, exchanges, or conversations with the police.

Miranda itself indicated that the assertion of the right to counsel was a significant event and that once exercised by the accused, "the interrogation must cease until an attorney is present." 384 U.S. at 474, 86 S. Ct. at 1627. Our later cases have not abandoned that view. In *Michigan v. Mosley*, 423 U.S. 96, 96 S. Ct. 321, 46 L. Ed. 2d 313 (1975), the Court noted that *Miranda* had distinguished between the procedural safeguards triggered by a request to remain silent and a request for an attorney and had required that interrogation cease until an attorney was present only if the individual stated that he wanted counsel. 423 U.S. at 104, n. 10, 96 S. Ct. at 326, n. 10. In *Fare v. Michael C., supra*, 442 U.S. at 719, 99 S. Ct. at 2569, the Court referred to *Miranda*'s "rigid rule that an accused's request for an attorney is *per se* an invocation of his Fifth Amendment rights, requiring that all interrogation cease." And just last Term, in a case where a suspect in custody had invoked his *Miranda* right to counsel, the Court again referred to the "undisputed right" under *Miranda* to remain silent and to be free of interrogation "until he had consulted with a lawyer." *Rhode Island v. Innis*, 446 U.S. 291, 298, 100 S. Ct. 1682, 1688, 64 L. Ed. 2d 297 (1980). We reconfirm these views and, to lend them substance, emphasize that it is inconsistent with *Miranda* and its progeny for the authorities, at their instance, to reinterrogate an accused in custody if he has clearly asserted his right to counsel.

In concluding that the fruits of the interrogation initiated by the police on January 20 could not be used against Edwards, we do not hold or imply that Edwards was powerless to countermand his election or that the authorities could in no event use any incriminating statements made by Edwards prior to his having access to counsel. Had Edwards initiated the meeting on January 20, nothing in the Fifth and Fourteenth Amendments would prohibit the police from merely listening to his voluntary, volunteered statements and using them against him at the trial. The Fifth Amendment right identified in *Miranda* is the right to have counsel present at any custodial interrogation. Absent such interrogation, there would have been no infringement of the right that Edwards invoked and there would be no occasion to determine whether there had been a valid waiver. *Rhode Island v. Innis, supra*, makes this sufficiently clear.[9]

---

9. If, as frequently would occur in the course of a meeting initiated by the accused, the conversation is not wholly one-sided, it is likely that the officers will say or do something that clearly would be "interrogation." In that event, the question would be whether a valid waiver of the right to counsel and the right to silence had occurred, that is, whether the purported waiver was knowing and intelligent and found to be so under the totality of the circumstances, including the necessary fact that the accused, not the police, reopened the dialogue with the authorities . . . .

But this is not what the facts of this case show. Here, the officers conducting the interrogation on the evening of January 19 ceased interrogation when Edwards requested counsel as he had been advised he had the right to do. The Arizona Supreme Court was of the opinion that this was a sufficient invocation of his *Miranda* rights, and we are in accord. It is also clear that without making counsel available to Edwards, the police returned to him the next day. This was not at his suggestion or request. Indeed, Edwards informed the detention officer that he did not want to talk to anyone. At the meeting, the detectives told Edwards that they wanted to talk to him and again advised him of his *Miranda* rights. Edwards stated that he would talk, but what prompted this action does not appear. He listened at his own request to part of the taped statement made by one of his alleged accomplices and then made an incriminating statement, which was used against him at his trial. We think it is clear that Edwards was subjected to custodial interrogation on January 20 within the meaning of *Rhode Island v. Innis, supra,* and that this occurred at the instance of the authorities. His statement, made without having had access to counsel, did not amount to a valid waiver and hence was inadmissible.

Accordingly, the holding of the Arizona Supreme Court that Edwards had waived his right to counsel was infirm, and the judgment of that court is reversed.

So ordered.

Chief Justice Burger, concurring in the judgment.

I concur only in the judgment because I do not agree that either any constitutional standard or the holding of *Miranda v. Arizona*, 384 U.S. 436, 86 S. Ct. 1602, 16 L. Ed. 2d 694 (1966) — as distinguished from its dicta — calls for a special rule as to how an accused in custody may waive the right to be free from interrogation. The extraordinary protections afforded a person in custody suspected of criminal conduct are not without a valid basis, but as with all "good" things they can be carried too far. The notion that any "prompting" of a person in custody is somehow evil *per se* has been rejected. *Rhode Island v. Innis*, 446 U.S. 291, 100 S. Ct. 1682, 64 L. Ed. 2d 297 (1980). For me, the inquiry in this setting is whether resumption of interrogation is a result of a voluntary waiver, and that inquiry should be resolved under the traditional standards established in *Johnson v. Zerbst*, 304 U.S. 458, 464, 58 S. Ct. 1019, 1023, 82 L. Ed. 1461 (1938):

> A waiver is ordinarily an intentional relinquishment or abandonment of a known right or privilege. The determination of whether there has been an intelligent waiver ... must depend, in each case, upon the particular facts and circumstances surrounding that case, including the background, experience, and conduct of the accused.

In this case, the Supreme Court of Arizona described the situation as follows:

> When the detention officer told Edwards that the detectives were there to see him, he told the officer that he did not wish to speak to anyone. The officer told him *that he had to.*

122 Ariz. 206, 209, 594 P.2d 72, 75 (1979) (emphasis added). This is enough for me, and on this record the Supreme Court of Arizona erred in holding that the resumption of interrogation was the product of a voluntary waiver, such as I found to be the situation in both *Innis* and *Brewer v. Williams*.

JUSTICE POWELL, with whom JUSTICE REHNQUIST joins, concurring in the result.

Although I agree that the judgment of the Arizona Supreme Court must be reversed, I do not join the Court's opinion because I am not sure what it means.

I can agree with much of the opinion. It states the settled rule:

> It is reasonably clear under our cases that waivers of counsel must not only be voluntary, but must also constitute a knowing and intelligent relinquishment or abandonment of a known right or privilege, a matter which depends in each case "upon the particular facts and circumstances surrounding that case, including the background, experience and conduct of the accused."

Johnson v. Zerbst, 304 U.S. 458, 464, 58 S. Ct. 1019, 1023, 82 L. Ed. 1461 (1938). I have thought it settled law, as these cases tell us, that one accused of crime may waive *any* of the constitutional safeguards — including the right to remain silent, to jury trial, to call witnesses, to cross-examine one's accusers, to testify in one's own behalf, and — of course — to have counsel. Whatever the right, the standard for waiver is whether the actor fully understands the right in question and voluntarily intends to relinquish it.

In its opinion today, however, the Court — after reiterating the familiar principles of waiver — goes on to say:

> We further hold that an accused, such as Edwards, having expressed his desire to deal with the police only through counsel, is not subject to further interrogation by the authorities until counsel has been made available to him, *unless the accused [has] himself initiate[d] further communication, exchanges, or conversations with the police. . . .*

(Emphasis added). In view of the emphasis placed on "initiation," I find the Court's opinion unclear. If read to create a new *per se* rule, requiring a threshold inquiry as to precisely who opened any conversation between an accused and state officials, I cannot agree. I would not superimpose a new element of proof on the established doctrine of waiver of counsel.

Perhaps the Court's opinion can be read as not departing from established doctrine. Accepting the formulation quoted above, two questions are identifiable: (i) was there in fact "interrogation," *see Rhode Island v. Innis*, 446 U.S. 291, 100 S. Ct. 1682, 64 L. Ed. 2d 297 (1980), and (ii) did the police "initiate" it? Each of these questions is, of course, relevant to the admissibility of a confession. In this case, for example, it is clear that Edwards was taken from his cell against his will and subjected to renewed interrogation. Whether this is described as police-"initiated" interrogation or in some other way, it clearly was questioning under circumstances incompatible with a voluntary waiver of the fundamental right to counsel.

But few cases will be as clear as this one. Communications between police and a suspect in custody are commonplace. It is useful to contrast the circumstances of this case with typical, and permissible, custodial communications between police and a suspect who has asked for counsel. For example, police do not impermissibly "initiate" renewed interrogation by engaging in routine conversations with suspects about unrelated matters. And police legitimately may inquire whether a suspect has changed his mind about speaking to them without an attorney. It is not unusual for a person in custody who previously has expressed an unwillingness to talk or a desire to have a lawyer, to change his mind and even welcome an opportunity to talk. Nothing in the Constitution erects obstacles that preclude police from ascertaining whether a suspect has reconsidered his original decision. As Justice White has observed, this Court consistently has "rejected any paternalistic rule protecting a defendant from his intelligent and voluntary decisions about his own criminal case." *Michigan v. Mosley*, 423 U.S. 96, 109, 96 S. Ct. 321, 329, 46 L. Ed. 2d 313 (1975) (White, J., concurring in result).

In sum, once warnings have been given and the right to counsel has been invoked, the relevant inquiry — whether the suspect now desires to talk to police without counsel — is a question of fact to be determined in light of all of the circumstances. Who "initiated" a conversation may be relevant to the question of waiver, but it is not the *sine qua non* to the inquiry. The ultimate question is whether there was a free and knowing waiver of counsel before interrogation commenced.

If the Court's opinion does nothing more than restate these principles, I am in agreement with it. I hesitate to join the opinion only because of what appears to be an undue, and undefined, emphasis on a single element: "initiation." As Justice White has noted, the Court in *Miranda v. Arizona*, 384 U.S. 436, 86 S. Ct. 1602, 16 L. Ed. 2d 694 (1966), imposed a general prophylactic rule that is not manifestly required by anything in the text of the Constitution. *Miranda* itself recognized, moreover, that counsel's assistance can be waived. Waiver always has been evaluated under the general formulation of the *Zerbst* standard quoted above. My concern is that the Court's opinion today may be read as "constitutionalizing" not the generalized *Zerbst* standard but a *single element of fact* among the various facts that may be relevant to determining whether there has been a valid waiver.[2]

Notes and Questions

Is it constitutionally appropriate to provide more protection for the suspect who asserts the right to have an attorney present at questioning than for the suspect who asserts the right to remain silent? The Model Pre-Arraignment Code 104.8(2)(d), adopted prior to *Mosley*, makes no distinction between invocation of

---

2. Such a step should be taken only if it is demonstrably clear that the traditional waiver standard is ineffective. There is no indication, in the multitude of cases that come to us each Term, that *Zerbst* and its progeny have failed to protect constitutional rights.

the two rights but provides that, if either of them is asserted, "no law enforcement officer shall seek a waiver or interrogate the suspect in any way until the suspect meets with counsel."

Davis v. United States

United States Supreme Court

512 U.S. 452, 114 S. Ct. 2350, 129 L. Ed. 2d 362 (1994)

JUSTICE O'CONNOR delivered the opinion of the Court.

In *Edwards v. Arizona*, 451 U.S. 477, 101 S. Ct. 1880, 68 L. Ed. 2d 378 (1981), we held that law enforcement officers must immediately cease questioning a suspect who has clearly asserted his right to have counsel present during custodial interrogation. In this case we decide how law enforcement officers should respond when a suspect makes a reference to counsel that is insufficiently clear to invoke the *Edwards* prohibition on further questioning.

I

Pool brought trouble not to River City, but to the Charleston Naval Base. Petitioner, a member of the United States Navy, spent the evening of October 2, 1988, shooting pool at a club on the base. Another sailor, Keith Shackleford, lost a game and a $30 wager to petitioner, but Shackleford refused to pay. After the club closed, Shackleford was beaten to death with a pool cue on a loading dock behind the commissary. The body was found early the next morning.

The investigation by the Naval Investigative Service (NIS) gradually focused on petitioner. Investigative agents determined that petitioner was at the club that evening, and that he was absent without authorization from his duty station the next morning. The agents also learned that only privately owned pool cues could be removed from the club premises, and that petitioner owned two cues — one of which had a bloodstain on it. The agents were told by various people that petitioner either had admitted committing the crime or had recounted details that clearly indicated his involvement in the killing.

On November 4, 1988, petitioner was interviewed at the NIS office. As required by military law, the agents advised petitioner that he was a suspect in the killing, that he was not required to make a statement, that any statement could be used against him at a trial by court-martial, and that he was entitled to speak with an attorney and have an attorney present during questioning. Petitioner waived his rights to remain silent and to counsel, both orally and in writing.

About an hour and a half into the interview, petitioner said, "Maybe I should talk to a lawyer." According to the uncontradicted testimony of one of the interviewing agents, the interview then proceeded as follows:

[We m]ade it very clear that we're not here to violate his rights, that if he wants a lawyer, then we will stop any kind of questioning with him, that we weren't going to pursue the matter unless we have it clarified is he asking for a lawyer or is he just making a comment about a lawyer, and he said, "No, I'm not asking for a lawyer," and then he continued on, and said, "No, I don't want a lawyer."

After a short break, the agents reminded petitioner of his rights to remain silent and to counsel. The interview then continued for another hour, until petitioner said, "I think I want a lawyer before I say anything else." At that point, questioning ceased.

At his general court-martial, petitioner moved to suppress statements made during the November 4 interview. The military judge denied the motion, holding that "the mention of a lawyer by [petitioner] during the course of the interrogation [was] not in the form of a request for counsel and . . . the agents properly determined that [petitioner] was not indicating a desire for or invoking his right to counsel." Petitioner was convicted on one specification of unpremeditated murder, in violation of Art. 118, UCMJ, 10 U.S.C. § 918. He was sentenced to confinement for life, a dishonorable discharge, forfeiture of all pay and allowances, and a reduction in rank to the lowest pay grade. The convening authority approved the findings and sentence. The Navy-Marine Corps Court of Military Review affirmed.

The United States Court of Military Appeals granted discretionary review and affirmed. . . .

. . . .

II

The Sixth Amendment right to counsel attaches only at the initiation of adversary criminal proceedings, and before proceedings are initiated a suspect in a criminal investigation has no constitutional right to the assistance of counsel. Nevertheless, we held in *Miranda v. Arizona*, 384 U.S. 436, 469–473, 86 S. Ct. 1602, 1625–1627, 16 L. Ed. 2d 694 (1966), that a suspect subject to custodial interrogation has the right to consult with an attorney and to have counsel present during questioning, and that the police must explain this right to him before questioning begins. The right to counsel established in *Miranda* was one of a "series of recommended 'procedural safeguards' . . . [that] were not themselves rights protected by the Constitution but were instead measures to insure that the right against compulsory self-incrimination was protected." *Michigan v. Tucker*, 417 U.S. 433, 443–444, 94 S. Ct. 2357, 2363–2364, 41 L. Ed. 2d 182 (1974); *see* U.S. Const., Amdt. 5 ("No person . . . shall be compelled in any criminal case to be a witness against himself").

The right to counsel recognized in *Miranda* is sufficiently important to suspects in criminal investigations, we have held, that it "requir[es] the special protection of the knowing and intelligent waiver standard." *Edwards v. Arizona*, 451 U.S., at 483, 101 S. Ct., at 1884. *See Oregon v. Bradshaw*, 462 U.S. 1039, 1046–1047, 103 S. Ct. 2830, 2835–2836, 77 L. Ed. 2d 405 (1983) (plurality opinion); *id.*, at 1051, 103 S. Ct., at 2838 (Powell, J., concurring in judgment). If the suspect effectively waives his right to counsel after receiving the *Miranda* warnings, law enforcement officers are free to question him. *North Carolina v. Butler*, 441 U.S. 369, 372–376, 99 S. Ct. 1755, 1756–1759, 60 L. Ed. 2d 286 (1979). But if a suspect requests counsel at any time during the interview, he is not subject to further questioning until a lawyer has been made available or the suspect himself reinitiates conversation. *Edwards v. Arizona, supra,* 451 U.S., at 484–485, 101 S. Ct., at 1884–1885. This "second layer of prophylaxis for the *Miranda* right to counsel," *McNeil v. Wisconsin,* 501 U.S. 171, 176, 111 S. Ct. 2204, 2208, 115 L. Ed. 2d 158 (1991), is "designed to prevent police from badgering a defendant into waiving his previously asserted *Miranda* rights," *Michigan v. Harvey,* 494 U.S. 344, 350, 110 S. Ct. 1176, 1180, 108 L. Ed. 2d 293 (1990). . . .

The applicability of the "'rigid' prophylactic rule" of *Edwards* requires courts to "determine whether the accused *actually invoked* his right to counsel." *Smith v. Illinois, supra,* 469 U.S., at 95, 105 S. Ct., at 492 (emphasis added), quoting *Fare v. Michael C.,* 442 U.S. 707, 719, 99 S. Ct. 2560, 2569, 61 L. Ed. 2d 197 (1979). To avoid difficulties of proof and to provide guidance to officers conducting interrogations, this is an objective inquiry. *See Connecticut v. Barrett, supra,* 479 U.S., at 529, 107 S. Ct., at 832. Invocation of the *Miranda* right to counsel "requires, at a minimum, some statement that can reasonably be construed to be an expression of a desire for the assistance of an attorney." *McNeil v. Wisconsin, supra,* 501 U.S., at 178, 111 S. Ct., at 2209. But if a suspect makes a reference to an attorney that is ambiguous or equivocal in that a reasonable officer in light of the circumstances would have understood only that the suspect *might* be invoking the right to counsel, our precedents do not require the cessation of questioning. *See ibid.* ("the *likelihood* that a suspect would wish counsel to be present is not the test for applicability of *Edwards*"); *Edwards v. Arizona, supra,* 451 U.S., at 485, 101 S. Ct., at 1885 (impermissible for authorities "to reinterrogate an accused in custody if he has *clearly asserted* his right to counsel") (emphasis added).

Rather, the suspect must unambiguously request counsel. As we have observed, "a statement either is such an assertion of the right to counsel or it is not." *Smith v. Illinois,* 469 U.S., at 97–98, 105 S. Ct., at 494 (brackets and internal quotation marks omitted). Although a suspect need not "speak with the discrimination of an Oxford don," *Post,* at 2364 (SOUTER, J., concurring in judgment), he must articulate his desire to have counsel present sufficiently clearly that a reasonable police officer in the circumstances would understand the statement to be a request for an attorney. If the statement fails to meet the requisite level of clarity, *Edwards* does not require that the officers stop questioning the suspect.

We decline petitioner's invitation to extend *Edwards* and require law enforcement officers to cease questioning immediately upon the making of an ambiguous or equivocal reference to an attorney. . . . The rationale underlying *Edwards* is that the police must respect a suspect's wishes regarding his right to have an attorney present during custodial interrogation. But when the officers conducting the questioning reasonably do not know whether or not the suspect wants a lawyer, a rule requiring the immediate cessation of questioning "would transform the *Miranda* safeguards into wholly irrational obstacles to legitimate police investigative activity," *Michigan v. Mosley,* 423 U.S. 96, 102, 96 S. Ct. 321, 326, 46 L. Ed. 2d 313 (1975), because it would needlessly prevent the police from questioning a suspect in the absence of counsel even if the suspect did not wish to have a lawyer present. Nothing in

Edwards requires the provision of counsel to a suspect who consents to answer questions without the assistance of a lawyer. In *Miranda* itself, we expressly rejected the suggestion "that each police station must have a 'station house lawyer' present at all times to advise prisoners," 384 U.S., at 474, 86 S. Ct., at 1628, and held instead that a suspect must be told of his right to have an attorney present and that he may not be questioned after invoking his right to counsel. We also noted that if a suspect is "indecisive in his request for counsel," the officers need not always cease questioning. *See id.*, at 485, 86 S. Ct., at 1633.

We recognize that requiring a clear assertion of the right to counsel might disadvantage some suspects who because of fear, intimidation, lack of linguistic skills, or a variety of other reasons will not clearly articulate their right to counsel although they actually want to have a lawyer present. But the primary protection afforded suspects subject to custodial interrogation is the *Miranda* warnings themselves. "[F]ull comprehension of the rights to remain silent and request an attorney [is] sufficient to dispel whatever coercion is inherent in the interrogation process." *Moran v. Burbine, supra*, 475 U.S., at 427, 106 S. Ct., at 1144. A suspect who knowingly and voluntarily waives his right to counsel after having that right explained to him has indicated his willingness to deal with the police unassisted. Although *Edwards* provides an additional protection — if a suspect subsequently requests an attorney, questioning must cease — it is one that must be affirmatively invoked by the suspect.

In considering how a suspect must invoke the right to counsel, we must consider the other side of the *Miranda* equation: the need for effective law enforcement. Although the courts ensure compliance with the *Miranda* requirements through the exclusionary rule, it is police officers who must actually decide whether or not they can question a suspect. The *Edwards* rule — questioning must cease if the suspect asks for a lawyer — provides a bright line that can be applied by officers in the real world of investigation and interrogation without unduly hampering the gathering of information. But if we were to require questioning to cease if a suspect makes a statement that *might* be a request for an attorney, this clarity and ease of application would be lost. Police officers would be forced to make difficult judgment calls about whether the suspect in fact wants a lawyer even though he hasn't said so, with the threat of suppression if they guess wrong. We therefore hold that, after a knowing and voluntary waiver of the *Miranda* rights, law enforcement officers may continue questioning until and unless the suspect clearly requests an attorney.

Of course, when a suspect makes an ambiguous or equivocal statement it will often be good police practice for the interviewing officers to clarify whether or not he actually wants an attorney. That was the procedure followed by the NIS agents in this case. Clarifying questions help protect the rights of the suspect by ensuring that he gets an attorney if he wants one, and will minimize the chance of a confession being suppressed due to subsequent judicial second-guessing as to the meaning of the suspect's statement regarding counsel. But we decline to adopt a rule requiring officers to ask clarifying questions. If the suspect's statement is not an unambiguous or unequivocal request for counsel, the officers have no obligation to stop questioning him. . . .

The courts below found that petitioner's remark to the NIS agents "Maybe I should talk to a lawyer" was not a request for counsel, and we see no reason to disturb that conclusion. The NIS agents therefore were not required to stop questioning petitioner, though it was entirely proper for them to clarify whether petitioner in fact wanted a lawyer. Because there is no ground for suppression of petitioner's statements, the judgment of the Court of Military Appeals is

Affirmed.

[The concurring opinion of JUSTICE SCALIA has been omitted.]

JUSTICE SOUTER, with whom JUSTICE BLACKMUN, JUSTICE STEVENS, and JUSTICE GINSBURG join, concurring in the judgment.

. . . .

I agree with the majority that the Constitution does not forbid law enforcement officers to pose questions (like those directed at Davis) aimed solely at clarifying whether a suspect's ambiguous reference to counsel was meant to assert his Fifth Amendment right. Accordingly I concur in the judgment affirming Davis's conviction, resting partly on evidence of statements given after agents ascertained that he did not wish to deal with them through counsel. I cannot, however, join in my colleagues' further conclusion that if the investigators here had been so inclined, they were at liberty to disregard Davis's reference to a lawyer entirely, in accordance with a general rule that interrogators have no legal obligation to discover what a custodial subject meant by an ambiguous statement that could reasonably be understood to express a desire to consult a lawyer.

Our own precedent, the reasonable judgments of the majority of the many courts already to have addressed the issue before us, and the advocacy of a considerable body of law enforcement officials are to the contrary. All argue against the Court's approach today, which draws a sharp line between interrogated suspects who "clearly" assert their right to counsel, and those who say something that may, but may not, express a desire for counsel's presence, the former suspects being assured that questioning will not resume without counsel present, the latter being left to fend for themselves. The concerns of fairness and practicality that have long anchored our *Miranda* case law point to a different response: when law enforcement officials "reasonably do not know whether or not the suspect wants a lawyer," they should stop their interrogation and ask him to make his choice clear.

I

A

While the question we address today is an open one, its answer requires coherence with nearly three decades of case law addressing the relationship between police and criminal suspects in custodial interrogation. Throughout that period, two precepts have commanded broad assent: that the *Miranda* safeguards exist "to assure that *the individual's right to choose* between speech and silence remains unfettered throughout the interrogation process," see *Connecticut v. Barrett*, 479 U.S. 523,

528, 107 S. Ct. 828, 831, 93 L. Ed. 2d 920 (1987) (quoting *Miranda*, 384 U.S., at 469, 86 S. Ct., at 1625, and supplying emphasis), and that the justification for *Miranda* rules, intended to operate in the real world, "must be consistent with . . . practical realities." *Arizona v. Roberson*, 486 U.S. 675, 688, 108 S. Ct. 2093, 2102, 100 L. Ed. 2d 704 (1988) (Kennedy, J., dissenting). A rule barring government agents from further interrogation until they determine whether a suspect's ambiguous statement was meant as a request for counsel fulfills both ambitions. It assures that a suspect's choice whether or not to deal with police through counsel will be "scrupulously honored," *Miranda, supra*, 384 U.S., at 479, 86 S. Ct., at 1630; *cf. Michigan v. Mosley*, 423 U.S. 96, 110, n. 2, 96 S. Ct. 321, 324, n. 2, 46 L. Ed. 2d 313 (1975) (White, J., concurring in result), and it faces both the real-world reasons why misunderstandings arise between suspect and interrogator and the real-world limitations on the capacity of police and trial courts to apply fine distinctions and intricate rules.

B

Tested against the same two principles, the approach the Court adopts does not fare so well. First, as the majority expressly acknowledges, criminal suspects who may (in *Miranda's* words) be "thrust into an unfamiliar atmosphere and run through menacing police interrogation procedures," 384 U.S., at 457, 86 S. Ct., at 1618, would seem an odd group to single out for the Court's demand of heightened linguistic care. A substantial percentage of them lack anything like a confident command of the English language, *see, e.g., United States v. De la Jara*, 973 F.2d 746, 750 (9th Cir. 1992); many are "woefully ignorant," *Miranda, supra*, 384 U.S., at 468, 86 S. Ct., at 1624; and many more will be sufficiently intimidated by the interrogation process or overwhelmed by the uncertainty of their predicament that the ability to speak assertively will abandon them.[4] Indeed, the awareness of just these realities has, in the past, dissuaded the Court from placing any burden of clarity upon individuals in custody, but has led it instead to require that requests for counsel be "give[n] a broad, rather than a narrow, interpretation," *see Michigan v. Jackson*, 475 U.S. 625, 633, 106 S. Ct. 1404, 1409, 89 L. Ed. 2d 631 (1986); *Barrett*, 479 U.S., at 529, 107 S. Ct., at 832, and that courts "indulge every reasonable presumption," *Johnson v. Zerbst*, 304 U.S. 458, 464, 58 S. Ct. 1019, 1023, 82 L. Ed. 1461 (1938) (internal quotation marks omitted), that a suspect has not waived his right to counsel under *Miranda*. . . .

---

4. Social science confirms what common sense would suggest, that individuals who feel intimidated or powerless are more likely to speak in equivocal or nonstandard terms when no ambiguity or equivocation is meant. *See* W. O'Barr, LINGUISTIC EVIDENCE: LANGUAGE, POWER AND STRATEGY IN THE COURTROOM 61–71 (1982). Suspects in police interrogation are strong candidates for these effects. Even while resort by the police to the "third degree" has abated since *Miranda*, the basic forms of psychological pressure applied by police appear to have changed less. *Compare, e.g., Miranda*, 384 U.S., at 449, 86 S. Ct., at 1615 ("'[T]he principal psychological factor contributing to a successful interrogation is *privacy*'") (quoting F. Inbau & J. Reid, Criminal Interrogations and Confessions 1 (1962)), *with* F. Inbau, J. Reid, & J. Buckley, CRIMINAL INTERROGATION AND CONFESSIONS 24 (3d ed. 1986) ("The principal psychological factor contributing to a successful interrogation is privacy").

Nor may the standard governing waivers as expressed in these statements be deflected away by drawing a distinction between initial waivers of *Miranda* rights and subsequent decisions to reinvoke them, on the theory that so long as the burden to demonstrate waiver rests on the government, it is only fair to make the suspect shoulder a burden of showing a clear subsequent assertion. *Miranda* itself discredited the legitimacy of any such distinction. The opinion described the object of the warning as being to assure "a continuous opportunity to exercise [the right of silence]," *id.*, 384 U.S. at 444, 86 S. Ct., at 1612. "[C]ontinuous opportunity" suggests an unvarying one, governed by a common standard of effectiveness. The suggestion is confirmed by the very first statement that follows, that "there can be no questioning" if the suspect "indicates in any manner and at any stage of the process that he wishes to consult with an attorney," *Miranda*, 384 U.S. at 444–445, 86 S. Ct., at 1612. "[A]t any stage" obviously includes the stage after initial waiver and the commencement of questioning, and "indicates in any manner" is a rule plainly in tension with the indication "with a vengeance," *see id.*, at 505, 86 S. Ct., at 1644 (Harlan, J., dissenting), that the Court would require for exercise of the "continuous" right at some point after initial waiver.

The Court defends as tolerable the certainty that some poorly expressed requests for counsel will be disregarded on the ground that *Miranda* warnings suffice to alleviate the inherent coercion of the custodial interrogation. But, "a once-stated warning, delivered by those who will conduct the interrogation cannot itself suffice" to "assure that the . . . right to choose between silence and speech remains unfettered throughout the interrogation process," [*Miranda*], 384 U.S. at 469, 86 S. Ct., at 1625. . . .

Indeed, it is easy, amidst the discussion of layers of protection, to lose sight of a real risk in the majority's approach, going close to the core of what the Court has held that the Fifth Amendment provides. . . . When a suspect understands his (expressed) wishes to have been ignored (and by hypothesis, he has said something that an objective listener could "reasonably," although not necessarily, take to be a request), in contravention of the "rights" just read to him by his interrogator, he may well see further objection as futile and confession (true or not) as the only way to end his interrogation. . . .

. . . While it might be fair to say that every statement is meant either to express a desire to deal with police through counsel or not, this fact does not dictate the rule that interrogators who hear a statement consistent with either possibility may presume the latter and forge ahead; on the contrary, clarification is the intuitively sensible course.

The other justifications offered for the "requisite level of clarity" rule, are that, whatever its costs, it will further society's strong interest in "effective law enforcement," and maintain the "ease of application," that has long been a concern of our *Miranda* jurisprudence. With respect to the first point, the margin of difference between the clarification approach advocated here and the one the Court adopts is defined by the class of cases in which a suspect, if asked, would make it plain that he meant to request counsel (at which point questioning would cease). While these lost confessions do extract a real price from society, it is one that *Miranda* itself determined should be borne. . . .

As for practical application, while every approach, including the majority's, will involve some "difficult judgment calls,"[7] the rule argued for here would relieve the officer of any responsibility for guessing "whether the suspect in fact wants a lawyer even though he hasn't said so." To the contrary, it would assure that the "judgment call" will be made by the party most competent to resolve the ambiguity, who our case law has always assumed should make it: the individual suspect.

II

Although I am convinced that the Court has taken the wrong path, I am not persuaded by the petitioner's contention that even ambiguous statements require an end to all police questioning. I recognize that the approach petitioner urges on us can claim some support from our case law, most notably in the "indicates in any manner" language of *Miranda*, and I do not deny that the rule I endorse could be abused by "clarifying" questions that shade subtly into illicitly badgering a suspect who wants counsel. . . . But the petitioner's proposal is not entirely in harmony with all the major themes of *Miranda* case law, its virtues and demerits being the reverse images of those that mark the Court's rule. While it is plainly wrong, for example, to continue interrogation when the suspect wants it to stop (and so indicates), the strong bias in favor of individual choice may also be disserved by stopping questioning when a suspect wants it to continue (but where his statement might be understood otherwise). The costs to society of losing confessions would, moreover, be especially

---

7. In the abstract, nothing may seem more clear than a "clear statement" rule, but in police stations and trial courts the question, "how clear is clear?" is not so readily answered. When a suspect says, "uh, yeah, I'd like to do that" after being told he has a right to a lawyer, has he "clearly asserted" his right? *Compare Smith v. Illinois*, 469 U.S. 91, 97, 105 S. Ct. 490, 493, 83 L. Ed. 2d 488 (1984) (per curiam) (statement was "'neither indecisive nor ambiguous'") (citation omitted)), *with id.* at 101, 105 S. Ct., at 495–496 (Rehnquist, J., dissenting) (questioning clarity); *see also Oregon v. Bradshaw*, 462 U.S. 1039, 1041–1042, 103 S. Ct. 2830, 2832–2833, 77 L. Ed. 2d 405 (1983) (plurality opinion) ("I do want an attorney before it goes very much further"); *Edwards*, 451 U.S., at 479, 101 S. Ct., at 1882 ("'I want an attorney before making a deal'"); *cf.* n. 3, *supra*. Indeed, in this case, when Davis finally said, "I think I want a lawyer before I say anything else," the agents ceased questioning; *but see People v. Kendricks*, 121 Ill. App. 3d 442, 446, 77 Ill. Dec. 41, 43, 459 N.E.2d 1137, 1139 (1984) (agents need not stop interrogation when suspect says, "I think I might need a lawyer"); *cf. People v. Santiago*, 133 App. Div. 2d 429, 430–431, 519 N.Y.S.2d 413, 414–415 (1987) ("'Will you supply [a lawyer] now so that I may ask him should I continue with this interview at this moment?'" held "not . . . an unequivocal invocation"). *See generally Smith, supra*, 469 U.S., at 101, 105 S. Ct., at 495–496 (Rehnquist, J., dissenting) (noting that statements are rarely "crystal-clear . . . [D]ifferences between certainty and hesitancy may well turn on the inflection with which words are spoken, especially where [a] statement is isolated from the statements surrounding it"). As a practical matter, of course, the primary arbiters of "clarity" will be the interrogators themselves, who tend as well to be courts' preferred source in determining the precise words a suspect used. And when an inculpatory statement has been obtained as a result of an unrecorded, incommunicado interrogation, these officers rarely lose "swearing matches" against criminal defendants at suppression hearings.

hard to bear where the suspect, if asked for his choice, would have chosen to continue. One need not sign the majority's opinion here to agree that resort to the rule petitioner argues for should be had only if experience shows that less drastic means of safeguarding suspects' constitutional rights are not up to the job. . . .

. . . .

Our cases are best respected by a rule that when a suspect under custodial interrogation makes an ambiguous statement that might reasonably be understood as expressing a wish that a lawyer be summoned (and questioning cease), interrogators' questions should be confined to verifying whether the individual meant to ask for a lawyer. While there is reason to expect that trial courts will apply today's ruling sensibly (without requiring criminal suspects to speak with the discrimination of an Oxford don) and that interrogators will continue to follow what the Court rightly calls "good police practice" (compelled up to now by a substantial body of state and Circuit law), I believe that the case law under *Miranda* does not allow them to do otherwise.

Notes and Questions

(1) INVOKING THE RIGHT TO COUNSEL: (a) In *Smith v. Illinois*, 469 U.S. 91, 105 S. Ct. 490, 83 L. Ed. 2d 488 (1984) (*per curiam*), a detective began reading the defendant his *Miranda* rights. When the detective came to the part of the warnings dealing with the right to a lawyer, the following occurred:

> Q. You have a right to consult with a lawyer and to have a lawyer present with you when you're being questioned. Do you understand that?
>
> A. Uh, yeah. I'd like to do that.
>
> Q. Okay
>
> Q. . . . If you want a lawyer and you're unable to pay for one a lawyer will be appointed to represent you free of cost, do you understand that?
>
> A. Okay.
>
> Q. Do you wish to talk to me at this time without a lawyer being present?
>
> A. Yeah and no, uh, I don't know what's what, really.
>
> Q. Well. You either have to talk to me this time without a lawyer being present and if you do agree to talk with me without a lawyer being present you can stop at any time you want to.
>
> A. All right. I'll talk to you then.

By a 6–3 majority, the Court held that the defendant's initial request for counsel was "unambiguous." Emphasizing that its holding was "a narrow one," the majority then stated that "an accused's *post-request* responses to further interrogation may not be used to cast retrospective doubt on the clarity of the initial request itself."

(b) In *McNeil v. Wisconsin*, 501 U.S. 171, 111 S. Ct. 2204, 115 L. Ed. 2d 158 (1991), a defendant who had been charged with armed robbery made an appearance in court with counsel — an event that was treated as an invocation of his Sixth Amendment right to counsel for proceedings pertaining to that robbery charge. Under *Michigan v. Jackson*, 475 U.S. 625, 106 S. Ct. 1404, 89 L. Ed. 2d 631 (1986), (which governed at the time but has since been overturned), this request for assistance did protect the defendant against officer-initiated interrogation regarding the robbery. However, officers initiated custodial interrogation with respect to three *uncharged* crimes — a murder, an attempted murder, and an armed burglary. As will be seen in Chapter Nine, the Sixth Amendment right to counsel attaches *only after* formal charges are initiated and is "offense specific" — that is, it attaches *only for* those offenses that have been formally charged. Consequently, the defendant in *McNeil* had no Sixth Amendment entitlement for the murder, attempted murder, and burglary. After being given full *Miranda* warnings, the defendant waived his rights and made inculpatory statements about the uncharged offenses. Subsequently, he claimed that his statements were inadmissible to prove those crimes because his waiver was invalid under *Edwards v. Arizona*. More specifically, he argued that his invocation of the Sixth Amendment right to assistance regarding the armed robbery also served to invoke his *Miranda* entitlement to assistance for custodial interrogation regarding the uncharged offenses. A six-Justice majority rejected the argument, holding that a request for the "offense-specific" Sixth Amendment right to assistance in proceedings pertaining to a charged offense does *not* constitute an invocation of *Miranda*'s Fifth Amendment-based entitlement to assistance for custodial interrogation concerning separate, uncharged crimes. Thus, to trigger the special protection of the *Edwards* rule, a suspect must make an unambiguous request for assistance with custodial interrogation.

(c) What if the suspect who has been given the *Miranda* warnings asks the police if he needs an attorney? Or asks some other question that has a bearing on his decision whether to assert his right to an attorney? For example, suppose a suspect says, "If I ask to have an attorney present, what attorney would I get? And how soon will he or she be able to talk to me?" Are the police required to answer such questions? May they ignore them in the same way that they are permitted to disregard ambiguous requests for counsel?

(2) INVOKING THE RIGHT TO REMAIN SILENT: In *Berghuis v. Thompkins*, 560 U.S. 370, 130 S. Ct. 2250, 176 L. Ed. 2d 1098 (2010), a defendant argued that he had invoked his right "to remain silent by not saying anything" for a considerable period of time while officers attempted to interrogate him. A five-Justice majority found this contention "unpersuasive," concluding that a suspect must unambiguously invoke the right to remain silent. In the majority's view, "there is no principled reason to adopt different standards for determining when an accused has invoked the *Miranda* right to remain silent and the *Miranda* right to counsel." Both rights "protect the privilege against compulsory self-incrimination by requiring an interrogation to cease when either right is invoked." Moreover, a requirement that the

right to remain silent be invoked "unambiguously" yields "an objective inquiry" that avoids problems of proof and provides guidance for officers. A rule that officers must stop interrogation after ambiguous acts or statements would require them "to make difficult decisions." Moreover, such a rule could lead to the "[s]uppression of a voluntary confession," which "would place a significant burden on society's interest in prosecuting criminal activity" while only adding "'marginally to *Miranda*'s goal of dispelling the compulsion.'" In *Thompkins*, the suspect "did not say that he wanted to remain silent or that he did not want to talk with the police[,] . . . simple, unambiguous statements" that "would have invoked his '"right to cut off questioning."'"

In a dissent authored by Justice Sotomayor, four Justices asserted that the majority's "clear-statement rule . . . invites police to question a suspect at length — notwithstanding his persistent refusal to answer questions — in the hope of eventually obtaining a single inculpatory response which will suffice to prove waiver of rights." They maintained that the "clear-statement rule is . . . a poor fit for the right to silence" because a warning of the right to remain silent is "unlikely to convey that [a suspect] must speak (and must do so in some particular fashion) to ensure the right will be protected." The majority's decision "turn[ed] *Miranda* upside down" by requiring "suspects [to] . . . unambiguously invoke their right to remain silent — which, counterintuitively, requires them to speak." According to the dissenters, when a suspect ambiguously invokes the right to remain silent, the appropriate question is whether officers "scrupulously honored" the suspect's right to cut off questioning.

(3) THE CONSEQUENCES OF A CLEAR INVOCATION OF THE *MIRANDA* RIGHT TO COUNSEL: When a suspect clearly invokes the right to have counsel present during custodial interrogation, when may officers interrogate him outside of counsel's presence? *Miranda* stated that "the interrogation must cease *until an attorney is present*." (Emphasis added.) In later decisions, however, the Court has recognized two situations in which a waiver of the right to counsel can be valid and interrogation can proceed in counsel's absence. On the other hand, the Court has not been receptive to every claim that officers should be able to obtain a valid waiver from a suspect who has unambiguously requested assistance.

(a) INITIATION OF COMMUNICATION BY A SUSPECT: In *Edwards*, the Court did indicate that officers may secure a valid waiver if a suspect who has invoked the right to counsel "initiates further communication, exchanges, or conversations with the police." *Davis* confirmed this option, asserting that officers may proceed if "the suspect himself reinitiates conversation." What is the meaning of "initiation of communication" in this context? Will any communication suffice?

Oregon v. Bradshaw, 462 U.S. 1039, 103 S. Ct. 2830, 77 L. Ed. 2d 405 (1983), is the only case in which the Justices have discussed the meaning of this important doctrinal criterion. The defendant in *Bradshaw* was arrested for furnishing liquor to a minor. He was also suspected of driving a truck that left a roadway and struck a tree and embankment, causing a minor's death. An officer recited the *Miranda* warnings to him and then suggested that he had been behind the wheel of the truck at the time of the accident. The defendant invoked his right to the presence of an attorney, and the officer immediately terminated the interrogation.

A few minutes later, the defendant asked the officer, "'Well, what is going to happen to me now?'" The officer responded by reminding him that he had requested an attorney and telling him, "'I don't want you to talk to me unless you so desire because anything you say . . . since you have requested an attorney, you know, it has to be at your own free will.'" General conversation followed in which the defendant agreed to take a lie detector test. The next day, after he received a new set of *Miranda* warnings, the defendant took the lie detector test. When the examiner informed the defendant "that he did not believe [he] was telling the truth," the defendant made incriminating admissions.

The Court split 4 to 4 over whether the defendant's initial question, "Well, what is going to happen to me now?" constituted the "initiation" of communication within the meaning of *Edwards*. Speaking for four Justices, Justice Rehnquist concluded that it was an initiation because "[a]lthough ambiguous, the . . . question in this case as to what was going to happen to him *evinced a willingness and a desire for a generalized discussion about the investigation. . . .*" (Emphasis added.) The defendant did initiate communication because even though his question was "ambiguous, . . . [i]t could reasonably have been interpreted by the officer as relating generally to the investigation." Justice Rehnquist observed that some inquiries by a suspect would not qualify as initiation of communication because they are "so routine that they cannot be fairly said to represent *a desire* on the part of [a suspect] *to open up a more generalized discussion relating directly or indirectly to the investigation.*" (Emphasis added.) "[I]nquiries or statements, by either [a suspect] or a police officer, [that relate to] routine incidents of the custodial relationship"—including, for example, a request for a drink of water or a request to make a telephone call—do not eliminate the additional protection against coerced waivers triggered by a clear request for counsel.

The Rehnquist plurality concluded that the defendant, after initiating further communications with the officer, had validly waived his rights under *Miranda*. Justice Powell concurred in the result, agreeing that a valid waiver was proven but declining to accept the *Edwards* rule that a valid waiver cannot be secured unless a suspect initiates communication. He adhered to the position that he had taken in *Edwards*—that the only relevant inquiry, even when there is an invocation of the right to counsel, is whether the suspect knowingly and intelligently waived that right.

Four dissenting Justices concluded that there was no initiation in *Bradshaw*. According to Justice Marshall, "[w]hen . . . *Edwards* spoke of 'initiat[ing] further communication' with the police and 'reopen[ing] the dialogue with the authorities,' it obviously had in mind communication or dialogue about the subject matter of the criminal investigation. The [*Edwards*] rule . . . was designed to ensure that any interrogation subsequent to an invocation of the right to counsel be at the instance of the accused, not the authorities. Thus, a question or statement which does not invite further interrogation before an attorney is present cannot qualify as 'initiation' under *Edwards*." [Emphasis omitted.] The dissenters "agree[d] with the plurality that, in order to constitute 'initiation' . . . , an . . . inquiry must demonstrate a desire to discuss the subject matter of the criminal investigation." They were "baffled, however, at the plurality's application of that standard to the facts of" *Bradshaw*.

(b) BREAKS IN CUSTODY: In *Maryland v. Shatzer*, 559 U.S. 98, 130 S. Ct. 1213, 175 L. Ed. 2d 1045 (2010), the question was "whether a break in custody ends the presumption of involuntariness established in *Edwards v. Arizona*." In 2003, while incarcerated for an unrelated offense, the accused was interviewed about allegations that he had sexually abused his three-year-old son. Upon being given *Miranda* warnings, he "declined to speak without an attorney," and the detective "ended the interview." In 2006, two and a half years later, after the police department had received additional allegations concerning "the same incident," another detective interviewed the defendant at the prison. After receiving *Miranda* warnings, the defendant waived his rights and made an incriminating admission in response to interrogation. Five days later, after another set of warnings and a written waiver, he submitted to a polygraph examination and made another incriminating statement in response to questioning before requesting an attorney. He was charged with a number of sex offenses. Before trial, the judge denied a motion to suppress the statements made on both occasions. After a bench trial, the judge "found Shatzer guilty of sexual child abuse of his son." The Court of Appeals reversed, holding that the incriminating statements were barred by the *Edwards* doctrine.

The Supreme Court held that *Edwards* did not require exclusion of the statements in these circumstances. According to the Court, the "rationale" of *Edwards* is that after a suspect requests counsel, a waiver prompted by the authorities "'is itself the product of the "inherently compelling pressures" and not the purely voluntary choice of the suspect.'" It rests on an "assumption . . . that the subsequent requests for interrogation" after a request for counsel "pose a significantly greater risk of coercion." The "increased risk" is the product of two factors — "the police's persistence in trying to get the suspect to talk" *and* "the continued pressure that begins when the individual is taken into custody as a suspect and sought to be interrogated — pressure likely to 'increase as custody is prolonged.'" Because "the *Edwards* rule is not a constitutional mandate, but judicially prescribed prophylaxis," the Court must "'justify its expansion'. . . . 'by reference to its prophylactic purpose'" and must apply it "only" to situations "where its benefits outweigh its costs."

The presumption announced in *Edwards* has two benefits: it conserves judicial resources, and it preserves "'the integrity of an accused's choice to communicate with police only through counsel'" by preventing the authorities from "'badgering'" a suspect who has asked for counsel into waiving his right. The latter benefit is "measured by the number of coerced confessions [the rule] suppresses that otherwise would have been admitted." The Court found it "easy to believe that a suspect may be coerced or badgered" into a waiver in cases where a suspect is "held in uninterrupted pretrial custody." However, when "a suspect has been released from his pretrial custody" after a request for counsel "and has returned to his normal life for some time before [a subsequent] attempted interrogation, there is little reason to think that his change of heart regarding interrogation without counsel has been coerced." When released, a suspect has not remained "isolated," has "likely been able to seek advice from an attorney, family members, and friends," and "knows . . . that he need only demand counsel" to end the interrogation "and that investigative custody does not last indefinitely." To think that a suspect in those circumstances would be worn down by an inquiry about whether he wishes to waive his right to counsel "is far fetched." A "change of heart is less likely" the result of "badgering" than of "further deliberation in familiar surroundings [that] has caused him to believe . . . that cooperating with the investigation is in his interest." Consequently, the "extension of *Edwards* . . . would not significantly increase the number of genuinely coerced confessions excluded." On the other hand, extension would increase the costs of the rule by excluding some voluntary confessions and deterring "officers from even trying to obtain" others.

In the Court's view, the "only logical endpoint of *Edwards* disability is termination of *Miranda* custody and any of its lingering effects." Without that endpoint, there would be an "eternal" bar to officer-initiated interrogation following requests for counsel, a bar with "disastrous" consequences. (The Court highlighted another possible endpoint — a "purely arbitrary time-limit" — but refused to address whether the passage of time alone could extinguish *Edwards* protection.) Ordinary *Miranda* protections, rather than the extra prophylaxis furnished by *Edwards*, will "adequately ensure" respect for a "suspect's desire to have an attorney present . . . when a suspect who initially requested counsel is reinterrogated after a break in custody that is of sufficient duration to dissipate its coercive effects." The Court deemed "it appropriate to specify" the minimal time needed, selecting "14 days" because that period "provides plenty of time for the suspect to get reacclimated to his normal life, to consult with friends and counsel, and to shake off any residual coercive effects of his prior custody." In addition, a "14-day limitation" is sufficient to discourage "police abuse" of "a break-in-custody rule."

Shatzer presented "an additional issue" — whether a suspect's "release[] back into the general prison population . . . constitutes a break in *Miranda* custody." After observing that it had "never decided whether incarceration constitutes custody for *Miranda* purposes," the Court concluded, for a number of reasons, that "lawful imprisonment imposed upon conviction of a crime does not create the coercive pressures identified in *Miranda*." When "released back into the general prison population," convicts who "live in prison" merely "return to . . . accustomed surroundings and daily routine," regaining the "control they had over their lives prior to the interrogation." They "are not isolated with their accusers," but, instead, "live among other inmates, guards, and workers, and often can receive visitors and communicate with" outsiders. In addition, the "detention . . . is relatively disconnected from their prior unwillingness to cooperate in an investigation." Put simply, the "'inherently compelling pressures' of custodial interrogation end[] when [a prisoner] return[s] to his normal life."

In sum, "[b]ecause Shatzer experienced a break in *Miranda* custody lasting more than two weeks between the first and second attempts at interrogation, *Edwards* [did] not mandate suppression of his . . . statements."

Justice Thomas concurred in part and in the judgment but rejected "the Court's arbitrary 14-day rule," concluding that even this extension of *Edwards* was not justifiable. He would have terminated the "presumption of involuntariness" as soon as "custody ends."

Justice Stevens concurred in the judgment but also disagreed "with the Court's newly announced rule." He did not believe that a 14-day break should always eliminate the presumption created by *Edwards*, and he concluded that the "many problems with the Court's new rule [were] exacerbated" in situations involving incarcerated suspects.

(c) INITIATION OF COMMUNICATION BY DIFFERENT OFFICERS ABOUT DIFFERENT OFFENSES: In *Arizona v. Roberson*, 486 U.S. 675, 108 S. Ct. 2093, 100 L. Ed. 2d 704 (1988), the question was whether the protection afforded by the *Edwards* rule applies when different officers seek to interrogate a suspect about different offenses. After Roberson was arrested at the scene of a burglary, the arresting officer recited *Miranda* warnings. Roberson "replied that he 'wanted a lawyer before answering any questions.' This fact was duly recorded in the officer's written report of the incident." (Roberson was subsequently convicted of this burglary.) Three days after the arrest, while Roberson "was still in custody . . . , a different officer" sought to interrogate "him about a different burglary that had occurred" one day before the burglary for which he had been arrested. "That officer was not aware of the fact that [Roberson] had requested the assistance of counsel. . . ." The officer issued *Miranda* warnings and interrogated Roberson, obtaining a statement that incriminated him in the earlier burglary. A trial judge ruled that the statement was not admissible at the trial for that offense, relying on a state court interpretation of *Edwards*. The Arizona Court of Appeals affirmed, and the Arizona Supreme Court denied review.

Justice Stevens, speaking for six Justices, concluded that a suspect who invokes the right to counsel during custodial interrogation after being given *Miranda* warnings as to one offense may not be questioned by a different officer about a separate offense unless the suspect initiates further communications or exchanges with the authorities. According to the *Roberson* majority, "to a suspect who has indicated his inability to cope with the pressures of custodial interrogation by requesting counsel, any further [police-initiated] interrogation without counsel having been provided will surely exacerbate whatever compulsion to speak the suspect may be feeling." The Justices did not believe that a "fresh set[] of *Miranda* warnings" by an officer pursuing a different investigation would " 'reassure' a suspect who has been denied the counsel he has clearly requested that his rights have remained untrammeled."

In addition, Justice Stevens asserted that "no significance" could be attached "to the fact that the officer who conducted the second interrogation did not know that [the suspect] had made a request for counsel. . . . *Edwards* focuses on the state of mind of the suspect and not of the police, custodial interrogation must be conducted pursuant to established procedures, and those procedures in turn must enable an officer who proposes to initiate an interrogation to determine whether the suspect has previously requested counsel. . . . Whether a contemplated reinterrogation concerns the same or a different offense, or whether the same or different law enforcement authorities are involved in the second investigation, the same need to determine whether the suspect has requested counsel exists."

Justice Kennedy and Chief Justice Rehnquist dissented. In their view, "[t]he majority's rule [was] not necessary to protect the rights of suspects, and it [would] in many instances deprive our nationwide law enforcement network of a legitimate investigative technique now routinely used to resolve major crimes." The "extension of" the protection afforded by *Edwards* "to separate and independent investigations" would bar "law enforcement officials, even those from some other city or . . . jurisdiction, from questioning a suspect about an unrelated matter if he is in custody and has requested counsel to assist in answering questions put to him about the crime for which he was arrested." The dissenters would have allowed officers conducting "a separate investigation" to warn a suspect "and ask him whether he wishes to invoke" his rights. This approach, in their view, "strikes an appropriate balance" of the suspect's and law enforcement's interests.

(d) CONSULTATION WITH COUNSEL BY A SUSPECT: In *Minnick v. Mississippi*, 498 U.S. 146, 111 S. Ct. 486, 112 L. Ed. 2d 489 (1990), Minnick and another man escaped from jail in Mississippi. They broke into a mobile home to steal weapons and ultimately killed two men. Four months later, Minnick was arrested in California. In the course of an interview with FBI agents, he asked for counsel. Thereafter, an appointed attorney met with him and he "spoke with the lawyer on two or three occasions." Three days after the interview with the FBI, a Mississippi law enforcement officer arrived to question Minnick. Although Minnick refused "to sign a rights waiver form," he did tell the officer about events that occurred at the mobile home, making incriminating statements in the course of his account. The trial judge refused to suppress his statements, and, after trial, he "was convicted on two counts of capital murder and sentenced to death."

The question was whether *Miranda* barred the use of his statements. More specifically, the issue was whether a waiver of the right to counsel made by a suspect who has clearly invoked his right to assistance during custodial interrogation can be valid if officers initiate communication with the suspect *after he has consulted with a lawyer*. By a 6-2 vote, the Court held that mere consultation with a lawyer does not terminate the protection *Edwards* affords against officer-initiated interrogation following a request for counsel. Consequently, the statements should not have been admitted at Minnick's trial.

The majority observed that "*Edwards* is 'designed to prevent police from badgering a defendant into waiving his previously asserted *Miranda* rights.' The rule ensures that any statement made in subsequent interrogation is not the result of coercive pressures. *Edwards* conserves judicial resources which would otherwise be expended in making difficult determinations of voluntariness, and implements the protections of *Miranda* in practical and straightforward terms."

The *Minnick* majority stressed that both *Miranda* and *Edwards* granted a "'right to have counsel *present* during custodial interrogation.'" (Emphasis in original.) Moreover, *Edwards* held that once a suspect asks for assistance, "the authorities may not initiate questioning . . . in counsel's absence." It erected a "bar [to] police-initiated interrogation unless the accused has counsel with him at the time of questioning." Following a request for counsel, "officials may not reinitiate interrogation without counsel present, whether or not the accused has consulted with his attorney."

This rule is "appropriate and necessary" because a "single consultation with an attorney does not remove the suspect from persistent attempts by officials to persuade him to waive his rights, or from the coercive pressures that accompany custody and that may increase as custody is prolonged." For that reason, the Justices "decline[d] to remove protection from police-initiated questioning based on isolated consultations with counsel who is absent when the interrogation resumes."

In addition, the "exception proposed . . . would undermine" the clarity *Edwards* provides. If consultation lowered the bar to police-initiated interrogation, a second request for counsel would raise the bar again. The consequence would be that "*Edwards*'[s] protection could pass in and out of existence multiple times," a "regime" that could "spread confusion" and "lead to a . . . loss of respect for the underlying constitutional principle." Furthermore, the "sort of consultation" that would suffice to permit police efforts to initiate communication and secure a waiver would be "far from certain."

Justice Scalia, along with Chief Justice Rehnquist, dissented. They asserted that *Edwards*'s "irrebutable presumption" of invalidity for waivers given after the authorities initiate communication should not "continue after a suspect has actually consulted with his attorney." Moreover, "any discussion between [the suspect] and an attorney" should be sufficient "to eliminate the suspect's feeling of isolation and to assure him the presence of legal assistance." Under those circumstances, the "prophylaxis" provided by *Edwards* should be suspended.

Invocation Problems

8E–1: Around midnight, police officers arrested Arthur for first-degree robbery and placed him in a holding cell near Detective Trick's desk. At 5:30 a.m., Detective Towel executed a warrant to search defendant's house. At 8:30 a.m., while the search was still in progress, Trick heard Arthur knocking on his cell door. When Trick responded, Arthur asked if he could use the restroom and when he could call his attorney. Trick called Detective Towel to advise him that Arthur had asked when he would be able to call his attorney. Trick then entered, "Request for restroom & wants to call attorney. Called Towel." in the prisoner log.

At 9:15 a.m., Arthur made a second request to speak with counsel. The precise language used by Arthur is unknown, but Detective Trick entered in the log, "Again demanding call. Called Towel." Trick called Towel a second time to reiterate Arthur's request. He also told Towel that Arthur was "upset" and "being troublesome" because he wanted to know why he was being held. Towel instructed Trick to inform Arthur that he was under arrest for first-degree robbery.

Towel completed the search of Arthur's house at 10:00 a.m., then went to the Detective Division to interview Arthur. At 10:45 a.m., Towel asked Arthur to read a form that provided advice about the right to counsel and the right to remain silent. Towel also read the form aloud. When Towel asked Arthur if he understood his rights, Arthur acknowledged that he did and signed the form. Arthur asked Towel about the robbery that he had been arrested for, and Towel shared some details of the robbery with Arthur. Arthur responded by admitting his involvement. Towel then returned Arthur to his holding cell. Shortly thereafter, Trick asked Towel whether he had addressed Arthur's requests regarding when he could speak with an attorney. Towel said he had forgotten about the requests. He then went to ask Arthur whether he would like to give a tape-recorded statement of his confession, "to put it in his own words." Arthur agreed to do so.

Towel resumed the interview shortly after 1:00 p.m., initially asking Arthur what he meant when he asked Trick when he could speak to his attorney. Arthur replied, "I just wanted to know what was going on." When Towel asked whether Arthur intended not to talk to the police, Arthur said, "No, not at any time did I intend not to talk to you." Towel then asked Arthur whether he had "any issue with talking to us without an attorney now," and Arthur responded, "No." Arthur then gave a tape-recorded confession of his involvement in the robbery. After his second confession, Towel asked Arthur whether his answer to the question of what he meant when he asked when he could speak to his attorney would have been different if Towel had asked at the beginning of the interview. Arthur replied that his answer would have been the same. Towel concluded the interview sometime after 2:00 p.m.

Arthur was charged with numerous counts of robbery. He moved to suppress his statements to Officer Towel.

Should the trial court grant Arthur's motion?

8E–2: Robert Van met David at a gay bar in Ohio. The two men went to David's apartment, where Van brutally stabbed David to death. He took several items from David's apartment and fled, making his way to Florida. Two months later, Van was arrested by local police, who read him his *Miranda* rights. Van initially agreed to talk, but then stated, "Maybe I should have an attorney present." The officers did not question him further. Van then had a conversation with his mother, who told him to cooperate with the police and to tell the truth. Based on this conversation, Van changed his mind and decided to talk.

Detective Williams, an Ohio police officer, was assigned the task of going to Florida to facilitate Van's extradition and transportation back to Ohio. Williams decided to speak to Van's mother before traveling to Florida. She told the detective that she had spoken with her son and indicated that he was now willing to talk to the police. Upon arriving in Florida, Williams met with Van, confirming first that Van wished to waive any objection he might have to extradition. The detective then told Van, "We have a lot to talk about, but we cannot talk unless you want to make a statement." Williams also informed Van that he had recently had a conversation with Van's mother. Van confirmed that he had spoken to his mother, that she had told him to "just tell the truth," and that he now wanted to make a statement. Williams then recited the *Miranda* warnings to Van, who replied that he would waive his rights and answer the detective's questions. Van ultimately provided a full and graphic confession.

A grand jury indicted Van for aggravated murder and aggravated robbery. Prior to trial, the defense moved to suppress Van's confession. The trial court denied the motion, and the confession was introduced at trial. Van was convicted of aggravated murder and was sentenced to death. He has appealed the denial of his motion to suppress.

What arguments should Van make on appeal? How should the government respond? How should the court of appeals rule?

8E–3: Clayton Bane was arrested for the murder of his wife. The interrogating officer, Detective Whitlow, advised Bane of his *Miranda* warnings. Bane stated he understood his rights and was willing to tell them "what he did." When Whitlow handed him the waiver of rights form and asked him to sign it, Bane shook his head. Whitlow then asked if he was correct in understanding that Bane did not want to sign a rights waiver form at that time. The following exchange then took place:

Bane: Not 'til you know? . . . When I talk to my lawyer, I'll—

Whitlow: O.K. But you don't want a lawyer at this time is what I'm saying. O.K.?

Bane: I will get a lawyer.

Whitlow: But you don't want one now? Is that correct?

Bane: I'd like to have one but you know . . . it would be hard to get hold of one right now.

Whitlow: Well what I am asking you, Clayton, is do you want to give me a statement at this time without having a lawyer present?

Bane: Well I can tell you what I did.

Whitlow: O.K. That's what I am asking.

In response to Whitlow's questions, Bane then made a statement admitting the killing of his wife.

Will Bane's statement be admissible?

8E–4: Martin was arrested for the robbery of a pizza delivery man and taken to the police station where he was advised of his *Miranda* warnings by Detective

Matthews. Martin told the Detective that he did not want to make a statement and would not sign the waiver of rights form.

At about the same time, the victim, who was also at the police station, identified Martin as the robber from a photo line-up. Another officer came into the room with Martin and Detective Matthews and stated that the identification had been made. Detective Matthews then said to Martin, "I've got no further questions. There's nothing else I need from you." He told Martin the other officers would take him downstairs to his cell unless "you have a statement or something you want to tell me." Martin then stated that he did wish to make a statement. Detective Matthews again advised Martin of his *Miranda* rights and received both oral and written waivers. Martin then made a statement admitting the robbery.

Will Martin's statement be admissible?

8E–5: Alex and Lon, friends and inmates at the Federal Correctional Institute (FCI), planned an attack on Curt, another inmate. Lon initiated the assault, persuading Alex to participate by describing persistent abuse he had suffered from Curt. One evening, Lon and Alex waited until Curt was returning alone from a shower. Lon repeatedly struck Curt with a belt to which he attached two padlocks. Alex restrained Curt and ensured that no other inmates could assist him. Alex never beat Curt with the belt, but he punched him, tackled him to the ground and kicked him in the head with steel-toed work boots.

The FBI attempted to question Alex first, but after he heard the *Miranda* warnings he invoked his right to remain silent and was returned to his cell. Alex did not ask for a lawyer. The FBI next questioned Lon, who waived his *Miranda* rights and confessed. After implicating Alex, Lon expressed concern that Alex's refusal to cooperate might adversely affect his chances of receiving a reduced sentence. He stressed that Alex had refused only because "prison code" forbade him from speaking with the authorities until *after* Lon's confession. Lon requested an opportunity to speak with Alex to convince him to give a statement. The FBI acquiesced and placed the two men in adjoining cells that night. Agents told Lon that they would not resume any questioning of Alex unless Alex volunteered.

In their cells that night, Alex and Lon discussed their plight. The conversation focused on Lon's concern with being labeled a "snitch," based on his confession to authorities that detailed Alex's role in the attack. Worried that inmates might harass Lon as a consequence of this confession, Alex agreed to contact the FBI and to give them a statement. FBI agents returned the following morning and again read the *Miranda* warnings to Alex. He waived his rights then made a statement admitting that he had been a lookout and that he had restrained, tackled, and kicked Curt.

What arguments should Alex make in support of exclusion of his statements from trial? What arguments should the government make in response? How should a judge rule?

8E–6: In the early morning hours of August 15, Anthony stopped his semitrailer at a state Motor Transportation Department inspection station. Officers inspecting the cargo inside found nearly 300 kilograms of marijuana. After handcuffing Anthony to a bench inside the station, Sergeant Roberts read the *Miranda* rights. When Border Operations Agents Chad and Atkins arrived two hours later, Roberts informed them that he had read Anthony the required warnings. Atkins and Chad awoke a sleeping Anthony and led him into an office for an interview. The following exchange took place:

> AGENT CHAD: Alright. Just wanted to let you know that ... Did you invoke your rights, or did you tell them that you didn't want to talk to anybody or that you wanted an attorney present or anything like that?
>
> ANTHONY: I don't want any ... I don't want nothing to say to anyone.
>
> CHAD: You don't have anything to say to anybody?
>
> ANTHONY: No.
>
> CHAD: Okay. Did, did they read you your *Miranda* warnings?
>
> ANTHONY: What rights do I have?
>
> CHAD: Okay. We'll get through that right now.

Chad began to re-read the *Miranda* warnings, but was interrupted. Atkins, Chad, and Anthony then discussed possible consequences of cooperating and refusing to cooperate. When Anthony attempted to speak about the details of his case, the agents repeatedly told him that they could not discuss these matters unless Anthony waived his rights. Around 6:00 a.m., more than 30 minutes after Chad's failed effort to re-read the *Miranda* warnings, Anthony signed a waiver form and made incriminating statements. During this 30-minute period, Anthony asked at least twice to be put in jail.

A grand jury indicted Anthony on one count of possession with intent to distribute 100 kilograms or more of marijuana and one count of conspiracy to possess with intent to distribute 100 kilograms or more of marijuana. Anthony filed a motion to suppress all of his statements, arguing that the agents violated his *Miranda* rights.

What arguments should Anthony make in support of his motion? How should the prosecution respond? Should the court suppress the statements?

8E–7: Clyde was arrested for murder. At the police station, a detective read him his *Miranda* rights from a card. After finishing the *Miranda* litany, the detective said to Clyde, "Understanding these rights, do you wish to talk to us now?" Clyde responded with a simple "No." The detective said, "You don't want to talk?" This time, Clyde responded, "Yes, I will talk." In response to questions, Clyde then confessed.

Did the detective's questioning of Clyde violate *Miranda*?

8E–8: Two weeks after Michael Malt's parents disappeared, Malt agreed to take a polygraph test at the police station. Sergeant Paul recited *Miranda* warnings, then administered the test. Malt denied knowing his parents' whereabouts. After "scoring" the polygraph test, Sergeant Paul told Malt, "no doubt you know exactly where your parents are." He told Malt that his family was at the station and needed to know "exactly where the bodies are." The following exchange then ensued:

MALT: At this point I have to talk to my uncle. I need to talk to my uncle.

PAUL: What exactly do you want to talk to your uncle about?

MALT: I don't know where to go, what to do from here.

PAUL: Okay, so before you go sit out there and talk to your uncle, let's get this clarified.

MALT: I'd like to talk to my uncle first.

PAUL: As you're sitting here, you're thinking to yourself, I want to tell them. No doubt about it. You realize it's the right thing to do. Let's just clear the air now.

MALT: I'd like to talk to my uncle first.

PAUL: I understand what you're saying.

MALT: I don't think you do. I want his opinion.

PAUL: His opinion as far as what?

MALT: As far as what I do. You're saying I failed the polygraph.

PAUL: I understand what you're saying, but the point is this is the opportunity for you to tell me the truth. Do you see what I'm saying?

MALT: And I might just do that. But I'd like to talk to my uncle first. I gotta talk to him. I can't say anything to anybody before I talk to him, you know what I mean? My uncle is even better than a freaking attorney.

Paul then left the room. He confirmed with a prosecutor that the camera could be left on as long as Malt's uncle knew that the camera was on. Paul then told Malt's uncle that Malt had failed the polygraph test, that he knew where his parents were, and that the camera would be on while he talked to his nephew. Malt's uncle agreed to help.

Before allowing Malt's uncle to enter the room, Sergeant Paul told Malt, "Your uncle knows the polygraph results and that you are responsible for your parents' disappearance." He falsely promised that "as soon as I open this door, the camera and recording will be going off." Detectives Ryun and Mullen then watched as Malt admitted to his uncle that he knew where his parents' bodies were buried. After Malt was permitted a cigarette break outside the interview room, Ryun and Mullen returned to the interview room with him. Mullen recited *Miranda* warnings and informed Malt that they knew what he had told his uncle. Malt then admitted that he had strangled his parents and buried them in the woods. The police discovered their bodies buried in a shallow grave.

Does *Miranda* bar the admission of Malt's statements to his uncle and to the detectives at his murder trial?

8E–9: On November 30, the police found Bryan lying in an alley. He had suffered a fatal gunshot wound. The same day, officers arrested Will and recited *Miranda* warnings. Will waived his rights and agreed to talk. After speaking with the officers, Will stated, "I need a lawyer, man. I would talk to y'all if I had a lawyer. I promise." The officers then explained what would happen next in the investigation — that they would take Will home, that they would investigate the crime, and that he would be assigned a lawyer. One officer then stated, "You already asked for a lawyer, right?" Will replied that he had not asked for a lawyer but that he would "take" one, adding that he "did not do anything wrong." One of the officers stated that if Will wanted to talk, Will could reaffirm his rights; otherwise, the officers could not talk to him anymore. Will responded that he was talking. Will asked who he was suspected of murdering. The officers showed Will a photograph of Bryan. The officers asked Will if he was ready to talk. Will responded that he did not have anything to do with the murder, and one of the officers asked Will to tell what he knew. Will claimed that the officers were trying to incriminate him, stating either "If I had a lawyer, I'd tell you everything," or "If I had a lawyer, if I just had a lawyer, I'd tell you everything," or "May I have a lawyer, if I had a lawyer, I'd tell you everything." The officers left the room.

Shortly thereafter, a police sergeant entered the interview room and asked if Will was willing to answer a few questions or if he was absolutely invoking his right to counsel. Will expressed his frustration with the officers who had been questioning him previously and said that they were trying to incriminate him. The sergeant told Will that the detectives wanted to hear Will's story and that he would be released if the story checked out, that he had not been charged with anything, and that the evidence indicated that Will was involved in Bryan's murder. Will made incriminating statements.

Early on December 14, Detective Eric, one of the officers who had originally questioned Will on November 30, resumed the interrogation. After he recited the *Miranda* warnings, Will agreed to talk. In response to interrogation, Will made incriminating statements. According to Eric, he resumed the interrogation because members of Will's family had informed him that Will wanted to talk to him. Eric could not remember the names of those family members. Will himself had not told Eric that he wanted to talk to him. At Will's trial for murdering Brian, over a defense objection, the police sergeant was allowed to testify to the incriminating statements Will made on November 30, and Detective Eric was allowed to testify to the incriminating statements he made on December 14. Will was convicted of capital murder and has appealed, claiming that his statements were inadmissible under *Miranda*.

How should the court rule?

8E–10: At 5:30 a.m., federal agents arrested Mills for participation in a cocaine conspiracy. While transporting Mills to the Federal Building in Chicago, one of the arresting officers read Mills the *Miranda* warnings from a printed form. The officer asked Mills if he understood his rights and Mills replied that he did. The officer then showed him a waiver of those rights and asked Mills if he would be willing to sign the waiver. Mills replied, "Get the f___ out of my face. I don't have nothing to say. I refuse to sign."

During the drive to the Federal Building, Agent Grapenthien told Mills he was facing a potential sentence of 20 years to life imprisonment. Grapenthien then asked Mills if he knew the nickname his co-conspirators had for him. When Mills said he didn't, Grapenthien told him that his co-conspirators had been calling him "Big Dumbo" in his absence.

At approximately 8:00 a.m., Mills was interviewed at the Federal Building. Grapenthien again read him his *Miranda* rights. Mills again stated he understood his rights. This time, Grapenthien did not present Mills with a waiver form or ask him to sign it but proceeded to ask Mills questions which Mills answered. During the interview, Grapenthien showed Mills the transcript of a telephone conversation in which his alleged co-conspirators referred to him as "Big Dumbo." After seeing the transcript, Mills made statements that incriminated both himself and his alleged co-conspirators.

Did Grapenthien's interactions with Mills violate *Miranda*?

8E–11: Doris, a 65-year-old woman, was found dead in her townhome, her throat cut from ear to ear. DNA taken from her fingernails matched that of 19-year-old Randy Viney. Officer Otter asked Viney if he would come to the police station to discuss Doris's murder. Viney consented. Without handcuffs, Viney rode to the police station in the front seat of Otter's car. Otter took Viney to an interview room where detectives were waiting. The detectives told Viney that he was not in custody or under arrest and that he could leave at any time. They then recited *Miranda* warnings. Following some small talk, they questioned Viney about Doris's murder. Viney said he knew "Ms. Doris" and had heard about her death but did not know who killed her. He stated that he had followed the murder investigation because "Ms. Doris was like my Godmother." He said he was at home and did not go to Doris's townhome on the night she was killed. He said, "I really cared about Ms. Doris." After Viney consented to a DNA swab of his cheek, the following exchange then occurred:

> Detective: Randy, the results of the investigation clearly show you killed Ms. Doris.
>
> Viney: No. No. Hell no. I don't see how you all see that.

The detectives then told him of the evidence they had found, including the DNA match, and the exchange continued:

> Viney: How much better can I explain, I did not do this.
>
> Detective: Listen, listen to me. That's not the question. You did do it. Randy—

Viney: I'm done. I'm done.

Detective: What does that mean, I'm done?

Viney: I'm done. I'm ready to go home and I did not do this and if I did do it, I want you all to show me that I did do it.

Detective: Why would your DNA be on her?

Viney: My DNA wasn't on her.

Detective: Oh, it was. You cared about this lady, Randy.

Viney: I'm done. I'm ready to go home. Can I leave?

Detective: No. You murdered this lady. You're not leaving.

Viney: You all said I could leave whenever I wanted to.

Detective: That was before.

Several additional times Viney said that he wanted to leave, standing and attempting to leave at one point. Repeatedly, the detectives told him that he could not leave and was being legally detained. Subsequently, Viney confessed to murdering Doris, claiming that he "did not remember the night" and that "when I was there, it wasn't me there." He said that he was visiting with her and that when she asked him about his childhood, "I lost my mind. I can't stand when somebody talks about my childhood." He admitted to cutting her throat with a fish fileting knife from his tackle box that he kept with him. Prior to trial for first-degree murder, Viney moved to suppress his statements under *Miranda*.

What arguments should Viney make in support of his motion? How should the prosecution respond? How should the trial judge rule?

8E–12: After Stewart was arrested for murder, Detective Young advised him of his *Miranda* rights and Stewart invoked his right to remain silent. As Detective Young started to take Stewart to the cellblock in the building's basement, they met Detective Treadwell, another member of the homicide unit who had worked on the case. Treadwell knew Stewart personally because they belonged to the same church. Treadwell went with Stewart and Young to the cellblock. Upon learning that Stewart had elected not to make a statement, Treadwell met with Stewart privately in the cellblock. Treadwell later described their conversation as follows: "I gave him words of encouragement. I was telling him that we all make mistakes and not to feel bad about this situation. I had told him that the situation that he was in was not a good situation, but that it was a situation that I was not judging him by and that I felt no one else, meaning other church members, would judge him by. I told him to be strong, keep his head up, and to remember what we believe in." At the conclusion of the conversation, Treadwell gave Stewart a picture of their Bishop to give him "inspiration and encouragement." Treadwell then asked Stewart if he wanted to talk to him again. Stewart said that he did.

Several hours later, Treadwell, accompanied by Detective Young, returned to Stewart's cell. After they exchanged greetings, Treadwell asked Stewart, "What happened?" Stewart began confessing to the crime. In response to further questions, Stewart gave a full confession.

Will Stewart's confession be admissible?

8E–13: At 10:40 p.m., Midkiff was arrested for arson and double homicide. Shortly after his arrest, a detective read him his *Miranda* rights and Midkiff indicated that he understood his rights. Midkiff then agreed to take a polygraph test. Before taking the test, he was again given his *Miranda* rights.

After completing the polygraph test, Midkiff met with Special Agent Svard. During the early part of their interview, the following exchanges took place:

> Svard: This is the only job I've had in 23 years where I can actually help people. You can't help them in uniform. You can't help them out there. Here, I can help them, help them. So I want you to tell me what happened.
>
> Midkiff: I'll be honest with you. I'm scared to say anything without talking to a lawyer.
>
> Svard: Well, that entirely up to you, but, but . . .
>
> Midkiff: Because I got hoodooed big time back in, when I was in, now don't get me wrong, I ain't . . .
>
> Svard: I'm not here to hoodoo you. I'm here to help you. Let's talk about it. Be up front with me. I'll be up front with you. I'll get you every bit of help I can. Was you over there? Talk to me.
>
> Midkiff: I don't got to answer that, Dick, you know.
>
> Svard: No. But you've got to tell me if you want me to help you. I've got to listen to you. I'm here to help you and the only way that I can get you help is for you to tell me.

Svard and other officers continued interrogating Midkiff throughout the night, during which time Midkiff made several incriminating admissions. At about 6:00 a.m. the next morning, Midkiff confessed to his involvement in the arson and homicides. At his trial, the prosecution seeks to introduce Midkiff's confession into evidence.

What objections can Midkiff make to the admission of his confession? Should the confession be admitted?

8E–14: Following a shooting at the "La Tomba" bar, the police learned that individuals involved in the shooting were hiding in a nearby neighborhood. Upon arriving in the neighborhood, Officer Rodriguez saw Enrique and Jose standing outside a residence. When Enrique removed a firearm from beneath his shirt, Officer Rodriguez identified himself as a police officer and ordered the men not to move. Enrique and Jose ran upstairs to a second floor residence. Upon pursuing them, Rodriguez saw Enrique throw a firearm through a gap between the roof and a structural wall. He saw Jose attempt to conceal two loaded firearms and two ammunition magazines in a clothes hamper.

Assisted by Officer Roberto, Rodriguez handcuffed the two men and moved them to a sofa in the rear of the room. Rodriguez then asked them if they had licenses to carry firearms. When both replied that they did not, he arrested them and recited *Miranda* warnings in Spanish. Enrique and Jose said they understood the warnings and, in Spanish, admitted that the weapons belonged to them. They asserted that neither they nor the weapons had anything to do with the shooting at the bar. Officer Rodríguez retrieved two firearms — one with an obliterated serial number — and two ammunition clips from the clothes hamper. He also retrieved the firearm Enrique had thrown between the roof and wall.

Two hours later, Rodriguez took Enrique and Jose to headquarters. At 4:50 p.m., upon being given written *Miranda* warnings in Spanish, Enrique indicated in writing that he did not wish to speak. Officer Rodríguez did not ask Enrique any questions. Soon thereafter, Federal ATF Agent Julio arrived at headquarters. Rodríguez informed Julio about the events that had occurred. The two men discussed whether state or federal charges should be filed.

Around 5:10 p.m., Agent Julio spoke with Enrique. He introduced himself as an ATF special agent working for the federal government and gave Enrique a copy of an ATF document that contained Spanish *Miranda* warnings and included a waiver form. Enrique read the document and made a notation: "No entiendo eso. Mi abogado habla." In English, this means: "I don't understand that. My lawyer speaks." Agent Julio then asked Enrique what part of the waiver he didn't understand. Enrique responded that he would speak about the events of that day, but not about La Tomba. Upon request, Enrique then signed the waiver form. During a 15-20 minute interview, he admitted to Julio that the firearm found outside the residence did belong to him, that he had paid $3,100 for the gun, and that it was loaded with 10 rounds of ammunition. When Julio asked, Enrique admitted that he knew that one of Jose's guns had an obliterated serial number. The government wishes to use all of Enrique's statements at his trial for a number of firearms-related offenses.

Does *Miranda* bar the use of any or all of Enrique's statements to prove his guilt?

8E–15: On February 22, Brian Harman was taken into custody on burglary charges and transported to the county jail. Detective Douglas sought to interview him, intending to inquire about Brian's father, Ellis Harman, who was missing at the time. When Douglas advised Brian of his *Miranda* rights, however, Brian requested an attorney. Consequently, Douglas ended the interview.

The following afternoon, Detective Thomas executed two search warrants at a residence located on property owned by Ellis Harman. He discovered the body of Ellis Harman inside the residence. (Brian Harman did not live in the residence, but lived in a "pole barn" located on the same property.) Early the following day, February 24, at approximately 1:00 in the morning, Detective Thomas had Brian brought to the jail's intake area and informed him that "by law I must read these search warrants to you." (In fact, there was no legal or other requirement that executed warrants be read to anyone.) After Thomas read the content of the search warrants, he asked if Brian had "any questions." Brian responded by asking if the house had been searched and if anything had been found. Thomas then asked Brian whether he wanted to speak with the detective, and Brian indicated that he did. Thomas took Brian to an interview room where he recited *Miranda* warnings. Brian indicated that he understood his rights and had no questions. In response to questions, he confessed to killing his father.

Prior to his murder trial, Brian sought to suppress his confession on the grounds that the statements were obtained as a result of an interrogation that occurred after he had invoked his right to an attorney. The trial judge denied the motion to suppress, finding that the reading of the search warrants "more than a day after the initial interview was clearly not of a coercive nature, which might cause [Brian] to feel pressure to answer questions. Rather, it was [Brian's] conduct and questions that led to his giving the incriminating statement. He may have simply wanted to come clean and be truthful with the officers. He may have hoped to obtain favor from the authorities by providing helpful information. This is only speculation. What is clear is that he voluntarily chose to initiate this conversation and, regardless of his motivation, chose to give the incriminating statement." Brian has appealed the suppression ruling.

How should the court of appeals rule?

8E–16: A real estate agent called the police and reported that as she was giving a man a tour of a home that was for sale, the man grabbed her, dragged her into the laundry room, and demanded her credit cards. According to the agent, he took her to the bedroom and ordered her to write out six separate checks in the amount of $1000 each, payable to Brad Brandon. He then sexually assaulted her. Later that day, she identified Brandon from a photographic lineup as the man who attacked her.

Two days later, Brandon was found in a hotel and was arrested. Detective Allen came to the jail, identified himself as an investigator with the Sheriff's Office and told Brandon that he wanted to ask him some questions "regarding a sexual assault." Allen then advised Brandon of his *Miranda* rights. When Brandon said he understood his rights and was willing to talk, Allen asked Brandon to tell him what had happened. Brandon said that he met the agent to tour the house and that they ended up having sex in the empty house. He said that the agent freely wrote him three checks for $1,000 each because he needed the money.

The following exchange then occurred:

Allen: The lady told us you grabbed her.

Brandon: I never grabbed her.

Allen: Let's backtrack a little bit. Tell me from beginning to end what happened.

Brandon: You know, if she's, if she's got some other different story, I'm going to have to talk to an attorney about this, because this is, you know, this obviously is a serious thing.

Allen: This is a serious thing.

Brandon: You know, I mean, I don't know what class felony it is, but you know, obviously this is serious if she's saying something different.

Allen: So are you telling me that this was consensual sex?

Brandon: Yes, it was.

Allen: And are you telling me that you want to talk to a lawyer now?

Brandon: Well, yeah. I mean, you're telling me she said something different.

Allen: Okay. Well, what I need to know is whether you want to continue talking to me in here or not. If you want to speak to a lawyer then I will stop my questions, okay? If you want to continue to talk to me, it needs to be voluntary and you need to tell me the truth.

Brandon: Well, I want to know what I'm facing here.

Allen: Well, I'm investigating a sexual assault, and I think you did it.

Brandon: Okay, but I mean what are we looking at? Obviously it's a felony.

Allen: So, do you want to continue talking to me or not or do you . . . ?

Brandon: I'll talk to you.

During the ensuing 45-minute interrogation, Brandon made incriminating statements. Before trial, relying on the *Miranda* doctrine, he filed a motion to suppress all of his inculpatory statements.

Should the judge grant Brandon's motion?

8E–17: Wolf was arrested for murder. Lieutenant Brown warned him of his *Miranda* rights. Wolf signed a card stating he voluntarily and intelligently waived his rights. After Brown presented the evidence and asked a few questions, the following exchange occurred:

Brown: Why did you kill your grandmother?

Wolf: I didn't kill my grandmother.

Brown: Yes, you did.

Wolf: I did not.

Brown: Yes, you did.

Wolf: Did not and that's my final statement.

Brown: Why did you try to burn up the guns?

Wolf: I didn't try to burn. . . .

In response to further questions, Wolf confessed to killing his grandmother.

What is Wolf's best argument for excluding his confession? Should it prevail?

8E–18: Peracchi was arrested for various charges, including DUI and Reckless Driving. An officer read him his *Miranda* rights and asked him if he understood them. Peracchi said he did. The conversation then proceeded as follows:

Officer: Having those rights in mind, do you want to talk to us now about the charges?

Peracchi: At this point, I don't think so. At this point, I don't think I can talk.

Officer: Why is that?

Peracchi: I just feel like my mind is not clear enough to discuss this. My mind is not clear enough right now. I need to be able to think. Right now isn't a good time.

Officer: Okay. And you're saying the reason is because —

Peracchi: Uh — somethin' — uh, I guess I don't want to discuss it right now. I guess I want —

Officer: You want what?

Peracchi: I don't want to discuss it right now.

Officer: Is it because you're too tired?

Peracchi: Not really. To be honest with you, not really. I mean, I'll give — I — I'll give you a little rundown maybe, but it's not going to be — go too deep about — that's what you want. It's not going — I didn't stop and that was it. Do you know what I mean?

Officer: Why didn't —

Peracchi: I lost control.

The officer proceeded to ask further questions and Peracchi made additional incriminating admissions.

Were Peracchi's admissions obtained in violation of *Miranda*?

8E–19: Hannon was arrested for arson and murder. A detective informed him of his *Miranda* rights and he signed a card waiving his rights. The interrogating officers then confronted Hannon with information they had obtained from the investigation. After the officers told him that the victim — Debbie Tolhurst — was dead, the following exchange took place:

Hannon: What are you saying here?

Detective: What are we saying? We're saying that you took Deb's life.

Hannon: You're saying I killed Deb?

Detective: Absolutely. There's no doubt about that. OK? We know that.

Hannon: You think I killed her?

Detective: Kevin, it's not that we think that, we know that. We need to know why you did that. That's all, OK? That — it's no question as to did you do that. That's not a question here, Kevin, OK? So —

Hannon: Can I have a drink of water and then lock me up — I think we really should have an attorney.

Detective: We'll get you a drink of water.

Hannon: I don't want to talk anymore please. (Pause). This is — this is really wrong. This woman has scars all over her from this Paul Mackey. He's calling her 50 times a week.

Detective: Okay. If you want to talk to an attorney, you understand that we have to stop talking to you. OK? And — and then your side of this story will never be known. That's your choice. That's a choice you're making.

Hannon: So, that means what?

Detective: That means we're gonna put this thing together and we're gonna convict you of murder.

Hannon: Of murder?

Detective: Absolutely. Yup.

Hannon: Convict me of murdering her?

The interrogation continued and Hannon eventually gave the police a formal statement in which he admitted his involvement in Tolhurst's death. Hannon was subsequently charged with murder. At his trial, the judge held that his formal statement could properly be admitted into evidence.

Was the judge's ruling correct?

Selected Bibliography

Liva Baker, MIRANDA: CRIME, LAW AND POLITICS (1983)

Paul G. Cassell & Richard Fowles, *Handcuffing the Cops? A Thirty-Year Perspective on* Miranda's *Harmful Effects on Law Enforcement*, 50 Stan. L. Rev. 1055 (1998)

Paul G. Cassell, *The Paths Not Taken: The Supreme Court's Failures in* Dickerson, 99 Mich. L. Rev. 898 (2001)

Steven D. Clymer, *Are Police Free To Disregard* Miranda, 112 Yale L.J. 447 (2002)

Geoffrey S. Corn, *The Missing* Miranda *Warning: Why What You Don't Know Really Can Hurt You*, 2011 Utah L. Rev. 761 (2011)

Geoffrey Corn & Chris Jenks, *Strange Bedfellows: How Expanding the Public Safety Exception to* Miranda *Benefits Counterterrorism Suspects*, 41 Fordham Urb. L. J. 1 (2013)

Alfredo Garcia, *Regression to the Mean: How* Miranda *Has Become a Tragicomical Farce*, 25 St. Thomas L. Rev. 293 (2012)

Mark A. Godsey, *Reformulating the* Miranda *Warnings in Light of Contemporary Law and Understandings*, 90 Minn. L. Rev. 781 (2006)

Steven P. Grossman, *Separate but Equal:* Miranda's *Rights to Silence and Counsel*, 96 Marq. L. Rev. 151 (2012)

Yale Kamisar, *Foreword: From* Miranda *To § 3501 To* Dickerson *To . . .* , 99 Mich. L. Rev. 879 (2001)

Yale Kamisar, Miranda *Thirty-Five Years Later: A Close Look at the Majority and Dissenting Opinions in* Dickerson, 33 Ariz. St. L.J. 387 (2001)

Yale Kamisar, POLICE INTERROGATION AND CONFESSIONS: ESSAYS IN LAW AND POLICY (1980)

Yale Kamisar, *The Rise, Decline, and Fall (?) of* Miranda, 87 Wash. L. Rev. 965 (2012)

Kit Kinports, *The Supreme Court's Love-Hate Relationship with* Miranda, 101 J. Crim. L. & Criminology 375 (2011)

Susan R. Klein, *Identifying and (Re)formulating Prophylactic Rules, Safe Harbors, and Incidental Rights in Constitutional Criminal Procedure*, 99 Mich. L. Rev. 1030 (200l)

Richard A. Leo, *Questioning the Relevance of* Miranda *in the Twenty-First Century*, 99 Mich. L. Rev. 1000 (2001)

Tracey Maclin, *Comprehensive Analysis of the History of Interrogation Law: With Some Shots Directed at* Miranda v. Arizona, 95 B.U. L. Rev. 1387 (2015)

John T. Parry, *Constitutional Interpretation, Coercive Interrogation, and Civil Rights Litigation After* Chavez v. Martinez, 39 Ga. L. Rev. 733 (2005)

William T. Pizzi & Morris B. Hoffman, *Taking* Miranda's *Pulse*, 58 Vand. L. Rev. 813 (2005)

Stephen J. Schulhofer, Miranda, Dickerson, *and the Puzzling Persistence of Fifth Amendment Exceptionalism*, 99 Mich. L. Rev. 941 (2001)

David A. Strauss, Miranda, *the Constitution, and Congress*, 99 Mich. L. Rev. 958 (2001)

William J. Stuntz, Miranda's *Mistake*, 99 Mich. L. Rev. 975 (2001)

George C. Thomas III, *Separated at Birth But Siblings Nonetheless:* Miranda *and the Due Process Notice Cases*, 99 Mich. L. Rev. 1081 (2001)

George C. Thomas III, *Stories About* Miranda, 102 Mich. L. Rev. 1959 (2004)

Charles D. Weisselberg, *Mourning* Miranda, 96 Cal. L. Rev. 1519 (2008)

Welsh S. White, Miranda's *Failure to Restrain Pernicious Interrogation Practices*, 99 Mich. L. Rev. 1211 (2001)

Welsh S. White, MIRANDA'S WANING PROTECTIONS: POLICE INTERROGATION PRACTICES AFTER DICKERSON (2001)

Jonathan Witmer-Rich, *Interrogation and the Roberts Court*, 63 Fla. L. Rev. 1189 (2011)

Chapter 9

Confessions and the Right to Assistance of Counsel

Introductory Note

The Sixth Amendment prescribes a number of rights considered necessary for a fair adjudication of guilt or innocence in American systems of criminal justice. Perhaps the most critical of those rights is the right to the assistance of counsel. As Justice Black famously said in *Gideon v. Wainwright*, discussed below, "[t]he right . . . to counsel may not be deemed fundamental and essential to fair trials in some countries, but it is in ours." The emergence of this right as a means of regulating government efforts to secure incriminating statements from defendants and to use those statements to prove guilt at trial occurred in 1964. In *Massiah v. United States*, 377 U.S. 201, 84 S. Ct. 1199, 12 L. Ed. 2d 246 (1964), the foundational case in this chapter — and *Miranda*'s Sixth Amendment equal — the Justices concluded that the accused's constitutional right to the assistance of counsel barred the prosecution from introducing at trial incriminating statements secured from him by a government agent. Thus, the recognition of this particular "confessions" safeguard occurred two years *before Miranda v. Arizona*, 384 U.S. 436, 86 S. Ct. 1602, 16 L. Ed. 2d 694 (1966), held that the privilege against compelled self-incrimination regulates the admissibility of confessions obtained by means of custodial interrogation.

Massiah's holding, although controversial, was not entirely unexpected. Just a few years earlier, in *Crooker v. California*, 357 U.S. 433, 78 S. Ct. 1287, 2 L. Ed. 2d 1448 (1958), Justice Douglas, speaking for four dissenting Justices, maintained that "[t]he right to have counsel at the pretrial stage is often necessary to give meaning and protection to the right to be heard at the trial itself. It may also be necessary as a restraint on the coercive power of the police . . . . The demands of our civilization expressed in the Due Process Clause require that the accused who wants counsel should have one at any time after the moment of arrest." Moreover, in *Spano v. New York*, 360 U.S. 315, 79 S. Ct. 1202, 3 L. Ed. 2d 1265 (1959), presented in Chapter Seven, four concurring Justices endorsed the view that the Sixth Amendment right to the assistance of counsel prevented the admission of a confession obtained from an indicted defendant after the police failed to comply with his request to consult with a lawyer.

Genuine understanding and thoughtful assessment of the merits of the Supreme Court's decision in *Massiah* require an appreciation of the historical background of the constitutional right that is the decision's foundation. The text of the Sixth Amendment provides that "[i]n all criminal prosecutions, the accused shall enjoy the right . . . to have the Assistance of Counsel for his defence." It seems clear that the scope of this fundamental entitlement to counsel was originally restricted in two very significant ways. First, the Sixth Amendment was intended to grant a defendant the right *to retain* a lawyer to represent him or her. See James J. Tomkovicz, THE RIGHT TO THE ASSISTANCE OF COUNSEL 20–21 (2002). Second, the right was meant to encompass representation for the *trial* of criminal charges. See *id*. at 81. Twentieth-century interpretations of the Sixth Amendment (and its Fourteenth Amendment counterpart for state prosecutions) have eliminated both of these constraints upon the breadth of the right to counsel today. Between the late 1930s and the late 1960s, the Justices concluded that the constitutional guarantee includes both an entitlement of indigent defendants to *appointed counsel* and an entitlement of all defendants to representation for purposes of certain *pretrial proceedings*.

INDIGENTS' RIGHT TO APPOINTED COUNSEL: In 1938, in *Johnson v. Zerbst*, 304 U.S. 458, 58 S. Ct. 1019, 82 L. Ed. 1461 (1938), the Court concluded that in *federal* prosecutions indigent defendants who could not afford to hire lawyers were entitled to have the government furnish counsel to represent them. Characterizing the right to counsel as one of the "essential barriers against arbitrary or unjust deprivation of human rights," the Justices declared that the Sixth Amendment required judges to "provid[e] counsel for an accused who is unable to obtain counsel." The right to appointed assistance for indigent *state* defendants, which today is identical to the right in federal proceedings, evolved gradually over the course of a number of years. In a landmark ruling in *Powell v. Alabama*, 287 U.S. 45, 53 S. Ct. 55, 77 L. Ed. 158 (1932), six years before *Zerbst*, the Court decided that the Fourteenth Amendment promise of due process did guarantee some indigent state defendants an entitlement to appointed counsel. (The scope of the *Powell* holding was uncertain. The opinion could be read narrowly to extend an appointed counsel entitlement to disadvantaged defendants charged with capital offenses, or more broadly to grant the right to all indigents accused of capital crimes or even to some charged with noncapital offenses.) Ten years later, in *Betts v. Brady*, 316 U.S. 455, 62 S. Ct. 1252, 86 L. Ed. 1595 (1942), the Justices rejected the contention that the right to due process of law contained "an inexorable command" that indigent defendants have state-funded counsel in every case. Instead, the Fourteenth Amendment mandated appointed assistance only when the specific circumstances demonstrated that counsel was essential to fundamental fairness. Case-by-case determinations based on a variety of considerations were required to decide whether an indigent accused had a constitutional right to appointed assistance in state prosecutions. Relevant considerations included, for example, the seriousness of the accusation, the complexity of the trial, and the capabilities of the particular defendant. Almost 20 years later, in *Gideon v. Wainwright*, 372 U.S. 335, 83 S. Ct. 792, 9 L. Ed. 2d 799 (1963), one of the Warren Court's most renowned criminal procedure rulings, the Justices overruled *Betts*, concluding that lawyers were generally essential to fair trials and, consequently, that indigent state defendants enjoyed the same entitlement to appointed counsel that federal defendants had been accorded in *Zerbst*.

In a subsequent ruling, a majority of Justices decided that the Sixth and Fourteenth Amendment holdings in *Zerbst* and *Gideon* governed only those charged with felonies. According to *Scott v. Illinois*, 440 U.S. 367, 99 S. Ct. 1158, 59 L. Ed. 2d 383 (1979), indigents accused of misdemeanor-level offenses (presumably offenses with maximum authorized punishment of no more than one year in jail) have a constitutional right to appointed assistance *only* if they are sentenced upon conviction to some amount of actual incarceration. According to *Scott*'s "actual imprisonment" standard, an accused may be tried without counsel for a misdemeanor as long as the sentence ultimately imposed does not entail jail time. More recently, a divided Court held that after a misdemeanor trial at which an accused had not been provided with appointed assistance, a judge violated the right to counsel by imposing a 30-day prison sentence that was then *suspended*. See *Alabama v. Shelton*, 535 U.S. 654, 122 S. Ct. 1764, 152 L. Ed. 2d 888 (2002). A deprivation of the constitutional right to counsel occurred even without "activation" of the term of incarceration imposed. Put otherwise, the Justices held that the right to appointed assistance is triggered by "a suspended sentence that may 'end up in the actual deprivation of a person's liberty.'"

Federal and state defendants who have a right to appointed assistance for purposes of trial under *Zerbst*, *Gideon*, and *Scott* surely have the same right for purposes of the pretrial encounters governed by the ruling in *Massiah*. Those who have no right for purposes of trial, however, surely have no right at the pretrial encounters governed by *Massiah*.

THE RIGHT TO ASSISTANCE FOR PRETRIAL PROCEEDINGS: As noted earlier, the Sixth Amendment right to counsel was originally an entitlement to retain counsel in connection with *trials* of criminal charges. At the time the Constitution was adopted, confrontations between the accused and the government occurred only at trial. As justice systems developed, however, significant pretrial encounters between the government and the accused became routine parts of the criminal process. The Justices concluded that some of these formal courtroom confrontations between defendants and the government were "critical stages" of prosecutions because what occurred could threaten the fairness of subsequent trials. To ensure that the guarantee of counsel at trial was not eroded and that the fairness of the trial was not undermined at pretrial stages in which defendants lacked assistance, the Justices held that the rights to retained and appointed assistance extended to these critical pretrial proceedings. Thus, in *Hamilton v. Alabama*, 368 U.S. 52, 82 S. Ct. 157, 7 L. Ed. 2d 114 (1961), the Court held that a defendant had a right to assistance at an arraignment and in both *White v. Maryland*, 373 U.S. 59, 83 S. Ct. 1050, 10 L. Ed. 2d.

193 (1963), and *Coleman v. Alabama*, 399 U.S. 1, 90 S. Ct. 1999, 26 L. Ed. 2d 387 (1970), the Court deemed "preliminary hearings" critical stages that triggered entitlements to counsel.

The extension of counsel to such formal, in-court proceedings was not controversial. These pretrial courtroom stages bore obvious similarities to trials. The spirit and purposes of the Sixth Amendment guarantee dictated assistance in courtroom confrontations with prosecutors — legally trained adversaries — during proceedings requiring legal knowledge that laypersons typically do not possess. The Warren Court, however, concluded that the right to counsel also applied to two types of confrontations with government representatives that took place outside the judicial process. The extensions of the trial right to the assistance of counsel to these "informal" encounters with government operatives outside courtrooms were controversial. Some Justices maintained that the encounters at issue were nothing like trial and that the justifications for granting a right to assistance at trial did not support extension to these out-of-court confrontations because the accused was not confronted by a trained adversary and faced no questions requiring legal expertise. In sum, the Court divided over whether these extra-judicial encounters between government agents and accused individuals involved risks of unfairness that called for the protective shield of the Sixth Amendment right. One of the informal pretrial stages that provoked disagreement over expansion of the right to assistance is identified and defined by *Massiah* and its progeny, and is the entire focus of this final "confessions" chapter. The other controversial stage involves recognition of an entitlement to assistance at certain kinds of "identification" processes, and is the sole topic addressed in Chapter 10.

Those who agree with the Court's decisions to stretch the counsel guarantee to these extra-judicial phases of the criminal process draw some support from *Gideon*'s recognition — one year before *Massiah* — that lawyers are "necessities, not luxuries," and are "fundamental and essential to fair trials" in our adversarial systems of criminal justice. If the assistance of a trained lawyer at trial is necessary to ensure fairness, then, arguably, such assistance is necessary to ensure fairness at pretrial stages where law enforcement is seeking to obtain incriminating statements from or eyewitness identifications of defendants. If the police were not constrained by counsel in these situations, by engaging in practices that would never be permitted in a courtroom they could secure highly persuasive evidence of guilt that might well seal a defendant's fate, ensuring conviction and rendering the right to assistance at trial an empty formality. *See generally* Yale Kamisar, *Equal Justice in the Gatehouses and Mansions of American Criminal Procedure*, in CRIMINAL JUSTICE IN OUR TIME 11–38 (A. Howard ed. 1965), *reprinted in* Yale Kamisar, ESSAYS 27–40.

Those who disagree with the extensions of counsel to law enforcement efforts to secure confessions or identifications have a notably different perspective. In their view, even if government agents obtain admissions from or identifications of uncounseled defendants before trial by means that would be impermissible at trial, the right to a fair trial is not necessarily jeopardized. An accused will still have the assistance of counsel at the trial where guilt or innocence is determined. The trial lawyer's opportunities to explore and reveal the means by which a confession or identification was obtained and to highlight for the trier of fact any potential inaccuracies or unreliability in the evidence secured in the absence of counsel adequately preserve the fairness of the prosecution. *See generally* H. Friendly, BENCHMARKS 254–56 (1967).

After the Court's decision in *Miranda v. Arizona*, 384 U.S. 436, 86 S. Ct. 1602, 16 L. Ed. 2d 694 (1966), it was widely believed that the Fifth Amendment privilege against compulsory self-incrimination might have supplanted the Sixth Amendment right to counsel as a means of controlling police questioning and regulating the use of incriminating admissions at trial. For the 11 years following *Miranda*, the Supreme Court virtually ignored the *Massiah* doctrine. (In fact, it relied on *Massiah* in only one insignificant *per curiam* decision. See *Beatty v. United States*, 389 U.S. 45, 88 S. Ct. 234, 19 L. Ed. 2d 48 (1967).) In the final main case in this chapter, however, *Brewer v. Williams*, 430 U.S. 387, 97 S. Ct. 1232, 51 L. Ed. 2d 424 (1977), the Justices made it clear that *Massiah*'s right to counsel-based protection in confession contexts had not been eliminated by *Miranda*. *Brewer v. Williams* proved that the *Massiah* right to pretrial assistance continues to provide independent constitutional shelter against efforts to obtain admissible incriminating statements from accused persons. Several later decisions establish that the Sixth Amendment protection afforded by *Massiah* is different from, and in some respects more potent than, the Fifth Amendment safeguards afforded by *Miranda*. Thus, a defendant who may be unable to challenge a confession on the grounds that it was obtained in violation of *Miranda* or the Fourteenth Amendment right to due process might nevertheless be able to establish that it is inadmissible as a result of the Sixth Amendment right to counsel.

This chapter begins with the seminal opinion regarding confessions and the right to counsel — *Massiah v. United States*. Subsections B and C correspond to and explain the two basic requisites for the pretrial entitlement to counsel — "attachment" of the Sixth Amendment right and confrontation by the government at a "critical stage" of the prosecution. The final subsection of this chapter explores the standards governing waivers of the right to counsel recognized in *Massiah*. Throughout the chapter, students should reflect on the following general issues: (1) whether the Sixth Amendment right to counsel should play any role in the regulation of pretrial efforts by the government to secure incriminating admissions; (2) how the doctrinal requirements imposed by *Massiah*'s Sixth Amendment doctrine are different from those prescribed by *Miranda*'s Fifth Amendment doctrine; and (3) whether the doctrinal requirements deemed necessary to trigger the pretrial right to assistance recognized by *Massiah* are appropriate constraints on that right.

[A] The Basic Doctrine

Massiah v. United States

United States Supreme Court

377 U.S. 201, 84 S. Ct. 1199, 12 L. Ed. 2d 246 (1964)

Mr. Justice Stewart delivered the opinion of the Court.

The petitioner was indicted for violating the federal narcotics laws. He retained a lawyer, pleaded not guilty, and was released on bail. While he was free on bail a federal agent succeeded by surreptitious means in listening to incriminating statements made by him. Evidence of these statements was introduced against the petitioner at his trial over his objection. He was convicted, and the Court of Appeals affirmed. We granted certiorari to consider whether, under the circumstances here presented, the prosecution's use at the trial of evidence of the petitioner's own incriminating statements deprived him of any right secured to him under the Federal Constitution.

The petitioner, a merchant seaman, was in 1958 a member of the crew of the S.S. *Santa Maria*. In April of that year federal customs officials in New York received information that he was going to transport a quantity of narcotics aboard that ship from South America to the United States. As a result of this and other information, the agents searched the *Santa Maria* upon its arrival in New York and found in the afterpeak of the vessel five packages containing about three and a half pounds of cocaine. They also learned of circumstances, not here relevant, tending to connect the petitioner with the cocaine. He was arrested, promptly arraigned, and subsequently indicted for possession of narcotics aboard a United States vessel. In July a superseding indictment was returned, charging the petitioner and a man named Colson with the same substantive offense, and in separate counts charging the petitioner, Colson, and others with having conspired to possess narcotics aboard a United States vessel, and to import, conceal, and facilitate the sale of narcotics. The petitioner, who had retained a lawyer, pleaded not guilty and was released on bail, along with Colson.

A few days later, and quite without the petitioner's knowledge, Colson decided to cooperate with the government agents in their continuing investigation of the narcotics activities in which the petitioner, Colson, and others had allegedly been engaged. Colson permitted an agent named Murphy to install a Schmidt radio transmitter under the front seat of Colson's automobile, by means of which Murphy, equipped with an appropriate receiving device, could overhear from some distance away conversations carried on in Colson's car.

On the evening of November 19, 1959, Colson and the petitioner held a lengthy conversation while sitting in Colson's automobile, parked on a New York street. By prearrangement with Colson, and totally unbeknown to the petitioner, the agent Murphy sat in a car parked out of sight down the street and listened over the radio to the entire conversation. The petitioner made several incriminating statements during the course of this conversation. At the petitioner's trial these incriminating statements were brought before the jury through Murphy's testimony, despite the insistent objection of defense counsel. The jury convicted the petitioner of several related narcotics offenses, and the convictions were affirmed by the Court of Appeals.

The petitioner argues that it was an error of constitutional dimensions to permit the agent Murphy at the trial to testify to the petitioner's incriminating statements which Murphy had overheard under the circumstances disclosed by this record. This argument is based upon two distinct and independent grounds. First, we are told that Murphy's use of the radio equipment violated the petitioner's rights under the Fourth Amendment, and, consequently, that all evidence which Murphy thereby obtained was, under the rule of *Weeks v. United States*, 232 U.S. 383, 34 S. Ct. 341, 58 L. Ed. 652, inadmissible against the petitioner at the trial. Secondly, it is said that the petitioner's Fifth and Sixth Amendment rights were violated by the use in evidence against him of incriminating statements which government agents had deliberately elicited from him after he had been indicted and in the absence of his retained counsel. Because of the way we dispose of the case, we do not reach the Fourth Amendment issue.

In *Spano v. New York*, 360 U.S. 315, 79 S. Ct. 1202, 3 L. Ed. 2d 1265, this Court reversed a state criminal conviction because a confession had been wrongly admitted into evidence against the defendant at his trial. In that case the defendant had already been indicted for first-degree murder at the time he confessed. The Court held that the defendant's conviction could not stand under the Fourteenth Amendment. While the Court's opinion relied upon the totality of the circumstances under which the confession had been obtained, four concurring Justices pointed out that the Constitution required reversal of the conviction upon the sole and specific ground that the confession had been deliberately elicited by the police after the defendant had been indicted, and therefore at a time when he was clearly entitled to a lawyer's help. It was pointed out that under our system of justice the most elemental concepts of due process of law contemplate that an indictment be followed by a trial, "in an orderly courtroom, presided over by a judge, open to the public, and protected by all the procedural safeguards of the law." 360 U.S. at 327, 79 S. Ct. at 1209, 3 L. Ed. 2d 1265 (Stewart, J., concurring). It was said that a Constitution which guarantees a defendant the aid of counsel at such a trial could surely vouchsafe no less to an indicted defendant under interrogation by the police in a completely extrajudicial proceeding. Anything less, it was said, might deny a defendant's "effective representation by counsel at the only stage when legal aid and advice would help him." 360 U.S. at 326, 79 S. Ct. at 1209, 3 L. Ed. 2d 1265 (Douglas, J., concurring).

Ever since this Court's decision in the *Spano* case, the New York courts have unequivocally followed this constitutional rule. "Any secret interrogation of the defendant, from and after the finding of the indictment, without the protection afforded by the presence of counsel, contravenes the basic dictates of fairness in the conduct of criminal causes and the fundamental rights of persons charged with crime." *People v. Waterman*, 9 N.Y.2d 561, 565, 216 N.Y.S.2d 70, 75, 175 N.E.2d 445, 448.

This view no more than reflects a constitutional principle established as long ago as *Powell v. Alabama*, 287 U.S. 45, 53 S. Ct. 55, 77 L. Ed. 158, where the Court noted that ". . . during perhaps the most critical period of the proceedings . . . that is to say, from the time of their arraignment until the beginning of their trial, when consultation, thoroughgoing investigation and preparation [are] vitally important, the defendants . . . [are] as much entitled to such aid [of counsel] during that period as at the trial itself." *Id.* at 57, 53 S. Ct. at 59, 77 L. Ed. 158. And since the *Spano* decision the same basic constitutional principle has been broadly reaffirmed by this Court.

Here we deal not with a state court conviction, but with a federal case, where the specific guarantee of the Sixth Amendment directly applies. We hold that the petitioner was denied the basic protections of that guarantee when there was used against him at his trial evidence of his own incriminating words, which federal agents had deliberately elicited from him after he had been indicted and in the absence of his counsel. It is true that in the *Spano* case the defendant was interrogated in a police station, while here the damaging testimony was elicited from the defendant without his knowledge while he was free on bail. But, as Judge Hays pointed out in his dissent in the Court of Appeals, "if such a rule is to have any efficacy it must apply to indirect and surreptitious interrogations as well as those conducted in the jailhouse. In this case, Massiah was more seriously imposed upon . . . because he did not even know that he was under interrogation by a government agent." 307 F.2d at 72–73.

The Solicitor General, in his brief and oral argument, has strenuously contended that the federal law enforcement agents had the right, if not indeed the duty, to continue their investigation of the petitioner and his alleged criminal associates even though the petitioner had been indicted. He points out that the Government was continuing its investigation in order to uncover not only the source of narcotics found on the *S.S. Santa Maria*, but also their intended buyer. He says that the quantity of narcotics involved was such as to suggest that the petitioner was part of a large and well-organized ring, and indeed that the continuing investigation confirmed this suspicion, since it resulted in criminal charges against many defendants. Under these circumstances the Solicitor General concludes that the Government agents were completely "justified in making use of Colson's cooperation by having Colson continue his normal associations and by surveilling them."

We may accept and, at least for present purposes, completely approve all that this argument implies, Fourth Amendment problems to one side. We do not question that in this case, as in many cases, it was entirely proper to continue an investigation of the suspected criminal activities of the defendant and his alleged confederates, even though the defendant had already been indicted. All that we hold is that the defendant's own incriminating statements, obtained by federal agents under the circumstances here disclosed, could not constitutionally be used by the prosecution as evidence against *him* at his trial.

Reversed.

Mr. Justice White, with whom Mr. Justice Clark and Mr. Justice Harlan join, dissenting.

. . . .

I am unable to see how this case presents an unconstitutional interference with Massiah's right to counsel. Massiah was not prevented from consulting with counsel as often as he wished. No meetings with counsel were disturbed or spied upon. Preparation for trial was in no way obstructed. It is only a sterile syllogism — an unsound one, besides — to say that because Massiah had a right to counsel's aid before and during the trial, his out-of-court conversations and admissions must be excluded if obtained without counsel's consent or presence.

. . . .

The Court presents no facts, no objective evidence, no reasons to warrant scrapping the voluntary-involuntary test for admissibility in this area. Without such evidence I would retain it in its present form.

This case cannot be analogized to the American Bar Association's rule forbidding an attorney to talk to the opposing party litigant outside the presence of his counsel. Aside from the fact that the Association's canons are not of constitutional dimensions, the specific canon argued is inapposite because it deals with the conduct of lawyers and not with the conduct of investigators. Lawyers are forbidden to interview the opposing party because of the supposed imbalance of legal skill and acumen between the lawyer and the party litigant; the reason for the rule does not apply to non-lawyers and certainly not to Colson, Massiah's codefendant.

Applying the new exclusionary rule is peculiarly inappropriate in this case. At the time of the conversation in question, petitioner was not in custody but free on bail. He was not questioned in what anyone could call an atmosphere of official coercion. What he said was said to his partner in crime who had also been indicted. There was no suggestion or any possibility of coercion. What petitioner did not know was that Colson had decided to report the conversation to the police. Had there been no prior arrangements between Colson and the police, had Colson simply gone to the police after the conversation had occurred, his testimony relating Massiah's statements would be readily admissible at the trial, as would a recording which he might have made of the conversation. In such event, it would simply be said that Massiah risked talking to a friend who decided to disclose what he knew of Massiah's criminal activities. But, if, as occurred here, Colson had been cooperating with the police prior to his meeting with Massiah, both his evidence and the recorded conversation are somehow transformed into inadmissible evidence despite the fact that the hazard to Massiah remains precisely the same — the defection of a confederate in crime.

Reporting criminal behavior is expected or even demanded of the ordinary citizen. Friends may be subpoenaed to testify about friends, relatives about relatives and partners about partners. I therefore question the soundness of insulating Massiah from the apostasy of his partner in crime and of furnishing constitutional sanction for the strict secrecy and discipline of criminal organizations. Neither the ordinary citizen nor the confessed criminal should be discouraged from reporting what he knows to the authorities and from lending his aid to secure evidence of crime. Certainly after this case the Colsons will be few and far between; and the Massiahs can breathe much more easily, secure in the knowledge that the Constitution furnishes an important measure of protection against faithless compatriots and guarantees sporting treatment for sporting peddlers of narcotics.

Meanwhile, of course, the public will again be the loser and law enforcement will be presented with another serious dilemma. The general issue lurking in the background of the Court's opinion is the legitimacy of penetrating or obtaining confederates in criminal organizations. For the law enforcement agency, the answer for the time being can only be in the form of a prediction about the future application of today's new constitutional doctrine. More narrowly, and posed by the precise situation involved here, the question is this: when the police have arrested and released on bail one member of a criminal ring and another member, a confederate, is cooperating with the police, can the confederate be allowed to continue his association with the ring or must he somehow be withdrawn to avoid challenge to trial evidence on the ground that it was acquired after rather than before the arrest, after rather than before the indictment?

Defendants who are out on bail have been known to continue their illicit operations. *See Rogers v. United States*, 325 F.2d 485 (C.A. 10th Cir.). That an attorney is advising them should not constitutionally immunize their statements made in furtherance of these operations and relevant to the question of their guilt at the pending prosecution. In this very case there is evidence that after indictment defendant Aiken tried to persuade Agent Murphy to go into the narcotics business with him. Under today's decision, Murphy may neither testify as to the content of this conversation nor seize for introduction in evidence any narcotics whose location Aiken may have made known.

Undoubtedly, the evidence excluded in this case would not have been available but for the conduct of Colson in cooperation with Agent Murphy, but is it this kind of conduct which should be forbidden to those charged with law enforcement? It is one thing to establish safeguards against procedures fraught with the potentiality of coercion and to outlaw "easy but self-defeating ways in which brutality is substituted for brains as an instrument of crime detection." *McNabb v. United States*, 318 U.S. 332, 344, 63 S. Ct. 608, 615, 87 L. Ed. 819. But here there was no substitution of brutality for brains, no inherent danger of police coercion justifying the prophylactic effect of another exclusionary rule. Massiah was not being interrogated in a police station, was not surrounded by numerous officers or questioned in relays, and was not forbidden access to others. Law enforcement may have the elements of a contest about it, but it is not a game. Massiah and those like him receive ample protection from the long line of precedents in this Court holding that confessions may not be introduced unless they are voluntary. In making these determinations the courts must consider the absence of counsel as one of several factors by which voluntariness is to be judged. This is a wiser rule than the automatic rule announced by the Court, which requires courts and juries to disregard voluntary admissions which they might well find to be the best possible evidence in discharging their responsibility for ascertaining truth.

Notes and Questions

(1) Solicitor General Archibald Cox argued on behalf of the government in *Massiah*. One of his arguments was that, even if the concurring opinions in *Spano* were accepted, Massiah's incriminating statements should be admissible because, unlike Spano, he was not subjected to "official pressure." He was not in custody, he was not subjected to police interrogation, and "Colson, a layman unskilled in the art of interrogation, did not and probably could not utilize any of the standard techniques to persuade or otherwise induce Massiah to incriminate himself." Yale Kamisar, Brewer v. Williams, Massiah, *and* Miranda: *What is "Interrogation"? When Does it Matter?*, 67 Geo. L.J. 1, 37 (1978), *reprinted in* Kamisar, ESSAYS 139, 171–72. Is there force to this argument? How does the Court respond to it?

(2) For an article strongly criticizing the Court's decision in *Massiah*, see H. Richard Uviller, *Evidence from the Mind of the Criminal Suspect: A Reconsideration of the Current Rules of Access and Restraint*, 87 Colum. L. Rev. 1137 (1987). For an article defending the Court's result, see James J. Tomkovicz, *An Adversary System Defense of the Right to Counsel Against Informants: Truth, Fair Play, and the* Massiah *Doctrine*, 22 U.C. Davis L. Rev. 1 (1988).

(3) A significant question is *when* the right to counsel violation occurs. Does the government transgress the Constitution *when it elicits* admissions at a pretrial encounter with an unassisted defendant or *when it introduces* the elicited incriminating statements at trial to prove guilt? The *Massiah* majority endorsed the latter position. In response to the government's argument that it was justified in conducting a further investigation of Massiah's drug transactions, the majority pointedly observed that it was holding *only* that the Constitution forbade the *use* of his statements "as evidence against *him* at his trial." The Sixth Amendment was not offended by an uncounseled pretrial confrontation, but only by the prosecution's introduction at trial of statements obtained at such a confrontation. Many years later, a different majority adopted the contrary view. Without acknowledging that it was radically modifying a fundamental premise underlying *Massiah*, the Justices concluded that a right to counsel deprivation occurs, and is completed, when the government elicits inculpatory statements in the absence of counsel. The use of the statements to prove guilt does not violate the Sixth Amendment right. See *Kansas v. Ventris*, 556 U.S. 586, 129 S. Ct. 1841, 173 L. Ed. 2d 801 (2009), (discussed in Chapters 12 and 13 — which address the justifications for and the scopes of constitutional doctrines dictating the exclusion of evidence). Considering the reasons why a defendant has a constitutional right to the assistance of counsel at trial and in critical pretrial confrontations with the government, does the original understanding or the subsequent explanation of when a right to counsel violation occurs make more constitutional sense? For a

detailed exploration of this issue, see James J. Tomkovicz, *Sacrificing* Massiah*: Confusion over Exclusion and Erosion of the Right to Counsel*, 16 Lewis & Clark L. Rev. 1 (2012).

[B] Attachment of the Right to Counsel

Notes on the Attachment Requirement

Two opinions prior to *Massiah* had rejected Sixth Amendment claims because the individuals claiming deprivation had not been charged with offenses when government agents secured their inculpatory statements. *See Crooker v. California*, 357 U.S. 433, 78 S. Ct. 1287, 2 L. Ed. 2d 1448 (1958) and *Cicenia v. LaGay*, 357 U.S. 504, 508–09, 78 S. Ct. 1297, 2 L. Ed. 2d 1523 (1958). In *Massiah* and in *Spano*, the case upon which Justice Stewart relied heavily in recognizing a right to pretrial assistance, the individuals claiming violations of the right to counsel were under indictment at the time statements were obtained from them. In dissent, Justice White suggested that the right recognized by the majority might apply as soon as an individual was arrested. Moreover, in *Escobedo v. Illinois*, 378 U.S. 478, 84 S. Ct. 1758, 12 L. Ed. 2d 977 (1964), decided the same year as *Massiah*, a majority of the Court held that an individual who was in custody, but had *not* been formally charged with an offense, did have an entitlement to the assistance of counsel.

Escobedo, however, proved to be unique — the sole decision in which the Court has ever recognized an entitlement to counsel prior to a formal government accusation. Moreover, the Justices subsequently reformulated *Escobedo*'s foundations, asserting that the decision had actually been a precursor of *Miranda* — that is, that it was rooted in the Fifth Amendment privilege, not the Sixth Amendment entitlement to assistance. *See Kirby v. Illinois*, 406 U.S. 682, 689, 92 S. Ct. 1877, 32 L. Ed. 2d 411 (1972) (asserting that "the Court in retrospect [had] perceived that the 'prime purpose' of *Escobedo* was not to vindicate the constitutional right to counsel as such, but, like *Miranda*, 'to guarantee full effectuation of the privilege against self-incrimination'") (quoting *Johnson v. New Jersey*, 384 U.S. 719, 729, 86 S. Ct. 1772, 1779, 16 L. Ed. 2d 882 (1966)).

(1) THE "FORMAL CHARGE" REQUIREMENT: In a number of opinions since *Massiah* and *Escobedo*, the Justices have made it unmistakably clear that the Sixth Amendment right has no application prior to the time an individual is formally accused by the government. In *Moran v. Burbine*, 475 U.S. 412, 106 S. Ct. 1135, 89 L. Ed. 2d 410 (1986) (discussed in Chapter 8, section [D]), the Court rejected an uncharged suspect's right to counsel claim. According to the majority, "[b]y its very terms, [the Sixth Amendment] becomes applicable *only* when the government's role shifts from investigation to accusation . . . . [L]ooking to *the initiation of adversary judicial proceedings*, far from being mere formalism, is fundamental to the proper application of the Sixth Amendment right to counsel." Consequently, the right to the assistance of

counsel "*does not attach until after the initiation of formal charges.*" (Emphasis added). *See also United States v. Gouveia*, 467 U.S. 180, 104 S. Ct. 2292, 81 L. Ed. 2d 146 (1984), ("[G]iven the *plain language* of the [Sixth] Amendment and its *purpose* of protecting the unaided layman at critical confrontations with his adversary, our conclusion that the right to counsel attaches at the initiation of adversary judicial criminal proceedings 'is far from a mere formalism.'") (emphasis added).

(2) THE MEANING OF "INITIATION OF ADVERSARY JUDICIAL PROCEED-INGS": An arrest, even one that is pursuant to a warrant, is not a formal charge that triggers attachment of the Sixth Amendment right. On the other hand, a grand jury indictment is not necessary to satisfy the formal charge requirement. In *Brewer v. Williams*, 430 U.S. 387, 97 S. Ct. 1232, 51 L. Ed. 2d 424 (1977), the Court indicated the sorts of formal steps that suffice, stating that: "[T]he right to counsel granted by the Sixth and Fourteenth Amendments means . . . that a person is entitled to the help of a lawyer at or after the time that judicial proceedings have been initiated against him 'whether by way of formal charge, preliminary hearing, indictment, information, or arraignment.'"

In *Rothgery v. Gillespie County, Texas*, 554 U.S. 191, 128 S. Ct. 2578, 171 L. Ed. 2d 366 (2008), the Court further explored the meaning of the "initiation of adversary judicial proceedings" threshold for attachment of the Sixth Amendment right to counsel. Rothgery was arrested for being a felon in possession of a firearm. He made an initial appearance before a magistrate who concluded that there was probable cause to believe he had committed the offense. The County did not appoint counsel for him until six months later, after he had been indicted. Soon thereafter, his attorney demonstrated that he had not previously been convicted of a felony, and the indictment was dismissed. Rothgery filed a federal civil rights claim, alleging that his right to counsel had attached upon his initial appearance and that the County's failure to appoint counsel within a reasonable time thereafter had violated the Sixth Amendment. The district court ruled that Rothgery's right to counsel had not attached at his initial appearance because prosecutors were not aware of or involved in the process at that stage.

The Supreme Court disagreed. According to the Court, it was "wrong" to conclude that the initiation of adversary proceedings depends "on whether the prosecutor had a hand in starting" the process. In prior decisions, including *Brewer v. Williams*, the Court had concluded that the act of "bringing a defendant before a court for initial appearance signals a sufficient commitment to prosecute and marks the start of adversary judicial proceedings." Whether or not a prosecutor is involved, the relationship between the state and an individual is sufficiently adversarial to trigger attachment of the right to legal assistance when an individual makes an "initial appearance before a judicial officer, where he learns the charge against him and his liberty is subject to restriction." This point in the criminal process, in fact, "marks the start of adversary judicial proceedings that trigger attachment of the Sixth Amendment right to counsel." Because Rothgery had appeared before a magistrate, had been informed of the charge contained in the complaint filed by the police, and had been released on bond, his constitutional right to the assistance of counsel had attached.

The Court noted that the question of whether attachment occurs at a particular event is entirely distinct from the question of whether that event qualifies as a "critical stage" of the prosecution at which an accused is entitled to assistance. (The "critical stage" requirement is discussed in the next subsection of this chapter.) The Court also observed that once the right has attached, "counsel must be appointed within a reasonable time . . . to allow for adequate representation at any critical stage before trial, as well as at trial itself."

(3) THE "OFFENSE SPECIFIC" NATURE OF THE RIGHT TO COUNSEL: When the right to counsel attaches because a person has been formally charged with an offense, does the right apply to government efforts to secure statements regarding other uncharged offenses? The Court answered that question in *Texas v. Cobb*, 532 U.S. 162, 121 S. Ct. 1335, 149 L. Ed. 2d 321 (2001).

In *Cobb*, a home was burglarized, and the woman and young child who lived there were missing. The defendant confessed to the burglary but denied involvement in the disappearance of the woman and child. After the defendant was indicted for burglary, the court appointed counsel to represent him. Defense counsel permitted the police to question the defendant, who repeatedly denied having any knowledge about the disappearance of the woman and child. After a considerable time had passed, the defendant's father informed the police that his son had admitted murdering the woman and child. The defendant, who at the time was released on bond in the burglary case, was arrested and given *Miranda* warnings. In response to police questioning, he confessed to killing the victims and led the police to the place where he had buried their bodies. The defendant was convicted of capital murder and received a death sentence. The Texas Court of Criminal Appeals reversed, holding that his confession should have been suppressed because it was obtained in violation of the Sixth Amendment right to counsel, which had attached because the murder charge was "'very closely related factually to'" and "'factually interwoven with'" the charged burglary.

A five-Justice Supreme Court majority rejected the Texas court's interpretation of the Sixth Amendment. Adhering to the view that the Sixth Amendment right to counsel is "offense specific" — i.e., that it attaches only for formally charged offenses — the Court held that the defendant's right to counsel had not attached for the murder charge. The Court offered two responses to the defendant's prediction that "the offense-specific rule [would] prove 'disastrous' to suspects' constitutional rights and [would] 'permit law enforcement officers almost complete and total license to conduct unwanted and uncounseled interrogations.'" First, suspects are not left unprotected because the authorities must honor the dictates of *Miranda*. Second, the Constitution must be construed with a recognition that society has an "interest in the ability of police to talk to witnesses and suspects, even those who have been charged with other offenses."

The majority also observed that, while the Sixth Amendment right to counsel attaches only for offenses with which an individual has been formally charged, "the definition of an 'offense' is not necessarily limited to the four corners of a charging instrument." Under *Blockburger v. United States*, 284 U.S. 299, 52 S. Ct. 180, 76 L. Ed.

306 (1932) — a decision that defines the scope of protection afforded by the Fifth Amendment Double Jeopardy Clause — " 'where the same act or transaction' " violates two statutes, the offenses defined by those statutes are the " 'same offence' " unless " 'each provision requires proof of a fact which the other does not.' " In other words, two offenses are the "same" under *Blockburger* when (and only when) all of the statutory elements of one offense are included within the statutory elements of the other offense. Seeing "no . . . difference between the meaning of the term 'offense' " in the double jeopardy and counsel contexts, the majority held "that when the Sixth Amendment right to counsel attaches, it does encompass offenses that, even if not formally charged, would be considered the same offense under the *Blockburger* test."

Justice Breyer, joined in dissent by Justices Stevens, Souter, and Ginsburg, observed that the *Cobb* majority's holding permitted law enforcement "to question those charged with a crime without first approaching counsel, through the simple device of asking questions about any other related crime not actually charged in the indictment" — unless an uncharged offense is the same under the narrow *Blockburger* standard. The dissenters predicted that this restriction upon the scope of the right to counsel would "undermine the lawyer's role as 'medium' between the defendant and the government." They considered it inappropriate to employ *Blockburger's* Fifth Amendment test to define the breadth of the right to counsel's assistance. That test "does nothing to address the substantial concerns about the circumvention of the Sixth Amendment right that are raised by the majority's rule" and is "extraordinarily difficult to administer in practice." The dissenting Justices would have interpreted the word "offense" more broadly, holding that once the right to counsel attaches it extends to all "criminal acts that are 'closely related to' or 'inextricably intertwined with' " a formally charged offense.

For another illustration of the "offense-specific" nature of right to counsel, *see Illinois v. Perkins*, 496 U.S. 292, 110 S. Ct. 2394, 110 L. Ed. 2d 243 (1990) (included in Chapter 8, section [C]) (concluding that the Court's "Sixth Amendment precedents [we]re not applicable" to the defendant's case because "no charges had been filed *on the subject of the interrogation*" at the time officers interrogated him) (emphasis added).

[C] *Massiah's* "Critical Stage"

Introductory Note

After the right to counsel attaches, accused individuals are entitled to assistance only at "critical stages" of the prosecution. Only certain types of confrontation between the accused and his governmental adversary give rise to an entitlement to counsel's aid. In *Massiah*, the Court held that the accused had been "denied the basic protections of th[e Sixth Amendment] guarantee when there was used against him at his trial evidence of his own incriminating words, which federal agents had *deliberately elicited* from him . . . in the absence of his counsel." (Emphasis added). It is important to note that the Court found deliberate elicitation when the record showed that the informant, his codefendant, had merely engaged in a "conversation" with Massiah.

When the Court revived the *Massiah* right in *Brewer v. Williams*, a case that involved a confrontation with a known police officer, Justice Stewart (the author of *Massiah*) confused the "critical stage" question. He first asserted that the detective who secured Williams's statements had "deliberately and designedly set out to elicit information from" him, "just as surely as . . . if he had formally interrogated him." Justice Stewart then declared that the "entitle[ment] to the assistance of counsel . . . would [not] have come into play if there had been no *interrogation*" and that "the clear rule of *Massiah* is that once adversary proceedings have commenced against an individual, he has a right to legal representation *when the government interrogates him*." (Emphasis added).

Subsequently, Justice Stewart sought to clarify the ambiguity created by his opinion in *Brewer v. Williams*. In *Rhode Island v. Innis*, 446 U.S. 291, 100 S. Ct. 1682, 64 L. Ed. 2d 297 (1980), he asserted that the Sixth Amendment right to counsel "prohibits law enforcement officers from 'deliberately elicit[ing]' incriminating information from a defendant in the absence of counsel" and indicated that "the term 'interrogation'" was not "apt in the Sixth Amendment context" because "the policies underlying the [Fifth and Sixth Amendments] are quite distinct." The next three opinions— *United States v. Henry, Kuhlmann v. Wilson*, and *Fellers v. United States*— provide additional insights into the nature of the encounters with government operatives that entitle an accused to legal assistance.

United States v. Henry

United States Supreme Court

447 U.S. 264, 100 S. Ct. 2183, 65 L. Ed. 2d 115 (1980)

Mr. Chief Justice Burger delivered the opinion of the Court.

. . . .

I

The Janaf Branch of the United Virginia Bank/Seaboard National in Norfolk, Va., was robbed in August 1972. Witnesses saw two men wearing masks and carrying guns enter the bank while a third man waited in the car. No witnesses were able to identify respondent Henry as one of the participants. About an hour after the robbery, the getaway car was discovered. Inside was found a rent receipt signed by one "Allen R. Norris" and a lease, also signed by Norris, for a house in Norfolk. Two men, who were subsequently convicted of participating in the robbery, were arrested at the rented house. Discovered with them were the proceeds of the robbery and the guns and masks used by the gunmen.

Government agents traced the rent receipt to Henry; on the basis of this information, Henry was arrested in Atlanta, Ga., in November 1972. Two weeks later he was indicted for armed robbery under 18 U.S.C. §§ 2113(a) and (d). He was held pending trial in the Norfolk city jail. Counsel was appointed on November 27.

On November 21, 1972, shortly after Henry was incarcerated, Government agents working on the Janaf robbery contacted one Nichols, an inmate at the Norfolk city jail, who for some time prior to this meeting had been engaged to provide confidential information to the Federal Bureau of Investigation as a paid informant. Nichols was then serving a sentence on local forgery charges. The record does not disclose whether the agent contacted Nichols specifically to acquire information about Henry or the Janaf robbery.

Nichols informed the agent that he was housed in the same cellblock with several federal prisoners awaiting trial, including Henry. The agent told him to be alert to any statements made by the federal prisoners, but not to initiate any conversation with or question Henry regarding the bank robbery. In early December, after Nichols had been released from jail, the agent again contacted Nichols, who reported that he and Henry had engaged in conversation and that Henry had told him about the robbery of the Janaf bank.[2] Nichols was paid for furnishing the information.

When Henry was tried in March 1973, an agent of the Federal Bureau of Investigation testified concerning the events surrounding the discovery of the rental slip and the evidence uncovered at the rented house. Other witnesses also connected Henry to the rented house, including the rental agent who positively identified Henry as the "Allen R. Norris" who had rented the house and had taken the rental receipt described earlier. A neighbor testified that prior to the robbery she saw Henry at the rented house with John Luck, one of the two men who had by the time of Henry's trial been convicted for the robbery. In addition, palm prints found on the lease agreement matched those of Henry.

Nichols testified at trial that he had "an opportunity to have some conversations with Mr. Henry while he was in the jail,"[3] and that Henry told him that on several occasions he had gone to the Janaf Branch to see which employees opened the vault. Nichols also testified that Henry described to him the details of the robbery and

---

2. Henry also asked Nichols if he would help him once Nichols was released. Henry requested Nichols to go to Virginia Beach and contact a woman there. He prepared instructions on how to find the woman and wanted Nichols to tell her to visit Henry in the Norfolk jail. He explained that he wanted to ask the woman to carry a message to his partner, who was incarcerated in the Portsmouth city jail. Henry also gave Nichols a telephone number and asked him to contact an individual named "Junior" or "Nail." In addition Henry asked Nichols to provide him with a floor plan of the United States Marshals' office and a handcuff key because Henry intended to attempt an escape.

3. Joseph Sadler, another of Henry's cellmates, also testified at trial. He stated that Henry had told him that Henry had robbed a bank with a man named "Lucky" or "Luck." Sadler testified that on advice of counsel he informed Government agents of the conversation with Henry. Sadler was not a paid informant and had no arrangement to monitor or report on conversations with Henry.

stated that the only evidence connecting him to the robbery was the rental receipt. The jury was not informed that Nichols was a paid Government informant.

On the basis of this testimony, Henry was convicted of bank robbery and sentenced to a term of imprisonment of 25 years. On appeal he raised no Sixth Amendment claims. His conviction was affirmed, and his petition to this Court for a writ of certiorari was denied.

On August 28, 1975, Henry moved to vacate his sentence pursuant to 28 U.S.C. § 2255. At this stage, he stated that he had just learned that Nichols was a paid Government informant and alleged that he had been intentionally placed in the same cell with Nichols so that Nichols could secure information about the robbery. Thus, Henry contended that the introduction of Nichols' testimony violated his Sixth Amendment right to the assistance of counsel. The District Court denied the motion without a hearing. The Court of Appeals, however, reversed and remanded for an evidentiary inquiry into "whether the witness [Nichols] was acting as a government agent during his interviews with Henry."

On remand, the District Court requested affidavits from the Government agents. An affidavit was submitted describing the agent's relationship with Nichols and relating the following conversation:

> I recall telling Nichols at this time to be alert to any statements made by these individuals [the federal prisoners] regarding the charges against them. I specifically recall telling Nichols that he was not to question Henry or these individuals about the charges against them, however, if they engaged him in conversation or talked in front of him, he was requested to pay attention to their statements. I recall telling Nichols not to initiate any conversations with Henry regarding the bank robbery charges against Henry, but that if Henry initiated the conversations with Nichols, I requested Nichols to pay attention to the information furnished by Henry.

The agent's affidavit also stated that he never requested anyone affiliated with the Norfolk city jail to place Nichols in the same cell with Henry.

The District Court again denied Henry's § 2255 motion, concluding that Nichols' testimony at trial did not violate Henry's Sixth Amendment right to counsel. The Court of Appeals reversed and remanded, holding that the actions of the Government impaired the Sixth Amendment rights of the defendant under *Massiah v. United States*, 377 U.S. 201, 84 S. Ct. 1199, 12 L. Ed. 2d 246 (1964). The court noted that Nichols had engaged in conversation with Henry and concluded that if by association, by general conversation, or both, Nichols had developed a relationship of trust and confidence with Henry such that Henry revealed incriminating information, this constituted interference with the right to the assistance of counsel under the Sixth Amendment.

II

This Court has scrutinized post-indictment confrontations between Government agents and the accused to determine whether they are "critical stages" of the prosecution at which the Sixth Amendment right to the assistance of counsel attaches. The present case involves incriminating statements made by the accused to an undisclosed and undercover Government informant while in custody and after indictment. The Government characterizes Henry's incriminating statements as voluntary and not the result of any affirmative conduct on the part of Government agents to elicit evidence. From this, the Government argues that Henry's rights were not violated, even assuming the Sixth Amendment applies to such surreptitious confrontations; in short, it is contended that the Government has not interfered with Henry's right to counsel.

This Court first applied the Sixth Amendment to post-indictment communications between the accused and agents of the Government in *Massiah v. United States, supra.* There, after the accused had been charged, he made incriminating statements to his codefendant, who was acting as an agent of the Government. In reversing the conviction, the Court held that the accused was denied "the basic protections of [the Sixth Amendment] when there was used against him at his trial evidence of his own incriminating words, which federal agents had deliberately elicited from him." *Id.* at 206, 84 S. Ct. at 1203. The *Massiah* holding rests squarely on interference with his right to counsel.

The question here is whether under the facts of this case a Government agent "deliberately elicited" incriminating statements from Henry within the meaning of *Massiah.* Three factors are important. First, Nichols was acting under instructions as a paid informant for the Government; second, Nichols was ostensibly no more than a fellow inmate of Henry; and third, Henry was in custody and under indictment at the time he was engaged in conversation by Nichols.

The Court of Appeals viewed the record as showing that Nichols deliberately used his position to secure incriminating information from Henry when counsel was not present and held that conduct attributable to the Government. Nichols had been a paid Government informant for more than a year; moreover, the FBI agent was aware that Nichols had access to Henry and would be able to engage him in conversations without arousing Henry's suspicion. The arrangement between Nichols and the agent was on a contingent-fee basis; Nichols was to be paid only if he produced useful information.[7] This combination of circumstances is sufficient to support the Court of Appeals' determination. Even if the agent's statement that he did not intend that

_____

7. The affidavit of the agent discloses that "Nichols had been paid by the FBI for expenses and services in connection with information he had provided" as an informant for at least a year. The only reasonable inference from this statement is that Nichols was paid when he produced information, not that Nichols was continuously on the payroll of the FBI. Here, the service requested of Nichols was that he obtain incriminating information from Henry; there is no indication that Nichols would have been paid if he had not performed the requested service.

Nichols would take affirmative steps to secure incriminating information is accepted, he must have known that such propinquity likely would lead to that result.

The Government argues that the federal agents instructed Nichols not to question Henry about the robbery.[8] Yet according to his own testimony, Nichols was not a passive listener; rather, he had "some conversations with Mr. Henry" while he was in jail and Henry's incriminatory statements were "the product of this conversation." While affirmative interrogation, absent waiver, would certainly satisfy *Massiah*, we are not persuaded, as the Government contends, that *Brewer v. Williams*, 430 U.S. 387, 97 S. Ct. 1232, 51 L. Ed. 2d 424 (1977), modified *Massiah*'s "deliberately elicited" test. *See Rhode Island v. Innis*, 446 U.S. 291 at 300, n. 4, 100 S. Ct. 1682 at 1689, n. 4, 64 L. Ed. 2d 297 (1980).[9] In *Massiah*, no inquiry was made as to whether Massiah or his codefendant first raised the subject of the crime under investigation.[10]

It is quite a different matter when the Government uses undercover agents to obtain incriminating statements from persons not in custody but suspected of criminal activity prior to the time charges are filed. In *Hoffa v. United States*, 385 U.S. 293, 302, 87 S. Ct. 408, 413, 17 L. Ed. 2d 374 (1966), for example, this Court held that "no interest legitimately protected by the Fourth Amendment is involved" because "the Fourth Amendment [does not protect] a wrongdoer's misplaced belief that a person to whom he voluntarily confides his wrongdoing will not reveal it." *See also United States v. White*, 401 U.S. 745, 91 S. Ct. 1122, 28 L. Ed. 2d 453 (1971). Similarly, the Fifth Amendment has been held not to be implicated by the use of undercover Government agents before charges are filed because of the absence of the potential

---

8. Two aspects of the agent's affidavit are particularly significant. First, it is clear that the agent in his discussions with Nichols singled out Henry as the inmate in whom the agent had a special interest. Thus, the affidavit relates that "I specifically recall telling Nichols that he was not to question *Henry* or these individuals" and "I recall telling Nichols not to initiate any conversations *with Henry* regarding the bank robbery charges," but to "pay attention to the information furnished *by Henry*." (Emphasis added.) Second, the agent only instructed Nichols not to question Henry or to initiate conversations regarding the bank robbery charges. Under these instructions, Nichols remained free to discharge his task of eliciting the statements in myriad less direct ways.

9. The situation where the "listening post" is an inanimate electronic device differs; such a device has no capability of leading the conversation into any particular subject or prompting any particular replies. *See e.g., United States v. Hearst*, 563 F.2d 1331, 1347–1348 (9th Cir. 1977), *cert. denied*, 435 U.S. 1000, 98 S. Ct. 1656, 56 L. Ed. 2d 90 (1978). However, that situation is not presented in this case, and there is no occasion to treat it; nor are we called upon to pass on the situation where an informant is placed in close proximity but makes no effort to stimulate conversations about the crime charged.

10. No doubt the role of the agent at the time of the conversations between Massiah and his codefendant was more active than that of the federal agents here. Yet the additional fact in *Massiah* that the agent was monitoring the conversations is hardly determinative. In both *Massiah* and this case, the informant was charged with the task of obtaining information from an accused. Whether *Massiah*'s codefendant questioned Massiah about the crime or merely engaged in general conversation about it was a matter of no concern to the *Massiah* Court. Moreover, we deem it irrelevant that in *Massiah* the agent had to arrange the meeting between Massiah and his codefendant while here the agents were fortunate enough to have an undercover informant already in close proximity to the accused.

for compulsion. *See Hoffa v. United States, supra*, 385 U.S. at 303–304, 87 S. Ct. at 414–415. But the Fourth and Fifth Amendment claims made in those cases are not relevant to the inquiry under the Sixth Amendment here — whether the Government has interfered with the right to counsel of the accused by "deliberately eliciting" incriminating statements. Our holding today does not modify *White* or *Hoffa*.

It is undisputed that Henry was unaware of Nichols' role as a Government informant. The government argues that this Court should apply a less rigorous standard under the Sixth Amendment where the accused is prompted by an undisclosed undercover informant than where the accused is speaking in the hearing of persons he knows to be Government officers. That line of argument, however, seeks to infuse Fifth Amendment concerns against compelled self-incrimination into the Sixth Amendment protection of the right to the assistance of counsel. An accused speaking to a known Government agent is typically aware that his statements may be used against him. The adversary positions at that stage are well established; the parties are then "arm's-length" adversaries.

When the accused is in the company of a fellow inmate who is acting by prearrangement as a Government agent, the same cannot be said. Conversation stimulated in such circumstances may elicit information that an accused would not intentionally reveal to persons known to be Government agents. Indeed, the *Massiah* Court noted that if the Sixth Amendment "is to have any efficacy it must apply to indirect and surreptitious interrogations as well as those conducted in the jailhouse." The Court pointedly observed that Massiah was more seriously imposed upon because he did not know that his codefendant was a Government agent.

Moreover, the concept of a knowing and voluntary waiver of Sixth Amendment rights does not apply in the context of communications with an undisclosed undercover informant acting for the Government. *See Johnson v. Zerbst*, 304 U.S. 458, 58 S. Ct. 1019, 82 L. Ed. 1461 (1938). In that setting, Henry, being unaware that Nichols was a Government agent expressly commissioned to secure evidence, cannot be held to have waived his right to the assistance of counsel.

Finally, Henry's incarceration at the time he was engaged in conversation by Nichols is also a relevant factor.[11] As a ground for imposing the prophylactic requirements in *Miranda v. Arizona*, 384 U.S. 436, 467, 86 S. Ct. 1602, 1624, 16 L. Ed. 2d 694 (1966), this Court noted the powerful psychological inducements to reach for aid when a person is in confinement. While the concern in *Miranda* was limited to custodial police interrogation, the mere fact of custody imposes pressures on the accused; confinement may bring into play subtle influences that will make him particularly susceptible to the ploys of undercover Government agents. The Court of Appeals determined that on this record the incriminating conversations between

---

11. This is not to read a "custody" requirement, which is a prerequisite to the attachment of *Miranda* rights, into this branch of the Sixth Amendment. Massiah was in no sense in custody at the time of his conversation with his codefendant. Rather, we believe the fact of custody bears on whether the Government "deliberately elicited" the incriminating statements from Henry.

Henry and Nichols were facilitated by Nichols' conduct and apparent status as a person sharing a common plight. That Nichols had managed to gain the confidence of Henry, as the Court of Appeals determined, is confirmed by Henry's request that Nichols assist him in his escape plans when Nichols was released from confinement.[12]

Under the strictures of the Court's holdings on the exclusion of evidence, we conclude that the Court of Appeals did not err in holding that Henry's statements to Nichols should not have been admitted at trial. By intentionally creating a situation likely to induce Henry to make incriminating statements without the assistance of counsel, the Government violated Henry's Sixth Amendment right to counsel. This is not a case where, in Justice Cardozo's words, "the constable . . . blundered," *People v. DeFore*, 242 N.Y. 13, 21, 150 N.E. 585, 587 (1926); rather, it is one where the "constable" planned an impermissible interference with the right to the assistance of counsel.[14]

The judgment of the Court of Appeals for the Fourth Circuit is

Affirmed.

MR. JUSTICE POWELL, concurring.

. . . .

II

I view this as a close and difficult case on its facts because no evidentiary hearing has been held on the *Massiah* claim. Normally, such a hearing is helpful to a reviewing court and should be conducted. On balance, however, I accept the view of the Court of Appeals and of the Court that the record adequately demonstrates the existence of a *Massiah* violation. I could not join the Court's opinion if it held that the mere presence or incidental conversation of an informant in a jail cell would violate *Massiah.** To demonstrate an infringement of the Sixth Amendment, a defendant

---

12. This is admittedly not a case such as *Massiah* where the informant and the accused had a prior longstanding relationship. Nevertheless, there is ample evidence in the record which discloses that Nichols had managed to become more than a casual jailhouse acquaintance. That Henry could be induced to discuss his past crime is hardly surprising in view of the fact that Nichols had so ingratiated himself that Henry actively solicited his aid in executing his next crime — his planned attempt to escape from the jail.

14. Although it does not bear on the constitutional question in this case, we note that Disciplinary Rule 7–104(A)(1) of the Code of Professional Responsibility provides:

> (A) During the course of his representation of a client a lawyer shall not:
> (1) Communicate or cause another to communicate on the subject of the representation with a party he knows to be represented by a lawyer in that matter unless he has the prior consent of the lawyer representing such other party or is authorized by law to do so.

See also ETHICAL CONSIDERATION 7–18.

* By reserving the question whether the mere presence of an informant in a jail cell violates *Massiah*, the Court demonstrates that its holding is not premised upon such a theory.

must show that the government engaged in conduct that, considering all of the circumstances, is the functional equivalent of interrogation. *See Brewer v. Williams*, 430 U.S. at 399, 97 S. Ct. at 1239; *id.* at 411, 412, 97 S. Ct. at 1245, 1246 (Powell, J., concurring). *See also Rhode Island v. Innis*, 446 U.S. 291, 100 S. Ct. 1682, 64 L. Ed. 2d 297 (1980).

Because I understand that the decision today rests on a conclusion that this informant deliberately elicited incriminating information by such conduct, I join the opinion of the Court.

MR. JUSTICE BLACKMUN, with whom MR. JUSTICE WHITE joins, dissenting.

. . . .

I

Massiah mandates exclusion only if a federal agent "deliberately elicited" statements from the accused in the absence of counsel. The word "deliberately" denotes intent. *Massiah* ties this intent to the act of elicitation, that is, to conduct that draws forth a response. Thus *Massiah*, by its own terms, covers only action undertaken with the specific intent to evoke an inculpatory disclosure.

Faced with Agent Coughlin's unequivocal expression of an intent *not* to elicit statements from respondent Henry, but merely passively to receive them, the Court, in its decision to affirm the judgment of the Court of Appeals, has no choice but to depart from the natural meaning of the *Massiah* formulation. The Court deems it critical that informant Nichols had been a paid informant; that Agent Coughlin was aware that Nichols "had access" to Henry and "would be able to engage him in conversations without arousing Henry's suspicion"; and that payment to Nichols was on a contingent-fee basis. Thus, it is said, even if Coughlin's "statement is accepted . . . he must have known that such propinquity likely would lead to that result" (that is, that Nichols would take "affirmative steps to secure incriminating information"). Later, the Court goes even further, characterizing this as a case of "intentionally creating a situation *likely to induce* Henry to make incriminating statements." (Emphasis added.) This determination, coupled with the statement that Nichols "prompted" respondent Henry's remarks, leads the Court to find a *Massiah* violation.

Thus, while claiming to retain the "deliberately elicited" test, the Court really forges a new test that saps the word "deliberately" of all significance. The Court's extension of *Massiah* would cover even a "negligent" triggering of events resulting in reception of disclosures. This approach, in my view, is unsupported and unwise.

. . . .

The unifying theme of *Massiah* cases . . . is the presence of deliberate, designed, and purposeful tactics, that is, the agent's use of an investigatory tool with the specific intent of extracting information in the absence of counsel. Thus, the Court's "likely to induce" test fundamentally restructures *Massiah*. Even if the agent engages in no "overreaching," and believes his actions to be wholly innocent and passive, evidence he comes by must be excluded if a court, with the convenient benefit of 20/20 hindsight, finds it likely that the agent's actions would induce the statements.

. . . .

. . . I note the limits, placed in other Sixth Amendment cases, of providing counsel to counterbalance prosecutorial expertise and to aid defendants faced with complex and unfamiliar proceedings. While not out of line with the Court's prior right-to-counsel cases, *Massiah* certainly is the decision in which Sixth Amendment protections have been extended to their outermost point. I simply do not perceive any good reason to give *Massiah* the expansion it receives in this case.

II

In my view, the Court not only missteps in forging a new *Massiah* test; it proceeds to misapply the very test it has created. The new test requires a showing that the agent created a situation "likely to induce" the production of incriminatory remarks, and that the informant in fact "prompted" the defendant. Even accepting the most capacious reading of both this language and the facts, I believe that neither prong of the Court's test is satisfied.

. . . .

MR. JUSTICE REHNQUIST, dissenting.

The Court today concludes that the Government through the use of an informant "deliberately elicited" information from respondent after formal criminal proceedings had begun, and thus the statements made by respondent to the informant are inadmissible because counsel was not present. The exclusion of respondent's statements has no relationship whatsoever to the reliability of the evidence, and it rests on a prophylactic application of the Sixth Amendment right to counsel that in my view entirely ignores the doctrinal foundation of that right. The Court's ruling is based on *Massiah v. United States*, 377 U.S. 201, 84 S. Ct. 1199, 12 L. Ed. 2d 246 (1964), which held that a postindictment confrontation between the accused and his accomplice, who had turned State's evidence and was acting under the direction of the Government, was a "critical" stage of the criminal proceedings at which the Sixth Amendment right to counsel attached. While the decision today sets forth the factors that are "important" in determining whether there has been a *Massiah* violation, I think that *Massiah* constitutes such a substantial departure from the traditional concerns that underlie the Sixth Amendment guarantee that its language, if not its actual holding, should be re-examined.

. . . .

I

The doctrinal underpinnings of *Massiah* have been largely left unexplained, and the result in this case, as in *Massiah*, is difficult to reconcile with the traditional notions of the role of an attorney. Here, as in *Massiah*, the accused was not prevented from consulting with his counsel as often as he wished. No meetings between the accused and his counsel were disturbed or spied upon. And preparation for trial was not obstructed . . . .

A

Our decisions recognize that after formal proceedings have commenced an accused has a Sixth Amendment right to counsel at "critical stages" of the criminal proceedings. This principle derives from *Powell v. Alabama*, 287 U.S. 45, 53 S. Ct. 55, 77 L. Ed. 158 (1932), which held that a trial court's failure to appoint counsel until the trial began violated the Due Process Clause of the Fourteenth Amendment . . . .

Powell was based on the rationale that an unaided layman, who has little or no familiarity with the law, requires assistance in the preparation and presentation of his case and in coping with procedural complexities in order to assure a fair trial . . . . More recently this Court has again observed that the concerns underlying the Sixth Amendment right to counsel are to provide aid to the layman in arguing the law and in coping with intricate legal procedure, and to minimize the imbalance in the adversary system that otherwise resulted with the creation of the professional prosecuting official. Thus, in examining whether a stage of the proceedings is a "critical" one at which the accused is entitled to legal representation, it is important to recognize that the theoretical foundation of the Sixth Amendment right to counsel is based on the traditional role of an attorney as a legal expert and strategist.

"Deliberate elicitation" after formal proceedings have begun is thus not by itself determinative . . . . If the event is not one that requires knowledge of legal procedure, involves a communication between the accused and his attorney concerning investigation of the case or the preparation of a defense, or otherwise interferes with the attorney-client relationship, there is in my view simply no constitutional prohibition against the use of incriminating information voluntarily obtained from an accused despite the fact that his counsel may not be present . . . .

Once the accused has been made aware of his rights, it is his responsibility to decide whether or not to exercise them. If he voluntarily relinquishes his rights by talking to authorities, or if he decides to disclose incriminating information to someone whom he mistakenly believes will not report it to the authorities, *cf. Hoffa v. United States*, 385 U.S. 293, 87 S. Ct. 408, 17 L. Ed. 2d 374 (1966), he is normally accountable for his actions and must bear any adverse consequences that result. Such information has not in any sense been obtained because the accused's will has been overborne, nor does it result from any "unfair advantage" that the State has over the accused: the accused is free to keep quiet and to consult with his attorney if he so chooses. In this sense, the decision today and the result in *Massiah* are fundamentally inconsistent with traditional notions of the role of the attorney that underlie the Sixth Amendment right to counsel.

. . . .

Notes and Questions

(1) In *Maine v. Moulton*, 474 U.S. 159, 106 S. Ct. 477, 88 L. Ed. 2d 481 (1985), the Court dealt with a case in which the facts were in some respects strikingly similar to those in *Massiah*. The defendant was indicted on four charges of theft. As in *Massiah*, the defendant had a co-defendant named Colson and both were released on bail. According to Colson, when Moulton and Colson met to plan for their upcoming trial, Moulton suggested the possibility of killing a state witness (Elwell), and they talked about how the murder might be committed.

Subsequently, Colson and his attorney met with the police. In the course of their discussions, the police and Colson agreed to a deal. No further charges would be brought against Colson if he would cooperate in the prosecution of the pending charges against Moulton.

About six weeks later, Moulton asked Colson to meet with him and plan their defense. Colson agreed. At the meeting, Colson was equipped with a body wire transmitter to record what was said. Police Chief Keating testified that he proposed this arrangement for Colson's safety, in case Moulton realized that his co-defendant was cooperating with the police, and to record any further conversation concerning threats to witnesses.

At the meeting, the idea of eliminating witnesses was briefly discussed but quickly dismissed by Moulton as unworkable. During the remainder of the lengthy meeting, Moulton and Colson discussed the pending case. Apologizing for his faulty memory, Colson repeatedly asked Moulton to remind him about the details of what had happened. This led Moulton to make numerous incriminating statements. These statements were later admitted against Moulton at his trial.

The government argued that *Moulton* was distinguishable from *Massiah* on two grounds: first, in this case, unlike *Massiah*, the defendant initiated the meeting with his co-defendant; second, the police had legitimate reasons for listening to Moulton's conversations with Colson. In an opinion written by Mr. Justice Brennan, a bare majority of the Court rejected both of these distinctions and held that Moulton's statements were inadmissible under the holding of *Massiah*.

As to the first distinction, the majority stated that "the identity of the party who instigated the meeting at which the Government obtained incriminating statements was not decisive or even important" to its *Massiah* decision. It added that, after the initiation of formal charges, "*knowing exploitation* by the State of an opportunity to confront the accused without counsel being present is as much a breach of the State's obligation not to circumvent the right to the assistance of counsel as is the *intentional creation* of such an opportunity." (Emphasis added.)

With respect to the second argument, the majority saw no distinction between *Moulton* and *Massiah*. In *Massiah* the government had also contended that law enforcement agents "had the right, if not indeed the duty, to continue their investigation of [Massiah] and his alleged criminal associates . . . ." The *Moulton* Court reaffirmed that "incriminating statements pertaining to pending charges are inadmissible at the trial of those charges, notwithstanding the fact that the police were also investigating other crimes, if, in obtaining this evidence, the State violated the Sixth Amendment by knowingly circumventing the accused's right to the assistance of counsel." In a footnote, the majority stated that "[d]irect proof of the State's knowledge will seldom be available to the accused. However, as *Henry* makes clear, proof that the State 'must have known' that its agent was likely to obtain incriminating statements from the accused in the absence of counsel suffices to establish a Sixth Amendment violation."

The dissent, written by Chief Justice Burger, objected that nothing in the Constitution or the Court's prior decisions supports the Court's holding "that the Sixth Amendment prohibits the use at trial of post-indictment statements made to a government informant, even where those statements were recorded as part of a good-faith investigation of entirely separate crimes."

(2) In determining whether a defendant's Sixth Amendment Right to Counsel has been violated, how should courts differentiate a government agent or informer from a private person who discloses incriminating statements made by a cellmate (or other associate) to the government? Should the criteria for determining whether a person is a government agent be the same in this context as those used when the defense of entrapment is at issue? For consideration of the standard applied in entrapment cases, see Chapter 6, *supra*.

Kuhlmann v. Wilson

United States Supreme Court

477 U.S. 436, 106 S. Ct. 2616, 91 L. Ed. 2d 364 (1986)

JUSTICE POWELL announced the judgment of the Court and delivered the opinion of the Court with respect to Parts I, IV, and V, and an opinion with respect to Parts II and III in which THE CHIEF JUSTICE, JUSTICE REHNQUIST, and JUSTICE O'CONNOR join.

. . . .

I

In the early morning of July 4, 1970, respondent and two confederates robbed the Star Taxicab Garage in the Bronx, New York, and fatally shot the night dispatcher. Shortly before, employees of the garage had observed respondent, a former employee there, on the premises conversing with two other men. They also witnessed respondent fleeing after the robbery, carrying loose money in his arms. After eluding the police for four days, respondent turned himself in. Respondent admitted that he had been present when the crimes took place, claimed that he had witnessed the robbery, gave the police a description of the robbers, but denied knowing them. Respondent also denied any involvement in the robbery or murder, claiming that he had fled because he was afraid of being blamed for the crimes.

After his arraignment, respondent was confined in the Bronx House of Detention, where he was placed in a cell with a prisoner named Benny Lee. Unknown to respondent, Lee had agreed to act as a police informant. Respondent made incriminating statements that Lee reported to the police. Prior to trial, respondent moved to suppress the statements on the ground that they were obtained in violation of his right to counsel. The trial court held an evidentiary hearing on the suppression motion, which revealed that the statements were made under the following circumstances.

Before respondent arrived in the jail, Lee had entered into an arrangement with Detective Cullen, according to which Lee agreed to listen to respondent's conversations and report his remarks to Cullen. Since the police had positive evidence of respondent's participation, the purpose of placing Lee in the cell was to determine the identities of respondent's confederates. Cullen instructed Lee not to ask respondent any questions, but simply to "keep his ears open" for the names of the other perpetrators. Respondent first spoke to Lee about the crimes after he looked out the cellblock window at the Star Taxicab Garage, where the crimes had occurred. Respondent said, "someone's messing with me," and began talking to Lee about the robbery, narrating the same story that he had given the police at the time of his arrest. Lee advised respondent that this explanation "didn't sound too good,"[1] but respondent did not alter his story. Over the next few days, however, respondent changed details of his original account. Respondent then received a visit from his brother, who mentioned that members of his family were upset because they believed that respondent had murdered the dispatcher. After the visit, respondent again described the crimes to Lee. Respondent now admitted that he and two other men, whom he never identified, had planned and carried out the robbery, and had murdered the dispatcher. Lee informed Cullen of respondent's statements and furnished Cullen with notes that he had written surreptitiously while sharing the cell with respondent.

After hearing the testimony of Cullen and Lee, the trial court found that Cullen had instructed Lee "to ask no questions of [respondent] about the crime but merely to listen as to what [respondent] might say in his presence." The court determined that Lee obeyed these instructions, that he "at no time asked any questions with respect to the crime," and that he "only listened to [respondent] and made notes regarding what [respondent] had to say." The trial court also found that respondent's statements to Lee were "spontaneous" and "unsolicited". . . . The trial court accordingly denied the suppression motion.

The jury convicted respondent of common law murder and felonious possession of a weapon. On May 18, 1972, the trial court sentenced him to a term of 20 years to life on the murder count and to a concurrent term of up to 7 years on the weapons count.

. . . .

---

1. At the suppression hearing, Lee testified that, after hearing respondent's initial version of his participation in the crimes, "I think I remember telling him that the story wasn't — it didn't sound too good. Things didn't look too good for him." At trial, Lee testified to a somewhat different version of his remark: "Well, I said, look, you better come up with a better story than that because that one doesn't sound too cool to me, that's what I said."

IV

. . . .

A

The decision in *Massiah* had its roots in two concurring opinions written in *Spano v. New York*, 360 U.S. 315, 79 S. Ct. 1202, 3 L. Ed. 2d 1265 (1959). *See Maine v. Moulton*, 474 U.S. 159, 172, 106 S. Ct. 477, 485, 88 L. Ed. 2d 481 (1985). Following his indictment for first-degree murder, the defendant in *Spano* retained a lawyer and surrendered to the authorities. Before leaving the defendant in police custody, counsel cautioned him not to respond to interrogation. The prosecutor and police questioned the defendant, persisting in the face of his repeated refusal to answer and his repeated request to speak with his lawyer. The lengthy interrogation involved improper police tactics, and the defendant ultimately confessed. Following a trial at which his confession was admitted in evidence, the defendant was convicted and sentenced to death. Agreeing with the Court that the confession was involuntary and thus improperly admitted in evidence under the Fourteenth Amendment, the concurring Justices also took the position that the defendant's right to counsel was violated by the secret interrogation. As Justice Stewart observed, an indicted person has the right to assistance of counsel throughout the proceedings against him. The defendant was denied that right when he was subjected to an "all-night inquisition," during which police ignored his repeated requests for his lawyer.

The Court in *Massiah* adopted the reasoning of the concurring opinions in *Spano* and held that, once a defendant's Sixth Amendment right to counsel has attached, he is denied that right when federal agents "deliberately elicit" incriminating statements from him in the absence of his lawyer. 377 U.S. at 206, 84 S. Ct. at 1203. The Court adopted this test, rather than one that turned simply on whether the statements were obtained in an "interrogation," to protect accused persons from "indirect and surreptitious interrogations as well as those conducted in the jailhouse. In this case, Massiah was more seriously imposed upon . . . because he did not even know that he was under interrogation by a government agent." *Id.*, quoting *United States v. Massiah*, 307 F.2d 62, 72–73 (1962) (Hays, J., dissenting in part). Thus, the Court made clear that it was concerned with interrogation or investigative techniques that were equivalent to interrogation, and that it so viewed the technique in issue in *Massiah*.

In *United States v. Henry*, the Court applied the *Massiah* test to incriminating statements made to a jailhouse informant. The Court of Appeals in that case found a violation of *Massiah* because the informant had engaged the defendant in conversations and "had developed a relationship of trust and confidence with [the defendant] such that [the defendant] revealed incriminating information." 447 U.S. at 269, 100 S. Ct. at 2186. This Court affirmed, holding that the Court of Appeals reasonably concluded that the government informant "deliberately used his position to secure incriminating information from [the defendant] when counsel was not present." *Id.* at 270, 100 S. Ct. at 2186. Although the informant had not questioned the defendant, the informant had "stimulated" conversations with the defendant in order to "elicit" incriminating information. The Court emphasized that those facts, like the facts of *Massiah*, amounted to "'indirect and surreptitious interrogatio[n]'" of the defendant. 447 U.S. at 273, 100 S. Ct. at 2188.

Earlier this Term, we applied the *Massiah* standard in a case involving incriminating statements made under circumstances substantially similar to the facts of *Massiah* itself. In *Maine v. Moulton*, 474 U.S. 159, 106 S. Ct. 477, 88 L. Ed. 2d 481 (1985), the defendant made incriminating statements in a meeting with his accomplice, who had agreed to cooperate with the police. During that meeting, the accomplice, who wore a wire transmitter to record the conversation, discussed with the defendant the charges pending against him, repeatedly asked the defendant to remind him of the details of the crime, and encouraged the defendant to describe his plan for killing witnesses. The Court concluded that these investigatory techniques denied the defendant his right to counsel on the pending charges. Significantly, the Court emphasized that, because of the relationship between the defendant and the informant, the informant's engaging the defendant "in active conversation about their upcoming trial was certain to elicit" incriminating statements from the defendant. *Id.* at 177, n. 13, 106 S. Ct. at 488, n. 13. Thus, the informant's participation "in this conversation was 'the functional equivalent of interrogation.'" *Id.* (quoting *United States v. Henry*, 447 U.S. at 277, 100 S. Ct. at 2190 (Powell, J., concurring)).

As our recent examination of this Sixth Amendment issue in *Moulton* makes clear, the primary concern of the *Massiah* line of decisions is secret interrogation by investigatory techniques that are the equivalent of direct police interrogation. Since "the Sixth Amendment is not violated whenever — by luck or happenstance — the State obtains incriminating statements from the accused after the right to counsel has attached," 474 U.S. at 176, 106 S. Ct. at 487, citing *United States v. Henry, supra*, at 276, 100 S. Ct. at 2189 (Powell, J., concurring), a defendant does not make out a violation of that right simply by showing that an informant, either through prior arrangement or voluntarily, reported his incriminating statements to the police. Rather, the defendant must demonstrate that the police and their informant took some action, beyond merely listening, that was designed deliberately to elicit incriminating remarks.

B

It is thus apparent that the Court of Appeals erred in concluding that respondent's right to counsel was violated under the circumstances of this case. Its error did not stem from any disagreement with the District Court over appropriate resolution of the question reserved in *Henry*, but rather from its implicit conclusion that this case did not present that open question. That conclusion was based on a fundamental mistake, namely, the Court of Appeals' failure to accord to the state trial court's factual findings the presumption of correctness expressly required by 28 U.S.C. § 2254(d). [28 U.S.C. § 2254(d) provides that certain findings of fact made by a state court of competent jurisdiction must be presumed to be correct by a federal court considering a state prisoner's attack on a state court conviction via federal habeas corpus.]

The state court found that Officer Cullen had instructed Lee only to listen to respondent for the purpose of determining the identities of the other participants in the robbery and murder. The police already had solid evidence of respondent's participation.[22] The court further found that Lee followed those instructions, that he "at no time asked any questions" of respondent concerning the pending charges, and that he "only listened" to respondent's "spontaneous" and "unsolicited" statements. The only remark made by Lee that has any support in this record was his comment that respondent's initial version of his participation in the crimes "didn't sound too good." Without holding that any of the state court's findings were not entitled to the presumption of correctness under § 2254(d), the Court of Appeals focused on that one remark and gave a description of Lee's interaction with respondent that is completely at odds with the facts found by the trial court. In the Court of Appeals' view, "[s]ubtly and slowly, but surely, Lee's ongoing verbal intercourse with [respondent] served to exacerbate [respondent's] already troubled state of mind."[24] 742 F.2d at 745. After thus revising some of the trial court's findings, and ignoring other more relevant findings, the Court of Appeals concluded that the police "deliberately elicited" respondent's incriminating statements. This conclusion conflicts with the decision of every other state and federal judge who reviewed this record, and is clear error in light of the provisions and intent of § 2254(d).

V

The judgment of the Court of Appeals is reversed, and the case is remanded for further proceedings consistent with this opinion.

It is so ordered.

CHIEF JUSTICE BURGER, concurring.

I agree fully with the Court's opinion and judgment. This case is clearly distinguishable from *United States v. Henry*, 447 U.S. 264, 100 S. Ct. 2183, 65 L. Ed. 2d 115 (1980). There is a vast difference between placing an "ear" in the suspect's cell and placing a voice in the cell to encourage conversation for the "ear" to record.

. . . .

JUSTICE BRENNAN, with whom JUSTICE MARSHALL joins, dissenting.

. . . .

---

22. Eyewitnesses had identified respondent as the man they saw fleeing from the garage with an armful of money.

24. Curiously, the Court of Appeals expressed concern that respondent was placed in a cell that overlooked the scene of his crimes. For all the record shows, however, that fact was sheer coincidence. Nor do we perceive any reason to require police to isolate one charged with crime so that he cannot view the scene, whatever it may be, from his cell window.

The state trial court simply found that Lee did not ask respondent any direct questions about the crime for which respondent was incarcerated. The trial court considered the significance of this fact only under State precedents, which the court interpreted to require affirmative "interrogation" by the informant as a prerequisite to a constitutional violation. The court did not indicate whether it referred to a Fifth Amendment or to a Sixth Amendment violation in identifying "interrogation" as a precondition to a violation; it merely stated that "the utterances made by [respondent] to Lee were unsolicited, and voluntarily made and did not violate the defendant's Constitutional rights."

The Court of Appeals did not disregard the state court's finding that Lee asked respondent no direct questions regarding the crime. Rather, the Court of Appeals *expressly accepted* that finding, *Wilson v. Henderson*, 742 F.2d 741, 745 (2d Cir. 1984) ("[e]ven accepting that Lee did not ask Wilson any direct questions . . ."), but concluded that, as a matter of law, the deliberate elicitation standard of *Henry, supra,* and *Massiah, supra,* encompasses other, more subtle forms of stimulating incriminating admissions than overt questioning. The court suggested that the police deliberately placed respondent in a cell that overlooked the scene of the crime, hoping that the view would trigger an inculpatory comment to respondent's cellmate. The court also observed that, while Lee asked respondent no questions, Lee nonetheless stimulated conversation concerning respondent's role in the Star Taxicab Garage robbery and murder by remarking that respondent's exculpatory story did not "sound too good" and that he had better come up with a better one. 742 F.2d at 745. Thus, the Court of Appeals concluded that the respondent's case did not present the situation reserved in *Henry*, where an accused makes an incriminating remark within the hearing of a jailhouse informant, who "makes no effort to stimulate conversations about the crime charged." 447 U.S. at 271, n. 9, 100 S. Ct. at 2187, n. 9. Instead, the court determined this case to be virtually indistinguishable from *Henry*.

The Sixth Amendment guarantees an accused, at least after the initiation of formal charges, the right to rely on counsel as the "medium" between himself and the State. *Maine v. Moulton*, 474 U.S. 159, 176, 106 S. Ct. 477, 487, 88 L. Ed. 2d 481 (1985). Accordingly, the Sixth Amendment "imposes on the State an affirmative obligation to respect and preserve the accused's choice to seek [the assistance of counsel]," *id.* at 171, 106 S. Ct. at 485, and therefore "[t]he determination whether particular action by state agents violates the accused's right to . . . counsel must be made in light of this obligation." *Id.* at 176, 106 S. Ct. at 487. To be sure, the Sixth Amendment is not violated whenever, "by luck or happenstance," the State obtains incriminating statements from the accused after the right to counsel has attached. It is violated, however, when "the State obtains incriminating statements by knowingly circumventing the accused's right to have counsel present in a confrontation between the accused and a state agent." *Id.* (footnote omitted). As we explained in *Henry*, where the accused has not waived his right to counsel, the government knowingly circumvents the defendant's right to counsel where it "deliberately elicit[s]" inculpatory admissions, 447 U.S. at 270, 100 S. Ct. at 2186, that is, "intentionally creat[es] a situation likely to induce [the accused] to make incriminating statements without the assistance of counsel." *Id.* at 274, 100 S. Ct. at 2187.

. . . .

In the instant case, as in *Henry*, the accused was incarcerated and therefore was "susceptible to the ploys of undercover Government agents." *Id.* Like Nichols, Lee was a secret informant, usually received consideration for the services he rendered the police, and therefore had an incentive to produce the information which he knew the police hoped to obtain. Just as Nichols had done, Lee obeyed instructions not to question respondent and to report to the police any statements made by the respondent in Lee's presence about the crime in question. And, like Nichols, Lee encouraged respondent to talk about his crime by conversing with him on the subject over the course of several days and by telling respondent that his exculpatory story would not convince anyone without more work. However, unlike the situation in *Henry*, a disturbing visit from respondent's brother, rather than a conversation with the informant, seems to have been the immediate catalyst for respondent's confession to Lee. While it might appear from this sequence of events that Lee's comment regarding respondent's story and his general willingness to converse with respondent about the crime were not the *immediate* causes of respondent's admission, I think that the deliberate-elicitation standard requires consideration of the entire course of government behavior.

The State intentionally created a situation in which it was foreseeable that respondent would make incriminating statements without the assistance of counsel — it assigned respondent to a cell overlooking the scene of the crime and designated a secret informant to be respondent's cellmate. The informant, while avoiding direct questions, nonetheless developed a relationship of cellmate camaraderie with respondent and encouraged him to talk about his crime. While the *coup de grace* was delivered by respondent's brother, the groundwork for respondent's confession was laid by the State. Clearly the State's actions had a sufficient nexus with respondent's admission of guilt to constitute deliberate elicitation within the meaning of *Henry*. I would affirm the judgment of the Court of Appeals.

[The dissenting opinion of JUSTICE STEVENS has been omitted.]

Fellers v. United States

United States Supreme Court

540 U.S. 519, 124 S. Ct. 1019, 157 L. Ed. 2d 1016 (2004)

JUSTICE O'CONNOR delivered the opinion of the Court.

. . . .

I

On February 24, 2000, after a grand jury indicted petitioner for conspiracy to distribute methamphetamine, Lincoln Police Sergeant Michael Garnett and Lancaster County Deputy Sheriff Jeff Bliemeister went to petitioner's home in Lincoln,

Nebraska, to arrest him. The officers knocked on petitioner's door and, when petitioner answered, identified themselves and asked if they could come in. Petitioner invited the officers into his living room.

The officers advised petitioner they had come to discuss his involvement in methamphetamine distribution. They informed petitioner that they had a federal warrant for his arrest and that a grand jury had indicted him for conspiracy to distribute methamphetamine. The officers told petitioner that the indictment referred to his involvement with certain individuals, four of whom they named. Petitioner then told the officers that he knew the four people and had used methamphetamine during his association with them.

After spending about 15 minutes in petitioner's home, the officers transported petitioner to the Lancaster County jail. There, the officers advised petitioner for the first time of his rights under *Miranda v. Arizona*, 384 U.S. 436, 86 S. Ct. 1602, 16 L. Ed. 2d 694 (1966), and *Patterson v. Illinois*, 487 U.S. 285, 108 S. Ct. 2389, 101 L. Ed. 2d 261 (1988). Petitioner and the two officers signed a *Miranda* waiver form, and petitioner then reiterated the inculpatory statements he had made earlier, admitted to having associated with other individuals implicated in the charged conspiracy, and admitted to having loaned money to one of them even though he suspected that she was involved in drug transactions.

Before trial, petitioner moved to suppress the inculpatory statements he made at his home and at the county jail. A Magistrate Judge conducted a hearing and recommended that the statements petitioner made at his home be suppressed because the officers had not informed petitioner of his *Miranda* rights. The Magistrate Judge found that petitioner made the statements in response to the officers' "implici[t] questions," noting that the officers had told petitioner that the purpose of their visit was to discuss his use and distribution of methamphetamine. The Magistrate Judge further recommended that portions of petitioner's jailhouse statement be suppressed as fruits of the prior failure to provide *Miranda* warnings.

The District Court suppressed the "unwarned" statements petitioner made at his house but admitted petitioner's jailhouse statements pursuant to *Oregon v. Elstad*, 470 U.S. 298, 105 S. Ct. 1285, 84 L. Ed. 2d 222 (1985), concluding petitioner had knowingly and voluntarily waived his *Miranda* rights before making the statements.

Following a jury trial at which petitioner's jailhouse statements were admitted into evidence, petitioner was convicted of conspiring to possess with intent to distribute methamphetamine. Petitioner appealed, arguing that his jailhouse statements should have been suppressed as fruits of the statements obtained at his home in violation of the Sixth Amendment. The Court of Appeals affirmed. 285 F.3d 721 (C.A.8 2002). With respect to petitioner's argument that the officers' failure to administer *Miranda* warnings at his home violated his Sixth Amendment right to counsel . . . the Court of Appeals stated: "[The Sixth Amendment] is not applicable here . . . for the officers did not interrogate [petitioner] at his home." 285 F.3d, at 724. The Court of Appeals also concluded that the statements from the jail were properly admitted under [*Oregon v. Elstad*].

. . . .

II

The Sixth Amendment right to counsel is triggered "at or after the time that judicial proceedings have been initiated . . . 'whether by way of formal charge, preliminary hearing, indictment, information, or arraignment.'" *Brewer v. Williams*, 430 U.S. 387, 398, 97 S. Ct. 1232, 51 L. Ed. 2d 424 (1977) (quoting *Kirby v. Illinois*, 406 U.S. 682, 689, 92 S. Ct. 1877, 32 L. Ed. 2d 411 (1972)). We have held that an accused is denied "the basic protections" of the Sixth Amendment "when there [is] used against him at his trial evidence of his own incriminating words, which federal agents . . . deliberately elicited from him after he had been indicted and in the absence of his counsel." *Massiah v. United States*, 377 U.S. 201, 206, 84 S. Ct. 1199, 12 L. Ed. 2d 246 (1964).

We have consistently applied the deliberate-elicitation standard in subsequent Sixth Amendment cases, see *United States v. Henry*, 447 U.S. 264, 270, 100 S. Ct. 2183, 65 L. Ed. 2d 115 (1980), and we have expressly distinguished this standard from the Fifth Amendment custodial-interrogation standard.

The Court of Appeals erred in holding that the absence of an "interrogation" foreclosed petitioner's claim that the jailhouse statements should have been suppressed as fruits of the statements taken from petitioner at his home. First, there is no question that the officers in this case "deliberately elicited" information from petitioner. Indeed, the officers, upon arriving at petitioner's house, informed him that their purpose in coming was to discuss his involvement in the distribution of methamphetamine and his association with certain charged co-conspirators. 285 F.3d, at 723. Because the ensuing discussion took place after petitioner had been indicted, outside the presence of counsel, and in the absence of any waiver of petitioner's Sixth Amendment rights, the Court of Appeals erred in holding that the officers' actions did not violate the Sixth Amendment standards established in *Massiah, supra*, and its progeny.

Second, because of its erroneous determination that petitioner was not questioned in violation of Sixth Amendment standards, the Court of Appeals improperly conducted its "fruits" analysis under the Fifth Amendment. Specifically, it applied *Elstad*[, a Fifth Amendment precedent] . . . . The Court of Appeals did not reach the question whether the Sixth Amendment requires suppression of petitioner's jailhouse statements on the ground that they were the fruits of previous questioning conducted in violation of the Sixth Amendment deliberate-elicitation standard. We have not had occasion to decide whether the rationale of *Elstad* applies when a suspect makes incriminating statements after a knowing and voluntary waiver of his right to counsel notwithstanding earlier police questioning in violation of Sixth Amendment standards. We therefore remand to the Court of Appeals to address this issue in the first instance.

Accordingly, the judgment of the Court of Appeals is reversed, and the case is remanded for further proceedings consistent with this opinion.

It is so ordered.

Notes and Questions

(1) After *Henry, Wilson,* and *Fellers,* what is the meaning of "deliberate elicitation," the official conduct governed by the *Massiah* doctrine? How does it differ from "custodial interrogation," the conduct regulated by *Miranda*?

(2) In the jailhouse context, is it realistic to distinguish between active and passive government agents? Assuming the distinction is tenable in theory, will there be practical problems in recreating the precise context in which the defendant's incriminating disclosure arose? In assessing the credibility of either the government informer or the defendant, both of whom have obvious incentives to fabricate? *See* Welsh S. White, *Interrogation Without Questions:* Rhode Island v. Innis *and* United States v. Henry, 78 Mich. L. Rev. 1209, 1241 n. 192 (1980).

(3) Assuming a suspect's cellmate is a government informer, will the determination of whether the informer's conduct implicated the suspect's Sixth Amendment right to counsel be made on the basis of the government's relationship to the informer (including the instructions given), the informer's conduct towards the suspect, or both? Why should the government's relationship or instructions to the informer have any relevance to this determination?

[D] Waiver of the Right to Counsel

Brewer v. Williams

United States Supreme Court

430 U.S. 387, 97 S. Ct. 1232, 51 L. Ed. 2d 424 (1977)

Mr. Justice Stewart delivered the opinion of the Court.

. . . .

I

On the afternoon of December 24, 1968, a 10-year-old girl named Pamela Powers went with her family to the YMCA in Des Moines, Iowa, to watch a wrestling tournament in which her brother was participating. When she failed to return from a trip to the washroom, a search for her began. The search was unsuccessful.

Robert Williams, who had recently escaped from a mental hospital, was a resident of the YMCA. Soon after the girl's disappearance Williams was seen in the YMCA lobby carrying some clothing and a large bundle wrapped in a blanket. He obtained help from a 14-year-old boy in opening the street door of the YMCA and the door to his automobile parked outside. When Williams placed the bundle in the front seat of his car the boy "saw two legs in it and they were skinny and white." Before anyone could see what was in the bundle Williams drove away. His abandoned car was found the following day in Davenport, Iowa, roughly 160 miles east of Des Moines. A warrant was then issued in Des Moines for his arrest on a charge of abduction.

On the morning of December 26, a Des Moines lawyer named Henry McKnight went to the Des Moines police station and informed the officers present that he had just received a long-distance call from Williams, and that he had advised Williams to turn himself in to the Davenport police. Williams did surrender that morning to the police in Davenport, and they booked him on the charge specified in the arrest warrant and gave him the warnings required by *Miranda v. Arizona*, 384 U.S. 436, 86 S. Ct. 1602, 16 L. Ed. 2d 694. The Davenport police then telephoned their counterparts in Des Moines to inform them that Williams had surrendered. McKnight, the lawyer, was still at the Des Moines police headquarters, and Williams conversed with McKnight on the telephone. In the presence of the Des Moines chief of police and a police detective named Leaming, McKnight advised Williams that Des Moines police officers would be driving to Davenport to pick him up, that the officers would not interrogate him or mistreat him, and that Williams was not to talk to the officers about Pamela Powers until after consulting with McKnight upon his return to Des Moines. As a result of these conversations, it was agreed between McKnight and the Des Moines police officials that Detective Leaming and a fellow officer would drive to Davenport to pick up Williams, that they would bring him directly back to Des Moines, and that they would not question him during the trip.

In the meantime Williams was arraigned before a judge in Davenport on the outstanding arrest warrant. The judge advised him of his *Miranda* rights and committed him to jail. Before leaving the courtroom, Williams conferred with a lawyer named Kelly, who advised him not to make any statements until consulting with McKnight back in Des Moines.

Detective Leaming and his fellow officer arrived in Davenport about noon to pick up Williams and return him to Des Moines. Soon after their arrival they met with Williams and Kelly, who, they understood, was acting as Williams' lawyer. Detective Leaming repeated the *Miranda* warnings, and told Williams:

> "[W]e both know that you're being represented here by Mr. Kelly and you're being represented by Mr. McKnight in Des Moines, and . . . I want you to remember this because we'll be visiting between here and Des Moines."

Williams then conferred again with Kelly alone, and after this conference Kelly reiterated to Detective Leaming that Williams was not to be questioned about the disappearance of Pamela Powers until after he had consulted with McKnight back in Des Moines. When Leaming expressed some reservations, Kelly firmly stated that the agreement with McKnight was to be carried out — that there was to be no interrogation of Williams during the automobile journey to Des Moines. Kelly was denied permission to ride in the police car back to Des Moines with Williams and the two officers.

The two detectives, with Williams in their charge, then set out on the 160-mile drive. At no time during the trip did Williams express a willingness to be interrogated in the absence of an attorney. Instead, he stated several times that "[w]hen I get to Des Moines and see Mr. McKnight, I am going to tell you the whole story." Detective Leaming knew that Williams was a former mental patient, and knew also that he was deeply religious.

The detective and his prisoner soon embarked on a wide-ranging conversation covering a variety of topics, including the subject of religion. Then, not long after leaving Davenport and reaching the interstate highway, Detective Leaming delivered what has been referred to in the briefs and oral arguments as the "Christian burial speech." Addressing Williams as "Reverend," the detective said:

> "I want to give you something to think about while we're traveling down the road.... Number one, I want you to observe the weather conditions, it's raining, it's sleeting, it's freezing, driving is very treacherous, visibility is poor, it's going to be dark early this evening. They are predicting several inches of snow for tonight, and I feel that you yourself are the only person that knows where this little girl's body is, that you yourself have only been there once, and if you get a snow on top of it you yourself may be unable to find it. And, since we will be going right past the area on the way into Des Moines, I feel that we could stop and locate the body, that the parents of this little girl should be entitled to a Christian burial for the little girl who was snatched away from them on Christmas [E]ve and murdered. And I feel we should stop and locate it on the way in rather than waiting until morning and trying to come back out after a snow storm and possibly not being able to find it at all."

Williams asked Detective Leaming why he thought their route to Des Moines would be taking them past the girl's body, and Leaming responded that he knew the body was in the area of Mitchellville — a town they would be passing on the way to Des Moines.[1] Leaming then stated: "I do not want you to answer me. I don't want to discuss it any further. Just think about it as we're riding down the road."

As the car approached Grinnell, a town approximately 100 miles west of Davenport, Williams asked whether the police had found the victim's shoes. When Detective Leaming replied that he was unsure, Williams directed the officers to a service station where he said he had left the shoes; a search for them proved unsuccessful. As they continued towards Des Moines, Williams asked whether the police had found the blanket, and directed the officers to a rest area where he said he had disposed of the blanket. Nothing was found. The car continued towards Des Moines, and as it approached Mitchellville, Williams said that he would show the officers where the body was. He then directed the police to the body of Pamela Powers.

---

1. The fact of the matter, of course, was that Detective Leaming possessed no such knowledge.

Williams was indicted for first-degree murder. Before trial, his counsel moved to suppress all evidence relating to or resulting from any statements Williams had made during the automobile ride from Davenport to Des Moines. After an evidentiary hearing the trial judge denied the motion. He found that "an agreement was made between defense counsel and the police officials to the effect that the Defendant was not to be questioned on the return trip to Des Moines," and that the evidence in question had been elicited from Williams during "a critical stage in the proceedings requiring the presence of counsel on his request." The judge ruled, however, that Williams had "waived his right to have an attorney present during the giving of such information."

The evidence in question was introduced over counsel's continuing objection at the subsequent trial. The jury found Williams guilty of murder, and the judgment of conviction was affirmed by the Iowa Supreme Court, a bare majority of whose members agreed with the trial court that Williams had "waived his right to the presence of his counsel" on the automobile ride from Davenport to Des Moines. *State v. Williams*, 182 N.W.2d 396, 402. . . . .

Williams then petitioned for a writ of habeas corpus in the United States District Court for the Southern District of Iowa. . . . . The District Court made findings of fact as summarized above, and concluded as a matter of law that the evidence in question had been wrongly admitted at Williams' trial. This conclusion was based on three alternative and independent grounds: (1) that Williams had been denied his constitutional right to the assistance of counsel; (2) that he had been denied the constitutional protections defined by this Court's decisions in *Escobedo v. Illinois*, 378 U.S. 478, 84 S. Ct. 1758, 12 L. Ed. 2d 977, and *Miranda v. Arizona*, 384 U.S. 436, 86 S. Ct. 1602, 16 L. Ed. 2d 694; and (3) that in any event, his self-incriminatory statements on the automobile trip from Davenport to Des Moines had been involuntarily made. Further, the District Court ruled that there had been no waiver by Williams of the constitutional protections in question.

The Court of Appeals for the Eighth Circuit, with one judge dissenting, affirmed this judgment and denied a petition for rehearing en banc. We granted certiorari to consider the constitutional issues presented.

II

. . . .

B

As stated above, the District Court based its judgment in this case on three independent grounds. The Court of Appeals appears to have affirmed the judgment on two of those grounds.[5] We have concluded that only one of them need be considered here.

---

5. The Court of Appeals did not address the District Court's ruling that Williams' statements had been made involuntarily.

Specifically, there is no need to review in this case the doctrine of *Miranda v. Arizona*, a doctrine designed to secure the constitutional privilege against compulsory self-incrimination. It is equally unnecessary to evaluate the ruling of the District Court that Williams' self-incriminating statements were, indeed, involuntarily made. For it is clear that the judgment before us must in any event be affirmed upon the ground that Williams was deprived of a different constitutional right — the right to the assistance of counsel.

This right, guaranteed by the Sixth and Fourteenth Amendments, is indispensable to the fair administration of our adversary system of criminal justice. Its vital need at the pretrial stage has perhaps nowhere been more succinctly explained than in Mr. Justice Sutherland's memorable words for the Court 44 years ago in *Powell v. Alabama*, 287 U.S. 45, 57, 53 S. Ct. 55, 59, 77 L. Ed. 158:

> "[D]uring perhaps the most critical period of the proceedings against these defendants, that is to say, from the time of their arraignment until the beginning of their trial, when consultation, thorough-going investigation and preparation were vitally important, the defendants did not have the aid of counsel in any real sense, although they were as much entitled to such aid during that period as at the trial itself."

There has occasionally been a difference of opinion within the Court as to the peripheral scope of this constitutional right. *See Kirby v. Illinois*, 406 U.S. 682, 92 S. Ct. 1877, 32 L. Ed. 2d 411. But its basic contours, which are identical in state and federal contexts, are too well established to require extensive elaboration here. Whatever else it may mean, the right to counsel granted by the Sixth and Fourteenth Amendments means at least that a person is entitled to the help of a lawyer at or after the time that judicial proceedings have been initiated against him "whether by way of formal charge, preliminary hearing, indictment, information, or arraignment." *Kirby v. Illinois, supra*, 406 U.S. at 689, 92 S. Ct. at 1882.

There can be no doubt in the present case that judicial proceedings had been initiated against Williams before the start of the automobile ride from Davenport to Des Moines. A warrant had been issued for his arrest, he had been arraigned on that warrant before a judge in a Davenport courtroom, and he had been committed by the court to confinement in jail. The State does not contend otherwise.

There can be no serious doubt, either, that Detective Leaming deliberately and designedly set out to elicit information from Williams just as surely as — and perhaps more effectively than — if he had formally interrogated him. Detective Leaming was fully aware before departing for Des Moines that Williams was being represented in Davenport by Kelly and in Des Moines by McKnight. Yet he purposely sought during Williams' isolation from his lawyers to obtain as much incriminating information as possible. Indeed, Detective Leaming conceded as much when he testified at Williams' trial:

> "Q. In fact, Captain, whether he was a mental patient or not, you were trying to get all the information you could before he got to his lawyer, weren't you?

"A. I was sure hoping to find out where that little girl was, yes, sir.

"Q. Well, I'll put it this way: You was (sic) hoping to get all the information you could before Williams got back to McKnight, weren't you?

"A. Yes, sir."

. . . .

III

The Iowa courts recognized that Williams had been denied the constitutional right to the assistance of counsel. They held, however, that he had waived that right during the course of the automobile trip from Davenport to Des Moines. The state trial court explained its determination of waiver as follows:

> "The time element involved on the trip, the general circumstances of it, and more importantly the absence on the Defendant's part of any assertion of his right or desire not to give information absent the presence of his attorney, are the main foundations for the Court's conclusion that he voluntarily waived such right."

In its lengthy opinion affirming this determination, the Iowa Supreme Court applied "the totality-of-circumstances test for a showing of waiver of constitutionally-protected rights in the absence of an express waiver," and concluded that "evidence of the time element involved on the trip, the general circumstances of it, and the absence of any request or expressed desire for the aid of counsel before or at the time of giving information, were sufficient to sustain a conclusion that defendant did waive his constitutional rights as alleged." 182 N.W.2d, at 401, 402.

In the federal habeas corpus proceeding the District Court, believing that the issue of waiver was not one of fact but of federal law, held that the Iowa courts had "applied the wrong constitutional standards" in ruling that Williams had waived the protections that were his under the Constitution. 375 F. Supp., at 182. The court held "that it is the *government* which bears a heavy burden . . . but that is the burden which explicitly was placed on [Williams] by the state courts." *Ibid.* (emphasis in original). After carefully reviewing the evidence, the District Court concluded:

> "[U]nder the proper standards for determining waiver, there simply is no evidence to support a waiver. . . ."

Id., at 182–183.

The Court of Appeals approved the reasoning of the District Court. . . .

The District Court and the Court of Appeals were correct in the view that the question of waiver was not a question of historical fact, but one which, in the words of Mr. Justice Frankfurter, requires "application of constitutional principles to the facts as found. . . ." *Brown v. Allen*, 344 U.S. 443, 507, 73 S. Ct. 397, 446, 97 L. Ed. 469 (separate opinion).

The District Court and the Court of Appeals were also correct in their understanding of the proper standard to be applied in determining the question of waiver as a matter of federal constitutional law — that it was incumbent upon the State to prove "an intentional relinquishment or abandonment of a known right or privilege." *Johnson v. Zerbst*, 304 U.S., at 464, 58 S. Ct., at 1023. That standard has been reiterated in many cases. We have said that the right to counsel does not depend upon a request by the defendant, and that courts indulge in every reasonable presumption against waiver. This strict standard applies equally to an alleged waiver of the right to counsel whether at trial or at a critical stage of pretrial proceedings.

We conclude, finally that the Court of Appeals was correct in holding that, judged by these standards, the record in this case falls far short of sustaining petitioner's burden. It is true that Williams had been informed of and appeared to understand his right to counsel. But waiver requires not merely comprehension but relinquishment, and Williams' consistent reliance upon the advice of counsel in dealing with the authorities refutes any suggestion that he waived that right. He consulted McKnight by long-distance telephone before turning himself in. He spoke with McKnight by telephone again shortly after being booked. After he was arraigned, Williams sought out and obtained legal advice from Kelly. Williams again consulted with Kelly after Detective Leaming and his fellow officer arrived in Davenport. Throughout, Williams was advised not to make any statements before seeing McKnight in Des Moines, and was assured that the police had agreed not to question him. His statements while in the car that he would tell the whole story *after* seeing McKnight in Des Moines were the clearest expressions by Williams himself that he desired the presence of an attorney before any interrogation took place. But even before making these statements, Williams had effectively asserted his right to counsel by having secured attorneys at both ends of the automobile trip, both of whom, acting as his agents, had made clear to the police that no interrogation was to occur during the journey. Williams knew of that agreement and, particularly in view of his consistent reliance on counsel, there is no basis for concluding that he disavowed it.[10]

Despite Williams' express and implicit assertions of his right to counsel, Detective Leaming proceeded to elicit incriminating statements from Williams. Leaming did not preface this effort by telling Williams that he had a right to the presence of a lawyer, and made no effort at all to ascertain whether Williams wished to relinquish that right. The circumstances of record in this case thus provide no reasonable basis for finding that Williams waived his right to the assistance of counsel.

---

10. Cf. *Michigan v. Mosley*, 423 U.S. 96, 110 n. 2, 96 S. Ct. 321, 329, 46 L. Ed. 2d 313 (White, J., concurring in result):

> [T]he reasons to keep the lines of communication between the authorities and the accused open when the accused has chosen to make his own decisions are not present when he indicates instead that he wishes legal advice with respect thereto. The authorities may then communicate with him through an attorney. More to the point, the accused having expressed his own view that he is not competent to deal with the authorities without legal advice, a later decision at the authorities' insistence to make a statement without counsel's presence may properly be viewed with skepticism.

The Court of Appeals did not hold, nor do we, that under the circumstances of this case Williams *could not*, without notice to counsel, have waived his rights under the Sixth and Fourteenth Amendments. It only held, as do we, that he did not.

IV

The crime of which Williams was convicted was senseless and brutal, calling for swift and energetic action by the police to apprehend the perpetrator and gather evidence with which he could be convicted. No mission of law enforcement officials is more important. Yet "[d]isinterested zeal for the public good does not assure either wisdom or right in the methods it pursues." *Haley v. Ohio*, 332 U.S. 596, 605, 68 S. Ct. 302, 306, 92 L. Ed. 224 (Frankfurter, J., concurring in judgment). Although we do not lightly affirm the issuance of a writ of habeas corpus in this case, so clear a violation of the Sixth and Fourteenth Amendments as here occurred cannot be condoned. The pressures on state executive and judicial officers charged with the administration of the criminal law are great, especially when the crime is murder and the victim a small child. But it is precisely the predictability of those pressures that makes imperative a resolute loyalty to the guarantees that the Constitution extends to us all.

The judgment of the Court of Appeals is affirmed.[12]

It is so ordered.

[The concurring opinions of Mr. Justice Marshall and Mr. Justice Powell have been omitted.]

Mr. Justice Stevens, concurring.

. . . .

Nothing that we write, no matter how well reasoned or forcefully expressed, can bring back the victim of this tragedy or undo the consequences of the official neglect which led to the respondent's escape from a state mental institution. The emotional aspects of the case make it difficult to decide dispassionately, but do not qualify our obligation to apply the law with an eye to the future as well as with concern for the result in the particular case before us.

---

12. The District Court stated that its decision "does not touch upon the issue of what evidence, if any, beyond the incriminating statements themselves must be excluded as 'fruit of the poisonous tree.'" 375 F. Supp. 170, 185. We, too, have no occasion to address this issue, and in the present posture of the case there is no basis for the view of our dissenting Brethren that any attempt to retry the respondent would probably be futile. While neither Williams' incriminating statements themselves nor any testimony describing his having led the police to the victim's body can constitutionally be admitted into evidence, evidence of where the body was found and of its condition might well be admissible on the theory that the body would have been discovered in any event, even had incriminating statements not been elicited from Williams. In the event that a retrial is instituted, it will be for the state courts in the first instance to determine whether particular items of evidence may be admitted.

Underlying the surface issues in this case is the question whether a fugitive from justice can rely on his lawyer's advice given in connection with a decision to surrender voluntarily. The defendant placed his trust in an experienced Iowa trial lawyer who in turn trusted the Iowa law enforcement authorities to honor a commitment made during negotiations which led to the apprehension of a potentially dangerous person. Under any analysis, this was a critical stage of the proceeding in which the participation of an independent professional was of vital importance to the accused and to society. At this stage — as in countless others in which the law profoundly affects the life of the individual — the lawyer is the essential medium through which the demands and commitments of the sovereign are communicated to the citizen. If, in the long run, we are seriously concerned about the individual's effective representation by counsel, the State cannot be permitted to dishonor its promise to this lawyer.

MR. CHIEF JUSTICE BURGER, dissenting.

The result in this case ought to be intolerable in any society which purports to call itself an organized society. It continues the Court — by the narrowest margin — on the much-criticized course of punishing the public for the mistakes and misdeeds of law enforcement officers, instead of punishing the officer directly, if in fact he is guilty of wrongdoing. It mechanically and blindly keeps reliable evidence from juries whether the claimed constitutional violation involves gross police misconduct or honest human error.

Williams is guilty of the savage murder of a small child; no member of the Court contends he is not. While in custody, and after no fewer than five warnings of his rights to silence and to counsel, he led police to the concealed body of his victim. The Court concedes Williams was not threatened or coerced and that he spoke and acted voluntarily and with full awareness of his constitutional rights. In the face of all this, the Court now holds that because Williams was prompted by the detective's statement — not interrogation but a statement — the jury must not be told how the police found the body.

Today's holding fulfills Judge (later Mr. Justice) Cardozo's grim prophecy that someday some court might carry the exclusionary rule to the absurd extent that its operative effect would exclude evidence relating to the body of a murder victim because of the means by which it was found.[1] In so ruling the Court regresses to playing a grisly game of "hide and seek," once more exalting the sporting theory of criminal justice which has been experiencing a decline in our jurisprudence. With JUSTICES WHITE, BLACKMUN, and REHNQUIST, I categorically reject the remarkable notion that the police in this case were guilty of unconstitutional misconduct, or any conduct justifying the bizarre result reached by the Court. . . . .

---

1. "The criminal is to go free because the constable has blundered . . . . A room is searched against the law, and the body of a murdered man is found . . . . The privacy of the home has been infringed, and the murderer goes free." *People v. Defore*, 242 N.Y. 13, 21, 23–24, 150 N.E. 585, 587, 588 (1926). . . .

(1)

The Court Concedes Williams' Disclosures Were Voluntary

Under well-settled precedents which the Court freely acknowledges, it is very clear that Williams had made a valid waiver of his Fifth Amendment right to silence and his Sixth Amendment right to counsel when he led police to the child's body. Indeed, even under the Court's analysis I do not understand how a contrary conclusion is possible.

The Court purports to apply as the appropriate constitutional waiver standard the familiar "intentional relinquishment or abandonment of a known right or privilege" test of *Johnson v. Zerbst*, 304 U.S. 458, 464, 58 S. Ct. 1019, 1023, 12 L. Ed. 2d 246 (1938). The Court assumes, without deciding, that Williams' conduct and statements were voluntary. It concedes, as it must, that Williams had been informed of and fully understood his constitutional rights and the consequences of their waiver. Then, having either assumed or found every element necessary to make out a valid waiver under its own test, the Court reaches the astonishing conclusion that no valid waiver has been demonstrated.

This remarkable result is compounded by the Court's failure to define what evidentiary showing the State failed to make. Only recently, in *Schneckloth v. Bustamonte*, 412 U.S. 218, 238 n. 25, 93 S. Ct. 2041, 2053, n. 25, 36 L. Ed. 2d 854 (1973), the Court analyzed the distinction between a voluntary act and the waiver of a right; there Mr. Justice Stewart stated for the Court:

> "[T]he question whether a person has acted 'voluntarily' is quite distinct from the question whether he has 'waived' a trial right. The former question, as we made clear in *Brady v. United States*, 397 U.S. [742], at 749, 90 S. Ct. [1463], at 1469, [25 L. Ed. 2d 747,] can be answered only by examining all the relevant circumstances to determine if he has been coerced. The later question turns on the extent of his knowledge."

Similarly, in *McMann v. Richardson*, 397 U.S. 759, 766, 90 S. Ct. 1441, 1446, 25 L. Ed. 2d 763 (1970), we said that since a guilty plea constituted a waiver of a host of constitutional rights, "it must be an intelligent act 'done with sufficient awareness of the relevant circumstances and likely consequences.'" If the Court today applied these standards with fidelity to the *Schneckloth* and *McMann* holdings it could not reach the result now announced.

The evidence is uncontradicted that Williams had abundant knowledge of his right to have counsel present and of his right to silence. Since the Court does not question his mental competence, it boggles the mind to suggest that Williams could not understand that leading police to the child's body would have other than the most serious consequences. All of the elements necessary to make out a valid waiver are shown by the record and acknowledged by the Court; we thus are left to guess how the Court reached its holding.

One plausible but unarticulated basis for the result reached is that once a suspect has asserted his right not to talk without the presence of an attorney, it becomes legally impossible for him to waive that right until he has seen an attorney. But constitutional rights are *personal*, and an otherwise valid waiver should not be brushed aside by judges simply because an attorney was not present. The Court's holding operates to "imprison a man in his privileges," *Adams v. United States ex rel. McCann*, 317 U.S. 269, 280, 63 S. Ct. 236, 242, 87 L. Ed. 268 (1942); it conclusively presumes a suspect is legally incompetent to change his mind and tell the truth until an attorney is present. It denigrates an individual to a nonperson whose free will has become hostage to a lawyer so that until the lawyer consents, the suspect is deprived of any legal right or power to decide for himself that he wishes to make a disclosure. It denies that the rights to counsel and silence are personal, nondelegable, and subject to a waiver only by that individual. The opinions in support of the Court's judgment do not enlighten us as to why police conduct — whether good or bad — should operate to suspend Williams' right to change his mind and "tell all" at once rather than waiting until he reached Des Moines.

. . . . The Court seems to be saying that since Williams said he would "tell the whole story" at Des Moines, the police should have been content and waited; of course, that would have been the wiser course, especially in light of the nuances of constitutional jurisprudence applied by the Court, but a murder case ought not turn on such tenuous strands.

In any case, the Court assures us, this is not at all what it intends, and that a valid waiver was *possible* in these circumstances, but was not quite made. Here, of course, Williams did not confess to the murder in so many words; it was his conduct in guiding police to the body, not his words, which incriminated him. And the record is replete with evidence that Williams knew precisely what he was doing when he guided police to the body. The human urge to confess wrongdoing is, of course, normal in all save hardened, professional criminals, as psychiatrists and analysts have demonstrated. T. Reik, The Compulsion to Confess (1972).

. . . .

MR. JUSTICE WHITE, with whom MR. JUSTICE BLACKMUN and MR. JUSTICE REHNQUIST join, dissenting.

. . . .

II

The strictest test of waiver which might be applied to this case is that set forth in *Johnson v. Zerbst*, 304 U.S. 458, 464, 58 S. Ct. 1019, 1023, 82 L. Ed. 1461 (1938), and quoted by the majority. In order to show that a right has been waived under this test, the State must prove "an intentional relinquishment or abandonment of a known right or privilege." The majority creates no new rule preventing an accused who has retained a lawyer from waiving his right to the lawyer's presence during questioning. The majority simply finds that no waiver was proved in this case. I disagree. That respondent knew of his right not to say anything to the officers without advice and presence of counsel is established on this record to a moral certainty. He was advised of the right by three officials of the State — telling at least one that he understood the right—and by two lawyers.[4] Finally, he further demonstrated his knowledge of the right by informing the police that he would tell them the story in the presence of McKnight when they arrived in Des Moines. The issue in this case, then, is whether respondent relinquished that right intentionally.

Respondent relinquished his right not to talk to the police about his crime when the car approached the place where he had hidden the victim's clothes. Men usually intend to do what they do, and there is nothing in the record to support the proposition that respondent's decision to talk was anything but an exercise of his own free will. Apparently, without any prodding from the officers, respondent—who had earlier said that he would tell the whole story when he arrived in Des Moines—spontaneously changed him mind about the timing of his disclosures when the car approached the places where he had hidden the evidence. However, even if his statements were influenced by Detective Leaming's above-quoted statement, respondent's decision to talk in the absence of counsel can hardly be viewed as the product of an overborne will. The statement by Leaming was not coercive; it was accompanied by a request that respondent not respond to it; and it was delivered hours before respondent decided to make any statement. Respondent's waiver was thus knowing and intentional.

The majority's contrary conclusion seems to rest on the fact that respondent "asserted" his right to counsel by retaining and consulting with one lawyer and by consulting with another. How this supports the conclusion that respondent's later relinquishment of his right not to talk in the absence of counsel was unintentional is a mystery. The fact that respondent consulted with counsel on the question whether he should talk to the police in counsel's absence makes his later decision to talk in counsel's absence *better* informed and, if anything, more intelligent.

The majority recognizes that even after this "assertion" of his right to counsel, it would have found that respondent waived his right not to talk in counsel's absence if his waiver had been express—*i.e.*, if the officers had asked him in the car whether he would be willing to answer questions in counsel's absence and if he had answered "yes." But waiver is not a formalistic concept. Waiver is shown whenever the facts establish that an accused knew of a right and intended to relinquish it. Such waiver, even if not express, was plainly shown here. The only other conceivable basis for the majority's holding is the implicit suggestion that the right involved in *Massiah v. United States*, 377 U.S. 201, 84 S. Ct. 1199, 12 L. Ed. 2d 246 (1964), as distinguished from the right involved in *Miranda v. Arizona*, 384 U.S. 436, 86 S. Ct. 1602, 16 L. Ed. 2d 694 (1966), is a right not to be *asked* any questions in counsel's absence rather than a right not to *answer* any questions in counsel's absence, and that the right not to be *asked* questions must be waived *before* the questions are asked. Such wafer-thin distinctions cannot determine whether a guilty murderer should go free. The only conceivable purpose for the presence of counsel during questioning is to protect an

---

4. Moreover, he in fact received advice of counsel on at least two occasions on the question whether he should talk to the police on the trip to Des Moines.

accused from making incriminating answers. Questions, unanswered, have no significance at all. Absent coercion — no matter how the right involved is defined — an accused is amply protected by a rule requiring waiver before or simultaneously with the giving by him of an answer or the making by him of a statement.

III

The consequence of the majority's decision is, as the majority recognizes, extremely serious. A mentally disturbed killer whose guilt is not in question may be released. Why? Apparently the answer is that the majority believes that the law enforcement officers acted in a way which involves some risk of injury to society and that such conduct should be deterred. However, the officers' conduct did not, and was not likely to, jeopardize the fairness of respondent's trial or in any way risk the conviction of an innocent man — the risk against which the Sixth Amendment guarantee of assistance of counsel is designed to protect. The police did nothing "wrong," let alone anything "unconstitutional." To anyone not lost in the intricacies of the prophylactic rules of *Miranda v. Arizona*, the result in this case seems utterly senseless; and for the reasons stated in Part II, *supra*, even applying those rules as well as the rule of *Massiah v. United States, supra*, the statements made by respondent were properly admitted. In light of these considerations, the majority's protest that the result in this case is justified by a "clear violation" of the Sixth and Fourteenth Amendments has a distressing hollow ring. I respectfully dissent.

[The dissenting opinion of MR. JUSTICE BLACKMUN has been omitted.]

Notes and Questions

(1) *Massiah*'s pretrial extension of the Sixth Amendment right to the assistance of counsel, like the core right to trial assistance, may be waived by an accused. What must the prosecution prove to establish a valid waiver of the *Massiah* entitlement? What was the failure of proof in *Brewer v. Williams*? As discussed in Chapter 8, waivers of *Miranda*'s counsel safeguard need not be express but can be inferred from the circumstances. Does *Brewer v. Williams* suggest that waivers of the Sixth Amendment right to assistance must be made expressly, either orally or in writing? Should an express waiver be required or should inferred waivers be acceptable?

(2) THE "KNOWLEDGE" REQUIRED: According to *Johnson v. Zerbst*, the landmark ruling that set forth the waiver standard endorsed in *Brewer v. Williams*, to prove a waiver, the government must show "an intentional relinquishment or abandonment of a known right or privilege." What must an accused "know" to validly relinquish the *Massiah* entitlement?

In *Patterson v. Illinois*, 487 U.S. 285, 108 S. Ct. 2389, 101 L. Ed. 2d 261 (1988), the Court rejected a claim that "waiver of an accused's Sixth Amendment right to counsel should be 'more difficult' to effectuate than waiver of a suspect's Fifth Amendment [*Miranda*] rights." The case involved an arrest of Patterson and other street gang members for a murder. After receiving *Miranda* warnings, Patterson agreed to answer questions but denied knowing anything about the murder. He was held in a lock-up during the continuing investigation. Two days later, Patterson and other gang members were indicted for the murder. An officer who had questioned Patterson earlier removed him from lock-up and told him that because he had been indicted he was being transferred to the county jail. Patterson asked the officer which gang members had not been charged. Upon learning that one particular member had not been indicted, he said, "[W]hy wasn't he indicted, he did everything." Patterson also began to explain that a witness would support his account of the crime.

At this point, the officer interrupted Patterson and handed him a *Miranda* waiver form. The officer read the complete *Miranda* warnings aloud as Patterson read along. Patterson initialed each warning, signed the waiver form, and made a lengthy incriminating admission. Subsequently, he made additional statements to a prosecutor. The statements were introduced at his trial and he was convicted of murder.

A majority of the Justices held that Patterson had validly waived his right to counsel, concluding that "[a]s a general matter . . . an accused who is [given the *Miranda* warnings] has been sufficiently apprised of the nature of his Sixth Amendment rights, and of the consequences of abandoning those rights, so that his waiver on this basis will be considered a knowing and intelligent one."

In a footnote, the majority indicated that there are some situations in which the standards for waivers under *Miranda* and the Sixth Amendment would differ. "For example, we have permitted a *Miranda* waiver to stand where a suspect was not told that his lawyer was trying to reach him during questioning; in the *Sixth Amendment* context, *this waiver would not be valid*." (Emphasis added). Moreover, "a surreptitious conversation between an undercover police officer and an unindicted suspect would not give rise to any *Miranda* violation as long as the 'interrogation' was not in a custodial setting; however, once the accused is indicted, such questioning would be prohibited."

The Court left *undecided* whether "an accused must be told that he has been indicted before a postindictment Sixth Amendment waiver would be valid." It was unnecessary to resolve the question in *Patterson* because the accused conceded that he had been so informed.

(3) THE "VOLUNTARINESS" REQUIREMENT: As is always the case, a waiver must not only be sufficiently knowing, it must also be "voluntary." As in other contexts where voluntariness assessments are essential — consent searches and waivers of *Miranda* safeguards, for example — Sixth Amendment voluntariness determinations must be based on all of the relevant facts. Both official pressures and attributes that render an individual more susceptible to those pressures are surely relevant. Moreover, it seems likely that the holding of *Colorado v. Connelly* (see Chapter 8, subsection [D]) would be extended to this context. The Court would almost certainly conclude that a waiver is voluntary as long as it is "uncoerced," and that a decision to forgo assistance cannot be involuntary, for constitutional purposes, without some amount of official coercion. A purely internal psychological compulsion or pressures exerted by private parties could not, by themselves, render a decision to waive the *Massiah* right invalid.

(4) INVOCATION OF THE RIGHT TO COUNSEL AND WAIVERS: In the *Miranda* context, *Edwards v. Arizona* and its progeny hold that once a suspect clearly invokes the entitlement to counsel during custodial interrogation, no waiver of that entitlement can be valid unless the suspect initiates communications with the authorities or a 14-day break in custody ensues. Just five years after the decision in *Edwards*, in *Michigan v. Jackson*, 475 U.S. 625, 106 S. Ct. 1404, 89 L. Ed. 2d 631 (1986), the Court extended the *Edwards* rule to situations in which accused individuals assert the Sixth Amendment right to assistance.

More specifically, *Jackson* held that an indigent defendant's request for the appointment of counsel *at an arraignment* constitutes an invocation of the *Massiah* right for purposes of government efforts to deliberately elicit statements. Following such an invocation, according to the *Jackson* majority, a waiver of the *Massiah* right is not valid unless the accused initiated further communications with the authorities. The Court asserted that "the reasons for prohibiting the interrogation of an uncounseled prisoner who has asked for the help of a lawyer are even stronger after he has been formally charged with an offense than before."

In *Montejo v. Louisiana*, 556 U.S. 778, 129 S. Ct. 2079, 173 L. Ed. 2d 955 (2009), the Court reconsidered "the scope and continued viability of the [*Michigan v. Jackson*] rule" — which it described as "forbidding police to initiate interrogation of a criminal defendant once he has requested counsel at an arraignment or similar proceeding." A five-Justice majority decided that the *Jackson* rule should be overruled because the "marginal benefits of" its "prophylactic rule" were "dwarfed by its substantial costs." The holding of *Jackson* had actually been two-pronged. First, the Court had determined that a request for counsel at an arraignment was an effective invocation of *Massiah*'s Sixth Amendment right to pretrial assistance. Second, the Court had decided that once an accused invoked his Sixth Amendment entitlement, a waiver of the right to counsel was not possible if the subsequent encounter was initiated by the authorities.

In "overruling" *Jackson*, the *Montejo* majority definitively rejected the conclusion that a request for counsel at an arraignment is an invocation of the right to counsel for purposes of police questioning. A suspect's request for counsel at an arraignment no longer impedes the ability of law enforcement officers to initiate efforts to obtain a waiver of counsel and secure disclosures from an unassisted accused. More important, it seems clear that the *Montejo* majority abandoned *Jackson*'s bar to official-initiated waivers following clear requests for counsel during interactions with the police. After *Montejo*, for Sixth Amendment purposes an unambiguous invocation of the right to counsel does not erect any additional barrier to the validity of a waiver. The only question is whether the accused knowingly and voluntarily relinquished the right to assistance. According to the Justices, there was simply no need for "*Jackson*'s fourth story of prophylaxis." By barring waivers when police initiate custodial interrogation after a suspect clearly invokes the right to counsel, the rule of *Edwards v. Arizona* adequately serves *Jackson*'s only defensible purpose — to prevent officers from "badgering" suspects into changing their minds about relying on counsel.

Is there any difference between the protection provided by *Edwards* and the protection furnished by an analogous Sixth Amendment constraint upon efforts to secure waivers of the *Massiah* right to counsel from defendants who have clearly requested counsel? In thinking about this question, keep in mind that the protection of the *Edwards* rule, a branch of the *Miranda* doctrine, is restricted to cases involving custodial interrogation.

Confessions and Right to Counsel Problems

9–1: On August 30, the Decatur Police Department received a report that Melodie Dove was a missing person. On September 11, Officer Mowen of the Decatur Police Department received an anonymous phone call from an unknown male who said that Melodie's husband, Gerald Wayne Dove, had tied and gagged Melodie, taken her outside of the county and was bringing food and water to her. Subsequently, the police learned that the caller was Gerald Alsup, a long-time friend of Gerald Dove.

Following another conversation between the police and Alsup, the prosecutor issued an arrest warrant for Gerald Wayne Dove. After the Decatur police received the arrest warrant, Officer Mowen recruited Alsup to obtain evidence from Dove. Alsup agreed to wear an electronic listening device and to engage Dove in a conversation regarding Melodie's location and condition. During this conversation, Alsup asked Dove numerous questions about Melodie's condition. Dove told Alsup that Melodie was alive and in good condition despite the fact that he had repeatedly struck her. He did not disclose Melodie's location.

Dove was arrested at 8:00 p.m. on September 11, shortly after his conversation with Alsup. When the police sought to interrogate him, Dove requested counsel and the interrogation was terminated. A week later, after Dove had been transferred to the county prison, the prosecutor filed a three-count information against Dove, charging him with murder, and counsel was appointed to represent him. On September 15, Alsup notified the Decatur police that Dove had telephoned Alsup at home and asked Alsup to visit him in jail. The Decatur police arranged Alsup's visit but, after discussing the case with the State's Attorney, told Alsup that "he would be strictly on his own, that he could not question Dove on behalf of the police, that he was not being asked to interrogate Dove, and that he was under no obligation to report the content of any conversation with Dove." The police also requested Alsup to inform them if Melodie was still alive so they might rescue her.

During the September 15th conversation with Alsup, Dove admitted that he had killed Melodie, told Alsup where the body was located, and asked Alsup to move the body to avoid its discovery by the police. Alsup met with the police and negotiated a deal under which he would receive immunity from prosecution in exchange for information regarding Melodie's murder. Based on that information, the police located Melodie's body.

976 9 · CONFESSIONS AND THE RIGHT TO ASSISTANCE OF COUNSEL

At Dove's trial, Alsup testified to the two conversations between himself and Dove. Dove was convicted. On appeal, Dove claims that Alsup's testimony was admitted in violation of his Sixth Amendment Right to Counsel.

How should the appellate court rule?

9–2: In order to sexually abuse nine-year-old Molly, Jack led her to believe that a fictitious organization named "Brockenridge" would kill her and her family if she did not follow the group's instructions. Jack sent email messages from a "Brockenridge" member named "Charles," telling Molly that Jack was her "sexual trainer" and advising her to engage in sex acts with him. Jack proceeded to sexually abuse Molly for five years. When she was 14 years old, an email message informed Molly that she should invite 12-year-old Janice to a party. On the morning of the supposed party, Jack and Molly picked Janice up in his car, dropped her off at a convenience store, and then picked her up again. According to the government, Jack then drugged, raped, and murdered Janice. Four days later, after police determined that the emails to Molly had come from Jack's computer, Jack was arrested. A criminal complaint was filed charging Jack with kidnapping and raping Janice. Soon thereafter, the police discovered Janice's body.

While in jail, Jack sent letters to his friend Michael asserting his innocence and asking for help. He asked Michael to visit, suggesting that he pose as Jack's attorney in a civil matter. Michael contacted the authorities. A team consisting of agents not working on the case pending against Jack was assigned to investigate. Subsequently, Jack called Michael and asked him to call on the "attorney line," which was not monitored. He followed up with a letter stressing that Michael's help was essential and that all he needed was "a few emails and text messages."

A few days later, agents met with Michael and helped him place a recorded phone call to Jack on the attorney line. They instructed Michael not to ask Jack anything about the crimes charged. During the call, Jack told Michael that he was being framed by some "bad guys" and that he needed Michael to send messages informing Molly that "the bad guys were still out there." About a week later, after Jack expressed concern at Michael's inaction, Michael made another recorded phone call to Jack. Jack stated that Michael had to contact Molly soon and that he had mailed a package to Michael explaining the steps he should take. This "package of instructions" told Michael to send Molly emails from Eric and Charles instructing her to tell the police and the media that Jack was innocent and had been framed.

A week later, Michael visited Jack. Prior to the visit, agents instructed Michael not to initiate any inquiries about the pending charges. During recorded conversations, Jack told Michael to expect to be contacted by the authorities. He asserted that he was innocent, had merely dropped Janice off at a convenience store, and that Brockenridge had framed him by planting evidence. During the meeting Michael asked, "What did they [Brockenridge] do? What kind of evidence?" and "Were you arrested at the time the girl's body was found?" Michael also told Jack that he would assist with the plan. Out of curiosity, Michael also asked Jack about criminal conduct he had engaged in 20 years earlier.

Prior to trial for kidnapping, rape, and murder, Jack moved, on Sixth Amendment grounds, to suppress statements he made during the telephone calls, in the package of instructions, and during the meeting at the jail.

Should the trial judge grant Jack's motion?

9–3: Johnson, Bullard, and several other individuals were arrested and indicted for various narcotics offenses. Bullard entered into a plea agreement with the government. Upon learning that Bullard was pleading guilty, Johnson called Bullard and asked to meet with him. Bullard responded that they both should check with their attorneys before having a meeting. Johnson called his attorney who advised him against meeting with Bullard. Bullard called the prosecutor who referred him to the IRS agent in charge of the case. The agent asked Bullard if he would be willing to be wired and talk to Johnson. Bullard agreed. The agent knew that Johnson was represented by counsel. He nevertheless advised Bullard to meet with Johnson and see what he wanted.

A few days later, Bullard phoned Johnson and told him he could visit him at his home. When they met at Johnson's home, Bullard "acted sympathetic to Johnson, his plight, and his fears." At Johnson's request, he showed Johnson a copy of the statement he had made to the police. In the course of pointing out inaccuracies in Bullard's statement, Johnson made numerous incriminating admissions. Some of these admissions were made in response to specific questions from Bullard. All of Johnson's admissions were recorded.

Throughout the meeting, Johnson stated that he knew meeting with Bullard was risky. At one point, he referred to the possibility that Bullard was "setting him up" but said he had concluded that Bullard would not do that to him. Bullard told Johnson he was meeting with him in defiance of the government's wishes. When Johnson expressed concern about government surveillance, Bullard replied, "I know. I'm paranoid too." Throughout the conversation, Bullard made statements portraying the government as his adversary.

May Bullard testify about Johnson's admissions?

9-4: On May 8, the state filed a criminal complaint against Brad charging him with attempted second-degree sexual assault and false imprisonment. A warrant was issued for his arrest. Brad was arrested in a neighboring state and made a court appearance there with his brother, Scott, who was licensed to practice law in that state. Brad waived extradition and was transported to the state where the complaint was pending in the early morning hours of May 16. The district attorney's office was notified that Brad was represented by counsel, and his brother contacted Sheriff's Department Detective Webb.

On the morning of May 16, Sheriff's Department Detective Lander, who had reviewed Detective Webb's notes, questioned Brad. He first recited the *Miranda* warnings. After 28 minutes of inquiry regarding whether Brad was willing to waive his right to have counsel present, Lander repeatedly told Brad that he would like to hear his side of the story; that it was usually better if law enforcement knew both sides of the story; and that Lander knew only one side of the story, but that he could not hear Brad's side unless Brad signed the waiver of rights form. Brad gave a verbal waiver and completed a waiver of rights form. Throughout the remainder of the interrogation, Brad made incriminating statements.

Immediately after the interrogation, Brad was taken to court for an initial appearance. Rebecca, an attorney with a local law firm, was present to represent Brad. Brad was, in fact, represented by both the law firm and his brother, Scott, prior to the interrogation. Before trial, Brad moved to suppress his statements to Lander on right to counsel grounds.

Does Brad have a valid Sixth Amendment claim?

9–5: On September 22, 1969, eight-year-old Susan Nason disappeared from her home. In December 1969, her body was found in a mountainous area several miles away. She had been beaten to death. The investigation of her murder remained open for many years. In November 1989, Eileen Franklin, who had been a schoolmate of Susan's, told the police that she had seen her father, George Franklin, murder Susan. Based on this information, George Franklin was arrested for Susan's murder and given *Miranda* warnings. In response, Franklin invoked his right to an attorney. After conferring with his attorney, he told the police that he would not discuss the case with anyone unless counsel was present. Franklin was then formally charged with the crime and placed in a cell of the County Jail, pending trial. At that time, he was informed that anything he said to a visitor over the jail telephone could be monitored by jail officials.

Soon thereafter, Eileen Franklin contacted Deputy District Attorney Martin Murray and told him she would visit the jail and try to get her father to confess. Murray replied, "I can't ask you to do that." Eileen then said, "You are not asking me. It's entirely my idea." Murray responded, "It's not a bad idea." He then gave her the name of a jail official who could arrange the visit.

The jail official arranged to have Eileen visit her father at a time when visiting was not generally allowed. During the visit, Eileen suggested to her father that "he should tell the truth." In response, George Franklin pointed to a sign in the visiting room that stated "Conversations May be Monitored."

At trial, Eileen testified that her father had been silent when she suggested that he tell the truth. In closing argument, the prosecutor argued that Franklin's response to his daughter was an adoptive admission that "compellingly" proved his guilt. The judge instructed the jury that they could properly consider Franklin's silence as evidence of his guilt. The jury convicted him of murder. On appeal, Franklin claims his conviction should be reversed because Eileen's testimony relating to his silence violated his Fifth and Sixth Amendment rights.

Should Franklin's conviction be reversed?

9–6: Late on the night of October 1, state and federal law enforcement officers were conducting joint surveillance of a motel after receiving a tip that cocaine would be delivered. They arrested Francisco after he entered the motel. When federal agent Jordi interrogated Francisco, he stated that he had recently returned from another state with 500 grams of cocaine, that the cocaine was in Room 333, that an individual wearing a red t-shirt was in the room, and that a white truck was associated with the drug ring. When officers saw Samuel, clad in a red t-shirt, exit Room 333 and climb into a white truck, they arrested him.

Agent Jordi recited the *Miranda* warnings and Samuel agreed to talk. He stated that he was staying in Room 338, and gave Jordi permission to search the room. Officers recovered 250 grams of cocaine from Room 333 and a suitcase full of marijuana and a handgun from Room 338. Early in the morning of October 2, Samuel was taken to the police station. Agent Jordi again recited the *Miranda* warnings and interrogated him there.

Later that same day, the state issued arrest warrants for Samuel, charging him with possession with intent to manufacture, sell, give, or distribute cocaine, and with conspiracy to manufacture, sell, give, or distribute cocaine. According to the warrants, these charges concerned only the events of October 1 and 2. Samuel requested counsel, and the state appointed a lawyer. The state retained custody of Samuel until a December 5 preliminary hearing at which all the charges were dismissed. On December 4, the day prior to the preliminary hearing in state court, federal agents had filed a federal criminal complaint against Samuel, and had obtained a warrant for his arrest. Agent Jordi was present at the courthouse when the state charges were dismissed. He immediately took Samuel into federal custody and took him to a local police station.

At the station, Samuel told Agent Jordi that he was glad to see him and wanted to give his side of the story. After *Miranda* warnings, the two men had a 45 minute conversation. Samuel made incriminating statements and provided several details about his involvement in the drug conspiracy. After the conversation ended, Agent Jordi took Samuel before a judge for an initial appearance.

Are the statements made to Agent Jordi admissible under Sixth Amendment standards?

9–7: Con met a group of friends at "Dolls," a strip bar. At closing time, a racial confrontation erupted in the Dolls parking lot between a large group of white males (Con's group) and a smaller group of black males. The brawl lasted several minutes and involved between 25 and 40 people. During the fighting, Mandel cut Con with a knife. Con and his friend, Rob, went to a car and retrieved a semiautomatic handgun. Con began shooting at Mandel, emptying his 8-shot weapon. Mandel died of multiple gunshot wounds.

On February 23, Con was arrested. He was jailed in the same cellblock as Ronald, a man who had been in jail for six months before Con's arrest. The two men had not previously known each other. On March 5, Con was indicted for aggravated murder. Around the time he was indicted, Con discovered that Ronald was his distant cousin. At some point, Con confided to Ronald that he was the shooter in the incident at Dolls. Con also attempted to enlist Ronald to kill a witness to the Dolls shooting and to stage a false confession by coercing someone else to admit on videotape to the Dolls shooting. Con promised Ronald $30,000 for killing a witness and arranged for $5,000 to be deposited in Ronald's jail commissary account as an advance payment.

On April 4, Ronald wrote a letter to a prosecutor in the Dolls shooting case, informing her that he had information regarding Con's involvement in the shooting. Ronald wrote her a second letter, dated April 10, reiterating that Con was involved in the Dolls shooting and adding that Con had offered him a contract to kill a witness. On April 25, detectives interviewed Ronald. Ronald provided information about the Dolls shooting, about Con's plan to murder a witness, and about his effort to stage a false confession. Ronald and law enforcement officials discussed a plan to record Ronald's subsequent conversations with Con.

On May 16, the state placed Ronald on work release from jail, and he began working with the Sheriff's Office in its investigation of Con. Between May 17 and May 24, a series of conversations was recorded in which Ronald and Con talked about Con's plans to kill a witness and stage a false confession.

Before his trial for aggravated murder, Con moved to suppress the statements he made to Ronald. After an evidentiary hearing, the trial judge denied the motion. During the state's case-in-chief, Ronald testified about conversations with Con both before and after he began working with the detectives. Con was convicted and sentenced to death. He appealed, claiming that the judge erred in denying his motion to suppress.

How should the court of appeals rule?

9–8: On February 23, 1992, Russell was shot 23 times. He died as a result. After several eyewitnesses identified Lind as the shooter, he was arrested in connection with the Russell murder. Lind was informed of his *Miranda* rights, and signed a form indicating that he was not willing to talk to police without an attorney present. After detaining Lind for several months, the government dismissed the charges against him.

Lind was arrested again in May of 1994 — this time on federal drug charges. He agreed to cooperate with law enforcement agents and pleaded guilty to distribution of cocaine pursuant to a plea agreement. Until his sentencing about a year later, Lind continued to cooperate with law enforcement authorities.

In August of 1997, Officer Hera visited Lind at the federal minimum security facility where he was serving his sentence on the cocaine charge. Lind was in a work-release program. While he was taking a GED test, Lind was summoned to meet with Hera in a conference room. After some initial pleasantries, the officer told Lind that he had new evidence relating to the Russell murder and that he believed Lind was involved. Hera provided "a detailed synopsis" of the events before, during and after the murder. Hera did not read Lind his *Miranda* rights, but notified him that he was not under arrest and did not have to talk about the murder. Hera did indicate, however, that he wanted Lind to cooperate on a new drug investigation and that it could be easier on him if he assisted in the investigation. Lind confessed to killing Russell.

Several months later, while he was still serving his federal sentence, Lind was arrested for the murder of Russell. In August of 1998, a grand jury indicted Lind for the murder. Prior to trial, he filed a motion to suppress his confession. After a three-day hearing, the trial judge stated: "I don't believe that the accused was in custody at the time he confessed. I also believe his confession was voluntary."

Does Lind have a valid *Massiah* doctrine claim for suppression?

9–9: The Ronde, an apartment complex owned and managed by the Metropolitan Housing Authority (MHA), serves elderly and disabled residents. Dorothy, a 76-year-old resident, was found dead in her apartment at 2:45 p.m. on December 17. She had suffered numerous serious injuries, several of which were "defensive." The police arrived at The Ronde at approximately 3:13 p.m. David was standing outside Dorothy's unit in a highly agitated state. According to one officer, he was "bawling," and his hands shook as he answered officers' questions. Officers learned that David was employed by MHA as a special police officer to provide security at The Ronde. As partial compensation, he was allowed to live at The Ronde for $50 per month. David knew Dorothy fairly well and had been in her apartment on several occasions. In the early morning hours of December 17, at approximately 2:00 a.m., he had gone to Dorothy's apartment to assist her because she had fallen and was unable to get up.

On March 14, David was arrested for murdering Dorothy. He was indicted on March 27. While awaiting trial, David was assigned to the same pod in the county jail as Donald, who was incarcerated for "passing bad checks." Donald introduced himself to David on his first day in jail during Bible class. According to Donald, David spoke frequently about his case from the very beginning of their association. At first, he denied murdering Dorothy, but later his story changed and he confessed to the murder. About one week after this confession, Donald contacted the police and met with the detectives assigned to investigate Dorothy's murder. Donald told them of David's confession and indicated that he would be willing to testify at a trial. The detectives informed him that prosecutors would likely be contacting him, then sent him back to the jail pod that he shared with David. In their report, the detectives specifically noted that Donald had not provided significant details about the murder weapon and the amount of money taken from Dorothy's apartment.

Within an hour of meeting with the detectives, Donald questioned David about the murder weapon and the sum of money stolen. David allegedly told him that he had used a small, black iron to kill Dorothy and that he had stolen $700 from her. The next day, Donald telephoned his wife and asked her to contact the police on his behalf. Soon thereafter, the police placed him in protective custody.

Prior to trial, David moved to suppress Donald's testimony regarding his statements about the murder weapon and amount of money stolen. The motion was denied. Based largely on Donald's testimony, David was convicted of murder. He appealed, claiming that Donald's testimony was inadmissible under the *Massiah* doctrine.

How should the appellate court rule?

9–10: On July 26, the State issued an arrest warrant for Anson and charged him with three counts of sexual contact with a child under the age of 16. On August 3, two police officers went to Anson's workplace. Their goal was to obtain a statement from Anson relating to the charges and then to arrest him.

The officers asked Anson if they could speak with him and Anson agreed. Anson then said, "I haven't been charged with anything yet." One of the officers responded, "Right," and added, "You understand you are not under arrest right now?" Anson responded affirmatively.

After a preliminary discussion, the officers told Anson about the alleged victim's allegations. One of the officers then asked Anson, "Why would she make up such a story?" Anson responded that the alleged victim had some grounds for her allegations. He went on to admit that he had had some sexual contact with her. After the interview, the officers arrested Anson.

At his trial, Anson's statements were admitted into evidence and he was convicted on one of the three counts. On appeal, Anson claims that the admission of his statements violated his Sixth Amendment right to counsel.

How should the appellate court rule?

Selected Bibliography

Craig Bradley, *What's Left of* Massiah? 45 Tex. Tech L. Rev. 247 (2012)

Martin R. Gardner, *The Right to Be Free from Uncounseled Interrogation: A Sixth Amendment Doctrine in Search of a Rationale*, 63 Baylor L. Rev. 80 (2011)

Brooks Holland, *A Relational Sixth Amendment During Interrogation*, 99 J. Crim. L. & Criminology 381 (2009)

Yale Kamisar, Police Interrogation and Confessions: Essays in Law and Policy (1980)

Carol S. Steiker, *Counter-Revolution in Constitutional Criminal Procedure? Two Audiences, Two Answers*, 94 Mich. L. Rev. 2466 (1996)

Eda Katharine Tinto, *Wavering on Waiver:* Montejo v. Louisiana *and the Sixth Amendment Right to Counsel*, 48 Am. Crim. L. Rev. 1335 (2011)

James J. Tomkovicz, *An Adversary System Defense of the Right to Counsel Against Informants: Truth, Fair Play, and the* Massiah *Doctrine*, 22 U.C. Davis L. Rev. 1 (1988)

James J. Tomkovicz, *Reaffirming the Right to Pretrial Assistance: The Surprising Little Case of* Fellers v. United States, 15 Wm. & Mary Bill Rts. J. 501 (2006)

James J. Tomkovicz, *Sacrificing* Massiah: *Confusion Over Exclusion and Erosion of the Right to Counsel,* 16 Lewis & Clark L. Rev. 1 (2012)

H. Richard Uviller, *Evidence from the Mind of the Criminal Suspect: A Reconsideration of the Current Rules of Access and Restraint,* 87 Colum. L. Rev. 1137 (1987)

Welsh S. White, *Interrogation Without Questions:* Rhode Island v. Innis *and* United States v. Henry, 78 Mich. L. Rev. 1209 (1980)

Jonathan Witmer-Rich, *Interrogation and the Roberts Court,* 63 Fla. L. Rev. 1189 (2011)

Part IV
Identifications

Chapter 10

Identifications and the Right to Assistance of Counsel

Introductory Note

Prior to the late 1960s, there was no constitutional regulation of eyewitness identification processes or of identification evidence secured by means of such processes. On a single, momentous day in 1967, the Supreme Court dramatically changed the landscape. In three significant and somewhat controversial opinions, the Justices announced that the Constitution did have quite a bit to say about official efforts to secure identifications and about the admissibility of eyewitness identification evidence in the courtroom. In the first two opinions, the Court declared that the Sixth Amendment right to the assistance of counsel imposed some controls. In the third of the trilogy, the Justices announced that the Due Process Clause also constrained the government's efforts to generate and use identification evidence. The right to counsel doctrine is the subject of this chapter. The due process restrictions are considered in Chapter 11. Unlike the rights discussed in other Parts of this text, the constitutional protections against efforts to identify individuals as the perpetrators of crimes have not been the subject of ongoing development by the Supreme Court. The last time the Justices addressed an issue involving the Sixth Amendment safeguard against eyewitness identification evidence was 1977. See *Moore v. Illinois*, 434 U.S. 220, 98 S. Ct. 458, 54 L. Ed. 2d 424 (1977), discussed *infra*. And since 1977, the due process safeguard has been the subject of only one relatively minor 2012 ruling. See *Perry v. New Hampshire*, 565 U.S. ____, 132 S. Ct. 716, 181 L. Ed. 2d 694 (2012), which appears in the notes at the end of Chapter 11. Thus, the evolution of the Warren Court's revolutionary constitutional identification safeguards occurred within a mere 10-year span following their arrival.

Before beginning this chapter, students may find it useful to reread the Introductory Note to Chapter 9, which offers a thorough summary of the background and development of the Sixth Amendment right to counsel. That note highlights that this fundamental right has been interpreted to include a right to appointed assistance for indigent defendants, and that it has been expanded to apply not only to trials but also to critical pretrial stages of prosecutions. As pointed out in Chapter 9, the Warren Court extended the right to counsel to two types of "informal" pretrial confrontation between the government and the accused that occur outside courtrooms. One informal critical stage is defined by the *Massiah* doctrine, which, as was seen in Chapter 9, recognizes a right to assistance when a government agent "deliberately elicits" incriminating statements after a formal charge. The other informal critical stage is the one addressed in the instant chapter. In *United States v. Wade*, 388 U.S. 218, 87 S. Ct. 1926, 18 L. Ed. 2d 1149 (1967), the initial and foundational case in this chapter, a majority of the Justices concluded that a lineup for purposes of identification is a critical stage that triggers an accused's right to counsel. Like the decision in *Massiah*, the *Wade* Court's decision to recognize a right to counsel at an entirely extra-judicial phase of the criminal process was quite controversial. It divided the Court, provoking dissenters to object that extension of the Sixth Amendment guarantee to lineups was a serious constitutional misstep, an entirely unjustifiable interpretation of the reach and function of the right to counsel.

In considering the meaning and merits of *Wade*, students should focus on several basic questions. First, what did the *Wade* Court perceive as the dangers posed by government identification procedures and how did it attempt to alleviate those dangers? Second, to what extent was *Wade* likely to eliminate the perceived dangers? Third, what role did the Court expect counsel to play at pretrial identifications? Fourth, what was the constitutional basis for assigning counsel this role? And, finally, is the *Wade* decision consistent with the underlying purposes and objectives of the Sixth Amendment right to counsel, or is there merit to the dissenters' view that there is neither need nor justification for extending the counsel guarantee to law enforcement procedures designed to secure eyewitness identifications?

In reading the later cases in this chapter, students should try to identify the specific circumstances necessary for exclusion of identification evidence on Sixth Amendment grounds. In addition, students should consider whether these later decisions are consistent with either *Wade* or the Sixth Amendment right to counsel.

United States v. Wade

United States Supreme Court

388 U.S. 218, 87 S. Ct. 1926, 18 L. Ed. 2d 1149 (1967)

MR. JUSTICE BRENNAN delivered the opinion of the Court.

The question here is whether courtroom identifications of an accused at trial are to be excluded from evidence because the accused was exhibited to the witnesses before trial at a post-indictment lineup conducted for identification purposes without notice to and in the absence of the accused's appointed counsel.

The federally insured bank in Eustace, Texas, was robbed on September 21, 1964. A man with a small strip of tape on each side of his face entered the bank, pointed a pistol at the female cashier and the vice president, the only persons in the bank at the time, and forced them to fill a pillowcase with the bank's money. The man then drove away with an accomplice who had been waiting in a stolen car outside the bank. On March 23, 1965, an indictment was returned against respondent, Wade, and two others for conspiring to rob the bank, and against Wade and the accomplice for the robbery itself. Wade was arrested on April 2, and counsel was appointed to represent him on April 26. Fifteen days later an FBI agent, without notice to Wade's lawyer, arranged to have the two bank employees observe a lineup made up of Wade and five or six other prisoners and conducted in a courtroom of the local county courthouse. Each person in the line wore strips of tape such as allegedly worn by the robber and upon direction each said something like "put the money in the bag," the words allegedly uttered by the robber. Both bank employees identified Wade in the lineup as the bank robber.

At trial the two employees, when asked on direct examination if the robber was in the courtroom, pointed to Wade. The prior lineup identification was then elicited from both employees on cross-examination. At the close of testimony, Wade's counsel moved for a judgment of acquittal or, alternatively, to strike the bank officials' courtroom identifications on the ground that conduct of the lineup, without notice to and in the absence of his appointed counsel, violated his Fifth Amendment privilege against self-incrimination and his Sixth Amendment right to the assistance of counsel. The motion was denied, and Wade was convicted. The Court of Appeals for the Fifth Circuit reversed the conviction and ordered a new trial at which the in-court identification evidence was to be excluded, holding that, though the lineup did not violate Wade's Fifth Amendment rights, "the lineup, held as it was, in the absence of counsel, already chosen to represent appellant, was a violation of his Sixth Amendment rights. . . ." 358 F.2d 557, 560. . . .

I

Neither the lineup itself nor anything shown by this record that Wade was required to do in the lineup violated his privilege against self-incrimination. We have only recently reaffirmed that the privilege "protects an accused only from being compelled to testify against himself, or otherwise provide the State with evidence of a testimonial or communicative nature. . . ." *Schmerber v. California*, 384 U.S. 757, 761, 86 S. Ct. 1826, 1830, 16 L. Ed. 2d 908. We there held that compelling a suspect to submit to a withdrawal of a sample of his blood for analysis for alcohol content and the admission in evidence of the analysis report were not compulsion to those ends. That holding was supported by the opinion in *Holt v. United States*, 218 U.S. 245, 31 S. Ct. 2, 54 L. Ed. 1021, in which case a question arose as to whether a blouse belonged to the defendant. A witness testified at trial that the defendant put on the blouse and it had fit him. The defendant argued that the admission of the testimony was error because compelling him to put on the blouse was a violation of his privilege. The Court rejected the claim as "an extravagant extension of the Fifth Amendment," Mr. Justice Holmes saying for the Court:

> [T]he prohibition of compelling a man in a criminal court to be witness against himself is a prohibition of the use of physical or moral compulsion

to extort communications from him, not an exclusion of his body as evidence when it may be material.

218 U.S. at 252–253, 31 S. Ct. at 6. The Court in *Holt*, however, put aside any constitutional questions which might be involved in compelling an accused, as here, to exhibit himself before victims of or witnesses to an alleged crime; the Court stated, "we need [not] consider how far a court would go in compelling a man to exhibit himself." *Id.* at 253, 31 S. Ct. at 6.

We have no doubt that compelling the accused merely to exhibit his person for observation by a prosecution witness prior to trial involves no compulsion of the accused to give evidence having testimonial significance. It is compulsion of the accused to exhibit his physical characteristics, not compulsion to disclose any knowledge he might have. It is no different from compelling Schmerber to provide a blood sample or Holt to wear the blouse, and, as in those instances, is not within the cover of the privilege. Similarly, compelling Wade to speak within hearing distance of the witnesses, even to utter words purportedly uttered by the robber, was not compulsion to utter statements of a "testimonial" nature; he was required to use his voice as an identifying physical characteristic, not to speak his guilt. We held in *Schmerber, supra,* 384 U.S. at 761, 86 S. Ct. at 1830, that the distinction to be drawn under the Fifth Amendment privilege against self-incrimination is one between an accused's "communications" in whatever form, vocal or physical, and "compulsion which makes a suspect or accused the source of 'real or physical evidence,'" *Schmerber, supra* at 764, 86 S. Ct. at 1832. We recognized that "both federal and state courts have usually held that . . . [the privilege] offers no protection against compulsion to submit to fingerprinting, photography, or measurements, to write or speak for identification, to appear in court, to stand, to assume a stance, to walk, or to make a particular gesture." *Id.* at 764, 86 S. Ct. at 1832. None of these activities becomes testimonial within the scope of the privilege because required of the accused in a pretrial lineup.

Moreover, it deserves emphasis that this case presents no question of the admissibility in evidence of anything Wade said or did at the lineup which implicates his privilege. The Government offered no such evidence as part of its case, and what came out about the lineup proceedings on Wade's cross-examination of the bank employees involved no violation of Wade's privilege.

II

The fact that the lineup involved no violation of Wade's privilege against self-incrimination does not, however, dispose of his contention that the courtroom identifications should have been excluded because the lineup was conducted without notice to and in the absence of his counsel. Our rejection of the right to counsel claim in *Schmerber* rested on our conclusion in that case that "[n]o issue of counsel's ability to assist petitioner in respect of any rights he did possess is presented." 384 U.S. at 766, 86 S. Ct. at 1833. In contrast, in this case it is urged that the assistance of counsel at the lineup was indispensable to protect Wade's most basic right as a criminal defendant — his right to a fair trial at which the witnesses against him might be meaningfully cross-examined.

The Framers of the Bill of Rights envisaged a broader role for counsel than under the practice then prevailing in England of merely advising his client in "matters of law," and eschewing any responsibility for "matters of fact." The constitutions in at least 11 of the 13 States expressly or impliedly abolished this distinction. "Though the colonial provisions about counsel were in accord on few things, they agreed on the necessity of abolishing the facts-law distinction; the colonists appreciated that if a defendant were forced to stand alone against the state, his case was foredoomed." 73 Yale L.J. 1000, 1033–1034. This background is reflected in the scope given by our decisions to the Sixth Amendment's guarantee to an accused of the assistance of counsel for his defense. When the Bill of Rights was adopted, there were no organized police forces as we know them today. The accused confronted the prosecutor and the witnesses against him, and the evidence was marshalled, largely at the trial itself. In contrast, today's law enforcement machinery involves critical confrontations of the accused by the prosecution at pretrial proceedings where the results might well settle the accused's fate and reduce the trial itself to a mere formality. In recognition of these realities of modern criminal prosecution, our cases have construed the Sixth Amendment guarantee to apply to "critical" stages of the proceedings. The guarantee reads: "In all criminal prosecutions, the accused shall enjoy the right . . . to have the Assistance of Counsel *for his defence.*" (Emphasis supplied.) The plain wording of this guarantee thus encompasses counsel's assistance whenever necessary to assure a meaningful "defence."

As early as *Powell v. Alabama*, 287 U.S. 45, 53 S. Ct. 55, 77 L. Ed. 158 (1932), we recognized that the period from arraignment to trial was "perhaps the most critical period of the proceedings . . . ," *id.* at 57, 53 S. Ct. at 59, during which the accused "requires the guiding hand of counsel . . . ," *id.* at 69, 53 S. Ct. at 64, if the guarantee is not to prove an empty right. That principle has since been applied to require the assistance of counsel at the type of arraignment — for example, that provided by Alabama — where certain rights might be sacrificed or lost: "What happens there may affect the whole trial. Available defenses may be irretrievably lost, if not then and there asserted. . . ." *Hamilton v. Alabama*, 368 U.S. 52, 54, 82 S. Ct. 157, 159, 7 L. Ed. 2d 114. The principle was also applied in *Massiah v. United States*, 377 U.S. 201, 84 S. Ct. 1199, 12 L. Ed. 2d 246, where we held that incriminating statements of the defendant should have been excluded from evidence when it appeared that they were overheard by federal agents who, without notice to the defendant's lawyer, arranged a meeting between the defendant and an accomplice turned informant. We said, quoting a concurring opinion in *Spano v. New York*, 360 U.S. 315, 326, 79 S. Ct. 1202, 1209, 3 L. Ed. 2d 1265, that "[a]nything less . . . might deny a defendant 'effective representation by counsel at the only stage when legal aid and advice would help him.'" 377 U.S. at 204, 84 S. Ct. at 1202.

In *Escobedo v. Illinois*, 378 U.S. 478, 84 S. Ct. 1758, 12 L. Ed. 2d 977, we drew upon the rationale of *Hamilton* and *Massiah* in holding that the right to counsel was guaranteed at the point where the accused, prior to arraignment, was subjected to secret interrogation despite repeated requests to see his lawyer. We again noted the necessity of counsel's presence if the accused was to have a fair opportunity to present a defense at the trial itself:

> The rule sought by the State here, however, would make the trial no more than an appeal from the interrogation; and the "right to use counsel at the formal trial [would be] a very hollow thing [if], for all practical purposes, the conviction is already assured by pretrial examination".... "One can imagine a cynical prosecutor saying: 'Let them have the most illustrious counsel, now. They cannot escape the noose. There is nothing that counsel can do for them at the trial.'"

378 U.S. at 487–488, 84 S. Ct. at 1763.

Finally in *Miranda v. Arizona*, 384 U.S. 436, 86 S. Ct. 1602, 16 L. Ed. 2d 694, the rules established for custodial interrogation included the right to the presence of counsel. The result was rested on our finding that this and the other rules were necessary to safeguard the privilege against self-incrimination from being jeopardized by such interrogation.

Of course, nothing decided or said in the opinions in the cited cases links the right to counsel only to protection of Fifth Amendment rights. Rather, those decisions "no more than [reflect] a constitutional principle established as long ago as *Powell v. Alabama*...." *Massiah v. United States, supra*, 377 U.S. at 205, 84 S. Ct. at 1202. It is central to that principle that in addition to counsel's presence at trial, the accused is guaranteed that he need not stand alone against the State at any stage of the prosecution, formal or informal, in court or out, where counsel's absence might derogate from the accused's right to a fair trial. The security of that right is as much the aim of the right to counsel as it is of the other guarantees of the Sixth Amendment — the right of the accused to a speedy and public trial by an impartial jury, his right to be informed of the nature and cause of the accusation, and his right to be confronted with the witnesses against him and to have compulsory process for obtaining witnesses in his favor. The presence of counsel at such critical confrontations, as at the trial itself, operates to assure that the accused's interests will be protected consistently with our adversary theory of criminal prosecution.

In sum, the principle of *Powell v. Alabama* and succeeding cases requires that we scrutinize *any* pretrial confrontation of the accused to determine whether the presence of his counsel is necessary to preserve the defendant's basic right to a fair trial as affected by his right meaningfully to cross-examine the witnesses against him and to have effective assistance of counsel at the trial itself. It calls upon us to analyze whether potential substantial prejudice to defendant's rights inheres in the particular confrontation and the ability of counsel to help avoid that prejudice.

III

The Government characterizes the lineup as a mere preparatory step in the gathering of the prosecution's evidence, not different — for Sixth Amendment purposes — from various other preparatory steps, such as systematized or scientific analyzing of the accused's fingerprints, blood sample, clothing, hair, and the like. We think there are differences which preclude such stages being characterized as critical stages at which the accused has the right to the presence of his counsel. Knowledge of the techniques of science and technology is sufficiently available, and the variables in techniques few enough, that the accused has the opportunity for a meaningful confrontation of the Government's case at trial through the ordinary processes of cross-examination of the Government's expert witnesses and the presentation of the evidence of his own experts. The denial of a right to have his counsel present at such analyses does not therefore violate the Sixth Amendment; they are not critical stages since there is minimal risk that his counsel's absence at such stages might derogate from his right to a fair trial.

IV

But the confrontation compelled by the State between the accused and the victim or witnesses to a crime to elicit identification evidence is peculiarly riddled with innumerable dangers and variable factors which might seriously, even crucially, derogate from a fair trial. The vagaries of eyewitness identification are well-known; the annals of criminal law are rife with instances of mistaken identification.[6] Mr. Justice Frankfurter once said: "What is the worth of identification testimony even when uncontradicted? The identification of strangers is proverbially untrustworthy. The hazards of such testimony are established by a formidable number of instances in the records of English and American trials. These instances are recent — not due to the brutalities of ancient criminal procedure." THE CASE OF SACCO AND VANZETTI 30 (1927). A major factor contributing to the high incidence of miscarriage of justice from mistaken identification has been the degree of suggestion inherent in the manner in which the prosecution presents the suspect to witnesses for pretrial identification. A commentator has observed that "[t]he influence of improper suggestion upon identifying witnesses probably accounts for more miscarriages of justice than any other single factor — perhaps it is responsible for more such errors than all other factors combined." Wall, EYE-WITNESS IDENTIFICATION IN CRIMINAL CASES 26. Suggestion can be created intentionally or unintentionally in many subtle ways. And the dangers for the suspect are particularly grave when the witness' opportunity for observation was insubstantial, and thus his susceptibility to suggestion the greatest.

---

6. Borchard, CONVICTING THE INNOCENT; Frank & Frank, NOT GUILTY; Wall, EYE-WITNESS IDENTIFICATION IN CRIMINAL CASES; 3 Wigmore, EVIDENCE § 786a (3d ed. 1940); Rolph, PERSONAL IDENTITY; Gross, CRIMINAL INVESTIGATION 47–54 (Jackson ed. 1962); Williams, PROOF OF GUILT 83–98 (1955); Wills, CIRCUMSTANTIAL EVIDENCE 192–205 (7th ed. 1937); Wigmore, THE SCIENCE OF JUDICIAL PROOF §§ 250–253 (3d ed. 1937).

Moreover, "[i]t is a matter of common experience that, once a witness has picked out the accused at the line-up, he is not likely to go back on his word later on, so that in practice the issue of identity may (in the absence of other relevant evidence) for all practical purposes be determined there and then, before the trial."[8]

The pretrial confrontation for purpose of identification may take the form of a lineup, also known as an "identification parade" or "showup," as in the present case, or presentation of the suspect alone to the witness, as in *Stovall v. Denno, supra*. It is obvious that risks of suggestion attend either form of confrontation and increase the dangers inhering in eyewitness identification. But as is the case with secret interrogations, there is serious difficulty in depicting what transpires at lineups and other forms of identification confrontations. "Privacy results in secrecy and this in turn results in a gap in our knowledge as to what in fact goes on. . . ." *Miranda v. Arizona, supra*, 384 U.S. at 448, 86 S. Ct. at 1614. For the same reasons, the defense can seldom reconstruct the manner and mode of lineup identification for judge or jury at trial. Those participating in a lineup with the accused may often be police officers; in any event, the participants' names are rarely recorded or divulged at trial. The impediments to an objective observation are increased when the victim is the witness. Lineups are prevalent in rape and robbery prosecutions and present a particular hazard that a victim's understandable outrage may excite vengeful or spiteful motives. In any event, neither witnesses nor lineup participants are apt to be alert for conditions prejudicial to the suspect. And if they were, it would likely be of scant benefit to the suspect since neither witnesses nor lineup participants are likely to be schooled in the detection of suggestive influences.[13] Improper influences may go undetected by a suspect, guilty or not, who experiences the emotional tension which we might expect in one being confronted with potential accusers. Even when he does observe abuse, if he has a criminal record he may be reluctant to take the stand and open up the admission of prior convictions. Moreover, any protestations by the suspect of the fairness of the lineup made at trial are likely to be in vain; the jury's choice is between the accused's unsupported version and that of the police officers present. In short, the accused's inability effectively to reconstruct at trial any unfairness that occurred at the lineup may deprive him of his only opportunity meaningfully to attack the credibility of the witness' courtroom identification.

. . . .

The potential for improper influence is illustrated by the circumstances, insofar as they appear, surrounding the prior identifications in the three cases we decide today. In the present case, the testimony of the identifying witnesses elicited on

---

8. Williams & Hammelmann, *Identification Parades, Part I*, [1963] Crim. L. Rev. 479, 482.

13. An additional impediment to the detection of such influences by participants, including the suspect, is the physical conditions often surrounding the conduct of the lineup. In many, lights shine on the stage in such a way that the suspect cannot see the witness. In some a one-way mirror is used and what is said on the witness' side cannot be heard.

cross-examination revealed that those witnesses were taken to the courthouse and seated in the courtroom to await assembly of the lineup. The courtroom faced on a hallway observable to the witnesses through an open door. The cashier testified that she saw Wade "standing in the hall" within sight of an FBI agent. Five or six other prisoners later appeared in the hall. The vice president testified that he saw a person in the hall in the custody of the agent who "resembled the person that we identified as the one that had entered the bank."

The lineup in *Gilbert*, 388 U.S. 263, 87 S. Ct. 1951, was conducted in an auditorium in which some 100 witnesses to several alleged state and federal robberies charged to Gilbert made wholesale identifications of Gilbert as the robber in each other's presence, a procedure said to be fraught with dangers of suggestion. And the vice of suggestion created by the identification in *Stovall*, 388 U.S. 293, 87 S. Ct. 1967, was the presentation to the witness of the suspect alone handcuffed to police officers. It is hard to imagine a situation more clearly conveying the suggestion to the witness that the one presented is believed guilty by the police.

The few cases that have surfaced therefore reveal the existence of a process attended with hazards of serious unfairness to the criminal accused and strongly suggest the plight of the more numerous defendants who are unable to ferret out suggestive influences in the secrecy of the confrontation. We do not assume that these risks are the result of police procedures intentionally designed to prejudice an accused. Rather we assume they derive from the dangers inherent in eyewitness identification and the suggestibility inherent in the context of the pretrial identification. Williams & Hammelmann, in one of the most comprehensive studies of such forms of identification, said, "[T]he fact that the police themselves have, in a given case, little or no doubt that the man put up for identification has committed the offense, and that their chief pre-occupation is with the problem of getting sufficient proof, because he has not 'come clean,' involves a danger that this persuasion may communicate itself even in a doubtful case to the witness in some way. . . ." *Identification Parades, Part I*, [1963] Crim. L. Rev. 479, 483.

Insofar as the accused's conviction may rest on a courtroom identification in fact the fruit of a suspect pretrial identification which the accused is helpless to subject to effective scrutiny at trial, the accused is deprived of that right of cross-examination which is an essential safeguard to his right to confront the witnesses against him. *Pointer v. Texas*, 380 U.S. 400, 85 S. Ct. 1065, 13 L. Ed. 2d 923. And even though cross-examination is a precious safeguard to a fair trial, it cannot be viewed as an absolute assurance of accuracy and reliability. Thus in the present context, where so many variables and pitfalls exist, the first line of defense must be the prevention of unfairness and the lessening of the hazards of eyewitness identification at the lineup itself. The trial which might determine the accused's fate may well not be that in the courtroom but that at the pretrial confrontation, with the State aligned against the accused, the witness the sole jury, and the accused unprotected against the overreaching, intentional or unintentional, and with little or no effective appeal from the judgment there rendered by the witness — "that's the man."

Since it appears that there is grave potential for prejudice, intentional or not, in the pretrial lineup, which may not be capable of reconstruction at trial, and since presence of counsel itself can often avert prejudice and assure a meaningful confrontation at trial,[26] there can be little doubt that for Wade the post-indictment lineup was a critical stage of the prosecution at which he was "as much entitled to such aid [of counsel] . . . as at the trial itself." *Powell v. Alabama*, 287 U.S. 45, at 57, 53 S. Ct. 55, at 60, 77 L. Ed. 158. Thus both Wade and his counsel should have been notified of the impending lineup, and counsel's presence should have been a requisite to conduct of the lineup, absent an "intelligent waiver." *See Carnley v. Cochran*, 369 U.S. 506, 82 S. Ct. 884, 8 L. Ed. 2d 70. No substantial countervailing policy considerations have been advanced against the requirement of the presence of counsel. Concern is expressed that the requirement will forestall prompt identifications and result in obstruction of the confrontations. As for the first, we note that in the two

---

26. One commentator proposes a model statute providing not only for counsel, but other safeguards as well:

> Most, if not all, of the attacks on the lineup process could be averted by a uniform statute modeled upon the best features of the civilian codes. Any proposed statute should provide for the right to counsel during any lineup or during any confrontation. Provision should be made that any person, whether a victim or a witness, must give a description of the suspect before he views any arrested person. A written record of this description should be required, and the witness should be made to sign it. This written record would be available for inspection by defense counsel for copying before the trial and for use at the trial in testing the accuracy of the identification made during the lineup and during the trial.

> This ideal statute would require at least six persons in addition to the accused in a lineup, and these persons would have to be of approximately the same height, weight, coloration of hair and skin, and bodily types as the suspect. In addition, all of these men should, as nearly as possible, be dressed alike. If distinctive garb was used during the crime, the suspect should not be forced to wear similar clothing in the lineup unless all of the other persons are similarly garbed. A complete written report of the names, addresses, descriptive details of the other persons in the lineup, and of everything which transpired during the identification would be mandatory. This report would include everything stated by the identifying witness during this step, including any reasons given by him as to what features, etc., have sparked his recognition.

> This statute should permit voice identification tests by having each person in the lineup repeat identical innocuous phrases, and it would be impermissible to force the use of words allegedly used during a criminal act.

> The statute would enjoin the police from suggesting to any viewer that one or more persons in the lineup had been arrested as a suspect. If more than one witness is to make an identification, each witness should be required to do so separately and should be forbidden to speak to another witness until all of them have completed the process.

> The statute could require the use of movie cameras and tape recorders to record the lineup process in those states which are financially able to afford these devices. Finally, the statute should provide that any evidence obtained as the result of a violation of this statute would be inadmissible.

Murray, *The Criminal Lineup at Home and Abroad*, 1966 Utah L. Rev. 610, 627–628.

cases in which the right to counsel is today held to apply, counsel had already been appointed and no argument is made in either case that notice to counsel would have prejudicially delayed the confrontations. Moreover, we leave open the question whether the presence of substitute counsel might not suffice where notification and presence of the suspect's own counsel would result in prejudicial delay.[27] And to refuse to recognize the right to counsel for fear that counsel will obstruct the course of justice is contrary to the basic assumptions upon which this Court has operated in Sixth Amendment cases. We rejected similar logic in *Miranda v. Arizona* concerning presence of counsel during custodial interrogation. . . . In our view counsel can hardly impede legitimate law enforcement; on the contrary, for the reasons expressed, law enforcement may be assisted by preventing the infiltration of taint in the prosecution's identification evidence. That result cannot help the guilty avoid conviction but can only help assure that the right man has been brought to justice.[29]

Legislative or other regulations, such as those of local police departments, which eliminate the risks of abuse and unintentional suggestion at lineup proceedings and the impediments to meaningful confrontation at trial may also remove the basis for regarding the stage as "critical."[30] But neither Congress nor the federal authorities have seen fit to provide a solution. What we hold today "in no way creates a constitutional

---

27. Although the right to counsel usually means a right to the suspect's own counsel, provision for substitute counsel may be justified on the ground that the substitute counsel's presence may eliminate the hazards which render the lineup a critical stage for the presence of the suspect's *own* counsel.

29. Many other nations surround the lineup with safeguards against prejudice to the suspect. In England the suspect must be allowed the presence of his solicitor or a friend, Napley, [*Problems of Effecting the Presentation of the Case for a Defendant*, 66 Col. L. Rev. 94 (1966)] *supra*, n. 7, at 98–99; Germany requires the presence of retained counsel; France forbids the confrontation of the suspect in the absence of his counsel; Spain, Mexico, and Italy provide detailed procedures prescribing the conditions under which confrontation must occur under the supervision of a judicial officer who sees to it that the proceedings are officially recorded to assure adequate scrutiny at trial. Murray, *The Criminal Lineup at Home and Abroad*, 1966 Utah L. Rev. 610, 621–627.

30. Thirty years ago Wigmore suggested a "scientific method" of pretrial identification "to reduce the risk of error hitherto inherent in such proceedings." Wigmore, THE SCIENCE OF JUDICIAL PROOF 541 (3d ed. 1937). Under this approach, at least 100 talking films would be prepared of men from various occupations, races, etc. Each would be photographed in a number of stock movements, with and without hat and coat, and would read aloud a standard passage. The suspect would be filmed in the same manner. Some 25 of the films would be shown in succession in a special projection room in which each witness would be provided an electric button which would activate a board backstage when pressed to indicate that the witness had identified a given person. Provision would be made for the degree of hesitancy in the identification to be indicated by the number of presses. Of course, the more systematic and scientific a process or proceeding, including one for purposes of identification, the less the impediment to reconstruction of the conditions bearing upon the reliability of that process or proceeding at trial. See discussion of fingerprint and like tests, Part III, *supra*, and of handwriting exemplars in *Gilbert v. California, supra*.

straitjacket which will handicap sound efforts at reform, nor is it intended to have this effect." *Miranda v. Arizona, supra* at 467, 86 S. Ct. at 1624.

V

We come now to the question whether the denial of Wade's motion to strike the courtroom identification by the bank witnesses at trial because of the absence of his counsel at the lineup required, as the Court of Appeals held, the grant of a new trial at which such evidence is to be excluded. We do not think this disposition can be justified without first giving the Government the opportunity to establish by clear and convincing evidence that the in-court identifications were based upon observations of the suspect other than the lineup identification. Where, as here, the admissibility of evidence of the lineup identification itself is not involved, a *per se* rule of exclusion of courtroom identification would be unjustified.[32] A rule limited solely to the exclusion of testimony concerning identification at the lineup itself, without regard to admissibility of the courtroom identification, would render the right to counsel an empty one. The lineup is most often used, as in the present case, to crystallize the witnesses' identification of the defendant for future reference. We have already noted that the lineup identification will have that effect. The State may then rest upon the witnesses' unequivocal courtroom identifications, and not mention the pretrial identification as part of the State's case at trial. Counsel is then in the predicament in which Wade's counsel found himself — realizing that possible unfairness at the lineup may be the sole means of attack upon the unequivocal courtroom identification, and having to probe in the dark in an attempt to discover and reveal unfairness, while bolstering the government witness' courtroom identification by bringing out and dwelling upon his prior identification. Since counsel's presence at the lineup would equip him to attack not only the lineup identification but the courtroom identification as well, limiting the impact of violation of the right to counsel to exclusion of evidence only of identification at the lineup itself disregards a critical element of that right.

We think it follows that the proper test to be applied in these situations is that quoted in *Wong Sun v. United States*, 371 U.S. 471, 488, 83 S. Ct. 407, 417, 9 L. Ed. 2d 441, "'[W]hether, granting establishment of the primary illegality, the evidence to which instant objection is made has been come at by exploitation of that illegality or instead by means sufficiently distinguishable to be purged of the primary taint.' Maguire, EVIDENCE OF GUILT 221 (1959)." Application of this test in the present context requires consideration of various factors; for example, the prior opportunity to observe the alleged criminal act, the existence of any discrepancy between any pre-lineup description and the defendant's actual description, any identification prior to lineup of another person, the identification by picture of the defendant prior to the lineup, failure to identify the defendant on a prior occasion, and the lapse of time between the alleged act and the lineup identification. It is also relevant to consider

---

32. We reach a contrary conclusion in *Gilbert v. California, supra* as to the admissibility of the witness' testimony that he also identified the accused at the lineup.

those facts which, despite the absence of counsel, are disclosed concerning the conduct of the lineup.[33]

. . . .

On the record now before us we cannot make the determination whether the in-court identifications had an independent origin. This was not an issue at trial, although there is some evidence relevant to a determination. That inquiry is most properly made in the District Court. We therefore think the appropriate procedure to be followed is to vacate the conviction pending a hearing to determine whether the in-court identifications had an independent source, or whether, in any event, the introduction of the evidence was harmless error, *Chapman v. California*, 386 U.S. 18, 87 S. Ct. 824, 17 L. Ed. 2d 705, and for the District Court to reinstate the conviction or order a new trial, as may be proper.

The judgment of the Court of Appeals is vacated and the case is remanded to that court with direction to enter a new judgment vacating the conviction and remanding the case to the District Court for further proceedings consistent with this opinion. It is so ordered.

Judgment of Court of Appeals vacated and case remanded with direction.

THE CHIEF JUSTICE joins the opinion of the Court except for Part I, from which he dissents for the reasons expressed in the opinion of MR. JUSTICE FORTAS.

MR. JUSTICE DOUGLAS joins the opinion of the Court except for Part I. On that phase of the case he adheres to the dissenting views in *Schmerber v. California*, 384 U.S. 757, 772–779, 86 S. Ct. 1826, 16 L. Ed. 2d 908, since he believes that compulsory lineup violates the privilege against self-incrimination contained in the Fifth Amendment.

MR. JUSTICE CLARK, concurring.

With reference to the lineup point involved in this case I cannot, for the life of me, see why a lineup is not a critical stage of the prosecution. Identification of the suspect — a prerequisite to establishment of guilt — occurs at this stage, and with *Miranda v. Arizona*, 384 U.S. 436, 86 S. Ct. 1602, 16 L. Ed. 2d 694 (1966), on the books, the requirement of the presence of counsel arises, unless waived by the suspect. I dissented in *Miranda* but I am bound by it now, as we all are. *Schmerber v. California*, 384 U.S. 757, 86 S. Ct. 1826, 16 L. Ed. 2d 908 (1966), precludes petitioner's claim of self-incrimination. I therefore join the opinion of the Court.

---

33. Thus it is not the case that "[i]t matters not how well the witness knows the suspect, whether the witness is the suspect's mother, brother, or long-time associate, and no matter how long or well the witness observed the perpetrator at the scene of the crime." Such factors will have an important bearing upon the true basis of the witness' in-court identification. Moreover, the State's inability to bolster the witness' courtroom identification by introduction of the lineup identification itself, *see Gilbert v. California, supra,* will become less significant the more the evidence of other opportunities of the witness to observe the defendant. Thus where the witness is a "kidnap victim who has lived for days with his abductor" the value to the State of admission of the lineup identification is indeed marginal, and such identification would be a mere formality.

[The opinion of Mr. Justice Black, dissenting in part and concurring in part has been omitted.]

Mr. Justice White, whom Mr. Justice Harlan and Mr. Justice Stewart join, dissenting in part and concurring in part.

The Court has again propounded a broad constitutional rule barring the use of a wide spectrum of relevant and probative evidence, solely because a step in its ascertainment or discovery occurs outside the presence of defense counsel. This was the approach of the Court in *Miranda v. Arizona*, 384 U.S. 436, 86 S. Ct. 1602, 16 L. Ed. 2d 694. I objected then to what I thought was an uncritical and doctrinaire approach without satisfactory factual foundation. I have much the same view of the present ruling and therefore dissent from the judgment and from Parts II, IV, and V of the Court's opinion.

The Court's opinion is far-reaching. It proceeds first by creating a new *per se* rule of constitutional law: a criminal suspect cannot be subjected to a pretrial identification process in the absence of his counsel without violating the Sixth Amendment. If he is, the State may not buttress a later courtroom identification of the witness by any reference to the previous identification. Furthermore, the courtroom identification is not admissible at all unless the State can establish by clear and convincing proof that the testimony is not the fruit of the earlier identification made in the absence of defendant's counsel — admittedly a heavy burden for the State and probably an impossible one. To all intents and purposes, courtroom identifications are barred if pretrial identifications have occurred without counsel being present.

The rule applies to any lineup, to any other techniques employed to produce an identification and *a fortiori* to a face-to-face encounter between the witness and the suspect alone, regardless of when the identification occurs, in time or place, and whether before or after indictment or information. It matters not how well the witness knows the suspect, whether the witness is the suspect's mother, brother, or long-time associate, and no matter how long or well the witness observed the perpetrator at the scene of the crime. The kidnap victim who has lived for days with his abductor is in the same category as the witness who has had only a fleeting glimpse of the criminal. Neither may identify the suspect without defendant's counsel being present. The same strictures apply regardless of the number of other witnesses who positively identify the defendant and regardless of the corroborative evidence showing that it was the defendant who had committed the crime.

The premise for the Court's rule is not the general unreliability of eyewitness identifications nor the difficulties inherent in observation, recall, and recognition. The Court assumes a narrower evil as the basis for its rule — improper police suggestion which contributes to erroneous identifications. The Court apparently believes that improper police procedures are so widespread that a broad prophylactic rule must be laid down, requiring the presence of counsel at all pretrial identifications, in order to detect recurring instances of police misconduct. I do not share this pervasive distrust of all official investigations. None of the materials the Court relies upon supports it. Certainly, I would bow to solid fact, but the Court quite obviously does not have before it any reliable, comprehensive survey of current police practices on which to base its new rule. Until it does, the Court should avoid excluding relevant evidence from state criminal trials.

The Court goes beyond assuming that a great majority of the country's police departments are following improper practices at pretrial identifications. To find the lineup a "critical" stage of the proceeding and to exclude identifications made in the absence of counsel, the Court must also assume that police "suggestion," if it occurs at all, leads to erroneous rather than accurate identifications and that reprehensible police conduct will have an unavoidable and largely undiscoverable impact on the trial. This in turn assumes that there is now no adequate source from which defense counsel can learn about the circumstances of the pretrial identification in order to place before the jury all of the considerations which should enter into an appraisal of courtroom identification evidence. But these are treacherous and unsupported assumptions resting as they do on the notion that the defendant will not be aware, that the police and the witnesses will forget or prevaricate, that defense counsel will be unable to bring out the truth and that neither jury, judge, nor appellate court is a sufficient safeguard against unacceptable police conduct occurring at a pretrial identification procedure. I am unable to share the Court's view of the willingness of the police and the ordinary citizen witness to dissemble, either with respect to the identification of the defendant or with respect to the circumstances surrounding a pretrial identification.

There are several striking aspects to the Court's holding. First, the rule does not bar courtroom identifications where there have been no previous identifications in the presence of the police, although when identified in the courtroom, the defendant is known to be in custody and charged with the commission of a crime. Second, the Court seems to say that if suitable legislative standards were adopted for the conduct of pretrial identifications, thereby lessening the hazards in such confrontations, it would not insist on the presence of counsel. But if this is true, why does not the Court simply fashion what it deems to be constitutionally acceptable procedures for the authorities to follow? Certainly the Court is correct in suggesting that the new rule will be wholly inapplicable where police departments themselves have established suitable safeguards.

Third, courtroom identification may be barred, absent counsel at a prior identification, regardless of the extent of counsel's information concerning the circumstances of the previous confrontation between witness and defendant—apparently even if there were recordings or sound-movies of the events as they occurred. But if the rule is premised on the defendant's right to have his counsel know, there seems little basis for not accepting other means to inform. A disinterested observer, recordings, photographs—any one of them would seem adequate to furnish the basis for a meaningful cross-examination of the eyewitness who identifies the defendant in the courtroom.

I share the Court's view that the criminal trial, at the very least, should aim at truthful factfinding, including accurate eyewitness identifications. I doubt, however, on the basis of our present information, that the tragic mistakes which have occurred in criminal trials are as much the product of improper police conduct as they are the consequence of the difficulties inherent in eyewitness testimony and in resolving evidentiary conflicts by court or jury. I doubt that the Court's new rule will obviate these difficulties, or that the situation will be measurably improved by inserting defense counsel into the investigative processes of police departments everywhere.

But, it may be asked, what possible state interest militates against requiring the presence of defense counsel at lineups? After all, the argument goes, he *may* do some good, he *may* upgrade the quality of identification evidence in state courts and he can scarcely do any harm. Even if true, this is a feeble foundation for fastening an ironclad constitutional rule upon state criminal procedures. Absent some reliably established constitutional violation, the processes by which the States enforce their criminal laws are their own prerogative. The States *do* have an interest in conducting their own affairs, an interest which cannot be displaced simply by saying that there are no valid arguments with respect to the merits of a federal rule emanating from this Court.

Beyond this, however, requiring counsel at pretrial identifications as an invariable rule trenches on other valid state interests. One of them is its concern with the prompt and efficient enforcement of its criminal laws. Identifications frequently take place after arrest but before an indictment is returned or an information is filed. The police may have arrested a suspect on probable cause but may still have the wrong man. Both the suspect and the State have every interest in a prompt identification at that stage, the suspect in order to secure his immediate release and the State because prompt and early identification enhances *accurate* identification and because it must know whether it is on the right investigative track. Unavoidably, however, the absolute rule requiring the presence of counsel will cause significant delay and it may very well result in no pretrial identification at all. Counsel must be appointed and a time arranged convenient for him and the witnesses. Meanwhile, it may be necessary to file charges against the suspect who may then be released on bail, in the federal system very often on his own recognizance, with neither the State nor the defendant having the benefit of a properly conducted identification procedure.

Nor do I think the witnesses themselves can be ignored. They will now be required to be present at the convenience of counsel rather than their own. Many may be much less willing to participate if the identification stage is transformed into an adversary proceeding not under the control of a judge. Others may fear for their own safety if their identity is known at an early date, especially when there is no way of knowing until the lineup occurs whether or not the police really have the right man.

Finally, I think the Court's new rule is vulnerable in terms of its own unimpeachable purpose of increasing the reliability of identification testimony.

Law enforcement officers have the obligation to convict the guilty and to make sure they do not convict the innocent. They must be dedicated to making the criminal trial a procedure for the ascertainment of the true facts surrounding the commission of the crime. To this extent, our so-called adversary system is not adversary at all; nor should it be. But defense counsel has no comparable obligation to ascertain or present the truth. Our system assigns him a different mission. He must be and is interested in preventing the conviction of the innocent, but, absent a voluntary plea of guilty, we also insist that he defend his client whether he is innocent or guilty. The State has the obligation to present the evidence. Defense counsel need present nothing, even if he knows what the truth is. He need not furnish any witnesses to the police, or reveal any confidences of his client, or furnish any other information to help the prosecution's case. If he can confuse a witness, even a truthful one, or make him appear at a disadvantage, unsure or indecisive, that will be his normal course. Our interest in not convicting the innocent permits counsel to put the State to its proof, to put the State's case in the worst possible light, regardless of what he thinks or knows to be the truth. Undoubtedly there are some limits which defense counsel must observe but more often than not, defense counsel will cross-examine a prosecution witness, and impeach him if he can, even if he thinks the witness is telling the truth, just as he will attempt to destroy a witness who he thinks is lying. In this respect, as part of our modified adversary system and as part of the duty imposed on the most honorable defense counsel, we countenance or require conduct which in many instances has little, if any, relation to the search for truth.

I would not extend this system, at least as it presently operates, to police investigations and would not require counsel's presence at pretrial identification procedures. Counsel's interest is in not having his client placed at the scene of the crime, regardless of his whereabouts. Some counsel may advise their clients to refuse to make any movements or to speak any words in a lineup or even to appear in one. To that extent the impact on truthful factfinding is quite obvious. Others will not only observe what occurs and develop possibilities for later cross-examination but will hover over witnesses and begin their cross-examination then, menacing truthful factfinding as thoroughly as the Court fears the police now do. Certainly there is an implicit invitation to counsel to suggest rules for the lineup and to manage and produce it as best he can. I therefore doubt that the Court's new rule, at least absent some clearly defined limits on counsel's role, will measurably contribute to more reliable pretrial identifications. My fears are that it will have precisely the opposite result. It may well produce fewer convictions, but that is hardly a proper measure of its long-run acceptability. In my view, the State is entitled to investigate and develop its case outside the presence of defense counsel. This includes the right to have private conversations with identification witnesses, just as defense counsel may have his own consultations with these and other witnesses without having the prosecutor present.

Whether today's judgment would be an acceptable exercise of supervisory power over federal courts is another question. But as a constitutional matter, the judgment in this case is erroneous and although I concur in Parts I and III of the Court's opinion I respectfully register this dissent.

[The opinion of MR. JUSTICE FORTAS, with whom THE CHIEF JUSTICE and MR. JUSTICE DOUGLAS join, concurring in part and dissenting in part has been omitted.]

Notes and Questions

(1) In *Wade*, the government had not sought to introduce the witness's pretrial identification into evidence at trial. In *Gilbert v. California*, 388 U.S. 263, 87 S. Ct. 1951, 18 L. Ed. 2d 1178 (1967), however, government witnesses who identified the defendant in the courtroom also testified on direct examination that they had identified the defendant at a pretrial lineup. The Court ruled that testimony relating to the pretrial identifications "is the direct result of the illegal lineup 'come at by exploitation of [the primary] illegality.' *Wong Sun v. United States*, 371 U.S. 471, 488, 83 S. Ct. 407, 417, 9 L. Ed. 2d 441. The State is therefore not entitled to an opportunity to show that that testimony had an independent source. Only a *per se* exclusionary rule as to such testimony can be an effective sanction to assure that law enforcement authorities will respect the accused's constitutional right to the presence of his counsel at the critical line-up."

(2) What will be the role of the defense lawyer at a police-conducted line-up? Consider the Commentary to the American Law Institute's Model Code of Pre-Arraignment Procedure (1975) at 429–33:

> The two extreme positions might be stated thus:
>
> (1) Counsel is to be present merely as an observer to assure against abuse and bad faith by law enforcement officers, and to provide the basis for any attack he might wish to make on the identification at trial.
>
> (2) The lineup procedure is to be a fully adversary proceeding in which the counsel for the suspect may make objections and proposals, which if they are proper or even reasonable must be respected.
>
> The cases and commentaries, as well as the practice since *Wade*, would indicate that the first interpretation of the counsel's role comes closer to describing the general interpretation of the constitutional requirement and to describing the practice under it. The major difficulty with this interpretation is that by forcing counsel into the role of a merely passive observer it gives him a job which at best can be accomplished in a large variety of ways including video recording and at worst is uncomfortable or demeaning. . . .
>
> On the other hand, any attempt to give counsel at identification a more active role is fraught with difficulties not only for the police but for counsel himself. For the police the difficulty is that a procedure which is often under the supervision not of lawyers but of police officers will be subject to manipulation and objection by a trained legal counsel for one side only.

. . . .

The assigning of a more active role to counsel has perils for counsel as well. If he is entitled to make objections at the lineup procedure, will he be held to have waived these objections if he does not make them at the procedure and he wishes later to question the fairness or accuracy of the identification at trial? If such a possibility of waiver exists will he not almost be under an obligation to raise every conceivable objection lest he find that he has waived his objections? Moreover, this hard choice would be imposed on a lawyer at a very early stage of his contact with the case. Indeed the lawyer who did this work is often likely to be a junior member of the public defender's staff assigned on rotation to do "lineup work," and thus would not likely be the lawyer to handle the case at trial.

Where a lawyer is present he should not be obliged to make his objections or be deemed to have waived them. The lawyer's intervention here is too early. Similarly, there does not appear to be any reason to require the police to abide by any objections or suggestions that the lawyer makes. All the Code would require is that any objections that the lawyer might have be made part of the record of the identification procedure. In this way if something has taken place to which defense counsel objects and which the record might not otherwise clearly show, the fact of the lawyer's objection will make this issue prominently available for use at the trial. At the same time, the police in hearing the objection would have the opportunity to remedy the situation if they chose. To be sure, the absence of any objection might possibly carry some factual implication that the defendant and his counsel acquiesced in an identification procedure to which they then find themselves subsequently objecting at trial. This possibility may be thought to provide just the right degree of incentive for defense counsel to make reasonable objections which the police might heed, rather than sitting back and hoping to trap the police in error.

(3) When a witness is prepared to identify the defendant in court after having previously identified him at an improper pretrial confrontation, how difficult will it be for the prosecution to establish by clear and convincing evidence that the in-court identification is not tainted by the pretrial identification?

Empirical studies lend some support to Justice White's assertion that it will be difficult, if not impossible, for the prosecution to prove that an in-court identification had an independent source. The studies indicate that a witness's ability to perceive and recall an event depends upon a variety of complex factors — including, for example, the stress produced by the event, the time the witness was exposed to the event, the time elapsed since the event, and the questions posed to the witness concerning the event. *See, e.g.,* Loftus, Eyewitness Testimony 20–109 (1979). Considering the complexity of the factors involved, it would be surprising if the witness would be able to determine with a high degree of confidence that the recollection of the defendant stemmed from the original encounter with the defendant rather than a later and presumably less stressful encounter arranged by the police.

In practice, however, lower courts confronted with an invalid pretrial identification have "easily found an 'independent source' for an in-court identification." Note, 55 Minn. L. Rev. 779, 818 (1971). *See generally* Grano, Kirby, Biggers, *and* Ash: *Do Any Constitutional Safeguards Remain Against the Danger of Convicting the Innocent?*, 72 Mich. L. Rev. 717, 760 (1974).

With respect to the lower courts' propensity for finding independent sources, consider the remarks made one year after the *Wade* decision by A.J. Davis of the Philadelphia District Attorney's Office:

> How [is the defense lawyer] going to prove that the in-court identification that the victim is about to make is the fruit of [the invalid police lineup]? The Supreme Court may say the burden of proof is on the prosecution, but you know and I know that the attitude of the trial judge is going to be that the burden of proof is on [the defense lawyer] as a practical matter to convince that judge. He is not going to be terribly sympathetic to these cases.

> What is the prosecution going to do? The prosecution is going to put the victim on the stand and the victim is going to say, "When this robber came to me and put that gun in my face, I looked at him and I formed a mental picture. . . . Then, I had this lineup and I compared this portrait in my mind with the people in the lineup and I picked out that defendant. Now I am in court and what am I doing? I am not paying any attention to the lineup. I am again conjuring up that [mental picture] which I evolved in my mind at the time of the robbery, and I am taking that [picture] and putting it next to this defendant at the counsel table and I am saying that they are precisely the same," and the judge is going to say, "Whoopie, there's an independent origin," and you can attempt to prove from today to tomorrow that the pretrial identification was unfair, but the trial court has a finding of fact to make here, and nine times out of ten, unless you have a very exceptional trial court, he is going to find against you on this issue.

See Panel Discussion, *The Role of the Defense Lawyer at a Line-up in Light of the* Wade, Gilbert, *and* Stovall *Decisions*, 4 Crim. Law Bull. 273, 293–94 (1968) (comments of A.J. Davis).

Kirby v. Illinois

United States Supreme Court

406 U.S. 682, 92 S. Ct. 1877, 32 L. Ed. 2d 411 (1972)

Mr. Justice Stewart announced the judgment of the Court and an opinion in which The Chief Justice, Mr. Justice Blackmun, and Mr. Justice Rehnquist join.

. . . .

On February 21, 1968, a man named Willie Shard reported to the Chicago police that the previous day two men had robbed him on a Chicago street of a wallet containing, among other things, traveler's checks and a Social Security card. On February 22, two police officers stopped the petitioner and a companion, Ralph Bean, on West Madison Street in Chicago.[1] When asked for identification, the petitioner produced a wallet that contained three traveler's checks and a Social Security card, all bearing the name of Willie Shard. Papers with Shard's name on them were also found in Bean's possession. When asked to explain his possession of Shard's property, the petitioner first said that the traveler's checks were "play money," and then told the officers that he had won them in a crap game. The officers then arrested the petitioner and Bean and took them to a police station.

Only after arriving at the police station, and checking the records there, did the arresting officers learn of the Shard robbery. A police car was then dispatched to Shard's place of employment, where it picked up Shard and brought him to the police station. Immediately upon entering the room in the police station where the petitioner and Bean were seated at a table, Shard positively identified them as the men who had robbed him two days earlier. No lawyer was present in the room, and neither the petitioner nor Bean had asked for legal assistance, or been advised of any right to the presence of counsel.

More than six weeks later, the petitioner and Bean were indicted for the robbery of Willie Shard. Upon arraignment, counsel was appointed to represent them, and they pleaded not guilty. A pretrial motion to suppress Shard's identification testimony was denied, and at the trial Shard testified as a witness for the prosecution. In his testimony he described his identification of the two men at the police station on February 22,[2] and identified them again in the courtroom as the men

---

1. The officers stopped the petitioner and his companion because they thought the petitioner was a man named Hampton, who was "wanted" in connection with an unrelated criminal offense. The legitimacy of this stop and the subsequent arrest is not before us.

2. **Q.** All right. Now, Willie, calling your attention to February 22, 1968, did you receive a call from the police asking you to come down to the station?

A. Yes, I did.

. . . .

Q. When you went down there, what if anything, happened, Willie?

A. Well, I seen the two men was down there who robbed me.

. . . .

Q. Who took you to the police station?

A. The policeman picked me up.

. . . .

MR. POMARO: Q. When you went to the police station did you see the two defendants?

A. Yes, I did.

Q. Do you see them in Court today?

A. Yes, sir.

who had robbed him on February 20.[3] He was cross-examined at length regarding the circumstances of his identification of the two defendants. The jury found both defendants guilty, and the petitioner's conviction was affirmed on appeal . . . .

. . . .

I

. . . .

In a line of constitutional cases in this Court stemming back to the Court's landmark opinion in *Powell v. Alabama*, 287 U.S. 45, 53 S. Ct. 55, 77 L. Ed. 158, it has been firmly established that a person's Sixth and Fourteenth Amendment right to counsel attaches only at or after the time that adversary judicial proceedings have been initiated against him.

This is not to say that a defendant in a criminal case has a constitutional right to counsel only at the trial itself. The *Powell* case makes clear that the right attaches at

---

Q. Point them out, please?

A. Yes, that one there and the other one. (Indicating.)

MR. POMARO: Indicating for the record the defendants Bean and Kirby.

Q. And you positively identified them at the police station, is that correct?

A. Yes.

Q. Did any police officer make any suggestion to you whatsoever?

. . .

THE WITNESS: No, they didn't.

3.

Q. Willie, when you looked back, when you were walking down the street and first saw the defendants, when you looked back, did you see them then?

A. Yes, I seen them.

Q. Did you get a good look at them then?

A. Yes, I did.

Q. All right. Now, when they grabbed you and took your money, did you see them then?

A. Yes, I did.

Q. Did you get a good look at them then?

A. Yes.

Q. Both of them?

A. Correct.

Q. When they walked away did you see them then?

A. Yes.

Q. Did you look at them, Willie?

A. Yes.

Q. Did you get a good look at them?

A. Yes.

Q. Are those the same two fellows? Look at them, Willie.

A. Correct.

Q. Are those the same two that robbed you?

A. Yes.

Q. You are sure, Willie?

A. Yes.

the time of arraignment, and the Court has recently held that it exists also at the time of a preliminary hearing. *Coleman v. Alabama, supra.* But the point is that, while members of the Court have differed as to existence of the right to counsel in the contexts of some of the above cases, all of those cases have involved points of time at or after the initiation of adversary judicial criminal proceedings — whether by way of formal charge, preliminary hearing, indictment, information, or arraignment.

The only seeming deviation from this long line of constitutional decisions was *Escobedo v. Illinois*, 378 U.S. 478, 84 S. Ct. 1758, 12 L. Ed. 2d 977. But *Escobedo* is not apposite here for two distinct reasons. First, the Court in retrospect perceived that the "prime purpose" of *Escobedo* was not to vindicate the constitutional right to counsel as such, but, like *Miranda*, "to guarantee full effectuation of the privilege against self-incrimination. . . ." *Johnson v. New Jersey*, 384 U.S. 719, 729, 86 S. Ct. 1772, 1779, 16 L. Ed. 2d 882. Secondly, and perhaps even more important for purely practical purposes, the Court has limited the holding of *Escobedo* to its own facts, *Johnson v. New Jersey, supra*, at 733–734, 86 S. Ct. at 1780, and those facts are not remotely akin to the facts of the case before us.

The initiation of judicial criminal proceedings is far from a mere formalism. It is the starting point of our whole system of adversary criminal justice. For it is only then that the government has committed itself to prosecute, and only then that the adverse positions of government and defendant have solidified. It is then that a defendant finds himself faced with the prosecutorial forces of organized society, and immersed in the intricacies of substantive and procedural criminal law. It is this point, therefore, that marks the commencement of the "criminal prosecutions" to which alone the explicit guarantees of the Sixth Amendment are applicable.

In this case we are asked to import into a routine police investigation an absolute constitutional guarantee historically and rationally applicable only after the onset of formal prosecutorial proceedings. We decline to do so. Less than a year after *Wade* and *Gilbert* were decided, the Court explained the rule of those decisions as follows: "The rationale of those cases was that an accused is entitled to counsel at any 'critical stage of the *prosecution*,' and that a post-indictment lineup is such a 'critical stage.'" (Emphasis supplied.) *Simmons v. United States*, 390 U.S. 377, 382–383, 88 S. Ct. 967, 970, 19 L. Ed. 2d 1247. We decline to depart from that rationale today by imposing a *per se* exclusionary rule upon testimony concerning an identification that took place long before the commencement of any prosecution whatever.

II

What has been said is not to suggest that there may not be occasions during the course of a criminal investigation when the police do abuse identification procedures. Such abuses are not beyond the reach of the Constitution. As the Court pointed out in *Wade* itself, it is always necessary to "scrutinize *any* pretrial confrontation. . . ."

388 U.S. at 227, 87 S. Ct. at 1932. The Due Process Clause of the Fifth and Fourteenth Amendments forbids a lineup that is unnecessarily suggestive and conducive to irreparable mistaken identification.[8] When a person has not been formally charged with a criminal offense, *Stovall* strikes the appropriate constitutional balance between the right of a suspect to be protected from prejudicial procedures and the interest of society in the prompt and purposeful investigation of an unsolved crime.

The judgment is *affirmed*.

MR. CHIEF JUSTICE BURGER, concurring.

I agree that the right to counsel attaches as soon as criminal charges are formally made against an accused and he becomes the subject of a "criminal prosecution." Therefore, I join in the plurality opinion and in the judgment.

MR. JUSTICE POWELL, concurring in the result.

As I would not extend the *Wade-Gilbert per se* exclusionary rule, I concur in the result reached by the Court.

MR. JUSTICE BRENNAN, with whom MR. JUSTICE DOUGLAS and MR. JUSTICE MARSHALL join, dissenting.

After petitioner and Ralph Bean were arrested, police officers brought Willie Shard, the robbery victim, to a room in a police station where petitioner and Bean were seated at a table with two other police officers. Shard testified at trial that the officers who brought him to the room asked him if petitioner and Bean were the robbers and that he indicated they were. The prosecutor asked him, "And you positively identified them at the police station, is that correct?" Shard answered, "Yes." Consequently, the question in this case is whether, under *Gilbert v. California*, 388 U.S. 263, 87 S. Ct. 1951, 18 L. Ed. 2d 1178 (1967), it was constitutional error to admit Shard's testimony that he identified petitioner at the pretrial station-house showup when that showup was conducted by the police without advising petitioner that he might have counsel present. *Gilbert* held, in the context of a post-indictment lineup, that "[o]nly a *per se* exclusionary rule as to such testimony can be an effective sanction to assure that law enforcement authorities will respect the accused's constitutional right to the presence of his counsel at the critical lineup." *Id.* at 273, 87 S. Ct. at 1957. I would apply *Gilbert* and the principles of its companion case, *United States v. Wade*, 388 U.S. 218, 87 S. Ct. 1926, 18 L. Ed. 2d 1149 (1967), and reverse.

While it should go without saying, it appears necessary, in view of the plurality opinion today, to re-emphasize that *Wade* did not require the presence of counsel at pretrial confrontations for identification purposes simply on the basis of an abstract consideration of the words "criminal prosecutions" in the Sixth Amendment. Counsel is required at those confrontations because "the dangers inherent in eyewitness identification and the suggestibility inherent in the context of the pretrial identifica-

---

8. In view of our limited grant of certiorari, we do not consider whether there might have been a deprivation of due process in the particularized circumstances of this case. That question remains open for inquiry in a federal habeas corpus proceeding.

tion," *id.*, at 235, 18 L. Ed. 2d at 1162, means that protection must be afforded to the "most basic right [of] a criminal defendant — his right to a fair trial at which the witnesses against him might be meaningfully cross-examined," *id.*, at 224, 18 L. Ed. 2d at 1155. Indeed, the Court expressly stated that "[l]egislative or other regulations, such as those of local police departments, which eliminate the risks of abuse and unintentional suggestion at lineup proceedings and the impediments to meaningful confrontation at trial may also remove the basis for regarding the stage as 'critical.'" *Id.*, at 239, 18 L. Ed. 2d at 1164; *see id.*, at 239 n. 30, 18 L. Ed. 2d at 1164. Hence, "the initiation of adversary judicial criminal proceedings," *ante*, at 689, 32 L. Ed. 2d at 417, is completely irrelevant to whether counsel is necessary at a pretrial confrontation for identification in order to safeguard the accused's constitutional rights to confrontation and the effective assistance of counsel at his trial.

. . . .

In view of *Wade*, it is plain, and the plurality today does not attempt to dispute it, that there inhere in a confrontation for identification conducted after arrest the identical hazards to a fair trial that inhere in such a confrontation conducted "after the onset of formal prosecutional proceedings." The plurality apparently considers an arrest, which for present purposes we must assume to be based upon probable cause, to be nothing more than part of "a routine police investigation," and thus not "the starting point of our whole system of adversary criminal justice." An arrest, according to the plurality, does not face the accused "with the prosecutorial forces of organized society," nor immerse him "in the intricacies of substantive and procedural criminal law." Those consequences ensue, says the plurality, only with "[t]he initiation of judicial criminal proceedings," "[f]or it is only then that the government has committed itself to prosecute, and only then that the adverse positions of government and defendant have solidified." If these propositions do not amount to "mere formalism," it is difficult to know how to characterize them.[8] An arrest evidences the belief of the police that the perpetrator of a crime has been caught. A post-arrest confrontation for identification is not "a mere preparatory step in the gathering of the prosecution's evidence." *Wade, supra,* at 227, 87 S. Ct. at 1932. A primary, and frequently sole, purpose of the confrontation for identification at that stage is to accumulate proof to buttress the conclusion of the police that they have the offender in hand. The plurality offers no reason, and I can think of none, for concluding that a post-arrest confrontation for identification, unlike a post-charge confrontation, is not among those "critical confrontations of the accused by the prosecution at pretrial proceedings where the results might well settle the accused's fate and reduce the trial itself to a mere formality." *Id.* at 224, 87 S. Ct. at 1930.

---

8. As the California Supreme Court pointed out, with an eye toward the real world, "the establishment of the date of formal accusation as the time wherein the right to counsel at lineup attaches could only lead to a situation wherein substantially all lineups would be conducted prior to indictment or information." *People v. Fowler*, 1 Cal. 3d 335, 344, 82 Cal. Rptr. 363, 370, 461 P.2d 643, 650 (1969).

The highly suggestive form of confrontation employed in this case underscores the point. This showup was particularly fraught with the peril of mistaken identification. In the setting of a police station squad room where all present except petitioner and Bean were police officers, the danger was quite real that Shard's understandable resentment might lead him too readily to agree with the police that the pair under arrest, and the only persons exhibited to him, were indeed the robbers. "It is hard to imagine a situation more clearly conveying the suggestion to the witness that the one presented is believed guilty by the police." *Id.* at 234, 87 S. Ct. at 1936. The State had no case without Shard's identification testimony, and safeguards against that consequence were therefore of critical importance. Shard's testimony itself demonstrates the necessity for such safeguards. On direct examination, Shard identified petitioner and Bean not as the alleged robbers on trial in the courtroom, but as the pair he saw at the police station. His testimony thus lends strong support to the observation, quoted by the Court in *Wade*, 388 U.S. at 229, 87 S. Ct. at 1933, 18 L. Ed. 2d 1149, that "[i]t is a matter of common experience that, once a witness has picked out the accused at the line-up, he is not likely to go back on his word later on, so that in practice the issue of identity may (in the absence of other relevant evidence) for all practical purposes be determined there and then, before the trial." Williams & Hammelmann, *Identification Parades, Part I*, [1963] Crim. L. Rev. 479, 482.

. . . .

Mr. Justice White, dissenting.

United States v. Wade, 388 U.S. 218, 87 S. Ct. 1926, 18 L. Ed. 2d 1149 (1967), and *Gilbert v. California*, 388 U.S. 263, 87 S. Ct. 1951, 18 L. Ed. 2d 1178 (1967), govern this case and compel reversal of the judgment below.

United States v. Ash

United States Supreme Court

413 U.S. 300, 93 S. Ct. 2568, 37 L. Ed. 2d 619 (1973)

Mr. Justice Blackmun delivered the opinion of the Court.

. . . .

I

On the morning of August 26, 1965, a man with a stocking mask entered a bank in Washington, D.C., and began waving a pistol. He ordered an employee to hang up the telephone and instructed all others present not to move. Seconds later a second man, also wearing a stocking mask, entered the bank, scooped up money from the tellers' drawers into a bag, and left. The gunman followed, and both men escaped through an alley. The robbery lasted three or four minutes.

A Government informer, Clarence McFarland, told authorities that he had discussed the robbery with Charles J. Ash, Jr., the respondent here. Acting on this information, an FBI agent, in February 1966, showed five black-and-white mug shots of Negro males of generally the same age, height, and weight, one of which was of Ash, to four witnesses. All four made uncertain identifications of Ash's picture. At this time Ash was not in custody and had not been charged. On April 1, 1966, an indictment was returned charging Ash and a codefendant, John L. Bailey, in five counts related to this bank robbery . . . .

Trial was finally set for May 1968, almost three years after the crime. In preparing for trial, the prosecutor decided to use a photographic display to determine whether the witnesses he planned to call would be able to make in-court identifications. Shortly before the trial, an FBI agent and the prosecutor showed five color photographs to the four witnesses who previously had tentatively identified the black-and-white photograph of Ash. Three of the witnesses selected the picture of Ash, but one was unable to make any selection. None of the witnesses selected the picture of Bailey which was in the group. This post-indictment identification provides the basis for respondent Ash's claim that he was denied the right to counsel at a "critical stage" of the prosecution.

No motion for severance was made, and Ash and Bailey were tried jointly. The trial judge held a hearing on the suggestive nature of the pretrial photographic displays.[4] The judge did not make a clear ruling on suggestive nature, but held that the Government had demonstrated by "clear and convincing" evidence that in-court identifications would be "based on observation of the suspect other than the intervening observation."

At trial, the three witnesses who had been inside the bank identified Ash as the gunman, but they were unwilling to state that they were certain of their identifications. None of these made an in-court identification of Bailey. The fourth witness, who had been in a car outside the bank and who had seen the fleeing robbers after they had removed their masks, made positive in-court identifications of both Ash and Bailey. Bailey's counsel then sought to impeach this in-court identification by calling the FBI agent who had shown the color photographs to the witnesses immediately before trial. Bailey's counsel demonstrated that the witness who had identified Bailey in court had failed to identify a color photograph of Bailey. During the course of the examination, Bailey's counsel also, before the jury, brought out the fact that this witness had selected another man as one of the robbers. At this point the prosecutor became concerned that the jury might believe that the witness had selected a third person when, in fact, the witness had selected a photograph of Ash. After a conference at the bench, the trial judge ruled that all five color photographs would be admitted into evidence. The Court of Appeals held that this constituted the introduction of a post-indictment identification at the prosecutor's request and over the objection of defense counsel.

McFarland testified as a Government witness. He said he had discussed plans for the robbery with Ash before the event and, later, had discussed the results of the

---

4. At this hearing both the black-and-white and color photographs were introduced as exhibits. The FBI agents who conducted the pretrial displays were called as witnesses and were cross-examined fully. Two of the four witnesses who were expected to make in-court identifications also testified and were cross-examined concerning the photographic identifications.

robbery with Ash in the presence of Bailey. McFarland was shown to possess an extensive criminal record and a history as an informer.

The jury convicted Ash on all counts. It was unable to reach a verdict on the charges against Bailey, and his motion for acquittal was granted. Ash received concurrent sentences on the several counts, the two longest being 80 months to 12 years.

The five-member majority of the Court of Appeals held that Ash's right to counsel, guaranteed by the Sixth Amendment, was violated when his attorney was not given the opportunity to be present at the photographic displays conducted in May 1968 before the trial.

. . . .

II

. . . .

. . . The right to counsel in Anglo-American law has a rich historical heritage, and this Court has regularly drawn on that history in construing the counsel guarantee of the Sixth Amendment. We re-examine that history in an effort to determine the relationship between the purposes of the Sixth Amendment guarantee and the risks of a photographic identification.

. . . .

A concern of . . . lasting importance was the recognition and awareness that an unaided layman had little skill in arguing the law or in coping with an intricate procedural system. The function of counsel as a guide through complex legal technicalities long has been recognized by this Court . . . . The Court frequently has interpreted the Sixth Amendment to assure that the "guiding hand of counsel" is available to those in need of its assistance.

Another factor contributing to the colonial recognition of the accused's right to counsel was the adoption of the institution of the public prosecutor from the Continental inquisitorial system. . . . Thus, an additional motivation for the American rule was a desire to minimize imbalance in the adversary system that otherwise resulted with the creation of a professional prosecuting official. . . .

. . . .

This historical background suggests that the core purpose of the counsel guarantee was to assure "Assistance" at trial, when the accused was confronted with both the intricacies of the law and the advocacy of the public prosecutor. Later developments have led this Court to recognize that "Assistance" would be less than meaningful if it were limited to the formal trial itself.

This extension of the right to counsel to events before trial has resulted from changing patterns of criminal procedure and investigation that have tended to generate pretrial events that might appropriately be considered to be parts of the trial itself. At these newly emerging and significant events, the accused was confronted, just as at trial, by the procedural system, or by his expert adversary, or by both . . . .

The Court consistently has applied an historical interpretation of the guarantee, and has expanded the constitutional right to counsel only when new contexts appear presenting the same dangers that gave birth initially to the right itself.

. . . .

Throughout this expansion of the counsel guarantee to trial-like confrontations, the function of the lawyer has remained essentially the same as his function at trial. In all cases considered by the Court, counsel has continued to act as a spokesman for, or advisor to, the accused. The accused's right to the "Assistance of Counsel" has meant just that, namely, the right of the accused to have counsel acting as his assistant.

. . . .

The function of counsel in rendering "Assistance" continued at the lineup under consideration in *Wade* and its companion cases. Although the accused was not confronted there with legal questions, the lineup offered opportunities for prosecuting authorities to take advantage of the accused. Counsel was seen by the Court as being more sensitive to, and aware of, suggestive influences than the accused himself, and as better able to reconstruct the events at trial. Counsel present at lineup would be able to remove disabilities of the accused in precisely the same fashion that counsel compensated for the disabilities of the layman at trial. Thus, the Court mentioned that the accused's memory might be dimmed by "emotional tension," that the accused's credibility at trial would be diminished by his status as defendant, and that the accused might be unable to present his version effectively without giving up his privilege against compulsory self-incrimination. It was in order to compensate for these deficiencies that the Court found the need for the assistance of counsel.

This review of the history and expansion of the Sixth Amendment counsel guarantee demonstrates that the test utilized by the Court has called for examination of the event in order to determine whether the accused required aid in coping with legal problems or assistance in meeting his adversary. Against the background of this traditional test, we now consider the opinion of the Court of Appeals.

III

Although the Court of Appeals' majority recognized the argument that "a major purpose behind the right to counsel is to protect the defendant from errors that he himself might make if he appeared in court alone," the court concluded that "other forms of prejudice," mentioned and recognized in *Wade*, could also give rise to a right to counsel. These forms of prejudice were felt by the court to flow from the possibilities for mistaken identification inherent in the photographic display. . . .

. . . .

We conclude that the dangers of mistaken identification, mentioned in *Wade*, were removed from context by the Court of Appeals and were incorrectly utilized as a sufficient basis for requiring counsel. Although *Wade* did discuss possibilities for suggestion and the difficulty for reconstructing suggestivity, this discussion occurred only after the Court had concluded that the lineup constituted a trial-like confrontation, requiring the "Assistance of Counsel" to preserve the adversary process by compensating for advantages of the prosecuting authorities.

The above discussion of *Wade* has shown that the traditional Sixth Amendment test easily allowed extension of counsel to a lineup. The similarity to trial was apparent, and counsel was needed to render "Assistance" in counterbalancing any "overreaching" by the prosecution.

After the Court in *Wade* held that a lineup constituted a trial-like confrontation requiring counsel, a more difficult issue remained in the case for consideration. The same changes in law enforcement that led to lineups and pretrial hearings also generated other events at which the accused was confronted by the prosecution. The Government had argued in *Wade* that if counsel was required at a lineup, the same forceful considerations would mandate counsel at other preparatory steps in the "gathering of the prosecution's evidence," such as, for particular example, the taking of fingerprints or blood samples.

The Court concluded that there were differences. Rather than distinguishing these situations from the lineup in terms of the need for counsel to assure an equal confrontation at the time, the Court recognized that there were times when the subsequent trial would cure a one-sided confrontation between prosecuting authorities and the uncounseled defendant. In other words, such stages were not "critical." Referring to fingerprints, hair, clothing, and other blood samples, the Court explained:

> Knowledge of the techniques of science and technology is sufficiently available, and the variables in techniques few enough, that the accused has the opportunity for a meaningful confrontation of the Government's case at trial through the ordinary processes of cross-examination of the Government's expert witnesses and the presentation of the evidence of his own experts.

388 U.S. at 227–228, 87 S. Ct. at 1932.

The structure of *Wade*, viewed in light of the careful limitation of the Court's language to "confrontations," makes it clear that lack of scientific precision and inability to reconstruct an event are not the tests for requiring counsel in the first instance. These are, instead, the tests to determine whether confrontation with counsel at trial can serve as a substitute for counsel at the pretrial confrontation. If accurate reconstruction is possible, the risks inherent in any confrontation still remain, but the opportunity to cure defects at trial causes the confrontation to cease to be "critical." . . .

. . . .

The Court of Appeals considered its analysis complete after it decided that a photographic display lacks scientific precision and ease of accurate reconstruction at trial. That analysis, under *Wade*, however, merely carries one to the point where one must establish that the trial itself can provide no substitute for counsel if a pretrial confrontation is conducted in the absence of counsel. . . .

None of the classical analyses of the assistance to be given by counsel . . . suggests that counsel must be present when the prosecution is interrogating witnesses in the defendant's absence even when, as here, the defendant is under arrest; counsel is rather to be provided to prevent the defendant himself from falling into traps devised by a lawyer on the other side and to see to it that all available defenses are proffered. Many other aspects of the prosecution's interviews with a victim or a witness to a crime afford just as much opportunity for undue suggestion as the display of photographs; so, too, do the defense's interviews, notably with alibi witnesses.

[*United States v. Bennett*, 409 F.2d 888, 899–900 (2d Cir. 1969)]. We now undertake the threshold analysis that must be addressed.

IV

A substantial departure from the historical test would be necessary if the Sixth Amendment were interpreted to give Ash a right to counsel at the photographic identification in this case. Since the accused himself is not present at the time of the photographic display, and asserts no right to be present, no possibility arises that the accused might be misled by his lack of familiarity with the law or overpowered by his professional adversary. Similarly, the counsel guarantee would not be used to produce equality in a trial-like adversary confrontation. Rather, the guarantee was used by the Court of Appeals to produce confrontation at an event that previously was not analogous to an adversary trial.

Even if we were willing to view the counsel guarantee in broad terms as a generalized protection of the adversary process, we would be unwilling to go so far as to extend the right to a portion of the prosecutor's trial-preparation interviews with witnesses. Although photography is relatively new, the interviewing of witnesses before trial is a procedure that predates the Sixth Amendment. In England in the 16th and 17th centuries counsel regularly interviewed witnesses before trial. 9 W. Holdsworth, HISTORY OF ENGLISH LAW 226–228 (1926). The traditional counterbalance in the American adversary system for these interviews arises from the equal ability of defense counsel to seek and interview witnesses himself.

That adversary mechanism remains as effective for a photographic display as for other parts of pretrial interviews. . . . No greater limitations are placed on defense counsel in constructing displays, seeking witnesses, and conducting photographic identifications than those applicable to the prosecution. . . . Selection of the picture of a person other than the accused, or the inability of a witness to make any selection, will be useful to the defense in precisely the same manner that the selection of a picture of the defendant would be useful to the prosecution. In this very case, for example, the initial tender of the photographic display was by Bailey's counsel, who sought to demonstrate that the witness had failed to make a photographic identification. Although we do not suggest that equality of access to photographs removes all potential for abuse, it does remove any inequality in the adversary process itself and thereby fully satisfies the historical spirit of the Sixth Amendment's counsel guarantee.

The argument has been advanced that requiring counsel might compel the police to observe more scientific procedures or might encourage them to utilize corporeal rather than photographic displays. This Court has recognized that improved procedures can minimize the dangers of suggestion. *Simmons v. United States*, 390 U.S. 377, 386 n. 6, 88 S. Ct. 967, 972, 19 L. Ed. 2d 1247 (1968). Commentators have also proposed more accurate techniques.[15]

Pretrial photographic identifications, however, are hardly unique in offering possibilities for the actions of the prosecutor unfairly to prejudice the accused. Evidence favorable to the accused may be withheld; testimony of witnesses may be manipulated; the results of laboratory tests may be contrived. In many ways the prosecutor, by accident or by design, may improperly subvert the trial. The primary safeguard against abuses of this kind is the ethical responsibility of the prosecutor, who, as so often has been said, may "strike hard blows" but not "foul ones." *Berger v. United States*, 295 U.S. 78, 88, 55 S. Ct. 629, 633, 79 L. Ed. 1314 (1935); *Brady v. Maryland*, 373 U.S. 83, 87–88, 83 S. Ct. 1194, 1196–1197, 10 L. Ed. 2d 215 (1963). If that safeguard fails, review remains available under due process standards. These same safeguards apply to misuse of photographs.

We are not persuaded that the risks inherent in the use of photographic displays are so pernicious that an extraordinary system of safeguards is required.

We hold, then, that the Sixth Amendment does not grant the right to counsel at photographic displays conducted by the Government for the purpose of allowing a witness to attempt an identification of the offender. This holding requires reversal of the judgment of the Court of Appeals. Although respondent Ash has urged us to examine this photographic display under the due process standard enunciated in *Simmons v. United States*, 390 U.S. at 384, 88 S. Ct. at 971, the Court of Appeals, expressing the view that additional findings would be necessary, refused to decide the issue. We decline to consider this question on this record in the first instance. It remains open, of course, on the Court of Appeals' remand to the District Court.

Reversed and remanded.

MR. JUSTICE STEWART, concurring in the judgment.

. . . .

[*Wade*] held . . . that counsel was required at a lineup, primarily as an observer, to ensure that defense counsel could effectively confront the prosecution's evidence at trial. Attuned to the possibilities of suggestive influences, a lawyer could see any unfairness at a lineup, question the witnesses about it at trial, and effectively reconstruct what had gone on for the benefit of the jury or trial judge.*

---

15. *E.g.*, P. Wall, EYE-WITNESS IDENTIFICATION IN CRIMINAL CASES 77–85 (1965). . . .

* I do not read *Wade* as requiring counsel because a lineup is a "trial-type" situation, nor do I understand that the Court required the presence of an attorney because of the advice or assistance he could give to his client at the lineup itself. Rather, I had thought the reasoning of *Wade* was that the right to counsel is essentially a protection for the defendant at trial, and that counsel is necessary at a lineup in order to ensure a meaningful confrontation and the effective assistance of counsel at trial.

A photographic identification is quite different from a lineup, for there are substantially fewer possibilities of impermissible suggestion when photographs are used, and those unfair influences can be readily reconstructed at trial. It is true that the defendant's photograph may be markedly different from the others displayed, but this unfairness can be demonstrated at trial from an actual comparison of the photographs used or from the witness' description of the display. Similarly, it is possible that the photographs could be arranged in a suggestive manner, or that by comment or gesture the prosecuting authorities might single out the defendant's picture. But these are the kinds of overt influence that a witness can easily recount and that would serve to impeach the identification testimony. In short, there are few possibilities for unfair suggestiveness — and those rather blatant and easily reconstructed. Accordingly, an accused would not be foreclosed from an effective cross-examination of an identification witness simply because his counsel was not present at the photographic display. For this reason, a photographic display cannot fairly be considered a "critical stage" of the prosecution . . . .

MR. JUSTICE BRENNAN, with whom MR. JUSTICE DOUGLAS and MR. JUSTICE MARSHALL join, dissenting.

The Court holds today that a pretrial display of photographs to the witnesses of a crime for the purpose of identifying the accused, unlike a lineup, does not constitute a "critical stage" of the prosecution at which the accused is constitutionally entitled to the presence of counsel. In my view, today's decision is wholly unsupportable in terms of such considerations as logic, consistency, and, indeed, fairness. As a result, I must reluctantly conclude that today's decision marks simply another step towards the complete evisceration of the fundamental constitutional principles established by this Court, only six years ago, in *United States v. Wade*, 388 U.S. 218, 87 S. Ct. 1926, 18 L. Ed. 2d 1149 (1967); *Gilbert v. California*, 388 U.S. 263, 87 S. Ct. 1951, 18 L. Ed. 2d 1178 (1967); and *Stovall v. Denno*, 388 U.S. 293, 87 S. Ct. 1967, 18 L. Ed. 2d 1199 (1967). I dissent.

. . . .

II

In June 1967, this Court decided a trilogy of "lineup" cases which brought into sharp focus the problems of pretrial identification. In essence, those decisions held (1) that a pretrial lineup is a "critical stage" in the criminal process at which the accused is constitutionally entitled to the presence of counsel; (2) that evidence of an identification of the accused at such an uncounseled lineup is *per se* inadmissible; and (3) that evidence of a subsequent in-court identification of the accused is likewise inadmissible unless the Government can demonstrate by clear and convincing evidence that the in-court identification was based upon observations of the accused independent of the prior uncounseled lineup identification. The considerations relied upon by the Court in reaching these conclusions are clearly applicable to photographic as well as corporeal identifications.

. . . .

III

As the Court of Appeals recognized, "the dangers of mistaken identification . . . set forth in *Wade* are applicable in large measure to photographic as well as corporeal identifications." 149 U.S. App. D.C. at 9, 461 F.2d at 100. To the extent that misidentification may be attributable to a witness' faulty memory or perception, or inadequate opportunity for detailed observation during the crime, the risks are obviously as great at a photographic display as at a lineup. But "[b]ecause of the inherent limitations of photography, which presents its subject in two dimensions rather than the three dimensions of reality, . . . a photographic identification, even when properly obtained, is clearly inferior to a properly obtained corporeal identification." P. Wall, Eye-Witness Identification in Criminal Cases 70 (1965). Indeed, noting "the hazards of initial identification by photograph," we have expressly recognized that "a corporeal identification . . . is normally more accurate" than a photographic identification. *Simmons v. United States*, 390 U.S. 377, 384, 386 n. 6, 88 S. Ct. 967, 971, 972, 19 L. Ed. 2d 1247 (1968). Thus, in this sense at least, the dangers of misidentification are even greater at a photographic display than at a lineup.

Moreover, as in the lineup situation, the possibilities for impermissible suggestion in the context of a photographic display are manifold. Such suggestion, intentional or unintentional, may derive from three possible sources. First, the photographs themselves might tend to suggest which of the pictures is that of the suspect. For example, differences in age, pose, or other physical characteristics of the persons represented, and variations in the mounting, background, lighting, or markings of the photographs all might have the effect of singling out the accused.

Second, impermissible suggestion may inhere in the manner in which the photographs are displayed to the witness. The danger of misidentification is, of course, "increased if the police display to the witness . . . the pictures of several persons among which the photograph of a single such individual recurs or is in some way emphasized." *Id.* at 383, 88 S. Ct. at 970. And, if the photographs are arranged in an asymmetrical pattern, or if they are displayed in a time sequence that tends to emphasize a particular photograph, "any identification of the photograph which stands out from the rest is no more reliable than an identification of a single photograph, exhibited alone." P. Wall, *supra*, at 81.

Third, gestures or comments of the prosecutor at the time of the display may lead an otherwise uncertain witness to select the "correct" photograph. For example, the prosecutor might "indicate to the witness that [he has] other evidence that one of the persons pictured committed the crime,"[11] and might even point to a particular photograph and ask whether the person pictured "looks familiar." More subtly, the prosecutor's inflection, facial expressions, physical motions, and myriad other almost imperceptible means of communication might tend, intentionally or unintentionally,

---

11. *Simmons v. United States, supra*, at 383, 88 S. Ct. at 971.

to compromise the witness' objectivity. Thus, as is the case with lineups, "[i]mproper photographic identification procedures, . . . by exerting a suggestive influence upon the witnesses, can often lead to an erroneous identification. . . ." P. Wall, *supra*, at 89.[12] And "[r]egardless of how the initial misidentification comes about, the witness thereafter is apt to retain in his memory the image of the photograph rather than of the person actually seen. . . ." *Simmons v. United States, supra*, 390 U.S. at 383–384, 88 S. Ct. at 971. As a result, "the issue of identity may (in the absence of other relevant evidence) for all practical purposes be determined there and then, before the trial." *United States v. Wade, supra*, 388 U.S. at 229, 87 S. Ct. at 1933, quoting Williams & Hammelmann, *supra*, at 482.

Moreover, as with lineups, the defense can "seldom reconstruct" at trial the mode and manner of photographic identification. It is true, of course, that the photographs used at the pretrial display might be preserved for examination at trial. But "it may also be said that a photograph can preserve the record of a lineup; yet this does not justify a lineup without counsel." 149 U.S. App. D.C. at 9–10, 461 F.2d at 100–101. Indeed, in reality, preservation of the photographs affords little protection to the unrepresented accused. For, although retention of the photographs may mitigate the dangers of misidentification due to the suggestiveness of the photographs themselves, it cannot in any sense reveal to defense counsel the more subtle, and therefore more dangerous, suggestiveness that might derive from the manner in which the photographs were displayed or any accompanying comments or gestures. Moreover, the accused cannot rely upon the witnesses themselves to expose these latter sources of suggestion, for the witnesses are not "apt to be alert for conditions prejudicial to the suspect. And if they were, it would likely be of scant benefit to the suspect" since the witnesses are hardly "likely to be schooled in the detection of suggestive influences." *Id.* at 230, 87 S. Ct. at 1934.

Finally, and *unlike* the lineup situation, the accused himself is not even present at the photographic identification, thereby reducing the likelihood that irregularities in the procedures will ever come to light.

. . . .

---

12. The Court maintains that "the ethical responsibility of the prosecutor" is in itself a sufficient "safeguard" against impermissible suggestion at a photographic display. The same argument might, of course, be made with respect to lineups. Moreover, it is clear that the "prosecutor" is not always present at such pretrial displays. Indeed, in this very case, one of the four eyewitnesses was shown the color photographs on the morning of trial by an agent of the FBI, *not* in the presence of the "prosecutor." *See* 149 U.S. App. D.C. at 5, 461 F.2d at 96. And even though "the ethical responsibility of the prosecutor" might be an adequate "safeguard" against *intentional* suggestion, it can hardly be doubted that a "prosecutor" is, after all, only human. His behavior may be fraught with wholly *unintentional* and indeed unconscious nuances that might effectively suggest the "proper" response. And, of course, as *Wade* itself makes clear, unlike other forms of unintentional prosecutorial "manipulation," even unintentional suggestiveness at an identification procedure involves serious risks of "freezing" the witness' mistaken identification and creates almost insurmountable obstacles to reconstruction at trial.

IV

. . . .

The fundamental premise underlying *all* of this Court's decisions holding the right to counsel applicable at "critical" pretrial proceedings, is that a "stage" of the prosecution must be deemed "critical" for the purposes of the Sixth Amendment if it is one at which the presence of counsel is necessary "to protect the fairness of *the trial itself.*" *Schneckloth v. Bustamonte*, 412 U.S. 218, 239, 93 S. Ct. 2041, 2054, 36 L. Ed. 2d 854 (1973) (emphasis added). . . .

This established conception of the Sixth Amendment guarantee is, of course, in no sense dependent upon the physical "presence of the accused," at a "trial-like confrontation" with the Government, at which the accused requires the "guiding hand of counsel." On the contrary, in *Powell v. Alabama*, 287 U.S. 45, 53 S. Ct. 55, 77 L. Ed. 158 (1932), the seminal decision in this area, we explicitly held the right to counsel applicable at a stage of the pretrial proceedings involving *none* of the three criteria set forth by the Court today. In *Powell*, the defendants in a state felony prosecution were not appointed counsel until the very eve of trial. This Court held, in no uncertain terms, that such an appointment could not satisfy the demands of the Sixth Amendment, for "[i]t is vain . . . to guarantee [the accused] counsel without giving the latter any opportunity to acquaint himself with the facts or law of the case." *Id.* at 59, 53 S. Ct. at 60. In other words, *Powell* made clear that, in order to preserve the accused's right to a fair trial and to "effective and substantial"[18] assistance of counsel at that trial, the Sixth Amendment guarantee necessarily encompasses a reasonable period of time before trial during which counsel might prepare the defense. Yet it can hardly be said that this preparatory period of research and investigation involves the physical "presence of the accused," at a "trial-like confrontation" with the Government, at which the accused requires the "guiding hand of counsel."

. . . .

. . . [C]ontrary to the suggestion of the Court, the conclusion in *Wade* that a pretrial lineup is a "critical stage" of the prosecution did not in any sense turn on the fact that a lineup involves the physical "presence of the accused" at a "trial-like confrontation" with the Government. And that conclusion most certainly did not turn on the notion that presence of counsel was necessary so that counsel could offer legal advice or "guidance" to the accused at the lineup. On the contrary, *Wade* envisioned counsel's function at the lineup to be primarily that of a trained observer, able to detect the existence of any suggestive influences and capable of understanding the legal implications of the events that transpire. Having witnessed the proceedings, counsel would then be in a position effectively to reconstruct at trial any unfairness that occurred at the lineup, thereby preserving the accused's fundamental right to a fair trial on the issue of identification.

---

18. 287 U.S. at 53, 53 S. Ct. at 58.

There is something ironic about the Court's conclusion today that a pretrial lineup identification is a "critical stage" of the prosecution because counsel's presence can help to compensate for the accused's deficiencies as an observer, but that a pretrial photographic identification is not a "critical stage" of the prosecution because the accused is not able to observe at all. In my view, there simply is no meaningful difference, in terms of the need for attendance of counsel, between corporeal and photographic identifications. And applying established and well-reasoned Sixth Amendment principles, I can only conclude that a pretrial photographic display, like a pretrial lineup, is a "critical stage" of the prosecution at which the accused is constitutionally entitled to the presence of counsel.

Notes and Questions

(1) In *Moore v. Illinois*, 434 U.S. 220, 98 S. Ct. 458, 54 L. Ed. 2d 424 (1977), the Court held that the defendant's right to have a lawyer present at a pretrial identification was violated when the victim identified the defendant at a preliminary hearing in which he was not represented by counsel. The identification in *Moore* occurred after the defendant was told to stand before the bench and the prosecutor recited evidence that incriminated him. The victim was then asked whether she saw her assailant in the courtroom. In response, she pointed to defendant. At trial, the victim testified on direct that she had identified the defendant at the preliminary hearing. The State conceded that the preliminary hearing marked the "initiation of adversary judicial criminal proceedings" against the defendant. Nevertheless, it argued that the defendant had no right to counsel at the identification procedure because "it was conducted in the course of a judicial proceeding."

The Court unanimously rejected this argument. In an opinion by Justice Powell, it concluded that "[t]he reasons supporting *Wade*'s holding that a corporeal identification is a critical stage of a criminal prosecution for Sixth Amendment purposes apply with equal force to this identification. It is difficult to imagine a more suggestive manner in which to present a suspect to a witness for their critical first confrontation than was employed in this case.... Had [defendant] been represented by counsel, some or all of this suggestiveness could have been avoided."

(2) Unlike the other constitutional restrictions on investigation and proof treated in this text, the Sixth Amendment right to counsel constraints upon eyewitness identification processes and evidence have not been the subject of continuous development and evolution. As noted at the outset of this chapter, the Court first addressed the topic in 1967. The decision in *Moore v. Illinois*, in 1977, was the last time the Justices have considered any issue in the area. The Court completed all of its work in a mere 10-year span. The following excerpt from *Wood v. State*, 196 Md. App. 146, 7 A.3d 1115 (2011), provides a colorful summary of the "meteoric rise and fall" of the relationship between the right to counsel and eyewitness identifications:

> Constitutional identification law ... enjoyed a precise decade (plus four days) of high-profile celebrity between 1967 and 1977. During that decade,

it rivaled confession law and search and seizure law in the national spotlight. It commanded the attention of academic seminars and law reviews. It began with a sunburst on June 12, 1967 as the *Wade-Gilbert-Stovall* trilogy rocketed onto the national stage.

Initially, the big stars of that trio were *United States v. Wade*, 388 U.S. 218, 87 S. Ct. 1926, 18 L. Ed. 2d 1149 (1967), and *Gilbert v. California*, 388 U.S. 263, 87 S. Ct. 1951, 18 L. Ed. 2d 1178 (1967). The constitutional principle which they championed was the Sixth Amendment's guarantee of the assistance of counsel to a defendant. For the first time in constitutional history, the placing of a suspect in a police line-up for identification purposes was deemed to be a "critical stage." These are classic Sixth Amendment code words. If a defendant were placed in such a line-up without a lawyer having been provided and present, exclusion of the identification was automatically called for. Such exclusion was in high vogue, and everyone was talking about identification procedures.

Within five years, however, a Thermidorean Reaction set in. *Kirby v. Illinois*, 406 U.S. 682, 92 S. Ct. 1877, 32 L. Ed. 2d 411 (1972), first held that a suspect placed in a pre-indictment, as opposed to a post-indictment, line-up did not yet enjoy the protection of the Sixth Amendment because such a suspect was not yet an "accused." Being at a critical stage would qualify an "accused" for Sixth Amendment assistance, but if you are not yet "accused" even a critical stage would not help. Whatever little wind still propelled the exclusionary sails after *Kirby*, it was largely wafted away by the subsequent holding in *United States v. Ash*, 413 U.S. 300, 93 S. Ct. 2568, 37 L. Ed. 2d 619 (1973), that even a post-indictment exhibition of a photograph of a subject, either in a group picture or as part of an array of individual photographs, was, unlike standing the suspect in a live line-up, not a critical stage. Whereas *Kirby* had diminished the ranks of the "accused," *Ash* diminished the incidence of a "critical stage." As a basis for challenging extrajudicial identification, the Sixth Amendment essentially disappeared from the scene within five years of its initial appearance. As this Court noted in *Turner v. State*, 184 Md. App. at 179, 964 A.2d 695:

> Under the combined impact of *Kirby* and *Ash, the post-indictment line-up essentially disappeared from the world of criminal investigation, and with it any significant exclusion of identification evidence based on the Sixth Amendment's right to counsel.* The once familiar line-up parade of stage and screen has been retired to the Smithsonian. *Creative law enforcement procedures effectively finessed the Sixth Amendment.* (Emphasis supplied).

Wade and *Gilbert* are has-beens; they are yesterday's stars.

(3) For a critical examination of the cases dealing with the right to counsel at identification, see Joseph D. Grano, Kirby, Biggers, *and* Ash, *Do Any Constitutional*

Safeguards Remain Against the Danger of Convicting the Innocent?, 72 Mich. L. Rev. 717 (1974).

Identifications and Right to Counsel Problems

10–1: After Defendant was indicted for charges relating to illegal gambling, he had three conversations with Agent Fiano. At least one of these conversations was initiated by Agent Fiano while defendant was incarcerated awaiting trial. The other two conversations also occurred while Defendant was incarcerated or in police custody. All three conversations were short and limited to pleasantries. In one, for example, the two men exchanged greetings and Defendant then remarked that Agent Fiano had lost some weight and had shaved his beard.

At Defendant's trial, the government introduces tapes of several incriminating telephone conversations. Agent Fiano is prepared to testify that, based on his knowledge of the defendant's voice, he recognizes the defendant as one of the participants in these conversations. Defendant moves to suppress Agent Fiano's testimony on the ground that Fiano's identification of Defendant's voice stems from post-indictment confrontations with Defendant at which Defendant was not represented by counsel.

Is defendant's motion to suppress likely to succeed?

10–2: Shortly after Appellant's arrest for rape and robbery, the police conducted a "live" voice line-up at which the victim observed Appellant and several other individuals. At the direction of the police, Appellant and the other participants in the line-up also repeated the words spoken by the victim's attacker. Since the victim's eyes were covered during the attack, she was unable to make a visual identification. Based on the voices she heard, however, she concluded that her attacker could have been either Appellant or one other participant in the line-up. Appellant was not represented by counsel at this line-up.

Over two months later, after Appellant had been indicted for the charges, the victim listened to an audio tape of the original line-up and positively identified Appellant as her assailant. Neither Appellant nor his attorney was present at the audio tape replay. At trial, the prosecution presented a video tape (with sound) of the line-up to the jury; again, the victim identified Appellant on the basis of his voice. Appellant was convicted of rape and robbery.

Does defendant have a valid Sixth Amendment claim on appeal?

10–3: LaPierre was indicted for bank robbery. His line-up was scheduled for 1:00 p.m. on August 2. His attorney, Bervar, arrived at the police station at approximately 12:45 p.m. Bervar told FBI agent Reneer that he was there for the LaPierre line-up and asked where the lineup was going to be held. Reneer responded that he did not know, but indicated that Bervar could wait on a bench outside the hallway leading to the line-up room. Bervar did so.

Sometime after 1:00 p.m., Reneer escorted LaPierre from the cell block to the lineup room. Shortly thereafter, FBI agents Kent and Pikus entered the lineup room with the witnesses. Kent and Pikus were aware that Bervar was waiting for the lineup outside the room but apparently thought he would come in on his own when the lineup was ready to start. Inside the lineup room, the six members of the lineup stood on one side of the one-way window, while the witnesses gathered on the other side, in the viewing area. The presentation began, and the first lineup member stepped forward for inspection. At some point during the presentation of the first two lineup members, Agent Pikus noticed that attorney Bervar was not in the viewing area. Pikus left the room to get Bervar, and the two returned to the viewing area while the third lineup member was being presented. LaPierre was the fourth member of the lineup. Bervar was present for the rest of the lineup, including the presentation of LaPierre.

The entire line-up was videotaped. During the line-up, some of the witnesses identified LaPierre. LaPierre now claims that his right to have an attorney present at the lineup was violated because Bervar was not present for the entire lineup.

Should LaPierre's claim be accepted?

10–4: Defendant, who was indicted for robbery, was incarcerated for failure to make bail. The police informed him that a lineup would take place on March 10, approximately seven months after the date of the alleged crime. Defendant informed the police that he was represented by an attorney and wanted to have his attorney present at the lineup. When the defendant's attorney was informed that the lineup would be held on March 10, he called the police and told them that he would be unable to attend that day because he would be out of town and requested that the lineup be held March 11 so that he could be present. An officer told the defendant's attorney that changing the date of the lineup would be inconvenient for the witnesses. He said, "The lineup is scheduled for March 10 at 1:00 p.m. and that time will not be changed." The lineup took place as scheduled. Defendant's attorney was not present and several witnesses identified defendant as the robber.

Was the defendant's right to counsel violated?

10–5: On three occasions in February and March of 1990, a South Carolina Law Enforcement Division (SLED) officer purchased crack cocaine from a man she knew only as "Glasses." A Deputy Sheriff's officer had personal knowledge that defendant was known as "Glasses." Based on this information, a warrant was issued for defendant's arrest.

After defendant's arrest, he was housed in the county jail. He was appointed counsel on June 29, 1990. On September 3, 1990, the assistant County Solicitor had the jailer deliver defendant to a room in the County Courthouse. The only persons present were the defendant, the assistant solicitor, and the SLED officer. Neither defendant nor his attorney were given prior notice of the meeting. At trial, the SLED officer testified that the purpose of the meeting with the defendant prior to trial was not for identification, but to explain to him the charges against him. She identified the defendant as "Glasses," the person who had sold her crack cocaine. Defendant was convicted.

What argument can the defendant make on appeal? Will it be successful?

10–6: On July 29, three people were shot, two of whom died. The surviving victim gave the police a description of the shooter. Because he believed that the defendant matched the victim's description, Detective Pesavanto tried to contact the defendant. Subsequently, defendant's lawyer, Charles Ingles, contacted the police and arranged for a meeting at which Detective Pesavanto could talk to the defendant in his presence. After asking the defendant a few questions, Detective Pesavanto asked if the defendant would be willing to appear in a line-up. Ingles replied that the defendant would agree to appear in the line-up if Ingles could also be present. Pesavanto agreed.

At the line-up, the witness and several police officers were in the viewing room where they could observe the participants in the line-up. The defendant and the four other participants in the line-up were not able to see or hear the people in the viewing room. Ingles told the police that he wanted to be in the viewing room so that he could observe the witness. Detective Karl told Ingles that he could not be in the viewing room, but that he could only be with the defendant. During the line-up, Ingles stayed in a nearby conference room where he could observe the defendant. He was unable to observe anyone in the viewing room. The witness identified the defendant as the one who had shot him and the other two victims.

Did the police violate the defendant's right to have an attorney present at the line-up?

10–7: In November, 2000, Officer Rubin responded to an armed robbery call and observed a white car matching the description of the suspect's car fleeing from the scene. As the car passed Rubin, he observed the driver for approximately one second before making a U-turn and giving chase. The chase ended when Rubin crashed his police cruiser. One week later, Rubin saw a "career criminal auto theft" BOLO flyer distributed by the auto theft task force. The flyer had six photographs, including a photograph of Nathaniel. Rubin recognized Nathaniel as the driver of the fleeing white car.

Subsequently, Nathaniel was charged with crimes unrelated to the armed robbery and was appointed counsel. Based on facts learned about the armed robbery, the State arranged for Nathaniel to participate in a live lineup that was viewed by the victims of that crime. His court-appointed lawyer was present. After Nathaniel was identified by a victim of the robbery, he was charged with robbery and armed assault. The lineup procedure was videotaped.

Prior to trial, Nathaniel disclosed six alibi witnesses. In February, 2002, after deposing Nathaniel's alibi witnesses, the state attorney called Officer Rubin to his office and showed him the videotape of the lineup in which Nathaniel had participated. Rubin identified Nathaniel as the man he saw speeding away in the white car when he responded to the armed robbery call.

Nathaniel moved to suppress Rubin's identification. After holding an evidentiary hearing, the trial judge suppressed Rubin's identification of Nathaniel at the showing of the videotape, but ruled that the officer could testify at trial based on what he personally observed in November, 2000.

Did the trial judge rule correctly?

10–8: Anton was arrested for and charged with robbery. Detective More arranged lineups at which Anton was identified by the robbery victims. Subsequently, Anton pleaded guilty to the robbery and was sentenced to serve a prison term. While incarcerated, Anton filed a civil rights action against Detective More, claiming that More had violated his constitutional rights in the conduct of the lineups. Specifically, Anton alleged that Detective More had violated his Fourteenth Amendment right to due process by using unduly and unnecessarily suggestive identification procedures and had violated his Sixth Amendment right to counsel by holding the lineups in the absence of counsel or a valid waiver of counsel.

Detective More filed a motion to dismiss Anton's claims.

What arguments support More's motion? Should the trial judge dismiss the claims?

Selected Bibliography

Joseph D. Grano, Kirby, Biggers, *and* Ash: *Do Any Constitutional Safeguards Remain Against the Danger of Convicting the Innocent?*, 72 Mich. L. Rev. 717 (1974)

Felice J. Levine & June Louin Tapp, *The Psychology of Criminal Identifications: The Gap from* Wade *to* Kirby, 121 U. Pa. L. Rev. 1079 (1973)

Elizabeth F. Loftus, Eyewitness Testimony (1979)

Patrick M. Wall, Eyewitness Identification in Criminal Cases (1965)

Gary L. Wells & Eric P. Seelau, *Eyewitness Identification: Psychological Research and Legal Policy on Line-ups*, 1 Psych. Pub. Pol. & L. 765 (1995)

Daniel A. Yarmey, The Psychology of Eyewitness Testimony (1979)

Chapter 11

The Due Process Clause and Identifications

Introductory Note

When the Court promulgated its three identification decisions in 1967, the majority undoubtedly believed that the right to counsel granted by *Wade* and *Gilbert* would be the primary constitutional protection against suggestive identification procedures. The majority probably viewed the due process right afforded by *Stovall* as a right that would have limited significance because it would be important only in those relatively rare instances in which the right to counsel was inapplicable.

As we saw in Chapter 10, however, the *Wade* and *Gilbert* decisions have been sharply limited. After the decisions in *Kirby* and *Ash*, it is clear that the police have the power to arrange pretrial identifications that are not subject to the Sixth Amendment. As a result, the Due Process Clause has become the primary constitutional means of controlling police practices used to obtain identifications and regulating the admissibility of identification evidence.

In considering the cases in this chapter, students should try to delineate the elements of the current due process test and to determine how that test is likely to be applied in practice. In addition, they should consider how the due process test announced in *Stovall v. Denno*, 388 U.S. 293, 87 S. Ct. 1967, 18 L. Ed. 2d 1199 (1967), has been changed by the Court's later decisions and whether those changes are consistent with the purposes of either the Court's decisions in *Wade, Stovall* and *Gilbert* or those of the Due Process Clause itself. Finally, students should analyze and reflect upon the constitutional justifications for the Due Process Clause prohibition on the introduction of eyewitness identification evidence at trial.

Stovall v. Denno

United States Supreme Court

388 U.S. 293, 87 S. Ct. 1967, 18 L. Ed. 2d 1199 (1967)

MR. JUSTICE BRENNAN delivered the opinion of the Court.

. . . .

Dr. Paul Behrendt was stabbed to death in the kitchen of his home in Garden City, Long Island, about midnight August 23, 1961. Dr. Behrendt's wife, also a physician, had followed her husband to the kitchen and jumped at the assailant. He knocked her to the floor and stabbed her 11 times. The police found a shirt on the kitchen floor and keys in a pocket which they traced to petitioner. They arrested him on the afternoon of August 24. An arraignment was promptly held but was postponed until petitioner could retain counsel.

Mrs. Behrendt was hospitalized for major surgery to save her life. The police, without affording petitioner time to retain counsel, arranged with her surgeon to permit them to bring petitioner to her hospital room about noon of August 25, the day after the surgery. Petitioner was handcuffed to one of five police officers who, with two members of the staff of the District Attorney, brought him to the hospital room. Petitioner was the only Negro in the room. Mrs. Behrendt identified him from her hospital bed after being asked by an officer whether he "was the man" and after petitioner repeated at the direction of an officer a "few words for voice identification." None of the witnesses could recall the words that were used. Mrs. Behrendt and the officers testified at the trial to her identification of the petitioner in the hospital room, and she also made an in-court identification of petitioner in the courtroom.

Petitioner was convicted and sentenced to death. The New York Court of Appeals affirmed without opinion. Petitioner *pro se* sought federal habeas corpus in the District Court for the Southern District of New York. He claimed that among other constitutional rights allegedly denied him at his trial, the admission of Mrs. Behrendt's identification testimony violated his rights under the Fifth, Sixth, and Fourteenth Amendments because he had been compelled to submit to the hospital room confrontation without the help of counsel and under circumstances which unfairly focused the witness' attention on him as the man believed by the police to be the guilty person. The District Court dismissed the petition after hearing argument on an unrelated claim of an alleged invalid search and seizure. On appeal to the Court of Appeals for the Second Circuit a panel of that court initially reversed the dismissal after reaching the issue of the admissibility of Mrs. Behrendt's identification evidence and holding it inadmissible on the ground that the hospital room identification violated petitioner's constitutional right to the assistance of counsel. The Court of Appeals thereafter heard the case *en banc*, vacated the panel decision, and affirmed the District Court. We granted certiorari.

. . . .

I

We turn now to the question whether petitioner, although not entitled to the application of *Wade* and *Gilbert* to his case, is entitled to relief on his claim that in any event the confrontation conducted in this case was so unnecessarily suggestive and conducive to irreparable mistaken identification that he was denied due process of law. This is a recognized ground of attack upon a conviction independent of any right to counsel claim. *Palmer v. Peyton*, 359 F.2d 199 (C.A. 4th Cir. 1966). The practice of showing suspects singly to persons for the purpose of identification, and not as part of a lineup, has been widely condemned.[6] However, a claimed violation of due process of law in the conduct of a confrontation depends on the totality of the circumstances surrounding it, and the record in the present case reveals that the showing of Stovall to Mrs. Behrendt in an immediate hospital confrontation was imperative. The Court of Appeals, *en banc*, stated, 355 F.2d at 735,

> Here was the only person in the world who could possibly exonerate Stovall. Her words, and only her words, "He is not the man" could have resulted in freedom for Stovall. The hospital was not far distant from the courthouse and jail. No one knew how long Mrs. Behrendt might live. Faced with the responsibility of identifying the attacker, with the need for immediate action and with the knowledge that Mrs. Behrendt could not visit the jail, the police followed the only feasible procedure and took Stovall to the hospital room. Under these circumstances, the usual police station line-up, which Stovall now argues he should have had, was out of the question.

The judgment of the Court of Appeals is affirmed. It is so ordered.

Affirmed.

[The opinions of MR. JUSTICE DOUGLAS and MR. JUSTICE FORTAS have been omitted.]

MR. JUSTICE WHITE, whom MR. JUSTICE HARLAN and MR. JUSTICE STEWART join.

For the reasons stated in my separate opinion in *United States v. Wade*, 388 U.S. 250, 87 S. Ct. 1944, I perceive no constitutional error in the identification procedure to which the petitioner was subjected. I concur in the result and in that portion of the Court's opinion which limits application of the new Sixth Amendment rule.

[The dissenting opinion of MR. JUSTICE BLACK has been omitted.]

Notes and Questions

(1) The first issue considered in *Stovall* was whether the Sixth Amendment holdings in *United States v. Wade*, 388 U.S. 218, 87 S. Ct. 1926, 18 L. Ed. 2d 1149 (1967), and *Gilbert v. California*, 388 U.S. 263, 87 S. Ct. 1951, 18 L. Ed. 2d 1178 (1967), would

---

6. *See* Wall, EYE-WITNESS IDENTIFICATION IN CRIMINAL CASES 26–40; Paul, *Identification of Accused Persons*, 12 Austl. L.J. 42, 44 (1938); Williams & Hammelmann, *Identification Parades, Part I*, [1963] Crim. L. Rev. 479, 480–481; Frankfurter, THE CASE OF SACCO AND VANZETTI 31–32.

apply to Stovall's case. The Court held that the decisions in *Wade* and *Gilbert* would "affect only [*Wade* and *Gilbert*] and all future cases which involve confrontations for identification purposes conducted in the absence of counsel after" June 12, 1967, the date of the *Wade, Gilbert* and *Stovall* decisions. Since the confrontation in *Stovall* occurred prior to June 12, 1967, the *Wade* and *Gilbert* decisions did not apply to that case.

Why shouldn't a new constitutional decision apply to all cases regardless of whether they arose before the time of the Court's decision? Assuming some constitutional decisions should not be retroactively applied, what should be the basis for determining a decision's retroactivity? For recent cases dealing with the issue of a constitutional decision's retroactivity, see *Teague v. Lane*, 489 U.S. 288, 109 S. Ct. 1060, 103 L. Ed. 2d 334 (1989); *Griffith v. Kentucky*, 479 U.S. 314, 107 S. Ct. 708, 93 L. Ed. 2d 649 (1987); *Shea v. Louisiana*, 470 U.S. 51, 105 S. Ct. 1065, 84 L. Ed. 2d 38 (1985). For articles considering the issues raised by the retroactivity cases, see, *e.g.*, James S. Liebman, *More Than "Slightly Retro": The Rehnquist Court's Rout of Habeas Corpus Jurisdiction in* Teague v. Lane, 18 N.Y.U. Rev. L. & Soc. Change 537 (1991); John B. Corr, *Retroactivity: A Study in Supreme Court Doctrine "As Applied,"* 61 N.C. L. Rev. 745 (1983); Paul M. Mishkin, *The High Court, the Great Writ, and the Due Process of Time and Law*, 79 Harv. L. Rev. 56 (1965).

(2) Two years after its decision in *Stovall*, the Court in *Foster v. California*, 394 U.S 440, 89 S. Ct. 1127, 22 L. Ed. 2d 402 (1969), held that a pretrial identification was so unnecessarily suggestive and conducive to irreparable mistaken identification that the introduction of testimony regarding that identification violated due process. In *Foster*, the sole witness to a robbery of a Western Union office identified the defendant only after he had viewed him in two line-ups and attempted to make an identification at a one-on-one confrontation.

At the first line-up, the witness observed the defendant, who was close to six feet in height, and two other men who were at least five or six inches shorter. The defendant was wearing a leather jacket which the witness said was similar to the one he had seen underneath the coveralls worn by one of the robbers. After seeing this line-up, the witness said he "thought" the defendant was one of the robbers but he was not sure. The defendant was then brought into an office and seated at a table across from the witness. The witness was still uncertain whether defendant was one of the robbers. A week or 10 days later, the police arranged a second line-up in which the witness viewed the defendant and four other men. The defendant was the only person in the second line-up who had appeared in the first line-up. This time, the witness positively identified the defendant as one of the robbers. At trial, the witness testified to his pretrial identifications of the defendant and also identified him in court.

In his opinion for a bare majority of the Court, Justice Fortas stated: "The suggestive elements in this identification procedure made it all but inevitable that [the witness] would identify [the defendant] whether or not he was in fact 'the man.' In effect, the police repeatedly said to the witness, 'This is the man.' This procedure so undermined the reliability of the eyewitness identification as to violate due process." Justices White, Harlan, Stewart, and Black dissented.

Foster is the only case in which the Supreme Court has held that admission of identification evidence violated due process.

(3) In *Foster*, the Court did not make it clear whether on remand the witness's in-court identification would be admissible if the prosecution could establish that the in-court identification did not stem from the suggestive pretrial confrontations but had an independent source. In *Coleman v. Alabama*, 399 U.S. 1, 90 S. Ct. 1999, 26 L. Ed. 2d 387 (1970), however, the Court indicated that a courtroom identification following a pretrial identification so unnecessarily suggestive as to violate due process would still be admissible as long as the courtroom identification did not stem from the pretrial identification. For consideration of the lower courts' treatment of this issue prior to the Supreme Court's decision in *Manson v. Brathwaite*, see Charles A. Pulaski, Neil v. Biggers: *The Supreme Court Dismantles the* Wade *Trilogy's Due Process Protection*, 26 Stan. L. Rev. 1097, 1111–13 (1974).

Manson v. Brathwaite

United States Supreme Court

432 U.S. 98, 97 S. Ct. 2243, 53 L. Ed. 2d 140 (1977)

MR. JUSTICE BLACKMUN delivered the opinion of the Court.

. . . .

I

Jimmy D. Glover, a full-time trooper of the Connecticut State Police, in 1970 was assigned to the Narcotics Division in an undercover capacity. On May 5 of that year, about 7:45 p.m., e.d.t., and while there was still daylight, Glover and Henry Alton Brown, an informant, went to an apartment building at 201 Westland, in Hartford, for the purpose of purchasing narcotics from "Dickie Boy" Cicero, a known narcotics dealer. Cicero, it was thought, lived on the third floor of that apartment building. Glover and Brown entered the building, observed by back-up Officers D'Onofrio and Gaffey, and proceeded by stairs to the third floor. Glover knocked at the door of one of the two apartments served by the stairway.[2] The area was illuminated by natural light from a window in the third floor hallway. The door was opened 12 to 18 inches in response to the knock. Glover observed a man standing at the door and, behind him, a woman. Brown identified himself. Glover then asked for "two things" of narcotics. The man at the door held out his hand, and Glover gave him two $10 bills. The door closed. Soon the man returned and handed Glover two

---

2. It appears that the door on which Glover knocked may not have been that of the Cicero apartment. Petitioner concedes, in any event, that the transaction effected "was with some other person than had been intended."

glassine bags.[3] While the door was open, Glover stood within two feet of the person from whom he made the purchase and observed his face. Five to seven minutes elapsed from the time the door first opened until it closed the second time.

Glover and Brown then left the building. This was about eight minutes after their arrival. Glover drove to headquarters where he described the seller to D'Onofrio and Gaffey. Glover at that time did not know the identity of the seller. He described him as being "a colored man, approximately five feet eleven inches tall, dark complexion, black hair, short Afro style, and having high cheekbones, and of heavy build. He was wearing at the time blue pants and a plaid shirt." D'Onofrio, suspecting from this description that respondent might be the seller, obtained a photograph of respondent from the Records Division of the Hartford Police Department. He left it at Glover's office. D'Onofrio was not acquainted with respondent personally but did know him by sight and had seen him "[s]everal times" prior to May 5. Glover, when alone, viewed the photograph for the first time upon his return to headquarters on May 7; he identified the person shown as the one from whom he had purchased the narcotics.

The toxicological report on the contents of the glassine bags revealed the presence of heroin. The report was dated July 16, 1970.

Respondent was arrested on July 27 while visiting at the apartment of a Mrs. Ramsey on the third floor of 201 Westland. This was the apartment at which the narcotics sale had taken place on May 5.[4]

Respondent was charged, in a two-count information, with possession and sale of heroin, in violation of Conn. Gen. Stat. (Rev. of 1958, as amended in 1969), §§ 19–481a and 19–480a (1977). At his trial in January 1971, the photograph from which Glover had identified respondent was received in evidence without objection on the part of the defense. Glover also testified that, although he had not seen respondent in the eight months that had elapsed since the sale, "there [was] no doubt whatsoever" in his mind that the person shown on the photograph was respondent. Glover also made a positive in-court identification without objection.

No explanation was offered by the prosecution for the failure to utilize a photographic array or to conduct a lineup.

Respondent, who took the stand in his own defense, testified that on May 5, the day in question, he had been ill at his Albany Avenue apartment ("a lot of back pains,

---

3. This was Glover's testimony. Brown later was called as a witness for the prosecution. He testified on direct examination that, due to his then use of heroin, he had no clear recollection of the details of the incident. On cross-examination, as in an interview with defense counsel the preceding day, he said that it was a woman who opened the door, received the money, and thereafter produced the narcotics. On redirect, he acknowledged that he was using heroin daily at the time, that he had had some that day, and that there was "an inability to recall and remember events."

4. Respondent testified: "Lots of times I have been there before in that building." He also testified that Mrs. Ramsey was a friend of his wife, that her apartment was the only one in the building he ever visited, and that he and his family, consisting of his wife and five children, did not live there but at 453 Albany Avenue, Hartford.

muscle spasms . . . a bad heart . . . high blood pressure . . . neuralgia in my face, and sinus") and that at no time on that particular day had he been at 201 Westland. His wife testified that she recalled, after her husband had refreshed her memory, that he was home all day on May 5. Doctor Wesley M. Vietzke, an internist and assistant professor of medicine at the University of Connecticut, testified that respondent had consulted him on April 15, 1970, and that he took a medical history from him, heard his complaints about his back and facial pain, and discovered that he had high blood pressure. The physician found respondent, subjectively, "in great discomfort." Respondent in fact underwent surgery for a herniated disc at L5 and S1 on August 17.

The jury found respondent guilty on both counts of the information. He received a sentence of not less than six nor more than nine years. His conviction was affirmed *per curiam* by the Supreme Court of Connecticut. . . .

Fourteen months later, respondent filed a petition for habeas corpus in the United States District Court for the District of Connecticut. He alleged that the admission of the identification testimony at his state trial deprived him of due process of law to which he was entitled under the Fourteenth Amendment. The District Court, by an unreported written opinion based on the court's review of the state trial transcript, dismissed respondent's petition. On appeal, the United States Court of Appeals for the Second Circuit reversed, with instructions to issue the writ unless the State gave notice of a desire to retry respondent and the new trial occurred within a reasonable time to be fixed by the District Judge.

In brief summary, the court felt that evidence as to the photograph should have been excluded, regardless of reliability, because the examination of the single photograph was unnecessary and suggestive. And, in the court's view, the evidence was unreliable in any event. We granted certiorari.

. . . .

IV

Petitioner at the outset acknowledges that "the procedure in the instant case was suggestive [because only one photograph was used] and unnecessary" [because there was no emergency or exigent circumstance]. The respondent, in agreement with the Court of Appeals, proposes a *per se* rule of exclusion that he claims is dictated by the demands of the Fourteenth Amendment's guarantee of due process. He rightly observes that this is the first case in which this Court has had occasion to rule upon strictly post-*Stovall* out-of-court identification evidence of the challenged kind.

Since the decision in [*Neil v. Biggers*, 409 U.S. 188, 93 S. Ct. 375, 34 L. Ed. 2d 401 (1972)], the Courts of Appeals appear to have developed at least two approaches to such evidence. *See* Pulaski, *Neil v. Biggers: The Supreme Court Dismantles the Wade Trilogy's Due Process Protection*, 26 Stan. L. Rev. 1097, 1111–1114 (1974). The first, or *per se* approach, employed by the Second Circuit in the present case, focuses on the procedures employed and requires exclusion of the out-of-court identification evidence, without regard to reliability, whenever it has been obtained through unnecessarily suggested confrontation procedures.[10] The justifications advanced are the elimination of evidence of uncertain reliability, deterrence of the police and prosecutors, and the stated "fair assurance against the awful risks of misidentification." 527 F.2d at 371.

The second, or more lenient, approach is one that continues to rely on the totality of the circumstances. It permits the admission of the confrontation evidence if, despite the suggestive aspect, the out-of-court identification possesses certain features of reliability. Its adherents feel that the *per se* approach is not mandated by the Due Process Clause of the Fourteenth Amendment. This second approach, in contrast to the other, is *ad hoc* and serves to limit the societal costs imposed by a sanction that excludes relevant evidence from consideration and evaluation by the trier of fact.

. . . .

There are, of course, several interests to be considered and taken into account. The driving force behind *United States v. Wade*, 388 U.S. 218, 87 S. Ct. 1926, 18 L. Ed. 2d 1149 (1967), *Gilbert v. California*, 388 U.S. 263, 87 S. Ct. 1951, 18 L. Ed. 2d 1178 (1967) (right to counsel at a post-indictment line-up), and *Stovall*, all decided on the same day, was the Court's concern with the problems of eyewitness identification. Usually the witness must testify about an encounter with a total stranger under circumstances of emergency or emotional stress. The witness' recollection of the stranger can be distorted easily by the circumstances or by later actions of the police. Thus, *Wade* and its companion cases reflect the concern that the jury not hear eyewitness testimony unless that evidence has aspects of reliability. It must be observed that both approaches before us are responsive to this concern. The *per se* rule, however, goes too far since its application automatically and peremptorily, and without consideration of alleviating factors, keeps evidence from the jury that is reliable and relevant.

The second factor is deterrence. Although the *per se* approach has the more significant deterrent effect, the totality approach also has an influence on police behavior. The police will guard against unnecessarily suggestive procedures under the totality rule, as well as the *per se* one, for fear that their actions will lead to the exclusion of identifications as unreliable.[12]

The third factor is the effect on the administration of justice. Here the *per se* approach suffers serious drawbacks. Since it denies the trier reliable evidence, it may result, on occasion, in the guilty going free. Also, because of its rigidity, the *per se*

---

10. Although the *per se* approach demands the exclusion of testimony concerning unnecessarily suggestive identifications, it does permit the admission of testimony concerning a subsequent identification, including an in-court identification, if the subsequent identification is determined to be reliable. The totality approach, in contrast, is simpler: if the challenged identification is reliable, then testimony as to it and any identification in its wake is admissible.

12. The interest in obtaining convictions of the guilty also urges the police to adopt procedures that show the resulting identification to be accurate. Suggestive procedures often will vitiate the weight of the evidence at trial and the jury may tend to discount such evidence. *Cf.* McGowan, *Constitutional Interpretation and Criminal Identification*, 12 Wm. & Mary L. Rev. 235, 241 (1970).

approach may make error by the trial judge more likely than the totality approach. And in those cases in which the admission of identification evidence is error under the *per se* approach but not under the totality approach — cases in which the identification is reliable despite an unnecessarily suggestive identification procedure — reversal is a Draconian sanction.[13] Certainly, inflexible rules of exclusion that may frustrate rather than promote justice have not been viewed recently by this Court with unlimited enthusiasm.

. . . .

The standard, after all, is that of fairness as required by the Due Process Clause of the Fourteenth Amendment. *Stovall*, with its reference to "the totality of the circumstances," 388 U.S. at 302, 87 S. Ct. at 1972, and *Biggers*, with its continuing stress on the same totality, did not, singly or together, establish a strict exclusionary rule or new standard of due process. Judge Leventhal, although speaking pre-*Biggers* and of a pre-*Wade* situation, correctly has described *Stovall* as protecting an *evidentiary* interest and, at the same time, as recognizing the limited extent of that interest in our adversary system.[14]

We therefore conclude that reliability is the linchpin in determining the admissibility of identification testimony for both pre- and post-*Stovall* confrontations. The factors to be considered are set out in *Biggers*. These include the opportunity of the witness to view the criminal at the time of the crime, the witness' degree of attention, the accuracy of his prior description of the criminal, the level of certainty demonstrated at the confrontation, and the time between the crime and the confrontation. Against these factors is to be weighed the corrupting effect of the suggestive identification itself.

V

We turn, then, to the facts of this case and apply the analysis:

1. *The opportunity to view.* Glover testified that for two to three minutes he stood at the apartment door, within two feet of the respondent. The door opened twice, and each time the man stood at the door. The moments passed, the conversation took place, and payment was made. Glover looked directly at his vendor. It was near sunset, to be sure, but the sun had not yet

---

13. Unlike a warrantless search, a suggestive preindictment identification procedure does not in itself intrude upon a constitutionally protected interest. Thus, considerations urging the exclusion of evidence deriving from a constitutional violation do not bear on the instant problem.

14. "In essence what the *Stovall* due process right protects is an evidentiary interest . . . . "It is part of our adversary system that we accept at trial much evidence that has strong elements of untrustworthiness — an obvious example being the testimony of witnesses with a bias. While identification testimony is significant evidence, such testimony is still only evidence, and, unlike the presence of counsel, is not a factor that goes to the very heart — the 'integrity' — of the adversary process. "Counsel can both cross-examine the identification witnesses and argue in summation as to factors causing doubts as to the accuracy of the identification — including reference to both any suggestibility in the identification procedure and any countervailing testimony such as alibi." *Clemons v. United States*, 408 F.2d 1230, 1251, 133 U.S. App. D.C. 27, 48 (1968)(concurring opinion) (footnote omitted), *cert. denied,* 394 U.S. 964, 89 S. Ct. 1318, 22 L. Ed. 2d 567 (1969).

set, so it was not dark or even dusk or twilight. Natural light from outside entered the hallway through a window. There was natural light, as well, from inside the apartment.

2. *The degree of attention.* Glover was not a casual or passing observer, as is so often the case with eyewitness identification. Trooper Glover was a trained police officer on duty—and specialized and dangerous duty—when he called at the third floor of 201 Westland in Hartford on May 5, 1970. Glover himself was a Negro and unlikely to perceive only general features of "hundreds of Hartford black males," as the Court of Appeals stated. It is true that Glover's duty was that of ferreting out narcotics offenders and that he would be expected in his work to produce results. But it is also true that, as a specially trained, assigned, and experienced officer, he could be expected to pay scrupulous attention to detail, for he knew that subsequently he would have to find and arrest his vendor. In addition, he knew that his claimed observations would be subject later to close scrutiny and examination at any trial.

3. *The accuracy of the description.* Glover's description was given to D'Onofrio within minutes after the transaction. It included the vendor's race, his height, his build, the color and style of his hair, and the high cheekbone facial feature. It also included clothing the vendor wore. No claim has been made that respondent did not possess the physical characteristics so described. D'Onofrio reacted positively at once. Two days later, when Glover was alone, he viewed the photograph D'Onofrio produced and identified its subject as the narcotics seller.

4. *The witness' level of certainty.* There is no dispute that the photograph in question was that of respondent. Glover, in response to a question whether the photograph was that of the person from whom he made the purchase, testified: "There is no question whatsoever." This positive assurance was repeated.

5. *The time between the crime and the confrontation.* Glover's description of his vendor was given to D'Onofrio within minutes of the crime. The photographic identification took place only two days later. We do not have here the passage of weeks or months between the crime and the viewing of the photograph.

These indicators of Glover's ability to make an accurate identification are hardly outweighed by the corrupting effect of the challenged identification itself. Although identifications arising from single-photograph displays may be viewed in general with suspicion, *see Simmons v. United States,* 390 U.S. at 383, 88 S. Ct. at 970–971, we find in the instant case little pressure on the witness to acquiesce in the suggestion that such a display entails. D'Onofrio had left the photograph at Glover's office and was not present when Glover first viewed it two days after the event. There thus was little urgency and Glover could view the photograph at his leisure. And since Glover examined the photograph alone, there was no coercive pressure to make an identification arising from the presence of another. The identification was made in circumstances allowing care and reflection.

Although it plays no part in our analysis, all this assurance as to the reliability of the identification is hardly undermined by the facts that respondent was arrested in the very apartment where the sale had taken place, and that he acknowledged his frequent visits to that apartment.

Surely, we cannot say that under all the circumstances of this case there is "a very substantial likelihood of irreparable misidentification." *Id.* at 384, 88 S. Ct. at 971. Short of that point, such evidence is for the jury to weigh. We are content to rely upon the good sense and judgment of American juries, for evidence with some element of untrustworthiness is customary grist for the jury mill. Juries are not so susceptible that they cannot measure intelligently the weight of identification testimony that has some questionable feature.

Of course, it would have been better had D'Onofrio presented Glover with a photographic array including "so far as practicable . . . a reasonable number of persons similar to any person then suspected whose likeness is included in the array." Model Code, § 160.2(2). The use of that procedure would have enhanced the force of the identification at trial and would have avoided the risk that the evidence would be excluded as unreliable. But we are not disposed to view D'Onofrio's failure as one of constitutional dimension to be enforced by a rigorous and unbending exclusionary rule. The defect, if there be one, goes to weight and not to substance.

We conclude that the criteria laid down in *Biggers* are to be applied in determining the admissibility of evidence offered by the prosecution concerning a post-*Stovall* identification, and that those criteria are satisfactorily met and complied with here.

The judgment of the Court of Appeals is *reversed.*

It is so ordered.

MR. JUSTICE STEVENS, concurring.

While I join the Court's opinion, I would emphasize two points.

First, as I indicated in my opinion in *United States ex rel. Kirby v. Sturges*, 510 F.2d 397, 405–406 (7th Cir. 1975), the arguments in favor of fashioning new rules to minimize the danger of convicting the innocent on the basis of unreliable eyewitness testimony carry substantial force. Nevertheless, for the reasons stated in that opinion, as well as those stated by the Court today, I am persuaded that this rulemaking function can be performed "more effectively by the legislative process than by a somewhat clumsy judicial fiat," *id.* at 408, and that the Federal Constitution does not foreclose experimentation by the States in the development of such rules.

Second, in evaluating the admissibility of particular identification testimony it is sometimes difficult to put other evidence of guilt entirely to one side.* MR. JUSTICE

---

* In this case, for example, the fact that the defendant was a regular visitor to the apartment where the drug transaction occurred tends to confirm his guilt. In the *Kirby* case, where the conviction was for robbery, the fact that papers from the victim's wallet were found in the possession of the defendant made it difficult to question the reliability of the identification. These facts should

BLACKMUN's opinion for the Court carefully avoids this pitfall and correctly relies only on appropriate indicia of the reliability of the identification itself. Although I consider the factual question in this case extremely close, I am persuaded that the Court has resolved it properly.

MR. JUSTICE MARSHALL, with whom MR. JUSTICE BRENNAN joins, dissenting.

Today's decision can come as no surprise to those who have been watching the Court dismantle the protections against mistaken eyewitness testimony erected a decade ago in *United States v. Wade*, 388 U.S. 218, 87 S. Ct. 1926, 18 L. Ed. 2d 1149 (1967); *Gilbert v. California*, 388 U.S. 263, 87 S. Ct. 1951, 18 L. Ed. 2d 1178 (1967); and *Stovall v. Denno*, 388 U.S. 293, 87 S. Ct. 1967, 18 L. Ed. 2d 1199 (1967). But it is still distressing to see the Court virtually ignore the teaching of experience embodied in those decisions and blindly uphold the conviction of a defendant who may well be innocent.

I

The magnitude of the Court's error can be seen by analyzing the cases in the *Wade* trilogy and the decisions following it. The foundation of the *Wade* trilogy was the Court's recognition of the "high incidence of miscarriage of justice" resulting from the admission of mistaken eyewitness identification evidence at criminal trials. *United States v. Wade, supra* at 228, 87 S. Ct. at 1933. Relying on numerous studies made over many years by such scholars as Professor Wigmore and Mr. Justice Frankfurter, the Court concluded that "[t]he vagaries of eyewitness identification are well-known; the annals of criminal law are rife with instances of mistaken identification." *Id.* It is, of course, impossible to control one source of such errors — the faulty perceptions and unreliable memories of witnesses — except through vigorously contested trials conducted by diligent counsel and judges. The Court in the *Wade* cases acted, however, to minimize the more preventable threat posed to accurate identification by "the degree of suggestion inherent in the manner in which the prosecution presents the suspect to witnesses for pretrial identification." *Id.*

. . . .

Stovall . . . established a due process right of criminal suspects to be free from confrontations that, under all the circumstances, are unnecessarily suggestive. The right was enforceable by exclusion at trial of evidence of the constitutionally invalid identification. Comparison with *Wade* and *Gilbert* confirms this interpretation. Where their Sixth Amendment holding did not apply, *Stovall* found an analogous Fourteenth Amendment right to a lineup conducted in a fundamentally fair manner. This interpretation is reinforced by the Court's statement that "a claimed viola-

---

not, however, be considered to support the admissibility of eyewitness testimony when applying the criteria identified in *Neil v. Biggers*, 409 U.S. 188, 93 S. Ct. 375, 34 L. Ed. 2d 401. Properly analyzed, however, such facts would be relevant to a question whether error, if any, in admitting identification testimony was harmless.

tion of due process of law *in the conduct of a confrontation* depends on the totality of the circumstances surrounding it." 388 U.S. at 302, 87 S. Ct. at 1972 (emphasis added). Significantly, several years later, *Stovall* was viewed in precisely the same way, even as the Court limited *Wade* and *Gilbert* to post-indictment confrontations: "The Due Process Clause . . . *forbids a lineup* that is unnecessarily suggestive and conducive to irreparable mistaken identification. *Stovall v. Denno*, 388 U.S. 293, 87 S. Ct. 1967, 18 L. Ed. 2d 1199; *Foster v. California*, 394 U.S. 440, 89 S. Ct. 1127, 22 L. Ed. 2d 402." *Kirby v. Illinois*, 406 U.S. 682, 691, 92 S. Ct. 1877, 1883, 32 L. Ed. 2d 411 (1972) (emphasis added).

. . . .

The development of due process protections against mistaken identification evidence, begun in *Stovall*, was continued in *Simmons v. United States*, 390 U.S. 377, 88 S. Ct. 967, 19 L. Ed. 2d 1247 (1968). There, the Court developed a different rule to deal with the admission of in-court identification testimony that the accused claimed had been fatally tainted by a previous suggestive confrontation. In *Simmons*, the exclusionary effect of *Stovall* had already been accomplished, since the prosecution made no use of the suggestive confrontation. *Simmons*, therefore, did not deal with the constitutionality of the pretrial identification procedure. The only question was the impact of the Due Process Clause on an in-court identification that was not itself unnecessarily suggestive. *Simmons* held that due process was violated by the later identification if the pretrial procedure had been "so impermissibly suggestive as to give rise to a very substantial likelihood of irreparable misidentification." 390 U.S. at 384, 88 S. Ct. at 971. This test focused, not on the necessity for the challenged pretrial procedure, but on the degree of suggestiveness that it entailed. In applying this test, the Court understandably considered the circumstances surrounding the witnesses' initial opportunity to view the crime. Finding that any suggestion in the pretrial confrontation had not affected the fairness of the in-court identification, *Simmons* rejected petitioner's due process attack on his conviction.

Again, comparison with the *Wade* cases is instructive. The inquiry mandated by *Simmons* is similar to the independent-source test used in *Wade* where an in-court identification is sought following an uncounseled lineup. In both cases, the issue is whether the witness is identifying the defendant solely on the basis of his memory of events at the time of the crime, or whether he is merely remembering the person he picked out in a pretrial procedure. Accordingly, in both situations, the relevant inquiry includes factors bearing on the accuracy of the witness' identification, including his opportunity to view the crime.

Thus, *Stovall* and *Simmons* established two different due process tests for two very different situations. Where the prosecution sought to use evidence of a questionable pretrial identification, *Stovall* required its exclusion, because due process had been violated by the confrontation, unless the necessity for the unduly suggestive procedure outweighed its potential for generating an irreparably mistaken identification. The *Simmons* test, on the other hand, was directed to ascertaining due process violations in the introduction of in-court identification testimony that the defendant claimed was tainted by pretrial procedures. In the latter situation, a court could consider the reliability of the identification under all the circumstances.

. . . .

. . . [I]n determining the admissibility of the post-*Stovall* identification in this case, the Court considers two alternatives, a *per se* exclusionary rule and a totality-of-the-circumstances approach. The Court weighs three factors in deciding that the totality approach . . . should be applied. In my view, the Court wrongly evaluates the impact of these factors.

First, the Court acknowledges that one of the factors, deterrence of police use of unnecessarily suggestive identification procedures, favors the *per se* rule. Indeed, it does so heavily, for such a rule would make it unquestionably clear to the police they must never use a suggestive procedure when a fairer alternative is available. I have no doubt that conduct would quickly conform to the rule.

Second, the Court gives passing consideration to the dangers of eyewitness identification recognized in the *Wade* trilogy. It concludes, however, that the grave risk of error does not justify adoption of the *per se* approach because that would too often result in exclusion of relevant evidence. In my view, this conclusion totally ignores the lessons of *Wade*. The dangers of mistaken identification are, as *Stovall* held, simply too great to permit unnecessarily suggestive identifications. Neither *Biggers* nor the Court's opinion today points to any contrary empirical evidence. Studies since *Wade* have only reinforced the validity of its assessment of the dangers of identification testimony.[8] While the Court is "content to rely on the good sense and judgment of American juries," the impetus for *Stovall* and *Wade* was repeated miscarriages of justice resulting from juries' willingness to credit inaccurate eyewitness testimony.

Finally, the Court errs in its assessment of the relative impact of the two approaches on the administration of justice. The Court relies most heavily on this factor, finding that "reversal is a Draconian sanction" in cases where the identification is reliable despite an unnecessarily suggestive procedure used to obtain it. Relying on little more than a strong distaste for "inflexible rules of exclusion," the Court rejects the *per se* test. In so doing, the Court disregards two significant distinctions between the *per se* rule advocated in this case and the exclusionary remedies for certain other constitutional violations.

---

8. *See e.g., People v. Anderson*, 389 Mich. 155, 172–180, 192–220, 205 N.W.2d 461, 468–472, 479–494, 485 (1973); Levine & Tapp, *The Psychology of Criminal Identification: The Gap From Wade to Kirby*, 121 U. Pa. L. Rev. 1079 (1973); O'Connor, *"That's the Man": A Sobering Study of Eyewitness Identification and the Polygraph*, 49 St. John's L. Rev. 1 (1974); McGowan, [*Constitutional Interpretation and Criminal Identification*, 12 Wm. & Mary L. Rev. 235, 240 (1970)], *supra* n. 4, at 238–239; Grano, [*Kirby, Biggers, and Ash: Do Any Constitutional Safeguards Remain Against the Danger of Convicting the Innocent?* 72 Mich. L. Rev. 717 (1974)], *supra* n. 7, at 723–724, 768–770; *Recent Developments*, [*Identification: Unnecessary Suggestiveness May Not Violate Due Process*, 73 Colum. L. Rev. 1168 (1973)], *supra* n. 7, at 1169 n. 11. . . .

First, the *per se* rule here is not "inflexible." Where evidence is suppressed, for example, as the fruit of an unlawful search, it may well be forever lost to the prosecution. Identification evidence, however, can by its very nature be readily and effectively reproduced. The in-court identification, permitted under *Wade* and *Simmons* if it has a source independent of an uncounseled or suggestive procedure, is one example. Similarly, when a prosecuting attorney learns that there has been a suggestive confrontation, he can easily arrange another lineup conducted under scrupulously fair conditions. Since the same factors are evaluated in applying both the Court's totality test and the *Wade-Simmons* independent-source inquiry, any identification which is "reliable" under the Court's test will support admission of evidence concerning such a fairly conducted lineup. The evidence of an additional, properly conducted confrontation will be more persuasive to a jury, thereby increasing the chance of a justified conviction where a reliable identification was tainted by a suggestive confrontation. At the same time, however, the effect of an unnecessarily suggestive identification — which has no value whatsoever in the law enforcement process — will be completely eliminated.

Second, other exclusionary rules have been criticized for preventing jury consideration of relevant and usually reliable evidence in order to serve interests unrelated to guilt or innocence, such as discouraging illegal searches or denial of counsel. Suggestively obtained eyewitness testimony is excluded, in contrast, precisely because of its unreliability and concomitant irrelevance. Its exclusion both protects the integrity of the truth-seeking function of the trial and discourages police use of needlessly inaccurate and ineffective investigatory methods.

Indeed, impermissibly suggestive identifications are not merely worthless law enforcement tools. They pose a grave threat to society at large in a more direct way than most governmental disobedience of the law, *see Olmstead v. United States*, 277 U.S. 438, 471, 485, 48 S. Ct. 564, 570, 575, 72 L. Ed. 944 (1928) (Brandeis, J., dissenting). For if the police and the public erroneously conclude, on the basis of an unnecessarily suggestive confrontation, that the right man has been caught and convicted, the real outlaw must still remain at large. Law enforcement has failed in its primary function and has left society unprotected from the depredations of an active criminal.

For these reasons, I conclude that adoption of the *per se* rule would enhance, rather than detract from, the effective administration of justice. In my view, the Court's totality test will allow seriously unreliable and misleading evidence to be put before juries. Equally important, it will allow dangerous criminals to remain on the streets while citizens assume that police action has given them protection. According to my calculus, all three of the factors upon which the Court relies point to acceptance of the *per se* approach.

Even more disturbing than the Court's reliance on the totality test, however, is the analysis it uses, which suggests a reinterpretation of the concept of due process of law in criminal cases. The decision suggests that due process violations in identification procedures may not be measured by whether the government employed procedures violating standards of fundamental fairness. By relying on the probable accuracy of a challenged identification, instead of the necessity for its use, the Court seems to be ascertaining whether the defendant was probably guilty. Until today, I had thought that "Equal justice under law" meant that the existence of constitutional violations did not depend on the race, sex, religion, nationality, or likely guilt of the accused. The Due Process Clause requires adherence to the same high standard of fundamental fairness in dealing with every criminal defendant, whatever his personal characteristics and irrespective of the strength of the State's case against him. . . .

III

Despite my strong disagreement with the Court over the proper standards to be applied in this case, I am pleased that its application of the totality test does recognize the continuing vitality of *Stovall*. In assessing the reliability of the identification, the Court mandates weighing "the corrupting effect of the suggestive identification itself" against the "indicators of [a witness'] ability to make an accurate identification." The Court holds, as *Neil v. Biggers* failed to, that a due process identification inquiry must take account of the suggestiveness of a confrontation and the likelihood that it led to misidentification, as recognized in *Stovall* and *Wade*. Thus, even if a witness did have an otherwise adequate opportunity to view a criminal, the later use of a highly suggestive identification procedure can render his testimony inadmissible. Indeed, it is my view that, assuming applicability of the totality test enunciated by the Court, the facts of the present case require that result.

I consider first the opportunity that Officer Glover had to view the suspect. Careful review of the record shows that he could see the heroin seller only for the time it took to speak three sentences of four or five short words, to hand over some money, and later after the door reopened, to receive the drugs in return. The entire face-to-face transaction could have taken as little as 15 or 20 seconds. But during this time, Glover's attention was not focused exclusively on the seller's face. He observed that the door was opened 12 to 18 inches, that there was a window in the room behind the door, and, most importantly, that there was a woman standing behind the man. Glover was, of course, also concentrating on the details of the transaction — he must have looked away from the seller's face to hand him the money and receive the drugs. The observation during the conversation thus may have been as brief as 5 or 10 seconds.

As the Court notes, Glover was a police officer trained in and attentive to the need for making accurate identifications. Nevertheless, both common sense and scholarly study indicate that while a trained observer such as a police officer "is somewhat less likely to make an erroneous identification than the average untrained observer, the mere fact that he has been so trained is no guarantee that he is correct in a specific case. His identification testimony should be scrutinized just as carefully as that of the normal witness." Wall, [Eye-Witness Identification in Criminal Cases 19-23 (1965)], *supra* n. 1, at 14; *see also* Levine & Tapp, [*The Psychology of Criminal Identification: The Gap From* Wade *to* Kirby, 121 U. Pa. L. Rev. 1079 (1973)], *supra* n. 8, at 1088. Moreover, "identifications made by policemen in highly competitive activities, such as undercover narcotic agents . . . , should be scrutinized with special care." Wall, *supra* n. 1, at 14. Yet it is just such a searching inquiry that the Court fails to make here.

Another factor on which the Court relies — the witness' degree of certainty in making the identification — is worthless as an indicator that he is correct. Even if Glover had been unsure initially about his identification of respondent's picture, by the time he was called at trial to present a key piece of evidence for the State that paid his salary, it is impossible to imagine his responding negatively to such questions as "is there any doubt in your mind whatsoever" that the identification was correct. As the Court noted in *Wade:* "It is a matter of common experience that, once a witness has picked out the accused at the [pretrial confrontation], he is not likely to go back on his word later on." 388 U.S. at 229, 87 S. Ct. at 1933, quoting Williams & Hammelmann, *Identification Parades — I*, Crim. L. Rev. 479, 482 (1963).

Next, the Court finds that because the identification procedure took place two days after the crime, its reliability is enhanced. While such temporal proximity makes the identification more reliable than one occurring months later, the fact is that the greatest memory loss occurs within hours after an event. After that, the dropoff continues much more slowly. Thus, the reliability of an identification is increased only if it was made within several hours of the crime. If the time gap is any greater, reliability necessarily decreases.

Finally, the Court makes much of the fact that Glover gave a description of the seller to D'Onofrio shortly after the incident. Despite the Court's assertion that because "Glover himself was a Negro and unlikely to perceive only general features of 'hundreds of Hartford black males,' as the Court of Appeals stated," the description given by Glover was actually no more than a general summary of the seller's appearance. We may discount entirely the seller's clothing, for that was of no significance later in the proceeding. Indeed, to the extent that Glover noticed clothes, his attention was diverted from the seller's face. Otherwise, Glover merely described vaguely the seller's height, skin color, hairstyle, and build. He did say that the seller had "high cheekbones," but there is no other mention of facial features, nor even an estimate of age. Conspicuously absent is any indication that the seller was a native of the West Indies, certainly something which a member of the black community could immediately recognize from both appearance and accent.[12]

From all of this, I must conclude that the evidence of Glover's ability to make an accurate identification is far weaker than the Court finds it. In contrast, the procedure used to identify respondent was both extraordinarily suggestive and strongly conducive to error. In dismissing "the corrupting effect of the suggestive identification" procedure here, the Court virtually grants the police license to convict the innocent. By displaying a single photograph of respondent to the witness Glover under

---

12. Brathwaite had come to the United States from his native Barbados as an adult. It is also noteworthy that the informant who witnessed the transaction and was described by Glover as "trustworthy" disagreed with Glover's recollection of the event. The informant testified that it was a woman in the apartment who took the money from Glover and gave him the drugs in return.

the circumstances in this record almost everything that could have been done wrong was done wrong.

In the first place, there was no need to use a photograph at all. Because photos are static, two-dimensional, and often outdated, they are "clearly inferior in reliability" to corporeal procedures. While the use of photographs is justifiable and often essential where the police have no knowledge of an offender's identity, the poor reliability of photos makes their use inexcusable where any other means of identification is available. Here, since Detective D'Onofrio believed that he knew the seller's identity, further investigation without resort to a photographic showup was easily possible. With little inconvenience, a corporeal lineup including Brathwaite might have been arranged. Properly conducted, such a procedure would have gone far to remove any doubt about the fairness and accuracy of the identification.

Worse still than the failure to use an easily available corporeal identification was the display to Glover of only a single picture, rather than a photo array. With good reason, such single-suspect procedures have "been widely condemned." *Stovall v. Denno*, 388 U.S. at 302, 87 S. Ct. at 1973. They give no assurance that the witness can identify the criminal from among a number of persons of similar appearance, surely the strongest evidence that there was no misidentification. In *Simmons v. United States*, our first decision involving photographic identification, we recognized the danger that a witness seeing a suggestively displayed picture will "retain in his memory the image of the photograph rather than of the person actually seen." 390 U.S. at 383–384, 88 S. Ct. at 971. "Subsequent identification of the accused then shows nothing except that the picture was a good likeness." Williams & Hammelmann, *supra*, at 484. As *Simmons* warned, the danger of error is at its greatest when "the police display to the witness only the picture of a single individual . . . [and] is also heightened if the police indicate to the witness that they have other evidence that . . . the perso[n] pictured committed the crime." 390 U.S. at 383, 88 S. Ct. at 971. *See also* ALI, Model Code of Pre-Arraignment Procedure §§ 160.2(2), (5) (1975).

The use of a single picture (or the display of a single live suspect, for that matter) is a grave error, of course, because it dramatically suggests to the witness that the person shown must be the culprit. Why else would the police choose the person? And it is deeply ingrained in human nature to agree with the expressed opinions of others — particularly others who should be more knowledgeable — when making a difficult decision. In this case, moreover, the pressure was not limited to that inherent in the display of a single photograph. Glover, the identifying witness, was a state police officer on special assignment. He knew that D'Onofrio, an experienced Hartford narcotics detective, presumably familiar with local drug operations, believed respondent to be the seller. There was at work, then, both loyalty to another police officer and deference to a better-informed colleague. Finally, of course, there was Glover's knowledge that without an identification and arrest, government funds used to buy heroin had been wasted.

The Court discounts this overwhelming evidence of suggestiveness, however. It reasons that because D'Onofrio was not present when Glover viewed the photograph, there was "little pressure on the witness to acquiesce in the suggestion." That conclusion blinks psychological reality. There is no doubt in my mind that even in D'Onofrio's absence, a clear and powerful message was telegraphed to Glover as he looked at respondent's photograph. He was emphatically told that "*this* is the man," and he responded by identifying respondent then and at trial "whether or not he was in fact 'the man.'" *Foster v. California*, 394 U.S. at 443, 89 S. Ct. at 1129.

I must conclude that this record presents compelling evidence that there was "a very substantial likelihood of misidentification" of respondent Brathwaite. The suggestive display of respondent's photograph to the witness Glover likely erased any independent memory that Glover had retained of the seller from his barely adequate opportunity to observe the criminal.

IV

Since I agree with the distinguished panel of the Court of Appeals that the legal standard of *Stovall* should govern this case, but that even if it does not, the facts here reveal a substantial likelihood of misidentification in violation of respondent's right to due process of law, I would affirm the grant of habeas corpus relief. Accordingly, I dissent from the Court's reinstatement of respondent's conviction.

Notes and Questions

(1) In what respect is the due process test in *Manson* different from the test in *Stovall*? To what extent will the difference in the tests lead to different results? For articles addressing these issues, see Steven P. Grossman, *Suggestive Identifications: The Supreme Court's Due Process Test Fails to Meet Its Own Criteria*, 11 U. Balt. L. Rev. 53 (1981); Charles A. Pulaski, Neil v. Biggers: *The Supreme Court Dismantles the Wade Trilogy's Due Process Protection*, 26 Stan. L. Rev. 1097 (1974).

(2) Drawing upon such works as Elizabeth F. Loftus, Eyewitness Testimony (1979) and Daniel A. Yarmey, The Psychology of Eyewitness Testimony (1979), Randolph N. Jonakait, *Reliable Identification: Could the Supreme Court Tell in* Manson v. Brathwaite?, 52 U. Colo. L. Rev. 511 (1981), questions some of the *Manson* majority's assumptions. For example, "studies do not support the idea that police make more reliable witnesses than civilians or that their training in any way improves their ability to make identifications," Jonakait, *supra*, at 519. Moreover, although "[i]t would seem logical that one who is able to give a highly detailed and accurate description of another would be more likely to recognize the other person than somebody who cannot give such a description ... [, t]his common sense conclusion has no scientific support, and indeed may be false." Jonakait, *supra*, at 520. Most importantly, perhaps, the studies show "no relationship" between the expressed confidence of an eyewitness and the accuracy of his or her identification. Jonakait, *supra*, at 521.

(3) Thirty-five years after *Brathwaite*, the Court decided *Perry v. New Hampshire*, 565 U.S. ____, 132 S. Ct. 716, 181 L. Ed. 2d 694 (2012). In *Perry*, an officer who was responding to a report that "an African-American male was trying to break into cars parked in" an apartment building's parking lot found Perry in the lot. A man who

resided in the building soon approached the officer and told her that his neighbor had informed him that "she had just seen someone break into his car." The man had found a rear window of his car shattered and had "discovered that the speakers and amplifiers from his car stereo were missing." After asking Perry to stay in the lot with another officer, the first officer went with the resident to talk to his neighbor. They met her "in the hallway just outside the open door to her apartment." She reported what she had witnessed and then, when "asked . . . for a more specific description of the man" she had seen, she "pointed to her kitchen window and said the person she saw breaking into [her neighbor's] car was standing in the parking lot, next to the police officer." Perry was charged with theft and criminal mischief. He moved to suppress the witness's identification on due process grounds. The trial judge denied the motion, and both the officer and the victim testified to her "out-of-court identification" of Perry. A jury convicted him of theft.

In the Supreme Court, Perry conceded that officers "did not arrange the suggestive circumstances surrounding [the] identification," but claimed that the "rationale" of the due process decisions required a reliability assessment "any time an identification is made under suggestive circumstances." The issue was whether a judge must assess "the reliability of an eyewitness identification made under suggestive circumstances not arranged by the police." By an 8-1 majority, the Court held that the Fourteenth Amendment "Due Process Clause does not require a preliminary judicial inquiry into the reliability of an eyewitness identification . . . *not procured under unnecessarily suggestive circumstances arranged by law enforcement*." (Emphasis added.) The Justices explained that "what triggers due process concerns is police use of an unnecessarily suggestive procedure, whether or not they intended the arranged procedure to be suggestive."

According to the majority, *Brathwaite* had decided that a determination of reliability was "the appropriate remedy *when the police use an unnecessarily suggestive identification procedure*. . . . The due process check for reliability . . . comes into play only after the defendant establishes improper police conduct. The very purpose of the check . . . was to avoid depriving the jury of identification evidence that is reliable, *notwithstanding* improper police conduct." (Emphasis in original.) The "contention that improper police action was not essential" ignored "a key premise of . . . *Brathwaite*" — that a "primary aim of excluding identification evidence obtained under unnecessarily suggestive circumstances . . . is to deter law enforcement use of improper" identification procedures "in the first place."

The Justices feared that a conclusion that police arrangement of suggestive identification processes is not required "would open the door to judicial preview, under the banner of due process, of most, if not all, eyewitness identifications." In their view, "[t]he fallibility of eyewitness evidence does not, without the taint of improper state conduct, warrant a due process rule requiring a trial court to screen such evidence for reliability before allowing the jury to assess its creditworthiness." In large part, the majority's "unwillingness to enlarge the domain of due process . . . rest[ed] . . . on [a] recognition that the jury, not the judge, traditionally determines the reliability of evidence" and also on the fact that the adversary system provides safeguards "that caution juries against placing undue weight on eyewitness testimony of questionable reliability" — including, among other things, the right to confront and cross-examine witnesses, the right to effective assistance of counsel, specific jury instructions counseling care in evaluating such testimony, and the constitutional demand that guilt be proven beyond a reasonable doubt.

Justice Sotomayor dissented.

(4) In 2011, the Supreme Court of New Jersey issued a major opinion reviewing the ongoing problems with eyewitness identification processes, highlighting the continuing risks of identification evidence, and describing perceived inadequacies in the *Stovall v. Denno-Manson v. Brathwaite* due process doctrine as a solution for the problems and a safeguard against the risks. In *State v. Henderson*, 208 N.J. 208, 27 A.3d 872 (2011), a unanimous court described the current legal framework, surveyed the scientific research on the subject at great length, and ultimately concluded that additional legal controls were necessary. The brief excerpt that follows captures the essence of the court's concerns and the new regulations it announced:

> [W]e conclude that the current standard for assessing eyewitness identification evidence does not . . . offer an adequate measure for reliability or sufficiently deter inappropriate police conduct. It also overstates the jury's inherent ability to evaluate evidence offered by eyewitnesses who honestly believe their testimony is accurate.

> Two principal steps are needed to remedy those concerns. First, when defendants can show *some evidence of suggestiveness*, all relevant system and estimator variables should be explored at pretrial hearings. [According to the court, "[s]ystem variables are factors like lineup procedures which are within the control of the criminal justice system" while "[e]stimator variables are factors related to the witness, the perpetrator, or the event itself — like distance, lighting, or stress — over which the legal system has no control."] A trial court can end the hearing at any time, however, if the court concludes from the testimony that defendant's threshold allegation of suggestiveness is groundless. Otherwise, the trial judge should weigh both sets of variables to decide if the evidence is admissible.

> Up until now, courts have only considered estimator variables if there was a finding of *impermissibly suggestive police conduct*. In adopting this broader approach, we decline to order pretrial hearings in every case, as opposed to cases in which there is some evidence of suggestiveness. We also reject a bright-line rule that would require suppression of reliable evidence any time a law enforcement officer missteps.

> Second, the court system should develop enhanced jury charges on eyewitness identification for trial judges to use. We anticipate that identification evidence will continue to be admitted in the vast majority of cases.

To help jurors weigh that evidence, they must be told about relevant factors and their effect on reliability.... With the use of more focused jury charges on those issues, there will be less need to call expert witnesses at trial. Trial courts will still have discretion to admit expert testimony when warranted.

The factors that both judges and juries will consider are not etched in stone. We expect that the scientific research underlying them will continue to evolve, as it has in the more than thirty years since *Manson*. For the same reason, police departments are not prevented from improving their practices as we learn more about variables that affect memory. New approaches, though, must be based on reliable scientific evidence that experts generally accept.

The changes outlined in this decision are significant because eyewitness identifications bear directly on guilt or innocence. At stake is the very integrity of the criminal justice system and the courts' ability to conduct fair trials. Ultimately, we believe that the framework [adopted in this opinion] will both protect the rights of defendants, by minimizing the risk of misidentification, and enable the State to introduce vital evidence. (Emphasis added.)

The opinion in *Henderson* provides perceptive insights into the issues underlying the legal regulation of identification processes and evidence. It makes excellent reading for anyone interested in pursuing the topic further. For another recent state court opinion that sheds light on the subject, see *Commonwealth v. Walker*, 460 Mass. 590, 953 N.E.2d 195 (2011).

Due Process Identification Problems

11–1: According to the victim, a 15-year-old girl, she was walking through the park to a shopping mall in the afternoon when she noticed a man sitting on a log near the path. On her way back a short time later, she noticed the same man in the park. As she passed him, he told her to stop or he would kill her. As she started to scream, the man took her by the throat, choked her, dragged her into the woods and raped her.

The victim reported that after her assailant began choking her she lost consciousness and remained unconscious during much of the episode. She did, however, observe her assailant for a brief time while he was attacking her. When she regained consciousness, he was gone. As she left the park, however, she saw him again at a distance talking with another man. She ran home immediately, reported the rape, and was taken to a hospital.

That same afternoon, the victim gave a description of her assailant to an investigating officer. She described him as white, 30–35 years old, with dark hair and a mustache. The next day, while the victim was still at the hospital, an officer conducted a photo identification, presenting the victim with more than 150 photographs of white sex offenders. At one point, the victim selected one of the photographs, telling the officer that the man in the photograph was "skinnier" than her assailant but had the same type of mustache. The officer then told her that this particular man was in jail.

The victim subsequently selected Appellant's photograph as the one most likely to be her attacker. The photo depicted Appellant without a mustache. The victim told the officer that she thought this was "the man" but that she needed to see him with a mustache.

Appellant, who had a mustache, was then taken into custody and brought to the hospital. The victim was very apprehensive, so arrangements were made for her to stay in a darkened room and to observe Appellant in the hallway through a glass panel in the door without being seen herself. Appellant was brought down the hall to stand in front of the glass panel and then was led away.

When the officer returned to the victim's room, she said, "That's not him." According to the officer, at this moment she was very frightened. He told her to take a longer look to be certain. When Appellant was brought into the hallway again, the victim asked the officers to have him place his hands around the officer's throat. After Appellant did so, the victim stated that she was sure that Appellant was her attacker.

At trial, the victim testified to the hospital room identification and made an in-court identification of Appellant. Appellant was convicted. On appeal, he claims that the admission of the identification evidence violated due process.

How should the appellate court rule?

11–2: In September 2006, the DEA legally found 13 bricks of cocaine in Lavega's luggage and arrested him. He agreed to cooperate in exchange for a promise not to indict his wife for conspiracy. His cooperation led the authorities to arrest and charge Carlos Torres with conspiracy to distribute and possession with intent to distribute cocaine.

At Torres's trial in 2011, Lavega testified for three days. On the second day, he was asked by the prosecutor about a 2006 visit to the home of Santana, one of the leaders of the conspiracy. Lavega said that while he was at Santana's home, he had loaded six suitcases into the trunk of "El Ron's" car and that Santana had told him that "El Ron" was in charge of taking bags to the airport. The prosecutor asked, "if 'El Ron' is in the courtroom, can you describe him or her?" Lavega replied: "Yes. He is the gentleman with the long-sleeved shirt." Torres's lawyer conceded, for the record, that "the witness is referring to my client." However, he raised a due process objection to the courtroom identification, requesting that the judge instruct the jury to disregard it. The judge overruled the objection. Lavega also testified that later in 2006, while he was riding in a car, he had seen "El Ron" working at the airport, loading bags onto an airplane. Lavega claimed that on another occasion in 2006 he and another conspirator, Jose, had gone to "El Ron's" house to deliver a bag. As Jose handed "El Ron" the bag, Lavega heard Jose tell "El Ron" that it contained $90,000.

On cross-examination, Torres's counsel asked Lavega if he had met with DEA agents and prosecutors to "discuss what you were going to testify to." "Yes," Lavega answered. In an effort to undermine Lavega's courtroom identification of Torres, defense counsel got Lavega to assert that "El Ron" had braided hair (reminiscent of a look favored by a Puerto Rican rapper known as "Don Diego"). He later called Torres to testify that he did not have braids in 2006. In closing argument, counsel contended that Lavega had simply "confused my client with somebody else." He stressed that Lavega had an obvious motive to lie — his wife's freedom.

Torres was convicted. On appeal, he maintains that the judge should not have allowed the in-court identification by Lavega.

Does the Due Process Clause protection against eyewitness identifications support Torres's claim on appeal?

11–3: On a morning in June, Virginia stopped at K-Mart. After making her purchases, she left the store and walked toward her Jeep. As she was getting into her vehicle, a man approached her from behind and said, "Hey." Virginia turned around and "saw a gun in the man's hand." While standing face to face with the man, Virginia "told him to get away from me." He told her to get out of the car, and aimed the gun at her chest. She stepped out, handed the man her keys, and then ran back to the K-Mart and called the police. She reported that the suspect was black and was wearing a dark t-shirt and a baseball cap.

Mary, another K-Mart shopper, stated that as she was approaching her car in the parking lot, she saw a black male dressed in a dark navy blue t-shirt and a baseball cap "walk very quickly towards a Jeep." She heard a woman say, "Leave me alone. Leave me alone." The woman and the man then engaged in what was "basically a fight. She was trying to get him away from her." Then the woman started screaming for help. Mary saw the man drive the Jeep out of the parking lot at a high rate of speed.

Daniel was traveling across a nearby bridge shortly after the incident. He saw a man in a Jeep speed past him on the right. The man "lost control of the vehicle and it fishtailed, then rolled over several times before coming to rest against a utility pole." After Daniel saw the driver get out of the car and run in the direction of Tarent, a small town nearby, he called the police. Scott, who was driving in the vicinity, also witnessed the crash and saw the man "get out of the car and start running down Sixth Avenue. The man stumbled to the ground once, then got up and continued to run." Robert, another witness, approached the overturned Jeep as the driver was climbing out. According to Robert, "his baseball cap fell off of his head. He then ran off at a pretty good clip."

By this time, the local police had issued a BOLO (Be On Lookout) broadcast concerning the carjacking. The suspect was described as "a black male with a dark blue shirt and baseball cap." Officers Tim Duggan and Clint Lock were responding to the BOLO when they heard a report that a suspect was "running east from the bridge on Sixth Avenue." Upon proceeding to that area, they saw Lee — a black male wearing a dark shirt — running toward First Avenue. Lee ran directly in front of their vehicle and into the backyard of a house. The two officers got out of their car, followed Lee into the yard, and arrested him there. They then put him in their cruiser and took him to the accident scene, where both Robert and Scott identified him as the man who had crashed and run from the Jeep. According to Scott, "I recognized him. I kind of went to see who was in the back seat of the police car and I was one hundred percent sure the guy in the back seat of the police car was the guy who crawled out of the vehicle." Lee was handcuffed at the time. The accident had occurred approximately 25 minutes earlier.

Shortly after that, police officers brought Mary and Virginia to the accident scene. Both women identified Lee as the man who had taken Virginia's car. According to Mary, "The policeman asked can we identify anyone. And the man was standing there, and we did." Virginia remarked, "There is no doubt in my mind that he's the man who took my Jeep." Lee was handcuffed, surrounded by police, and standing beside the police cruiser at the time of these two identifications.

At the accident scene, the police found a Yankees baseball cap on one side of the Jeep. On the other side of the vehicle, a damaged, but operative, firearm was lying on the ground. Neither the car nor its contents were tested for fingerprints, and the car was subsequently destroyed. The firearm and cartridge were tested for prints, but none were found. The identification evidence, therefore, proved to be critical. At Lee's trial for carjacking, the state planned to call each of the four witnesses to testify to his or her on-the-scene identification of Lee. Lee moved to suppress the identifications, relying on the Due Process Clause.

What arguments should Lee make? How should the prosecution respond? Does Lee have a valid claim for suppression?

11-4: On March 25, at 10:20 p.m., Abdul, his brother, Omar, and Evan arrived at an apartment where William, Joanne, and their two sons, Derek and Bert, lived. Abdul, Omar, and Evan entered the apartment, and engaged in a five-minute conversation with William and Joanne. Suddenly, Evan jumped up, held a gun to William's head and asked him for money. William resisted, and, during a scuffle that ensued, Evan stabbed William, Abdul stabbed Joanne, and Omar stabbed Derek. Both William and Joanne died of the stab wounds they suffered, but Derek survived.

On April 6, Abdul was indicted for two counts of aggravated murder. At trial, Bert, who was seven years old, testified to the following: He had gone to bed at nine o'clock on the night of the murders. He came out of his bedroom later in the evening upon hearing some loud noises. He was able to see over the couch, and there was light coming from his mother's room. He watched as Abdul (known to Bert by the nickname "Twin") stabbed his mother 30 times. (In fact, Joanne suffered 32 stab wounds.) Twin had kicked his father while his father was lying on the ground. Twin had then motioned to him to go back to his bedroom. He did so and stayed there until the police came. He had been concerned for his own safety.

Bert also identified Abdul as "Twin" by pointing to him in the courtroom. He testified that after the incident he had picked Twin out of a lineup as the man who had killed his mother and kicked his father. Although he could not remember the exact number of days between the murder and the lineup, when asked whether it was a short or long time, Bert stated that it was "short." According to Bert, he had seen Twin on four separate occasions before the murders. He said that he thought that Twin's "real name" was Omar (the name of Abdul's brother).

Evidence showed that the lineup at which Bert made his identification contained five males of the same race who were all of approximately the same age and stature. Adbul was the only one who was bandaged and dressed in prison clothing.

Does Abdul have a valid due process objection to Bert's identifications of him?

11–5: Jones was charged with armed robbery. Krystal LeBlanc, a key government witness, testified that Jones was in the company of other participants in the robbery shortly before it occurred. Jones challenged LeBlanc's testimony on the ground that it was influenced by two incidents that occurred after the crime but prior to trial. Three months after the crime, LeBlanc was summoned by counsel for a co-defendant to attend a probable cause hearing. She wound up sitting in the courtroom in which Jones and a co-defendant were present, handcuffed, and shackled together. LeBlanc had the opportunity to watch them for more than an hour. Neither the prosecutor nor the police planned or participated in arranging this confrontation.

Several months later, LeBlanc again encountered Jones shackled to a co-defendant. While LeBlanc was waiting in a hallway to testify at a suppression hearing on behalf of the government, Jones and a co-defendant were brought past her into the courtroom. Anyone going into the courtroom had to go down the hallway. The prosecutor had not told LeBlanc to sit in the hallway, had not pointed anyone out to LeBlanc, and had not facilitated her opportunity for observation. On both occasions, Jones was the only black person in shackles that LeBlanc saw that day. LeBlanc also saw Jones and his co-defendant sitting together at the counsel table when she testified.

The trial judge rejected the defense claim that LeBlanc's testimony should be excluded as violative of due process. According to the judge, the suggestive pretrial confrontations between LeBlanc and Jones did not violate due process because the prosecutor played no part in arranging them. The judge also concluded that if a due process violation did occur, the prosecution did not meet its burden of showing that LeBlanc had an independent basis for her identification of Jones. The jury convicted Jones of armed robbery.

Should Jones's conviction be upheld on appeal?

11–6: On February 20, an armed man entered the First Federal Savings Bank and attempted to rob it. Laurie Gervasio and Jeanie Mizher, employees of the bank, witnessed the attempted robbery. They described the gunman as approximately six feet tall, slender, and fair-skinned, and said that he had a long thin face, an extremely large nose, and very distinctive nervous mannerisms. Subsequently, Gervasio assisted a police officer in making a composite drawing of the robber. Both Gervasio and Mizher looked at numerous color photographs of suspects but were unable to identify any of them as the robber.

On February 23, another bank robbery occurred. The robber was not apprehended, but the robbery was recorded by the bank's surveillance camera. The police watched the videotape of the robbery and concluded that the robber resembled Gervasio's composite drawing of the man who committed the February 20 robbery.

On February 24, the police showed the videotape of the February 23 robbery to Gervasio, warning her to remain "unbiased" as she watched it. Within seconds of observing the man on the videotape, Gervasio positively identified him as the man who committed the February 20 robbery. The police later showed the videotape to Mizher who made a similar identification.

Austin was subsequently identified by police officers as the man who appeared in the February 23 videotape. The police arrested Austin and placed him in a line-up with four other individuals. At the line-up, both Gervasio and Mizher identified Austin as the man who committed the February 20 robbery. Austin's attorney moved to suppress the two witnesses' identifications on the ground that they were tainted by the unnecessarily suggestive displays of the February 23 videotape.

Should the attorney's motion be granted?

11–7: At 10:00 p.m. on June 6, a man entered Eileen Olson's apartment through a patio door and robbed her. According to Olson, the robber was in her apartment for 10 to 15 minutes. During that time, he threatened her with a knife and threatened to kill her. Olson described her assailant as 45-year-old white male wearing a baseball hat, a dark plaid shirt, and blue jeans.

While Olson was being treated for her injuries at a hospital, the police showed her a picture of Norrid, a suspect they had detained and photographed near her apartment. Olson at first said she could not tell whether the man in the picture was the robber because she did not have her glasses at the hospital. After the police retrieved her glasses, she was still unable to make an identification. She stated that it was hard for her to look at the picture "cause my glasses were so bent out of shape."

At approximately 12:30 a.m., the police took Olson to a location near the scene of the crime so she could personally view Norrid. According to Olson, the police "put a spot light on him and asked me if that was the man that had assaulted me. And I said I was 99 percent sure, I said, I just — I hated to think that I would get an innocent man or anything and I wanted to stay and make sure. So we sat for a long time until I was positive it was him."

Norrid's attorney moved to suppress Olson's identification of Norrid, arguing that the identification procedure was unduly suggestive and the resulting identification violated Norrid's right to due process. The judge ruled that the identification procedure, while suggestive, was not "unnecessarily suggestive." The judge, therefore, ruled it was unnecessary to consider the factors identified as relevant in *Manson v. Brathwaite*. Norrid's due process claim was denied on the basis of his failure to show that the procedure leading to his identification was "unnecessarily suggestive."

Was the judge's ruling correct?

11–8: On Labor Day weekend in 1989, Robert Nuchereno and his girlfriend Jennifer Zielinski were guests at a New York motel. An intruder entered the room, knocked Zielinski unconscious and stole her wallet. Nuchereno, hearing the disturbance, emerged from the bathroom. The robber fled from the room to his car, which was parked in a nearby parking lot. Nuchereno gave chase and caught the robber as he entered his car. After a brief struggle inside the car, Nuchereno retreated, allowing the robber to escape. Nuchereno later gave the police a detailed description of both the robber and the car he was driving.

Zielinski's wallet contained her ATM card and the card's personal identification number. Soon after the theft, someone attempted to use her ATM card to withdraw funds on numerous occasions. Some of these attempts were recorded by security cameras. After being notified of the ATM card's theft, a Key Bank security investigator made more than 30 pictures from the ATM videotapes and asked Nuchereno and Zielinski to view these pictures. Each picture appeared to be of the same man wearing a sweatshirt bearing the words "Number One Dad." After viewing these pictures and no others, Nuchereno immediately and unequivocally identified the man in the picture as the robber.

The pictures were then circulated to law enforcement agents in the New York area. In October, a New York parole officer identified the man in the pictures as Richard Dunnigan. Based on this information, Dunnigan was arrested. During a search of his residence, police found a sweatshirt bearing the words "Number One Dad."

In a pretrial motion, Dunnigan claimed that Nuchereno's identification should be suppressed on due process grounds and requested a hearing for the purpose of showing (1) that the pretrial showing of pictures was unnecessarily suggestive and (2) that Nuchereno's resulting identification was substantially likely to be mistaken.

Should the court conduct the requested hearing? If so, how is it likely to rule?

11–9: Giulio and Maria lived together in Maria's apartment. Giulio planned to marry Maria and gain American citizenship, but she wanted to end their relationship. During the week prior to her death, Maria and Giulio argued, prompting Maria to leave the apartment and temporarily move in with a friend. A few days later, while visiting Maria at the friend's home, Giulio made threatening statements. At 2:30 p.m. that day, Maria went to work. She did not return to her friend's home that night.

Around 4:30 in the afternoon the next day, the police found Maria's dead body inside her automobile, which was parked on the side of a road near the hospital where she worked. She had suffered multiple stab wounds to her hands, head, and neck. After a brief investigation, the police arrested Giulio. He said that he had not seen Maria on the previous night and denied having been near the hospital where she worked. After a thorough investigation, the police assembled a considerable amount of evidence that Giulio had stabbed Maria to death.

At Giulio's trial for murder, a woman who had been delivering newspapers in the vicinity of the hospital early in the morning of the day Maria's body was found testified as a witness for the prosecution. She stated that around 5:00 a.m. she saw a man walking near the location where Maria's car and body were found. Over defense objection, she identified Giulio as the man she had seen. The witness also testified that she had identified a photograph of Giulio before testifying. Because it was "unusual to see somebody on that road at that time of day," she had mentioned the sighting to her husband when she had returned from her newspaper route. Two days later, her husband asked whether she had seen the daily newspaper. The witness had not seen it yet. When she looked at the front page she saw a photograph of Giulio. She immediately remarked to her husband, "Oh my God, that's the man that I saw." She then contacted the police. In the photograph, which was not introduced at trial, Giulio is in handcuffs. A caption over the photograph reads, "A brutal, horrific murder." In much smaller print below the photo, the text reads, "Giulio ____ of Bricktown is arraigned in District Court yesterday for a vicious stabbing slaying." On cross-examination, the witness testified that she had actually observed the man for "a short span of time" and that when she saw him it was "before dawn." When asked whether she had noticed a caption over the newspaper photograph, the witness stated, "I don't remember seeing any words on — I'm sure there was a caption, but don't remember ever reading it."

Giulio has appealed his murder conviction, claiming that the witness's photographic identification tainted her courtroom identification, rendering it constitutionally impermissible.

Does Giulio have a valid claim for exclusion of the courtroom identification?

11–10: A man called 911 and told the operator that he had seen two African American men leaving his neighbor's house and carrying black or silver garbage bags. He did not recognize the men and suspected that they were burglars. The man stated that one of the men was wearing a jersey with orange stripes. The other, who was approximately 5' 10" and had an afro, was wearing a dark jacket and dark pants.

Officers McMahon and Swanson heard the broadcast of the reported burglary and drove to the area. When they were a few blocks from the burglarized residence, they spotted Anderson, an African American male wearing a dark denim jacket with matching pants and carrying a silver garbage bag containing computer equipment. The officers arrested Anderson and drove him back to the scene of the alleged burglary for a show-up. Prior to having the witness observe Anderson face-to-face, the police told the witness that they thought they had one of the men the witness had described and that he had been caught carrying a silver bag. The witness then observed Anderson and identified him as one of the men he had seen leaving his neighbor's house. He told the police that his identification was based mainly on Anderson's clothing, but he was sure that he was right.

Anderson was charged with second-degree burglary. Before trial, the defense moved to suppress the witness's show-up identification of Anderson on the ground that it was unnecessarily suggestive. The judge denied the motion.

At trial, the witness was unable to identify Anderson. Over defense objection, the judge then permitted the witness to testify about his pretrial identification. The jury found Anderson guilty of second-degree burglary. On appeal, Anderson claims that his conviction should be reversed because the witness should not have been permitted to testify to his pretrial identification.

How should the appellate court rule?

11–11: After the defendant was charged with first-degree robbery, the prosecutor asked the trial court to sign an order requiring the defendant to appear in a line-up. In response, the defendant filed a motion requesting an order that required the prosecution to conduct a double-blind, sequential line-up if the court granted the prosecution's motion for a line-up. In a double-blind line-up, the investigators conducting the procedure do not know the identity of the suspect and are thus unable to indicate to the witness which participant is the suspect. In a sequential line-up, potential suspects are individually displayed to the witness in an attempt to prevent an identification by comparison — i.e., where the witness compares the potential suspects against one another and then selects the one who most closely resembles the perpetrator. The prosecutor opposed the defendant's motion.

At the hearing on the defendant's motion, the defense introduced articles showing that in some controlled studies, sequential line-ups have been shown to reduce misidentifications by as much as 50 percent. The prosecutor argued, however, that using a sequential line-up rather than the ordinary comparative line-up would reduce the number of correct identifications. The prosecutor also directed the court to language in an article indicating that there may not be "100 percent agreement among all experts on the desirability of sequential lineups under all circumstances."

As to double-blind line-ups, the defense introduced an article stating that experts uniformly favor this approach because "numerous scientific studies suggest that officers who know the identity of a true suspect in a lineup might influence the decision of a witness, even unintentionally, through suggestive words or movements." The prosecutor did not dispute the article's conclusion, but nevertheless argued that a court order to conduct a double-blind line-up would improperly interfere with the prosecutor's discretionary authority to investigate and prepare cases for trial.

How should the court rule on the defendant's motion?

11–12: In early May, Brian spent 10 days at the apartment of Cora, his brother's on-again-off-again girlfriend. When he mentioned to Cora that he wanted to rob a Western Union office, she told him that it would be "a stupid thing to do" and that he would "end up going to jail." On May 5, a man wearing a gray hooded sweatshirt entered a market, approached a clerk working at the Western Union desk, pulled out a knife, and demanded "all the money." The clerk handed over a wad of bills totaling between $2,000 and $3,000. As the robber ran out the door, the clerk exclaimed, "I've been robbed!" John Rye, a market manager, and Tony Runo, another employee, pursued the robber on foot. When the robber dropped some of the money and stopped to pick it up, Rye and Runo caught up to him. The robber punched Rye in the mouth and broke free from his pursuers. He then ran toward a vehicle being driven by Gavin Thomson, which was stopped at a red light. He tried forcibly to enter the vehicle but fell off when Thomson accelerated and made a right turn. The robber then got back to his feet and ran into a nearby housing complex. Anthony Vega, a young man who was on his way to school at the time, also witnessed the robber's flight from the store with the money and his efforts to get into Thomson's car.

The robber ran into an apartment inside the housing complex. When an elderly man who lived there ordered him to leave, he stabbed the man. He then stabbed an elderly woman who lived in the apartment and set fire to the apartment. Both of the occupants died of the stab wounds.

Later that day, both Thomson and Vega went to the detective bureau. Vega viewed a series of several photographs on a computer terminal in an effort to identify the robber. After he finished looking at the photographs without making an identification, Vega got up from the computer terminal. As he was being led out of the detective bureau, he happened to look at the computer terminal being viewed by Thomson. A photograph of Brian was on the screen at the time. Upon looking at the photograph of Brian, Vega remarked, "That looks like the guy that I saw." The police did not do or say anything to direct Vega's attention to the computer screen being viewed by Thomson. Moreover, there is no evidence that Vega overheard Thomson making any comments regarding Brian's photograph.

Brian was arrested on May 6. He was charged with armed robbery, felony-murder, arson, and assault and battery. Prior to trial, he moved to suppress Vega's identification of his photograph, claiming that it was the product of unnecessarily suggestive police procedures.

Does due process bar introduction of Vega's photographic identification?

Selected Bibliography

Noah Clements, *Flipping a Coin: A Solution for the Inherent Unreliability of Eyewitness Identification Testimony*, 40 Ind. L. Rev. 271 (2007)

Jules Epstein, *Irreparable Misidentifications and Reliability: Reassessing the Threshold for Admissibility of Eyewitness Identification*, 58 Vill. L. Rev. 69 (2013)

Brandon L. Garrett, *Eyewitnesses and Exclusion*, 65 Vand. L. Rev. 451 (2012)

Rudolf Koch, Note, *Process v. Outcome: The Proper Role of Corroborative Evidence in Due Process Analysis of Eyewitness Identification Testimony*, 88 Cornell L. Rev. 1097 (2003)

Margery Malkin Koosed, *Reforming Eyewitness Identification Law and Practices to Protect the Innocent*, 42 Creighton L. Rev. 595 (2009)

Elizabeth F. Loftus, Eyewitness Testimony (1979)

Amy Luria, *Showup Identifications: A Comprehensive Overview of the Problems and a Discussion of Necessary Changes*, 86 Neb. L. Rev. 515 (2008)

Evan J. Mandery, *Legal Development: Due Process Considerations of In-Court Identifications*, 60 Alb. L. Rev. 389 (1996)

Connie Mayer, *Due Process Challenges to Eyewitness Identification Based on Pretrial Photographic Arrays*, 13 Pace L. Rev. 815 (1994)

Radha Natarajan, Note, *Racialized Memory and Reliability: Due Process Applied to Cross-Racial Eyewitness Identifications*, 78 N.Y.U. L. Rev. 1821 (2003)

Timothy P. O'Toole & Giovanna Shay, Manson v. Brathwaite *Revisited: Towards a New Rule of Decision for Due Process Challenges to Eyewitness Identification Procedures*, 41 Val. U. L. Rev. 109 (2006)

Charles A. Pulaski, Neil v. Biggers: *The Supreme Court Dismantles the* Wade *Trilogy's Due Process Protection*, 26 Stan. L. Rev. 1097 (1974)

Ofer Raban, *On Suggestive and Necessary Identification Processes*, 37 Am. J. Crim. L. 53 (2009)

Benjamin E. Rosenberg, *Rethinking the Right to Due Process in Connection with Pretrial Identification Procedures: An Analysis and a Proposal*, 79 Ky. L.J. 259 (1991)

Wallace W. Sherwood, *The Erosion of Constitutional Safeguards in the Area of Eyewitness Identification*, 30 How. L.J. 731 (1987)

David A. Sonenshein & Robin Nilon, *Eyewitness Errors and Wrongful Convictions: Let's Give Science a Chance*, 89 Or. L. Rev. 263 (2010)

Sandra Guerra Thompson, *Beyond a Reasonable Doubt? Reconsidering Uncorroborated Eyewitness Identification Testimony*, 41 U.C. Davis L. Rev. 1487 (2008)

Sandra Guerra Thompson, *Judicial Blindness to Eyewitness Misidentification*, 93 Marq. L. Rev. 639 (2009)

Daniel A. Yarmey, The Psychology of Eyewitness Testimony (1979)

Part V

Exclusionary Rules

Chapter 12

The Sources of and Rationales for the Exclusionary Rules

Introductory Note

In the first eleven chapters of this text, students have encountered seven different constitutional constraints upon the government's efforts to investigate criminal activity. Six of these constraints — all but the due process guarantee against official involvement in manufacturing crimes — are enforced by means of "exclusionary rules." (They might also be enforced by civil suits seeking compensation for violations of constitutional rights.) These exclusionary rules prevent prosecutors from introducing evidence that has been obtained by violating constitutional restrictions upon investigatory activity and thereby constrain, and impede, efforts to prove guilt at trial.

Chapters 12 and 13 address the exclusionary rules in considerable depth. The instant chapter, which is relatively brief, has a primarily theoretical orientation and focus. It addresses the constitutional roots of and justifications for the suppression of what is typically highly relevant and probative evidence. Chapter 13, which is much longer, has a more pragmatic focus. It is concerned with the scope and operation of the exclusionary rules. More particularly, that chapter considers a wide variety of concrete limitations imposed upon constitutional suppression doctrines.

The main opinions in this chapter, and the first note following those opinions, explore the rationales for the most prominent and frequently invoked exclusionary rule, the rule that bars evidence secured by means of unreasonable searches and seizures. One important note briefly describes the justifications offered to support the suppression of statements obtained in violation of the dictates of *Miranda v. Arizona*. Another significant note summarizes the rationales for the *Massiah* doctrine's right to counsel-based exclusionary rule. The justifications underlying other exclusion doctrines are not addressed in this chapter. Opinions in previous chapters and in Chapter 13 provide insights into the underpinnings of those suppression mandates. *See, e.g., Ashcraft v. Tennessee, Spano v. New York,* and *Colorado v. Connelly, supra* Chapter Seven (Due Process Clause protection against coerced confessions); *United States v. Wade* and *Gilbert v. California, supra* Chapter 10 (Sixth Amendment right to counsel safeguard against eyewitness identification evidence); *Manson v. Brathwaite, supra* Chapter 11 (Due Process Clause bar to eyewitness identifications).

In reading the materials in this chapter, students should reflect upon the different possible justifications for excluding evidence acquired unlawfully. They should identify and analyze the Supreme Court's conclusions regarding the rationales for the various exclusionary rules and should make their own assessments of the legitimacy of the exclusion doctrines.

Weeks v. United States

United States Supreme Court

232 U.S. 383, 34 S. Ct. 341, 58 L. Ed. 652 (1914)

MR. JUSTICE DAY delivered the opinion of the court:

An indictment was returned against the plaintiff in error, defendant below, and herein so designated, in the District Court of the United States for the Western District of Missouri, containing nine counts. The seventh count, upon which a conviction was had, charged the use of the mails for the purpose of transporting certain coupons or tickets representing chances or shares in a lottery or gift enterprise, in violation of § 213 of the Criminal Code. Sentence of fine and imprisonment was imposed. This writ of error is to review that judgment.

The defendant was arrested by a police officer, so far as the record shows, without warrant, at the Union Station in Kansas City, Missouri, where he was employed by an express company. Other police officers had gone to the house of the defendant, and being told by a neighbor where the key was kept, found it and entered the house. They searched the defendant's room and took possession of various papers and articles found there, which were afterwards turned over to the United States Marshal. Later in the same day police officers returned with the Marshal, who thought he might find additional evidence, and, being admitted by someone in the house, probably a boarder, in response to a rap, the Marshal searched the defendant's room and carried away certain letters and envelopes found in the drawer of a chiffonier. Neither the marshal nor the police officers had a search warrant.

The defendant filed in the cause before the time for trial the following petition:

"Petition to Return Private Papers, Books, and Other Property.

"Now comes defendant and states that he is a citizen and resident of Kansas City, Missouri, and that he resides, owns, and occupies a home at 1834 Penn Street in said City;

"That on the 21st day of December, 1911, while plaintiff was absent at his daily vocation, certain officers of the government whose names are to plaintiff unknown, unlawfully and without warrant or authority so to do, broke open the door to plaintiff's said home and seized all of his books, letters, money, papers, notes, evidences of indebtedness, stock, certificates, insurance policies, deeds, abstracts, and other muniments of title, bonds, candies, clothes, and other property in said home, and this in violation of Sections 11 and 23 to the Constitution of Missouri, and of the 4th and 5th Amendments to the Constitution of the United States:

"That the District Attorney, Marshal, and Clerk of the United States Court for the Western District of Missouri took the above-described property so seized into their possession, and have failed and refused to return to defendant portion of same. . . . :

. . . .

"That said property is being unlawfully and improperly held by said District Attorney, Marshal, and Clerk in violation of defendant's rights under the Constitution of the United States and the State of Missouri:

"That said District Attorney purposes [sic] to use said books, letters, papers, certificates of stock, etc., at the trial of the above-entitled cause, and that by reason thereof and of the facts above set forth defendant's rights under the amendments aforesaid to the Constitution of Missouri and the United States have been and will be violated unless the Court order the return prayed for:

"Wherefore, defendant prays that said District Attorney, Marshal, and Clerk be notified, and that the Court direct and order said District Attorney, Marshal, and Clerk to return said property to said defendant."

Upon consideration of the petition the court entered in the cause an order directing the return of such property as was not pertinent to the charge against the defendant, but denied the petition as to pertinent matter, reserving the right to pass upon the pertinency at a later time. In obedience to the order the District Attorney returned part of the property taken and retained the remainder, concluding a list of the latter with the statement that, "all of which last above described property is to be used in evidence in the trial of the above-entitled cause, and pertains to the alleged sale of lottery tickets of the company above named."

After the jury had been sworn and before any evidence had been given, the defendant again urged his petition for the return of his property, which was denied by the court. Upon the introduction of such papers during the trial, the defendant objected on the ground that the papers had been obtained without a search warrant and by breaking open his home, in violation of the Fourth and Fifth Amendments to the Constitution of the United States, which objection was overruled by the court. Among the papers retained and put in evidence were a number of lottery tickets and statements with reference to the lottery, taken at the first visit of the police to the defendant's room, and a number of letters written to the defendant in respect to the lottery, taken by the Marshal upon his search of defendant's room.

The defendant assigns error, among other things, in the court's refusal to grant his petition for the return of his property and in permitting the papers to be used at the trial.

. . . .

The history of [the Fourth] Amendment is given with particularity in the opinion of Mr. Justice Bradley, speaking for the court in *Boyd v. United States*, 116 U.S. 616, 6 S. Ct. 524, 29 L. Ed. 746. As was there shown, it took its origin in the determination of the framers of the Amendments to the Federal Constitution to provide for that instrument a Bill of Rights, securing to the American people, among other things, those safeguards which had grown up in England to protect the people from unreasonable searches and seizures, such as were permitted under the general warrants issued under authority of the Government by which there had been invasions of the home and privacy of the citizens and the seizure of their private papers in support of charges, real or imaginary, made against them. Such practices had also received sanction under warrants and seizures under the so-called writs of assistance, issued in the American colonies. Resistance to these practices had established the principle which was enacted into the fundamental law in the Fourth Amendment, that a man's house was his castle and not to be invaded by any general authority to search and seize his goods and papers. Judge Cooley, in his Constitutional Limitations, pp. 425, 426, in treating of this feature of our Constitution, said: "The maxim that 'every man's house is his castle' is made a part of our constitutional law in the clauses prohibiting unreasonable searches and seizures, and has always been looked upon as of high value to the citizen." "Accordingly," says Lieber in his work on CIVIL LIBERTY AND SELF-GOVERNMENT, 62, in speaking of the English law in this respect, "no man's house can be forcibly opened, or he or his goods be carried away after it has thus been forced, except in cases of felony; and then the sheriff must be furnished with a warrant, and take great care lest he commit a trespass. This principle is jealously insisted upon."

. . . .

The effect of the Fourth Amendment is to put the courts of the United States and Federal officials, in the exercise of their power and authority, under limitations and restraints as to the exercise of such power and authority, and to forever secure the people, their persons, houses, papers, and effects against all unreasonable searches and seizures under the guise of law. This protection reaches all alike, whether accused of crime or not, and the duty of giving to it force and effect is obligatory upon all entrusted under our Federal system with the enforcement of the laws. The tendency of those who execute the criminal laws of the country to obtain conviction by means of unlawful seizures and enforced confessions, the latter often obtained after subjecting accused persons to unwarranted practices destructive of rights secured by the Federal Constitution, should find no sanction in the judgments of the courts, which are charged at all times with the support of the Constitution, and to which people of all conditions have a right to appeal for the maintenance of such fundamental rights.

What, then, is the present case? . . .

The case in the aspect in which we are dealing with it involves the right of the court in a criminal prosecution to retain for the purposes of evidence the letters and correspondence of the accused, seized in his house in his absence and without his authority, by a United States Marshal holding no warrant for his arrest and none for the search of his premises. The accused, without awaiting his trial, made timely application to the court for an order for the return of these letters, as well as other property. This application was denied, the letters retained and put in evidence, after a further application at the beginning of the trial, both applications asserting the rights of the accused under the Fourth and Fifth Amendments to the Constitution. If letters and private documents can thus be seized and held and used in evidence against a citizen accused of an offense, the protection of the Fourth Amendment declaring his right to be secure against such searches and seizures is of no value, and, so far as those thus placed are concerned, might as well be stricken from the Constitution. The efforts of the courts and their officials to bring the guilty to punishment, praiseworthy as they are, are not to be aided by the sacrifice of those great principles established by years of endeavor and suffering which have resulted in their embodiment in the fundamental law of the land. The United States Marshal could only have invaded the house of the accused when armed with a warrant issued as required by the Constitution, upon sworn information and describing with reasonable particularity the thing for which the search was to be made. Instead, he acted without sanction of law, doubtless prompted by the desire to bring further proof to the aid of the Government, and under color of his office undertook to make a seizure of private papers in direct violation of the constitutional prohibition against such action. . . . To sanction such proceedings would be to affirm by judicial decision a manifest neglect, if not an open defiance, of the prohibitions of the Constitution, intended for the protection of the people against such unauthorized action.

"If this can happen, the 4th Amend means nothing"

The court before which the application was made in this case recognized the illegal character of the seizure, and ordered the return of property not in its judgment competent to be offered at the trial, but refused the application of the accused to turn over the letters, which were afterwards put in evidence on behalf of the Government. While there is no opinion in the case, the court in this proceeding doubtless relied upon what is now intended by the Government to be the correct rule of law under such circumstances, that the letters having come into the control of the court, it would not inquire into the manner in which they were obtained, but, if competent, would keep them and permit their use in evidence. Such proposition, the Government asserts, is conclusively established by certain decisions of this court. . . .

. . . .

We . . . reach the conclusion that the letters in question were taken from the house of the accused by an official of the United States, acting under color of his office, in direct violation of the constitutional rights of the defendant; that having made a seasonable application for their return, which was heard and passed upon by the court, there was involved in the order refusing the application a denial of the constitutional rights of the accused, and that the court should have restored these letters to the accused. In holding them and permitting their use upon the trial, we think prejudicial error was committed. . . .

It results that the judgment of the court below must be reversed, and the case remanded for further proceedings in accordance with this opinion.

Reversed.

Mapp v. Ohio

United States Supreme Court

367 U.S. 643, 81 S. Ct. 1684, 6 L. Ed. 2d 1081 (1961)

Mr. Justice Clark delivered the opinion of the Court.

. . . .

On May 23, 1957, three Cleveland police officers arrived at appellant's residence in that city pursuant to information that "a person [was] hiding out in the home, who was wanted for questioning in connection with a recent bombing, and that there was a large amount of policy paraphernalia being hidden in the home." Miss Mapp and her daughter by a former marriage lived on the top floor of the two-family dwelling. Upon their arrival at that house, the officers knocked on the door and demanded entrance but appellant, after telephoning her attorney, refused to admit them without a search warrant. They advised their headquarters of the situation and undertook a surveillance of the house.

The officers again sought entrance some three hours later when four or more additional officers arrived on the scene. When Miss Mapp did not come to the door immediately, at least one of the several doors to the house was forcibly opened and the policemen gained admittance. Meanwhile Miss Mapp's attorney arrived, but the officers, having secured their own entry, and continuing in their defiance of the law, would permit him neither to see Miss Mapp nor to enter the house. It appears that Miss Mapp was halfway down the stairs from the upper floor to the front door when the officers, in this highhanded manner, broke into the hall. She demanded to see the search warrant. A paper, claimed to be a warrant, was held up by one of the officers. She grabbed the "warrant" and placed it in her bosom. A struggle ensued in which the officers recovered the piece of paper and as a result of which they handcuffed appellant because she had been "belligerent" in resisting their official rescue of the "warrant" from her person. Running roughshod over appellant, a policeman "grabbed" her, "twisted [her] hand," and she "yelled [and] pleaded with him" because "it was hurting." Appellant, in handcuffs, was then forcibly taken upstairs to her bedroom where the officers searched a dresser, a chest of drawers, a closet and some suitcases. They also looked into a photo album and through personal papers belonging to the appellant. The search spread to the rest of the second floor including the child's bedroom, the living room, the kitchen and a dinette. The basement of the building and a trunk found therein were also searched. The obscene materials for possession of which she was ultimately convicted were discovered in the course of that widespread search.

At the trial no search warrant was produced by the prosecution, nor was the failure to produce one explained or accounted for. At best, "There is, in the record, considerable doubt as to whether there ever was any warrant for the search of defendant's home." 170 Ohio St., at 430, 166 N.E.2d, at 389. . . .

The State says that even if the search were made without authority, or otherwise unreasonably, it is not prevented from using the unconstitutionally seized evidence at trial, citing *Wolf v. Colorado*, 338 U.S. 25, 33, 69 S. Ct. 1359, 1364, 93 L. Ed. 1782 (1949), in which this Court did indeed hold "that in a prosecution in a State court for a State crime the Fourteenth Amendment does not forbid the admission of evidence obtained by an unreasonable search and seizure." On this appeal . . . it is urged once again that we review that holding.

I

. . . .

. . . [I]n the *Weeks* case, this Court "for the first time" held that "in a federal prosecution the Fourth Amendment barred the use of evidence secured through an illegal search and seizure." *Wolf v. Colorado*, 338 U.S. at 28, 69 S. Ct. at 1361. This Court has ever since required of federal law officers a strict adherence to that command which this Court has held to be a clear, specific, and constitutionally required — even if judicially implied — deterrent safeguard without insistence upon which the Fourth Amendment would have been reduced to "a form of words." Holmes J., *Silverthorne Lumber Co. v. United States*, 251 U.S. 385, 392, 40 S. Ct. 182, 183, 64 L. Ed. 319 (1920). It meant, quite simply, that "conviction by means of unlawful seizures and enforced confessions . . . should find no sanction in the judgments of the courts . . . ," *Weeks v. United States*, 232 U.S. at 392, 34 S. Ct. at 344, and that such evidence "shall not be used at all." *Silverthorne Lumber Co. v. United States*, 251 U.S. at 392, 40 S. Ct. at 183.

There are in the cases of this Court some passing references to the *Weeks* rule as being one of evidence. But the plain and unequivocal language of *Weeks* — and its later paraphrase in *Wolf* — to the effect that the *Weeks* rule is of constitutional origin, remains entirely undisturbed.

. . . .

II

In 1949, 35 years after *Weeks* was announced, this Court, in *Wolf v. Colorado*, again for the first time, discussed the effect of the Fourth Amendment upon the States through the operation of the Due Process Clause of the Fourteenth Amendment. It said:

> We have no hesitation in saying that were a State affirmatively to sanction such police incursion into privacy it would run counter to the guaranty of the Fourteenth Amendment.

338 U.S. at 28, 69 S. Ct. at 1361.

Nevertheless, after declaring that the "security of one's privacy against arbitrary intrusion by the police" is "implicit in 'the concept of ordered liberty' and as such enforceable against the States through the Due Process Clause," *cf. Palko v. Connecticut*,

302 U.S. 319, 58 S. Ct. 149, 82 L. Ed. 288 (1937), and announcing that it "stoutly adhere[d]" to the *Weeks* decision, the Court decided that the *Weeks* exclusionary rule would not then be imposed upon the States as "an essential ingredient of the right." 338 U.S. at 27–29, 69 S. Ct. at 1362. The Court's reasons for not considering essential to the right to privacy, as a curb imposed upon the States by the Due Process Clause, that which decades before had been posited as part and parcel of the Fourth Amendment's limitations upon federal encroachment of individual privacy, were bottomed on factual considerations.

While they are not basically relevant to a decision that the exclusionary rule is an essential ingredient of the Fourth Amendment as the right it embodies is vouchsafed against the States by the Due Process Clause, we will consider the current validity of the factual grounds upon which *Wolf* was based.

The Court in *Wolf* first stated that "the contrariety of views of the States" on the adoption of the exclusionary rule of *Weeks* was "particularly impressive" (338 U.S. at 29, 69 S. Ct. at 1362); and, in this connection, that it could not "brush aside the experience of States which deem the incidence of such conduct by the police too slight to call for a deterrent remedy . . . by overriding the [States'] relevant rules of evidence." 338 U.S. at 31–32, 69 S. Ct. at 1363. While in 1949, prior to the *Wolf* case, almost two-thirds of the States were opposed to the use of the exclusionary rule, now, despite the *Wolf* case, more than half of those since passing upon it, by their own legislative or judicial decision, have wholly or partly adopted or adhered to the *Weeks* rule. Significantly, among those now following the rule is California, which, according to its highest court, was "compelled to reach that conclusion because other remedies have completely failed to secure compliance with the constitutional provisions. . . ." *People v. Cahan*, 44 Cal. 2d 434, 445, 282 P.2d 905, 911 (1955). In connection with this California case, we note that the second basis elaborated in *Wolf* in support of its failure to enforce the exclusionary doctrine against the States was that "other means of protection" have been afforded "the right to privacy." 338 U.S. at 30, 69 S. Ct. at 1362. The experience of California that such other remedies have been worthless and futile is buttressed by the experience of other States. The obvious futility of relegating the Fourth Amendment to the protection of other remedies has, moreover, been recognized by this Court since *Wolf*.

Likewise, time has set its face against what *Wolf* called the "weighty testimony" of *People v. Defore*, 242 N.Y. 13, 150 N.E. 585 (1926). There Justice (then Judge) Cardozo, rejecting adoption of the *Weeks* exclusionary rule in New York, had said that "[t]he Federal rule as it stands is either too strict or too lax." 242 N.Y. at 22, 150 N.E. at 588. However, the force of that reasoning has been largely vitiated by later decisions of this Court. These include the recent discarding of the "silver platter" doctrine which allowed federal judicial use of evidence seized in violation of the Constitution by state agents; the relaxation of the formerly strict requirements as to standing to challenge the use of evidence thus seized, so that now the procedure of exclusion, "ultimately referable to constitutional safeguards," is available to anyone even "legitimately on [the] premises" unlawfully searched, *Jones v. United States*, 362 U.S. 257, 266–267,

80 S. Ct. 725, 734, 4 L. Ed. 2d 697 (1960); and finally, the formulation of a method to prevent state use of evidence unconstitutionally seized by federal agents. . . .

It, therefore, plainly appears that the factual considerations supporting the failure of the *Wolf* Court to include the *Weeks* exclusionary rule when it recognized the enforceability of the right to privacy against the States in 1949, while not basically relevant to the constitutional consideration, could not, in any analysis, now be deemed controlling.

III

. . . .

Today we once again examine *Wolf*'s constitutional documentation of the right to privacy free from unreasonable state intrusion, and, after its dozen years on our books, are led by it to close the only courtroom door remaining open to evidence secured by official lawlessness in flagrant abuse of that basic right, reserved to all persons as a specific guarantee against that very same unlawful conduct. We hold that all evidence obtained by searches and seizures in violation of the Constitution is, by that same authority, inadmissible in a state court. NOT coming in !

IV

Since the Fourth Amendment's right of privacy has been declared enforceable against the States through the Due Process Clause of the Fourteenth, it is enforceable against them by the same sanction of exclusion as is used against the Federal Government. Were it otherwise, then just as without the *Weeks* rule the assurance against unreasonable federal searches and seizures would be "a form of words," valueless and undeserving of mention in a perpetual charter of inestimable human liberties, so too, without that rule the freedom from state invasions of privacy would be so ephemeral and so neatly severed from its conceptual nexus with the freedom from all brutish means of coercing evidence as not to merit this Court's high regard as a freedom "implicit in the concept of ordered liberty." At the time that the Court held in *Wolf* that the Amendment was applicable to the States through the Due Process Clause, the cases of this Court, as we have seen, had steadfastly held that as to federal officers the Fourth Amendment included the exclusion of the evidence seized in violation of its provisions. Even *Wolf* "stoutly adhered" to that proposition. The right to privacy, when conceded operatively enforceable against the States, was not susceptible of destruction by avulsion of the sanction upon which its protection and enjoyment had always been deemed dependent under the *Boyd*, *Weeks* and *Silverthorne* cases. Therefore, in extending the substantive protections of due process to all constitutionally unreasonable searches — state or federal — it was logically and constitutionally necessary that the exclusion doctrine — an essential part of the right to privacy — be also insisted upon as an essential ingredient of the right newly recognized by the *Wolf* case. In short, the admission of the new constitutional right by *Wolf* could not consistently tolerate denial of its most important constitutional privilege, namely, the exclusion of the evidence which an accused had been forced to give by reason of the unlawful seizure. To hold otherwise is to grant the right but in reality to withhold its privilege and enjoyment. Only last year the Court itself recognized that the purpose of the exclusionary rule "is to deter — to compel respect for the constitutional guaranty in the only effectively available way — by removing the incentive to disregard it." *Elkins v. United States*, 364 U.S. 206, 217, 80 S. Ct. 1437, 1444.

Indeed, we are aware of no restraint, similar to that rejected today, conditioning the enforcement of any other basic constitutional right. The right to privacy, no less important than any other right carefully and particularly reserved to the people, would stand in marked contrast to all other rights declared as "basic to a free society." *Wolf v. Colorado*, 338 U.S. at 27, 69 S. Ct. at 1361. This Court has not hesitated to enforce as strictly against the States as it does against the Federal Government the rights of free speech and of a free press, the rights to notice and to a fair, public trial, including, as it does, the right not to be convicted by use of a coerced confession, however logically relevant it be, and without regard to its reliability. And nothing could be more certain than that when a coerced confession is involved, "the relevant rules of evidence" are overridden without regard to "the incidence of such conduct by the police," slight or frequent. Why should not the same rule apply to what is tantamount to coerced testimony by way of unconstitutional seizure of goods, papers, effects, documents, etc.? We find that, as to the Federal Government, the Fourth and Fifth Amendments and, as to the States, the freedom from unconscionable invasions of privacy and the freedom from convictions based upon coerced confessions do enjoy an "intimate relation" in their perpetuation of "principles of humanity and civil liberty [secured] . . . only after years of struggle." *Bram v. United States*, 168 U.S. 532, 543–544, 18 S. Ct. 183, 187, 42 L. Ed. 568 (1897). They express "supplementing phases of the same constitutional purpose — to maintain inviolate large areas of personal privacy." *Feldman v. United States*, 322 U.S. 487, 489–490, 64 S. Ct. 1082, 1083, 88 L. Ed. 1408 (1944). The philosophy of each Amendment and of each freedom is complementary to, although not dependent upon, that of the other in its sphere of influence — the very least that together they assure in either sphere is that no man is to be convicted on unconstitutional evidence. *Cf. Rochin v. California*, 342 U.S. 165, 173, 72 S. Ct. 205, 210, 96 L. Ed. 183 (1952).

V

Moreover, our holding that the exclusionary rule is an essential part of both the Fourth and Fourteenth Amendments is not only the logical dictate of prior cases, but it also makes very good sense. There is no war between the Constitution and common sense. Presently, a federal prosecutor may make no use of evidence illegally seized, but a State's attorney across the street may, although he supposedly is operating under the enforceable prohibitions of the same Amendment. Thus the State, by admitting evidence unlawfully seized, serves to encourage disobedience to the Federal Constitution which it is bound to uphold. Moreover, as was said in *Elkins*, "[t]he very essence of a healthy federalism depends upon the avoidance of needless conflict between state and federal courts." 364 U.S. at 221, 80 S. Ct. at 1446.

. . . .

There are those who say, as did Justice (then Judge) Cardozo, that under our constitutional exclusionary doctrine "the criminal is to go free because the constable has blundered." *People v. Defore*, 242 N.Y. at 21, 150 N.E. at 587. In some cases this will undoubtedly be the result. But, as was said in *Elkins*, "there is another consideration — the imperative of judicial integrity." 364 U.S. at 222, 80 S. Ct. at 1447. The criminal goes free, if he must, but it is the law that sets him free. Nothing can destroy a government more quickly than its failure to observe its own laws, or worse, its disregard of the charter of its own existence. As Mr. Justice Brandeis, dissenting, said in *Olmstead v. United States*, 277 U.S. 438, 485, 48 S. Ct. 564, 575, 72 L. Ed. 944 (1928): "Our Government is the potent, the omnipresent teacher. For good or for ill, it teaches the whole people by its example . . . . If the Government becomes a lawbreaker, it breeds contempt for law; it invites every man to become a law unto himself; it invites anarchy." Nor can it lightly be assumed that, as a practical matter, adoption of the exclusionary rule fetters law enforcement. Only last year this Court expressly considered that contention and found that "pragmatic evidence of a sort" to the contrary was not wanting. *Elkins v. United States*, 364 U.S. at 218, 80 S. Ct. at 1444. The Court noted that

> The federal courts themselves have operated under the exclusionary rule of *Weeks* for almost half a century; yet it has not been suggested either that the Federal Bureau of Investigation has thereby been rendered ineffective, or that the administration of criminal justice in the federal courts has thereby been disrupted. Moreover, the experience of the states is impressive. . . . The movement towards the rule of exclusion has been halting but seemingly inexorable.

Id. at 218–219, 80 S. Ct. at 1444–1445.

The ignoble shortcut to conviction left open to the State tends to destroy the entire system of constitutional restraints on which the liberties of the people rest. Having once recognized that the right to privacy embodied in the Fourth Amendment is enforceable against the States, and that the right to be secure against rude invasions of privacy by state officers is, therefore, constitutional in origin, we can no longer permit that right to remain an empty promise. Because it is enforceable in the same manner and to like effect as other basic rights secured by the Due Process Clause, we can no longer permit it to be revocable at the whim of any police officer who, in the name of law enforcement itself, chooses to suspend its enjoyment. Our decision, founded on reason and truth, gives to the individual no more than that which the Constitution guarantees him, to the police officer no less than that to which honest law enforcement is entitled, and, to the courts, that judicial integrity so necessary in the true administration of justice.

The judgment of the Supreme Court of Ohio is reversed and the cause remanded for further proceedings not inconsistent with this opinion.

Reversed and remanded.

MR. JUSTICE BLACK, concurring.

. . . .

I am still not persuaded that the Fourth Amendment, standing alone, would be enough to bar the introduction into evidence against an accused of papers and effects seized from him in violation of its commands. For the Fourth Amendment does not itself contain any provision expressly precluding the use of such evidence, and I am extremely doubtful that such a provision could properly be inferred from nothing more than the basic command against unreasonable searches and seizures. Reflection on the problem, however, in the light of cases coming before the Court since *Wolf*, has led me to conclude that when the Fourth Amendment's ban against unreasonable searches and seizures is considered together with the Fifth Amendment's ban against compelled self-incrimination, a constitutional basis emerges which not only justifies but actually requires the exclusionary rule.

. . . .

MR. JUSTICE DOUGLAS, concurring.

. . . .

We held in *Wolf v. Colorado*, 338 U.S. 25, 69 S. Ct. 1359, 93 L. Ed. 1782, that the Fourth Amendment was applicable to the States by reason of the Due Process Clause of the Fourteenth Amendment. But a majority held that the exclusionary rule of the *Weeks* case was not required of the States, that they could apply such sanctions as they chose. That position had the necessary votes to carry the day. But with all respect it was not the voice of reason or principle. As stated in the *Weeks* case, if evidence seized in violation of the Fourth Amendment can be used against an accused, "his right to be secure against such searches and seizures is of no value, and . . . might as well be stricken from the Constitution." 232 U.S. at 393, 34 S. Ct. at 344.

When we allowed States to give constitutional sanction to the "shabby business" of unlawful entry into a home (to use an expression of Mr. Justice Murphy, *Wolf v. Colorado*, 338 U.S. at 46, 69 S. Ct. at 1371), we did indeed rob the Fourth Amendment of much meaningful force. There are, of course, other theoretical remedies. One is disciplinary action within the hierarchy of the police system, including prosecution of the police officer for a crime. Yet as Mr. Justice Murphy said in *Wolf v. Colorado*, 338 U.S. at 42, 69 S. Ct. at 1369, "Self-scrutiny is a lofty ideal, but its exaltation reaches new heights if we expect a District Attorney to prosecute himself or his associates for well-meaning violations of the search and seizure clause during a raid the District Attorney or his associates have ordered."

The only remaining remedy, if exclusion of the evidence is not required, is an action of trespass by the homeowner against the offending officer. Mr. Justice Murphy showed how onerous and difficult it would be for the citizen to maintain that action and how meagre the relief even if the citizen prevails. The truth is that trespass actions against officers who make unlawful searches and seizures are mainly illusory remedies.

Without judicial action making the exclusionary rule applicable to the States, *Wolf v. Colorado* in practical effect reduced the guarantee against unreasonable searches and seizures to "a dead letter," as Mr. Justice Rutledge said in his dissent. *Wolf v. Colorado* was decided in 1949. The immediate result was a storm of constitutional controversy which only today finds its end. I believe that this is an appropriate case in which to put an end to the asymmetry which *Wolf* imported into the law.

. . . .

[The Memorandum of Mr. Justice Stewart has been omitted.]

Mr. Justice Harlan, with whom Mr. Justice Frankfurter and Mr. Justice Whittaker join, dissenting.

In overruling the *Wolf* case the Court, in my opinion, has forgotten the sense of judicial restraint which, with due regard for *stare decisis*, is one element that should enter into deciding whether a past decision of this Court should be overruled. Apart from that I also believe that the *Wolf* rule represents sounder Constitutional doctrine than the new rule which now replaces it.

. . . .

II

Essential to the majority's argument against *Wolf* is the proposition that the rule of *Weeks v. United States*, 232 U.S. 383, 34 S. Ct. 341, 58 L. Ed. 362, excluding in federal criminal trials the use of evidence obtained in violation of the Fourth Amendment, derives not from the "supervisory power" of this Court over the federal judicial system, but from Constitutional requirement. This is so because no one, I suppose, would suggest that this Court possesses any general supervisory power over the state courts. Although I entertain considerable doubt as to the soundness of this foundational proposition of the majority, I shall assume, for present purposes, that the *Weeks* rule "is of constitutional origin."

At the heart of the majority's opinion in this case is the following syllogism: (1) the rule excluding in federal criminal trials evidence which is the product of all illegal search and seizure is a "part and parcel" of the Fourth Amendment; (2) *Wolf* held that the "privacy" assured against federal action by the Fourth Amendment is also protected against state action by the Fourteenth Amendment; and (3) it is therefore "logically and constitutionally necessary" that the *Weeks* exclusionary rule should also be enforced against the States.

This reasoning ultimately rests on the unsound premise that because *Wolf* carried into the States, as part of "the concept of ordered liberty" embodied in the Fourteenth Amendment, the principle of "privacy" underlying the Fourth Amendment, it must follow that whatever configurations of the Fourth Amendment have been developed in the particularizing federal precedents are likewise to be deemed a part of "ordered liberty," and as such are enforceable against the States. For me, this does not follow at all.

It cannot be too much emphasized that what was recognized in *Wolf* was not that the Fourth Amendment *as such* is enforceable against the States as a facet of due process, a view of the Fourteenth Amendment which, as *Wolf* itself pointed out, has long since been discredited, but the principle of privacy "which is at the core of the Fourth Amendment." *Id.*, 338 U.S. at 27, 69 S. Ct. at 1361. It would not be proper to expect or impose any precise equivalence, either as regards the scope of the right or the means of its implementation, between the requirements of the Fourth and Fourteenth Amendments. . . .

. . . Since there is not the slightest suggestion that Ohio's policy is "affirmatively to sanction . . . police incursion into privacy," what the Court is now doing is to impose upon the States not only federal substantive standards of "search and seizure" but also the basic federal remedy for violation of those standards. For I think it entirely clear that the *Weeks* exclusionary rule is but a remedy which, by penalizing past official misconduct, is aimed at deterring such conduct in the future.

I would not impose upon the States this federal exclusionary remedy. The reasons given by the majority for now suddenly turning its back on *Wolf* seem to me notably unconvincing.

First, it is said that "the factual grounds upon which *Wolf* was based" have since changed, in that more States now follow the *Weeks* exclusionary rule than was so at the time *Wolf* was decided. While that is true, a recent survey indicates that at present one-half of the States still adhere to the common-law non-exclusionary rule, and one, Maryland, retains the rule as to felonies. But in any case surely all this is beside the point, as the majority itself indeed seems to recognize. Our concern here, as it was in *Wolf*, is not with the desirability of that rule but only with the question whether the States are Constitutionally free to follow it or not as they may themselves determine, and the relevance of the disparity of views among the States on this point lies simply in the fact that the judgment involved is a debatable one. Moreover, the very fact on which the majority relies, instead of lending support to what is now being done, points away from the need of replacing voluntary state action with federal compulsion.

The preservation of a proper balance between state and federal responsibility in the administration of criminal justice demands patience on the part of those who might like to see things move faster among the States in this respect. Problems of criminal law enforcement vary widely from State to State. One State, in considering the totality of its legal picture, may conclude that the need for embracing the *Weeks* rule is pressing because other remedies are unavailable or inadequate to secure compliance with the substantive Constitutional principle involved. Another, though equally solicitous of Constitutional rights, may choose to pursue one purpose at a time, allowing all evidence relevant to guilt to be brought into a criminal trial, and dealing with Constitutional infractions by other means. Still another may consider the exclusionary rule too rough-and-ready a remedy, in that it reaches only unconstitutional intrusions which eventuate in criminal prosecution of the victims. Further, a State after experimenting with the *Weeks* rule for a time may, because of unsatisfactory experience with it, decide to revert to a non-exclusionary rule. And so on. From the standpoint of Constitutional permissibility in pointing a State in one direction or another, I do not see at all why "time has set its face against" the considerations which led Mr. Justice Cardozo, then chief judge of the New York Court of Appeals, to reject for New York in *People v. Defore*, 242 N.Y. 13, 150 N.E. 585, the *Weeks* exclusionary rule. For us the question remains, as it has always been, one of state power, not one of passing judgment on the wisdom of one state course or another. In my view this Court should continue to forbear from fettering the States with an adamant rule which may embarrass them in coping with their own peculiar problems in criminal law enforcement.

Further, we are told that imposition of the *Weeks* rule on the States makes "very good sense," in that it will promote recognition by state and federal officials of their "mutual obligation to respect the same fundamental criteria" in their approach to law enforcement, and will avoid "needless conflict between state and federal courts." Indeed the majority now finds an incongruity in *Wolf*'s discriminating perception between the demands of "ordered liberty" as respects the basic right of "privacy" and the means of securing it among the States. That perception, resting both on a sensitive regard for our federal system and a sound recognition of this Court's remoteness from particular state problems, is for me the strength of that decision.

An approach which regards the issue as one of achieving procedural symmetry or of serving administrative convenience surely disfigures the boundaries of this Court's functions in relation to the state and federal courts.

. . . .

Finally, it is said that the overruling of *Wolf* is supported by the established doctrine that the admission in evidence of an involuntary confession renders a state conviction Constitutionally invalid. Since such a confession may often be entirely reliable, and therefore of the greatest relevance to the issue of the trial, the argument continues, this doctrine is ample warrant in precedent that the way evidence was obtained, and not just its relevance, is Constitutionally significant to the fairness of a trial. I believe this analogy is not a true one. The "coerced confession" rule is certainly not a rule that any illegally obtained statements may not be used in evidence.

. . . .

. . . [I]n requiring exclusion of an involuntary statement of an accused, we are concerned not with an appropriate remedy for what the police have done, but with something which is regarded as going to the heart of our concepts of fairness in judicial procedure. The operative assumption of our procedural system is that "Ours is the accusatorial as opposed to the inquisitorial system. Such has been the characteristic of Anglo-American criminal justice since it freed itself from practices borrowed by the Star Chamber from the Continent whereby an accused was interrogated in secret for hours on end." *Watts v. Indiana*, 338 U.S. 49, 54, 69 S. Ct. 1347, 1350, 93 L. Ed. 1801. The pressures brought to bear against an accused leading to a confession, unlike an unconstitutional violation of privacy, do not, apart from the use of the confession at trial, necessarily involve independent Constitutional violations. What is crucial is that the trial defense to which an accused is entitled should not be rendered an empty formality by reason of statements wrung from him, for then "a prisoner ... [has been] made the deluded instrument of his own conviction." 2 Hawkins, PLEAS OF THE CROWN (8th ed., 1824), c. 46, § 34. That this is a *procedural right*, and that its violation occurs at the time his improperly obtained statement is admitted at trial, is manifest. For without this right all the careful safeguards erected around the giving of testimony, whether by an accused or any other witness, would become empty formalities in a procedure where the most compelling possible evidence of guilt, a confession, would have already been obtained at the unsupervised pleasure of the police.

This, and not the disciplining of the police, as with illegally seized evidence, is surely the true basis for excluding a statement of the accused which was unconstitutionally obtained. In sum, I think the coerced confession analogy works strongly against what the Court does today.

. . . .

I regret that I find so unwise in principle and so inexpedient in policy a decision motivated by the high purpose of increasing respect for Constitutional rights. But in the last analysis I think this Court can increase respect for the Constitution only if it rigidly respects the limitations which the Constitution places upon it, and respects as well the principles inherent in its own processes. In the present case I think we exceed both, and that our voice becomes only a voice of power, not of reason.

Notes and Questions

(1) *Weeks* and *Mapp* introduce the Fourth and Fourteenth Amendment exclusionary rules. Since *Mapp*, the Court has had numerous opportunities to discuss and refine the rationales for excluding evidence acquired by means of an illegal search or seizure. The understanding that evolved and that continues to command majority support on the Court is captured by the following excerpt from *United States v. Calandra*, 414 U.S. 338, 94 S. Ct. 613, 38 L. Ed. 2d 561 (1974):

> The purpose of the exclusionary rule is not to redress the injury to the privacy of the search victim:
>
> "[T]he ruptured privacy of the victims' homes and effects cannot be restored. Reparation comes too late." *Linkletter v. Walker*, 381 U.S. 618, 637, 85 S. Ct. 1731, 1742, 14 L. Ed. 2d 601 (1965). Instead, the rule's prime purpose is to deter future unlawful conduct and thereby effectuate the guarantee of the Fourth Amendment against unreasonable searches and seizures:
>
> "The rule is calculated to prevent, not to repair. Its purpose is to deter—to compel respect for the constitutional guaranty in the only effectively available way—by removing the incentive to disregard it." *Elkins v. United States*, 364 U.S. 206, 217, 80 S. Ct. 1437, 1444, 4 L. Ed. 2d 1669 (1960).

In sum, the rule is a judicially created remedy designed to safeguard Fourth Amendment rights generally through its deterrent effect, rather than a personal constitutional right of the party aggrieved.

Is the *Calandra* Court's conception of the *Weeks* and *Mapp* exclusionary rules consistent with the reasoning and conclusions of the *Weeks* and *Mapp* opinions? For a fuller exposition of the prevailing views concerning the underpinnings of the Fourth Amendment rule, see *United States v. Leon*, 468 U.S. 897, 104 S. Ct. 3405, 82 L. Ed. 2d 677 (1984), *infra* Chapter 13[D].

(2) In 1995, the Senate Judiciary Committee held a hearing on the following proposed legislation:

Evidence obtained as a result of a search or seizure that is otherwise admissible in a Federal criminal proceeding shall not be excluded in a proceeding in a court of the United States on the ground that the search or seizure was in violation of the Fourth Amendment to the Constitution.

In place of the exclusion of evidence, the proposed legislation authorized *civil suits* against the federal government for damages resulting from a search or seizure conducted by an investigative or law enforcement officer, acting within the scope of the officer's office or employment, in violation of the Fourth Amendment to the Constitution.

The legislation provided that this would be the *only* civil remedy. It specifically abolished civil actions for violations of constitutional rights authorized by *Bivens v. Six Unknown Named Agents*, 403 U.S. 388 (1971). Under the proposed legislation, those whose Fourth Amendment rights were violated could recover actual and punitive damages, but punitive damages could not exceed $10,000, and the combined actual and punitive damages ordinarily could not exceed $30,000. Criteria for assessing punitive damages were specified. In addition, courts were given discretion to order the government to pay a prevailing plaintiff's attorney's fees.

The proposed legislation also provided that an officer who conducted an unconstitutional search or seizure would be

subject to appropriate discipline in the discretion of the Federal agency employing the officer, if that agency determines, after notice and hearing, that the officer conducted the search and seizure lacking a good faith belief that the search and seizure was constitutional.

Suppose that this legislation had been enacted by Congress and challenged in court on constitutional grounds. What arguments should be made in support of that challenge? How should defenders of the legislation respond? How should a court rule?

(3) The *Mapp* majority observed that coerced confessions, "however logically relevant," are suppressed under the command of the Due Process Clause. It relied in part on that fact in concluding that the products of illegal searches and seizures had

to be excluded. Dissenting Justice Harlan maintained that the Court's "analogy [to coerced confessions] is not a true one." Is the majority's reliance upon the prohibition against coerced confessions sound? What is the logic behind the Due Process Clause's exclusion of coerced statements?

(4) What are the premises for barring the use of evidence obtained in violation of *Miranda*?

(a) In *Miranda v. Arizona*, the Court held that "the prosecution may not use statements . . . stemming from custodial interrogation . . . unless it demonstrates the use of procedural safeguards effective to secure the privilege against self-incrimination." Chief Justice Warren observed that without "adequate protective devices . . . to dispel the compulsion inherent in custodial surroundings, no statement . . . can truly be the product of . . . free choice." He later added that because statements used "to impeach [a defendant's] testimony at trial . . . are incriminating in any meaningful sense of the word[, they] may not be used without the full warnings and effective waiver required for any other statement." As Justice Scalia would suggest much later, in *Dickerson v. United States*, the "fairest reading of" the original *Miranda* opinion was that exclusion was required because "the admission at trial of un-*Mirandized* confessions . . . violate[d] the Constitution." Put otherwise, exclusion under *Miranda* was initially thought to be part and parcel of the Fifth Amendment right not to be compelled to be a witness against oneself. As is clear from post-*Miranda* opinions discussed in Chapter Eight, that view of *Miranda*'s evidentiary bar was not destined to prevail.

(b) In *Michigan v. Tucker*, 417 U.S. 433, 94 S. Ct. 2357, 41 L. Ed. 2d 182 (1974), the defendant sought to suppress the testimony of a witness who was discovered as a result of statements the defendant made in response to custodial interrogation without full *Miranda* warnings. The Supreme Court concluded that the defendant's *statements* had to be excluded under *Miranda*. The *testimony of the witness*, however, was deemed admissible even though it had been derived from the inadmissible statements.

Justice Rehnquist, for a five-member majority, observed that the typical *Miranda* violation involves no actual compulsion and emphasized that the *Miranda* requirements are merely "procedural safeguards" that "provide practical reinforcement for the right against compulsory self-incrimination" and are "not themselves rights protected by the Constitution." He then considered three potential rationales for the *Miranda* exclusionary rule: (1) deterring police misconduct; (2) preventing reliance upon untrustworthy evidence; and (3) preserving the adversary system principle that requires the government to shoulder the burden of conviction. With respect to the *voluntary* statements produced by a typical *Miranda* violation, the Court indicated that the only defensible reason for exclusion is *to deter* transgressions of the *Miranda* rules — i.e., to encourage compliance with the Warren Court's prophylactic scheme. Moreover, in deciding whether to exclude evidence derived from *Miranda* violations, "the need to provide an effective sanction to a constitutional right" must be balanced against "the strong interest . . . in making available to the trier of fact all concededly relevant and trustworthy evidence" and "society's interest in the effective prosecution of criminals." If the costs of losing probative evidence outweigh the deterrent gains from suppression, the evidence should be admitted. An application of this balancing process led the *Tucker* Court to conclude that the witness's testimony did not have to be suppressed.

Does it make constitutional sense to conclude that *Miranda* exclusion, like Fourth Amendment exclusion, is deterrent in nature? For consideration of this question, see Arnold H. Loewy, *Police-Obtained Evidence and the Constitution: Distinguishing Unconstitutionally Obtained Evidence From Unconstitutionally Used Evidence*, 87 Mich. L. Rev. 907, 916–28 (1989).

(c) Subsequently, in *Withrow v. Williams*, 507 U.S. 680, 113 S. Ct. 1745, 123 L. Ed. 2d 407 (1993), a five-person majority evinced a somewhat different attitude toward *Miranda* exclusion. The issue in *Withrow v. Williams* was whether the rule of *Stone v. Powell*, 428 U.S. 465, 96 S. Ct. 3037, 49 L. Ed. 2d 1067 (1976), applies to *Miranda*-based claims. *Stone v. Powell* had held that federal habeas corpus relief is unavailable for a state prisoner who claims that his conviction rests on evidence obtained in violation of the Fourth Amendment if the state has afforded him a full and fair opportunity to litigate that contention. The *Withrow* majority concluded that *Stone*'s holding should not be extended to *Miranda* claims.

In reaching that conclusion, Justice Souter's opinion for the majority contrasted the rationales for the *Mapp* and *Miranda* exclusionary rules as follows:

> [T]he *Mapp* rule "is not a personal constitutional right," but serves to deter future constitutional violations; although it mitigates the juridical consequences of invading the defendant's privacy, the exclusion of evidence at trial can do nothing to remedy the completed and wholly extrajudicial Fourth Amendment violation. Nor can the *Mapp* rule be thought to enhance the soundness of the criminal process by improving the reliability of evidence introduced at trial. Quite the contrary, . . . the evidence excluded under *Mapp* "is typically reliable and often the most probative information bearing on the guilt or innocence of the defendant."

> *Miranda* differs from *Mapp* in both respects. "Prophylactic" though it may be, in protecting a defendant's Fifth Amendment privilege against self-incrimination *Miranda* safeguards a "fundamental *trial* right." The privilege embodies "principles of humanity and civil liberty . . ." and reflects [fundamental values, including our preference for an accusatorial system, our fear of inhumane treatment, our sense that fair play dictates a balance in which the government shoulders the load, our respect for the inviolability of the human personality, our distrust of self-deprecatory statements, and our realization that the privilege often provides protection for innocent persons.]

> Nor does the Fifth Amendment "trial right" protected by *Miranda* serve some value necessarily divorced from the correct ascertainment of guilt. . . .

By bracing against the "possibility of unreliable statements in every instance of in-custody interrogation," *Miranda* serves to guard against "the use of unreliable statements at trial." (Citations omitted).

The *Withrow* majority's view that *Miranda* exclusion ensures the preservation of vital values underlying the Fifth Amendment privilege and safeguards against untrustworthy evidence that could lead to conviction of the innocent contrasts dramatically with the perspective of the *Tucker* Court and with intimations contained in other pre-*Withrow* discussions of *Miranda* exclusion. *See, e.g., Oregon v. Elstad*, 470 U.S. 298, 105 S. Ct. 1285, 84 L. Ed. 2d 222 (1985), *infra* Chapter 13[C]; *New York v. Quarles*, 467 U.S. 649, 104 S. Ct. 2626, 81 L. Ed. 2d 550 (1984), *supra* Chapter 8[A].

For more recent decisions that provide insights into the Court's conception of the rationales for the *Miranda* exclusionary rule, see *Missouri v. Seibert* and *United States v. Patane, infra* Chapter 13[E]. In *Patane*, the three Justices who joined the lead opinion rejected the deterrent rationale for suppression that was relied upon by the *Tucker* majority and that was not disavowed in *Withrow*. The two other Justices essential to the majority in that case declined to express a view on the question of whether deterrence is a justification for *Miranda*'s bar to confessions.

(5) The Court has only rarely reflected upon the underpinnings of the *Massiah* exclusion doctrine. Before 2009, the justifications for *Massiah*'s Sixth Amendment bar were not entirely clear.

(a) In *Massiah* itself, the Court held that the defendant "was denied the basic protections of [the Sixth Amendment right to counsel] *when there was used against him at his trial evidence of his own incriminating words*, which federal agents had deliberately elicited from him after he had been indicted and in the absence of his counsel." (Emphasis added.) Moreover, the Court did "not question that . . . it was entirely proper to continue an investigation of the suspected criminal activities of the defendant and his alleged confederates, even though [he] had already been indicted," thereby indicating that there was no Sixth Amendment problem with efforts to investigate criminal activity by eliciting information from charged individuals. The majority pointedly declared: "All that we hold is that the defendant's own incriminating statements . . . *could not constitutionally be used by the prosecution as evidence against him at his trial*." (Emphasis added.) The message seemed quite clear — that the right to counsel was at risk of violation *only* when the government introduced at trial statements deliberately elicited from an accused in the absence of counsel. Exclusion was essential to prevent an in-court deprivation of that fundamental guarantee.

(b) *Nix v. Williams*, 467 U.S. 431, 104 S. Ct. 2501, 81 L. Ed. 2d 377 (1984), which is considered in Chapter 13[B], was the first *Massiah* decision focused exclusively on the Sixth Amendment suppression doctrine. Therein, the Court assumed that the deterrence of pretrial efforts to secure statements in the absence of counsel was an objective of the *Massiah* exclusionary rule. The Court justified an exception to that rule by engaging in the same sort of deterrent analysis that has governed the resolution of Fourth Amendment exclusionary rule issues ever since *United States v. Calandra*. The Court, however, did not reject a claim that suppression under the right to counsel is also essential to ensure the fair trial guaranteed by the Sixth Amendment. In other words, the Court continued to entertain the possibility that the admission of evidence obtained in violation of *Massiah's* pretrial constraints could deny an accused his or her constitutional entitlement and, therefore, that suppression was essential to prevent courtroom violation of the Sixth Amendment.

(c) Finally, in 2009, the Court addressed the rationales for *Massiah's* evidentiary bar directly. In *Kansas v. Ventris*, 556 U.S. 586, 129 S. Ct. 1841, 173 L. Ed. 2d 801 (2009), considered in Chapter 13[F], a seven-Justice majority rejected the view that the introduction of deliberately elicited statements constitutes a deprivation of an accused's right to the assistance of counsel. According to the Justices, the suppression of such statements serves to enforce the Sixth Amendment by deterring officers from confronting uncounseled defendants prior to trial. A violation of the constitutional right can occur only during such a confrontation, not when the evidence obtained is used to convict an accused.

(d) Is the *Ventris* Court's understanding of *Massiah's* bar to inculpatory admissions constitutionally defensible? For a critical view of the Court's position, see James J. Tomkovicz, *Sacrificing* Massiah: *Confusion over Exclusion and Erosion of the Right to Counsel*, 16 Lewis & Clark L. Rev. 1 (2012).

(6) What are the reasons for excluding evidence secured in violation of the Sixth Amendment right to counsel protection against corporeal identification processes? What justifications support the due process bar to eyewitness identifications resulting from unnecessarily suggestive identification methods? The only insights into the rationales for those two evidentiary bars are those provided by the opinions studied in Chapters 10 and 11. What do those opinions suggest?

Selected Bibliography

Craig M. Bradley, Mapp *Goes Abroad*, 52 Case W. Res. L. Rev. 375 (2001)

Guido Calabresi, *The Exclusionary Rule*, 26 Harv. J.L. & Pub. Pol'y 111 (2003)

H. Mitchell Caldwell, *Fixing the Constable's Blunder: Can One Trial Judge in One County in One State Nudge a Nation Beyond the Exclusionary Rule?*, 2006 B.Y.U. L. Rev. 1

Lawrence Crocker, *Can the Exclusionary Rule Be Saved?*, 84 J. Crim. L. & Criminology 310 (1993)

Sharon L. Davies, *The Penalty of Exclusion—A Price or Sanction?*, 73 S. Cal. L. Rev. 1275 (2000)

Donald Dripps, *The Case for the Contingent Exclusionary Rule*, 38 Am. Crim. L. Rev. 1 (2001)

David A. Harris, *How Accountability-Based Policing Can Reinforce—Or Replace— The Fourth Amendment Exclusionary Rule*, 7 Ohio St. J. Crim. L. 149 (2009)

William C. Heffernan, *Foreword — The Fourth Amendment Exclusionary Rule as a Constitutional Remedy*, 88 Geo. L.J. 799 (2000)

Yale Kamisar, *In Defense of the Search and Seizure Exclusionary Rule*, 26 Harv. J.L. & Pub. Pol'y 119 (2003)

Yale Kamisar, *On the Fruits of* Miranda *Violations, Coerced Confessions, and Compelled Testimony*, 93 Mich. L. Rev. 929 (1995)

Yale Kamisar, *The Writings of John Barker Waite and Thomas Davies on the Search and Seizure Exclusionary Rule*, 100 Mich. L. Rev. 1821 (2002)

Lewis R. Katz, Mapp *After Forty Years: Its Impact on Race in America*, 52 Case W. Res. L. Rev. 471 (2001)

Arnold H. Loewy, *Police-Obtained Evidence and the Constitution: Distinguishing Unconstitutionally Obtained Evidence from Unconstitutionally Used Evidence*, 87 Mich. L. Rev. 907 (1989)

Timothy Lynch, *In Defense of the Exclusionary Rule*, 23 Harv. J.L. & Pub. Pol'y 711 (2000)

Eugene Milhizer, *The Exclusionary Rule Lottery Revisited*, 59 Cath. U. L. Rev. 747 (2010)

Jerry E. Norton, *The Exclusionary Rule Reconsidered: Restoring the Status Quo Ante*, 33 Wake Forest L. Rev. 261 (1998)

Timothy L. Perrin, Mitchell H. Caldwell, Carol A. Chase & Ronald W. Fagan, *If It's Broken, Fix It: Moving Beyond the Exclusionary Rule and a Call for a Civil Administrative Remedy to Partially Replace It*, 83 Iowa L. Rev. 669 (1998)

Barry S. Pollack & George C. Thomas III, *Saving Rights From a Remedy: A Societal View of the Fourth Amendment*, 73 B.U. L. Rev. 147 (1993)

Jeffrey Standen, *The Exclusionary Rule and Damages: An Economic Comparison of Private Remedies for Unconstitutional Police Conduct*, 2000 B.Y.U. L. Rev. 1443

Scott E. Sundby & Lucy B. Ricca, *The Majestic and the Mundane: The Two Creation Stories of the Exclusionary Rule*, 43 Tex. Tech L. Rev. 391 (2010)

James J. Tomkovicz, CONSTITUTIONAL EXCLUSION: THE RULES, RIGHTS, AND REMEDIES THAT STRIKE THE BALANCE BETWEEN FREEDOM AND ORDER (2011)

Chapter 13

The Scope of and Exceptions to the Exclusionary Rules

Introductory Note

As mentioned in the Introduction to Chapter 12, this final chapter focuses upon the operational details of the exclusionary rules. It is primarily concerned with doctrines that define the scope of, limitations upon, and exceptions to those rules. Contrary to popular misconceptions, a constitutional (or *Miranda*) violation does not inevitably lead to the permanent suppression of all evidence discovered. The reality is that much improperly obtained evidence is admissible in court. The cases and materials that follow discuss the standards that dictate when illegally acquired evidence must be excluded and when it may be introduced at trial. As will be seen, the Supreme Court has developed a number of doctrines that restrict the reach of the exclusion sanction. As a result, there are many situations in which the prosecution is able to make use of the evidentiary products of official improprieties.

This chapter is divided into a number of subsections. Most of these subsections are concerned with a specific limitation on the ambit of the exclusionary rules. The first subsection addresses the "standing" limitation, a constraint based on the "status" of the individual claiming exclusion. The second and third subsections are concerned with "exceptions" to the exclusionary rules that are based on the connections between illegalities and the acquisition of evidence sought to be suppressed — the "independent source," "inevitable discovery," and "attenuation" doctrines. The third subsection also includes a significant opinion that announces a unique qualification on Fourth Amendment suppression — the Court's decision to preclude exclusion for violations of the "knock and announce" rule. The fourth subsection is devoted to the "good faith" exceptions to the exclusionary rule, doctrines that are rooted in the character and culpability of the government transgression. The penultimate subsection includes decisions that provide significant insights into the uniquely narrow reach of *Miranda*'s evidentiary bar. The final subsection addresses the "impeachment" limitation, a stricture rooted in the nature of the proposed use of the evidence sought to be barred.

Students should identify and evaluate the character of and the justifications for each of the restrictions on exclusion presented in this chapter. Moreover, they should analyze whether the various doctrinal constraints are consistent with the basic rationales for suppressing probative evidence of guilt.

[A] The "Standing" Limitation

Note on *Alderman v. United States*

In *Alderman v. United States*, 394 U.S. 165, 89 S. Ct. 961, 22 L. Ed. 2d 176 (1969), the Government admitted that it had overheard conversations by means of unconstitutional electronic eavesdropping. The defendants claimed that any evidence that was the product of that surveillance had to be excluded from trial "regardless of whose Fourth Amendment rights the surveillance violated." Alternatively, they "urged that if evidence [was] inadmissible against one defendant or conspirator, because tainted by electronic surveillance illegal as to him, it [was] also inadmissible against his codefendant or coconspirator."

The Supreme Court "reject[ed]" the defendants' "expansive reading . . . of the exclusionary rule." According to the Court:

> The established principle is that *suppression of the product of a Fourth Amendment violation can be successfully urged only by those whose rights were violated by the search itself, not by those who are aggrieved solely by the introduction of damaging evidence.* Coconspirators and codefendants have been accorded no special standing.

> We adhere to . . . the general rule that Fourth Amendment rights are personal rights, which . . . may not be vicariously asserted. There is no necessity to exclude evidence against one defendant in order to protect the rights of another. No rights of the victim of an illegal search are at stake when the evidence is offered against some other party. The victim can and very probably will object for himself when and if it becomes important for him to do so.

> What petitioners appear to assert is an independent constitutional right of their own to exclude relevant and probative evidence because it was seized from another in violation of the Fourth Amendment. But we think there is a substantial difference for constitutional purposes between preventing the incrimination of a defendant through the very evidence illegally seized from him and suppressing evidence on the motion of a party who cannot claim this predicate for exclusion.

> The necessity for that predicate was not eliminated by recognizing and acknowledging the deterrent aim of the rule. Neither those cases nor any others hold that anything which deters illegal searches is thereby commanded by the Fourth Amendment. The deterrent values of preventing the

incrimination of those whose rights the police have violated have been considered sufficient to justify the suppression of probative evidence even though the case against the defendant is weakened or destroyed. We adhere to that judgment. But we are not convinced that the additional benefits of extending the exclusionary rule to other defendants would justify further encroachment upon the public interest in prosecuting those accused of crime and having them acquitted or convicted on the basis of all the evidence which exposes the truth.

. . . .

Of course, Congress or state legislatures may extend the exclusionary rule and provide that illegally seized evidence is inadmissible against anyone for any purpose. But for constitutional purposes, we are not now inclined to expand the existing rule that unlawful wiretapping or eavesdropping, whether deliberate or negligent, can produce nothing usable against the person aggrieved by the invasion. (Emphasis added.)

. . . .

Based on these premises, the Court concluded that each of the defendants in *Alderman* was "entitled to the suppression of government evidence originating in electronic surveillance violative of his own Fourth Amendment right to be free of unreasonable searches and seizures. [I]f the United States unlawfully overheard conversations of a [defendant] himself or conversations occurring on his premises, whether or not he was present or participated in those conversations," the defendant was entitled to have those conversations suppressed.

Rakas v. Illinois

United States Supreme Court

439 U.S. 128, 99 S. Ct. 421, 58 L. Ed. 2d 387 (1978)

MR. JUSTICE REHNQUIST delivered the opinion of the Court.

. . . .

I

Because we are not here concerned with the issue of probable cause, a brief description of the events leading to the search of the automobile will suffice. A police officer on a routine patrol received a radio call notifying him of a robbery of a clothing store in Bourbonnais, Ill., and describing the getaway car. Shortly thereafter, the officer spotted an automobile which he thought might be the getaway car. After following the car for some time and after the arrival of assistance, he and several other officers stopped the vehicle. The occupants of the automobile, petitioners and two female companions, were ordered out of the car and, after the occupants had left the car, two officers searched the interior of the vehicle. They discovered a box of rifle shells in the glove compartment, which had been locked, and a sawed-off rifle under the front passenger seat. After discovering the rifle and the shells, the officers took petitioners to the station and placed them under arrest.

Before trial petitioners moved to suppress the rifle and shells seized from the car on the ground that the search violated the Fourth and Fourteenth Amendments. They conceded that they did not own the automobile and were simply passengers; the owner of the car had been the driver of the vehicle at the time of the search. Nor did they assert that they owned the rifle or the shells seized. The prosecutor challenged petitioners' standing to object to the lawfulness of the search of the car because neither the car, the shells nor the rifle belonged to them. The trial court agreed that petitioners lacked standing and denied the motion to suppress the evidence.

. . . .

II

Petitioners first urge us to relax or broaden the rule of standing enunciated in *Jones v. United States*, 362 U.S. 257, 80 S. Ct. 725, 4 L. Ed. 2d 697 (1960), so that any criminal defendant at whom a search was "directed" would have standing to contest the legality of that search and object to the admission at trial of evidence obtained as a result of the search. Alternatively, petitioners argue that they have standing to object to the search under *Jones* because they were "legitimately on [the] premises" at the time of the search.

The concept of standing discussed in *Jones* focuses on whether the person seeking to challenge the legality of a search as a basis for suppressing evidence was himself the "victim" of the search or seizure. Adoption of the so-called "target" theory advanced by petitioners would in effect permit a defendant to assert that a violation of the Fourth Amendment rights of a third party entitled him to have evidence suppressed at his trial. If we reject petitioners' request for a broadened rule of standing such as this, and reaffirm the holding of *Jones* and other cases that Fourth Amendment rights are personal rights that may not be asserted vicariously, we will have occasion to re-examine the "standing" terminology emphasized in *Jones*. For we are not at all sure that the determination of a motion to suppress is materially aided by labeling the inquiry identified in *Jones* as one of standing, rather than simply recognizing it as one involving the substantive question of whether or not the proponent of the motion to suppress has had his own Fourth Amendment rights infringed by the search and seizure which he seeks to challenge. We shall therefore consider in turn petitioners' target theory, the necessity for continued adherence to the notion of standing discussed in *Jones* as a concept that is theoretically distinct from the merits of a defendant's Fourth Amendment claim, and, finally, the proper disposition of petitioners' ultimate claim in this case.

A

We decline to extend the rule of standing in Fourth Amendment cases in the manner suggested by petitioners. As we stated in *Alderman v. United States*, 394 U.S. 165, 174, 89 S. Ct. 961, 966, 22 L. Ed. 2d 176 (1969), "Fourth Amendment rights are personal rights which, like some other constitutional rights, may not be vicariously asserted." A person who is aggrieved by an illegal search and seizure only through the introduction of damaging evidence secured by a search of a third person's premises or property has not had any of his Fourth Amendment rights infringed. And since the exclusionary rule is an attempt to effectuate the guarantees of the Fourth Amendment, it is proper to permit only defendants whose Fourth Amendment rights have been violated to benefit from the rule's protections. There is no reason to think that a party whose rights have been infringed will not, if evidence is used against him, have ample motivation to move to suppress it. Even if such a person is not a defendant in the action, he may be able to recover damages for the violation of his Fourth Amendment rights, or seek redress under state law for invasion of privacy or trespass.

. . . .

Conferring standing to raise vicarious Fourth Amendment claims would necessarily mean a more widespread invocation of the exclusionary rule during criminal trials. . . .

Each time the exclusionary rule is applied it exacts a substantial social cost for the vindication of Fourth Amendment rights. Relevant and reliable evidence is kept from the trier of fact and the search for truth at trial is deflected. Since our cases generally have held that one whose Fourth Amendment rights are violated may successfully suppress evidence obtained in the course of an illegal search and seizure, misgivings as to the benefit of enlarging the class of persons who may invoke that rule are properly considered when deciding whether to expand standing to assert Fourth Amendment violations.

B

. . . [H]aving rejected petitioners' target theory and reaffirmed the principle that the "rights assured by the Fourth Amendment are personal rights, [which] . . . may be enforced by exclusion of evidence only at the instance of one whose own protection was infringed by the search and seizure," *Simmons v. United States*, 390 U.S., at 389, 88 S. Ct., at 974, the question necessarily arises whether it serves any useful analytical purpose to consider this principle a matter of standing, distinct from the merits of a defendant's Fourth Amendment claim. We can think of no decided cases of this Court that would have come out differently had we concluded, as we do now, that the type of standing requirement discussed in *Jones* and reaffirmed today is more properly subsumed under substantive Fourth Amendment doctrine. Rigorous application of the principle that the rights secured by this Amendment are personal, in place of a notion of "standing," will produce no additional situations in which evidence must be excluded. The inquiry under either approach is the same. But we think the better analysis forthrightly focuses on the extent of a particular defendant's rights under the Fourth Amendment, rather than on any theoretically separate, but invariably intertwined concept of standing. The Court in *Jones* also may have been aware that there was a certain artificiality in analyzing this question in terms of standing because in at least three separate places in its opinion the Court placed that term within quotation marks.

It should be emphasized that nothing we say here casts the least doubt on cases which recognize that, as a general proposition, the issue of standing involves two inquiries: first, whether the proponent of a particular legal right has alleged "injury in fact," and, second, whether the proponent is asserting his own legal rights and interests rather than basing his claim for relief upon the rights of third parties. But this Court's long history of insistence that Fourth Amendment rights are personal in nature has already answered many of these traditional standing inquiries, and we think that definition of those rights is more properly placed within the purview of substantive Fourth Amendment law than within that of standing.

Analyzed in these terms, the question is whether the challenged search or seizure violated the Fourth Amendment rights of a criminal defendant who seeks to exclude the evidence obtained during it. That inquiry in turn requires a determination of whether the disputed search and seizure has infringed an interest of the defendant which the Fourth Amendment was designed to protect. We are under no illusion that by dispensing with the rubric of standing used in *Jones* we have rendered any simpler the determination of whether the proponent of a motion to suppress is entitled to contest the legality of a search and seizure. But by frankly recognizing that this aspect of the analysis belongs more properly under the heading of substantive Fourth Amendment doctrine than under the heading of standing, we think the decision of this issue will rest on sounder logical footing.

C

Here petitioners, who were passengers occupying a car which they neither owned nor leased, seek to analogize their position to that of the defendant in *Jones v. United States*. In *Jones*, petitioner was present at the time of the search of an apartment which was owned by a friend. The friend had given Jones permission to use the apartment and a key to it, with which Jones had admitted himself on the day of the search. He had a suit and shirt at the apartment and had slept there "maybe a night," but his home was elsewhere. At the time of the search, Jones was the only occupant of the apartment because the lessee was away for a period of several days. Under these circumstances, this Court stated that while one wrongfully on the premises could not move to suppress evidence obtained as a result of searching them, "anyone legitimately on premises where a search occurs may challenge its legality." Petitioners argue that their occupancy of the automobile in question was comparable to that of Jones in the apartment and that they therefore have standing to contest the legality of the search — or as we have rephrased the inquiry, that they, like Jones, had their Fourth Amendment rights violated by the search.

We do not question the conclusion in *Jones* that the defendant in that case suffered a violation of his personal Fourth Amendment rights if the search in question was unlawful. Nonetheless, we believe that the phrase "legitimately on premises" coined in *Jones* creates too broad a gauge for measurement of Fourth Amendment rights. For example, applied literally, this statement would permit a casual visitor who has never seen, or been permitted to visit, the basement of another's house to object to a search of the basement if the visitor happened to be in the kitchen of the house at the time of the search. Likewise, a casual visitor who walks into a house one minute before a search of the house commences and leaves one minute after the search ends would be able to contest the legality of the search. The first visitor would have absolutely no interest or legitimate expectation of privacy in the basement, the second would have none in the house, and it advances no purpose served by the Fourth Amendment to permit either of them to object to the lawfulness of the search.[11]

. . . .

We think that *Jones* on its facts merely stands for the unremarkable proposition that a person can have a legally sufficient interest in a place other than his own home so that the Fourth Amendment protects him from unreasonable governmental intrusion into that place. In defining the scope of that interest, we adhere to the view expressed in *Jones* and echoed in later cases that arcane distinctions developed in property and tort law between guests, licensees, invitees, and the like, ought not to control. But the *Jones* statement that a person need only be "legitimately on premises" in order to challenge the validity of the search of a dwelling place cannot be taken in its full sweep beyond the facts of that case.

. . . [T]he holding in *Jones* can best be explained by the fact that Jones had a legitimate expectation of privacy in the premises he was using and therefore could claim the protection of the Fourth Amendment with respect to a governmental invasion of those premises, even though his "interest" in those premises might not have been a recognized property interest at common law.[12]

---

11. This is not to say that such visitors could not contest the lawfulness of the seizure of evidence or the search if their own property were seized during the search.

12. Obviously, however, a "legitimate" expectation of privacy by definition means more than a subjective expectation of not being discovered. A burglar plying his trade in a summer cabin during the off season may have a thoroughly justified subjective expectation of privacy, but it is not one which the law recognizes as "legitimate." His presence, in the words of *Jones*, 362 U.S., at 267, 80 S. Ct., at 734, is "wrongful"; his expectation is not "one that society is prepared to recognize as 'reasonable.'" *Katz v. United States*, 389 U.S., at 361, 88 S. Ct., at 516 (Harlan, J., concurring). And it would, of course, be merely tautological to fall back on the notion that those expectations of privacy which are legitimate depend primarily on cases deciding exclusionary-rule issues in criminal cases. Legitimation of expectations of privacy by law must have a source outside of the Fourth Amendment, either by reference to concepts of real or personal property law or to understandings that are recognized and permitted by society. One of the main rights attaching to property is the right to exclude others, and one who owns or lawfully possesses or controls property will in all likelihood have a legitimate expectation of privacy by virtue of this right to exclude. Expectations of privacy protected by the Fourth Amendment, of course, need not be based on a common-law interest in real or personal property, or on the invasion of such an interest. These ideas were rejected both in *Jones* and *Katz*. But by focusing on legitimate expectations of privacy in Fourth Amendment jurisprudence, the Court has not altogether abandoned use of property concepts in determining the presence or absence of the privacy interests protected by that Amendment. No better demonstration of

Our Brother White in dissent expresses the view that by rejecting the phrase "legitimately on [the] premises" as the appropriate measure of Fourth Amendment rights, we are abandoning a thoroughly workable, "bright line" test in favor of a less certain analysis of whether the facts of a particular case give rise to a legitimate expectation of privacy. If "legitimately on premises" were the successful litmus test of Fourth Amendment rights that he assumes it is, his approach would have at least the merit of easy application, whatever it lacked in fidelity to the history and purposes of the Fourth Amendment. But a reading of lower court cases that have applied the phrase "legitimately on premises," and of the dissent itself, reveals that this expression is not a shorthand summary for a bright-line rule which somehow encapsulates the "core" of the Fourth Amendment's protections.

The dissent itself shows that the facile consistency it is striving for is illusory. The dissenters concede that "there comes a point when use of an area is shared with so many that one simply cannot reasonably expect seclusion." But surely the "point" referred to is not one demarcating a line which is black on one side and white on another; it is inevitably a point which separates one shade of gray from another. We are likewise told by the dissent that a person "legitimately on *private* premises . . . , though his privacy is *not absolute*, is entitled to expect that he is sharing it only with those persons [allowed there] and that governmental officials will intrude only with *consent* or by complying with the Fourth Amendment." (emphasis added). This single sentence describing the contours of the supposedly easily applied rule virtually abounds with unanswered questions: What are "private" premises? Indeed, what are the "premises"? It may be easy to describe the "premises" when one is confronted with a 1-room apartment, but what of the case of a 10-room house, or of a house with an attached garage that is searched? Also, if one's privacy is not absolute, how is it bounded? If he risks governmental intrusion "with consent," who may give that consent?

Again, we are told by the dissent that the Fourth Amendment assures that "*some* expectations of privacy are justified and will be protected from official intrusion" (emphasis added). But we are not told which of many possible expectations of privacy are embraced within this sentence. And our dissenting Brethren concede that "perhaps the Constitution provides some degree less protection for the personal freedom from unreasonable governmental intrusion when one does not have a possessory interest in the invaded private place." But how much "less" protection is available when one does not have such a possessory interest?

Our disagreement with the dissent is not that it leaves these questions unanswered, or that the questions are necessarily irrelevant in the context of the analysis

---

this proposition exists than the decision in *Alderman v. United States*, 394 U.S. 165, 89 S. Ct. 961, 22 L. Ed. 2d 176 (1969), where the Court held that an individual's property interest in his own home was so great as to allow him to object to electronic surveillance of conversations emanating from his home, even though he himself was not a party to the conversations. On the other hand, even a property interest in premises may not be sufficient to establish a legitimate expectation of privacy with respect to particular items located on the premises or activity conducted thereon.

contained in this opinion. Our disagreement is rather with the dissent's bland and self-refuting assumption that there will not be fine lines to be drawn in Fourth Amendment cases as in other areas of the law, and that its rubric, rather than a meaningful exegesis of Fourth Amendment doctrine, is more desirable or more easily resolves Fourth Amendment cases. In abandoning "legitimately on premises" for the doctrine that we announce today, we are not forsaking a time-tested and workable rule, which has produced consistent results when applied, solely for the sake of fidelity to the values underlying the Fourth Amendment. Rather, we are rejecting blind adherence to a phrase which at most has superficial clarity and which conceals underneath that thin veneer all of the problems of line drawing which must be faced in any conscientious effort to apply the Fourth Amendment. Where the factual premises for a rule are so generally prevalent that little would be lost and much would be gained by abandoning case-by-case analysis, we have not hesitated to do so. But the phrase "legitimately on premises" has not been shown to be an easily applicable measure of Fourth Amendment rights so much as it has proved to be simply a label placed by the courts on results which have not been subjected to careful analysis. We would not wish to be understood as saying that legitimate presence on the premises is irrelevant to one's expectation of privacy, but it cannot be deemed controlling.

D

Judged by the foregoing analysis, petitioners' claims must fail. They asserted neither a property nor a possessory interest in the automobile, nor an interest in the property seized. And as we have previously indicated, the fact that they were "legitimately on [the] premises" in the sense that they were in the car with the permission of its owner is not determinative of whether they had a legitimate expectation of privacy in the particular areas of the automobile searched. It is unnecessary for us to decide here whether the same expectations of privacy are warranted in a car as would be justified in a dwelling place in analogous circumstances. We have on numerous occasions pointed out that cars are not to be treated identically with houses or apartments for Fourth Amendment purposes. But here petitioners' claim is one which would fail even in an analogous situation in a dwelling place, since they made no showing that they had any legitimate expectation of privacy in the glove compartment or area under the seat of the car in which they were merely passengers. Like the trunk of an automobile, these are areas in which a passenger *qua* passenger simply would not normally have a legitimate expectation of privacy.

. . . Katz and Jones could legitimately expect privacy in the areas which were the subject of the search and seizure each sought to contest. No such showing was made by these petitioners with respect to those portions of the automobile which were searched and from which incriminating evidence was seized.[17]

---

17. For reasons which they do not explain, our dissenting Brethren repeatedly criticize our "holding" that unless one has a common-law property interest in the premises searched, one cannot object to the search. We have rendered no such "holding," however. To the contrary, we have

III

The Illinois courts were therefore correct in concluding that it was unnecessary to decide whether the search of the car might have violated the rights secured to someone else by the Fourth and Fourteenth Amendments to the United States Constitution. Since it did not violate any rights of these petitioners, their judgment of conviction is

Affirmed.

MR. JUSTICE POWELL, with whom THE CHIEF JUSTICE joins, concurring.

. . . .

The ultimate question . . . is whether one's claim to privacy from government intrusion is reasonable in light of all the surrounding circumstances. As the dissenting opinion states, this standard "will not provide law enforcement officials with a bright line between the protected and the unprotected." Whatever the application of this standard may lack in ready administration, it is more faithful to the purposes of the Fourth Amendment than a test focusing solely or primarily on whether the defendant was legitimately present during the search.[1]

In considering the reasonableness of asserted privacy expectations, the Court has recognized that no single factor invariably will be determinative. . . .

. . . The petitioners' Fourth Amendment rights were not abridged here because none of the factors relied upon by this Court on prior occasions supports petition-

---

taken pains to reaffirm the statements in *Jones* and *Katz* that "arcane distinctions developed in property . . . law . . . ought not to control." In a similar vein, the dissenters repeatedly state or imply that we now "hold" that a passenger lawfully in an automobile "may not invoke the exclusionary rule and challenge a search of that vehicle unless he happens to own or have a possessory interest in it." It is not without significance that these statements of today's "holding" come from the dissenting opinion, and not from the Court's opinion. The case before us involves the search of and seizure of property from the glove compartment and area under the seat of a car in which petitioners were riding as passengers. Petitioners claimed only that they were "legitimately on [the] premises" and did not claim that they had any legitimate expectation of privacy in the areas of the car which were searched. We cannot, therefore, agree with the dissenters' insistence that our decision will encourage the police to violate the Fourth Amendment.

1. Allowing anyone who is legitimately on the premises searched to invoke the exclusionary rule extends the rule far beyond the proper scope of Fourth Amendment protections, as not all who are legitimately present invariably have a reasonable expectation of privacy. And, as the Court points out, the dissenters' standard lacks even the advantage of easy application. I do not share the dissenters' concern that the Court's ruling will "invit[e] police to engage in patently unreasonable searches every time an automobile contains more than one occupant." A police officer observing an automobile carrying several passengers will not know the circumstances surrounding each occupant's presence in the automobile, and certainly will not know whether an occupant will be able to establish that he had a reasonable expectation of privacy. Thus, there will continue to be a significant incentive for the police to comply with the requirements of the Fourth Amendment, lest otherwise valid prosecutions be voided. Moreover, any marginal diminution in this incentive that might result from the Court's decision today is more than justified by society's interest in restricting the scope of the exclusionary rule to those cases where in fact there is a reasonable expectation of privacy.

ers' claim that their alleged expectation of privacy from government intrusion was reasonable.

We are concerned here with an automobile search. Nothing is better established in Fourth Amendment jurisprudence than the distinction between one's expectation of privacy in an automobile and one's expectation when in other locations.

. . . .

A distinction also properly may be made in some circumstances between the Fourth Amendment rights of passengers and the rights of an individual who has exclusive control of an automobile or of its locked compartments. In *South Dakota v. Opperman*, 428 U.S. 364, 96 S. Ct. 3092, 49 L. Ed. 2d 1000 (1976), for example, we considered "the citizen's interest in the privacy of the contents of his automobile" where its doors were locked and windows rolled up. *See id.*, at 379, 96 S. Ct., at 3102 (Powell, J., concurring). Here there were three passengers and a driver in the automobile searched. None of the passengers is said to have had control of the vehicle or the keys. It is unrealistic — as the shared experience of us all bears witness — to suggest that these passengers had any reasonable expectation that the car in which they had been riding would not be searched after they were lawfully stopped and made to get out. The minimal privacy that existed simply is not comparable to that, for example, of an individual in his place of abode; of one who secludes himself in a telephone booth; or of the traveler who secures his belongings in a locked suitcase or footlocker.[4]

. . . .

This is not an area of the law in which any "bright line" rule would safeguard both Fourth Amendment rights and the public interest in a fair and effective criminal justice system. The range of variables in the fact situations of search and seizure is almost infinite. Rather than seek facile solutions, it is best to apply principles broadly faithful to Fourth Amendment purposes. I believe the Court has identified these principles.

Mr. Justice White, with whom Mr. Justice Brennan, Mr. Justice Marshall, and Mr. Justice Stevens join, dissenting.

The Court today holds that the Fourth Amendment protects property, not people, and specifically that a legitimate occupant of an automobile may not invoke the exclusionary rule and challenge a search of that vehicle unless he happens to own or have a possessory interest in it. Though professing to acknowledge that the primary purpose of the Fourth Amendment's prohibition of unreasonable searches is the pro-

---

4. The sawed-off rifle in this case was merely pushed beneath the front seat, presumably by one of the petitioners. In that position, it could have slipped into full or partial view in the event of an accident, or indeed upon any sudden stop. As the rifle shells were in the locked glove compartment, this might have presented a closer case if it had been shown that one of the petitioners possessed the keys or if a rifle had not been found in the automobile. . . .

tection of privacy — not property — the Court nonetheless effectively ties the application of the Fourth Amendment and the exclusionary rule in this situation to property law concepts. Insofar as passengers are concerned, the Court's opinion today declares an "open season" on automobiles. However unlawful stopping and searching a car may be, absent a possessory or ownership interest, no "mere" passenger may object, regardless of his relationship to the owner. Because the majority's conclusion has no support in the Court's controlling decisions, in the logic of the Fourth Amendment, or in common sense, I must respectfully dissent. If the Court is troubled by the practical impact of the exclusionary rule, it should face the issue of that rule's continued validity squarely instead of distorting other doctrines in an attempt to reach what are perceived as the correct results in specific cases.

I

Two intersecting doctrines long established in this Court's opinions control here. The first is the recognition of some cognizable level of privacy in the interior of an automobile. Though the reasonableness of the expectation of privacy in a vehicle may be somewhat weaker than that in a home, "[a] search, even of an automobile, is a substantial invasion of privacy. To protect that privacy from official arbitrariness, the Court always has regarded probable cause as the minimum requirement for a lawful search." *United States v. Ortiz*, 422 U.S. 891, 896, 95 S. Ct. 2585, 2588, 45 L. Ed. 2d 623 (1975) (footnote omitted). So far, the Court has not strayed from this application of the Fourth Amendment.

The second tenet is that when a person is legitimately present in a private place, his right to privacy is protected from unreasonable governmental interference even if he does not own the premises. . . . The Court in *Jones* itself was unanimous in this regard, and its holding is not the less binding because it was an alternative one.

These two fundamental aspects of Fourth Amendment law demand that petitioners be permitted to challenge the search and seizure of the automobile in this case. It is of no significance that a car is different for Fourth Amendment purposes from a house, for if there is some protection for the privacy of an automobile then the only relevant analogy is between a person legitimately in someone else's vehicle and a person legitimately in someone else's home. If both strands of the Fourth Amendment doctrine adumbrated above are valid, the Court must reach a different result. Instead, it chooses to eviscerate the *Jones* principle, an action in which I am unwilling to participate.

. . . .

III

. . . Our starting point is "[t]he established principle . . . that suppression of the product of a Fourth Amendment violation can be successfully urged only by those whose rights were violated by the search itself. . . ." *Alderman v. United States*, 394 U.S. 165, 171–172, 89 S. Ct. 961, 965, 22 L. Ed. 2d 176 (1969). Though the Amendment protects one's liberty and property interests against unreasonable seizures of self[5] and effects,[6] "the primary object of the Fourth Amendment [is] . . . the protection of privacy." *Cardwell v. Lewis*, 417 U.S. 583, 589, 94 S. Ct. 2464, 2469, 41 L. Ed. 2d 325 (1974) (plurality opinion). And privacy is the interest asserted here, so the first step is to ascertain whether the premises searched "fall within a protected zone of privacy." *United States v. Miller*, 425 U.S. 435, 440, 96 S. Ct. 1619, 1623, 48 L. Ed. 2d 71 (1976). My Brethren in the majority assertedly do not deny that automobiles warrant at least some protection from official interference with privacy. Thus, the next step is to decide who is entitled, vis-a-vis the State, to enjoy that privacy. The answer to that question must be found by determining "whether petitioner had an interest in connection with the searched premises that gave rise to 'a reasonable expectation [on his part] of freedom from governmental intrusion' upon those premises." *Combs v. United States*, 408 U.S., at 227, 92 S. Ct., at 2286, quoting *Mancusi v. DeForte*, 392 U.S., at 368, 88 S. Ct., at 2123 (bracketed material in original).

Not only does *Combs* supply the relevant inquiry, it also directs us to the proper answer. We recognized there that *Jones* had held that one of those protected interests is created by legitimate presence on the searched premises, even absent any possessory interest. This makes unquestionable sense. We have concluded on numerous occasions that the entitlement to an expectation of privacy does not hinge on ownership:

> What a person knowingly exposes to the public, even in his own home or office, is not a subject of Fourth Amendment protection. . . . But what he seeks to preserve as private, even in an area accessible to the public, may be constitutionally protected.

Katz v. United States, 389 U.S. 347, 351–352, 88 S. Ct. 507, 511, 19 L. Ed. 2d 576 (1967).

---

5. *See United States v. Brignoni-Ponce*, 422 U.S. 873, 878, 95 S. Ct. 2574, 2578, 45 L. Ed. 2d 607 (1975) ("The Fourth Amendment applies to all seizures of the person, including seizures that involve only a brief detention short of traditional arrest"); *Terry v. Ohio*, 392 U.S. 1, 88 S. Ct. 1868, 20 L. Ed. 2d 889 (1968). Thus, petitioners of course have standing to challenge the legality of the stop, and the evidence found may be a fruit of that stop. *See United States v. Martinez-Fuerte*, 428 U.S. 543, 548, 556, 96 S. Ct. 3074, 3078, 3082, 49 L. Ed. 2d 1116 (1976). Petitioners have not argued that theory here, perhaps because the justification necessary for such a stop is less than that needed for a search. Nor have petitioners chosen to argue that they were "arrested" in constitutional terms as soon as they were ordered from the vehicle and that the search was a fruit of that infringement on their personal rights.

6. Petitioners never asserted a property interest in the items seized from the automobile. The evidence found was useful to the prosecution solely on the theory that petitioners' possession of the items was probative of petitioners' identity as the robbers. In *Jones* the Court recognized automatic standing in possessory crimes because the prosecution should not be allowed to take contradictory positions in the suppression hearing and then at trial, and also because of the dilemma that the defendant would face if he were forced to assert possession to challenge a search. In *Simmons* we eliminated the dilemma by holding that the accused's testimony at the suppression hearing could not be used against him at trial. We also noted that the question whether automatic standing should be recognized for possessory evidence in nonpossessory crimes was an open one. Finally, in *Brown v. United States*, 411 U.S. 223, 229, 93 S. Ct. 1565, 1569, 36 L. Ed. 2d 208 (1973), we reserved the question whether prosecutorial self-contradiction by itself warrants automatic standing.

. . . .

. . . [T]he Court's opinion in *Katz* reemphasized that "[t]he premise that property interests control the right of the Government to search and seize has been discredited." 389 U.S., at 353, 88 S. Ct., at 512, quoting *Warden v. Hayden*, 387 U.S. 294, 304, 87 S. Ct. 1642, 1648, 18 L. Ed. 2d 782 (1967). That logic led us inescapably to the conclusion that "[n]o less than an individual in a business office, in a friend's apartment, or in a taxicab, a person in a telephone booth may rely upon the protection of the Fourth Amendment." 389 U.S., at 352, 88 S. Ct., at 511 (footnotes omitted). And if all of those situations are protected, surely a person riding in an automobile next to his friend the owner, or a child or wife with the father or spouse, must have some protection as well.

The same result is reached by tracing other lines of our Fourth Amendment decisions. If a nonowner may consent to a search merely because he is a joint user or occupant of a "premises," *Frazier v. Cupp*, 394 U.S. 731, 740, 89 S. Ct. 1420, 1425, 22 L. Ed. 2d 684 (1969), then that same nonowner must have a protected privacy interest. The scope of the authority sufficient to grant a valid consent can hardly be broader than the contours of protected privacy. And why should the owner of a vehicle be entitled to challenge the seizure from it of evidence even if he is absent at the time of the search, *see Coolidge v. New Hampshire*, 403 U.S. 443, 91 S. Ct. 2022, 29 L. Ed. 2d 564 (1971), while a nonowner enjoying in person, and with the owner's permission, the privacy of an automobile is not so entitled?

In sum, one consistent theme in our decisions under the Fourth Amendment has been, until now, that "the Amendment does not shield only those who have title to the searched premises." *Mancusi v. DeForte*, 392 U.S., at 367, 88 S. Ct., at 2123. Though there comes a point when use of an area is shared with so many that one simply cannot reasonably expect seclusion, short of that limit a person legitimately on private premises knows the others allowed there and, though his privacy is not absolute, is entitled to expect that he is sharing it only with those persons and that governmental officials will intrude only with consent or by complying with the Fourth Amendment.

It is true that the Court asserts that it is not limiting the Fourth Amendment bar against unreasonable searches to the protection of property rights, but in reality it is doing exactly that.[14] Petitioners were in a private place with the permission of the owner, but the Court states that that is not sufficient to establish entitlement to a le-

---

14. The Court's reliance on property law concepts is additionally shown by its suggestion that visitors could "contest the lawfulness of the seizure of evidence or the search if their own property were seized during the search." What difference should that property interest make to constitutional protection against unreasonable searches, which is concerned with privacy? Contrary to the Court's suggestion, a legitimate passenger in a car expects to enjoy the privacy of the vehicle whether or not he happens to carry some item along for the ride. We have never before limited our concern for a person's privacy to those situations in which he is in possession of personal property. Even a person living in a barren room without possessions is entitled to expect that the police will not intrude without cause.

gitimate expectation of privacy. But if that is not sufficient, what would be? We are not told, and it is hard to imagine anything short of a property interest that would satisfy the majority. Insofar as the Court's rationale is concerned, no passenger in an automobile, without an ownership or possessory interest and regardless of his relationship to the owner, may claim Fourth Amendment protection against illegal stops and searches of the automobile in which he is rightfully present. The Court approves the result in *Jones*, but it fails to give any explanation why the facts in *Jones* differ, in a fashion material to the Fourth Amendment, from the facts here. More importantly, how is the Court able to avoid answering the question why presence in a private place with the owner's permission is insufficient? If it is "tautological to fall back on the notion that those expectations of privacy which are legitimate depend primarily on cases deciding exclusionary rule issues in criminal cases," then it surely must be tautological to decide that issue simply by unadorned fiat.

As a control on governmental power, the Fourth Amendment assures that some expectations of privacy are justified and will be protected from official intrusion.

. . . .

IV

The Court's holding is contrary not only to our past decisions and the logic of the Fourth Amendment but also to the everyday expectations of privacy that we all share. Because of that, it is unworkable in all the various situations that arise in real life. If the owner of the car had not only invited petitioners to join her but had said to them, "I give you a temporary possessory interest in my vehicle so that you will share the right to privacy that the Supreme Court says that I own," then apparently the majority would reverse. But people seldom say such things, though they may mean their invitation to encompass them if only they had thought of the problem. If the nonowner were the spouse or child of the owner,[20] would the Court recognize a sufficient interest? If so, would distant relatives somehow have more of an expectation of privacy than close friends? What if the nonowner were driving with the owner's permission? Would nonowning drivers have more of an expectation of privacy than mere passengers? What about a passenger in a taxicab? *Katz* expressly recognized protection for such passengers. Why should Fourth Amendment rights be present when one pays a cabdriver for a ride but be absent when one is given a ride by a friend?

The distinctions the Court would draw are based on relationships between private parties, but the Fourth Amendment is concerned with the relationship of one of those parties to the government. Divorced as it is from the purpose of the Fourth Amendment, the Court's essentially property-based rationale can satisfactorily answer none of the questions posed above. That is reason enough to reject it. The *Jones*

---

20. In fact, though it was not brought out at the suppression hearing, one of the petitioners is the former husband of the owner and driver of the car. He did testify at the suppression hearing that he was with her when she purchased it.

rule is relatively easily applied by police and courts; the rule announced today will not provide law enforcement officials with a bright line between the protected and the unprotected.[21] Only rarely will police know whether one private party has or has not been granted a sufficient possessory or other interest by another private party. Surely in this case the officers had no such knowledge. The Court's rule will ensnare defendants and police in needless litigation over factors that should not be determinative of Fourth Amendment rights.

More importantly, the ruling today undercuts the force of the exclusionary rule in the one area in which its use is most certainly justified — the deterrence of bad-faith violations of the Fourth Amendment. This decision invites police to engage in patently unreasonable searches every time an automobile contains more than one occupant. Should something be found, only the owner of the vehicle, or of the item, will have standing to seek suppression, and the evidence will presumably be usable against the other occupants. The danger of such bad faith is especially high in cases such as this one where the officers are only after the passengers and can usually infer accurately that the driver is the owner. The suppression remedy for those owners in whose vehicles something is found and who are charged with crime is small consolation for all those owners and occupants whose privacy will be needlessly invaded by officers following mistaken hunches not rising to the level of probable cause but operated on in the knowledge that someone in a crowded car will probably be unprotected if contraband or incriminating evidence happens to be found. After this decision, police will have little to lose by unreasonably searching vehicles occupied by more than one person.

Of course, most police officers will decline the Court's invitation and will continue to do their jobs as best they can in accord with the Fourth Amendment. But the very purpose of the Bill of Rights was to answer the justified fear that governmental agents cannot be left totally to their own devices, and the Bill of Rights is enforceable in the courts because human experience teaches that not all such officials will otherwise adhere to the stated precepts. Some policemen simply do act in bad faith, even if for understandable ends, and some deterrent is needed. In the rush to limit the applicability of the exclusionary rule somewhere, anywhere, the Court ignores precedent, logic, and common sense to exclude the rule's operation from situations in which, paradoxically, it is justified and needed.

---

21. Contrary to the assertions in the majority and concurring opinions, I do not agree that the Court's rule is faithful to the purposes of the Fourth Amendment but reject it only because it fails to provide a "bright line." As the discussion indicates, this dissent disagrees with the Court's view that petitioners lack a reasonable expectation of privacy. The Court's *ipse dixit* is not only unexplained but also is unjustified in light of what persons reasonably do, and should be entitled to, expect. My point in this portion of the opinion is that the Court's lack of faithfulness to the purposes of the Fourth Amendment does not have even the saving grace of providing an easily applied rule.

Notes and Questions

(1) Why shouldn't *any* individual be entitled to object to the introduction of incriminating evidence that has been obtained in violation of the Fourth Amendment? Why shouldn't those *legitimately on premises* that have been illegally searched be entitled to exclude evidence found during that search? After *Rakas*, what is needed to establish "standing" to object to the search of a place?

The Court's decision in *Minnesota v. Olson*, 495 U.S. 91, 110 S. Ct. 1684, 109 L. Ed. 2d 85 (1990), sheds additional light on the subject. In *Olson*, the issue was whether a suspect's Fourth Amendment rights had been violated when the "police . . . made a warrantless, nonconsensual entry into a house where [he] was an overnight guest and arrested him." The Court first rejected the State's suggestion that, under *Rakas's* interpretation of *Jones*, an overnight guest can only have a legitimate expectation of privacy when his host is away and he has a key with which he can come and go and admit and exclude others. It then held that, in general, "an overnight guest has a legitimate expectation of privacy in his host's home," an expectation that entitles the guest to object to a warrantless entry to arrest him. Because "society recognizes that a houseguest has a legitimate expectation of privacy in his host's home[,]" such overnight guests "are entitled to a legitimate expectation of privacy despite the fact that they have no legal interest in the premises and do not have the legal authority to determine who may or may not enter the household."

(2) The *Rakas* dissenters criticized the majority for demanding a "property" or "possessory" interest in a vehicle as a necessary predicate for "standing" to object to the search of that vehicle. The majority rejected that characterization of its holding. Under *Rakas*, can an individual without a property or possessory interest successfully object to an illegal search?

The Court observed more than once that the *Rakas* defendants did not claim an interest in the property seized. If they had done so, would they have had "standing"?

In *Rawlings v. Kentucky*, 448 U.S. 98, 100 S. Ct. 2556, 65 L. Ed. 2d 633 (1980), the police discovered a considerable amount of illegal narcotics in a purse belonging to the defendant's acquaintance. The Kentucky Supreme Court held that the defendant "could not challenge the legality of the search of [the] purse" because he did not have a reasonable expectation of privacy in the purse. In the United States Supreme Court, the defendant contended that "because he claimed ownership of the drugs in [the] purse, he should be entitled to challenge the search regardless of his expectation of privacy."

The Court rejected that contention, holding that ownership of the property seized as a result of a search does not by itself entitle an individual to challenge the search. To contest the legality of the search, the individual must demonstrate that his or her legitimate expectation of privacy was violated by the search. Ownership of the seized property "is undoubtedly one fact to be considered" in determining whether a person had a legitimate privacy expectation, but, like legitimate presence on premises, it is not a dispositive fact.

According to the Court, there was "no reason to overturn" the Kentucky court's "conclusion that [the defendant] had no legitimate expectation of privacy in [the] purse." He had suddenly and precipitously "dumped thousands of dollars of illegal drugs into [the] purse," an action that "hardly supports a reasonable inference that [he] took normal precautions to maintain his privacy." He had known the owner of the purse for "only a few days," had "never [before] sought or received access to" the purse, and "did not have any right to exclude others from" the purse. Moreover, he had admitted that he "had no subjective expectation that [the] purse would remain free from governmental intrusion." The fact that the defendant owned the contraband that was found did not contradict these powerful indicia that he had no legitimate expectation of privacy in his acquaintance's purse.

(3) In *Jones v. United States*, 362 U.S. 257, 80 S. Ct. 725, 4 L. Ed. 2d 697 (1960), the Court had ruled that defendants who are "legitimately on premises" when a search occurs have "standing" to challenge the search. This principle was discarded in *Rakas. Jones* also had held that a defendant who is charged with the criminal possession of an item at the time of an allegedly illegal search and seizure would have "automatic standing." The reasons for granting "automatic standing" (and, therefore, not requiring that a defendant demonstrate "actual standing") were twofold. First, defendants charged with possession were confronted with an unacceptable "dilemma." They had to either admit possession for standing purposes and risk use of that admission to prove guilt at trial, or give up the opportunity to challenge an illegal search and seizure in order to avoid making inculpatory admissions regarding possession. Second, it was not considered "consonant with the amenities of criminal justice" to allow the government "to have the advantage of contradictory positions as a basis for conviction." The government should not be permitted to "deny possession in order to defeat a standing claim, but to claim possession in order to prove guilt."

In *United States v. Salvucci*, 448 U.S. 83, 100 S. Ct. 2547, 65 L. Ed. 2d 619 (1980), the Court abolished the "automatic standing" rule. A majority concluded that the "dilemma" described in *Jones* had been eliminated by the holding of *Simmons v. United States*, 390 U.S. 377, 88 S. Ct. 967, 19 L. Ed. 2d 1247 (1968). *Simmons* had held that a defendant's admissions at a suppression hearing could not be used as substantive proof of guilt at trial. In addition, *Salvucci* concluded that standing law, as modified by *Rakas* and *Rawlings*, does not necessitate any unseemly "self-contradiction" by the government. A prosecutor can contest standing without denying possession and then, with perfect consistency, assert possession for purposes of the trial.

(4) In *Rakas*, if the officers had *illegally stopped* the car in which they were riding, would the passengers have been entitled to object to the constitutionality of that stop? In *Brendlin v. California*, 551 U.S. 249, 127 S. Ct. 2400, 168 L. Ed. 2d 132 (2007), a unanimous Court held that a typical "reasonable passenger" in a vehicle stopped by the police is, like the driver, "seized" within the meaning of the Fourth Amendment. *See supra*, Chapter 5[A][2]. Consequently, it is clear that a passenger is entitled to object to the stop of the vehicle. If the stop is unreasonable, it violates the passenger's

rights. The Court did not resolve the question of whether such an illegality entitles a passenger to the suppression of evidence found in a subsequent search of the illegally stopped vehicle. After concluding that the passenger in that case had been seized, the Court remanded the case, observing that it would be up to "the state courts to consider in the first instance whether suppression turns on any other issue." In the course of its opinion, the Court did quote a treatise's assertion that "'[i]f either the stopping of [a] car, the length of [a] passenger's detention thereafter, or [a] passenger's removal from it are unreasonable . . . , then surely the passenger *has standing to object* to those constitutional violations *and to have suppressed any evidence found in the car which is their fruit.*'" (Quoting 6 W. LaFave, SEARCH AND SEIZURE § 11.3(e), pp. 194, 195, and n. 277 (4th ed. 2004 and Supp. 2007); emphasis added.) Is evidence found in an illegally stopped vehicle the "fruit" of the unconstitutional seizure of a passenger? Lower courts have struggled with this question and have reached inconsistent conclusions.

(5) The *Rakas* dissenters contended that the majority had "exclude[d] the [exclusionary] rule's operation from situations in which, paradoxically, it is justified and needed." Is their contention valid? Why?

(6) In *United States v. Payner*, 447 U.S. 727, 100 S. Ct. 2439, 65 L. Ed. 2d 468 (1980), the Internal Revenue Service (IRS) had affirmatively counseled agents to disregard Fourth Amendment commands. Specifically, the operation in *Payner* involved the deliberate illegal search of a banker's briefcase for the specific purpose of discovering information about the financial dealings of bank customers. The IRS agents involved were aware that the customer, the individual who would be criminally charged, would not have "standing" to challenge the illegal search and that the banker, the individual who would have standing to seek suppression, would not be charged with a criminal offense.

The trial judge recognized that, under *Rakas*, the defendant was not entitled to challenge the illegal search. Nevertheless, he decided that both the Fifth Amendment Due Process Clause and the inherent supervisory power of the federal courts mandated the exclusion of the evidence that had been tainted by the government's "knowing and purposeful *bad faith hostility*" to constitutional rights.

Justice Powell, for a six-member majority, observed that he "certainly [could] understand the District Court's commendable desire to deter deliberate intrusions into the privacy of persons who are unlikely to become defendants in a criminal prosecution. No court should condone the unconstitutional and possibly criminal behavior of those who planned and executed the 'briefcase caper.'" Nevertheless, he concluded

> that the supervisory power does not authorize a federal court to suppress otherwise admissible evidence on the ground that it was seized unlawfully from a third party not before the court. Our Fourth Amendment decisions have established beyond any doubt that the interest in deterring illegal searches does not justify the exclusion of tainted evidence at the instance of a party who was not the victim of the challenged practices.

Justice Powell also concluded that the "same difficulty attend[ed]" the Fifth Amendment Due Process Clause basis for the trial court's decision. Even if the search and seizure were "outrageous" and violative of due process values, "the fact remains that '[t]he limitations of the Due Process Clause . . . come into play only when the Government activity in question violates some protected right of the *defendant.*'" (citation omitted; emphasis in original).

Justices Marshall, Brennan, and Blackmun dissented.

Minnesota v. Carter

United States Supreme Court

525 U.S. 83, 119 S. Ct. 469, 142 L. Ed. 2d 373 (1998)

CHIEF JUSTICE REHNQUIST delivered the opinion of the Court.

Respondents and the lessee of an apartment were sitting in one of its rooms, bagging cocaine. While so engaged they were observed by a police officer, who looked through a drawn window blind. The Supreme Court of Minnesota held that the officer's viewing was a search which violated respondents' Fourth Amendment rights. We hold that no such violation occurred.

James Thielen, a police officer in the Twin Cities' suburb of Eagan, Minnesota, went to an apartment building to investigate a tip from a confidential informant. The informant said that he had walked by the window of a ground-floor apartment and had seen people putting a white powder into bags. The officer looked in the same window through a gap in the closed blind and observed the bagging operation for several minutes. He then notified headquarters, which began preparing affidavits for a search warrant while he returned to the apartment building. When two men left the building in a previously identified Cadillac, the police stopped the car. Inside were respondents Carter and Johns. As the police opened the door of the car to let Johns out, they observed a black zippered pouch and a handgun, later determined to be loaded, on the vehicle's floor. Carter and Johns were arrested, and a later police search of the vehicle the next day discovered pagers, a scale, and 47 grams of cocaine in plastic sandwich bags.

After seizing the car, the police returned to Apartment 103 and arrested the occupant, Kimberly Thompson, who is not a party to this appeal. A search of the apartment pursuant to a warrant revealed cocaine residue on the kitchen table and plastic baggies similar to those found in the Cadillac. Thielen identified Carter, Johns, and Thompson as the three people he had observed placing the powder into baggies. The police later learned that while Thompson was the lessee of the apartment, Carter and Johns lived in Chicago and had come to the apartment for the sole purpose of packaging the cocaine. Carter and Johns had never been to the apartment before and were only in the apartment for approximately 2-1/2 hours. In return for the use of the apartment, Carter and Johns had given Thompson one-eighth of an ounce of the cocaine.

Carter and Johns were charged with conspiracy to commit controlled substance crime in the first degree and aiding and abetting in a controlled substance crime in the first degree, in violation of Minn. Stat. § 152.021, subd. 1(1), subd. 3(a) (1996); § 609.05. They moved to suppress all evidence obtained from the apartment and the Cadillac, as well as to suppress several post-arrest incriminating statements they had made. They argued that Thielen's initial observation of their drug packaging activities was an unreasonable search in violation of the Fourth Amendment and that all evidence obtained as a result of this unreasonable search was inadmissible as fruit of the poisonous tree. The Minnesota trial court held that since, unlike the defendant in *Minnesota v. Olson*, 495 U.S. 91, 110 S. Ct. 1684, 109 L. Ed. 2d 85 (1990), Carter and Johns were not overnight social guests but temporary out-of-state visitors, they were not entitled to claim the protection of the Fourth Amendment against the government intrusion into the apartment. The trial court also concluded that Thielen's observation was not a search within the meaning of the Fourth Amendment. After a trial, Carter and Johns were each convicted of both offenses. The Minnesota Court of Appeals [upheld the convictions]. . . .

A divided Minnesota Supreme Court reversed, holding that respondents had "standing" to claim the protection of the Fourth Amendment because they had "'a legitimate expectation of privacy in the invaded place.'" 569 N.W.2d 169, 174 (Minn. 1997) (quoting *Rakas v. Illinois*, 439 U.S. 128, 143, 99 S. Ct. 421, 58 L. Ed. 2d 387 (1978). . . . Based upon its conclusion that the respondents had "standing" to raise their Fourth Amendment claims, the court went on to hold that Thielen's observation constituted a search of the apartment under the Fourth Amendment, and that the search was unreasonable. *Id.* at 176–179. We granted certiorari, and now reverse.

The Minnesota courts analyzed whether respondents had a legitimate expectation of privacy under the rubric of "standing" doctrine, an analysis which this Court expressly rejected 20 years ago in *Rakas*, 439 U.S. at 139–140. In that case, we held that automobile passengers could not assert the protection of the Fourth Amendment against the seizure of incriminating evidence from a vehicle where they owned neither the vehicle nor the evidence. *Ibid.* Central to our analysis was the idea that in determining whether a defendant is able to show the violation of his (and not someone else's) Fourth Amendment rights, the "definition of those rights is more properly placed within the purview of substantive Fourth Amendment law than within that of standing." 439 U.S., at 140. Thus, we held that in order to claim the protection of the Fourth Amendment, a defendant must demonstrate that he personally has an expectation of privacy in the place searched, and that his expectation is reasonable; *i.e.*, one which has "a source outside of the Fourth Amendment, either by reference to concepts of real or personal property law or to understandings that are recognized and permitted by society." *Id.*, at 143–144, and n. 12.

. . . The [Fourth] Amendment protects persons against unreasonable searches of "their persons [and] houses" and thus indicates that the Fourth Amendment is a personal right that must be invoked by an individual. But the extent to which the Fourth Amendment protects people may depend upon where those people are. . . .

The text of the Amendment suggests that its protections extend only to people in "their" houses. But we have held that in some circumstances a person may have a legitimate expectation of privacy in the house of someone else. In *Minnesota v. Olson*, 495 U.S. 91, 110 S. Ct. 1684, 109 L. Ed. 2d 85 (1990), for example, we decided that an overnight guest in a house had the sort of expectation of privacy that the Fourth Amendment protects. We said:

> "To hold that an overnight guest has a legitimate expectation of privacy in his host's home merely recognizes the every day expectations of privacy that we all share. Staying overnight in another's home is a longstanding social custom that serves functions recognized as valuable by society. We stay in others' homes when we travel to a strange city for business or pleasure, we visit our parents, children, or more distant relatives out of town, when we are in between jobs or homes, or when we house-sit for a friend. . . .

> "From the overnight guest's perspective, he seeks shelter in another's home precisely because it provides him with privacy, a place where he and his possessions will not be disturbed by anyone but his host and those his host allows inside. We arc at our most vulnerable when we are asleep because we cannot monitor our own safety or the security of our belongings. It is for this reason that, although we may spend all day in public places, when we cannot sleep in our own home we seek out another private place to sleep, whether it be a hotel room, or the home of a friend." *Id.*, at 98–99.

. . . Thus an overnight guest in a home may claim the protection of the Fourth Amendment, but one who is merely present with the consent of the householder may not.

Respondents here were obviously not overnight guests, but were essentially present for a business transaction and were only in the home a matter of hours. There is no suggestion that they had a previous relationship with Thompson, or that there was any other purpose to their visit. Nor was there anything similar to the overnight guest relationship in *Olson* to suggest a degree of acceptance into the household.[1] While the apartment was a dwelling place for Thompson, it was for these respondents simply a place to do business.

Property used for commercial purposes is treated differently for Fourth Amendment purposes than residential property. "An expectation of privacy in commercial

---

1. JUSTICE GINSBURG's dissent would render the operative language in *Minnesota v. Olson* almost entirely superfluous. There, we explained the justification for extending Fourth Amendment protection to the overnight visitor: "Staying overnight in another's home is a long-standing social custom that serves functions recognized as valuable by society . . . . We are at our most vulnerable when we are asleep because we cannot monitor our own safety or the security of our belongings." 495 U.S. at 98–99. If any short-term business visit by a stranger entitles the visitor to share the Fourth Amendment protection of the lease holder's home, the Court's explanation of its holding in *Olson* was quite unnecessary.

premises, however, is different from, and indeed less than, a similar expectation in an individual's home." *New York v. Burger*, 482 U.S. 691, 700, 107 S. Ct. 2636, 96 L. Ed. 2d 601 (1987). And while it was a "home" in which respondents were present, it was not their home. Similarly, the Court has held that in some circumstances a worker can claim Fourth Amendment protection over his own workplace. *See, e.g., O'Connor v. Ortega*, 480 U.S. 709, 107 S. Ct. 1492, 94 L. Ed. 2d 714 (1987). But there is no indication that respondents in this case had nearly as significant a connection to Thompson's apartment as the worker in *O'Connor* had to his own private office. *See id.* at 716–17.

If we regard the overnight guest in *Minnesota v. Olson* as typifying those who may claim the protection of the Fourth Amendment in the home of another, and one merely "legitimately on the premises" as typifying those who may not do so, the present case is obviously somewhere in between. But the purely commercial nature of the transaction engaged in here, the relatively short period of time on the premises, and the lack of any previous connection between respondents and the householder, all lead us to conclude that respondents' situation is closer to that of one simply permitted on the premises. We therefore hold that any search which may have occurred did not violate their Fourth Amendment rights.

Because we conclude that respondents had no legitimate expectation of privacy in the apartment, we need not decide whether the police officer's observation constituted a "search." The judgment of the Supreme Court of Minnesota is accordingly reversed, and the cause is remanded for proceedings not inconsistent with this opinion.

It is so ordered.

Justice Scalia, with whom Justice Thomas joins, concurring.

I join the opinion of the Court because I believe it accurately applies our recent case law, including *Minnesota v. Olson*, 495 U.S. 91, 110 S. Ct. 1684, 109 L. Ed. 2d 85 (1990). I write separately to express my view that that case law — like the submissions of the parties in this case — gives short shrift to the text of the Fourth Amendment, and to the well and long understood meaning of that text. Specifically, it leaps to apply the fuzzy standard of "legitimate expectation of privacy" — a consideration that is often relevant to whether a search or seizure covered by the Fourth Amendment is "unreasonable" — to the threshold question whether a search or seizure covered by the Fourth Amendment *has occurred*. If that latter question is addressed first and analyzed under the text of the Constitution as traditionally understood, the present case is not remotely difficult.

The Fourth Amendment protects "[t]he right of the people to be secure in *their* persons, houses, papers, and effects, against unreasonable searches and seizures...." U.S. Const., Amdt. 4 (emphasis added). It must be acknowledged that the phrase "their ... houses" in this provision is, in isolation, ambiguous. It could mean "their respective houses" so that the protection extends to each person only in his *own* house. But it could also mean "their respective and each other's houses," so that each person would be protected even when visiting the house of someone else. As today's opinion for the Court suggests, however, it is not linguistically possible to give the provision the latter, expansive interpretation with respect to "houses" without giving it the same interpretation with respect to the nouns that are parallel to "houses" — "persons, . . . papers, and effects" — which would give me a constitutional right not to have your person unreasonably searched. This is so absurd that it has to my knowledge never been contemplated. The obvious meaning of the provision is that *each* person has the right to be secure against unreasonable searches and seizures in *his own* person, house, papers, and effects.

The Founding-era materials that I have examined confirm that this was the understood meaning. . . . Like most of the provisions of the Bill of Rights, the Fourth Amendment was derived from provisions already existing in state constitutions. Of the four of those provisions that contained language similar to that of the Fourth Amendment, two used the same ambiguous "their" terminology. *See* Pa. Const., Art. X (1776); Vt. Const., ch. I, § XI (1777). The other two, however, avoided the ambiguity by using the singular instead of the plural. *See* Mass. Const., pt. I, Art. XIV (1780) ("Every subject has a right to be secure from all unreasonable searches, and seizures of his person, his houses, his papers, and all his possessions"); N.H. Const. § XIX (1784) ("Every subject hath a right to be secure from all unreasonable searches and seizures of his person, his houses, his papers, and all his possessions"). The New York Convention that ratified the Constitution proposed an amendment that would have given every freeman "a right to be secure from all unreasonable searches and seizures of *his* person *his* papers or *his* property," 4 B. Schwartz, The Roots of the Bill of Rights 913 (1980) (reproducing New York proposed amendments, 1778) (emphases added), and the Declaration of Rights that the North Carolina Convention demanded prior to its ratification contained a similar provision protecting a freeman's right against "unreasonable searches and seizures of *his* person, *his* papers and property," *id.*, at 968 (reproducing North Carolina proposed Declaration of Rights, 1778) (emphases added). There is no indication anyone believed that [these state] texts, by using the word "his" rather than "their," narrowed the protections contained in the Pennsylvania and Vermont Constitutions.

That "their . . . houses" was understood to mean "their respective houses" would have been clear to anyone who knew the English and early American law of arrest and trespass that underlay the Fourth Amendment. The people's protection against unreasonable search and seizure in their "houses" was drawn from the English common-law maxim, "A man's home is *his* castle." As far back as *Semayne's Case* of 1604, the leading English case for that proposition . . . , the King's Bench proclaimed that "the house of any one is not a castle or privilege but for himself, and shall not extend to protect any person who flies to his house." *Semayne v. Gresham*, 5 Co. Rep. 91a, 93a, 77 Eng. Rep. 194, 198 (K.B. 1604). Thus Cooley, in discussing Blackstone's statement that a bailiff could not break into a house to conduct an arrest because "every man's house is looked upon by the law to be his castle," 3 W. Blackstone, Commentaries on the Laws of England 288 (1768), added the explanation:

"[I]t is the defendant's own dwelling which by law is said to be his castle; for if he be in the house of another, the bailiff or sheriff may break and enter it to effect his purpose. . . ." 3 W. Blackstone, Commentaries on the Laws of England 287, n. 5 (T. Cooley 2d rev. ed. 1872).[2]

Of course this is not to say that the Fourth Amendment protects only the Lord of the Manor who holds his estate in fee simple. People call a house "their" home when legal title is in the bank, when they rent it, and even when they merely occupy it rent-free — *so long as they actually live there.* That this is the criterion of the people's protection against government intrusion into "their" houses is established by the leading American case of *Oystead v. Shed*, 13 Mass. 520 (1816), which held it a trespass for the sheriff to break into a dwelling to capture a boarder who lived there. . . .

Thus, in deciding the question presented today we write upon a slate that is far from clean. The text of the Fourth Amendment, the common-law background against which it was adopted, and the understandings consistently displayed after its adoption make the answer clear. . . . We went to the absolute limit of what text and tradition permit in *Minnesota v. Olson*, 495 U.S. 91, 110 S. Ct. 1684, 109 L. Ed. 2d 85 (1990), when we protected a mere overnight guest against an unreasonable search of his hosts' apartment. But whereas it is plausible to regard a person's overnight lodging as at least his "temporary" residence, it is entirely impossible to give that characterization to an apartment that he uses to package cocaine. Respondents here were not searched in "their . . . hous[e]" under any interpretation of the phrase that bears the remotest relationship to the well-understood meaning of the Fourth Amendment.

The dissent believes that "[o]ur obligation to produce coherent results" requires that we ignore this clear text and four-century-old tradition, and apply instead the notoriously unhelpful test adopted in a "benchmar[k]" decision that is 31 years old. *Post*, at 110, citing *Katz v. United States*, 389 U.S. 347, 88 S. Ct. 507, 19 L. Ed. 2d 576 (1967). In my view, the only thing the past three decades have established about the *Katz* test (which has come to mean the test enunciated by Justice Harlan's separate

---

2. . . . JUSTICE KENNEDY . . . attempts to distinguish *Semayne's Case* on the ground that it arose in "the context of civil process," and so may be "of limited application to enforcement of the criminal law." But of course the distinction cuts in precisely the opposite direction from the one that would support JUSTICE KENNEDY's case: if one man's house is not another man's castle for purposes of serving civil process, it is *a fortiori* not so for purposes of resisting the government's agents in pursuit of crime. . . . . . . JUSTICE KENNEDY [also] suggests that, whatever the Fourth Amendment meant at the time it was adopted, it does not matter, since "the axiom that a man's home is his castle . . . has acquired over time a power and an independent significance justifying a more general assurance of personal security in one's home, an assurance which has become part of our constitutional tradition." The issue in this case, however, is not "personal security in one's home," but personal security in someone else's home, as to which JUSTICE KENNEDY fails to identify *any* "constitutional tradition" other than the one I have described — leaving us with nothing but his personal assurance that some degree of protection higher than that (and higher than what the people have chosen to provide by law) is "justif[ied]."

concurrence in *Katz, see id.*, at 360) is that, unsurprisingly, those "actual (subjective) expectation[s] of privacy" "that society is prepared to recognize as 'reasonable,' " *id.*, at 361, bear an uncanny resemblance to those expectations of privacy that this Court considers reasonable. When that self-indulgent test is employed (as the dissent would employ it here) to determine whether a "search or seizure" within the meaning of the Constitution has *occurred* (as opposed to whether that "search or seizure" is an "unreasonable" one), it has no plausible foundation in the text of the Fourth Amendment. That provision did not guarantee some generalized "right of privacy" and leave it to this Court to determine which particular manifestations of the value of privacy "society is prepared to recognize as 'reasonable.' " *Ibid.* Rather, it enumerated ("persons, houses, papers, and effects") the objects of privacy protection to which the *Constitution* would extend, leaving further expansion to the good judgment, not of this Court, but of the people through their representatives in the legislature.

The dissent may be correct that a person invited into someone else's house to engage in a common business (even common monkey business, so to speak) *ought* to be protected against government searches of the room in which that business is conducted; and that persons invited in to deliver milk or pizza (whom the dissent dismisses as "classroom hypotheticals," as opposed, presumably, to flesh-and-blood hypotheticals) ought *not* to be protected against government searches of the rooms that they occupy. I am not sure of the answer to those policy questions. But I am sure that the answer is not remotely contained in the Constitution, which means that it is left — as *many*, indeed *most*, important questions are left — to the judgment of state and federal legislators. We go beyond our proper role as judges in a democratic society when we restrict the people's power to govern themselves over the full range of policy choices that the Constitution has left available to them.

JUSTICE KENNEDY, concurring.

I join the Court's opinion, for its reasoning is consistent with my view that almost all social guests have a legitimate expectation of privacy, and hence protection against unreasonable searches, in their host's home.

The Fourth Amendment protects "[t]he right of the people to be secure in their . . . houses," and it is beyond dispute that the home is entitled to special protection as the center of the private lives of our people. Security of the home must be guarded by the law in a world where privacy is diminished by enhanced surveillance and sophisticated communication systems. As is well established, however, Fourth Amendment protection, though dependent upon spatial definition, is in essence a personal right. Thus, as the Court held in *Rakas v. Illinois*, 439 U.S. 128, 99 S. Ct. 421, 58 L. Ed. 2d 387 (1978), there are limits on who may assert it.

. . . The [*Rakas*] Court's premise was . . . [that] Fourth Amendment rights are personal, and when a person objects to the search of a place and invokes the exclusionary rule, he or she must have the requisite connection to that place. The analysis in *Rakas* must be respected with reference to dwellings unless that precedent is to be overruled or so limited to its facts that its underlying principle is, in the end, repudiated.

. . . .

. . . Our cases establish . . . that respondents have no independent privacy right, the violation of which results in exclusion of evidence against them, unless they can establish a meaningful connection to Thompson's apartment.

The settled rule is that the requisite connection is an expectation of privacy that society recognizes as reasonable. The application of that rule involves consideration of the kind of place in which the individual claims the privacy interest and what expectations of privacy are traditional and well recognized. I would expect that most, if not all, social guests legitimately expect that, in accordance with social custom, the homeowner will exercise her discretion to include or exclude others for the guests' benefit. As we recognized in *Minnesota v. Olson*, 495 U.S. 91, 110 S. Ct. 1684, 109 L. Ed. 2d 85 (1990), where these social expectations exist — as in the case of an overnight guest — they are sufficient to create a legitimate expectation of privacy, even in the absence of any property right to exclude others. In this respect, the dissent must be correct that reasonable expectations of the owner are shared, to some extent, by the guest. This analysis suggests that, as a general rule, social guests will have an expectation of privacy in their host's home. That is not the case before us, however.

In this case respondents have established nothing more than a fleeting and insubstantial connection with Thompson's home. For all that appears in the record, respondents used Thompson's house simply as a convenient processing station, their purpose involving nothing more than the mechanical act of chopping and packing a substance for distribution. There is no suggestion that respondents engaged in confidential communications with Thompson about their transaction. Respondents had not been to Thompson's apartment before, and they left it even before their arrest. . . .

If respondents here had been visiting twenty homes, each for a minute or two, to drop off a bag of cocaine and were apprehended by a policeman wrongfully present in the nineteenth home; or if they had left the goods at a home where they were not staying and the police had seized the goods in their absence, we would have said that *Rakas* compels rejection of any privacy interest respondents might assert. So it does here, given that respondents have established no meaningful tie or connection to the owner, the owner's home, or the owner's expectation of privacy.

We cannot remain faithful to the underlying principle in *Rakas* without reversing in this case, and I am not persuaded that we need depart from it to protect the homeowner's own privacy interests. Respondents have made no persuasive argument that we need to fashion a *per se* rule of home protection, with an automatic right for all in the home to invoke the exclusionary rule, in order to protect homeowners and their guests from unlawful police intrusion. With these observations, I join the Court's opinion.

JUSTICE BREYER, concurring in the judgment.

I agree with JUSTICE GINSBURG that respondents can claim the Fourth Amendment's protection. Petitioner, however, raises a second question, whether under the circumstances Officer Thielen's observation made "from a public area outside the curtilage of the residence" violated respondents' Fourth Amendment rights. *See* Pet. for Cert. i. In my view, it did not.

. . . .

JUSTICE GINSBURG, with whom JUSTICE STEVENS and JUSTICE SOUTER join, dissenting.

The Court's decision undermines not only the security of short-term guests, but also the security of the home resident herself. In my view, when a homeowner or lessor personally invites a guest into her home to share in a common endeavor, whether it be for conversation, to engage in leisure activities, or for business purposes licit or illicit, that guest should share his host's shelter against unreasonable searches and seizures.

I do not here propose restoration of the "legitimately on the premises" criterion.

. . . First, the disposition I would reach in this case responds to the unique importance of the home — the most essential bastion of privacy recognized by the law. Second, even within the home itself, the position to which I would adhere would not permit "a casual visitor who has never seen, or been permitted to visit, the basement of another's house to object to a search of the basement if the visitor happened to be in the kitchen of the house at the time of the search." *Rakas*, 439 U.S., at 142. Further, I would here decide only the case of the homeowner who chooses to share the privacy of her home and her company with a guest, and would not reach classroom hypotheticals like the milkman or pizza deliverer.

My concern centers on an individual's choice to share her home and her associations there with persons she selects. Our decisions indicate that people have a reasonable expectation of privacy in their homes in part because they have the prerogative to exclude others. The power to exclude implies the power to include. Our Fourth Amendment decisions should reflect these complementary prerogatives.

A home dweller places her own privacy at risk, the Court's approach indicates, when she opens her home to others, uncertain whether the duration of their stay, their purpose, and their "acceptance into the household" will earn protection. It remains textbook law that "[s]earches and seizures inside a home without a warrant are presumptively unreasonable absent exigent circumstances." *Karo*, 468 U.S. at 714–715. The law in practice is less secure. Human frailty suggests that today's decision will tempt police to pry into private dwellings without warrant, to find evidence incriminating guests who do not rest there through the night. *Rakas* tolerates that temptation with respect to automobile searches. I see no impelling reason to extend this risk into the home. As I see it, people are not genuinely "secure in their . . . houses . . . against unreasonable searches and seizures," U.S. Const., Amdt. 4, if their invitations to others increase the risk of unwarranted governmental peering and prying into their dwelling places.

Through the host's invitation, the guest gains a reasonable expectation of privacy in the home. *Minnesota v. Olson*, 495 U.S. 91, 110 S. Ct. 1684, 109 L. Ed. 2d 85 (1990), so held with respect to an overnight guest. The logic of that decision extends to shorter term guests as well. Visiting the home of a friend, relative, or business associate, whatever the time of day, "serves functions recognized as valuable by society." *Olson*, 495 U.S., at 98. One need not remain overnight to anticipate privacy in another's home, "a place where [the guest] and his possessions will not be disturbed by anyone but his host and those his host allows inside." *Id.*, at 99. In sum, when a homeowner chooses to share the privacy of her home and her company with a short-term guest, the twofold requirement "emerg[ing] from prior decisions" has been satisfied: Both host and guest "have exhibited an actual (subjective) expectation of privacy"; that "expectation [is] one [our] society is prepared to recognize as 'reasonable.'" *Katz v. United States*, 389 U.S. 347, 361, 88 S. Ct. 507, 19 L. Ed. 2d 576 (1967) (Harlan, J., concurring).[2]

As the Solicitor General acknowledged, the illegality of the host-guest conduct, the fact that they were partners in crime, would not alter the analysis. In *Olson*, for example, the guest whose security this Court's decision shielded stayed overnight while the police searched for him. 495 U.S., at 93–94. The Court held that the guest had Fourth Amendment protection against a warrantless arrest in his host's home despite the guest's involvement in grave crimes (first-degree murder, armed robbery, and assault). Other decisions have similarly sustained Fourth Amendment pleas despite the criminality of the defendants' activities. Indeed, it must be this way. If the illegality of the activity made constitutional an otherwise unconstitutional search, such Fourth Amendment protection, reserved for the innocent only, would have little force in regulating police behavior toward either the innocent or the guilty.

Our leading decision in *Katz* is key to my view of this case. . . . The Court's decision in this case veers sharply from the path marked in *Katz*. I do not agree that we have a more reasonable expectation of privacy when we place a business call to a

---

2. In his concurring opinion, Justice Kennedy maintains that respondents here lacked "an expectation of privacy that society recognizes as reasonable" because they "established nothing more than a fleeting and insubstantial connection" with the host's home. As the Minnesota Supreme Court reported, however, the stipulated facts showed that respondents were inside the apartment with the host's permission, remained inside for at least 2-1/2 hours, and, during that time, engaged in concert with the host in a collaborative venture. *See* 569 N.W.2d 169, 175–176 (1997). These stipulated facts — which scarcely resemble a stop of a minute or two at the 19th of 20 homes to drop off a packet — securely demonstrate that the host intended to share her privacy with respondents, and that respondents, therefore, had entered into the homeland of Fourth Amendment protection. While I agree with the Minnesota Supreme Court that, under the rule settled since *Katz*, the reasonableness of the expectation of privacy controls, not the visitor's status as social guest, invitee, licensee, or business partner, 569 N.W.2d at 176, I think it noteworthy that five Members of the Court would place under the Fourth Amendment's shield, at least, "almost all social guests," *ante*, at 478 (Kennedy, J., concurring).

person's home from a public telephone booth on the side of the street, see *Katz*, 389 U.S., at 353, than when we actually enter that person's premises to engage in a common endeavor.[3]

For the reasons stated, I dissent from the Court's judgment, and would retain judicial surveillance over the warrantless searches today's decision allows.

Notes and Questions

(1) After *Carter*, what "guests" are entitled to object to the searches of homes they are visiting? Are those guests entitled to contest every search that takes place in those homes? If not, which searches may they challenge?

(2) The *Rakas* majority noted that it was "unnecessary" in that case "to decide . . . whether the same expectations of privacy are warranted in a car as would be justified in a dwelling place in analogous circumstances." Nevertheless, after observing that "on numerous occasions" the Court had "pointed out that cars are not to be treated identically with houses or apartments for Fourth Amendment purposes," the majority asserted that the claim raised by the passengers in *Rakas* was "one which *would fail even in an analogous situation in a dwelling place.*" (Emphasis added.) In light of the opinions in *Carter*, are guests in homes and guests in automobiles equally likely to have "legitimate expectations of privacy" in those places? Are there any plausible bases for treating such guests differently?

(3) The dissenters in *Carter* expressed concern that the "Court's decision undermines not only the security of short-term guests, but also the security of the home resident herself." Is there reason to fear that the legitimate expectations of home dwellers will be seriously jeopardized by refusing to recognize protected interests for short-term guests? Is that fear an adequate reason to extend Fourth Amendment protection to all guests?

(4) Should a defendant have "standing" to claim exclusion of inculpatory evidence:

(a) secured by violating the *Miranda* "rights" of another person? *See United States v. Fredericks*, 586 F.2d 470 (5th Cir. 1978).

---

3. JUSTICE SCALIA's lively concurring opinion deplores our adherence to *Katz*. In suggesting that we have elevated Justice Harlan's concurring opinion in *Katz* to first place, JUSTICE SCALIA undervalues the clear opinion of the Court that "the Fourth Amendment protects people, not places," 389 U.S., at 351. That core understanding is the *leitmotif* of JUSTICE HARLAN's concurring opinion. One cannot avoid a strong sense of *deja vu* on reading JUSTICE SCALIA's elaboration. It so vividly recalls the opinion of JUSTICE BLACK in dissent in *Katz*. JUSTICE SCALIA relies on what he deems "clear text" to argue that the Fourth Amendment protects people from searches only in the places where they live. Again, as JUSTICE STEWART emphasized in the majority opinion in *Katz*, which *stare decisis* and reason require us to follow, "the Fourth Amendment protects people, not places." 389 U.S., at 351.

(b) acquired by means of actual official coercion of another person to speak? *See United States v. Fredericks, supra.*

(c) obtained in violation of another individual's *Massiah* right to counsel? *See United States v. Shapiro,* 669 F.2d 593 (9th Cir. 1982).

"Standing" Problems

13A–1: On the morning of December 14, Officer James Canberry and two fellow officers were on duty in a yellow cab located outside the Dante Bar in a high crime area. At 12:15 a.m., the officers noticed two males exit the bar. The two men, later identified as Jud and Keels, entered another yellow cab. The officers followed in their cab. As they followed, the officers observed that the men continued to turn their heads around, looking backward through the rear window of the cab. Both seemed to be looking in the officers' direction.

After following the cab for two blocks, the officers pulled alongside it, showed identification to the driver, and told him to pull over to the side. The driver complied. The officers exited their cab and asked Jud and Keels to step out of theirs. Both got out on the driver's side, near Officer Canberry. As the other two officers began to search the cab, Jud and Keels volunteered inculpatory statements to Canberry. Soon thereafter, the two officers searching the cab found a gun under the seat. Both Jud and Keels were placed under arrest.

Do Jud and Keels have standing to object to the admission of their statements and the gun?

13A–2: Lorenzo arrived at his brother's house at 7:00 p.m. His brother asked him to take care of his young son while he went to the store. Lorenzo agreed to babysit the boy. He intended to go home to sleep in his own house when his brother returned. Lorenzo's nephew was asleep in the living room, and Lorenzo was sitting on the living room sofa when police officers entered and searched the house without a warrant. In two of the bedrooms, the officers found cocaine and narcotics paraphernalia. Lorenzo had not gone into the bedrooms that evening. The officers also found items with the contraband that furnished a connection to Lorenzo.

Lorenzo was charged with narcotics offenses. He moved to suppress the cocaine and paraphernalia found in the house. The trial judge denied the motion, concluding that Lorenzo could not object to any illegality that might have occurred. Lorenzo appealed that ruling.

Should the trial court's decision be reversed? Why?

13A–3: Quick solicited Hunt to assist in a drug smuggling scheme. He then purchased a 54-foot vessel — the Sea Otter — and gave possession to Hunt. Hunt took the Sea Otter to Colombia and picked up roughly 12,000 pounds of marijuana, which he then delivered to Quick's ranch in California. On June 27, California Fish and

Game officials, suspecting that the Sea Otter had been engaged in unlawful fishing operations, boarded the vessel. They observed marijuana "debris" in plain view. They left and notified the United States Coast Guard and the Customs Service of their suspicion that the Sea Otter had been used in a marijuana smuggling operation.

Federal officials intercepted and boarded the Sea Otter at sea. The crew could not produce documentation for the boat. Hunt admitted that he had not contacted either the Coast Guard or the Immigration and Naturalization Service when the vessel arrived at the California coast as required by law. The officials took the vessel to a nearby Coast Guard station. The forward holds were emptied and material later identified as marijuana was discovered.

Quick had purchased the vessel for the specific purpose of having others operate it to smuggle drugs into the United States. He had never kept private quarters on the boat or used it as a repository of personal effects. Moreover, he did not exert any control over the boat. His partner, Hunt, had complete control over the vessel at all times prior to the search.

Quick was arrested and charged with importation and possession of marijuana. He moved to suppress all evidence obtained as a result of the stop and search of the Sea Otter.

Should Quick be able to assert a Fourth Amendment claim?

13A–4: On the night of October 28, Robert was driven to the Diamond Dolls night club by his nephew, Jerome. While they were at the club, Jerome received a telephone call from a romantic acquaintance. He told Robert that he was leaving. Not wanting to leave Robert without a ride home, Jerome introduced Robert to his friend Julian, who agreed to drop Robert off on his way home. At around 1:30 a.m., Robert left the club with Julian. Julian and Scott got in the front seat of Julian's vehicle, a green SUV, and Robert got in the back.

At about the same time, a police radio call went out advising officers to be on the lookout for a black man with dreadlocks driving a green SUV. The source of the information relayed in the radio call is unknown. Police officers on patrol in the neighborhood of the nightclub heard the call and shortly thereafter saw Julian's SUV — a green SUV with a black driver — as it was pulling away from the nightclub. They immediately pulled the car over. Upon approaching the car, the officers observed a gun on the floor under the driver's seat. They then ordered Julian, Scott, and Robert to get out of the car, and searched it, recovering a second gun from the front seat, two from the floorboards of the back seat area, and one from the back seat itself. Julian and Robert were arrested and charged with gun possession.

The prosecution conceded that the stop of the SUV was illegal, and dropped all charges against Julian. The prosecution, however, proceeded with the gun possession case against Robert. After the trial court denied Robert's motion to suppress the guns found in the back seat of the SUV, they were admitted into evidence, and Robert was convicted. He now appeals, challenging the suppression ruling.

Should the court of appeals reverse the trial court's ruling?

13A–5: Josh Hill was charged with manufacturing methamphetamine. He filed a motion to suppress inculpatory evidence obtained during an allegedly unlawful search of an apartment. The trial judge ruled that Hill could not contest the legality of the search of the apartment. Hill has appealed that ruling. The facts underlying the motion to suppress were as follows:

Hill was present at the apartment at the time the police conducted the contested search. The tenant of the apartment had neither invited Hill into the apartment nor granted him permission to enter the apartment. Instead, without the tenant's knowledge, Hill's friend, who was an overnight guest of the tenant, had invited Hill into the apartment. Hill and his friend testified at the motion to suppress hearing that Hill had intended to stay in the apartment overnight. The trial judge concluded that Hill had not intended to stay overnight. The bases for this conclusion were that Hill did not have clothes, that he did not have a toothbrush, and that the only bag in his possession contained materials used in manufacturing methamphetamine.

Should the trial court's ruling be overturned on appeal?

13A–6: Through Expedia.com, 21-year-old Mark reserved a room at a privately-owned hotel for three nights — from Friday, June 17, to Monday, June 20. He prepaid for the 3-day stay by credit card. On June 17, Mark arrived and was assigned to room 718. He signed a registration card containing the following notice:

> This hotel is privately-owned. The management reserves the right to lawfully refuse service to anyone. Guests must comply with all federal, state, and local laws as well as the hotel's rules and regulations. If a guest does not comply with the above, the guest may be asked to leave and/or be evicted.

At 2:30 a.m., on June 18, two women and four men entered the lobby. They appeared to be intoxicated and carried alcoholic beverages. Night Manager Gerry Goodman explained that three guests could visit Mark's room at a time if Mark registered them. When the visitors became verbally abusive, Goodman summoned Mark and informed him that if his friends continued to misbehave, he would call the police and eject them and Mark from the hotel. Mark asked the visitors to leave, and they complied. Goodman warned Mark that if there was one more complaint from guests or staff concerning his occupancy, he would be "gone."

That day, guests complained of an odor of marijuana in the hall outside room 718, which is on a nonsmoking floor. At 7 p.m., Goodman went to investigate. Because he could smell marijuana in the vicinity of room 718, he knocked on the door. After receiving no response to several knocks, he used a master key to enter. No one was inside. Goodman saw a scale, what appeared to be marijuana residue, and rolling papers on a table. He saw more marijuana in a bag on the bed. After deciding that Mark would no longer be allowed to use the room, Goodman had a security officer "double-lock" the door so that Mark could not enter. He then contacted the police.

At 7:30 p.m., Officer Tracy arrived and Goodman told him what had taken place. Using his master key, Goodman let Tracy into room 718, where the officer found what Goodman had observed earlier. Tracy also detected a strong aroma of marijuana from the bathroom. He determined that the smell was coming from an unzipped and open backpack on the bathroom floor. At the top of the backpack, Tracy saw clear plastic bags of marijuana. He moved the bags and just underneath them found a loaded nine millimeter handgun. After removing the weapon, he saw a clear bag of cocaine and bundles of cash totaling $10,860. Tracy confiscated the backpack, gun, cash, and drugs and left the room. Goodman again had the door double-locked. At approximately 11 p.m., Mark returned to the hotel and attempted unsuccessfully to enter room 718 with his pass key. After Goodman notified police that Mark had returned, Officer Tracy came back and arrested him. Mark was charged with a number of narcotics offenses.

If Mark moves to suppress the evidence found in room 718, can he establish that his Fourth Amendment rights were violated?

13A–7: On April 9, Bart and his wife, Deb, were working at a residential construction site. Bart asked Deb to take his car to fill a water container. The car was titled in Bart's name, but Deb had a key and often drove the car when Bart didn't need it. Not long after Deb left the site, she was pulled over by Officer Bouch for speeding. After advising Deb that she had exceeded the speed limit, Bouch asked to see her license. He noticed that Deb was "shaking violently" and that her voice seemed "a little bit nervous." Bouch asked Deb for proof of insurance, but she could not find it in the glove compartment. The officer then returned to his car. As he was completing the citations he intended to issue, he saw Deb lean over several times in the front seat out of his view. Because he had seen similar sorts of movements in past cases involving narcotics arrests, Bouch decided to radio for the assistance of a second police unit.

Officer Bouch then returned to Deb's car and asked her to step out so he could explain the citations and show her the radar reading. In fact, he wanted to see how Deb would behave. After walking Deb back to his car and issuing the citations, the officer began to question her and asked for consent to pat her down and search the car. Whether she freely gave consent is disputed. The officer patted Deb down, but found nothing. Inside the car, he found drugs in the pocket of a jacket on the back seat. He also found drug paraphernalia in the glove compartment and in the front console. When asked, Deb said that the jacket belonged to Bart.

Bart was charged with drug offenses. He moved to suppress the evidence found in the car, claiming that Officer Bouch had illegally detained Deb and had illegally searched the car. The trial judge concluded that Bart lacked standing to assert these Fourth Amendment claims.

Was the judge's ruling correct?

13A–8: Gary's single-family home is located on 0.9 acres, with the majority of the land in the back yard. A sidewalk runs along the eastern border of the property, in front of the house and parallel to the street. There is no path or sidewalk leading into the backyard. A one- to-two-foot-high rock wall runs along the south side of the property. Several trees line this wall but do not block views of the backyard and side of the house. The north side of the property has a short wire fence that consists of three posts connected by wire. This fence does not inhibit an onlooker from seeing the backyard from the adjacent property. An alleyway runs along the western border at the rear of the property. A "No Trespassing" sign and a "No Soliciting" sign are affixed to the front of the house.

Around 4:30 p.m. on June 22, Deputy Sheriff Cory and Police Officer D.J. drove to Gary's home to arrest Michael Rucker on an outstanding warrant. When they arrived, the two officers parked and got out of their vehicle. As they approached the property, they observed Gary and Kingston, each with a leashed dog, walking along the south side of the house inside the short rock wall. Kingston was a long-time acquaintance who had come to Gary's home on numerous occasions to visit and to work on cars and mopeds in the backyard. Upon seeing the officers, the men dropped their dogs' leashes. The dogs ran toward the officers, while Gary and Kingston ran to the back of the house. Shortly thereafter, they returned to the front of the house and restrained their dogs. The officers asked if Rucker was at the residence. Gary said he was not. Kingston said that he did not know Rucker.

Officer D.J. stayed with the men while Deputy Sheriff Cory walked to the backyard. Because there was no sidewalk leading to the rear, Cory walked on an adjacent lot and then crossed back onto Gary's property. Cory was looking for "Rucker or any weapons that could be used to ambush" the officers. In the back yard, Cory found a baggie of methamphetamine near a PVC pipe protruding from the ground. The baggie was partially covered by insulation on the ground and was about three to five feet from the back door of the residence. The baggie was about 20 yards inside the property line. Cory did not realize what it was until he was approximately five to 10 feet away from it.

Based on facts connecting both men to the baggie of methamphetamine, the officers arrested Kingston and Gary. Prior to his trial for possession with intent to distribute methamphetamine, Kingston filed a motion to suppress the baggie, alleging that Deputy Sheriff Cory discovered it by violating the Fourth Amendment.

Should the trial judge grant Kingston's suppression motion?

13A–9: Michael Barr, a Drug Enforcement Agency ("DEA") task force officer, received a tip that Roshon had been renting cars — or instructing others to rent them for him — which he would use to transport crack cocaine from Long Beach, California, to Spokane, Washington. According to the tipster, in November, McGuff and Roshon had driven to Long Beach. Roshon had purchased crack there, and the two men had then transported the crack from Long Beach to Spokane. The tipster reported that McGuff had rented the vehicle that had been used and that he usually rented cars from "Dollar" or "Budget" at the Spokane Airport. Spokane Gang Unit Officers confirmed that McGuff was a "known associate" of Roshon. A check with Budget Car Rental at the Spokane Airport showed that McGuff had rented a car at that location in November and had returned it with almost 3000 additional miles on the odometer — a distance consistent with a round trip to Long Beach. At the request of authorities, Budget employees alerted other rental car services at the airport about Roshon and McGuff.

On March 4, a representative from National Car Rental ("National") at the Spokane Airport called Agent Barr and reported that McGuff had just made a four-day rental reservation. McGuff was scheduled to pick up the car — a white Dodge Intrepid — at noon the following day. National's manager agreed to allow the police to install a tracking device in the car while the car was in National's garage. On March 5, McGuff signed a rental contract with National. McGuff's signature on the agreement was below text which states: "Only I and authorised driver(s) may drive the vehicle." The contract did not list Roshon as an authorized driver.

On March 8, the tracking device alerted the authorities that the car rented by McGuff had returned to Washington State. On March 9, at 1:30 a.m., State Troopers stopped a car that matched the description of the car rented by McGuff. Roshon, who was alone in the vehicle, presented the Troopers with a driver's license bearing the name "Roland Phillippe." After they confirmed Roshon's true identity by checking his tattoos, officers arrested him based on an outstanding warrant. They then searched the Intrepid and found, among other items, nearly 600 grams of cocaine in what police described as "a small telephone bag," located next to the spare tire in the vehicle's trunk. They also found $1000 and 25 grams of heroin in the trunk.

Roshon's counsel moved to suppress the evidence seized from the rental car. During the suppression hearing, Roshon did not testify or present other evidence that McGuff had given him permission to use or to drive the car.

Is Roshon entitled to raise a Fourth Amendment objection to the search of the car? If not, would the answer be different if he had proven that McGuff had given him permission to use the car?

13A–10: Based on the report of an informant who had bought marijuana from Dom Ami in the past, the police contacted a postal inspector and asked him to be on the lookout for a package sent to Dom's address. The inspector spotted and seized a package addressed to "Gabe Ami" at Dom's address. After a drug-sniffing dog alerted to the package, the inspector opened the package and found five bundles of marijuana inside. The police resealed the package after enclosing a device that would signal them when the package was opened. The postal inspector took the package to Dom's house. When Dom answered the door, the inspector informed him that he had "a package for Gabe Ami." Dom responded that he was Mr. Ami, and accepted the package. Officers immediately applied for and obtained a search warrant for Dom's residence.

When the device signaled that the package had been opened, the police entered Dom's home, found the marijuana, and arrested him. Dom was convicted of possession of marijuana after the trial judge denied his motion to suppress the marijuana on the ground that he did not have "standing" to object to the seizure and search of the package by the postal inspector.

Was Dom entitled to object to the seizure and search of the package?

[B] The "Independent Source" and "Inevitable Discovery" Doctrines

Silverthorne Lumber Co. v. United States

United States Supreme Court

251 U.S. 385, 40 S. Ct. 182, 64 L. Ed. 319 (1920)

MR. JUSTICE HOLMES delivered the opinion of the Court.

. . . .

The facts are simple. An indictment upon a single specific charge having been brought against the two Silverthornes mentioned, they both were arrested at their homes early in the morning of February 25, and were detained in custody a number of hours. While they were thus detained representatives of the Department of Justice and the United States marshal without a shadow of authority went to the office of their company and made a clean sweep of all the books, papers and documents found there. All the employees were taken or directed to go to the office of the District Attorney of the United States to which also the books, etc., were taken at once. An application was made as soon as might be to the District Court for a return of what thus had been taken unlawfully. It was opposed by the District Attorney so far as he had found evidence against the plaintiffs in error, and it was stated that the evidence so obtained was before the grand jury. Color had been given by the District Attorney to the approach of those concerned in the act by an invalid subpoena for certain documents relating to the charge in the indictment then on file. Thus the case is not that of knowledge acquired through the wrongful act of a stranger, but it must be assumed that the Government planned or at all events ratified the whole performance. Photographs and copies of material papers were made and a new indictment was framed based upon the knowledge thus obtained. The District Court ordered a return of the originals but impounded the photographs and copies. Subpoenas to produce the originals then were served and on the refusal of the plaintiffs in error to produce them the Court made an order that the subpoenas should be complied with, although it had found that all the papers had been seized in violation of the parties' constitutional rights. The refusal to obey this order is the contempt alleged. The Government now, while in form repudiating and condemning the illegal seizure, seeks to maintain its right to avail itself of the knowledge obtained by that means which otherwise it would not have had.

The proposition could not be presented more nakedly. It is that although of course its seizure was an outrage which the Government now regrets, it may study the papers before it returns them, copy them, and then may use the knowledge that it has gained to call upon the owners in a more regular form to produce them; that the protection of the Constitution covers the physical possession but not any advantages that the Government can gain over the object of its pursuit by doing the forbidden act. *Weeks v. United States*, 232 U.S. 383, 34 Sup. Ct. 341, 58 L. Ed. 652, to be sure, had established that laying the papers directly before the grand jury was unwarranted, but it is taken to mean only that two steps are required instead of one. In our opinion such is not the law. It reduces the Fourth Amendment to a form of words. 232 U.S. 393, 34 Sup. Ct. 341, 58 L. Ed. 652. The essence of a provision forbidding the acquisition of evidence in a certain way is that not merely evidence so acquired shall not be used before the Court but that it shall not be used at all. Of course this does not mean that the facts thus obtained become sacred and inaccessible. If knowledge of them is gained from an independent source they may be proved like any others, but the knowledge gained by the Government's own wrong cannot be used by it in the way proposed. . . .

Judgment reversed.

Murray v. United States

United States Supreme Court

487 U.S. 533, 108 S. Ct. 2529, 101 L. Ed. 2d 472 (1988)

JUSTICE SCALIA delivered the opinion of the Court.

In *Segura v. United States*, 468 U.S. 796, 104 S. Ct. 3388, 82 L. Ed. 2d 599 (1984), we held that police officers' illegal entry upon private premises did not require suppression of evidence subsequently discovered at those premises when executing a search warrant obtained on the basis of information wholly unconnected with the initial entry. In these consolidated cases we are faced with the question whether, again assuming evidence obtained pursuant to an independently obtained search warrant, the portion of such evidence that had been observed in plain view at the time of a prior illegal entry must be suppressed.

I

Both cases arise out of the conviction of petitioner Michael F. Murray, petitioner James D. Carter, and others for conspiracy to possess and distribute illegal drugs. Insofar as relevant for our purposes, the facts are as follows: Based on information received from informants, federal law enforcement agents had been surveilling petitioner Murray and several of his co-conspirators. At about 1:45 p.m. on April 6, 1983, they observed Murray drive a truck and Carter drive a green camper, into a warehouse in South Boston. When the petitioners drove the vehicles out about 20 minutes later, the surveilling agents saw within the warehouse two individuals and a tractor-trailer rig bearing a long, dark container. Murray and Carter later turned over the truck and camper to other drivers, who were in turn followed and ultimately arrested, and the vehicles lawfully seized. Both vehicles were found to contain marijuana.

After receiving this information, several of the agents converged on the South Boston warehouse and forced entry. They found the warehouse unoccupied, but observed in plain view numerous burlap-wrapped bales that were later found to contain marijuana. They left without disturbing the bales, kept the warehouse under surveillance, and did not reenter it until they had a search warrant. In applying for the warrant, the agents did not mention the prior entry, and did not rely on any observations made during that entry. When the warrant was issued — at 10:40 p.m., approximately eight hours after the initial entry — the agents immediately reentered the warehouse and seized 270 bales of marijuana and notebooks listing customers for whom the bales were destined.

Before trial, petitioners moved to suppress the evidence found in the warehouse. The District Court denied the motion, rejecting petitioners' arguments that the warrant was invalid because the agents did not inform the Magistrate about their prior warrantless entry, and that the warrant was tainted by that entry. The First Circuit affirmed, assuming for purposes of its decision that the first entry into the warehouse was unlawful. Murray and Carter then separately filed petitions for certiorari, which we granted, and have consolidated here.

II

The exclusionary rule prohibits introduction into evidence of tangible materials seized during an unlawful search and of testimony concerning knowledge acquired during an unlawful search. Beyond that, the exclusionary rule also prohibits the introduction of derivative evidence, both tangible and testimonial, that is the product of the primary evidence, or that is otherwise acquired as an indirect result of the unlawful search, up to the point at which the connection with the unlawful search becomes "so attenuated as to dissipate the taint," *Nardone v. United States*, 308 U.S. 338, 341, 60 S. Ct. 266, 268, 84 L. Ed. 307 (1939).

[margin note:] exclusionary rule

[margin note:] Derivative evidence

Almost simultaneously with our development of the exclusionary rule, in the first quarter of this century, we also announced what has come to be known as the "independent source" doctrine. *See Silverthorne Lumber Co. v. United States*, 251 U.S. 385, 392, 40 S. Ct. 182, 183, 64 L. Ed. 319 (1920). . . .

The dispute here is over the scope of this doctrine. Petitioners contend that it applies only to evidence obtained for the first time during an independent lawful search. The Government argues that it applies also to evidence initially discovered during, or as a consequence of, an unlawful search, but later obtained independently from activities untainted by the initial illegality. We think the Government's view has better support in both precedent and policy.

*[margin note: * Issue — Scope of Ind. source Doc.]*

Our cases have used the concept of "independent source" in a more general and a more specific sense. The more general sense identifies all evidence acquired in a fashion untainted by the illegal evidence-gathering activity. Thus, where an unlawful entry has given investigators knowledge of facts x and y, but fact z has been learned by other means, fact z can be said to be admissible because derived from an "independent source." This is how we used the term in *Segura v. United States*, 468 U.S. 796, 104 S. Ct. 3380, 82 L. Ed. 2d 599 (1984). In that case, agents unlawfully entered the defendant's apartment and remained there until a search warrant was obtained. The admissibility of what they discovered while waiting in the apartment was not before us, but we held that the evidence found for the first time during the execution

[margin note: unlawful search gives knowledge to x + y but z comes from diff. Independ source!]

of the valid and untainted search warrant was admissible because it was discovered pursuant to an "independent source," *id.*, at 813–814, 104 S. Ct., at 3389–90.

The original use of the term, however, and its more important use for purposes of this case, was more specific. It was originally applied in the exclusionary rule context, by Justice Holmes, with reference to that particular category of evidence acquired by an untainted search *which is identical to the evidence unlawfully acquired* — that is, in the example just given, to knowledge of facts x and y derived from an independent source:

> The essence of a provision forbidding the acquisition of evidence in a certain way is that not merely evidence so acquired shall not be used before the Court but that it shall not be used at all. Of course this does not mean that the facts thus obtained become sacred and inaccessible. If knowledge of them is gained from an independent source they may be proved like any others.

Silverthorne Lumber, 251 U.S., at 392, 40 S. Ct., at 183.

. . . .

Petitioners' asserted policy basis for excluding evidence which is initially discovered during an illegal search, but is subsequently acquired through an independent and lawful source, is that a contrary rule will remove all deterrence to, and indeed positively encourage, unlawful police searches. As petitioners see the incentives, law enforcement officers will routinely enter without a warrant to make sure that what they expect to be on the premises is in fact there. If it is not, they will have spared themselves the time and trouble of getting a warrant; if it is, they can get the warrant and use the evidence despite the unlawful entry. We see the incentives differently. An officer with probable cause sufficient to obtain a search warrant would be foolish to enter the premises first in an unlawful manner. By doing so, he would risk suppression of all evidence on the premises, both seen and unseen, since his action would add to the normal burden of convincing a magistrate that there is probable cause the much more onerous burden of convincing a trial court that no information gained from the illegal entry affected either the law enforcement officers' decision to seek a warrant or the magistrate's decision to grant it. Nor would the officer without sufficient probable cause to obtain a search warrant have any added incentive to conduct an unlawful entry, since whatever he finds cannot be used to establish probable cause before a magistrate.[2]

. . . .

---

2. JUSTICE MARSHALL argues, in effect, that where the police cannot point to some historically verifiable fact demonstrating that the subsequent search pursuant to a warrant was wholly unaffected by the prior illegal search — *e.g.*, that they had already sought the warrant before entering the premises — we should adopt a *per se* rule of inadmissibility. We do not believe that such a prophylactic exception to the independent source rule is necessary. To say that a district court must be satisfied that a warrant would have been sought without the illegal entry is not to give dispositive effect to police officers' assurances on the point. Where the facts render those assurances implausible, the independent source doctrine will not apply. . . .

III

To apply what we have said to the present case: Knowledge that the marijuana was in the warehouse was assuredly acquired at the time of the unlawful entry. But it was also acquired at the time of entry pursuant to the warrant, and if that later acquisition was not the result of the earlier entry there is no reason why the independent source doctrine should not apply. Invoking the exclusionary rule would put the police (and society) not in the same position they would have occupied if no violation occurred, but in a worse one.

We think this is also true with respect to the tangible evidence, the bales of marijuana. . . . The First Circuit has discerned a difference between tangible and intangible evidence that has been tainted, in that objects "once seized cannot be cleanly reseized without returning the objects to private control." *United States v. Silvestri*, 787 F.2d 736, 739 (1st Cir. 1986). It seems to us, however, that reseizure of tangible evidence already seized is no more impossible than rediscovery of intangible evidence already discovered. The independent source doctrine does not rest upon such metaphysical analysis, but upon the policy that, while the government should not profit from its illegal activity, neither should it be placed in a worse position than it would otherwise have occupied. So long as a later, lawful seizure is genuinely independent of an earlier, tainted one (which may well be difficult to establish where the seized goods are kept in the police's possession) there is no reason why the independent source doctrine should not apply.

The ultimate question, therefore, is whether the search pursuant to warrant was in fact a genuinely independent source of the information and tangible evidence at issue here. This would not have been the case if the agents' decision to seek the warrant was prompted by what they had seen during the initial entry,[3] or if information obtained during that entry was presented to the Magistrate and affected his decision to issue the warrant. On this point the Court of Appeals said the following:

> [W]e can be absolutely certain that the warrantless entry in no way contributed in the slightest either to the issuance of a warrant or to the discovery of the evidence during the lawful search that occurred pursuant to the warrant.

. . . .

---

3. JUSTICE MARSHALL argues that "the relevant question [is] whether, even if the initial entry uncovered no evidence, the officers would return immediately with a warrant to conduct a second search." We do not see how this is "relevant" at all. To determine whether the warrant was independent of the illegal entry, one must ask whether it would have been sought even if what actually happened had not occurred — not whether it would have been sought if something else had happened. That is to say, what counts is whether the actual illegal search had any effect in producing the warrant, not whether some hypothetical illegal search would have aborted the warrant. Only that much is needed to assure that what comes before the court is not the product of illegality; to go further than that would be to expand our existing exclusionary rule.

This is as clear a case as can be imagined where the discovery of the contra-band in plain view was totally irrelevant to the later securing of a warrant and the successful search that ensued. As there was no causal link whatever between the illegal entry and the discovery of the challenged evidence, we find no error in the court's refusal to suppress.

United States v. Moscatiello, 771 F.2d 589, 603, 604 (1st Cir. 1985).

Although these statements can be read to provide emphatic support for the Government's position, it is the function of the District Court rather than the Court of Appeals to determine the facts, and we do not think the Court of Appeals' conclusions are supported by adequate findings. The District Court found that the agents did not reveal their warrantless entry to the Magistrate, and that they did not include in their application for a warrant any recitation of their observations in the warehouse. It did not, however, explicitly find that the agents would have sought a warrant if they had not earlier entered the warehouse. The Government concedes this in its brief. To be sure, the District Court did determine that the purpose of the warrantless entry was in part "to guard against the destruction of possibly critical evidence," and one could perhaps infer from this that the agents who made the entry already planned to obtain that "critical evidence" through a warrant-authorized search. That inference is not, however, clear enough to justify the conclusion that the District Court's findings amounted to a determination of independent source.

Accordingly, we vacate the judgments and remand these cases to the Court of Appeals with instructions that it remand to the District Court for determination whether the warrant-authorized search of the warehouse was an independent source of the challenged evidence in the sense we have described.

It is so ordered.

JUSTICE BRENNAN and JUSTICE KENNEDY took no part in the consideration or decision of this litigation.

JUSTICE MARSHALL, with whom JUSTICE STEVENS and JUSTICE O'CONNOR join, dissenting.

The Court today holds that the "independent source" exception to the exclusionary rule may justify admitting evidence discovered during an illegal warrantless search that is later "rediscovered" by the same team of investigators during a search pursuant to a warrant obtained immediately after the illegal search. I believe the Court's decision, by failing to provide sufficient guarantees that the subsequent search was, in fact, independent of the illegal search, emasculates the Warrant Clause and undermines the deterrence function of the exclusionary rule. I therefore dissent.

. . . The independent source exception . . . is primarily based on a practical view that under certain circumstances the beneficial deterrent effect that exclusion will have on future constitutional violations is too slight to justify the social cost of excluding probative evidence from a criminal trial. When the seizure of the evidence at issue is "wholly independent of" the constitutional violation, then exclusion argu-ably will have no effect on a law enforcement officer's incentive to commit an unlaw-ful search.

Given the underlying justification for the independent source exception, any inquiry into the exception's application must keep sight of the practical effect ad-mission will have on the incentives facing law enforcement officers to engage in unlawful conduct. The proper scope of the independent source exception, and guidelines for its application, cannot be divined in a factual vacuum; instead, they must be informed by the nature of the constitutional violation and the deterrent effect of exclusion in particular circumstances. In holding that the inde-pendent source exception may apply to the facts of this case, I believe the Court loses sight of the practical moorings of the independent source exception and cre-ates an affirmative incentive for unconstitutional searches. This holding can find no justification in the purposes underlying both the exclusionary rule and the in-dependent source exception.

. . . .

Under the circumstances of this case, the admission of the evidence "reseized" during the second search severely undermines the deterrence function of the ex-clusionary rule. Indeed, admission in this case affirmatively encourages illegal searches. The incentives for such illegal conduct are clear. Obtaining a warrant is inconvenient and time-consuming. Even when officers have probable cause to sup-port a warrant application, therefore, they have an incentive first to determine whether it is worthwhile to obtain a warrant. Probable cause is much less than cer-tainty, and many "confirmatory" searches will result in the discovery that no evi-dence is present, thus saving the police the time and trouble of getting a warrant. If contraband is discovered, however, the officers may later seek a warrant to shield the evidence from the taint of the illegal search. The police thus know in advance that they have little to lose and much to gain by foregoing the bother of obtaining a war-rant and undertaking an illegal search.

The Court, however, "see[s] the incentives differently." Under the Court's view, today's decision does not provide an incentive for unlawful searches, because the of-ficer undertaking the search would know that "his action would add to the normal burden of convincing a magistrate that there is probable cause the much more oner-ous burden of convincing a trial court that no information gained from the illegal entry affected either the law enforcement officers' decision to seek a warrant or the magistrate's decision to grant it." The Court, however, provides no hint of why this risk would actually seem significant to the officers. Under the circumstances of this case, the officers committing the illegal search have both knowledge and control of the factors central to the trial court's determination. First, it is a simple matter, as was done in this case, to exclude from the warrant application any information gained from the initial entry so that the magistrate's determination of probable cause is not influenced by the prior illegal search. Second, today's decision makes the application of the independent source exception turn entirely on an evaluation of the officers' intent. It normally will be difficult for the trial court to verify, or the defendant to rebut, an assertion by officers that they always intended to obtain a warrant, regardless of the results of the illegal search.[2] The testimony of the officers conducting the illegal search is the only direct evidence of intent, and the defendant will be relegated simply to arguing that the officers should not be believed. Under these circumstances, the litigation risk described by the Court seems hardly a risk at all; it does not significantly dampen the incentive to conduct the initial illegal search.

The strong Fourth Amendment interest in eliminating these incentives for illegal entry should cause this Court to scrutinize closely the application of the independent source exception to evidence obtained under the circumstances of the instant case; respect for the constitutional guaranty requires a rule that does not undermine the deterrence function of the exclusionary rule. When, as here, the same team of investigators is involved in both the first and second search, there is a significant danger that the "independence" of the source will in fact be illusory, and that the initial search will have affected the decision to obtain a warrant notwithstanding the officers' subsequent assertions to the contrary. It is therefore crucial that the factual premise of the exception — complete independence — be clearly established before the exception can justify admission of the evidence. I believe the Court's reliance on the intent of the law enforcement officers who conducted the warrantless search provides insufficient guarantees that the subsequent legal search was unaffected by the prior illegal search.

To ensure that the source of the evidence is genuinely independent, the basis for a finding that a search was untainted by a prior illegal search must focus . . . on "demonstrated historical facts capable of ready verification or impeachment." *Nix v. Williams*, 467 U.S., at 445, n. 5, 104 S. Ct., at 2509, n. 5. In the instant case, there are no "demonstrated historical facts" capable of supporting a finding that the subsequent warrant search was wholly unaffected by the prior illegal search. The same team of investigators was involved in both searches. The warrant was obtained immediately after the illegal search, and no effort was made to obtain a warrant prior to the discovery of the marijuana during the illegal search. The only evidence available that the warrant search was wholly independent is the testimony of the agents who conducted the illegal search. Under these circumstances, the threat that the subsequent search was tainted by the illegal search is too great to allow for the application of the

---

2. Such an intent-based rule is of dubious value for other reasons as well. First, the intent of the officers prior to the illegal entry often will be of little significance to the relevant question: whether, even if the initial entry uncovered no evidence, the officers would return immediately with a warrant to conduct a second search. Officers who have probable cause to believe contraband is present genuinely might intend later to obtain a warrant, but after the illegal search uncovers no such contraband, those same officers might decide their time is better spent than to return with a warrant. . . .

independent source exception.[4] The Court's contrary holding lends itself to easy abuse, and offers an incentive to bypass the constitutional requirement that probable cause be assessed by a neutral and detached magistrate before the police invade an individual's privacy.

. . . .

In sum, under circumstances as are presented in this case, when the very law enforcement officers who participate in an illegal search immediately thereafter obtain a warrant to search the same premises, I believe the evidence discovered during the initial illegal entry must be suppressed. Any other result emasculates the Warrant Clause and provides an intolerable incentive for warrantless searches. I respectfully dissent.

[The dissenting opinion of JUSTICE STEVENS has been omitted.]

Notes and Questions

What does it mean for evidence or knowledge of facts to be "gained from an independent source"? Why did *Silverthorne* and *Murray* hold that information or evidence gained from such sources need not be excluded? Is the application of the "independent source" doctrine to cases like *Murray* consistent with the deterrent objectives of the exclusionary rule?

Nix v. Williams

United States Supreme Court

467 U.S. 431, 104 S. Ct. 2501, 81 L. Ed. 2d 377 (1984)

CHIEF JUSTICE BURGER delivered the opinion of the Court.

[The Chief Justice began his opinion by recounting the factual and procedural history of the case prior to Williams' second murder trial. First, he related the facts regarding the disappearance of 10-year-old Pamela Powers from the Des Moines YMCA in 1968, Williams' subsequent surrender to the police, and the "Christian Burial Speech" that resulted in Williams' decision to lead the police to the body of the child. He then observed that an independent official search for the body had been in progress at the time, but had been called off when Williams began to reveal information; that one search team was only two and one-half miles from the location

---

4. To conclude that the initial search had no effect on the decision to obtain a warrant, and thus that the warrant search was an "independent source" of the challenged evidence, one would have to assume that even if the officers entered the premises and discovered no contraband, they nonetheless would have gone to the Magistrate, sworn that they had probable cause to believe that contraband was in the building, and then returned to conduct another search. Although such a scenario is possible, I believe it is more plausible to believe that the officers would not have chosen to return immediately to the premises with a warrant to search for evidence had they not discovered evidence during the initial search.

where the body was found; and that the body was found next to a culvert beside a gravel road, "essentially within the area to be searched."

The Chief Justice described Williams' first trial and appeal and the habeas corpus petition that ultimately led to the decision in *Brewer v. Williams*, 430 U.S. 387, 97 S. Ct. 1232, 51 L. Ed. 2d 424 (1977). He concluded by noting that the *Brewer v. Williams* majority had observed "that although Williams' incriminating statements could not be introduced into evidence at a second trial, evidence of the body's location and condition 'might well be admissible on the theory that the body would have been discovered in any event even had incriminating statements not been elicited from Williams.' *Id.*, at 407, n. 12, 97 S. Ct., at 1243, n. 12."]

I

. . . .

C

Second Trial

At Williams' second trial in 1977 in the Iowa court, the prosecution did not offer Williams' statements into evidence, nor did it seek to show that Williams had directed the police to the child's body. However, evidence of the condition of her body as it was found, articles and photographs of her clothing, and the results of *post mortem* medical and chemical tests on the body were admitted. The trial court concluded that the State had proved by a preponderance of the evidence that, if the search had not been suspended and Williams had not led the police to the victim, her body would have been discovered "*within a short time*" in essentially the same condition as it was actually found. The trial court also ruled that if the police had not located the body, "the search would clearly have been taken up again where it left off, given the extreme circumstances of this case and the body would [have] been found *in short order.*" (emphasis added).

In finding that the body would have been discovered in essentially the same condition as it was actually found, the court noted that freezing temperatures had prevailed and tissue deterioration would have been suspended. The challenged evidence was admitted and the jury again found Williams guilty of first-degree murder; he was sentenced to life in prison.

On appeal, the Supreme Court of Iowa again affirmed. That court held that there was in fact a "hypothetical independent source" exception to the Exclusionary Rule. . . .

The Iowa court then reviewed the evidence *de novo* and concluded that the State had shown by a preponderance of the evidence that, even if Williams had not guided police to the child's body, it would inevitably have been found by lawful activity of the search party before its condition had materially changed.

In 1980 Williams renewed his attack on the state-court conviction by seeking a writ of habeas corpus in the United States District Court for the Southern District of Iowa. The District Court conducted its own independent review of the evidence and concluded, as had the state courts, that the body would inevitably have been found by the searchers in essentially the same condition it was in when Williams led police to its discovery. The District Court denied Williams' petition.

The Court of Appeals for the Eighth Circuit reversed. . . . [A]n equally divided court denied rehearing *en banc*. That court assumed, without deciding, that there is an inevitable discovery exception to the Exclusionary Rule and that the Iowa Supreme Court correctly stated that exception to require proof that the police did not act in bad faith and that the evidence would have been discovered absent any constitutional violation. In reversing the District Court's denial of habeas relief, the Court of Appeals stated:

> We hold that the State has not met the first requirement. It is therefore unnecessary to decide whether the state courts' finding that the body would have been discovered anyway is fairly supported by the record. It is also unnecessary to decide whether the State must prove the two elements of the exception by clear and convincing evidence, as defendant argues, or by a preponderance of the evidence, as the state courts held.

. . . .

II
A

. . . .

Williams contends that evidence of the body's location and condition is "fruit of the poisonous tree," *i.e.*, the "fruit" or product of Detective Leaming's plea to help the child's parents give her "a Christian burial," which this Court had already held equated to interrogation. He contends that admitting the challenged evidence violated the Sixth Amendment whether it would have been inevitably discovered or not. Williams also contends that, if the inevitable discovery doctrine is constitutionally permissible, it must include a threshold showing of police good faith.

B

The doctrine requiring courts to suppress evidence as the tainted "fruit" of unlawful governmental conduct had its genesis in *Silverthorne Lumber Co. v. United States*, 251 U.S. 385, 40 S. Ct. 182, 64 L. Ed. 319 (1920); there, the Court held that the Exclusionary Rule applies not only to the illegally obtained evidence itself, but also to other incriminating evidence derived from the primary evidence.

. . . .

The core rationale consistently advanced by this Court for extending the Exclusionary Rule to evidence that is the fruit of unlawful police conduct has been that this admittedly drastic and socially costly course is needed to deter police from violations of constitutional and statutory protections. This Court has accepted the argument that the way to ensure such protections is to exclude evidence seized as a result of such violations notwithstanding the high social cost of letting persons obviously guilty go unpunished for their crimes. On this rationale, the prosecution is not to be put in a better position than it would have been in if no illegality had transpired.

By contrast, the derivative evidence analysis ensures that the prosecution is not put in a *worse* position simply because of some earlier police error or misconduct. The independent source doctrine allows admission of evidence that has been discovered by means wholly independent of any constitutional violation. That doctrine, although closely related to the inevitable discovery doctrine, does not apply here; Williams' statements to Leaming indeed led police to the child's body, but that is not the whole story. The independent source doctrine teaches us that the interest of society in deterring unlawful police conduct and the public interest in having juries receive all probative evidence of a crime are properly balanced by putting the police in the same, not a *worse*, position than they would have been in if no police error or misconduct had occurred. When the challenged evidence has an independent source, exclusion of such evidence would put the police in a worse position than they would have been in absent any error or violation. There is a functional similarity between these two doctrines in that exclusion of evidence that would inevitably have been discovered would also put the government in a worse position, because the police would have obtained that evidence if no misconduct had taken place. Thus, while the independent source exception would not justify admission of evidence in this case, its rationale is wholly consistent with and justifies our adoption of the ultimate or inevitable discovery exception to the Exclusionary Rule.

It is clear that the cases implementing the Exclusionary Rule "begin with the premise that the challenged evidence is *in some sense* the product of illegal governmental activity." *United States v. Crews*, 445 U.S. 463, 471, 100 S. Ct. 1244, 1250, 63 L. Ed. 2d 537 (1980) (emphasis added). Of course, this does not end the inquiry. If the prosecution can establish by a preponderance of the evidence that the information ultimately or inevitably would have been discovered by lawful means — here the volunteers' search — then the deterrence rationale has so little basis that the evidence should be received.[5] Anything less would reject logic, experience, and common sense.

---

5. As to the quantum of proof, we have already established some relevant guidelines. In *United States v. Matlock*, 415 U.S. 164, 178, n. 14, 94 S. Ct. 988, 996, n. 14, 39 L. Ed. 2d 242 (1974) (emphasis added), we stated that "the controlling burden of proof at suppression hearings should impose *no greater burden* than proof by a preponderance of the evidence." In *Lego v. Twomey*, 404 U.S. 477, 488, 92 S. Ct. 619, 626, 30 L. Ed. 2d 618 (1972), we observed "from our experience [that] no substantial evidence has accumulated that federal rights have suffered from determining admissibility by a preponderance of the evidence" and held that the prosecution must prove by a preponderance of the evidence that a confession sought to be used at trial was voluntary. We are unwilling to impose added burdens on the already difficult task of proving guilt in criminal cases by enlarging the barrier to placing evidence of unquestioned truth before juries. Williams argues that the preponderance of the evidence standard used by the Iowa courts is inconsistent with *United States v. Wade*, 388 U.S. 218, 87 S. Ct. 1926, 18 L. Ed. 2d 1149 (1967). In requiring clear and convincing evidence of an independent source for an in-court identification, the Court gave weight to the effect an uncounseled pre-trial identification has in "crystalliz[ing] the witnesses' identification of the defendant for the

The requirement that the prosecution must prove the absence of bad faith, imposed here by the Court of Appeals, would place courts in the position of withholding from juries relevant and undoubted truth that would have been available to police absent any unlawful police activity. Of course, that view would put the police in a worse position than they would have been in if no unlawful conduct had transpired. And, of equal importance, it wholly fails to take into account the enormous societal cost of excluding truth in the search for truth in the administration of justice. Nothing in this Court's prior holdings supports any such formalistic, pointless, and punitive approach.

The Court of Appeals concluded, without analysis, that if an absence-of-bad-faith requirement were not imposed, "the temptation to risk deliberate violations of the Sixth Amendment would be too great, and the deterrent effect of the Exclusionary Rule reduced too far." 700 F.2d, at 1169, n. 5. We reject that view. A police officer who is faced with the opportunity to obtain evidence illegally will rarely, if ever, be in a position to calculate whether the evidence sought would inevitably be discovered. . . . On the other hand, when an officer is aware that the evidence will inevitably be discovered, he will try to avoid engaging in any questionable practice. In that situation, there will be little to gain from taking any dubious "shortcuts" to obtain the evidence. Significant disincentives to obtaining evidence illegally — including the possibility of departmental discipline and civil liability — also lessen the likelihood that the ultimate or inevitable discovery exception will promote police misconduct. In these circumstances, the societal costs of the Exclusionary Rule far outweigh any possible benefits to deterrence that a good-faith requirement might produce.

Williams contends that because he did not waive his right to the assistance of counsel, the Court may not balance competing values in deciding whether the challenged evidence was properly admitted. He argues that, unlike the Exclusionary Rule in the Fourth Amendment context, the essential purpose of which is to deter police misconduct, the Sixth Amendment Exclusionary Rule is designed to protect the right to a fair trial and the integrity of the factfinding process. Williams contends that, when those interests are at stake, the societal costs of excluding evidence obtained from responses presumed involuntary are irrelevant in determining whether such evidence should be excluded. We disagree.

Exclusion of physical evidence that would inevitably have been discovered adds nothing to either the integrity or fairness of a criminal trial. The Sixth Amendment right to counsel protects against unfairness by preserving the adversary process in

---

future reference." *Id.*, at 240, 87 S. Ct., at 1939. The Court noted as well that possible unfairness at the lineup "may be the sole means of attack upon the unequivocal courtroom identification," *ibid.*, and recognized the difficulty of determining whether an in-court identification was based on independent recollection unaided by the lineup identification, *id.*, at 240–241, 87 S. Ct., at 1939–1940. By contrast, inevitable discovery involves no speculative elements but focuses on demonstrated historical facts capable of ready verification or impeachment and does not require a departure from the usual burden of proof at suppression hearings.

which the reliability of proffered evidence may be tested in cross-examination. Here, however, Detective Leaming's conduct did nothing to impugn the reliability of the evidence in question — the body of the child and its condition as it was found, articles of clothing found on the body, and the autopsy. No one would seriously contend that the presence of counsel in the police car when Leaming appealed to Williams' decent human instincts would have had any bearing on the reliability of the body as evidence. Suppression, in these circumstances, would do nothing whatever to promote the integrity of the trial process, but would inflict a wholly unacceptable burden on the administration of criminal justice.

Nor would suppression ensure fairness on the theory that it tends to safeguard the adversary system of justice. To assure the fairness of trial proceedings, this Court has held that assistance of counsel must be available at pretrial confrontations where "the subsequent trial [cannot] cure a[n otherwise] one-sided confrontation between prosecuting authorities and the uncounseled defendant." *United States v. Ash*, 413 U.S. at 315, 93 S. Ct., at 2576. Fairness can be assured by placing the State and the accused in the same positions they would have been in had the impermissible conduct not taken place. However, if the government can prove that the evidence would have been obtained inevitably and, therefore, would have been admitted regardless of any overreaching by the police, there is no rational basis to keep that evidence from the jury in order to ensure the fairness of the trial proceedings. In that situation, the State has gained no advantage at trial and the defendant has suffered no prejudice. Indeed, suppression of the evidence would operate to undermine the adversary system by putting the State in a worse position than it would have occupied without any police misconduct. Williams' argument that inevitable discovery constitutes impermissible balancing of values is without merit.

. . . .

C

The Court of Appeals did not find it necessary to consider whether the record fairly supported the finding that the volunteer search party would ultimately or inevitably have discovered the victim's body. However, three courts independently reviewing the evidence have found that the body of the child inevitably would have been found by the searchers. Williams challenges these findings, asserting that the record contains only the "*post hoc* rationalization" that the search efforts would have proceeded two and one-half miles into Polk County where Williams had led police to the body.

When that challenge was made at the suppression hearing preceding Williams' second trial, the prosecution offered the testimony of Agent Ruxlow of the Iowa Bureau of Criminal Investigation. Ruxlow had organized and directed some 200 volunteers who were searching for the child's body. The searchers were instructed "to check all the roads, the ditches, any culverts. . . . If they came upon any abandoned farm buildings, they were instructed to go onto the property and search those abandoned farm buildings or any other places where a small child could be secreted." Ruxlow testified that he marked off highway maps of Poweshiek and Jasper Counties in grid fashion, divided the volunteers into teams of four to six persons, and assigned each team to search specific grid areas. Ruxlow also testified that, if the search had not been suspended because of Williams' promised cooperation, it would have continued into Polk County, using the same grid system. Although he had previously marked off into grids only the highway maps of Poweshiek and Jasper Counties, Ruxlow had obtained a map of Polk County, which he said he would have marked off in the same manner had it been necessary for the search to continue.

The search had commenced at approximately 10 a.m. and moved westward through Poweshiek County into Jasper County. At approximately 3 p.m., after Williams had volunteered to cooperate with the police, Officer Leaming, who was in the police car with Williams, sent word to Ruxlow and the other Special Agent directing the search to meet him at the Grinnell truck stop and the search was suspended at that time. Ruxlow also stated that he was "under the impression that there was a possibility" that Williams would lead them to the child's body at that time. The search was not resumed once it was learned that Williams had led the police to the body, which was found two and one-half miles from where the search had stopped in what would have been the easternmost grid to be searched in Polk County. There was testimony that it would have taken an additional three to five hours to discover the body if the search had continued; the body was found near a culvert, one of the kinds of places the teams had been specifically directed to search.

On this record it is clear that the search parties were approaching the actual location of the body and we are satisfied, along with three courts earlier, that the volunteer search teams would have resumed the search had Williams not earlier led the police to the body and the body inevitably would have been found. . . .

The judgment of the Court of Appeals is reversed, and the case is remanded for further proceedings consistent with this opinion.

It is so ordered.

[The concurring opinion of JUSTICE WHITE has been omitted.]

JUSTICE STEVENS, concurring in the judgment.

. . . .

II

The constitutional violation that gave rise to the decision in *Williams I* is neither acknowledged nor fairly explained in the Court's opinion. Yet the propriety of admitting evidence relating to the victim's body can only be evaluated if that constitutional violation is properly identified.

. . . .

The Sixth Amendment guarantees that the conviction of the accused will be the product of an adversarial process, rather than the *ex parte* investigation and determination by the prosecutor. *Williams I* grew out of a line of cases in which this Court made it clear that the adversarial process protected by the Sixth Amendment may not be undermined by the strategems of the police.

. . . .

The "Christian burial speech" was nothing less than an attempt to substitute an *ex parte*, inquisitorial process for the clash of adversaries commanded by the Constitution. Thus the now-familiar plaint that "[t]he criminal is to go free because the constable has blundered," is entirely beside the point. More pertinent is what THE CHIEF JUSTICE wrote for the Court on another occasion: "This is not a case where, in Justice Cardozo's words, 'the constable . . . blundered,' rather, it is one where the 'constable' planned an impermissible interference with the right to the assistance of counsel." *United States v. Henry*, 447 U.S. 264, 274–275, 100 S. Ct. 2183, 2188–2189, 65 L. Ed. 2d 115 (1980) (footnote and citation omitted).

III

Once the constitutional violation is properly identified, the answers to the questions presented in this case follow readily. Admission of the victim's body, if it would have been discovered anyway, means that the trial in this case was not the product of an inquisitorial process; that process was untainted by illegality. The good or bad faith of Detective Leaming is therefore simply irrelevant. If the trial process was not tainted as a result of his conduct, this defendant received the type of trial that the Sixth Amendment envisions. Generalizations about the Exclusionary Rule employed by the majority simply do not address the primary question in the case.

The majority is correct to insist that any rule of exclusion not provide the authorities with an incentive to commit violations of the Constitution. If the inevitable discovery rule provided such an incentive by permitting the prosecution to avoid the uncertainties inherent in its search for evidence, it would undermine the constitutional guarantee itself, and therefore be inconsistent with the deterrent purposes of the Exclusionary Rule. But when the burden of proof on the inevitable discovery question is placed on the prosecution, it must bear the risk of error in the determination made necessary by its constitutional violation. The uncertainty as to whether the body would have been discovered can be resolved in its favor here only because, as the Court explains, petitioner adduced evidence demonstrating that at the time of the constitutional violation an investigation was already under way which, in the natural and probable course of events, would have soon discovered the body. This is not a case in which the prosecution can escape responsibility for a constitutional violation through speculation; to the extent uncertainty was created by the constitutional violation the prosecution was required to resolve that uncertainty through proof. Even if Detective Leaming acted in bad faith in the sense that he deliberately violated the Constitution in order to avoid the possibility that the body would not be discovered, the prosecution ultimately does not avoid that risk; its burden of proof forces it to assume the risk. The need to adduce proof sufficient to discharge its burden, and the difficulty in predicting whether such proof will be available or sufficient, means that the inevitable discovery rule does not permit state officials to avoid the uncertainty they would have faced but for the constitutional violation.

The majority refers to the "societal cost" of excluding probative evidence. In my view, the more relevant cost is that imposed on society by police officers who decide to take procedural shortcuts instead of complying with the law. What is the consequence of the shortcut that Detective Leaming took when he decided to question Williams in this case and not to wait an hour or so until he arrived in Des Moines? The answer is years and years of unnecessary but costly litigation. Instead of having a 1969 conviction affirmed in routine fashion, the case is still alive 15 years later. Thanks to Detective Leaming, the State of Iowa has expended vast sums of money and countless hours of professional labor in his defense. That expenditure surely provides an adequate deterrent to similar violations; the responsibility for that expenditure lies not with the Constitution, but rather with the constable.

Accordingly, I concur in the Court's judgment.

JUSTICE BRENNAN, with whom JUSTICE MARSHALL joins, dissenting.

. . . .

To the extent that today's decision adopts th[e] "inevitable discovery" exception to the exclusionary rule, it simply acknowledges a doctrine that is akin to the "independent source" exception first recognized by the Court in *Silverthorne Lumber Co. v. United States*, 251 U.S. 385, 392, 40 S. Ct. 182, 183, 64 L. Ed. 319 (1920). In particular, the Court concludes that unconstitutionally obtained evidence may be admitted at trial if it inevitably would have been discovered in the same condition by an independent line of investigation that was already being pursued when the constitutional violation occurred. As has every federal Court of Appeals previously addressing this issue, I agree that in these circumstances the "inevitable discovery" exception to the exclusionary rule is consistent with the requirements of the Constitution.

In its zealous efforts to emasculate the exclusionary rule, however, the Court loses sight of the crucial difference between the "inevitable discovery" doctrine and the "independent source" exception from which it is derived. When properly applied, the "independent source" exception allows the prosecution to use evidence only if it was, in fact, obtained by fully lawful means. It therefore does no violence to the constitutional protections that the exclusionary rule is meant to enforce. The "inevitable discovery" exception is likewise compatible with the Constitution, though it differs in one key respect from its next of kin: specifically, the evidence sought to be introduced at trial has not actually been obtained from an independent source, but rather would have been discovered as a matter of course if independent investigations were allowed to proceed.

In my view, this distinction should require that the government satisfy a heightened burden of proof before it is allowed to use such evidence. The inevitable discovery exception necessarily implicates a hypothetical finding that differs in kind from the factual finding that precedes application of the independent source rule. To ensure that this hypothetical finding is narrowly confined to circumstances that are functionally equivalent to an independent source, and to protect fully the fundamental rights served by the exclusionary rule, I would require clear and convincing evidence before concluding that the government had met its burden of proof on this issue. Increasing the burden of proof serves to impress the factfinder with the importance of the decision and thereby reduces the risk that illegally obtained evidence will be admitted. Because the lower courts did not impose such a requirement, I would remand this case for application of this heightened burden of proof by the lower courts in the first instance. I am therefore unable to join either the Court's opinion or its judgment.

Notes and Questions

(1) In *Nix*, the Court reasoned that the objects of the exclusionary rule require that the government not "be put in a better position than it would have been in if no illegality had transpired." It concluded that the application of the exclusionary rule to evidence that "would inevitably have been discovered" is inappropriate because the result would be to put "the police in a *worse* position than they would have been in if no unlawful conduct had transpired." Is it clear that the government is never "put in a better position" when it obtains by unconstitutional means evidence it would have gained through constitutional means? Assume, for example, that Detective Leaming had intentionally violated Williams's constitutional right to counsel because he was fairly certain that the constitutional alternative, the ongoing search that would have inevitably discovered the body, would consume a considerable amount of official time and resources. Should the "nonevidentiary" gains in that situation bear upon the applicability of the exclusionary rule? Should "bad faith" really be irrelevant?

(2) *Nix* involved a violation of the *Massiah* right to counsel. Is the "inevitable discovery" exception announced in *Nix* equally applicable to evidence derived from unconstitutional searches and seizures? From *Miranda* violations? From confessions coerced in violation of the Due Process Clause?

(3) In *Nix*, the *immediate* product of the violation — the defendant's statement revealing the location of Pamela Powers's body — had to be suppressed. The *derivative* fruits of the violation — the victim's body and evidence related thereto — fell within the inevitable discovery exception. Assuming that it could be shown that the immediate evidentiary products of unconstitutional conduct "would inevitably have been discovered," would there be any reason not to apply the "inevitable discovery" exception to them? For example, suppose it could have been shown that the defendant in *Nix v. Williams* personally would have revealed the location of Pamela Powers's body to the police after he had consulted with his lawyer in Des Moines. Would his initial statement have been admissible?

Independent Source and Inevitable Discovery Problems

13B–1: As a police surveillance team watched, a confidential informer purchased cocaine from Gene Herr at Herr's trailer home. Afterwards, the informer told the team that Herr intended to take his remaining cocaine to a bar that night in order to sell it. The officers abandoned their plan to obtain a warrant because they were concerned that the proximity of the neighboring residences would not allow them to maintain undetected surveillance during the three or four hours they believed it would take to obtain a search warrant. On the basis of the information they had, the officers decided to arrest Herr in his trailer.

Trooper Hill knocked on the trailer door. When Herr came to the door, Hill and other officers forced their way inside. They arrested Herr, took away a pistol he was carrying, and secured the trailer. Though the officers observed cocaine and drug paraphernalia in plain view, they did not search the trailer. Instead, Hill went to get a search warrant while the other officers remained at the trailer. After Hill obtained the warrant, the officers searched the trailer and seized cocaine and drug paraphernalia.

Herr was charged with possession of a firearm by a felon and drug trafficking. At a hearing on Herr's motion to suppress the evidence, the district court concluded that the application in support of the warrant contained some facts that were discovered during the entry to arrest Herr. The court ruled that the pistol, cocaine, and paraphernalia had to be suppressed.

What arguments should the defense and prosecution make on appeal of the trial court's ruling? How should the appellate court rule?

13B–2: At approximately 10:00 a.m. on September 9, the police received a telephone call from Louise Monroe. She reported that her father, Edgar Holl, had just come to her home and told her that he had killed her mother that morning. Ms. Monroe informed the police that Holl had since left her home. She provided them with a description of his vehicle. The police chief proceeded to the Holl residence where he found Shirley Holl's body in the kitchen. She had been shot to death.

Edgar Holl was stopped and arrested while driving along Route 101 at approximately 11:00 a.m. He appeared highly intoxicated. The arresting officer advised Holl of his *Miranda* rights and took him directly to the police station. During the ride to the station, Holl voluntarily told the officer that he had shot his wife.

Shortly after 11:00 a.m., the arresting officer arrived with Holl at the police station. Lieutenant Buxton advised Holl of his rights for a second time and asked whether he wished to waive them. Holl responded that he did not, then added: "But let me tell you, I killed Shirley because I loved her more than life itself." After making other unsolicited incriminating statements, Holl asked for Attorney Gordon Snyder. The police telephoned Snyder, who requested that they not question the defendant. Lieutenant Buxton then left to obtain a warrant to search the Holl residence and vehicle.

Prior to the arrival of Holl's attorney, Detective Wiggin approached him and asked where the murder weapon was. In response, Holl agreed to show the police the location of the gun. Wiggin and another officer then took Holl to his residence, where they met Captain Beaudoin and other members of the state crime laboratory. Together, they entered the house without a warrant. Holl pointed out the gun, which was protruding from under a couch. Without disturbing the scene, the officers left the residence. Wiggin took Holl back to the police station. Beaudoin and his crime lab associates remained outside the residence.

At about 12:30 p.m., Lieutenant Buxton obtained a search warrant for Holl's residence and vehicle. He radioed ahead and told Beaudoin and the crime lab team to begin the search of the house. When the crime lab team entered the house, Beaudoin pointed out the location of the gun, which they then seized.

Is the gun admissible at Holl's murder trial?

13B–3: Detective Anderson was eating lunch at a McDonald's restaurant when he saw a Hispanic man walking north on 82nd Avenue. Several minutes later, Anderson thought he saw the "same Hispanic man" drive past the McDonald's in a red Toyota. Anderson saw the Toyota circling around the area in a manner that led him to believe that the man might be involved in drug sales. Subsequently, he saw the man in a nearby supermarket parking lot known for "daily drug transactions." As Anderson watched, a gray Jeep Cherokee arrived. The man spoke to the driver, then got into the back seat.

When the Jeep drove out of the parking lot, the driver failed to use a turn signal. Anderson stopped and approached the Jeep. The driver, Marie, and a passenger, Dennis, were in the front seat. The man Anderson had been watching and Marie's four-year-old nephew were in the back seat. While he was talking to Marie, it "appeared" to Anderson that the man in the back seat "had swallowed, which is real common for street-level deliverers, who sometimes keep drugs in balloons in their mouths and swallow them in order to avoid being caught with the drugs." Anderson asked the man to step out of the car.

In response to questions, the man said that his name was "Jorge Valdez." When Anderson asked the man if he had ever sold drugs, he replied, "No." Detective Anderson then strip searched the man in the coffee shop restroom, but found no drugs or evidence that he was selling drugs. He then formally arrested the man for attempted delivery of a controlled substance and took him to the police station. At the station, Anderson arranged for a telephone interview with an Immigration and Naturalization Service (INS) agent because he assumed that the man "was most likely wanted." The interview produced no incriminating information. Anderson then arranged for fingerprinting. When the man's fingerprints were run through the Automated Fingerprint Identification System, he was identified as "Jose Luis Hernandez." From a computer check of this name, Anderson discovered that the man had previous convictions for eluding examination and inspection by immigration officials, and for drug possession and delivery and that he had been deported to Mexico six months earlier.

State drug charges against Jose were dropped, but he was indicted by a federal grand jury for illegal reentry into the United States. Before trial, Jose moved to suppress the fingerprints taken from him after his arrest by Detective Anderson. The government filed a motion requesting that Jose be compelled to provide another set of fingerprints to prove his identity at his trial. The court granted Jose's motion, but denied the government's motion, ruling that because of the "egregious and race-based illegal arrest" the government would not be able to introduce the compelled set of fingerprints at Jose's trial.

Were these rulings correct?

13B–4: On May 23, the Cedar Rapids Police Department (CRPD) received word from Chicago officers that Mark Lanell, a suspect in a shooting death in Chicago the day before, could be on his way to Cedar Rapids on a particular bus. Three CRPD officers met the bus upon its arrival in Cedar Rapids. Among others, two African-American males not matching Lanell's description exited the bus, and were not stopped. Craig then exited the bus. Officers thought that he matched a photograph they had of Lanell. They approached and handcuffed him, then performed a pat-down search. An officer felt a metal object and what he believed to be a large bundle of currency in Craig's front pants pockets, and left them where they were. He also found some paperwork in Craig's back left pocket, which he left there.

Craig told officers his name was Tom Donald (his brother's name) and said he did not have any identification. He said he was unemployed and did not know his Social Security number. He gave his address as being in an affluent Chicago suburb. The officers did not believe him. They asked if he had any relatives they could contact to confirm his identity. He gave a phone number but no name for his mother and said his brother, "Craig," also lived in Chicago. After he denied consent for officers to search his person and his bag, an officer reached into his back pocket, and pulled out a bus ticket assigned to "Donald, C."

Officers ran a search on both Craig and Tom Donald's names. They discovered a description of Tom Donald that did not match the man they had handcuffed. They also learned of an outstanding arrest warrant for Craig Donald. The officers then came up with a plan. One officer began to walk away while another officer remained with Craig. The officer who was walking away suddenly called out "Craig!" According to the officers, Craig reacted by "snapping his neck towards our direction looking at us, acknowledging the word 'Craig.'" After being confronted with his reaction, Craig admitted that he was indeed Craig Donald and had a warrant outstanding. He was then arrested on the warrant and for providing false information to a police officer.

Incident to the arrest, officers subsequently searched Craig and his bag, and found two tin-foil wrapped objects in a pair of brown shoes. The objects turned out to be 240 grams of crack cocaine. The encounter had taken about 10 minutes. Craig was charged with possession with the intention of distributing 50 grams or more of crack cocaine. At a hearing on Craig's motion to suppress the bus ticket found in his back pocket, he testified that his head had not snapped around when the officer called out "Craig!" He asserted that he had merely turned to the other officer and asked, "What did he say?"

What arguments should Craig make in support of his motion to suppress the ticket? How should the government respond? How should the judge rule?

13B–5: Officer Gregory of the Gardens Police Department was on patrol in the early morning of October 19. He encountered a white Ford truck driven by Johnny. Officer Gregory searched the license plate number on his computer and discovered that the registered owner of the truck was deceased. When Johnny failed to properly signal a turn, Officer Gregory stopped the truck and asked Johnny for his driver's license. Johnny replied that it had been suspended. He showed Gregory a state identification card. Officer Gregory then searched Johnny's license history and learned that his license had been suspended six times and was currently suspended. He issued Johnny a traffic citation for driving with a suspended license, and decided that he might well arrest Johnny for the infraction. Gregory, however, did not execute the arrest immediately.

Officer Gregory approached Johnny's truck to determine if anyone else was inside. While peering inside the truck, he noticed an item wrapped in a clean white cloth. He removed the cloth and discovered a sawed-off shotgun. Officer Gregory then arrested Johnny. After the arrest, he conducted a detailed inventory search of the truck, including its bed and containers. Officer Gregory further researched the truck by computer, but he was unable to find another registered owner. About 20 minutes after he inventoried the truck, Officer Gregory completed a vehicle storage receipt and requested that the truck be towed. He marked "license suspended" as the reason.

A grand jury indicted Johnny on charges of possessing a firearm as a felon and knowingly possessing an unregistered firearm. Before trial, Johnny moved to suppress the shotgun as the fruit of an unconstitutional search.

Should the trial court exclude the shotgun from Johnny's trial?

13B–6: In May, a confidential informant told Drug Enforcement Administration (DEA) special agent James that he had known a person named Manny for approximately six months and that he had heard from others on the street that Manny was "involved in a narcotics distribution operation." The informant described Manny. He also informed James that Manny had been in jail for a violent crime, that he kept weapons, and that he ran his drug business from an apartment at 158 East 119th Street.

A few weeks later, the informant told James that he had visited Manny at his apartment on 119th Street in order to discuss a purchase of cocaine. He gave James a telephone number where Manny could be reached. When James checked the number, he found that it was registered to a woman who resided at 158 119th Street, apartment 4F.

In mid-June, the informant told James that Manny had a kilogram of cocaine at his apartment and wanted to sell it "right away." The next day, James and other agents met at DEA headquarters. When he arrived, James was told that Special Agent Neimer had already gone to the United States Attorney's office to prepare an application for a search warrant. Neimer arrived at the U.S. Attorney's office around 12:30 p.m. At 2:30 p.m., James and a team of DEA agents went to the apartment building at 158 119th Street to maintain surveillance until a warrant was issued. Neimer was supposed to call James when the warrant was procured.

Around 3:00 p.m., James began to worry that Manny would leave or become aware of their presence because the agents were "white people" who "stuck out like a sore thumb." He decided that they should enter the apartment. In the lobby of the building, the agents encountered Roland, the building superintendent. Roland agreed to accompany them to Manny's apartment. After Roland knocked on the door of 4F and identified himself, Manny opened the door and saw the DEA agents. He tried to close the door again, but the agents forced their way inside and handcuffed him. While sweeping the apartment for security purposes, the agents found cocaine and automatic weapon ammunition.

Once the sweep was completed, James received a call from Neimer, who was still at the U.S. Attorney's office. To complete the warrant application, Neimer needed to know how many times the informant had met with Manny. James gave Neimer the information, then told him that they had already entered the apartment. James then told Manny that a warrant was being obtained and that the "best thing [he] could do to help [him]self was to consent to a search prior to the arrival of the warrant." Manny consented to a search. The agents found nine weapons, a silencer, drug paraphernalia, ammunition, and a kilogram of cocaine in the apartment.

At approximately 3:30, James called Neimer and informed him that Manny had consented to a search. At that point, Neimer stopped working on the warrant application. Manny was charged with narcotics and weapons offenses.

Will the items found in the apartment be admissible at Manny's trial?

13B–7: On June 2, at about 5:30 p.m., State Trooper John Thompson stopped Len on the interstate for driving with a cracked windshield and broken taillight. When Thompson asked for his license, Len said he did not have it. Thompson understood Len to mean that he was not carrying it with him. Len also was unable to produce proof of insurance. He did provide a state welfare identification card bearing his name and photograph. Thompson recognized the name on the card because he had seen it when he was employed with a jail in the vicinity. However, he could not recall the nature of Len's offense. Because the card provided by Len was not sufficient identification for purposes of the traffic stop, Thompson asked him to come back to his patrol car so he could run a computer check on Len's driving record. Len complied with the request.

Because he intended to put Len in the backseat of the patrol car, Officer Thompson patted him down for weapons. He found a loaded, semi-automatic handgun in Len's pants pocket, arrested Len for carrying a concealed weapon, and handcuffed him. He then removed Len's wallet to locate additional identification and found inside a driver's license with the name "George Roper" and Len's photograph. Thompson placed Len in the back of his car and asked him some routine identification questions. Len volunteered that he had a felony record, whereupon Thompson remembered that Len had been in the jail for a drive-by shooting. He ran a computer check on Len, learning that he did not have a valid driver's license. Under applicable state law, an officer must arrest a suspect for a misdemeanor when it "reasonably appears to the officer that arrest or detention is necessary to prevent further criminal conduct."

Len was charged with being a felon in possession of a firearm. He moved to suppress the gun, contending that the patdown violated his Fourth Amendment rights.

If the trial court agrees that the patdown violated Len's rights, should the gun be suppressed?

13B–8: Around 8:30 a.m., on June 20, a highway patrol officer stopped Mr. and Mrs. Ham as they were driving a rental car east through Missouri. Mr. Ham had been driving in the passing lane of the interstate without changing into the center or left lane, and traffic had begun to back up behind him. When the officer asked Mr. Ham for identification, Mr. Ham gave him a state identification card and admitted that his California driver's license had been suspended. Ham explained that his wife, who was sitting next to him in the passenger's seat, had been driving. He had taken over, however, because she had grown tired.

The officer took Mr. Ham back to his patrol car while Mrs. Ham waited in the rental car. He checked to make sure that Mrs. Ham's driver's license was valid. He also examined the Hams' car rental agreement, learning that the vehicle had been rented in Las Vegas in Mrs. Ham's name. After he wrote a ticket and summons for Mr. Ham, the officer asked him why he and his wife had rented a car in Las Vegas when they lived in California. Mr. Ham said that flying to Las Vegas and renting a car there was less expensive than renting a car in California.

The officer then returned to the rental car to speak with Mrs. Ham, leaving Mr. Ham by the front door of his patrol car. He told Mrs. Ham that she would have to drive. As she slid over into the driver's seat, she seemed very nervous. The officer motioned to Mr. Ham to return to the rental car, telling him that he was "free to go." He turned back to Mrs. Ham and asked whether there were any drugs or guns in the car. When she said "No," he asked if he could search the vehicle to make sure she was telling the truth. Mrs. Ham agreed to the search and gave the officer the keys to the trunk. Upon opening the trunk, the officer found several pieces of luggage, a box of shirts, a briefcase, and a silver garment bag. Working his way toward the front of the trunk, he found a brown garment bag. When he felt the outside of the bag, he detected a hard rectangular object inside. He opened the garment bag and pulled out a black jacket. Inside the jacket was a large manila envelope, stapled shut.

At that point, Mr. Ham, who had walked back to the rental car, was standing near the open trunk. The officer asked him what was in the envelope, and Ham said he didn't know. The officer asked him if the garment bag was his, and Ham acknowledged that it was. The officer asked twice if he could open the envelope, but Ham simply stared at the ground. The officer told him that he could answer "yes" or "no," and Ham said that he did not want to say yes. The officer said that he thought the envelope contained drugs and that he was going to call for a drug dog to sniff it. Ham replied that he did not want his wife to get in trouble. During further exchanges with the officer, he admitted that there was "contraband" in the envelope. Upon being asked again, Ham consented to a search of the envelope. Inside were four packages of cocaine.

Prior to trial for possession of cocaine with intent to distribute it, Ham moved to suppress the contraband and the statements he made to the officer. The trial judge suppressed the statements, but permitted the government to introduce the cocaine.

Did the trial court rule correctly?

13B–9: At 9:00 p.m., Officer Rattman, while on routine patrol, noticed a vehicle without an illuminated rear license plate, a violation of state law. Rattman stopped the vehicle, which pulled into a grocery store parking lot, stopping between two rows of parking spaces but not in a designated spot. The car was occupied by the driver, Dwayne Wright; a front-seat passenger, Sierra Holliday, who owned the car; and in the back seat, Holliday's three-year-old child. Rattman asked Wright for his license, but Wright replied that he did not have it in his possession. When Rattman asked him for his name, Wright gave a name that Rattman could not confirm. Based on his nervous demeanor and refusal to identify himself, Rattman removed Wright from the car, handcuffed him, and placed him under arrest. ("Intentionally refusing to provide one's name or license to a law enforcement officer who has stopped the person for an infraction" is a Class C misdemeanor.)

In the meantime, Officer James arrived on the scene and removed Holliday and her child from the car. After Wright's arrest, James searched the back seat and found a loaded Ruger semi-automatic pistol, which he removed and secured. He completed the search, finding nothing else other than some old clothing inside the vehicle. Because Wright was under arrest and Holliday did not have a driver's license, pursuant to departmental policy, Rattman arranged to have the car towed. Also in accord with policy, James searched the car prior to the towing. He found nothing of value and filled out a "tow slip," listing the reason for impoundment as "arrest."

Because Holliday lacked the funds to reclaim her vehicle from impoundment, upon learning that it was going to be towed she had asked the officers to allow her to have someone else move it. The officers had refused her request. She later stated that she would have allowed anyone, even a stranger, to move the car in order to avoid the impoundment. Wright was subsequently charged with "possession of a firearm by a felon." He moved to suppress the gun found in the vehicle.

What arguments should the government make against suppression of the gun? How should the court rule?

[C] The "Attenuation" Doctrine

Wong Sun v. United States
United States Supreme Court
371 U.S. 471, 83 S. Ct. 407, 9 L. Ed. 2d 441 (1963)

Mr. Justice Brennan delivered the opinion of the Court.

. . . .

About 2 a.m. on the morning of June 4, 1959, federal narcotics agents in San Francisco, after having had one Hom Way under surveillance for six weeks, arrested him and found heroin in his possession. Hom Way, who had not before been an informant, stated after his arrest that he had bought an ounce of heroin the night before from one known to him only as "Blackie Toy," proprietor of a laundry on Leavenworth Street.

About 6 a.m. that morning six or seven federal agents went to a laundry at 1733 Leavenworth Street. The sign above the door of this establishment said "Oye's Laundry." It was operated by the petitioner James Wah Toy. There is, however, nothing in the record which identifies James Wah Toy and "Blackie Toy" as the same person. The other federal officers remained nearby out of sight while Agent Alton Wong, who was of Chinese ancestry, rang the bell. When petitioner Toy appeared and opened the door, Agent Wong told him that he was calling for laundry and dry cleaning. Toy replied that he didn't open until 8 o'clock and told the agent to come back at that time. Toy started to close the door. Agent Wong thereupon took his badge from his pocket and said, "I am a federal narcotics agent." Toy immediately "slammed the door and started running" down the hallway through the laundry to his living quarters at the back where his wife and child were sleeping in a bedroom. Agent Wong and the other federal officers broke open the door and followed Toy down the hallway to the living quarters and into the bedroom. Toy reached into a nightstand drawer. Agent Wong thereupon drew his pistol, pulled Toy's hand out of the drawer, placed him under arrest and handcuffed him. There was nothing in the drawer and a search of the premises uncovered no narcotics.

One of the agents said to Toy ". . . [Hom Way] says he got narcotics from you." Toy responded, "No, I haven't been selling any narcotics at all. However, I do know somebody who has." When asked who that was, Toy said, "I only know him as Johnny. I don't know his last name." However, Toy described a house on Eleventh Avenue where he said Johnny lived; he also described a bedroom in the house where he said "Johnny kept about a piece" of heroin, and where he and Johnny had smoked some of the drug the night before. The agents left immediately for Eleventh Avenue and located the house. They entered and found one Johnny Yee in the bedroom. After a discussion with the agents, Yee took from a bureau drawer several tubes containing in all just less than one ounce of heroin, and surrendered them. Within the hour Yee and Toy were taken to the Office of the Bureau of Narcotics. Yee there stated that the heroin had been brought to him some four days earlier by petitioner Toy and another Chinese known to him only as "Sea Dog."

Toy was questioned as to the identity of "Sea Dog" and said that "Sea Dog" was Wong Sun. Some agents, including Agent Alton Wong, took Toy to Wong Sun's neighborhood where Toy pointed out a multifamily dwelling where he said Wong Sun lived. Agent Wong rang a downstairs door bell and a buzzer sounded, opening the door. The officer identified himself as a narcotics agent to a woman on the landing and asked "for Mr. Wong." The woman was the wife of petitioner Wong Sun. She said that Wong Sun was "in the back room sleeping." Alton Wong and some six other officers climbed the stairs and entered the apartment. One of the officers went into the back room and brought petitioner Wong Sun from the bedroom in handcuffs. A thorough search of the apartment followed, but no narcotics were discovered.

Petitioner Toy and Johnny Yee were arraigned before a United States Commissioner on June 4 on a complaint charging a violation of 21 U.S.C. § 174. Later that day, each was released on his own recognizance. Petitioner Wong Sun was arraigned on a similar complaint filed the next day and was also released on his own recognizance. Within a few days, both petitioners and Yee were interrogated at the office of the Narcotics Bureau by Agent William Wong, also of Chinese ancestry. The agent advised each of the three of his right to withhold information which might be used against him, and stated to each that he was entitled to the advice of counsel, though it does not appear that any attorney was present during the questioning of any of the three. The officer also explained to each that no promises or offers of immunity or leniency were being or could be made.

The agent interrogated each of the three separately. After each had been interrogated the agent prepared a statement in English from rough notes. The agent read petitioner Toy's statement to him in English and interpreted certain portions of it for him in Chinese. Toy also read the statement in English aloud to the agent, said there were corrections to be made, and made the corrections in his own hand. Toy would not sign the statement, however; in the agent's words "he wanted to know first if the other persons involved in the case had signed theirs." Wong Sun had considerable difficulty understanding the statement in English and the agent restated its substance in Chinese. Wong Sun refused to sign the statement although he admitted the accuracy of its contents.

Hom Way did not testify at petitioners' trial. The Government offered Johnny Yee as its principal witness but excused him after he invoked the privilege against self-incrimination and flatly repudiated the statement he had given to Agent William Wong. That statement was not offered in evidence nor was any testimony elicited from him identifying either petitioner as the source of the heroin in his possession, or otherwise tending to support the charges against the petitioners.

The statute expressly provides that proof of the accused's possession of the drug will support a conviction under the statute unless the accused satisfactorily explains the possession. The Government's evidence tending to prove the petitioners' possession (the petitioners offered no exculpatory testimony) consisted of four items which the trial court admitted over timely objections that they were inadmissible as "fruits" of unlawful arrests or of attendant searches: (1) the statements made orally by petitioner Toy in his bedroom at the time of his arrest; (2) the heroin surrendered to the agents by Johnny Yee; (3) petitioner Toy's pretrial unsigned statement; and (4) petitioner Wong Sun's similar statement. The dispute below and here has centered around the correctness of the rulings of the trial judge allowing these items in evidence.

. . . .

I.

The Court of Appeals found there was neither reasonable grounds nor probable cause for Toy's arrest. Giving due weight to that finding, we think it is amply justified by the facts clearly shown on this record.

. . . .

It remains to be seen what consequences flow from this conclusion.

II.

It is conceded that Toy's declarations in his bedroom are to be excluded if they are held to be "fruits" of the agents' unlawful action.

In order to make effective the fundamental constitutional guarantees of sanctity of the home and inviolability of the person, this Court held nearly half a century ago that evidence seized during an unlawful search could not constitute proof against the victim of the search. *Weeks v. United States*, 232 U.S. 383, 34 S. Ct. 341, 58 L. Ed. 652. The exclusionary prohibition extends as well to the indirect as the direct products of such invasions. *Silverthorne Lumber Co. v. United States*, 251 U.S. 385, 40 S. Ct. 182, 64 L. Ed. 319. . . .

The exclusionary rule has traditionally barred from trial physical, tangible materials obtained either during or as a direct result of an unlawful invasion. It follows from our holding in *Silverman v. United States*, 365 U.S. 505, 81 S. Ct. 679, 5 L. Ed. 2d 734, that the Fourth Amendment may protect against the overhearing of verbal statements as well as against the more traditional seizure of "papers and effects." Similarly, testimony as to matters observed during an unlawful invasion has been excluded in order to enforce the basic constitutional policies. Thus, verbal evidence which derives so immediately from an unlawful entry and an unauthorized arrest as the officers' action in the present case is no less the "fruit" of official illegality than the more common tangible fruits of the unwarranted intrusion. Nor do the policies underlying the exclusionary rule invite any logical distinction between physical and verbal evidence. Either in terms of deterring lawless conduct by federal officers or of closing the doors of the federal courts to any use of evidence unconstitutionally obtained, the danger in relaxing the exclusionary rules in the case of verbal evidence would seem too great to warrant introducing such a distinction.

The Government argues that Toy's statements to the officers in his bedroom, although closely consequent upon the invasion which we hold unlawful, were nevertheless admissible because they resulted from "an intervening independent act of a free will." This contention, however, takes insufficient account of the circumstances. Six or seven officers had broken the door and followed on Toy's heels into the bedroom where his wife and child were sleeping. He had been almost immediately handcuffed and arrested. Under such circumstances it is unreasonable to infer that Toy's response was sufficiently an act of free will to purge the primary taint of the unlawful invasion.

The Government also contends that Toy's declarations should be admissible because they were ostensibly exculpatory rather than incriminating. There are two answers to this argument. First, the statements soon turned out to be incriminating, for they led directly to the evidence which implicated Toy. Second, when circumstances are shown such as those which induced these declarations, it is immaterial whether the declarations be termed "exculpatory." Thus we find no substantial reason to omit Toy's declarations from the protection of the exclusionary rule.

III.

We now consider whether the exclusion of Toy's declarations requires also the exclusion of the narcotics taken from Yee, to which those declarations led the police. The prosecutor candidly told the trial court that "we wouldn't have found those drugs except that Mr. Toy helped us to." Hence this is not the case envisioned by this Court where the exclusionary rule has no application because the Government learned of the evidence "from an independent source," *Silverthorne Lumber Co. v. United States*, 251 U.S. 385, 392, 40 S. Ct. 182, 183, 64 L. Ed. 319; nor is this a case in which the connection between the lawless conduct of the police and the discovery of the challenged evidence has "become so attenuated as to dissipate the taint." *Nardone v. United States*, 308 U.S. 338, 341, 60 S. Ct. 266, 268, 84 L. Ed. 307. We need not hold that all evidence is "fruit of the poisonous tree" simply because it would not have come to light but for the illegal actions of the police. Rather, the more apt question in such a case is "whether, granting establishment of the primary illegality, the evidence to which instant objection is made has been come at by exploitation of that illegality or instead by means sufficiently distinguishable to be purged of the primary taint." Maguire, EVIDENCE OF GUILT, 221 (1959). We think it clear that the narcotics were "come at by the exploitation of that illegality" and hence that they may not be used against Toy.

. . . .

V.

We turn now to the case of the other petitioner, Wong Sun. We have no occasion to disagree with the finding of the Court of Appeals that his arrest, also, was without probable cause or reasonable grounds. At all events no evidentiary consequences turn upon that question. For Wong Sun's unsigned confession was not the fruit of that arrest, and was therefore properly admitted at trial. On the evidence that Wong Sun had been released on his own recognizance after a lawful arraignment, and had returned voluntarily several days later to make the statement, we hold that the connection between the arrest and the statement had "become so attenuated as to dissipate the taint." *Nardone v. United States*, 308 U.S. 338, 341, 60 S. Ct. 266, 84 L. Ed. 307. The fact that the statement was unsigned, whatever bearing this may have upon its weight and credibility, does not render it inadmissible; Wong Sun understood and adopted its substance, though he could not comprehend the English words. The petitioner has never suggested any impropriety in the interrogation itself which would require the exclusion of this statement.

We must then consider the admissibility of the narcotics surrendered by Yee. Our holding, that this ounce of heroin was inadmissible against Toy does not compel a like result with respect to Wong Sun. The exclusion of the narcotics as to Toy was required solely by their tainted relationship to information unlawfully obtained from Toy, and not by any official impropriety connected with their surrender by Yee. The seizure of this heroin invaded no right of privacy of person or premises which would entitle Wong Sun to object to its use at his trial.

. . . .

The judgment of the Court of Appeals is reversed and the case is remanded to the District Court for further proceedings consistent with this opinion.

It is so ordered.

[The concurring opinion of Mr. Justice Douglas has been omitted.]

[The dissenting opinion of Mr. Justice Clark has been omitted.]

Brown v. Illinois

United States Supreme Court

422 U.S. 590, 95 S. Ct. 2254, 45 L. Ed. 2d 416 (1975)

Mr. Justice Blackmun delivered the opinion of the Court.

This case lies at the crossroads of the Fourth and the Fifth Amendments. Petitioner was arrested without probable cause and without a warrant. He was given, in full, the warnings prescribed by *Miranda v. Arizona*, 384 U.S. 436, 86 S. Ct. 1602, 16 L. Ed. 2d 694 (1966). Thereafter, while in custody, he made two inculpatory statements. The issue is whether evidence of those statements was properly admitted, or should have been excluded, in petitioner's subsequent trial for murder in state court. Expressed another way, the issue is whether the statements were to be excluded as the fruit of the illegal arrest, or were admissible because the giving of the *Miranda* warnings sufficiently attenuated the taint of the arrest. *See Wong Sun v. United States*, 371 U.S. 471, 83 S. Ct. 407, 9 L. Ed. 2d 441 (1963). The Fourth Amendment, of course, has been held to be applicable to the states through the Fourteenth Amendment. *Mapp v. Ohio*, 367 U.S. 643, 81 S. Ct. 1684, 6 L. Ed. 2d 1081 (1961).

I

As petitioner Richard Brown was climbing the last of the stairs leading to the rear entrance of his Chicago apartment in the early evening of May 13, 1968, he happened to glance at the window near the door. He saw, pointed at him through the window, a revolver held by a stranger who was inside the apartment. The man said: "Don't move, you are under arrest." Another man, also with a gun, came up behind Brown and repeated the statement that he was under arrest. It was about 7:45 p.m. The two men turned out to be Detectives William Nolan and William Lenz of the Chicago police force. It is not clear from the record exactly when they advised Brown of their identity, but it is not disputed that they broke into his apartment, searched it, and then arrested Brown, all without probable cause and without any warrant, when he arrived. They later testified that they made the arrest for the purpose of questioning Brown as part of their investigation of the murder of a man named Roger Corpus.

Corpus was murdered one week earlier, on May 6, with a .38-caliber revolver in his Chicago West Side second-floor apartment. Shortly thereafter, Detective Lenz obtained petitioner's name, among others, from Corpus' brother. Petitioner and the others were identified as acquaintances of the victim, not as suspects.[1]

On the day of petitioner's arrest, Detectives Lenz and Nolan, armed with a photograph of Brown, and another officer arrived at petitioner's apartment about 5 p.m. While the third officer covered the front entrance downstairs, the two detectives broke into Brown's apartment and searched it. Lenz then positioned himself near the rear door and watched through the adjacent window which opened onto the back porch. Nolan sat near the front door. He described the situation at the later suppression hearing:

> After we were there for a while, Detective Lenz told me that somebody was coming up the back stairs. I walked out the front door through the hall and around the corner, and I stayed there behind a door leading on to the back porch. At this time I heard Detective Lenz say, "Don't move, you are under arrest." I looked out. I saw Mr. Brown backing away from the window. I walked up behind him, I told him he is under arrest, come back inside the apartment with us.

---

1. The brother, however, when asked at the trial whether any of the victim's family suggested to the police that petitioner was possibly responsible for the victim's death, answered: "Nobody asked."

As both officers held him at gunpoint, the three entered the apartment. Brown was ordered to stand against the wall and was searched. No weapon was found. He was asked his name. When he denied being Richard Brown, Detective Lenz showed him the photograph, informed him that he was under arrest for the murder of Roger Corpus, handcuffed him, and escorted him to the squad car.

The two detectives took petitioner to the Maxwell Street police station. During the 20-minute drive Nolan again asked Brown, who then was sitting with him in the back seat of the car, whether his name was Richard Brown and whether he owned a 1966 Oldsmobile. Brown alternately evaded these questions or answered them falsely. Upon arrival at the station house Brown was placed in the second-floor central interrogation room. The room was bare, except for a table and four chairs. He was left alone, apparently without handcuffs, for some minutes while the officers obtained the file on the Corpus homicide. They returned with the file, sat down at the table, one across from Brown and the other to his left, and spread the file on the table in front of him.

The officers warned Brown of his rights under *Miranda.* They then informed him that they knew of an incident that had occurred in a poolroom on May 5, when Brown, angry at having been cheated at dice, fired a shot from a revolver into the ceiling. Brown answered: "Oh, you know about that." Lenz informed him that a bullet had been obtained from the ceiling of the poolroom and had been taken to the crime laboratory to be compared with bullets taken from Corpus' body. Brown responded: "Oh, you know that, too." At this point — it was about 8:45 p.m. — Lenz asked Brown whether he wanted to talk about the Corpus homicide. Petitioner answered that he did. For the next 20 to 25 minutes Brown answered questions put to him by Nolan, as Lenz typed.

This questioning produced a two-page statement in which Brown acknowledged that he and a man named Jimmy Claggett visited Corpus on the evening of May 5; that the three for some time sat drinking and smoking marihuana; that Claggett ordered him at gunpoint to bind Corpus' hands and feet with cord from the headphone of a stereo set; and that Claggett, using a .38-caliber revolver sold to him by Brown, shot Corpus three times through a pillow. The statement was signed by Brown.

About 9:30 p.m. the two detectives and Brown left the station house to look for Claggett in an area of Chicago Brown knew him to frequent. They made a tour of that area but did not locate their quarry. They then went to police headquarters where they endeavored, without success, to obtain a photograph of Claggett. They resumed their search — it was now about 11 p.m. — and they finally observed Claggett crossing at an intersection. Lenz and Nolan arrested him. All four, the two detectives and the two arrested men, returned to the Maxwell Street station about 12:15 a.m.

Brown was again placed in the interrogation room. He was given coffee and was left alone, for the most part, until 2 a.m. when Assistant State's Attorney Crilly arrived.

Crilly, too, informed Brown of his *Miranda* rights. After a half hour's conversation, a court reporter appeared. Once again the *Miranda* warnings were given: "I read him the card." Crilly told him that he "was sure he would be charged with murder." Brown gave a second statement, providing a factual account of the murder substantially in accord with his first statement, but containing factual inaccuracies with respect to his personal background. When the statement was completed, at about 3 a.m., Brown refused to sign it. An hour later he made a phone call to his mother. At 9:30 that morning, about 14 hours after his arrest, he was taken before a magistrate.

On June 20 Brown and Claggett were jointly indicted by a Cook County grand jury for Corpus' murder. Prior to trial, petitioner moved to suppress the two statements he had made. He alleged that his arrest and detention had been illegal and that the statements were taken from him in violation of his constitutional rights. After a hearing, the motion was denied.

The case proceeded to trial. The State introduced evidence of both statements. Detective Nolan testified as to the contents of the first, but the writing itself was not placed in evidence. The second statement was introduced and was read to the jury in full. Brown was 23 at the time of the trial.

The jury found petitioner guilty of murder. He was sentenced to imprisonment for not less than 15 years nor more than 30 years.

On appeal, the Supreme Court of Illinois affirmed the judgment of conviction. The court refused to accept the State's argument that Brown's arrest was lawful. "Upon review of the record, we conclude that the testimony fails to show that at the time of his apprehension there was probable cause for defendant's arrest, [and] that his arrest was, therefore, unlawful." But it went on to hold in two significant and unembellished sentences:

> [W]e conclude that the giving of the *Miranda* warnings, in the first instance by the police officer and in the second by the assistant State's Attorney, served to break the causal connection between the illegal arrest and the giving of the statements, and that defendant's act in making the statements was "sufficiently an act of free will to purge the primary taint of the unlawful invasion." (*Wong Sun v. United States*, 371 U.S. 471, at 486, 83 S. Ct. at 416, 9 L. Ed. 2d 441.) We hold, therefore, that the circuit court did not err in admitting the statements into evidence.

Aside from its reliance upon the presence of the *Miranda* warnings, no specific aspect of the record or of the circumstances was cited by the court in support of its conclusion. The court, in other words, appears to have held that the *Miranda* warnings in and of themselves broke the causal chain so that any subsequent statement, even one induced by the continuing effects of unconstitutional custody, was admissible so long as, in the traditional sense, it was voluntary and not coerced in violation of the Fifth and Fourteenth Amendments.

Because of our concern about the implication of our holding in *Wong Sun v. United States*, 371 U.S. 471, 83 S. Ct. 407, 9 L. Ed. 2d 441 (1963), to the facts of Brown's case, we granted certiorari.

II

In *Wong Sun*, the Court pronounced the principles to be applied where the issue is whether statements and other evidence obtained after an illegal arrest or search should be excluded. . . .

This Court ruled that Toy's declarations and the contraband taken from Yee were the fruits of the agents' illegal action and should not have been admitted as evidence against Toy. It held that the statement did not result from "an intervening independent act of a free will," and that it was not "sufficiently an act of free will to purge the primary taint of the unlawful invasion." With respect to Wong Sun's confession, however, the Court held that in the light of his lawful arraignment and release on his own recognizance, and of his return voluntarily several days later to make the statement, the connection between his unlawful arrest and the statement "had 'become so attenuated as to dissipate the taint.' *Nardone v. United States*, 308 U.S. 338, 341, 60 S. Ct. 266, 84 L. Ed. 307. . . .'"

The exclusionary rule thus was applied in *Wong Sun primarily* to protect Fourth Amendment rights. Protection of the Fifth Amendment right against self-incrimination was not the Court's paramount concern there. To the extent that the question whether Toy's statement was voluntary was considered, it was only to judge whether it "was *sufficiently* an act of free will to purge the primary taint of the unlawful invasion."

The Court in *Wong Sun*, as is customary, emphasized that application of the exclusionary rule on Toy's behalf protected Fourth Amendment guarantees in two respects: "in terms of deterring lawless conduct by federal officers," and by "closing the doors of the federal courts to any use of evidence unconstitutionally obtained." These considerations of deterrence and of judicial integrity, by now, have become rather commonplace in the Court's cases. "The rule is calculated to prevent, not to repair. Its purpose is to deter — to compel respect for the constitutional guaranty in the only effectively available way — by removing the incentive to disregard it." *Elkins v. United States*, 364 U.S. 206, 217, 80 S. Ct. 1437, 1444, 4 L. Ed. 2d 1669 (1960). But "[d]espite its broad deterrent purpose, the exclusionary rule has never been interpreted to proscribe the use of illegally seized evidence in all proceedings or against all persons." *United States v. Calandra*, 414 U.S., at 348, 94 S. Ct. at 620.

III

The Illinois courts refrained from resolving the question, as apt here as it was in *Wong Sun*, whether Brown's statements were obtained by exploitation of the illegality of his arrest. They assumed that the *Miranda* warnings, by themselves, assured that the statements (verbal acts, as contrasted with physical evidence) were of sufficient free will as to purge the primary taint of the unlawful arrest. *Wong Sun*, of course, preceded *Miranda*.

This Court has described the *Miranda* warnings as a "prophylactic rule," *Michigan v. Payne*, 412 U.S. 47, 53, 93 S. Ct. 1966, 1969, 36 L. Ed. 2d 736 (1973), and as a "procedural safeguard," *Miranda v. Arizona*, 384 U.S., at 457, 478, 86 S. Ct. at 1629, employed to protect Fifth Amendment rights against "the compulsion inherent in custodial surroundings." *Id.*, at 458, 86 S. Ct. at 1619. The function of the warnings relates to the Fifth Amendment's guarantee against coerced self-incrimination, and the exclusion of a statement made in the absence of the warnings, it is said, serves to deter the taking of an incriminating statement without first informing the individual of his Fifth Amendment rights.

Although, almost 90 years ago, the Court observed that the Fifth Amendment is in "intimate relation" with the Fourth, *Boyd v. United States*, 116 U.S. 616, 633, 6 S. Ct. 524, 533, 29 L. Ed. 746 (1886), the *Miranda* warnings thus far have not been regarded as a means either of remedying or deterring violations of Fourth Amendment rights. Frequently, as here, rights under the two Amendments may appear to coalesce since "the 'unreasonable searches and seizures' condemned in the Fourth Amendment are almost always made for the purpose of compelling a man to give evidence against himself, which in criminal cases is condemned in the Fifth Amendment." *Id.*; *see Mapp v. Ohio*, 367 U.S., at 646 n. 5, 81 S. Ct. at 1687. The exclusionary rule, however, when utilized to effectuate the Fourth Amendment, serves interests and policies that are distinct from those it serves under the Fifth. It is directed at all unlawful searches and seizures, and not merely those that happen to produce incriminating material or testimony as fruits. In short, exclusion of a confession made without *Miranda* warnings might be regarded as necessary to effectuate the Fifth Amendment, but it would not be sufficient fully to protect the Fourth. *Miranda* warnings, and the exclusion of a confession made without them, do not alone sufficiently deter a Fourth Amendment violation.[6]

Thus, even if the statements in this case were found to be voluntary under the Fifth Amendment, the Fourth Amendment issue remains. In order for the causal chain, between the illegal arrest and the statements made subsequent thereto, to be broken, *Wong Sun* requires not merely that the statement meet the Fifth Amendment standard of voluntariness but that it be "sufficiently an act of free will to purge the primary taint." 371 U.S. at 486, 83 S. Ct. at 416. *Wong Sun* thus mandates consideration of a statement's admissibility in light of the distinct policies and interests of the Fourth Amendment.

If *Miranda* warnings, by themselves, were held to attenuate the taint of an unconstitutional arrest, regardless of how wanton and purposeful the Fourth Amendment violation, the effect of the exclusionary rule would be substantially diluted. Arrests made without warrant or without probable cause, for questioning or "investigation," would be encouraged by the knowledge that evidence derived therefrom could well be made admissible at trial by the simple expedient of giving *Miranda* warnings. Any incentive to avoid Fourth Amendment violations would be eviscerated by making

---

6. The *Miranda* warnings in no way inform a person of his Fourth Amendment rights, including his right to be released from unlawful custody following an arrest made without a warrant or without probable cause.

the warnings, in effect, a "cure-all," and the constitutional guarantee against unlawful searches and seizures could be said to be reduced to "a form of words." *See Mapp v. Ohio*, 367 U.S., at 648, 81 S. Ct. at 1687.

It is entirely possible, of course, as the State here argues, that persons arrested illegally frequently may decide to confess, as an act of free will unaffected by the initial illegality. But the *Miranda* warnings, alone and *per se*, cannot always make the act sufficiently a product of free will to break, for Fourth Amendment purposes, the causal connection between the illegality and the confession. They cannot assure in every case that the Fourth Amendment violation has not been unduly exploited.

While we therefore reject the *per se* rule which the Illinois courts appear to have accepted, we also decline to adopt any alternative *per se* or "but for" rule. The petitioner himself professes not to demand so much. The question whether a confession is the product of a free will under *Wong Sun* must be answered on the facts of each case. No single fact is dispositive. The workings of the human mind are too complex, and the possibilities of misconduct too diverse, to permit protection of the Fourth Amendment to turn on such a talismanic test. The *Miranda* warnings are an important factor, to be sure, in determining whether the confession is obtained by exploitation of an illegal arrest. But they are not the only factor to be considered. The temporal proximity of the arrest and the confession, the presence of intervening circumstances, and, particularly, the purpose and flagrancy of the official misconduct are all relevant. The voluntariness of the statement is a threshold requirement. And the burden of showing admissibility rests, of course, on the prosecution.

IV

Although the Illinois courts failed to undertake the inquiry mandated by *Wong Sun* to evaluate the circumstances of this case in the light of the policy served by the exclusionary rule, the trial resulted in a record of amply sufficient detail and depth from which the determination may be made. We therefore decline the suggestion of the United States, as *amicus curiae*, to remand the case for further factual findings. We conclude that the State failed to sustain the burden of showing that the evidence in question was admissible under *Wong Sun*.

Brown's first statement was separated from his illegal arrest by less than two hours, and there was no intervening event of significance whatsoever. In its essentials, his situation is remarkably like that of James Wah Toy in *Wong Sun*.[11] We could hold Brown's first statement admissible only if we overrule *Wong Sun*. We decline to do so. And the second statement was clearly the result and the fruit of the first.[12]

---

11. The situation here is thus in dramatic contrast to that of Wong Sun himself. Wong Sun's confession, which the Court held admissible, came several days after the illegality, and was preceded by a lawful arraignment and a release from custody on his own recognizance.

12. The fact that Brown had made one statement, believed by him to be admissible, and his cooperation with the arresting and interrogating officers in the search for Claggett, with his anticipation of leniency, bolstered the pressures for him to give the second, or at least vitiated any incentive on his part to avoid self-incrimination.

The illegality here, moreover, had a quality of purposefulness. The impropriety of the arrest was obvious; awareness of that fact was virtually conceded by the two detectives when they repeatedly acknowledged, in their testimony, that the purpose of their action was "for investigation" or for "questioning." The arrest, both in design and in execution, was investigatory. The detectives embarked upon this expedition for evidence in the hope that something might turn up. The manner in which Brown's arrest was effected gives the appearance of having been calculated to cause surprise, fright, and confusion.

We emphasize that our holding is a limited one. We decide only that the Illinois courts were in error in assuming that the *Miranda* warnings, by themselves, under *Wong Sun* always purge the taint of an illegal arrest.

The judgment of the Supreme Court of Illinois is reversed and the case is remanded for further proceedings not inconsistent with this opinion.

It is so ordered.

[The concurrence in the judgment of MR. JUSTICE WHITE has been omitted.]

MR. JUSTICE POWELL, with whom MR. JUSTICE REHNQUIST joins, concurring in part.

I join the Court insofar as it holds that the *per se* rule adopted by the Illinois Supreme Court for determining the admissibility of petitioner's two statements inadequately accommodates the diverse interests underlying the Fourth Amendment exclusionary rule. I would, however, remand the case for reconsideration under the general standards articulated in the Court's opinion and elaborated herein.

A

The issue presented in this case turns on proper application of the policies underlying the Fourth Amendment exclusionary rule, not on the Fifth Amendment or the prophylaxis added to that guarantee by *Miranda v. Arizona*, 384 U.S. 436, 86 S. Ct. 1602, 16 L. Ed. 2d 694 (1966). The Court recognized in *Wong Sun v. United States*, 371 U.S. 471, 83 S. Ct. 407, 9 L. Ed. 2d 441 (1963), that the Fourth Amendment exclusionary rule applies to statements obtained following an illegal arrest just as it does to tangible evidence seized in a similar manner or obtained pursuant to an otherwise illegal search and seizure. *Wong Sun* squarely rejected, however, the suggestion that the admissibility of statements so obtained should be governed by a simple "but for" test that would render inadmissible all statements given subsequent to an illegal arrest. In a similar manner, the Court today refrains from according dispositive weight to the single factor of *Miranda* warnings. I agree with each holding. Neither of the rejected extremes adequately recognizes the competing considerations involved in a determination to exclude evidence after finding that official possession of that evidence was to some degree caused by a violation of the Fourth Amendment.

On this record, I cannot conclude as readily as the Court that admission of the statements here at issue would constitute an effective overruling of *Wong Sun*. Although *Wong Sun* establishes the boundaries within which this case must be decided, the incompleteness of the record leaves me uncertain that it compels the exclusion of petitioner's statements. The statements at issue in *Wong Sun* were on the temporal extremes in relation to the illegal arrest. . . .

Like most cases in which the admissibility of statements obtained subsequent to an illegal arrest is contested, this case concerns statements more removed than that of Toy from the time and circumstances of the illegal arrest. Petitioner made his first statement some two hours following his arrest, after he had been given *Miranda* warnings. The Court is correct in noting that no other significant intervening event altered the relationship established between petitioner and the officers by the illegal arrest. . . .

B

The Court's rejection in *Wong Sun* of a "but for" test, reaffirmed today, recognizes that in some circumstances strict adherence to the Fourth Amendment exclusionary rule imposes greater cost on the legitimate demands of law enforcement than can be justified by the rule's deterrent purposes. The notion of the "dissipation of the taint" attempts to mark the point at which the detrimental consequences of illegal police action become so attenuated that the deterrent effect of the exclusionary rule no longer justifies its cost. Application of the *Wong Sun* doctrine will generate fact-specific cases bearing distinct differences as well as similarities, and the question of attenuation inevitably is largely a matter of degree. The Court today identifies the general factors that the trial court must consider in making this determination. I think it appropriate, however, to attempt to articulate the possible relationships of those factors in particular, broad categories of cases.

All Fourth Amendment violations are, by constitutional definition, "unreasonable." There are, however, significant practical differences that distinguish among violations, differences that measurably assist in identifying the kinds of cases in which disqualifying the evidence is likely to serve the deterrent purposes of the exclusionary rule. In my view, the point at which the taint can be said to have dissipated should be related, in the absence of other controlling circumstances, to the nature of that taint.

That police have not succeeded in coercing the accused's confession through willful or negligent misuse of the power of arrest does not remove the fact that they may have tried. The impermissibility of the attempt, and the extent to which such attempts can be deterred by the use of the exclusionary rule, are of primary relevance in determining whether exclusion is an appropriate remedy. The basic purpose of the rule, briefly stated, is to remove possible motivations for illegal arrests. Given this purpose the notion of voluntariness has practical value in deciding whether the rule should apply to statements removed from the immediate circumstances of the illegal arrest. If an illegal arrest merely provides the occasion of initial contact between the police and the accused, and because of time or other intervening factors the accused's eventual statement is the product of his own reflection and free will, application of the exclusionary rule can serve little purpose: the police normally will not make an illegal arrest in the hope of eventually obtaining such a truly volunteered statement. In a similar manner, the role of the *Miranda* warnings in the *Wong Sun* inquiry is indirect. To the extent that they dissipate the psychological pressures of custodial interrogation, *Miranda* warnings serve to assure that the accused's decision to make a statement has been relatively unaffected by the preceding illegal arrest. Correspondingly, to the extent that the police perceive *Miranda* warnings to have this equalizing potential, their motivation to abuse the power of arrest is diminished. Bearing these considerations in mind, and recognizing that the deterrent value of the Fourth Amendment exclusionary rule is limited to certain kinds of police conduct, the following general categories can be identified.

Those most readily identifiable are on the extremes: the flagrantly abusive violation of Fourth Amendment rights, on the one hand, and "technical" Fourth Amendment violations, on the other. In my view, these extremes call for significantly different judicial responses.

I would require the clearest indication of attenuation in cases in which official conduct was flagrantly abusive of Fourth Amendment rights. If, for example, the factors relied on by the police in determining to make the arrest were so lacking in indicia of probable cause as to render official belief in its existence entirely unreasonable, or if the evidence clearly suggested that the arrest was effectuated as a pretext for collateral objectives, or the physical circumstances of the arrest unnecessarily intrusive on personal privacy, I would consider the equalizing potential of *Miranda* warnings rarely sufficient to dissipate the taint. In such cases the deterrent value of the exclusionary rule is most likely to be effective, and the corresponding mandate to preserve judicial integrity most clearly demands that the fruits of official misconduct be denied. I thus would require some demonstrably effective break in the chain of events leading from the illegal arrest to the statement, such as actual consultation with counsel or the accused's presentation before a magistrate for a determination of probable cause, before the taint can be deemed removed.

At the opposite end of the spectrum lie "technical" violations of Fourth Amendment rights where, for example, officers in good faith arrest an individual in reliance on a warrant later invalidated or pursuant to a statute that subsequently is declared unconstitutional. As we noted in *Michigan v. Tucker*, 417 U.S. 433, 447, 94 S. Ct. 2357, 2365, 41 L. Ed. 2d 182 (1974): "The deterrent purpose of the exclusionary rule necessarily assumes that the police have engaged in willful, or at the very least negligent, conduct which has deprived the defendant of some right." In cases in which this underlying premise is lacking, the deterrence rationale of the exclusionary rule does not obtain, and I can see no legitimate justification for depriving the prosecution of reliable and probative evidence. Thus, with the exception of statements given in the immediate circumstances of the illegal arrest—a constraint I think is imposed by existing exclusionary-rule law—I would not require more than proof that effective *Miranda* warnings were given and that the ensuing statement was voluntary in the Fifth Amendment sense. Absent aggravating circumstances, I would consider a statement given at the station house after one has been advised of *Miranda* rights to be sufficiently removed from the immediate circumstances of the illegal arrest to justify its admission at trial.

Between these extremes lies a wide range of situations that defy ready categorization, and I will not attempt to embellish on the factors set forth in the Court's opinion other than to emphasize that the *Wong Sun* inquiry always should be conducted with the deterrent purpose of the Fourth Amendment exclusionary rule sharply in focus. . . .

C

On the facts of record as I view them, it is possible that the police may have believed reasonably that there was probable cause for petitioner's arrest. Although the trial court conducted hearings on petitioner's motion to suppress and received his testimony and that of the arresting officers, its inquiry focused on determining whether petitioner's statements were preceded by adequate *Miranda* warnings and were made voluntarily. The court did not inquire into the possible justification, actual or perceived, for the arrest. . . .

. . . .

The trial court made no determination as to whether probable cause existed for petitioner's arrest. The Illinois Supreme Court resolved that issue, but did not consider whether the officers might reasonably, albeit erroneously, have thought that probable cause existed. Rather than decide those matters for the first time at this level, I think it preferable to allow the state courts to reconsider the case under the general guidelines expressed in today's opinions. I therefore would remand for reconsideration with directions to conduct such further factual inquiries as may be necessary to resolve the admissibility issue.

Notes and Questions

(1) How does the "attenuation" doctrine explained in *Wong Sun* and *Brown* differ from the "independent source" doctrine discussed in *Silverthorne* and *Murray*? From the "inevitable discovery" doctrine explained in *Nix*? When is evidence acquired as a result of an illegality "attenuated" and, therefore, outside the presumptive ban on the government's use of derivative evidence?

(2) The *Brown* Court lists three factors that are pertinent to application of the attenuation doctrine: (1) the temporal proximity of the illegality and the acquisition of evidence; (2) the presence of intervening events and circumstances; and (3) the purpose and flagrancy of the particular official misconduct. Should each of these factors be significant in attenuation analysis? Why? Should any other factors be considered relevant?

(3) In *United States v. Ceccolini*, 435 U.S. 268, 98 S. Ct. 1054, 55 L. Ed. 2d 268 (1978), a police officer casually, but without probable cause or a search warrant,

opened an envelope on the counter of the defendant's place of business. Upon discovering "policy slips" and money indicative of gambling activity, the officer asked the defendant's employee to whom the envelope belonged. She informed him that it was the defendant's. Ultimately, the employee became a key witness at defendant's perjury trial. The trial court, however, suppressed her testimony because she had first come to the government's attention as a consequence of the illegal search of the envelope, and because there was no showing by the government that she would have been found without the unconstitutional search.

The Supreme Court did not deny the causal connection between the illegal search and the employee's testimony, but concluded that the connection was sufficiently attenuated to dissipate the Fourth Amendment taint. The Court rejected the government's argument for a "*per se* rule that testimony of a live witness should not be excluded at trial no matter how close and proximate the connection between it and a violation of the Fourth Amendment," and reaffirmed the *Wong Sun* holding that "verbal evidence" derived from an illegality can be "fruit of the poisonous tree." Nevertheless, the majority suggested that in deciding whether a connection is attenuated the policies underlying the exclusionary rule require a distinction between physical and verbal evidence. According to the majority:

> The greater the willingness of the witness to freely testify, the greater the likelihood that he or she will be discovered by legal means and, concomitantly, the smaller the incentive to conduct an illegal search to discover the witness. Witnesses are not like guns or documents which remain hidden from view until one turns over a sofa or opens a filing cabinet. Witnesses can, and often do, come forward and offer evidence entirely of their own volition. And evaluated properly, the degree of free will necessary to dissipate the taint will very likely be found more often in the case of live-witness testimony than other kinds of evidence. The time, place and manner of the initial questioning of the witness may be such that any statements are truly the product of detached reflection and a desire to be cooperative on the part of the witness. And the illegality which led to the discovery of the witness very often will not play any meaningful part in the witness's willingness to testify.

Furthermore, another relevant factor that

> differentiate[s] the [exclusion of] testimony of all live witnesses — even putative defendants — from the exclusion of the typical documentary evidence, is that such exclusion would perpetually disable a witness from testifying about relevant and material facts, regardless of how unrelated such testimony might be to the purpose of the originally illegal search or the evidence discovered thereby. . . . In short, since the cost of excluding live-witness testimony often will be greater, a closer, more direct link between the illegality and that kind of testimony is required.

Ultimately, the Court concluded that

> the exclusionary rule should be invoked with much greater reluctance where the claim is based on a causal relationship between a constitutional violation and the discovery of a live witness than when a similar claim is advanced to support suppression of an inanimate object.

Applying these principles to the facts of *Ceccolini*, the Court held that the employee-witness's testimony fell within the attenuation exception. In support of this conclusion, the Court relied on the free will of the witness, the substantial periods of time between the illegality and the initial contact with the witness and between the initial contact and her testimony at trial, and the absence of official intent to find any evidence of gambling, "much less . . . the intent of finding a willing and knowledgeable witness to testify against" the defendant.

Chief Justice Burger, concurring in the judgment, opined that he would "resolve the case of a living witness on a *per se* basis, holding that such testimony is always admissible, provided it meets all other traditional evidentiary requirements." Justices Marshall and Brennan dissented. In their view, when properly applied, attenuation analysis already took into account the differences between live-witness testimony and physical evidence, and the Court's insistence upon additional distinctions involved "a form of judicial 'double-counting.'"

(4) In *Utah v. Strieff*, 579 U.S. ____, 136 S. Ct. 2056, 195 L. Ed. 2d 400 (2016), by a 5–3 vote, the Justices held that the attenuation exception dictated the admission of evidence found after an officer illegally detained a man who had left a house under surveillance for suspected drug activity. After stopping the man, obtaining his name, and running a warrant check, the officer discovered "an outstanding arrest warrant for a traffic violation." He arrested the man and searched his person incident to the arrest, finding contraband. The majority observed that, under "the attenuation doctrine," illegally acquired "[e]vidence is admissible when the connection between the unconstitutional police conduct and the evidence is remote or has been interrupted by some intervening circumstance." The majority then evaluated "the causal link" in this case by analyzing the "three factors articulated in *Brown v. Illinois*." Because the evidence was found "only minutes after the illegal stop," the "temporal proximity" factor "favor[ed] suppressing the evidence." The "intervening circumstances" factor, however, "strongly favor[ed]" attenuation. Between the stop and obtaining the evidence, the officer discovered a valid arrest warrant that "predated" and "was entirely unconnected with the stop," a warrant that obligated him to arrest the man. The search that followed "was undisputedly lawful." In addition, the "purpose and flagrancy of the official misconduct" factor "also strongly favor[ed]" attenuation. Observing that deterrence is most needed when "misconduct . . . is purposeful and flagrant," the Court concluded that this case involved, at most, "an isolated instance of negligence . . . in connection with a bona fide investigation of a suspected drug house." Although the officer had mistakenly initiated a stop, "his conduct thereafter was lawful," and he had not conducted an entirely "suspicionless fishing expedition." Neither his "purpose nor the flagrancy of the violation [rose] to a level of mis-

conduct to warrant suppression." In response to the concern that "the prevalence of outstanding arrest warrants in many jurisdictions" could induce the police to "engage in dragnet searches if the exclusionary rule is not applied," the majority observed that "[s]uch wanton conduct would expose police to civil liability" and that "evidence of a dragnet search . . . could" yield a "different" assessment of the "purpose and flagrancy" factor.

Justices Sotomayor, Kagan, and Ginsburg dissented. In their view, the majority's assessments of the intervening circumstance and purposeful and flagrant misconduct variables were misguided. According to Justice Kagan, the "majority's misapplication of *Brown*'s three-part inquiry create[d] unfortunate incentives for the police — indeed, practically invite[d] them to" seize individuals they wish to stop "for investigative reasons" when they do "not have . . . reasonable suspicion." By not applying the exclusionary rule, the Court "place[d] Fourth Amendment protections at risk."

(5) In *New York v. Harris*, 495 U.S. 14, 110 S. Ct. 1640, 109 L. Ed. 2d 13 (1990), police officers developed probable cause to arrest the defendant for murder. Three officers went to his apartment without an arrest warrant. They knocked, displayed their guns and badges, and entered. The officers read the defendant his *Miranda* rights. He said he understood the warnings and agreed to answer questions. In the course of doing so, he admitted to killing the victim. The defendant was taken to the police station where he was again informed of his *Miranda* rights. At the station, he signed a written inculpatory statement. After a third reading of the *Miranda* warnings, the defendant "indicated he wanted to end the interrogation." Nevertheless, the district attorney interviewed him, and the defendant made additional incriminating statements.

The "sole issue" before the Supreme Court was "whether [the] second statement — the written statement made at the station house — should have been suppressed because the police" had entered the defendant's home in violation of the holding in *Payton v. New York* that police must generally obtain an arrest warrant to enter a home to arrest a suspected felon. By a narrow 5-4 majority, the Court held that "where the police have probable cause to arrest a suspect, the exclusionary rule does not bar the State's use of a statement made by a defendant outside of his home, even though the statement is taken after an arrest made in the home in violation of *Payton*."

According to the majority, "the rule in *Payton* was designed to protect the physical integrity of the home," not "to grant criminal suspects . . . protection for statements made outside their premises." Moreover, the reasoning of the *Payton* Court did not suggest "that an arrest in a home without a warrant but with probable cause somehow renders unlawful continued custody of the suspect once he is removed from the house." The existence of probable cause to arrest makes that continued custody lawful. There is no need to engage in "attenuation analysis" to determine the admissibility of a statement made outside a home after officers enter in violation of *Payton* because attenuation analysis is necessary only when "'evidence is in some sense the product of illegal government activity.'" (Quoting *United States v. Crews*, 445. U.S. 463, 471 (1980)). A statement that is made outside a home is *not* the product of the unconstitutional entry—that is, it has not been obtained by "exploitation of the illegal entry" into the suspect's home and is "not the fruit of the fact that the arrest was made in the house rather than someplace else." In sum, there is no causal connection between a home entry in violation of *Payton* and a statement made by an arrestee outside the home.

The majority also observed that excluding a statement made outside a home "would not serve the purpose" of the *Payton* rule—i.e., "to protect the home" against unjustified entry. The purpose of that rule is vindicated by the exclusion of "anything incriminating gathered from arresting [a suspect] in his home." Police still have adequate incentive to obey the *Payton* rule because they "know that a warrantless entry will lead to the suppression of any evidence found or statements taken inside the home."

The four dissenters characterized the majority's reasoning as "analytical sleight-of-hand." In their view, statements made outside the home are the product of an illegal entry to arrest a suspect. They should be admissible *only* if the government shows that the connection between the entry and the statements is sufficiently attenuated to justify the conclusion that the statements are not the "fruits" of that entry.

Hudson v. Michigan

United States Supreme Court

547 U.S. 586, 126 S. Ct. 2159, 165 L. Ed. 2d 56 (2006)

JUSTICE SCALIA delivered the opinion of the Court, except as to Part IV.

We decide whether violation of the "knock-and-announce" rule requires the suppression of all evidence found in the search.

I

Police obtained a warrant authorizing a search for drugs and firearms at the home of petitioner Booker Hudson. They discovered both. Large quantities of drugs were found, including cocaine rocks in Hudson's pocket. A loaded gun was lodged between the cushion and armrest of the chair in which he was sitting. Hudson was charged under Michigan law with unlawful drug and firearm possession.

This case is before us only because of the method of entry into the house. When the police arrived to execute the warrant, they announced their presence, but waited only a short time—perhaps "three to five seconds,"—before turning the knob of the unlocked front door and entering Hudson's home. Hudson moved to suppress all the inculpatory evidence, arguing that the premature entry violated his Fourth Amendment rights.

The Michigan trial court granted his motion. On interlocutory review, the Michigan Court of Appeals reversed. . . . The Michigan Supreme Court denied leave to appeal. Hudson was convicted of drug possession. He renewed his Fourth Amendment claim on appeal, but the Court of Appeals rejected it and affirmed the conviction. The Michigan Supreme Court again declined review. We granted certiorari.

II

The common-law principle that law enforcement officers must announce their presence and provide residents an opportunity to open the door is an ancient one. *See Wilson v. Arkansas*, 514 U.S. 927, 931–932, 115 S. Ct. 1914, 131 L. Ed. 2d 976 (1995). . . . [I]n *Wilson*, we were asked whether the rule was . . . a command of the Fourth Amendment. Tracing its origins in our English legal heritage, 514 U.S., at 931–936, 115 S. Ct. 1914, we concluded that it was.

We recognized that the new constitutional rule we had announced is not easily applied. *Wilson* and cases following it have noted the many situations in which it is not necessary to knock and announce. . . .

When the knock-and-announce rule does apply, it is not easy to determine precisely what officers must do. How many seconds' wait are too few? Our "reasonable wait time" standard, *see United States v. Banks*, 540 U.S. 31, 41, 124 S. Ct. 521, 157 L. Ed. 2d 343 (2003), is necessarily vague. *Banks* (a drug case, like this one) held that the proper measure was not how long it would take the resident to reach the door, but how long it would take to dispose of the suspected drugs — but that such a time (15 to 20 seconds in that case) would necessarily be extended when, for instance, the suspected contraband was not easily concealed. If our *ex post* evaluation is subject to such calculations, it is unsurprising that, *ex ante*, police officers about to encounter someone who may try to harm them will be uncertain how long to wait.

Happily, these issues do not confront us here. From the trial level onward, Michigan has conceded that the entry was a knock-and-announce violation. The issue here is remedy. . . .

III
A

In *Weeks v. United States*, 232 U.S. 383, 34 S. Ct. 341, 58 L. Ed. 652 (1914), we adopted the federal exclusionary rule for evidence that was unlawfully seized from a home without a warrant in violation of the Fourth Amendment. We began applying the same rule to the States, through the Fourteenth Amendment, in *Mapp v. Ohio*, 367 U.S. 643, 81 S. Ct. 1684, 6 L. Ed. 2d 1081 (1961).

Suppression of evidence, however, has always been our last resort, not our first impulse. The exclusionary rule generates "substantial social costs," *United States v. Leon*, 468 U.S. 897, 907, 104 S. Ct. 3405 (1984), which sometimes include setting the guilty free and the dangerous at large. We have therefore been "cautio[us] against expanding" it, *Colorado v. Connelly*, 479 U.S. 157, 166, 107 S. Ct. 515, 93 L. Ed. 2d 473 (1986), and "have repeatedly emphasized that the rule's 'costly toll' upon truth-seeking and law enforcement objectives presents a high obstacle for those urging [its] application," *Pennsylvania Bd. of Probation and Parole v. Scott*, 524 U.S. 357, 364–365, 118 S. Ct. 2014, 141 L. Ed. 2d 344 (1998) (citation omitted). We have rejected "[i]ndiscriminate application" of the rule, *Leon, supra,* at 908, 104 S. Ct. 3405, and have held it to be applicable only "where its remedial objectives are thought most efficaciously served," *United States v. Calandra,* 414 U.S. 338, 348, 94 S. Ct. 613, 38 L. Ed. 2d 561 (1974) — that is, "where its deterrence benefits outweigh its 'substantial social costs,'" *Scott, supra,* at 363, 118 S. Ct. 2014 (quoting *Leon, supra,* at 907, 104 S. Ct. 3405).

We did not always speak so guardedly. Expansive dicta in *Mapp,* for example, suggested wide scope for the exclusionary rule. . . . But we have long since rejected that approach. . . .

In other words, exclusion may not be premised on the mere fact that a constitutional violation was a "but-for" cause of obtaining evidence. Our cases show that but-for causality is only a necessary, not a sufficient, condition for suppression. In this case, of course, the constitutional violation of an illegal *manner* of entry was *not* a but-for cause of obtaining the evidence. Whether that preliminary misstep had occurred *or not*, the police would have executed the warrant they had obtained, and would have discovered the gun and drugs inside the house. But even if the illegal entry here could be characterized as a but-for cause of discovering what was inside, we have "never held that evidence is 'fruit of the poisonous tree' simply because 'it would not have come to light but for the illegal actions of the police.'" *Segura v. United States,* 468 U.S. 796, 815, 104 S. Ct. 3380, 82 L. Ed. 2d 599 (1984). Rather, but-for cause, or "causation in the logical sense alone," *United States v. Ceccolini,* 435 U.S. 268, 274, 98 S. Ct. 1054, 55 L. Ed. 2d 268 (1978), can be too attenuated to justify exclusion, *id.,* at 274–275, 98 S. Ct. 1054. . . .

Attenuation can occur, of course, when the causal connection is remote. Attenuation also occurs when, even given a direct causal connection, the interest protected by the constitutional guarantee that has been violated would not be served by suppression of the evidence obtained. "The penalties visited upon the Government, and in turn upon the public, because its officers have violated the law must bear some relation to the purposes which the law is to serve." *Ceccolini, supra,* at 279, 98 S. Ct. 1054. . . . For this reason, cases excluding the fruits of unlawful warrantless searches say nothing about the appropriateness of exclusion to vindicate the interests protected by the knock-and-announce requirement. Until a valid warrant has issued, citizens are entitled to shield "their persons, houses, papers, and effects," U.S. Const., Amdt. 4, from the government's scrutiny. Exclusion of the evidence obtained by a warrantless search vindicates that entitlement. The interests protected by the knock-and-announce requirement are quite different — and do not include the shielding of potential evidence from the government's eyes.

One of those interests is the protection of human life and limb, because an unannounced entry may provoke violence in supposed self-defense by the surprised resident. Another interest is the protection of property. . . . The knock-and-announce rule gives individuals "the opportunity to comply with the law and to avoid the destruction of property occasioned by a forcible entry." *Richards,* 520 U.S., at 393, n. 5,

117 S. Ct. 1416. And thirdly, the knock-and-announce rule protects those elements of privacy and dignity that can be destroyed by a sudden entrance. It gives residents the "opportunity to prepare themselves for" the entry of the police. *Richards*, 520 U.S., at 393, n. 5, 117 S. Ct. 1416. "The brief interlude between announcement and entry with a warrant may be the opportunity that an individual has to pull on clothes or get out of bed." *Ibid.* In other words, it assures the opportunity to collect oneself before answering the door.

What the knock-and-announce rule has never protected, however, is one's interest in preventing the government from seeing or taking evidence described in a warrant. Since the interests that *were* violated in this case have nothing to do with the seizure of the evidence, the exclusionary rule is inapplicable.

B

Quite apart from the requirement of unattenuated causation, the exclusionary rule has never been applied except "where its deterrence benefits outweigh its 'substantial social costs,'" *Scott*, 524 U.S., at 363, 118 S. Ct. 2014 (quoting *Leon*, 468 U.S., at 907, 104 S. Ct. 3405). The costs here are considerable. In addition to the grave adverse consequence that exclusion of relevant incriminating evidence always entails (viz., the risk of releasing dangerous criminals into society), imposing that massive remedy for a knock-and-announce violation would generate a constant flood of alleged failures to observe the rule, and claims that any asserted *Richards* justification for a no-knock entry had inadequate support. The cost of entering this lottery would be small, but the jackpot enormous: suppression of all evidence, amounting in many cases to a get-out-of-jail-free card. Courts would experience as never before the reality that "[t]he exclusionary rule frequently requires extensive litigation to determine whether particular evidence must be excluded." *Scott, supra*, at 366, 118 S. Ct. 2014. Unlike the warrant or *Miranda* requirements, compliance with which is readily determined (either there was or was not a warrant; either the *Miranda* warning was given, or it was not), what constituted a "reasonable wait time" in a particular case, *Banks, supra*, at 41, 124 S. Ct. 521 (or, for that matter, how many seconds the police in fact waited), or whether there was "reasonable suspicion" of the sort that would invoke the *Richards* exceptions, is difficult for the trial court to determine and even more difficult for an appellate court to review.

Another consequence of the incongruent remedy Hudson proposes would be police officers' refraining from timely entry after knocking and announcing. As we have observed, the amount of time they must wait is necessarily uncertain. If the consequences of running afoul of the rule were so massive, officers would be inclined to wait longer than the law requires — producing preventable violence against officers in some cases, and the destruction of evidence in many others. . . .

Next to these "substantial social costs" we must consider the deterrence benefits, existence of which is a necessary condition for exclusion. . . . To begin with, the value of deterrence depends upon the strength of the incentive to commit the forbidden act. Viewed from this perspective, deterrence of knock-and-announce violations is not worth a lot. Violation of the warrant requirement sometimes produces incriminating evidence that could not otherwise be obtained. But ignoring knock-and-announce can realistically be expected to achieve absolutely nothing except the prevention of destruction of evidence and the avoidance of life-threatening resistance by occupants of the premises—dangers which, if there is even "reasonable suspicion" of their existence, *suspend the knock-and-announce requirement anyway.* Massive deterrence is hardly required.

It seems to us not even true . . . that without suppression there will be no deterrence of knock-and-announce violations at all. Of course even if this assertion were accurate, it would not necessarily justify suppression. Assuming (as the assertion must) that civil suit is not an effective deterrent, one can think of many forms of police misconduct that are similarly "undeterred." When, for example, a confessed suspect in the killing of a police officer, arrested (along with incriminating evidence) in a lawful warranted search, is subjected to physical abuse at the station house, would it seriously be suggested that the evidence must be excluded, since that is the only "effective deterrent"? And what, other than civil suit, is the "effective deterrent" of police violation of an already-confessed suspect's Sixth Amendment rights by denying him prompt access to counsel? Many would regard these violated rights as more significant than the right not to be intruded upon in one's nightclothes—and yet nothing but "ineffective" civil suit is available as a deterrent. And the police incentive for those violations is arguably greater than the incentive for disregarding the knock-and-announce rule.

We cannot assume that exclusion in this context is necessary deterrence simply because we found that it was necessary deterrence in different contexts and long ago. That would be forcing the public today to pay for the sins and inadequacies of a legal regime that existed almost half a century ago. Dollree Mapp could not turn to 42 U.S.C. § 1983 for meaningful relief; *Monroe v. Pape*, 365 U.S. 167, 81 S. Ct. 473, 5 L. Ed. 2d 492 (1961), which began the slow but steady expansion of that remedy, was decided the same Term as *Mapp*. It would be another 17 years before the § 1983 remedy was extended to reach the deep pocket of municipalities, *Monell v. New York City Dept. of Social Servs.*, 436 U.S. 658, 98 S. Ct. 2018, 56 L. Ed. 2d 611 (1978). Citizens whose Fourth Amendment rights were violated by federal officers could not bring suit until 10 years after *Mapp*, with this Court's decision in *Bivens v. Six Unknown Fed. Narcotics Agents*, 403 U.S. 388, 91 S. Ct. 1999, 29 L. Ed. 2d 619 (1971).

Hudson complains that "it would be very hard to find a lawyer to take a case such as this," but 42 U.S.C. § 1988(b) answers this objection. Since some civil-rights violations would yield damages too small to justify the expense of litigation, Congress has authorized attorney's fees for civil-rights plaintiffs. This remedy was unavailable in the heydays of our exclusionary-rule jurisprudence, because it is tied to the availability of a cause of action. For years after *Mapp*, "very few lawyers would even consider representation of persons who had civil rights claims against the police," but now "much has changed. Citizens and lawyers are much more willing to seek relief in the courts for police misconduct." M. Avery, D. Rudovsky, & K. Blum, Police Misconduct: Law and Litigation, p. v (3d ed.2005); *see generally* N. Aron, Liberty and Justice for All: Public Interest Law in the 1980s and Beyond (1989) (describing the growth of public-interest law). The number of public-interest law firms and lawyers who specialize in civil-rights grievances has greatly expanded.

Hudson points out that few published decisions to date announce huge awards for knock-and-announce violations. But this is an unhelpful statistic. Even if we thought that only large damages would deter police misconduct (and that police somehow are deterred by "damages" but indifferent to the prospect of large § 1988 attorney's fees), we do not know how many claims have been settled, or indeed how many violations have occurred that produced anything more than nominal injury. It is clear, at least, that the lower courts are allowing colorable knock-and-announce suits to go forward, unimpeded by assertions of qualified immunity. As far as we know, civil liability is an effective deterrent here, as we have assumed it is in other contexts. *See, e.g., Correctional Services Corp. v. Malesko*, 534 U.S. 61, 70, 122 S. Ct. 515, 151 L. Ed. 2d 456 (2001) ("[T]he threat of litigation and liability will adequately deter federal officers for *Bivens* purposes no matter that they may enjoy qualified immunity" (as violators of knock-and-announce do not)); *see also Nix v. Williams*, 467 U.S. 431, 446, 104 S. Ct. 2501, 81 L. Ed. 2d 377 (1984).

Another development over the past half-century that deters civil-rights violations is the increasing professionalism of police forces, including a new emphasis on internal police discipline. Even as long ago as 1980 we felt it proper to "assume" that unlawful police behavior would "be dealt with appropriately" by the authorities, *United States v. Payner*, 447 U.S. 727, 733–734, n. 5, 100 S. Ct. 2439, 65 L. Ed. 2d 468 (1980), but we now have increasing evidence that police forces across the United States take the constitutional rights of citizens seriously. There have been "wide-ranging reforms in the education, training, and supervision of police officers." S. Walker, Taming the System: The Control of Discretion in Criminal Justice 1950–1990, p. 51 (1993). Numerous sources are now available to teach officers and their supervisors what is required of them under this Court's cases, how to respect constitutional guarantees in various situations, and how to craft an effective regime for internal discipline. *See, e.g.,* D. Waksman & D. Goodman, The Search and Seizure Handbook (2d ed.2006); A. Stone & S. DeLuca, Police Administration: An Introduction (2d ed.1994); E. Thibault, L. Lynch, & R. McBridge, Proactive Police Management (4th ed.1998). Failure to teach and enforce constitutional requirements exposes municipalities to financial liability. *See Canton v. Harris*, 489 U.S. 378, 388, 109 S. Ct. 1197, 103 L. Ed. 2d 412 (1989). Moreover, modern police forces are staffed with professionals; it is not credible to assert that internal discipline, which can limit successful careers, will not have a deterrent effect. There is also evidence that the increasing use of various forms of citizen review can enhance police accountability.

In sum, the social costs of applying the exclusionary rule to knock-and-announce violations are considerable; the incentive to such violations is minimal to begin with, and the extant deterrences against them are substantial — incomparably greater than the factors deterring warrantless entries when *Mapp* was decided. Resort to the massive remedy of suppressing evidence of guilt is unjustified.

IV

A trio of cases — *Segura v. United States*, 468 U.S. 796, 104 S. Ct. 3380, 82 L. Ed. 2d 599 (1984); *New York v. Harris*, 495 U.S. 14, 110 S. Ct. 1640, 109 L. Ed. 2d 13 (1990); and *United States v. Ramirez*, 523 U.S. 65, 118 S. Ct. 992, 140 L. Ed. 2d 191 (1998) — confirms our conclusion that suppression is unwarranted in this case.

Like today's case, *Segura* involved a concededly illegal entry. Police conducting a drug crime investigation waited for Segura outside an apartment building; when he arrived, he denied living there. The police arrested him and brought him to the apartment where they suspected illegal activity. An officer knocked. When someone inside opened the door, the police entered, taking Segura with them. They had neither a warrant nor consent to enter, and they did not announce themselves as police — an entry as illegal as can be. Officers then stayed in the apartment for *19 hours* awaiting a search warrant. 468 U.S., at 800–801, 104 S. Ct. 3380; *id.*, at 818–819, 104 S. Ct. 3380 (Stevens, J., dissenting). Once alerted that the search warrant had been obtained, the police — still inside, having secured the premises so that no evidence could be removed — conducted a search. *Id.*, at 801, 104 S. Ct. 3380. We refused to exclude the resulting evidence. We recognized that only the evidence gained from the particular violation could be excluded, *see id.*, at 799, 804–805, 104 S. Ct. 3380, and therefore distinguished the effects of the illegal entry from the effects of the legal search: "None of the information on which the warrant was secured was derived from or related in any way to the initial entry into petitioners' apartment. . . ." *Id.*, at 814, 104 S. Ct. 3380. It was therefore "beyond dispute that the information possessed by the agents before they entered the apartment constituted an independent source for the discovery and seizure of the evidence now challenged." *Ibid.*

If the search in *Segura* could be "wholly unrelated to the prior entry," *ibid.*, when the only entry was warrantless, it would be bizarre to treat more harshly the actions in this case, where the only entry was *with* a warrant. If the probable cause backing a warrant that was issued *later in time* could be an "independent source" for a search that proceeded after the officers illegally entered and waited, a search warrant obtained *before* going in must have at least this much effect.

In the second case, *Harris*, the police violated the defendant's Fourth Amendment rights by arresting him at home without a warrant, contrary to *Payton v. New York*, 445 U.S. 573, 100 S. Ct. 1371, 63 L. Ed. 2d 639 (1980). Once taken to the station house, he gave an incriminating statement. *See* 495 U.S., at 15–16, 110 S. Ct. 1640. We refused to exclude it. Like the illegal entry which led to discovery of the evidence in today's case, the illegal arrest in *Harris* began a process that culminated in acquisition of the evidence sought to be excluded. While Harris's statement was "the product of an arrest and being in custody," it "was not the fruit of the fact that the arrest was made in the house rather than someplace else." *Id.*, at 20, 110 S. Ct. 1640. Likewise here: While acquisition of the gun and drugs was the product of a search pursuant to warrant, it was not the fruit of the fact that the entry was not preceded by knock and announce.

United States v. Ramirez, supra, involved a claim that police entry violated the Fourth Amendment because it was effected by breaking a window. We ultimately concluded that the property destruction was, under all the circumstances, reasonable, but in the course of our discussion we unanimously said the following: "[D]estruction of property in the course of a search may violate the Fourth Amendment, even though the entry itself is lawful and the fruits of the search are not subject to suppression." *Id.*, at 71, 118 S. Ct. 992. Had the breaking of the window been unreasonable, the Court said, it would have been necessary to determine whether there had been a "sufficient causal relationship between the breaking of the window and the discovery of the guns to warrant suppression of the evidence." *Id.*, at 72, n. 3, 118 S. Ct. 992. What clearer expression could there be of the proposition that an impermissible manner of entry does not necessarily trigger the exclusionary rule?

. . . .

For the foregoing reasons we affirm the judgment of the Michigan Court of Appeals.

It is so ordered.

Justice Kennedy, concurring in part and concurring in the judgment.

Two points should be underscored with respect to today's decision. First, the knock-and-announce requirement protects rights and expectations linked to ancient principles in our constitutional order. *See Wilson v. Arkansas,* 514 U.S. 927, 934, 115 S. Ct. 1914, 131 L. Ed. 2d 976 (1995). The Court's decision should not be interpreted as suggesting that violations of the requirement are trivial or beyond the law's concern. Second, the continued operation of the exclusionary rule, as settled and defined by our precedents, is not in doubt. Today's decision determines only that in the specific context of the knock-and-announce requirement, a violation is not sufficiently related to the later discovery of evidence to justify suppression.

As to the basic right in question, privacy and security in the home are central to the Fourth Amendment's guarantees as explained in our decisions and as understood since the beginnings of the Republic. This common understanding ensures respect for the law and allegiance to our institutions, and it is an instrument for transmitting our Constitution to later generations undiminished in meaning and force. It bears repeating that it is a serious matter if law enforcement officers violate the sanctity of the home by ignoring the requisites of lawful entry. Security must not be subject to erosion by indifference or contempt.

Our system, as the Court explains, has developed procedures for training police officers and imposing discipline for failures to act competently and lawfully. If those measures prove ineffective, they can be fortified with more detailed regulations or legislation. Supplementing these safeguards are civil remedies . . . that provide restitution for discrete harms. These remedies apply to all violations, including, of course, exceptional cases in which unannounced entries cause severe fright and humiliation.

Suppression is another matter. Under our precedents the causal link between a violation of the knock-and-announce requirement and a later search is too attenuated to allow suppression. When, for example, a violation results from want of a 20-second pause but an ensuing, lawful search lasting five hours discloses evidence of criminality, the failure to wait at the door cannot properly be described as having caused the discovery of evidence.

Today's decision does not address any demonstrated pattern of knock-and-announce violations. If a widespread pattern of violations were shown, and particularly if those violations were committed against persons who lacked the means or voice to mount an effective protest, there would be reason for grave concern. Even then, however, the Court would have to acknowledge that extending the remedy of exclusion to all the evidence seized following a knock-and-announce violation would mean revising the requirement of causation that limits our discretion in applying the exclusionary rule. That type of extension also would have significant practical implications, adding to the list of issues requiring resolution at the criminal trial questions such as whether police officers entered a home after waiting 10 seconds or 20.

In this case the relevant evidence was discovered not because of a failure to knock-and-announce, but because of a subsequent search pursuant to a lawful warrant. The Court in my view is correct to hold that suppression was not required. While I am not convinced that *Segura v. United States*, 468 U.S. 796, 104 S. Ct. 3380, 82 L. Ed. 2d 599 (1984), and *New York v. Harris*, 495 U.S. 14, 110 S. Ct. 1640, 109 L. Ed. 2d 13 (1990), have as much relevance here as JUSTICE SCALIA appears to conclude, the Court's holding is fully supported by Parts I through III of its opinion. I accordingly join those Parts and concur in the judgment.

JUSTICE BREYER, with whom JUSTICE STEVENS, JUSTICE SOUTER, and JUSTICE GINSBURG join, dissenting.

In *Wilson v. Arkansas*, 514 U.S. 927, 115 S. Ct. 1914, 131 L. Ed. 2d 976 (1995), a unanimous Court held that the Fourth Amendment normally requires law enforcement officers to knock and announce their presence before entering a dwelling. Today's opinion holds that evidence seized from a home following a violation of this requirement need not be suppressed.

As a result, the Court destroys the strongest legal incentive to comply with the Constitution's knock-and-announce requirement. And the Court does so without significant support in precedent. . . .

Today's opinion is thus doubly troubling. It represents a significant departure from the Court's precedents. And it weakens, perhaps destroys, much of the practical value of the Constitution's knock-and-announce protection.

I

This Court has set forth the legal principles that ought to have determined the outcome of this case in two sets of basic Fourth Amendment cases. I shall begin by describing that underlying case law.

A

The first set of cases describes the constitutional knock-and-announce requirement, a requirement that this Court initially set forth only 11 years ago in *Wilson v. Arkansas, supra.* . . .

. . . .

[In *Wilson,*] we held that the "common-law 'knock and announce' principle forms a part of the reasonableness inquiry under the Fourth Amendment." *Id.*, at 929, 115 S. Ct. 1914. Thus, "a search or seizure of a dwelling might be constitutionally defective if police officers enter without prior announcement." *Id.*, at 936, 115 S. Ct. 1914.

B

The second set of cases sets forth certain well-established principles that are relevant here. They include:

. . . .

Weeks, supra. This case . . . originated the exclusionary rule. The Court held that the Federal Government could not retain evidence seized unconstitutionally and use that evidence in a federal criminal trial. . . .

Silverthorne Lumber Co. v. United States, 251 U.S. 385, 40 S. Ct. 182, 64 L. Ed. 319 (1920). This case created an exception to (or a qualification of) *Weeks'* exclusionary rule. The Court held that the Government could not use information obtained during an illegal search to subpoena documents that they illegally viewed during that search. . . . *Silverthorne* . . . stands for the proposition that the exclusionary rule does not apply if the evidence in question (or the "fruits" of that evidence) was obtained through a process unconnected with, and untainted by, the illegal search.

Wolf v. Colorado, 338 U.S. 25, 69 S. Ct. 1359, 93 L. Ed. 1782 (1949), and *Mapp v. Ohio*, 367 U.S. 643, 81 S. Ct. 1684, 6 L. Ed. 2d 1081 (1961). Both of these cases considered whether *Weeks'* exclusionary rule applies to the States. In *Wolf*, the Court held that it did not. . . . In *Mapp*, the Court overruled *Wolf*. Experience, it said, showed that alternative methods of enforcing the Fourth Amendment's requirements had failed. *See* 367 U.S., at 651–653, 81 S. Ct. 1684. The Court consequently held that "all evidence obtained by searches and seizures in violation of the Constitution is, by that same authority, inadmissible in a state court." *Mapp*, 367 U.S., at 655, 81 S. Ct. 1684. . . .

II

Reading our knock-and-announce cases in light of this foundational Fourth Amendment case law, it is clear that the exclusionary rule should apply. For one thing, elementary logic leads to that conclusion. We have held that a court must "conside[r]" whether officers complied with the knock-and-announce requirement "in assessing the *reasonableness* of a search or seizure." *Wilson*, 514 U.S., at 934, 115 S. Ct. 1914 (emphasis added). The Fourth Amendment insists that an unreasonable search or seizure is, constitutionally speaking, an illegal search or seizure. And ever since *Weeks* (in respect to federal prosecutions) and *Mapp* (in respect to state prosecutions), "the use of evidence secured through an illegal search and seizure" is "barred" in criminal trials. *Wolf, supra*, at 28, 69 S. Ct. 1359 (citing *Weeks*); *see Mapp, supra*, at 655, 81 S. Ct. 1684.

For another thing, the driving legal purpose underlying the exclusionary rule, namely, the deterrence of unlawful government behavior, argues strongly for suppression. . . . [T]his Court in *Mapp* held that the exclusionary rule applies to the States in large part due to its belief that alternative state mechanisms for enforcing the Fourth Amendment's guarantees had proved "worthless and futile." 367 U.S., at 652, 81 S. Ct. 1684.

Why is application of the exclusionary rule any the less necessary here? Without such a rule, as in *Mapp*, police know that they can ignore the Constitution's requirements without risking suppression of evidence discovered after an unreasonable entry. As in *Mapp*, some government officers will find it easier, or believe it less risky, to proceed with what they consider a necessary search immediately and without the requisite constitutional (say, warrant or knock-and-announce) compliance.

Of course, the State or the Federal Government may provide alternative remedies for knock-and-announce violations. But that circumstance was true of *Mapp* as well. What reason is there to believe that those remedies (such as private damages actions under 42 U.S.C. § 1983), which the Court found inadequate in *Mapp*, can adequately deter unconstitutional police behavior here?

The cases reporting knock-and-announce violations are legion. Indeed, these cases of reported violations seem sufficiently frequent and serious as to indicate "a widespread pattern." *Ante*, at 604, 126 S. Ct. at 2171 (Kennedy, J., concurring in part and concurring in judgment). Yet the majority, like Michigan and the United States, has failed to cite a single reported case in which a plaintiff has collected more than nominal damages solely as a result of a knock-and-announce violation. Even Michigan concedes that, "in cases like the present one . . . , damages may be virtually nonexistent." Brief for Respondent 35, n. 66. . . .

. . . . The upshot is that the need for deterrence—the critical factor driving this Court's Fourth Amendment cases for close to a century—argues with at least comparable strength for evidentiary exclusion here.

To argue, as the majority does, that new remedies . . . make suppression unnecessary is to argue that *Wolf*, not *Mapp*, is now the law. . . . To argue that there may be few civil suits because violations may produce nothing "more than nominal injury" is to confirm, not to deny, the inability of civil suits to deter violations. *See ante*, at 598, 126 S. Ct. at 2167. And to argue without evidence (and despite myriad reported cases of violations, no reported case of civil damages, and Michigan's concession of their nonexistence) that civil suits may provide deterrence because claims *may* "have been settled" is, perhaps, to search in desperation for an argument. *See ibid.* Rather, the majority, as it candidly admits, has simply "assumed" that, "[a]s far as [it] know[s], civil liability is an effective deterrent," *ibid.*, a support-free assumption that *Mapp* and subsequent cases make clear does not embody the Court's normal approach to difficult questions of Fourth Amendment law.

It is not surprising, then, that after looking at virtually every pertinent Supreme Court case decided since *Weeks*, I can find no precedent that might offer the majority support for its contrary conclusion. . . . [T]he class of Fourth Amendment violations that do not result in suppression of the evidence seized . . . is limited.

The Court has declined to apply the exclusionary rule only:

(1) where there is a specific reason to believe that application of the rule would "not result in appreciable deterrence," *United States v. Janis*, 428 U.S. 433, 454, 96 S. Ct. 3021, 49 L. Ed. 2d 1046 (1976); *see, e.g., United States v. Leon*, 468 U.S. 897, 919–920, 104 S. Ct. 3405, 82 L. Ed. 2d 677 (1984) (exception where searching officer executes defective search warrant in "good faith"); *Arizona v. Evans*, 514 U.S. 1, 14, 115 S. Ct. 1185, 131 L. Ed. 2d 34 (1995) (exception for clerical errors by court employees); *Walder v. United States*, 347 U.S. 62, 74 S. Ct. 354, 98 L. Ed. 503 (1954) (exception for impeachment purposes), or

(2) where admissibility in proceedings other than criminal trials was at issue, *see, e.g., Pennsylvania Bd. of Probation and Parole v. Scott*, 524 U.S. 357, 364, 118 S. Ct. 2014, 141 L. Ed. 2d 344 (1998) (exception for parole revocation proceedings); *INS v. Lopez-Mendoza*, 468 U.S. 1032, 1050, 104 S. Ct. 3479, 82 L. Ed. 2d 778 (1984) (plurality opinion) (exception for deportation proceedings); *Janis, supra*, at 458, 96 S. Ct. 3021 (exception for civil tax proceedings); *United States v. Calandra*, 414 U.S. 338, 348–350, 94 S. Ct. 613, 38 L. Ed. 2d 561 (1974) (exception for grand jury proceedings); *Stone v. Powell*, 428 U.S. 465, 493–494, 96 S. Ct. 3037, 49 L. Ed. 2d 1067 (1976) (exception for federal habeas proceedings).

Neither of these two exceptions applies here. The second does not apply because this case is an ordinary criminal trial. The first does not apply because (1) officers who violate the rule are not acting "as a reasonable officer would and should act in similar circumstances," *Leon, supra*, at 920, 104 S. Ct. 3405, (2) this case does not involve government employees other than police, *Evans, supra*, and (3), most importantly, the key rationale for any exception, "lack of deterrence," is missing. That critical latter rationale, which underlies *every* exception, does not apply here, as there is no reason to think that, in the case of knock-and-announce violations by the police, "the exclusion of evidence at trial would not sufficiently deter future errors," *Evans, supra*, at 14, 115 S. Ct. 1185, or "'further the ends of the exclusionary rule in any appreciable way,'" *Leon, supra*, at 919–920, 104 S. Ct. 3405.

I am aware of no other basis for an exception. . . .

. . . .

Neither can the majority justify its failure to respect the need for deterrence . . . through its claim of "substantial social costs" — at least if it means that those "social costs" are somehow special here. The only costs it mentions are those that typically accompany *any* use of the Fourth Amendment's exclusionary principle: (1) that where the constable blunders, a guilty defendant may be set free (consider *Mapp* itself); (2) that defendants may assert claims where Fourth Amendment rights are uncertain (consider the Court's qualified immunity jurisprudence), and (3) that sometimes it is difficult to decide the merits of those uncertain claims. *See ante*, at ____, 126 S. Ct. at 2165–2166. In fact, the "no-knock" warrants that are provided by many States, by diminishing uncertainty, may make application of the knock-and-announce principle less "cost[ly]" on the whole than application of comparable Fourth Amendment principles, such as determining whether a particular warrantless search was justified by exigency. The majority's "substantial social costs" argument is an argument against the Fourth Amendment's exclusionary principle itself. And it is an argument that this Court, until now, has consistently rejected.

III

The majority, Michigan, and the United States make several additional arguments. In my view, those arguments rest upon misunderstandings of the principles underlying this Court's precedents.

A

The majority first argues that "the constitutional violation of an illegal *manner* of entry was *not* a but-for cause of obtaining the evidence." *Ante*, at ____, 126 S. Ct. at 2164. But taking causation as it is commonly understood in the law, I do not see how that can be so. Although the police might have entered Hudson's home lawfully, they did not in fact do so. Their unlawful behavior inseparably characterizes their actual entry; that entry was a necessary condition of their presence in Hudson's home; and their presence in Hudson's home was a necessary condition of their finding and seizing the evidence. . . .

Moreover, separating the "manner of entry" from the related search slices the violation too finely. As noted, we have described a failure to comply with the knock-and-announce rule, not as an independently unlawful event, but as a factor that renders the *search* "constitutionally defective." *Wilson*, 514 U.S., at 936, 115 S. Ct. 1914.

The Court nonetheless accepts Michigan's argument that the requisite but-for causation is not satisfied in this case because, whether or not the constitutional violation occurred (what the Court refers to as a "preliminary misstep"), "the police would have executed the warrant they had obtained, and would have discovered the gun and drugs inside the house." *Ante*, at 592, 126 S. Ct. at 2164. . . .

. . . .

[T]he Court's opinion reflects a misunderstanding . . . when it says, "[i]n this case, of course, the constitutional violation of an illegal *manner* of entry was *not* a but-for cause of obtaining the evidence." *Ante*, at 592, 126 S. Ct. at 2164. The majority rests this conclusion on its next statement: "Whether that preliminary misstep has occurred *or not*, the police ... would have discovered the gun and the drugs inside the house." *Ibid.* Despite the phrase "of course," neither of these statements is correct. It is not true that, had the illegal entry not occurred, "police would have discovered the guns and drugs inside the house." Without that unlawful entry they would not have been inside the house; so there would have been no discovery.

Of course, had the police entered the house lawfully, they would have found the gun and drugs. But that fact is beside the point. The question is not what police might have done had they not behaved unlawfully. The question is what they did do. Was there set in motion an independent chain of events that would have inevitably led to the discovery and seizure of the evidence despite, and independent of, that behavior? The answer here is "no."

B

. . . .

C

. . . .

The majority ... says that evidence should not be suppressed once the causal connection between unlawful behavior and discovery of the evidence becomes too "attenuated." *Ante*, at 592, 126 S. Ct. at 2164. But the majority then makes clear that it is not using the word "attenuated" to mean what this Court's precedents have typically used that word to mean, namely, that the discovery of the evidence has come about long after the unlawful behavior took place or in an independent way, *i.e.*, through " 'means sufficiently distinguishable to be purged of the primary taint.' " *Wong Sun v. United States*, 371 U.S. 471, 487–488, 83 S. Ct. 407, 9 L. Ed. 2d 441 (1963); *see Brown v. Illinois*, 422 U.S. 590, 603–604, 95 S. Ct. 2254, 45 L. Ed. 2d 416 (1975).

Rather, the majority gives the word "attenuation" a new meaning. ... "Attenuation," it says, "also occurs when, even given a direct causal connection, the interest protected by the constitutional guarantee that has been violated would not be served by suppression of the evidence obtained." *Ante*, at 593, 126 S. Ct. at 2164. The interests the knock-and-announce rule seeks to protect, the Court adds, are "human life" (at stake when a householder is "surprised"), "property" (such as the front door), and "those elements of privacy and dignity that can be destroyed by a sudden entrance," namely, "the opportunity to collect oneself before answering the door." *Ante*, at 594, 126 S. Ct. at 2165. Since none of those interests led to the discovery of the evidence seized here, there is no reason to suppress it.

There are three serious problems with this argument. First, it does not fully describe the constitutional values, purposes, and objectives underlying the knock-and-announce requirement. That rule does help to protect homeowners from damaged doors; it does help to protect occupants from surprise. But it does more than that. It protects the occupants' privacy by assuring them that government agents will not enter their home without complying with those requirements (among others) that diminish the offensive nature of any such intrusion. . . .

. . . The knock-and-announce requirement is no less a part of the "centuries-old principle" of special protection for the privacy of the home than the warrant requirement. *See* [*Georgia v. Randolph,*] 547 U.S., at 115, 126 S. Ct., at 1523 (citing *Miller, supra*, at 307, 78 S. Ct. 1190). The Court is therefore wrong to reduce the essence of its protection to "the right not to be intruded upon in one's nightclothes." *Ante*, at 597, 126 S. Ct. at 2167.

Second, whether the interests underlying the knock-and-announce rule are implicated in any given case is, in a sense, beside the point. As we have explained, failure to comply with the knock-and-announce rule renders the related search unlawful. *Wilson, supra*, at 936, 115 S. Ct. 1914. And where a search is unlawful, the law insists upon suppression of the evidence consequently discovered, even if that evidence or its possession has little or nothing to do with the reasons underlying the unconstitutionality of a search. . . .

Third, the majority's interest-based approach departs from prior law. Ordinarily a court will simply look to see if the unconstitutional search produced the evidence. . . .

D

The United States . . . has argued that suppression is "an especially harsh remedy given the nature of the violation in this case." Brief for United States as *Amicus Curiae* 28; see also *id.*, at 24. This argument focuses upon the fact that entering a house after knocking and announcing can, in some cases, prove dangerous to a police officer. Perhaps someone inside has a gun, as turned out to be the case here. The majority adds that police officers about to encounter someone who may try to harm them will be "uncertain" as to how long to wait. *Ante*, at 595, 126 S. Ct. at 2166. It says that, "[i]f the consequences of running afoul" of the knock-and-announce "rule were so massive," *i.e.*, would lead to the exclusion of evidence, then "officers would be inclined to wait longer than the law requires — producing preventable violence against officers in some cases." *Ante*, at 595, 126 S. Ct. at 2165–2166.

To argue that police efforts to assure compliance with the rule may prove dangerous, however, is not to argue against evidence suppression. It is to argue against the validity of the rule itself. Similarly, to argue that enforcement means uncertainty, which in turn means the potential for dangerous and longer-than-necessary delay, is (if true) to argue against meaningful compliance with the rule.

The answer to the first argument is that the rule itself does not require police to knock or to announce their presence where police have a "reasonable suspicion" that doing so "would be dangerous or futile" or "would inhibit the effective investigation of the crime by, for example, allowing the destruction of evidence." *Richards, supra*, at 394, 117 S. Ct. 1416.

The answer to the second argument is that States can, and many do, reduce police uncertainty while assuring a neutral evaluation of concerns about risks to officers or the destruction of evidence by permitting police to obtain a "no-knock" search warrant from a magistrate judge, thereby assuring police that a prior announcement is not necessary. *Richards*, 520 U.S., at 396, n. 7, 117 S. Ct. 1416 (collecting state statutes). While such a procedure cannot remove all uncertainty, it does provide an easy way for officers to comply with the knock-and-announce rule.

. . . .

Consider this very case. The police obtained a search warrant that authorized a search, not only for drugs, but also for *guns*. If probable cause justified a search for guns, why would it not also have justified a no-knock warrant, thereby diminishing any danger to the officers? Why (in a State such as Michigan that lacks no-knock warrants) would it not have justified the very no-knock entry at issue here? Indeed, why did the prosecutor not argue in this very case that, given the likelihood of guns, the no-knock entry was lawful? From what I have seen in the record, he would have won. And had he won, there would have been no suppression here.

That is the right way to win. The very process of arguing the merits of the violation would help to clarify the contours of the knock-and-announce rule, contours that the majority believes are too fuzzy. That procedural fact, along with no-knock warrants, back up authority to enter without knocking regardless, and use of the "reasonable suspicion" standard for doing so should resolve the government's problems with the knock-and-announce rule while reducing the "uncertain[ty]" that the majority discusses to levels beneath that found elsewhere in Fourth Amendment law (*e.g.*, exigent circumstances). *Ante*, at 595, 126 S. Ct. at 2166. Regardless, if the Court fears that effective enforcement of a constitutional requirement will have harmful consequences, it should face those fears directly by addressing the requirement itself. It should not argue, "the requirement is fine, indeed, a serious matter, just don't enforce it."

E

[In this subsection, JUSTICE BREYER explained why, in his view, the three cases relied upon by Justice Scalia — *Segura v. United States, New York v. Harris*, and *Ramirez v. United States* — did "not support his conclusion."]

IV

There is perhaps one additional argument implicit in the majority's approach. The majority says, for example, that the "cost" to a defendant of "entering this lottery," *i.e.*, of claiming a "knock-and-announce" violation, "would be small, but the jackpot enormous" — namely, a potential "get-out-of-jail-free card." *Ante*, at 594, 126 S. Ct. at 2166. It adds that the "social costs" of applying the exclusionary rule here are not worth the deterrence benefits. *Ante*, at 599, 126 S. Ct. at 2168. Leaving aside what I believe are invalid arguments based on precedent or the majority's own estimate that suppression is not necessary to deter constitutional violations, one is left with a simple unvarnished conclusion, namely, that in this kind of case, a knock-and-announce case, "[r]esort to the massive remedy of suppressing evidence of guilt is unjustified." *Ibid.* Why is that judicial judgment, taken on its own, inappropriate?

Could it not be argued that the knock-and-announce rule, a subsidiary Fourth Amendment rule, is simply not important enough to warrant a suppression remedy? Could the majority not simply claim that the suppression game is not worth the candle?

The answer, I believe, is "no." That "no" reflects history, a history that shows the knock-and-announce rule is important. That "no" reflects precedent, precedent that shows there is no pre-existing legal category of exceptions to the exclusionary rule into which the knock-and-announce cases might fit. That "no" reflects empirical fact, experience that provides confirmation of what common sense suggests: without suppression there is little to deter knock-and-announce violations.

. . . [O]ur Fourth Amendment traditions place high value upon protecting privacy in the home. They emphasize the need to assure that its constitutional protections are effective, lest the Amendment "sound the word of promise to the ear but break it to the hope." They include an exclusionary principle, which since *Weeks* has formed the centerpiece of the criminal law's effort to ensure the practical reality of those promises. That is why the Court should assure itself that any departure from that principle is firmly grounded in logic, in history, in precedent, and in empirical fact. It has not done so. That is why, with respect, I dissent.

Notes and Questions

(1) In *Hudson*, a majority held that evidence should not be excluded on the ground that officers have unreasonably entered a home in violation of the Fourth Amendment knock-and-announce requirement. One reason that exclusion was not justified was that the "illegal *manner* of entry" involved in the failure to honor the knock-and-announce rule in *Hudson* was "*not* a but-for cause of obtaining the evidence" discovered during the ensuing search. There was no causal link because officers would have discovered the evidence whether or not they had entered prematurely. The dissent maintained that a but-for connection was evident if one takes "causation as it is commonly understood in the law." Which understanding of causation is constitutionally preferable?

(2) The Court suggests that the "attenuation" exception to the exclusionary rule can apply "even" when there is a "direct causal connection" between an illegality and the discovery of evidence. Is this view consistent with prior explanations of the "attenuation" doctrine in *Wong Sun* and *Brown*? Does it make sense to extend the "attenuation" exception to evidence found as a direct, immediate result of a Fourth Amendment violation?

(3) According to the dissent, the holding of *Hudson* "destroys the strongest legal incentive to comply with" the knock-and-announce requirement and "weakens, perhaps destroys, much of the practical value of the Constitution's knock-and-announce protection." Knowing that a failure to comply will not have adverse evidentiary consequences, what reasons do officers have to abide by the knock-and-announce requirement? Are those reasons likely to counterbalance the law enforcement advantages of entering premises unannounced?

Attenuation Problems

13C–1: On March 13, the body of Joe Merri was found near 9440 South Vernon Avenue. Merri had been killed by a single gunshot wound. On March 15, while De-mar Buff, Ed Capp, and John Leming were visiting Mario Jenn's house, Jenn admit-ted that he had shot Merri — whom he believed to be a member of a gang known as the "Gangster Disciples" — when Merri had tried to take his jacket. Jenn showed the others the gun he had used. The four boys then decided to go to Capp's girlfriend's house, which was located near 95th Street and Vernon Avenue, in Gangster Disciple territory. They took Jenn's gun along, agreeing that Buff should carry it.

The same day, Detectives Hess and Lynn were investigating the Merri homicide. While in the area of 95th and Vernon, traveling in an unmarked car, the officers saw the four boys walking in an alley. As the officers approached, they saw Buff remove the gun from his waistband and run. The detectives chased and caught Buff and brought him back to where the other three were standing. Because they had not recovered the gun, the detectives handcuffed all four boys and placed them in the police car. While in the car, Jenn told Buff that if the gun was found and the police asked about it, he should tell them that Jenn had given it to him. Jenn said that Buff should not worry about going to jail for Merri's murder because Jenn would admit to the killing if he was questioned.

After the detectives recovered the gun from the alley, they took the boys to the police station. Hess and Lynn were aware that a witness had reported that Merri's killer had worn a "black and orange Miami Hurricanes jacket with a big bird on it." The detectives decided to interview Buff first. After hearing the *Miranda* warnings, Buff stated that he had been given the gun to hold. The detectives then noticed that Buff's jacket did not match the description of the killer's jacket. They decided to talk to Jenn. As they were taking him to an interrogation room, they noticed that he was wearing a Miami Hurricanes jacket turned inside out. They asked Jenn to remove the jacket and took it from him. After being read the *Miranda* warnings, Jenn waived his rights and admitted his involvement in Merri's murder. Prior to his trial for second-degree murder, Jenn moved to suppress the jacket and his admission.

How should the trial judge rule?

13C–2: Tony Friars was stopped at a traffic light. Officer Steven Mills was stopped behind Friars's vehicle. When the light turned green, without using his blinker or giving a hand signal, Friars made a left hand turn. According to Officer Mills, nei-ther he nor the drivers of other vehicles were affected by Friars's failure to use a turn signal. In addition, Mills spotted a crack in the plastic lens covering the left taillight of Friars's vehicle. A white light emanated from that crack. Because of the failure to signal and because of the crack in the taillight cover, Officer Mills stopped Friars's vehicle.

When Mills ran a check on the identification provided by Friars, he learned that there was an outstanding warrant for Friars's arrest for failure to appear in another proceeding. He arrested Friars based on that warrant. A search incident to this arrest uncovered a firearm in Friars's vehicle. Friars was charged with possession of a firearm by a convicted felon.

Friars moved to suppress the firearm, alleging that both the traffic stop and arrest were unconstitutional. He submitted two controlling holdings of the State Supreme Court, a seven-year-old holding that a failure to use a turn signal is not a violation unless it creates a "reasonable safety concern," and a nine-year-old holding that a cracked taillight alone does not violate the law. He also proved that the warrant on which he had been arrested had been issued when another man who had been issued a notice to appear had falsely given Friars's name and date of birth.

What arguments support Friars's motion to suppress the firearm? What arguments should the prosecution make in response? How should the trial court rule?

13C–3: Police investigating a recent hit-and-run accident suspected that Martin Eisler had been driving the vehicle involved. Acting without a warrant, they went to his home. They observed Eisler's car in the driveway. The car had minor damage, its key was in the ignition, and its door was open. The officers rang the doorbell, knocked on the doors and windows, and shouted through the screen, but received no response. They then entered the house, found Eisler within, and placed him under arrest. At the time of Eisler's arrest, the officers properly warned him of his *Miranda* rights and then asked him some questions. Eisler made inculpatory statements in response.

The officers then took Eisler to police headquarters, where he was again warned and questioned. He made additional statements and was subjected to tests to determine whether he was intoxicated. Prior to his trial, Eisler filed a motion to suppress all of his statements and the evidence resulting from the tests.

At the hearing on the motion to suppress, the government admitted that the arresting officers had not secured a warrant for Eisler's arrest, but established that the officers had been in possession of facts sufficient to establish probable cause to believe that he had been involved in the hit-and-run accident.

Should the trial court grant Eisler's motion to suppress? Why?

13C–4: Detective Evans was assigned to investigate multiple robberies in a five-block area of Los Angeles. Tony Shawn was a victim of one of the robberies. He claimed that Dom Giston was the man who had robbed him. When Detective Evans arrested Giston, Giston told him that Kevin Herry had actually robbed Tony Shawn. He provided Herry's nickname and his address, and volunteered that Herry had also been involved in robberies at a gas station located at Cienega Street and Cadillac Avenue. The description of the suspect in these robberies was consistent with Herry's appearance.

On November 29, Officer Jenny Hicks, of the Los Angeles Police Department, was patrolling the area near Cadillac Avenue and Chariton Street. Detective Evans had informed her that Kevin Herry was wanted for robberies. He provided a description of Herry, and told her that Herry frequented the area that she would be patrolling.

While on patrol, Officer Hicks observed Herry on the west side of Garth Street, just north of Cadillac Avenue. She took him into custody. At the station, Herry was formally arrested for the robbery of Tony Shawn.

The day after Herry's arrest, Detective Evans took his picture. He showed it to Tony Shawn as part of a photographic array. Shawn said that he knew Herry and that Herry was not the man who had robbed him. Evans then showed the same photographic array to victims of other robberies he was investigating. Two victims identified Herry as the man who had robbed each of them. Herry was eventually charged with six counts of robbery and two counts of attempted robbery. None of the charges involved the Shawn robbery for which he had been arrested. Prior to trial, Herry's motion to suppress the photograph taken by Detective Evans and the identifications made from that photograph was denied. Herry has appealed that ruling.

How should the appellate court rule?

13C–5: A task force of federal and local officers (the agents) suspected Adrian Bowling of drug trafficking. On the morning of March 1, they followed her to a residence where she pulled in the driveway and parked. Shortly after, Ronnie Wise exited the house and entered Bowling's car. The agents saw Wise and Bowling bend down near an area of the car that contained a hidden compartment. Wise then carried a grocery bag back to his house. Shortly after Bowling drove away, the agents stopped her for a traffic violation. She refused consent to search her car. After a canine alerted to the car, the agents searched it and discovered approximately $73,000 in the hidden compartment.

That afternoon, the agents returned to Wise's house. They were aware that one occupant of the house had a criminal record for guns and drugs. While watching the house, the agents saw a woman wearing a correctional officer uniform exit and walk toward a car. The agents approached and asked the woman if they could search the house. She said that she would have to ask her husband, Wise, the owner of the house. Explaining that he was in the shower, she went back inside the house. About 30 seconds later, in part because they were concerned for their safety, the agents knocked on the door. When Wise's wife opened it, they pushed her back and, with guns drawn, entered the home.

Once inside, the agents directed Wise to sit on the couch as they conducted a protective sweep. After the sweep, the agents asked Wise for consent to search. Wise did not respond. Still sitting on the couch, Wise asked the agents if he could smoke a cigarette. The agents permitted him to smoke, and, as he finished, the agents again asked him if they could search the house. Once again Wise did not respond. The agents informed Wise that they would obtain a search warrant if he did not consent. Wise and the agents then discussed whether the agents were going to tear up his house. After that discussion, 15 minutes after the agents had entered his home, Wise consented to the search, both orally and through a written consent form. The signed consent form stated that he "ha[d] been informed by [the agents] of [his] right to refuse consent to a search of [his] property," he "voluntarily and intentionally consent[ed] to allow [the agents] to search [his] property," and his consent was "freely given and not the result of any promises, threats, coercion, or other intimidation." As a result of the search, the agents seized two firearms, more than $100,000 in cash, and other drug evidence.

Wise was indicted for various crimes. He moved to suppress the evidence the officers found in his home, alleging that they had entered illegally. The government contended that, if the entry was illegal, the attenuation exception justified admission of the evidence.

Should the trial judge admit or suppress the evidence?

13C–6: On October 31, around 10:00 pm, Lieutenant Stevens of the University Police Department stopped a vehicle for making an illegal left turn against a red light. Antoine was driving. The vehicle was registered to Jennifer, Antoine's girlfriend, who was a passenger at the time of the stop. Stevens approached Antoine and asked for his driver's license. He then ran Antoine's name through the computer system and discovered a federal arrest warrant for Antoine for drug offenses. When additional officers arrived, Antoine was arrested on the outstanding warrant and searched. Officers found $2,600 in cash on his person.

The police officers at the scene searched the car and found nothing. A drug dog was then called to the scene, sniffed the vehicle, and alerted officers to the presence of controlled substances by sitting down and staring at the passenger side car door. Stevens searched the area near the glove compartment again and discovered a hiding place behind the glove compartment, where he found crack and heroin hidden in a sock. Antoine, who was aware of the discovery of the hidden drugs, was removed from the patrol car. After an officer administered *Miranda* warnings, Antoine waived his rights and made statements that connected him to the drugs in the car.

Before trial, Antoine moved to suppress the evidence found and the statements he made after he was stopped on October 31. After watching a video of the stop, the district judge agreed with Antoine's contention that Lieutenant Stevens did not have probable cause or reasonable suspicion to stop Antoine's car because he had not, in fact, committed a traffic violation. The prosecution claimed that the evidence was nonetheless admissible because of the "attenuation" exception to the exclusionary rule.

Should the judge suppress the evidence?

13C–7: In January, officials at a school discovered that a laptop computer, valued at $1,500, was missing. The computer was equipped with tracking software designed to facilitate its recovery. Using that software, the police were able to trace the computer to an address in the city. Police officers went to the address, a single-family dwelling, in the middle of the afternoon. Once there, they entered the vestibule of the house without ringing the doorbell or otherwise announcing their presence. Inside the vestibule, one of the officers knocked on an inner door separating the vestibule from the rest of the home. LeRoi's sister, who had heard the officers enter the vestibule, welcomed the officers inside, saying "Thank God you're all here." When asked whether LeRoi was at home, she answered affirmatively, explaining that her brother had been "acting up" and cursing at her mother, and that she "was going to call [the police] anyway, if [her brother] kept it up." The sister then directed the officers up the stairs to a bedroom where they encountered a young man, not LeRoi, with a laptop. When asked whether it was his laptop, the young man answered that it was not. At this point, LeRoi entered the room and said, "That's my laptop. My friend stole it."

LeRoi, who was 15 years old, was arrested and charged with fourth-degree criminal possession of stolen property. LeRoi moved to suppress all evidence obtained by the police at his residence on the ground that they had entered without a warrant.

What claims should the prosecution make in response to the motion to suppress? Should the evidence be excluded from trial?

13C–8: Michelle Ray told the police that she had gone to Kenny's house to confront him with her belief that he was supplying drugs to their 18-year-old son. Kenny responded by choking and kicking her. He then ran to another floor of the house and returned waving a semi-automatic handgun. Ray reported that other people, including an infant and a prison associate of Kenny, were living in Kenny's house. Officers learned that there were several outstanding warrants for Kenny's arrest and that he had an extensive criminal history which included convictions for possession and delivery of controlled substances, attempting to elude a police officer, escape, felon in possession of a firearm, and robbery. He had also been charged with assault on a police officer and aggravated assault.

Believing that a street arrest would threaten the public safety because of Kenny's lengthy record of violence and hostility toward police, officers decided that it was necessary to arrest him at his home. The "Special Emergency Reaction Team" secured a search warrant and proceeded to Kenny's home around 5:30 a.m. The house was dark, and there was no noise or movement within. Of the 44 officers who participated in executing the warrant, 13 were assigned to enter the home.

Between one and two seconds after an officer pounded on Kenny's door and yelled, "Police! Search Warrant!" the police used a battering ram to break it open. Kenny, who had been sleeping on a recliner near the front door, stood up as the officers broke his door down. One officer instructed him to show his hands and get down while another threw a flash-bang device with a two-second fuse into the center of the room. The device exploded near Kenny, inflicting first and second-degree burns on his face, chest, and upper arms. Meanwhile, officers outside the house shot out the second-story windows with rubber bullets. Officers securing the second level threw another flash-bang device into an open area. A man and a woman were lying in bed in that area, and the explosion caused the bed to catch fire. After attempting to extinguish the fire, officers threw the mattress and box spring out of a window. Extensive damage was done to the house during the entry. The police shot out approximately

10 windows, kicked in many doors, burned carpet, and made holes in the walls and ceilings with the rubber bullets.

In a search, officers recovered a 9mm semiautomatic handgun from the crack between the arm and the bottom cushion of the recliner in which Kenny had been sitting. They recovered another semiautomatic handgun on an adjacent chair. Elsewhere in the house, they found and seized a 12-gauge sawed-off shotgun, two .22-caliber rifles, and illegal narcotics. Kenny was indicted on four counts of being a felon in possession of a firearm and one count of possession of an unregistered sawed-off shotgun. Kenny moved to suppress the items found in his home, claiming that officers had executed the search warrant in an unreasonable manner.

Does Kenny's claim have merit?

[D] The "Good Faith" Exceptions

United States v. Leon

United States Supreme Court

468 U.S. 897, 104 S. Ct. 3405, 82 L. Ed. 2d 677 (1984)

JUSTICE WHITE delivered the opinion of the Court.

This case presents the question whether the Fourth Amendment exclusionary rule should be modified so as not to bar the use in the prosecution's case-in-chief of evidence obtained by officers acting in reasonable reliance on a search warrant issued by a detached and neutral magistrate but ultimately found to be unsupported by probable cause. . . .

I

In August 1981, a confidential informant of unproven reliability informed an officer of the Burbank Police Department that two persons known to him as "Armando" and "Patsy" were selling large quantities of cocaine and methaqualone from their residence at 620 Price Drive in Burbank, Cal. The informant also indicated that he had witnessed a sale of methaqualone by "Patsy" at the residence approximately five months earlier and had observed at that time a shoebox containing a large amount of cash that belonged to "Patsy." He further declared that "Armando" and "Patsy" generally kept only small quantities of drugs at their residence and stored the remainder at another location in Burbank.

On the basis of this information, the Burbank police initiated an extensive investigation focusing first on the Price Drive residence and later on two other residences as well. Cars parked at the Price Drive residence were determined to belong to respondents Armando Sanchez, who had previously been arrested for possession of marihuana, and Patsy Stewart, who had no criminal record. During the course of the investigation, officers observed an automobile belonging to respondent Ricardo Del Castillo, who had previously been arrested for possession of 50 pounds of mari-huana, arrive at the Price Drive residence. The driver of that car entered the house, exited shortly thereafter carrying a small paper sack, and drove away. A check of Del Castillo's probation records led the officers to respondent Alberto Leon, whose tele-phone number Del Castillo had listed as his employer's. Leon had been arrested in 1980 on drug charges, and a companion had informed the police at that time that Leon was heavily involved in the importation of drugs into this country. Before the current investigation began, the Burbank officers had learned that an informant had told a Glendale police officer that Leon stored a large quantity of methaqualone at his residence in Glendale. During the course of this investigation, the Burbank offi-cers learned that Leon was living at 716 South Sunset Canyon in Burbank.

Subsequently, the officers observed several persons, at least one of whom had prior drug involvement, arriving at the Price Drive residence and leaving with small pack-ages; observed a variety of other material activity at the two residences as well as at a condominium at 7902 Via Magdalena; and witnessed a variety of relevant activity involving respondents' automobiles. The officers also observed respondents Sanchez and Stewart board separate flights for Miami. The pair later returned to Los Angeles together, consented to a search of their luggage that revealed only a small amount of marihuana, and left the airport. Based on these and other observations summarized in the affidavit, Officer Cyril Rombach of the Burbank Police Department, an expe-rienced and well-trained narcotics investigator, prepared an application for a war-rant to search 620 Price Drive, 716 South Sunset Canyon, 7902 Via Magdalena, and automobiles registered to each of the respondents for an extensive list of items be-lieved to be related to respondents' drug-trafficking activities. Officer Rombach's ex-tensive application was reviewed by several Deputy District Attorneys.

A facially valid search warrant was issued in September 1981 by a state superior court judge. The ensuing searches produced large quantities of drugs at the Via Magdalena and Sunset Canyon addresses and a small quantity at the Price Drive residence. Other evidence was discovered at each of the residences and in Stewart's and Del Castillo's automobiles. Respondents were indicted by a grand jury in the District Court for the Central District of California and charged with conspiracy to possess and distribute cocaine and a variety of substantive counts.

The respondents then filed motions to suppress the evidence seized pursuant to the warrant. The District Court held an evidentiary hearing and, while recogniz-ing that the case was a close one, granted the motions to suppress in part. It con-cluded that the affidavit was insufficient to establish probable cause, but did not suppress all of the evidence as to all of the respondents because none of the respon-dents had standing to challenge all of the searches. In response to a request from the Government, the court made clear that Officer Rombach had acted in good faith, but it rejected the Government's suggestion that the Fourth Amendment exclusionary rule should not apply where evidence is seized in reasonable, good-faith reliance on a search warrant.

The District Court denied the Government's motion for reconsideration, and a divided panel of the Court of Appeals for the Ninth Circuit affirmed. . . .

The Government's petition for certiorari expressly declined to seek review of the lower courts' determinations that the search warrant was unsupported by probable cause and presented only the question "[w]hether the Fourth Amendment exclusionary rule should be modified so as not to bar the admission of evidence seized in reasonable, good-faith reliance on a search warrant that is subsequently held to be defective. . . ."

II

. . . .

A

The Fourth Amendment contains no provision expressly precluding the use of evidence obtained in violation of its commands, and an examination of its origin and purposes makes clear that the use of fruits of a past unlawful search or seizure "work[s] no new Fourth Amendment wrong." *United States v. Calandra*, 414 U.S. 338, 354, 94 S. Ct. 613, 623, 38 L. Ed. 2d 561 (1974). The wrong condemned by the Amendment is "fully accomplished" by the unlawful search or seizure itself, *ibid.*, and the exclusionary rule is neither intended nor able to "cure the invasion of the defendant's rights which he has already suffered." *Stone v. Powell*, 428 U.S., at 540, 96 S. Ct., at 3073 (White, J., dissenting). The rule thus operates as "a judicially created remedy designed to safeguard Fourth Amendment rights generally through its deterrent effect, rather than a personal constitutional right of the person aggrieved." *United States v. Calandra*, 414 U.S., at 348, 94 S. Ct., at 620.

Whether the exclusionary sanction is appropriately imposed in a particular case, our decisions make clear, is "an issue separate from the question whether the Fourth Amendment rights of the party seeking to invoke the rule were violated by police conduct." *Illinois v. Gates*, 462 U.S., at 223, 103 S. Ct., at 2324. Only the former question is currently before us, and it must be resolved by weighing the costs and benefits of preventing the use in the prosecution's case-in-chief of inherently trustworthy tangible evidence obtained in reliance on a search warrant issued by a detached and neutral magistrate that ultimately is found to be defective.

The substantial social costs exacted by the exclusionary rule for the vindication of Fourth Amendment rights have long been a source of concern. "Our cases have consistently recognized that unbending application of the exclusionary sanction to enforce ideals of governmental rectitude would impede unacceptably the truth-finding functions of judge and jury." *United States v. Payner*, 447 U.S. 727, 734, 100 S. Ct. 2439, 2445, 65 L. Ed. 2d 468 (1980). An objectionable collateral consequence of this interference with the criminal justice system's truth-finding function is that some guilty defendants may go free or receive reduced sentences as a result of favorable plea bargains. Particularly when law enforcement officers have acted in objective good faith or their transgressions have been minor, the magnitude of the benefit conferred on such guilty defendants offends basic concepts of the criminal justice system. *Stone v. Powell*, 428 U.S., at 490, 96 S. Ct., at 3050. Indiscriminate application of the exclusionary rule, therefore, may well "generat[e] disrespect for the law and the administration of justice." *Id.*, at 491, 96 S. Ct., at 3051. Accordingly, "[a]s with any remedial device, the application of the rule has been restricted to those areas where its remedial objectives are thought most efficaciously served." *United States v. Calandra*, 414 U.S., at 348, 94 S. Ct., at 670.

B

Close attention to those remedial objectives has characterized our recent decisions concerning the scope of the Fourth Amendment exclusionary rule. The Court has, to be sure, not seriously questioned, "in the absence of a more efficacious sanction, the continued application of the rule to suppress evidence from the [prosecution's] case where a Fourth Amendment violation has been substantial and deliberate. . . ." *Franks v. Delaware*, 438 U.S. 154, 171, 98 S. Ct. 2674, 2684, 57 L. Ed. 2d 667 (1978); *Stone v. Powell*, 428 U.S., at 492, 96 S. Ct., at 3051. Nevertheless, the balancing approach that has evolved in various contexts — including criminal trials — "forcefully suggest[s] that the exclusionary rule be more generally modified to permit the introduction of evidence obtained in the reasonable good-faith belief that a search or seizure was in accord with the Fourth Amendment." *Illinois v. Gates*, 462 U.S., at 255, 103 S. Ct., at 2341 (White, J., concurring in the judgment).

. . . .

As cases considering the use of unlawfully obtained evidence in criminal trials themselves make clear, it does not follow from the emphasis on the exclusionary rule's deterrent value that "anything which deters illegal searches is thereby commanded by the Fourth Amendment." *Alderman v. United States*, 394 U.S., at 174, 89 S. Ct., at 967.

. . . .

As yet, we have not recognized any form of good-faith exception to the Fourth Amendment exclusionary rule. But the balancing approach that has evolved during the years of experience with the rule provides strong support for the modification currently urged upon us. As we discuss below, our evaluation of the costs and benefits of suppressing reliable physical evidence seized by officers reasonably relying on a warrant issued by a detached and neutral magistrate leads to the conclusion that such evidence should be admissible in the prosecution's case-in-chief.

III
A

Because a search warrant "provides the detached scrutiny of a neutral magistrate, which is a more reliable safeguard against improper searches than the hurried judgment of a law enforcement officer 'engaged in the often competitive enterprise of ferreting out crime,'" *United States v. Chadwick*, 433 U.S. 1, 9, 97 S. Ct. 2476, 2482, 53 L. Ed. 2d 538 (1971) (quoting *Johnson v. United States*, 333 U.S. 10, 14, 68 S. Ct. 367, 369, 92 L. Ed. 436 (1948)), we have expressed a strong preference for warrants and declared that "in a doubtful or marginal case a search under a warrant may be sustainable where without one it would fail." *United States v. Ventresca*, 380 U.S. 102, 106, 85 S. Ct. 741, 744, 13 L. Ed. 2d 687 (1965). Reasonable minds frequently may differ on the question whether a particular affidavit establishes probable cause, and we have thus concluded that the preference for warrants is most appropriately effectuated by according "great deference" to a magistrate's determination. *Spinelli v. United States*, 393 U.S., at 419, 89 S. Ct., at 590.

Deference to the magistrate, however, is not boundless. It is clear, first, that the deference accorded to a magistrate's finding of probable cause does not preclude inquiry into the knowing or reckless falsity of the affidavit on which that determination was based. *Franks v. Delaware*, 438 U.S. 154, 98 S. Ct. 2674, 57 L. Ed. 2d 667 (1978). Second, the courts must also insist that the magistrate purport to "perform his 'neutral and detached' function and not serve merely as a rubber stamp for the police." *Aguilar v. Texas*, 378 U.S., at 111, 84 S. Ct., at 1512. A magistrate failing to "manifest that neutrality and detachment demanded of a judicial officer when presented with a warrant application" and who acts instead as "an adjunct law enforcement officer" cannot provide valid authorization for an otherwise unconstitutional search. *Lo-Ji Sales, Inc. v. New York*, 442 U.S. 319, 326–327, 99 S. Ct. 2319, 2324–2325, 60 L. Ed. 2d 920 (1979).

Third, reviewing courts will not defer to a warrant based on an affidavit that does not "provide the magistrate with a substantial basis for determining the existence of probable cause." *Illinois v. Gates*, 462 U.S., at 239, 103 S. Ct., at 2332. "Sufficient information must be presented to the magistrate to allow that official to determine probable cause; his action cannot be a mere ratification of the bare conclusions of others." *Id*. Even if the warrant application was supported by more than a "bare bones" affidavit, a reviewing court may properly conclude that, notwithstanding the deference that magistrates deserve, the warrant was invalid because the magistrate's probable-cause determination reflected an improper analysis of the totality of the circumstances, or because the form of the warrant was improper in some respect.

Only in the first of these three situations, however, has the Court set forth a rationale for suppressing evidence obtained pursuant to a search warrant; in the other areas, it has simply excluded such evidence without considering whether Fourth Amendment interests will be advanced. To the extent that proponents of exclusion rely on its behavioral effects on judges and magistrates in these areas, their reliance is misplaced. First, the exclusionary rule is designed to deter police misconduct rather than to punish the errors of judges and magistrates. Second, there exists no evidence suggesting that judges and magistrates are inclined to ignore or subvert the

Fourth Amendment or that lawlessness among these actors requires application of the extreme sanction of exclusion.[14]

Third, and most important, we discern no basis, and are offered none, for believing that exclusion of evidence seized pursuant to a warrant will have a significant deterrent effect on the issuing judge or magistrate. Many of the factors that indicate that the exclusionary rule cannot provide an effective "special" or "general" deterrent for individual offending law enforcement officers apply as well to judges or magistrates. And, to the extent that the rule is thought to operate as a "systemic" deterrent on a wider audience, it clearly can have no such effect on individuals empowered to issue search warrants. Judges and magistrates are not adjuncts to the law enforcement team; as neutral judicial officers, they have no stake in the outcome of particular criminal prosecutions. The threat of exclusion thus cannot be expected significantly to deter them. Imposition of the exclusionary sanction is not necessary meaningfully to inform judicial officers of their errors, and we cannot conclude that admitting evidence obtained pursuant to a warrant while at the same time declaring that the warrant was somehow defective will in any way reduce judicial officers' professional incentives to comply with the Fourth Amendment, encourage them to repeat their mistakes, or lead to the granting of all colorable warrant requests.[18]

B

If exclusion of evidence obtained pursuant to a subsequently invalidated warrant is to have any deterrent effect, therefore, it must alter the behavior of individual law enforcement officers or the policies of their departments. One could argue that applying the exclusionary rule in cases where the police failed to demonstrate probable cause in the warrant application deters future inadequate presentations or "magistrate shopping" and thus promotes the ends of the Fourth Amendment. Suppressing evidence obtained pursuant to a technically defective warrant supported by probable cause also might encourage officers to scrutinize more closely the form of the warrant and to point out suspected judicial errors. We find such arguments speculative and conclude that suppression of evidence obtained pursuant to a warrant should

---

14. Although there are assertions that some magistrates become rubber stamps for the police and others may be unable effectively to screen police conduct, *see, e.g.,* 2 W. LaFave, SEARCH AND SEIZURE § 4.1 (1978); Kamisar, *Does (Did) (Should) the Exclusionary Rule Rest on a "Principled Basis" Rather than an "Empirical Proposition"?,* 16 Creighton L. Rev. 565, 569–571 (1983); Schroeder, *Deterring Fourth Amendment Violations: Alternatives to the Exclusionary Rule,* 69 Geo. L.J. 1361, 1412 (1981), we are not convinced that this is a problem of major proportions.

18. Limiting the application of the exclusionary sanction may well increase the care with which magistrates scrutinize warrant applications. We doubt that magistrates are more desirous of avoiding the exclusion of evidence obtained pursuant to warrants they have issued than of avoiding invasions of privacy. Federal magistrates, moreover, are subject to the direct supervision of district courts. They may be removed for "incompetency, misconduct, neglect of duty, or physical or mental disability." 28 U.S.C. § 631(i). If a magistrate serves merely as a "rubber stamp" for the police or is unable to exercise mature judgment, closer supervision or removal provides a more effective remedy than the exclusionary rule.

be ordered only on a case-by-case basis and only in those unusual cases in which exclusion will further the purposes of the exclusionary rule.[19]

We have frequently questioned whether the exclusionary rule can have any deterrent effect when the offending officers acted in the objectively reasonable belief that their conduct did not violate the Fourth Amendment. "No empirical researcher, proponent or opponent of the rule, has yet been able to establish with any assurance whether the rule has a deterrent effect. . . ." *United States v. Janis*, 428 U.S., at 452, n. 22, 96 S. Ct., at 3031, n. 22. But even assuming that the rule effectively deters some police misconduct and provides incentives for the law enforcement profession as a whole to conduct itself in accord with the Fourth Amendment, it cannot be expected, and should not be applied, to deter objectively reasonable law enforcement activity.[20]

. . . In short, where the officer's conduct is objectively reasonable,

> excluding the evidence will not further the ends of the exclusionary rule in any appreciable way; for it is painfully apparent that . . . the officer is acting as a reasonable officer would and should act under the circumstances. Excluding the evidence can in no way affect his future conduct unless it is to make him less willing to do his duty.

Stone v. Powell, 428 U.S., at 539–540, 96 S. Ct., at 3073–3074 (White, J., dissenting).

This is particularly true, we believe, when an officer acting with objective good faith has obtained a search warrant from a judge or magistrate and acted within its scope. In most such cases, there is no police illegality and thus nothing to deter. It is the magistrate's responsibility to determine whether the officer's allegations estab-

---

19. Our discussion of the deterrent effect of excluding evidence obtained in reasonable reliance on a subsequently invalidated warrant assumes, of course, that the officers properly executed the warrant and searched only those places and for those objects that it was reasonable to believe were covered by the warrant.

20. We emphasize that the standard of reasonableness we adopt is an objective one. Many objections to a good-faith exception assume that the exception will turn on the subjective good faith of individual officers. "Grounding the modification in objective reasonableness, however, retains the value of the exclusionary rule as an incentive for the law enforcement profession as a whole to conduct themselves in accord with the Fourth Amendment." *Illinois v. Gates*, 462 U.S., at 261, n. 15, 103 S. Ct., at 2344, n. 15 (White, J., concurring in the judgment). The objective standard we adopt, moreover, requires officers to have a reasonable knowledge of what the law prohibits. As Professor Jerold Israel has observed: "The key to the [exclusionary] rule's effectiveness as a deterrent lies, I believe, in the impetus it has provided to police training programs that make officers aware of the limits imposed by the fourth amendment and emphasize the need to operate within those limits. [An objective good-faith exception] . . . is not likely to result in the elimination of such programs, which are now viewed as an important aspect of police professionalism. Neither is it likely to alter the tenor of those programs; the possibility that illegally obtained evidence may be admitted in borderline cases is unlikely to encourage police instructors to pay less attention to fourth amendment limitations. Finally, [it] . . . should not encourage officers to pay less attention to what they are taught, as the requirement that the officer act in 'good faith' is inconsistent with closing one's mind to the possibility of illegality." Israel, *Criminal Procedure, the Burger Court, and the Legacy of the Warren Court*, 75 Mich. L. Rev. 1319, 1412–1413 (footnotes omitted).

lish probable cause and, if so, to issue a warrant comporting in form with the requirements of the Fourth Amendment. In the ordinary case, an officer cannot be expected to question the magistrate's probable-cause determination or his judgment that the form of the warrant is technically sufficient. "[O]nce the warrant issues, there is literally nothing more the policeman can do in seeking to comply with the law." *Id.*, 428 U.S., at 498, 96 S. Ct., at 3054 (Burger, C.J., concurring). Penalizing the officer for the magistrate's error, rather than his own, cannot logically contribute to the deterrence of Fourth Amendment violations.[22]

C

We conclude that the marginal or nonexistent benefits produced by suppressing evidence obtained in objectively reasonable reliance on a subsequently invalidated search warrant cannot justify the substantial costs of exclusion. We do not suggest, however, that exclusion is always inappropriate in cases where an officer has obtained a warrant and abided by its terms. . . . "[S]earches pursuant to a warrant will rarely require any deep inquiry into reasonableness," *Illinois v. Gates*, 462 U.S., at 267, 103 S. Ct., at 2347 (White, J., concurring in the judgment), for "a warrant issued by a magistrate normally suffices to establish" that a law enforcement officer has "acted in good faith in conducting the search." *United States v. Ross*, 456 U.S. 798, 823, n. 32, 102 S. Ct. 2157, 2172, n. 32, 72 L. Ed. 2d 572 (1982). Nevertheless, the officer's reliance on the magistrate's probable-cause determination and on the technical sufficiency of the warrant he issues must be objectively reasonable, *cf. Harlow v. Fitzgerald*, 457 U.S. 800, 815–819, 102 S. Ct. 2727, 2737–2739, 73 L. Ed. 2d 396 (1982),[23] and it is clear that in some circumstances the officer will have no reasonable grounds for believing that the warrant was properly issued.

---

22. To the extent that JUSTICE STEVENS' conclusions concerning the integrity of the courts rest on a foundation other than his judgment, which we reject, concerning the effects of our decision on the deterrence of police illegality, we find his argument unpersuasive. "Judicial integrity clearly does not mean that the courts must never admit evidence obtained in violation of the Fourth Amendment." *United States v. Janis*, 428 U.S. 433, 458, n. 35, 96 S. Ct. 3021, 3034, n. 35, 49 L. Ed. 2d 1046 (1976). "While courts, of course, must ever be concerned with preserving the integrity of the judicial process, this concern has limited force as a justification for the exclusion of highly probative evidence." *Stone v. Powell*, 428 U.S., at 485, 96 S. Ct., at 3048. Our cases establish that the question whether the use of illegally obtained evidence in judicial proceedings represents judicial participation in a Fourth Amendment violation and offends the integrity of the courts "is essentially the same as the inquiry into whether exclusion would serve a deterrent purpose. . . . The analysis showing that exclusion in this case has no demonstrated deterrent effect and is unlikely to have any significant such effect shows, by the same reasoning, that the admission of the evidence is unlikely to encourage violations of the Fourth Amendment." *United States v. Janis*, 428 U.S., at 459, n. 35, 96 S. Ct., at 3034, n. 35. Absent unusual circumstances, when a Fourth Amendment violation has occurred because the police have reasonably relied on a warrant issued by a detached and neutral magistrate but ultimately found to be defective, "the integrity of the courts is not implicated." *Illinois v. Gates*, 462 U.S., at 259, n. 14, 103 S. Ct., at 2343, n. 14 (White, J., concurring in the judgment).

23. In *Harlow*, we eliminated the subjective component of the qualified immunity public officials enjoy in suits seeking damages for alleged deprivations of constitutional rights. The situations are not perfectly analogous, but we also eschew inquiries into the subjective beliefs of law enforcement

Suppression therefore remains an appropriate remedy if the magistrate or judge in issuing a warrant was misled by information in an affidavit that the affiant knew was false or would have known was false except for his reckless disregard of the truth. *Franks v. Delaware*, 438 U.S. 154, 98 S. Ct. 2674, 57 L. Ed. 2d 667 (1978). The exception we recognize today will also not apply in cases where the issuing magistrate wholly abandoned his judicial role in the manner condemned in *Lo-Ji Sales, Inc. v. New York*, 442 U.S. 319, 99 S. Ct. 2319, 60 L. Ed. 2d 920 (1979); in such circumstances, no reasonably well-trained officer should rely on the warrant. Nor would an officer manifest objective good faith in relying on a warrant based on an affidavit "so lacking in indicia of probable cause as to render official belief in its existence entirely unreasonable." *Brown v. Illinois*, 422 U.S., at 610–611, 95 S. Ct., at 2265–2266 (Powell, J., concurring in part); see *Illinois v. Gates*, 462 U.S., at 263–264, 103 S. Ct., at 2345–2346 (White, J., concurring in the judgment). Finally, depending on the circumstances of the particular case, a warrant may be so facially deficient — *i.e.*, in failing to particularize the place to be searched or the things to be seized — that the executing officers cannot reasonably presume it to be valid.

In so limiting the suppression remedy, we leave untouched the probable-cause standard and the various requirements for a valid warrant. Other objections to the modification of the Fourth Amendment exclusionary rule we consider to be insubstantial. . . .

Nor are we persuaded that application of a good-faith exception to searches conducted pursuant to warrants will preclude review of the constitutionality of the search or seizure, deny needed guidance from the courts, or freeze Fourth Amendment law in its present state. . . .

If the resolution of a particular Fourth Amendment question is necessary to guide future action by law enforcement officers and magistrates, nothing will prevent reviewing courts from deciding that question before turning to the good-faith issue. Indeed, it frequently will be difficult to determine whether the officers acted reasonably without resolving the Fourth Amendment issue. Even if the Fourth Amendment question is not one of broad import, reviewing courts could decide in particular cases that magistrates under their supervision need to be informed of their errors and so evaluate the officers' good faith only after finding a violation. In other cir-

---

officers who seize evidence pursuant to a subsequently invalidated warrant. Although we have suggested that "[o]n occasion, the motive with which the officer conducts the illegal search may have some relevance in determining the propriety of applying the exclusionary rule," *Scott v. United States*, 436 U.S. 128, 139, n. 13, 98 S. Ct. 1717, 1724, n. 13, 56 L. Ed. 2d 168 (1978), we believe that "[s]ending state and federal courts into the minds of police officers would produce a grave and fruitless misallocation of judicial resources." *Massachusetts v. Painten*, 389 U.S. 560, 565, 88 S. Ct. 660, 663, 19 L. Ed. 2d 770 (1968) (White, J., dissenting). Accordingly, our good-faith inquiry is confined to the objectively ascertainable question whether a reasonably well-trained officer would have known that the search was illegal despite the magistrate's authorization. In making this determination, all of the circumstances — including whether the warrant application had previously been rejected by a different magistrate — may be considered.

cumstances, those courts could reject suppression motions posing no important Fourth Amendment questions by turning immediately to a consideration of the officers' good faith. We have no reason to believe that our Fourth Amendment jurisprudence would suffer by allowing reviewing courts to exercise an informed discretion in making this choice.

IV

When the principles we have enunciated today are applied to the facts of this case, it is apparent that the judgment of the Court of Appeals cannot stand. The Court of Appeals applied the prevailing legal standards to Officer Rombach's warrant application and concluded that the application could not support the magistrate's probable-cause determination. In so doing, the court clearly informed the magistrate that he had erred in issuing the challenged warrant. This aspect of the court's judgment is not under attack in this proceeding.

. . . .

In the absence of an allegation that the magistrate abandoned his detached and neutral role, suppression is appropriate only if the officers were dishonest or reckless in preparing their affidavit or could not have harbored an objectively reasonable belief in the existence of probable cause. Only respondent Leon has contended that no reasonably well-trained police officer could have believed that there existed probable cause to search his house; significantly, the other respondents advance no comparable argument. Officer Rombach's application for a warrant clearly was supported by much more than a "bare bones" affidavit. The affidavit related the results of an extensive investigation and, as the opinions of the divided panel of the Court of Appeals make clear, provided evidence sufficient to create disagreement among thoughtful and competent judges as to the existence of probable cause. Under these circumstances, the officers' reliance on the magistrate's determination of probable cause was objectively reasonable, and application of the extreme sanction of exclusion is inappropriate.

Accordingly, the judgment of the Court of Appeals is

Reversed.

Justice Blackmun, concurring.

. . . I join the Court's opinion in this case and the one in *Massachusetts v. Sheppard* because I believe that the rule announced today advances the legitimate interests of the criminal justice system without sacrificing the individual rights protected by the Fourth Amendment. I write separately, however, to underscore what I regard as the unavoidably provisional nature of today's decisions.

As the Court's opinion in this case makes clear, the Court has narrowed the scope of the exclusionary rule because of an empirical judgment that the rule has little appreciable effect in cases where officers act in objectively reasonable reliance on search warrants. Because I share the view that the exclusionary rule is not a constitutionally compelled corollary of the Fourth Amendment itself, I see no way to avoid making an empirical judgment of this sort, and I am satisfied that the Court has made the correct one on the information before it. Like all courts, we face institutional limitations on our ability to gather information about "legislative facts," and the exclusionary rule itself has exacerbated the shortage of hard data concerning the behavior of police officers in the absence of such a rule. Nonetheless, we cannot escape the responsibility to decide the question before us, however imperfect our information may be, and I am prepared to join the Court on the information now at hand.

What must be stressed, however, is that any empirical judgment about the effect of the exclusionary rule in a particular class of cases necessarily is a provisional one. By their very nature, the assumptions on which we proceed today cannot be cast in stone. To the contrary, they now will be tested in the real world of state and federal law enforcement, and this Court will attend to the results. If it should emerge from experience that, contrary to our expectations, the good faith exception to the exclusionary rule results in a material change in police compliance with the Fourth Amendment, we shall have to reconsider what we have undertaken here. The logic of a decision that rests on untested predictions about police conduct demands no less.

If a single principle may be drawn from this Court's exclusionary rule decisions, from *Weeks* through *Mapp v. Ohio*, 367 U.S. 643, 81 S. Ct. 1684, 6 L. Ed. 2d 1081 (1961), to the decisions handed down today, it is that the scope of the exclusionary rule is subject to change in light of changing judicial understanding about the effects of the rule outside the confines of the courtroom. It is incumbent on the Nation's law enforcement officers, who must continue to observe the Fourth Amendment in the wake of today's decisions, to recognize the double-edged nature of that principle.

JUSTICE BRENNAN, with whom JUSTICE MARSHALL joins, dissenting [in both *Leon* and *Massachusetts v. Sheppard, infra*].

Ten years ago in *United States v. Calandra*, 414 U.S. 338, 94 S. Ct. 613, 38 L. Ed. 2d 561 (1974), I expressed the fear that the Court's decision "may signal that a majority of my colleagues have positioned themselves to reopen the door (to evidence secured by official lawlessness) still further and abandon altogether the exclusionary rule in search-and-seizure cases." *Id.*, at 365, 94 S. Ct., at 628 (Brennan, J., dissenting). Since then, in case after case, I have witnessed the Court's gradual but determined strangulation of the rule. It now appears that the Court's victory over the Fourth Amendment is complete. That today's decision represents the *piece de resistance* of the Court's past efforts cannot be doubted, for today the Court sanctions the use in the prosecution's case-in-chief of illegally obtained evidence against the individual whose rights have been violated — a result that had previously been thought to be foreclosed.

. . . .

A proper understanding of the broad purposes sought to be served by the Fourth Amendment demonstrates that the principles embodied in the exclusionary rule rest upon a far firmer constitutional foundation than the shifting sands of the Court's deterrence rationale. But even if I were to accept the Court's chosen method of analyzing the question posed by these cases, I would still conclude that the Court's decision cannot be justified.

I

. . . .

A

At bottom, the Court's decision turns on the proposition that the exclusionary rule is merely a "judicially created remedy designed to safeguard Fourth Amendment rights generally through its deterrent effect, rather than a personal constitutional right." quoting *United States v. Calandra*, 414 U.S., at 348, 94 S. Ct., at 620. The germ of that idea is found in *Wolf v. Colorado*, 338 U.S. 25, 69 S. Ct. 1359, 93 L. Ed. 1782 (1949), and although I had thought that such a narrow conception of the rule had been forever put to rest by our decision in *Mapp v. Ohio*, 367 U.S. 643, 81 S. Ct. 1684, 6 L. Ed. 2d 1081 (1961), it has been revived by the present Court and reaches full flower with today's decision. The essence of this view, as expressed initially in the *Calandra* opinion and as reiterated today, is that the sole "purpose of the Fourth Amendment is to prevent unreasonable governmental intrusions into the privacy of one's person, house, papers, or effects. The wrong condemned is the unjustified governmental invasion of these areas of an individual's life. That wrong . . . is *fully accomplished* by the original search without probable cause." 414 U.S., at 354, 94 S. Ct., at 623 (emphasis added). This reading of the Amendment implies that its proscriptions are directed solely at those government agents who may actually invade an individual's constitutionally protected privacy. The courts are not subject to any direct constitutional duty to exclude illegally obtained evidence, because the question of the admissibility of such evidence is not addressed by the Amendment. This view of the scope of the Amendment relegates the judiciary to the periphery. Because the only constitutionally cognizable injury has already been "fully accomplished" by the police by the time a case comes before the courts, the Constitution is not itself violated if the judge decides to admit the tainted evidence. Indeed, the most the judge can do is wring his hands and hope that perhaps by excluding such evidence he can deter future transgressions by the police.

. . . .

Because seizures are executed principally to secure evidence, and because such evidence generally has utility in our legal system only in the context of a trial supervised by a judge, it is apparent that the admission of illegally obtained evidence implicates the same constitutional concerns as the initial seizure of that evidence. Indeed, by admitting unlawfully seized evidence, the judiciary becomes a part of what is in fact a single governmental action prohibited by the terms of the Amendment. Once that connection between the evidence-gathering role of the police and the evidence-admitting function of the courts is acknowledged, the plausibility of the Court's interpretation becomes more suspect. Certainly nothing in the language or history of the Fourth Amendment suggests that a recognition of this evidentiary link between the police and the courts was meant to be foreclosed. It is difficult to give any meaning at all to the limitations imposed by the Amendment if they are read to proscribe only certain conduct by the police but to allow other agents of the same government to take advantage of evidence secured by the police in violation of its requirements. The Amendment therefore must be read to condemn not only the initial unconstitutional invasion of privacy — which is done, after all, for the purpose of securing evidence — but also the subsequent use of any evidence so obtained.

. . . .

For my part, "[t]he right of the people to be secure in their persons, houses, papers, and effects, against unreasonable searches and seizures" comprises a personal right to exclude all evidence secured by means of unreasonable searches and seizures. The right to be free from the initial invasion of privacy and the right of exclusion are coordinate components of the central embracing right to be free from unreasonable searches and seizures.

. . . .

In contrast to the present Court's restrictive reading, the Court in *Weeks* recognized that, if the Amendment is to have any meaning, police and the courts cannot be regarded as constitutional strangers to each other; because the evidence-gathering role of the police is directly linked to the evidence-admitting function of the courts, an individual's Fourth Amendment rights may be undermined as completely by one as by the other.

B

. . . .

The various arguments advanced by the Court in this campaign have only strengthened my conviction that the deterrence theory is both misguided and unworkable. First, the Court has frequently bewailed the "cost" of excluding reliable evidence. In large part, this criticism rests upon a refusal to acknowledge the function of the Fourth Amendment itself. If nothing else, the Amendment plainly operates to disable the government from gathering information and securing evidence in certain ways. In practical terms, of course, this restriction of official power means that some incriminating evidence inevitably will go undetected if the government obeys these constitutional restraints. It is the loss of that evidence that is the "price" our society pays for enjoying the freedom and privacy safeguarded by the Fourth Amendment. Thus, some criminals will go free *not*, in Justice (then Judge) Cardozo's misleading epigram, "because the constable has blundered," *People v. Defore*, 242 N.Y. 13, 21, 150 N.E. 585, 587 (1926), but rather because official compliance with Fourth Amendment requirements makes it more difficult to catch criminals. Understood in this way, the Amendment directly contemplates that some reliable and incriminating evidence will be lost to the government; therefore, it is not the exclusionary rule, but the Amendment itself that has imposed this cost.

In addition, the Court's decisions over the past decade have made plain that the entire enterprise of attempting to assess the benefits and costs of the exclusionary rule in various contexts is a virtually impossible task for the judiciary to perform honestly or accurately. Although the Court's language in those cases suggests that some specific empirical basis may support its analyses, the reality is that the Court's opinions represent inherently unstable compounds of intuition, hunches, and occasional pieces of partial and often inconclusive data. In *Calandra*, for example, the Court, in considering whether the exclusionary rule should apply in grand jury proceedings, had before it no concrete evidence whatever concerning the impact that application of the rule in such proceedings would have either in terms of the long-term costs or the expected benefits. To the extent empirical data is available regarding the general costs and benefits of the exclusionary rule, it has shown, on the one hand, as the Court acknowledges today, that the costs are not as substantial as critics have asserted in the past, and, on the other hand, that while the exclusionary rule may well have certain deterrent effects, it is extremely difficult to determine with any degree of precision whether the incidence of unlawful conduct by police is now lower than it was prior to *Mapp*. . . .

By remaining within its redoubt of empiricism and by basing the rule solely on the deterrence rationale, the Court has robbed the rule of legitimacy. A doctrine that is explained as if it were an empirical proposition but for which there is only limited empirical support is both inherently unstable and an easy mark for critics. The extent of this Court's fidelity to Fourth Amendment requirements, however, should not turn on such statistical uncertainties. I share the view, expressed by JUSTICE STEWART for the Court in *Faretta v. California*, 422 U.S. 806, 95 S. Ct. 2525, 45 L. Ed. 2d 562 (1975), that "[p]ersonal liberties are not based on the law of averages." *Id.*, at 834, 95 S. Ct., at 2540. Rather than seeking to give effect to the liberties secured by the Fourth Amendment through guesswork about deterrence, the Court should restore to its proper place the principle framed 70 years ago in *Weeks* that an individual whose privacy has been invaded in violation of the Fourth Amendment has a right grounded in that Amendment to prevent the government from subsequently making use of any evidence so obtained.

II

Application of that principle clearly requires affirmance in the two cases decided today. In the first, *United States v. Leon*, 468 U.S. 897, 104 S. Ct. 3405, 81 L. Ed. 2d 677, it is conceded by the Government and accepted by the Court that the affidavit filed by the police officers in support of their application for a search warrant failed to provide a sufficient basis on which a neutral and detached magistrate could conclude that there was probable cause to issue the warrant. . . . The warrant, therefore, should never have issued. Stripped of the authority of the warrant, the conduct of these officers was plainly unconstitutional — it amounted to nothing less than a naked invasion of the privacy of respondents' homes without the requisite justification demanded by the Fourth Amendment. In order to restore the Government to the position it would have occupied had this unconstitutional search not occurred, therefore, it was necessary that the evidence be suppressed.

. . . .

In the second case before the Court, *Massachusetts v. Sheppard*, 468 U.S. 981, 104 S. Ct. 3424, 81 L. Ed. 2d 737, the State concedes and the Court accepts that the warrant issued to search respondent's home completely failed to state with particularity the things to be seized. Indeed, the warrant expressly and particularly described things such as "controlled substances" and "other paraphernalia used in, for, or in connection with the unlawful possession or use of any controlled substance" that the police had no reason whatsoever to believe were to be found in respondent's home. Given the Fourth Amendment's requirement that "no Warrants shall issue, but upon probable cause . . . and particularly describing . . . the things to be seized," this warrant should never have been issued. The police who entered respondent's home, therefore, were without constitutional authority to do so.

Although the Court's opinion tends to overlook this fact, the requirement of particularity is not a mere "technicality," it is an express constitutional command. The purpose of that requirement is to prevent precisely the kind of governmental conduct that the faulty warrant at issue here created a grave risk of permitting—namely, a search that was not narrowly and particularly limited to the things that a neutral and detached magistrate had reason to believe might be found at respondent's home. Although it is true, as JUSTICE STEVENS observes, that the affidavit submitted by the police set forth with particularity those items that they sought authority to search for, it is nevertheless clear that the warrant itself—the document which actually gave the officers legal authority to invade respondent's privacy—made no mention of these items. And, although it is true that the particular officers who applied for the warrant also happened to execute it and did so in accordance with the limits proposed in their affidavit, this happenstance should have no bearing on the central question whether these officers secured that prior judicial authority to conduct their search required by the Fourth Amendment. . . . I therefore fail to see how a search pursuant to such a fundamentally defective warrant can be characterized as "reasonable."

. . . I am convinced that it is not too much to ask that an attentive magistrate take those minimum steps necessary to ensure that every warrant he issues describes with particularity the things that his independent review of the warrant application convinces him are likely to be found in the premises. And I am equally convinced that it is not too much to ask that well-trained and experienced police officers take a moment to check that the warrant they have been issued at least describes those things for which they have sought leave to search. These convictions spring not from my own view of sound criminal law enforcement policy, but are instead compelled by the language of the Fourth Amendment and the history that led to its adoption.

III

Even if I were to accept the Court's general approach to the exclusionary rule, I could not agree with today's result. There is no question that in the hands of the present Court the deterrence rationale has proved to be a powerful tool for confining the scope of the rule.

. . . .

At the outset, the Court suggests that society has been asked to pay a high price—
in terms either of setting guilty persons free or of impeding the proper functioning
of trials—as a result of excluding relevant physical evidence in cases where the police, in conducting searches and seizing evidence, have made only an "objectively
reasonable" mistake concerning the constitutionality of their actions. But what evidence is there to support such a claim?

Significantly, the Court points to none, and, indeed, as the Court acknowledges, recent studies have demonstrated that the "costs" of the exclusionary rule—calculated in
terms of dropped prosecutions and lost convictions—are quite low. Contrary to the
claims of the rule's critics that exclusion leads to "the release of countless guilty
criminals," *Bivens v. Six Unknown Federal Narcotics Officers*, 403 U.S. 388, 416, 91 S.
Ct. 1999, 2014, 29 L. Ed. 2d 619 (Burger, C.J., dissenting), these studies have demonstrated that federal and state prosecutors very rarely drop cases because of potential search and seizure problems. . . . Of course, these data describe only the
costs attributable to the exclusion of evidence in all cases; the costs due to the exclusion of evidence in the narrower category of cases where police have made objectively reasonable mistakes must necessarily be even smaller. The Court, however,
ignores this distinction and mistakenly weighs the aggregated costs of exclusion in
all cases, irrespective of the circumstances that led to exclusion, against the potential benefits associated with only those cases in which evidence is excluded because
police reasonably but mistakenly believe that their conduct does not violate the
Fourth Amendment. When such faulty scales are used, it is little wonder that the
balance tips in favor of restricting the application of the rule.

What then supports the Court's insistence that this evidence be admitted? Apparently, the Court's only answer is that even though the costs of exclusion are not very
substantial, the potential deterrent effect in these circumstances is so marginal that
exclusion cannot be justified. The key to the Court's conclusion in this respect is its
belief that the prospective deterrent effect of the exclusionary rule operates only in
those situations in which police officers, when deciding whether to go forward with
some particular search, have reason to know that their planned conduct will violate
the requirements of the Fourth Amendment. If these officers in fact understand (or
reasonably should understand because the law is well-settled) that their proposed
conduct will offend the Fourth Amendment and that, consequently, any evidence
they seize will be suppressed in court, they will refrain from conducting the planned
search. In those circumstances, the incentive system created by the exclusionary rule
will have the hoped-for deterrent effect. But in situations where police officers reasonably (but mistakenly) believe that their planned conduct satisfies Fourth Amendment requirements—presumably either (a) because they are acting on the basis of
an apparently valid warrant, or (b) because their conduct is only later determined to
be invalid as a result of a subsequent change in the law or the resolution of an unsettled question of law—then such officers will have no reason to refrain from conducting the search and the exclusionary rule will have no effect.

At first blush, there is some logic to this position. Undoubtedly, in the situation hypothesized by the Court, the existence of the exclusionary rule cannot be expected to have any deterrent effect on the particular officers at the moment they are deciding whether to go forward with the search. Indeed, the subsequent exclusion of any evidence seized under such circumstances appears somehow "unfair" to the particular officers involved. As the Court suggests, these officers have acted in what they thought was an appropriate and constitutionally authorized manner, but then the fruit of their efforts is nullified by the application of the exclusionary rule.

The flaw in the Court's argument, however, is that its logic captures only one comparatively minor element of the generally acknowledged deterrent purposes of the exclusionary rule. To be sure, the rule operates to some extent to deter future misconduct by individual officers who have had evidence suppressed in their own cases. But what the Court overlooks is that the deterrence rationale for the rule is not designed to be, nor should it be thought of as, a form of "punishment" of individual police officers for their failures to obey the restraints imposed by the Fourth Amendment. Instead, the chief deterrent function of the rule is its tendency to promote institutional compliance with Fourth Amendment requirements on the part of law enforcement agencies generally. Thus, as the Court has previously recognized, "over the long term, [the] demonstration [provided by the exclusionary rule] that our society attaches serious consequences to violation of constitutional rights is thought to encourage those who formulate law enforcement policies, and the officers who implement them, to incorporate Fourth Amendment ideals into their value system." *Stone v. Powell*, 428 U.S., at 492, 96 S. Ct., at 3051. It is only through such an institution-wide mechanism that information concerning Fourth Amendment standards can be effectively communicated to rank and file officers.

If the overall educational effect of the exclusionary rule is considered, application of the rule to even those situations in which individual police officers have acted on the basis of a reasonable but mistaken belief that their conduct was authorized can still be expected to have a considerable long-term deterrent effect. If evidence is consistently excluded in these circumstances, police departments will surely be prompted to instruct their officers to devote greater care and attention to providing sufficient information to establish probable cause when applying for a warrant, and to review with some attention the form of the warrant that they have been issued, rather than automatically assuming that whatever document the magistrate has signed will necessarily comport with Fourth Amendment requirements.

After today's decision, however, that institutional incentive will be lost. Indeed, the Court's "reasonable mistake" exception to the exclusionary rule will tend to put a premium on police ignorance of the law. Armed with the assurance provided by today's decision that evidence will always be admissible whenever an officer has "reasonably" relied upon a warrant, police departments will be encouraged to train officers that if a warrant has simply been signed, it is reasonable, without more, to rely on it. Since in close cases there will no longer be any incentive to err on the side of constitutional behavior, police would have every reason to adopt a "let's-wait-until-it's-decided" approach in situations in which there is a question about a warrant's validity or the basis for its issuance.

Although the Court brushes these concerns aside, a host of grave consequences can be expected to result from its decision to carve this new exception out of the exclusionary rule. A chief consequence of today's decision will be to convey a clear and unambiguous message to magistrates that their decisions to issue warrants are now insulated from subsequent judicial review. Creation of this new exception for good faith reliance upon a warrant implicitly tells magistrates that they need not take much care in reviewing warrant applications, since their mistakes will from now on have virtually no consequence: If their decision to issue a warrant was correct, the evidence will be admitted; if their decision was incorrect but the police relied in good faith on the warrant, the evidence will also be admitted. Inevitably, the care and attention devoted to such an inconsequential chore will dwindle. Although the Court is correct to note that magistrates do not share the same stake in the outcome of a criminal case as the police, they nevertheless need to appreciate that their role is of some moment in order to continue performing the important task of carefully reviewing warrant applications. Today's decision effectively removes that incentive.[15]

Moreover, the good-faith exception will encourage police to provide only the bare minimum of information in future warrant applications. The police will now know that if they can secure a warrant, so long as the circumstances of its issuance are not "entirely unreasonable," all police conduct pursuant to that warrant will be protected from further judicial review. The clear incentive that operated in the past to establish probable cause adequately because reviewing courts would examine the magistrate's judgment carefully has now been so completely vitiated that the police need only show that it was not "entirely unreasonable" under the circumstances of a particular case for them to believe that the warrant they were issued was valid. The long-run effect unquestionably will be to undermine the integrity of the warrant process.

Finally, even if one were to believe, as the Court apparently does, that police are hobbled by inflexible and hypertechnical warrant procedures, today's decision cannot be justified. This is because, given the relaxed standard for assessing probable cause established just last Term in *Illinois v. Gates*, 462 U.S. 213, 103 S. Ct. 2317, 76 L. Ed. 2d 527 (1983), the Court's newly fashioned good faith exception, when applied in

---

15. Just last Term in *Illinois v. Gates*, 462 U.S. 213, 103 S. Ct. 2317, 76 L. Ed. 2d 527 (1983), the Court noted: "Sufficient information must be presented to the magistrate to allow that official to determine probable cause; his action cannot be a mere ratification of the bare conclusions of others. In order to ensure that such an abdication of the magistrate's duty does not occur, courts must continue to conscientiously review the sufficiency of affidavits on which warrants are issued." *Id.*, at 239, 103 S. Ct., at 2332. After today's decision, there will be little reason for reviewing courts to conduct such a conscientious review; rather, these courts will be more likely to focus simply on the question of police good faith. Despite the Court's confident prediction that such review will continue to be conducted, it is difficult to believe that busy courts faced with heavy dockets will take the time to render essentially advisory opinions concerning the constitutionality of the magistrate's decision before considering the officer's good faith.

the warrant context, will rarely, if ever, offer any greater flexibility for police than the *Gates* standard already supplies. In *Gates*, the Court held that "the task of an issuing magistrate is simply to make a practical, common-sense decision whether, given all the circumstances set forth in the affidavit before him, . . . there is a fair probability that contraband or evidence of a crime will be found in a particular place." *Id.*, at 238, 103 S. Ct., at 2332. The task of a reviewing court is confined to determining whether "the magistrate had a 'substantial basis' for concluding that probable cause existed." *Id.* Given such a relaxed standard, it is virtually inconceivable that a reviewing court, when faced with a defendant's motion to suppress, could first find that a warrant was invalid under the new *Gates* standard, but then, at the same time, find that a police officer's reliance on such an invalid warrant was nevertheless "objectively reasonable" under the test announced today. Because the two standards overlap so completely, it is unlikely that a warrant could be found invalid under *Gates* and yet the police reliance upon it could be seen as objectively reasonable; otherwise, we would have to entertain the mind-boggling concept of objectively reasonable reliance upon an objectively unreasonable warrant.

This paradox, as JUSTICE STEVENS suggests, perhaps explains the Court's unwillingness to remand [*Leon*] for reconsideration in light of *Gates*, for it is quite likely that on remand the Court of Appeals would find no violation of the Fourth Amendment, thereby demonstrating that the supposed need for the good faith exception in this context is more apparent than real. Therefore, although the Court's decisions are clearly limited to the situation in which police officers reasonably rely upon an apparently valid warrant in conducting a search, I am not at all confident that the exception unleashed today will remain so confined. Indeed, the full impact of the Court's regrettable decision will not be felt until the Court attempts to extend this rule to situations in which the police have conducted a warrantless search solely on the basis of their own judgment about the existence of probable cause and exigent circumstances. When that question is finally posed, I for one will not be surprised if my colleagues decide once again that we simply cannot afford to protect Fourth Amendment rights.

. . . .

I dissent.

JUSTICE STEVENS, concurring in the judgment in [*Sheppard*] and dissenting in [*Leon*].

. . . .

III

. . . .

In [*Leon*] . . . the Government now admits — at least for the tactical purpose of achieving what it regards as a greater benefit — that the substance, as well as the letter, of the Fourth Amendment was violated. The Court therefore assumes that the warrant in that case was not supported by probable cause, but refuses to suppress the evidence obtained thereby because it considers the police conduct to satisfy a "new-fangled" nonconstitutional standard of reasonableness. Yet if the Court's assumption is correct — if there was no probable cause — it must follow that it was "unreasonable" for the authorities to make unheralded entries into and searches of private dwellings and automobiles. The Court's conclusion that such searches undertaken without probable cause can nevertheless be "reasonable" is totally without support in our Fourth Amendment jurisprudence.

. . . .

. . . [I]f the majority's assumption is correct, that even after paying heavy deference to the magistrate's finding and resolving all doubt in its favor, there is no probable cause here, then by definition — as a matter of constitutional law — the officers' conduct was unreasonable. The Court's own hypothesis is that there was no fair likelihood that the officers would find evidence of a crime, and hence there was no reasonable law enforcement justification for their conduct.

The majority's contrary conclusion rests on the notion that it must be reasonable for a police officer to rely on a magistrate's finding. Until today that has plainly not been the law; it has been well-settled that even when a magistrate issues a warrant there is no guarantee that the ensuing search and seizure is constitutionally reasonable.

. . . .

The notion that a police officer's reliance on a magistrate's warrant is automatically appropriate is one the Framers of the Fourth Amendment would have vehemently rejected. The precise problem that the Amendment was intended to address was the *unreasonable issuance of warrants*. As we have often observed, the Amendment was actually motivated by the practice of issuing general warrants — warrants which did not satisfy the particularity and probable cause requirements. The resentments which led to the Amendment were directed at the issuance of warrants unjustified by particularized evidence of wrongdoing. Those who sought to amend the Constitution to include a Bill of Rights repeatedly voiced the view that the evil which had to be addressed was the issuance of warrants on insufficient evidence. . . .

In short, the Framers of the Fourth Amendment were deeply suspicious of warrants; in their minds the paradigm of an abusive search was the execution of a warrant not based on probable cause. The fact that colonial officers had magisterial authorization for their conduct when they engaged in general searches surely did not make their conduct "reasonable." The Court's view that it is consistent with our Constitution to adopt a rule that it is presumptively reasonable to rely on a defective warrant is the product of constitutional amnesia.

IV

. . . .

The exclusionary rule is designed to prevent violations of the Fourth Amendment. "Its purpose is to deter — to compel respect for the constitutional guaranty in the only effectively available way, by removing the incentive to disregard it." *Elkins v.*

United States, 364 U.S. 206, 217, 80 S. Ct. 1437, 1444, 4 L. Ed. 2d 1669 (1960). If the police cannot use evidence obtained through warrants issued on less than probable cause, they have less incentive to seek those warrants, and magistrates have less incentive to issue them.

Today's decisions do grave damage to that deterrent function. Under the majority's new rule, even when the police know their warrant application is probably insufficient, they retain an incentive to submit it to a magistrate, on the chance that he may take the bait. No longer must they hesitate and seek additional evidence in doubtful cases. . . .

The Court is of course correct that the exclusionary rule cannot deter when the authorities have no reason to know that their conduct is unconstitutional. But when probable cause is lacking, then by definition a reasonable person under the circumstances would not believe there is a fair likelihood that a search will produce evidence of a crime. Under such circumstances well-trained professionals must know that they are violating the Constitution. The Court's approach — which, in effect, encourages the police to seek a warrant even if they know the existence of probable cause is doubtful — can only lead to an increased number of constitutional violations.

Thus, the Court's creation of a double standard of reasonableness inevitably must erode the deterrence rationale that still supports the exclusionary rule. But we should not ignore the way it tarnishes the role of the judiciary in enforcing the Constitution. . . .

. . . As the Court correctly notes, we have refused to apply the exclusionary rule to collateral contexts in which its marginal efficacy is questionable; until today, however, every time the police have violated the applicable commands of the Fourth Amendment a court has been prepared to vindicate that Amendment by preventing the use of evidence so obtained in the prosecution's case-in-chief against those whose rights have been violated. Today, for the first time, this Court holds that although the Constitution has been violated, no court should do anything about it at any time and in any proceeding. In my judgment, the Constitution requires more. Courts simply cannot escape their responsibility for redressing constitutional violations if they admit evidence obtained through unreasonable searches and seizures, since the entire point of police conduct that violates the Fourth Amendment is to obtain evidence for use at trial. If such evidence is admitted, then the courts become not merely the final and necessary link in an unconstitutional chain of events, but its actual motivating force.

. . . .

While I concur in the Court's judgment in [*Sheppard*] I would vacate the judgment in [*Leon*] and remand the case to the Court of Appeals for reconsideration in the light of *Gates*. Accordingly, I respectfully dissent from the disposition in [*Leon*].

Massachusetts v. Sheppard

United States Supreme Court

468 U.S. 981, 104 S. Ct. 3424, 82 L. Ed. 2d 737 (1984)

JUSTICE WHITE delivered the opinion of the Court.

This case involves the application of the rules articulated today in *United States v. Leon* to a situation in which police officers seize items pursuant to a warrant subsequently invalidated because of a technical error on the part of the issuing judge.

I

The badly burned body of Sandra Boulware was discovered in a vacant lot in the Roxbury section of Boston at approximately 5 a.m., Saturday, May 5, 1979. An autopsy revealed that Boulware had died of multiple compound skull fractures caused by blows to the head. After a brief investigation, the police decided to question one of the victim's boyfriends, Osborne Sheppard. Sheppard told the police that he had last seen the victim on Tuesday night and that he had been at a local gaming house (where card games were played) from 9 p.m. Friday until 5 a.m. Saturday. He identified several people who would be willing to substantiate the latter claim.

By interviewing the people Sheppard had said were at the gaming house on Friday night, the police learned that although Sheppard was at the gaming house that night, he had borrowed an automobile at about 3 a.m. Saturday morning in order to give two men a ride home. Even though the trip normally took only fifteen minutes, Sheppard did not return with the car until nearly 5 a.m.

On Sunday morning, police officers visited the owner of the car Sheppard had borrowed. He consented to an inspection of the vehicle. Bloodstains and pieces of hair were found on the rear bumper and within the trunk compartment. In addition, the officers noticed strands of wire in the trunk similar to wire strands found on and near the body of the victim. The owner of the car told the officers that when he last used the car on Friday night, shortly before Sheppard borrowed it, he had placed articles in the trunk and had not noticed any stains on the bumper or in the trunk.

On the basis of the evidence gathered thus far in the investigation, Detective Peter O'Malley drafted an affidavit designed to support an application for an arrest warrant and a search warrant authorizing a search of Sheppard's residence. The affidavit set forth the results of the investigation and stated that the police wished to search for

> [a] fifth bottle of amaretto liquor, 2 nickel bags of marijuana, a woman's jacket that has been described as black-grey (charcoal), any possessions of Sandra D. Boulware, similar type wire and rope that match those on the body of Sandra D. Boulware, or in the above [T]hunderbird. A blunt instrument that might have been used on the victim, men's or women's clothing that may have blood, gasoline, burns on them. Items that may have fingerprints of the victim.

Detective O'Malley showed the affidavit to the District Attorney, the District Attorney's first assistant, and a sergeant, who all concluded that it set forth probable cause for the search and the arrest.

Because it was Sunday, the local court was closed, and the police had a difficult time finding a warrant application form. Detective O'Malley finally found a warrant form previously in use in the Dorchester District. The form was entitled "Search Warrant — Controlled Substance G.L. c. 276 §§ 1 through 3A." Realizing that some changes had to be made before the form could be used to authorize the search requested in the affidavit, Detective O'Malley deleted the subtitle "controlled substance" with a typewriter. He also substituted "Roxbury" for the printed "Dorchester" and typed Sheppard's name and address into blank spaces provided for that information. However, the reference to "controlled substance" was not deleted in the portion of the form that constituted the warrant application and that, when signed, would constitute the warrant itself.

Detective O'Malley then took the affidavit and the warrant form to the residence of a judge who had consented to consider the warrant application. The judge examined the affidavit and stated that he would authorize the search as requested. Detective O'Malley offered the warrant form and stated that he knew the form as presented dealt with controlled substances. He showed the judge where he had crossed out the subtitles. After unsuccessfully searching for a more suitable form, the judge informed O'Malley that he would make the necessary changes so as to provide a proper search warrant. The judge then took the form, made some changes on it, and dated and signed the warrant. However, he did not change the substantive portion of the warrant, which continued to authorize a search for controlled substances; nor did he alter the form so as to incorporate the affidavit. The judge returned the affidavit and the warrant to O'Malley, informing him that the warrant was sufficient authority in form and content to carry out the search as requested. O'Malley took the two documents and, accompanied by other officers, proceeded to Sheppard's residence. The scope of the ensuing search was limited to the items listed in the affidavit, and several incriminating pieces of evidence were discovered. Sheppard was then charged with first-degree murder.

At a pretrial suppression hearing, the trial judge concluded that the warrant failed to conform to the commands of the Fourth Amendment because it did not particularly describe the items to be seized. The judge ruled, however, that the evidence could be admitted notwithstanding the defect in the warrant because the police had acted in good faith in executing what they reasonably thought was a valid warrant. At the subsequent trial, Sheppard was convicted.

On appeal, Sheppard argued that the evidence obtained pursuant to the defective warrant should have been suppressed. The Supreme Judicial Court of Massachusetts agreed. . . .

II

Having already decided [in *Leon*] that the exclusionary rule should not be applied when the officer conducting the search acted in objectively reasonable reliance on a warrant issued by a detached and neutral magistrate that subsequently is determined to be invalid, the sole issue before us in this case is whether the officers reasonably believed that the search they conducted was authorized by a valid warrant.[5] There is no dispute that the officers believed that the warrant authorized the search that they conducted. Thus, the only question is whether there was an objectively reasonable basis for the officers' mistaken belief. Both the trial court and a majority of the Supreme Judicial Court concluded that there was. We agree.

The officers in this case took every step that could reasonably be expected of them. Detective O'Malley prepared an affidavit which was reviewed and approved by the District Attorney. He presented that affidavit to a neutral judge. The judge concluded that the affidavit established probable cause to search Sheppard's residence, and informed O'Malley that he would authorize the search as requested. O'Malley then produced the warrant form and informed the judge that it might need to be changed. He was told by the judge that the necessary changes would be made. He then observed the judge make some changes and received the warrant and the affidavit. At this point, a reasonable police officer would have concluded, as O'Malley did, that the warrant authorized a search for the materials outlined in the affidavit.

Sheppard contends that since O'Malley knew the warrant form was defective, he should have examined it to make sure that the necessary changes had been made. However, that argument is based on the premise that O'Malley had a duty to disregard the judge's assurances that the requested search would be authorized and the necessary changes would be made. Whatever an officer may be required to do when he executes a warrant without knowing beforehand what items are to be seized,[6] we refuse to rule that an officer is required to disbelieve a judge who has just

---

5. Both the trial court and a majority of the Supreme Judicial Court concluded that the warrant was constitutionally defective because the description in the warrant was completely inaccurate and the warrant did not incorporate the description contained in the affidavit. Petitioner does not dispute this conclusion. Petitioner does argue, however, that even though the warrant was invalid, the search was constitutional because it was reasonable within the meaning of the Fourth Amendment. The uniformly applied rule is that a search conducted pursuant to a warrant that fails to conform to the particularity requirement of the Fourth Amendment is unconstitutional. That rule is in keeping with the well-established principle that "except in certain carefully defined classes of cases, a search of private property without proper consent is 'unreasonable' unless it has been authorized by a valid warrant." *Camara v. Municipal Court*, 387 U.S. 523, 528–529, 87 S. Ct. 1727, 1730–1731, 18 L. Ed. 2d 930 (1967). Whether the present case fits into one of those carefully defined classes is a fact-bound issue of little importance since similar situations are unlikely to arise with any regularity.

6. Normally, when an officer who has not been involved in the application stage receives a warrant, he will read it in order to determine the object of the search. In this case, Detective O'Malley, the officer who directed the search, knew what items were listed in the affidavit presented to the judge, and he had good reason to believe that the warrant authorized the seizure of those items. Whether an officer who is less familiar with the warrant application or who has unalleviated concerns about the proper scope of the search would be justified in failing to notice a defect like the one in the warrant in this case is an issue we need not decide. We hold only that it was not unreasonable for the police in this case to rely on the judge's assurances that the warrant authorized the search they had requested.

advised him, by word and by action, that the warrant he possesses authorizes him to conduct the search he has requested. In Massachusetts, as in most jurisdictions, the determinations of a judge acting within his jurisdiction, even if erroneous, are valid and binding until they are set aside under some recognized procedure. If an officer is required to accept at face value the judge's conclusion that a warrant form is invalid, there is little reason why he should be expected to disregard assurances that everything is all right, especially when he has alerted the judge to the potential problems.

In sum, the police conduct in this case clearly was objectively reasonable and largely error-free. An error of constitutional dimensions may have been committed with respect to the issuance of the warrant, but it was the judge, not the police officers, who made the critical mistake. "[T]he exclusionary rule was adopted to deter unlawful searches by police, not to punish the errors of magistrates and judges." *Illinois v. Gates*, 462 U.S. 213, 263, 103 S. Ct. 2317, 2345, 76 L. Ed. 2d 527 (1983) (White, J., concurring in the judgment). Suppressing evidence because the judge failed to make all the necessary clerical corrections despite his assurances that such changes would be made will not serve the deterrent function that the exclusionary rule was designed to achieve. Accordingly, federal law does not require the exclusion of the disputed evidence in this case. The judgment of the Supreme Judicial Court is therefore reversed, and the case is remanded for further proceedings not inconsistent with this opinion.

It is so ordered.

Notes and Questions

(1) Suppose an officer honestly and sincerely, although misguidedly, believes that her affidavit provides probable cause for issuance of a search warrant. A magistrate erroneously agrees. Will the evidence obtained pursuant to the warrant be admissible under *Leon* and *Sheppard*? Suppose, instead, that the officer correctly believes that she lacks probable cause for the issuance of a search warrant. Nevertheless, she submits an affidavit in application for a search warrant to a magistrate. The magistrate incorrectly finds probable cause, and the officer conducts a warranted search. Must the evidence discovered be excluded?

(2) Does the Court's analysis in *Leon* and *Sheppard* dictate a similar result in situations where officers' conduct unconstitutional warrantless searches but reasonably believe those searches to be legal? Suppose, for example, that an officer searches an automobile incident to the arrest of a passenger. The officer reasonably, but erroneously, believes that the search is sufficiently contemporaneous with the arrest to be a valid warrantless search. A trial judge upholds the validity of the search, but a divided appellate court disagrees, holding that the search, although close to the line, was just outside the permissible temporal scope of searches incident to arrests. Would the benefits of excluding the products of that search outweigh the costs of doing so? Why?

(3) In their dissents, both Justice Brennan and Justice Stevens imply that it is inconceivable that an officer could reasonably rely on a magistrate's issuance of a warrant if the information furnished by the officer in fact failed to support a probable

cause finding under the liberal probable cause standard of *Illinois v. Gates*. Similarly, Professor Yale Kamisar has concluded that to "impose a 'good faith' or 'reasonable belief' exception on *Gates'*[s] soft standard for upholding search warrants" is "incomprehensible" and "mind boggling." Yale Kamisar, Gates, *"Probable Cause," "Good Faith," and Beyond*, 69 Iowa L. Rev. 551, 589 (1984). Is there an inherent, unavoidable contradiction in the *Leon* majority's notion of "reasonable reliance" upon a warrant that fails the *Gates* test for probable cause?

(4) In interpreting their own constitutions, a fair number of state courts have decided to reject the *Leon-Sheppard* exception. What is it about the "good faith" doctrine that has made it decidedly less popular than other modern exceptions to the exclusionary rule?

(5) In two additional situations, the Court has relied on the reasoning of *Leon* and *Sheppard* to justify additional, albeit limited, "good faith" exceptions to the Fourth Amendment exclusionary rule.

(a) In *Illinois v. Krull*, 480 U.S. 340, 107 S. Ct. 1160, 94 L. Ed. 2d 364 (1987), the Court concluded that even though a statutorily-authorized search was constitutionally unreasonable, the evidence obtained as a result of that search was admissible because the officers conducting the search had acted in "objectively reasonable reliance upon the statute authorizing" the search. According to the Court, in cases like *Krull*, the error is that of legislators, who, like judges, do not need to be and are not likely to be deterred by the exclusion of evidence. Moreover, when officers have acted in "reasonable reliance" upon a statute, there is no police error to deter. Consequently, the deterrent premises of the exclusionary rule do not support suppression.

(b) In *Arizona v. Evans*, 514 U.S. 1, 115 S. Ct. 1185, 131 L. Ed. 2d 34 (1995), the Court concluded that if an officer arrests an individual based on a computer record that erroneously indicates the existence of an outstanding arrest warrant, evidence found as a result of that "unreasonable" arrest is admissible *if* the officer acted in "objectively reasonable reliance" on the erroneous computer record and *if* "court employees [are] responsible for the erroneous computer record." The Court decided that another extension of the "good faith" exception was justified because the exclusionary rule is not designed to affect the behavior of court employees and because there is no reason to attempt to deter "objectively reasonable" behavior by law enforcement officers. Consequently, "the *Leon* framework supports a categorical exception to the exclusionary rule for clerical errors of court employees."

Although the Government argued that the same result ought to follow even if "police personnel were responsible for the error" in the computer record, the Court "decline[d] to address that question." Because the trial court in *Evans* had not determined whether a court employee or sheriff's office employee was responsible for the erroneous computer record, the Court remanded the case for further consideration.

Herring v. United States

United States Supreme Court

555 U.S. 135, 129 S. Ct. 695, 172 L. Ed. 2d 496 (2009)

CHIEF JUSTICE ROBERTS delivered the opinion of the Court.

The Fourth Amendment forbids "unreasonable searches and seizures," and this usually requires the police to have probable cause or a warrant before making an arrest. What if an officer reasonably believes there is an outstanding arrest warrant, but that belief turns out to be wrong because of a negligent bookkeeping error by another police employee? The parties here agree that the ensuing arrest is still a violation of the Fourth Amendment, but dispute whether contraband found during a search incident to that arrest must be excluded in a later prosecution.

Our cases establish that such suppression is not an automatic consequence of a Fourth Amendment violation. Instead, the question turns on the culpability of the police and the potential of exclusion to deter wrongful police conduct. Here the error was the result of isolated negligence attenuated from the arrest. We hold that in these circumstances the jury should not be barred from considering all the evidence.

I

On July 7, 2004, Investigator Mark Anderson learned that Bennie Dean Herring had driven to the Coffee County Sheriff's Department to retrieve something from his impounded truck. Herring was no stranger to law enforcement, and Anderson asked the county's warrant clerk, Sandy Pope, to check for any outstanding warrants for Herring's arrest. When she found none, Anderson asked Pope to check with Sharon Morgan, her counterpart in neighboring Dale County. After checking Dale County's computer database, Morgan replied that there was an active arrest warrant for Herring's failure to appear on a felony charge. Pope relayed the information to Anderson and asked Morgan to fax over a copy of the warrant as confirmation. Anderson and a deputy followed Herring as he left the impound lot, pulled him over, and arrested him. A search incident to the arrest revealed methamphetamine in Herring's pocket, and a pistol (which as a felon he could not possess) in his vehicle.

There had, however, been a mistake about the warrant. The Dale County sheriff's computer records are supposed to correspond to actual arrest warrants, which the office also maintains. But when Morgan went to the files to retrieve the actual warrant to fax to Pope, Morgan was unable to find it. She called a court clerk and learned that the warrant had been recalled five months earlier. Normally when a warrant is recalled the court clerk's office or a judge's chambers calls Morgan, who enters the information in the sheriff's computer database and disposes of the physical copy. For whatever reason, the information about the recall of the warrant for Herring did not appear in the database. Morgan immediately called Pope to alert her to the mixup, and Pope contacted Anderson over a secure radio. This all unfolded in 10 to 15 minutes, but Herring had already been arrested and found with the gun and drugs, just a few hundred yards from the sheriff's office.

Herring was indicted in the District Court for the Middle District of Alabama for illegally possessing the gun and drugs, violations of 18 U.S.C. § 922(g)(1) and 21 U.S.C. § 844(a). He moved to suppress the evidence on the ground that his initial arrest had been illegal because the warrant had been rescinded. The Magistrate Judge recommended denying the motion because the arresting officers had acted in a good-faith belief that the warrant was still outstanding. . . . . The District Court adopted the Magistrate Judge's recommendation, and the Court of Appeals for the Eleventh Circuit affirmed.

The Eleventh Circuit found that the arresting officers in Coffee County "were entirely innocent of any wrongdoing or carelessness." The court assumed that whoever failed to update the Dale County sheriff's records was also a law enforcement official, but noted that "the conduct in question [wa]s a negligent failure to act, not a deliberate or tactical choice to act." . . . [T]he Eleventh Circuit concluded that . . . the evidence was . . . admissible under the good-faith rule of *United States v. Leon*, 468 U.S. 897, 104 S. Ct. 3405 (1984).

. . . .

II

. . . For purposes of deciding this case . . . we accept the parties' assumption that there was a Fourth Amendment violation. The issue is whether the exclusionary rule should be applied.

A

The Fourth Amendment protects "[t]he right of the people to be secure in their persons, houses, papers, and effects, against unreasonable searches and seizures," but "contains no provision expressly precluding the use of evidence obtained in violation of its commands," *Arizona v. Evans*, 514 U.S. 1, 10, 115 S. Ct. 1185, 131 L. Ed. 2d 34 (1995). Nonetheless, our decisions establish an exclusionary rule that, when applicable, forbids the use of improperly obtained evidence at trial. . . .

In analyzing the applicability of the rule, *Leon* admonished that we must consider the actions of all the police officers involved. 468 U.S., at 923, n. 24, 104 S. Ct. 3405 ("It is necessary to consider the objective reasonableness, not only of the officers who eventually executed a warrant, but also of the officers who originally obtained it or who provided information material to the probable-cause determination"). The Coffee County officers did nothing improper. Indeed, the error was noticed so quickly because Coffee County requested a faxed confirmation of the warrant.

The Eleventh Circuit concluded, however, that somebody in Dale County should have updated the computer database to reflect the recall of the arrest warrant. The court also concluded that this error was negligent, but did not find it to be reckless or deliberate. That fact is crucial to our holding that this error is not enough by itself to require "the extreme sanction of exclusion." *Leon, supra*, at 916, 104 S. Ct. 3405.

B

1. The fact that a Fourth Amendment violation occurred — *i.e.*, that a search or arrest was unreasonable — does not necessarily mean that the exclusionary rule applies. *Illinois v. Gates*, 462 U.S. 213, 223, 103 S. Ct. 2317, 76 L. Ed. 2d 527 (1983). Indeed, exclusion "has always been our last resort, not our first impulse," *Hudson v. Michigan*, 547 U.S. 586, 591, 126 S. Ct. 2159, 165 L. Ed. 2d 56 (2006), and our precedents establish important principles that constrain application of the exclusionary rule.

First, the exclusionary rule is not an individual right and applies only where it "'result[s] in appreciable deterrence.'" *Leon, supra*, at 909, 104 S. Ct. 3405 (quoting *United States v. Janis*, 428 U.S. 433, 454, 96 S. Ct. 3021, 49 L. Ed. 2d 1046 (1976)). . . .

In addition, the benefits of deterrence must outweigh the costs. *Leon, supra*, at 910, 104 S. Ct. 3405. . . . . The principal cost of applying the rule is, of course, letting guilty and possibly dangerous defendants go free — something that "offends basic concepts of the criminal justice system." *Leon, supra*, at 908, 104 S. Ct. 3405. . . .

. . . .

. . . [I]n [*Arizona v.*] *Evans*, 514 U.S. 1, 115 S. Ct. 1185, 131 L. Ed. 2d 34 [(1995)], we applied th[e] good-faith rule to police who reasonably relied on mistaken information in a court's database that an arrest warrant was outstanding. . . . *Evans* left unresolved "whether the evidence should be suppressed if police personnel were responsible for the error," an issue . . . that we now confront.

2. The extent to which the exclusionary rule is justified by . . . deterrence principles varies with the culpability of the law enforcement conduct. As we said in *Leon*, "an assessment of the flagrancy of the police misconduct constitutes an important step in the calculus" of applying the exclusionary rule. 468 U.S., at 911, 104 S. Ct. 3405. Similarly, in [*Illinois v.*] *Krull* we elaborated that "evidence should be suppressed 'only if it can be said that the law enforcement officer had knowledge, or may properly be charged with knowledge, that the search was unconstitutional under the Fourth Amendment.'" [480 U.S. 340, 348–349, 107 S. Ct. 1160, 94 L. Ed. 2d 364 (1987)] (quoting *United States v. Peltier*, 422 U.S. 531, 542, 95 S. Ct. 2313, 45 L. Ed. 2d 374 (1975)).

Anticipating the good-faith exception to the exclusionary rule, Judge Friendly wrote that "[t]he beneficent aim of the exclusionary rule to deter police misconduct can be sufficiently accomplished by a practice . . . outlawing evidence obtained by flagrant or deliberate violation of rights." The Bill of Rights as a Code of Criminal Procedure, 53 Calif. L. Rev. 929, 953 (1965) (footnotes omitted); see also *Brown v. Illinois*, 422 U.S. 590, 610–611, 95 S. Ct. 2254, 45 L. Ed. 2d 416 (1975) (Powell, J., concurring in part) ("[T]he deterrent value of the exclusionary rule is most likely to be effective" when "official conduct was flagrantly abusive of Fourth Amendment rights").

Indeed, the abuses that gave rise to the exclusionary rule featured intentional conduct that was patently unconstitutional. In *Weeks*, 232 U.S. 383, 34 S. Ct. 341, 58 L.

Ed. 652, a foundational exclusionary rule case, the officers had broken into the defendant's home (using a key shown to them by a neighbor), confiscated incriminating papers, then returned again with a U.S. Marshal to confiscate even more. *Id.*, at 386, 34 S. Ct. 341. Not only did they have no search warrant, which the Court held was required, but they could not have gotten one had they tried. They were so lacking in sworn and particularized information that "not even an order of court would have justified such procedure." *Id.*, at 393–394, 34 S. Ct. 341. *Silverthorne Lumber Co. v. United States*, 251 U.S. 385, 40 S. Ct. 182, 64 L. Ed. 319 (1920), on which petitioner repeatedly relies, was similar; federal officials "without a shadow of authority" went to the defendants' office and "made a clean sweep" of every paper they could find. *Id.*, at 390, 40 S. Ct. 182. Even the Government seemed to acknowledge that the "seizure was an outrage." *Id.*, at 391, 40 S. Ct. 182.

Equally flagrant conduct was at issue in *Mapp v. Ohio*, 367 U.S. 643, 81 S. Ct. 1684, 6 L. Ed. 2d 1081 (1961), which . . . extended the exclusionary rule to the States. Officers forced open a door to Ms. Mapp's house, kept her lawyer from entering, brandished what the court concluded was a false warrant, then forced her into handcuffs and canvassed the house for obscenity. 367 U.S., at 644–645, 81 S. Ct. 1684. An error that arises from nonrecurring and attenuated negligence is thus far removed from the core concerns that led us to adopt the rule in the first place. And in fact since *Leon*, we have never applied the rule to exclude evidence obtained in violation of the Fourth Amendment, where the police conduct was no more intentional or culpable than this.

3. To trigger the exclusionary rule, police conduct must be sufficiently deliberate that exclusion can meaningfully deter it, and sufficiently culpable that such deterrence is worth the price paid by the justice system. As laid out in our cases, the exclusionary rule serves to deter deliberate, reckless, or grossly negligent conduct, or in some circumstances recurring or systemic negligence. The error in this case does not rise to that level.[4]

. . . .

Both this case and *Franks* [*v. Delaware*, 438 U.S. 154, 98 S. Ct. 2674, 57 L. Ed. 2d 667 (1978),] concern false information provided by police. Under *Franks*, negligent police miscommunications in the course of acquiring a warrant do not provide a basis to rescind a warrant and render a search or arrest invalid. Here, the miscommunications occurred in a different context — after the warrant had been issued and recalled — but that fact should not require excluding the evidence obtained.

---

4. We do not quarrel with JUSTICE GINSBURG's claim that "liability for negligence . . . creates an incentive to act with greater care," and we do not suggest that the exclusion of this evidence could have no deterrent effect. But our cases require any deterrence to "be weighed against the 'substantial social costs exacted by the exclusionary rule,'" *Illinois v. Krull*, 480 U.S. 340, 352–353, 107 S. Ct. 1160, 94 L. Ed. 2d 364 (1987) (quoting *Leon*, 468 U.S., at 907, 104 S. Ct. 3405), and here exclusion is not worth the cost.

The pertinent analysis of deterrence and culpability is objective, not an "inquiry into the subjective awareness of arresting officers," Reply Brief for Petitioner 4–5. We have already held that "our good-faith inquiry is confined to the objectively ascertainable question whether a reasonably well trained officer would have known that the search was illegal" in light of "all of the circumstances." *Leon*, 468 U.S., at 922, n. 23, 104 S. Ct. 3405. These circumstances frequently include a particular officer's knowledge and experience, but that does not make the test any more subjective than the one for probable cause, which looks to an officer's knowledge and experience, *Ornelas v. United States*, 517 U.S. 690, 699–700, 116 S. Ct. 1657, 134 L. Ed. 2d 911 (1996), but not his subjective intent, *Whren v. United States*, 517 U.S. 806, 812–813, 116 S. Ct. 1769, 135 L. Ed. 2d 89 (1996).

4. We do not suggest that all recordkeeping errors by the police are immune from the exclusionary rule. In this case, however, the conduct at issue was not so objectively culpable as to require exclusion. In *Leon* we held that "the marginal or nonexistent benefits produced by suppressing evidence obtained in objectively reasonable reliance on a subsequently invalidated search warrant cannot justify the substantial costs of exclusion." 468 U.S., at 922, 104 S. Ct. 3405. The same is true when evidence is obtained in objectively reasonable reliance on a subsequently recalled warrant.

If the police have been shown to be reckless in maintaining a warrant system, or to have knowingly made false entries to lay the groundwork for future false arrests, exclusion would certainly be justified under our cases should such misconduct cause a Fourth Amendment violation. We said as much in *Leon*, explaining that an officer could not "obtain a warrant on the basis of a 'bare bones' affidavit and then rely on colleagues who are ignorant of the circumstances under which the warrant was obtained to conduct the search." *Id.*, at 923, n. 24, 104 S. Ct. 3405 (citing *Whiteley v. Warden, Wyo. State Penitentiary*, 401 U.S. 560, 568, 91 S. Ct. 1031, 28 L. Ed. 2d 306 (1971)). . . . [F]ears that our decision will cause police departments to deliberately keep their officers ignorant are thus unfounded.

The dissent also adverts to the possible unreliability of a number of databases not relevant to this case. In a case where systemic errors were demonstrated, it might be reckless for officers to rely on an unreliable warrant system. But there is no evidence that errors in Dale County's system are routine or widespread. Officer Anderson testified that he had never had reason to question information about a Dale County warrant, and both Sandy Pope and Sharon Morgan testified that they could remember no similar miscommunication ever happening on their watch. . . . Because no such showings were made here, the Eleventh Circuit was correct to affirm the denial of the motion to suppress.

Petitioner's claim that police negligence automatically triggers suppression cannot be squared with the principles underlying the exclusionary rule, as they have been explained in our cases. In light of our repeated holdings that the deterrent effect of suppression must be substantial and outweigh any harm to the justice system, *e.g., Leon*, 468 U.S., at 909–910, 104 S. Ct. 3405, we conclude that when police mistakes are the result of negligence such as that described here, rather than systemic error or reckless disregard of constitutional requirements, any marginal deterrence does not "pay its way." *Id.*, at 907–908, n. 6, 104 S. Ct. 3405 (internal quotation marks omitted). In such a case, the criminal should not "go free because the constable has blundered." *People v. Defore*, 242 N.Y. 13, 21, 150 N.E. 585, 587 (1926) (opinion of the Court by Cardozo, J.).

The judgment of the Court of Appeals for the Eleventh Circuit is affirmed.

It is so ordered.

JUSTICE GINSBURG, with whom JUSTICE STEVENS, JUSTICE SOUTER, and JUSTICE BREYER join, dissenting.

Petitioner Bennie Dean Herring was arrested, and subjected to a search incident to his arrest, although no warrant was outstanding against him, and the police lacked probable cause to believe he was engaged in criminal activity. The arrest and ensuing search therefore violated Herring's Fourth Amendment right "to be secure . . . against unreasonable searches and seizures." The Court of Appeals so determined, and the Government does not contend otherwise. The exclusionary rule provides redress for Fourth Amendment violations by placing the government in the position it would have been in had there been no unconstitutional arrest and search. The rule thus strongly encourages police compliance with the Fourth Amendment in the future. The Court, however, holds the rule inapplicable because careless recordkeeping by the police — not flagrant or deliberate misconduct — accounts for Herring's arrest.

I would not so constrict the domain of the exclusionary rule and would hold the rule dispositive of this case: "[I]f courts are to have any power to discourage [police] error of [the kind here at issue], it must be through the application of the exclusionary rule." *Arizona v. Evans*, 514 U.S. 1, 22–23, 115 S. Ct. 1185, 131 L. Ed. 2d 34 (1995) (Stevens, J., dissenting). The unlawful search in this case was contested in court because the police found methamphetamine in Herring's pocket and a pistol in his truck. But the "most serious impact" of the Court's holding will be on innocent persons "wrongfully arrested based on erroneous information [carelessly maintained] in a computer data base." *Id.*, at 22, 115 S. Ct. 1185.

I

A warrant for Herring's arrest was recalled in February 2004, apparently because it had been issued in error. The warrant database for the Dale County Sheriff's Department, however, does not automatically update to reflect such changes. A member of the Dale County Sheriff's Department — whom the parties have not identified — returned the hard copy of the warrant to the County Circuit Clerk's office, but did not correct the Department's database to show that the warrant had been recalled. The erroneous entry for the warrant remained in the database, undetected, for five months.

On a July afternoon in 2004, Herring came to the Coffee County Sheriff's Department to retrieve his belongings from a vehicle impounded in the Department's lot.

Investigator Mark Anderson, who was at the Department that day, knew Herring from prior interactions: Herring had told the district attorney, among others, of his suspicion that Anderson had been involved in the killing of a local teenager, and Anderson had pursued Herring to get him to drop the accusations. Informed that Herring was in the impoundment lot, Anderson asked the Coffee County warrant clerk whether there was an outstanding warrant for Herring's arrest. The clerk, Sandy Pope, found no warrant.

Anderson then asked Pope to call the neighboring Dale County Sheriff's Department to inquire whether a warrant to arrest Herring was outstanding there. Upon receiving Pope's phone call, Sharon Morgan, the warrant clerk for the Dale County Department, checked her computer database. As just recounted, that Department's database preserved an error. Morgan's check therefore showed — incorrectly — an active warrant for Herring's arrest. Morgan gave the misinformation to Pope, who relayed it to Investigator Anderson. Armed with the report that a warrant existed, Anderson promptly arrested Herring and performed an incident search minutes before detection of the error.

. . . The sole question presented . . . is whether evidence the police obtained through the unlawful search should have been suppressed. The Court holds that suppression was unwarranted because the exclusionary rule's "core concerns" are not raised by an isolated, negligent recordkeeping error attenuated from the arrest. In my view, the Court's opinion underestimates the need for a forceful exclusionary rule and the gravity of recordkeeping errors in law enforcement.

II

A

The Court states that the exclusionary rule is not a defendant's right; rather, it is simply a remedy applicable only when suppression would result in appreciable deterrence that outweighs the cost to the justice system.

The Court's discussion invokes a view of the exclusionary rule famously held by renowned jurists Henry J. Friendly and Benjamin Nathan Cardozo. Over 80 years ago, Cardozo . . . suggested that in at least some cases the rule exacted too high a price from the criminal justice system. See *People v. Defore*, 242 N.Y. 13, 24–25, 150 N.E. 585, 588–589 (1926). [He] questioned whether the criminal should "go free because the constable has blundered." *Id.*, at 21, 150 N.E., at 587.

Judge Friendly later elaborated on Cardozo's query. . . . Judge Friendly suggested that deterrence of police improprieties could be "sufficiently accomplished" by confining the rule to "evidence obtained by flagrant or deliberate violation of rights." [The Bill of Rights as a Code of Criminal Procedure, 53 Calif. L. Rev. 929, 953 (1965)].

B

Others have described "a more majestic conception" of the Fourth Amendment and its adjunct, the exclusionary rule. *Evans*, 514 U.S., at 18, 115 S. Ct. 1185 (Stevens, J., dissenting). Protective of the fundamental "right of the people to be secure in their persons, houses, papers, and effects," the Amendment "is a constraint on the power of the sovereign, not merely on some of its agents." *Ibid.* (internal quotation marks omitted); see Stewart, The Road to *Mapp v. Ohio* and Beyond: The Origins, Development and Future of the Exclusionary Rule in Search-and-Seizure Cases, 83 Colum. L. Rev. 1365 (1983). I share that vision of the Amendment.

The exclusionary rule is "a remedy necessary to ensure that" the Fourth Amendment's prohibitions "are observed in fact." *Id.*, at 1389; see Kamisar, Does (Did) (Should) The Exclusionary Rule Rest On A "Principled Basis" Rather Than An "Empirical Proposition"? 16 Creighton L. Rev. 565, 600 (1983). The rule's service as an essential auxiliary to the Amendment earlier inclined the Court to hold the two inseparable. See *Whiteley v. Warden, Wyo. State Penitentiary,* 401 U.S. 560, 568–569, 91 S. Ct. 1031, 28 L. Ed. 2d 306 (1971).

Beyond doubt, a main objective of the rule "is to deter — to compel respect for the constitutional guaranty in the only effectively available way — by removing the incentive to disregard it." *Elkins v. United States,* 364 U.S. 206, 217, 80 S. Ct. 1437, 4 L. Ed. 2d 1669 (1960). But the rule also serves other important purposes: It "enabl[es] the judiciary to avoid the taint of partnership in official lawlessness," and it "assur[es] the people — all potential victims of unlawful government conduct — that the government would not profit from its lawless behavior, thus minimizing the risk of seriously undermining popular trust in government." *United States v. Calandra,* 414 U.S. 338, 357, 94 S. Ct. 613, 38 L. Ed. 2d 561 (1974) (Brennan, J., dissenting).

The exclusionary rule, it bears emphasis, is often the only remedy effective to redress a Fourth Amendment violation. See *Mapp v. Ohio,* 367 U.S. 643, 652, 81 S. Ct. 1684, 6 L. Ed. 2d 1081 (1961) (noting "the obvious futility of relegating the Fourth Amendment to the protection of other remedies"). Civil liability will not lie for "the vast majority of [F]ourth [A]mendment violations — the frequent infringements motivated by commendable zeal, not condemnable malice." Stewart, 83 Colum. L. Rev., at 1389. Criminal prosecutions or administrative sanctions against the offending officers and injunctive relief against widespread violations are an even farther cry. See *id.*, at 1386–1388.

III

The Court maintains that Herring's case is one in which the exclusionary rule could have scant deterrent effect and therefore would not "pay its way." (internal quotation marks omitted). I disagree.

A

The exclusionary rule, the Court suggests, is capable of only marginal deterrence when the misconduct at issue is merely careless, not intentional or reckless. The suggestion runs counter to a foundational premise of tort law — that liability for negligence, *i.e.,* lack of due care, creates an incentive to act with greater care. . . .

That the mistake here involved the failure to make a computer entry hardly means that application of the exclusionary rule would have minimal value. "Just as the risk of *respondeat superior* liability encourages employers to supervise . . . their employees' conduct [more carefully], so the risk of exclusion of evidence encourages policymakers and systems managers to monitor the performance of the systems they install and the personnel employed to operate those systems." *Evans*, 514 U.S., at 29, n. 5, 115 S. Ct. 1185 (Ginsburg, J., dissenting).

Consider the potential impact of a decision applying the exclusionary rule in this case. As earlier observed, the record indicates that there is no electronic connection between the warrant database of the Dale County Sheriff's Department and that of the County Circuit Clerk's office, which is located in the basement of the same building. When a warrant is recalled, one of the "many different people that have access to th[e] warrants," must find the hard copy of the warrant in the "two or three different places" where the department houses warrants, return it to the Clerk's office, and manually update the Department's database. The record reflects no routine practice of checking the database for accuracy, and the failure to remove the entry for Herring's warrant was not discovered until Investigator Anderson sought to pursue Herring five months later. Is it not altogether obvious that the Department could take further precautions to ensure the integrity of its database? The Sheriff's Department "is in a position to remedy the situation and might well do so if the exclusionary rule is there to remove the incentive to do otherwise." 1 W. LaFave, Search and Seizure § 1.8(e), p. 313 (4th ed. 2004).

B

Is the potential deterrence here worth the costs it imposes? In light of the paramount importance of accurate recordkeeping in law enforcement, I would answer yes, and next explain why, as I see it, Herring's motion presents a particularly strong case for suppression.

Electronic databases form the nervous system of contemporary criminal justice operations. In recent years, their breadth and influence have dramatically expanded. Police today can access databases that include not only the updated National Crime Information Center (NCIC), but also terrorist watchlists, the Federal Government's employee eligibility system, and various commercial databases. Moreover, States are actively expanding information sharing between jurisdictions. As a result, law enforcement has an increasing supply of information within its easy electronic reach.

The risk of error stemming from these databases is not slim. Herring's *amici* warn that law enforcement databases are insufficiently monitored and often out of date. Brief for *Amicus* EPIC 13–28. Government reports describe, for example, flaws in NCIC databases, terrorist watchlist databases, and databases associated with the Federal Government's employment eligibility verification system.

Inaccuracies in expansive, interconnected collections of electronic information raise grave concerns for individual liberty. "The offense to the dignity of the citizen who is arrested, handcuffed, and searched on a public street simply because some bureaucrat has failed to maintain an accurate computer data base" is evocative of the use of general warrants that so outraged the authors of our Bill of Rights. *Evans*, 514 U.S., at 23, 115 S. Ct. 1185 (Stevens, J., dissenting).

C

The Court assures that "exclusion would certainly be justified" if "the police have been shown to be reckless in maintaining a warrant system, or to have knowingly made false entries to lay the groundwork for future false arrests." This concession provides little comfort.

First, by restricting suppression to bookkeeping errors that are deliberate or reckless, the majority leaves Herring, and others like him, with no remedy for violations of their constitutional rights. . . .

Second, I doubt that police forces already possess sufficient incentives to maintain up-to-date records. The Government argues that police have no desire to send officers out on arrests unnecessarily, because arrests consume resources and place officers in danger. The facts of this case do not fit that description of police motivation. Here the officer wanted to arrest Herring and consulted the Department's records to legitimate his predisposition.[6]

Third, even when deliberate or reckless conduct is afoot, the Court's assurance will often be an empty promise: How is an impecunious defendant to make the required showing? If the answer is that a defendant is entitled to discovery (and if necessary, an audit of police databases), see Tr. of Oral Arg. 57–58, then the Court has imposed a considerable administrative burden on courts and law enforcement.[7]

IV

Negligent recordkeeping errors by law enforcement threaten individual liberty, are susceptible to deterrence by the exclusionary rule, and cannot be remedied effectively through other means. Such errors present no occasion to further erode the exclusionary rule. The rule "is needed to make the Fourth Amendment something real; a guarantee that does not carry with it the exclusion of evidence obtained by its violation is a chimera." *Calandra*, 414 U.S., at 361, 94 S. Ct. 613 (Brennan, J., dissenting). . . .

JUSTICE BREYER, whom JUSTICE SOUTER joins, dissenting.

I agree with JUSTICE GINSBURG and join her dissent. I write separately to note one additional supporting factor that I believe important. In *Arizona v. Evans,* 514 U.S. 1, 115 S. Ct. 1185, 131 L. Ed. 2d 34 (1995), we held that recordkeeping errors made by

---

6. It has been asserted that police departments have become sufficiently "professional" that they do not need external deterrence to avoid Fourth Amendment violations. See Tr. of Oral Arg. 24–25; cf. *Hudson v. Michigan*, 547 U.S. 586, 598–599, 126 S. Ct. 2159, 165 L. Ed. 2d 56 (2006). But professionalism is a sign of the exclusionary rule's efficacy — not of its superfluity.

7. It is not clear how the Court squares its focus on deliberate conduct with its recognition that application of the exclusionary rule does not require inquiry into the mental state of the police.

1222   13 · THE SCOPE OF AND EXCEPTIONS TO THE EXCLUSIONARY RULES

a court clerk do not trigger the exclusionary rule, so long as the police reasonably relied upon the court clerk's recordkeeping. *Id.*, at 14, 115 S. Ct. 1185; *id.*, at 16–17, 115 S. Ct. 1185 (O'Connor, J., concurring). The rationale for our decision was premised on a distinction between judicial errors and police errors, and we gave several reasons for recognizing that distinction.

. . . .

Distinguishing between police recordkeeping errors and judicial ones not only is consistent with our precedent, but also is far easier for courts to administer than THE CHIEF JUSTICE's case-by-case, multifactored inquiry into the degree of police culpability. I therefore would apply the exclusionary rule when police personnel are responsible for a recordkeeping error that results in a Fourth Amendment violation.

. . . .

Notes and Questions

(1) In *Davis v. United States*, 564 U.S. 229, 131 S. Ct. 2419, 180 L. Ed. 2d 285 (2011), the Court recognized another variety of good-faith exception to Fourth Amendment suppression, holding "that searches conducted in objectively reasonable reliance on binding appellate precedent are not subject to the exclusionary rule." In *Davis*, officers searched a vehicle incident to the arrests of recent occupants. At the time, extant Eleventh Circuit precedent interpreting *New York v. Belton* authorized that vehicle search. Two years later, the Supreme Court decided *Arizona v. Gant*, which interpreted *Belton* narrowly, thereby restricting the scope of vehicle searches incident to arrest. Under *Gant*, the search in *Davis* violated the Fourth Amendment. The question before the Court was whether the evidence obtained from that search was subject to exclusion.

All members of the Court agreed that the Fourth Amendment rule announced in *Gant* was retroactively applicable to *Davis*, which was not yet final on appeal when *Gant* was decided. Thus, the vehicle search in *Davis* was unconstitutional. A six-Justice majority, however, concluded that *Gant*'s retroactive application did not mean that exclusion was an appropriate remedy for the violation in *Davis*. Whether the exclusionary rule was applicable depended on whether the deterrent benefits of suppression outweighed the social costs. Relying on prior good-faith exception decisions, the majority decided that when officers rely upon binding appellate precedent authorizing a search, the deterrent premises of the exclusionary rule and the balance of costs and benefits dictate the admission of any evidence obtained. Consequently, "when the police conduct a search in objectively reasonable reliance on binding appellate precedent, the exclusionary rule does not apply." (The majority did reserve the question of whether the Court might, "in a future case, . . . recognize a limited exception to the good-faith exception for a defendant who obtains a judgment over-ruling one of [the Supreme Court's] Fourth Amendment precedents." In other words, a defendant who persuades the Court to overturn its own previously binding decision that authorized an officer's search might be entitled to exclusion even though the officer was objectively reasonable in relying on that precedent.)

In the course of endorsing this new variation on the good-faith theme, the majority relied upon and reaffirmed dicta in *Herring v. United States* regarding the need for official "culpability" as a predicate for suppression. According to the majority, "'deliberate,' 'reckless,' or 'grossly negligent' disregard for Fourth Amendment rights" can justify suppression, but when conduct is either objectively reasonable or "involves only simple, 'isolated' negligence ... exclusion cannot 'pay its way.'" "'[I]solated,' 'nonrecurring' police negligence ... lacks the culpability required to justify the harsh sanction of exclusion." The Fourth Amendment violation in *Davis* was neither "deliberate enough" nor "culpable enough" to justify suppression. Because the "behavior" of the officers "was not wrongful," the exclusionary rule could "have no application."

Justice Sotomayor concurred in the judgment, agreeing that a limited good-faith exception was justifiable when officers rely upon binding appellate precedent specifically authorizing or sanctioning their conduct. In her view, however, "whether an officer's conduct can be characterized as 'culpable' is not itself dispositive." She expressed concern that the culpability criterion endorsed in the majority opinion could result in suspension of the exclusionary rule in cases "where its application would appreciably deter Fourth Amendment violations." According to Justice Sotomayor, whether suppression is justified "when the governing law is unsettled" is "a different question" not resolved in *Davis*.

Justice Breyer authored a dissent joined by Justice Ginsburg. He contended that the retroactive applicability of *Gant* meant that the remedy of exclusion was applicable in *Davis*. In addition, he observed that what constitutes "binding appellate precedent" for purposes of the new exception was far from clear and raised issues of "workability." Finally, and most significantly, the dissent took issue with the implications of the majority's culpability premise, expressing a "fear that the Court's opinion will undermine the exclusionary rule." According to Justice Breyer, "if the Court means what it now says, if it would place determinative weight upon the culpability of an individual officer's conduct, and if it would apply the exclusionary rule only where a Fourth Amendment violation was 'deliberate, reckless, or grossly negligent,' then the 'good faith' exception will swallow the exclusionary rule." The ultimate result will be "a watered-down Fourth Amendment [that] offer[s] its protection against only those searches and seizures that are *egregiously* unreasonable." (Emphasis in original.)

(2) Read most broadly, how do the majority opinions in *Herring* and *Davis* restrict the reach of the Fourth Amendment exclusionary rule? Is that limitation upon the scope of suppression consistent with precedent? Is it justifiable and consistent with the objectives of suppression?

1224   13 · THE SCOPE OF AND EXCEPTIONS TO THE EXCLUSIONARY RULES

"Good Faith" Problems

13D–1: On June 13, two Drug Enforcement Administration (DEA) agents reported to Officer Paul Land of the Collins Police Department that two white males had purchased hydroponic growing equipment of the type commonly used for indoor marijuana cultivation and had transported the equipment in a rental car to 508 Maple Street in Collins. Over the next three weeks, Officer Land conducted an investigation. He discovered that the rental car used to transport the equipment had been rented by Robert Newton for 10 days, beginning on June 10. Newton had told the rental agent that he lived on Young Street. When the agents called the telephone number Newton had given to the rental company, a man identifying himself as Newton informed them that he now lived at 508 Maple. On June 14 and 15, Officer Land saw the rental car parked in the driveway of 508 Maple. Land also saw two additional vehicles that were owned by Newton and registered in his name parked at 508 Maple.

Officer Land also checked utility records for the house. He discovered that Damian Tallman had been paying utility bills for the residence since October of the prior year. Since the time the utilities were put in Tallman's name, electrical usage had been two to three times higher than usage for surrounding residences and two to three times higher than the previous resident's usage. Upon checking police department records, Land found out that Tallman had several prior contacts with the Collins police and that there was an outstanding warrant for Tallman's arrest on misdemeanor charges. Land also checked city sales tax records and found no record of a business registered at 508 Maple that might explain high electrical usage.

Based on all he had learned, Officer Land, a 14-year veteran with training and experience in controlled substance investigations, suspected that marijuana was being cultivated at the house. He submitted an affidavit containing all that he had learned in support of an application for a search warrant. A magistrate issued a search warrant for 508 Maple. When Land executed the warrant, he found a 96-plant marijuana "farm" in the basement. He also discovered "psilocybin mushrooms" (a controlled substance), marijuana, and evidence connecting Tallman to the residence on the ground floor. The state charged Tallman with cultivation of marijuana and unlawful possession of a controlled substance. Prior to trial, he moved to suppress the evidence, alleging that the warrant authorizing the search of his residence was invalid.

Was the warrant invalid? Should the trial judge grant the motion to suppress?

13D–2: Officer Foy obtained a warrant based on a form affidavit with information inserted in the blanks on the form. The affidavit provided as follows:

> David M. Foy, Investigator, having been duly sworn in the form and manner required by law, on oath states:

I have probable cause to believe that on or in the residence, grounds, and outbuildings located at Rt. 4, Box 405, Crossett, or the 1981 Chev. pickup with Arizona license IWE-892 in the charge or possession of Michael Herrington, the following items or property is/are contained or concealed — marijuana and other controlled substances — and that such items or property is/are contraband.

The facts upon which I base my request for a Search Warrant are:

An informant whom I have used several times and whose information has been accurate advised me that at times in the past he had seen marijuana and other controlled substances in the house and on the premises occupied by Herrington.

Upon executing the warrant, Foy found marijuana and other controlled substances.

Should the contraband obtained pursuant to the warrant be excluded?

13D–3: Deputy George Johnson, a deputy sheriff for 16 years who had been assigned to the narcotics division for two years, prepared an affidavit in support of an application for a warrant to search Salvador's home. Johnson had previously applied for over a hundred search warrants. In the affidavit he prepared to support the warrant for Salvador's home, Deputy Johnson "discussed" a "confidential reliable informer" who had told him that "drugs were being sold out of Salvador's residence."

Johnson was aware that the informer had been used on prior occasions to make "controlled narcotics buys." In these previous controlled buys, the informer was searched and found not to be in possession of narcotics. He then met with suspects and returned with narcotics. Deputy Johnson did not include this information in the affidavit, however, because he was afraid of revealing the identity of his informer. Nor did he include the facts that the informer had provided Johnson with information in other cases and that the information had proven to be truthful.

A magistrate issued a search warrant for Salvador's home. Sometime after the warrant had been signed, Deputy Johnson obtained surveillance information that tended to corroborate his informant's tip. Johnson then searched Salvador's residence pursuant to the warrant. He found cocaine, narcotics paraphernalia, and a firearm. Salvador moved to suppress the items that were found.

How should the trial court rule on Salvador's motion to suppress?

13D–4: On September 13, at approximately 7:40 p.m., Special Officer Anthony stopped a group of individuals for riding their bicycles on the sidewalk, in violation of a city ordinance. Officer Anthony called for back-up, and Officer Drago, who was on routine patrol, responded. Because none of the bicyclists had identification, Drago asked for their names and dates of birth. Germayne A. Hand, one of the individuals questioned, spelled out his name, along with his address — 218 East Broad Street, Millville, and his date of birth — March 18, 1973. Drago recorded Hand's information and radioed police dispatch with Hand's name and date of birth for a warrant check. The police dispatcher informed Drago that there was an outstanding warrant for Hand. Based on that information, Drago placed Hand under arrest and hand-cuffed him. A search incident to the arrest led to the discovery of drugs.

Subsequently, the police dispatcher informed Drago that there was a discrepancy between the date of birth Hand had given (March 18, 1973) and the date of birth listed on the warrant (March 14, 1971). When Drago arrived at headquarters with Hand, he attempted to verify the existence of the warrant himself. In doing so, he ascertained that, in addition to the birth-date discrepancy, the warrant, which was about 10 years old, had been issued for Jermayne O. Hand with an address on W. 73rd Street, Los Angeles. Drago then called the Municipal Court which had issued the warrant, reached an automated voicemail, and left a message but did not receive a reply. In light of what he had learned, Drago did not process Hand on the warrant, concluding that Hand was not the subject of the warrant. Instead, he charged Hand with drug offenses based on the contraband found on his person and released him.

Hand was indicted for possession of cocaine. Hand moved to suppress the evidence against him. The trial court found, as a matter of fact, that the dispatcher was aware of the discrepancies between the warrant and the information conveyed by Drago.

Should the evidence be suppressed from Hand's trial?

13D–5: On November 11, Detective Violetta filed three criminal complaints and requests for warrants to arrest in municipal court, charging Harv Brandon with theft, criminal damaging, and "house stripping," all first-degree misdemeanors. Each complaint merely cited the relevant statute and the statutory elements for each offense, and, in a brief narrative statement, identified the victim, the location of the offense, and the property taken or removed. The complaints did not state that Detective Violetta witnessed any of the acts described or otherwise explain how Violetta came to believe that Brandon committed the offenses she alleged. In sum, the source of the information was entirely unidentified. A deputy court clerk who had been employed for 17 years issued the warrants without asking Violetta any questions.

On November 26, police responded to a "call for service" to a residential address. Inside the residence, they found the dead body of Scott Holtz. A gun safe in an adjacent area was open. Neighbors stated that someone named Harv had recently visited Holtz and had been interested in purchasing guns from him. When further information identified this Harv as Harv Brandon, a computer check revealed that he had active misdemeanor arrest warrants.

The police decided to execute the arrest warrants. At the address listed in the warrants, officers looked through a window and observed Brandon lying on the floor inside, apparently sleeping. They knocked on the front door, and a man let them in. When they arrested Brandon, they discovered a .45–caliber Ruger semi-automatic on the floor where Brandon was lying. The gun was later identified as belonging to Holtz. Two cell phones were nearby, in plain view, and when an officer used her own phone to call Holtz's cell-phone number, one of the phones immediately rang. Officers found additional evidence linking Brandon to Holtz.

Brandon was charged in a two-count indictment with aggravated murder. He filed a motion to suppress the evidence found as a result of his arrest, claiming that the arrest warrants were constitutionally infirm. At a hearing on the motion to suppress, the deputy clerk who issued the arrest warrants testified that when an officer comes in for a warrant, she verifies that the complaint includes the offender's correct name and address, the violation codes, the charge, the offense classification, the date of the offense, a description of the offense, and the signature of the officer. She stated that she never asks an officer any questions. With regard to the warrants issued against Brandon, the deputy clerk specifically testified that she did not make a probable-cause determination. When asked if she knew what probable cause is, she said, "No, I don't." She denied that it was part of her job responsibility to make a finding of probable cause. She simply gave the officer the oath, issued the warrants, and placed them into the computer system.

Approximately 10 years earlier, a state intermediate appellate court had ruled that warrants virtually identical in form and substance to the arrest warrants in this case are consistent with the Fourth Amendment.

Should the evidence be suppressed from Harv's murder trial?

13D–6: At 1:10 a.m., Sergeant Barber of the Sheriff's Department advised Deputy Darin Mecham that at 12:45 a.m., he and Deputy Atkins had responded to the report of a fire in an outbuilding located at 333 Road #252, in North Fork. By the time the officers had arrived, the outbuilding had burned to the ground. Inside the burned structure were hoods from lights. Twenty yards away was a double-wide mobile home with an attached wood shed. A tarp was over the door to the wood shed, and the lights inside were on. A fireman reported to Barber that a citizen who had been concerned by the fire had gone to the wood shed in case there were residents inside who might be endangered. The citizen had seen about 20 six-foot tall marijuana plants inside the wood shed. Based on this information, Deputy Mecham believed marijuana plants were inside the wood shed, that the burned outbuilding may have contained a marijuana cultivation operation, and that evidence in the mobile home would indicate who was involved in the operation.

Deputy Mecham immediately went to his home computer and began to prepare an affidavit in support of a warrant to search the mobile home and wood shed. He completed the affidavit between 2:00 and 3:00 a.m. Because the officers who had investigated the fire were waiting at the scene, Mecham felt pressure to present the affidavit to a judge as soon as possible. There were only two judges in the area, Deputy Mecham's father, the Honorable Richard Mecham, who lived next door to him, and Judge Thomas Fletcher, who lived in Bass Lake. Deputy Mecham concluded that if he had to awaken a judge in the wee hours of the morning, his father was the better choice.

Upon reviewing the affidavit prepared by his son, Judge Mecham issued a search warrant at approximately 3:00 a.m. Deputy Mecham served the warrant that morning. Upon searching the mobile home, he found evidence that Connor lived there. He also found several bags of marijuana, three loaded firearms, and evidence of marijuana sales. Inside the wood shed, he found a garden that consisted of 14 growing marijuana plants. The state charged Connor with possession of marijuana for sale and cultivation of marijuana and alleged that he was armed with a firearm during the commission of the offenses. Connor moved to suppress the evidence found pursuant to the search warrant.

Should the trial judge grant the motion?

13D–7: On August 1, agents of the Drug Enforcement Administration (DEA), in conjunction with local police officers, initiated an investigation of Ying Tsao, after he arrived on a flight from Hong Kong. The next day, the agents sought a warrant to search the residence of Tung Luo, a man Tsao had met with earlier in the day. DEA Agent Lori Burns swore out an affidavit which asserted:

> A multi-agency investigation of Ying Tsao is underway. The Hong Kong office of the DEA informed the local DEA office that "a suspect known as a chemist" would be arriving at the local airport on a flight from Hong Kong to "set up and manufacture methamphetamine." When Tsao arrived on an August 1 flight, local agents followed him to a hotel where he checked in.

> On August 2, an Asian male, later identified as Luo, arrived at Tsao's hotel and went into his room. Minutes later, Tsao and Luo left the room, got into Luo's car, and drove to a residence. They entered and walked back and forth several times between the front door and the back yard. Several hours later, they left the residence and drove to a Home Depot store. Tsao was carrying a red high pressure hose, and Luo asked an employee "how to insert a new adapter fitting into this hose." Luo then purchased a small adapter fitting, and he and Tsao returned to the residence. The hose is a common tool used during methamphetamine production.

On August 3, at 2:45 a.m., a magistrate issued a warrant to search Luo's residence for evidence of methamphetamine manufacturing. Agents executed the warrant at 5:45 a.m., discovering evidence of a meth lab and 60 pounds of methamphetamine. Luo was indicted for manufacturing and possessing methamphetamine with intent to distribute.

Before trial, Luo filed a motion to suppress, contending that the search warrant was not supported by probable cause. The government argued that the agents had relied on the warrant in good faith. At a hearing, Agent Burns testified that she had been under time pressure to prepare the warrant because she believed Tsao and Luo were fixing a potentially explosive, broken drug lab. She asserted that she had had "technical difficulties" in printing and typing the warrant due to a broken thumb. She also stated that while she was preparing the affidavit she had two unrecorded and unsworn phone conversations with the magistrate in which she had informed him of three facts not included in her affidavit: (1) that a DEA wiretap in Hong Kong had been the source of the tip relayed to the local DEA office; (2) that Tsao had been identified based on this tip as he passed through customs; and (3) that agents had observed "counter-surveillance activity" during their investigation of Tsao and Luo. Burns acknowledged that this information "should have been included in the affidavit but was not because I was rushed."

The judge suppressed the evidence seized from Luo's residence, and the government now appeals.

Should the appellate court reverse the ruling?

13D–8: James Poll was at Yvonne Dane's apartment when Val Smith (a deaf man), Howard, and Vincent arrived. Smith and Poll argued. Vincent gave Smith a gun, and Smith fired three shots at Poll, killing him. Smith then handed the gun back to Vincent and left the apartment. After Smith's wallet was found at the scene, he was arrested. Through a sign language interpreter, Cheryl Fern, Smith was told he was being questioned about the shooting and was advised of his *Miranda* rights. The following exchange then took place:

Detective Frisk: Keeping these rights in mind, do you wish to talk to me about this?

Smith (Through Fern): I don't really. I prefer to go to court and see what happens. In the case. In the case. In the case? What I mean . . . is if you sue me, or not sue me, but to have a . . . a lawyer in court.

Frisk: OK. And do I understand that he does not want to discuss this at all.

Fern (For herself): Wait! Slow down! Please wait until I finish because if not it will change the meaning of what he is saying. OK?

Frisk: Do I understand him correctly in that he doesn't want to explain to us what happened?

Smith (Through Fern): Oh! I get it! OK, yeah. I'll go ahead and talk!

Frisk: Did I misunderstand at first?

Smith (Through Fern): Yes. Yeah, now I understand clearly. OK, let's go ahead.

Smith first told Frisk that one of the other men had fought with Poll and shot him. After Frisk said he knew Smith was the shooter, Smith said that Howard had given guns to him and to Vincent, that he had shot Poll in the leg twice, but that Vincent had shot Poll in the head and killed him. After Smith was charged with first-degree murder, he moved to suppress his statements.

After an evidentiary hearing, the trial judge agreed with the defense's sign language experts that Fern had not accurately understood Smith's sign language and that Smith had actually said that he "wanted a lawyer right here, right now." He also found that Frisk had asked his "clarifying questions" in good faith and had believed that Smith had waived his rights. The judge then denied Smith's motion to suppress. Smith was convicted and has appealed the judge's ruling.

Should the trial judge's ruling be affirmed?

13D–9: On June 25, as part of an undercover investigation, Officer Michael Bard bought six prescription pills for $10 from Cheryl Popp at Popp's home. On September 11, Bard received an unsupported anonymous tip that Popp was cooking methamphetamine. The tip had nothing to do with prescription drugs. The next day Bard began to draft an affidavit in support of a warrant — the first of his career — to search Popp's home for prescription drugs. In the affidavit, he related the facts surrounding his undercover buy from Popp. Bard stayed at work past midnight preparing his affidavit, slept a few hours, then timed his trip to a state magistrate's home to arrive at seven o'clock the next morning.

Bard did not inform the magistrate that the true reason for wanting to search Popp's house was to look for evidence of a meth lab. He attested under oath that he was applying for "a search warrant for the purpose of obtaining evidence of a crime that has already been committed — a prescription-drug buy." The magistrate issued the warrant requested. Accompanied by a team of officers fully dressed in the kind of protective gear used to search for meth labs, Bard proceeded to Popp's home to execute the warrant for prescription drugs. When he found evidence of a meth lab in plain view, Bard immediately left the premises to obtain a second warrant to search for additional evidence of the meth lab. Additional evidence of meth manufacturing was found during the execution of this second warrant. No prescription drugs were seized.

Popp sought to suppress all the evidence found in his home, asserting that Bard's initial affidavit did not provide probable cause for the search. The government claimed that the affidavit did provide probable cause. The government also argued that even if the affidavit did not furnish probable cause, the evidence was admissible under the good faith exception to the exclusionary rule. At a hearing, Officer Bard admitted that he had applied for and obtained the warrant because of the tip that Popp was conducting "a meth cook."

The judge found that the "sole purpose" of the issuance of the initial warrant was to authorize a search for prescription drugs; that this warrant "was not based on probable cause to search for prescription drugs"; and that "Officer Bard consciously withheld from the magistrate all information about the meth lab, because he knew that he did not have probable cause for a warrant to search for evidence of a meth operation." The judge then denied Popp's motion to suppress, agreeing with the government that the good faith exception was applicable.

Was the court's ruling correct?

13D–10: In 2000, while investigating Hacker's suspected marijuana cultivation and distribution, Narcotics Agent Helen and Sheriff Wick scanned Hacker's house with a thermal imager without obtaining a search warrant. At the time, a controlling appellate opinion had held that thermal imaging was not a Fourth Amendment "search." Agent Helen concluded that uneven heat fields radiating from the house were consistent with an indoor marijuana growing operation.

Sheriff Wick prepared an affidavit in support of a warrant to search Hacker's house. In addition to the thermal imaging data, the affidavit stated: (1) that an informant had told Wick in August 1999 that "Charlie Hacker sells a lot of marijuana"; (2) that, in December 1999, another informant had stated that a neighbor had purchased marijuana from "Charlie," a young man who lived near the county line, and that Hacker's home was within two miles of the county line; (3) that Hacker's electrical records for a six-month period in 1998 showed high usage consistent with an indoor growing operation; (4) that Hacker's father cultivated orchids using a hydroponic system; and (5) that Hacker's basement windows were "blocked out" — a measure consistent with efforts of marijuana growers to prevent heat emanation. Based on Wick's affidavit, a judge issued a search warrant.

While executing the warrant, officers seized 40 cannabis plants, 3000 grams of harvested marijuana, 88.5 grams of processed marijuana in plastic bags, seven bags of starter soil, four 1000-watt lights, five light timers, two exhaust fans, a triple-beam scale, notes, and a notebook describing the growing operation. Hacker waived his rights, then stated that he had grown marijuana for the previous 18 months and had sold 30 to 40 ounces per harvest cycle for $175 per ounce.

The federal government charged Hacker with manufacturing and distributing marijuana. While the charges were pending, the United States Supreme Court ruled that thermal imaging of a home is a search and that a search warrant is required. Hacker filed a motion to suppress the evidence found as a result of the thermal imaging and the subsequent search of his home.

What arguments support suppression of the evidence? What arguments support admission of the evidence? How should the trial court rule?

13D–11: Sometime before 6:00 p.m., Masso landed his single-engine airplane at Midville International Airport en route from Las Vegas to Orlando. Several minutes after the landing, United States Customs and Border Protection (USCBP) contacted the Midville Police Department (MPD) and requested a "ramp check" of Masso's airplane. During a "ramp check" agents ask for consent to search, ask for the identities of passengers, and check FAA records. Three facts triggered the USCBP request: the airplane had flown from Orlando to Las Vegas, making six refueling stops, staying in Las Vegas for about 12 hours, before returning to Orlando with Midville as a refueling stop; the registered owner of the airplane had been convicted of drug trafficking 20 years earlier; and Masso had "recently" crossed from Tijuana into the United States.

Two MPD officers approached Masso near the aircraft and questioned him, requesting documents and identification. Masso complied with the requests. Homeland Security Agents Knight and Garnett, upon request from USCBP, were dispatched to the site around 6:20. They arrived soon after the initial questioning by the MPD officers. After speaking to the MPD officers, Knight and Garrett questioned Masso. They then examined the exterior of the airplane. At some point, they summoned a canine unit to conduct a sniff of the airplane's exterior, including the luggage that

Masso had set on the wing. The canine, Gus, did not alert. Masso then refused to consent to a search of the interior of the airplane.

During the inspection of the airplane's exterior, Agent Knight saw a cardboard box through the window behind the rear seat. When asked about the box, Masso first denied any knowledge, then admitted that it was his box and asked for an attorney. At 7:30, Homeland Security Agent Howard arrived. For the next two hours he collected facts about what had happened prior to his arrival and gathered additional information. During this time, Masso was required to remain near the airplane.

Agent Howard left the airport around 9:30 p.m. At his office, he prepared an affidavit in support of an application for a warrant to search the plane. He included information gathered during the ramp check investigation and additional facts he had learned. A federal magistrate issued a warrant at 11:30 p.m. Agent Howard returned to the airport at approximately midnight and searched the airplane, finding 19 sealed bags of marijuana weighing 10.50 kilograms inside the cardboard box. Masso was arrested.

Prior to trial, Masso moved to suppress the marijuana. The trial judge agreed that his detention at the airport became a *de facto* arrest that was not supported by probable cause. The government contended that the marijuana was nonetheless admissible because Agent Howard had relied in good faith on the search warrant.

What arguments should the defense make in support of the motion to suppress? What responses should the government make? Should the judge suppress the marijuana?

[E] The *Miranda* Exclusion Doctrine

Oregon v. Elstad

United States Supreme Court

470 U.S. 298, 105 S. Ct. 1285, 84 L. Ed. 2d 222 (1985)

JUSTICE O'CONNOR delivered the opinion of the Court.

This case requires us to decide whether an initial failure of law enforcement officers to administer the warnings required by *Miranda v. Arizona*, 384 U.S. 436, 86 S. Ct. 1602, 16 L. Ed. 2d 694 (1966), without more, "taints" subsequent admissions made after a suspect has been fully advised of and has waived his *Miranda* rights. . . .

I

In December 1981, the home of Mr. and Mrs. Gilbert Gross, in the town of Salem, Polk County, Ore., was burglarized. Missing were art objects and furnishings valued at $150,000. A witness to the burglary contacted the Polk County Sheriff's office, implicating respondent Michael Elstad, an 18-year-old neighbor and friend of the Grosses' teenage son. Thereupon, Officers Burke and McAllister went to the home of respondent Elstad, with a warrant for his arrest. Elstad's mother answered the door. She led the officers to her son's room where he lay on his bed, clad in shorts and listening to his stereo. The officers asked him to get dressed and to accompany them into the living room. Officer McAllister asked respondent's mother to step into the kitchen, where he explained that they had a warrant for her son's arrest for the burglary of a neighbor's residence. Officer Burke remained with Elstad in the living room. He later testified:

> "I sat down with Mr. Elstad and I asked him if he was aware of why Detective McAllister and myself were there to talk with him. He stated no, he had no idea why we were there. I then asked him if he knew a person by the name of Gross, and he said yes, he did, and also added that he heard that there was a robbery at the Gross house. And at that point I told Mr. Elstad that I felt he was involved in that, and he looked at me and stated, 'Yes, I was there.'"

The officers then escorted Elstad to the back of the patrol car. As they were about to leave for the Polk County Sheriff's office, Elstad's father arrived home and came to the rear of the patrol car. The officers advised him that his son was a suspect in the burglary. Officer Burke testified that Mr. Elstad became quite agitated, opened the rear door of the car and admonished his son: "I told you that you were going to get into trouble. You wouldn't listen to me. You never learn."

Elstad was transported to the Sheriff's headquarters and approximately one hour later, Officers Burke and McAllister joined him in McAllister's office. McAllister then advised respondent for the first time of his *Miranda* rights, reading from a standard card. Respondent indicated he understood his rights, and, having these rights in mind, wished to speak with the officers. Elstad gave a full statement, explaining that he had known that the Gross family was out of town and had been paid to lead several acquaintances to the Gross residence and show them how to gain entry through a defective sliding glass door. The statement was typed, reviewed by respondent, read back to him for correction, initialed and signed by Elstad and both officers. As an afterthought, Elstad added and initialed the sentence, "After leaving the house Robby & I went back to [the] van & Robby handed me a small bag of grass." Respondent concedes that the officers made no threats or promises either at his residence or at the Sheriff's office.

Respondent was charged with first-degree burglary. He was represented at trial by retained counsel. . . .

Elstad was found guilty of burglary in the first degree. He received a 5-year sentence and was ordered to pay $18,000 in restitution.

. . . .

. . . . This Court granted certiorari to consider the question whether the Self-Incrimination Clause of the Fifth Amendment requires the suppression of a confession, made after proper *Miranda* warnings and a valid waiver of rights, solely because the police had obtained an earlier voluntary but unwarned admission from the defendant.

II

The arguments advanced in favor of suppression of respondent's written confession rely heavily on metaphor. One metaphor, familiar from the Fourth Amendment context, would require that respondent's confession, regardless of its integrity, voluntariness, and probative value, be suppressed as the "tainted fruit of the poisonous tree" of the *Miranda* violation. A second metaphor questions whether a confession can be truly voluntary once the "cat is out of the bag." Taken out of context, each of these metaphors can be misleading. They should not be used to obscure fundamental differences between the role of the Fourth Amendment exclusionary rule and the function of *Miranda* in guarding against the prosecutorial use of compelled statements as prohibited by the Fifth Amendment. . . .

A

Prior to *Miranda*, the admissibility of an accused's in-custody statements was judged solely by whether they were "voluntary" within the meaning of the Due Process Clause. If a suspect's statements had been obtained by "techniques and methods offensive to due process," *Haynes v. Washington*, 373 U.S., at 515, 83 S. Ct., at 1344, or under circumstances in which the suspect clearly had no opportunity to exercise "a free and unconstrained will," *id.*, at 514, 83 S. Ct., at 1343, the statements would not be admitted. The Court in *Miranda* required suppression of many statements that would have been admissible under traditional due process analysis by presuming that statements made while in custody and without adequate warnings were protected by the Fifth Amendment. The Fifth Amendment, of course, is not concerned with nontestimonial evidence. Nor is it concerned with moral and psychological pressures to confess emanating from sources other than official coercion. Voluntary statements "remain a proper element in law enforcement." *Miranda v. Arizona*, 384 U.S., at 478, 86 S. Ct., at 1630. "Indeed, far from being prohibited by the Constitution, admissions of guilt by wrongdoers, if not coerced, are inherently desirable. . . . Absent some officially coerced self-accusation, the Fifth Amendment privilege is not violated by even the most damning admissions." *United States v. Washington*, 431 U.S. 181, 187, 97 S. Ct. 1814, 1818, 52 L. Ed. 2d 238 (1977). As the Court noted last Term in *New York v. Quarles*, 467 U.S. 649, 654, 104 S. Ct. 2626, 2630, 81 L. Ed. 2d 550 (1984) (footnote omitted):

> "The *Miranda* Court, however, presumed that interrogation in certain custodial circumstances is inherently coercive and . . . that statements made under those circumstances are inadmissible unless the suspect is specifically informed of his *Miranda* rights and freely decides to forgo those rights. The prophylactic *Miranda* warnings therefore are 'not themselves rights protected by the Constitution but [are] instead measures to insure that the right against compulsory self-incrimination [is] protected.' *Michigan v. Tucker*, 417 U.S. 433, 444, 94 S. Ct. 2357, 2364, 41 L. Ed. 2d 182 (1974). Re-

quiring *Miranda* warnings before custodial interrogation provides 'practical reinforcement' for the Fifth Amendment right."

Respondent's contention that his confession was tainted by the earlier failure of the police to provide *Miranda* warnings and must be excluded as "fruit of the poisonous tree" assumes the existence of a constitutional violation. This figure of speech is drawn from *Wong Sun v. United States*, 371 U.S. 471, 83 S. Ct. 407, 9 L. Ed. 2d 441 (1963), in which the Court held that evidence and witnesses discovered as a result of a search in violation of the Fourth Amendment must be excluded from evidence. The *Wong Sun* doctrine applies as well when the fruit of the Fourth Amendment violation is a confession. . . .

But as we explained in *Quarles* and *Tucker*, a procedural *Miranda* violation differs in significant respects from violations of the Fourth Amendment, which have traditionally mandated a broad application of the "fruits" doctrine. The purpose of the Fourth Amendment exclusionary rule is to deter unreasonable searches, no matter how probative their fruits. . . . Where a Fourth Amendment violation "taints" the confession, a finding of voluntariness for the purposes of the Fifth Amendment is merely a threshold requirement in determining whether the confession may be admitted in evidence. Beyond this, the prosecution must show a sufficient break in events to undermine the inference that the confession was caused by the Fourth Amendment violation.

The *Miranda* exclusionary rule, however, serves the Fifth Amendment and sweeps more broadly than the Fifth Amendment itself. It may be triggered even in the absence of a Fifth Amendment violation.[1] The Fifth Amendment prohibits use by the prosecution in its case in chief only of *compelled* testimony. Failure to administer *Miranda* warnings creates a presumption of compulsion. Consequently, unwarned statements that are otherwise voluntary within the meaning of the Fifth Amendment must nevertheless be excluded from evidence under *Miranda*. Thus, in the individual case, *Miranda*'s preventive medicine provides a remedy even to the defendant who has suffered no identifiable constitutional harm.

But the *Miranda* presumption, though irrebuttable for purposes of the prosecution's case in chief, does not require that the statements and their fruits be discarded as inherently tainted. . . .

---

1. Justice Stevens expresses puzzlement at our statement that a simple failure to administer *Miranda* warnings is not in itself a violation of the Fifth Amendment. Yet the Court so held in *New York v. Quarles,* 467 U.S. 649, 654, 104 S. Ct. 2626, 2630, 81 L. Ed. 2d 550 (1983), and *Michigan v. Tucker,* 417 U.S. 433, 444, 94 S. Ct. 2357, 2363, 41 L. Ed. 2d 182 (1974). The *Miranda* Court itself recognized this point when it disclaimed any intent to create a "constitutional straitjacket" and invited Congress and the States to suggest "potential alternatives for protecting the privilege." 384 U.S., at 467, 86 S. Ct., at 1624. A *Miranda* violation does not constitute coercion but rather affords a bright-line, legal presumption of coercion, requiring suppression of all unwarned statements. It has never been remotely suggested that any statement taken from Mr. Elstad without benefit of *Miranda* warnings would be admissible.

In *Michigan v. Tucker, supra*, the Court was asked to extend the *Wong Sun* fruits doctrine to suppress the testimony of a witness for the prosecution whose identity was discovered as the result of a statement taken from the accused without benefit of full *Miranda* warnings. As in respondent's case, the breach of the *Miranda* procedures in *Tucker* involved no actual compulsion. The Court concluded that the unwarned questioning "did not abridge respondent's constitutional privilege . . . but departed only from the prophylactic standards later laid down by this Court in *Miranda* to safeguard that privilege." 417 U.S., at 446, 94 S. Ct., at 2364. Since there was no actual infringement of the suspect's constitutional rights, the case was not controlled by the doctrine expressed in *Wong Sun* that fruits of a constitutional violation must be suppressed. In deciding "how sweeping the judicially imposed consequences" of a failure to administer *Miranda* warnings should be, 417 U.S., at 445, 94 S. Ct., at 2364, the *Tucker* Court noted that neither the general goal of deterring improper police conduct nor the Fifth Amendment goal of assuring trustworthy evidence would be served by suppression of the witness' testimony. The unwarned confession must, of course, be suppressed, but the Court ruled that introduction of the third-party witness' testimony did not violate Tucker's Fifth Amendment rights.

We believe that this reasoning applies with equal force when the alleged "fruit" of a noncoercive *Miranda* violation is neither a witness nor an article of evidence but the accused's own voluntary testimony. As in *Tucker*, the absence of any coercion or improper tactics undercuts the twin rationales — trustworthiness and deterrence — for a broader rule. Once warned, the suspect is free to exercise his own volition in deciding whether or not to make a statement to the authorities. . . .

. . . If errors are made by law enforcement officers in administering the prophylactic *Miranda* procedures, they should not breed the same irremediable consequences as police infringement of the Fifth Amendment itself. It is an unwarranted extension of *Miranda* to hold that a simple failure to administer the warnings, unaccompanied by any actual coercion or other circumstances calculated to undermine the suspect's ability to exercise his free will, so taints the investigatory process that a subsequent voluntary and informed waiver is ineffective for some indeterminate period. Though *Miranda* requires that the unwarned admission must be suppressed, the admissibility of any subsequent statement should turn in these circumstances solely on whether it is knowingly and voluntarily made.

B

The Oregon court, however, believed that the unwarned remark compromised the voluntariness of respondent's later confession. It was the court's view that the prior *answer* and not the unwarned questioning impaired respondent's ability to give a valid waiver and that only lapse of time and change of place could dissipate what it termed the "coercive impact" of the inadmissible statement. When a prior statement is actually coerced, the time that passes between confessions, the change in place of interrogations, and the change in identity of the interrogators all bear on whether that coercion has carried over into the second confession. The failure of police to administer *Miranda* warnings does not mean that the statements received have actually been coerced, but only that courts will presume the privilege against compulsory self-incrimination has not been intelligently exercised. Of the courts that have considered whether a properly warned confession must be suppressed because it was preceded by an unwarned but clearly voluntary admission, the majority have explicitly or implicitly recognized that [the] requirement of a break in the stream of events is inapposite. In these circumstances, a careful and thorough administration of *Miranda* warnings serves to cure the condition that rendered the unwarned statement inadmissible. The warning conveys the relevant information and thereafter the suspect's choice whether to exercise his privilege to remain silent should ordinarily be viewed as an "act of free will." *Wong Sun v. United States*, 371 U.S., at 486, 83 S. Ct., at 416.

The Oregon court nevertheless identified a subtle form of lingering compulsion, the psychological impact of the suspect's conviction that he has let the cat out of the bag and, in so doing, has sealed his own fate. But endowing the psychological effects of *voluntary* unwarned admissions with constitutional implications would, practically speaking, disable the police from obtaining the suspect's informed cooperation even when the official coercion proscribed by the Fifth Amendment played no part in either his warned or unwarned confessions. . . .

. . . .

This Court has never held that the psychological impact of voluntary disclosure of a guilty secret qualifies as state compulsion or compromises the voluntariness of a subsequent informed waiver. The Oregon court, by adopting this expansive view of Fifth Amendment compulsion, effectively immunizes a suspect who responds to pre-*Miranda* warning questions from the consequences of his subsequent informed waiver of the privilege of remaining silent. This immunity comes at a high cost to legitimate law enforcement activity, while adding little desirable protection to the individual's interest in not being *compelled* to testify against himself. When neither the initial nor the subsequent admission is coerced, little justification exists for permitting the highly probative evidence of a voluntary confession to be irretrievably lost to the factfinder.

There is a vast difference between the direct consequences flowing from coercion of a confession by physical violence or other deliberate means calculated to break the suspect's will and the uncertain consequences of disclosure of a "guilty secret" freely given in response to an unwarned but noncoercive question, as in this case. JUSTICE BRENNAN's contention that it is impossible to perceive any causal distinction between this case and one involving a confession that is coerced by torture is wholly unpersuasive.[3] Certainly, in respondent's case, the causal connection between any psycho-

---

3. Most of the 50 cases cited by JUSTICE BRENNAN in his discussion of consecutive confessions concern an initial unwarned statement obtained through overtly or inherently coercive methods which raise serious Fifth Amendment and due process concerns. . . . . JUSTICE BRENNAN cannot seriously mean to equate such situations with the case at bar. Likewise inapposite are the cases the dissent cites concerning suspects whose invocation of their rights to remain silent and to have

logical disadvantage created by his admission and his ultimate decision to cooperate is speculative and attenuated at best. It is difficult to tell with certainty what motivates a suspect to speak. A suspect's confession may be traced to factors as disparate as "a prearrest event such as a visit with a minister," *Dunaway v. New York*, 442 U.S., at 220, 99 S. Ct., at 2261 (Stevens J., concurring), or an intervening event such as the exchange of words respondent had with his father. We must conclude that, absent deliberately coercive or improper tactics in obtaining the initial statement, the mere fact that a suspect has made an unwarned admission does not warrant a presumption of compulsion. A subsequent administration of *Miranda* warnings to a suspect who has given a voluntary but unwarned statement ordinarily should suffice to remove the conditions that precluded admission of the earlier statement. In such circumstances, the finder of fact may reasonably conclude that the suspect made a rational and intelligent choice whether to waive or invoke his rights.

III

Though belated, the reading of respondent's rights was undeniably complete. McAllister testified that he read the *Miranda* warnings aloud from a printed card and recorded Elstad's responses. There is no question that respondent knowingly and voluntarily waived his right to remain silent before he described his participation in the burglary. It is also beyond dispute that respondent's earlier remark was voluntary, within the meaning of the Fifth Amendment. . . .

The State has conceded the issue of custody and thus we must assume that Burke breached *Miranda* procedures in failing to administer *Miranda* warnings before initiating the discussion in the living room. This breach may have been the result of confusion as to whether the brief exchange qualified as "custodial interrogation" or it may simply have reflected Burke's reluctance to initiate an alarming police procedure before McAllister had spoken with respondent's mother. Whatever the reason for Burke's oversight, the incident had none of the earmarks of coercion. Nor did the officers exploit the unwarned admission to pressure respondent into waiving his right to remain silent.

Respondent, however, has argued that he was unable to give a fully *informed* waiver of his rights because he was unaware that his prior statement could not be used against him. Respondent suggests that Officer McAllister, to cure this deficiency, should have added an additional warning to those given him at the Sheriff's office. Such a requirement is neither practicable nor constitutionally necessary. In many cases, a breach of *Miranda* procedures may not be identified as such until

---

counsel present were flatly ignored while police subjected them to continued interrogation. Finally, many of the decisions JUSTICE BRENNAN claims require that the "taint" be "dissipated" simply recite the stock "cat" and "tree" metaphors but go on to find the second confession voluntary without identifying any break in the stream of events beyond the simple administration of a careful and thorough warning. Out of the multitude of decisions JUSTICE BRENNAN cites, no more than half a dozen fairly can be said to suppress confessions on facts remotely comparable to those in the instant case and some of these decisions involved other elements not present here. . . . .

long after full *Miranda* warnings are administered and a valid confession obtained. . . . .

This Court has never embraced the theory that a defendant's ignorance of the full consequences of his decisions vitiates their voluntariness. . . . Thus we have not held that the *sine qua non* for a knowing and voluntary waiver of the right to remain silent is a full and complete appreciation of all of the consequences flowing from the nature and the quality of the evidence in the case.

IV

When police ask questions of a suspect in custody without administering the required warnings, *Miranda* dictates that the answers received be presumed compelled and that they be excluded from evidence at trial in the State's case in chief. The Court has carefully adhered to this principle, permitting a narrow exception only where pressing public safety concerns demanded. The Court today in no way retreats from the bright-line rule of *Miranda*. We do not imply that good faith excuses a failure to administer *Miranda* warnings; nor do we condone inherently coercive police tactics or methods offensive to due process that render the initial admission involuntary and undermine the suspect's will to invoke his rights once they are read to him. A handful of courts have, however, applied our precedents relating to confessions obtained under coercive circumstances to situations involving wholly voluntary admissions, requiring a passage of time or break in events before a second, fully warned statement can be deemed voluntary. Far from establishing a rigid rule, we direct courts to avoid one; there is no warrant for presuming coercive effect where the suspect's initial inculpatory statement, though technically in violation of *Miranda*, was voluntary. The relevant inquiry is whether, in fact, the second statement was also voluntarily made. As in any such inquiry, the finder of fact must examine the surrounding circumstances and the entire course of police conduct with respect to the suspect in evaluating the voluntariness of his statements. The fact that a suspect chooses to speak after being informed of his rights is, of course, highly probative. We find that the dictates of *Miranda* and the goals of the Fifth Amendment proscription against use of compelled testimony are fully satisfied in the circumstances of this case by barring use of the unwarned statement in the case in chief. No further purpose is served by imputing "taint" to subsequent statements obtained pursuant to a voluntary and knowing waiver. We hold today that a suspect who has once responded to unwarned yet uncoercive questioning is not thereby disabled from waiving his rights and confessing after he has been given the requisite *Miranda* warnings.

The judgment of the Court of Appeals of Oregon is reversed, and the case is remanded for further proceedings not inconsistent with this opinion.

It is so ordered.

JUSTICE BRENNAN, with whom JUSTICE MARSHALL joins, dissenting.

. . . .

... [T]he Court has engaged of late in a studied campaign to strip the *Miranda* decision piecemeal and to undermine the rights *Miranda* sought to secure. Today's decision not only extends this effort a further step, but delivers a potentially crippling blow to *Miranda* and the ability of courts to safeguard the rights of persons accused of crime. For at least with respect to successive confessions, the Court today appears to strip remedies for *Miranda* violations of the "fruit of the poisonous tree" doctrine prohibiting the use of evidence presumptively derived from official illegality.[2]

. . . .

. . . . If violations of constitutional rights may not be remedied through the well-established rules respecting derivative evidence, as the Court has held today, there is a critical danger that the rights will be rendered nothing more than a mere "form of words." *Silverthorne Lumber Co. v. United States*, 251 U.S. 385, 392, 40 S. Ct. 182, 183, 64 L. Ed. 319 (1920).

. . . .

Today's decision, in short, threatens disastrous consequences far beyond the outcome in this case. As the Court has not seen fit to provide a full explanation for this result, I believe it essential to consider in detail the premises, reasoning, and implications of the Court's opinion.

I

The threshold question is this: What effect should an admission or confession of guilt obtained in violation of an accused's *Miranda* rights be presumed to have upon the voluntariness of subsequent confessions that are preceded by *Miranda* warnings? . . . .

If this Court's reversal of the judgment below reflected mere disagreement with the Oregon court's application of the "cat out of the bag" presumption to the particular facts of this case, the outcome, while clearly erroneous, would be of little lasting consequence. But the Court rejects the "cat out of the bag" presumption *entirely* and instead adopts a new rule presuming that "ordinarily" there is *no* causal connection between a confession extracted in violation of *Miranda* and a subsequent confession preceded by the usual *Miranda* warnings. The Court suggests that it is merely following settled lower-court practice in adopting this rule and that the analysis followed by the Oregon Court of Appeals was aberrant. This is simply not so. Most federal courts have rejected the Court's approach and instead held that (1) there is a rebuttable presumption that a confession obtained in violation of *Miranda* taints subsequent confessions, and (2) the taint cannot be dissipated solely by giving *Miranda* warnings. . . .

---

2. The Court repeatedly casts its analysis in terms of the "fruits" of a *Miranda* violation, but its dicta nevertheless surely should not be read as necessarily foreclosing application of derivative-evidence rules where the *Miranda* violation produces evidence other than a subsequent confession by the accused.

The Court today sweeps aside this common-sense approach as "speculative" reasoning, adopting instead a rule that "the psychological impact of *voluntary* disclosure of a guilty secret" neither "qualifies as state compulsion" nor "compromises the voluntariness" of subsequent confessions. ([E]mphasis added). So long as a suspect receives the usual *Miranda* warnings before further interrogation, the Court reasons, the fact that he "is free to exercise his own volition in deciding whether or not to make" further confessions "ordinarily" is a sufficient "cure" and serves to break any causal connection between the illegal confession and subsequent statements.

The Court's marble-palace psychoanalysis is tidy, but it flies in the face of our own precedents, demonstrates a startling unawareness of the realities of police interrogation, and is completely out of tune with the experience of state and federal courts over the last 20 years. Perhaps the Court has grasped some psychological truth that has eluded persons far more experienced in these matters; if so, the Court owes an explanation of how so many could have been so wrong for so many years.

A
(1)

This Court has had long experience with the problem of confessions obtained after an earlier confession has been illegally secured. Subsequent confessions in these circumstances are not *per se* inadmissible, but the prosecution must demonstrate facts "sufficient to insulate the [subsequent] statement from the effect of all that went before." *Clewis v. Texas*, 386 U.S. 707, 710, 87 S. Ct. 1338, 1340, 18 L. Ed. 2d 423 (1967). . . .

One of the factors that can vitiate the voluntariness of a subsequent confession is the hopeless feeling of an accused that he has nothing to lose by repeating his confession, even where the circumstances that rendered his first confession illegal have been removed. As the Court observed in *United States v. Bayer*, 331 U.S., at 540, 67 S. Ct., at 1398:

> "[A]fter an accused has once let the cat out of the bag by confessing, no matter what the inducement, he is never thereafter free of the psychological and practical disadvantages of having confessed. He can never get the cat back in the bag. The secret is out for good. In such a sense, a later confession always may be looked upon as a fruit of the first."

. . . . Although we have . . . rejected a *per se* rule forbidding the introduction of subsequent statements in these circumstances, we have emphasized that the psychological impact of admissions and confessions of criminal guilt nevertheless can have a decisive impact in undermining the voluntariness of a suspect's responses to continued police interrogation and must be accounted for in determining their admissibility. . . .

(2)

Our precedents . . . reflect an understanding of the realities of police interrogation and the everyday experience of lower courts. Expert interrogators, far from dismissing a first admission or confession as creating merely a "speculative and attenuated" disadvantage for a suspect, understand that such revelations frequently lead directly to a full confession. Standard interrogation manuals advise that "[t]he securing of the first admission is the biggest stumbling block . . . ." A. Aubry & R. Caputo, Criminal Interrogation 290 (3d ed. 1980). If this first admission can be obtained, "there is every reason to expect that the first admission will lead to others, and eventually to the full confession." *Ibid.*

. . . .

The practical experience of state and federal courts confirms the experts' understanding. From this experience, lower courts have concluded that a first confession obtained without proper *Miranda* warnings, far from creating merely some "speculative and attenuated" disadvantage for the accused, frequently enables the authorities to obtain subsequent confessions on a "silver platter." *Cagle v. State*, 45 Ala. App. 3, 4, 221 So.2d 119, 120, cert. denied, 284 Ala. 727, 221 So.2d 121 (1969).

. . . .

. . . [T]he underlying problem is always the same: after hearing the witness testimony and considering the practical realities, courts have confirmed the time-honored wisdom of presuming that a first illegal confession "taints" subsequent confessions, and permitting such subsequent confessions to be admitted at trial *only* if the prosecution convincingly rebuts the presumption. They have discovered that frequently, "[h]aving once confessed [the accused] was ready to confess some more." *State v. Lekas*, 201 Kan. 579, 587–588, 442 P.2d 11, 19 (1968). For all practical purposes, the prewarning and post-warning questioning are often but stages of one overall interrogation. . . .

I would have thought that the Court, instead of dismissing the "cat out of the bag" presumption out of hand, would have accounted for these practical realities. Expert interrogators and experienced lower-court judges will be startled, to say the least, to learn that the connection between multiple confessions is "speculative" and that a subsequent rendition of *Miranda* warnings "ordinarily" enables the accused in these circumstances to exercise his "free will" and to make "a rational and intelligent choice whether to waive or invoke his rights."

(3)

The Court's new view about the "psychological impact" of prior illegalities also is at odds with our Fourth Amendment precedents. For example, it is well established that a confession secured as a proximate result of an illegal arrest must be suppressed. . . .

. . . If the Court so quickly dismisses the notion of a multiple-confession taint as nothing more than a "speculative and attenuated" disadvantage, what is to prevent it in the future from deciding that, contrary to the settled understanding, the fact of a proximate illegal arrest is presumptively nothing but a "speculative and attenuated" disadvantage to a defendant who is asked to confess?

. . . .

B

The correct approach . . . is to presume that an admission or confession obtained in violation of *Miranda* taints a subsequent confession unless the prosecution can show that the taint is so attenuated as to justify admission of the subsequent confession. Although the Court warns against the "irremediable consequences" of this presumption, it is obvious that a subsequent confession, just like any other evidence that follows upon illegal police action, does not become "sacred and inaccessible." *Silverthorne Lumber Co. v. United States*, 251 U.S., at 392, 40 S. Ct., at 183. As with any other evidence, the inquiry is whether the subsequent confession "'has been come at by exploitation of [the] illegality or instead by means sufficiently distinguishable to be purged of the primary taint.'" *Wong Sun v. United States*, 371 U.S., at 488, 83 S. Ct., at 417 (citation omitted).

Until today the Court has recognized that the dissipation inquiry requires the prosecution to demonstrate that the official illegality did not taint the challenged confession, and we have rejected the simplistic view that abstract notions of "free will" are alone sufficient to dissipate the challenged taint.

. . . .

Nor have we ever allowed *Miranda* warnings alone to serve talismanically to purge the taint of prior illegalities. In *Brown v. Illinois*, for example, we emphasized that "*Miranda* warnings, *alone* and *per se*, cannot always make [a confession] sufficiently a product of free will to break . . . the causal connection between [an illegal arrest] and the confession." 422 U.S., at 603, 95 S. Ct., at 2261 (emphasis in original). . . . .

. . . . Where an accused believes that it is futile to resist because the authorities already have elicited an admission of guilt, the mere rendition of *Miranda* warnings does not convey the information most critical at that point to ensuring his informed and voluntary decision to speak again: that the earlier confession may not be admissible and thus that he need not speak out of any feeling that he already has sealed his fate. The Court therefore is flatly wrong in arguing, as it does repeatedly, that the mere provision of *Miranda* warnings prior to subsequent interrogation supplies the accused with "the relevant information" and ensures that a subsequent confession "ordinarily" will be the product of "a rational and intelligent choice" and "'an act of free will.'"

. . . .

C

Perhaps because the Court is discomfited by the radical implications of its failure to apply the settled derivative-evidence presumption to violations of *Miranda*, it grudgingly qualifies its sweeping pronouncements with the acknowledgment that its new presumption about so-called "ordinary" *Miranda* violations can be overcome by the accused. Explicitly eschewing "a *per se* rule," the Court suggests that its approach should not be followed where the police have employed "improper tactics" or "inherently coercive methods" that are "calculated to undermine the suspect's ability to exercise his free will." The Court thus concedes that lower courts must continue to be free to "examine the surrounding circumstances and the entire course of police conduct with respect to the suspect in evaluating the voluntariness of his statements."

The Court's concessions are potentially significant, but its analysis is wholly at odds with established dissipation analysis. To begin with, the Court repeatedly suggests that a confession may be suppressed only if the police have used "improper tactics"; this obscure reasoning overlooks the fact that a violation of *Miranda* is obviously *itself* an "improper tactic," one frequently used precisely to undermine the voluntariness of subsequent confessions. The Court's negative implication that *Miranda* violations are *not* "improper tactics" is, to say the least, disquieting. Second, the Court reasons that the fact that the accused gave a subsequent confession is *itself* "highly probative" evidence that he was able to exercise his free will. This inaccurate premise follows from the Court's erroneous rejection of the "cat out of the bag" presumption in these circumstances and its inexplicable assertion that the previous extraction of a "guilty secret" neither constitutes compulsion nor compromises the voluntariness of later confessions. Finally, the foundation of the derivative-evidence doctrine has always been that, where the authorities have acted illegally, *they* must bear the "ultimate burden" of proving that their misconduct did not "taint" subsequently obtained evidence. That is precisely the point of the derivative-evidence presumption. By rejecting this presumption in *Miranda* cases, the Court today appears to adopt a "go ahead and try to prove it" posture toward citizens whose Fifth Amendment *Miranda* rights have been violated, an attitude that marks a sharp break from the Court's traditional approach to official lawlessness.

. . . .

In sum, today's opinion marks an evisceration of the established fruit of the poisonous tree doctrine, but its reasoning is sufficiently obscure and qualified as to leave state and federal courts with continued authority to combat obvious flouting by the authorities of the privilege against self-incrimination. I am confident that lower courts will exercise this authority responsibly, as they have for the most part prior to this Court's intervention.

II

. . . [T]he Court goes on to assert that nothing in the Fifth Amendment or the general judicial policy of deterring illegal police conduct "ordinarily" requires the suppression of evidence derived proximately from a confession obtained in violation of *Miranda*. The Court does not limit its analysis to successive confessions, but recurrently refers generally to the "fruits" of the illegal confession. Thus the potential impact of the Court's reasoning might extend far beyond the "cat out of the bag" context to include the discovery of physical evidence and other derivative fruits of *Miranda* violations as well.[29]

. . . .

C

Even if I accepted the Court's conclusion that the Fifth Amendment does not command the suppression of evidence proximately derived from a *Miranda* violation, I would nevertheless dissent from the Court's refusal to recognize the importance of deterring *Miranda* violations in appropriate circumstances. . . .

The Court today refuses to apply the derivative-evidence rule even to the extent necessary to deter objectively unreasonable failures by the authorities to honor a suspect's *Miranda* rights. Incredibly, faced with an obvious violation of *Miranda*, the Court asserts that it will not countenance suppression of a subsequent confession in such circumstances where the authorities have acted "legitimate[ly]" and have not used "improper tactics." One can only respond: whither went *Miranda*?

. . . .

The Court clearly errs in suggesting that suppression of the "unwarned admission" alone will provide meaningful deterrence. The experience of lower courts demonstrates that the police frequently have refused to comply with *Miranda* precisely in order to obtain incriminating statements that will undermine the voluntariness of the accused's decision to speak again once he has received the usual warnings; in such circumstances, subsequent confessions often follow on a "silver platter." *Cagle v. State*, 45 Ala. App., at 4, 221 So.2d, at 120. Expert interrogators themselves recognize the direct connection between such statements. And the Court's suggestion that its analysis might apply generally to "fruits" of illegal interrogations, blinks reality even further. For example, expert interrogators acknowledge that confessions are "'the prime source of other evidence.'" If the police through illegal interrogation could discover contraband and be confident that the contraband "ordinarily" would not be suppressed, what possible incentive would they have to obey *Miranda*?

. . . .

. . . How can the Court possibly expect the authorities to obey *Miranda* when they have every incentive now to interrogate suspects without warnings or an effective waiver, knowing that the fruits of such interrogations "ordinarily" will be admitted, that an admissible subsequent confession "ordinarily" can be obtained simply by reciting the *Miranda* warnings shortly after the first has been procured and asking the accused to repeat himself, and that unless the accused can demonstrate otherwise

---

29. Notwithstanding the sweep of the Court's language, today's opinion surely ought not be read as also foreclosing application of the traditional derivative-evidence presumption to physical evidence obtained as a proximate result of a *Miranda* violation. The Court relies heavily on individual "volition" as an insulating factor in successive-confession cases. Although the Court's reliance on this factor is clearly misplaced, the factor is altogether missing in the context of inanimate evidence. . . . .

his confession will be viewed as an "act of free will" in response to "legitimate law enforcement activity"? By condoning such a result, the Court today encourages practices that threaten to reduce *Miranda* to a mere "form of words," *Silverthorne Lumber Co. v. United States*, 251 U.S., at 392, 40 S. Ct., at 183, and it is shocking that the Court nevertheless disingenuously purports that it "in no way retreats" from the *Miranda* safeguards.

. . . .

I dissent.

JUSTICE STEVENS, dissenting.

The Court concludes its opinion with a carefully phrased statement of its holding:

> "We hold today that a suspect who has once responded to unwarned yet uncoercive questioning is not thereby disabled from waiving his rights and confessing after he has been given the requisite *Miranda* warnings."

I find nothing objectionable in such a holding. Moreover, because the Court expressly endorses the "bright-line rule of *Miranda*," which conclusively presumes that incriminating statements obtained from a suspect in custody without administering the required warnings are the product of compulsion, and because the Court places so much emphasis on the special facts of this case, I am persuaded that the Court intends its holding to apply only to a narrow category of cases in which the initial questioning of the suspect was made in a totally uncoercive setting and in which the first confession obviously had no influence on the second. I nevertheless dissent because even such a narrowly confined exception is inconsistent with the Court's prior cases, because the attempt to identify its boundaries in future cases will breed confusion and uncertainty in the administration of criminal justice, and because it denigrates the importance of one of the core constitutional rights that protects every American citizen from the kind of tyranny that has flourished in other societies.

. . . .

I respectfully dissent.

Notes and Questions

(1) The violation of *Miranda* at issue in *Elstad* was a failure to administer the requisite warnings. Should the analysis and result differ if the violation that led to an initial statement — followed by a subsequent, *Mirandized* statement — was:

(a) a failure to "scrupulously honor" a suspect's express desire to remain silent?

(b) an "initiation of communications" by officials after a suspect has made a clear request for the assistance of counsel?

(c) obtainment of a "waiver" of *Miranda* rights that was either insufficiently knowing or involuntary?

(d) the actual coercion of an involuntary confession from the suspect?

(2) Why is a confession obtained without *Miranda* warnings inadmissible at trial? Why do the justifications for excluding such a statement not extend to a successive confession obtained after compliance with *Miranda*'s warnings and waiver requirements?

(3) The tenor of the *Elstad* majority's attitude toward *Miranda*'s exclusion doctrine seems distinctly different from the tenor of the majority's attitude toward such exclusion in *Withrow v. Williams, supra* Chapter 12. Whether the two are reconcilable or, instead, reflect a change in the Court's thinking about *Miranda*'s evidentiary bar is an interesting and significant question. The two opinions that follow shed additional light on the prevailing understanding of and disposition toward the *Miranda* exclusionary rule.

Missouri v. Seibert

United States Supreme Court

542 U.S. 600, 124 S. Ct. 2601, 159 L. Ed. 2d 643 (2004)

JUSTICE SOUTER announced the judgment of the Court and delivered an opinion, in which JUSTICE STEVENS, JUSTICE GINSBURG, and Justice BREYER join.

. . . .

I

Respondent Patrice Seibert's 12-year-old son Jonathan had cerebral palsy, and when he died in his sleep she feared charges of neglect because of bedsores on his body. In her presence, two of her teenage sons and two of their friends devised a plan to conceal the facts surrounding Jonathan's death by incinerating his body in the course of burning the family's mobile home, in which they planned to leave Donald Rector, a mentally ill teenager living with the family, to avoid any appearance that Jonathan had been unattended. Seibert's son Darian and a friend set the fire, and Donald died.

Five days later, the police awakened Seibert at 3 a.m. at a hospital where Darian was being treated for burns. In arresting her, Officer Kevin Clinton followed instructions from Rolla, Missouri, Officer Richard Hanrahan that he refrain from giving *Miranda* warnings. After Seibert had been taken to the police station and left alone in an interview room for 15 to 20 minutes, Officer Hanrahan questioned her without *Miranda* warnings for 30 to 40 minutes, squeezing her arm and repeating "Donald was also to die in his sleep." After Seibert finally admitted she knew Donald was meant to die in the fire, she was given a 20-minute coffee and cigarette break. Officer Hanrahan then turned on a tape recorder, gave Seibert the *Miranda* warnings, and obtained a signed waiver of rights from her. He resumed the questioning with "Ok, 'trice, we've been talking for a little while about what happened on Wednesday the twelfth, haven't we?," and confronted her with her prewarning statements:

Hanrahan: "Now, in discussion you told us, you told us that there was a[n] understanding about Donald."

Seibert: "Yes."

Hanrahan: "Did that take place earlier that morning?"

Seibert: "Yes."

Hanrahan: "And what was the understanding about Donald?"

Seibert: "If they could get him out of the trailer, to take him out of the trailer."

Hanrahan: "And if they couldn't?"

Seibert: "I, I never even thought about it. I just figured they would."

Hanrahan: "'Trice, didn't you tell me that he was supposed to die in his sleep?"

Seibert: "If that would happen, 'cause he was on that new medicine, you know. . . . ."

Hanrahan: "The Prozac? And it makes him sleepy. So he was supposed to die in his sleep?"

Seibert: "Yes."

After being charged with first-degree murder for her role in Donald's death, Seibert sought to exclude both her prewarning and postwarning statements. At the suppression hearing, Officer Hanrahan testified that he made a "conscious decision" to withhold *Miranda* warnings, thus resorting to an interrogation technique he had been taught: question first, then give the warnings, and then repeat the question "until I get the answer that she's already provided once." He acknowledged that Seibert's ultimate statement was "largely a repeat of information . . . obtained" prior to the warning.

The trial court suppressed the prewarning statement but admitted the responses given after the *Miranda* recitation. A jury convicted Seibert of second-degree murder. On appeal, the Missouri Court of Appeals affirmed. . . .

The Supreme Court of Missouri reversed, holding that "[i]n the circumstances here, where the interrogation was nearly continuous, . . . the second statement, clearly the product of the invalid first statement, should have been suppressed." 93 S.W.3d 700, 701 (2002). . . .

. . . .

II

. . . .

In *Miranda* [*v. Arizona*, 384 U.S. 436 (1966)], we explained that the "voluntariness doctrine in the state cases . . . encompasses all interrogation practices which are likely to exert such pressure upon an individual as to disable him from making a free and rational choice," *id.*, at 464–465. We appreciated the difficulty of judicial enquiry *post hoc* into the circumstances of a police interrogation, *Dickerson v. United States*, 530 U.S. 428, 444, 120 S. Ct. 2326, 147 L. Ed. 2d 405 (2000), and recognized that "the coercion inherent in custodial interrogation blurs the line between voluntary and involuntary statements, and thus heightens the risk" that the privilege against self-incrimination will not be observed, *id.*, at 435. Hence our concern that the "traditional totality-of-the-circumstances" test posed an "unacceptably great" risk that involuntary custodial confessions would escape detection. *Id.*, at 442.

Accordingly, "to reduce the risk of a coerced confession and to implement the Self-Incrimination Clause," *Chavez v. Martinez*, 538 U.S. 760, 790, 123 S. Ct. 1994, 155 L. Ed. 2d 984 (2003) (Kennedy, J., concurring in part and dissenting in part), this Court in *Miranda* concluded that "the accused must be adequately and effectively apprised of his rights and the exercise of those rights must be fully honored," 384 U.S., at 467. *Miranda* conditioned the admissibility at trial of any custodial confession on warning a suspect of his rights: failure to give the prescribed warnings and obtain a waiver of rights before custodial questioning generally requires exclusion of any statements obtained. Conversely, giving the warnings and getting a waiver has generally produced a virtual ticket of admissibility; maintaining that a statement is involuntary even though given after warnings and voluntary waiver of rights requires unusual stamina, and litigation over voluntariness tends to end with the finding of a valid waiver. To point out the obvious, this common consequence would not be common at all were it not that *Miranda* warnings are customarily given under circumstances allowing for a real choice between talking and remaining silent.

III

There are those, of course, who preferred the old way of doing things, giving no warnings and litigating the voluntariness of any statement in nearly every instance. In the aftermath of *Miranda*, Congress even passed a statute seeking to restore that old regime, 18 U.S.C. § 3501, although the Act lay dormant for years until finally invoked and challenged in *Dickerson v. United States, supra. Dickerson* reaffirmed *Miranda* and held that its constitutional character prevailed against the statute.

The technique of interrogating in successive, unwarned and warned phases raises a new challenge to *Miranda*. Although we have no statistics on the frequency of this practice, it is not confined to Rolla, Missouri. An officer of that police department testified that the strategy of withholding *Miranda* warnings until after interrogating and drawing out a confession was promoted not only by his own department, but by a national police training organization and other departments in which he had worked. Consistently with the officer's testimony, the Police Law Institute, for example, instructs that "officers may conduct a two-stage interrogation. . . . At any point during the pre-*Miranda* interrogation, usually after arrestees have confessed, officers may then read the *Miranda* warnings and ask for a waiver. If the arrestees waive their *Miranda* rights, officers will be able to repeat any *subsequent* incriminating statements later in court." Police Law Institute, Illinois Police Law Manual 83 (Jan.

2001–Dec. 2003), http:// www.illinoispolicelaw.org/training/lessons/ILPLMIR.pdf (available in the Clerk of Court's case file) (hereinafter Police Law Manual) (emphasis in original).[2] The upshot of all this advice is a question-first practice of some popularity, as one can see from the reported cases describing its use, sometimes in obedience to departmental policy.

IV

When a confession so obtained is offered and challenged, attention must be paid to the conflicting objects of *Miranda* and question-first. *Miranda* addressed "interrogation practices ... likely ... to disable [an individual] from making a free and rational choice" about speaking, 384 U.S., at 464–465, and held that a suspect must be "adequately and effectively" advised of the choice the Constitution guarantees, *id.*, at 467, 86 S. Ct. 1602. The object of question-first is to render *Miranda* warnings ineffective by waiting for a particularly opportune time to give them, after the suspect has already confessed.

Just as "no talismanic incantation [is] required to satisfy [*Miranda*'s] strictures," *California v. Prysock*, 453 U.S. 355, 359, 101 S. Ct. 2806, 69 L. Ed. 2d 696 (1981) (*per curiam*), it would be absurd to think that mere recitation of the litany suffices to satisfy *Miranda* in every conceivable circumstance. "The inquiry is simply whether the warnings reasonably 'conve[y] to [a suspect] his rights as required by *Miranda*.'" *Duckworth v. Eagan*, 492 U.S. 195, 203, 109 S. Ct. 2875, 106 L. Ed. 2d 166 (1989) (quoting *Prysock, supra*, at 361, 101 S. Ct. 2806). The threshold issue when interrogators question first and warn later is thus whether it would be reasonable to find that in these circumstances the warnings could function "effectively" as *Miranda* requires. Could the warnings effectively advise the suspect that he had a real choice about giving an admissible statement at that juncture? Could they reasonably convey that he could choose to stop talking even if he had talked earlier? For unless the warnings could place a suspect who has just been interrogated in a position to make such an informed choice, there is no practical justification for accepting the formal warnings as compliance with *Miranda*, or for treating the second stage of interrogation as distinct from the first, unwarned and inadmissible segment.[4]

---

2. Emphasizing the impeachment exception to the *Miranda* rule approved by this Court, *Harris v. New York*, 401 U.S. 222, 91 S. Ct. 643, 28 L. Ed. 2d 1 (1971), some training programs advise officers to omit *Miranda* warnings altogether or to continue questioning after the suspect invokes his rights. This training is reflected in the reported cases involving deliberate questioning after invocation of *Miranda* rights. Scholars have noted the growing trend of such practices. It is not the case, of course, that law enforcement educators en masse are urging that *Miranda* be honored only in the breach. Most police manuals do not advocate the question-first tactic, because they understand that *Oregon v. Elstad*, 470 U.S. 298, 105 S. Ct. 1285, 84 L. Ed. 2d 222 (1985), involved an officer's good-faith failure to warn.

4. Respondent Seibert argues that her second confession should be excluded from evidence under the doctrine known by the metaphor of the "fruit of the poisonous tree," developed in the Fourth Amendment context in *Wong Sun v. United States*, 371 U.S. 471, 83 S. Ct. 407, 9 L. Ed. 2d 441 (1963): evidence otherwise admissible but discovered as a result of an earlier violation is excluded as

There is no doubt about the answer that proponents of question-first give to this question about the effectiveness of warnings given only after successful interrogation, and we think their answer is correct. By any objective measure, applied to circumstances exemplified here, it is likely that if the interrogators employ the technique of withholding warnings until after interrogation succeeds in eliciting a confession, the warnings will be ineffective in preparing the suspect for successive interrogation, close in time and similar in content. After all, the reason that question-first is catching on is as obvious as its manifest purpose, which is to get a confession the suspect would not make if he understood his rights at the outset; the sensible underlying assumption is that with one confession in hand before the warnings, the interrogator can count on getting its duplicate, with trifling additional trouble. Upon hearing warnings only in the aftermath of interrogation and just after making a confession, a suspect would hardly think he had a genuine right to remain silent, let alone persist in so believing once the police began to lead him over the same ground again.[5] A more likely reaction on a suspect's part would be perplexity about the reason for discussing rights at that point, bewilderment being an unpromising frame of mind for knowledgeable decision. What is worse, telling a suspect that "anything you say can and will be used against you," without expressly excepting the statement just given, could lead to an entirely reasonable inference that what he has just said will be used, with subsequent silence being of no avail. Thus, when *Miranda* warnings are inserted in the midst of coordinated and continuing interrogation, they are likely to mislead and "depriv[e] a defendant of knowledge essential to his ability to understand the nature of his rights and the consequences of abandoning them." *Moran v. Burbine*, 475 U.S. 412, 424, 106 S. Ct. 1135, 89 L. Ed. 2d 410 (1986). By the same token, it would ordinarily be unrealistic to treat two spates of integrated and proximately conducted questioning as independent interrogations subject to independent evaluation simply because *Miranda* warnings formally punctuate them in the middle.

---

tainted, lest the law encourage future violations. But the Court in *Elstad* rejected the *Wong Sun* fruits doctrine for analyzing the admissibility of a subsequent warned confession following "an initial failure . . . to administer the warnings required by *Miranda*." *Elstad*, 470 U.S., at 300, 105 S. Ct. 1285. . . . In a sequential confession case, clarity is served if the later confession is approached by asking whether in the circumstances the *Miranda* warnings given could reasonably be found effective. If yes, a court can take up the standard issues of voluntary waiver and voluntary statement; if no, the subsequent statement is inadmissible for want of adequate *Miranda* warnings, because the earlier and later statements are realistically seen as parts of a single, unwarned sequence of questioning.

5. It bears emphasizing that the effectiveness *Miranda* assumes the warnings can have must potentially extend through the repeated interrogation, since a suspect has a right to stop at any time. It seems highly unlikely that a suspect could retain any such understanding when the interrogator leads him a second time through a line of questioning the suspect has already answered fully. The point is not that a later unknowing or involuntary confession cancels out an earlier, adequate warning; the point is that the warning is unlikely to be effective in the question-first sequence we have described.

V

Missouri argues that a confession repeated at the end of an interrogation sequence envisioned in a question-first strategy is admissible on the authority of *Oregon v. Elstad*, 470 U.S. 298, 105 S. Ct. 1285, 84 L. Ed. 2d 222 (1985), but the argument disfigures that case. In *Elstad*, the police went to the young suspect's house to take him into custody on a charge of burglary. Before the arrest, one officer spoke with the suspect's mother, while the other one joined the suspect in a "brief stop in the living room," *id.*, at 315, where the officer said he "felt" the young man was involved in a burglary, *id.*, at 301, 105 S. Ct. 1285 (internal quotation marks omitted). The suspect acknowledged he had been at the scene. *Ibid.* This Court noted that the pause in the living room "was not to interrogate the suspect but to notify his mother of the reason for his arrest," *id.*, at 315, 105 S. Ct. 1285, and described the incident as having "none of the earmarks of coercion," *id.*, at 316, 105 S. Ct. 1285. The Court, indeed, took care to mention that the officer's initial failure to warn was an "oversight" that "may have been the result of confusion as to whether the brief exchange qualified as 'custodial interrogation' or . . . may simply have reflected . . . reluctance to initiate an alarming police procedure before [an officer] had spoken with respondent's mother." *Id.*, at 315–316, 105 S. Ct. 1285. At the outset of a later and systematic station house interrogation going well beyond the scope of the laconic prior admission, the suspect was given *Miranda* warnings and made a full confession. *Elstad, supra*, at 301, 314–315, 105 S. Ct. 1285. In holding the second statement admissible and voluntary, *Elstad* rejected the "cat out of the bag" theory that any short, earlier admission, obtained in arguably innocent neglect of *Miranda*, determined the character of the later, warned confession, *Elstad*, 470 U.S., at 311–314, 105 S. Ct. 1285; on the facts of that case, the Court thought any causal connection between the first and second responses to the police was "speculative and attenuated," *id.*, at 313, 105 S. Ct. 1285. Although the *Elstad* Court expressed no explicit conclusion about either officer's state of mind, it is fair to read *Elstad* as treating the living room conversation as a good-faith *Miranda* mistake, not only open to correction by careful warnings before systematic questioning in that particular case, but posing no threat to warn-first practice generally.

The contrast between *Elstad* and this case reveals a series of relevant facts that bear on whether *Miranda* warnings delivered midstream could be effective enough to accomplish their object: the completeness and detail of the questions and answers in the first round of interrogation, the overlapping content of the two statements, the timing and setting of the first and the second, the continuity of police personnel, and the degree to which the interrogator's questions treated the second round as continuous with the first. In *Elstad*, it was not unreasonable to see the occasion for questioning at the station house as presenting a markedly different experience from the short conversation at home; since a reasonable person in the suspect's shoes could have seen the station house questioning as a new and distinct experience, the *Miranda* warnings could have made sense as presenting a genuine choice whether to follow up on the earlier admission.

At the opposite extreme are the facts here, which by any objective measure reveal a police strategy adapted to undermine the *Miranda* warnings.[6] The unwarned interrogation was conducted in the station house, and the questioning was systematic, exhaustive, and managed with psychological skill. When the police were finished there was little, if anything, of incriminating potential left unsaid. The warned phase of questioning proceeded after a pause of only 15 to 20 minutes, in the same place as the unwarned segment. When the same officer who had conducted the first phase recited the *Miranda* warnings, he said nothing to counter the probable misimpression that the advice that anything Seibert said could be used against her also applied to the details of the inculpatory statement previously elicited. In particular, the police did not advise that her prior statement could not be used.[7] Nothing was said or done to dispel the oddity of warning about legal rights to silence and counsel right after the police had led her through a systematic interrogation, and any uncertainty on her part about a right to stop talking about matters previously discussed would only have been aggravated by the way Officer Hanrahan set the scene by saying "we've been talking for a little while about what happened on Wednesday the twelfth, haven't we?" The impression that the further questioning was a mere continuation of the earlier questions and responses was fostered by references back to the confession already given. It would have been reasonable to regard the two sessions as parts of a continuum, in which it would have been unnatural to refuse to repeat at the second stage what had been said before. These circumstances must be seen as challenging the comprehensibility and efficacy of the *Miranda* warnings to the point that a reasonable person in the suspect's shoes would not have understood them to convey a message that she retained a choice about continuing to talk.

VI

Strategists dedicated to draining the substance out of *Miranda* cannot accomplish by training instructions what *Dickerson* held Congress could not do by statute. Because the question-first tactic effectively threatens to thwart *Miranda*'s purpose of reducing the risk that a coerced confession would be admitted, and because the facts here do not reasonably support a conclusion that the warnings given could have served their purpose, Seibert's postwarning statements are inadmissible. The judgment of the Supreme Court of Missouri is affirmed.

It is so ordered.

Justice Breyer, concurring.

---

6. Because the intent of the officer will rarely be as candidly admitted as it was here (even as it is likely to determine the conduct of the interrogation), the focus is on facts apart from intent that show the question-first tactic at work.

7. We do not hold that a formal addendum warning that a previous statement could not be used would be sufficient to change the character of the question-first procedure to the point of rendering an ensuing statement admissible, but its absence is clearly a factor that blunts the efficacy of the warnings and points to a continuing, not a new, interrogation.

In my view, the following simple rule should apply to the two-stage interrogation technique: Courts should exclude the "fruits" of the initial unwarned questioning unless the failure to warn was in good faith. Cf. *Oregon v. Elstad*, 470 U.S. 298, 309, 318, n. 5, 105 S. Ct. 1285, 84 L. Ed. 2d 222 (1985); *United States v. Leon*, 468 U.S. 897, 104 S. Ct. 3405, 82 L. Ed. 2d 677 (1984). I believe this is a sound and workable approach to the problem this case presents. Prosecutors and judges have long understood how to apply the "fruits" approach, which they use in other areas of law. See *Wong Sun v. United States*, 371 U.S. 471, 83 S. Ct. 407, 9 L. Ed. 2d 441 (1963). . . .

I believe the plurality's approach in practice will function as a "fruits" test. The truly "effective" *Miranda* warnings on which the plurality insists will occur only when certain circumstances — a lapse in time, a change in location or interrogating officer, or a shift in the focus of the questioning — intervene between the unwarned questioning and any postwarning statement.

I consequently join the plurality's opinion in full. I also agree with JUSTICE KENNEDY's opinion insofar as it is consistent with this approach and makes clear that a good-faith exception applies.

JUSTICE KENNEDY, concurring in the judgment.

The interrogation technique used in this case is designed to circumvent *Miranda v. Arizona*, 384 U.S. 436, 86 S. Ct. 1602, 16 L. Ed. 2d 694 (1966). It undermines the *Miranda* warning and obscures its meaning. The plurality opinion is correct to conclude that statements obtained through the use of this technique are inadmissible. Although I agree with much in the careful and convincing opinion for the plurality, my approach does differ in some respects, requiring this separate statement.

The *Miranda* rule has become an important and accepted element of the criminal justice system. See *Dickerson v. United States*, 530 U.S. 428, 120 S. Ct. 2326, 147 L. Ed. 2d 405 (2000). At the same time, not every violation of the rule requires suppression of the evidence obtained. Evidence is admissible when the central concerns of *Miranda* are not likely to be implicated and when other objectives of the criminal justice system are best served by its introduction. . . . [The] admission of evidence is proper when it would further important objectives without compromising *Miranda*'s central concerns. . . . [T]he scope of the *Miranda* suppression remedy depends on a consideration of those legitimate interests and on whether admission of the evidence under the circumstances would frustrate *Miranda*'s central concerns and objectives.

Oregon v. Elstad, 470 U.S. 298, 105 S. Ct. 1285, 84 L. Ed. 2d 222 (1985), reflects this approach. . . .

In my view, *Elstad* was correct in its reasoning and its result. *Elstad* reflects a balanced and pragmatic approach to enforcement of the *Miranda* warning. An officer may not realize that a suspect is in custody and warnings are required. The officer may not plan to question the suspect or may be waiting for a more appropriate time. Skilled investigators often interview suspects multiple times, and good police work may involve referring to prior statements to test their veracity or to refresh recollection. In light of these realities it would be extravagant to treat the presence of one statement that cannot be admitted under *Miranda* as sufficient reason to prohibit subsequent statements preceded by a proper warning. . . .

This case presents different considerations. The police used a two-step questioning technique based on a deliberate violation of *Miranda*. The *Miranda* warning was withheld to obscure both the practical and legal significance of the admonition when finally given. As JUSTICE SOUTER points out, the two-step technique permits the accused to conclude that the right not to respond did not exist when the earlier incriminating statements were made. The strategy is based on the assumption that *Miranda* warnings will tend to mean less when recited midinterrogation, after inculpatory statements have already been obtained. This tactic relies on an intentional misrepresentation of the protection that *Miranda* offers and does not serve any legitimate objectives that might otherwise justify its use.

Further, the interrogating officer here relied on the defendant's prewarning statement to obtain the postwarning statement used against her at trial. The postwarning interview resembled a cross-examination. The officer confronted the defendant with her inadmissible prewarning statements and pushed her to acknowledge them. This shows the temptations for abuse inherent in the two-step technique. Reference to the prewarning statement was an implicit suggestion that the mere repetition of the earlier statement was not independently incriminating. The implicit suggestion was false.

The technique used in this case distorts the meaning of *Miranda* and furthers no legitimate countervailing interest. The *Miranda* rule would be frustrated were we to allow police to undermine its meaning and effect. The technique simply creates too high a risk that postwarning statements will be obtained when a suspect was deprived of "knowledge essential to his ability to understand the nature of his rights and the consequences of abandoning them." *Moran v. Burbine*, 475 U.S. 412, 423–424, 106 S. Ct. 1135, 89 L. Ed. 2d 410 (1986). When an interrogator uses this deliberate, two-step strategy, predicated upon violating *Miranda* during an extended interview, postwarning statements that are related to the substance of prewarning statements must be excluded absent specific, curative steps.

The plurality concludes that whenever a two-stage interview occurs, admissibility of the postwarning statement should depend on "whether [the] *Miranda* warnings delivered midstream could have been effective enough to accomplish their object" given the specific facts of the case. This test envisions an objective inquiry from the perspective of the suspect, and applies in the case of both intentional and unintentional two-stage interrogations. In my view, this test cuts too broadly. *Miranda*'s clarity is one of its strengths, and a multifactor test that applies to every two-stage interrogation may serve to undermine that clarity. I would apply a narrower test applicable only in the infrequent case, such as we have here, in which the two-step interrogation technique was used in a calculated way to undermine the *Miranda* warning.

The admissibility of postwarning statements should continue to be governed by the principles of *Elstad* unless the deliberate two-step strategy was employed. If the deliberate two-step strategy has been used, postwarning statements that are related to the substance of prewarning statements must be excluded unless curative measures are taken before the postwarning statement is made. Curative measures should be designed to ensure that a reasonable person in the suspect's situation would understand the import and effect of the *Miranda* warning and of the *Miranda* waiver. For example, a substantial break in time and circumstances between the prewarning statement and the *Miranda* warning may suffice in most circumstances, as it allows the accused to distinguish the two contexts and appreciate that the interrogation has taken a new turn. Alternatively, an additional warning that explains the likely inadmissibility of the prewarning custodial statement may be sufficient. No curative steps were taken in this case, however, so the postwarning statements are inadmissible and the conviction cannot stand.

For these reasons, I concur in the judgment of the Court.

JUSTICE O'CONNOR, with whom THE CHIEF JUSTICE, JUSTICE SCALIA, and JUSTICE THOMAS join, dissenting.

The plurality devours *Oregon v. Elstad*, 470 U.S. 298, 105 S. Ct. 1285, 84 L. Ed. 2d 222 (1985), even as it accuses petitioner's argument of "disfigur[ing]" that decision. I believe that we are bound by *Elstad* to reach a different result. . . .

I

On two preliminary questions I am in full agreement with the plurality. First, the plurality appropriately follows *Elstad* in concluding that Seibert's statement cannot be held inadmissible under a "fruit of the poisonous tree" theory. Second, the plurality correctly declines to focus its analysis on the subjective intent of the interrogating officer.

A

This Court has made clear that there simply is no place for a robust deterrence doctrine with regard to violations of *Miranda v. Arizona*, 384 U.S. 436, 86 S. Ct. 1602, 16 L. Ed. 2d 694 (1966). Consistent with that view, the Court today refuses to apply the traditional "fruits" analysis to the physical fruit of a claimed *Miranda* violation. [*United States v.*] *Patane*, [542 U.S.630, 124 S. Ct. 2620, 159 L. Ed. 2d 667 (2004)]. The plurality correctly refuses to apply a similar analysis to testimonial fruits.

Although the analysis the plurality ultimately espouses examines the same facts and circumstances that a "fruits" analysis would consider (such as the lapse of time between the two interrogations and change of questioner or location), it does so for entirely different reasons. The fruits analysis would examine those factors because they are relevant to the balance of deterrence value versus the "drastic and socially costly course" of excluding reliable evidence. *Nix v. Williams*, 467 U.S. 431, 442–443, 104 S. Ct. 2501, 81 L. Ed. 2d 377 (1984). The plurality, by contrast, looks to those factors to inform the *psychological* judgment regarding whether the suspect has been informed effectively of her right to remain silent. The analytical underpinnings of the two approaches are thus entirely distinct, and they should not be conflated just because they function similarly in practice.

B

The plurality's rejection of an intent-based test is also, in my view, correct. Freedom from compulsion lies at the heart of the Fifth Amendment, and requires us to assess whether a suspect's decision to speak truly was voluntary. Because voluntariness is a matter of the suspect's state of mind, we focus our analysis on the way in which suspects experience interrogation.

Thoughts kept inside a police officer's head cannot affect that experience. . . . A suspect who experienced exactly the same interrogation as Seibert, save for a difference in the undivulged, subjective intent of the interrogating officer when he failed to give *Miranda* warnings, would not experience the interrogation any differently. . . .

Because the isolated fact of Officer Hanrahan's intent could not have had any bearing on Seibert's "capacity to comprehend and knowingly relinquish" her right to remain silent, it could not by itself affect the voluntariness of her confession. Moreover, recognizing an exception to *Elstad* for intentional violations would require focusing constitutional analysis on a police officer's subjective intent, an unattractive proposition that we all but uniformly avoid. . . . This case presents the uncommonly straightforward circumstance of an officer openly admitting that the violation was intentional. But the inquiry will be complicated in other situations probably more likely to occur. For example, different officers involved in an interrogation might claim different states of mind regarding the failure to give *Miranda* warnings. Even in the simple case of a single officer who claims that a failure to give *Miranda* warnings was inadvertent, the likelihood of error will be high.

These evidentiary difficulties have led us to reject an intent-based test in several criminal procedure contexts. . . .

For these reasons, I believe that the approach espoused by JUSTICE KENNEDY is ill advised. JUSTICE KENNEDY would extend *Miranda*'s exclusionary rule to any case in which the use of the "two-step interrogation technique" was "deliberate" or "calculated." . . .

II

The plurality's adherence to *Elstad*, and mine to the plurality, end there. Our decision in *Elstad* rejected two lines of argument advanced in favor of suppression. The first was based on the "fruit of the poisonous tree" doctrine, discussed above. The second was the argument that the "lingering compulsion" inherent in a defendant's having let the "cat out of the bag" required suppression. 470 U.S., at 311, 105 S. Ct. 1285. The Court of Appeals of Oregon, in accepting the latter argument, had endorsed a theory indistinguishable from the one today's plurality adopts: "[T]he coercive impact of the unconstitutionally obtained statement remains, because in a defendant's mind it has sealed his fate. It is this impact that must be dissipated in order to make a subsequent confession admissible." *State v. Elstad*, 61 Or. App. 673, 677, 658 P.2d 552, 554 (1983).

We rejected this theory outright. We did so not because we refused to recognize the "psychological impact of the suspect's conviction that he has let the cat out of the bag," but because we refused to "endo[w]" those "psychological effects" with "constitutional implications." 470 U.S., at 311, 105 S. Ct. 1285. To do so, we said, would "effectively immuniz[e] a suspect who responds to pre-*Miranda* warning questions from the consequences of his subsequent informed waiver," an immunity that "comes at a high cost to legitimate law enforcement activity, while adding little desirable protection to the individual's interest in not being *compelled* to testify against himself." *Id.*, at 312. The plurality might very well think that we struck the balance between Fifth Amendment rights and law enforcement interests incorrectly in *Elstad*; but that is not normally a sufficient reason for ignoring the dictates of *stare decisis*.

I would analyze the two-step interrogation procedure under the voluntariness standards central to the Fifth Amendment and reiterated in *Elstad*. *Elstad* commands that if Seibert's first statement is shown to have been involuntary, the court must examine whether the taint dissipated through the passing of time or a change in circumstances. . . . In addition, Seibert's second statement should be suppressed if she showed that it was involuntary despite the *Miranda* warnings. Although I would leave this analysis for the Missouri courts to conduct on remand, I note that, unlike the officers in *Elstad*, Officer Hanrahan referred to Seibert's unwarned statement during the second part of the interrogation when she made a statement at odds with her unwarned confession. Such a tactic may bear on the voluntariness inquiry.

Because I believe that the plurality gives insufficient deference to *Elstad* and that JUSTICE KENNEDY places improper weight on subjective intent, I respectfully dissent.

Notes and Questions

(1) The plurality opinion asserted that Missouri's argument that Seibert's confession was "admissible on the authority of *Oregon v. Elstad* . . . disfigure[d] that case." In dissent, Justice O'Connor, the author of *Elstad*, accused the plurality of "devour[ing] *Oregon v. Elstad*." Is the plurality opinion in *Seibert* consistent or incompatible with the reasoning and result of *Elstad*?

(2) In *Seibert*, a "second" confession made after *Miranda* warnings was inadmissible while in *Elstad*, a "second" confession following *Miranda* warnings was deemed admissible. What are the critical distinctions that led to these different outcomes? In future cases, when should a court admit such a confession?

United States v. Patane

United States Supreme Court

542 U.S. 630, 124 S. Ct. 2620, 159 L. Ed. 2d 667 (2004)

JUSTICE THOMAS announced the judgment of the Court and delivered an opinion, in which THE CHIEF JUSTICE and JUSTICE SCALIA join.

In this case we must decide whether a failure to give a suspect the warnings prescribed by *Miranda v. Arizona*, 384 U.S. 436, 86 S. Ct. 1602, 16 L. Ed. 2d 694 (1966), requires suppression of the physical fruits of the suspect's unwarned but voluntary statements.... Because the *Miranda* rule protects against violations of the Self-Incrimination Clause, which, in turn, is not implicated by the introduction at trial of physical evidence resulting from voluntary statements, we answer the question presented in the negative.

I

In June 2001, respondent, Samuel Francis Patane, was arrested for harassing his ex-girlfriend, Linda O'Donnell. He was released on bond, subject to a temporary restraining order that prohibited him from contacting O'Donnell. Respondent apparently violated the restraining order by attempting to telephone O'Donnell. On June 6, 2001, Officer Tracy Fox of the Colorado Springs Police Department began to investigate the matter. On the same day, a county probation officer informed an agent of the Bureau of Alcohol, Tobacco, and Firearms (ATF), that respondent, a convicted felon, illegally possessed a .40 Glock pistol. The ATF relayed this information to Detective Josh Benner, who worked closely with the ATF. Together, Detective Benner and Officer Fox proceeded to respondent's residence.

After reaching the residence and inquiring into respondent's attempts to contact O'Donnell, Officer Fox arrested respondent for violating the restraining order. Detective Benner attempted to advise respondent of his *Miranda* rights but got no further than the right to remain silent. At that point, respondent interrupted, asserting that he knew his rights, and neither officer attempted to complete the warning.

Detective Benner then asked respondent about the Glock. Respondent was initially reluctant to discuss the matter, stating: "I am not sure I should tell you anything about the Glock because I don't want you to take it away from me." Detective Benner persisted, and respondent told him that the pistol was in his bedroom. Respondent then gave Detective Benner permission to retrieve the pistol. Detective Benner found the pistol and seized it.

A grand jury indicted respondent for possession of a firearm by a convicted felon, in violation of 18 U.S.C. § 922(g)(1). The District Court granted respondent's motion to suppress the firearm, reasoning that the officers lacked probable cause to arrest respondent for violating the restraining order. It therefore declined to rule on respondent's alternative argument that the gun should be suppressed as the fruit of an unwarned statement.

The Court of Appeals reversed the District Court's ruling with respect to probable cause but affirmed the suppression order on respondent's alternative theory. . . . We granted certiorari.

As we explain below, the *Miranda* rule is a prophylactic employed to protect against violations of the Self-Incrimination Clause. The Self-Incrimination Clause, however, is not implicated by the admission into evidence of the physical fruit of a voluntary statement. Accordingly, there is no justification for extending the *Miranda* rule to this context. And just as the Self-Incrimination Clause primarily focuses on the criminal trial, so too does the *Miranda* rule. The *Miranda* rule is not a code of police conduct, and police do not violate the Constitution (or even the *Miranda* rule, for that matter) by mere failures to warn. For this reason, the exclusionary rule articulated in cases such as *Wong Sun* [*v. United States*, 371 U.S. 471 (1963)] does not apply. Accordingly, we reverse the judgment of the Court of Appeals and remand the case for further proceedings.

II

The Self-Incrimination Clause provides: "No person . . . shall be compelled in any criminal case to be a witness against himself." U.S. Const., Amdt. 5. We need not decide here the precise boundaries of the Clause's protection. For present purposes, it suffices to note that the core protection afforded by the Self-Incrimination Clause is a prohibition on compelling a criminal defendant to testify against himself at trial. The Clause cannot be violated by the introduction of nontestimonial evidence obtained as a result of voluntary statements.

To be sure, the Court has recognized and applied several prophylactic rules designed to protect the core privilege against self-incrimination. . . . We have explained that "[t]he natural concern which underlies [these] decisions is that an inability to protect the right at one stage of a proceeding may make its invocation useless at a later stage." [*Michigan v.*] *Tucker*, 417 U.S. [433,] 440–441 [(1974)].

Similarly, in *Miranda*, the Court concluded that the possibility of coercion inherent in custodial interrogations unacceptably raises the risk that a suspect's privilege against self-incrimination might be violated. See *Dickerson* [*v. United States*], 530 U.S. [428,] 434–435 [(2000)]; *Miranda*, 384 U.S., at 467. To protect against this danger, the *Miranda* rule creates a presumption of coercion, in the absence of specific warnings, that is generally irrebuttable for purposes of the prosecution's case in chief.

But because these prophylactic rules (including the *Miranda* rule) necessarily sweep beyond the actual protections of the Self-Incrimination Clause, see, *e.g., Withrow* [*v. Williams*, 507 U.S. 680,] 690–691 [(1993)]; [*Oregon v.*] *Elstad*, [470 U.S. 298,] 306 [(1985)], any further extension of these rules must be justified by its necessity for the protection of the actual right against compelled self-incrimination. Indeed, at times the Court has declined to extend *Miranda* even where it has perceived a need to protect the privilege against self-incrimination. See, *e.g.,* [*New York v.*] *Quarles*, [467 U.S. 649,] 657 [(1984)] (concluding "that the need for answers to questions in a situation posing a threat to the public safety outweighs the need for the prophylactic rule protecting the Fifth Amendment's privilege against self-incrimination").

It is for these reasons that statements taken without *Miranda* warnings (though not actually compelled) can be used to impeach a defendant's testimony at trial, see *Elstad, supra,* at 307–308; *Harris v. New York,* 401 U.S. 222, 91 S. Ct. 643, 28 L. Ed. 2d 1 (1971), though the fruits of actually compelled testimony cannot, see *New Jersey v. Portash,* 440 U.S. 450, 458–459, 99 S. Ct. 1292, 59 L. Ed. 2d 501 (1979). More generally, the *Miranda* rule "does not require that the statements [taken without complying with the rule] and their fruits be discarded as inherently tainted," *Elstad,* 470 U.S., at 307. Such a blanket suppression rule could not be justified by reference to the "Fifth Amendment goal of assuring trustworthy evidence" or by any deterrence rationale, *id.,* at 308; see *Tucker, supra,* at 446–449; *Harris* [*v. New York,* 401 U.S. 222,] 225–226, and n. 2 [(1971)], and would therefore fail our close-fit requirement.

Furthermore, the Self-Incrimination Clause contains its own exclusionary rule. It provides that "[n]o person . . . shall be compelled in any criminal case to be a witness against himself." Amdt. 5. Unlike the Fourth Amendment's bar on unreasonable searches, the Self-Incrimination Clause is self-executing. We have repeatedly explained "that those subjected to coercive police interrogations have an *automatic* protection from the use of their involuntary statements (or evidence derived from their statements) in any subsequent criminal trial." *Chavez* [*v. Martinez*], 538 U.S. [760,] 769 [(2003)] (plurality opinion) (citing, for example, *Elstad, supra,* at 307–308). This explicit textual protection supports a strong presumption against expanding the *Miranda* rule any further.

Finally, nothing in *Dickerson*, including its characterization of *Miranda* as announcing a constitutional rule, 530 U.S., at 444, changes any of these observations. Indeed, in *Dickerson*, the Court specifically noted that the Court's "subsequent cases have reduced the impact of the *Miranda* rule on legitimate law enforcement while reaffirming [*Miranda*]'s core ruling that unwarned statements may not be used as evidence in the prosecution's case in chief." *Id.,* at 443–444. This description of *Miranda*, especially the emphasis on the use of "unwarned statements . . . in the prosecution's case in chief," makes clear our continued focus on the protections of the Self-Incrimination Clause. The Court's reliance on our *Miranda* precedents, including both *Tucker* and *Elstad*, see, *e.g., Dickerson, supra,* at 438, 441, further demonstrates the continuing validity of those decisions. In short, nothing in *Dickerson* calls into question our continued insistence that the closest possible fit be maintained between the Self-Incrimination Clause and any rule designed to protect it.

III

Our cases also make clear the related point that a mere failure to give *Miranda* warnings does not, by itself, violate a suspect's constitutional rights or even the *Miranda* rule. So much was evident in many of our pre-*Dickerson* cases, and we have adhered to this view since *Dickerson*. See *Chavez, supra,* at 772–773 (plurality opinion) (holding that a failure to read *Miranda* warnings did not violate the respondent's constitutional rights); 538 U.S., at 789. (Kennedy, J., concurring in part and dissenting in part) (agreeing "that failure to give a *Miranda* warning does not, without more, establish a completed violation when the unwarned interrogation ensues"); *Elstad, supra,* at 308; *Quarles,* 467 U.S., at 654; cf. *Chavez, supra,* at 777–779 (Souter, J., concurring in judgment). . . .

It follows that police do not violate a suspect's constitutional rights (or the *Miranda* rule) by negligent or even deliberate failures to provide the suspect with the full panoply of warnings prescribed by *Miranda.* Potential violations occur, if at all, only upon the admission of unwarned statements into evidence at trial. And, at that point, "[t]he exclusion of unwarned statements . . . is a complete and sufficient remedy" for any perceived *Miranda* violation. *Chavez, supra,* at 790.[3]

Thus, unlike unreasonable searches under the Fourth Amendment or actual violations of the Due Process Clause or the Self-Incrimination Clause, there is, with respect to mere failures to warn, nothing to deter. There is therefore no reason to apply the "fruit of the poisonous tree" doctrine of *Wong Sun,* 371 U.S., at 488. It is not for this Court to impose its preferred police practices on either federal law enforcement officials or their state counterparts.

IV

In the present case, the Court of Appeals, relying on *Dickerson,* wholly adopted the position that the taking of unwarned statements violates a suspect's constitutional rights. 304 F.3d, at 1028–1029. And, of course, if this were so, a strong deterrence-based argument could be made for suppression of the fruits.

But *Dickerson*'s characterization of *Miranda* as a constitutional rule does not lessen the need to maintain the closest possible fit between the Self-Incrimination Clause and any judge-made rule designed to protect it. And there is no such fit here. Introduction of the nontestimonial fruit of a voluntary statement, such as respondent's Glock, does not implicate the Self-Incrimination Clause. The admission of such fruit presents no risk that a defendant's coerced statements (however defined) will be used against him at a criminal trial. In any case, "[t]he exclusion of unwarned statements . . . is a complete and sufficient remedy" for any perceived *Miranda* violation. *Chavez,* [538 U.S.], at 790 (KENNEDY, J., concurring in part and dissenting in

---

3. We acknowledge that there is language in some of the Court's post-*Miranda* decisions that might suggest that the *Miranda* rule operates as a direct constraint on police. See, *e.g., Stansbury v. California,* 511 U.S. 318, 322, 114 S. Ct. 1526, 128 L. Ed. 2d 293 (1994) (*per curiam*); *Moran v. Burbine,* 475 U.S. 412, 420, 106 S. Ct. 1135, 89 L. Ed. 2d 410 (1986) (stating that "*Miranda* imposed on the police an obligation to follow certain procedures"); cf. *Edwards v. Arizona,* 451 U.S. 477, 485, 101 S. Ct. 1880, 68 L. Ed. 2d 378 (1981). But *Miranda* itself made clear that its focus was the admissibility of statements, see, e.g., 384 U.S., at 439, 467, a view the Court reaffirmed in *Dickerson v. United States,* 530 U.S. 428, 443–444, 120 S. Ct. 2326, 147 L. Ed. 2d 405 (2000) (equating the *Miranda* rule with the proposition that "unwarned statements may not be used as evidence in the prosecution's case in chief" (emphasis added)).

part). There is simply no need to extend (and therefore no justification for extending) the prophylactic rule of *Miranda* to this context.

Similarly, because police cannot violate the Self-Incrimination Clause by taking unwarned though voluntary statements, an exclusionary rule cannot be justified by reference to a deterrence effect on law enforcement, as the Court of Appeals believed, 304 F.3d, at 1028–1029. Our decision not to apply *Wong Sun* to mere failures to give *Miranda* warnings was sound at the time *Tucker* and *Elstad* were decided, and we decline to apply *Wong Sun* to such failures now.

The Court of Appeals ascribed significance to the fact that, in this case, there might be "little [practical] difference between [respondent's] confessional statement" and the actual physical evidence. 304 F.3d, at 1027. The distinction, the court said, "appears to make little sense as a matter of policy." *Ibid.* But, putting policy aside, we have held that "[t]he word 'witness' in the constitutional text limits the" scope of the Self-Incrimination Clause to testimonial evidence. *Hubbell*, 530 U.S., at 34–35. The Constitution itself makes the distinction. And although it is true that the Court requires the exclusion of the physical fruit of actually coerced statements, it must be remembered that statements taken without sufficient *Miranda* warnings are presumed to have been coerced only for certain purposes and then only when necessary to protect the privilege against self-incrimination. For the reasons discussed above, we decline to extend that presumption further.

Accordingly, we reverse the judgment of the Court of Appeals and remand the case for further proceedings.

It is so ordered.

Justice Kennedy, with whom Justice O'Connor joins, concurring in the judgment.

In *Oregon v. Elstad*, 470 U.S. 298, 105 S. Ct. 1285, 84 L. Ed. 2d 222 (1985), *New York v. Quarles*, 467 U.S. 649, 104 S. Ct. 2626, 81 L. Ed. 2d 550 (1984), and *Harris v. New York*, 401 U.S. 222, 91 S. Ct. 643, 28 L. Ed. 2d 1 (1971), evidence obtained following an unwarned interrogation was held admissible. This result was based in large part on our recognition that the concerns underlying the *Miranda v. Arizona*, 384 U.S. 436, 86 S. Ct. 1602, 16 L. Ed. 2d 694 (1966), rule must be accommodated to other objectives of the criminal justice system. I agree with the plurality that *Dickerson v. United States*, 530 U.S. 428, 120 S. Ct. 2326, 147 L. Ed. 2d 405 (2000), did not undermine these precedents and, in fact, cited them in support. Here, it is sufficient to note that the Government presents an even stronger case for admitting the evidence obtained as the result of Patane's unwarned statement. Admission of nontestimonial physical fruits (the Glock in this case), even more so than the postwarning statements to the police in *Elstad* and *Michigan v. Tucker*, 417 U.S. 433, 94 S. Ct. 2357, 41 L. Ed. 2d 182 (1974), does not run the risk of admitting into trial an accused's coerced incriminating statements against himself. In light of the important probative value of reliable physical evidence, it is doubtful that exclusion can be justified by a deterrence rationale sensitive to both law enforcement interests and a suspect's rights during an in-custody interrogation. Unlike the plurality, however, I find it unnecessary to decide whether the detective's failure to give Patane the full *Miranda* warnings should be characterized as a violation of the *Miranda* rule itself, or whether there is "[any]thing to deter" so long as the unwarned statements are not later introduced at trial.

With these observations, I concur in the judgment of the Court.

Justice Souter, with whom Justice Stevens and Justice Ginsburg join, dissenting.

The plurality repeatedly says that the Fifth Amendment does not address the admissibility of nontestimonial evidence, an overstatement that is beside the point. The issue actually presented today is whether courts should apply the fruit of the poisonous tree doctrine lest we create an incentive for the police to omit *Miranda* warnings, see *Miranda v. Arizona*, 384 U.S. 436, 86 S. Ct. 1602, 16 L. Ed. 2d 694 (1966), before custodial interrogation. In closing their eyes to the consequences of giving an evidentiary advantage to those who ignore *Miranda*, the plurality adds an important inducement for interrogators to ignore the rule in that case.

Miranda rested on insight into the inherently coercive character of custodial interrogation and the inherently difficult exercise of assessing the voluntariness of any confession resulting from it. Unless the police give the prescribed warnings meant to counter the coercive atmosphere, a custodial confession is inadmissible, there being no need for the previous time-consuming and difficult enquiry into voluntariness. That inducement to forestall involuntary statements and troublesome issues of fact can only atrophy if we turn around and recognize an evidentiary benefit when an unwarned statement leads investigators to tangible evidence. There is, of course, a price for excluding evidence, but the Fifth Amendment is worth a price, and in the absence of a very good reason, the logic of *Miranda* should be followed: a *Miranda* violation raises a presumption of coercion, *Oregon v. Elstad*, 470 U.S. 298, 306–307, and n. 1, 105 S. Ct. 1285, 84 L. Ed. 2d 222 (1985), and the Fifth Amendment privilege against compelled self-incrimination extends to the exclusion of derivative evidence. That should be the end of this case.

The fact that the books contain some exceptions to the *Miranda* exclusionary rule carries no weight here. In *Harris v. New York*, 401 U.S. 222, 91 S. Ct. 643, 28 L. Ed. 2d 1 (1971), it was respect for the integrity of the judicial process that justified the admission of unwarned statements as impeachment evidence. But Patane's suppression motion can hardly be described as seeking to "perver[t]" *Miranda* "into a license to use perjury" or otherwise handicap the "traditional truth-testing devices of the adversary process." 401 U.S., at 225–226. Nor is there any suggestion that the officers' failure to warn Patane was justified or mitigated by a public emergency or other exigent circumstance, as in *New York v. Quarles*, 467 U.S. 649, 104 S. Ct. 2626, 81 L. Ed. 2d 550 (1984). And of course the premise of *Oregon v. Elstad, supra*, is not on point; although a failure to give *Miranda* warnings before one individual statement does not necessarily bar the admission of a subsequent statement given after adequate warnings, 470 U.S. 298, 105 S. Ct. 1285, 84 L. Ed. 2d 222; cf. *Missouri v. Seibert*, [542 U.S. 600, 124 S. Ct. 2601, 159 L. Ed. 2d 643 (2004)] (plurality opinion), that rule obviously does not apply to physical evidence seized once and for all.

There is no way to read this case except as an unjustifiable invitation to law enforcement officers to flout *Miranda* when there may be physical evidence to be gained. The incentive is an odd one, coming from the Court on the same day it decides *Missouri v. Seibert*. I respectfully dissent.

JUSTICE BREYER, dissenting.

... I would extend to this context the "fruit of the poisonous tree" approach, which I believe the Court has come close to adopting in *Seibert*. Under that approach, courts would exclude physical evidence derived from unwarned questioning unless the failure to provide *Miranda* warnings ... was in good faith. ...

Notes and Questions

(1) After *Elstad*, *Seibert*, and *Patane*, should a judge ever exclude evidence that the authorities have obtained as a result of a statement secured in violation of *Miranda*? Does it matter that the discovery of the derivative evidence was immediate? That the officer was following a departmental protocol that encourages officers to deliberately refrain from reciting warnings when there is a chance that a suspect will lead them to probative evidence?

(2) What purposes are served by excluding statements secured in violation of *Miranda*? Is the limitation on exclusion imposed by *Patane* reconcilable with those purposes?

(3) Justices Kennedy and O'Connor concurred in the Court's judgment, refusing to join Justice Thomas's opinion. Does the concurrence limit the scope of the ruling in *Patane*? If so, how?

(4) Some state courts have interpreted their state constitutions to provide more protection than the Fifth Amendment-based *Miranda* doctrine, as interpreted in *Patane*, provides. Specifically, they have held that evidentiary fruits of statements obtained in violation of *Miranda*'s dictates are subject to suppression. *See Commonwealth v. Martin*, 444 Mass. 213, 827 N.E.2d 198 (2005); *State v. Farris*, 109 Ohio St. 3d 519, 849 N.E.2d 985 (2006); *State v. Peterson*, 181 Vt. 436, 923 A.2d 585 (2007); *State v. Knapp*, 285 Wis.2d 86, 700 N.W.2d 899 (2005) (limited to physical fruits of "deliberate" *Miranda* violations).

Miranda Exclusion Problems

13E–1: As part of an investigation of John Longo for murder, police officers came to Weet's house on May 17. The officers were aware that Weet knew Longo, who was in hiding as the result of an earlier police raid. They went to Weet's residence hoping to learn where Longo was hiding. While sitting in Weet's living room, the officers asked him about Longo's location. When Weet denied knowing where Longo was, they threatened that they were going to lock Weet, his girlfriend, and his girlfriend's nephew up for obstruction of justice if Weet didn't take them to Longo. In response, Weet agreed to do so. He led the officers to the hotel where Longo was hiding. They arrested Longo pursuant to a warrant and found drugs in his hotel room. Longo subsequently pleaded guilty to drug charges and agreed that he would testify against Weet concerning their involvement in drug trafficking.

In mid-November, 2004, officers again came to Weet's house with an arrest warrant. Before formally arresting Weet, they handcuffed him and asked about the whereabouts of Maurice. Weet said he would take the police to Maurice. When he did so, they arrested Maurice. Weet was then taken to the police station where, at a little after 12:20 a.m., Detective Michael began questioning him. Weet made an incriminating statement, admitting that Longo had fronted him crack cocaine. At 1:40 a.m., Weet agreed to and did repeat the incriminating statement on tape.

According to Detective Michael, as soon as he approached Weet at 12:20 a.m., he recited *Miranda* warnings, and Weet then signed a waiver form. He then questioned Weet and, after receiving an inculpatory statement, brought in a tape recorder to record it. Prior to the taped statement, Michael recited the *Miranda* warnings for the second time. According to Weet, however, Detective Michael did not give *Miranda* warnings when first questioning him at 12:20 a.m. The first statement he gave was unwarned. Then, at 1:40 a.m., before his second, taped statement, he was given the *Miranda* warnings for the first time. He signed a waiver form at that time.

Before his trial in September, 2005, Weet filed a motion to suppress the testimony of John Longo at his trial, the evidence of drugs and drug paraphernalia obtained from Longo's hotel room on May 17, 2004, and both the unrecorded and recorded statements given to Detective Michael on November 19, 2004.

How should the trial judge rule?

13E–2: On June 25, just before 10 p.m., two men entered a convenience store in Delray Beach, Florida, where Patricia Greenfield, a college student, was employed. The men, later identified as Nollie Tin and Gary Forbes, robbed Greenfield at knifepoint of approximately $90 and two cases of beer and abducted her from the store. They drove her back to Tin's apartment, blindfolding her along the way. At the apartment, both men committed sexual battery on her.

Tin and Forbes then transported Greenfield away from the apartment, keeping her blindfolded and assuring her that she would be released at a remote area. After driving some distance, they arrived at the vicinity of the Lantana Dump. Tin walked the victim out of Forbes's sight and stabbed her to death.

On July 4, Tin and Forbes were arrested by detectives from the County Sheriff's Office on charges unrelated to the Greenfield murder. Beginning at about 2:30 p.m., Tin was interrogated, off and on, until 7:55 p.m., when he finally confessed to killing Patricia Greenfield. Tin was read and waived his *Miranda* rights prior to the start of the interrogation. At one point during the interrogation, Tin had asked whether questioning could wait until later. Detective Anderson, however, had said, "Let's go on."

On July 11, Tin was interrogated again. At the beginning of the interrogation, Detective Glover read another complete set of *Miranda* warnings to Tin. Tin said that he understood his rights, then provided another confession in response to the detective's interrogation.

Should either or both of the confessions be excluded from Tin's trial?

13E–3: On August 22, Detective Irvin obtained an arrest warrant for Timothy, an 18-year-old male, relating to the murder of Mr. Johns. Irvin advised his fellow officers that if they saw Timothy they should arrest him but should not advise him of his rights. He did this because he "wanted to be the one to speak with Timothy when he was arrested." On September 26, at 10:00 p.m., Irvin was informed that Timothy had been arrested and "was being transported to the Homicide Branch" by Sergeant Kirk. Irvin instructed Kirk to "place Timothy in the interview room and to leave him alone," saying that he would be there shortly.

Detective Irvin arrived between 11:00 p.m. and 11:30 p.m. Timothy was alone in a small interview room on the third floor, handcuffed to a chain that was attached to the floor. He had been restrained there for approximately one and a half hours. He had not been given *Miranda* warnings. Irvin sat down at the table across from Timothy and introduced himself. He advised Timothy that he was under arrest for murder, and he was interested in hearing Timothy's side of the story as to what happened to Mr. Johns. Irvin began to outline some of the facts he knew about Timothy's involvement — in particular, that Timothy was in a van that drove to the scene of the crime around the time Johns was shot. Irvin did not immediately advise Timothy of his *Miranda* rights. Rather, he related some of the details of Mr. Johns's death — describing the van used and naming some of the people who were also involved in the murder. Irvin told Timothy "I just want you to listen, because I just want you to be aware of some of the facts." If Timothy did attempt to speak, Irvin planned to emphasize that he wanted him to listen and not to talk at that time.

According to Irvin, he did not advise Timothy of his *Miranda* rights at this time because he "wanted to speak to him and didn't want to run the risk of Timothy invoking his right to remain silent or his right to counsel." His goal was "to get whatever information he could get out of" Timothy. He did not recite the *Miranda* warnings because he wanted Timothy to understand that "I had a lot of knowledge about the case, and that if he wanted to help himself, that he should tell me what happened, and I told him that there were two sides to every story, and I may not have had the whole story."

While recounting the facts of the murder to Timothy, Irvin mentioned that he had already spoken with Amos Chan, another suspect. He told Timothy that Chan had "already been placed under arrest" and that Chan had "already given me a statement." When Timothy told Irvin that he did not believe that Chan had given a statement, Irvin asked, "Do you want to see the proof?" When Timothy said he did, Irvin had a videotape machine set up. He then played a video recording of his interview with Chan with the volume turned down. Timothy, who could not hear what was being said on the recording, watched for "a little under a minute." Irvin then asked if he wanted any help and if he wanted to tell his side of the story. Timothy replied, "Yes." Irvin then administered the *Miranda* warnings, saying, "Before you tell me your side of the story I have to advise you of your rights." At 12:50 a.m., after having been with Irvin for approximately one hour, Timothy initialed a card indicating he understood and wanted to waive his rights.

According to Irvin, "I started up the interview again." In a questioning session that lasted for an hour, Timothy gave details about his involvement in the murder of Johns. Eventually, he signed a five-page statement prepared by Irvin. Prior to trial, relying on the *Miranda* doctrine, Timothy moved to suppress all of his incriminating statements.

Should Timothy's statements be excluded from his trial?

13E–4: Owen was killed by multiple gunshots to the head and chest from a .22 caliber gun. A gray Pontiac belonging to Owen was seen leaving the area where his body was found. The next day, Harry was seen driving Owen's car and using Owen's credit card. Based on these facts, on evidence obtained from Harry's mother, and on a statement given by James Malo, the police arrested Harry.

The same day, Kathy Still, a public defender who had previously represented Harry, called the police station where he was being held. Upon Still's advice, Harry indicated to the police that he did not desire to make any statements to the authorities outside the presence of counsel. The next day, a complaint charging Harry with first-degree murder and armed robbery was issued. Harry was arraigned on the complaint, and he again informed the authorities that he would make no statements without the assistance of counsel.

The following day, Detectives Ucik and Lazer, who were aware that Harry had said that he would not make a statement without counsel's assistance, came to the station to talk with Harry. Without providing *Miranda* warnings, Lazer initiated a 45-minute conversation. During the conversation, Lazer mentioned that he had spoken with Harry's mother. When Harry asked what his mother had said, Ucik warned him about "getting into the offense itself" because of his request for an attorney.

Shortly thereafter, Ucik left the room. Lazer proceeded to inform Harry that his mother had surrendered property belonging to the victim. When Lazer also truthfully told Harry that James Malo had been charged in connection with Owen's murder, Harry replied that Malo "had nothing to do with it," and said that he wanted to tell the detectives about the offense. After Lazer recited *Miranda* warnings, Harry said he would waive his right to counsel. He then admitted that he had killed Owen and told the detectives how and where he had disposed of the murder weapon.

Based on Harry's admissions, the detectives found the murder weapon, .22 caliber ammunition, and the victim's keys in a sewer approximately two blocks from Harry's home. After Harry's motion to suppress his confession, the gun, the ammunition, and the keys was denied, a jury convicted him of first-degree murder and armed robbery. Harry has appealed, challenging the denial of his motion.

How should the appellate court rule?

13E–5: On November 25, Ben Holly was shot and killed. At 4:00 p.m., on January 14, Dave, an 18-year-old with a tenth-grade education and several juvenile arrests, was arrested for the killing. He was taken to an office at the police station. Around 5:30 p.m., Detectives Sully and Call arrived at the office. Dave was seated in a chair with his left arm handcuffed to a bolt affixed to the floor. The detectives informed Dave that he was under arrest for the Holly murder, then left the room for 15 to 20 minutes to prepare paperwork. When they returned around 6:00 p.m., the officers made a conscious decision not to recite the *Miranda* warnings. They were aware that no other officer had given Dave the warnings. The detectives told Dave that they had learned that he and Angel Daniel (a.k.a. "Peanut") had shot Holly. They said that officers had recovered the weapons that had been used and that Dave could get "35 years to life" for the crime. They falsely reported that they had spoken to "Peanut" and that they understood that "Peanut had the nine millimeter and that [Dave] had the AK." Dave blurted out, "Peanut had the AK, I had the nine." Shortly thereafter, Dave asked Sully to leave the room, and Sully did so. Later, Dave asserted that he had done so because Sully seemed aggravated with his answers and hostile toward him.

Detective Call continued to talk to Dave until about 6:45 p.m., while Sully watched on a video monitor. Dave told Call that he had shot Holly with the nine millimeter weapon and that Daniels had shot him with the AK-47. Dave mentioned that his sister was a police officer. Call said that he knew her and had a "pretty close working relationship" with her. Call also told Dave that this day would change his life and that he should "stand up and be a man and accept whatever comes down the road." Around 7:00 p.m., Call advised Dave of his *Miranda* rights. Dave signed a waiver and gave a videotaped statement that contained basically the same information that he had already provided. Dave then telephoned his sister and told her that he had shot a man.

Dave filed a motion to suppress his statements from his trial for second-degree murder.

Should the trial judge grant Dave's motion?

13E–6: The United States Postal Service suspected Cappers, a mail handler, of stealing money orders from Express Mail envelopes. Postal Inspectors decided to conduct a sting operation. They planted two Express Mail envelopes in the mail-sorting facility where Cappers worked. One contained $30 cash, and the other contained two $80 money orders and was equipped with an alarm device. The alarm was set to trigger automatically if the contents of the envelope were removed. After planting the envelopes, the inspectors set up surveillance. At approximately 5:00 p.m.,

Cappers noticed the envelopes. He soon entered a trailer holding mail containers, disappearing briefly from the inspectors' view. One minute later, the alarm sounded.

The inspectors rushed into the trailer and apprehended Cappers. Inspector Hott handcuffed him and, along with Inspector Chow, escorted him to a supervisor's office. Without reciting *Miranda* warnings, Hott said, "Look, you know, talk to me or don't talk to me, I don't care but I'm telling you right now that I'm going to do my best to make you go away. And I've been watching you all day. I know everything that you did tonight." Hott then asked Cappers where the contents of the Express Mail envelope were located. Cappers gestured toward his pants pocket. Hott asked Cappers what was in his pocket and Cappers replied, "the money orders." Hott asked for permission to "grab" them. When Cappers said "yes," Hott removed the money orders from Cappers's pocket. Hott asked if the money orders belonged to him, and Cappers said "No," admitting that he got the money orders from the Express Mail envelope. The questioning took less than five minutes. According to Hott, he did not read Cappers his rights because he was in a hurry to track down the missing money orders so that they did not get lost in the large mail-sorting facility and because he needed to question another suspect to determine his level of involvement in Cappers's crime.

Postal Inspector Good escorted Cappers to a van to transport him to another Postal Service facility ("the Domicile") for further questioning. During the 35-minute drive to the Domicile, Good engaged Cappers in conversation—mainly about Cappers's automobile. Good placed Cappers in an interview room at the Domicile, handcuffing him to a chair. Cappers asked about the possibility of being fired, and Good told him, "It's in your best interest to tell the truth when Inspector Hott arrives. Be honest. It's always better if you're honest." Cappers and Good waited in the room for 30 to 40 minutes until Hott arrived. Hott advised Cappers of his *Miranda* rights. He did not refer to the statements Cappers had made during the initial interrogation. After Cappers signed a waiver form, Hott questioned him about the events of the evening, specifically asking about what he had done with the Express Mail envelopes. Cappers confessed to taking the money orders.

Cappers was charged with one count of theft of mail matter by a postal employee. He moved to suppress the inculpatory statements he made to Inspector Hott both before and after receiving the *Miranda* warnings.

Should the court suppress Cappers's statements?

13E-7: James was suspected of killing his former lover, Shari Nugget. On the evening of March 20, nine police officers took James from a hotel and transported him to the police station. At 11:30 p.m., James was read his *Miranda* rights and placed in the "Blue Room"—a 10 by 10, windowless and clockless chamber furnished with three chairs, a table, and a one-way mirror. Except for trips to the restroom, James was locked in the room for the next 49½ hours. With only relatively brief intervals, four rotating pairs of detectives aggressively interrogated him, relieving each other pursuant to a schedule devised by the supervising sergeant. James did not sleep and during the entire period ate only a sandwich. He stared at the floor and often wept. During the questioning, he made several statements that were not directly inculpatory but did suggest that he was involved in the disappearance of Ms. Nugget. For example, he said, that "[o]nly me, God, and Shari know what happened to her."

On the evening of March 22, the supervising sergeant told James that he would be charged with murder. When James became distraught, the sergeant urged him to disclose the location of the body. James said that he would "give everybody what they want," pledging that the police would have the body if he could confer with the Assistant District Attorney (ADA) and if he was provided with an attorney. The sergeant contacted the ADA, who, set in motion the process to have counsel appointed.

Upon his arrival at the station, James's assigned attorney spoke with the ADA. He was not told how long James had been questioned, but was told that if James disclosed the location of the body and pled guilty, his sentence would be capped at 18 years to life. After he met with an "emotional and distraught" James for two hours, counsel informed the authorities that his client should not be questioned further. At 1:30 a.m. on March 23, officers formally arrested and booked James.

At 9:30 a.m., James was arraigned in court. He was then returned to the police station, conferred briefly with his counsel, and was again placed in the Blue Room. With his counsel and the ADA present, the supervising sergeant asked James, "What happened?" James replied, "I killed her," then said he had placed the body in a dumpster at a specified location. No dumpster was found at the location and Ms. Nugget's body was never recovered. Over objection, James's admissions on the morning of March 23 were admitted at trial. He was convicted of murder and sentenced to 25 years to life. James has appealed, claiming that the judge should have excluded his admissions.

What arguments support James's claim? How should the court of appeals rule?

13E-8: FBI Agent John Eck recruited an informant, Craig, to take part in the purchase of illegal drugs from Mike Barrie at the local airport. Craig made the arrangements to buy the drugs during a recorded telephone call. The FBI agents were delayed and did not make it to the airport in time to either search Craig before the transaction with Barrie or to monitor the drug transaction. When the agents did arrive, they met with Craig, who gave them a package of methamphetamine he said that he had received from Barrie.

A few months later, at the request of the FBI agents, Barrie's parole officer, Andrea Kertz, scheduled a meeting with Barrie. She did not inform Barrie, who was required by the terms of his parole to attend the meeting, that FBI agents would be there. Kertz normally meets with parolees at the window to the lobby of her office, without requiring them to be searched or escorted into the secure area. However, upon arrival at the parole office, Barrie was searched and escorted into the interior of the building through an electronically locked door.

When Barrie arrived at Kertz's office, two FBI agents were waiting to question him about the transaction with Craig. Without informing Barrie of his *Miranda* rights, the agents told Barrie that they knew he had been involved in a drug distribution at the airport. Barrie denied the agents' allegations. The agents then played a portion of one of the recorded phone calls between Barrie and Craig. After hearing the recording, Barrie admitted that he had engaged in the drug transaction with Craig. Because Agent Eck thought Barrie "looked like he was going to continue talking," the FBI agents recited *Miranda* warnings. Barrie then waived his rights, and confessed involvement in the drug transaction. Before trial, Barrie filed a motion to suppress his statements, claiming that all of them were inadmissible under *Miranda*.

Does the *Miranda* exclusionary rule require supression of Barrie's statements?

[F] The "Impeachment" Limitation

Harris v. New York

United States Supreme Court

401 U.S. 222, 91 S. Ct. 643, 28 L. Ed. 2d 1 (1971)

Mr. Chief Justice Burger delivered the opinion of the Court.

. . . .

The State of New York charged petitioner in a two-count indictment with twice selling heroin to an undercover police officer. At a subsequent jury trial the officer was the State's chief witness, and he testified as to details of the two sales. A second officer verified collateral details of the sales, and a third offered testimony about the chemical analysis of the heroin.

Petitioner took the stand in his own defense. He admitted knowing the undercover police officer but denied a sale on January 4, 1966. He admitted making a sale of contents of a glassine bag to the officer on January 6 but claimed it was baking powder and part of a scheme to defraud the purchaser.

On cross-examination petitioner was asked seriatim whether he had made specified statements to the police immediately following his arrest on January 7 — statements that partially contradicted petitioner's direct testimony at trial. In response to the cross-examination, petitioner testified that he could not remember virtually any of the questions or answers recited by the prosecutor. At the request of petitioner's counsel the written statement from which the prosecutor had read questions and answers in his impeaching process was placed in the record for possible use on appeal; the statement was not shown to the jury.

The trial judge instructed the jury that the statements attributed to petitioner by the prosecution could be considered only in passing on petitioner's credibility and not as evidence of guilt. In closing summations both counsel argued the substance of the impeaching statements. The jury then found petitioner guilty on the second count of the indictment. The New York Court of Appeals affirmed in a *per curiam* opinion.

At trial the prosecution made no effort in its case in chief to use the statements allegedly made by petitioner, conceding that they were inadmissible under *Miranda v. Arizona*, 384 U.S. 436, 86 S. Ct. 1602, 16 L. Ed. 2d 694 (1966). The transcript of the interrogation used in the impeachment, but not given to the jury, shows that no warning of a right to appointed counsel was given before questions were put to petitioner when he was taken into custody. Petitioner makes no claim that the statements made to the police were coerced or involuntary.

Some comments in the *Miranda* opinion can indeed be read as indicating a bar to use of an uncounseled statement for any purpose, but discussion of that issue was not at all necessary to the Court's holding and cannot be regarded as controlling. *Miranda* barred the prosecution from making its case with statements of an accused made while in custody prior to having or effectively waiving counsel. It does not follow from *Miranda* that evidence inadmissible against an accused in the prosecution's case in chief is barred for all purposes, provided of course that the trustworthiness of the evidence satisfies legal standards.

In *Walder v. United States*, 347 U.S. 62, 744 S. Ct. 354, 98 L. Ed. 503 (1954), the Court permitted physical evidence, inadmissible in the case in chief, to be used for impeachment purposes. . . .

It is true that Walder was impeached as to collateral matters included in his direct examination, whereas petitioner here was impeached as to testimony bearing more directly on the crimes charged. We are not persuaded that there is a difference in principle that warrants a result different from that reached by the Court in *Walder*. Petitioner's testimony in his own behalf concerning the events of January 7 contrasted sharply with what he told the police shortly after his arrest. The impeachment process here undoubtedly provided valuable aid to the jury in assessing petitioner's credibility, and the benefits of this process should not be lost, in our view, because of the speculative possibility that impermissible police conduct will be encouraged thereby. Assuming that the exclusionary rule has a deterrent effect on proscribed police conduct, sufficient deterrence flows when the evidence in question is made unavailable to the prosecution in its case in chief.

Every criminal defendant is privileged to testify in his own defense, or to refuse to do so. But that privilege cannot be construed to include the right to commit perjury. Having voluntarily taken the stand, petitioner was under an obligation to speak truthfully and accurately, and the prosecution here did no more than utilize the traditional truth-testing devices of the adversary process.[2] Had inconsistent state-

---

2. If, for example, an accused confessed fully to a homicide and led the police to the body of the victim under circumstances making his confession inadmissible, the petitioner would have us al-

ments been made by the accused to some third person, it could hardly be contended that the conflict could not be laid before the jury by way of cross-examination and impeachment.

The shield provided by *Miranda* cannot be perverted into a license to use perjury by way of a defense, free from the risk of confrontation with prior inconsistent utterances. We hold, therefore, that petitioner's credibility was appropriately impeached by use of his earlier conflicting statements.

Affirmed.

Mr. Justice Black dissents.

Mr. Justice Brennan, with whom Mr. Justice Douglas and Mr. Justice Marshall, join, dissenting.

. . . .

The State's case against Harris depended upon the jury's belief of the testimony of the undercover agent that petitioner "sold" the officer heroin on January 4 and again on January 6. Petitioner took the stand and flatly denied having sold anything to the officer on January 4. He countered the officer's testimony as to the January 6 sale with testimony that he had sold the officer two glassine bags containing what appeared to be heroin, but that actually the bags contained only baking powder intended to deceive the officer in order to obtain $12. The statement contradicted petitioner's direct testimony as to the events of both days. The statement's version of the events on January 4 was that the officer had used petitioner as a middleman to buy some heroin from a third person with money furnished by the officer. The version of the events on January 6 was that petitioner had again acted for the officer in buying two bags of heroin from a third person for which petitioner received $12 and a part of the heroin. Thus, it is clear that the statement was used to impeach petitioner's direct testimony not on collateral matters but on matters directly related to the crimes for which he was on trial.

Walder v. United States was not a case where tainted evidence was used to impeach an accused's direct testimony on matters directly related to the case against him. In *Walder* the evidence was used to impeach the accused's testimony on matters collateral to the crime charged. Walder had been indicted in 1950 for purchasing and possessing heroin. When his motion to suppress use of the narcotics as illegally seized was granted, the Government dismissed the prosecution. Two years later Walder was indicted for another narcotics violation completely unrelated to the 1950 one. Testifying in his own defense, he said on direct examination that he had never in his life possessed narcotics. On cross-examination he denied that law enforcement

---

low that accused to take the stand and blandly deny every fact disclosed to the police or discovered as a "fruit" of his confession, free from confrontation with his prior statements and acts. The voluntariness of the confession would, on this thesis, be totally irrelevant. We reject such an extravagant extension of the Constitution.

officers had seized narcotics from his home two years earlier. The Government was then permitted to introduce the testimony of one of the officers involved in the 1950 seizure, that when he had raided Walder's home at that time he had seized narcotics there. The Court held that on facts where "the defendant went beyond a mere denial of complicity in the crimes of which he was charged and made the sweeping claim that he had never dealt in or possessed any narcotics," 347 U.S., at 65, 74 S. Ct., at 356, the exclusionary rule of *Weeks v. United States*, 232 U.S. 383, 34 S. Ct. 341, 58 L. Ed. 652 (1914), would not extend to bar the Government from rebutting this testimony with evidence, although tainted, that petitioner had in fact possessed narcotics two years before. The Court was careful, however, to distinguish the situation of an accused whose testimony, as in the instant case, was a "denial of complicity in the crimes of which he was charged," that is, where illegally obtained evidence was used to impeach the accused's direct testimony on matters directly related to the case against him. As to that situation, the Court said:

> Of course, the Constitution guarantees a defendant the fullest opportunity to meet the accusation against him. He must be free to deny all the elements of the case against him without thereby giving leave to the Government to introduce by way of rebuttal evidence illegally secured by it, and therefore not available for its case in chief.

347 U.S., at 65, 74 S. Ct., at 356.

. . . .

While *Walder* did not identify the constitutional specifics that guarantee "a defendant the fullest opportunity to meet the accusation against him . . . [and permit him to] be free to deny all the elements of the case against him," in my view *Miranda v. Arizona*, 384 U.S. 436, 86 S. Ct. 1602, 16 L. Ed. 2d 694 (1966), identified the Fifth Amendment's privilege against self-incrimination as one of those specifics. That privilege has been extended against the States. It is fulfilled only when an accused is guaranteed the right "to remain silent unless he chooses to speak in the *unfettered* exercise of his own will," *id.*, at 8, 84 S. Ct., at 1493 (emphasis added). The choice of whether to testify in one's own defense must therefore be "unfettered," since that choice is an exercise of the constitutional privilege, *Griffin v. California*, 380 U.S. 609, 85 S. Ct. 1229, 14 L. Ed. 2d 106 (1965). *Griffin* held that comment by the prosecution upon the accused's failure to take the stand or a court instruction that such silence is evidence of guilt is impermissible because it "fetters" that choice — "[i]t cuts down on the privilege by making its assertion costly." *Id.*, at 614, 85 S. Ct., at 1233. For precisely the same reason the constitutional guarantee forbids the prosecution to use a tainted statement to impeach the accused who takes the stand: The prosecution's use of the tainted statement "cuts down on the privilege by making its assertion costly." *Id.* Thus, the accused is denied an "unfettered" choice when the decision whether to take the stand is burdened by the risk that an illegally obtained prior statement may be introduced to impeach his direct testimony denying complicity in the crime charged against him. We settled this proposition in *Miranda* where we said:

The privilege against self-incrimination protects the individual from being compelled to incriminate himself in *any* manner.... [S]tatements merely intended to be exculpatory by the defendant are often *used to impeach his testimony at trial.... These statements are incriminating in any meaningful sense of the word and may not be used without the full warnings and effective waiver required for any other statement.*

384 U.S., at 476–477, 86 S. Ct., at 1629 (emphasis added).

. . . .

The objective of deterring improper police conduct is only part of the larger objective of safeguarding the integrity of our adversary system. The "essential mainstay" of that system, *Miranda v. Arizona*, 384 U.S., at 460, 86 S. Ct. 1602, is the privilege against self-incrimination, which for that reason has occupied a central place in our jurisprudence since before the Nation's birth.... The Court today tells the police that they may freely interrogate an accused incommunicado and without counsel and know that although any statement they obtain in violation of *Miranda* cannot be used on the State's direct case, it may be introduced if the defendant has the temerity to testify in his own defense. This goes far toward undoing much of the progress made in conforming police methods to the Constitution. I dissent.

Notes and Questions

Harris involved a confession obtained after a failure to give proper *Miranda* warnings. *Oregon v. Hass*, 420 U.S. 714, 95 S. Ct. 1215, 43 L. Ed. 2d 570 (1975), involved a confession obtained after the police gave the defendant *Miranda* warnings but failed to honor his request for counsel. The Court in *Hass* held that, although the confession was inadmissible in the prosecution's case-in-chief, it could be used to impeach the defendant's testimony. The majority did acknowledge that "when proper *Miranda* warnings have been given, and the officer then continues his interrogation after the suspect asks for an attorney, the officer may be said to have little to lose and perhaps something to gain by way of possibly uncovering impeachment material." It nonetheless concluded that the principles underlying *Harris* were controlling.

United States v. Havens

United States Supreme Court

446 U.S. 620, 100 S. Ct. 1912, 64 L. Ed. 2d 559 (1980)

Mr. Justice White delivered the opinion of the Court.

. . . .

I

Respondent was convicted of importing, conspiring to import, and intentionally possessing a controlled substance, cocaine. According to the evidence at his trial, Havens and John McLeroth, both attorneys from Ft. Wayne, Ind., boarded a flight from Lima, Peru, to Miami, Fla. In Miami, a customs officer searched McLeroth and found cocaine sewed into makeshift pockets in a T-shirt he was wearing under his outer clothing. McLeroth implicated respondent, who had previously cleared customs and who was then arrested. His luggage was seized and searched without a warrant. The officers found no drugs but seized a T-shirt from which pieces had been cut that matched the pieces that had been sewn to McLeroth's T-shirt. The T-shirt and other evidence seized in the course of the search were suppressed on motion prior to trial.

Both men were charged in a three-count indictment, but McLeroth pleaded guilty to one count and testified against Havens. Among other things, he asserted that Havens had supplied him with the altered T-shirt and had sewed the makeshift pockets shut. Havens took the stand in his own defense and denied involvement in smuggling cocaine. His direct testimony included the following:

Q. And you heard Mr. McLeroth testify earlier as to something to the effect that this material was taped or draped around his body and so on, you heard that testimony?

A. Yes, I did.

Q. Did you ever engage in that kind of activity with Mr. McLeroth and Augusto or Mr. McLeroth and anyone else on that fourth visit to Lima, Peru?

A. I did not.

On cross-examination, Havens testified as follows:

Q. Now, on direct examination, sir, you testified that on the fourth trip you had absolutely nothing to do with the wrapping of any bandages or tee shirts or anything involving Mr. McLeroth; is that correct?

A. I don't — I said I had nothing to do with any wrapping or bandages or anything, yes. I had nothing to do with anything with McLeroth in connection with this cocaine matter.

. . . .

Q. And your testimony is that you had nothing to do with the sewing of the cotton swatches to make pockets on that tee shirt?

A. Absolutely not.

Q. Sir, when you came through Customs, the Miami International Airport, on October 2, 1977, did you have in your suitcase Size 38–40 medium tee shirts?

An objection to the latter question was overruled and questioning continued:

Q. On that day, sir, did you have in your luggage a Size 38–40 medium man's tee shirt with swatches of clothing missing from the tail of that tee shirt?

A. Not to my knowledge.

. . . .

Q. Mr. Havens, I'm going to hand you what is Government's Exhibit 9 for identification and ask you if this tee shirt was in your luggage on October 2nd, 1975 [*sic*]?

A. Not to my knowledge. No.

Respondent Havens also denied having told a Government agent that the T-shirts found in his luggage belonged to McLeroth.

On rebuttal, a Government agent testified that Exhibit 9 had been found in respondent's suitcase and that Havens claimed the T-shirts found in his bag, including Exhibit 9, belonged to McLeroth. Over objection, the T-shirt was then admitted into evidence, the jury being instructed that the rebuttal evidence should be considered only for impeaching Havens' credibility.

The Court of Appeals reversed, relying on *Agnello v. United States*, 269 U.S. 20, 46 S. Ct. 4, 70 L. Ed. 145 (1925), and *Walder v. United States*, 347 U.S. 62, 74 S. Ct. 354, 98 L. Ed. 503 (1954). The court held that illegally seized evidence may be used for impeachment only if the evidence contradicts a particular statement made by a defendant in the course of his direct examination. We reverse.

II

In *Agnello v. United States*, a defendant charged with conspiracy to sell a package of cocaine testified on direct examination that he had possessed the packages involved but did not know what was in them. On cross-examination, he denied ever having seen narcotics and ever having seen a can of cocaine which was exhibited to him and which had been illegally seized from his apartment. The can of cocaine was permitted into evidence on rebuttal. Agnello was convicted and his conviction was affirmed by the Court of Appeals. This Court reversed, holding that the Fourth Amendment required exclusion of the evidence. The Court pointed out that "[i]n his direct examination, Agnello was not asked and did not testify concerning the can of cocaine" and "did nothing to waive his constitutional protection or to justify cross-examination in respect of the evidence claimed to have been obtained by the search." 269 U.S., at 35, 46 S. Ct., at 7. The Court also said, quoting from *Silverthorne Lumber Co. v. United States*, 251 U.S. 385, 392, 40 S. Ct. 182, 183, 64 L. Ed. 319 (1920), that the exclusionary rule not only commands that illegally seized evidence "shall not be used before the Court but that it shall not be used at all." 269 U.S., at 35, 46 S. Ct., at 7.

The latter statement has been rejected in our later cases, however, and *Agnello* otherwise limited. In *Walder v. United States*, the use of evidence obtained in an illegal search and inadmissible in the Government's case in chief was admitted to impeach the direct testimony of the defendant. This Court approved, saying that it would pervert the rule of *Weeks v. United States*, 232 U.S. 383, 34 S. Ct. 341, 58 L. Ed. 652 (1914), to hold otherwise. Similarly, in *Harris v. New York*, 401 U.S. 222, 91 S. Ct. 643, 28 L. Ed. 2d 1 (1971), and *Oregon v. Hass*, 420 U.S. 714, 95 S. Ct. 1215, 43 L. Ed. 2d 570 (1975), statements taken in violation of *Miranda v. Arizona*, 384 U.S. 436, 86 S. Ct. 1602, 16 L. Ed. 2d 694 (1966), and unusable by the prosecution as part of its own case, were held admissible to impeach statements made by the defendant in the course of his direct testimony. *Harris* also made clear that the permitted impeachment by otherwise inadmissible evidence is not limited to collateral matters.

. . . .

It is true that *Agnello* involved the impeachment of testimony first brought out on cross-examination and that in *Walder, Harris*, and *Hass*, the testimony impeached was given by the defendant while testifying on direct examination. In our view, however, a flat rule permitting only statements on direct examination to be impeached misapprehends the underlying rationale of *Walder, Harris* and *Hass*. These cases repudiated the statement in *Agnello* that no use at all may be made of illegally obtained evidence. Furthermore, in *Walder*, the Court said that in *Agnello*, the Government had "smuggled in" the impeaching opportunity in the course of cross-examination. The Court also relied on the statement in *Agnello*, 269 U.S. at 35, 46 S. Ct., at 7, that *Agnello* had done nothing "to justify cross-examination in respect of the evidence claimed to have been obtained by the search." The implication of *Walder* is that *Agnello* was a case of cross-examination having too tenuous a connection with any subject opened upon direct examination to permit impeachment by tainted evidence.

In reversing the District Court in the case before us, the Court of Appeals did not stop to consider how closely the cross-examination about the T-shirt and the luggage was connected with matters gone into in direct examination. If these questions would have been suggested to a reasonably competent cross-examiner by Havens' direct testimony, they were not "smuggled in"; and forbidding the Government to impeach the answers to these questions by using contrary and reliable evidence in its possession fails to take account of our cases, particularly *Harris* and *Hass*. In both cases, the Court stressed the importance of arriving at the truth in criminal trials, as well as the defendant's obligation to speak the truth in response to proper questions. We rejected the notion that the defendant's constitutional shield against having illegally seized evidence used against him could be "perverted into a license to use perjury by way of a defense, free from the risk of confrontation with prior inconsistent utterances." 401 U.S., at 226, 91 S. Ct., at 646. Both cases also held that the deterrent function of the rules excluding unconstitutionally obtained evidence is sufficiently served by denying its use to the government on its direct case. It was only a "speculative possibility" that also making it unavailable to the government for otherwise proper impeachment would contribute substantially in this respect. *Harris v. New York*, [401 U.S.] at 225, 91 S. Ct., at 645.

Neither *Harris* nor *Hass* involved the impeachment of assertedly false testimony first given on cross-examination, but the reasoning of those cases controls this one. There is no gainsaying that arriving at the truth is a fundamental goal of our legal system. We have repeatedly insisted that when defendants testify, they must testify truthfully or suffer the consequences. This is true even though a defendant is compelled to testify against his will. It is essential, therefore, to the proper functioning of the adversary system that when a defendant takes the stand, the government be permitted proper and effective cross-examination in an attempt to elicit the truth. The defendant's obligation to testify truthfully is fully binding on him when he is cross-examined. His privilege against self-incrimination does not shield him from proper questioning. He would unquestionably be subject to a perjury prosecution if he knowingly lies on cross-examination. In terms of impeaching a defendant's seemingly false statements with his prior inconsistent utterances or with other reliable evidence available to the government, we see no difference of constitutional magnitude between the defendant's statements on direct examination and his answers to questions put to him on cross-examination that are plainly within the scope of the defendant's direct examination. Without this opportunity, the normal function of cross-examination would be severely impeded.

We also think that the policies of the exclusionary rule no more bar impeachment here than they did in *Walder, Harris,* and *Hass.* In those cases, the ends of the exclusionary rules were thought adequately implemented by denying the government the use of the challenged evidence to make out its case in chief. The incremental furthering of those ends by forbidding impeachment of the defendant who testifies was deemed insufficient to permit or require that false testimony go unchallenged, with the resulting impairment of the integrity of the factfinding goals of the criminal trial. We reaffirm this assessment of the competing interests, and hold that a defendant's statements made in response to proper cross-examination reasonably suggested by the defendant's direct examination are subject to otherwise proper impeachment by the government, albeit by evidence that has been illegally obtained and that is inadmissible on the government's direct case, or otherwise, as substantive evidence of guilt.

. . . The Court of Appeals did not suggest that either the cross-examination or the impeachment of Havens would have been improper absent the use of illegally seized evidence, and we cannot accept respondent's suggestions that because of the illegal search and seizure, the Government's questions about the T-shirt were improper cross-examination. McLeroth testified that Havens had assisted him in preparing the T-shirt for smuggling. Havens, in his direct testimony, acknowledged McLeroth's prior testimony that the cocaine "was taped or draped around his body and so on" but denied that he had "ever engage[d] in that kind of activity with Mr. McLeroth. . . ." This testimony could easily be understood as a denial of any connection with McLeroth's T-shirt and as a contradiction of McLeroth's testimony. Quite reasonably, it seems to us, the Government on cross-examination called attention to his answers on direct and then asked whether he had anything to do with sewing the cotton swatches on McLeroth's T-shirt. This was cross-examination growing out of Havens' direct testimony; and, as we hold above, the ensuing impeachment did not violate Havens' constitutional rights.

We reverse the judgment of the Court of Appeals and remand the case to that court for further proceedings consistent with this opinion.

So ordered.

Mr. Justice Brennan, joined by Mr. Justice Marshall and joined in Part I by Mr. Justice Stewart and Mr. Justice Stevens, dissenting.

. . . .

I

The question before us is not of first impression. The identical issue was confronted in *Agnello v. United States*, 269 U.S. 20, 46 S. Ct. 4, 70 L. Ed. 145 (1925), which determined — contrary to the instant decision — that it was constitutionally impermissible to admit evidence obtained in violation of the Fourth Amendment to rebut a defendant's response to a matter first raised during the Government's cross-examination. Subsequently, *Walder v. United States*, 347 U.S. 62, 74 S. Ct. 354, 98 L. Ed. 503 (1954), affirmed the introduction of unlawfully acquired evidence to impeach an accused's false assertions about previous conduct that had been offered during direct testimony. But *Walder* took pains to draw the distinction between its own holding and *Agnello*, noting that "the defendant [Walder] went beyond a mere denial of complicity in the crimes of which he was charged and made the sweeping [and untrue] claim that he had never dealt in or possessed any narcotics." 347 U.S., at 65, 74 S. Ct., at 356. In "shar[p] contras[t]," in *Agnello*, "the Government . . . tried to smuggle [the tainted evidence] . . . in on cross-examination," and "elicit[ed] the expected denial. . . ." 347 U.S., at 66, 74 S. Ct., at 356.

The Court's recent decisions have left *Agnello* undisturbed. *Harris v. New York*, 401 U.S. 222, 91 S. Ct. 643, 28 L. Ed. 2d 1 (1971), allowed the government to use inadmissible uncounseled statements to impeach direct examination. So, too, *Oregon v. Hass*, 420 U.S. 714, 95 S. Ct. 1215, 43 L. Ed. 2d 570 (1975), reaffirmed *Harris* in the context of impeachment of the defendant's direct testimony. Significantly, neither decision intimated that *Agnello* had lost vitality, or that the distinction emphasized by *Walder* had been effaced.

The Court's opinion attempts to discredit *Agnello* by casting a strawman as its holding, and then demolishing the pitiful scarecrow of its own creation. Specifically, the Court cites *Agnello*'s quotation of language from *Silverthorne Lumber Co. v. United States*, 251 U.S. 385, 392, 40 S. Ct. 182, 183, 64 L. Ed. 319 (1920), that "illegally seized evidence 'shall not . . . be used at all,'" and then refers to the subsequent decisions that indeed permit limited use of that evidence for impeachment. But the actual principle of *Agnello*, as discerned by *Walder*, is that the Government may not employ its power of cross-examination to predicate the admission of illegal evidence. In other words, impeachment by cross-examination about — or introduction of — suppressible evidence must be warranted by defendant's statements upon direct questioning. That principle is not at all inconsistent with later cases holding that the defendant may not take advantage of evidentiary suppression to advance specific perjurious claims as part of his direct case.

. . . .

Finally, the rationale of *Harris v. New York* and *Oregon v. Hass* does not impel the decision at hand. The exclusionary rule exception established by *Harris* and *Hass* may be fairly easily cabined by defense counsel's willingness to forgo certain areas of questioning. But the rule prescribed by the Court in this case passes control of the exception to the Government, since the prosecutor can lay the predicate for admitting otherwise suppressible evidence with his own questioning. To be sure, the Court requires that cross-examination be "proper"; however, traditional evidentiary principles accord parties fairly considerable latitude in cross-examining opposing witnesses. *See* C. McCormick, Law of Evidence §§ 21–24 (2d ed. 1972).[1] In practical terms, therefore, today's holding allows even the moderately talented prosecutor to "work in . . . evidence on cross-examination [as it would] in its case in chief. . . ." *Walder v. United States*, 347 U.S., at 66, 74 S. Ct., at 356. To avoid this consequence, a defendant will be compelled to forgo testifying on his own behalf.

. . . "[T]he Constitution guarantees a defendant the fullest opportunity to meet the accusation against him." *Id.*, at 65, 74 S. Ct., at 356. Regrettably, surrender of that guarantee is the price the Court imposes for the defendant to claim his right not to be convicted on the basis of evidence obtained in violation of the Constitution. I cannot agree that one constitutional privilege must be purchased at the expense of another.

II

The foregoing demonstration of its break with precedent provides a sufficient ground to condemn the present ruling — unleashing, as it does, a hitherto relatively confined exception to the exclusionary rule. But I have a more fundamental difference with the Court's holding here, which culminates the approach taken in *Harris v. New York*, and *Oregon v. Hass*. For this sequence of decisions undercuts the constitutional canon that convictions cannot be procured by governmental lawbreaking.

. . . .

Of course, "[t]here is no gainsaying that arriving at the truth is a fundamental goal of our legal system." But it is also undeniable that promotion of that objective must be consonant with other ends, in particular those enshrined in our Constitution. I still hope that the Court would not be prepared to acquiesce in torture or other police conduct that "shocks the conscience" even if it demonstrably advanced the fact-finding process. At any rate, what is important is that the Constitution does not countenance police misbehavior, even in the pursuit of truth. The processes of our judicial system may not be fueled by the illegalities of government authorities.

---

1. Federal Rule of Evidence 611 does provide for limitation of the scope of cross-examination "to the subject matter of the direct examination and matters affecting the credibility of the witness." But even these constraints need not be adopted by the States, which are generally free to fashion their own rules of evidence.

Nevertheless, the Court has undertaken to strike a "balance" between the "policies" it finds in the Bill of Rights and the "competing interes[t]" in accurate trial determinations. This balancing effort is completely freewheeling. Far from applying criteria intrinsic to the Fourth and Fifth Amendments, the Court resolves succeeding cases simply by declaring that so much exclusion is enough to deter police misconduct. That hardly conforms to the disciplined analytical method described as "legal reasoning," through which judges endeavor to formulate or derive principles of decision that can be applied consistently and predictably.

Ultimately, I fear, this *ad hoc* approach to the exclusionary rule obscures the difference between judicial decisionmaking and legislative or administrative policymaking. More disturbingly, by treating Fourth and Fifth Amendment privileges as mere incentive schemes, the Court denigrates their unique status as *constitutional* protections. Yet the efficacy of the Bill of Rights as the bulwark of our national liberty depends precisely upon public appreciation of the special character of constitutional prescriptions. The Court is charged with the responsibility to enforce constitutional guarantees; decisions such as today's patently disregard that obligation.

Accordingly, I dissent.

James v. Illinois

United States Supreme Court

493 U.S. 307, 110 S. Ct. 648, 107 L. Ed. 2d 676 (1990)

JUSTICE BRENNAN delivered the opinion of the Court.

. . . .

I

On the night of August 30, 1982, eight young boys returning home from a party were confronted by a trio of other boys who demanded money. When the eight boys refused to comply, one member of the trio produced a gun and fired into the larger group, killing one boy and seriously injuring another. When the police arrived, the remaining members of the larger group provided eyewitness accounts of the event and descriptions of the perpetrators.

The next evening, two detectives of the Chicago Police Department took 15-year-old Darryl James into custody as a suspect in the shooting. James was found at his mother's beauty parlor sitting under a hair dryer; when he emerged, his hair was black and curly. After placing James in their car, the detectives questioned him about his prior hair color. He responded that the previous day his hair had been reddish-brown, long, and combed straight back. The detectives questioned James again later at the police station, and he further stated that he had gone to the beauty parlor in order to have his hair "dyed black and curled in order to change his appearance."

The State subsequently indicted James for murder and attempted murder. Prior to trial, James moved to suppress the statements regarding his hair, contending that they were the fruit of a Fourth Amendment violation because the detectives lacked probable cause for his warrantless arrest. After an evidentiary hearing, the trial court sustained this motion and ruled that the statements would be inadmissible at trial.

At trial, five members of the larger group of boys testified for the State, and each made an in-court identification of the defendant. Each testified that the person responsible for the shooting had "reddish" hair, worn shoulder length in a slicked-back "butter" style. Each also recalled having seen James several weeks earlier at a parade, at which time James had the aforementioned hair color and style. At trial, however, his hair was black and worn in a "natural" style. Despite the discrepancy between the witnesses' description and his present appearance, the witnesses stood firm in their conviction that James had been present and had fired the shots.

James did not testify in his own defense. He called as a witness Jewel Henderson, a friend of his family. Henderson testified that on the day of the shooting she had taken James to register for high school and that, at that time, his hair was black. The State then sought, over James' objection, to introduce his illegally obtained statements as a means of impeaching the credibility of Henderson's testimony. After determining that the suppressed statements had been made voluntarily, the trial court overruled James' objection. One of the interrogating detectives then reported James' prior admissions that he had reddish hair the night of the shooting and he dyed and curled his hair the next day in order to change his appearance. James ultimately was convicted of both murder and attempted murder and sentenced to 30 years' imprisonment.

On appeal, the Illinois Appellate Court reversed James' convictions and ordered a new trial. The appellate court held that the exclusionary rule barred admission of James' illegally obtained statements for the purpose of impeaching a defense witness' testimony and that the resulting constitutional error was not harmless. However, the Illinois Supreme Court reversed. The court reasoned that, in order to deter the defendant from engaging in perjury "by proxy," the impeachment exception to the exclusionary rule ought to be expanded to allow the State to introduce illegally obtained evidence to impeach the testimony of defense witnesses other than the defendant himself. The court therefore ordered James' convictions reinstated. We granted certiorari.

II

"There is no gainsaying that arriving at the truth is a fundamental goal of our legal system." *United States v. Havens*, 446 U.S. 620, 626 (1980). But various constitutional rules limit the means by which government may conduct this search for truth in order to promote other values embraced by the Framers and cherished throughout our Nation's history. "Ever since its inception, the rule excluding evidence seized in violation of the Fourth Amendment has been recognized as a principal mode of discouraging lawless police conduct. . . . [W]ithout it the constitutional guarantee against unreasonable searches and seizure would be a mere 'form of words.'" *Terry v. Ohio*, 392 U.S. 1, 12 (1968), quoting *Mapp v. Ohio*, 367 U.S. 643, 655 (1961). The occasional suppression of illegally obtained yet probative evidence has long been considered a necessary cost of preserving overriding constitutional values: "[T]here is nothing new in the realization that the Constitution sometimes insulates the criminality of a few in order to protect the privacy of us all." *Arizona v. Hicks*, 480 U.S. 321, 329 (1987).

This Court has carved out exceptions to the exclusionary rule, however, where the introduction of reliable and probative evidence would significantly further the truth-seeking function of a criminal trial and the likelihood that admissibility of such evidence would encourage police misconduct is but a "speculative possibility." *Harris v. New York*, 401 U.S. 222, 225 (1971). One exception to the rule permits prosecutors to introduce illegally obtained evidence for the limited purpose of impeaching the credibility of the defendant's own testimony . . . . In *Harris v. New York* and *Oregon v. Hass*, 420 U.S. 714 (1975), the Court applied the exception to permit prosecutors to impeach defendants using incriminating yet voluntary and reliable statements elicited in violation of *Miranda* requirements. [I]n *United States v. Havens*, the Court expanded the exception to permit prosecutors to introduce illegally obtained evidence in order to impeach a defendant's "answers to questions put to him on cross-examination that are plainly within the scope of the defendant's direct examination." *Id.*, at 627.

. . . .

III

. . . Expanding the class of impeachable witnesses from the defendant alone to all defense witnesses would create different incentives affecting the behavior of both defendants and law enforcement officers. As a result, this expansion would not promote the truth-seeking function to the same extent as did creation of the original exception, and yet it would significantly undermine the deterrent effect of the general exclusionary rule. Hence, we believe that this proposed expansion would frustrate rather than further the purposes underlying the exclusionary rule.

The previously recognized exception penalizes defendants for committing perjury by allowing the prosecution to expose their perjury through impeachment using illegally obtained evidence. Thus defendants are discouraged in the first instance from "affirmatively resort[ing] to perjurious testimony." *Walder v. United States*, 347 U.S. 62, 65 (1954). But the exception leaves defendants free to testify truthfully on their own behalf; they can offer probative and exculpatory evidence to the jury without opening the door to impeachment by carefully avoiding any statements that directly contradict the suppressed evidence. The exception thus generally discourages perjured testimony without discouraging truthful testimony.

In contrast, expanding the impeachment exception to encompass the testimony of all defense witnesses would not have the same beneficial effects. First, the mere threat of a subsequent criminal prosecution for perjury is far more likely to deter a witness from intentionally lying on a defendant's behalf than to deter a defendant, already facing conviction for the underlying offense, from lying on his own behalf. Hence the Illinois Supreme Court's underlying premise that a defendant frustrated by our previous impeachment exception can easily find a witness to engage in "perjury by proxy" is suspect.[4]

More significantly, expanding the impeachment exception to encompass the testimony of all defense witnesses likely would chill some defendants from presenting their best defense — and sometimes any defense at all — through the testimony of others. Whenever police obtained evidence illegally, defendants would have to assess prior to trial the likelihood that the evidence would be admitted to impeach the otherwise favorable testimony of any witness they call. Defendants might reasonably fear that one or more of their witnesses, in a position to offer truthful and favorable testimony, would also make some statement in sufficient tension with the tainted evidence to allow the prosecutor to introduce that evidence for impeachment. First, defendants sometimes need to call "reluctant" or "hostile" witnesses to provide reliable and probative exculpatory testimony, and such witnesses likely will not share the defendants' concern for avoiding statements that invite impeachment through contradictory evidence. Moreover, defendants often cannot trust even "friendly" witnesses to testify without subjecting themselves to impeachment, simply due to insufficient care or attentiveness. This concern is magnified in those occasional situations when defendants must call witnesses to testify despite having had only a limited opportunity to consult with or prepare them in advance. For these reasons, we have recognized in a variety of contexts that a party "cannot be absolutely certain that his witnesses will testify as expected." *Brooks v. Tennessee*, 406 U.S. 605, 609 (1972). As a result, an expanded impeachment exception likely would chill some defendants from calling witnesses who would otherwise offer probative evidence.

This realization alters the balance of values underlying the current impeachment exception governing defendants' testimony. Our prior cases make clear that defendants ought not be able to "pervert" the exclusion of illegally obtained evidence into a shield for perjury, but it seems no more appropriate for the State to brandish such evidence as a sword with which to dissuade defendants from presenting a meaningful defense through other witnesses. Given the potential chill created by expanding the impeachment exception, the conceded gains to the truth-seeking process from discouraging or disclosing perjured testimony would be offset to some extent by the concomitant loss of probative witness testimony. Thus, the truth-seeking rationale supporting the impeachment of defendants in *Walder* and its progeny does not apply to other witnesses with equal force.

Moreover, the proposed expansion of the current impeachment exception would significantly weaken the exclusionary rule's deterrent effect on police misconduct.

---

4. The dissent concedes, as it must, that "of course, false testimony can result from faulty recollection" as opposed to intentional lying. Even assuming that Henderson's testimony in this case (as opposed to the detective's contrary testimony) was indeed false, nothing in the record suggests that Henderson intentionally committed perjury rather than honestly provided her best (even if erroneous) perception and recollection of events.

This Court has characterized as a mere "speculative possibility," *Harris v. New York*, 401 U.S., at 225, the likelihood that permitting prosecutors to impeach defendants with illegally obtained evidence would encourage police misconduct. Law enforcement officers will think it unlikely that the defendant will first decide to testify at trial and will also open the door inadvertently to admission of any illegally obtained evidence. Hence, the officers' incentive to acquire evidence through illegal means is quite weak.

In contrast, expanding the impeachment exception to *all* defense witnesses would significantly enhance the expected value to the prosecution of illegally obtained evidence. First, this expansion would vastly increase the number of occasions on which such evidence could be used. Defense witnesses easily outnumber testifying defendants, both because many defendants do not testify themselves and because many if not most defendants call multiple witnesses on their behalf. Moreover, due to the chilling effect identified above, illegally obtained evidence holds even greater value to the prosecution for each individual witness than for each defendant. The prosecutor's access to impeachment evidence would not just deter perjury; it would also deter defendants from calling witnesses in the first place, thereby keeping from the jury much probative exculpatory evidence. For both of these reasons, police officers and their superiors would recognize that obtaining evidence through illegal means stacks the deck heavily in the prosecution's favor. It is thus far more than a "speculative possibility" that police misconduct will be encouraged by permitting such use of illegally obtained evidence.

The United States argues that this result is constitutionally acceptable because excluding illegally obtained evidence solely from the prosecution's case in chief would still provide a quantum of deterrence sufficient to protect the privacy interests underlying the exclusionary rule. We disagree. Of course, a police officer might in certain situations believe that obtaining particular evidence through illegal means, resulting in its suppression from the case in chief, would prevent the prosecution from establishing a *prima facie* case to take to a jury. In such situations, the officer likely would be deterred from obtaining the evidence illegally for fear of jeopardizing the entire case. But much if not most of the time, police officers confront opportunities to obtain evidence illegally after they have already legally obtained (or know that they have other means of legally obtaining) sufficient evidence to sustain a *prima facie* case. In these situations, a rule requiring exclusion of illegally obtained evidence from only the government's case in chief would leave officers with little to lose and much to gain by overstepping constitutional limits on evidence gathering.[8] Narrowing the exclusionary rule in this manner, therefore, would significantly undermine

---

8. Indeed, the detectives who unlawfully detained James and elicited his incriminating statements already knew that there were several eyewitnesses to the shooting. Because the detectives likely believed that the exclusion of any statement they obtained from James probably would not have precluded the prosecution from making a *prima facie* case, an exclusionary rule applicable only to the prosecution's case in chief likely would have provided little deterrent effect in this case.

the rule's ability "to compel respect for the constitutional guaranty in the only effectively available way — by removing the incentive to disregard it." *Elkin v. United States*, 364 U.S. 206, 217 (1960). So long as we are committed to protecting the people from the disregard of their constitutional rights during the course of criminal investigations, inadmissibility of illegally obtained evidence must remain the rule, not the exception.

IV

The cost to the truth-seeking process of evidentiary exclusion invariably is perceived more tangibly in discrete prosecutions than is the protection of privacy values through deterrence of future police misconduct. When defining the precise scope of the exclusionary rule, however, we must focus on systemic effects of proposed exceptions to ensure that individual liberty from arbitrary or oppressive police conduct does not succumb to the inexorable pressure to introduce all incriminating evidence, no matter how obtained, in each and every criminal case. Our previous recognition of an impeachment exception limited to the testimony of defendants reflects a careful weighing of the competing values. Because expanding the exception to encompass the testimony of all defense witnesses would not further the truth-seeking value with equal force but would appreciably undermine the deterrent effect of the exclusionary rule, we adhere to the line drawn in our previous cases.

Accordingly, we hold that the Illinois Supreme Court erred in affirming James' convictions despite the prosecutor's use of illegally obtained statements to impeach a defense witness' testimony. The court's judgment is reversed, and the case is remanded for further proceedings not inconsistent with this opinion.

It is so ordered.

[The concurring opinion of JUSTICE STEVENS has been omitted.]

JUSTICE KENNEDY, with whom CHIEF JUSTICE REHNQUIST, JUSTICE O'CONNOR and JUSTICE SCALIA join, dissenting.

. . . .

Our precedents establish that the exclusionary rule does not apply where the interest in pursuing truth or other important values outweighs any deterrence of unlawful conduct that the rule might achieve. One instance is a defendant's attempt to take advantage by presenting testimony in outright contradiction of excluded facts, secure in the knowledge that the inconsistency will not be revealed to the jury.

. . . .

The interest in protecting the truth-seeking function of the criminal trial is every bit as strong in this case as in our earlier cases that allowed rebuttal with evidence that was inadmissible as part of the prosecution's case in chief. Here a witness who knew the accused well took the stand to testify about the accused's personal appearance. The testimony could be expected to create real doubt in the minds of jurors concerning the eyewitness identifications by persons who did not know the accused. To deprive the jurors of knowledge that statements of the defendant himself revealed the witness' testimony to be false would result in a decision by triers of fact who were not just kept in the dark as to excluded evidence, but positively misled. The potential for harm to the truth-seeking process resulting from the majority's new rule in fact will be greater than if the defendant himself had testified. It is natural for jurors to be skeptical of self-serving testimony by the defendant. Testimony by a witness said to be independent has the greater potential to deceive. And if a defense witness can present false testimony with impunity, the jurors may find the rest of the prosecution's case suspect, for ineffective and artificial cross-examination will be viewed as a real weakness in the State's case. Jurors will assume that if the prosecution had any proof the statement was false, it would make the proof known. The majority does more than deprive the prosecution of evidence. The State must also suffer the introduction of false testimony and appear to bolster the falsehood by its own silence.

The majority's fear that allowing the jury to know the whole truth will chill defendants from putting on any defense seems to me far too speculative to justify the rule here announced. No restriction on the defense results if rebuttal of testimony by witnesses other than the defendant is confined to the introduction of excludable evidence that is in direct contradiction of the testimony. If mere "tension with the tainted evidence" opened the door to introduction of *all* the evidence subject to suppression, then the majority's fears might be justified. But in this context rebuttal can and should be confined to situations where there is direct conflict, which is to say where, within reason, the witness' testimony and the excluded testimony cannot both be true.

Also missing from the majority's analysis is the almost certain knowledge that the testimony immunized from rebuttal is false. The majority's apparent assumption that defense witnesses protected by today's rule have only truth-telling in mind strikes me as far too sanguine to support acceptance of a rule that controls the hard reality of contested criminal trials. The majority expresses the common sense of the matter in saying that presentation of excluded evidence must sometimes be allowed because it "penalizes defendants for committing perjury."

In some cases, of course, false testimony can result from faulty recollection. But the majority's ironclad rule is one that applies regardless of the witness' motives, and may be misused as a license to perjure. Even if the witness testifies in good faith, the defendant and his lawyer, who offer the testimony, know the facts. Indeed, it is difficult here to imagine the defense attorney's reason for asking Henderson about petitioner's hair color if he did not expect her to cast doubt on the eyewitness identification of petitioner by giving a description of petitioner's hair color contrary to that contained in his own (suppressed) statement.

The suggestion that the threat of a perjury prosecution will provide sufficient deterrence to prevent false testimony is not realistic. A heightened proof requirement applies in Illinois and other States, making perjury convictions difficult to sustain. Where testimony presented on behalf of a friend or family member is involved, the threat that a future jury will convict the witness may be an idle one.

The damage to the truth-seeking process caused by the majority's rule is certain to be great whether the testimony is perjured or merely false. In this case there can be little doubt of the falsity, since petitioner's description of his own hair was at issue. And as a general matter the alternative to rebuttal is endorsement of judicial proceedings conducted in reliance on information known to be untrue. Suppressed evidence is likely to consist of either voluntary statements by the defendant himself or physical evidence. Both have a high degree of reliability, and testimony in direct conflict to such evidence most often will represent an attempt to place falsehoods before the jury.

The suggestion that all this is so far beyond the control of the defendant that he will put on no defense is not supported. As to sympathetic witnesses, such as the family friend here, it should not be too hard to assure the witness does not volunteer testimony in contradiction of the facts. The defendant knows the content of the suppressed evidence. Even in cases where the time for consultation is limited, the defense attorney can take care not to elicit contradicting testimony. And in the case of truly neutral witnesses, or witnesses hostile to the accused, it is hard to see the danger that they will present false testimony for the benefit of the defense.

The majority's concerns may carry greater weight where contradicting testimony is elicited from a defense witness on cross-examination. In that situation there might be a concern that the prosecution would attempt to produce such testimony as the foundation to put excluded evidence before the jury. We have found that possibility insufficient to justify immunity for a defendant's own false testimony on cross-examination. *United States v. Havens*, 446 U.S. 620 (1980). As to cross-examination of other witnesses, perhaps a different rule could be justified. Rather than wait for an appropriate case to consider this or similar measures, however, the majority opts for a wooden rule immunizing all defense testimony from rebuttal, without regard to knowledge that the testimony introduced at the behest of the defendant is false or perjured.

I also cannot agree that admission of excluded evidence on rebuttal would lead to the "disregard of . . . constitutional rights," by law enforcement officers that the majority fears. This argument has been raised in our previous cases in this area of the law. To date we have rejected it. Now the spectre appears premised on an assumption that a single slip of the tongue by any defense witness will open the door to any suppressed evidence at the prosecutor's disposal. If this were so, the majority's concern that officers would be left with little to lose from conducting an illegal search would be understandable. And the argument might hold more force if, as the majority speculates, police confront the temptation to seize evidence illegally "much if not most of the time" after gathering sufficient evidence to present proof of guilt beyond a reasonable doubt in the case in chief. Again, however, I disagree with the predictions.

It is unrealistic to say that the decision to make an illegal search turns on a precise calculation of the possibilities of rebuttal at some future trial. There is no reason to believe a police officer, unschooled in the law, will assess whether evidence already in his possession would suffice to survive a motion for acquittal following the case in chief. The officer may or may not even know the identity of the ultimate defendant.[3] He certainly will not know anything about potential defense witnesses, much less what the content of their testimony might be. What he will know for certain is that evidence from an illegal search or arrest (which may well be crucial to securing a conviction) will be lost to the case in chief. Our earlier assessments of the marginal deterrent effect are applicable here. "Assuming that the exclusionary rule has a deterrent effect on proscribed police conduct, sufficient deterrence flows when the evidence in question is made unavailable to the prosecution in its case in chief." *Harris, supra*, at 225.

In this case, the defense witness, one Jewel Henderson, testified that petitioner's hair was black on the date of the offense. Her statement, perjured or not, should not have been offered to the jurors without giving them the opportunity to consider the unequivocal and contradicting description by the person whose own hair it was. I would allow the introduction of petitioner's statement that his hair was red on the day of the shootings. The result is consistent with our line of cases from *Walder* to *Havens*, and compelled by their reasoning.

. . . .

Where the jury is misled by false testimony, otherwise subject to flat contradiction by evidence illegally seized, the protection of the exclusionary rule is "perverted into a license to use perjury by way of a defense, free from the risk of confrontation with prior inconsistent utterances." *Havens, supra*, at 626 (quoting *Harris, supra*, at 226). The perversion is the same where the perjury is by proxy. I would affirm the judgment of the Illinois Supreme Court.

Notes and Questions

(1) Should the government be allowed to introduce a statement that is the product of "actual coercion" to impeach the trial testimony of an accused? How is the impeachment use of such a statement constitutionally distinguishable from the impeachment use of a statement that is "presumed" to have been compelled because it was obtained in violation of *Miranda*?

In *Mincey v. Arizona*, 437 U.S. 385, 98 S. Ct. 2408, 57 L. Ed. 2d 290 (1978), the Court held that the Fourteenth Amendment forbade the use of a statement that was

---

3. In this case, contrary to the impression conveyed by the majority, the arresting officers knew almost nothing of the state of a future prosecution case. The officers did know there were several eyewitnesses to the shooting. But these eyewitnesses had made no identification of any suspect. The officers did not know petitioner's real name or his true appearance, but had sought him out at the beauty parlor on an anonymous tip. They could not know what physical evidence, such as the murder weapon, they might find on petitioner, or might lose to the case in chief as a result of illegal conduct. The suggestion that the officers' calculated assessment of a future trial allowed them to ignore the exclusionary rule finds no support in the record and, in fact, is pure speculation.

coerced from an accused for impeachment purposes. According to the Court, "*any* criminal trial use against a defendant of his *involuntary* statement is a denial of due process of law." (Emphasis in original). In addition, in *New Jersey v. Portash*, 440 U.S. 450, 99 S. Ct. 1292, 59 L. Ed. 2d 501 (1979), the Justices made it clear that impeachment use of statements forced from the mind of a defendant is also forbidden by the Fifth Amendment. According to the *Portash* Court, interest balancing of the sort that supported the holdings in *Harris* and *Hass* is "impermissible" when a genuinely compelled statement is involved. A statement that is the product of actual compulsion "cannot be used to impeach" a defendant because such use at trial would violate the "privilege against compulsory self-incrimination."

(2) In *Kansas v. Ventris*, 556 U.S. 586, 129 S. Ct. 1841, 173 L. Ed. 2d 801 (2009), the Court held that incriminating statements obtained by a jailhouse informant in violation of the *Massiah* doctrine — statements the informant deliberately elicited from an accused — were admissible to impeach the defendant's trial testimony. According to the majority, "[w]hether otherwise excluded evidence can be admitted for purposes of impeachment depends upon the nature of the constitutional guarantee that is violated." Unlike the impeachment use of a coerced confession, which itself violates both the right to due process of law and the Fifth Amendment privilege against compulsory self-incrimination, the introduction of statements obtained in violation of *Massiah* does not itself deprive the defendant of a constitutional entitlement. The *Massiah* Court extended the trial right to counsel to pretrial confrontations "to ensure that police manipulation does not render counsel entirely impotent — depriving the defendant of" effective representation prior to the ultimate confrontation at trial. "[T]he *Massiah* right is a right to be free of uncounseled interrogation, and is infringed at the time of the interrogation." Put otherwise, deprivation of the Sixth Amendment right to assistance of counsel occurs when and *only* when the government confronts an accused without counsel before trial and secures incriminating admissions.

Like the Fourth Amendment exclusionary rule, *Massiah*'s suppression doctrine is a deterrent sanction. Whether exclusion is called for is a question about "the scope of the remedy for a violation that has already occurred." As under the Fourth Amendment and *Miranda*, the balance of interests tips in favor of an exception for impeachment use. Suppression from the government's case in chief furnishes ample deterrence of future right to counsel deprivations, and the costs to the truth-finding process of suppression for impeachment purposes outweigh any additional deterrent benefits that might result. "[T]he game of excluding tainted evidence for impeachment purposes is not worth the candle."

Two Justices dissented. In their view, *Massiah* had held that the *use* of deliberately elicited statements constituted a violation of the Sixth Amendment and that holding was a correct interpretation of the right to the assistance of counsel. "While the constitutional breach beg[ins] at the time of interrogation, the State's use of th[e] evidence [it obtains] at trial compound[s] the violation. The logic that compels the exclusion of the evidence during the State's case in chief extends to any attempt by the State to rely on the evidence, even for impeachment. The use of ill-gotten evidence during any phase of criminal prosecution does damage to the adversarial process — the fairness of which the Sixth Amendment was designed to protect." According to the dissenters, the majority's refusal to recognize that the "constitutional harm" occurs upon admission of the evidence at trial was, quite simply, "[i]nexplicabl[e]" and "lamentable." The majority had "privileged the prosecution at the expense of the Constitution."

(3) The Court has grounded some additional limitations of the operation of the exclusionary rule upon the "context" in which the defendant has sought suppression. *See, e.g., Pennsylvania Board of Probation and Parole v. Scott*, 524 U.S. 357, 118 S. Ct. 2014, 141 L. Ed. 2d 344 (1998) (Fourth Amendment exclusionary rule does not bar introduction of illegally obtained evidence at parole revocation hearings); *Immigration and Naturalization Service v. Lopez-Mendoza*, 468 U.S. 1032, 104 S. Ct. 3479, 82 L. Ed. 2d 778 (1984) (Fourth Amendment exclusionary rule inapplicable in civil deportation proceeding); *Stone v. Powell*, 428 U.S. 465, 96 S. Ct. 3037, 49 L. Ed. 2d 1067 (1976) (Fourth Amendment exclusionary rule claim may not be raised in a habeas corpus challenge to a state conviction if the state court has afforded a full and fair opportunity to litigate the claim); *United States v. Calandra*, 414 U.S. 338, 94 S. Ct. 613, 38 L. Ed. 2d 561 (1974) (Fourth Amendment exclusionary rule inapplicable in grand jury proceeding).

Impeachment Use Problems

13F–1: Immediately following an attempted shooting, John was arrested and taken to local police headquarters in the custody of federal agents and D.C. police. The group arrived at 2:40 p.m. John was read the *Miranda* warnings on three separate occasions, during the last of which he was given a waiver-of-rights card. In response, John asked to speak with "Joe Bates, my father's attorney in Dallas." The police pursued no interrogation.

John remained in police custody until 4:50 p.m., during which time he provided information necessary for the booking process and the police attempted to contact Joe Bates. He was transferred to the FBI field office at approximately 5:15. John was again advised of his *Miranda* rights by the FBI. He was told that Joe Bates had been contacted and had recommended that John retain Vincent Fuller, a D.C. lawyer. John said he would like the assistance of Fuller.

At 7:00 p.m., prior to Fuller's arrival, FBI Agent Ragle approached John and asked him to respond to certain "background" questions. John agreed to answer questions. For the next 25 minutes, in response to questioning, he provided information about his life up until his arrival in Washington, including his family history, his criminal record, his erratic travel patterns, his psychiatric treatment, his lack of a sense of direction, and his relationship with his parents. When asked specifically whether he had a girlfriend, John described his one-sided relationship with the actress Jodie Foster. After this, the interview ended. Three minutes later, Vincent Fuller arrived.

At his trial for attempted murder, John interposed an insanity defense. Once such a claim was raised, the government had the burden of proving sanity beyond a reasonable doubt. To rebut the insanity claim and carry its burden on the sanity issue, the prosecution sought to introduce John's statements. John objected to their admission.

Should the prosecution be able to use John's statements to rebut his insanity defense?

13F–2: Stanley's family was homeless. His wife used their government assistance checks to support her drug habit. In despair, Stanley stabbed his two handicapped sons and then himself.

While Stanley was in the hospital recovering from his injuries, he was visited repeatedly by Detective Schwartz. The third visit occurred after his indictment for first-degree murder. Schwartz knew that counsel had been appointed to represent Stanley at the time, and knew that an interrogation in the absence of counsel was impermissible. Nonetheless, he believed that any statements he obtained could be used to impeach Stanley if he took the stand at his trial.

Without advising Stanley of his rights, Schwartz questioned him about the killings. Stanley stated that because he had only wanted to kill the boys and had not wanted to hurt them, he had waited until they had fallen asleep and had been careful about where and how he had stabbed them.

At trial, Stanley testified about his frustration and despair and claimed that he had killed the boys in an unthinking rage. The government sought permission to introduce his prior statements to impeach him, and Stanley's counsel objected. The court allowed the introduction of the statements. Stanley was convicted and appealed.

What arguments should Stanley raise on appeal? How should the government respond? How should the trial court rule?

13F–3: On January 19, 1998, Brim sold 100 grams of heroin to a witness cooperating with the FBI. Subsequent to this sale, the FBI sought a search warrant for Brim's condominium unit. The search warrant covered both the condominium and Brim's storage locker in the basement of the building. While agents were searching the storage locker, they noticed an air conditioner box located next to it. They decided to search the box. Inside, they discovered a black bag that belonged to Brim. The bag contained 443 grams of heroin.

At trial, Brim moved to suppress the 443 grams of heroin found in the bag. The district judge agreed with his contention that the search warrant did not cover the air conditioner box. Consequently, the judge granted Brim's motion to suppress the heroin from the trial.

On February 12, 1999, a jury found Brim guilty of distribution of heroin based on the 100 grams that he had sold to the FBI's cooperating witness. In preparation for

Brim's sentencing, the Probation Office issued a Presentence Report that included as "relevant conduct" his possession of the 443 grams of heroin that had been illegally obtained. Brim objected to the Report, maintaining that the 443 grams of heroin had to be excluded from the sentencing proceeding. The district judge overruled the objection. Under the United States Sentencing Guidelines, the judge concluded that Brim's offense level was "twenty-eight." In part, this determination was founded on the fact that Brim had possessed the 443 grams of heroin. The judge sentenced Brim to 81 months in prison and four years of supervised release. Brim appealed the sentence, challenging the court's reliance on the contraband discovered during the illegal search.

How should the appellate court rule?

13F–4: On the morning of August 29, Valerie discovered the naked body of her roommate, Anna, in the bedroom of their West Virginia apartment. Valerie called the authorities. Detectives Davies and Pole responded to the call. Davies noticed that the transom above the front door was open and smeared with blood. He also saw blood spots beside a chair that was outside the door. Detective Pole lifted two bloody shoe prints from the apartment. The disarray in the victim's bedroom indicated that a struggle had occurred.

According to Valerie, Floyd and Anna were friends. At one time, Floyd had lived in the same building. After he moved out, he continued to visit regularly. The detectives went to see Barbara, Floyd's mother. Barbara reported that her son had gotten home around 7:00 a.m. on August 29, that he had a butcher knife in his hand and blood on his shirt and pant leg. He told his mother that he had stabbed Anna, then left, saying he was going to the State Hospital for treatment.

Floyd was subsequently arrested in Michigan. The herringbone pattern on his shoes proved to be "consistent with" the pattern of the prints lifted from the murder scene. Moreover, blood samples taken from Floyd proved to be "consistent with" blood found at the crime scene. The state charged Floyd with first degree murder.

Floyd raised a "diminished capacity" defense, claiming that he was too impaired by the effects of intoxication and mental illness to premeditate the killing. His mother testified to his "hysterical" condition on the morning of the slaying. Floyd's friends testified that shortly before the killing Floyd had ingested a considerable amount of alcohol. A pharmacist testified about various prescriptions he had filled for Floyd and the potential effects of those drugs.

Dr. Welan, a psychiatrist, testified via videotaped deposition that Floyd suffered from bipolar disorder or manic depression; that Floyd had told him that he had taken three Percocets on the night of the crime; that in his opinion Floyd's ability to reflect on his actions would have been "drastically affected" by his mental illness and the drugs; and that "it would be consistent" with the facts for Floyd to have had a loss of memory or period of blackout. On cross-examination, Welan gave a detailed account of Floyd's statements regarding his inability to recall events on the morning of the murder and testified that his opinion of Floyd's condition on the 29th was "primarily based on what Floyd told" him.

In rebuttal, the state called Detective Davies. Over defense objection, Davies testified that when he and Detective Pole were bringing Floyd back from Michigan, Pole looked at Floyd's hand and said, "I know how you got that." Floyd responded, "You've talked to mama." A casual conversation concerning the roads on the way back from Michigan then ensued. Floyd remarked that "the way I came up, the way I went to Michigan, was shorter than the way we are going back. There were no tolls the way I came." At no time was Floyd given the *Miranda* warnings.

Floyd was convicted of first-degree murder and has appealed, challenging the admission of Detective Davies' testimony on rebuttal.

Was it proper to admit Davies' rebuttal testimony?

13F–5: James Boy was arrested at 2:00 p.m., on March 6, and was taken to the Los Angeles Police Department's South Bureau. There is no holding tank at that facility and the policy is to handcuff prisoners by one hand to a bench. At 6:00 p.m., two detectives came to interrogate Boy. They led him to an interview room for an interview that lasted 15 minutes. Boy was not in handcuffs at the time.

Detective Ben began the interrogation before advising Boy of his rights. After obtaining Boy's name, address, and other background information, Ben asked if he knew why he was there. Boy responded that he had an idea — that he was a suspect in the murder of a woman who had been in his house. He stated that she had left his house alive and that she had come to his house with a man named Gary.

At that point, Ben asked Detective Cosby: "Before we go further, you want to advise him?" Boy was given the *Miranda* warnings and asked whether he wished to give up the right to remain silent. The following exchange then occurred:

> Boy: Am I being charged with murder? If I'm being charged, then I won't have another word until I have an attorney.
>
> Ben: Is that your feelings?
>
> Boy: If you read me those rights, you must be gonna charge me, so I'll wait and see what happens. I won't say another word until I have an attorney.
>
> Ben: Okay. Let me explain something to you, James. I'm going to continue to ask you questions. Now you realize that you didn't waive your rights, so we can't use 'em in court. I think you're familiar with *Miranda*, right, James?
>
> Boy: I don't know much about the law. I'm just telling you I know to keep my mouth shut.

The detectives then told Boy that they had found incriminating evidence in his apartment. Boy responded that he would not say anything without his attorney. Ben then asked, "Why don't you tell me what happened that night?" In response to numerous questions from the detectives, Boy gave an account of the events of the night of the murder. He never confessed to the murder.

At a hearing prior to Boy's murder trial, Detective Ben testified that he had continued to question Boy "so that if he did take the stand, his testimony could be impeached." Defense counsel asked, "Have you attended seminars where it was suggested as a tactic to keep addressing questions to a suspect after they invoke their rights?" Ben answered, "Yes," and explained the instruction he received at the seminar as follows: "In essence, you do want to get a statement for the expressed purpose that I just stated."

At the trial, evidence of Boy's guilt was overwhelming. Boy testified in his own defense. He admitted that the victim died in his apartment, that he disposed of her body, and that he tried to clean up the blood. He claimed that she was murdered by another person while he was sleeping. He did admit, however, that the victim had stolen money from him on three occasions and that he had been angry and upset. He also admitted having a dispute with the victim over drugs on the night of the murder.

The statements Ben had made to the detectives were inconsistent with his trial testimony in some respects. Over defense objection, the state was permitted to introduce those statements to impeach Boy's testimony.

Were Boy's statements properly admitted?

13F–6: On January 30, at 6:30 a.m., Jack McBray collected the receipts from the Kentucky Fried Chicken restaurant he managed in Hesper. He intended to deposit the receipts in the bank. As he got into his truck, McBray saw two persons in his side-view mirror. One was wearing a gorilla mask. McBray locked his doors and started his truck. He then noticed that the two men were trying to open the truck's doors. As he drove away, McBray saw the man in the mask, who was later identified as Josh Jenks, put a gun in his waistband. The two men then got into a car. McBray decided to pursue their vehicle, but soon lost track of it. He immediately provided the police with descriptions of the men and with the license plate number of their vehicle.

Shortly after receiving McBray's report, police officers detained Jenks and Reevy. McBray identified them as the men he had seen. He recognized Jenks as a Kentucky Fried Chicken employee. Officers arrested the two men, and, in a search of their vehicle, found a gorilla mask, a pair of gloves, and a BB gun. After Jenks and Reevy were taken to the Hesper police station, Deputy Sheriff Comb advised Reevy of his *Miranda* rights. Reevy said he did not wish to speak. Reevy was then taken to Detective Henderson's office and again given the *Miranda* warnings. He said that he wanted an attorney. Knowing that he was violating *Miranda*'s dictates, Henderson kept talking to Reevy "for impeachment purposes." He understood that statements obtained in violation of *Miranda* could be used to impeach a testifying defendant at trial. Henderson asked Reevy why he was at the Kentucky Fried Chicken restaurant. Reevy said that he and Jenks were "there for the money." The interrogation took place in Henderson's office and lasted 10 minutes. Henderson was three feet away from Reevy at all times. He spoke in a conversational tone, made no threats or promises, and did not indicate to Reevy that his statements could not be used at his trial.

Jenks and Reevy were charged with attempted robbery. At trial, Reevy testified in his own defense. He claimed that Jenks had asked him to help "frighten" McBray in revenge for his poor treatment of the Kentucky Fried Chicken employees. Reevy said that there had been no plan to rob McBray. He also testified that he had feigned willingness to participate in the attempt to frighten him because he intended to have "revenge" against Jenks by "leaving him in the lurch" at the scene. He added that he and Jenks had hidden in the bushes outside the restaurant, and that he had turned and headed toward his car while Jenks had approached McBray's truck. Jenks denied telling officers that he was there "for the money."

In rebuttal, Detective Henderson testified that he had interviewed Reevy after his arrest, that he had advised Reevy of his rights, and that Reevy had asked for a lawyer. Despite the request, Henderson had asked Reevy why he and Jenks were at the restaurant. According to Henderson, Reevy had said he was "there for the money." Reevy denied making the statement. He also contested its admissibility and moved to strike Henderson's testimony about the incriminating statement. The government opposed the motion to strike, contending that the statement was admissible to impeach Reevy's trial testimony.

How should the trial court rule?

13F–7: On February 3, Theodore True was scheduled to appear in County Court in Golden. When he failed to appear in court, a warrant was issued for his arrest. On February 12, True was arrested. The two arresting officers questioned True without giving him *Miranda* warnings. True told the officers that he understood there was a warrant for his arrest and that on the day of the arrest, "I was fleeing to California." True was charged with "violating bail bond conditions." To establish guilt, the prosecution had to show that True "knew" about the scheduled court date at the time he failed to appear.

True did not testify at his trial. His mother, Alice True, testified that her son has a poor memory, that he had taken Ritalin in the past, and that he took special education classes in school. True's wife, Shelly True, testified that her husband is very forgetful and that she organizes the household and keeps track of her husband's obligations, such as court dates. Shelly True's day-timer page for February 3, which was admitted into evidence, reflected that her husband had a court appearance scheduled in Woodlake on February 3, but not that he was scheduled to appear in Golden. Shelly testified that either True did not tell her the correct date or that she had recorded it incorrectly. At one point, True's attorney asked Shelly if her husband told her the date he had to be in court when he returned home from his preliminary hearing. Shelly indicated that her husband had not told her anything about the date. She stated that he usually tells her about court dates after a hearing and that if he did not tell her a date, she would write the date in the day-timer when she learned about it later.

After the close of the defense case, the prosecution offered the testimony of Sergeant Fish "to impeach Shelly's testimony and to rebut the defense that True is generally unable to keep track of his appointments and that he did not know, due to cognitive disabilities, of his scheduled court appearance on February 3." Over a defense objection, the trial judge allowed Sergeant Fish to testify that during a post-arrest interview True had said that he knew there was a warrant for his arrest and that on the day of his arrest he was in the process of fleeing to California.

The jury convicted True of violating bail bond conditions. He was also adjudicated a habitual criminal and sentenced to imprisonment for six years. A court of appeals reversed the conviction and vacated the habitual criminal adjudication, holding that True's statements were improperly admitted at trial. The prosecution then appealed to the state supreme court.

How should the state supreme court rule?

13F–8: On March 13, Nick entered the First Citizens Bank and handed a bank teller a note stating, "This Is A Robbery Give Up The Money Or I Shoot." The teller gave Nick $5000. Shortly after the robbery, Nick's father informed the police that his son may have committed the robbery. A few days later, Detective James telephoned Nick and arranged for him to surrender. According to Nick and his father, during this conversation Nick informed James that he wanted an attorney, and James assured Nick he would receive one. Nick and his father then met Detective James at an agreed-upon location, and Nick returned what was left of the robbery proceeds. According to Nick and his father, Nick again informed Detective James that he wanted an attorney, and James again responded that Nick would receive one.

After his arrival at the police station. Detective James took Nick to an interview room and reviewed with him an "Waiver of Rights" form. Nick initialed statements acknowledging that he had the rights to consult with an attorney, to have an attorney present during questioning, and to stop answering questions until he spoke with an attorney. Nick also circled, initialed, and signed a portion of the form indicating that he voluntarily agreed to answer questions without an attorney present. Detective James then interviewed Nick, who confessed to robbing the bank and to carrying a pistol in his pocket during the robbery.

Nick was indicted by a federal grand jury on charges of bank robbery, armed bank robbery, and using or carrying a firearm during and in relation to a crime of violence. He moved to suppress his confession — specifically, his admission to carrying a firearm during the robbery. He claimed that he had requested an attorney and had been assured that counsel would be made available to him. After an evidentiary hearing at which Nick, his father, and Detective James testified, a judge found that the testimony of Nick and his father "credibly establishes that an attorney was requested not once but twice." The judge decided that Nick's confession had to be suppressed.

Because Nick's admission was the only evidence that he had carried a firearm during the robbery, the Government dismissed the armed bank robbery and firearm charges. Nick then pleaded guilty to the bank robbery charge. At Nick's sentencing, the Government argued that Nick's admission that he had carried a pistol could be introduced and relied upon to "enhance" his sentence for the bank robbery. The sentencing judge disagreed and excluded Nick's admission from the sentencing proceeding.

Did the judge rule correctly?

Selected Bibliography

Jose Felipe Anderson, *Reflections on Standing: Challenges to Searches and Seizures in a High Technology World*, 75 Miss. L.J. 1099 (2006)

Robert M. Bloom & David H. Fentin, *"A More Majestic Conception": The Importance of Judicial Integrity in Preserving the Exclusionary Rule*, 13 U. Pa. J. Const. L. 47 (2010)

Thomas K. Clancy, *The Fourth Amendment's Exclusionary Rule as a Constitutional Right*, 10 Ohio St. J. Crim. L. 357 (2013)

Donald Dripps, *Living With* Leon, 95 Yale L.J. 906 (1986)

Donald Dripps, *The "New" Exclusionary Rule Debate: From "Still Preoccupied with 1985" to "Virtual Deterrence,"* 37 Fordham Urb. L.J. 743 (2010)

Steven Duke, *Making* Leon *Worse*, 95 Yale L.J. 1405 (1986)

Andrew Guthrie Ferguson, *Constitutional Culpability: Questioning the New Exclusionary Rules*, 66 Fla. L. Rev. 623 (2014)

James P. Fleissner, *Glide Path to an "Inclusionary Rule": How Expansion of the Good Faith Exception Threatens to Fundamentally Change the Exclusionary Rule*, 48 Mercer L. Rev. 1023 (1997)

David Gray, Meagan Cooper & David McAloon, *The Supreme Court's Contemporary Silver Platter Doctrine*, 91 Tex. L. Rev. 7 (2012)

John P. Gross, *Dangerous Criminals, the Search for the Truth and Effective Law Enforcement: How the Supreme Court Overestimates the Social Costs of the Exclusionary Rule*, 51 Santa Clara L. Rev. 545 (2011)

Tonya Jacobi, *The Law and Economics of the Exclusionary Rule*, 87 Notre Dame L. Rev. 585 (2011)

James L. Kainen, *The Impeachment Exception to the Exclusionary Rules: Policies, Principles, and Politics*, 44 Stan. L. Rev. 1301 (1992)

Yale Kamisar, Gates, *"Probable Cause," "Good Faith," and Beyond*, 69 Iowa L. Rev. 551 (1984)

Yale Kamisar, *Postscript: Another Look at* Patane *and* Seibert, *the 2004 Miranda "Poisoned Fruit" Cases*, 2 Ohio St. J. Crim. L. 97 (2004)

Orin S. Kerr, *Good Faith, New Law, and the Scope of the Exclusionary Rule*, 99 Geo. L.J. 1077 (2011)

Wayne R. LaFave, *The Smell of* Herring: *A Critique of the Supreme Court's Latest Assault on the Exclusionary Rule*, 99 J. Crim. Law & Criminology 757 (2009)

Jennifer E. Laurin, *Trawling for* Herring: *Lessons in Doctrinal Borrowing and Convergence*, 111 Colum. L. Rev. 670 (2011)

Tracey Maclin, *No More Chipping Away: The Roberts Court Uses an Axe to Take Out the Fourth Amendment Exclusionary Rule*, 81 Miss. L. J. 1183 (2012)

Joelle Anne Moreno, *Faith-Based* Miranda?: *Why the New* Missouri v. Seibert *Police "Bad Faith" Test Is a Terrible Idea*, 47 Ariz. L. Rev. 395 (2005)

Lawrence Rosenthal, *Seven Theses in Grudging Defense of the Exclusionary Rule*, 10 Ohio St. J. Crim L. 525 (2013)

Andrew E. Taslitz, *The Expressive Fourth Amendment: Rethinking the Good Faith Exception to the Exclusionary Rule*, 76 Miss. L.J. 483 (2006)

Sandra Guerra Thompson, *Evading* Miranda: *How* Seibert *and* Patane *Failed to "Save"* Miranda, 40 Val. U. L. Rev. 645 (2006)

James J. Tomkovicz, Constitutional Exclusion: The Rules, Rights, and Remedies That Strike the Balance Between Freedom and Order (2011)

James J. Tomkovicz, Davis v. United States: *The Exclusion Revolution Continues*, 9 Ohio St. J. Crim L. 381 (2011)

James J. Tomkovicz, Hudson v. Michigan *and the Future of Fourth Amendment Exclusion*, 93 Iowa L. Rev. 1819 (2008)

James J. Tomkovicz, *The* Massiah *Right to Exclusion: Constitutional Premises and Doctrinal Implications*, 67 N.C. L. Rev. 751 (1989)

Appendix A

The Constitution of the United States of America

We the People of the United States, in Order to form a more perfect Union, establish Justice, insure domestic Tranquility, provide for the common defence, promote the general Welfare, and secure the Blessings of Liberty to ourselves and our Posterity, do ordain and establish this Constitution for the United States of America.

* * *

ARTICLES IN ADDITION TO, AND AMENDMENT OF,
THE CONSTITUTION OF THE UNITED STATES OF AMERICA,
PROPOSED BY CONGRESS, AND RATIFIED BY THE SEVERAL
STATES, PURSUANT TO THE FIFTH ARTICLE OF THE
ORIGINAL CONSTITUTION.[*]

AMENDMENT I [1791].

Congress shall make no law respecting an establishment of religion, or prohibiting the free exercise thereof; or abridging the freedom of speech, or of the press; or the right of the people peaceably to assemble, and to petition the Government for a redress of grievances.

AMENDMENT II [1791].

A well regulated Militia, being necessary to the security of a free State, the right of the people to keep and bear Arms, shall not be infringed.

AMENDMENT III [1791].

No Soldier shall, in time of peace be quartered in any house, without the consent of the Owner, nor in time of war, but in a manner to be prescribed by law.

AMENDMENT IV [1791].

The right of the people to be secure in their persons, houses, papers, and effects, against unreasonable searches and seizures, shall not be violated, and no Warrants

---

[*] The first ten Amendments to the United States Constitution are commonly referred to as the "Bill of Rights."

shall issue, but upon probable cause, supported by Oath or affirmation, and particularly describing the place to be searched, and the persons or things to be seized.

AMENDMENT V [1791].

No person shall be held to answer for a capital, or otherwise infamous crime, unless on a presentment or indictment of a Grand Jury, except in cases arising in the land or naval forces, or in the Militia, when in actual service in time of War or public danger; nor shall any person be subject for the same offence to be twice put in jeopardy of life or limb; nor shall be compelled in any criminal case to be a witness against himself, nor be deprived of life, liberty, or property, without due process of law; nor shall private property be taken for public use, without just compensation.

AMENDMENT VI [1791].

In all criminal prosecutions, the accused shall enjoy the right to a speedy and public trial, by an impartial jury of the State and district wherein the crime shall have been committed, which district shall have been previously ascertained by law, and to be informed of the nature and cause of the accusation; to be confronted with the witnesses against him; to have compulsory process for obtaining witnesses in his favor, and to have the Assistance of Counsel for his defence.

AMENDMENT VII [1791].

In Suits at common law, where the value in controversy shall exceed twenty dollars, the right of trial by jury shall be preserved, and no fact tried by a jury, shall be otherwise re-examined in any Court of the United States, than according to the rules of the common law.

AMENDMENT VIII [1791].

Excessive bail shall not be required, nor excessive fines imposed, nor cruel and unusual punishments inflicted.

AMENDMENT IX [1791].

The enumeration in the Constitution, of certain rights, shall not be construed to deny or disparage others retained by the people.

AMENDMENT X [1791].

The powers not delegated to the United States by the Constitution, nor prohibited by it to the States, are reserved to the States respectively, or to the people.

* * *

AMENDMENT XIV [1868].
SECTION 1.

All persons born or naturalized in the United States, and subject to the jurisdiction thereof, are citizens of the United States and of the State wherein they reside. No State shall make or enforce any law which shall abridge the privileges or immunities of citizens of the United States; nor shall any State deprive any person of life, liberty, or property, without due process of law; nor deny to any person within its jurisdiction the equal protection of the laws.

* * *

SECTION 5.

The Congress shall have power to enforce, by appropriate legislation, the provisions of this article.

Table of Cases

References are to page numbers

Index

References are to sections